STRATEGY AND POLICY:
Concepts and Cases

CONSULTING EDITOR IN MANAGEMENT

John M. Ivancevich
University of Houston

STRATEGY AND POLICY
Concepts and Cases

ARTHUR A. THOMPSON, JR.
and
A. J. STRICKLAND, III
Both of The University of Alabama

. 1981

Revised Edition

BUSINESS PUBLICATIONS, INC.
Plano, Texas   75075
Irwin-Dorsey Limited
Georgetown, Ontario   L7G 4B3

© BUSINESS PUBLICATIONS, INC., 1978 and 1981

All rights reserved. No part of this publication may be
reproduced, stored in a retrieval system, or transmitted,
in any form or by any means, electronic, mechanical,
photocopying, recording, or otherwise, without the prior
written permission of the publisher.

ISBN 0-256-02385-9
Library of Congress Catalog Card No. 80–70445

Printed in the United States of America

2 3 4 5 6 7 8 9 0 MP 7 6 5 4 3 2 1

To
Hasseline and Kitty

PREFACE

This book is intended for capstone courses in "business policy." It features a thorough, up-to-date survey of strategy/policy concepts and a strong, diverse collection of cases. The focus throughout is on strategy management—all those entrepreneurial and administrative tasks that a general manager is responsible for in formulating and implementing strategy and in directing the total enterprise. The text portion offers a fresh, expansive treatment of the fundamental ideas and analytical techniques of strategic management: It captures and reflects the numerous changes in content and emphasis which are sweeping the business policy field. The cases were selected not only with the aim of reinforcing application of the text material but also with an eye toward providing students an opportunity to wrestle with contemporary strategic problems and issues. The combination of text and cases creates, we think, a most powerful pedagogy for the study of strategy and policy. Our objective has been to assemble a text-case package that presents a comprehensive picture of the tasks, functions, and responsibilities inherent in managing the total enterprise.

The Text Portion: Orientation and Content

Since 1970, the field of business policy has made major strides in becoming a discipline of its own with a distinctive literature of its own. This literature is fast becoming a standard part of the business policy course—and with good reason. Concepts and techniques for assessing corporate strategy, competitive position, and internal strengths and weaknesses have grown in use and are having managerial impact. More attention is consciously being given to strategy formulation and strategy implementation. There is widespread appreciation for the managerial importance of (1) a creative, insightful determination of an organization's overall strategic game plan and (2) a careful, deliberate pursuit of this game plan in ways that will enhance performance and results. While the concept of corporate strategy and the attendant methods of formal strategic analysis do not constitute a "theory" of how to manage, they very definitely do represent a "way of thinking" that illuminates the basic economics of a business, that identifies the requirements for success, and, ultimately that addresses whether a firm is doing the right things. Now academics and practitioners alike are much more alert to the whys and hows of strategic management.

In a very real sense, therefore, it is not stretching things too far to suggest that the fundamentals of strategic management are a fundamental *part* of management and managing. This applies, we think, to all levels of the management process and to all types of managers. Hence, even though many business school graduates may never reach positions of top management or have a general-manager type job, they will be in a better position to contribute to the organization as staff specialists, department heads, and lower and middle managers if they have an accurate sense of their organization's character, the direction it is heading, and how it is going to get there—in other words, if they are better able to grasp all that is meant by corporate strategy and why it is important. How to acquire this perspective and how to weigh things from an overall company point of view are the unique contributions of the business policy course.

Changes and Additions to the Text Portion. As with the first edition, the text portion of the book continues to stress the basic aspects of the process of strategic management—the tasks of defining business purpose and setting strategic objectives; deciding what businesses to enter, to get out of, and to continue with; the specifics of formulating and implementing a comprehensive strategic plan; monotoring performance and results; and reevaluating organization direction and strategy. However, this edition features some significant improvements in coverage:

1. The former six chapters of text material have been expanded to seven chapters.
2. The basic phases of the *process* of strategic management have been delineated more sharply.
3. Core concepts and methods of strategic analysis are explored in greater detail—in line with the fast-moving pace reflected in the literature.
4. Considerably more attention has been devoted to the levels of strategy and how the hierarchical web of strategies interfaces with the hierarchy of organizational objectives.
5. Chapter 3 now includes a wide-ranging discussion of both corporate-level and business-level strategy alternatives. We think it contains an unusually thorough rundown of what strategies firms have used in what situations and why.
6. The techniques for analyzing and evaluating strategy at the corporate level have been accorded chapter-length treatment. Discussions of business portfolio matrices, how to assess long-run industry attractiveness, portfolio evaluation, and the role of performance gap analysis are featured.

7. Strategy analysis at the line of business level is also organized into a separate chapter. Here the spotlight is on the strategic aspects of competition, determining a firm's competitive strength and position in a given market, and what to look for in deciding how to try to compete in a given line of business.
8. The managerial aspects of strategy implementation are addressed in two chapters, one focusing on relating structure to strategy and the other dealing with the day-to-day details of successful strategy execution.

All in all, we think you will find the text material fresh, completely updated, and better presented.

The Collection of Cases

This edition includes 34 cases and an industry note. Twenty-one of the cases are new to this edition and 13 were included in the previous edition (however, three of the holdovers—Exxon, Mobil, and Alabama Power—plus the Note on the World Petroleum Industry have been extensively revised and updated). Although we prepared several of the cases, most were written by seasoned case researchers across the country and were generously contributed to this volume.

The cases represent what we feel is a very attractive collection, especially for senior-level students. All cases been tested and found worthy in the classroom. Together they offer a solid, well-balanced mix of strategic issues and organizational circumstances. There are short cases, long cases, multiple-part cases, "two-day" cases, cases about big companies and about small companies, cases about not-for-profit organizations, cases that students will closely identify with, "change-of-pace" cases, and cases that allow intraindustry comparison. We think you will find the case package stimulating, pedagogically sound, and durable.

While the cases have been arranged in a structured sequence that generally follows the order of text discussion, the arrangement is flexible. You will have no difficulty in adjusting the sequence of cases to fit your approach. The *Instructor's Manual* contains a breakdown of topics and issues featured in each case, as well as offering suggested course outlines, alternatives on case use and case sequencing, and comprehensive teaching notes.

Additional Pedagogical Features

As in the first edition, special pains have been taken to illustrate the use of strategic management concepts in actual practice. All seven chapters of text are laced with concrete examples of the triumphs and failures of companies and their managements—what has worked, what hasn't, and why. The use of in-depth *illustration capsules* to further highlight application and of core concepts was well-received in the earlier edition and has been continued. The number of capsules has been increased from 15 to 17; and 10 are brand new. As before, the capsules aim at keeping the bridge between concept and application always open to the reader without disjointing the discussion. They have been boxed to permit a relatively detailed and extended discussion of the ways in which managers and companies rely upon the concepts of strategic management, thereby giving the reader a richer flavor and feel for how strategy/policy fundamentals are utilized in real-world management circumstances. None of the capsules is "trumped up" or a "cute attention grabber"; rather, they are no-nonsense practical applications of concepts discussed in the text. We think students will find the illustration capsules worthwhile, enjoyable, and informative. Most involve companies or people which the student will have heard of previously; and several are suitable for use as case incidents. The liberal use of examples and the illustration capsules, together with the conceptual framework, should give students a useful package of ideas and tools for the case analysis part of the course.

A chapter-length appendix is devoted to giving students positive direction in how to size up and evaluate a company and to orienting them to the pedagogy of the case method. In our experience, many students are unsure about how to conduct a full-blown analysis of a company from a strategic management and policy point of view. Appendix A is intended to lessen any student uncertainties about case analysis by focusing attention on the traditional analytical sequence of (1) identify, (2) evaluate, and (3) recommend. We have specifically included a thorough checklist of areas to examine in sizing up economic and market trends, what to look for in identifying company strengths and weaknesses, a brief review of how to calculate and interpret key financial ratios, a discussion of the nature of cases and the case method, pointers on how to learn from cases, how to prepare a case for oral class discussion, and guidelines for written case analyses. These discussions should be particularly useful for students who want assistance in making the transition from the lecture method to the case method of teaching/learning. Moreover, this chapter in conjunction with the conceptual framework, the examples, and the illustration capsules should give students a solid package of ideas and clues for doing a good job of case analysis.

Acknowledgments

Our intellectual debt to the writers and academicians upon whose concepts and contributions we have leaned heavily will be obvious to any reader familiar with the literature of strategy and policy. So also is our debt to the case researchers whose efforts appear herein and to the companies and organizations whose experiences and situations comprise the case studies.

To the case contributors, especially, go our thanks and appreciation. The importance of good, comprehensive business policy cases cannot be overestimated in contributing to a substantive study of strategy and policy. From a research standpoint, cases in strategic management are invaluable in forming hypotheses about strategic behavior and in drawing limited generalizations. Pedagogically, strategy/policy cases give students essential practice in diagnosing and evaluating strategic situations, in applying strategy/policy concepts and analytical approaches, and in developing recommendations to deal with strategy/policy problems. Without an ample supply of current cases, the discipline of business policy would indeed be in sad disrepair. We trust, therefore, that writing business policy cases will be "a growth industry" and that appropriate recognition will continue to be given to such efforts.

The following reviewers offered insightful comments and helpful suggestions for improving earlier drafts of the manuscript: W. Harvey Hegarty, Indiana University; Roger Evered, Penn State University; Charles B. Saunders, The University of Kansas; Rhae M. Swisher, Troy State University; Claude I. Shell, Eastern Michigan University; R. Thomas Lenz, Indiana University–Purdue University at Indianapolis; James B. Thurman, George Washington University; Michael C. White, Texas Tech University; Dennis W. Callahan, University of Rhode Island; R. Duane Ireland, Oklahoma State University; William E. Burr, II, University of Oregon; C. W. Millard, Iowa State University; and Richard Mann, University of Southern California. Many of their valued recommendations have been incorporated.

Naturally, as custom properly dictates, we accept responsibility for whatever errors of fact, deficiencies in logic or in exposition, and oversights that remain. Your comments about coverage and emphasis will be most welcome, as will your calling our attention to specific errors. Please write us at P.O. Box J, University, AL 35486.

Arthur A. Thompson, Jr.
A. J. Strickland, III

A SPECIAL NOTE TO STUDENTS

The topics of strategy and policy make for a challenging and exciting course. But they also make for a truly different kind of course—one which serves a unique function in the overall business school curriculum. Most of the other required and elective courses taken by business students revolve around a highly structured and well-developed body of knowledge. Many are quite "theoretical" and/or quantitative. Some relate to general knowledge and information you need to have. A few others concentrate on proven management practices, specific problems you may encounter, or special skills you may need. This course shares few of these traits. It focuses instead on the broad sweep of managerial actions and decisions which bear directly on the *total* enterprise. The center of attention is the organization in its totality—its operating environment, its corporate strategy, and its internal administrative activities. The emphasis, specifically, is on the kinds of strategic problems and issues which go to the heart of an organization's business and which determine whether it will be outstanding or mediocre or an outright failure.

Thus, where other courses in the business curriculum achieve their power by leaving out complicating variables and constraints and then zeroing in on those fairly specific kinds of concepts and problems that dovetail with well-structured models, this course attempts to wrestle with all of the determining factors at once, with what differences they make, and with how they shape what actions need to be taken. Where other courses often simplify the complexity of management's overall tasks and responsibilities and force particular issues into the Procrustean bed of their discipline (so as to make learning about the subject much easier), this course cuts across and draws upon all these other courses and disciplines. It is a "big picture" course.

The central task of the strategy/policy course is to examine how an organization must in fact deal with all the constraints and complexities of the real world, why these cannot be assumed away or ignored, and how they impact managerial decisions and actions. This means teaching you to use the knowledge gained elsewhere as tools for analysis and evaluation. It means learning to grapple with the dilemma of figuring out what is best for the total enterprise. It means helping you learn to weigh the pros and cons and to develop a stronger sense of business judgment. It means putting all the pieces of the business puzzle together and assessing the overall picture of how managerial effectiveness and organization performance might be improved. Suffice it to say, then, that this book is predicated on the thesis that the role of the strategy/policy course, in addition to offering an integrating experience, is (1) to develop your ability to see the enterprise as a whole; and (2) to understand how and why the pieces and functions of a business are interdependent and must be carefully managed for the organization to perform well.

If you are to make the most out of this book and this course you must do two things: (1) dig in and get involved, and (2) approach things from the standpoint of a practicing, professional manager rather than as a mildly curious student. Such a posture is not only conducive to the study of strategy and policy; it will also contribute (more than you might suspect) to your future development as a manager. This course is deliberately positioned in the curriculum to build your self-confidence in what has been learned from previous courses and to "put it all together" (probably for the first time). The study of concepts and cases in strategic management should start you thinking seriously about your own management style and approaches. It should instill a sense of pride and professionalism that will launch your career on a positive note.

The opportunity exists here to make this the most exciting and the best course in your curriculum. The glamour and grand sweep of strategy/policy issues will keep the course interesting and lively. Make the most of it. And ponder Ralph Waldo Emerson's acute observation, "Commerce is a game of skill which many people play, but which few play well." We hope you will be among these few.

A. A. T.
A. J. S.

CONTENTS

PART III
CASES IN STRATEGIC MANAGEMENT

LIST OF CASE CONTRIBUTORS

Case:
1. Jeffrey C. Shuman
2. Richard I. Levin and Ian Cooper
3.1 Melvin J. Stanford
3.2 Melvin J. Stanford
4. Terry Allen under the direction of Philip Thurston
5. James D. Taylor, Robert L. Johnson, and Gene B. Iverson
6. B. G. Bizzell and Ed D. Roach
7. Charles F. Douds
8. Carle M. Hunt and Richard C. Johanson
9. Jean-Pierre Jeannet
10. J. W. Brown under the direction of John Thiel
11. William R. Boulton and Phyllis G. Holland
12. Eleanor Casebier and Manning Hanline
13. Richard S. Harrigan and Burnard H. Sord
14. William E. Fulmer
15. Douglas J. Workman, Neil H. Snyder, Rich Bonaventura, John Cary, Scott McMasters, and Karen Cook
16. Arthur A. Thompson, Jr. with the assistance of Victor Gray
17. Arthur A. Thompson, Jr. with the assistance of Victor Gray
18. Arthur A. Thompson, Jr. and Victor Gray
19. A. J. Strickland with the assistance of Ken Voelker
20. Melvin J. Stanford with the collaboration of J. Weldon Moffitt
21. Richard Hamermesh
22. Arthur A. Thompson
23. Louis K. Bragaw and William R. Allen in collaboration with Daniel J. McCarthy and Robert Ames
24. Dennis M. Crites and James M. Kenderdine
25. Leon Joseph Rosenberg
26. Jeremy F. Plant
27. Ed D. Roach and Jack D. Eure
28. John R. Russel with the help of Terrence Briggs
29. Diana Johnston, Russ King, and Jay T. Knippen
30. W. Harvey Hegarty
31. Frank Leonard under the direction of J. A. Barach
32. Roger M. Atherton and Dennis M. Crites
33. William B. Callarman, Denzil Strickland, and Victor J. LaPorte, Jr.
34. Herman Gadon and Dwight R. Ladd
35. Terry Allen under the supervision of Neil H. Borden, Jr.

THE PROCESS OF STRATEGY MANAGEMENT

PART I

1 STRATEGY AND POLICY: THE FRAMEWORK OF GENERAL MANAGEMENT

"Cheshire Puss," she [Alice] began . . . "would you please tell me which way I ought to go from here?"
"That depends on where you want to get to," said the cat.

Lewis Carroll

Why are some enterprises outstanding successes, while others are only moderately or marginally successful and still others are dismal failures? What is it about an organization that tends to make it a winner or a loser? These are intriguing questions and they have attracted serious study.[1] Although what we have learned to date has produced neither a proven set of step-by-step management procedures which guarantee business success nor a genuine theory of management, the evidence does point directly to the conclusion that management and managers have a heavy hand in making organizations perform. Some of the managerial differences between successful and unsuccessful organizations are worth attention here:

1. The managers of successful organizations work hard at developing a clear sense of direction and at shaping the organization's present and

[1] Joel Ross and Michael Kami, *Corporate Management in Crisis: Why the Mighty Fall* (Englewood Cliffs, N.J.: Prentice-Hall, Inc., 1973); Seymour Tilles, "How to Evaluate Corporate Strategy," *Harvard Business Review,* vol. 41, no. 4 (July–August 1963), pp. 111–21; Dan Schendel, G. R. Patton, and James Riggs, "Corporate Turnaround Strategies," *Journal of General Management,* vol. 3, no. 3 (Spring 1976), pp. 3–11; H. Igor Ansoff et al., "Does Planning Pay? The Effect of Planning on Success of Acquisitions in American Firms," *Long-Range Planning* (December 1970), pp. 2–7; D. M. Herold, "Long-Range Planning and Organizational Performance: A Cross Validation Study," *Academy of Management Journal,* vol. 14, no. 1 (March 1971), pp. 92–102; L. W. Rue and R. M. Fulmer, "Is Long-Range Planning Profitable?" *Proceedings: Academy of Management Meetings, 1973,* pp. 66–73; S. Schoeffler, R. D. Buzzell, and D. F. Heany, "Impact of Strategic Planning on Profit Performance," *Harvard Business Review,* vol. 52, no. 2 (March–April 1974), pp. 137–45; S. S. Thune and R. T. House, "Where Long-Range Planning Pays Off," *Business Horizons,* vol. 13, no. 3 (August 1970), pp. 81–87; and Alfred D. Chandler, *The Visible Hand* (Cambridge, Mass.: Harvard University Press, 1977).

future mix of activities. The managers of unsuccessful organizations are so consumed with "putting out brush fires" and tending to administrative detail that they neglect the tasks of assessing where the organization is now and where it is headed.

2. The managers of successful organizations emphasize the formulation of an astute and opportune *strategy* for achieving target objectives and then effectively implement the chosen strategy through unified policy actions. The managers of unsuccessful organizations seldom have a comprehensive game plan which is being deliberately and systematically pursued.

3. The managers of successful organizations concentrate on gaining an insightful understanding of what business they are in, who their customers are, and why buyers want or need the organization's product/service. The managers of unsuccessful organizations are less perceptive about the hows and whys of "the market" for their product/service.

4. The managers of successful organizations exhibit a skill in engineering an effective, results-oriented system for creating, performing, and delivering the organization's product/service. In less successful organizations, management tends to be preoccupied with various sorts of internal bottlenecks, operating problems, coordinating mechanisms, and control procedures; their activities seem to be problem-focused instead of opportunity-focused and results-focused.

In short, differences among firms in sales growth, in market share, in profitability, in product innovation, in technological prowess, in quality of manufacture, in customer loyalty and satisfaction, in image and reputation, and in capacity to adapt and respond to change all seem based, to some significant degree, upon how well managers perform the related tasks of formulating an astute, timely organization strategy and then figuring out how to execute the strategic plan in ways that will produce the desired performance and results.

Where Strategy and Policy Fit in

Just why managerial skill in carrying out strategy-policy activities contributes mightily to an organization's success or failure is rooted in the familiar expression "if you don't know where you are going, any road will take you there." The point, very simply, is that *managers must consciously shape the totality of what an enterprise is and does* if the organization is to improve its chances for long-term success. This means more than just seeing that the traditional functions of manufacturing, finance, marketing, personnel, accounting, and so on are performed efficiently and then coordinated. It means more than being concerned with the nuts and bolts of daily activities, with seeing that the necessary administrative details are taken care of and that operations flow smoothly. These are obviously important but doing them well is not a surefire recipe for successful performance.

The task of managing the *total* enterprise goes beyond everyday operations and the problems and crises of the moment and takes account of how the growth and development of the organization can be sustained and enhanced. Successfully managing the totality of an organization's activities requires conscious, shrewd consideration of such crucial direction-setting actions as (1) deciding what new businesses to get into, which ones to abandon, and which ones to continue, (2) establishing long-range and short-range objectives, (3) allocating resources among the enterprise's various divisions and activities, and (4) evaluating merger and acquisition possibilities. At the same time, management must be alert for how the enterprise can develop the staying power to survive and win out over competition, product-market-technological changes, and the winds of economic uncertainty. The choices thus made are central to the molding of an organization's identity and character and to the unending definition of what needs to be done to make the organization perform.

The managerial decisions and skills that bear directly upon an organization's capacity to survive, to adapt to market and environmental changes, to grow profitably, and to perhaps move in new directions and fundamentally alter its mix of business interests form the core of what managerial strategy and policy are all about. Thus when we speak of *strategy* and *policy*, we are expressly concerned with the managerial activities associated with giving an organization purposeful direction, formulating a comprehensive strategy for accomplishing the chosen goals and objectives, marshalling and allocating the resources requisite for strategic accomplishment, and directing pursuit of the strategic plan so as to produce the desired performance and results. The concern of strategy and policy is, therefore, with the management of the *total enterprise*. It is with the nature of the forest, not of the trees.

General Management: Concept and Function

Taking a balanced, overall look at how a particular event, problem, market change, or course of action could impact the *total* organization is commonly referred to as a *general management point of view*. In fact, the term *general management* has become synonomous with the tasks of managing the total enterprise and with the particular managerial perspective and skills associated with evaluating things in terms of their impact upon the *whole* organization. In the same vein, persons charged with overall responsibility for the activities and results of an organization (or autonomous organization subunit) can be referred to as *general managers*. Because of their position, general managers are necessarily concerned with strategy-policy issues—that is to say, with the performance of the organization as a whole and with defining, deciding, and putting into effect a conscious purpose and direction appropriate to emerging opportunities, threats, and internal capabilities.

Obviously, strategy-policy decisions are matters of "top" management concern. But the strategy-policy domain does not belong exclusively to a small group of senior executives. Most large organizations and many medium-sized organizations now have general management positions at the product group level, the division level, and the departmental level—a direct outgrowth of decentralized approaches to organization. Furthermore, the strategy-policy pronouncements of higher-level managers are seldom definitive enough to provide unambiguous guidance through an uncertain future and the one-of-a-kind situations that constantly crop up. At the very least, lower-level managers must work out the details of organizational strategies and policies to meet the circumstances of daily operations. This means that a significant amount of strategy-policy discretion resides below the senior executive level. Consequently, whether in a line or a staff position, lower and middle managers influence the strategy-policy process through their everyday activities, and the ways they use to deal with day-to-day operating problems contribute to keener strategy-policy definition.

The point here is that *all* managers need to be acquainted with strategy-policy concepts and how to apply them in the context of their respective area of management responsibility. Strategy-policy issues cut through the performance of the entire management function and go to the heart of organization success or failure. The study of strategy, policy, and general management is thus not as remote from the immediate realm of lower-level managers and students of management as a first impression might indicate.

General Management Is Common to All Organizations

One final introductory observation deserves mention. How well management performs its strategy-policy functions is vital in *all types* of *organizations,* whether they be large or small, profit or not for profit. The study of managerial strategy and policy is fundamentally as applicable to a local real estate firm, a small manufacturer of chemicals, a chain of drugstores, or the Pittsburgh Steelers as to IBM and U.S. Steel. It speaks to the effective management of hospitals, educational institutions, a local YMCA, the National Organization for Women, a state department of public safety, the Ford Foundation, Sigma Chi Fraternity, the Roman Catholic Church, and the U.S. Postal Service just as much as to privately owned, profit-motivated enterprises.

In succeeding pages a serious attempt will be made to elaborate on the *general* applicability of the strategy-policy discipline to all sizes and types of organizations (although the major emphasis will focus on profit-seeking enterprises operating in a competitive market environment). We shall endeavor to stress how and why the study of strategy and policy is important, how it relates to the problems of general managers, and how it represents a way of thinking and a perspective view that zeros in on what and where an organization is now, where it is headed, and how its performance might be improved.

BASIC CONCEPTS OF STRATEGY MANAGEMENT

It will prove useful if, at the outset, we get a firmer grip on some of the key concepts and terminology that serve as the foundation for the management of strategy and policy. This is especially important because in talking and writing about management such terms as purpose, objectives, goals, strategy, and policy are variously defined and interpreted.

Organization Purpose and Mission

Simply stated, *purpose* and *mission* refer to a long-term vision of what an organization seeks to do and the markets and customers it seeks to serve. Purpose is management's concept of the organization's character, image, and range of business interests. An organization's purpose, when expressed in managerially meaningful terms, provides a view of what activities the organization as a whole intends to pursue now and in the future. It says something about what kind of organization it is now and is to become and, by omission, what it is not to do and not to become.[2] It depicts an organization's business character and does so in ways that are detailed enough to distinguish the organization from other types of organizations.

Presented below are examples of how several prominent companies describe themselves and their business role (all taken from their respective annual reports):

Standard Oil of Ohio

The Standard Oil Company is an integrated domestic petroleum company engaged in all phases of the petroleum business including the production of crude oil and natural gas and the transportation, refining and marketing of crude oil and petroleum products. Through its ownership of oil and gas leases at Prudhoe Bay on the North Slope of Alaska and the development of the Prudhoe Bay oil reserves, the Company is the largest holder of domestic proved crude oil reserves and it is one of the leading producers of domestic crude oil. In addition, the Company is engaged in the mining and marketing of coal and uranium and the manufacture and marketing of chemical and plastic products.

Wendy's International, Inc.

Wendy's International, Inc. operates and franchises a chain of quick service hamburger restaurants under the name of "Wendy's Old Fashioned Hamburgers." . . .

Restaurant decor and food are in keeping with the theme of "old-fashioned hamburgers." The menu consists of large size ($\frac{1}{4}$, $\frac{1}{2}$, $\frac{3}{4}$ pound), cooked-to-order, fresh meat hamburgers, enough condiments to provide 256 combina-

---

[2] C. Roland Christensen, Kenneth R. Andrews, and Joseph L. Bower, *Business Policy: Text and Cases,* 4th ed. (Homewood, Ill.: Richard D. Irwin, 1978), p. 125. For a more extended discussion see Kenneth R. Andrews, *The Concept of Corporate Strategy,* rev. ed. (Homewood, Ill.: Richard D. Irwin, Inc., 1980), chaps. 1 and 2.

tions, chili, Frosty dairy dessert, french fries, and beverages. A warm dining atmosphere is enhanced by Tiffany lamps, colorful beads, rosewood paneling, tabletops printed with reproductions of 19th century advertising, carpeted floors, and bentwood chairs.

General Motors

General Motors is a highly integrated business engaged primarily in the manufacture, assembly and sale of automobiles, trucks and related parts, and accessories classified as automotive products. Substantially all of General Motors' products are marketed through retail dealers and through distributors and jobbers in the United States and Canada and through distributors and dealers overseas. To assist in the merchandising of General Motors products, General Motors Acceptance Corporation and its subsidiaries offer financial services and certain types of automobile insurance to dealers and customers.

Fuqua Industries

. . . Fuqua Industries . . . is a multimarket manufacturing, distribution and service company with businesses in the areas of Recreational Products and Services, Farm and Home Products, Transportation, Petroleum Distribution, and Other Operations.

In each of these market areas, Fuqua prides itself upon providing high quality products and services. Recreational Products and Services include photofinishing, entertainment, and sporting goods. The Farm and Home Products segment covers lawn and garden equipment, shelter products, and retail farm, home and auto stores. Interstate Motor Freight System and the Direct System comprise Fuqua's Transportation group. In the area of Petroleum Distribution, Fuqua is a wholesale distributor of refined petroleum products. Fuqua's Other Operations include Industrial Services and Food Products . . .

Fuqua Industries has grown by acquiring well-managed businesses and providing them with the financial resources and management support for internal expansion. Although widely diversified, Fuqua's companies generally have a high market share and low capital intensity.

Tandy Corporation

Tandy Corporation is engaged in consumer electronics retailing and manufacturing with more than 6,500 Radio Shack retail outlets in all 50 United States and Canada. The Company also conducts retail operations in England, Belgium, Holland, West Germany, France, Australia and Japan through approximately 650 outlets under the Tandy name. The average Radio Shack store is slightly over 2,100 square feet and stocks more than 2,400 different items. Radio Shack stores carry a multitude of electronic products including antennas, radios, receivers, magnetic tape, speakers, turntables, public address systems, intercoms, calculators, electronic and scientific toys, games and kits, citizens band radios, scanners, and electronic parts. The TRS-80™ Microcomputer System introduced in August 1977 is the most successful product category innovation in Radio Shack's history.

Houston Oil & Minerals Corporation

Houston Oil & Minerals Corporation is engaged in the exploration for production of natural resources. Major emphasis is on domestic exploration for oil and gas on undeveloped properties. The domestic oil and gas exploration efforts are concentrated in the Texas and Louisiana Gulf Coast area, but exploration has expanded into the Rocky Mountains, West Texas, and the Atlantic and Gulf of Mexico outer continental shelf. The Company is also engaged in the domestic and foreign exploration for minerals, foreign exploration for oil and gas, interstate gas gathering operations, and products trading. The Company currently has no production of minerals and no foreign production of oil or gas.

Avon

Avon is the world's largest manufacturer and distributor of cosmetics, fragrances and costume jewelry . . . we offer approximately 600 products, all covered by the Avon Guarantee of satisfaction, and there are almost a million active independent Representatives worldwide.

Since our founding, Representatives have always sold our products on a person-to-person, direct-selling basis. These men and women operate their own businesses in their communities. Today, more than ever, their customers appreciate the friendly, reliable and personal service they offer.

Service to these Representatives was provided by 27,300 Avon employees worldwide. The top-quality products they manufacture, process and deliver, and the administrative and promotional support they provide help Representatives successfully conduct their businesses.

Observe that each of these statements is both broad and narrow. All are broad in the sense of cutting across several distinct types of products, customers, and markets to be served, but they are narrow in the sense of delimiting the nature and character of the organization's business interests. This is as it should be. It serves no useful function for business purpose to be so narrowly conceived that it confines the enterprise's growth and development or else restricts its adaptation to changing business and economic conditions.[3] On the other hand, there is little to be gained from management's conceiving organization purpose and mission in such broad and ambiguous language as to obscure what the firm's central character and range of operations really is and is going to be. An umbrella-like statement that "our purpose is to serve the food needs of the nation" can mean anything from growing wheat to operating a vegetable cannery to delivering milk to manufacturing farm machinery to running a Kentucky Fried Chicken franchise.

A sweeping statement of purpose may occasionally have public relations value, but it is certainly *too broad to guide management action*. It does not establish direction nor does it narrow down and focus management attention on what the firm is actually trying to do. It offers no guidance to the firm's

---

[3] Of course, any "danger" of an organization "locking itself in" with an overly narrow concept of purpose is contrived rather than real. Organization purpose is always subject to revision and is not something "carved in stone." Many, if not most, organizations fundamentally change the scope of their activities (and hence their purpose) from time to time. This is particularly true of firms which, for one reason or another, diversify into activities well outside their original business (as when a cigarette manufacturing company diversifies into brewing beer).

managers in developing sharply focused, results-oriented objectives, strategies, and policies—and this is where the real value of a carefully reasoned purpose comes into play. A clear understanding of organization purpose is the starting point for rational managerial action and for the effective design of organization structure, processes, and procedures. Said a bit differently, real management of the *total* enterprise begins with clarity of purpose—with an astute understanding of the central character of the organization, where it is now and where it is headed, and what it should and should not be doing and for whom.

Notice here that the focus of organization purpose is external rather than internal. While it is tempting to view the purpose of a business firm as one of "making a profit," this typifies all profit-seeking enterprises and thus distinguishes none.[4] Profit is more accurately a *result* of doing something; to look upon purpose as being to make a profit poses the immediate question of "what will we *do* to make a profit?" It is the answer to "make a profit doing what?" that identifies and defines business purpose. Ultimately, therefore, purpose is always found outside the organization in what it is undertaking and trying to accomplish. This means viewing purpose in terms of markets and customers to be served and, even more fundamentally, in terms of the wants or needs customers satisfy when they utilize the organization's product or service. In this regard, Peter Drucker, in *Management: Tasks, Responsibilities, Practices,* maintains:

> To know what a business is we have to start with its *purpose.* Its purpose must lie outside of the business itself. In fact, it must lie in society since business enterprise is an organ of society. There is only one valid definition of business purpose: *to create a customer.*[5]

Drucker's insightful point about purpose is that unless an organization can develop a sufficiently large clientele for its product/service, it is destined to wither and die. The customer is the foundation of an organization and keeps it in existence.[6] This alone is reason enough to define the purpose of an enterprise in terms of the clientele to be served and the customer wants and needs to be satisfied.

---

[4] Philip Kotler, *Marketing Management: Analysis, Planning, Control* (Englewood Cliffs, N.J.: Prentice-Hall, Inc. 1976), p. 52.

[5] (New York: Harper & Row, Publishers, 1974), p. 61.

[6] Ibid. Moreover, according to Drucker, every organization, profit seeking or not for profit, has an implied contract with society that calls not only for the organization's purpose to be ratified by its customers but also for the organization's activities to be consistent with the expectations of society at large. Society has, after all, entrusted a portion of its pool of scarce, productive resources to the organization and thus has a right to expect they not be misused. For this reason, failure to act in socially responsible ways or to perform socially useful functions quite properly tends to trigger serious societal scrutiny of an organization's activities and, usually, a reevaluation by the organization of its purpose and behavior.

Organization Objectives

Objectives refer to the specific kinds of results which an organization seeks to achieve in pursuing its purpose and mission.[7] Ideally, organizational objectives should relate (1) *externally* to the desired impact upon the organization's customers in terms of satisfaction, product performance, and meeting individual and societal wants and needs and (2) *internally* to the desired organizational performance and results—that is, market share, growth, profitability, cash flow, return on investment, and so on. By delineating the results which are to be achieved, objectives give concrete meaning to the general direction indicated in management's vision of purpose.

Unless and until an organization's purpose is converted into *specific* targets and *specific* actions, there is greater risk of it remaining a statement of good intentions and unrealized achievement. Setting objectives reduces this risk in managerially useful ways because when the desired results are made concrete and measurable, it is more likely that (1) resources can and will be allocated to their attainment, (2) priorities can be agreed upon and deadlines set, and (3) responsibility can be assigned and somebody held accountable for producing the desired results. Consequently, the managerial role of objectives is, first and foremost, to serve as a vehicle for transforming broad direction into *concrete, measurable action commitments.*[8] The specifications for properly formulated objectives include the following:

They must give explicit direction (and not take the form of vague abstractions and pious platitudes).

They must be measurable (stated in quantitative terms whenever feasible).

They must set forth organizational priorities.

---

[7] The literature of management is filled with references to *goals* and *objectives*. These terms are used in a variety of ways, many of them conflicting. Some writers use the term goals to refer to the *long-run* results which an organization seeks to achieve and use the term objectives to refer to immediate, *short-run* performance targets. Other writers reverse the usage, referring to objectives as the desired long-run results and goals as the desired short-run results. Still other writers use the terms interchangeably, as synonyms. And still others use the term goals to refer to *general* organization-wide performance targets and the term objectives to mean the specific targets set by subordinate managers in response to the broader, more inclusive goals of the whole organization. In our view, the semantical confusion over the usage of the terms goals and objectives is secondary; the important thing is to recognize that the results a firm seeks to attain vary both in scope and in time perspective. In nearly every instance, those organizations which are results-oriented will tend to establish a hierarchy of both long-range and short-range performance targets. Practically speaking, it makes no difference what labels one attaches to these targets. Thus we have deliberately chosen to use the single term *objectives* to refer to the performance targets and results which an organization seeks to attain. We will use the adjectives long-range (or long-run) and short-range (or short-run) to identify the relevant time frame and we will endeavor to describe objectives in such a way as to indicate their intended scope and level in the organization.

[8] Drucker, *Management,* p. 99.

They must be the real basis for management action and act as *the* guidelines for management decisions.

They must serve as the cornerstones for designing jobs and for organizing the activities to be performed.

They must be the yardstick of achievement.

They must serve as the standards against which individuals and groups are judged in terms of their having done a good job or not.[9]

Illustration Capsule 1 contains a number of possible organizational objectives, some clearly defined and some poorly phrased, so as to indicate the nature and features of properly formulated objectives.

Since the role of objectives is to guide the concentration of resources and efforts toward the desired ends, objectives should be selective as opposed to all-encompassing. But this by no means implies that management can or should rely upon just a single organizational objective. On the contrary, objectives are needed in *all areas* on which the *survival* and *success* of the organization depend and they are needed at all levels of management from the corporate level on down to the first level of supervision.[10] Moreover, it is normally desirable to develop both long-range objectives and short-range objectives. *Long-range objectives* keep management alert to what has to be done *now* to attain the desired results later. *Short-range objectives* serve to indicate the speed and momentum which management seeks to maintain in accomplishing longer range objectives and purpose; they direct the attention of managers and organizational subunits toward the desired standards of performance and behavior in the near term.

Long-Run Objectives. From a long-run corporatewide perspective, most organizations have need for:

1. *Sales, growth, and marketing objectives*—so as to create a viable, sustainable customer base and market for its products/services.
2. *Technology-innovation objectives*—so as to keep products/services up-to-date and competitive (thereby avoiding obsolescence).
3. *Profitability and financial objectives*—so as to cover the risks of economic activity, test the validity of the organization's contributions, and generate the financial capital requisite for preserving (and enhancing if necessary) the organization's productive capability.
4. *Efficiency objectives*—so as to remain cost competitive and to make judicious use of the economic resources entrusted by society to its care.
5. *Resource supply objectives*—so as to work toward the availability of whatever human, capital, and natural resources are needed for continuing to supply customers (society) with the organization's products/services.

---

[9] Ibid., pp. 99–102.

[10] Ibid., p. 100. See also Charles H. Granger, "The Hierarchy of Objectives," *Harvard Business Review,* vol. 42, no. 3 (May–June 1963), pp. 63–74.

Examples of "Good" and "Bad" Organizational Objectives

Examples of "good" (clearly defined) objectives

Remarks

1. "We plan to make Product X the number one selling brand in its field in terms of units sold by 1985."

   Leaves little doubt as to the intended sales objective and market standing.

2. "We strive to be a leader, not a follower, in introducing new products and in implementing new technologies by spending no less than 5% of sales revenue for R & D."

   Indicates an attempt to remain on or near technological frontiers and says how this attempt is to be financed.

3. "Our profit objective is to increase earnings per share by a minimum of 8% annually and to earn at least a 20% after-tax return on net worth."

   Clear, concrete, and readily measured.

4. "We seek to produce the most durable, maintenance-free product that money can buy."

   An obvious focus on being the leader with respect to high quality.

5. "It is our objective to help assure that the wood products needs of this country are met by planting two seedlings for every tree we cut and by following exemplary forest management practices."

   A specific commitment.

Examples of "bad" (poorly phrased) objectives

Remarks

1. "Our objective is to maximize sales revenue and unit volume?"

   Not subject to measurement. What dollar figure constitutes maximum sales? Also, may be inconsistent; the price and output which generate the greatest dollar revenue is almost certainly not the same as the combination which will yield the largest possible unit volume.

2. "No new idea is too extreme and we will go to great lengths to develop it."

   Too broad. No firm has the money or capability to investigate any and every idea that it comes across. To even try is to march in all directions at once.

3. "We seek to be the most profitable company in our industry."

   Vague. By what measures of profit—total dollars? earnings per share? return on sales? return on equity investment? all of these?

4. "In producing our products we strive to minimize costs and maximize efficiency."

   What are the standards by which costs will be said to be minimum and efficiency maximum? How will management know when the objective has been achieved?

5. "We intend to meet our responsibilities to stockholders, customers, employers, and the public."

   In what respects? As determined by whom? More a platitude than an action commitment.

6. *Social responsibility objectives*—so as to keep the organization in tune with societal expectations and priorities and, in particular, to keep management alert to the positive and negative impacts which organizational activities can have on the environment at large.

The foregoing list is, of course, by no means exhaustive. An organization may wish to have long-run objectives relating to industry leadership, competitive position, overall size and degree of diversification, technological capability, the financial payoffs it seeks to provide stockholders in the form of dividends and capital gains, and vulnerability to recession. The essential consideration is that the chosen *set* of objectives signify, in specific terms, just what kinds of performance and results management wants the organization to produce.

Because long-run objectives relate to the ongoing activities of an organization, their achievement tends to be open-ended in the sense of not being bounded by time. For example, the objective of survival is never completely attained since failure and bankruptcy are always future possibilities. A long-run objective of 10 percent growth in sales and profits continues on into the future even though it may have been successfully reached in the past.

Short-run Objectives. An organization's short-run objectives act as the intermediate quantitative and qualitative performance targets which management wishes to attain in moving toward long-run objectives. Because short-run objectives are inherently keyed to the pursuit of longer-run objectives, they should have five features: (1) they should relate to some specific long-run objective or set of long-run objectives; (2) they should be measurable and reflect the progress being made in achieving long-run objectives; (3) they should specify a time frame for accomplishment; (4) they should be internally consistent such that any conflicts that pit the achievement of one against another are resolved and the affected objectives revised; and (5) they should be realistic in the sense of being within the reach of organizational capability and within what market and competitive conditions will allow. Once short-run objectives are agreed upon both for the organization as a whole and for each subordinate level and activity, then they should be ranked according to priority. The following statements are illustrations of short-run objectives:

1. We have set our sights on a target market share of 15 percent this year and 17.5 percent next year.
2. Our objective every year is the same—to win the national championship.
3. The company's immediate objective is to open up at least two new sales territories each year for the next five years to boost our market coverage to eight states.
4. We intend to reduce new store openings by 10 percent this year.
5. Our immediate target is to increase donations and contributions by 20 percent.

6. Our aim is to cutback staffing requirements by 5 percent each of the next three years.
7. We seek to gain enough new accounts this year to reach our interim objective of $50 million in deposits.
8. We aim to reduce infant mortality rates to less than 1 per 1000 births within 12 months.
9. The plant's annual production objective is an output rate close to 95 percent of rated capacity.
10. The objective of this year's rush is to get 20 new pledges.

Observe that the statements all reflect a short-range target level of achievement. Contrast this with the longer term continuing focus of the stated objectives in Illustration Capsule 1.

The Hierarchy of Objectives. Correctly formulated and applied objectives are a potentially powerful management tool for keeping the whole organization's attention focused on achieving the right kinds of results. Objectives point to what is important and to where resources and energies should be aimed. Thus, from a management perspective, objectives should be formulated and stated in such a way that they decompose into work, into specific tasks, into assignment of responsibility, and into deadlines. Moreover, objectives are needed not only at the corporate level for the organization as a whole but also for each of the specific lines of business and products in which the organization has an interest and, further, for each division and department within the organization structure. When every manager, from the chief executive officer on down to the first-line supervisor, is (1) involved in formulating objectives at his/her level of job responsibility and (2) committed to achieving the agreed-upon objectives, then objectives can be used as rallying points for coordinating the activities of organizational subunits and as a basis for establishing common purpose in the performance of diverse tasks. Acceptance of organizational objectives by the people concerned promotes teamwork and a united approach to fulfilling the organization's purpose and mission. To the extent that this occurs the result is to turn the objectives hierarchy into a tool both for channeling resources and for appraising the performance of (1) the organization as a whole, (2) organizational subunits, and (3) individual managers. Illustration Capsule 2 provides an inside look at the managerial role and function of organizational objectives.

Organization Strategy

In almost every case, an organization will have several viable options for going about what it is trying to do—as the old adage goes "there's more than one way to skin a cat." *Strategy* serves the function of indicating *how* management has chosen to reach organizational objectives. It is a blueprint of the organizational game plan. It says in specific terms how the organization intends to get where it wants to go. It indicates what management's program

Illustration Capsule 2

The Role and Function of Objectives

The following remarks of a vice president of marketing for a small candy manufacturer illustrate the internal role and function of objectives. Observe that the
manager uses the terms *goals* and *objectives* interchangeably whereas we distinguish between short-run objectives and long-run objectives (see footnote 7).

Basically I'm trying to operate so my people will grow along with the company. I set high standards. I know they won't all be met, but at least people will
know what I'm looking for. I expect a subordinate to have ideas and to have
plans on what he wants to do and how. I may differ with him, and I'll explain why
I think another way is better, but I don't penalize people for doing things their
own way. What I want is results, and if a man has his own way, that's O.K.

Our regional men and brokers have quotas and also specific goals to reach
in each market. I ask them to set a quota for themselves, partly to get their
appraisal of a market and partly so I can appraise their motivation and judgment. I don't want them to promise pie in the sky, but neither do I want to see
them aiming low to be sure of hitting it and getting a bonus.

We give each regional manager a discretionary fund to spend as he pleases.
It's only $5,000, but it is important in a couple of ways. For one thing the way a
man uses it helps me appraise his judgment. Second, it makes him a much more
important part of the organization. The brokers look to him to use some of the
money for promotions in their territory—so it helps the regional man get the
broker's cooperation. And don't forget that it's the strength of our distribution
that has let us grow rapidly on so little money.

All this field work is done within the general framework of corporate marketing objectives. We write these up and send them out to each broker and regional man. Each month we send him a rundown on how he is doing compared
to the objectives (based on information from the IBM reports). At the end of the
year we go over the plan and each unfulfilled objective with every man. We try to
determine if we were unrealistic, if it was unavoidable, or if it was a lack of
something on his part. It isn't done to crucify someone; we want our objectives
and quotas to be realistic or they are worse than useless. We want each man to
believe he can hit them, so it's important that we all understand why they
weren't reached.*

* As quoted in George A. Smith, Jr., C. Roland Christensen, Norman A. Berg, and Malcolm S.
Salter, *Policy Formulation and Administration*, 6th ed. (Homewood, III.: Richard D. Irwin, 1972),
pp. 363–64. Copyright © 1972, Richard D. Irwin, Inc. Used with permission.

of action will be over both the short term and the long term. It is the guide for
the enterprise's development and indicates how management intends to
shape and align the organization's activities to take into account both the
external environment and internal constraints.

It should be obvious from this brief description that the concept of strategy bears directly on *how* an enterprise is to be managed—that is, how
management intends to go about achieving the target objectives and fulfilling
the organization's purpose and mission. In particular, strategy embraces four
areas of management concern:

1. The choice of products, markets, and types of businesses the organization will enter, stay in, and get out of.
2. How an organization's perhaps diverse range of activities will be integrated, coordinated, and otherwise fit together to make a workable whole.
3. What priorities and guidelines are to be observed in allocating organizational resources among various products, divisions, and activities.
4. How the organization intends to compete in each one of the businesses in which it engages.

General Electric, one of the pioneers in the development and use of the concept of strategy, has simplified these areas of strategic concern into the following capsule definition: strategy is a statement of how what resources are going to be used to take advantage of which opportunities to minimize which threats to produce a desired result. This view of strategy emphasizes that for organizations to survive, and certainly for them to perform, management must seek to position an organization in its environment such that it can be effective in utilizing internal competencies and resources to take advantage of external opportunities and/or to reduce the impact to externally imposed threats.

One example of how strategy is used to guide an enterprise's development is given by Beatrice Foods' transformation from a local dairy operation into a $5 billion company:

> Beginning as a local butter and egg company in Beatrice, Nebraska, the company began an effort to diversify its product line and reduce its dependence on local conditions. It started by acquiring a string of small dairies. From the outset, Beatrice followed two key principles—diversification and decentralization. Only firms headed by independent-minded entrepreneurs were brought into the fold. Although Beatrice found that the dairy business had the disadvantage of low profit margins, it had the advantage of generating a lot of excess cash (mainly because inventories of milk are provided by nature and do not require endless financing). Thus, having acquired dairies coast to coast and grown into a $200 million dairy company, Beatrice began to invest some of its cash in higher-margin food companies. LaChoy Food Products was the first acquisition and, when it worked out well, Beatrice began to push into other food lines at an accelerating rate. In the 1960s Beatrice acquired some non-food firms and by the 1970s owned several different kinds of manufacturing operations, a warehousing division, and an insurance company. Among its products are such brands as Samsonite (luggage), Meadow Gold (dairy products), Martha White (flour), Dannon (yogurt), Clark (candy bars), Eckrich (meats), Gebhardt's (chili and tamales), and LaChoy (Chinese foods).
>
> Beatrice's acquisition strategy followed some strict guidelines. Commodity-oriented firms were excluded because of the unpredictable price swings. Companies in head-on competition with such powerhouses as Kellogg's and Campbell Soups were avoided. In the non-food areas, Beatrice shied away from labor-intensive companies because of the risks of inflation of labor costs. Industries like steel and chemicals were avoided because of their heavy capital demands.

The basic acquisition strategy was to go after companies with at least five years of sales and profit increases, and to eliminate from consideration any firm so large that failure could seriously damage Beatrice's overall profitability. Between 1952 and 1962 most of the acquired firms had sales of about $2 million. While Beatrice sought companies with a growth rate higher than its own, it insisted on a purchase price keyed to a price-earnings multiple about one-third below Beatrice's own current price-earnings ratio. Beatrice was generally successful in buying firms it wanted at a "discount" because the Beatrice stock it was offering in return had performed so very well over the years.

In 1977, Beatrice Foods overtook Kraft and Esmark to become the nation's largest food processor.[11] Another example of the use of strategy to accomplish objectives is given in Illustration Capsule 3.

Illustration Capsule 3

Northwest Industries' Strategy for Coping with Inflation and Producing Real Growth

In November 1978, Northwest Industries explained what its strategies were for lessening the impact of inflation on its operations and on its stockholders:

No company can control or even completely foresee the rate of inflation. But at Northwest Industries we're always trying to lessen its influence on our operations. We do this by sticking with longstanding management strategies that are particularly helpful in uncertain times.

Our goal is to produce real growth. And that means to maximize the total return to our stockholders—including dividend income.

Vertical Integration

One tool we use is vertical integration. It doesn't just provide cost efficiencies. It also helps insulate our operating companies from price volatility in purchased materials and services. For instance, our General Battery Corporation's integrated production processes include everything from secondary lead smelting and plastic case manufacturing to the delivery of batteries by the company's own truck distribution system. This kind of control helps keep our product costs both reasonable and comparatively predictable.

We also have a conscious policy of making forward commitments on key raw materials well into the future—far longer than many of our competitors. Occasionally we guess wrong and miss out on falling prices. But we like the advantage of having known costs for an extended period of time. For instance, by settling now on future cotton costs, Union Underwear Company can stabilize an important cost element. This helps Union plan production and price its goods sensibly. But be sure of this: we are *not* speculators or commodity traders. We are manufacturers.

---

[11] For a more complete discussion of Beatrice's strategy and operating philosophy, see Linda Grant Martin, "How Beatrice Foods Sneaked Up on $5 Billion," *Fortune* (April 1976), pp. 118–29.

Illustration Capsule 3 (continued)

Efficient Production

Efficient production also helps us fight inflation. Almost all of our companies are industry leaders. That allows us advantages many competitors do not have, so we can make good products at lower costs. And when it comes to maintaining or increasing margins in an inflationary environment, our companies frequently do the job through cost reduction rather than by relying simply on price increases.

Another way our companies maintain margins without price increase is by upgrading product mix. They drop lower margin goods to concentrate on more profitable items. This ensures our facilities are utilized for maximum profitability. An example is Acme Boot Company getting out of the manufacturing of golf and dress shoes to make and sell more western boots. A simple move, but effective.

Acquisition Criteria

That we seek stability in an unstable economy is also evident in our acquisition criteria. These criteria generally rule out companies subject to unusually large cyclical swings. We avoid companies that are dependent on a single supplier or customer. We never want to be in a position where a customer or supplier can control our bottom line. Also, we avoid highly labor intensive businesses. We believe we can control the availability of capital more easily than the availability of labor.

U.S. Orientation

Another way we have tried to insulate our stockholders from uncertainty is by keeping Northwest's earnings coming essentially from the United States, and for good reason. With ninety-five percent of our earnings U.S.-based, we have avoided the comparatively high rates of inflation and the unstable economies of many countries, not to mention the damaging effects of fickle policy changes by foreign governments. In so doing, we have largely avoided the vagaries of foreign currency fluctuations.

Every policy we follow—whether it pertains to management, manufacturing, or marketing—seeks to add stability to our rates of growth. And not just growth at the rate of inflation, but at a considerably higher rate.

Source: Ad appearing in *Business Week*, November 20, 1978, pp. 168–69.

Organization Policy

Whereas strategy depicts how the organization's purpose and objectives are to be accomplished, it is the role of management policy to guide and channel the implementation of strategy and to prescribe how internal organization processes will function and be administered. Thus, the term *policy* refers to the organizational methods, procedures, rules, and administrative practices associated with converting the strategic plan into results.[12] In this sense, policies are internal procedural guides to carrying out strategy; they set boundaries and limit the kinds and directions of administrative actions which are to be taken. They are the result of institutionalizing and operationalizing the chosen strategy and of getting the organization into a position of being able to execute the strategic plan effectively and efficiently.

Plainly, in the managerial scheme of things, administrative policy is (or should be!) subordinate to and supportive of strategy and purpose, since it signals what should and should not be done to further achievement of the desired strategic performance and results. Examples of policies which an organization might adopt in support of its overall purpose and strategy include:

1. A retail grocery chain giving store managers authority to buy fresh produce locally when they can get a better buy, rather than ordering from the regional warehouse.
2. An oil company's deciding to lease the properties and buildings for its service station operations so as to minimize long-term capital requirements.
3. A graduate school of business deciding not to admit to its MBA program any applicant who does not have at least two years of business experience as well as a B average on all undergraduate coursework.
4. A firm's practice of requiring each of its product divisions and profit centers to file weekly sales and profit reports with headquarters as a means of monitoring and evaluating progress toward corporate goals.
5. A hospital's requiring all patients to make a $100 cash deposit upon being admitted, as part of its plan for maintaining financial solvency.

Policy make take the form of written statements, or it may consist of unwritten understandings of past actions (which may or may not be intended to establish precedent or frames of reference for future action). The need for both major and minor policy guides exists at all levels in the management structure. Thus, the scope of policy statements may range widely from such

---

[12] In management literature, definition and actual use of the term *policy* is far from uniform. In years past, it was common and customary to refer to "policy" to describe company purpose, company direction, and ways of doing business—a usage which makes policy and strategy indistinguishable. However, this overlap in usage is giving way to a conceptual difference between strategy and policy similar to the one we have been using here. Nonetheless, there are times when both academicians and practitioners use the term policy to refer to top management pronouncements on what course of action a company will follow (it is our "policy" not to diversify into markets where we lack technological proficiency) and on statements of management intent (it is our "policy" to pay dividends equal to 50 percent of net earnings per share). It is important for the reader to be alert, therefore, to the fact that policy is sometimes used in a much broader sense than we have defined it here; our definition is a relatively narrow one. The definition we presented tends to equate "policy" with those managerial actions and decisions relating specifically to strategy implementation and execution. We think this is advantageous since it permits a sharper conceptual distinction to be made between those actions and decisions relating primarily to strategy formulation and those relating to strategy administration. In practice, as we shall later point out, strategy and policy decisions blur and shade into one another.

lofty principles as "It is company policy to give our customers complete satisfaction or their money back" and "We are an equal opportunity employer" down to such mundane matters as "It is company policy not to accept personal checks for more than the amount of purchase" and "It is the policy of this organization to pay one-half of the tuition fees of any employee who wishes to further his education."

Some policies concern operating procedures and amount to little more than work rules, as in the case of statements specifying the length of coffee breaks and the methods for obtaining reimbursement for travel expenses. Yet, others may provide vital support to an organization's strategic plan—for example, General Motors' policy of trying to standardize as many parts as possible in producing its many different models of Chevrolets, Pontiacs, Buicks, Oldsmobiles, and Cadillacs was aimed at achieving greater mass production economies and minimizing the working capital tied up in parts inventories.

Whatever the scope and form, the managerial thrust of policy is to set organizational mechanisms in place that will support strategic success.

THE INTERRELATIONSHIPS AMONG PURPOSE, OBJECTIVES, STRATEGY, AND POLICY

Taken together, an organization's purpose and objectives set forth *exactly what the organization intends to do and to accomplish*—in both the short run and long run. Purpose delineates an organization's service mission to customers and to society; long- and short-run objectives serve to indicate the organization's priorities and commitments to specific results. Strategy, then, addresses the issue of precisely how the desired results are to be accomplished; it is the means to the end, the game plan, the outline of how things are to be done, the blueprint for getting the organization where it wants to go. Policy refers to strategy implementation—the organizational procedures, practices, and structure associated with administering the strategic plan and operating the organization on a day-to-day basis. In conjunction, organizational purpose, objectives, strategy, and policy define an overall grand design for the organization and indicate the guidelines and principles by which it is to be managed. Figure 1–1 depicts these relationships.

It should be emphasized at this point that in actual situations it is not always easy to distinguish sharply between purpose and objectives, between objectives and strategy, and between strategy and policy. We have tried to maintain a fairly clear-cut separation in our definitions and conceptual descriptions, so as to better expose the elements inherent in charting and following an organization's course and path of development. But, unfortunately, definitions are not always well-settled nor are they strictly adhered to in practice. Words like purpose, objectives, strategy, and policy are "accordianlike" in the sense that they include statements which can span the spectrum from broad to narrow, very important to comparatively unimportant,

FIGURE 1–1
Schematic of the Relationships among Purpose, Objectives, Strategy, and Policy

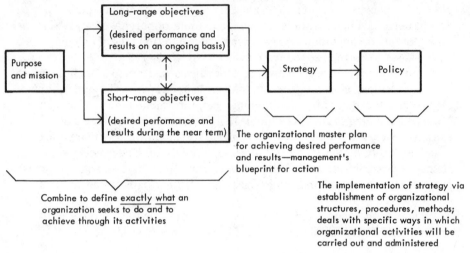

and general to specific. Moreover, statements of purpose and mission shade into objectives, objectives shade into strategies, and strategies shade into policies. An indication of the possibility for overlap and blurring is given by the statement "Our major objective is to be a diversified, growing, and profitable company with emphasis on manufacturing electronic products and components for worldwide use in industry, government, and the home." This statement, which is not unusual, contains an indication of what the company is trying to do (its purpose and mission); it suggests the existence of several objectives (diversification, growth, profitability); and it has hints of strategy (the emphasis on manufacturing electronic products and its identification of target markets).

The blurring and overlap among purpose, objectives, strategy, and policy suggest an even more important point, however. The sequence of steps from purpose to objectives to strategy to policy implied in Figure 1–1 is not something that managers actually do sequentially. In practice, the steps are interrelated and can be undertaken more or less simultaneously. This is particularly true of the three direction-setting components—purpose, objectives, and strategy. Strategy is plainly predicated upon and intertwined with an organization's purpose and objectives; at the same time, though, strategy (especially a highly successful one) bends back to influence objectives and purpose. There is two-way cause and effect. Thus, to consider purpose, objectives, and strategy as interconnected and integral parts of an overall strategic plan accurately lumps together the key direction-setting components of an organization's activities.

Summary Definitions of Terms

Purpose consists of a long-term vision of what an organization seeks to do and what kind of organization it intends to become.

Objectives define the specific kinds of performance and results which an organization seeks to produce through its activities.

Long-range objectives are the desired performance and results on an ongoing basis.

Short-range objectives are the near-term organizational performance targets which an organization desires to attain in progressing toward its long-range objectives.

Strategy refers to a blueprint of the organizational game plan; it indicates how the organization intends to get where it wants to go.

Policy concerns the implementation and execution of the chosen strategy via whatever organizational procedures, practices and mechanisms are helpful in carrying out and administering the organization's activities.

Strategy Formulation encompasses the process whereby management in effect develops an organization's purpose and mission, derives specific objectives, and chooses a strategy; includes all of the direction-setting components of managing the *total* organization.

Strategy Implementation embraces the full range of managerial activities associated with putting the chosen strategy into place and supervising its pursuit.

THE PROCESS OF STRATEGY MANAGEMENT

From a conceptual standpoint, the strategic functions of managers break down into four distinct categories: *strategy formulation, strategy implementation*, the *measurement of strategic performance*, and *strategy evaluation*. These are depicted in Figure 1–2 and together they comprise the *process of strategy management*.

Strategy Formulation and Entrepreneurship

The managerial task of formulating a timely strategy for an organization is primarily *entrepreneurial* in character and focus. The key strategy-formulating activities consist of an entrepreneurial size-up of whether an organization is *doing the right things* and how it can be *more effective in what it does*. It entails working at being shrewd and perceptive enough to move the enterprise in the right direction at the right time, to set the right priorities, and to fund their pursuit. The need here is to enhance the organization's capacity for producing *extraordinary* results, generating *superior* organization

FIGURE 1-2
The Process of Strategy Management

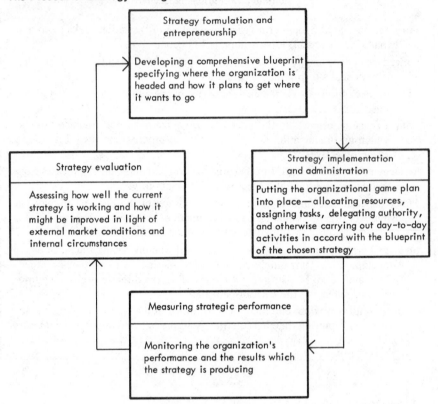

performance, and keeping the organization responsive to change and capable of further growth and success. This specifically means devoting managerial time and attention to such entrepreneurial matters as identifying opportunities to create and enter new markets, developing new and improved products and services, figuring out better ways to meet customer needs and wants, evaluating how to meet emerging environmental or competitive threats, deciding upon when and how to diversify, and, ultimately, choosing which businesses to get out of, which to continue with, and which new ones to enter. Of equal importance is an entrepreneurial alertness for opportunities to redirect resources away from areas of low or diminishing results toward areas of high or increasing results. The managerial posture in strategy formulation is not so much one of "how can we do better what we're already doing?" as it is one of "what sorts of *new* or *different* activities should we undertake?" The keynote is on insightful, timely, and creative opportunism.

Strategy Implementation and Administration

The next phase of strategy management—that of implementing and executing the strategic plan—has a sharply different flavor and is essentially *administrative* in character. Putting the strategy into place and building an organization which is capable of executing the chosen strategy entails a whole set of administrative activities:

1. Organizing and coordinating the technical tasks of research and development, production, manufacturing, marketing, finance, personnel, and so on in ways that are supportive of strategic accomplishment.
2. Attempting to develop internal proficiency and competence in carrying out the organization's activities.
3. Focusing organizational resources and energies on achieving the desired objectives and overall organizational performance.
4. Devising and administering policies, procedures, and internal controls.
5. Seeing that the day-to-day operations flow smoothly and that the work of the organization gets done.

The managerial thrust here is to try to make the strategy work successfully and to *do things right.* A smooth implementation and execution of the strategic plan, together with a high level of *administrative and operating efficiency,* are the optimal conditions.

Entrepreneurship versus Administration. At this point it is useful to pose the managerial question of which is the more crucial determinant of organization success: good entrepreneurship (strategy formulation) or good administration (strategy implementation)? This is a relevant question because it helps establish a perspective view about the relative importance and contribution of various facets of managerial work.

It is generally agreed that the entrepreneurial task of effective strategy formulation is more crucial to organization performance than is the administrative task of efficient strategy implementation.[13] The reasoning is straightforward: *An organization, however efficient and well-administered it may be, simply cannot be successful or outstanding or a winner if it is doing the wrong things.* An extreme example illustrates the point. A firm might well be the world's most efficient producer of buggy-whips, but in the absence of much demand for buggy-whips there is no way for efficiency alone to guarantee spectacular success in the marketplace. Consequently, it is fair to say that even the most efficient organization is unlikely to survive, much less succeed, if it is efficient doing the wrong things. True, efficiency *may* keep an enterprise successful for a time, but it takes *entrepreneurial effectiveness* and a strategy predicated on doing the right things at the right time to generate *superior* performance and results over the long term. Or, to put it a bit

---

[13] Drucker, *Management,* pp. 45–48; Chester I. Barnard, *The Functions of the Executive* (Cambridge, Mass.: Harvard University Press, 1938), pp. 26–32, 55–61.

differently, the foundations of organizational success rest *first* on an entre-preneurially astute strategy keyed to doing the right things; administrative efficiency and doing things right are optimal conditions once effectiveness is demonstrated.

It follows, then, that any manager of an organization (or major subunit) is well advised to take time for periodic strategy review and reappraisal. It is always appropriate to ask: Are we doing the right thing? Are we headed in the right direction? Are we in the right business (or mix of businesses)? How does our success compare with what we might be achieving in some other set of activities? When the answers to such questions come up short of satisfactory, it is time for management to evaluate whether the organization's strategy is entrepreneurially effective.

Measuring Strategic Performance

Obtaining timely and appropriate information about external conditions and internal operations is an obvious aspect of strategic management. Current performance has to be carefully and thoroughly monitored; this specifically includes looking at profitability, financial status, market share and sales growth, customer satisfaction, operating efficiency, employee morale and productivity, and other significant areas which indicate the tempo of performance. Such information is important because it gives direct indication of what results the strategy is producing and the extent to which objectives and purpose are being attained. Deviations from plan can thus be identified and corrective action taken. Measuring strategic performance is also a prerequisite for strategy evaluation and strategy reformulation.

Strategy Evaluation

It is always incumbent upon management to evaluate strategy. In the case of a new organization or a new strategy, evaluation precedes strategy selection and is a part of the initial task of strategy formulation. But once a strategy has been formulated, implemented, and the results begin coming in, then evaluation once again presents itself. Moreover, evaluation is called for because changing external conditions and emerging market developments make reappraisal of the present strategy a regular occurence. In this sense, strategy evaluation is both the end and the beginning of the continuous process of strategy management.

At this introductory stage it is sufficient to point out the central elements in strategy evaluation: (1) review of why the present strategy was selected, (2) identification of what new external and internal factors may call for altering the strategy, (3) reappraisal of external opportunities and threats, (4) reassessment of internal strengths, weaknesses, and resource constraints, (5) consideration of risk/reward trade-offs and timing aspects, and (6) a judgment of how (if at all) to modify strategy in light of present and expected future conditions.

Managing the Process

Although it is useful to describe the process of strategy management as a four-stage sequence, this is not meant to imply that managers actually undertake these tasks so systematically. The needs of strategy management are *irregular*.[14] Problems, opportunities, and "bright ideas" do not appear according to some neat timetable; they have to be dealt with as they arise, using both judgment and whatever analytical techniques may be handy. Hence, certain strategic decisions are motivated by problems forced on the manager; others result from an active, deliberate entrepreneurial search for new and better opportunities; and still others are the product of a good brainstorm.[15] At the same time, managers are busy people with many demands on their time; they are bombarded with information, surrounded by the press of daily events, and confronted with a variety of problems and brushfires. This makes it impractical for the job of strategy management to be done in planned, uninterrupted fashion, much less in logical sequence. Moreover, each strategic decision tends to be made in a different context at unpredictable intervals and with new information and changed circumstances; precise evaluation is seldom feasible.[16] The result is that *strategy evolves* as managers react to stimuli. It is fair to say that strategy stands more as the product of a Darwinist evolutionary approach than it does as a precise systematically analyzed Biblical grand design.[17]

Nonetheless, Figure 1–2 is a useful framework for thinking about strategy management. It pinpoints what kind of managerial thinking and what sorts of managerial functions comprise the task of strategy management. The four phases of strategy formulation, strategy implementation, measurement of strategic performance, and strategy evaluation may not be something management does systematically, sequentially, or precisely, but they do accurately depict what strategy management involves.

A Capsule Summary of the General Management Function

Our introductory survey of general management has stressed the basic elements involved in managing the total enterprise—and, in particular, what it takes to make an organization successful and effective in what it does. The

---

[14] Robert N. Anthony, *Planning and Control Systems: A Framework for Analysis* (Boston: Division of Research, Harvard Business School, 1965), pp. 38–39.

[15] Henry Mintzberg, "The Science of Strategy-Making," *Industrial Management Review*, vol. 8, no. 2 (Spring 1967), pp. 73–74.

[16] Ibid., p. 74.

[17] Ibid., p. 80.

work of a general manager in trying to make an organization entrepreneurially effective and results-focused concerns:

1. Developing a clear, carefully thought out concept of exactly what the organization seeks to do—its purpose and mission.
2. Deriving specific, measurable objectives from the definition of purpose. (In the case of multiproduct, multimarket, multinational enterprises, objectives will be needed for each product, market, and line of business, as well as for the whole organization.)
3. Developing a detailed strategy for achieving organizational objectives and purpose and setting priorities for concentrated effort.
4. Assigning responsibility and accountability for all of the organization's activities, and most especially for those activities crucial to strategic success.
5. Setting policies and administering the organization on a day-to-day basis.
6. Devising measures of performance, setting standards of accomplishment, indicating minimum acceptable results, and fixing deadlines.
7. Using the performance measures to set up an information system for monitoring strategy implementation and organization activities.
8. Evaluating strategy in light of new developments and new information with the express aim of
   a. Identifying any need for strategy change.
   b. Pinpointing areas of unsatisfactory results and the reasons therefore.
   c. Zeroing in on inefficient activities and areas of low performance.
   d. Revising and reformulating the current strategy to conform to expected future needs and conditions.

Items 1, 2, and 3 constitute the organization's direction-setting components and, taken together, cover the essentials of strategy formulation. The remaining five items encompass the tasks of implementing strategy, measuring strategic performance, and evaluating strategy. If the process of strategy management is done properly, then chances are good that the organization will be one which is effective, which performs, which is engaged in doing the right things, and which is successful. This is what management of the *total* enterprise is all about. In the succeeding chapters and readings, we shall add flesh to this skeletal outline of general management and the strategy-policy discipline.

SUGGESTED READINGS

Andrews, Kenneth R. *The Concept of Corporate Strategy*, Rev. ed. Homewood, Ill.: Dow Jones-Irwin, Inc., 1980, chap. 1.

Barnard, Chester I. *The Functions of the Executive*. Cambridge, Mass.: Harvard University Press, 1938, chaps. 15, 16, and 17.

Boettinger, Henry M. "Is Management Really an Art?" *Harvard Business Review*, vol. 53, no. 1 (January–February 1975), pp. 54–64.

Drucker, Peter F. *Management: Tasks, Responsibilities, Practices.* New York: Harper and Row, Publishers, Inc., 1974, chaps. 2, 4, 30, 31, and 50.

Granger, Charles H. "The Hierarchy of Objectives." *Harvard Business Review*, vol. 42, no. 3 (May–June 1964), pp. 63–74.

Katz, Robert L. "Skills of an Effective Administrator." *Harvard Business Review*, vol. 33, no. 1 (January–February 1955), pp. 33–42.

Koontz, Harold. "Making Strategic Planning Work." *Business Horizons*, vol. 19, no. 2 (April 1976), pp. 37–47.

Livingston, J. Sterling. "Myth of the Well-Educated Manager." *Harvard Business Review*, vol. 49, no. 1 (January–February 1971), pp. 79–87.

McConkey, Dale D. *How to Manage by Results.* New York: AMACOM, 1976, chaps. 4, 5, 10, 11, and 13.

Mintzberg, Henry. "The Manager's Job: Folklore and Fact." *Harvard Business Review*, vol. 53, no. 4 (July–August 1975), pp. 49–61.

Quinn, James B. "Strategic Goals: Process and Politics." *Sloan Management Review*, vol. 19, no. 1 (Fall 1977), pp. 21–37.

Raia, Anthony P. *Managing by Objectives.* Glenview, Ill.: Scott, Foresman & Co., 1974, chaps. 1 and 3.

Ross, Joel, and Kami, Michael. *Corporate Management in Crisis: Why the Mighty Fall.* Englewood Cliffs, N.J.: Prentice-Hall, Inc., 1973.

Tilles, Seymour. "The Manager's Job: A Systems Approach." *Harvard Business Review*, vol. 41, no. 1 (January–February 1963), pp. 73–81.

Wrapp, H. Edward. "Good Managers Don't Make Policy Decisions." *Harvard Business Review*, vol. 45, no. 5 (September–October 1967), pp. 91–99.

2 FORMULATING ORGANIZATION STRATEGY

. . . a business enterprise guided by a clear sense of purpose rationally arrived at and emotionally ratified by commitment is more likely to have a successful outcome, in terms of profit and social good, than a company whose future is left to guesswork and chance.

Kenneth R. Andrews

Without a strategy the organization is like a ship without a rudder, going around in circles. It's like a tramp; it has no place to go.

Joel Ross and Michael Kami

One can accurately conceptualize the entrepreneurial task of strategy formulation in any of several ways: as the development of a comprehensive game plan for managing an organization *or* as putting together a blueprint for where an organization is trying to go and how it is going to get there, *or* as choosing a set of directional signals regarding an organization's scope and conduct of its operations. All of these shorthand descriptions convey reasonably compatible notions and do so in language which make the basic thrust of strategy formulation easy enough to grasp.

But is is one thing to understand the concept of strategy formulation in its most elemental form and another thing to understand what a manager needs to think about and to do in order to forge a full-blown strategic plan of action. This chapter disassembles the task of strategy formulation and offers an in-depth look at the component pieces and how they join together. In addition, we will give specific attention to the idea of strategic fit, the levels of organization strategy, and the range of factors which act to shape strategy. Our intent is twofold: one, to make explicit the kinds of managerial work that go into the process of strategy formulation and, two, to portray an organization's strategic plan as an interconnected web of actions, decisions, objectives, plans, and policies which are formulated and pursued at all levels of the management hierarchy.

The Value of a Consciously Formulated Strategy

Every organization can be said to have a strategy, however imperfect or unconscious it may be. Its strategy may be openly stated by management or it may have to be deduced from management actions and the ways in which an organization operates and behaves. The present strategy may have been carefully calculated and regularly assessed from every angle or it may have emerged haphazardly and be mainly a product of chance and circumstance. Or, in the most frequent case, it may have evolved gradually over time, standing as a result of trial and error and market feedback regarding what worked and what didn't.

The key question, though, is whether a consciously formulated strategy is better than one which has been arrived at by "muddling through." Can better strategies and better performance result if management takes the time and trouble to do a thorough strategic review and analytically arrive at a strategic game plan? The answer may not be as obvious as it seems because some organizations have succeeded by relying mainly on ownership of key raw materials, superior finances and/or labor skills, good products (or services), key patents and unique technical knowhow, outstanding location, clever ads, the luck and coincidence of having been in the right place at the right time, and so on. Nonetheless, the current research evidence to date does point to effective strategy management and formal strategy analysis as having a positive impact on organization performance.[1] The significance of leading edge strategy management has been underscored by the chief executive officer of a very successful company which has been a longstanding leader in its industry:

> In the main, our competitors are acquainted with the same fundamental concepts and techniques and approaches that we follow, and they are as free to pursue them as we are. More often than not, the difference between their level of success and ours lies in the relative thoroughness and self-discipline with which we and they develop and execute our strategies for the future.[2]

---

[1] For a representative sample of studies, see Stanley Thune and Robert House, "Where Long-Range Planning Pays Off," *Business Horizons*, vol. 13, no. 4 (August 1970), pp. 81–87; Joseph O. Eastlack and Philip R. McDonald, "CEO's Role in Corporate Growth," *Harvard Business Review*, vol. 48, no. 3 (May–June 1970), pp. 150–63; David M. Herold, "Long-Range Planning and Organizational Performance: A Cross-Validation Study," *Academy of Management Journal*, vol. 15, no. 1 (March 1972), pp. 91–102; Dan Schendel, G. R. Patton, and James Riggs, "Corporate Turnaround Strategies," *Journal of General Management*, vol. 3, no. 3 (Spring 1976), pp. 2–11; S. Schoeffler, Robert Buzzell, and Donald Heany, "Impact of Strategic Planning on Profit Performance," *Harvard Business Review*, vol. 52, no. 2 (March–April 1974), pp. 137–45; and Alfred D. Chandler, *The Visible Hand* (Cambridge, Mass.: Harvard University Press, 1977).

[2] Dick Neuschel, "The Chief Executive's Strategic Role and Responsibilities," a special study prepared for The Presidents Association, the Chief Executive Officers' Division of the American Management Associations, 1977, p. 5.

The advantages of an organization having a consciously formulated strategy, rather than one which just evolves from freewheeling improvisation or drifting along, include: (1) the guidance it provides to the managers of organizational subunits, (2) the contribution it makes to identifying strategic issues and to coordinating management's direction-setting decisions, (3) the rationale it provides top management in deploying organizational resources among various activities and in evaluating competing requests from organizational subunits for corporate funds, and (4) the desirability of trying to *influence* rather than merely *respond* to product-market-technological-environmental change.[3] The fourth advantage is of acute importance. A well-managed enterprise will always seek to *impact* the market with a timely, perceptive, and opportunistic strategy. Indeed, a major thrust of business strategy formulation revolves around how to *initiate* and *influence* rather than just *respond* and *react*—although, obviously, it is sometimes useful to employ adaptive and defensive strategies as well as offensive strategies. But it can be fairly said that *the acid test of a powerful strategy is the extent to which it successfully impacts markets, buyers, rival firms, and the directions of product-market-technological changes.* The desired outcome is one where the firm's strategy becomes the *trend-setter* for the whole industry, with the added benefit that its products/services become differentiated and strong buyer preferences for them are created.

In the final analysis, of course, the value of conscious strategy formulation and careful strategy analysis hinges upon whether and how much organizational performance is improved. Whether better performance is realized depends upon how much is learned from the process of developing a full-blown organizational strategy, the quality of the strategy (the assumptions, predictions and business savvy on which it is based), and the skill with which it is implemented. By itself, strategy formulation—while clearly a step forward—is still only a prelude to effective action.

Where Strategy Formulation Begins

Management's logical starting point in formulating strategy is with what the scope and make-up of the organization's business interests will be, now and in the future—that is, with organizational purpose and mission. The following questions are fundamental: In what kinds of activities should we have a strategic interest? In what kinds of markets and technologies do we want to be involved? Who should our customers be and why should they buy *our* products or services? What products or services do we want to provide? What functions will they serve and are these functions marketable? What should the character of our organization be like? In what ways should we try

---

    [3] Kenneth R. Andrews, *The Concept of Corporate Strategy,* rev. ed. (Homewood, Ill.: Dow Jones-Irwin, 1980), pp. 46, 123–129; and Seymour Tilles, "How to Evaluate Corporate Strategy," *Harvard Business Review,* vol. 41, no. 4 (July–August 1963).

to be distinctive and uniquely good at what we do? Does our concept of the organization and its scope of activities mesh with competitive and market realities? And, in the case of diversified firms: Should our several lines of business be related? If so, in what ways? Not infrequently, the answers to these kinds of questions are far from clearcut—even for established or successful enterprises. Nor are the answers ever final—changing circumstances can and do cause firms to redefine their business scope and to reorient organization purpose.

In actuality, there are several ways for an organization to approach the question of "what is our business, what will it be, and what should it be?" Some organizations build the concept of their businesses around the dominant characteristics of their products or services. Thus, a trucking company may think of itself as being in the trucking business, a chemical company as in the chemicals business, and a shoe manufacturer as being in the shoe business. Similarly, in the nonprofit sector a university may relate its mission to the business of higher education; an agricultural extension service may define its business as agriculture-related technical assistance and information; and the local fire department may view its business as fire fighting and fire prevention. Other organizations describe their business by the principal ingredient in their products, as with steel companies, aluminum companies, and paper companies. Technology can also serve as the basis for conceptual definition, an example being General Electric, whose thousands of products are related in varying degrees to the technology of electricity.

Still other organizations prefer a concept based on a *broad* view of the customers or markets they serve. Thus, rural electric cooperatives often construe their business as one of supplying electrical service to residents of less-populated rural areas. A community college may view its mission as one of furnishing two-year college programs to graduates of high schools within a 50-mile radius of its campus. An agricultural machinery manufacturer may define its business as supplying farm equipment to farmers. The business of home appliance manufacturers may be thought of as one of offering effort-saving and time-saving devices to households.

Yet another alternative is for a firm to define its business in terms of a product aimed at a specific *market segment* or distinguishable group of customers having some common (and strategically relevant) characteristic— location, usage of product, timing of purchase, volume bought, service requirements, and so forth. For instance, typewriters sold as office equipment define a buyer segment quite distinct from portable typewriters sold to individuals through retail channels. Likewise the clientele of a major state university is fundamentally different from that of a small private liberal arts college. And the business of a neighborhood convenience food mart is different from that of a large supermarket. In such cases, an organization's concept of its business combines a definition of its product with a definition of the class of customer or market segment to which that product is sold. This approach to defining the business seeks a strategic match between a particular product (or service) and the more narrowly-focused target market for which it is primarily intended.

Finally, an enterprise may have a concept of itself that is predicated on the scope of its operations. For a small company, just part of an industry may constitute its sole field of endeavor; such would be the case of a firm whose entire business consists of drilling offshore oil wells. This type of firm is often labeled as "specialized" and such a firm may well perceive its economic mission as none other than a specialty-type enterprise performing a limited service. Larger firms may, for reasons of scale economies, have activities extending across several stages of the process of getting a product to the final consumer (mining, manufacturing, distribution) and are thus said to be "integrated." An example would be an oil company which drills its own oil wells, pipes crude oil to its own refineries, and sells gasoline through its own network of branded distributors and service station outlets. Still other firms, large or small, are said to be "diversified" because their operations extend into several different industries—either related or unrelated.

Strictly speaking, many organizations are in a variety of distinct businesses. Either they sell the same product to different types of customers in distinctly different ways, or they utilize a number of different distribution channels in gaining access to customers and markets, or they have a diversified product line. Consequently, to understand the overall concept of a multibusiness organization, one must look first at each line of business and then at whether and how these join together. However, in the case of true conglomerate organizations which, by design, are in a number of *unrelated* businesses, the overall definition of organizational concept tends to relate more to issues of risk, financial objectives of the owners, growth, and earnings stability than to unifying fit among its numerous product-market-technology activities.[4]

"What Is Our Business and What Should It Be?" For many years Peter Drucker has been the most noted and perceptive authority on the whys and hows of an organization clearly defining its purpose and mission. According to Drucker, while nothing may seem simpler or more obvious than "What is our business?" a neglect of this question is the most important single cause of organization frustration and failure. He argues quite forcefully, therefore, that the theory of an organization's business should be thought through and spelled out clearly; otherwise the organization will lack a solid foundation for establishing realistic objectives, strategies, plans, and work assignments.[5] Drucker offers the following approach to defining "what is our business":

A business is not defined by the company's name, statutes or articles of corporation. It is defined by the want the customer satisfies when he buys a

---

[4] See, for example, Richard F. Vancil and Peter Lorange, "Strategic Planning in Diversified Companies," *Harvard Business Review*, vol. 53, no. 1 (January–February 1975), pp. 81–90.

[5] Peter F. Drucker, *Management: Tasks, Responsibilities, Practices* (New York: Harper and Row, Publishers, 1974), pp. 77–79.

product or a service. To satisfy the customer is the mission and purpose of every business. The question "What is our business?" can, therefore, be answered only by looking at the business from the outside, from the point of view of customer and market. What the customer sees, thinks, believes, and wants, at any given time, must be accepted by management as an objective fact. . . .
. . . to the customers, no product or service, and certainly no company, is of much importance. . . . The customer only wants to know what the product or service will do for him tomorrow. All he is interested in are his own values, his own wants, his own reality. For this reason alone, any serious attempt to state "what our business is" must start with the customer, his realities, his situation, his behavior, his expectations, and his values.[6]

Following up on this rationale, Drucker advocates a searching inquiry into such questions as: Who is our customer and what are his needs?; Where is the customer? What does the customer buy? Is it status? Comfort? Satisfaction of a physical need? An ego need? Security? What is value to the customer? Is it price? Function? Quality? Service? Economy of use? Durability? Styling? Convenience?

These questions plainly need to be posed and answered at the inception of a business and whenever it gets in trouble. But every so often a successful operation should also ask them.[7] Sooner or later, even the most successful response to "what is our business?" becomes obsolete. Therefore, in periodically addressing the question of "what is our business?" management is well-advised to add "and what will it be?"[8] This latter question forces the organization to look ahead and try to anticipate the impact of environmental changes on the organization's business. It lays the basis for conscious redirection of the organization. It reduces the chances of becoming smug and complacent. Answering it also means doing some serious thinking about "What are the customer's *unsatisfied* wants?"—the response to which may offer clues as to what direction a firm ought to pursue in modifying, extending, and developing its existing business concept.

Finally, it is pertinent to inquire "What *should* our business be?"[9] How can innovations be converted into new businesses? What other opportunities are opening up or can be created that offer attractive prospects for transforming the organization into a *different* (and more desirable) business? Which things should the organization continue doing and which should it plan to abandon? For instance, should Exxon consider itself as primarily an oil company or an energy company? Should IBM's concept of its business be computers or information processing? Should the business of hospitals remain one of curing those persons who are sick enough to be patients or should they seek to become comprehensive centers for all types of medical and health care?

---

[6] Ibid., pp. 79–80.
[7] Ibid., pp. 87–88.
[8] Ibid., pp. 88–89.
[9] Ibid., p. 82.

By and large, if an organization follows Drucker's prescribed methodology for periodically thinking through its definition of purpose and mission, the outcome will be a clearer and more perceptive understanding of how the enterprise should be managed.

Avoiding an Overly Broad Concept of "What Is Our Business?"   In approaching the question of "what is our business and what will it be?" management should heed the dangers of descriptive labels that are too broad to be operationally useful and provide meaningful guidance.[10] While the widespread tendency of organizations to diversify has rendered the traditional identification of firms with particular industries obsolete and overly narrow, there is nothing to be gained from describing the firm's scope of interest in language so sweeping that it obscures what an organization's business really is and where it is headed. For example, if a hospital views its strategic mission as one of "providing comprehensive health care to the residents of the surrounding community," then questions immediately surface as to whether this broad definition is to include filling cavities and pulling teeth, examinations for eyeglasses, nursing of the aged, annual checkups, and rehabilitation services for the handicapped—all of which are typically performed by medical professionals outside hospitals. A state university is unquestionably in the business of "higher education," but is this to mean it should offer the *full* range of programs in "higher education"—including technical training, associate degrees similar to those of junior colleges, adult and continuing education, as well as undergraduate and graduate programs in *all* disciplines and professions? A railroad company may decide to view itself as a "transportation company," but does this mean it should get into long-haul trucking or air-freight services or fleet car leasing or intercity busing or rapid transit? The broader the language used to answer "what is our business and what will it be?" the less that is revealed about what the firm's real strategic interests are. Broad generalities may be okay from a public relations or annual report perspective but they are dysfunctional when it comes to giving managers a sharp understanding of the firm's business.

Generally speaking, top management's concept of the organization's business should (1) avoid the ambiguity of organizational direction that flows from broad statements about purpose and scope, (2) give *specific guidance* as to how the organization should be managed in terms of setting objectives and selecting strategy, and (3) not be so confining as to foreclose growth and adaptation to environmental change.

The Concept of Strategic Fit

In trying to define "what is our business, what will it be and what should it be?" there exists some dispute over the need to build an organization's scope of activities around some "common thread" or unifying conceptual

---

[10] H. Igor Ansoff, *Corporate Strategy* (New York: McGraw-Hill, 1965), pp. 105–8.

feature. In recent years the prevailing view seems to be that it is desirable for an organization's activities, however diversified, to contain some form of *strategic fit*.

Strategic fit is a measure of the synergistic effects—the mutually reinforcing impacts—that engaging in different activities have on an organization's overall effectiveness and efficiency.[11] To put it more simply, strategic fit is a 2 + 2 = 5 phenomenon. The fit can take several forms. *Product-market fit* exists when different products follow common distribution channels, utilize the same sales promotion techniques, are bought by the same customers, and/or can be sold by the same sales force. *Operating fit* results from purchasing and warehousing economies, joint utilization of plant and equipment, overlaps in technology and engineering design, carryover of R&D activities, and/or common manpower requirements. *Management fit* emerges when different kinds of activities present managers with comparable or similar types of technical, administrative or operating problems, thereby allowing the accumulated managerial knowhow associated with one line of business to spill over and be useful in managing another of the organization's activities. The value of having strategic fit in a diversified organization is the unifying focus and rationale it gives to management in directing and administering the organization's activities.

On the other hand, so-called conglomerate firms are built on the principle of *unrelated* diversification and thus are by design characterized by lack of product-market-technology fit and a common thread concept. Textron, for example, has built a successful sales-profit record with activities as diverse as Bell helicopters, Gorham silver, Homelite saws, Sheaffer pens, Fafnir bearings, Speidel watchbands, Polaris snowmobiles, Sprague gas meters and fittings, Bostitch staplers, air cushion vehicles, iron castings, milling machines, rolling mills, industrial fasteners, insurance, and missile and spacecraft propulsion systems—among others. (Illustration Capsule 4 describes the logic underlying Textron's diversity.)

Using an aggressive acquisition-merger strategy quarterbacked by Harold Geneen, International Telephone and Telegraph (ITT) in the short span of 15 years grew from a medium-sized telecommunications company in 1959 into the nation's eleventh largest industrial corporation with annual sales exceeding $17 billion in 1979. A congressional committee hearing in 1969 revealed that ITT's aggressive acquisition-merger strategy made "the world of ITT" a conglomerate structure of some 350 companies having an additional 700-plus lower-tier subsidiaries of their own. ITT products and companies run the gamut, including telephone equipment, Sheraton hotels, Wonder Bread, Smithfield Hams, Bobbs-Merrill Publishing Co., Hartford Insurance Co., Aetna Finance Co., Jabsco Pump Co., Gotham Lighting Co., Speedwriting Inc., Transportation Displays, Inc., Rayonier chemical cellulose, Bramwell

---

[11] David T. Kollat, Roger D. Blackwell, and James F. Robeson, *Strategic Marketing* (New York: Holt, Rinehart & Winston, Inc., 1972), pp. 23–24.

Illustration Capsule 4

How One Conglomerate Views the Concept of Its Business

In its 1976 and 1977 *Annual Reports,* Textron made the following statements about its corporate purpose, objectives, and strategy:

Textron is founded on the principle of balanced diversification, designed on the one hand to afford protection against economic cycles and product obsolescence and on the other to provide a means for participating in new markets and new technologies. The key elements are balance and flexibility in a rapidly changing world.

Textron, . . . , has established a versatile business organization with a presence in many markets, geographic areas and technologies, and a management style and philosophy that has generated a proven record.

Textron seeks to be distinctive in its products and services—distinctive as to technology, design, service and value. Superior performance will be achieved by way of excellence and quality. These, plus motivated people of high standards, are the essential ingredients for achievement of an overall goal of superior performance on a continuing basis.

Through more than two dozen Divisions in five Groups—Aerospace, Consumer, Industrial, Metal Product, and Creative Capital—Textron's decentralization of day-to-day operations is coupled with corporate coordination and control to assure consistency of standards and performance. The operating Divisions are provided with the capital and planning assistance to meet demonstrated needs for growth. This business structure combines the enthusiasm and quick response of moderate-sized enterprises with the planning and financial resources available on a consolidated basis.

Textron has three important priorities: *People development. Internal profit growth. New initiatives.* Emphasizing these priorities, Textron seeks to accomplish quantitative objectives set in 1972 for the ten-year period ending 1982. These specific targets for compound rates of growth are:

Sales: 8 percent per year, to $3.5 billion in 1982.
Progress, 1972 to date: 11 percent to 2.8 billion in 1977.

Net income: 10 percent per year, to $200 million in 1982.
Progress, 1972 to date: 11 percent to $137 million in 1977.

Net income per common share: 10 percent per year.
to $6.00 in 1982.
Progress, 1972 to date: 9 percent to $3.65 in 1977.

Business School, South Bend Window Cleaning Co., and Scott lawn care products.

Textron and ITT, along with several other conglomerates, have been successful enough to cast doubt upon the *necessity* of a unified theme and strategic fit. But the final verdict is not in yet.[12] Managing widely diversified companies effectively has proved to be something many corporate man-

---

[12] For an interesting discussion of some of the issues involved, see Lewis Meman, "What We Learned from the Great Merger Frenzy," *Fortune* (April 1973), pp. 70–73, 144–50.

agements are not able to do; acquisition-minded conglomerates have had serious difficulties in profitably operating so many unrelated businesses—chiefly because corporate managers, not having firsthand experience in each one of the firm's varied business interests, find themselves short on the grassroots product/market knowledge requisite for providing guidance on the diverse kinds of specific problems being encountered at the division and operating levels.[13]

Consequently, while it is not *absolutely essential* for a common thread or strategic fit to run through each of an organization's several activities, the experience thus far shows that only a few organizations have performed well over the long run without having a common denominator for at least most of its business interests. The reason, simply enough, is that from the standpoint of managerial knowhow the problems of managing diversification tend to get out of hand when an organization's range of operation spans many unrelated product markets and technologies.[14] The conglomerate's penchant for rate of return criteria as *the* decisive strategic guide thus runs the risk of deteriorating into mediocre long-run performance unless senior management is exceptionally good at keeping close watch over the real strategic issues in each line of business and thereby remaining in position to probe deeply into the recommendations of division-level managers. As one president of a diversified firm expressed it:

> . . . . we've got to make sure that our core businesses are properly managed for solid, long-term earnings. We can't just sit back and watch the numbers. We've got to know what the real issues are out there in the profit centers. Otherwise, we're not even in a position to check out our managers on the big decisions. And considering the pressures they're under, that's pretty dangerous for all concerned.[15]

The Levels of Strategy

Once an enterprise has gotten a firm grip on the kind of organization it wants to become, the direction-setting task turns toward the development of a hierarchical web of strategies that span the organization from top to bottom. Four major levels of organizational strategy are distinguishable: (1) *corporate strategy*, (2) *line of business* (or just *business*) *strategy*, (3) *functional area support strategy*, and (4) *operating-level strategy*.

---

[13] The confusion and uncertainty over corporate purpose, corporate objectives, and corporate strategy that is engendered by conglomerate diversification is evidenced by the number of firms which now designate themselves by initials—LTV, FMC, ACF Industries, SCM, NLT, MCA, AMAX, CPC International, AMP, A-T-O, TRW, GAF, NVF, DHJ Industries, UMC Industries, SCOA Industries, RLC, and NL Industries.

[14] As an illustration of some of the difficulties a conglomerate company may encounter see Dan Cordtz, "What Does U.S.I. Do: Why, Almost Everything," *Fortune* (February 1973), pp. 73–77.

[15] Carter F. Bales, "Strategic Control: The President's Paradox," *Business Horizons,* vol. 20, no. 4 (August 1977), p. 17.

Corporate Strategy. Corporate strategy is management's game plan for directing and running the organization as a whole over the next two to five years. It cuts across all of the organization's product lines, operating divisions, and business interests. Corporate strategy is the umbrella under which an organization's perhaps diverse activities are linked and it tackles head on the gut issue of "what *set* of businesses should we be in—now and in the future?" In effect, corporate strategy is composed of two main elements: (1) the firm's scope of activities and (2) the priorities and patterns whereby internal resources will be allocated among these activities. The strategic importance of a firm's scope of activities is that it determines how the organization will be positioned in the external environment—how well-situated it is to capitalize on opportunities and how vulnerable it may be to emerging threats. Scope may be described in terms of products, markets, service to customers, technology, distribution channels, geographic coverage, degree of vertical integration, degree of diversification, and any other relevant factor. The second element of corporate strategy—the priorities and patterns for internal resource deployment—is crucial because it supplies a much-needed rationale for management to use in evaluating competing requests for corporate resources. Furthermore, it forces some management consideration of how to develop the kind of match between internal resource capability and mix of business activities that will yield a level of performance and results commensurate with corporate objectives.

The concept of corporate strategy has classic application in multiproduct, multiindustry, multitechnology organizations since their top managements are continually under the gun to make a workable whole out of numerous activities, some or many of which are not related. But it also applies to single-business enterprises which are contemplating some kind of diversification and/or shift in corporate direction. In either case, the task of corporate strategy is heavily focused on what new businesses (if any) to get into, which current businesses to stay in, and which existing activities to divest or close down. Necessarily, then, corporate strategy is concerned with whether and to what extent different lines of business should be related or unrelated. It is concerned with how much and what kind of diversification to pursue. It is concerned with the whys and hows of acquisition and divestiture and, more generally, with a strategic rationale for evaluating a portfolio of businesses. And it is concerned with the criteria and priorities to be used in allocating financial capital and organizational skills among the chosen lines of business. The last concern is an important one because if a high level of performance is to be achieved, then both the availability of internal resources and the patterns with which they are deployed must be in close alignment with the success requirements of each line of business.

Table 2–1 provides abbreviated examples of some "good" and "bad" corporate strategy statements. Observe that the more specific and detailed the strategy statement is, the more clear it is what kind of organization is being described, where it is headed, and how it is going to get there. Unless

TABLE 2–1
Examples of "Good" and "Bad" Corporate Strategy Statements

Corporate Strategy Statement	Remarks
1. "The strategy of Company A is to become a growth company and to emphasize fast-growing product lines."	This statement is more an expression of an objective and some intentions rather than a delineation of how growth is to be achieved and what set of businesses that Company A seeks to engage in.
2. "Our strategy is to become the most efficient firm in the industry."	The statement is explicit as compared to statement 1, but it still describes an objective. No mention is made of how the enterprise intends to become the most efficient firm.
3. The strategy of Ajax Corp. is to become a fully integrated steel producer over the next five years.	This strategy statement indicates the direction the company will be moving and its intended scope of operations, but it is incomplete because it says nothing about resource allocation among the stages of vertical integration nor does it address how the firm intends to compete successfully and how a distinctive competence will be achieved.
4. PWB Company's strategy is to retain all of its profits to finance diversification into the leisure time industry and thereby raise its annual growth rate of sales and profits from 5 to 10 percent. Diversification will emphasize acquiring young, rapidly-growing companies which have proven management and which have demonstrated the ability to manufacture and market a quality product.	Although the strategy suggests a wider scope of operation and the means to finance it, as well as relating strategy to specific objectives, it omits mention of PWB's existing business. Also the notion of "leisure time industry" needs to be pinned down more specifically.
5. Our strategy for the next two years is to compete in the low price segment of the women's apparel business, with a limited line of fashion conscious items that can be sold on the basis of style and low price to national retail chains catering to budget-conscious women. During this period, no diversification efforts will be undertaken and all available internal funds will be allocated to debt retirement, increased marketing efforts, and improved production methods—in that order of priority.	This strategy statement is the most complete and detailed of the five statements. It describes the intended scope of operations, the deployment of resources, and the competitive approach to the market. Yet it could be improved upon by adding references to distinctive competence, sought for competitive advantages, and how the strategy relates to corporate objectives.

strategy reveals these things about an organization, it is too vague to provide guidance to lower-level managers and it may reflect a fuzzy or incompletely formulated strategic plan.

Line of Business Strategy.   Line of business (or business) strategy focuses on how a firm plans to conduct its activities in a single market or market segment. It addresses most particularly the issues of (1) how the organization intends to compete in that specific business and (2) how organizational resources will be allocated to various facets of that business so as to give the organization a viable competitive advantage and, if possible, a unique and distinctive competence in creating, producing, and delivering the product or service. The external aspects of line of business strategy deal with how the organization can be entrepreneurially effective in that particular business and with the specifics of adapting to the evolutionary aspects of both products and markets. The internal character of line of business strategy suggests how the different pieces of the business (manufacturing, marketing, finance, R&D, and so on) ought to be aligned and coordinated so as to be responsive to those market factors upon which competitive success depends. In this regard, line of business strategy provides guidance for organizing and funding the performance of subactivities within the business in ways which speak directly to what is needed for strategic success.

Obviously, for a single-product, single-business enterprise, corporate strategy and business strategy are one and the same—except for when new directions are being contemplated. Our distinction between corporate and business strategy is most relevant for multiproduct, multiindustry firms—that is, for firms which are sufficiently diversified to have more than one line of business or which have different strategies for each of its several products/market segments.

As an example of line of business strategy, consider the strategy Kellogg has employed in ready-to-eat cereals. Since 1906, when Will Keith Kellogg formed the company after accidentally discovering a way to make ready-to-eat cereal, Kellogg has aimed its strategy at being the dominant leader in the industry. Kellogg's strategy for competing is based on product differentiation and market segmentation. The company's product line features a diverse number of brands, differentiated according to grain, shape, form, flavor, color, and taste—a something for everyone approach. Competing on the basis of low price has been slighted in favor of nonprice strategies keyed to extensive product variety, regular product innovation, substantial TV advertising, periodic promotional offers and prizes, and maintaining more space on the grocery shelf than rivals have. Much of Kellogg's sales efforts are targeted at the under-25 age group (the biggest cereal eaters with an average annual consumption of 11 pounds per capita), and 33 percent of its cereal sales are in presweetened brands promoted almost totally through TV advertising to children. Kellogg endeavors to sidestep industry maturity and product saturation with introductions of fresh, "new" types of cereals (presweetened cereals in the 1940s, "nutritional" cereals in the 1950s, "natural" and health conscious cereals in the 1960s and early 1970s, and adult cereals in the late 1970s) and also by advertising a variety of times and places for eating cereals other than at the morning breakfast table. Product line freshness is additionally enhanced by introduction of brands which differ only slightly from existing brands (flaked versus shredded, plain versus sugar-frosted, puffed versus cocoa-flavored). In 1979, Kellogg introduced five new cereal brands—more than it had ever launched in a single year—as part of a stepped-up and redirected effort to attract consumers in the 25–50 age group (where consumption levels were only half those of the younger age groups). Kellogg also introduced its cereals in four additional countries in South America and the Middle East using campaigns that featured free samples, demonstration booths in food stores, and heavy local advertising so as to promote the use of ready-to-eat cereals as a substitute for traditional breakfast foods (corn meal and bulgar). This new strategic thrust aimed at changing the eating habits of adults who had shied away from cereals or had spurned breakfast altogether. In further support of this, Kellogg continued to up its research budget (already the industry's most extensive) by 15 percent annually in an effort to develop more nutritional, health conscious cereals and breakfast foods for the older consumer segment. The whole of Kellogg's strategy in cereals had three strategic objectives: (1) increasing Kellogg's 42 percent market share, (2) increasing sales by 5 percent annually (compared to an industry growth of 2 percent), and (3) boosting annual cereal consumption from 8.6 pounds per capita to 12 pounds by 1985.

Functional Area Support Strategy.   Functional area support strategy deals with the specifics of how the principal subordinate activities that make up the business (production, marketing, finance, R&D, personnel) should be managed and how resources allocated to each of these pieces of the business are to be made effective and efficient in their contribution to the accomplishment of the overall line of business strategy. Each of the principal activities within a single business, and most especially the activities crucial to successful strategy execution, need to be integrated and fit together to form a smoothly-functioning, consistent business unit. Thus, functional area support strategies are major corollaries of the line of business strategy; they give it substance, completeness, and concrete meaning as applied to a specific part of the business, whether it be sales or manufacturing, or a specific geographic market area, or a subset of the product line. They indicate how each major subactivity in the business is to be managed in support of accomplishing the strategy of the overall business unit.

Whereas formulation of line of business strategy is the responsibility of the manager of the business unit (in diversified corporations this is usually the head of the product division), responsibility for formulation of functional area support strategy is typically delegated by the business manager to his principal subordinates who are charged with running the functional areas in question. And just as the business-level manager is obliged to establish a set of objectives and a strategy that is deemed by corporate management to contribute adequately toward corporate-level performance objectives, so also the business manager's principal subordinates need to establish performance objectives and strategies for their areas of responsibility that will promote accomplishment of the chosen line of business strategy and the agreed-upon business-level performance objectives. Moreover, just as business-level strategies and objectives tend to be approved via negotiation between corporate managers and business managers, the close tie between line of business strategy and functional area support strategy argues for the business manager's ratification of the functional area objectives and support strategies which are proposed by his subordinates.

Illustration Capsule 5 provides a detailed look at a sample functional area support strategy—one that, interestingly enough, has not only received unusually wide attention but also has sparked some controversy (see Tandy's *1978 Annual Report*, p. 53.)

Illustration Capsule 5

Tandy Corporation's Financial Strategy

In its *1977* and *1978 Annual Reports,* Tandy Corporation discussed in considerable detail its corporate financial strategy and, in particular, the rationale underlying the company's decision to repurchase its common stock in lieu of making cash dividend payments. Tandy management's open discussion of its financial strategy offers an excellent example of what is meant by a functional area support strategy and how it is linked to a company's overall strategy and performance. What follows is excerpted and pieced together from Tandy's *1977, 1978,* and *1979 Annual Reports:*

On four occasions since 1973, Tandy Corporation has reduced its equity capitalization. In August 1974 the Company exchanged 1,219,000 shares (2,438,000 adjusted for a two-for-one stock split in 1976) for $35,337,000 face amount of 10 percent subordinated debentures maturing in 1994. In December 1976 the Company exchanged $98,039,000 of 10 percent subordinated debentures maturing in 1991 for an additional 2,450,975 shares of common stock. In July 1977, shares totaling 3,500,000 were repurchased through a cash tender offer at $29.00 per share. In 1979, internal cash flows were used to repurchase 1,246,000 shares of the Company's stock on the open market.

What is the rationale behind the decision to repurchase shares? Tandy management and directors believe the shares represent an attractive investment for the Company and its stockholders. At prices prevailing in recent years, which have been quite modest multiples of current earnings relative to historical norms, the purchase of shares with borrowed funds will enhance the future return on equity and earnings per share growth because the profit margins of the Company are in excess of the interest costs of the funds borrowed. What does that academic theoretical statement mean? The explanation lies in the interrelationship between the operating variables of an ongoing enterprise and its financial structure, or to put it in simpler terms, how efficiently a company employs its assets and how it finances the acquisition and carrying of those assets. A few definitions are in order before proceeding:

Illustration Capsule 5 (*continued*)

Asset Turnover (sometimes called operating leverage) is the ratio of sales per dollar of assets found by dividing net sales by the average assets. It is one standard measure of productivity used by financial analysts to gauge how efficiently a company utilizes the assets it holds.

Return on Sales (or net profit margin) is the percentage of profit earned on sales. It is calculated by dividing net income by net sales.

Return on Assets is the percentage of net profits earned on assets employed, calculated by dividing net income for the year by average assets.

Financial Leverage is the ratio of a company's asset base to its equity investment, or, stated another way, the ratio of how many dollars of assets held per dollar of stockholders' equity. It is calculated by dividing average assets by average stockholders' equity. This measurement gives an indication of how much of a company's assets are financed by stockholders' equity and how much with borrowed funds.

Return on Equity is the net income earned by a company expressed as a percentage return on the stockholders' investment. This figure is computed by dividing net income by average stockholders' equity. Return on equity is the ultimate measure of the profitability of an investment.

All the defined ratios and percentages are interrelated and a change in any one can and does affect the others. The interrelationship between the variables is expressed in the following classic investment formula:

$$\begin{matrix} \text{Asset} \\ \text{turnover} \\ \text{(operating} \\ \text{leverage)} \end{matrix} \times \begin{matrix} \text{Return} \\ \text{on sales} \\ \text{(net margin)} \end{matrix} = \begin{matrix} \text{Return} \\ \text{on assets} \end{matrix} \times \begin{matrix} \text{Financial} \\ \text{leverage} \end{matrix} = \begin{matrix} \text{Return} \\ \text{on equity} \end{matrix}$$

$$\frac{\text{Sales}}{\text{Average assets}} \times \frac{\text{Net income}}{\text{Sales}} = \frac{\text{Net income}}{\text{Average assets}} \times \frac{\text{Average assets}}{\text{Average equity}}$$

$$= \frac{\text{Net income}}{\text{Average equity}}$$

From the formula it can be seen that changes in the operating ratios of asset turnover or net margin can change the return on assets. A rise in operating leverage, for example, could increase the return on assets, and ultimately the return on equity, but not if the increase in asset turnover was achieved by reducing net margin.

Similarly, changing the financial leverage has a direct impact on the return on stockholders' equity, but also affects net margin. Increasing financial leverage through more borrowings to finance assets could increase the return on equity, but not if the added interest costs were such as to seriously erode the net profit margins earned on sales. The point is that management of a company must look at the various pieces of the return on investment equation, within the context of the whole, to earn the highest return for stockholders.

In relating the above discussion to the original question—"Why does management consider the repurchase of outstanding stock an attractive investment?"—two reasons emerge:

1.   The current net profit margin is considerably in excess of the interest cost of the funds borrowed to effect the transactions. The effective cost of our debt is

Illustration Capsule 5 (continued)

less than 5 percent in aftertax dollars, while our net profit margin in fiscal 1977 was 7.3 percent.
2.   Asset turnover or operating leverage should show gradual further improvement in future years.

If asset turnover continues to improve and profit margins do not significantly deteriorate, return on assets should remain at a high level and possibly show further improvement as well. By modestly increasing the financial leverage through substitution of long-term debt for a portion of outstanding stock, a further substantial gain in the percentage return on equity and growth in earnings per share should be achievable in the short-term future. If this occurs, the attractiveness of Tandy stock as an investment for its stockholders should be enhanced over the longer term.

Asset turnover could continue to rise for three principal reasons:

A.   More than half of the Radio Shack stores are less than four years old and likely have not as yet reached maturity. Average sales per store data, compiled by the Company by year for the North American stores, gives a 14-year history showing sales productivity increases as the store base matures.
B.   Virtually all of Radio Shack's 2,000-plus dealers have been added since fiscal 1972 and this business is continuing to grow. The dealer program requires no fixed asset investment by the Company, minimal incremental advertising and administration costs, and increases throughout for our manufacturing plants and distribution centers.
C.   The great bulk of our manufacturing capacity has been built within the last five years. New manufacturing plants tend to act as a temporary retardant on asset turnover while the plants are in a start-up phase. With the Company now self-manufacturing more than forty percent of its merchandise items, additional fixed asset commitments for new manufacturing capacity should be more modest relative to the total asset base, and throughput of existing factories should increase as the sales base grows.

Effect on the Balance Sheet

A potential fallacy in this rationale should be addressed, and that relates to the structural change of the Balance Sheet of the Company by such action. One of the cardinal tenets of financial theory is that investors determine the price they are willing to pay for a potential investment within the context of the risk inherent in making the investment. All else being equal, investors will pay a higher price for less risk. Or stated conversely, investors will pay less for an expected return as risk increases.

Within that context, investors equate increased financial leverage on a balance sheet with increased levels of risk and tend to pay less (or discount the investment to use the financial term) for stocks of highly leveraged companies. Thus, if the course of action discussed above were achieved only through permanent deterioration of the Balance Sheet of Tandy Corporation, management would be accomplishing little for the stockholder, even if the return on equity rises, because the higher return would tend to be offset by the higher risk.

This has not been the case with Tandy in the two prior exchange offers, as witnessed by the fact that the financial leverage factor has been relatively flat since fiscal 1974. Further, management does not expect that the recently com-

Illustration Capsule 5 (continued)

pleted cash tender offer will have a lasting negative effect on our financial structure, even though $100 million of revolving debt was assumed to buy the 3.5 million shares. While balance sheet leverage has increased temporarily each time we have repurchased shares, our growing retained earnings and internal cash flow have permitted rapid rebuilding of the stockholders' equity account and the timely repayment of debt. At the same time fixed asset additions have grown more modestly, which has created incremental cash flow available for debt repayment after normal additions to working capital. This pattern should continue. It is the current intention of management to repay the new revolving debt as soon as practicable. In summary, the program discussed here has been embarked upon after carefully considering the potential benefits to be achieved, the temporary impact the program will have on the Balance Sheet and the cash flow necessary to quickly return the Balance Sheet of the Company to its normal strength.

The Dividend Question

The above discussion leads directly to the issue of dividend policy. The accumulation of the capital required to pursue the business opportunities available to the Company has been a priority item for many years. Because of that continuing attention, our growth has been essentially self-financed and a sound financial position has been maintained. The resulting strong equity base has permitted the controlled management of debt in the Company's capital structure, while largely insulating Tandy Corporation from the hazards of credit crunch periods, which can be so damaging to the progress of a business. For these reasons a cash dividend has, to date, not been paid. Consistent with the rationale that the potential benefits to the stockholder of the stock repurchase program will be maximized by quickly restoring the stockholders' equity account and reducing the revolving debt, a cash dividend is unlikely in the immediate future.

To accelerate the repayment of debt, the Company has announced its intention to issue at least $75 million of convertible subordinated debentures, with the proceeds to be applied against outstanding debt. Not only will this course of action move forward the timetable of balance sheet restructuring, it should also result in significant interest savings over current rates—which in turn should enhance return on sales and assets in fiscal 1979.

With respect to how well this financial strategy is working, Tandy reported the following results through 1979:

June 30	Asset Turnover	×	Return on Sales	=	Return on Assets	×	Financial Leverage	=	Return on Equity
1972	1.39	×	3.9%	=	5.4%	×	1.61	=	8.7%
1973	1.34	×	4.4	=	5.9	×	2.06	=	12.1
1974	1.47	×	3.6	=	5.3	×	2.41	=	12.8
1975	1.71	×	5.1	=	8.7	×	2.53	=	22.0
1976	2.04	×	8.7	=	17.7	×	2.18	=	38.7
1977	2.16	×	7.3	=	15.7	×	2.37	=	37.2
1978	2.06	×	6.2	=	12.8	×	3.39	=	43.6
1979	2.09	×	6.9	=	14.3	×	3.35	=	47.9

Illustration Capsule 5 (concluded)

Tandy's management also cited financial performance comparisons relative to other high performing companies both in retailing and in the computer-electronics-instrument industry.

Measure of Financial Performance	Where Tandy Ranked among the Top Ten Highest Performing Companies	
	Retailing Companies	Computer-Electronics-Instrument Companies
Pretax return on average total operating assets	4	2
Pretax return on average invested capital	2	1
Pretax return on average common equity	1	1
Sales per employee	Unranked	2
Pretax income as percentage of sales	3	Unranked
Pretax income per employee	4	6
Sales per share of common stock	1	2
Pretax income per share of common stock (5-year growth rate)	1	2
Earnings per share (5-year growth rate)	1	2
Sales per dollar of total assets	Unranked	2
Cash flow per share of common stock (5-year growth rate)	1	1

As to whether and how long Tandy would stick with its financial strategy, management said:

> None of the discussion relating to the stock repurchase transactions or the dividend policy of Tandy Corporation should be construed as a projection that such programs will necessarily persist in the future. Rather, we have sought to explain why we have followed this course up until the present. The whole issue of financial structure, cash needs of a corporation, and maximizing return on investment in an inflationary business environment is a complex and multifaceted issue in an ever-changing environment. There may be a time when the capital requirements of the Company, dividend tax policy, and money market patterns will point to the adoption of a dividend program for the common stock. Until then, however, it appears the most effective service to shareholders will be the continued effort to provide capital appreciation through continued growth of our Company.

Source: Synthesized from Tandy's *1977, 1978,* and *1979 Annual Reports.*

Operating-Level Strategy.   Operating-level strategies refer to the strategic guidelines operating-level managers develop and use in carrying out the day-to-day requirements of functional area support strategies. Thus, operating strategy deals with the nuts and bolts of how the various facets of each functional area strategy will be carried out. The scope of the operating manager's job is, of course, more limited than that of the functional area manager to whom he reports and the operating strategy statement which he develops and proposes as a guide to his activities is accordingly more specific.[16] However, since the operating manager has the task of devising and executing actions that will partially implement the functional area strategy and, ultimately, the business strategy, the need for the operating manager to have his own specific game plan for his area of responsibility is every bit as great as it is for higher-ranking managers.[17]

Several examples of operating-level strategy are indicated below:

A cosmetics firm relies upon ads placed in magazines as an integral part of its marketing effort to inform women about its product line. The firm's advertising director elects to employ a media ad strategy which calls for a concentrated campaign during the month prior to each of the company's three peak sales periods of Christmas, Easter, and Mother's Day, with full page ads to be placed in *McCall's, Cosmopolitan,* and *Ladies' Home Journal* and quarter-page ads to be placed in *Seventeen, Family Circle,* and *Woman's Day.*

A company whose profitability depends upon selling in mass quantities at the lowest possible price supports this result at the manufacturing level with a production worker strategy that stresses achieving unusually high levels of labor efficiency via (1) careful selection and training of new employees, (2) unhesitating purchases of time-saving tools and equipment, and (3) a wage-fringe benefit package that promotes high morale and employee retention.

A distributor of heating and air-conditioning equipment emphasizes quick, reliable parts delivery as the feature component of its dealer service package. Accordingly, the inventory strategy of the warehouse manager is to maintain a sufficiently ample supply of parts that the chance of a stockout on a given item is virtually nil, and his warehouse staffing strategy is to maintain a large enough work force to service each order within 24 hours.

Note that in each example cited the logic of the operating-level strategy flowed directly from a higher-order strategic requirement and that responsibility for the operating strategy was assigned to the lower echelons of the

---

[16] Richard F. Vancil, "Strategy Formulation in Complex Organizations," *Sloan Management Review,* vol. 17, no. 2 (Winter 1976), p. 12.
[17] Ibid.

management hierarchy where the day-to-day details of a firm's activities are administered.

The Hierarchical Web of Strategy. Ideally, corporate strategy, business strategy, functional area support strategy, and operating-level strategy will be developed in sufficient detail that each manager in the organization has a confident understanding of how to manage his/her area of responsibility in accordance with the total game plan. This is why many layers of strategy are typically needed (especially in large, diversified organizations), with each layer being progressively more detailed to provide strategic guidance for the next level of subordinate managers. In addition, the separate pieces and layers of strategy should be consistent and interlock smoothly—like the pieces of a puzzle. When the elements of corporate strategy are in harmony and mutually supportive, then strategy can be a useful source of organizational cohesiveness. An effectively articulated strategy helps weld an organization's activities together and promotes a shared commitment among managers to accomplishing the game plan. It assists in keeping functional perspectives from blurring larger strategic priorities.[18]

Figure 2–1 depicts a hypothetical composite strategy and the several levels of directional actions and decisions requisite for making it operationally complete. Note the logical flow from business strategy to functional support strategies to operating-level strategies. It should be evident from an examination of this figure why an organization's strategic plan is the sum total of the directional actions and decisions it must make in trying to accomplish its objectives.

One final word about the levels of strategy. No matter how layered and specific a given strategy is, it should still be regarded as dynamic and temporal.[19] While an organization's fundamental purpose and long-term strategic objectives may not change significantly over long periods of time (particularly if they are carefully drawn), the strategic nature and scope of its product-market-technological activities are certain to change in material ways in response to a fairly constant flow of new environmental circumstances. As a consequence, finetuning the elements of the organization's strategic plan, and an occasional major change in strategic thrust, will be a normal and expected occurrence. The *inevitability of an evolving strategy* means that any strategy statement should be viewed as only *currently useful*—a fact which speaks loudly for regular review and revalidation of all levels of strategy.

---

[18] The ease with which functional areas can get at cross purposes with business strategy is illustrated by the case of a well-established foundry which initiated a strategy to build up a new customer base for industrial castings but found that work orders for castings were given the lowest priority in the milling and shipping departments because they were a new item and required different handling procedures; the strategic importance of the castings had simply not been impressed upon these two functional subunits.

[19] Vancil, "Strategy Formulation," pp. 2–5.

FIGURE 2-1
The Levels of Strategy for a Hypothetical Petroleum Company

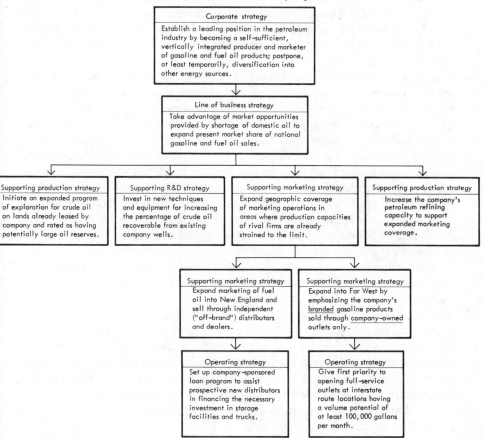

The Determinants of Strategy

An astute, timely strategy is typified by "goodness of fit" between the organization's internal skills, capabilities, and resources on the one hand and the external environment it confronts on the other hand. The evaluative process whereby an organization seeks an effective match between its internal and external environments highlights the factors which determine strategy.

Product-Market Opportunities. Opportunity is always a factor in determining strategy.[20] Most of the time it is a pivotal strategic consideration, for

---

[20] As cogently pointed out by Philip Kotler, there is a difference of opinion in the literature of management regarding whether the strategy formulation process should begin with the identification of opportunities or with the defining of purpose and objectives. Those who say the first

unless one perceives that an opportunity exists there is little point in proceeding. But on occasions, opportunity is just a necessary presence. For instance, when market demand is growing rapidly, it is virtually certain that firms in the industry will pursue the avenues for increased sales and profits; the gut issue is thus not whether opportunity exists but rather how to capture it.

In general terms, an organization's attempt to relate its strategy to opportunity consists of an assessment of any influence or trends in the external environment which may make a difference in what it elects to do or not do. This assessment of the external environment entails many facets: analyzing it, predicting it, attempting to change it, deciding how best to adapt to it, electing to get into or get out of some parts of it (in terms of specific products, markets, and technologies). It means looking at all relevant aspects of the external environment: customer needs and wants, resource availability, competitor's actions, trends in technology, R&D potentials, government policies and regulations, population and lifestyle characteristics, economic trends and conditions—essentially anything and everything that can have a bearing on the firm's market opportunities.

In viewing the role of opportunity in the strategy formulation process, it is important to distinguish between *environmental opportunities* and *company opportunities*.[21] It is fair to say that there are always product-market opportunities in an economy as long as there are unsatisfied needs and wants backed up by adequate purchasing power. But none of these necessarily represent opportunities for a specific company. New forms of health care delivery are probably not an opportunity for Texaco, nor is a growing popularity of skiing a likely opportunity for General Motors. The environmental opportunities that are most likely to be relevant to a particular company are those where the company in question will be able to enjoy some kind of strategic fit or competitive advantage.

---

step should be to identify opportunities argue that (1) many organizations have gotten their start because they recognized the existence of a major opportunity (Xerox, Polaroid, Holiday Inns, IBM, and Coca-Cola, among others); (2) many organizations which lack sharply-defined objectives and are unable to articulate what they are really trying to do have nonetheless compiled a good record of seizing opportunities; and (3) a number of organizations have changed their objectives when their opportunities change (as did the March of Dimes in shifting the problem to birth defects when the Salk vaccine virtually eliminated polio). Those who argue that the setting of purpose and objectives should logically precede a search for opportunity point out that (1) a number of organizations have been observed to look for opportunities that will allow them to achieve sales, profit, and growth objectives, (2) the environment is simply too full of opportunities for companies to look merely for opportunities without a guiding purpose and set of objectives, and (3) organizations can and do, from time to time, change their objectives—an event which, subsequently, leads them to search for new and different opportunities.

Both viewpoints have merit in theory and in practice. Quite clearly there is a close two-way link between an organization's search for opportunity and its definition of purpose and objectives. As long as this is recognized, there is little need to become embroiled in a "chicken-or-egg—which-comes-first" type of controversy.

See Philip Kotler, *Marketing Management: Analysis, Planning, and Control*, 3d ed. (Englewood Cliffs, N.J.: Prentice-Hall, Inc., 1976), p. 46.

[21] Ibid., p. 47.

A number of companies have been observed to pursue product/market growth opportunities in a particular strategic sequence. Starting from a single-product, limited-market base, a firm first seeks to increase its sales volume, improve its market share, and build customer loyalty. In essence, this step represents a more intensive implementation of the existing strategy. Price, quality, service, and promotion are fine-tuned to respond more precisely to a detailed market need, often including the introduction of a full product line to meet minor variations in customer tastes and preferences. As this strategy approaches its full exploitation, a growth-minded company will begin to assess the opportunities for geographical market expansion. Normally, the strategy of wider geographical coverage proceeds from local to regional to national to international markets, though the degree of penetration may be uneven from area to area because of varying profit potentials and may, of course, stop well short of global or even national proportions. When the opportunities for profitable market area expansion start to peter out, the organization's strategy may shift toward opportunities for vertical integration—either backward to sources of supply or forward to the ultimate consumer. For some companies this is a natural strategic move, owing to the close relationships to the organization's main line and to the potential for realizing economies of scale.

Once a firm has reached the limits of geographical market expansion for its original product line and has also come to terms with the possibilities of forward and backward integration, the strategic options are either to continue in the same lines of business and attempt a more intensive implementation or to shift the focus to diversification opportunities.

No set standard procedure can be prescribed for how an organization ought to conduct its search for opportunity. These remain somewhat unique to each organization and its particular circumstances. Suffice it to say that ferreting out and validating opportunities must be a constant concern of top management, and that the task requires daily enterpreneurial alertness to what is happening and what the implications are for the organization.

Organizational Competence and Resources. No matter how appealing or how abundant product-market opportunities may be, the strategist is forced to validate the viability of each "opportunity" by inquiring into whether the organization has the means to capitalize upon it, given the opposing forces of competition and organizational circumstance. Opportunity without the organizational competence to capture it is an illusion. An organization's strengths (demonstrated and potential) may make it particularly suited to seize some opportunities; likewise, its weaknesses may make the pursuit of other sorts of opportunities excessively risky or else disqualify it entirely. The strategist is thus well-advised to seek out a match between opportunity and competence which exploits or extends organizational strengths and which contains or minimizes dependence upon its weaknesses.

An organization's skills and strengths derive primarily from gradually-accumulated experience and sustained success in its business. Unique and occasional flashes of skill or strength are rarely as dependable as are those built up over a period of time and subjected to the tests of competitive pressure. It takes more than a year or two of experience and success to develop a level of expertise in which much confidence can be placed.

In practice, one finds that the strengths and capabilities of rival organizations vary significantly. Firms in the same industry will be ordinarily found to have different financial resources, different marketing skills, different degrees of technical knowhow, different costs, different morale, different images and market standing, different managerial depth—in short, different internal capabilities. Whether the internal differences prove to be important strengths or important weaknesses depend upon how they relate to the chosen strategy. But, clearly, significant differences between one organization and its major rivals have the potential for being the cornerstone of strategy.

Because of the strategic relevance of organizational strengths and weaknesses, it is always worthwhile for an organization to ponder what *distinctive* skills and capabilities it can bring to bear that will allow it to draw business away from rival organizations. Some organizations excel in manufacturing a "quality product," others in creative approaches to marketing, and still others in innovation and new product development. An organization's *distinctive competence* is thus more than just what it can do—it is what it can do *especially well* as compared to rival enterprises.[22] The importance of distinctive competence to strategy rests with the unique capability it gives an organization in developing a comparative advantage in the marketplace.

Typically, a key element in successful business strategy formulation is the ability to build into the strategic plan a product-market approach that will set the organization apart from others and give it some kind of strategic advantage. Generally, this means (1) following a different course from rival firms, (2) conceiving of a plan which will have quite different (and more favorable) consequences for one's own organization than for competitors, and (3) making it hard for other organizations to imitate the strategy should it succeed.[23] Obviously enough, these guidelines are easier to follow when an organization has some kind of distinctive competence around which to build its strategy. It is always easier to develop strategic advantage in a market where the success requirements correspond to the organization's distinctive competence, where other organizations do not have these competences, and where potential rivals are not able to attain these competences except at high cost and/or over an extended period of time.[24] But if an organization has no

---

[22] Philip Selznick, *Leadership in Administration* (Evanston, Ill.: Row, Peterson & Company, 1957), p. 42.

[23] Bruce D. Henderson, "Construction of a Business Strategy," reprinted in Daniel J. McCarthy, Robert J. Minichiello, and Joseph R. Curran, *Business Policy and Strategy: Concepts and Readings* (Homewood, Ill.: Richard D. Irwin, 1975), p. 290.

[24] Kollat, Blackwell, and Robeson, *Strategic Marketing*, p. 24. For a detailed description of how to evaluate internal competences and resources, see William E. Rothschild, *Putting It All Together: A Guide to Strategic Thinking* (New York: AMACOM, 1976), chap. 6.

particular distinctive competence upon which to try to capitalize, the next best bet is to focus on ways to exploit existing differences between the organization's product/service and those of its competitors.

Environmental Threats.   Very often, certain factors in the environment pose *threats* to an organization's strategic plans. These externally imposed threats may stem from possible new technological developments, the advent of new substitute products, adverse economic trends, government action, changing consumer values and lifestyles, projections of natural resource depletion, unfavorable demographic shifts, and the like. Such threats can be a major factor in shaping organizational strategy and a wise strategist is as much alert to the threats of environmental change as to the opportunities that it may present.

An example of the technological threat which solid-state digital watches presented to Timex is described in Illustration Capsule 6. Other instances of strategy-related environmental threats include:

The potential of nationalization and government takeover threatens the investment strategy of transnational corporations whenever they locate facilities in countries having a record of political instability.

The business of the manufacturers of coated copying paper was threatened and eventually ruined by technological developments which allowed the use of plain paper in copying equipment.

The emergence of gasohol as a partial substitute for gasoline threatened to alter the grip which oil companies had on the market for motor vehicle fuels.

Scientific discoveries that fluorocarbon-based aerosol sprays damaged the ozone layers on the earth's atmosphere (and the subsequent likelihood of future government bans) caused aerosol chemical manufacturers and aerosol can users to initiate a high priority search for substitute forms of technology and packaging.

Increased costs of regulatory compliance and public concerns about the safety of nuclear generation of electric power threatened both the viability of the business of the manufacturers of nuclear generating equipment and the financial ability of power companies to install and operate nuclear powered plants—indeed, during the 1975–1978 period no new nuclear facilities were ordered (many previously contracted-for units were cancelled), and several manufacturers were seriously considering withdrawal from the market for nuclear-powered equipment.

For the most part, organizations appear to *react* to environmental threats rather than to plan for or to anticipate them. Actually, this is not a strong criticism of managers; a great portion of the environmental changes having major strategic implications are not readily subject to prediction. Some occur without warning and with few, if any, advance clues; others are "bound to happen" but the uncertainty is when. Moreover, even when threatening

Strategic Implications of the Solid-State Technology Threat to Timex

In 1975, Timex ranked as the world's largest maker of finished watches. Its sales of some 40 million watches a year gave it a commanding 50 percent of the U.S. mechanical watch market and 70 percent of the electric watch market. The core of Timex's strategy was (1) to mass-produce a simple pin-levered movement watch in highly efficient plant facilities, and (2) to market them at rock-bottom prices through some 150,000 outlets—drugstores, variety stores, department stores, and even auto supply dealers. With eye-catching point-of-sale displays and skillful television advertising (the "torture test ads" narrated by John Cameron Swazy) to go with its low prices, Timex watches made steady market inroads to become the leading brand.

But, unexpectedly in 1975, Timex found itself confronted with a major technological challenge to its market position: how to develop a strategic response to the digital watch and the technology of solid-state electronics—a technology that was on the verge of sweeping the watch industry and undermining the cost advantage Timex enjoyed with its simple pin-levered mechanical watches. To complicate matters, Timex had little, if any, digital technology capability of its own.

The solid-state revolution in digital display watches was spearheaded not by established watch companies (Timex, Bulova, Benrus, Gruen, and others), but by semiconductor companies, including Texas Instruments, National Semiconductor, Litronix, Hughes Aircraft, and Fairchild Camera & Instrument. These firms, although newcomers to the watch industry, moved aggressively to dominate the market. Accustomed to competing in an industry where technological breakthroughs change things almost overnight, they quickly began to ignore traditional watch business practices (such as financing the watch inventories of retail jewelers and considering a 50 percent margin of selling price over cost as standard). They initiated bold price cuts even though demand seemed to be outstripping supply. Whereas the strategy of several semiconductor firms was, originally, to seek to enter into joint ventures with the traditional watchmakers, when the latter reacted so slowly, the strategy was changed to one of beating them head-on in the marketplace. Developments were so fast-paced that by mid-1975 jewelers were worried about the digital watch killing their watch business—not only because of the sharply lower profit margins but also because the semiconductor companies planned to furnish what little service or repair was needed on digitals from the factory, rather than at the point of sale.

Digital watch technology represented a radical departure from the Timex pin-levered watch. The digital watch had no moving parts to wear out and was far more accurate (within a minute per year) than even the most expensive mechanical watch. It operates with just four components: a battery, quartz crystal, an integrated circuit, and a digital display. The battery causes the quartz crystal to vibrate at 32,768 cycles per second (in most watches). The integrated circuit divides the vibrations into one pulse per second, accumulates the pulses to compute minutes, hours, days, and months, and transmits signals to the display to illuminate the digits showing the time and date.

When the first digital watches appeared in 1972, Timex was not unduly alarmed. It, together with most other watch manufacturers, viewed digitals as a fad or at most a specialty watch. Moreover, the first digitals were poorly designed, big and ugly, and experienced 60 percent defective returns. The biggest problem was in the digital time displays which were unreliable and often unreadable. Within three years, however, the semiconductor firms had made rapid progress in making the displays dependable and easy to read; styling was much sharper; and components had been made much smaller. Then in a move reminiscent of their strategy in the calculator business, the semiconductor firms in early 1975 slashed the prices of components in half—to as low as $20 per watch. Lower digital watch prices quickly followed (about half of what prices were in 1974). The move caught Timex and other traditional watch manufacturers offguard. The apparent pricing strategy of the semiconductor firms was based on the "cost learning curve" whereby the prices of watches and component modules were to be lowered as production efficiency increased. But, at the same time, the digital watch firms were finding ways to reduce the number of parts in the module, ways to squeeze more of the electronic circuitry onto the main circuit, and ways to cut assembly costs. These savings permitted large price cuts to be made even sooner than planned.

As late as 1975, Timex had done little more than dip its toe into the digital market, with mediocre results. Solid-state technology was new to Timex. The company had no in-house capacity to produce such components as integrated circuits and digital displays, although it had introduced a digital watch line back in 1972.

Previously, Timex had rejected several contractual offers from semiconductor firms to supply it with digital-watch components. Hughes Aircraft Company, for example, which produced integrated circuits for Timex analog quartz watches, offered in 1971 to build a digital watch to sell under the Timex label if Timex would guarantee a minimum production run of 1 million units. The Hughes offer was for watches with light-emitting diode readouts which have to be turned on by pushing a button. Timex rejected the offer. Meanwhile, Timex's own efforts to develop inhouse electronic watch capability progressed slowly. The head of its program to develop both digital and analog quartz watches left in 1973 to become director of watch operations at Rockwell International Corporation; his departure reportedly was due to Timex's failure to move rapidly in building up a digital capability.

The solid-state technology threat thus raised several strategy issues of vital concern to Timex's future:

1. Was the digital watch just a fad or was solid-state circuitry the wave of the future in watchmaking technology? (In 1974, digital watch sales totaled 650,000; some forecasts called for digital sales of 2.5 million units in 1975, and as much as 10 million in 1976.)
2. How quickly and to what extent would the rapidly falling prices of digital watches begin to create strong competitive pressures for Timex? (The prices of digital watches fell from $125 in 1974 to $50 in 1975, and to as low as $20 in early 1976.)
3. When and to what extent should Timex begin to push its own line of digital watches?
4. Should it purchase digital watch components from suppliers or should it develop its own digital component manufacturing capability? If the latter, then should the capability be developed internally or should Timex seek to acquire a firm with the technological know-how and experience?

In the minds of many observers, there was little doubt that Timex would soon have to offer a wide range of digital watches and, because of its carefully nurtured image as a producer of economy-priced watches, that the new digital watches would also have to be low priced. Otherwise, its market position would be in serious jeopardy.

Based upon information in "The Electronics Threat to Timex," *Business Week,* August 18, 1975, pp. 42 ff; "Digital Watches: Bringing Watchmaking Back to the U.S.," *Business Week,* October 27, 1975, pp. 78 ff; "Timex Corporation" in H. Uyterhoeven, R. W. Ackerman, and J. W. Rosenblum, *Strategy and Organization: Text and Cases in General Management* (Homewood, Ill.: Richard D. Irwin, Inc., 1973), pp. 309–20; and "The $20 Digital Watch Arrives a Year Early," *Business Week,* January 26, 1976, pp. 27–28.

signals are detected early, it is not always easy to assess the extent of their strategic significance. Trying to forecast those future events which have strategic significance is scarcely an exact science. But, this is not sufficient to provide excuses or alibis; an alert and responsible management will endeavor to stay in close touch with the possibilities of adverse environmental change and will have done some contingency planning.

Personal Values and Aspirations. Strategy formulation is rarely so objective an analytical process that the personal values and aspirations of managers are excluded. Both casual observation and systematic studies indicate that the firsthand influences, experiences, beliefs, and goals of managers can be important determinants of strategy.[25] As Professor Andrews has noted in characterizing why personal values are relevant to strategy, "Somebody has to have his heart in it."[26]

Most managers have their own concepts of what their organization's strategy is or ought to be. These concepts are certain to reflect, in part, a manager's own values and opinions—especially when he/she has had a hand in formulating the strategy. There is a natural human tendency for managers to draw upon their own personal values, background experiences, preferences, and ambitions when choosing among alternative strategies and when interpreting the strategic plan. Sometimes the influence of one's own values and experiences is conscious and deliberate, at other times it may be unconscious. Whichever, the important point is that managers do not dispassionately assess what their organization can do or should do; they often are influenced by what they personally want the company to do and to be.

The following examples illustrate how personal values and aspirations can influence strategy:

A minister aspires to be the pastor of the largest congregation in town so he launches a well-organized campaign to attract new members and, in turn, a fund-raising drive to build the biggest church in the area.

A corporate president has unswerving bias against dealing with unions, so he deliberately insists on locating plant facilities in geographical areas where workers have traditionally been indisposed toward unionism. In turn, he uses the ability to pay subunion wages as a tactic for gaining a competitive edge on costs and selling price.

A division manager in a diversified corporation wishes to make the business unit he heads "number one in sales and in the industry" so he pushes for a marketing strategy that calls for increasing volume and sales revenue even at the expense of slightly smaller (though acceptable) profit margins and returns on investment.

---

[25] See, for instance, William D. Guth and Renato Tagiuri, "Personal Values and Corporate Strategy," *Harvard Business Review*, vol. 43, no. 5 (September–October 1965), pp. 123–32; Kenneth R. Andrews, *The Concept of Corporate Strategy* (Homewood, Ill.: Dow Jones-Irwin, Inc., 1971, chap. 4; and Vancil, "Strategy Formulation, pp. 4–5.

[26] Andrews, *Corporate Strategy*, p. 117.

Being alert to where an organization's management is coming from in terms of backgrounds, lifestyles, experiences, and professional standards can therefore provide important clues to the nature and makeup of strategy. Two well-known instances can be cited.[27] The publishers and editors of the *New York Times* have a strong, long-standing commitment to reporting the news intelligently, accurately, and without bias or sensationalism. Their dedication to this style of journalism has caused them to reject changing the nature and character of the *New York Times,* even though their decision to preserve the *status quo* strategy has undoubtedly been costly in terms of less circulation and a lower return on investment. Hugh Hefner, the founder and publisher of *Playboy,* worked initially for several other magazines, but he found himself wanting to strike out on his own and create a magazine which reflected his own preferences and lifestyle. As he soon discovered, there was indeed a market for *Playboy* and Hefner, guided largely by his own sense of values and aspirations, pioneered a new concept in magazine publishing.

As indicated by Vancil, the personalization of strategy is not restricted to senior management and, indeed, is both feasible and desirable at lower levels of management:

> A personalized strategy is feasible in a complex organization if the statement of strategy is drafted carefully. As discussed earlier, the superior manager devises his strategy and expresses it in the form of constraints on the scope of the activities of his subordinates. However, he should take care to leave them some discretion as to how they operate within those constraints. Each subordinate manager will then accept (or challenge) those constraints, devise "his" strategy within them, and in turn express his strategy to his subordinates in the form of constraints on their activities. The resulting series of progressively detailed statements of strategy are personalized, in the sense that each manager can see his imprint on his part of the series. Furthermore, they are integrated throughout the organization as a whole, because each statement is consistent with the constraints imposed by higher authority.
>
> Two of the several advantages of personalized strategies deserve mention here. First, encouraging each manager to use his imagination to devise the best strategy he can increases the vitality and creativity of the organization. In a complex organization, no one man, not even the president, can identify all the opportunities that exist, and a framework of progressive constraints that elicits personalized strategies multiplies the sources of initiative in the corporation. Second, a personalized strategy engenders a personal commitment.[28]

Societal Obligations and Ethical Considerations. The ethical, political, social, and moral aspects of the external environment obviously enter into strategy formulation. Although the interaction between strategy and societal factors is a two-way street, here we wish to focus on how societal values and

---

[27] Guth and Tagiuri, "Personal Values," p. 128.

[28] Reprinted from "Strategy Formulation in Complex Organizations" by Richard F. Vancil, *Sloan Management Review,* Winter 1976, pp. 4–5, by permission of the publisher. Copyright © 1976 by the Sloan Management Review Association. All rights reserved.

expectations, together with a firm's perceived social and ethical obligations, impinge on strategy. That consumerism, truth-in-packaging, equal opportunity employment, occupational health and safety, open housing, product safety, beliefs about ethics and morals, ethics and moral values, and other similar societal-based factors have an impact on organization strategies requires no discussion. Adapting strategy to accommodate these factors is commonplace and generally accepted. Some firms, since they can exercise but little influence over societal values and expectations, view the ethical-moral-social value dimension of strategy formulation as a constraint and sometimes as a threat. This view is not without some justification; changes in social mores and preferences can indeed be potentially threatening to an organization's business. But, what is threatening to one enterprise may, at the same time, open new doors to another organization. For instance, while public concern about cancer-causing food additives poses obvious strategic threats to some food manufacturers, there arises simultaneously major new market opportunities for organizations with expertise in health and nutrition research and for producers of food items thought to be safe.

Irrespective of whether changes in societal values and requirements destroy or create strategic opportunities, managerial alertness to the corporation's societal and ethical obligations is an essential ingredient of effective strategy formulation. Indeed, the desirability (if not the imperative) of relating an organization to the needs and expectations of society is, today, a fairly noncontroversial issue. The notion of what management ought to do to make an organization "socially responsible" includes (1) adapting the organization to the changing requirements and expectations of society, (2) endeavoring to keep organizational activities in tune with what is generally perceived as the public interest, (3) responding positively to emerging societal priorities, (4) demonstrating a willingness to take needed action ahead of regulatory confrontation, (5) balancing stockholder interests against the larger interest of society as a whole, (6) being a "good citizen" in the community, and (7) making the corporation's social and ethical obligations an explicit and high priority consideration in the way the enterprise conducts its affairs.

Being "socially responsible" has both carrot and stick aspects. There is the positive appeal for all organizations to pursue strategies and policies that will improve their public standing at the same time that it enhances their own performance opportunities—and these are always inexorably tied to the generally healthy well-being of society.[29] And there is the negative burden of public criticism and onerous regulation if they come up short.

Strategy and Organizational "Personality". Every organization has a personality and modes of behavior which are somewhat unique to itself. Some

---

[29] Those who doubt the general principle that high levels of organization performance are closely tied to the general well-being of society should take note of the remarkably good correlation between changes in the levels of business profits and changes in the level of economic activity. Comparatively few businesses will be found to enjoy higher levels of performance during periods of social and economic decline. There is more truth to the view that "what's good for General Motors is good for the U.S.A." than it is currently fashionable to admit.

organizations are noted for being aggressive and exhibiting leadership; others are clearly more complacent and slow-moving, often quite content to assume a follow-the-leader role. A few older, long-established, family-dominated firms display the characteristics of paternalism toward employees or toward customers of long-standing. Companies may be variously noted for their "conservatism," or their pervasive preoccupation with technological virtuosity, or their financial wheeling and dealing, or their hard-hitting competitive style, or their emphasis on growth, or their social consciousness, or their desire to avoid risk. Quite clearly, these traits can spill over into, and even dominate, organization strategy at all levels.

How the Determinants of Strategy Combine to Affect Strategic Choice

Our discussion of the determinants of strategy raises the question of how the determinants interact with one another and in due course work their way into an organization's choice of strategy. Figure 2–2 presents a simple model of the strategy formulation process and indicates the role of the major strategy determinants in this process. As Figure 2–2 implies, we think it is appropriate to view strategy formulation as a special kind of problem-solving *process* for choosing an organization's strategy. The strategy formulation process entails five main steps or phases:

1. *Current strategy identification*—an assessment of where the company is now (in terms of scope of operations, current strategies, and overall performance) and how its present position has been shaped by personal aspirations and values of owners/managers, competition, opportunities and threats, societal expectations and government regulations, internal resources, and so on.
2. *External environment/market analysis*—an evaluation of product-market opportunities, competition, environmental threats, and other relevant external factors.
3. *Evaluation of internal resources, skills, and competences*—an assessment of what the organization can do, how hard it can be pushed, and an inventory of its skills, competences, and capabilities.
4. *Analysis of strategic alternatives*—identification and evaluation of each feasible strategic option, taking into account both the pressures for performance and results and the need to closely align the organization's responses to opportunities/threats with its internal resource capabilities.
5. *Selection of strategy*—arriving at a choice of one or more of the strategic options, after factoring in all of the considerations which are deemed relevant (specifically including opportunities, threats, values and aspirations, societal expectations, government regulations, competitive and market realities, and internal capabilities).

Except for organizations that are highly diversified and also experienced in the use of complex strategy formulation techniques, the model depicted in

FIGURE 2-2
Simple Model of How the Determinants of Strategy Impact upon Strategy Formulation

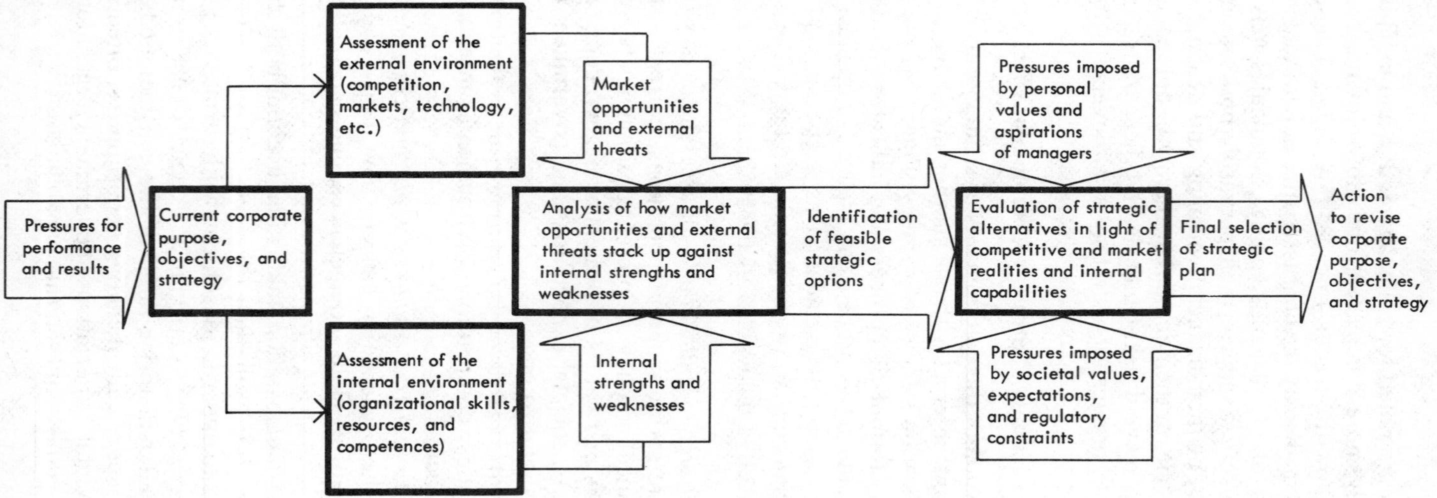

Pressures for performance and results

Current corporate purpose, objectives, and strategy

Assessment of the external environment (competition, markets, technology, etc.)

Assessment of the internal environment (organizational skills, resources, and competences)

Market opportunities and external threats

Analysis of how market opportunities and external threats stack up against internal strengths and weaknesses

Internal strengths and weaknesses

Identification of feasible strategic options

Pressures imposed by personal values and aspirations of managers

Evaluation of strategic alternatives in light of competitive and market realities and internal capabilities

Pressures imposed by societal values, expectations, and regulatory constraints

Final selection of strategic plan

Action to revise corporate purpose, objectives, and strategy

Figure 2–2 is a reasonably sufficient portrayal of the basic elements and considerations inherent in the task of formulating organization strategy.[30]

Much more elaborate diagrammatics are, of course, possible. In the typical case, however, probing deeply into the *methodology* of strategy formulation and intricately *modeling* the strategy formulation process offer less to the practicing manager (and to successful strategy analysis) than does consciously concentrating on creative, perceptive, insightful, and opportunistic entrepreneurship. Said a bit differently, the substance underlying good strategy is astute entrepreneurship and business judgment, not a detailed schematic of the steps to be followed. This is because the task of strategy formulation requires a heavy dose of "situational design"—that is to say, it must take into account all the relevant specifics of a particular organization's situation. Hence, emphasis upon some allegedly universal, off-the-shelf procedure for strategy formulation is misplaced for two very good reasons: one, the situation of each organization is different in terms of internal capability, managerial philosophy and objectives, competitive position in the marketplace, and diversity and scope of operations and, two, organizational strategy is inherently the product of managers and thus bears the mark of their character, perceptivity, analytical skills, and personal values. The primary value, therefore, of studying strategy formulation processes and procedures is to raise managerial consciousness about what kinds of considerations underlie a shrewd choice of organization strategy, rather than to offer a generalized or highly detailed presentation of what steps to follow and what to do at each step.

Characteristics of an Effective Strategy

The effectiveness of a particular strategy can be appraised from two angles.[31] One is from the perspective of whether the strategy is right for the organization in its particular situation. Does it offer a viable and potentially effective fit between the organization's internal and external environments? Does it allow the enterprise to exploit attractive product-market opportunities and/or to escape the impact of externally imposed threats? Is it compatible with the organization's perceived strengths and weaknesses? Does it fully utilize internal competences and resources? It is timely? In short, does the strategy exemplify "goodness of fit" among the relevant external/internal considerations?

The second angle is the more subtle issue of whether the strategy has been sufficiently delineated. Is the strategy complete enough to allow managers to proceed confidently in managing their areas of responsibility according to the game plan? Has the strategy been developed and articulated in sufficient

---

[30] For more elaborate strategy formulation models, see Ansoff, *Corporate Strategy*, p. 202; and Charles W. Hofer and Dan Schendel, *Strategy Formulation: Analytical Concepts* (St. Paul, Minn.: West Publishing Company, 1978), chap. 3.

[31] Vancil, "Strategy Formulation," p. 3.

detail, beginning at the corporate level and continuing in ever more detailed layers down to the operating level? The whole of an organization's strategy is always a compound of many distinct actions and decisions, rather than a single point of attack.

An effective and complete concept of strategy says a great deal about the organization involved—its present and future character. It reconciles the organization-wide response to the questions of: What might we do? What can we do? What do we want to do? What should we do? It supplies an answer to "what set of businesses should we be in?" Ultimately, it defines the organization's business in terms of products, markets, and geographic coverage. At the competitive level, these definitions are clear-cut enough to pinpoint product functions and uses, as well as the precise customer classes for which these products are intended. Strategy provides direction and guidance for administrative process and policies and for internal resource allocation. It speaks to whether and how the organization seeks a distinctive competence. It points toward the criteria for operating the organization on a day-to-day basis. It indicates organizational priorities and, because of its close relationship to the organization's long-run and short-run objectives, it is indicative of the kinds of performance and results to be achieved.

A Concluding Point

As Professor Vancil has said, strategy is the conceptual glue that binds an organization's activities together.[32] Yet, it is doubtful whether one can speak accurately of *the* strategy, except in very simple types of organization. In most organizations, and especially in diversified firms of some size, it is more correct to think of strategy as a collection of strategies— one for each facet of the organization's activities and perhaps one for each manager. These strategies form a hierarchical network, linked together by analysis and soul-searching as well as by an interactive, iterative process of negotiation and agreement on objectives, plans, policies, and constraints. To be effective, strategy must personally affect each manager, guiding what is to be done but in a manner which gives the manager enough elbow room to devise his/her unit's strategy within the broader context.[33]

Management may from time to time attempt to express strategy (or some parts thereof) in a written statement, but it is rare for such statements to be developed at the same time for every organization unit and every facet of the organization's activities. Consequently, the web of an organization's strategy is rarely delineated and written down as explicitly and comprehensively as has been described in this chapter. Much of strategy consists of verbal agreements and implied understandings between managers. Some pieces of strategy are readily deduced from visible management actions (acquisitions,

---

[32] Ibid., p. 18.
[33] Ibid.

divestiture, competitive behavior). Other pieces may appear in the forms of annual reports, speeches of top executives before meetings of securities analysts, internal memoranda, in-house studies and reports, minutes of meetings, and the like. Consequently, one should not expect an organization's strategy to be laid out boldly and regularly in some document called "the strategic plan." But, irrespective of whether an organization's strategy is written or oral, explicit or implicit, open or covert, the foregoing discussion should suffice to indicate that managerial alertness to the role of strategy and managerial understanding of the current strategy are of prime importance in the management of the total organization. It is the unity, coherence, and internal consistency of management's strategic decisions that position the organization in its environment and give the organization its identity, its power to mobilize its strengths, and its likelihood of economic success.[34] In this regard, we would urge that the concept of strategy is neither an empty academic box nor a managerially moot activity with little or no bottom-line impact.

SUGGESTED READINGS

Abell, Derek F. *Defining the Business: The Starting Point of Strategic Planning.* Englewood Cliffs, N.J.: Prentice–Hall, Inc., 1980.

Andrews, Kenneth R. *The Concept of Corporate Strategy.* Rev. ed. (Homewood, Ill.: Dow Jones-Irwin, Inc., 1980), chaps. 2, 3, 4, and 5.

Ansoff, H. Igor. *Corporate Strategy.* New York: McGraw-Hill, 1965, chap. 6.

Cannon, J. Thomas. *Business Strategy and Policy.* New York: Harcourt, Brace, and World, Inc., 1968, chaps. 1 and 2.

Drucker, Peter F. *Management: Tasks, Responsibilities, Practices.* New York: Harper & Row, Publishers, 1974, chaps. 6 and 7.

Hall, William K. "Strategic Planning, Product Innovation, and the Theory of the Firm." *Journal of Business Policy,* vol. 3, no. 3 (Spring 1973), pp. 19–27.

Hanan, Mack. "Reorganize Your Company Around Its Markets." *Harvard Business Review,* vol. 52, no. 6 (November–December 1974), pp. 63–74.

Hofer, Charles W., and Schendel, Dan. *Strategy Formulation: Analytical Concepts.* St. Paul, Minn.: West Publishing Co., 1978, chap. 2.

Leontiades, Milton. *Strategies for Diversification and Change.* Boston: Little, Brown and Co., 1980, chap. 1.

Levitt, Theodore. "Marketing Myopia." *Harvard Business Review,* vol. 38, no. 4 (July–August 1960), pp. 45–56.

Newman, William H. "Shaping the Master Strategy of Your Firm." *California Management Review,* vol. 9, no. 3 (Spring 1967), pp. 77–88.

Steiner, George A. *Strategic Planning: What Every Manager Must Know.* New York: Free Press, 1979, chaps. 1–3, 9.

---

[34] Andrews, *Corporate Strategy,* p. 20.

Stephenson, Howard H. "Defining Corporate Strengths and Weaknesses." *Sloan Management Review*, vol. 17, no. 3 (Spring 1976), pp. 51–68.

Tilles, Seymour. "Making Strategy Explicit." *Business Strategy*, ed. H. Igor Ansoff. New York: Penguin Books, 1970, pp. 180–209.

Vance, Jack O. "The Anatomy of a Corporate Strategy." *California Management Review*, vol. 13, no. 1 (Fall 1970), pp. 5–12.

Vancil, Richard F. "Strategy Formulation in Complex Organizations." *Sloan Management Review*, vol. 17, no. 2 (Winter 1976), pp. 1–18.

Vancil, Richard F., and Lorange, Peter. "Strategic Planning in Diversified Companies." *Harvard Business Review*, vol. 53, no. 1 (January–February 1975), pp. 81–90.

3 IDENTIFYING STRATEGIC ALTERNATIVES

Markets are not created by God, nature, or economic forces but by businessmen.

Peter F. Drucker

E very organization ought to be wary of becoming a prisoner of its present strategy. Sooner or later, all strategies grow stale or obsolete. They need either finetuning or major overhaul or radical surgery. Thus, while it is by no means necessary for the incumbent strategic plan to be shunted aside in favor of new alternatives at each time of reappraisal, an alert management will guard against letting strategic reevaluation be little more than a time for rationalizing why the status quo should be maintained.

The real managerial purpose behind regular reappraisal of strategy is to help management avoid the complacency of viewing the prevailing strategy as too much of a given rather than as only one among several viable, and perhaps more attractive, possibilities. True, taking a creative, entrepreneurial approach to strategy reformulation raises a possibility that the existing strategy will be deemphasized; this may threaten those in the organization who have vested interests in the current strategic plan. But for an enterprise which aspires to continued success and high performance, this is the way things must be. Imaginative strategy formulation and reformulation is virtually a prerequisite of sustained high performance. Nostalgic and inopportune adherence to existing strategy merely paves the way for other organizations which, lacking strong attachment to strategies of the past or present, will surely be less reluctant to seize upon a fresh strategy if they view the entrenched firms' strategies as vulnerable to attack. For this reason alone, a strong commitment to regular strategic reappraisals and, further, to creative identification of strategic alternatives is an essential ingredient of entrepreneurially effective management.

Corporate Strategy Alternatives versus Business Strategy Alternatives

As previously discussed, corporate strategy and business strategy are two very different animals. Business strategy relates to how an enterprise intends to conduct its business for a particular product, product line, or group of related products. It specifically is concerned with how to compete effectively and profitably in a distinct, identifiable, and strategically relevant line of business. On the other hand, corporate strategy is most relevant to diversified organizations whose activities cut across several lines of business and thus pose to management the ever-present issue of "what set of businesses should we be in—what should we continue to do, what existing businesses should we get out of, and what new businesses should we get into?" Corporate strategy aims at making a workable whole out of diverse activities and at giving directions to the total mix of organizational activities.

Because of the difference in scope and focus between corporate and business strategy, there necessarily is a difference in the kinds of strategy alternatives at each level. Corporate strategy alternatives deal directly with the different ways of (1) shaping what an organization does and does not do and (2) adjusting the makeup and emphasis among the organization's chosen business activities. Business strategy alternatives, on the other hand, concern the different ways of trying to compete in a given market and the different ways of handling a particular kind of business given its particular set of circumstances.

In identifying and discussing the various strategic alternatives open to an enterprise, it is therefore desirable to proceed at two levels: the basic alternatives of corporate strategy and the basic alternatives of business strategy. We begin with corporate strategy.

THE BASIC ALTERNATIVES OF CORPORATE STRATEGY

In trying to decide upon an overall strategy to accomplish its performance objectives, an organization has essentially nine basic corporate strategy options to select from (either singly or in combination):

1. Concentration on a single business.
2. Vertical integration.
3. Concentric diversification.
4. Conglomerate diversification.
5. Merger and acquisition.
6. Joint ventures.
7. Retrenchment.
8. Divestiture.
9. Liquidation.

Each of these merit discussion because it is useful to have a strong grasp on the full range of corporate strategies when addressing the issue of whether the present strategy is the most advantageous.

Concentration on a Single Business

The number of organizations which have made their mark parlaying a single-product, single-market, or single-technology strategy is impressively long. The power and achievement which attaches to concentrating on the right business at the right time is testified to by the blue-chip strategic performance of such familiar companies as McDonald's, Holiday Inn, Coca-Cola, BIC Pen Corp., Campbell Soup Co., Anheuser-Busch, Xerox, Dr Pepper, Gerber, and Polaroid.[1]

A concentration strategy offers numerous strengths and advantages. To begin with, a specialized business is more manageable. Simplicity breeds clarity and unity of purpose. With the efforts of the *total* organization aimed at successfully catering to a clearly identified target clientele, objectives can be made precise and results appraised more easily. There is less chance that limited organizational resources will be spread thinly over too many activities. Corporate management has ample opportunity to develop first-hand, in-depth knowledge of the business, the market, the organization, its customers, its technology, and major competitors. As a consequence, a concentration strategy offers excellent potential for an organization to:

1. Focus on doing *one* thing *very well*, thereby building a distinctive competence and promoting a high degree of efficiency and productivity.
2. Zero in on specific markets and market segments, thus gaining greater market visibility and even a leadership position.
3. Detect changes and trends in customer purchasing behavior and market conditions at an early stage and to respond quickly to them.
4. Achieve a high degree of effectiveness in meeting stiffer competition and in reacting to new market opportunities.
5. Create a differential strategic advantage via the market reputation and the competitive strength that come from having a distinctive competence.

The advantages of a concentration strategy cannot be taken lightly. That they are well recognized and important is acknowledged by the widespread attempt of diversified firms to decentralize their activities into well-defined lines of business so that a special opportunity in a significant market niche can be successfully pursued. The power of a concentration strategy is also suggested by the fact that the managers of large diversified companies often view their strongest competitors as being smaller, specialized enterprises with concentrated, in-depth expertise in particular products and market segments. When a given product or customer group is only one among many of a company's interests, then it may not receive the same degree of attention and management priority as when it is the organization's sole business.

It is important to recognize that a concentration strategy does not require

---

[1] In the nonprofit sector the specialist strategy has proved successful for the Boston Pops Orchestra, the Red Cross, the Girl Scouts, Phi Beta Kappa, and the American Civil Liberties Union.

an enterprise to continue to do the same thing in the same ways. There are numerous options for varying and finetuning a concentration strategy. One option is to pursue new ways to gain greater market penetration of the present product line. This could include one or more of the following:

1. Trying to increase current customers' usage of the product by:
   a. Increasing the size of units offered for sale.
   b. Incorporating more features into the basic unit.
   c. Creating and promoting more uses for the product.
   d. Using innovation to shorten the time span for the product to become obsolete.
   e. Giving price discounts for increased use.
2. Endeavoring to attract customers away from rival firms via:
   a. Increased advertising and promotional efforts.
   b. Sharper product differentiation and brand identification.
   c. Lower prices.
3. Attracting nonusers to buy the products by
   a. Inducing trial use through free samples, cents-off coupons, and low introductory price offers.
   b. Advertising new or different product uses and features.
   c. Repricing the product—up or down.

A second option is to expand into additional geographic markets—regional, national, or international. A third approach is to improve product quality, convenience of use, customer services, and the like. A fourth set of options aims at developing new product features and catering to distinct buyer preferences via any of the following:

1. Offering a wider variety of models and sizes.
2. Distributing the product line through other types of distribution channels.
3. Advertising in different kinds of media.
4. Developing new or different product features (by making the item shorter, lighter, smaller, stronger, thicker, longer, or more durable; or by changing the item's color, odor, taste, sound, components, styling, design, or packaging—as may be appropriate).

The corporate strategy of concentrating on a single business does pose a major business risk, however. By specializing, an enterprise puts all of its eggs in one basket. If the market for the enterprise's product or service declines, so does the enterprise's business. Changing customer needs, technological innovation, or new products can undermine or virtually wipe out a highly specialized, single-business firm in short order. One has only to recall what television did to the profitability and markets of the once-powerful Hollywood movie producers and what IBM electric typewriters did to the manual typewriter business formerly dominated by Royal-McBee, Underwood, and Smith Corona. And if the product/service is particularly vulnerable to recessionary influence in the economy, then the enterprises's fortunes are subject to wide swings and, consequently, a normally lower stock market appraisal.

Furthermore, by concentrating its expertise in a narrow area, an organization may find itself without the competence and knowhow to break out of its shell and develop alternatives if and when the time arrives to cast off a fast-obsolescing strategic plan. Every product, every service, every technology eventually loses its market grip.[2] Sales volume may still be there, but profitability and growth opportunities shrivel. If the specialist firm is to escape stagnation, it must keep some fresh options open. And like any habit, doing something new and different must be kept sharp by practice. Otherwise the capacity for shifting to new strategies and new businesses is never developed or else withers away.

Vertical Integration

Two factors tend to trigger serious corporate-level consideration of a vertical integration strategy: (1) diminishing profit prospects associated with further expansion of the main product line into new geographic markets and (2) being the wrong size to realize scale economies and performance potentials.[3] Market saturation and the impracticalities of an oversize market coverage give rise to the first factor cited. A variety of causes underlie being the wrong size but the symptom is easy enough to spot: one (or a few) of the organization's production or distribution activities are out of proportion to the remainder, thereby making it difficult for the organization to support the volume, the product line, or the market standing requisite for economical operations and long-run competitive survival.[4]

Vertical integration has much to recommend itself as a strategy for dealing with these two factors. Consider first the benefits of integrating backward. To begin with, backward integration offers the potential for converting a cost center into a profit producer. This potential may be very attractive when suppliers have wide profit margins. Moreover, integrating backward allows a firm to supercede market uncertainties associated with supplies of raw materials. Where a firm is dependent on a particular raw material or service furnished by other enterprises, the door is always open for requisite supplies to be disrupted by strikes, bad weather, production breakdowns, or delays in scheduled deliveries. Furthermore, the cost structure is vulnerable to untimely increases in the prices of critical component materials. Stockpiling,

---

[2] It has been estimated that 80 percent of today's products will have disappeared from the market ten years from now and that 80 percent of the products which will be sold in the next decade are as yet unknown. See E. E. Scheuing, *New Product Management* (Hinsdale, Ill.: The Dryden Press, 1974), p. 1.

[3] This section draws heavily from Arthur A. Thompson, *Economics of the Firm: Theory and Practice,* 2d ed. (Englewood Cliffs, N.J.: Prentice-Hall, Inc., 1977), chap. 2.

[4] Peter F. Drucker, *Management: Tasks, Responsibilities, Practices* (New York: Harper and Row, Publishers, 1974), pp. 666–67.

fixed-price contracts, or the use of substitute inputs may not be feasible ways for dealing with such market uncertainties. When this is the case, bringing supplies and costs under its own wings may be an organization's most profitable option for securing *reliable deliveries* of essential inputs at *reliable prices*. In short, sparing itself the uncertainties of being dependent upon suppliers permits an organization to coordinate and routinize its operating cycle, thereby (1) avoiding the transient, but upsetting, influences of unreliable suppliers and wide swings in supply prices, (2) realizing the cost efficiencies of a stable operating pattern, and (3) insulating itself from the tactical maneuvers of other firms regarding raw material sources. In so doing, an organization can become more a master of its own destiny than a slave to fortuitous market circumstances beyond its control.

While backward integration may be justified by an economic need to assure sources of supply, it may also be the best and most practical way to obtain a workable degree of commitment from suppliers. The case of Sears offers a prime example.[5] A large portion of the merchandise which Sears sells is made by manufacturers in which Sears has an ownership interest. While this might stem from Sears' desire to "control" its suppliers, it is as probable that Sears was concerned that it could not get reputable suppliers to commit themselves to making goods especially for Sears unless assured of a long-term relationship. The reasoning is not hard to understand: for a firm to become the chief supplier of one of Sears' big-ticket or volume items is likely to make Sears the supplier's main customer and major channel of distribution. For a supplier to allow itself to become a "captive company" of Sears without some sort of guarantee that the relationship would be a continuing one would be foolhardy and unduly risky. Thus for Sears to get major suppliers to forego their independence and agree to orient most or all of their business of manufacturing products to Sears' specifications to be sold under Sears' brand names and to be delivered according to Sears' demands very likely meant in some cases that Sears had to go beyond the offering of a "long-term" contract. Without ties as permanent as those of ownership, some key suppliers could have balked, leaving Sears with uncertain sources of supply or with unwanted gaps in its product line. Given Sears' merchandising strategy, being the "wrong size" to assure itself of dependable supplies of goods at the right price and quality could have been a serious strategic flaw.

The strategic impetus for forward integration has much the same roots. Undependable sales and distribution channels can give rise to costly inventory pileups and frequent production shutdowns, thereby undermining the economies of stable production operations. Loss of these economies may make it imperative for an organization to gain stronger market access in order to remain competitive. Sometimes even a few percentage point increases in the average rate of capacity utilization can make a substantial difference in price and profitability.

---

[5] Ibid., p. 686.

For a raw materials producer, integrating forward into manufacturing may help achieve greater product differentiation and thus allow for increased profit margins. In the early phases of the vertical product flow, intermediate goods are "commodities,"—that is, they have essentially identical technical specifications irrespective of producer (wheat, coal, sheet steel, cement, sulfuric acid, newsprint). Competition is extremely price-oriented. Yet, the closer the production stage is to the ultimate consumer, the greater are the opportunities for a firm to differentiate its end product via design, service, quality features, packaging, promotion, and so on. Marketing activities become more critical and the importance of price shrinks in comparison to other competitive variables.

For a manufacturer, integrating forward may take the form of building a chain of closely supervised dealer franchises or it may mean establishing company-owned and operated retail outlets. Alternatively, it could entail simply staffing regional and district sales offices instead of selling through manufacturer's agents of independent distributors. Whatever its specific format, forward integration is usually motivated by a desire to realize the higher profits that come with stable production, large-scale distribution, and product differentiation and to enjoy the security that comes with having one's own capability for accessing markets and customers.

There is, however, one other aspect of vertical integration which warrants mention. The large size that accompanies full integration puts a firm in a position to exert a measure of monopolistic control over its costs, its selling prices, its production technology, and its customers' buying propensities and attitudes. Size breeds power, and power gives management latitude in making decisions and setting policies. For instance, to the degree that an integrated firm is self-sufficient at each of the intermediate stages of the production process, it is also partially insulated from the impacts of competition and short-run price-quantity adjustments in the intermediate goods markets. Such freedom is not without design or social import. Max Weber, years ago, observed how complex organizations, moved by an instinct for self-protection and risk avoidance, acted to construct devices that would shield them from unwanted change while, at the same time, promoting a degree of order and stability conducive to achieving peak efficiency and profitability. Needless to say, the competitive latitude and discretion conferred on management by a firm's large size and market power merit close social scrutiny, if not outright attack, for it is a virtual certainty that an organization will have occasions to use them to serve its own interests.

Aside from the obvious social disadvantages that *may* accrue from extensive vertical integration, there are internal organizational shortcomings as well. The large capital requirements of vertical integration may place a heavy strain on an organization's financial resources. Second, integration introduces more complexity into the management process. It requires new skills and the assumption of additional risks since the effect is to extend the enterprise's scope of operations. It means bearing the burdens of learning a new business and coping with the problems of a larger organization. While this may all be justified if it remedies a disparity between costs and profits, it can so increase a firm's vested interests in its technology and production facilities that it becomes reluctant to abandon its heavy fixed investments. Because of this inflexibility a fully integrated firm is vulnerable to new technologies and new products. Either it has to write off large portions of its fixed investments or else it must endure a competitive disadvantage with innovative enterprises having no proprietary interests to protect.

Moreover, integration can pose problems of balancing capacity at each production stage. The most efficient sizes at each phase of the vertical product flow can be at substantial variance. This can mean exact self-sufficiency at each interface is the exception not the rule. Where internal capacity is deficient to supply the next stage, the difference will have to be bought externally. Where internal capacity is excessive, customers will need to be found for the surplus. And if by-products are generated, they will require arrangements for disposal.

All in all, therefore, vertical integration strategy has both important strengths and weaknesses. Which direction the scales tip on integration depends upon (1) how compatible it is with the organization's long-term strategic interests and performance objectives, (2) how much it strengthens an organization's position in its primary business, and (3) the extent to which it permits fuller exploitation of an organization's technical talents. Unless these issues are answered in the affirmative, vertical integration is likely to be an unattractive corporate strategy option.

Corporate Diversification Strategies

A number of wide-ranging factors account for the strategic appeal of corporate diversification:[6]

1. An organization may consider diversification because market saturation, competitive pressures, product line obsolescence, declining demand, or fear of antitrust action no longer allow profit objectives to be met solely through an expansion of its current product-market activities.
2. Even if appealing expansion opportunities still exist in its current business, an organization may diversify because its free cash flow exceeds the cash needs of expansion.
3. An organization's diversification opportunities may have a greater expected profitability than that of expanding its present business.

---

[6] H. Igor Ansoff, *Corporate Strategy* (New York: McGraw-Hill, 1965), pp. 129–30; Drucker, *Management,* p. 684; George A. Steiner, "Why and How to Diversify," *California Management Review,* vol. 6, no. 4 (Summer 1964), pp. 11–17; J. F. Weston and S. F. Mansinghka, "Tests of the Efficiency Performance of Conglomerate Firms," *Journal of Finance,* vol. 26, no. 4 (September 1971), pp. 919–36; and Ronald W. Melicher and David F. Rush, "Evidence on the Acquisition-Related Performance of Conglomerate Firms," *Journal of Finance,* vol. 29, no. 1 (March 1974), pp. 141–49.

4. An organization may consider diversification because of a desire to spread risk and increase the stability and security of its operations. This desire may stem from uneasiness about "overspecialization" in particular products or technologies, the risks of having a disproportionately large fraction of sales to a single customer, dwindling supplies of a key raw material, the threat of new technologies, or vulnerability to swings in the economy.

5. A firm may diversify because of a perceived financial serendipity associated with certain kinds of acquisitions. This search for financial-related advantages is said to account for (a) attempts by firms with depressed earnings to diversify into areas of higher average earnings performance level, (b) the pursuit of "instantaneous profits" whereby an acquiring firm buys out firms having lower pre-merger price-earnings ratio in an effort to immediately realize a higher stock price and earnings per share, and (c) the attempt to increase one's access to capital by acquiring enterprises with large cash flows and/or low debt to equity ratios.

6. An organization may pursue diversification because owners/managers enjoy the challenges of something new and something different.

One viewpoint even goes so far as to make diversification a condition of survival—"in the long run an organization must diversify or die."[7] The argument here is that a concentration strategy eventually falls victim to the new obsoleting the old. Be that as it may, the wealth of organizational experiences with diversification strategies clearly demonstrates that there is *right* diversification and *wrong* diversification.[8] Drucker's analogy to the musician illustrates the point well:

> An accomplished and well-established concert pianist will as a matter of course, add one new major piece to his repertoire each year. Every few years he will pick for his new piece something quite different from the repertoire through which he has made his name. This forces him to learn again, to hear new things in old and familiar pieces, and to become a better pianist altogether. At the same time, concert pianists have long known that they slough off an old piece as they add on one new major one. The total size of the repertoire remains the same. There are only so many pieces of music even the greatest pianist can play with excellence.[9]

If and when corporate diversification appears on the strategy agenda, the question of what kind of diversification—how exactly to apply the musician's rule—becomes paramount.

There are two basic kinds of corporate diversification: *concentric* and *conglomerate*. Concentric diversification is *related* diversification; that is, the organization's lines of business, although distinct, still possess some mean-

---

[7] Steiner, "Why and How to Diversify," p. 12.

[8] Drucker, *Management*, p. 692.

[9] Ibid., p. 685.

ingful kind of strategic fit. In concentric diversification, the related nature of the various lines of business can be keyed to common technology, customer usage, distribution channels, methods of operation, managerial knowhow, or product similarity—virtually any strategically meaningful facet. In contrast, conglomerate diversification is *unrelated* or *pure* diversification; there is no common thread or element of true strategic fit among the organization's several lines of business.

Concentric Diversification Strategies. Concentric diversification can be a very attractive corporate strategy. It allows an enterprise to preserve a common core of unity in its business activities, while at the same time spreading the risks out over a broader product base. But more importantly, perhaps, when an organization has some kind of distinctive competence in its present business, concentric diversification offers a way to build upon what it does best. Diversifying with the express intent of extending the firm's expertise to related businesses may carry with it a competitive advantage and above-average profit opportunities.

Specific types of concentric diversification include:

1. Moving into closely related products (a bread bakery getting into saltine crackers).
2. Building upon company technology or knowhow (a synthetic fibers manufacturer diversifying into the production of carpets).
3. Seeking to increase plant utilization (a coarse paper bag manufacturer deciding to utilize excess paper-making capacity by adding corrugated paperboard boxes to its product line).
4. Utilizing available sources of raw materials (a lumber products firm elects to devote some of its timberland to plywood production).
5. Making fuller utilization of the firm's sales force (a wholesaler of electrical supplies adds electric heating and cooling equipment to its line of products).
6. Building upon the organization's brand name and goodwill (a successful coffee firm diversifies into tea).

Numerous actual examples of concentric diversification abound. Procter and Gamble has been eminently successful in building a diversified product line (Crest toothpaste, Ivory Snow, Tide, Duncan Hines cake mixes, Folger's coffee, Jif peanut butter, Pringles potato chips, Head and Shoulders shampoo, Crisco shortening, Comet cleanser, Charmin toilet tissue—to mention a few) around its expertise in marketing household products through supermarket channels. Pepsi-Cola practiced concentric diversification when it bought Frito-Lay, Pizza Hut, and Taco Bell, as did Coca-Cola in purchasing Minute Maid orange juice and Taylor wine, and Lockheed in encircling the needs of the Department of Defense with its product line of airframes, rocket engines, missiles, electronics, defense research and development, and shipbuilding. Sears learned that the diverse nature of TV sets, auto repair centers, men's suits, draperies, refrigerators, paint, and home-owner's insurance posed no difficulty to its corporate strategy because the same customer buys them, in very much the same way, and with the same value expectations, thereby providing the essential link for its version of customer-based concentric diversification.[7]

Technology-based concentric diversification has proven successful in process industries (steel, aluminum, paper, and glass), where a single processing technique spawns a multitude of related products. The same paper machines which produce newsprint are equally adept at turning out stationery, notebook paper, and specialty printing paper for books and magazines. The line of products emerging from a single steel mill might include sheet steel, steel rails, reinforcing rods, I-beams, metal door frames, and wire products.

Other firms (in chemicals and electronics particularly) have pursued a technology-linked diversification strategy because their expertise in a given scientific area led to the discovery of new technological branches having practical market application. Often, in the early stages of a major technology, it is not feasible to exploit an innovation fully by concentrating on just one of a few product markets. Simultaneous, or else closely-sequenced, R&D efforts into several product areas may be optimal.[10]

A further indication of the use and preference for concentric diversification strategies is shown in Illustration Capsule 9.

Conglomerate Diversification Strategies.   While one might expect an overwhelming majority of organizations to favor concentric diversification because of the greater likelihood of good strategic fit, the conglomerate strategy has nonetheless attracted some important companies. A simple criterion of "will it meet our minimum standard for expected profitability?" captures the essence of the corporate diversification strategy of such firms as Textron, Whittaker, ITT, Litton, Gulf and Western, U.S. Industries, and Northwest Industries.

However, other organizations have opted for the conglomerate approach because their distinctive competence either was so narrow as to have little in common with other businesses or was so lacking in depth that any diversification move was inherently conglomerate in nature. And still others have

---

[10] However, beyond some stage the progressive branching out of a common technology can spread an enterprise so thin and push it in so many different directions that further technological-based diversification dilutes what once was clear advantage. According to Peter Drucker:

> That this might be the case is indicated by the fact that most of these giant extended technological families have a few areas in which they have strength and maintain their leadership position: GE and Westinghouse in heavy electrical apparatus, Philips in consumer electronics, Union Carbide in metallurgical chemistry, DuPont in textile fibers and so on. In these areas they also maintain their innovative capacity. The reason for the relative sluggishness and vulnerability of these companies is not "poor management" but "spotty management." It is not that they are in too few "good businesses" but that they are in too many that do not "fit."

See Drucker, *Management,* p. 705.

viewed a conglomerate approach as the optimal way of escaping a declining industry or overdependence on a single product-market area. Possible options for conglomerate diversification strategies include:

1. Seeking a match between a cash-rich, opportunity-poor company and an opportunity-rich, cash-poor firm.
2. Diversifying into areas with a counterseasonal or countercyclical sales pattern so as to smooth out sales and profit fluctuations.
3. Attempting to merge an opportunity-poor, skill-rich company with an opportunity-rich, skill-poor enterprise.
4. Seeking out a marriage of a highly leveraged firm and a debt-free firm so as to balance the capital structure of the former and increase its borrowing capacity.
5. Gaining entry into new product markets via licensing agreements or purchase of manufacturing or distribution rights.
6. Acquiring any firm in any line of business so long as the projected profit opportunities equal or exceed minimum criteria.

Aside from the pros and cons of being in businesses not having either a common thread or strategic fit, a purely conglomerate diversification strategy has several other advantages and limitations which should be set forth. First, a conglomerate strategy can lead to improved sales, profits, and growth when an organization diversifies into industries where the economic potential is stronger than its existing businesses. However, an organization should beware of being blinded by promising opportunities. Sooner or later every business gets into trouble. Thus, whenever management contemplates either acquisition or grass-roots diversification it should ask "if the new business got into trouble, would we know how to bail it out?" If the answer is no, it is surely diversification of the wrong kind even though the lure of above-average profitability is tempting.[11]

Second, despite the fact that its consolidated performance may improve, the price which a conglomerate pays to buy its way into a growth industry may impair stockholder earnings. This holds whether diversification takes place from within or through acquisition since some kind of $2 + 2 = 5$ effect is frequently needed to offset the premium price paid to get into the business. The high price-earnings multiples which many conglomerates have paid for their acquisitions, as well as the millions of dollars of purchased "goodwill" which appear on corporate financial statements, are ample evidence of the added costs of "buying in."

Third, unless some kind of $2 + 2 = 5$ benefits can be developed, the consolidated performance of a conglomerate enterprise will tend to be no better than if its divisions were independent firms, and it may be worse to the extent that centralized management policies hamstring the operating divisions. This

---

[11] Of course, management may be willing to assume the risk that trouble will not strike before it has had time to learn the business well enough to bail it out of most any difficulty. See Drucker, *Management*, p. 709.

implies that the best which conglomerates can generally expect is to be at no cost/efficiency disadvantage in trying to compete against nonconglomerates.[12] Fourth, although in theory a conglomerate strategy would seem to offer the potential of greater sales-profit stability over the course of the business cycle, in practice the attempts at countercyclical diversification appear to have fallen short of the mark. Conglomerate profits have evidenced no propensity to suffer milder reversals in periods of recession and economic stress.[13] In fact, during times of adversity, the staying power of conglomerates may be weaker than that of concentrically-diversified firms.[14] Finally, the "financial synergism" of trying to marry businesses with a high cash throw-off to businesses with a large cash appetite is more often than not an illusion. For a conglomerate strategy to be truly successful, a great deal more strategic fit is needed than money alone (see Illustration Capsule 7).[15]

Illustration Capsule 7

Pillsbury's Shift in Diversification Strategy

During the 60s many companies initiated strategies for broadly diversifying their activities. During the seventies, when it became painfully apparent that many of the newly-acquired businesses were not performing up to expectations or else did not "fit in" very well, a sizeable number of these very same companies changed their strategies from pure diversification to one of related diversification. Pillsbury was one of the companies which retreated from a conglomerate approach to a conceptual approach to diversification.

When William H. Spoor became chairman of the board of Pillsbury in January 1973, he moved quickly to narrow Pillsbury's product base to the area he felt the company knew best—food. In short order Pillsbury moved to divest its low-growth, cyclical business in poultry, its minority housing unit (Pentom Builders), its interest in magazine publishing (*Bon Appetit*), its computer services business, and its money-losing wine business (Souverain Winery). Mr. Spoor was quoted as saying, "I am only interested in businesses that fall into three categories. We should only be in consumer foods, food away from home, and agri-products."

Pillsbury's original base of businesses from which it first launched its diversification efforts revolved around flour milling (it is the largest miller in the United States),

---

[12] Evidence to this effect is given in Stanley E. Boyle, *Economic Report on Conglomerate Merger Performance: An Empirical Analysis of Nine Corporations,* Staff Report to the Federal Trade Commission, reprinted in *Mergers and Acquisitions,* vol. 8, no. 1 (Spring 1973), pp. 5–41; Ronald W. Melicher and David F. Rush, "The Performance of Conglomerate Firms: Recent Risk and Return Experience," *Journal of Finance,* vol. 28, no. 2 (May 1973), pp. 381–88; and Robert L. Coun, "The Performance of Conglomerate Firms: Comment," *Journal of Finance,* vol. 28, no. 3 (June 1973), pp. 754–58.

[13] Drucker, *Management,* p. 767.

[14] See H. I. Ansoff and J. F. Weston, "Merger Objectives and Organization Structure," *Quarterly Review of Economics and Business,* vol. 2, no. 3 (August 1962), pp. 49–58.

[15] Drucker, *Management,* pp. 707–8.

Illustration Capsule 7 (continued)

producing bakery mixes (some 300 varieties), commodity merchandising, grain exports, and grocery items for consumers (including flour, cake mixes and frostings, pancake mix, quick bread mixes, and a wide assortment of refrigerated dough products). Most of these businesses generated healthy profits and cash flows but were in markets where growth was slower. Volume gains, particularly in the consumer products categories, were largely dependent on taking business away from rival brands—a costly process with little prospect of major gains in profitability. This was what motivated the original diversification strategy.

Under its new chairman, Pillsbury's acquisitions took on a more focused direction and reflected the decision to become an international food company participating in the three major areas of agribusiness, household food items, and restaurants. Recent acquisitions bear this out:

1. Wilton Enterprises, Inc. (acquired in 1973)—the nation's leading marketer of cake decorating products.
2. Totino's Pizza (acquired in 1976)—the second largest maker of prepared pizzas, with just over a 20 percent market share.
3. Fox Deluxe Foods (acquired in 1976)—operator of a pizza manufacturing plant in Joplin, Missouri.
4. American Beauty Macaroni Company (acquired in 1977)—manufacturer of a broad line of quality pasta products.
5. Speas Company (acquired in 1978)—a manufacturer of apple juice, cider vinegar, and pectin.
6. Green Giant Co. (acquired in 1978)—maker of frozen and canned foods.

The Green Giant acquisition represents a major strategic effort by Pillsbury to gain a product mix that would put the company on a par with Kellogg Co. and H. J. Heinz, and to prepare it for a later capability to compete more broadly with General Mills and General Foods. By acquiring Green Giant, Pillsbury gained some strategic leverage in capturing shelf space in supermarkets for Pillsbury's less widely distributed lines (cake decorating sets, Funny Face and Squoze powdered drink mixes, Erasco food products, American Beauty pasta, and Sprinkle Sweet artificial sweetner). Green Giant's canned and frozen foods lines are popular and thus attractive lines for supermarkets to carry. A key to success in gaining distribution through supermarkets is for a manufacturer to have products with dominant first or second positions in fast-growing sales areas—something Pillsbury had not been able to accomplish as well as some other manufacturers. Green Giant products were tagged to fill this gap.

Besides its new acquisitions, Pillsbury has been active for some time in expanding its interests in the restaurant business. In 1967, Burger King Corp. was acquired; this unit is now the company's main revenue producer. When Burger King failed to keep pace with its fast-growing market, Spoor hired the No. 3 man at McDonald's, Donald Smith, to revitalize the chain—specifically to double the number of outlets and triple earnings by 1983. During the 1973–1978 period, 70 percent of Pillsbury's capital improvement budget, or $385 million, was allocated to the Burger King division. Expansion has also occurred in Pillsbury's Steak and Ale restaurants (some of which operate under the names of Jolly Ox and Bennigan's) where the number of outlets rose from 52 in 1973 to 165 in 1978. At the same time, Pillsbury has pushed forward in expanding its Poppin Fresh Pie shops business; the number of units open increased from 6 in 1974 to 45 in 1978. The pie shops are mid-priced family

Illustration Capsule 7 (concluded)

restaurants, seating about 135 persons, featuring 27 varieties of pies and offering a limited menu of sandwiches, soups, and salads.

In its *1977 Annual Report,* Pillsbury announced that the current corporate strategy and diversification program were aimed at producing a "repetitive, predictable, and growing" stream of earnings. The company's quantitative targets are (1) an average annual sales growth rate of 10 percent, (2) a minimum annual earnings per share growth rate of 10 percent, (3) a pretax return on average invested capital of 20 percent, (4) an aftertax return on stockholders' equity of 16 percent, and (5) an "A" credit rating.

A Perspective View on Corporate Diversification Strategies. Diversification—whether concentric or conglomerate—can be neither recommended nor condemned per se. Many organizations are actively pursuing diversification strategies of some sort, and doing so for what they view as good and sufficient business reasons. It plainly makes sense for a firm to *consider* diversification when its existing business has been expanded to its practical limits and/or when it is severely threatened by outside forces; it may or may not make sense to diversify before this occurs.

In addition, the pros and cons of what kind and how much diversification an organization needs to get the best performance and results weigh differently from case to case. A logical place for an organization's management to begin its evaluation of diversification alternatives is with a consideration of "what is the least diversification we need to attain our objectives and remain a healthy, viable entity, capable of competing successfully?" At the other extreme, though, management is equally obliged to examine the question of "what is the most diversification we can manage, given the complexity it adds?"[16] In all likelihood, the optimal answer lies in between. And after deciding what to include and what to exclude, the next step is to make the diversification strategy specific enough to define the role of each line of business within the total organization. The reverse approach of letting corporate strategy be merely an aggregation of each line of business strategy is risky—it can quickly deteriorate into marching in too many directions at once.

The investor disfavor which conglomerates have acquired, the poor performance of several prominent conglomerates, and the serious issue of how to manage a diverse number of businesses effectively have caused many highly diversified firms to avoid or discard the conglomerate label by developing "corporate unity themes." Multiproduct firms have come up with broad labels like leisure time, high technology, consumer products, materials processing, communication systems, and total service to mask the variety of

---

[16] Ibid., pp. 692–3.

distinct businesses they operate. The idea seems to be to convey the image of being diversified around a concept ("a conceptually oriented conglomerate") rather than projecting the image of a "pure" or "free-form" conglomerate.

Merger and Acquisition Strategies

A given merger or acquisition can reflect any or all of the three types of strategies previously discussed: it can be motivated by a desire to concentrate on a single business, by a move to integrate vertically, or by an effort at diversification. In this sense, merger/acquisition is not so much a fundamental strategy in its own right as it is a specific technique for accomplishing the larger target of entry into other businesses. But it is still a distinctive strategic act and one which is often used—sometimes with drama, stress, and marketwide impact. Some firms use merger/acquisition as the exclusive means for entering the business they want to be in; indeed, entire companies (nearly all of the large conglomerates) have been put together by mergers and acquisitions. For this reason, merger and acquisition can be looked upon as a corporate strategy in its own right.[17]

A *merger* can be thought of as combining two (or more) firms into one. An *acquisition* is when one firm (the parent) acquires another and absorbs it into its own operations, often as an operating subsidiary or division. Obviously, the difference is mainly one of who is acquiring whom; the terms are commonly used interchangeably.

From the standpoint of corporate strategy, there are five distinguishable types of acquisition strategies. *Horizontal acquisition* is when one firm acquires or merges with another firm in the same industry. Examples are National Steel's acquisition of Granite City Steel, Honeywell's acquisition of General Electric's computer division, and Atlantic Richfield's (ARCO) acquisition of Sinclair Oil Corporation. Horizontal acquisitions are an off-shoot of a concentration strategy since the acquiring firm remains in much the same business (unless the firm which is acquired has other business interests as well). The chief constraint in employing a horizontal acquisition strategy is staying clear of Section 7 of the Clayton Act which forbids acquisition of competitors where the effect "may be substantially to lessen competition, or to tend to create a monopoly." Horizontal mergers tend to raise issues of market power because they eliminate side-by-side competition between the two firms. Because the Antitrust Division of the Justice Department will normally challenge a horizontal merger when the firms involved have a combined market share greater than 10 percent, firms are constrained in their use of horizontal acquisition as a corporate strategy.

A second type of acquisition is the *vertical acquisition* aimed at creating a more vertically integrated enterprise. An example is U.S. Plywood's merger

---

[17] An excellent source of information on mergers and acquisitions is the periodical *Mergers and Acquisitions: The Journal of Corporate Venture*, published quarterly.

with Champion Paper to form U.S. Plywood-Champion Paper Corp. Although vertical mergers do not generally entail anticompetitive effects, there are instances where they have been held to raise barriers to entry, to produce unfair control over sources of critical inputs, and to allow vertically integrated firms to put a profit squeeze on nonintegrated firms. As a consequence, vertical acquisitions resulting in 10–20 percent market shares at both levels will usually be given close scrutiny by antitrust officials.

The third type of acquisition strategy aims at market extension. A *market extension acquisition* involves two firms in the same industry which do business in different *geographical* areas. This type of acquisition strategy is a common one; many firms seek to enter new geographical areas by acquiring a firm (young or mature, large or small, successful or not so successful) which operates in the desired location. Examples include Winn-Dixie's acquisition of a retail grocery chain in Texas, Standard Oil of California's acquisition of Standard Oil of Kentucky, and Philips' acquisition of Magnavox.

A fourth strategic type is that involving related product diversification or *product extension acquisition*. A product extension acquisition arises when Firm A adds a product related to its existing product line by acquiring Firm B. According to the Federal Trade Commission, these are the most common types of acquisitions and represent a form of concentric diversification.[18] Examples include Pepsico's acquisitions of Pizza Hut, Rheingold Beer, and Taco Bell, Colgate-Palmolive's acquisition of Helena Rubenstein, and American Motors' acquisition of Kaiser Jeep Corp.

The fifth type of acquisition strategy is the *conglomerate acquisition*—a strategy typically used to accomplish an organization's attempt at pure diversification. Roughly 30 percent of the merger activity of the 1960s and 1970s has consisted of conglomerate mergers—a direct reflection of the wide use of conglomerate diversification strategy. Some prominent examples include Beatrice Foods' acquisition of Samsonite, United Technologies' acquisition of Otis Elevator, Philip Morris' acquisition of Miller Brewing Co., American Tobacco's acquisition of Sunshine Biscuits, and Illinois Central's acquisition of Midas International.

Pros and Cons of Acquisition Strategies. There are several reasons why an organization may prefer acquisition of an existing enterprise to launching its own grassroots development of a new business. The factors involved are those implicit in any "buy or build" situation, but often the most important considerations are time and money.[19] Acquiring existing organizations,

---

[18] Federal Trade Commission, Bureau of Economics, *Statistical Report on Mergers and Acquisitions,* November 1977 (Washington, D.C.: U.S. Government Printing Office, 1977). This document contains statistical breakdown on various types of mergers and acquisitions since 1946.

[19] A study of firms' experiences with diversification from within is reported in Ralph Biggadike, "The Risky Business of Diversification," *Harvard Business Review,* vol. 57, no. 3 (May–June 1979), pp. 103–11. Methods for evaluating how much to pay for an acquisition are contained in Alfred Rappaport, "Strategic Analysis for More Profitable Acquisitions," *Harvard Business Review,* vol. 57, no. 4 (July–August 1979), pp. 99–110.

products, technologies, facilities, or talent and manpower has the strong advantage of much quicker entry into the target market while, at the same time, detouring such barriers to entry as patents, technological inexperience, lack of raw material supplies, substantial economies of scale, costly promotional expenses requisite for gaining market visibility and brand recognition, and establishment of distribution channels. Internally developing the knowledge, resources, and reputation necessary to become an effective competitor can take years and entails all the problems of startup. Internal entry can also result in oversupply conditions in the market. For instance, if existing firms already have the production capability to supply customers' needs and/or if entry must be on a large scale to take advantage of scale economies, then the added presence of a new, large supplier can produce an acute surplus of capacity. The likely outcome would be a spirited and profitless battle for market share. The prospect of such situations effectively reduces the number of viable options to two: entry via acquisition versus no entry at all.

Yet, acquisition is not without its own drawbacks. Finding the right kind of company to acquire can sometimes present a problem. Conceivably, an acquisitive-minded firm may face the dilemma of buying a successful company at a high price or a struggling company at a low price. In the first case, the seller is in position to demand a generous compensation for the risks that have been faced and for the effort expended in putting together a successful product, technology, market, organization or whatever key feature (distinctive competence) is being acquired. If the buying firm has very little knowledge about the industry it is seeking to enter but has ample capital, then it may be better off acquiring a capable firm—irrespective of the higher price. On the other hand, it can be advantageous to acquire a struggling firm at a bargain price when the new parent sees promising ways for transforming the weak firm into a strong one and has the money and knowhow to back up its turnaround strategy.

Mergers and acquisitions can be accomplished via any of several financial strategies: purchase of stock on the open market, tender offers, an exchange of stock, a purchase of assets, or a pooling of interests. They can occur amicably or with conflict and tension, intermingled with proxy fights, bidding wars, and complex legal maneuvering. One of the most dramatic of these is the takeover.

Takeover Strategies. A *takeover* is the surprise attempt of one firm to acquire ownership or control over the management of another firm against the wishes of the latter's management (and perhaps some of its stockholders). In recent years, takeover strategies have been used increasingly as a means of acquisition. The motives for takeover and the types of takeover mergers (horizontal, vertical, conglomerate, etc.) are the same as for any kind of merger/acquisition; what makes takeover unique is its unfriendly nature and the mechanics by which it is carried out.

A takeover strategy can follow many different paths and sequences. Typically, the acquiring firm or its investment banker conducts a search for likely takeover candidates which meet management's criteria; hundreds or even thousands of firms may be looked at via computerized procedures. When the takeover target is selected, an offer price is chosen—usually 20–30 percent above the current stock price, and other specific details are worked out. The takeover target may be approached openly at this point (in hope of a friendly merger or a quiet surrender) or the tender offer may be sprung publicly as a surprise. The terms of the tender offer are frequently announced at a news conference, followed up quickly with newspaper ads and personal contacts with known large shareholders of the target firm.

The takeover target may initiate a vigorous defensive strategy: denouncing the offer as too low, urging all shareholders not to accept the tender offer, making special attempts to convince major stockholders to reject the bid for their stock, requesting the Justice Department or other government agencies to intervene to stop the merger, seeking out a more attractive merger partner, filing lawsuits to block the takeover, and trying quickly to arrange some acquisitions of its own—to force a revision of the takeover offer. In launching its defense, top management may be trying both to get better offer terms and to protect its own jobs and independence.

The struggle may last a few days, a few weeks, or a few months. The original tender offer may be raised one or more times—especially if another bidder enters the fray, attracted by the action and seeing interesting takeover possibility of its own. The market price of the target firm's stock often fluctuates up and down as the tender offer changes and prospects of merger brighten or darken. Speculators may trade heavily in the stocks of the firms, buying, selling, or selling short according to their estimates of the situation. An actual takeover attempt is described in Illustration Capsule 8.

Illustration Capsule 8

Strategic Responses to a Takeover Bid—To Fight or to Bargain?

When W. R. Grace & Co. announced a takeover bid of $3.75 a share for the stock of Daylin, Inc., a West Coast health services and specialty retailing firm, Daylin's management wasted little time in developing a strategy to preserve its independence. Daylin was unimpressed with the Grace offer even though Daylin's stock was selling at $2.38 before the Grace bid. Daylin had cash on hand equal to $1.30 a share ($46 million); and it had a net tax-loss carryforward of $88 million of which $66 million expired in 1980 (worth an estimated $1.35 per share). This meant that Grace was offering barely over $1 per share for Daylin's basic business—at a time when earnings were expected to be nearly 40 cents a share.

Just 11 days after the Grace announcement, Daylin simultaneously filed suit to block Grace's takeover (on grounds that Grace had violated federal securities laws and had not disclosed possible antitrust implications with respect to Grace's and Daylin's home improvement centers) and proposed a tender offer of its own of $38 per share for the 1.8 million shares of Narco Scientific Inc., a communication and health care concern. Only five days before, Narco had agreed in principle to accept a

Illustration Capsule 8 (continued)

$28 a share offer to be acquired by Rorer Group Inc., a maker of pharmaceutical and surgical products; both Narco and Rorer are based in Fort Washington, Pa. Narco viewed Rorer's offer of $28 as fair, since the book value of Narco's stock was roughly $15.65 and since the market price of Narco's stock had recently traded in the $12.75–$14.00 range. Needless to say, Narco's management was surprised by the size of the Daylin offer, since the $38 bid was not only 36 percent higher than Rorer's but also represented a price 18 times Narco's 1978 earnings per share and 2.4 times its book value.

Daylin justified the $38 offer price as necessary "to demonstrate our sincerity and ensure a high probability of success." (Daylin failed on two acquisition attempts in 1978). Daylin's management further expressed the view that Narco's medical products complemented Daylin's and that Narco had proprietary and patented products with sufficient growth potential beyond 1980 to warrant a hefty price-earnings multiple.

Three days after the Daylin offer, Narco's board of directors announced it might be willing to support a takeover bid from Daylin if Daylin were serious rather than using the bid to fight Grace's takeover of Daylin, if Daylin could give assurance of its ability to finance the proposed purchase of Narco, and if Daylin would clear up certain other reservations (one of which was that if the Grace takeover of Daylin was successful, Grace might cancel Daylin's offer for Narco and, perhaps, foul up the chance for Narco's stockholders to benefit from the Rorer offer). Daylin immediately reaffirmed its position that the offer for Narco "really had nothing to do with Grace. We've been looking at the Narco acquisition for a long period of time, and the offer isn't being done for defensive purposes." Meanwhile, W. R. Grace officials offered no immediate public comment and adopted a wait-and-see posture on the Daylin-Narco deal.

Epilogue

Within a matter of days after these developments, W. R. Grace's management upped the offer bid for Daylin's stock from $3.75 to $4.065 a share. Daylin's management and board of directors agreed to support the offer, which was subject to stockholder approval. Daylin then promptly withdrew its offer to purchase Narco Scientific. Rorer Group, Inc. and Narco Scientific quickly agreed in principle to a slightly higher tender offer for Narco's shares than the $50.8 million in cash and stock which Rorer had earlier offered, but with the stipulation that Narco's three nonhealth subsidiaries be divested. Except for finalizing all the details, the strategic maneuvers among the four parties were over and the dust had settled within three weeks.

Sources: David G. Santry, "Staying Independent and Paying for It," *Business Week*, January 29, 1979, p. 100; and *The Wall Street Journal*, 1979 issues of January 5, January 16, January 22, and February 1.

The outcome can go either way and depends on many factors. If the takeover target escapes, its management is likely to make numerous changes in strategy and internal operations to avert future takeover attempts and, especially, to improve performance and results. Dividends may be increased to try to solidify stockholder support of present management. The firm may become bolder, more innovative, and more competitive in outlook. If the takeover is successful, the acquiring firm may absorb the acquired firm and parcel its activities among various subunits; or it may operate the acquired firm as a separate and fairly autonomous division, keeping the original management or replacing all or part of top management with its own team. Either way, changes in the acquired firm can be expected in the way of revised objectives, new strategies, attempts to improve operating efficiency and profit performance, transfers of assets, closing or selling of marginal plants, expansion or pruning of the product line, new policies and procedures—in general, new direction.

The significance of takeover strategies, for our purposes, is two-fold: one, it is a new and increasingly used vehicle for accomplishing a merger/acquisition that might otherwise not occur, thereby opening up strategic opportunities for giving an organization new direction and different focus. Two, fears of takeover are prompting managements to adjust corporate strategies so as to make their firms less vulnerable to takeover. Examples of defensive moves being undertaken to help thwart a takeover include (1) stock splits (to broaden and splinter ownership and thereby make it harder for an outsider to gain control by secretly negotiating the purchase of large blocks of shares), (2) keeping liquidity to a safe minimum (to avoid large cash reserves which may be viewed as a desirable target in itself by "cash-poor" or "opportunity-rich" firms), (3) discarding "conservative" policies and strategies in favor of more innovative, aggressive ones, and (4) making special efforts to remain efficient and as profitable as possible (thus eliminating takeover attempts motivated by the potential for sharply higher profits).

Joint Venture Strategies

A joint venture is the right strategy for several types of situations.[20] It is, first, a device for doing something which an organization is not well-suited to do alone. Entering into a "consortium" kind of arrangement is a means of making a workable whole out of otherwise undersized levels of activity. In such cases, the whole is greater than the sum of its parts because alone each part is smaller than the threshold size of effectiveness. The Alaskan pipeline, for instance, is a joint venture in raw material supply which not only is beyond the prudent financial strength of any one oil giant but which also is, in its most economic size, designed to carry more crude oil than one company could produce from its reserve holdings. For each oil company owning oil reserves on the Alaskan North Slope to build its own pipeline geared to the size of its own production capability would make little business or environmental sense. But for them all to contribute a jointly financed and jointly operated pipeline allows the group to make economic fits out of misfits and

---

[20] Drucker, *Management*, pp. 720–24. Information regarding the joint venture activities of firms can be found in *Mergers and Acquisitions: The Journal of Corporate Venture*.

thereby realize a profit of their Alaskan oil reserves. At the same time, the strategy of joint venturing carries the advantage that risk is shared and therefore reduced for each of the participating firms. This is no small matter in a relatively large undertaking.

A second type of joint venture emerges when the distinctive competence of two or more independent organizations is brought together to form a jointly owned business. In this joint venture format each company brings to the deal special talents which, when pooled, give rise to a new enterprise with features quite apart from the parents. The complementarity of two or more distinctive competences can create a degree of synergy that spells the difference between success and near-success. For example, when in the 1920s General Motors developed tetraethyl lead to cure engine knocking problems, it decided not to start its own gasoline production and distribution business to exploit the advantages of tetraethyl lead but, instead, it chose to enter into a joint venture with Standard Oil of New Jersey (now Exxon) which already knew the gasoline business and had the missing expertise. Thus was born Ethyl Corporation which grew into a worldwide supplier of tetraethyl lead for all the large gasoline marketers. With its joint venture strategy GM, in effect, made money on every gallon of tetraethyl lead gasoline sold—an effective outcome as compared to that of entering the gasoline business on its own and trying to compete directly against the oil companies.[21]

Last, there are joint ventures created chiefly to surmount political and cultural roadblocks.[22] The political realities of nationalism often require a foreign company to team up with a domestic company if it is to gain needed government approval for its activities. At the same time, there are added pressures for a foreign company to seek out a domestic partner to help it

---

[21] General Motors and Standard Oil, N.J. sold Ethyl Corporation in the 1960s largely because Ethyl had become too big and too successful to be continued as a joint venture. Likewise, when Sears decided it was time for Whirlpool not only to supply Sears but also to sell appliances under the Whirlpool brand, Sears took the company public while retaining a controlling majority interest; gradually, then, Sears sold its holdings of Whirlpool shares as the company began to make it on its own. Such a spinning off of joint ventures into independent companies is not uncommon—either with or without the parent companies retaining an ownership interest.

To extend the life of a successful joint venture beyond some point in its development can have the effect of stunting its growth. Moreover, conflicts begin to arise between objectives of the parent company and the mission of the joint venture. Hence, at some point it becomes propitious for a successful joint venture company to begin to develop its own mission, objectives, strategy, and policies and for its management to become truly autonomous.

Alternatively, the joint venture can be liquidated with the parents splitting up the business and absorbing it into their own operations. This was the fate of Standard Vaccuum, a joint venture of Standard Oil, N.J. and Mobil Oil begun in the WW I era to produce, refine, and market petroleum products in the Far East. In the 1950s Standard Vacuum's petroleum business in the Far East had expanded to a size where it was more desirable for each of the parents to proceed on their own rather than to continue a joint venture where their strategies and objectives were beginning to clash.

See Drucker, *Management*, pp. 722–24.

[22] Philip Kotler, *Marketing Management: Analysis, Planning, and Control*, 4th Ed. (Englewood Cliffs, N.J.: Prentice-Hall, Inc., 1980), pp. 671–73.

overcome language and cultural barriers. So powerful are nationalistic interests in the smaller developing nations such as Brazil, Chile, Peru, and India that it is not unusual for foreign companies to find themselves restricted to a minority ownership position. Indeed, local businesses in Brazil and India, even though deeply engaged in joint ventures with multinational corporations based in the United States and in Europe, have been quite vocal in demanding protection from multinational domination, advocating not just majority or at least controlling ownership but the closing off of whole economic sectors to multinationals as well.

Retrenchment Strategies

The conceptual thrust of a corporate retrenchment strategy is to fall back and regroup.[23] It is a common short-run strategy for organizations during periods of uncertainty about the economic future, recession, tight money and corporate financial strain, and poor corporate performance. Retrenchment at the corporate level can assume either of two variations: one, stringent internal economies aimed at wringing out organizational slack and improving efficiency and, two, a reduction in the corporation's scope of business activities.

In the first instance, an organization which finds itself in a defensive or overextended position elects to hold onto most or all of its business activities and weather the storm with various internal economy measures. Ordinarily this type of corporate retrenchment strategy is highlighted by corporatewide directives to reduce operating expenses, improve productivity, and increase profit margins. The specifics of retrenchment vary according to the situation but may include reduced hiring of new personnel, trimming the size of corporate staff, postponing capital expenditure projects, stretching out the use of equipment and delaying replacement purchases so as to economize on cash requirements, retiring obsolete equipment, dropping marginally profitable products, closing older and less efficient plants, internal reorganization of work flows, inventory reductions, revised purchasing procedures, and so on.

The second variation of corporate retrenchment is more fundamental and consists of reappraisal of the desirability of continuing in each one of the present lines of business. Reappraisal of the scope of corporate activities is nearly always a byproduct of poor overall corporate performance and /or persistently poor performance in one or more operating divisions. Many diversified firms have found it necessary to retrench because they had severe trouble managing so many different businesses which did not "fit," or because they encountered operating problems in one or more divisions which were intractable or beyond their expertise, or because they found them-

---

[23] A retrenchment strategy can be (and is) used at both the levels of corporate strategy and business strategy. This section focuses on retrenchment at the corporate level—primarily as concerns diversified firms; business strategy retrenchment is discussed later in this chapter along with the other types of business level strategies.

selves short of the cash needed to support the investment needs of all of their different lines of business.

Corporate retrenchment is a typical reaction to adversity from within or without the organization. Ordinarily, it is a temporary or short-run strategy for riding through bad times; once it becomes feasible to renew growth and pursue expansion opportunities, retrenchment strategies are usually discarded in favor of some other strategy.

Divestiture Strategies

Even a shrewd corporate diversification strategy can result in the acquisition of businesses that just do not work out. Misfits or partial fits cannot be completely avoided, if only because it is impossible to predict precisely how getting into a new line of business will actually work out. Moreover, market potentials change with the times and what once was a good diversification move may later turn sour. Subpar performance by some operating units is bound to occur, thereby raising questions of whether to continue. Other operating units may simply not mesh as well with the rest of the organization as was originally thought.

Sometimes, a diversification move which originally appeared to make good sense from the standpoint of common markets, technologies, or channels turns out to lack the compatibility of values essential to a *temperamental fit*.[24] The pharmaceutical companies had just this experience. When several tried to diversify into cosmetics and perfume they discovered that their personnel had little respect for the "frivolous" nature of such products as compared to the far nobler task of developing miracle drugs to cure the ill. The absence of "temperamental unity" between the chemical and compounding expertise of the pharmaceutical companies and the fashion-marketing orientation of the cosmetics business was the undoing of the pharmaceutical's diversification move into what otherwise was a business with related technology and logical product fit.

Partial misfits and poorly performing divisions can also occur, despite the presence of some strategic fit, owing to an organization's inability to manage the business or to the overload placed on internal cash resources. In still other cases, the market changes slowly but surely to where the product consumers want to buy differs from what the producer is trying to sell, thereby breaking up what once was a good strategic fit with the seller's other products. Likewise, technological branching can progress to a point where pruning becomes a wise course of action if not a necessary one.

When a particular line of business loses its appeal (for any of the preceding reasons), divestiture may be the most attractive corporate strategy for that part of the organization. Normally such businesses should be divested as fast as is practical. To drag things out in hopes of a breakthrough or a

---

[24] Drucker, *Management*, p. 709.

turnaround is liable to be futile and risks draining away valuable organization resources. This explains why every diversified organization needs a systematic "planned abandonment" strategy for divesting itself of poor performers, losers, and misfits. A useful guide for determining if and when to divest a particular line of business is to ask the question "If we were not in this business today, would we want to get into it now?"[25] When the answer is "no" or "probably not," then divestiture ought to become a strategic consideration.

Divestiture can take several forms. Successful misfits may be spun off into financially and managerially independent companies, with the parent company electing to maintain either a majority or minority ownership.[26] On the other hand, a business may not be able to survive as an independent operation, in which case a buyer needs to be found. This is a "marketing" rather than a "selling" problem.[27] As a rule, one should avoid approaching divestment with a view of "who can we pawn this business off into and how much can we get for it?" Instead, it is stronger to undertake divesture on the basis "for what sort of organization would this business be a good fit and under what conditions would it be viewed as a sound bet?" In identifying organizations for whom the business is a "perfect fit," one also finds the buyers who will pay the highest price.

Liquidation Strategy

Of all the strategic alternatives, liquidation is the most unpleasant and painful, especially for a single-product enterprise where it means terminating the organization's existence. For a multiproduct firm to liquidate one of its lines of business is much less traumatic; the hardships of suffering through layoffs, plant closings, and so on, while not to be minimized, still leaves an ongoing organization, and perhaps one that eventually will turn out to be healthier after its pruning than before. (See Illustration Capsule 9.)

In hopeless situations, an early liquidation effort often serves owner-stockholder interests better than an inevitable bankruptcy. Prolonging and pursuit of a lost cause merely exhausts an organization's resources and leaves less to liquidate; it can also mar reputations and ruin management careers. Unfortunately, of course, it is seldom simple for management to

---

[25] Ibid., p. 94.

[26] One of the more unique approaches to divestiture involved Ling-Temco-Vought's reorganization of the Wilson Company in 1967. Shortly after it acquired Wilson, LTV split Wilson into three separate corporations: Wilson and Company (meats and food products), Wilson Sporting Goods, and Wilson Pharmaceutical and Chemical Company. LTV then sold off a substantial minority portion of the stock of each of the three new companies at price-earnings ratios higher than it initially paid for the total Wilson operation. LTV was attracted to this approach because it allowed LTV to improve its return from the Wilson acquisition by recovering part of its initial investment, while retaining control over all three of the new Wilson companies. For a more complete discussion, see Robert S. Attiyeh, "Where Next for Conglomerates," *Business Horizons,* vol. 12, no. 6 (December 1968), p. 42.

[27] Drucker, *Management,* p. 719.

Illustration Capsule 9

Corporate Liquidation: A Case of Being Worth More Dead than Alive

Rarely does a healthy company pursue a liquidation strategy—especially if it is a large company listed No. 357 on the *Fortune 500*. But in early 1979 the board of directors of UV Industries, at the urging of board chairman and major stockholder Martin Horvitz, voted unanimously for a resolution to sell or distribute all of the company's assets to stockholders.

During the 1960s and 1970s UV Industries—formerly U.S. Smelting, Refining, and Mining Co.—used an aggressive acquisition strategy to increase sales from $31 million to over $600 million and profits from $2.3 million to nearly $40 million. After approval of the liquidation resolution, UV's stock price jumped from $19 a share to about $30 a share, and a successful liquidation was projected to yield shareholders $33 or more a share.

UV's business interests included copper, gold, and coal operations, oil and gas properties, a lead-refining company, and a manufacturer of electric generating equipment. The sale of the latter, Federal Pacific Electric Co., UV's largest business (60 percent of sales and earnings), was arranged in late 1978; Reliance Electric offered UV a handsome $345 million in cash for Federal Pacific, a price which represented a price-earnings ratio of 13 at a time when UV's common stock was selling at 5 times earnings. The sale price produced a sizeable capital gain—and a tax liability of some $45 million. Liquidation offered a way to avoid this tax since under Section 337 of the Internal Revenue Code any corporation that liquidates itself in the space of one year pays no *corporate* capital gains tax on the sale of its assets (however, shareholders are subject to capital gains taxes on any appreciation in the common stock price). Liquidation was also a good defensive strategy against a takeover, given that UV would be flush with some $500 million in cash from the Federal Pacific sale and from funds generated by various other securities transactions.

Management's liquidation plan was to sell off those divisions and businesses where attractive prices could be obtained and, where the offers to buy were deemed too low, to spin the divisions off into independent companies, distributing shares to current UV stockholders. Liquidation was not expected to produce a hardship because UV only had 40 employees at its New York City headquarters and its operating divisions would presumably continue to exist—albeit under new owners and managers.

Source: Peter W. Bernstein, "A Company That's Worth More Dead than Alive," *Fortune* (February 26, 1979), pp. 42–44.

differentiate between when a cause is lost and when a turnaround is achievable. This is particularly true when emotions and pride get mixed with sound managerial judgment—as often they do.

Combination Strategies

The nine corporate strategy alternatives discussed above are not mutually exclusive. They can be used in combination, either in whole or in part, and they can be chained together in whatever sequences may be appropriate for adjusting to changing internal and external circumstances. Moreover, there are endless variations of each of the nine "pure" alternatives themselves. These variations allow ample room for organizations to create their own individualized blend of corporate purpose, objectives, and strategies. As a consequence, the difficulty of determining corporate strategy concerns not so much figuring out what options are open as evaluating the various viable alternatives.

When Some Corporate Strategies Are More Logical than Others

A firm's market position and competitive strength is often such that some corporate strategy alternatives offer a stronger logical fit than do others.[28] Consider, for instance, Figure 3-1 where a firm's competitive position is

FIGURE 3-1
Identifying Strategic Alternatives that Fit a Firm's Market Circumstances

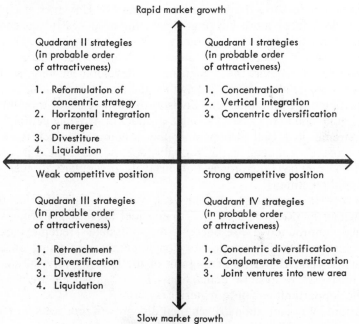

plotted against the rate of market growth to create four distinct strategic situations. Firms which fall into quadrant I (rapid market growth and strong competitive position) are in an excellent strategic position. In such circum-

---

[28] C. Roland Christensen, Norman A. Berg, and Malcolm S. Salter, *Policy Formulation and Administration*, 7th ed. (Homewood, Ill.: Richard D. Irwin, 1976), pp. 16–18.

stances a concentration strategy has powerful appeal and one can logically expect quadrant I firms to push hard to maintain or increase their market shares, to develop further their distinctive competences, and to make whatever capital investments may be necessary to continue in a leadership position. In addition, a quadrant I company may find it desirable to consider vertical integration as strategy for undergirding its market standing and protecting its profit margins. It may also make sense for an organization to look into concentric diversification as a means of spreading its business risks and capitalizing on its distinctive competence.

Firms falling into quadrant II should, first of all, direct their attention to a concentration strategy (given the high rate of market growth) and address the questions of (1) why their current approach to the market has resulted in a weak competitive position and (2) what it will take to become an effective competitor. With the market expanding rapidly, there should be ample opportunity for even a weak firm to carve out a viable market niche, provided strategic and organizational shortcomings can be overcome and the needed resource base developed. Certainly, a young, developing company has a better chance for survival in a growing market where there is plenty of new business than it does in a stable or declining industry. However, if a quadrant II firm lacks one or more key ingredients for a successful concentration strategy, then either horizontal merger with another company in the industry that has the missing pieces or else merger with an outsider having the cash and resources to support the organization's development may be the best corporate strategy alternative. Failing this, the most logical strategies would entail getting out of the industry: divestiture in the case of a multiproduct firm or liquidation in the case of a single-product firm. While getting out may seem extreme, it is well to remember that a company which is unable to make a profit in a booming market probably does not have the ability to make a profit at all and has little prospect of survival—particularly if recession hits or competition stiffens.

Quadrant III companies with their weak competitive position in a more or less stagnant market would do well to consider (1) retrenchment—so as to free up unproductive resources for possible redeployment, (2) diversification—either concentric or conglomerate, depending on existing opportunities elsewhere, (3) getting out of the industry (divestiture of this line of business), or even (4) liquidation—if profit prospects are nonexistent and other opportunities fail to materialize.

Quadrant IV organizations, given their dim growth prospects, are likely to be drawn toward using the excess cash flow from their existing business to begin a program of diversification. A concentric approach keyed to the distinctive competence that gave it its dominant position is an obvious option, but conglomerate diversification should be considered if concentric opportunities do not appear especially attractive. Joint ventures with other organizations into new fields of endeavor are another logical possibility. Whichever, the firm will likely wish to minimize new investments in its present facilities (to do little more than preserve the status quo), thereby freeing the maximum amount of funds for new endeavors.

Comparing firms on the basis of competitive position and market growth rate (or any other two variables) is useful for the insight it provides into why companies (even those in the same industry) may have good reason to pursue different corporate strategies. The nature of a firm's market standing, its competitive capabilities, its cash flow, its capital investment requirements, its ability to respond to emerging market opportunities, its distinctive competences, and so on all combine to shape its strategic position and its strategic alternatives. Sometimes a company's situation is such that a radical change in corporate strategy is called for; at other times, though, maintaining the status quo or just finetuning will suffice.

ALTERNATIVE LINE OF BUSINESS STRATEGIES

The focus of strategy at the business level is "how do we compete effectively in this particular business?" Strategic analysis at the business level consists primarily of (1) assessing opportunities and threats in particular markets and for particular products, (2) determining the keys to success in that particular business, (3) evaluating the competitive strategies of rival organizations, (4) searching for an effective competitive advantage, (5) identifying organizational strengths and weaknesses, and (6) trying to match specific product-market opportunities with internal skills, distinctive competences, and financial resources. The *essential* concern is finding an approach to the market and a competitive strategy that is capable of being effective and producing the desired performance and results.

Numerous types of business strategies abound. We shall discuss the following categories and classifications to indicate the rich array of varieties and options:

1. Strategies for underdog and low market share businesses.
2. Strategies for dominant firms.
3. Strategies for firms in growth markets.
4. Strategies for weak businesses.
5. Strategies for firms in mature or declining industries.
6. Turnaround strategies.
7. Strategies to be leery of.
8. Strategies to avoid.

Strategies for Underdog and Low Market Share Businesses

In many cases the most important strategic concern is how a firm can increase its market share and transform a trailing position into a more profitable position or a "middle-of-the-pack" position into a leadership position. A sizeable (10 percent or more) market share is sometimes necessary to realize scale economies, to generate an ample R&D budget, to gain good distribution, and, in general, to establish a viable long-run competitive niche in the industry. Normally, if an underdog firm is to be "outstandingly successful" it will need some sort of differentiating strategy aimed at building a competitive advantage; rarely can an underdog achieve real success by imitating what leading firms in the industry are doing.

The stage of the product-market life cycle often dictates just where the right kind of competitive advantage is likely to be located.[29] During the product development stage of a young industry, the competitive spotlight tends to center on product design, product quality positioning, and technical capability. Later, during the maturity-shakeout phase, the keys to competitive success tend to turn to product performance features, pricing, service, effectiveness of distribution channels, and market segmentation. Even so, underdog firms must still figure out just what strategic approach to product design, product positioning, product performance, market segmentation, and so on they ought to employ. No dependable generalizations can be offered. Each situation is sufficiently unique that creativity and sensitivity to market forces will be required. In some cases, a low market share business faces only two strategic options: fight to increase its share or withdraw from the business (gradually or quickly). In other cases, though, companies having a low market share may be able to remain small, compete effectively, and earn healthy profits.

There are several business strategies which can work well for underdog and low market share companies:[30]

1. *Vacant niche strategy.* Search out and cultivate profitable areas of the market that larger firms are not catering to or are ignoring or are not as

---

[29] Most discussions of product-market life cycles speak of five stages: (1) introduction and development, (2) take off and rapid growth, (3) maturity, (4) saturation, and (5) stagnation and decline. The period of introduction and development entails slow growth as initial inertia, product debugging, and start-up must all be overcome. Growth is a period of rapid market acceptance and substantial profit improvement. Many new firms may be drawn into the market to try to capitalize upon the opportunities present whereas other firms, unable to keep pace, fall by the wayside. Maturity is characterized by a slowing down in sales growth, proliferation of products, attempts at intense market segmentation, and increased competition; there is often an industrywide *shakeout* of weak, inefficient, and ineffective firms. Saturation brings on negligible sales growth and pressure on profit margins, as price cutting and competition heat up—the struggle is much like a "survival of the fittest" type of contest. Stagnation and decline is the period where new and better substitutes begin to appear, sales erode and begin a downward drift, and profits decline rapidly toward the zero level.

The point here is that the nature of competition shifts in important ways over the course of the cycle. What it takes to compete effectively in the early part of the product-market life cycle is not the same as in the latter part of the cycle. For an excellent treatment of product-market life cycles see Robert D. Buzzell, "Competitive Behavior and Product Life Cycles," in *New Ideas for Successful Marketing,* ed. by John S. Wright and Jac L. Goldstucker (Chicago: American Marketing Association, 1966), pp. 46–68; and Kotler, *Marketing Management,* pp. 289–309.

[30] For more details, see Kotler, *Marketing Management,* pp. 281–84, and R. G. Hamermesh, M. J. Anderson, Jr., and J. E. Harris, "Strategies for Low Market Share Businesses," *Harvard Business Review,* vol. 56, no. 3 (May–June 1978), pp. 95–102.

well equipped to serve. Examples include the small tire manufacturers which have managed to survive competing with Goodyear, Firestone, B. F. Goodrich, and Uniroyal.

2. *Specialist* or *concentration strategy.* Attempt to compete in only a few, carefully chosen market *segments,* rather than making a broad assault on the entire industry. Sell only to segments where the company has special expertise and where the company's strengths will be highly valued by customers. Be alert to the fact that a market can be segmented by location of plants, stage of production, price-quality-performance characteristics of the product, the cost and speed of distribution, credit and service arrangements, manufacturing capability—as well as by products and customers. Companies which have successfully used a specialist of concentration approach include Control Data (which developed a better computer for scientific research), Timex (which designed a cheap, but reliable, watch), and Crown Cork and Seal (which concentrated on metal cans for hard-to-hold products and on aerosol cans).

3. *"Ours-is-better-than-theirs" strategy.* Try to capitalize on opportunities to improve upon the products of dominant firms and develop an appeal to quality-conscious or performance-oriented buyers. Be more innovative. Work closely with major customers to develop a better product. Some examples: Chivas Regal's approach to selling scotch, Zenith's attempt to overtake RCA with its "the quality goes in, before the name goes on" strategy, and Mercedes-Benz's appeal to luxury car buyers.

4. *Channel innovation strategy.* Find a new way to distribute goods that offers substantial savings or that reaches particular groups of buyers more efficiently. Examples are Avon's door-to-door selling of cosmetics and Timex's use of drug stores and discount stores as outlets for its watches.

5. *Distinctive image strategy.* Seek to develop a differential competitive advantage via some distinctive, visible, and unique appeal. Examples include Dr. Pepper's combined strategy of distinctive taste and effective advertising slogans; Miller's introduction of Lite beer; and Avis' "We're No. 2, We Try Harder" campaign to provide cleaner rental cars and more personal attention.

Without a doubt, in some industries low market share companies have serious obstacles to overcome—less access to economies of scale in manufacturing or distribution or sales promotion, smaller R&D budgets, less opportunity to distribute through internal channels, difficulties in attracting capital, keeping good managerial and technical personnel, and gaining public and customer recognition.[31] But it is erroneous to classify all low share businesses as "dogs." The handicaps can be surmounted and a viable competitive position established. The most promising strategic guidelines seem

---

[31] Hamermesh, Anderson, and Harris, "Strategies for Low Market Share Business," p. 102.

to be: (1) compete only in carefully chosen market segments where particular strengths can be developed and avoid attacking dominant firms head on with price cuts and increased promotional expenditure; (2) focus R&D budgets on developing a distinctive competence in new product development or technical capabilities, but only for the target market segments; (3) be content to remain small and emphasize profits rather than sales growth or market share; (4) push specialization rather than diversification (but if diversification is needed, enter closely related markets); and (5) manage the business in an innovative/"dare to be different"/"beat-the-odds" type of mode. However if the economics of the business is such that market share is the key to profitability, then the preceding guidelines must be modified and emphasis placed upon developing a competitive advantage that extends over many market segments. Of course, a trailing firm may be able to make major market share gains without a real competitive advantage if it makes a sudden technological breakthrough, or if the leaders stumble or become complacent, or if it is willing to make major investments over long periods of time to secure incremental gains in its products and customer base.

Business Strategies for Dominant Firms

The strategic position of a dominant firm is more enviable. As a leader, it has a well-established and well-known position. The main issue of business strategy thus tends to revolve around how best to harvest what has been achieved and how to maintain or improve upon the present position. Several different strategic postures are open:[32]

1. *Keep-the-offensive strategy.* Refuse to be content with just being a leader. Seek to continue to outperform the industry by breaking records the firm itself has already set. Become firmly established as *the* source of new product ideas, cost-cutting discoveries, innovative customer services, and better means of distribution. In general, exercise initiative, set the pace, and exploit the weaknesses of rival firms.

2. *Fortification strategy.* Surround the chief products with patents; foreclose the attractiveness of entry by introducing more of the company's own brands to compete with the already-successful company brands; introduce additional items under current brand names.

3. *Confrontation strategy.* Defend the company's market base by being quick to launch massive promotional wars which underdog firms cannot hope to match; promptly meet all competitive price cuts of lesser-sized firms to neutralize any benefits to would-be price-cutters; make it hard for aggressive-minded smaller firms to grow by selling at prices so low that smaller firms are denied the profit margins and total earnings needed to make further expansion attractive.

---

[32] Kotler, *Marketing Management,* pp. 273–81.

4. *Maintenance strategy.* Peg the level of reinvestment in the business sufficiently high to maintain production capacity, operating efficiency, product quality, and customer service, thus avoiding any slippage in sales, market share, and profitability. Shift extra cash flow and retained earnings to other businesses where growth and profit potential may be greater. A maintenance strategy is appropriate for a dominant firm when the business occupies an important position in the organization's overall lineup and when it generates ample cash flow to support other ventures.

Business Strategies for Firms in Growth Markets

Two crucial strategic issues confront firms trying to participate in a rapidly growing market: (1) how to acquire the resources needed to grow with the market, so that the firm can maintain or improve its current position and (2) how to develop the sort of distinctive competence and competitive stamina that will be needed as growth slows and maturity-saturation begins.[33] Again, no neat prescriptions can be given for just how these two issues should be resolved. Strategy has to be geared to match the specifics of each growth market. Nonetheless, the following strategic guidelines can be offered:[34]

1. Manage the business in an entrepreneurial mode with the aim of building the business for its future potential.
2. Be alert for product development opportunities keyed to product quality, performance features, styling, additional models and sizes, and improved design.
3. Search out new market segments and new geographical areas to enter.
4. Shift the focus of advertising and promotion from building product awareness to increasing frequency of use and to creating brand loyalty.
5. Seek out new distribution channels to gain additional product exposure.
6. Watch for the right time to lower prices to attract the next layer of price-sensitive buyers into the market.
7. Although the priorities may be on growth, market share, and a strengthening of competitive position, recognize that during the growth stage market-expanding activities usually come at the expense of higher current profits. If the profits foregone now to capture growth are to be recaptured later, then any market share or dominant position gained at the expense of profitability in the growth stage should offer the prospect of a higher than otherwise return on investment.

However, one caution can be urged. The strategic imperative of how to maintain/improve competitive market position during the takeoff stage should not blind management to the longer-range strategic need to prepare

---

[33] Charles W. Hofer and Dan Schendel, *Strategy Formulation: Analytical Concepts* (St. Paul, Minn.: West Publishing Company, 1978), pp. 164–65.

[34] Kotler, *Marketing Management,* p. 296.

for the different types of competition that will occur when the market matures and a rigorous market share struggle sets in.[35] The temptation to neglect the latter for the former can be great when current market growth is in the 15–50 percent range and management must spend much of its energies figuring out ways to continue to achieve rapid growth—how to supplement internal cash flows with debt and equity capital, where to build new plants, how many personnel to add, which way to push R&D and market development efforts, how to respond to the product developments of rival firms, and so on. Moreover, it may be hard to foresee what twists competition may take as the market matures.

Nonetheless, the longer-range needs of strategy ought to be balanced against the immediate needs. This can be accomplished most easily in multi-industry enterprises that have had experience in managing young businesses through the early stages of product-market evolution. A single-business enterprise in a rapid growth situation does have some strategic substitutes for experience: it can gain guidance via wise selection of members for its board of directors; it can hire skilled management personnel from firms that have recently passed through the shakeout stage or else are in the early maturity phase; or it can try to gain functional skills via acquisition or merger.

Strategies for Weak Businesses

Management has essentially four options for handling a weak business (whether it be a division, product line, or product).[36] It can employ a *building strategy* and pour enough money and talent into the business to make it a stronger performer. It can use a *maintenance strategy* and budget enough funds to maintain sales and profitability at present levels. It can opt for a *divestment strategy* or a *liquidation strategy* and abandon the business— quickly or gradually. Or, it can resort to a *harvest strategy* whereby investment levels are reduced and efforts are made to "harvest" reasonable short-term profits and/or maximize short-term cash flow. The first three options are self-explanatory. The fourth deserves added treatment.

A harvesting strategy steers a middle course between maintenance and abandonment. It entails a level of resource support in between what is required for maintenance and a decision to divest or liquidate. It is a phasing down approach. Kotler has suggested seven indicators of when a business should become a candidate for harvesting:[37]

1. When the business is in a saturated or declining market.
2. When the business has gained only a small market share, and building it up would be too costly or not profitable enough; or when it has a re-

---

[35] Hofer and Schendel, *Strategy Formulation*, pp. 164–65.

[36] Ibid., p. 166.

[37] Philip Kotler, "Harvesting Strategies for Weak Products," *Business Horizons*, vol. 21, no. 5 (August 1978), pp. 17–18.

spectable market share that is becoming increasingly costly to maintain or defend.
3. When profits are not especially attractive.
4. When reduced levels of resource support will not entail sharp declines in sales and market position.
5. When the organization can redeploy the freed-up resources in higher opportunity areas.
6. When the business is not a major component of the organization's overall business portfolio.
7. When the business does not contribute other desired features (sales stability, prestige, a well-rounded product line) to the total business portfolio.

The more of these seven conditions which are present, the more ideal the business is for harvesting.

The features of a harvesting strategy are fairly clearcut. The operating budget is reduced to a bare-bones level; stringent cost cutting is undertaken. The business is given little, if any, capital expenditure priority—depending upon the current condition of fixed assets and upon whether the harvest is to be fast or slow. Price may be raised, promotional expenses cut, quality reduced, customer services curtailed, equipment maintenance decreased, and the like. The mandate, typically, is to maximize short-term cash flow—for redeployment to other parts of the organization. It is understood that sales will fall to some core level of demand, but it may be that costs can be cut such that profits do not suffer much—at least immediately. Ideally, though, sales and market share will not fall far below their preharvest level in the short run. If the business cannot make money and/or generate positive cash flow at the lower core level of demand, then it can be divested or liquidated. A harvesting strategy thus clearly implies the sunset or twilight stage of a product or business in its life cycle.

Although a harvesting strategy calls for reduced budgets and cost-cutting, it is useful to implement these moves in ways which do not alert competitors and customers to the harvesting intention.[38] To do so merely precipitates the decline in sales and reduces the potential harvest. Generally, the first cutbacks should be in expenditures for R&D and for plant and equipment. Later, marketing expenditures can be reduced and prices raised slightly. Still later, product quality and customer services can be trimmed. Management may also elect to splash some advertising occasionally, since such sporadic bursts will recapture customer and dealer attention, thereby slowing sales decay. Such an approach may result in a smaller gain in cash flow, but one which lasts over a longer period. A fast harvest, where deep cutbacks are made across the board, produces a large cash flow increase, but it doesn't last long.

Although it may not seem so at first, harvesting strategies have much to

---

[38] Ibid., p. 20.

recommend, especially in diversified companies having products in different stages of their life cycle. Different lines of business deserve different levels of resource support depending on their profit potential, their life cycle stage, and their rank in an organization's overall line of business portfolio. Businesses which are fading or on the verge of decline are logical candidates for a harvesting strategy. Reducing resource support and commitment to a line of business (or division or product) makes strategic sense when costs can be decreased without proportionate losses in sales. The result can be improved profitability and cash flow in the short run—the very things at which a harvesting strategy aims.

Strategies for Firms in Mature or Declining Industries

Many firms do business in industries where demand is declining or else growing at rates well below the economywide average. Although such businesses may be prime candidates for harvesting, divestiture, or even liquidation, other alternatives exist and may in fact be more appealing.[39] The difficulty of finding a buyer who will pay an acceptable price often makes divestiture impractical, and stagnant or declining demand by itself is not enough to warrant liquidation. For example, even though the demand for coffee has trended downward for over 15 years, General Foods still derives 40 percent of its sales and 33 percent of its profits from its line of coffee products. Even more important, a decision to drop certain product lines just because they are in tough, slow-growth markets is not always best, since without the contribution margin generated by the sales of such products a firm may find itself unable to cover overhead costs and its whole operation may become unprofitable.

A first step in formulating a successful strategy in slow-growth/declining business is to accept the difficult realities of a continuing stagnant demand and then adopt a set of target objectives consistent with market opportunities.[40] Cash flow and return on investment criteria are more appropriate than growth-oriented performance measures. Furthermore, head-to-head competition is usually more intense in markets where demand is stagnant than where expansion is vigorous. So long as industry demand grows rapidly, there tends to be enough new business that firms need not launch aggressive attacks on rivals to gain higher sales; the major concern is with how to take advantage of market growth, not with how to outmaneuver rival firms. However, as industry growth slows to a halt, increases in volume have to come at the expense of one's competitors. The ensuing battle for market share frequently drives weaker firms out of the market and market shares of

---

[39] R. G. Hamermesh and S. B. Silk, "How to Compete in Stagnant Industries," *Harvard Business Review*, vol. 57, no. 5 (September–October 1979), p. 161.

[40] Ibid., p. 162.

the remaining companies rise. For instance in the cigar industry, where unit volume has been declining at a 5 percent annual rate since the mid-60s, the number of manufacturers declined from 283 in 1958 to 132 in 1972; in coffee, not only did the number of companies decline but the combined market shares of the top 3 firms rose from 47 percent in 1960 to 67 percent in 1976.[41]

In general, three themes characterize the strategies of firms which have succeeded in stagnant industries:[42]

1. *They identify, create, and exploit the growth segments within their industries.* Most industries are composed of numerous segments and subsegments (whether the segments are best identified by price, product use, geographic location, customer type, product features, or service requirements varies from case to case). Nearly always at least one of these segments is growing rapidly. The skill, then, is to collect and analyze industry information in such a way as to seek out and identify the segments with faster growth potential. By concentrating its efforts in the emerging or growth segments, a firm thus escapes being victimized by the declining industrywide trends. Such a conscious redefinition of what business to compete in is precisely what the strategy formulation task is all about.

2. *They emphasize quality improvements and product innovation.* A key point to be recognized here is that stagnant demand does not preclude significant innovation; indeed, innovation can rejuvenate demand by creating important new growth segments or otherwise postponing further stagnation in sales. From the standpoint of competition, successful product innovation allows a firm to escape competing mainly on the basis of selling price. In addition, it can be difficult and expensive for rival firms to imitate. An example is General Foods' introduction of freeze-dried coffee. Because many people viewed freeze-dried instant coffee as better tasting, demand grew rapidly (even though total consumption of coffee declined). Yet, with the notable exception of Nestlé, other producers were unwilling or unable to invest in the more expensive freeze-dry technology; as a consequence, the profit margins which General Foods has earned on its freeze-dried business are the highest of all coffee products.

3. *They work diligently and persistently to improve production and distribution efficiency.* When increases in sales cannot be counted upon to generate increases in earnings, an alternative is to improve profit margins and return on investment by reducing operating costs. This can be achieved by (1) improving the manufacturing process via automation and increased specialization, (2) consolidating underutilized production

---

[41] Ibid.

[42] Ibid., pp. 163–65.

facilities, (3) adding more distribution channels to ensure the unit volume needed for low-cost production, and (4) shifting sales away from low-volume, high-cost distribution outlets to high-volume, low-cost outlets.

Plainly enough, these three strategic themes are not mutually exclusive. They can be used simultaneously and can reinforce one another.[43] For instance, attempts to introduce new innovative versions of a product can result in *creating* a fast growing market segment. Similarly, concentrating on operating efficiencies can stimulate an increased emphasis on catering to emerging growth segments.

In any event, since it is a rare company that competes only in rapidly growing markets, strategies for competing successfully in stagnant or declining industries warrant close management attention.

Turnaround Strategies

Turnaround strategies come into play when a business worth saving has fallen into disrepair and decline. The goal is to arrest and reverse the situation as quickly as possible. Assuming that it is possible to avoid failure and/or bankruptcy, the first task of a turnaround is diagnosis. What is the cause of the decline? Is it bad strategy? Or poor implementation and execution of an otherwise workable strategy? Is it weak management? Or are the causes of decline beyond management control? One must know what is wrong before a plan for cure can be formulated. Moreover, one must learn what internal skills and resources need to be protected so as to preserve them as a base for launching a turnaround strategy. Generally speaking, there are five approaches to turnaround: (1) a replacement of top management and other key personnel, (2) revenue-increasing strategies, (3) cost-reduction strategies, (4) asset reduction/retrenchment strategies, and (5) a combination of these. Replacing key management personnel is an obvious turnaround alternative. Management is responsible for successful performance of a business. It is obliged to take whatever actions are deemed advisable to accommodate internal and external changes and to ensure efficient, effective performance. It is reasonable to infer that when decay sets into a business, management has either taken no action to ward off poor performance or else it has taken inappropriate actions. Whichever, one corrective approach is to install new management.[44] Only when the circum-

---

[43]Ibid., p. 165.

[44] One study of corporate turnaround reports the occurrence of significant management changes, including chief executive officers, in 39 out of 54 firms attempting to reverse a downturn in performance. See Dan Schendel, G. R. Patton, and James Riggs, "Corporate Turnaround Strategies," *Journal of General Management*, vol. 3, no. 3 (Spring 1976), pp. 3–11.

stances underlying decline are beyond management control should no change in management be seriously contemplated.

Revenue-increasing turnaround strategy focuses on how to increase sales volume (increased promotion, more emphasis on marketing, added customer services) and whether and how much of a price increase can be instituted. It is a necessary strategic approach when there is little or no room in the operating budget to cut back on expenses and still reach breakeven and when the key to restoring profitability is an increased utilization of existing capacity.

Cost-reduction turnaround strategies work best when the firm's cost structure is flexible enough to permit radical surgery, when operating inefficiencies are identifiable and readily correctable, and when the firm is relatively close to its breakeven point. Accompanying a general belt-tightening can be an increased emphasis on budgeting and cost control, elimination of jobs and hirings, modernization of existing plant and equipment to gain greater productivity, and capital expenditure cutbacks.

Asset reduction/retrenchment turnaround strategies are necessary when cash flow is a critical consideration and when the most practical way to generate cash is (1) through sale of some of the firm's assets (plant and equipment, land, patents, divisions, or inventories) and (2) through retrenchment—pruning of marginal products from the product line, closing or sale of older plants, a reduced work force, withdrawal from outlying markets, cutbacks in customer service, and the like. A divestment of assets may not only be needed to improve cash flow but it may also represent the best way to unload money-losing activities and restore profitability. Thus asset reduction may not signify liquidation and retrenchment as much as it does an attempt to eliminate losses and cash drains.

Combination turnaround strategies are usually the most effective, especially in grim situations where fast action on a broad front is required. This is because the result to be gained from the best asset reduction and revenue increasing actions are greater than from the third or fourth best cost-reducing actions, and conversely.[45]

No matter which variety of turnaround strategy is chosen, attention will tend to center on those actions which have the greatest short-term cash flow impact and which will move the business toward breakeven the quickest. The urgency and limited resources of a near-bankrupt business make these considerations imperative. The key to turnaround is management action of the right kind. Specifically, it is important to diagnose whether the prevailing strategy is suitably matched to the external environment and to internal resources. If so, the difficulties probably lie in operating inefficiency and poor internal management. But if strategy is at the root of the decline in performance, the spotlight of turnaround must be on strategy reformulation.

---

[45] Hofer and Schendel, *Strategy Formulation*, p. 174.

Strategies to Be Leery of

On occasion management may be pulled toward the adoption of a strategy which is risky and lacks the potential for real success. This can occur out of desperation or poor analysis or simply lack of creativity. The following strategies are offered as examples of those which managers should be cautious about adopting:

1. *"Me too" or "copy-cat" strategy.* Imitating the strategy of leading or successful enterprises; trying to play catch-up by beating the leaders at their own game. *Weakness:* Ignores development of firm's own personality, image, strategy, and policies.
2. *Take-away strategy.* Trying to achieve greater market share and market penetration by attacking other firms head on and luring away their customers via a lower price, more advertising, and other attention-getting gimmicks. *Weakness:* Invites retaliation and risks precipitating a fierce and costly battle for market share in which no one wins—including the firm trying to play take-away.
3. *Glamour strategy.* When a firm gets seduced by the prospects of a new idea for a product or technology which it thinks will sweep the market. *Weakness:* The best laid plans. . . .
4. *Test-the-water strategy.* Often arises when an enterprise is engaged in developing new opportunities or is reacting to market-technological-environmental changes which call for a fundamental reformulation or redesign of strategy. In such cases, firms may "test the water" in venturing out into new fields of endeavor. *Weakness:* A half-way effort or "sideline stepchild" seldom succeeds for lack of adequate corporate commitment; it's usually best to either get in or stay out entirely.
5. *Hit-another-home-run strategy.* This strategy is typified by a firm which has hit one "home run" (pioneering a very successful product and strategy) and which is urgently looking for ways to hit a second home run (by getting into a new line of business either related or unrelated to its first home run), so as to continue to grow and prosper at its former rate. A second "home-run" business may be necessary because growth of the initial business is rapidly slowing down and becoming more competitive. *Weakness:* Trying to repeat the same strategy in a new business may not work out because the conditions and the requirements for success are not the same.
6. *Arms-race strategy.* May emerge when firms of relatively equal size enter into a spirited battle for increased market share. Commonly, such battles are waged with increased promotional and advertising expenditures and/or aggressive price cuts and/or increased R&D and new product development budgets and/or extra services to customers. As one firm pours more money into its efforts, other firms feel forced to do likewise for defensive reasons. The result is escalating costs, producing

a situation much like an arms race. *Weakness:* Seldom do such battles produce a substantial change in market shares, yet they almost certainly raise costs—costs which must either be absorbed in the form of lower profit margins or else passed on to customers via higher prices.[46]

Strategies to Avoid

Experience has shown that some business strategies seldom if ever work. An alert management, for obvious reasons, will seek to avoid use of the following strategies:

1. *Drift strategy.* When strategy is not consciously designed and coordinated but rather just evolves out of day-to-day decisions and actions at the operating level.
2. *Hope-for-a-better-day strategy.* Emerges from managerial inertia and tradition and is exemplified by firms which blame their subpar sales-profits-market share performance on bad luck, the economy, unexpected problems, and other circumstances "beyond their control." Such "entrepreneurial coasting" until good times arrive is a sure sign of a dim future and managerial ineptness.
3. *Losing hand strategy.* Arises in companies where a once successful (and perhaps spectacularly so) strategy is fading and no longer viable. Nonetheless, management, blinded by the success-breeds-success syndrome, continues to be reluctant to begin to reformulate its strategy, preferring instead to try to rekindle the old spark with cosmetic changes—in hopes of reversing a downhill slide.
4. *Popgun strategy.* Seeking to go into head-to-head competition with proven leaders when the firm has neither a differential competitive advantage nor adequate financial strength with which to do battle.[47]

Business Strategies: A Perspective View

The foregoing survey of business strategy alternatives is by no means exhaustive. For example, concentration or specialist strategies, joint venture strategies, retrenchment strategies, divestiture, and liquidation, all of which were discussed under the heading of corporate strategy, also have their counterparts in line of business strategy. Moreover, as has been pointed out, whether a particular business strategy is "right" for an organization depends upon the stage of product-market evolution, the competitive position a firm has, the competitive position it seeks, the business strategies being used

---

[46] Kotler, *Marketing Management,* Second Edition, chap. 8; and Joel Ross and Michael Kami, *Corporate Management in Crisis: Why the Mighty Fall* (Englewood Cliffs, N.J.: Prentice-Hall, Inc., 1973).

[47] Ibid.

by rival firms, and the internal resources and distinctive competences at a firm's disposal—to mention only the more important considerations.

How a firm should try to compete—the overriding issue in line of business strategy—is therefore variable from situation to situation and from time to time. Competition is a dynamic process which assumes many forms and comes in many different shades of intensity. Thus, there can be no nice, neat package of business strategy options to choose among; just as with corporate-level strategy, line of business strategy is something which must be tailor-made to fit the situation at hand. Our sampling of strategic alternatives is intended to highlight the variety of approaches and to demonstrate the need for creative strategy formulation.

SUGGESTED READINGS

Ansoff, H. Igor. *Corporate Strategy*. New York: McGraw-Hill, 1965, chap. 7.

Ansoff, H. Igor, and Stewart, John M. "Strategies for a Technology-Based Business." *Harvard Business Review*, vol. 45, no. 6 (November–December 1967), pp. 71–83.

Bettauer, Arthur. "Strategy for Divestments." *Harvard Business Review*, vol. 45, no. 2 (March–April 1967), pp. 116–24.

Bloom, Paul N., and Kotler, Philip. "Strategies for High Market Share Companies." *Harvard Business Review*, vol. 53, no. 6 (November–December 1975), pp. 63–72.

Bright, William M. "Alternative Strategies for Diversification." *Research Management*, vol. 12, no. 4 (July 1969), pp. 247–53.

Cooper, Arnold C., and Schendel, Dan. "Strategic Responses to Technological Threats." *Business Horizons*, vol. 19, no. 1 (February 1976), pp. 61–69.

Doutt, J. T. "Product Innovation in Small Business." *Business Topics*, vol. 8, no. 3 (Summer 1960), pp. 58–62.

Drucker, Peter. *Management: Tasks, Responsibilities, Practices*. New York: Harper Row, Publishers, 1974, chaps. 55–58, 60, and 61.

Hamermesh, R. G., Anderson, M. J., and Harris, J. E. "Strategies for Low Market Share Businesses." *Harvard Business Review*, vol. 56, no. 3 (May–June 1978), pp. 95–102.

Hamermesh, R. G., and Silk, S. B. "How to Compete in Stagnant Industries." *Harvard Business Review*, vol. 57, no. 5 (September–October 1979), pp. 161–68.

Hanan, Mack. "Corporate Growth through Internal Spinouts." *Harvard Business Review*, vol. 47, no. 6 (November–December 1969), pp. 55–66.

Kotler, Philip. "Harvesting Strategies for Weak Products." *Business Horizons*, vol. 21, no. 4 (August 1978), pp. 15–22.

Mason, R. S. "Product Diversification and the Small Firm." *Journal of Business Policy*, vol. 3, no. 3 (Spring 1973), pp. 28–39.

Steiner, George A. "Why and How to Diversify." *California Management Review*, vol. 6, no. 4 (Summer 1964), pp. 11–17.

Vancil, Richard F. and Lorange, Peter. "Strategic Planning in Diversified Companies." *Harvard Business Review*, vol. 53, no. 1 (January–February 1975), pp. 81–90.

Webster, Frederick A. "A Model of Vertical Integration Strategy." *California Management Review*, vol. 10, no. 2 (Winter 1967), pp. 49–58.

Woodward, Herbert N. "Management Strategies for Small Companies." *Harvard Business Review*, vol. 54, no. 1 (January–February 1976), pp. 113–21.

4 STRATEGY ANALYSIS AND EVALUATION AT THE CORPORATE LEVEL

If we can know where we are and something about how we got there, we might see where we are trending—and if the outcomes which lie naturally in our course are unacceptable, to make timely change.

Abraham Lincoln

The preceding chapter surveyed the major corporate and business strategy alternatives. The task of this and the next chapter is to examine the analytic considerations which make up a thoroughgoing strategy evaluation and which thus form the basis for deciding which strategy to choose. This chapter concentrates upon the analysis and evaluation of corporate-level strategy in a multibusiness organization; Chapter 5 deals with the task of analyzing business-level strategy.

Approaching the Task of Corporate Strategy Evaluation

A major contribution of top management in any organization is developing insightful answers to questions like: Where are we now? If we stay in the same activities we are in today and don't do anything new or different, where will we be in another five to ten years? Do we like the answer to this question? If not, what can we and what should we do about it? How top management deals with questions of this type sums up very neatly what strategic management at the corporate level is all about.[1]

Managerial approaches to strategy evaluation at the corporate level can and do vary to some extent with the type of company. In a diversified, multiindustry enterprise, the primary task of corporate strategy evaluation is one of (1) working out tentative corporate objectives and the desired portfolio lineup of businesses, (2) determining the relative attractiveness of each

---

[1] George Odiorne, *Management and the Activity Trap* (New York: Harper & Row, Publishers, 1974), p. 12.

of the firm's current businesses, and (3) figuring out how the performance of the total portfolio can be upgraded via better strategic management of existing businesses, further diversification, and/or divestiture. The development and evaluation of *business* strategies in multiindustry companies tend to be delegated to lower-level general managers who have profit-and-loss responsibility for particular divisions and product lines. Corporate and business strategies are then joined and dovetailed by negotiation between corporate managers and business-unit managers, usually according to the priorities and objectives of corporate strategy. Consequently, in a multiindustry enterprise business strategy tends to follow corporate strategy.

In contrast, in single-line or dominant-product-line companies, the strategy of the base business is the center of attention, after which diversification and other portfolio questions relating to corporate strategy are addressed. Such firms generally do not divorce corporate strategy evaluation and business strategy evaluation because (1) activities outside the base business contribute minimally to sales and profits and (2) the issue of "which way do we go from here" is so closely related to the main business. Thus in dominant-business companies corporate strategy is heavily keyed to business strategy instead of being the other way around. But whatever approach to corporate strategy formulation best fits a company, sound strategy evaluation starts with explicit and detailed information about the realities of the organization's present condition and situation.

Identifying the Present Corporate Strategy

Identifying an organization's present corporate strategy is an obvious first step in strategy analysis and evaluation. Understanding where a company is now and what strategy is being followed logically precedes any serious judgments as to whether the "right" strategy or an appropriate strategy is being pursued and whether any changes in corporate strategy are called for.

Although identifying "what the strategy is" comes before recommending "what the strategy should be," this is easier said than done. Seldom will management have formally articulated the firm's corporate strategy fully and completely. Some, or even much, of the strategy commonly has to be deduced or inferred from the ways the firm's operations have been and are being conducted—that is, from its past behavior and pattern of doing business and from its major policies, plans, and objectives. On occasions, there may be contradictions and inconsistencies between what is said and what is done, thus further confounding what the reality of the strategy is. The analyst thus has the task of interpreting and evaluating both the actions of the firm and the statements of various managers in identifying the current strategy.

Areas for Analysis in the Strategy Identification Process. A full identification of an organization's corporate strategy requires an assessment of both external and internal factors. The relevant external factors include:

1. The present scope and diversity of the firm's activities and business interests.
2. The nature of the firm's recent acquisitions and divestitures.
3. The *relative* proportions and blend of the firm's activities, together with the recent trends in these proportions and the apparent factors underlying any changes in the mix.
4. What "opportunities" the firm is apparently trying to pursue and capitalize upon.
5. How the firm seems to be trying to minimize the impact of perceived external "threats."

The most important internal factors include:

1. The firm's objectives (stated or implied), especially with respect to growth, profitability, and financial performance targets.
2. The stated criteria for allocating investment capital to proposed projects and the actual pattern of investment expenditures across the firm's various lines of business.
3. The organization's attitude toward risk, as stated by management and as reflected by policies governing debt-equity ratios, liquidity, financing of new investments and growth, and overall financial structure and financial condition.
4. Where the firm is focusing its R&D efforts.
5. Key functional area strategies, stated or implied, concerning product quality, technological competence, physical facilities, operating practices and procedures, personnel and staffing, marketing, and overall corporate image.

Figure 4–1 is a summary portrayal of these factors and considerations; the totality of how they interact constitutes a picture of the present corporate strategy and where the organization is now. As previously stated, this picture may reveal a company and a management which is simply "muddling through" or, at the other extreme, it may reflect a timely, opportunistic organizationwide game plan which gives every evidence of having been shrewdly thought out and carefully integrated into a consistent, powerful action plan. Whichever is the case, a skillful identification of the present corporate strategy lays the foundation for conducting a thoroughgoing strategy analysis and, subsequently, for reformulating the strategy as it "should be."

Corporate Portfolio Analysis

Our discussion of corporate strategy evaluation will focus upon *corporate portfolio analysis* which, currently at least, is the prevailing method of strategy analysis at the corporate level in diversified firms and in multiproduct firms. In less diversified firms, the portfolio approach is also applicable,

FIGURE 4-1
Angles from which to Determine and Evaluate Corporate Strategy

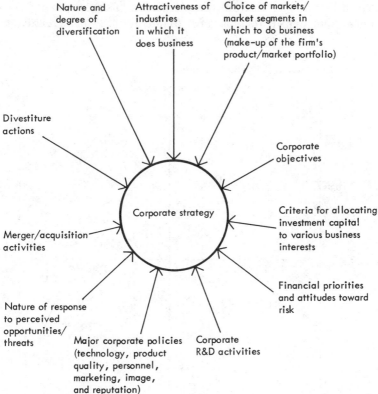

provided it is modified slightly to take account of the fact that the main strategic issue is not so much how to realign the mix and proportions of the firm's business to improve overall performance as it is what kind of new businesses—if any—the firm should attempt to get into to go along with its base business.[2]

The widespread popularity of the portfolio approach stems from the relative simplicity and clarity it offers in initiating an aggregate assessment of a firm's several lines of business. The distinguishing feature of this approach is the construction of a *business portfolio matrix*. Such a matrix facilitates comparisons of different businesses on the basis of such strategically relevant variables as growth rate in sales, relative competitive position, stage of product/market evolution, market share, and industry attractiveness. Any two-variable comparison can be used.

---

[2] However, the portfolio approach turns out to be just as valid for a multiproduct firm as for a multiindustry firm when the former manages each product and/or market segment as if they were independent businesses.

The Four-Cell BCG Matrix. The most publicized business portfolio matrix is a four-square grid pioneered by the Boston Consulting Group (BCG) and depicted in Figure 4-2.[3] Each of the company's businesses is plotted in the matrix according to its percentage growth rate in sales and its relative market

FIGURE 4–2
The BCG Business Portfolio Matrix

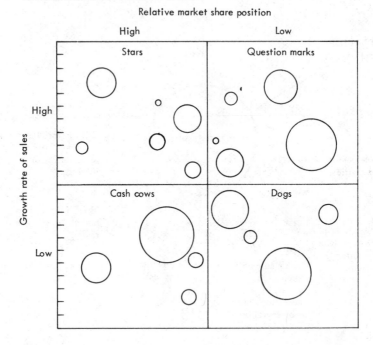

Relative market share position

Growth rate of sales

share position.[4] The size of each circle in the matrix is proportional to the sales revenues generated by each business.

Businesses with high growth rates and high market share positions are labeled as "stars" by BCG, because they usually represent the best profit and growth opportunities in the firm's portfolio. As such, they are the businesses that an enterprise needs to nurture and groom for the long run. Star-type businesses vary as to whether they need heavy infusions of investment funds to support continued rapid growth and high performance. According to BCG, some stars (usually those that are well-established and beginning to mature) are virtually self-sustaining in terms of cash flow and little investment will be needed from sources external to the business. Young

[3] For a more detailed discussion see Barry Hedley, "A Fundamental Approach to Strategy Development," *Long-Range Planning* (December 1976), pp. 2–11.

[4] Relative market share position is measured by the ratio of the business's market share to the market share held by the largest rival firm.

stars, however, often require substantial investment capital beyond what can be generated internally in order to secure and maintain their high growth/ high market share ranking.

Businesses with a high market share in a low growth market are called "cash cows" by BCG because their entrenched position tends to yield substantial *cash surpluses* over and above what is needed for reinvestment and growth in the business. Many of today's cash cows are yesterday's stars. Cash cows, though less attractive from a growth standpoint, are nonetheless a valuable corporate portfolio holding because they can be "milked" for the cash to pay corporate dividends and corporate overhead, they provide debt capacity, and they provide cash flow to support investment in the next round of stars and to make new acquisitions. "Strong cash cows" are not "harvested" but are maintained and managed for cash flow. The idea is to preserve market position while efficiently generating dollars to reallocate to business investments elsewhere. "Weak cash cows," however, may be prime candidates for harvesting and, eventually, divestiture.

Businesses with low growth and low market share are referred to as "dogs" by BCG because of their weak competitive position (owing, perhaps, to high costs, low quality products, less effective marketing, and the like) and the low profit potential that can be associated with slow growth and impending market saturation. Another characteristic of dogs is the lack of attractive cash flow on a long-term basis; sometimes they do not produce enough cash to maintain their existing position—especially if competition is stiff, profit margins are thin, or inflation is causing sharply higher costs. Consequently, except for unusual reasons, BCG recommends that dogs be harvested, divested, or liquidated, depending on which alternative will maximize short-term cash flow.

Businesses falling in the upper right quadrant of the matrix are tagged as "question marks." Rapid market growth makes the business attractive from an industry standpoint, but low market share makes it questionable whether the profit potential associated with growth can realistically be captured— hence, the "question mark" designation. According to BCG, question mark businesses are typically "cash hogs"—so labeled because their cash needs are high (owing to rapid growth) and their internal cash generation is low (owing to low market share). BCG reasons that the most rational strategic options for a question market business are (1) to grow it into a star or, if the costs of strengthening its competitive position do not warrant the effort, (2) to divest it.

The BCG business portfolio matrix has considerable appeal in evaluating different businesses and reaching strategic decisions on how to manage the corporate portfolio. Yet, several legitimate shortcomings exist:

1. A four-cell matrix based on high-low classifications gives scant attention to the many businesses that are in varying degrees of intermediate positions. All businesses cannot be neatly and accurately categorized as stars, dogs, cash cows, or question marks.

2. There are other relevant strategic factors besides just business growth rate and relative market share position—including stage of product-market evolution, strategic fit among the different businesses, the presence of competitive advantages and distinctive competences, emerging threats and opportunities, vulnerability to recession, market structure, capital requirements, and size of market. The BCG matrix does not give explicit consideration to these factors.

3. The variables of growth rate and market share are not always good proxies for a business's profitability, cash flow, and overall industry attractiveness. In many industries, companies with a low market share are able to earn consistently high profits and sometimes outperform larger rivals. High market share businesses in low growth industries may not generate cash surpluses since it is to be expected that competition will stiffen and profit margins will shrink during the maturity-saturation stages.

4. The BCG matrix is not very helpful in comparing relative investment opportunities across business units. For example, is every "star" better than a "cash cow"? How should one "question mark" be compared to another in terms of whether it should be built into a "star" or divested?[5]

The Nine-Cell GE Matrix. In recognition of these difficulties, General Electric, with help from McKinsey & Co., developed a nine-cell portfolio matrix based on long-term product-market attractiveness and business strength/competitive position. In this matrix, depicted in Figure 4–3, the area of the circles is proportional to the size of the industry, and the pie slices within the circle reflect the business's market share. At GE, product-market attractiveness is defined as a *composite projection* of market size, market growth rate (units and real dollars), competitive diversity, competitive structure, profitability, and technological, social, environmental, legal, and human impacts.[6] Business strength or competitive position is viewed as a function of market size and growth rate, market share, profitability, margins, technology position, skill or weaknesses, image, environmental impact, and calibre of management.

The strength of the Figure 4–3 approach is twofold. One, it allows for intermediate rankings between high and low and between strong and weak and, two, it incorporates explicit consideration of a much wider variety of strategically relevant variables. However, once each existing business has been evaluated and positioned in the matrix, the prescriptions for what to do with each business so as to improve the overall portfolio lineup are largely analogous to those for the four-cell matrix. The only difference concerns what to do with those that are "average"—and no generalized answers can

---

[5] Derek F. Abell and John S. Hammond, *Strategic Market Planning* (Englewood Cliffs, N.J.: Prentice-Hall, Inc., 1979), p. 212.

[6] William K. Hall, "SBUs: Hot, New Topic in the Management of Diversification," *Business Horizons,* vol. 21, no. 1 (February 1978), p. 20.

FIGURE 4–3
GE's Nine-Cell Business Portfolio Matrix

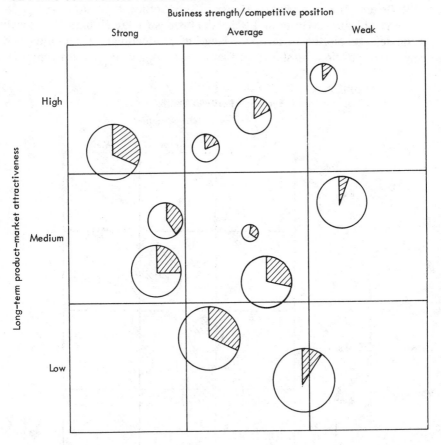

be given. Here lies the greatest shortcoming of the matrix approach: it provides no real clues or hints as to the right strategy for dealing with the vast number of businesses which, of statistical necessity, are "average" or close to average. Thus, while the business portfolio matrix is insightfully suggestive of the "right" strategies for managing stars, dogs, and cash cows, it suggests virtually nothing about the right strategy selection for average or near-average businesses. This is a very serious weakness given the direction-setting function of corporate strategy and given that every business needs a specific strategy that will lead to the best possible performance, regardless of its attractiveness and competitive position.[7] Another weakness has been pointed out by Hofer and Schendel: the GE approach does not

[7] For a discussion of these and other difficulties, see D. E. Hussey, "Portfolio Analysis: Practical Experiences with the Directional Policy Matrix," *Long-Range Planning,* vol. 11, no. 4 (August 1978), pp. 4–5.

depict as well as it might the positions of businesses that are about to emerge as winners because the product/market is entering the takeoff stage.[8]

The Product/Market Evolution Matrix.   To better identify a *developing winner* type of business, Hofer and Schendel propose a 15-cell matrix in which businesses are plotted in terms of stage of product/market evolution and competitive position, as shown in Figure 4–4.[9] Again, the circles represent

FIGURE 4–4
A Product/Market Evolution Portfolio Matrix

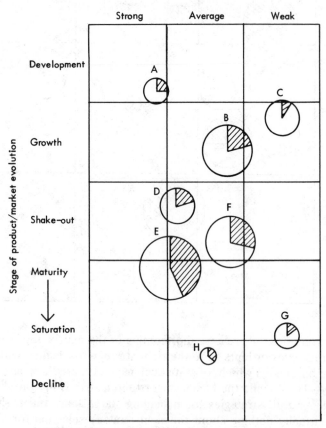

Source: Adapted from C. W. Hofer, "Conceptual Constructs for Formulating Corporate and Business Strategies." (Boston: Intercollegaite Case Clearing House, #9-378-754, 1977), p. 3.

---

[8] Charles W. Hofer and Dan Schendel, *Strategy Formulation: Analytical Concepts* (St. Paul Minn.: West Publishing Company, 1978), p. 33.

[9] Ibid., p. 34. This approach to business portfolio analysis was reportedly first used in actual practice by consultants at Arthur D. Little, Inc.

the sizes of the industries involved and pie wedges denote the business's market share. Looking at the plot in Figure 4–4, business A would appear to be a *developing winner,* business C might be classified as a *potential loser,* business E might be labeled an *established winner,* business F could be a cash cow, and business G a loser or a dog. The power of the Hofer-Schendel approach is the story it tells about the distribution of the firm's businesses across the stages of product-market evolution.

Actually, there is no need to force a choice as to which type of portfolio matrix to use; several types with various sets of variables can be constructed to gain insights from different perspectives. Each matrix type has its pros and cons. The important thing is not so much methodological procedure as it is completeness in describing the firm's current portfolio position.

Evaluating a Firm's Current Business Portfolio

While the construction of business portfolio matrices is a revealing way to identify the makeup and character of a firm's business portfolio, it by no means constitutes the whole evaluation process. As specifically pointed out by Hofer and Schendel, other relevant perspectives include:

1. A searching assessment of each industry in which the firm does business to determine key trends and market changes, the nature and direction of competition, important technological developments, cost and raw material supply conditions, labor relations, and, in particular, the overall attractiveness of the industry.
2. An evaluation of the firm's competitive position in each industry and how the business ranks on the key factors underlying successful performance.
3. An identification of opportunities and threats that might reasonably arise in each of the firm's businesses.
4. A consideration of what corporate resources and skills could improve the competitive strength of each business unit.
5. A comparison of the relative short-run and long-run attractiveness of each of the different businesses in the firm's portfolio.
6. An examination of the overall portfolio to determine whether the mix of businesses is adequately "balanced"—not too many losers or question marks, not so many mature businesses that corporate growth will be slow, enough cash producers to support the stars and developing winners, too few dependable profit performers, and so on.[10]

---

[10] Hofer and Schendel, *Strategy Formulation: Analytic Concepts,* p. 71 and pp. 81–86. The remainder of this section is drawn from Hofer and Schendel's discussion of their procedural approach, particularly pages 72–86.

Assessing Industry Attractiveness.   No business is likely to prove more attractive than the industry or industry segment of which it is a part.[11] Hence an important step in corporate strategy evaluation is a detailed assessment of the risks and potential of each industry in which the firm has a strategic interest. The main concerns here center around (1) whether the industry has enough of the positive attributes that management is looking for (such as growth, profitability, or export opportunities), (2) the extent to which the industry is characterized by traits that management wants to avoid (such as a history of labor strife, highly cyclical or seasonal demand, or major pollution control problems), and (3) the risk that industry conditions and trends will not be favorable enough to allow the firm's business to contribute its "fair share" toward the achievement of overall corporate objectives.

The method which Hofer and Schendel recommend for systematically assessing industry attractiveness entails the following:

1. Decide which traits and factors are most relevant and which should serve as the criteria for judging industry attractiveness. (Table 4–1 lists some of the commonly considered questions and issues; however, in looking at different industries, it is probably not practical to develop more than ten attractiveness criteria, so as to escape getting bogged down in detail.)
2. Attach priorities or weights to each of the factors on which overall attractiveness depends.
3. Gather information relevant to each one of the industry factors selected as being important considerations.
4. Rate the industry on each of the attractiveness factors and compute a weighted overall attractiveness "score." (The assigned rating may be a simple go/no go type or a numerical score that ranges from highly positive down to highly negative.)
5. Check the weighted overall ranking against informed managerial opinions and perceptions about the industry and its potential, and attempt to resolve any significant disparity.[12]

---

[11] As an example of the relevance of assessing industry attractiveness, consider the following long-range strategy issues now confronting the major oil companies in their oil business. Given the apparently dwindling world oil supplies and the rapidly rising price of crude oil, what is the long-range future of the petroleum industry? How soon and how fast can rising crude oil prices and a dependence on foreign oil imports be expected to propel a switch to other forms of energy? When and what kinds of new substitute energy sources are likely? What kinds of cost and supply advantages are they likely to have over currently known energy alternatives? Will the established oil companies have access to these new energy technologies or will antitrust factors make them the exclusive province of new companies? How probable is it that large industrial energy users will be able to integrate backward and supply their own energy needs? What should the oil companies be doing *today* to prepare for the future of the oil business? Predictive answers to these questions have obvious strategic value to energy suppliers and major energy users and can scarcely fail to weigh heavily in their strategic investment decisions.

[12] Hofer and Schendel, *Strategy Formulation: Analytic Concepts,* pp. 72–75. For some other approaches, see D. E. Hussey, "Portfolio Analysis: Practical Experience with the Directional Policy Matrix," *Long-Range Planning,* vol. 11, no. 4 (August 1978), pp. 4–5; Derek F. Abell and John S. Hammond, *Strategic Market Planning,* pp. 212–19; and William E. Rothschild, *Putting It All Together: A Guide to Strategic Thinking* (New York: AMACOM, 1976), chap. 8.

TABLE 4-1
A Checklist of Questions for Assessing Industry Attractiveness

A. *Product-Market Structure and Market Trends*
 1. What are the main products of the industry and where do they fit in the product-market life cycle?
 2. How big is the market? What is the forecasted growth rate in market demand?
 3. What are the sizes and numbers of buyers for the industry's products? Are there meaningful differences between types of buyers? Is the market becoming more segmented in terms of buyers and/or products? Which market segments are growing the fastest? Why?
 4. What are the basic determinants of market demand? To what degree is demand cyclical or seasonal? What is the relationship between industry demand and general economic conditions? Is the market overly susceptible to recessionary or inflationary influences?
 5. What motives and needs influence customers to buy the industry's products? To what degrees are buyers sensitive to price, to income changes, and to product differentiation?
 6. Are export or import considerations a significant factor in the industry?
 7. What market opportunities and threats are apparent?
B. *Industry Characteristics*
 1. At what stage is the industry in its life cycle—infancy? Early takeoff? Rapid growth? Early maturity? Steady-state? Decline?
 2. What is the present supply/demand balance in the industry? Has the industry been plagued with periodic excess capacity? To what extent is capacity utilization a key to profitability?
 3. Are there any major barriers to entry and exit?
 4. What is the role and importance of technology? What are the R&D requirements? Are patents or proprietary knowledge a factor? Are there any technological threats or opportunities on the horizon?
 5. What is the nature of economies of scale in the industry? What are the labor and capital requirements which it takes to compete successfully? What is the minimum entry size? How has the size of firms in the industry been changing and what are the underlying causes? What are the economies of vertical integration and automation?
 6. What are the numbers and sizes of firms which compete in the industry? Is the degree of seller concentration in the industry a negative factor?
 7. What is the price/cost structure in the industry? What price/cost trends are evident and how are these affecting profitability? To what extent is inflation a major factor in influencing costs and prices?
 8. What is the industry's profitability record? Are the industry's profits price sensitive? Volume sensitive?
 9. What substitutes exist for the industry's products? To what extent is competition from substitute products a factor?
 10. How do you make money in this industry?
C. *Financial and Operating Characteristics*
 1. Has innovation and changing technology produced major changes in costs and prices? Is having *new* plant facilities a factor? How difficult is it to achieve the necessary quality of manufacture?
 2. What is the expected life of plant and equipment? How adaptable are manufacturing facilities to other uses? Are there any special risks in facilities construction, plant locations, or plant operations?

Table 4–1 (*continued*)

3. What are the sizes, numbers, and locations of suppliers? Are raw material prices or availability a major problem area? Are energy requirements an important consideration?
4. Are there any reasons to be especially concerned about distribution channels, distribution access, warehousing and shipping, or available modes of transportation?
5. What is the union situation in the industry? Is enough of the right kind of labor available? Are labor conditions, labor costs, or productivity trends a major cause for concern?
6. Are there any special environmental concerns, pollution control problems, safety issues, or regulatory requirements which make the business unattractive?
7. How is the industry viewed by the banking industry and by Wall Street?
8. How attractive is the industry from the standpoint of capital structure, working capital requirements, investment payback, cash throw-off, inventory turnover, profit margins, and investment requirements for expansion?
9. What is necessary in terms of advertising, sales promotion, technical support for sales staff, sales force organization, and customer service?
10. What sort of marketing mix typifies firms in the industry? What are the expenses of adding new customers? What is the role of marketing research?

D. *Competitive Factors*
1. What makes a product competitive in the industry? Has the industry evidenced a capacity for exploiting new products and developing new market segments?
2. How significant is new product R&D? Brand consciousness? Trademarks and copyrights? Customer loyalty? Image and reputation of the seller?
3. What are the trends in market standing among the various firms and how do these vary by geographic area, customer type, and product application? Are there any gaps in geographic coverage? Which firms are considered the industry leaders and why?
4. What particular competitive features distinguish the poorly performing firms from the outstanding performers?
5. How strong are competitive pressures in the industry and what form do they take? Are these pressures equally strong in every market niche?
6. What must a firm do right and do well in order to compete successfully?

Table 4–2 provides a rundown of major sources of information for assessing industry attractiveness and for finding out about specific companies.

Evaluation of Competitive Position.   The value of competitive position analysis is to develop a better measure of a firm's potential in a business than is provided by an assessment of industry attractiveness.[13] A favorable judgment on industry attractiveness is necessary but not sufficient to warrant keeping a business in the firm's portfolio; in addition, a firm must be or be capable of becoming a viable competitor in that industry—being relegated to an also-ran in an attractive industry is usually not a "go" proposition.

---

[13] Hofer and Schendel, *Strategy Formulation: Analytical Concepts,* pp. 75–77.

TABLE 4–2
Sources of Information for Assessing Industry Attractiveness and
Evaluating Companies

A. Population, the Economy, and Current Business Conditions
1. U.S. Department of Commerce, Bureau of the Census, *Census of Population, Census of Housing, County Business Patterns, Census of Governments*—for periodic, but comprehensive and detailed, data on population characteristics, housing conditions, and various business and governmental statistics.
2. U.S. Department of Commerce, *Survey of Current Business* (monthly), *Business Conditions Digest* (monthly), *U.S. Industrial Outlook, Statistical Abstract of the United States* (annually)—for current and historical statistics on the economy and business conditions.
3. Council of Economic Advisors, *Economic Report of the President* (published annually)—contains a good variety of statistics relating to GNP, income, employment, prices, money supply, and governmental finance.
4. United Nations, *Statistical Yearbook*—for various economic statistics of foreign countries.
5. OECD, *Economic Outlook and Main Economic Indicators*——for international economic data.
6. Board of Governors of Federal Reserve System. *Federal Reserve Bulletin* (monthly)—for data on banking, money supply conditions, interest rates, and credit conditions.
7. U.S. Department of Labor, Bureau of Labor Statistics, *Monthly Labor Review* (monthly), *Employment and Earnings* (monthly), *Handbook of Labor Statistics* (annually)—for data on employment, hours worked and earnings, productivity, wholesale and consumer prices, labor turnover, and area unemployment characteristics.
8. Editor and Publisher, *Market Guide* (annually)—contains rankings of cities, counties, and SMSA areas based on individual income population, total retail sales, and food sales as well as pertinent local area information.
9. *Sales Management* magazine's "Annual Survey of Buying Power"—for rankings on the amount spent for selected products/services by geographical location.
B. Industry Information
1. U.S. Department of Commerce, Bureau of the Census, *Census of Manufactures, Annual Survey of Manufacturing, Census of Business, Census of Transportation*—for statistics relating to the volume of manufacturing activity, size and structure of firms, retail and wholesale trade, and transportation.
2. Federal Trade Commission, *Quarterly Financial Report for Manufacturing, Mining, and Trade Corporations* (quarterly)—for sales, profit, balance sheet, and income statement statistics by industry division and size of firm.
3. U.S. Department of the Treasury, Internal Revenue Service, *Business Income Tax Returns* (annually) and *Corporate Income Tax Returns* (annually)—for breakdowns on revenues, operating expenses, and profits by type of business organization and industry division.
4. National Industrial Conference Board: research and statistical reports issued periodically and the *Conference Board Record* (monthly).
5. Securities and Exchange Commmission: quarterly reports of finance and capital expenditures.
6. Trade association and industry publications such as *Commercial and Financial Chronicle, Banking, Advertising Age, Automotive News, Public*

Table 4-2 (continued)

Utilities Fortnightly, Engineering News Record, Best's Insurance Review, Progressive Grocer, and Electronic News.
C. Company-Oriented Information
1. Annual reports of companies.
2. Investment services and directories: Standard and Poor's, Moody's, Value Line.
3. Financial ratios: Dun & Bradstreet Annual Surveys, Robert Morris Associates Annual Statement Studies.
4. Securities and Exchange Commission, Form 10-K reports.
5. Periodicals: Fortune, Barron's, Forbes, Wall Street Transcript, Dun's Review, Business Week, Financial World, Over-the-Counter Securities Review.

For an additional classification and survey of information sources, see C. R. Goeldner and Laura M. Dirks, "Business Facts: Where to Find Them," *Business Topics*, vol. 24, no. 3 (Summer 1976), pp. 23–36.

There are two dimensions to an evaluation of competitive position. One involves a determination of where the firm's business stands in relation to that of its rivals, with particular emphasis on comparisons of market share, prices, breadth and quality of product line, profit margins, technology and cost differentials, facilities locations, proprietary and key account advantages, and overall image with buyers. The second involves an explicit identification of the key factors underlying competitive success in the industry and an evaluation of how well the firm rates on each of these *key success factors*. A clear understanding of what specific competences, competitive advantages, and strategic approaches have produced leading positions in the marketplace is an essential part of assessing the competitive potential of the firm's own business.

Key success factors, as the label implies, bear directly on those things which merit high priority and which must be done right if a business is to be truly successful. These factors vary from industry to industry but they usually relate either to certain economic and technological characteristics of the business or to those particular competitive variables which unlock the door to building a successful strategy. Examples of key success factors include manufacturing a superior quality product, developing unusually effective advertising campaigns, using low-cost manufacture as the basis for outcompeting rival firms on price, offering superior customer service, gaining a large enough market share to capitalize fully on scale economies, having a more complete product line, proficiency in R&D, having higher calibre personnel, having new facilities in the right locations, and developing better distribution channels and outlets. Ordinarily, there are only a few key success factors that have a substantial impact on competitive position; thus it is more useful to limit attention to the five or so most important factors, along with a hardnosed evaluation of how the firm's business ranks on each of them, than it is to attempt a comprehensive identification and evaluation of 10–15 factors.[14] A check against how the business ranks on the key success factors can be made by using the firm's current market share as a yardstick for judging the reasonableness of the evaluation results.

Identifying Opportunities and Threats in the Industry. Some of the opportunities and threats present in the industry environment may have been identified and included in the assessment of industry attractiveness. But there is merit in a separate and explicit identification and evaluation of industrywide opportunities and threats. Managerial alertness to the specific opportunities/threats in an industry is useful in two respects, namely in understanding how they impinge on and alter the industry's relative attractiveness and in suggesting the whys and hows of adjusting line of business strategy.

Needless to say, the thrust at this stage should be to concentrate on pinpointing those opportunities and threats that might significantly alter the judgments made earlier about the relative attractiveness of the industry.[15] If important new opportunities and threats come to the surface, the attractiveness rating of the industry should be modified accordingly. Otherwise, the entire group of opportunities and threats in the industry should be noted as strategic issues to be considered at the business-level strategy review stage.

Resource/Skills Analysis. This aspect of corporate strategy evaluation entails a realistic appraisal of whether the organization has any resources and skills that could materially alter the firm's competitive standing in the industry under study.[16] This is particularly important where the business is judged to be in a less than desirable competitive position and/or where improvement in some key success area is indicated. In particular, what needs to be considered is whether the organization has any skills, competences, or strengths that it is willing to devote to the business in an effort to develop a competitive edge and make its market position more viable.

Comparing the Attractiveness of Different Businesses. After each of the businesses in the firm's portfolio has been assessed in terms of overall industry attractiveness, competitive position in the industry, unique opportunities and threats, and the availability of special skills and resources, it is time to compare and rate their relative attractiveness and to factor any considerations about strategic fit into this assessment. The groundwork for this has been done in the form of the ratings and scores calculated in assessing each business. These scores could, of course, be used to construct any of several different types of business portfolio matrices. But the summary picture provided by such a matrix (or matrices) usually will need supplementing. This means more than considering "the intangibles" and explicitly examining some of the underlying details. Two additional factors are pertinent. One is whether any difference exists between the assessments of short-run and

---

[14] Ibid., p. 78.

[15] Ibid., p. 79.

[16] Ibid., p. 80.

long-run attractiveness and how this affects the comparisons across the portfolio. The second is the importance that management attaches to building a portfolio that has good strategic fit and how this will alter the relative rankings within the portfolio.

Overall "Balance" in the Portfolio. The focus here is on an evaluation of the *mix* of businesses in the portfolio.[17] The kinds of key questions to be answered include: Does the portfolio contain enough businesses in "attractive" or "very attractive" industries? Does it contain too many "losers" or "question marks?" Is the proportion of mature or declining businesses so great that corporate growth will be sluggish? Does the firm have enough "cash cows" to finance the "stars" and emerging winners? Are there enough businesses that generate dependable profits and/or cash flow? Is the portfolio overly vulnerable to inflation or recessionary influences? Are there any businesses which it is time to get out of or divest? Does the firm have a number of businesses with strong competitive positions or is it burdened with too many businesses having average to weak competitive standings?

Performance Gap Analysis

The final phase of the corporate strategy evaluation process involves determining whether the aggregate performance of the businesses in the portfolio can be expected to produce achievement of corporate objectives and, if not, what kinds of corporate strategy changes can be devised to close the performance gap. If a performance gap is found to exist, then there are at least five basic types of actions that top management can take to reduce or close the gap between the projected and desired levels of corporate performance.[18]

1. *Alter the business-level strategies of some (or all) of its businesses.* This option essentially involves special corporate efforts to improve the competitive position of selected business units. The attempt may entail not only a shift in business-level strategy but also shifts in corporate financial support of the business and in functional area support (R&D, manufacturing, marketing, and so on) so as to enhance the chances of building a distinctive competence and, in turn, an improved standing in the market.

2. *Add new business units to the corporate portfolio.* The alternative of an acquisition or internal start-up of a new business raises several corporate strategy issues; namely: (1) What kind and size of new business and having what kind of strategic fit? (2) How would the new business fit into the present corporate structure? (3) What specific features should it look

---

[17] Barry Hedley, "Strategy and the Business Portfolio," *Long-Range Planning,* vol. 10, no. 1 (February 1977), p. 13; and Hofer and Schendel, *Strategy Formulation: Analytical Concepts,* pp. 82–86.

[18] Hofer and Schendel, *Strategy Formulation: Analytical Concepts,* pp. 93–100.

for in an acquisition candidate? (4) Are acquisitions compatible with the present corporate strategy?

3. *Delete one or more businesses from the corporate portfolio.* The most likely candidates for divestiture are those businesses which are in a weak competitive position, or in a relatively unattractive industry, or in an industry which does not "fit."

4. *Use political action to alter conditions which are responsible for subpar performance potentials.* In some situations, concerted actions with rival firms, trade associations, suppliers, unions, customers, or other interested groups may help ameliorate adverse conditions and improve the business climate. Joining forces to form a political action group may be an effective way of dealing with import-export problems, tax disincentives, regulatory matters, or environmental requirements.

5. *Change corporate performance objectives.* On occasion, changing circumstances render corporate objectives unreachable. Closing the gap between actual and desired performance may then require revision of corporate objectives to bring them more in line with reality. As a practical matter, though, this tends to be a "last resort" option, being used only after other options have been explored and tried.

Illustration Capsule 10

Cooper Industries: Shifting Corporate Strategy Toward Diversification

Until 1967, Cooper Industries was basically a one-product, one-market company making engines and compressors for energy-producing companies. Its business was very cyclical and Cooper's economic forecast indicated that the next downward cycle would be especially steep. As a consequence, Cooper's management decided to put some of the company's eggs into a second basket in an effort to help smooth out the cyclical fluctuations in its main business.

Cooper decided on hand tools as its first diversification move, reasoning that all kinds of people use hand tools—wrenches, pliers, files—year in and year out so that the demand is steady and not very sensitive to major ups and downs of the company. The first hand tool company Cooper acquired was the Lufkin Rule Company, a leading maker of measuring tapes and rules. Interestingly, Lufkin's own strategic plan was to build one strong hand tool company from several smaller, complementary companies. The new company would offer hardware dealers a variety of tools from a single source.

When Cooper acquired Lufkin, two more criteria were set up as a basis for building a well-rounded tool company. In addition to helping Cooper smooth out its earning cycle, any candidates for acquisition would have to:

1. Have a quality image and a first-class brand name, and
2. Be just as interested in joining Cooper as Cooper was in acquiring them.

In going multiindustry, it was Cooper's plan to continue to be an operating company, not just a holding company.

Within a very short time, the Cooper group of tool companies grew to include Lufkin; Crescent wrenches, pliers, and screw drivers; Weller soldering equipment;

Illustration Capsule 10 (*continued*)

Nicholson files and saws; and Xcelite Electronics Tools. The sales strategy for Cooper's tool groups became "a single source for five great brands." By 1975 the Cooper tool division was an established leader in the hand tool industry with sales of $164 million.

Not long after the Nicholson File became a division of Cooper Industries the decision was made by Nicholson to drop 90 percent of its files from its product line. The reason? As long as Nicholson depended solely on files for its business, it felt it had to offer customers every kind of file imaginable; the strategy was "we've got 'em all." But when Nicholson joined forces with Cooper and became part of a group of companies boasting several top brand names in hand tools, the strategy of carrying every file under the sun became obsolete. Nicholson continued to manufacture almost 2,000 different types of files, including many specialty items. And despite dropping 90 percent of its files, Nicholson's sales and profits increased.

The same principle was applied to all the Cooper Industries tool companies. Low-margin and low-turnover items were dropped, averaging a 50 percent cut. All the emphasis went behind the bread and butter of the line; sales rose to new heights. Profits also went up for dealers and distributors, owing to a higher turnover of fewer items. At the same time, sales force economies were taken advantage of; five independent hand tool companies needed five salesmen to call on one customer. But when the five companies were put together, only one salesman per customer was required, thereby lowering the cost of selling. Besides combining sales forces, Cooper also combined warehousing, distribution, advertising, merchandising, and paperwork flows. Customers also benefited because they found it more convenient and less expensive to deal with one supplier instead of five.

In addition to the selling advantage of five companies in one, the tool companies benefited from becoming part of a multiindustry organization. For instance, the Energy Services Division of Cooper provided the tool companies with more than $50 million for modernization. Then, in 1975–76, the tool companies returned the favor, providing cash to take advantage of a sharp upswing in the markets for Cooper's energy products.

1971 was a bad year for Cooper's energy divisions and prompted a hard look at each product and each market to make sure it was worth staying in them. One of the decisions Cooper faced was especially tough: whether to keep making centrifugal compressors for certain process industries—mainly ammonia, ethylene, and methanol plants—or to drop out of that market and concentrate on natural gas compression. There were strong arguments on both sides. On the one hand, process industries were growing; to drop out would be to leave an expanding market. In addition, Cooper was a recognized quality leader in the market and Cooper felt that this gave prestige to the Cooper Industries name and professional pride to its engineers.

On the other hand, compressors for these plants required almost total custom design which meant high engineering costs. It also meant that Cooper found it hard to hold down costs by building several identical units, the way they did for the natural gas compression units. Moreover, Cooper Industries did not have as dominant a position in the process market as it had in natural gas compression. So when sales slacked off in the process market, Cooper was among the first companies to feel the squeeze. After a lot of soul-searching, Cooper decided to pull out of its business of making centrifugal compressors for the process industries. It was a controversial decision, but Cooper felt its commitment had to be to the long-term profitability of the company.

Illustration Capsule 10 (*concluded*)

The earnings of its energy division went up in 1972 despite the fact that sales fell even lower because of the decision to get out of centrifugal compressors. In 1976, Cooper boasted that the changes that were made in 1971 were really beginning to pay off. In 1976, almost 40 percent of the centrifugal horsepower used in natural gas was built by Cooper-Bessemer—worldwide. In addition, the company found that the excess capacity created by pulling out of the weak markets in 1971 was being gradually brought back into production as market penetration in natural gas energy services increased. This meant that Cooper Industries did not have to invest heavily in new facilities to keep pace with mushrooming energy demand.

The company's strategy also included one of emphasizing products that generated follow-on sales. More than one third of its energy-related revenue in 1976 was estimated to come from parts and services, steadier revenue sources than the sale of original equipment.

In 1976, Cooper Industries was touting itself as a "very well-balanced company with leadership positions in three different markets: hand tools, aircraft services, and energy services. This combination will help us ride out the economic ups and downs."

By business category the Cooper Industries companies as of 1976 were:

1. In hand tools—The Cooper Group (Lufkin, Crescent, Weller, Nicholson, Xcelite, Rotor tool).
2. In aircraft services—Cooper Airmotive.
3. In energy services—Cooper Energy Services (Cooper-Bessemer, Ajax, Penn Pump).

Sources: Cooper Industries *Annual Reports* and full-page advertisements placed by Cooper Industries in *The Wall Street Journal*, February 12, 1976, p. 17; March 11, 1976, p. 15; and March 24, 1976, p. 15.

A Concluding Perspective

To be successful, the process of evaluating corporate strategy must be iterative and ongoing, incorporating reappraisal of each business as it develops and takes a new position in the portfolio matrix. Moreover, reassessments of the mix of businesses in the corporate portfolio should be routinely conducted. At General Electric, reappraisal is initiated not just at regular intervals but also when a strategic "trigger point" (an external development projected to have a significant impact on a business's performance) occurs.[19] Such an approach is one way of keeping a close watch on whether a business will actually contribute its expected weight toward the achievement of corporate objectives.

One final point. Once the portfolio has been evaluated and strategic decisions reached on how to handle each business, the process is not concluded. Simply deciding to manage a business as a star or a cash cow will not make anything happen.[20] Detailed business strategies, functional area support

---

[19] Hall, "SBUs" p. 22.
[20] Ibid.

strategies, and operating-level strategies will need to be devised and·implemented. And numerous alternatives exist—there is more than one kind of cash cow and more than one way to harvest a dog. It is at this juncture that business strategy and corporate strategy come together and can be dovetailed.

SUGGESTED READINGS

Abell Derek F., and Hammond, John S. *Strategic Market Planning.* Englewood Cliffs, N.J.: Prentice-Hall, Inc., 1979, chaps. 4 and 5.

Aguilar, Francis. *Scanning the Business Environment.* New York: The Macmillan Company, 1967.

Bales, Carter F. "Strategic Control: The President's Paradox." *Business Horizons,* vol. 20, no. 4 (August 1977), pp. 17–28.

Emshoff, James R., and Finnel, Arthur. "Defining Corporate Strategy: A Case Study Using Strategic Assumptions Analysis." *Sloan Management Review,* vol. 20, no. 3 (Spring 1979), pp. 41–52.

Hall, William K. "SBUs: Hot, New Topic in the Management of Diversification." *Business Horizons,* vol. 21, no. 1 (February 1978), pp. 17–25.

Hedley, Barry. "A Fundamental Approach to Strategy Development." *Long-Range Planning,* vol. 9, no. 6 (December 1976), pp. 2–11.

————. "Strategy and the Business Portfolio." *Long-Range Planning,* vol. 10, no. 1 (February 1977), pp. 9–15.

Hofer, Charles W. and Schendel, Dan. *Strategy Formulation: Analytical Concepts.* St. Paul, Minn.: West Publishing Co., 1978, chaps. 2 and 4.

Hussey, D. E. "Portfolio Analysis: Practical Experience with the Directional Policy Matrix." *Long-Range Planning,* vol. 11, no. 4 (August 1978), pp. 2–8.

Kiechel, Walter. "Playing by the Rules of the Corporate Strategy Game." *Fortune* (September 24, 1979), pp. 110–18.

Koontz, Harold. "Making Strategic Planning Work." *Business Horizons,* vol. 19, no. 2 (April 1976), pp. 37–47.

Lorange, Peter. *Corporate Planning: An Executive Viewpoint* (Englewood Cliffs, N.J.: Prentice–Hall, Inc., 1980), chaps. 1–3.

Mason, R. Hal, Harris, Jerome, and McLoughlin, John. "Corporate Strategy: A Point of View." *California Management Review,* vol. 13, no. 3 (Spring 1971), pp. 5–12.

Paul, Ronald N., Donavan, Neil B., and Taylor, James W. "The Reality Gap in Strategic Planning." *Harvard Business Review,* vol. 56, no. 3 (May–June 1978), pp. 124–30.

Salter, Malcolm, and Weinhold, Wolf. *Diversification through Acquisition.* New York: The Macmillan Company, 1979.

Robinson, S. J. Q., Hitchens, R. E., and Wade, D. P. "The Directional Policy Matrix: Tool for Strategic Planning." *Long-Range Planning,* vol. 11, no. 3 (June 1978), pp. 8–15.

Vancil, Richard F. "Strategy Formulation in Complex Organizations." *Sloan Management Review,* vol. 17, no. 2 (Winter 1976), pp. 1–18.

5 STRATEGY ANALYSIS AND EVALUATION AT THE BUSINESS LEVEL

Never follow the crowd.

Bernard Baruch

Tomorrow's competitive environment is of more import than today's.

Anonymous

Once a "go" decision has been reached on continuing in or entering a particular industry, the action and work of strategy analysis and evaluation shifts to the business-unit level and below. Here, the formulator of strategy is on more familiar grounds. Much has been learned and written about analyzing a business, evaluating and forecasting such things as market growth, pricing, cost changes, and the impact of government regulations, and dealing with the moves of competitors, swings in market trends, and customer wants and needs. This chapter surveys the major considerations in selecting a business strategy that will "best" position the firm in its target market environment.

Identifying the Present Strategy

In an ongoing business, strategy evaluation ought logically to begin with what the present strategy is. As in the case of corporate strategy, identification of the current strategy of a business unit entails sorting out what management has said the strategy is, the firm's actual behavior in the marketplace, and various plans and actions in the main functional areas of the business. Figure 5–1 summarizes the major factors to be considered.

Performing a Competitive Audit

The first step in evaluating business-level strategy is an analysis of the competitive nature and structure of the industry and the competitive position

FIGURE 5-1
Angles from which to Determine and Evaluate Business Strategy

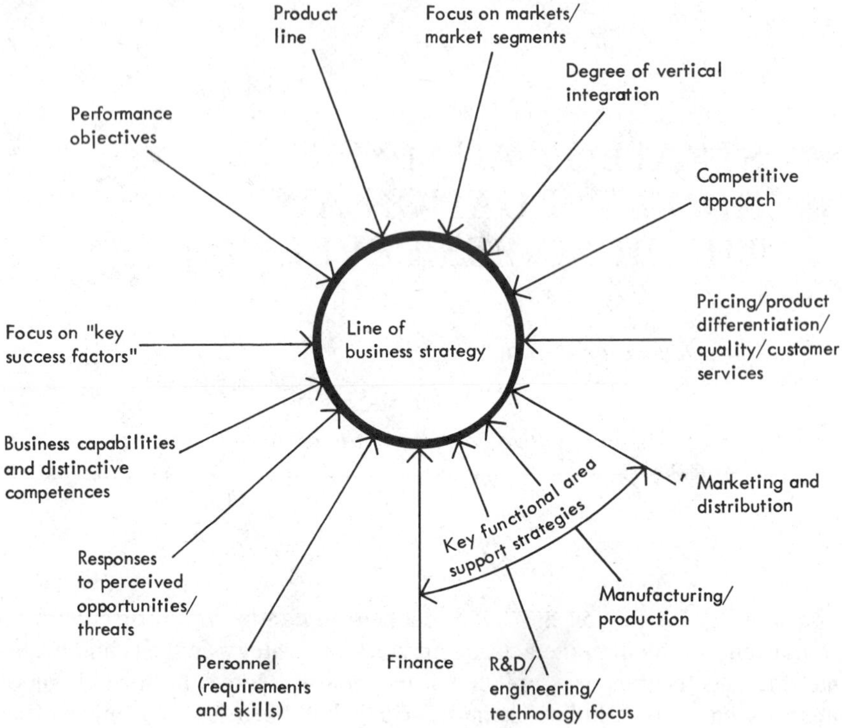

the business unit occupies (or is considering occupying) in that industry. A competitive audit serves several purposes: (1) to assess what the competitive environment of the industry is like and how/why it is changing, (2) to pinpoint the hows/whys of the firm's own competitive position in the industry, (3) to identify the key factors for profitably competing in the industry, and (4) to provide the backdrop against which to decide what the "best" competitive strategy for the firm's own business unit is.

There may be a temptation to short-circuit this phase of business strategy evaluation, especially when management considers itself knowledgeable about the economics of the industry or when the pressures of time and circumstance close in. The managements of some organizations may feel that their longtime industry experiences have programmed all of the key factors into their thinking. Supposedly, the reasoning goes, experience has been a good teacher, schooling them well in the whys and hows of being systematic in their evaluation of what competitors are doing and what that means for the firm's own best competitive course of action. But experience can also boomerang. Prior knowledge and a stubborn defensive pride in established ways of doing things may blind management to change; a management may assume it knows things about the industry or the overall competitive environment that are no longer accurate (see Illustration Capsule 11). Therefore, a periodic competitive audit in which "the facts" are updated is well worth doing and it is certainly worth doing when entry into a new industry, or product market, or geographic area is being contemplated.

Table 5–1 contains a checklist of questions which are part and parcel of a thorough competitive audit. All of the topics and issues may not be pivotal in each and every situation, but the list does suggest the range of competitive factors to be considered.

The Present Competitive Environment.   Answers to the questions posed in sections A and B of Table 5–1, if thoroughly developed, should spotlight what it takes to compete successfully (the strategic advantage factors), thereby revealing how and why firms in the industry occupy their relative competitive positions. However, where an industry has unusually diverse market segments, it may be necessary to conduct a detailed examination of

Illustration Capsule 11

A Failure in Business Strategy Evaluation

Recently, Greyhound and Trailways took on one another in a fierce and profitless strategic maneuver over passenger bus fares. Greyhound, in an effort to boost passenger traffic on its intercity bus routes, in early 1978 announced a $50 fare applying to all trips extending more than 1,000 miles. Trailways responded with a series of commercials on national television proclaiming the cheapest rates from New York to Los Angeles.

However, the promotional war drew in little new business, mainly because it took no account of the changing market for intercity bus service. The reduced fares were aimed at long-distance travelers—despite the fact that fewer than 5 percent of all bus passengers ride 1,000 miles or more. Most of the passenger market for distances over 500 miles is captured by the airlines. Even though air fares are roughly 50 percent higher than bus fares, the travel time is much less on long trips. For instance, at the height of the Greyhound-Trailways price war, the lowest one-way bus fare from Chicago to Miami was $69 and involved travel time of a day and a half; by airplane the fare was $99 and flight time was two and a half hours—a comparison which pinpoints the strategic folly of the bus lines' attempt to attract long-distance business.

At the same time, both Trailways and Greyhound failed to focus their business strategy on the short-haul market of less than 200 miles, the segment containing 40 percent of all intercity travel. Moreover, they ignored the airlines' long-standing and successful strategy of structuring their routes into networks of short-haul markets, where each major city serves as the hub for a series of spokes or corridor routes radiating out for 100–200 miles to smaller cities and other key hubs. Instead, buses were often run on a continuing schedule from one end of the country to the other, passing through many metropolitan areas in the middle of the night and not during prime-time travel hours.

Source: Rush Loving, Jr., "The Bus Lines Are on the Road to Nowhere," *Fortune* (December 31, 1978), pp. 58–64.

TABLE 5-1
Checklist of Questions/Issues in Performing a Competitive Audit

A. *Nature and Structure of Competition*
1. Who are the firms which compete in the industry and what are their respective market shares? How do these firms compare in terms of breadth of product line, market coverage, and rates of growth?
2. What are the *trends* in sales and market shares among the various rival firms and how do these vary by type of customer, use of the product, geographical area, or other relevant market segment dimensions?
3. What are the distinguishing features of each major firm's competitive strategy? What are the strengths and weaknesses inherent in each approach? How well do they appear to be executing their respective strategies? What is the image of each major competitor from the viewpoint of customers? Which firms are considered the leaders in product quality? In the introduction of new products? In pricing? In advertising and marketing effectiveness? In management knowhow?
4. Are there any identifiable "clusters" of firms which have common and strategically relevant features? Why and how are the strategic clusters of firms approaching the market differently—that is, what is the basis of the strategic clustering? Are there important differences in competition across the various strategic clusters? How does the nature of competition among the clusters compare with that within a cluster—especially within the cluster that the firm's own business is in?
5. What are the pivotal product features that prompt a buyer to purchase from one seller and not another?
B. *Evaluating a Firm's Own Competitive Position*
1. What is the firm's competitive strategy in the line of business under study? Does it contain any features which distinguish it from its closest rivals and, if so, what is the basis for these features?
2. What do buyers think of the company and its product line? How does this compare with what they think of rival firms? What is the company's trend in image and market standing—is its reputation improving or not and why?
3. What particular benefits do customers get when they buy the company's product instead of rivals' products? Which firm offers the most value for the money and how important is this?
4. To what extent do the company's products have the pivotal features that prompt buyers to select one seller over another? How successful has the company been at promoting the key features of its products?
5. When customers have a problem, do they look to this company for help or to its rivals?
6. In what segments of the market is the company strongest? Weakest? What potential customers are being missed or overlooked? What is its record in expanding its customer base and what are the reasons for this record?
7. What are the firm's biggest competitive strengths? Does it have an identifiable distinctive competence which is strategically important? Is this confirmed by customer perceptions?
8. What are the firm's biggest competitive weaknesses? How important are they? What is it doing and what more can it do about them in terms of competitive strategy?
9. What specific market opportunities/threats can be identified for this company? To what extent is the company's ability to respond to these opportunities/threats conditioned by its competitive strengths/weaknesses?

Table 5-1 (continued)

10. Is the firm considered to be a leader or a follower? On what is this judgment based?
11. Overall, how strong is the company's competitive position in the marketplace? What would it take to strengthen its position?

C. *Forecast of Future Competitive Trends and Conditions*
1. What market opportunities/threats appear to be on the horizon for this industry? How will these likely affect competition in the industry?
2. Are new products/services likely to emerge in the industry (or in other industries) which could materially alter competitive trends and pressures in this line of business?
3. What sorts of customer needs are presently *not* being met by existing products? Why is this? Are R&D activities under way to develop means for fulfilling these needs? What is their status?
4. What demographic and population-based changes can be anticipated and what do these portend for the size of the market and for competition in the industry?
5. Are there any reasons to expect major changes in costs or in supply conditions?
6. Is the probable future course of the economy (rates of inflation, unemployment, economic growth, interest rates, and so on) likely to produce any unusual change in competition or market direction?
7. What competitive changes are likely to stem from new or existing governmental policies on pollution control, product safety, consumer protection, antitrust, wage-price controls, foreign trade regulations, taxation, energy conservation, and other pertinent areas?
8. What uses can be made of such forecasting techniques as the Delphi method (researching the consensus views of experts), trend extrapolation, regression and correlation analysis, econometric models, and dynamic predictive models (e.g., simulation) to estimate how future events may influence market trends, competitive conditions, and strategic opportunities in the industry?

---

what the specific dimensions of competition are for the distinguishable product-customer segments, followed up with an analysis of how rival firms vary in their emphasis on these different segments. Determining what variations underlie the competitive strategies of major firms goes a long way toward accounting for why some firms in the industry are doing better than others.[1] Also, knowing what the strategic advantage factors are, together with how and by whom they have been used, is of obvious value in evaluating a firm's own competitive position in the industry.

The Future Competitive Environment. Although the specifics of what the future holds for competition in an industry, just like the specifics of a firm's

---

[1] See Jerry Wall, "What the Competition Is Doing: Your Need to Know," *Harvard Business Review*, vol. 52, no. 6 (November–December 1974), pp. 22 ff.; Michael E. Porter, *Competitive Strategy: Techniques for Analyzing Industries and Competitors* (New York: Free Press, 1980); and William E. Rothschild, *Putting It All Together: A Guide to Strategic Thinking* (New York: AMACOM, 1976), chap. 5.

present competitive position, vary from situation to situation, the general areas of inquiry do not vary greatly. The questions in section C of Table 5–1 illustrate what is involved. As with any assessment of the future, though, assumptions must be made and uncertainties will remain. Different people may view the same set of "facts" and reach significantly different judgments about where competition in the industry is headed and why. Nonetheless, judgmental errors based on serious analysis are more tolerable than flying blind with little or no preparation for changes in competitive conditions. At the very least, the "hard to call" areas can be made explicit and explored fully for the various probable scenarios. Moreover, a set of forecasts can be prepared to test the sensitivity of projected outcomes to changes in the underlying assumptions; this makes contingency planning for forecasting errors much easier. Consequently, a serious attempt at forecasting future industry and competitive conditions is better than no attempt despite the inaccuracies involved.

Arriving at judgments about the nature of the future competitive market environment is, however, not to be confused with simply extrapolating past trends into the future. Trend projections are inherently rooted in the past, and historical data may or may not be a reliable preview of coming events. Hence, while trends have a valid place in assessments of future conditions, by themselves they are neither trustworthy nor sufficient.

The Role of Competition in Business Strategy Evaluation

Auditing the competitive environment sets the stage for thoroughly analyzing the impact of competition on an organization's choice of strategy.[2] This is a fundamental issue because anytime two or more organizations operate in the same market there arises, more or less automatically, a gut competitive issue: Should rival firms' respective approaches to the market and prospective buyers be identical or different; and if it is the latter in what specific respects should they differ? Imitative or "me too" competitive strategies prove to be the most profitable and viable plan in some cases, but many (most?) markets tend to be large and diverse enough to warrant firms pursuing distinguishably different competitive strategies—some firms may choose to emphasize a lower price, others a higher quality; some may elect to integrate vertically, others may concentrate within a single stage; some may strive to become "full-line" producers whereas others deliberately limit themselves to a narrower offering; some may concentrate R&D expenditures on cost-saving process innovations whereas others search more for new and better products. For obvious reasons, each rival has motivations to formulate a competitive strategy aimed at outdoing the other firms, gaining a stronger foothold with buyers, and reaping the rewards of greater market

---

[2] This section parallels the discussion in Arthur A. Thompson, "Competition as a Strategic Process," *Antitrust Bulletin* (forthcoming).

success. In essence, a firm's business strategy can be viewed as its action plan for building a competitive advantage over rivals in the marketplace and for catering to market differences based on product use, customer location, channels of distribution, or some other relevant aspect of diversity.

Out of the motivation of rival firms to secure a competitive advantage, together with an awareness of the interactions of their approaches to the market, emerges a *strategic process* that, in turn, activates and produces competitive pressures of varying types and degrees. This process consists of an ongoing series of competitive strategies and counterstrategies, some offensive and some defensive, on the part of each seller in the market. Each firm's moves and countermoves are an integral part of its overall business strategy for improving its competitive position and for achieving a degree of market success sufficient to justify staying in the business over the long-run. Normally, a firm's overall competitive strategy can be expected to incorporate price and nonprice factors, with the exact mix being a function of management perceptions as to what combination will have the most desirable market impact, given the prevailing strategies (and anticipated counterstrategies) of rival firms. With the passage of time, a firm's overall line of business strategy and its product-specific or market segment-specific strategies will tend either to be finetuned or to undergo major overhaul, according to the firm's market successes (or failures) and the durability of its competitive approach in withstanding strategic challenges from rival firms.

When a firm makes a successful strategic move, it can expect increased rewards, largely at the expense of rivals' market shares and rates of sales growth. The speed and extent of the strategic encroachment varies with whether the product is standardized or differentiated, the initiator's competence and resources to capitalize on any advantage the strategy has produced, how difficult it is for sellers to shift buyer loyalties, and the ease with which the strategy can be copied. The pressures on rivals to respond are, in addition, a function of whether the initiator is (1) a major firm with considerable market visibility, (2) a fringe firm whose efforts can be ignored for some time, or (3) a firm in financial distress and thus whose strategy is predicated on desperation. For instance, if a firm's strategic offensive is keyed to a low price and quick market penetration but also carries with it a substantial risk that full costs will not be recovered, rivals may judge that the strategy will be short-lived; they may choose to respond or not, depending on their estimates of whether it will be better to meet the low price on a temporary basis or to ride out whatever buyer resistance may be encountered. If the initiating firm finds its move neutralized by rivals' countermoves, then it is challenged to seek out a better strategy not as easily defeated or else remain content with the stalemate it has encountered.

The ease with which a firm's alternative strategies can be neutralized is a major criterion of strategy selection; there is good reason to gravitate towards strategies which can be neither easily imitated nor easily defeated. Such considerations indicate why it is wise for a firm to push the development of a *distinctive competence* whereby it can differentiate its product in ways not susceptible to successful imitation. By developing a reputation and image on some key facet of its product offering, a firm may be able to set its product above and apart from those of rival firms—thereby acquiring a position of some useful advantage.

It may be that only a few firms (large or small) will tend to initiate fresh strategic moves, and they may not do it often. But to the extent that these few are able to set the pace for the others, the give-and-take of strategic move and competitive response spreads and continues.[3] A fresh move may come from a firm with ambitious growth objectives, from a firm with excess capacity, or from a firm under pressure to gain added business. More generally, though, the classic offensive strategies will be made by firms that see market opportunities and a chance to improve their profit performance. Such firms, whether they be actual leaders, would-be leaders, or mavericks, will likely be aware of the risks of undertaking a bold strategic move but they also are likely to have confidence, one, that they are shrewd enough to keep ahead of the game and, two, that they will be better off making a bold move than they would be by holding back and letting others take the lead.[4] Often, new marketing strategies are undertaken by sales force organizations under pressure from top management to improve sales-profit-growth performance or otherwise stave off stagnation. The defensive responses which follow aggressive moves will not only reflect time lags and uncertainties but their character will also tend to differ according to whether the new offensive consists of a new promotional campaign, introduction of a new product or product variation, a new channel of distribution, or an expansive move towards a new form of horizontal or vertical integration.

Typically the strategies of the participant firms cause the flow of competition to swing first in one direction and then another—in no certain pattern and mix. At any one time, the central focus of competition may be on price, new and improved products, a broader product offering, technical sophistication, the adoption of new cost-saving methods of manufacture, customer service, promotion, guarantees, styling, function, economy of use, convenience, and so on—either singly or in various combinations. This, together with the time sequence of strategic moves and the information base underlying them, act to shape the specific features of the competitive behavior and the competitive pressures that develop in a particular market or industry. Usually, initiatory moves come from a variety of firms acting out of a variety of motivations and circumstances, but at the same time it is not likely that all, or even most, firms will take a turn at starting a fresh round of moves.[5] It is to be expected that some firms will be bolder and more aggressive than others.

---

[3] J. M. Clark, *Competition as a Dynamic Process* (Washington: The Brookings Institution, 1961), p. 473. See also Michael E. Porter, *Interbrand Choice, Strategy, and Bilateral Market Power* (Cambridge, Mass.: Harvard University Press, 1976), chap. 4.

[4] Ibid., p. 474.

[5] Ibid.

The strategic patterns that give rise to the sort of competition which eliminates excess profits will tend to be different from the strategies that result in inefficient and poorly performing firms being driven from the market. Strategic behavior which has the effect of causing firms to increase the number of models and varieties in their product offering will have a character that is discernible from the strategic competition which leads firms to increase sales so as to capture scale economies. At the same time, because what is the best strategy for firm A may depend partly on firm B's choice, and because B, in turn, may elect to finetune its strategy in light of A's strategic behavior and options, the optimal strategy for a given firm at a given time is not necessarily clearcut and readily perceived. And, except in the case of distressed firms in dire straits, no strategic choice is ever final. The sequence of move and countermove is neverending, thus emphasizing the strategic process aspects of competition.

Any pause in this process is certain to be temporary, owing to the continuous stream of new strategic opportunities and threats which emerge from the possibilities for product variation, cost-related technological changes, new buyer tastes and preferences, changing demographics and lifestyles, shifts in buying power, new product availability, and general economic change. Apart from these market-related variables, periodic changes can be expected in the host of complex institutional factors that mold a firm's strategy choices from the outside and the intrafirm considerations which shape strategy from the inside. From a strategy evaluation standpoint, the main thing to remember is that from time to time there will be fresh strategic moves and these are likely to so stir competitive forces as to compel reactions and responses from other firms in the market. This is why the crux of business strategy centers around positioning the firm in its target market environment in ways intended to enhance its distinctive and competitive capabilities relative to rival firms.

Gathering Strategic Intelligence about Rival Firms

The move-countermove feature of competition makes gathering intelligence about rival firms an essential part of identifying a firm's own best strategy and whether/how it should respond to rivals' moves. Specifically, a perceptive analysis of rival firms ought to provide useful clues and predictions about (1) how a rival will likely react to market trends and broader environmental conditions, (2) which rivals will initiate what kinds of fresh strategic moves and why, (3) what each rival would probably do in response to the feasible strategic changes of other firms, and (4) the meaning and intent of a new strategic move and how seriously it should be taken.[6]
Diagnosing competitive responses has five dimensions: the priorities and performance objectives of each rival, each rival's assumptions and beliefs

[6] The discussion in this section is drawn largely from Michael E. Porter, *Competitive Strategy: Techniques for Analyzing Industries and Competitors* (New York: Free Press, 1980).

about the industry and about its competitors, each rival's current business strategy, the backgrounds and experiences of the rival's managers, and each firm's competitive capabilities.[7] Each is worth considering in some detail.

Rivals' Priorities and Performance Objectives. Doing the detective work to uncover a rival firm's priorities and performance objectives has several payoffs. It can reveal whether the rival is satisfied with its current performance and thus its current strategy. It can aid in assessing the likelihood of a shift in strategy, the reasons for and seriousness behind such a shift, and the speed and vigor of a rival's response to either changes in market conditions or new strategic moves of other firms. Developing answers to the following questions ought to prove particularly helpful:

1. What inferences can be made about the rival's performance objectives and its attitudes toward risks? Is there any evidence that the rival aspires to be the industry leader in pricing or technological proficiency or market share or product quality or some other aspect?

2. How do the rival's performance objectives in this industry compare with how it compensates business-level managers? With compensation of its sales force?

3. Does the rival have a parent company? If so, what are its performance objectives and how is the rival business unit expected to contribute to them in terms of profitability, growth, and cash flow? Does the parent view this business as one of its main strategic interests or is it a sideline or peripheral business? How does the business fit into the parent's corporate strategy and business portfolio? To what extent does the rival business command financial support and management attention from corporate headquarters? Does corporate management have an emotional attachment to the business?

4. Has the rival been involved in any antitrust actions that could condition its strategic responses or that could constrain its performance objectives? In the same vein, is it constrained by other regulatory, environmental, or social considerations?

5. Is the rival under any new pressures from headquarters, customers, or other competitors to improve its performance? Is the rival's future threatened in any way? Is the rival striving to regain lost ground? Can the rival meet its performance objectives without doing anything different or without launching a major strategic offensive? Is there reason to believe the rival is reasonably happy with its performance?

---

[7] In addition to the Porter reference cited in footnote 6, readers may wish to consult H. Kalff, "How Is Competition Performing?" *Long-Range Planning,* vol. 12, no. 3 (June 1979), p. 16; Jaime I. Rodriguez and William R. King, "Competitive Information Systems," *Long-Range Planning,* vol. 10, no. 6 (December 1979), pp. 46–47; Carter F. Bales, "Strategic Control: The President's Paradox," *Business Horizons,* vol. 20, no. 4 (August 1977), p. 23; Rothschild, *Putting It All Together,* chap. 5, George A. Steiner, *Strategic Planning: What Every Manager Must Know* (New York: Free Press, 1979), pp. 133–39; Derek F. Abell and John S. Hammond, *Strategic Market Planning* (Englewood Cliffs, N.J.: Prentice-Hall, Inc., 1979), chap. 2; and Robert Hershey, "Commercial Intelligence on a Shoestring," *Harvard Business Review,* vol. 58, no. 5 (September–October 1980), pp. 22–30.

Rivals' Assumptions and Beliefs. Every management operates on the assumptions and beliefs both about the industry and about how the business ought to be run. How a firm sees itself and its situation is often a good barometer of its strategic thinking. The relevant areas to probe into here are indicated in the following questions: What does the rival appear to believe (based on speeches, advertising claims, representations by its sales force to customers, and so on) about its standing in the marketplace relative to quality, cost, technological proficiency, and image with customers? Has the rival's reputation been traditionally identified with some key competitive aspect which will be strongly held to—like superior service, quality of manufacture, product innovation, breadth of product line, or focus on particular products or market segments? Does the management of the rival believe strongly in certain principles or values or ways of doing business that can be counted upon to condition what the rival does or does not do? Do the managers of the rival typically adhere to industry customs or rules of thumb or conventional wisdom (such as "you have to give customers great service," "buyers look for quality and performance not low price," "the key is low-cost manufacture and full utilization of capacity," and "you have to offer a full product line")? What does the rival's management appear to believe about industry trends, future competitive conditions, and the strengths and weaknesses of other firms in the industry? What patterns are evident in the way the rival conducts its business? What has the rival tried that succeeded, what has it tried that failed, and are these experiences likely to shape future strategic moves? What does it believe its competitive strengths and weaknesses are? Does the rival use certain consultants, advertising agencies, banks, or other advisors and are they known for particular techniques and approaches? Why did the rival get into this business, or what reason does it have to stay in the business? How accurate are the rival's perceptions about itself, about its competitive position, and about industry trends and conditions? Is the rival's management prone to misjudge or misestimate market conditions or competitors or the kind of shift in strategy which is needed?

Rivals' Current Business Strategy. An understanding of each rival's current business strategy and the way it is being implemented is fundamental to designing a winning strategy of one's own. It is difficult to outmaneuver one's rivals without first having keen insight into what they are doing in the marketplace. Thus diagnosing each rival's business strategy and determining how and why each of its functional area support strategies build or do not build upon the other is a relevant part of the intelligence-gathering process.

Insofar as possible, information is needed on the following: What is the apparent business strategy of each rival? What are the main markets of each rival in terms of products, customers, and geographic focus? What are the major functional area support strategies (especially in the areas of R&D, product development, product quality, and marketing) and the major operating-level strategies (especially as concerns maintaining volume and pricing)? Do these appear to be integrated and coordinated? What does the rival's organization structure indicate about the priorities and importance attached to the various functional areas and how they are coordinated? Who controls pricing? Where are key strategy decisions made—in the business unit itself (where?) or at corporate headquarters? Is the rival's business a free-standing unit or does it have to accommodate the requirements of sister units in the company? How influential is the rival unit in its parent organization? What flaws are evident in the rival's strategy? What are its pluses? How well is the strategy being executed? How flexible is their strategy? Are they locked into the strategy because of facilities commitments or some other factor? What are the implications for our own strategy?

Backgrounds and Experiences of Rival Managers.   One of the most important set of clues about the behavior and strategies of rival businesses can be gleaned from the personal experiences and backgrounds of their managers. Hence while the information may be hard to come by, it is worth exerting an effort to get. The most important areas of inquiry include:

1. What are the functional backgrounds of the key managers—accounting, finance, sales, production, R&D, and how likely is it that they will feel most comfortable with strategies which emphasize such functional areas? What other businesses have these managers worked in and what strategic approaches were characteristic of those businesses?
2. What types of strategies have/have not worked for them personally in their previous jobs?
3. Has the rival's current management been promoted from within (which may suggest continuation of the present strategy) or have those in charge come recently from outside the division or even outside the company? Is the manager in charge a person thought to be "on the way up" or is it someone who is about ready to retire? Is the rival known for selecting managers with a certain personality or educational background or managerial philosophy?
4. Is there reason to believe that the managers of the rival business will be influenced by some previous major event in their background or experience (a sharp recession, having managed a rapid growth business, a sudden drop in profitability, a severe strike, or a disruption in raw material supply)?
5. Have any of the rival's managers offered clues about their current thinking in their speeches to securities analysts, program appearances at trade associations, interviews with the media, or conversations with customers? Is there any evidence that they place a high value on industry leadership in market share or technology, stable pricing, quality manufacture, or on some other strategic feature that may suggest what courses of action they are apt to follow?

Rival's Capabilities to Compete Effectively.   Perhaps the really key issue about any rival firm is its capacity for competing effectively in the marketplace. Its strengths and weaknesses regarding product line, marketing and selling, dealer distribution network, R&D, engineering, manufacturing, cost and efficiency, financial condition, and managerial competence are all important in determining its ability to respond to competitive moves or to deal with industry trends. Special attention ought to be given to what a rival firm is best and worst at doing and what flexibility it has should a need arise to adapt to a price-cost squeeze, a shift to more emphasis on customer service, extensive product innovation, or some other relevant change in competitive conditions. Also pertinent is an appraisal of the degree to which it is likely to be a major factor in the marketplace over the long haul and why its market standing is likely to increase or decrease.

Pinning Down a Rival's Competitive Moves. Gaining useful answers to the kinds of questions and issues posed above is not a simple, short-run task. The needed information trickles in in bits and pieces and it takes both time and hard work to get a real "feel" for a rival's situation and how its management thinks. But it is a task worth doing and doing systematically. The result can be a good ability to predict:

- How a rival will respond to changes in market trends or economic conditions.
- How satisfied a rival firm is with its present market position and profitability, and thus whether it is likely to initiate a fresh strategic move.
- The most likely moves a rival will make, given its performance objectives, its assumptions and beliefs about the market, its current strategy, its management approach, and its competitive strengths and weaknesses.
- How vulnerable a rival would be to one's own strategic moves.
- How much the rival can be pushed before it will be provoked into retaliation.
- The nature and effectiveness of any such retaliatory action.

Such predictive ability is immensely valuable in choosing one's own best time, place, and method for fighting it out with competitors. Indeed, indepth familiarity with rivals' strategies and how they think is the key to astutely judging what competitive strategy is likely to meet with the greatest market success.

Screening out Alternative Strategies

Once management has performed a complete audit of the market and its main competitors, it ought to be fairly easy to come up with a realistic set of business strategy options. These must then be evaluated and the weaker alternatives screened out. Numerous considerations and criteria can be used to separate the stronger candidates from the weaker ones. Looking at the alternatives from the following angles is helpful:

Which alternative offers the best match with the organization's competence and financial resources? Do any of the business strategy alternatives call for greater competence and/or resources than can be mustered? Do any fall short of adequately exploiting the firm's distinctive competence and business strengths? Which strategy best fits what the company is good at doing?

Are any of the candidate strategies less attractive from the standpoint of profit outlook or return on investment criteria even though they meet minimum standards? Which strategy offers the best risk-reward tradeoffs?

Which of the candidate strategies offers the most dominant competitive edge? How vulnerable is each alternative to successful competitive counterattack?

How vulnerable are each of the alternatives to market and environmental threats now existing or on the horizon?

Which strategy appears most capable of succeeding in a variety of market and economic situations? Are any of the alternatives heavily dependent for their success on general economic prosperity and a "sellers' market"? If market conditions are likely to be volatile, which strategy offers the most flexibility and allows contingencies to be built in?

Which strategy appears best suited to management's philosophy and personality? Should any of the candidate strategies be ruled out because of a conflict with management's sense of social responsibilities or personal values?

Which option, if successfully executed, would provide the best platform for taking advantage of other market opportunities that might present themselves?

When an alternative scores well on some factors but negatively on others, the net effect is not simply a function of whether there are more pluses than minuses or vice versa. Some criteria are more critical than others—and which ones are the most important vary from case to case.

Ideally, one would like to be able to formulate a business strategy where all or most of the vital considerations were simultaneously optimized.[8] In practice, this objective proves much too utopian. Tradeoffs are inevitably necessary. Trying to minimize risk exposure, for example, nearly always entails a sacrifice of potential profits. Likewise, strategic attempts to exploit every opportunity to its fullest can mean concomitant increases in the number of failures; the criterion of catering to organizational strengths can be incompatible with a need to show up organizational weaknesses. In addition, compromises are necessary in order to fashion a strategy which meets the needs of various coalition groups in the management hierarchy (marketing,

---

[8] The discussion in this paragraph applies to corporate strategy evaluation as well as to business strategy evaluation.

manufacturing, finance) and which also is consonant with the interest of exogeneous groups (stockholders, labor, consumers, government, the general public). Hence, which strategy is "best" from one angle seldom turns out to be the "best" from other pertinent angles.

In the final analysis, strategic decisions, both at the corporate level and the business level, boil down to a matter of managerial and business judgment. Even after a lengthy and exhaustive strategic evaluation, management is often confronted with choosing among several close alternatives rather than merely confirming a clearcut choice. Very rarely is the issue of what to do so cut-and-dried as to eliminate the judgment/choice problem. Facts and analysis by themselves usually do not resolve the problem of conflicts and inconsistencies. For this reason, intuition, personal experience, judgment, qualitative trade-offs, value preferences, intangible situational factors, and compromise of opinion become an integral part of the process of making a strategic commitment. And no formula or how-to-do-it description is ever likely to take their place.

Three elements of the strategy selection problem frequently assume a pivotal import in reaching a decision: (1) the risk/reward trade-off, (2) timing the strategic move, and (3) contribution to performance and objectives.

Risk/Reward Considerations. The relevance of the profitability versus risk tradeoff is obvious. Risk-averters will be inclined toward "safe" strategies where external threats appear minimal, profits adequate but not spectacular, and in-house resources ample to meet the task ahead. Quite often, such firms insist upon following a financial approach that emphasizes internal financing rather than debt-financing; likewise they may opt to defer major financial commitments as long as possible or until the effects of uncertainty are deemed minimal. They may view pioneering-type innovations as "too chancy" relative to proven, well-established techniques, or else they may simply prefer to be followers rather than leaders. In general, the risk-averter places a high premium on "conservative" strategies which minimize the downside risk.

On the other hand, eager risk-takers lean more toward opportunistic strategies where the payoffs are greater, the challenges more demanding, and the glamour more appealing—despite the pitfalls which may exist. Innovation is preferred to imitation. Aggressive action ranks ahead of defensive conservatism. A confident optimism overrules pessimism. The organization's strengths, not its weaknesses, serve as a chief criterion for matching strategy and organizational capability.

Timing Considerations. Timing issues are partly a function of the risk-reward situation. For instance, where uncertainty is high, the risk-averter's tendency is to proceed with extreme caution or to stall. A defensive stance is likely to emerge. In contrast, the risk-taker is willing to move early and assume a trail-blazing role. Yet, the timing dilemma goes deeper than the risk/reward tradeoff and a preference for an active or reactive style. It also relates to whether market conditions are ripe for the strategies being contemplated. A "good" strategy undertaken at the wrong time can spell failure. Chrysler Corporation had this experience in 1974–1975 when it decided to put more emphasis on full-size, family cars and compete head on with General Motor's Chevrolet Impala and full-sized Pontiacs, Buicks, and Oldsmobiles. Chrysler redesigned its Plymouth, Dodge, and Chrysler cars along the styling lines of GM's medium-priced models but, unfortunately for Chrysler, they had barely hit the market when the Arab oil boycott and the subsequent steep climb in gasoline prices made customers wary of "big" cars. Chrysler found itself not only stuck with the high costs of having restyled its line of cars but also without an appealing selection of small cars to offer the growing number of economy-minded buyers.

In addition, there are several other timing-related issues which bear on strategy selection.[9] One pertains to the lead time between action and result and any difficulties which may ensue if the lead time is "too long" or "too short." In a closely related vein, whether management's attention is focused principally on the short-run or the long-run can prompt the selection of a strategy geared towards improving performance in whichever time interval is preferred. Still another involves whether the magnitude and rate of investment funding required to support a given strategy fits in with the organization's overall financial structure and cash flow requirements. Inasmuch as strategic investments commonly entail a stream of expenditures rather than a single lump-sum expenditure, the timing of the components may favor the selection of one strategy over another, especially if other factors are not decisive.

Contribution to Performance and Objectives.   Frequently, the real problem of strategy selection originates as a response to unsatisfactory performance. Thus it makes sense that the choice of strategy is heavily governed by the expected contribution to achieving high-priority performance objectives.

Consider, for example, the case where a firm is contemplating a new competitive strategy to improve its market position and its profits. One of the most relevant evaluative factors will be the sort of "counterattack" which may be expected from rivals and how this will likely affect the performance outcome. Typically, the performance potential of a given competitive strategy is stronger(1) the less vulnerable it is to the moves and countermoves of rivals and (2) the greater the chance that it will put an enterprise in a superior or at least equal competitive position vis-a-vis the strategies it confronts.

In weighing the competitive interplay of strategic moves and countermoves, several salient points merit consideration. To begin with, the posture of one's own proposed strategy has a bearing on the counterresponses of competitors. Attacking the positions of rival firms squarely will elicit an almost sure response—and maybe a vigorous one at that, unless the attack is deemed feeble or doomed to failure. But, ot choose a strategy that sidesteps

---

[9] Seymour Tilles, "Making Strategy Explicit," in H. Igor Ansoff, *Business Strategy* (Baltimore: Penguin Books, 1970), p. 197.

direct confrontation stands a fair chance of going ignored for a time period long enough to establish a lead over rivals. The comparative benefits of attacking competitors' strengths or weaknesses warrant careful assessment. Challenging rivals where they are strongest carries a higher risk of failure though, also, a greater performance improvement if the strategy succeeds. On the other hand, to attack weakness brings modest gain in overall performance unless competitive weakness is associated with strong market potential—as sometimes it is.

Illustration Capsule 12

Does Strategy Formulation Really Pay Off?

As an example of what the performance payoff can be when management takes the time to do a serious job of formulating corporate strategy, consider the case of a small manufacturer of industrial plastics (sales of $60 million). Acquired the previous year by a much larger diversified company, it suffered a serious business downturn and reported profits well below the corporate ROI target. According to one analyst:

The division had never developed a formal strategy, but management cherished ambitions of building the division into a major producer of commodity and specialty plastics. On the commodity plastics side, division management had counted on finding new applications in the construction industry. On the assumption that new Occupational Safety and Health Administration (OSHA) plant regulations would force at least a few of its competitors out of the market, it was planning an aggressive marketing program. In this way, management thought it could enlarge the division's operating base and eventually justify and "base load" a new world-scale plant to replace two older, relatively inefficient facilities. Meanwhile, on the specialty side, sales of the division's 200-odd patented plastics were limping badly, and a score of new items added over the past two years had so far failed to take off as expected.

It is not surprising that corporate headquarters was worried. Top management knew that the profit decline since 1974 was due partly to the rising price of one major raw material, a petroleum derivative, and partly to the deteriorating production economics of their old plants. They were less confident about the division's strategic assumptions. What if customers should begin shifting to substitute materials? And what if the maturation of some commodity plastics markets should lead to a more cyclical pattern of demand? Faced with these questions, corporate management decided to invest in a formal strategy development effort.

The initial situation analysis was an eye opener. First, division management's optimism about the commodity end of the business turned out to be ill founded: the specialty plastics side was clearly more promising. An analysis of end-use markets, coupled with detailed projections of likely profit economics, pointed to a slow-growing but genuine opportunity in selected segments. But to capitalize on that opportunity, the product line and marketing effort would have to be modified.

Accordingly, management decided to convert the division, over a five-year period, from a minor factor in many sectors of the industrial plastics market to a

Illustration Capsule 12 (*continued*)

strong competitor on a much narrower front. The specialty product line would be tailored to customer requirements, the sales force upgraded and the marketing approach refocused. As demand for the specialty line grew, the division would gradually withdraw from the commodity business. At the same time, exposure and risk would be reduced by closing the older of the two manufacturing plants, by cutting working capital and by eliminating near-term capital expenditures.

Eighteen months after these decisions were made, the division had already realized profit improvements of better than $4 million, almost doubling its profits and performing well above the corporate ROI target. It did so well, in fact, that a proposal to replace the remaining manufacturing plant with a modern, efficient facility had already been approved. The division's profitable new strategy had four characteristics that are present in most high-payoff strategies:

It focused on the sectors of highest potential yield. The plastics division concentrated on the most profitable and exploitable product families and types, customer industries and specific customers, and channels of distribution. Analysis showed that well over half of the division's 200 specialty plastics lines were making a marginal contribution to fixed costs or actually losing money. Nearly 40 had been competing in markets where they were clearly inferior; for example, one that was being pushed for outdoor application did not stand up well to weathering. And the many colors offered often meant short, uneconomic production runs.

By pruning unprofitable products and consolidating product recipes, the division reduced its line to 33 items that had above-average performance characteristics and were targeted at end-use markets where competition was not yet severe and demand was likely to grow. Prices were increased, based on the price differential with the nearest competitive material and the calculable effect on the customer's production costs. A special surcharge was instituted on low-volume purchases of nonstandard colors.

It balanced profit payoff and business risk. In its drive for expanded market share in the commodity sector, the plastics division had unwittingly embraced a high-risk strategy. Despite its precarious position as a marginal competitor, it had failed to plan for such contingencies as a proposed federal regulation that could have wiped out one major product application. Moreover, it would have sharply increased its financial exposure had it proceeded with the proposal to replace the two obsolete plants.

Management carefully examined a range of alternatives before settling on the strategy offering the most acceptable combination of risk and payoff. Risk was reduced by withdrawing from the commodity business, while the phaseout of the older factory shrank the asset base and cut working capital. To put the strategy on a pay-as-you-go basis, specific financial and market development objectives were set up for specialty plastics, and replacement of the second plant was tied to their attainment. At the same time, a targeted sales effort and a tough manufacturing cost reduction program were launched.

It emphasized both feasibility and consistency. Surprisingly often, businesses plan market and sales initiatives, product development programs and the like that are unrealistic or incompatible. The plastics division, for example, had been trying to penetrate the specialty market with a sales force that knew how to sell only commodity plastics to a few high-volume customers. Unable to help with new applications, they soon lost the few prospects that turned up for

Illustration Capsule 12 (concluded)

the specialty line. The new strategy, in contrast, explicitly identified target customers and analyzed their potential, and laid out programs for upgrading the sales force and providing applications support.

Again, though the division was plagued with cost problems and loaded with new products it couldn't sell, its R&D staff had been hard at work developing new specialty products. But four out of the twelve new products under development were technological long shots, and the total potential market for the rest was estimated at less than $50 million. Under the new strategy, a watchdog group of managers—from marketing, customer applications assistance and R&D—was set up to keep all new product and applications projects geared to the new market priorities.

It specified tasks, responsibilities, and timetables. Specific goals, responsibilities and completion dates were assigned to each major product group and business function for three years ahead. Volume, profit and market share objectives were translated into specific targets such as the percentage of trial customers to be converted into repeat purchasers and the amount and timing of price increases by product and customer. Performance criteria were established for successive six-month progress reviews, and contingency moves were mapped out, based on the results in hand and the market and competitive situation as each checkpoint was reached.

Source: Carter F. Bales, "Strategic Control: The President's Paradox," *Business Horizons*, vol. 20, no. 4 (August 1977), pp. 18–19. Copyright, 1977, by the Foundation for the School of Business at Indiana University. Reprinted by permission.

The Act of Strategic Commitment

The final component of strategy selection is the commitment decision. In fact, a strategic choice cannot be said to have been made until money and manpower have been committed. The act of commitment is what takes the issue of the strategic decision out of the category of an alternative and activates the chosen strategy to official organizational status. Commitment entails (1) directing some part of the organization to undertake the strategy selected, (2) assigning responsibility for implementing the strategic plan to the appropriate personnel, (3) allocating the resources necessary for implementation, (4) clarifying exactly where and under what circumstances implementation is to be undertaken, and (5) specifying the time interval for implementation. In effect, then, strategic commitment supplies answers to the obvious implementation issues of *who, where,* and *when* and thus lays a foundation for launching the task of putting the chosen strategy into place.

A final point. The process of evaluating strategic alternatives and arriving at a choice of strategy has elements of ambiguity. There are no infallible rules or procedures which, if followed to the letter, will lead to the "right" strategy choice. Strategy selection cannot be reduced to a precise, formula-like, analytic process. Intangible situational factors, astute entrepreneurship, and creativity must be judiciously interwoven with the quantifiable, concrete realities of a competitive marketplace. Thus, there is no substitute for the exercise of managerial business judgment and, consequently, no way of posing a strategy formulation methodology that will "guarantee" an effective strategic choice. In short, strategy selection is a managerial responsibility, not a technique; the process is not susceptible to a step-by-step "how to" set of answers. One can, at most, offer guidelines, indicate pitfalls, and pose some of the right kinds of questions to ask.

SUGGESTED READINGS

Abell, Derek F., and Hammond, John S. *Strategic Market Planning.* Englewood Cliffs, N.J.: Prentice-Hall, Inc., 1979, chap. 2.

Buchele, Robert B. "How to Evaluate a Firm." *California Management Review,* vol. 4, no. 1 (Fall 1962), pp. 5–17.

Cannon, J. Thomas. *Business Strategy and Policy.* New York: Harcourt, Brace & World, 1968, pp. 84–102.

Cohen, K. J. and Cyert, R. M. "Strategy: Formulation, Implementation, and Monitoring." *Journal of Business,* vol. 46, no. 3 (July 1973), pp. 349–67.

Gilmore, Frank. "Formulating Strategy in Smaller Companies." *Harvard Business Review,* vol. 49, no. 3 (May–June 1971), pp. 71–81.

Hussey, David E. "The Corporate Appraisal: Assessing Company Strengths and Weaknesses." *Long-Range Planning,* vol. 1, no. 2 (December 1968), pp. 19–25.

Kalff, H. "How Is Competition Performing?" *Long-Range Planning,* vol. 12, no. 3 (June 1979), pp. 16–21.

Lunneman, Robert E., and Kennell, John D. "Short-Sleeve Approach to Long-Range Planning." *Harvard Business Review,* vol. 55, no. 2 (March–April 1977), pp. 141–50.

Porter, Michael E. *Interbrand Choice, Strategy, and Bilateral Market Power.* Cambridge, Mass.: Harvard University Press, 1976, chap. 4.

————. "How Competitive Forces Shape Strategy." *Harvard Business Review,* vol. 57, no. 2 (March–April 1979), pp. 137–45.

————. *Competitive Strategy: Techniques for Analyzing Industries and Competitors.* New York: Free Press, 1980.

Rodriguez, Jaime I., and King, William R. "Competitive Information Systems." *Long-Range Planning,* vol. 10, no. 6 (December 1977), pp. 45–50.

Rothschild, William E. *Putting It All Together: A Guide to Strategic Thinking.* New York: AMACOM, 1976, chap. 5.

Steiner, George A. *Strategic Planning: What Every Manager Must Know.* New York: Free Press, 1979, chaps. 8, 11, 12, and 14.

Wall, Jerry. "What the Competition Is Doing: Your Need to Know." *Harvard Business Review,* vol. 52, no. 6 (November–December 1974), pp. 22 ff.

6 STRATEGY IMPLEMENTATION AND ADMINISTRATION: ORGANIZATIONAL CONSIDERATIONS

It doesn't matter what you do, just so long as you do it well.

J. Galbraith and D. Nathanson

. . . the purpose of formal organizations is to provide a framework for cooperation and to fix responsibilities, delineate authority, and provide for accountability. . . .

Edmund P. Learned

Strategy implementation has a fundamentally different managerial character than strategy formulation. The latter is largely intellectual and emphasizes the abilities to conceptualize, analyze, and evaluate; it requires shrewd judgment as to what constitutes an entrepreneurially effective strategy and what does not. But there is more to managing than being a good paper strategist; the acid test is being able to convert the strategic plan into effective performance and results. Indeed, it takes a lot more managerial time and energy to implement and administer strategy than it does to formulate it. And the managerial tasks involved sweep across a wider front.

Strategy implementation raises all kinds of administrative and policy issues concerning the specifics and details of what it will take to put the chosen strategy in place and make it work. In ongoing enterprises, management needs to determine whether the present organization is well-suited to implement the chosen strategy and, if not, what changes may have to be made. A new organization will have to decide how to build from the ground up. Internal operating policies and procedures will have to be developed to guide strategy implementation and to indicate "the way we do things around here;" this includes figuring out how to develop a distinctive competence, allocating resources to the various subunits, setting performance standards,

151

installing an information system, and devising an effective reward structure. Later, management will have to assess the progress being made in the implementation process and how well the strategy is working out. This chapter and the next focus on these aspects of the general manager's job.

Strategy and Organization

It goes almost without saying that one of the highest priorities of strategy implementation and administration is building an organization capable of effective strategy execution. Accomplishing the strategic mission requires that organization be consciously structured rather than allowed to evolve comfortably and expediently. As Drucker says, "the only things that evolve in an organization are disorder, friction, malperformance."[1]

A number of distinct subtasks are involved in conceiving and putting in motion an organization structure capable of seeing the chosen strategy through to a successful conclusion. Those activities that have to be done right and on time if the strategy is to succeed must be identified and responsibility for them assigned to individuals or groups having the appropriately specialized skills. A review of the formal organization structure, together with its informal relationships, will be needed to assure coordinated integration of separately-performed functions; here it may be useful not only to assess existing supervisory and line-staff relationships but also to be creative in setting up project staffs, task forces, teams, committees, and other *ad hoc* units. Ways must be found to instill organizational objectives in all subunits, while at the same time (if the organization behaviorists are to be believed) allowing room for the satisfaction of individual aspirations. Reporting channels and communication mechanisms must be made operational to keep each subunit posted on what it must know about other subunits and to let those in positions of authority know what is going on so that the task sequence can proceed without confusion and delay. Insofar as practical, it will be beneficial to contain interdepartmental rivalries, interpersonal conflicts, and the maneuvers of subunits with vested interests to protect, lest too much energy be spent on internal policies and playing the power game.

There are no hard and fast rules as how to build a strategically effective organization. However, a strong case can be made that the choice among alternative forms of organizational structure should be governed by the relative contribution of each alternative to the accomplishment of strategy. In other words, structural form and work flows should be closely aligned with the needs of strategy.[2] The logic behind the view that an organization's

---

[1] Peter Drucker, *Management: Tasks, Responsibilities, Practices* (New York: Harper and Row, Publishers, 1974), p. 523.

[2] Research evidence also supports the structure follows strategy thesis. The landmark study is Alfred Chandler's *Strategy and Structure*. According to Chandler, changes in an organization's strategy bring about new administrative problems which, in turn, require a new or refashioned structure if the new strategy is to be successfully implemented. In more specific

structure should be carefully linked to its strategy is relatively simple: how the work of an organization is structured is just a means to an end—not an end in itself. Structure is no more than a managerial device for facilitating the implementation and execution of the organization's strategy and, ultimately, for achieving the intended performance and results. Toward this end, the structural design of an organization acts not only as a "harness" that helps people pull together in their performance of diverse tasks but also as a means of tying the organizational building blocks together in ways that promote strategy accomplishment and improved performance. Without *deliberately* organizing functional responsibilities and activities so as to produce coordination between structure and strategy, the outcome is likely to be confusion, misdirection, and splintered efforts. Consequently, if structure is to be sound and effective, the task of organization-building needs to be viewed as one of figuring out *strategically effective ways* of weaving the total work effort together.

DuPont's experience offers a classic example of the rationale for the linkage between strategy and structure:

> The strategy of diversification quickly demanded a refashioning of the company's administrative structure if its resources, old and new, were to be used efficiently and therefore profitably; for diversification greatly intensified the administrative load carried by the functional departments and the central office. Once the functional needs and the activities of several rather than one product line had to be coordinated, once the work of several very different lines of businesses had to be appraised, once the policies and procedures had to be formulated for divisions handling a wide variety of products, and, finally, once the central office had to make critical decisions about what new lines of business to develop, then the old structure quickly showed signs of strain. To meet the new needs, the new organizational design provided several central offices, each responsible for one line of products. At the new general office, the Executive Committee and staff specialists concentrated on the overall administration of what had become a multiindustry enterprise. And in transforming the highly centralized, functionally departmentalized structure into a "decentralized," multi-divisional one, the major achievement had been the creation of the new divisions.[3]

The lesson of this example is that the choice of organization structure *does make a difference* in how an organization performs. All forms of organization structure are not equally effective in implementing a given strategy. In the

---

terms, Chandler found that structure tends to follow the growth strategy of the firm—but often not until inefficiency and internal operating problems provoke a structural adjustment. His studies of 70 large corporations revealed a sequence consisting of new strategy creation, emergence of new administrative problems, a decline in profitability and performance, a shift to a more appropriate organizational structure, and then recovery to more profitable levels and improved strategy execution. Chandler found this sequence to be oft-repeated as firms grew and modified their corporate strategies. For more details, see Alfred D. Chandler, *Strategy and Structure* (Cambridge, Mass.: M.I.T. Press, 1962).

[3] Chandler, *Strategy and Structure*, p. 113.

remaining sections of this chapter we will explore aspects of structuring a strategically effective organization.

How Structure Follows Strategy: The Stages Model

In a number of respects, the strategist's approach to organization-building is governed by the size and growth stage of the enterprise, together with the key strategic characteristics of the organization's business. For instance, the type of organization structure that suits a small specialty steel firm relying upon a concentration strategy in a regional market is not likely to be suitable for a large, vertically-integrated steel producer doing business in geographically diverse areas. The organization form that works best in a multiproduct, multitechnology, multibusiness corporation pursuing a conglomerate diversification strategy is, understandably, likely to be different yet again. Recognition of this characteristic has prompted several attempts to formulate a model linking changes in organizational structure to stages in an organization's strategic development.[4]

The underpinning of the stages concept is that enterprises can be arrayed along a continuum running from very simple to very complex organizational forms and that there is a tendency for an organization to move along this continuum toward more complex forms as it grows in size, market coverage, and product line scope and as the strategic aspects of its technology-product-market relationships become more intricate. Four distinct stages of strategy-related organization have been singled out.

Stage I.   A Stage I organization is essentially a small, single-business enterprise managed by one person. The owner-entrepreneur has close daily contact with employees and each phase of operations. Most employees report directly to the owner, who makes all the pertinent decisions about objectives, strategy, daily operations, and so on. As a consequence, the organization's strengths, vulnerabilities, and resources are closely allied with the entrepreneur's personality, management ability and style, and personal financial situation. Not only is a Stage I enterprise an extension of the interests, abilities, and limitations of its owner-entrepreneur but also its activities are typically concentrated in just one line of business. For the most part, today's Stage I enterprise is epitomized by small firms run by "independent businesspersons" who are "their own bosses" and, typically, such firms have a strategy which centers around a single product, market, technology, or channel of distribution.

Stage II.   Stage II organizations differ from Stage I enterprises in one essential respect: an increased scale and scope of operations create a perva-

---

[4] See, for example, Malcolm S. Salter, "Stages of Corporate Development," *Journal of Business Policy*, vol. 1, no. 1 (Spring 1970), pp. 23–27; Donald H. Thain, "Stages of Corporate Development," *The Business Quarterly* (Winter 1969), pp. 32–45; Bruce R. Scott, "The Industrial State: Old Myths and New Realities," *Harvard Business Review*, vol. 51, no. 2 (March–April 1973), pp. 133–48; and Chandler, *Strategy and Structure*, chap. 1.

sive strategic need for management specialization and force a transition from one-person management to group management. However, a Stage II enterprise, although run by a team of managers with functionally specialized responsibilities, remains fundamentally a single-business operation. This is not to imply, though, that the categories of management specialization are uniform among large, single-business enterprises. In practice, there is wide variation. Some Stage II organizations prefer to divide strategic responsibilities along classic functional lines—marketing, production, finance, personnel, control, engineering, public relations, procurement, planning, and so on. In other Stage II companies functional specialization is keyed to distinct production units; for example, the organizational building blocks of a vertically integrated oil company may consist of exploration, drilling, pipelines, refining, wholesale distribution, and retail sales. In a process-oriented Stage II company, the functionally sequenced units aim primarily at synchronizing the flow of output between them.

Stage III.   Stage III embraces those organizations whose operations, though concentrated in a single field or product line, are large enough and scattered over a wide geographical area to justify having *geographically decentralized* operating units. These units all report to corporate headquarters and conform to corporate policies but they are given the flexibility to tailor their unit's strategic plan to meet the specific needs of each respective geographic area. Ordinarily, each of the semiautonomous operating units of a Stage III organization is structured along functional lines. The key difference between Stage II and Stage III, however, is that while the functional units of a Stage II organization stand or fall together (in that they are built around one business and one end market), the operating units of a Stage III firm can stand alone (or nearly so) in the sense that the operations in each geographic unit are not rigidly tied to or dependent on those in other areas. Characteristic firms in this category would be breweries, cement companies, and steel mills having production capacity and sales organizations in several geographically separate market areas. Corey and Star cite Pfizer International as being a good example of a company whose strategic requirements in 1964 made geographic decentralization propitious:

> With sales of $223 million in 1964, Pfizer International operated plants in 27 countries and marketed in more than 100 countries. Its product lines included pharmaceuticals (antibiotics and other ethical prescription drugs), agriculture and veterinary products (such as animal feed supplements and vaccines, and pesticides), chemicals (fine chemicals, bulk pharmaceuticals, petrochemicals and plastics), and consumer products (cosmetics and toiletries).
>
> Ten geographic Area Managers reported directly to the President of Pfizer International and exercised line supervision over Country Managers. According to a company position description, it was "the responsibility of each Area Manager to plan, develop, and carry out Pfizer International's business in the assigned foreign area in keeping with company policies and goals."
>
> Country Managers had profit responsibility. In most cases a single Country

Manager managed all Pfizer activities in his country. In some of the larger, well-developed countries of Europe there were separate Country Managers for pharmaceutical and agricultural products and for consumer lines.

Except for the fact that New York headquarters exercised control over the to-the-market prices of certain products, especially prices of widely used pharmaceuticals, Area and Country Managers had considerable autonomy in planning and managing the Pfizer International business in their respective geographic areas. This was appropriate because each area, and some countries within areas, provided unique market and regulatory environments. In the case of pharmaceuticals and agriculture and veterinary products (Pfizer International's most important lines) national laws affected formulations, dosages, labeling, distribution, and often price. Trade restrictions affected the flow of bulk pharmaceuticals and chemicals and packages products, and might in effect require the establishment of manufacturing plants to supply local markets. Competition, too, varied significantly from area to area.[5]

Stage IV.   Stage IV is typified by large, multiproduct, multiunit, multimarket enterprises decentralized along product lines. Their corporate strategies emphasize diversification, concentric and/or conglomerate. As with Stage III companies, the semiautonomous operating units report to a corporate headquarters and conform to certain firm-wide policies, but the divisional units pursue their own respective line of business strategies. Typically, each separate business unit is headed by a general manager who has profit and loss responsibility and whose authority extends across all of the unit's functional areas except, perhaps, accounting and capital investment (both of which are traditionally subject to corporate approval). Both strategic decisions and operating decisions are thus concentrated at the divisional level rather than at the corporate level. The organizational structure of the business unit may be along the lines of Stage I, II, or III types of organizations. Characteristic Stage IV companies include General Electric, ITT, Procter & Gamble, General Foods, Textron, and DuPont.

Movement Through the Stages.   From our perspective, the stages model provides useful insights into why organization structure tends to change in accordance with product-market-technology relationships and new directions in corporate strategy. As firms have progressed from small, entrepreneurial enterprises following a basic concentration strategy to more complex strategic phases of volume expansion, vertical integration, geographic expansion, and product diversification, their organizational structures have evolved from unifunctional to functionally centralized to multidivisional decentralized organizational forms. Firms that remain single-line business almost always have some form of a centralized functional structure. Enterprises which are predominately in one industry but which are slightly diversified typically have a hybrid structure; the dominant business is managed via a functional organization and the diversified activities are handled

---

[5] E. Raymond Corey and Steven H. Star, *Organizational Strategy: A Marketing Approach* (Boston: Division of Research, Harvard Business School, 1971), pp. 23–24.

through a divisionalized form. The more diversified an organization becomes, irrespective of whether the diversification is along either concentric or conglomerate lines, the more it moves toward some form of decentralized divisional structure.

However, it is by no means imperative that organizations begin at Stage I and move sequentially toward Stage IV.[6] U.S. Rubber (now Uniroyal) moved from a Stage II organization to a Stage IV form without ever passing through Stage III. And some organizations exhibit characteristics of two or more stages simultaneously. Sears, at one time, was decentralized geographically for store operations, personnel, sales promotion, banking, inventory and warehousing, and maintenance, yet centralized for manufacturing and procurement of goods, thus overlapping the organization structures of Stages II and III. Furthermore, some companies have found it desirable to retreat into prior stages after entering a particular stage. For example, the DuPont Textile Fibers Department originated out of five separate, decentralized, fully-integrated fiber businesses—rayon, acetate, nylon, "Orlon," and "Dacron."[7] Many weavers and other industrial users bought one or more of these fibers and used them in significantly different ways that also required different application technologies. According to Corey and Star:

> Customers objected to being solicited by five DuPont salesmen each promoting a different type of synthetic fiber and each competing with the others. Users of synthetic fibers wanted sales representatives from DuPont who understood their product lines and production processes and who could serve as a source of useful technical ideas.[8]

As a consequence, DuPont consolidated all five units into a Textile Fibers Department in an effort to deal more effectively with these customers. The new department established a single multifiber field sales force and set up market programs for four broad market segments—men's wear, women's wear, home furnishings, and industrial products, each of which had a potential demand for all five fibers.

In general, then, owing to the several ways which product-market relationships and strategy may turn, the paths along which an organization's structure may develop are more complex and variable than is suggested by a pattern of movement from Stage I through Stage IV. Still, it does appear that as the strategic emphasis shifts from small, single-product businesses to large, dominant-product businesses and then on to concentric or conglomerate diversification, a firm's organizational structure evolves, in turn, from one-man management to large-group functional management to decentralized, divisional management. This is substantiated by the fact that about

---

[6] For a more thorough discussion of this point, see Salter, "Stages of Corporate Development," pp. 34–35.

[7] Corey and Star, *Organization Strategy*, p. 14.

[8] Ibid.

90 percent of the *Fortune 500* firms (nearly all of which are to some degree diversified) have a divisionalized organizational structure.

Guidelines for Linking Structure to Strategy

In evaluating whether an enterprise is organized to meet the needs of its strategy, two questions can usefully be posed: "What functions and activities need to be performed right and on time for the organization's strategy to succeed?" and "In what areas would malperformance seriously endanger or undermine strategic success?"[9] The answers to these two questions should point squarely at the *key activities* essential to strategic success. In general, an activity's contribution to strategy should determine its rank and placement in the organizational hierarchy. Key activities should never be subordinated to nonkey activities. Revenue-producing or results-producing activities should never be subordinated to support activities. By making key activities the major building blocks for organizational structure, the chances are greatly improved that strategy will be effectively executed. Toward this end, a reassessment of organization structure is always useful whenever strategy is changed.[10] A new strategy is likely to entail modifications in key activities, which if not formally recognized and properly restructured, could leave strategic performance unnecessarily short of its potential.

A second strategy-structure linkage concerns the ability of the organization to react to and cope with new external developments of either a threatening or opportunistic nature. Here the questions that need to be posed are: Is the organization structure suitable for dealing with the effects of either rapid expansion of sales or the contractionary forces of a recession? Is the present structure appropriate for dealing with market threats and opportunities now on the horizon? Do impending shifts in strategic emphasis make the present organization structure suspect or out of date? Are the firm's R&D activities attuned with the marketplace and with customer needs? Do strategic decisions have "to go looking for a home" or do managers know where strategic responsibility lies? Are the firm's key activities headed up by managers with the right skills and talents, and are they being given enough latitude and clout to do what needs to be done?

A Suggested Procedure. In addressing what structure is best suited to the achievement of strategy:[11]

1. Delineate as precisely and clearly as possible the relationships of customer needs and product-market aspects to the organization's strategy and performance objectives.

---

[9] Drucker, *Management*, pp. 530, 535.

[10] For an excellent documentation of how a number of well-known corporations revised their organization structure to meet the needs of strategy changes and specific product/market developments, see Corey and Star, *Organization Strategy*, chap. 3.

[11] The following is adapted from J. Thomas Cannon, *Business Strategy and Policy* (New York: Harcourt, Brace & World, 1968), p. 316.

2. Identify the key activities and functional skills requisite for strategic success.
3. Classify each of the key activities and skills according to (a) whether they are unique to the product/market being considered or analogous to those needed for other of the organization's product/markets and (b) their priority of contribution to strategic success.
4. Determine the degrees of authority and responsibility required to manage both the key and nonkey functions, keeping in mind two factors: (a) economy and (b) the degree of decentralization of decision-making best suited to each.
5. Design organizational ties around these principal building blocks so as to ensure adequate coordination and integration.

Step 4 is a crucial one. The economy factor is the basis for deciding whether to provide a major product/market subunit with the managerial backup it needs from other existing organizational units or to let it be self-sufficient and thereby have its own managerial staff to perform these functions. The decentralization factor, while partly economic, is mainly a matter of determining the appropriate managerial level at which to make the principal decisions that will confront the product/market subunit and figuring out how to align corporate strategy and line of business strategy. Taken together, steps 1–4 constitute a systematic way of identifying what the key activities are and where in the management hierarchy to perform them; once these steps are completed, the task of organizing the major strategic building blocks can proceed with less difficulty.

FORMS OF ORGANIZATION: WHAT THE OPTIONS ARE

The importance of the linkage between strategy and structure makes it worthwhile to scrutinize the strategy-related features of the major organizational alternatives. Currently, most forms of organization are based on (1) functional specialization, (2) geographic considerations, (3) departmentalization keyed to differences in processing stage, market channel, or customer class, (4) decentralized product divisions, (5) strategic business units, and (6) matrix structures featuring *dual* lines of authority and strategic priority. Each form relates structure to strategy in a different way and, consequently, has its own set of managerial pros and cons.

The Functional Organization Structure

Dividing key activities according to functional specialization takes as its premise the value of combining related effort and segregating unrelated effort. The resulting deeper specialization and focused concentration on functional problems can then enhance both efficiency and the development of distinctive competence. Generally speaking, organizing by function promotes full utilization of the most up-to-date technical skills and makes it more possible to capitalize on the efficiency gains to be had from using specialized manpower, facilities, and equipment. These are strategically important considerations for organizations that depend upon a single product line and/or are vertically integrated, and accounts for why such organizations favor some kind of centralized, functionally specialized structure.

However, just what form the functional specialization will take varies according to product-market-technology considerations. For instance, a large, technically-oriented manufacturing firm may be organized around research and development, engineering, materials management, production, quality control, marketing, personnel, finance and accounting, and public relations; further, some of the departments may be line and others staff, as shown in Figure 6–1. A municipal government may, on the other hand, be

FIGURE 6–1
A Functional Organization Structure (manufacturing company)

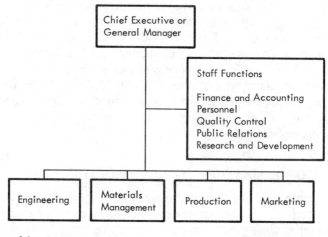

Advantages	Disadvantages
Enhances operating efficiency where tasks are routine and repetitive.	Poses problems of functional coordination.
Preserves centralized control of strategic results.	Can lead to interfunctional rivalry and conflict.
Allows benefits of specialization to be fully exploited.	May promote overspecialization and narrow management viewpoints.
Simplifies training of management specialists.	Limits development of general managers.
Promotes high emphasis on craftsmanship and professional standards.	Forces profit responsibility to the top.
	Not well-suited to situations requiring cross-functional problem solving.
	Conducive to empire building.
	More difficult for functional subunits to relate their tasks to corporate strategy and objectives.

departmentalized according to purposeful function—fire, public safety, health services, water and sewer, streets, parks and recreation, and education. A university may divide its organizational units into academic affairs, student services, alumni relations, athletics, buildings and grounds, institutional services, and budget control.

The Achilles heel of a functional structure is proper coordination of the separated functional units. Functional specialists, partly because of their training and the technical nature of their jobs, tend to develop their own mindset and ways of doing things. The more that functional specialists differ in their perspectives and their approaches to task accomplishment, the more difficult it becomes to achieve effective coordination between them. They neither "talk the same language" nor have an adequate understanding and appreciation for one another's problems and approaches. Each group is more interested in its own "empire" and sets its priorities accordingly. As a consequence, while there may be a free flow of communication and ideas up and down within functional units, there often emerges a strong built-in bias against horizontal movements—a bias which not only impedes coordination but also engenders conflict and rivalry (despite the lip service given to cooperation and "what's best for the company"). This, in turn, can create an excessive decision-making burden at the top of the management hierarchy where much time is spent resolving cross-functional differences, enforcing joint cooperation, and opening lines of communication.

Geographic Forms of Organization

Organizing according to geographic areas or territories is a rather common structural form for enterprises whose growth and expansion has caused their operations to become physically dispersed. As indicated in Figure 6–2, geographic organization has its advantages and disadvantages but the chief reason for its popularity is that, for one reason or another, it promotes improved performance. A geographic organization structure is especially attractive when the geographical differences are such that strategy has to be tailor-made to fit the particular needs and features of each area.

In the private sector, a territorial structure is typically utilized by chain store retailers, cement firms, railroads, airlines, the larger paper box and carton manufacturers, and large bakeries and dairy products enterprises; the member companies of American Telephone and Telegraph which make up the Bell Telephone System all represent geographically decentralized units. In the public sector, such organizations and agencies as the Internal Revenue Service, the Small Business Administration, the federal courts, the U.S. Postal Service, the state troopers, the Red Cross, and religious denominations have adopted territorial departmentation in their efforts to provide like services to geographically dispersed clienteles.

FIGURE 6-2
A Geographic Organizational Structure

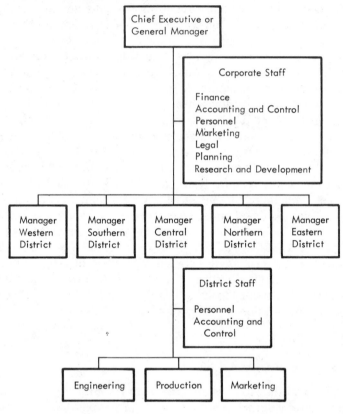

Advantages	Disadvantages
Allows tailoring of strategy to needs of area markets.	Greater difficulty in maintaining consistent and uniform companywide practices.
Delegates profit/loss responsibility to lowest strategic level.	Requires a larger management staff, especially general managers.
Improves functional coordination within the target market.	Leads to duplication of staff services.
Takes advantage of economies of local operations.	Poses a problem of headquarters control over local operations.
Area units make an excellent training ground for general managers.	

Process, Market Channel, or Customer Departmentation

Grouping an enterprise's activities around its several production stages, market channels, or customer groups is often employed where there are important operating economies or market advantages to be gained from a specialized approach. A metal parts manufacturer may find it operationally efficient to subdivide in series, thus having foundry, forging, machining, finishing, assembly, and painting departments. Firms with a diverse clientele may find it strategically useful to organize their marketing activities so as to cater to the requirements of each buyer segment. For example, some years ago Purex Corp. decided that neither product nor territorial departmentation was as well-suited to their operations as was a market channel departmentation which allowed it to focus separately on selling to supermarket chains and to drug chains. United Way drives are typically organized into a number of individual solicitation units with each assigned to canvass a particular segment of the community—commercial establishments, industrial plants, unions, local schools, county government, city government, hospitals, and agriculture. There are various departments of the federal government set up expressly for veterans, senior citizens, the unemployed, small businessmen, widows and dependent children, the poor, and others. Figure 6–3 illustrates departmentation by process, by market channel, and by customer category.

Decentralized Product Divisions

Grouping activities along product lines has been a clear-cut trend among diversified enterprises for the past half-century, beginning with the pioneering efforts of DuPont in the 1920s. Separate product divisions emerged because diversification made a functionally-specialized manager's job incredibly complex. Even with many immediate subordinates, a production executive cannot effectively manage the production of 10 to 20 different items being produced at as many as 50 different plant locations; similarly, the jobs of engineering, sales, and R&D executives become unwieldy when they have to be knowledgeable in so many different lines of business. Product decentralization thus aims at creating *manageable* product-oriented subunits that are responsive to customer needs, competitive behavior, and emerging market opportunities.

Organizing on a divisional or product group basis permits top management to delegate to a single executive extensive authority for formulating and implementing business-level, functional area, and operating strategies for specific products or product families. New semiautonomous divisions can then be created for each substantially different product-market grouping. By and large, the general managers of these divisions are given profit responsibility (which explains why such units are often called "profit centers") and are held accountable for both short-run results and long-run market development. They determine the appropriate tradeoffs in allocating resources between current operations and efforts for future growth. Within limits, they develop their own divisional staffs. The effect is to make the division general manager more like a semi-independent entrepreneur who specializes in a single line of business.

Figure 6–4 illustrates a typical divisionalized organization structure. One

FIGURE 6–3
Departmentation by Process, Market Channel, and Customer

A. Process departmentation

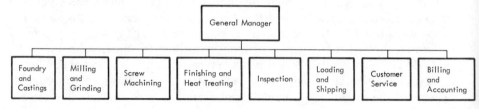

B. Market channel departmentation

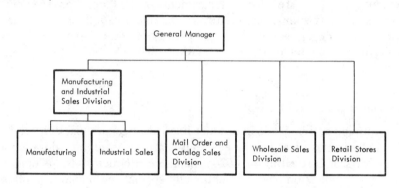

C. Customer departmentation

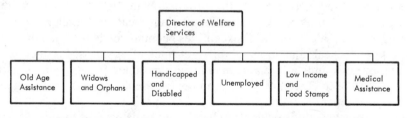

Advantages	*Disadvantages*
Structure is tied to performance of key activities.	Encourages pressure for special treatment.
Facilitates achievement of operating economies derived from use of specialized departments.	Poses problems of how to coordinate interdepartmental activities.
	May lead to uneconomically small units or underutilization of specialized facilities and manpower as demand shifts from unit to unit.

FIGURE 6-4
A Typical Divisionalized Organization Structure

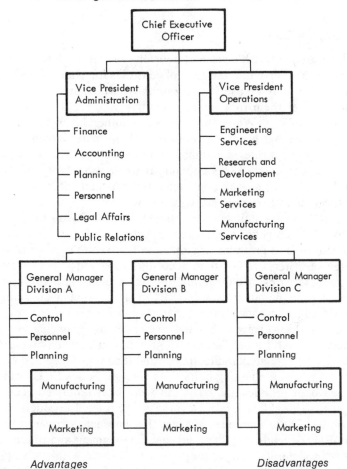

Advantages	Disadvantages
Offers a logical and workable means of decentralizing responsibility and delegating authority in diversified organizations.	Leads to proliferation of staff functions, policy inconsistencies between divisions, and problems of coordination of divisional operations.
Reduces layering of management.	Poses a problem of how much authority to centralize and how much to decentralize.
Improves coordination of functional activities for a specific product or product family.	
Brings line of business strategy into sharper organization focus.	
Facilitates profit/loss measurement by product line.	

of the most well-known product division structures is that of the Chevrolet, Oldsmobile, Cadillac and other divisions of General Motors.

Strategic Business Units

Sometimes an enterprise's product divisions and interindustry units are so numerous and so diverse that the span of control is too wide for a single chief executive. Then it may be useful to group those which are related and dele- gate authority over them to a senior executive who reports directly to the chief executive officer. While this imposes another layer of management between the divisional general managers and the chief executive, it may nonetheless improve strategic planning and top management coordination of diverse business interests. This explains both the popularity of the group vice president concept among conglomerate firms and the recent trend to- ward the formation of *strategic business units.*

A strategic business unit can be thought of as a clustering of discrete, product/divisional units based on some important strategic element common to each. The idea is to group an organization's activities according to strate- gically relevant criteria rather than according to size or span of control or product characteristics. At General Electric, a pioneer in the concept of decentralized strategic business units (SBUs), 48 divisions were reorganized into 43 SBUs; in one case, three separate divisions making various food preparation appliances were combined as a single SBU serving the "house- wares" market.[12] At Union Carbide 15 groups and divisions were decom- posed into 150 "strategic planning units" and then regrouped and combined into 9 new "aggregate planning units." At General Foods SBUs were origi- nally defined on a product line basis but were later redefined according to menu segments (breakfast foods, beverages, main meal products, desserts, and pet foods). These examples suggest that how management chooses to define its SBUs depends largely on managerial judgment and pragmatic con- siderations. In general, though, the aim is to include within a single SBU those kinds of products and activities which share an important strategic relationship—whether it be with regard to similarity in manufacturing or use of the same distribution channels, or overlap in customers and target mar- kets or some other pertinent strategic feature.

The managerial value of the concept of SBUs is that it provides diversified companies with a practical rationale for organizing what they do and with a workable approach to staying on top of the strategic performance of diverse operating units. It is particularly helpful in reducing the complexity of dovetailing corporate strategy and business strategy and in developing fo- cused product/market business strategies on a decentralized basis. Figure 6–5 illustrates the SBU concept of organizing diversification where each

---

[12] William K. Hall, "SBUs: Hot, New Topic in the Management of Diversification," *Busi- ness Horizons,* vol. 21, no. 1 (February 1978), p. 19.

FIGURE 6-5
A Product Group/SBU Type of Organization

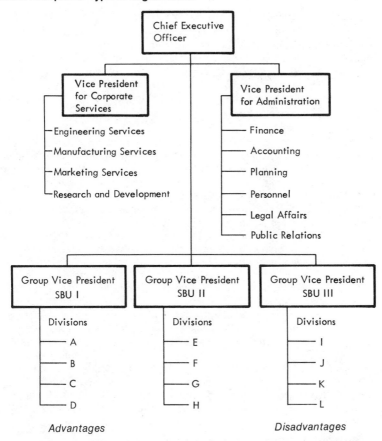

Advantages	Disadvantages
Provides a logical basis for top management to maintain close watch over divisional operations.	Adds another layer to top management.
Improves coordination between divisions with similar strategies, markets, and management problems.	The role and authority of the group v-p is often ambiguous and fleeting.

SBU is headed by a "group" vice president (see also Illustration Capsule 13).

Matrix Forms of Organization

A matrix form of organization is a structure with two (or more) channels of command, two lines of budget authority, two sources of performance and reward, and so forth. The key feature of the matrix is that product and functional lines of authority are overlaid (to form a matrix or grid) and

Illustration Capsule 13

Structuring Diversification: The Troublesome Role of the Group Executive

A recent survey showed that 70 percent of the *Fortune 500* firms used some form of a group vice president structure in managing diversification. This percentage was up sharply from 39 percent a few years previous. Yet, nearly two thirds of the group executives working in these companies view their jobs as more or less a "can of worms." The reasons given are interesting for what they reveal about the management problems of diversified organizations:

1. Some group vice presidents find themselves as being little more than a high-priced courier between the chief executive and the division heads.
2. The group head is in a no-man's land between operating units that expect maximum autonomy and presidents who judge his performance by the profits and losses of those same operating units. As a consequence, the group head is like an army corps commander, responsible for sector achievement but having limited control over limited resources.
3. The group vice president must walk a line between giving division managers enough elbow room to be effective entrepreneurs and maintaining enough control to keep corporate headquarters comfortable. The manager who is not politically expert at walking this line tends to be regarded as "the gestapo" by the divisions and "a nursemaid" by the CEO.
4. Although the job of group vice-president is often seen as a logical progression on the way to corporate president, in many companies a group vice-president either moves up, sideways, or out within five years. It is not the type of job that many people make a career out of.
5. For executives who enjoy "doing" rather than "coordinating and overseeing," the nebulous role of a group head is frustrating. It requires a low profile and behind the scenes influence, as opposed to being in the thick of the action. Recognition for performance gets blurred; credit for success tends to go first to the chief executive, then to the division head, and last to the group vice president.

From a corporate perspective, having a layer of group vice presidents to help the CEO direct and coordinate a growing, diversified company is almost a creation of necessity. The more operating divisions an enterprise has, the more important it becomes to have them report to someone besides the chief executive. So far, no more logical way has been devised than a group structure.

While it is generally agreed that there is a legitimate need for a group vice-president type structure in diversified companies, there are wide differences on what the group vice-president position should be like. At Textron group managers are regarded as "counselors" while at AMF a group head is held totally responsible for division performance. The prevailing view seems to be that, as a minimum, the group vice-president should (1) have heavy line responsibility for allocating financial resources within his group, (2) be brought into corporate operating committees, and (3) exercise primary responsibility for defining and directing the group's marketing, sales, and advertising priorities. This means that the chief executive must be willing to relax his own supervision over the divisions and to delegate a meaningful role to the group executive. In addition, it is important for the CEO to not deal directly with the divisions in a manner which undercuts the group manager's role and authority.

Illustration Capsule 13 (continued)

> The key to making the job of group vice president both attractive and effective is finding the middle ground in terms of delegating power to the divisions while at the same time fully utilizing the talents and energies of senior executives at the group level. The right balance needs to be found between the desire for autonomy at the division level and a need to hold the group vice-president at least partly accountable for division performance and group performance.
>
> Source: "The Frustrations of the Group Executive," *Business Week*, September 25, 1978, pp. 102ff.

managerial authority over the employees in each unit/cell of the matrix is shared between the product manager and the functional manager, as shown in Figure 6–6. In a matrix structure, subordinates have a continuing dual assignment: to the product and to their base function.[13] The outcome is a compromise between functional specialization (engineering, R&D, manufacturing, marketing, accounting) and product specialization (where all of the specialized talent needed to produce and sell a given product are assigned to the same divisional unit).

A matrix type organization is a genuinely different structural form and represents a "new way of life." One reason is that the unity of command principle is broken; two reporting channels, two bosses, and shared authority create a new kind of organizational climate. In essence, the matrix is a conflict resolution system through which strategic and operating priorities are negotiated, power is shared, and resources are allocated internally on a "strongest case for what is best overall for the unit" type basis.[14]

The list of companies using some form of a matrix includes General Electric, Texas Instruments, Citibank, Shell Oil, TRW, Bechtel, and Dow Chemical. Its growing popularity is founded on some solid business trends. Firms are turning more and more to strategies that add new sources of diversity (products, markets, technology) to their ranges of activities. Out of this diversity are coming product managers, functional managers, geographic area managers, division managers, and SBU managers—*all* of whom have important *strategic* responsibilities. When product, technology, geography, and business groups all have strategic importance and when their respective strategic priorities are roughly equal, then a matrix organization can be an effective structural form. A matrix form of organization allows for the management of multiple sources of diversity by creating multiple dimensions for

---

[13] A more thorough treatment of matrix organizational forms can be found in Jay R. Galbraith, "Matrix Organizational Designs," *Business Horizons,* vol. 15, no. 1 (February 1971), pp. 29–40.

[14] An excellent critique of matrix organizations is presented in Stanley M. Davis and Paul R. Lawrence, "Problems of Matrix Organizations," *Harvard Business Review,* vol. 56, no. 3 (May–June 1978), pp. 131–42.

FIGURE 6-6
Matrix Organization Structures

A. A defense contractor

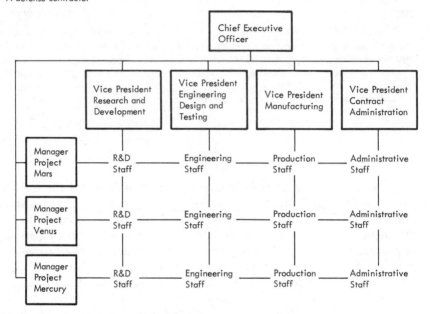

B. A college of business administration

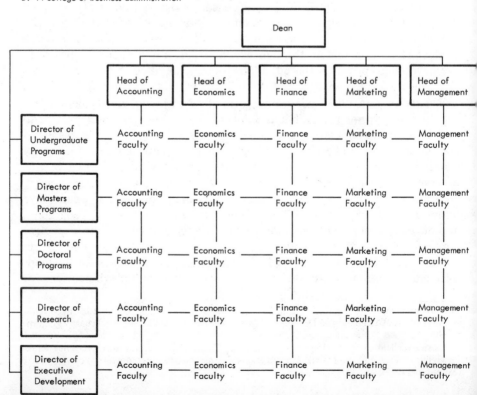

strategic management, with each dimensional manager being responsible for one dimension of strategic initiative. The matrix approach thus allows *each* of several strategic priorities to be managed directly and to be represented in discussions of how the total enterprise (or business unit) can best be managed. In this sense, it helps middle managers make trade-off decisions from a general management perspective.[15] Further, because a manager is assigned line responsibility for attending to an explicit area of strategic concern, a matrix organization can facilitate rapid management recognition of and response to new strategic product-market-technology developments.

Supplemental Methods of Organization

The foregoing structural designs have not proved sufficient to meet completely the diversity of situations and activities confronting contemporary organizations. Many enterprises have responded not only by mixing the basic forms in varying combinations but also by introducing some novel features that effect interesting compromises between the pros and cons of the primary organizational forms. Among these are

1. The *project manager* or *project staff* concept, where a separate, largely self-sufficient subunit is created to oversee the completion of a new activity (setting up a new technological process, bringing out a new product, starting up a new venture, consummating a merger with another company, seeing through the completion of a government contract, supervising the construction of a new plant).[16] Project management has become a relatively popular means of handling "one-of-a-kind" situations having a finite life expectancy and where the normal organization is deemed unable or ill-equipped to achieve the same results in addition to regular duties. On occasions, however, "temporary" projects have proved worthy of becoming made "ongoing," thus resulting in either the elevation of the project unit to "permanent" status or a parceling out of the project's functions to units of the regular organization.

2. The creation of *cross-functional teams* or *task forces* to work on unusual assignments of a problem-solving or innovative nature where there is a need for a pooling of talent and tight integration among specialists. Spe-

---

[15] Ibid., p. 132.

[16] For a more complete treatment of project management, see C. J. Middleton, "How to Set Up a Project Organization," *Harvard Business Review,* vol. 45, no. 2 (March–April 1967), pp. 73–82; George A. Steiner and William G. Ryan, *Industrial Project Management* (New York: The Macmillan Company, 1968); Ivar Avots, "Why Does Project Management Fail," *California Management Review,* vol. 12, no. 1 (Fall 1969), pp. 77–82; C. Reeser, "Human Problems of the Project Form of Organization," *Academy of Management Journal,* vol. 12, no. 4 (December 1969), pp. 459–67; R. A. Goodman, "Ambiguous Authority Definition in Project Management," *Academy of Management Journal,* vol. 10, no. 4 (December 1967), pp. 395–407; and D. L. Wilemon and J. P. Cicero, "The Project Manager-Anomalies and Ambiguities," *Academy of Management Journal,* vol. 13, no. 3 (September 1970), pp. 269–82.

cial task forces provide increased opportunity for creativity, open communication across lines of authority, expeditious conflict resolution, and common identification for coping with the problem at hand, while at the same time facilitating intensified access to the requisite expertise. However, according to Drucker, team organization is more than a temporary expedient for dealing with nonrecurring special problems; he argues that the team is a genuine design principle of organization and is especially good for such permanent organizing tasks as top-management work and innovating work.[17]

3. The *venture team* concept whereby a group is brought together specifically to bring a specific product to market or a specific new business into being. Dow, General Mills, Westinghouse, and Monsanto have used the venture team approach as a regenesis of the entrepreneurial spirit. One difficulty with venture teams is if and when to transfer control of the project back to the regular organization and the problems of discontinuity and shifting purpose which result.[18]

Perspectives on Organization Design

Organization theorists are agreed on two points: (1) there is no such thing as a perfect or ideal organization design and (2) there are no universally applicable panaceas for structuring an organization. Studies of organizations confirm that the same structural design which works well in one organization may not work well in another. What suits one type of strategy can be totally wrong for another. Structures that worked well in the past may not be as suitable for the future. Indeed, firms have a habit of regularly outgrowing their existing organizational form—either an internal shakeup is deemed periodically desirable or else changes in the size and scope of product-market-technology relationships make the firm's structure strategically obsolete. An organization's structure thus is dynamic; changes are not only inevitable but proper.

There is less agreement on whether organization design should commence with a conceptual framework or with a pragmatic consideration of the realities of the situation at hand—the special needs, the constraints imposed by the personalities involved and the way things have been done before. By and large, agonizing over which approach is best is counterproductive; both approaches should be used in parallel. A conceptual framework is essential if structure is to be firmly rooted in the organization's mission, objectives, strategy, and activities. But it must be adapted to the circumstances of the situation.

Yet, there is no one indisputably *best* structure or overriding principle of

---

[17] Drucker, *Management, pp. 564–71.*

[18] Philip Kotler, *Marketing Management: Analysis, Planning, and Control,* 3d ed. (Englewood Cliffs, N.J.: Prentice-Hall, Inc., 1976), pp. 200–201.

design—even for a particular organization at a single moment of time. All of the basic organizational forms have their strengths and weaknesses. Moreover, use of one organizational form does not preclude simultaneous use of others. Many organizations are large enough and diverse enough to employ departmentalization by functional specialty, by geographical area, by process sequence, by market channel, by customer type, and by product group at the same time. Therefore, there can be ample rhyme and reason in organization-building to depart from a slavish adherence to a basic conceptual framework and, thus, accommodate tailoring to the inevitable internal/external exceptions and special situations. Depending on an organization's strategy and stage of development, the general manager is confronted with different sorts of organizational problems and with a need to design a different sort of organizational structure. The critical element of organization building is figuring out how to support the execution of corporate and business strategies with an organization structure that is workable, efficient, pragmatic, and not just "theoretically sound" in terms of its strategy-supporting features.

The prevailing view about the strategic aspects of organization structure is basically a *contingency approach*.[19] Contingency theory states that choice of structure is dependent on the external/internal aspects of the environment in which the firm is operating. The greater the diversity among an organization's products-markets-technologies, the greater the likelihood that the most effective form of organization will be decentralized and multidivisional, as opposed to centralized and functional. Moreover, if an organization uses a continuous process or assembly-line type of technology, then the contingency approach would suggest a larger dose of functionally oriented, centralized principles of organization since common standards of performance as well as tightly sequenced integration is crucial. To use a more decentralized, "free form" organization style where highly interdependent subunits are individualized in their approaches to task accomplishment can make it more difficult to achieve a desirable degree of coordination and integration. Similarly, close and strict government regulation may prompt use of a more mechanistic organization structure, since there necessarily are more rules and procedures which must be observed and, consequently, less room for individualized discretion. On the other hand, if a firm's products are mostly custom-made, there is wide variety in the day-to-day work routine, or if the production process is almost completely automated, then a heavier mix of decentralized and individualized techniques can be more advantageous. From another view, the more uncertain and diverse the organization's product-market environment the more likely will a firm utilize a discretionary, "organic" type approach, the logic being that it is more con-

---

[19] The contingency approach to organization-building has been pioneered by Jay Lorsch and Paul Lawrence of the Harvard Business School. See, for example, P. R. Lawrence and J. W. Lorsch, *Organization and Environment: Managing Differentiation and Integration* (Boston: Division of Research, Harvard Business School, 1967).

Illustration Capsule 14

Selecting Managers to Fit Each Strategy

There is a growing practice in diversified companies to match a manager's personality and skills to the strategy of the line of business or operating division which the person is assigned to manage. The reason stems from a recognition that a manager, because of his own particular talents, experience, and approach to managing, is better suited for some strategic situations than for others. For instance, an entrepreneurial-type manager who has guided a business through the growth stage of the product-industry life cycle and transformed a 5 percent market share into a 25 percent market share might not be the right person to manage the division once demand matures and the division's product line has little growth potential. An entrepreneurial manager's forte is discerning opportunity, capitalizing on existing expansion potential, being creative in product development and innovation, and taking the necessary risks to outmaneuver the competition. But in a mature business, the strategic and operating emphasis tends to be on keeping costs to a minimum, improving productivity, increasing cash flows and profit margins, and maintaining competitive position and market share—managerial tasks which an entrepreneurially oriented manager may not be as skilled at or as well-suited personalitywise to tackle. In a sense, assigning an entrepreneurial manager to run a mature or declining business is akin to moving a star offensive halfback into a defensive guard's slot.

A recent *Business Week* article cited several examples where companies have explicitly tried to match managerial talents, personality, and orientation with the requirements of strategy.

General Electric—Using business portfolio matrix analysis, GE has identified three types of strategies as being appropriate for many of the company's products and businesses; the shorthand labels attached to these three strategies are "grow," "defend," and "harvest" (and are based largely on the perceived stage of the business in the product/industry life cycle). In attempting to match managerial talent and style with the needs of strategy, general managers at GE are being classified by their personalities and managerial orientations as "growers," "caretakers," and "undertakers." According to one "GE-watcher," the company is rumored to have a shortage of "growers" but is making a concerted effort to remove the "undertaker" types who are heading up units with a "grow" strategy.

United Vintners (A subsidiary of Heublein)—In 1977 the company split its wine operations into two divisions, forming a premium wine division to stress quality over volume and a standard wine division to emphasize competitive prices and efficient, high volume production. A wine professional, with previous marketing experience, was chosen to head the premium wine business; but as general manager of the standard wines division, the company brought in a personal products manager from Gillette. The former sales staff was also reorganized along quality versus quantity lines; moreover, in the premium wine group most of the people had wine backgrounds while those in the standard wine business often had backgrounds in consumer products and food companies.

Texas Instruments—According to the manager of strategic planning at TI, "As a product moves through different phases of its life cycle, different kinds of management skills become dominant." Corporate manpower policies reflect belief in this principle and TI takes special pains to match management style and expertise with job needs. TI's president personally reviews the backgrounds and records of the top 20 percent of TI's managers.

Illustration Capsule 14 (continued)

On the other hand, many companies do not accept the idea that strategic performance is improved by a careful matching of strategy and managerial skills. The chairman of Tenneco has expressed a preference for versatile, capable managers: "It doesn't make that much difference to us whether it's a growth business or a stable business per se. Most good managers can run any kind of business."

Source: "Wanted: A Manager to Fit Each Strategy," *Business Week*, February 25, 1980, pp. 166–73.

ducive to adapting organizational subunits to the unique features of their respective subenvironments.[20]

Drucker has summed up the intricacies of organization-building well:

> The simplest organization structure that will do the job is the best one. What makes an organization structure "good" are the problems it does not create. The simpler the structure, the less that can go wrong.
>
> Some design principles are more difficult and problematic than others. But none is without difficulties and problems. None is primarily people-focused rather than task-focused; none is more "creative," "free," or "more democratic." Design principles are tools; and tools are neither good nor bad in themselves. They can be used properly or improperly; and that is all. To obtain both the greatest possible simplicity and the greatest "fit," organization design has to start out with a clear focus on *key activities* needed to produce *key results*. They have to be structured and positioned in the simplest possible design. Above all, the architect of organization needs to keep in mind the purpose of the structure he is designing.[21]

NONSTRUCTURAL CONSIDERATIONS IN ORGANIZING FOR STRATEGIC ACCOMPLISHMENT

There are other organizational considerations besides structure which affect the success of strategy implementation. Two of the more important ones are the development of a distinctive competence and focusing organizational resources on achieving strategic objectives.

Building a Distinctive Competence

The strategic importance of deliberately trying to develop a distinctive competence within an organization stems from the extra contribution which special expertise and a competitive edge make both to performance and to strategic success. To the extent that an organization can build and nurture an

---

[20] Gene W. Dalton, Paul L. Lawrence, and Jay W. Lorsch, *Organization Structure and Design* (Homewood, Ill.: Irwin-Dorsey, 1970), p. 6.

[21] Drucker, *Management*, pp. 601–2.

astutely conceived distinctive competence in its chosen business domains, it creates a golden opportunity for achieving a competitive advantage, gaining market share, and posting a superior record of performance.

In the vast majority of strategically successful enterprises, management will be found to have worked hard at figuring out how to make the organization not just good at what it does but at how it can be *better* than its rivals. This may be accomplished by making special efforts to be more proficient in product development or quality of manufacture or calibre of technical services offered to customers or speed of response to changing customer requirements or any other strategically relevant factor. The point is that in building and staffing the organization, management should make a concerted effort to focus time and money on creating high-performance skills and capabilities in those few select internal areas and activities where superiority can make a real difference to strategic success. Once developed, these strengths become logical cornerstones for successful strategy implementation. Moreover, really distinctive internal skills and capabilities are not easily duplicated by other firms; this means that any differential advantage so gained is likely to have a lasting strategic impact and thus pave the way for above-average performance over the long term. Conscious managerial attention to the task of building strategically relevant internal skills and strengths into the overall organizational scheme is therefore a major element of organization building and effective strategy implementation.

Focusing Organizational Resources on Strategic Objectives

For management to keep an organization results-oriented and pointed in the direction of strategy accomplishment, organizational objectives should become the basis for work and for assignments. In a very real way, strategic objectives help identify the organization's key activities; they set forth organizational priorities; and, thus, they are suggestive of how funds should be allocated and where work efforts should be directed.

One of the guidelines a general manager can follow in determining who should do what is to define jobs and tasks in terms of the desired strategic results and performance rather than simply in terms of the functions to be performed. Specific objectives ought to be developed not only for the organization as a whole but also for each major organizational subunit and, through the efforts of subordinate managers, for each job. Every manager in the organization all the way down to the first-level supervisors needs to have his/her job spelled out in terms of expected results and the objectives to be achieved. While the objective/results setting process need not be an exclusively top-down approach, it is important that there be an emphasis on each person and each organizational unit doing their part to achieve strategic success. Such an approach has the advantage of putting the organizational spotlight on accomplishment of strategy and on achieving the intended performance. It makes clearer the kind of work and effort that can be strategically productive. It relates jobs to the needs of the organization as a whole. Further, it lets people know what is expected of them—from a results perspective instead of a functional effort perspective.

Using strategic objectives as the focal points for work and assignments therefore begins with the question "What sort of performance and results do we want to generate?" Next, it is asked, "What key activities, what organizational units, what tasks, what jobs need to be set up and organized to produce these results?" The answers should suggest the kinds of skills, expertise, staffing, and funding which will be needed to allow the various organizational units to accomplish the designated results. The advantage of a results-oriented approach to the design of organizational tasks and assignments is that it keeps the whole organization trained on implementing and executing strategy. It draws organizationwide attention to the right things to shoot for, rather than risking inadvertent drift and diversion to nonstrategic concerns.

In the final analysis, though, the test of whether an organization is strategically effective is not revealed by astuteness of structure and design or by the care with which the total work effort has been subdivided into jobs and then recombined into coordinated action or by the degree of reliance upon managing by objectives or by the efficiency of internal resource allocation. These things are important but not sufficient. The sufficient condition is that the organization perform up to potential and to expectations. This alone is the most telling measure of effective strategy implementation.

SUGGESTED READINGS

Ansoff, H. Igor, and Brandenberg, Richard.   "A Language for Organizational Design: Part II." *Management Science,* vol. 12, no. 12 (August 1971), pp. B-717–B-731.

Chandler, Alfred D.   *Strategy and Structure.* Cambridge: M.I.T. Press, 1962.

Corey, E. Raymond, and Star, Steven H.   *Organization Strategy: A Marketing Approach.* Boston: Division of Research, Harvard Business School, 1971, chaps. 2–5.

Daniel, D. Ronald.   "Reorganizing for Results." *Harvard Business Review,* vol. 44, no. 6 (November–December 1966), pp. 96–104.

Drucker, Peter.   *Management: Tasks, Responsibilities, Practices.* New York: Harper & Row, Publishers, 1974, chaps. 41–48.

Lawrence, Paul R., and Lorsch, Jay W.   *Organization and Environment: Managing Differentiation and Integration.* Boston: Division of Research, Harvard Business School, 1967.

Leontiades, Milton.   *Strategies for Diversification and Change.* Boston: Little, Brown and Co., 1980, chaps. 2, 3, and 6.

Lorange, Peter.   *Corporate Planning: An Executive Viewpoint.* Englewood Cliffs, N.J.: Prentice-Hall, Inc., 1980, chaps. 2, 4, and 7.

Lorsch, Jay W., and Walker, Arthur H.   "Organizational Choice: Product vs. Function." *Harvard Business Revieew*, vol. 46, no. 6 (November–December 1968), pp. 129–38.

Peters, Thomas J. "Beyond the Matrix Organization." *Business Horizons*, vol. 22, no. 5 (October 1979), pp. 15–27.

Rumelt, Richard. *Strategy, Structure, and Economic Performance.* Cambridge, Mass.: Harvard University Press, 1974.

Salter, Malcolm S. "Stages of Corporate Development." *Journal of Business Policy*, vol. 1, no. 1 (1970), pp. 23–37.

Scott, Bruce R. "The Industrial State: Old Myths and New Realities." *Harvard Business Review*, vol. 51, no. 2 (March–April 1973), pp. 133–48.

Slocum, John W., Jr., and Hellriegel, Don. "Using Organizational Designs to Cope with Change." *Business Horizons*, vol. 22, no. 6 (December 1979), pp. 65–76.

7

STRATEGY IMPLEMENTATION AND ADMINISTRATION: THE DAY-TO-DAY ASPECTS

. . . managerial ability is generally tied quite closely to the particular industry setting in which it develops and operates. A good manager's intuitions, like those of a good card player, come from his long experience with the special rules, technology, and markets of a particular industry.

Joel Dean and Winfield Smith

Nothing makes a prince so much esteemed as the undertaking of great enterprises and the setting of a noble example in his own person.

N. Machiavelli

Given that the organization's structure is suitably keyed to the needs of strategy, the general manager's priorities tend to focus on seeing that prescribed activities and processes are effectively carried out. This means measuring and evaluating organizational and individual performance, overseeing and coordinating day-to-day tasks, creating a timely flow of the right information to the right people, instituting controls to contain deviations from plan, and exercising appropriate leadership and communication skills. All of these functions are important and pose tests of a manager's basic administrative abilities. This chapter highlights how managerial performance of these functions relates to successful strategy implementation and policy administration.

Measuring and Evaluating Performance

A basic element in the job of every general manager is measuring and evaluating performance. Measurement and evaluation are essential to knowing where the organization is in terms of its strategic plan. The starting point is to define what sorts of results constitute effective strategy execution. From these, specific performance measures can be developed for the organization as a whole, for each major subunit, and, ultimately, through the efforts of lower-level managers, for each job. The job of each manager in the organization, from the "big boss" on down to the first-level supervisor, needs to be spelled out in terms of expected results and the objectives to be achieved. Usually, a number of performance criteria will be used, most of which typically are quantifiable but some of which may be subjective; rarely will a single standard suffice. For obvious reasons, the objectives and performance standards attached to each job and each organization unit should always derive from those objectives stressed and implied in the strategic plan.

To the extent that management properly defines the performance expected at each organizational level, the entire organization will tend to be performance and results oriented. Otherwise some degree of confusion and misdirection is guaranteed. Indeed, when managers *fail* to (1) devise ways to measure performance, (2) set standards of accomplishment, (3) indicate minimum acceptable results, (4) assign responsibility for results, and (5) fix deadlines, the stage is set for a shortfall in strategy execution and strategic accomplishment.

The performance standards, once established, must become the *real* basis for evaluating individual efforts and the performance of organizational units. Managers must insist that contributions and results be documented and rigorously compared against standards and objectives. They must be informed and ready to intervene when actual performance falls short of the performance targets specified in the overall strategic plan. Appropriate corrective actions are an obvious general management responsibility whenever negative deviations from plan are encountered. It is not, however, possible to generalize about the form these actions should take, since they ought to be tailored to fit the specifics of the situation. But one precaution can be urged. Management needs to guard against a tendency to acknowledge all activities/products/services as virtuous, worthy of more funding, and essential to continue. When the results and performance of a product/division/ activity are unsatisfactory (because it is out of date, poorly conceived, or ineffective), it should be scrutinized for ways to overhaul it, or, if circumstances demand, to phase it out or abandon it at once. It is in such instances that timely opportunity may exist to shift resources and energies into more productive endeavors. In addition, management is well-advised to use the time for evaluating actual performance also as a time for regularly reviewing and appraising whether the organization is doing the right things.

Motivation and Rewards.   Proper motivation and the rewarding of good performance are key ingredients of strategy implementation. Obviously it is important for organizational subunits and individuals to have a reasonably strong commitment to the achievement of the enterprise's objectives and overall strategy. Motivation is brought about most fundamentally by the organization's reward-punishment structure—salary raises, bonuses, stock options, fringe benefits, promotions (or fear of demotions), assurance of not being "sidelined" and ignored, praise, recognition, criticism, tension, fear, more (or less) responsibility, increased (or decreased) job control or autonomy, the promise of attractive locational assignments, and the bonds of group acceptance. As the foregoing suggests, motivational incentives can be positive or negative in nature. They may also be intrinsic, as in the case of the increased self-respect and gratification which comes with achieving an objective or solving a tough problem.

The prevailing view is that a good motivational system allows for blended fulfillment of both organizational and personal objectives. No doubt this is a useful guideline. But, in practice, it is a ticklish task to gear the size of an individual's rewards to a corresponding contribution to organization objectives; rewards may be excessive, target achievement levels set too low, or contributions unrecognized and mismeasured. More often, though, the opposite is true, as suggested by the way Harold Geneen, former president and chief executive officer of ITT, allegedly combined the use of money, tension, and fear:

> Geneen provides his managers with enough incentives to make them tolerate the system. Salaries all the way through ITT are higher than average—Geneen reckons 10 percent higher—so that few people can leave without taking a drop. As one employee put it: "We're all paid just a bit more than we think we're worth." At the very top, where the demands are greatest, the salaries and stock options are sufficient to compensate for the rigors. As someone said, "He's got them by their limousines."
>
> Having bound his men to him with chains of gold, Geneen can induce the tension that drives the machine. "The key to the system," one of his men explained, "is the profit forecast. Once the forecast has been gone over, revised and agreed on, the managing director has a personal commitment to Geneen to carry it out. That's how he produces the tension on which the success depends." The tension goes through the company, inducing ambition, perhaps exhilaration, but always with some sense of fear: what happens if the target is missed?[1]

It goes without saying that if and when an organization's structure of rewards and punishments induces too much tension, anxiety, and job insecurity that the results can be counterproductive. Yet, it is doubtful whether it is ever useful to completely eliminate tension, fear, anxiety and insecurity from the motivational system; there is, for example, no evidence that "the quiet life" is highly correlated with superior performance. On the contrary, high-performing organizations usually require an endowment of ambitious people who relish the opportunity to climb the ladder of success, who have a need for stimulation (or who want to avoid boredom), and who thus find some

---

[1] Anthony Sampson, *The Sovereign State of ITT* (New York: Stein and Day, Publishers, 1973), p. 132.

Illustration Capsule 15

The Mysteries of Motivation

The eminently successful Paul W. Bryant, head football coach at the University of Alabama, tells of the time he unwittingly motivated a team just prior to game time:

When I was at Kentucky I got booed one night by a group of students who came to the train to see us off for a game with Cincinnati. I had fired some of our star players and they didn't like that. And we'd lost three of our first five games and they didn't like that either, which I can understand. I didn't like it myself. In fact, I hated it. For a young coach—which I was then—so keyed up I couldn't get to work in the morning without vomiting along the way, it was not exactly heaven on earth. The Cincinnati game took on added importance.

Cincinnati had fine teams then, coached by Sid Gillman, who has been a big name in the pros and is with the Houston Oilers now. What I'm about to say should not be taken as a lack of respect for Sid. You have to appreciate that my collar was tighter than it is now.

We got to the stadium at Cincinnati and I sensed something was wrong. When we went out to warm up for the game there was nobody in the stands. Just a few handfuls scattered around. I thought for a minute I was in the wrong place. When we finished our warm-up and the Cincinnati team still hadn't made an appearance, I said to Carney Laslie, one of my original assistant coaches, "What's that no-good conniving smart-aleck"—meaning the eminent Coach Gillman—"up to now? What the hell is that damn thief trying to pull?"

Carney just shook his head. He was as dumbfounded as I was.

I ordered the team back into the locker room—and then it dawned on me. I'd screwed up the schedule. We were an hour early.

I was too embarrassed to tell what I knew. I just walked around, up and down the aisles where the players sat waiting, my big old farmer's boots making the only noise in there. I couldn't think of anything to say, so I didn't say a word. For an hour I clomped up and down. Finally, when I'd used up enough time I delivered a one-sentence pep talk, the only thing I could think to say:

"Let's go."

They almost tore the door down getting out. Cincinnati was favored that day, but it was no contest. We won, 27–7.

Bryant tells of a second instance when coaching at Texas A&M where an approach he tried worked on one occasion but apparently failed when someone else tried it.

They'd been dead all week in practice before the SMU game, and I wondered, what could we do? What was left to try? I'd run out of ways to motivate them. Elmer Smith, one of my assistants, said he remembered one time when he was playing for Ivan Grove at Hendrix College. Grove woke him up at midnight and read him something about how a mustard seed could move a mountain if you believed in it, something Norman Vincent Peale, or somebody, had taken from the Bible and written in a little pamphlet. It impressed me.

I didn't tell a soul. At 12 o'clock on Thursday night I called everyone on my staff and told them to meet me at the dormitory at 1 o'clock. When they got there, I said, OK, go get the players real quick, and they went around shaking them, and the boys came stumbling in there, rubbing their eyes, thinking I'd finally lost my mind. And I read 'em that little thing about the mustard seed—just three sentences—turned around, and walked out.

Illustration Capsule 15 (*continued*)

> Well, you never know if you are doing right or wrong, but we went out and played the best game we'd played all year. SMU should have beaten us by 40 points, but they were lucky to win, 6–3. In the last minute of play we had a receiver wide open inside their 20-yard line, but our passer didn't see him.
>
> Several years after that, Darrell Royal called me from Texas. He was undefeated, going to play Rice and worried to death. He said he'd never been in that position before, undefeated and all, and his boys were lazy and fatheaded, and he wanted to know what to do about it.
>
> I said, "Well, Darrell, there's no set way to motivate a team, and the way I do it may be opposite to your way but I can tell you a story." And I gave him that thing about the mustard seed. He said, by golly, he'd try it.
>
> Well, I don't know whether he did or not, but I remember the first thing I wanted to do Sunday morning was get that paper and see how Texas made out. Rice won, 34–7.
>
> Source: Paul W. Bryant and John Underwood, *Bear: The Hard Life and Good Times of Alabama's Coach Bryant* (Boston: Little, Brown and Company, 1974), pp. 3–4, 6–7.

degree of position anxiety useful in order to satisfy their own drives for personal recognition, accomplishment, and self-satisfaction.

Instilling a Spirit of Performance

One test of administrative effectiveness lies in management's ability to perceive what each employee can do well and what he or she cannot. A good manager works at developing employees' strengths, neutralizing their respective weaknesses, and building upon and blending the individual skills of employees in ways that cause employees to perform consistently at or near peak capability. When successfully done, the outcome is a spirit of high performance and an emphasis on excellence and achievement.

Such a spirit of performance, sometimes referred to as "morale," should not be confused with whether employees are "happy" or "satisfied" or whether they "get along well together." An organization whose approach to "human relations" and "dealing with people" is not grounded in high standards of performance actually has poor human relations and a management that is liable to produce a mean spirit.[2] Certainly, there is no greater indictment of an organization than that of allowing or fostering an atmosphere in which the outstanding performances of a few people become a threat to the whole group and a source of controversy, backstabbing, and attempts to enforce safe mediocrity.

For an organization to be instilled with and sustain a spirit of performance, it must maintain a focus on achievement and on excellence. It must

---

[2] Peter F. Drucker, *Management: Tasks, Responsibilities, Practices,* (New York: Harper & Row, Publishers, 1974), p. 455.

strive at developing a consistent ability to produce results over prolonged periods of time. It must be alert to opportunities and seek to capitalize upon them. It must succeed in utilizing the full range of rewards and punishment (pay, promotion, assignments, tension, pressure, job security, and so on) to establish and enforce standards of excellence.

Particularly must management have the courage and willingness to remove people who consistently render poor or mediocre performance. Such people should, if for no other reason, be removed for their own good since people who find themselves in a job they cannot handle are usually frustrated, anxiety-ridden, harassed, and unhappy.[3] One does not do a person a favor by keeping him in a job he is not equal to. Moreover, subordinates have a right to be managed with competence, dedication, and achievement; unless their boss performs well, they themselves cannot perform well.[4] In general, then, an organization should not have to tolerate managers who fail to perform; they should be "sidetracked," or in extreme cases dismissed, so as not to undercut either the implementation of strategy or the careers of subordinates. One well-known proponent of this approach was General George C. Marshall, chief of staff of the U.S. Army in World War II.[5] Marshall reportedly said, "I have a duty to the soldiers, their parents, and the country, to remove immediately any commander who does not satisfy the highest performance standards." He repeatedly upheld this duty, actually removing a number of commanders from assignments. But when he did, he followed it up with the recognition that, "It was my mistake to have put this or that man in a command that was not the right command for him. It is therefore *my* job to think through where he belongs."

The toughest cases, of course, concern the need to reassign people who have given long and loyal service to the organization but who are past their prime and unable to deal effectively with demanding situations. The decision in such cases should be objectively based upon what is best for the company—which usually means removing the person from his or her job. Yet, it can be done in a compassionate and human fashion. When Henry Ford II was trying to revive Ford Motor Company after World War II, he felt that none of the nine top-management people in one key division were competent enough to handle new jobs created by reorganization.[6] Not one was appointed to the newly created positions. But while their incompetence was undisputed and it would have been easy to fire them, the fact remained that they had served loyally through trying periods. Ford took the position that while no one should be allowed to hold a job he or she could not perform in superior fashion, neither should anyone be penalized for the mistakes of the previous regime. So, the nine men were assigned as experienced technicians

---

[3] Ibid., p. 457.

[4] Ibid.

[5] As cited by Drucker, *Management,* p. 459.

[6] This example is drawn from Drucker, *Management,* 459.

and experts to jobs they could be expected to do well. As things turned out, seven of the men did well in their new assignments—one so well that he was later promoted into a more important job than originally held. The other two failed; the older one was given early retirement and the younger one was dismissed. A management that is concerned with building excellent organizational spirit takes the cases of loyal nonperformers seriously because, while they are (or should be) few in number, they have a major impact on morale and how their cases are handled tells others in the organization much about management's character and respect for its employees.

Two additional considerations weigh heavily on whether an organization attains a spirit of high performance in implementing the chosen strategy.[7] The first concerns the extent to which an organization is pointed toward capitalizing on opportunity as opposed to solving existing problems. An organization is prone to have higher morale and an acceptance of challenge when top priority is given to converting opportunities into results. Concentrating on solving problems tends to detract from an organization's momentum and to put it on "hold" until the problems at hand are solved or else brought under control. In contrast, an attitude of "damn the torpedoes, full steam ahead" works to keep the attention of the organization focused on generating the greatest impact on results and performance—an orientation which, in many circumstances, acts to enhance strategy implementation.

The second consideration which affects an organization's spirit of performance is the reward-punishment structure. Decisions on pay, on assignments, and on promotion are management's *foremost* "control" device. These decisions signal who is getting ahead and who is not, who is climbing up the ladder fastest, and who is perceived as doing a good job. They signal what sort of behavior and performance management wants, values, and rewards. Such decisions seldom escape the closest scrutiny of every member of the organization. If anything, an organization will overreact to these kinds of management decisions. What management may view as an innocuous move to solve an interpersonal conflict or to bypass an organizational obstacle may be interpreted as a sign that management wants one kind of behavior while preaching another. Hence, a good manager must be ever alert to his or her decisions on placement, pay, and promotion. They should be based on a factual record of performance as measured against explicit standards—never on "potential" or friendship or expediency or casual opinions. They should reflect careful thinking, clear policy and procedures, and high standards of fairness and equity.

Drucker offers a number of personal characteristics in a manager which can undermine a spirit of high performance:

A lack of integrity.
A lack of character.
Cynicism.

---

[7] Ibid., pp. 460–61.

Emphasizing the negative aspect of what subordinates cannot do (their weaknesses) rather than the positive aspects of what they can do (their strengths).
Being more interested in "who is right?" than "what is right?"
Being afraid of strong (high-performing) subordinates.
Not setting high standards for one's own work.
Valuing intelligence more highly than integrity.[8]

Obviously a management interested in nurturing a spirit of high performance and accomplishment should endeavor to weed out managers and candidate managers who display such characteristics.

Finding the "Right" Style of Managerial Leadership

The litany of good leadership is simple enough: plan, decide, organize, direct, control, win![9] Obviously, any organization benefits from having people who are able to "take charge" and serve as both "spark plug" and "ramrod" in implementing strategy. Leadership is exemplified by those who are known as "the movers" and "the shakers" in the organization. Yet the ability to exercise extraordinary leadership is rare; not many managers are skilled in the art of inducing subordinates to accomplish their assignments with eagerness, enthusiasm, and to the maximum of their ability. Moreover, as head of an organization or organization subunit, a manager is called upon to play numerous roles: taskmaster, crisis solver, policymaker, decision-maker, spokesman, figurehead, resource allocator, negotiator, motivator, inspirationist, and so on. In carrying out these roles, no one leadership style or managerial approach is likely to suffice. For example, sometimes it will prove useful to be authoritarian and hardnosed; at other times a participative, collegial approach may work best.

In general, the problem of managerial leadership is one of devising effective ways to initiate, direct, facilitate, change, and inspire; the desired effect is to lift aspirations, raise performance to higher levels, and develop people to their fullest. But it is equally important to understand what managerial leadership is not. It is not *necessarily* having a magnetic personality or charisma. It is not winning friends and influencing people. It is not being likable, loved, and well thought of. On the contrary, history describes a number of renowned leaders as demanding, arrogant, obstreperous, or hard to get along with—Napoleon, Patton, and Queen Elizabeth I serve as examples. A study of noted business executives would, no doubt, yield similar conclusions. The key to understanding managerial leadership seems to hinge more on what leaders do rather than on their personal traits.

Studies of managerial leadership reveal four basic approaches: autocratic, participative, instrumental, and "great person." The autocratic manager tends to command, to be dogmatic, positive, and confident, and to rely upon

---

[8] Ibid., p. 462.

[9] Jay Hall, "To Achieve or Not: The Manager's Choice," *California Management Review*, vol. 18, no. 4 (Summer 1976), p. 5.

authority and discipline; he leads through his control over rewards and punishment. The participative manager believes that people will work hard and accomplish their assignments best when supervised in a manner that lets them use their own initiative, be independent, contribute their ideas, and participate in decisions; participative leaders act as "coordinators" instead of bosses and endeavor to treat subordinates as "self-starters." The instrumental-type manager is a pragmatist who favors using whatever approach or technique will best get the job done; the instrumental manager may use autocratic or participative approaches but the emphasis is on the central task of allocating human and organizational resources in the most effective, efficient manner. The instrumental leader is skillful in arousing support and developing a consensus, in working with people, in achieving objectives and results on schedule, and in making the right things happen. The essence of the instrumental approach is that those who manage well are also effective as leaders. The "great person" concept of leadership is a combination instrumental-participative pattern whereby the manager exhibits balanced concern both for people and for production, but does so in ways which exemplify vision, a grand design, and innovative plans calling for major changes and progress. The great person pattern is a heroic leadership style and suggests that such persons are "natural" or "born" leaders who most likely will be successful leaders in any situation.

Although the historical position of most behavioral scientists has been anti-authoritarian and pro-participative management, the increasingly widespread view is that for managers, as leaders, to be effective they should utilize whatever leadership posture or style is best for them in that situation quite irrespective of whether it is strongly authoritarian or strongly participative or somewhere in between.[10] More specifically, it is held that effective

---

[10] Drucker, for one, has launched a powerful attack on some of the psychological aspects underlying participative management styles (represented most prominently by McGregor's Theory Y) and suggests that managers are correct in being leery of it. Drucker describes Theory Y management as "enlightened psychological despotism" and a "repugnant form of tyranny." According to Drucker,

"Most, if not all, of the recent writers on industrial psychology profess allegiance to Theory Y. They use terms like 'self-fulfillment,' 'creativity,' and 'the whole man.' But what they talk and write about is control through psychological manipulation. They are led to this by their basic assumptions, which are precisely the Theory X assumptions: man is weak, sick and incapable of looking after himself. He is full of fears, anxieties, neuroses, inhibitions. Essentially he does not want to achieve but wants to fail. He therefore wants to be controlled. Indeed, for his own good he needs to be controlled—not by fear and incentive of material rewards but through his fear of psychological alienation and the incentive of 'psychological security.'
". . . The manager, if one listens to the psychologists, will have to have insight into all kinds of people. He will have to be in command of all kinds of psychological techniques. He will have to have empathy for all his subordinates. He will have to understand an infinity of individual personality structures, individual psychological needs, and individual psychological problems."

Such an approach, Drucker alleges, supposedly makes psychological control by the manager "unselfish" and in the worker's own interest but, more importantly, by becoming his workers'

managers will tend to vary their leadership techniques as people, tasks, organization environment, and the requirements of strategy vary. This "contingency approach" to leadership is based on growing research evidence (as well as intuitive management opinion) that different kinds of organization groups, given their different tasks and staffing "personalities," function best when they are structured and managed and led in quite different and distinct ways.[11] For example, it makes sense that a manager's leadership behavior in implementing organization strategy will be influenced according to whether:

He feels strongly that individuals should have a voice in making decisions which affect them.

He has confidence in subordinates' qualifications to handle the problem issue on their own.

He feels more comfortable functioning in a directive role or in a team role.

Subordinates exhibit relatively high needs for independence.

Subordinates are experienced enough to make responsible decisions.

Subordinates prefer to be given clear-cut directives or whether they wish to have wider areas of freedom.

Subordinates are interested in the problem and wish to have a voice in solving it.

Subordinates expect to share in decision making.

Subordinates work together as a unit effectively.

There is severe time pressure for immediate action.

The size of organizational subunits, their geographical distribution, and the degree of intraorganizational cooperation required to attain goals and objectives are such as to preclude use of authoritarian (or participative) practices.

There is a need for confidentiality.

The organizational climate is flexible enough to allow for deviation from what higher-ups have established as approved behavior.[12]

In deciding what kind of leadership pattern to employ in strategy implementation, the manager may find it useful to ask two questions of himself:

---

psychological servant the manager retains control as their boss. The effect, says Drucker, is to substitute persuasion for command, psychological manipulation for the carrot of financial rewards, and empathy for the fear of being punished.

Drucker maintains that such an approach is not only contemptuous but also will cause the manager-psychologist to undermine his own authority. Why? Because the integrity of the manager stems from his commitment to the work of the organization and any manager who pretends that the personal needs of subordinates, rather the objective needs of the task, determine what should be done is apt not to be believed and, therefore, risks losing his integrity and his subordinates' respect. See Drucker, *Management*, pp. 243–45.

[11] E. P. Learned and A. T. Sproat, *Organization Theory and Policy* (Homewood, Ill.: Richard D. Irwin, 1966), p. 61.

[12] Robert Tannenbaum and Warren H. Schmidt, "How to Choose a Leadership Pattern," *Harvard Business Review*, vol. 36, no. 2 (March–April 1958), pp. 98–100.

(1) Have I gotten the ideas and suggestions of everyone who has the necessary knowledge to make a significant contribution to the solution of the problem? and (2) What can the organization do and what can I do to help my subordinates the most in doing a superior job? He may also find it useful to ask subordinates what *they* can do to help him, as their manager, do the best job for the organization.

Two additional guidelines for managing in a leadership situation also deserve emphasis. First, a manager should always exhibit the traits of honesty and integrity in all of his dealings; without these, the respect of subordinates will not be long forthcoming. Second, the more a manager understands what motivates his subordinates and the more he uses these motivations in carrying out his managerial activities, the more effective as a leader he is likely to be.[13]

Instituting Management Controls

The role of management controls is to provide systematic verification of whether strategy implementation is proceeding in accordance with plan. Is the strategy being put in place on schedule? Are goals and objectives being met? Are the established policies being followed and are they effective? Have appropriate standards of performance been set? What sorts of deviations from these standards are being experienced? Is the strategy (and its accompanying set of policies) working?

The purpose of management controls is to provide feedback on the accomplishment of strategy: this includes pointing out weaknesses in standards (whether they are clear and realistic), uncovering and correcting negative deviations from agreed-upon standards, and preventing their recurrence. The desired effect is to carry out organizational activities smoothly, properly, and according to high standards. The whole concept of management control is therefore normative and concerned with what ought to be.

Controls are necessary because the structure of an organization, by itself, is never "tight" enough to ensure the proper commitment to and execution of organization strategy and policy. Organizational subunits have their own substrategies which are at least slightly deflected from the overall organizational strategy. Moreover, individuals have their own career goals and needs, as well as their own perceptions of strategy. Internal politics and rivalry among subunits and professional groups introduce still other possibilities for misdirection. Such happenings and considerations are all quite normal—even in high-performing organizations manned by people of competence and goodwill who are informed as to strategy and policy. As a consequence, the performance of individuals and subunits cannot be left to chance. And, understandably, the thrust of the control process is on goal-

---

[13] Harold Koontz and Cyril O'Donnell, *Principles of Management: An Analysis of Managerial Functions* (New York: McGraw-Hill, 1972), p. 559.

setting, standard-setting, measuring, comparing, and taking corrective action.

In designing a set of control devices, the manager should keep one principle firmly in mind—*controls follow strategy*. Unless controls are means to strategy accomplishment, there is undue risk of wrong action and "miscontrol." The following guidelines are recommended:[14]

1. Controls should be economical and involve only the *minimum* amount of information needed to give a reliable picture of what is going on. In general, the less effort and fewer control devices which have to be created to maintain the desired standards, the better and more effective the control design: too many controls create confusion.
2. Controls should seek to measure only meaningful events (sales volume, product mix, market standing, productivity rates) or symptoms of potentially significant developments (lower profit margins, higher rates of turnover, and absenteeism). Controls should relate to key objectives, key activities, and priority considerations rather that the mass of trivia and events which are marginal to strategic performance and results.
3. Controls should report the variables being measured in ways which reveal the real structure of the situation and which are grounds for action. For example, reporting the *number* of grievances per thousand employees does not indicate the *importance* of the grievances in terms of the impacts on morale and performance.
4. Controls should be geared to provide information on a timely basis—not too late to take corrective action nor so often as to confuse and overburden.
5. Controls should be kept simple. Voluminous control manuals and complicated reports are likely to misdirect and obscure because of the attention that has to be paid to mechanics, procedures, and interpretive guidelines instead of to what is being measured. Moreover, the measures reported should be in a form that is suitable for the recipient and tailored to his needs.
6. Controls should be oriented toward taking corrective action rather than just providing interesting information. It is debatable whether reports or studies should receive wide distribution ("for your information"), but they should without fail reach the persons who can take action by virtue of their position in the decision structure.
7. Controls should, for the most part, aim at pinpointing the "exceptions"; this allows management to zero in on the significant departures from norm.

---

[14] Drucker, *Management,* pp. 498–504; Harold Koontz, "Management Control: A Suggested Formulation of Principles." *California Management Review,* vol. 2, no. 2 (Winter 1959), pp. 50–55: William H. Sihler, "Toward Better Management Control Systems," *California Management Review,* vol. 14, no. 2 (Winter 1971), pp. 33–39.

When corrective action is required, it is better for management to respond in ways which do not dampen initiative and spirit of performance. To dwell on finding errors and mistakes in subordinates' work encourages them to play it safe, "cover up" difficulties, and use political tactics to stay on the boss's good side. Attention shifts from doing things better to avoiding doing things wrong. One approach to get around this pitfall is to give as much attention to favorable variances as to unfavorable variances in control reviews. In other words, positive reinforcement, incentives, and rewards for performance above standards may in some situations be as effective in reducing negative deviations as are various forms of criticism, punishment, and disciplinary action. This gets back to the most fundamental control device of all—management's use of the reward-punishment structure.

Communication and Management Control

It is management's job, of course, to communicate the organization's strategy and the plans and policies for implementing it to all members of the organization. That this must be done and done effectively requires no further elaboration. But it is worth noting that the control process provides a way of thinking about and approaching the task of informing members of the organization of the objectives to be achieved, how these relate to strategy, and the relative priorities that various tasks should have. Control devices should clearly signal the kinds of results and behavior expected. And periodic reviews of the organizational unit's performance, together with the manager's periodic reviews of individual job performance with his or her subordinates, offer a golden opportunity to (a) evaluate standards of performance with employees, (b) review results on the job, (c) analyze the reasons for these results, (d) discuss plans for increasing on-the-job effectiveness, (e) consider each job incumbent's potential for advancement, (f) prepare plans, programs, and budgets for the coming year, and (g) agree on specific standards and objectives for periods ahead.

Problem Areas in Managing People

How well, or how poorly a manager manages people, is a major factor in the implementation of strategy and, ultimately, in the strategy's success. Unfortunately, there is no neat formula of "five steps to follow" in managing people. Proper motivation and effective leadership, as discussed above, are plainly important. But during the course of strategy implementation there are also a number of questions relating to organization personnel and management which need to be asked regularly and the current practices reevaluated:

1. What type and quality of personnel does the organization now have and how does this compare with what it will need in the future? Is management competent to meet the challenges ahead? What are management's

Illustration Capsule 16

United Airline's System of Management Controls

As early as the mid-1950s, United Airlines had a computer-assisted system of reporting and controls which resulted not only in the chief executive officer having a profit and loss statement every 24 hours but also provided operating heads with up-to-the-hour information on how to respond to weather and passenger load patterns. According to an article in *Nation's Business* by Philip Gustafson:

The statement has its birth every day in the statistical production room at United's Denver operating base. Passenger and cargo volumes, collected from each flight, are combined at the end of the day. The results are wired to United's Chicago offices ready for processing at 8:30 A.M. Economic research employees apply revenue rates predetermined by experience and expense rates based on current operating budget requirements to the previous day's volume appearing on the wire. Within an hour, an operating profit or loss is estimated and passed on to top management.

The daily report shows the day's operating profit or loss along with a month and year to date accumulation. Also, daily revenue passenger-miles and the passenger load factor are given. Data are broken down in such a way as to give the passenger department information on which to decide whether to put more planes on the Chicago to San Francisco run or advertise to get additional passengers.

An intrinsic part of United's reporting system is what company executives like to call "the room with the 14,000-mile view." This is an information and planning center at Denver which is the business world's equivalent of the military briefing room. Facts funneled daily into this center present a clear picture of operations throughout United's 80-city system.

In keeping with the idea of expansive vision, the room has glass walls on one side. Modern white plastic chairs are grouped before a map of the United States, 8 feet high and 20 feet wide, on which United's routes are outlined. Colored lights (red for weather, green for maintenance, and white for passengers) at major terminals show current operating conditions. If the red light glows steadily, for example, it means adverse weather, if it is flashing, the weather is marginal. Electric clocks above the map show the time in each zone through which United operates.

The room is designed to provide management with operational facts in the most convenient form. Data, such as mileage flown, delays at terminals by type of plane and total number of departures, are posted on lucite panels, flanking the map. Dozens of supplementary charts deal with payload volumes and load factors, weather, actual performance as compared with schedule and related information.

Daily at 8:30 A.M., MST, United's operations executives meet in the room for a 14,000-mile view. Four briefing specialists review operations of the past 24 hours and outline what the next 24 are expected to bring. The opening summary is presented by a meterologist who analyzes the decisive factors in yesterday's weather conditions from the Atlantic seaboard to the Hawaiian Islands. He then gives his forecast for the next 24 hours, accenting developments which may affect operations.

A mechanical specialist follows with information on the status of the company's fleet. He reports the number and types of aircraft withdrawn from service

Illustration Capsule 16 (continued)

for overhaul and comments on the progress of various engineering projects at the San Francisco base.

A traffic specialist then gives a resumé of the previous day's performance in terms of any customer service problems which arose. Approximately 750 plane departures are scheduled daily. Those which deviate from schedule are spotlighted for management study to prevent possible recurrence.

The remaining gaps in the 14,000-mile view are filled in by a flight operations specialist who discusses the availability of equipment, and weather outlook on the line. The session then adjourns. Immediately afterwards, some department chiefs may call their staffs together to act on particular facets of the day's operating plan.

Source: Philip Gustafson, "Business Reports: How to Get Facts You Need," *Nation's Business*, vol. 44, no. 8 (August 1956), pp. 78–82.

strengths and weaknesses? What are the ages of key executives and personnel? Will there be adequate replacements at retirement?

2. How and from where will the organization recruit new personnel? Is the organization attracting the right kinds of people to fill entry level positions? Is the organization attracting and keeping qualified personnel? Is there a high turnover rate among good employees at lower levels? To what extent should the organization promote from within or recruit from the outside?

3. Does the organization have a "key executive" problem—i.e., an executive without a replacement? To what extent would operations be impaired if something happened to the key executive?

4. Are the organization's personnel adequately trained? Is formal on-the-job training needed? Do new employees have trouble understanding what is expected of them?

5. How well are employees, including managers, performing? Does the appraisal system really measure performance or is it simply an exercise which management goes through to comply with organization procedures? Are promotable persons being identified through the appraisal system? Are those who need more training or better training being identified?

6. In what ways should people be compensated? Is the compensation structure adequate? Are compensation rewards correctly geared to the sought-for results and performance? Are those employees (and managers) perceived as "high-performing" or as "key executives" better compensated than other employees at their level? Are material rewards relied upon too heavily as the main (or only) positive motivator?

7. How should the performance of managers be evaluated? (This is not a small matter when one considers that the manager's job description includes such phrases as "maintaining relationships with," "supervising

the operation of," "having responsibility for," and such activities as coordinating, problem solving, and administering—all of which lack concreteness and ready measurement.) To what extent should complexity of the work, general education and technical training required, the scope of responsibility for people and property, and the effect of the manager's decisions and activities upon profits (or other desired outcomes) be balanced against performance in determining the manager's compensation package? What relationship should the compensation of managers and executives have with the monetary reward paid to others in the organization?

8. To what extent should the general manager manage his subordinates through personal contact and direct intervention, offering his own ideas and inputs and getting involved in day-to-day matters? Or, should he reject the "playing coach" approach and place greater reliance on instituting the necessary guidelines via formal planning, budgeting, control, and compensation systems? How far should he go in staying out of daily operating activities by delegating authority to subordinates?

Playing "The Power Game"

All organizations are political. The drives and ambitions to climb the ladder of career achievement and success, the conflicts and coalitions that evolve in translating goals into action and on into results, and the hierarchical divisions of responsibility and authority combine to guarantee the existence of a political atmosphere. Positions of power and weakness are inevitable and the people involved are neither likely to be indifferent to power relationships nor passive in their own maneuvering and use of power. Jockeying for position is a normal activity. After all, careers, prestige, and egos are at stake, not to mention material rewards.

On occasions, therefore, ambition, personal biases, and favoritism may overrule "objective" analysis; conceivably, unscrupulous actions and unethical behavior may arise, together with selfish attempts to "feather one's own nest." One cannot assume that virtue guarantees rewards nor that doing a good job suffices for promotion. This is not to say that organizations are a political jungle with much effort put into political maneuvering and thinking up new power plays. Such can occur, but it is the exception not the rule. Usually, organizational politics is kept within bounds and does not deteriorate into wholesale plotting and schemes, backstabbing, and dissension. Yet, it would be naïve to presume that a manager can be effective and get ahead without being perceptive about internal politics and being adept at playing the power game. Like it or not, managers need to be sensitive to the political environment in the organization.

Middle-level managers are particularly susceptible to political considerations. Higher level executives measure success in terms of results; they tend to be less interested in how the results are produced. The middle manager's performance thus often hinges on how well the results of his or her actions match the general directives from above to get the job done.[15] But in the course of translating these general directives into concrete action to be followed by first-level managers and technical unit heads, middle managers are vulnerable to heavy flak from both sides. They are caught between pressure from above for results to make their bosses look good and the need for the goodwill and cooperation of their own subordinates (plus other organizational subunits on which they must rely for support) to carry out their assignments. It is difficult for middle managers to shift blame or make excuses when things do not work out well. Hence, they are thrust into walking a political tight-rope, seeking compromise and workability between the goals of subordinates (whose cooperation is required) and the goals of superiors (whose approval is needed to get ahead). If they want to maintain the loyalty and respect of subordinates, middle managers must represent their interests and be willing "to go to bat" for them when the occasion demands. Middle managers must understand the organization's power structure and be sensitive to the direction of political winds. They need to ask themselves a series of questions: Who are my friends and who are my enemies? Who can I count on in a showdown or when the going gets tough? Whose opinions really count and whose can be ignored? Which department and division heads have the most influence and the most clout in shaping decisions? With whom should I develop strong alliances? On what issues do I need to take a stand and be willing "to rock the boat" if necessary and on what should I accept the status quo? Given the way the system works, am I better off with a job assignment in a nonkey activity where I can be a "star performer" (perhaps outshining a weak boss) or with a job assignment in an area "where the action is" (perhaps working directly for someone who is reliably reported to be "on their way up")?[16] To what extent should I strive for positions with high visibility and exposure to higher level executives?

The Ingredients of Successful Strategy Implementation

By now it should be evident that the managerial tasks of implementing and executing the chosen strategic plan are expansive. Virtually every aspect of

---

[15] Middle managers are seldom told how to get their jobs done in specific terms. The guidelines they receive from higher-ups regarding sales or profits, carving out a bigger market share, or getting by on a smaller budget are mostly general and, so long as organizational policies are observed, the boss's attitude is most likely to be "I don't care how you do it, just get it done—and on time." In other words, the specifics are delegated to the next level down and it ends up the middle manager's job to figure out how what plans and concrete actions will be needed to generate the desired results. It is the middle manager, more than anyone else, who translates financial, sales, production, and strategic goals and objectives into a day-to-day operating plan and, then, communicates it in functional-specialist language to the technical, detail-oriented, first-line supervisors.

[16] For a discussion of how to climb to higher ranks in an organization, see Ross A. Webber, "Career Problems of Young Managers," *California Management Review*, vol. 18, no. 4 (Summer 1976), pp. 19–33.

Illustration Capsule 17

Playing the Power Game the Machiavellian Way

Niccolo Machiavelli, in his classic *The Prince,* presented a manual of methods and tactics in the acquisition and use of power. *The Prince* is full of straightforward, bitter truths about the drive for power and the realities of human motivation. Some say that *The Prince* is diabolical; others call it insightful and utterly realistic in its portrayal of human nature. Whatever adjectives one chooses to apply, there is no denying it as one of the most influential books ever written.

Although Machiavelli's study of power politics was addressed specifically to political rulers, the lessons apply equally well to management. Indeed, if in reading the excerpts below one will simply substitute "manager" for "prince" (or its equivalent), then the relevance of Machiavelli to modern management can be readily approached:

. . . men must either be cajoled or crushed; for they will revenge themselves for slight wrongs, while for grave ones thay cannot. The injury therefore that you do to a man should be such that you need not fear his revenge.

. . . in taking possession of a state the conqueror should well reflect as to the harsh measures that may be necessary, and then execute them at a single blow, so as not to be obliged to renew them every day; and by thus not repeating them, to assure himself of the support of the inhabitants, and win them over to himself by benefits bestowed. . . . Cruelties should be committed all at once, as in that way each separate one is less felt, and gives less offense; benefits, on the other hand, should be conferred one at a time, for in that way they will be more appreciated.

. . . he who, contrary to the will of the people, has become prince by favor of the nobles, should at once and before everything else strive to win the good will of the people, which will be easy for him, by taking them under his protection.

. . . it is much more safe to be feared than to be loved, when you have to choose between the two.

. . . there are two ways of carrying on a contest: the one by law, and the other by force. The first is practiced by men, and the other by animals; and as the first is often insufficient, it becomes necessary to resort to the second . . . It being necessary then for a prince to know well how to employ the nature of the beasts, he should be able to assume both that of the fox and that of the lion; for while the latter cannot escape the traps laid for him, the former cannot defend himself against the wolves. A prince should be a fox, to know the traps and snares; and a lion, to be able to frighten the wolves; for those who simply hold to the nature of the lion do not understand their business.

. . . a prince should seem to be merciful, faithful, humane, religious, and upright, and should even be so in reality; but he should have his mind so trained that, when occasion requires it, he may know how to change to the opposite.

. . . For the manner in which men live is so different from the way in which they ought to live, that he who leaves the common course for that which he ought to follow will find that it leads him to ruin rather than to safety. For a man who, in all respects, will carry out only his professions of good, will be apt to be ruined among so many who are evil. A prince therefore who desires to maintain himself must learn to be not always good, but to be so or not as necessity may require. . . . For all things considered, it will be found that some things that

Illustration Capsule 17 (continued)

seem like virtue will lead you to ruin if you follow them; while others, that apparently are vices, will, if followed, result in your safety and well-being.

. . . the dispositions of peoples are variable; it is easy to persuade them to anything, but difficult to confirm them in that belief. And therefore a prophet should be prepared, in case the people will not believe any more, to be able by force to compel them to that belief.

. . . The worst that a prince may expect of a people who are unfriendly to him is that they will desert him; but the hostile nobles he has to fear, not only lest they abandon him, but also because they will turn against him. For they, being more farsighted and astute, always save themselves in advance, and seek to secure the favor of him whom they hope may be successful.

We must bear in mind . . . that there is nothing more difficult and dangerous, or more doubtful of success, than an attempt to introduce a new order of things in any state. For the innovator has for enemies all those who derived advantages from the old order of things while those who expect to be benefited by the new institutions will be but lukewarm defenders. This indifference arises in part from fear of their adversaries who were favored by the existing laws, and partly from the incredulity of men who have no faith in anything new that is not the result of well-established experience. Hence it is that, whenever the opponents of the new order of things have the opportunity to attack it, they will do it with the zeal of partisans, while the others defend it but feebly, so that it is dangerous to rely upon the latter.

. . . a prince cannot depend upon what he observes in ordinary quiet times, when the citizens have need of his authority; for then everybody runs at his bidding, everybody promises, and everybody is willing to die for him, when death is very remote. But in adverse times, when the government has need of the citizens, then but few will be found to stand by the prince. And this experience is the more dangerous as it can only be made once.

A wise prince, therefore, will steadily pursue such a course that the citizens of his state will always and under all circumstances feel the need of his authority, and will therefore always prove faithful to him.

A prince . . . should always take counsel, but only when he wants it, and not when others wish to thrust it upon him; in fact, he should rather discourage persons from tendering him advice unsolicited by him. But he should be an extensive questioner, and a patient listener to the truth respecting the things inquired about, and should even show his anger in case any one should, for some reason, not tell him the truth.

It is obvious from the above quotations that a practicing Machiavellian divorces morals from power politics; indeed, moral considerations have no place in the Machiavellian system of power politics except where an evil reputation would be a political detriment. To many people, this is shocking if not abhorrent. But even if your own moral code totally rejects a Machiavellian use of power, the issue still remains what to do in your dealings with people who are Machiavellian in their attempts to acquire and use power. How would you deal with such a person? Do you not, in fact, know people who in your own experience are Machiavellians? What would your strategy be if you were one of the intended "victims?"

administrative work comes into play—planning, organizing, staffing, directing, coordinating, reporting, and budgeting. More importantly, there is no well-researched, well-understood set of implementation guidelines to follow. Usually, the set of organization circumstances under which strategy is implemented and executed are so unique and one-of-a-kind that most of what can be recommended is conceptually normative. Much of what can be offered is just basic "principles of management" and plain common sense.

However, in Chapters 6 and 7 we have tried to focus on those managerial aspects and principles which relate most directly to strategy implementation. These have been summarized and presented in the form of a checklist in Table 7–1. Suffice it to say at this point that in translating strategy into effective action and results the job of management centers on identifying the activities and operations which are crucial, organizing them to create a coordinated and economical flow of work, and instilling a spirit of high performance and achievement throughout the organization. If these things are well done, the chances of successful strategy implementation are much improved.

TABLE 7–1
Checklist for Successfully Implementing Strategy and Monitoring Strategic Performance

---

A. *Organization Structure and Management Capability*
  1. Does the firm's present management have a good track record in managing the aspects of strategy implementation? How well have administrative problems and crises been handled? In the past has top management been successful in adapting both structure and staffing to accommodate shifts in strategy, objectives, and competitive conditions?
  2. Is the present organization structure supportive of strategy? Have key activities been correctly identified and is the organization structure predicated upon these key activities?
  3. Do the qualifications and experience of key managers match up well with the managerial requirements of the chosen strategy? Have the right kinds of people been selected to fill new or vacant positions? Are recent structural and staffing changes in tune with what is needed for successful strategy execution? Is top management alert to what organizational resources and what staffing skills and expertise are called for? Is there an overdependence on one person or one group?
  4. Have key management personnel been delegated the right authority? Has power to make decisions been put in the right places? Are strategic priorities and objectives being made the basis for assignment of managerial responsibilities?
B. *Internal Operations*
  1. Does the company have the resources it will need to see its strategy through to a successful implementation? Will money and cash flow be a problem?
  2. Is there an apparent match between strategy and internal resources and capabilities? If not, are actions being taken to create a match?
  3. To what extent are functional area and operating strategies being coordinated and made compatible? Do managers in these areas understand what

---

TABLE 7-1 (continued)

performance and time schedule is required of them to make implementation successful?

4. Have ample provisions been made for R&D capability? Are there likely to be undue problems in manufacturing technology or threats from new technological developments?

5. Are there provisions for giving the firm a competitive degree of efficiency in its manufacturing and production activities? Are facilities and equipment in line with the requirements of strategy?

6. Are inventory controls and purchasing procedures adequate? Is the firm overly vulnerable to adverse shifts in raw material supply conditions? Do labor supplies or union-management relations pose an undue threat to successful strategy implementation? Is management doing what it can to address and solve any problems in these areas?

7. Is the firm missing any distinctive competence? Are any important strategy-related weaknesses not being corrected?

C. *Controls and Performance Appraisal*

1. Do policies and control procedures seem adequate? Are provisions in place (or being made) to furnish managers with solid, pertinent, and timely information on the status of current operations?

2. Is there evidence of sufficient planning and budgeting?

3. Have objectives and performance standards been made explicit, communicated, and agreed upon at each level in the management hierarchy? Have responsibilities been fixed and deadlines set?

4. Is the reward structure supportive of accomplishing strategy and achieving objectives? Are productivity and motivation problem areas?

D. *Managerial Leadership and Effectiveness*

1. Is top management's leadership style adequate for the firm's situation? Do they have the right temperament and personality orientation to implement the strategy successfully?

2. Do the firm's managers enjoy the respect of subordinates?

3. Do all the details of strategy implementation appear to be thought through? Do contingency plans exist where they are needed?

4. Does management seem to place too much reliance on unsupported opinion or hunch or seat-of-the-pants guesstimates?

5. In view of the firm's overall strengths and weaknesses, and the challenges it faces, what are the odds that the strategy can be implemented with an attractive degree of success?

SUGGESTED READINGS

Adizes, Ichak. "Mismanagement Styles." *California Management Review,* vol. 19, no. 2 (Winter 1976), pp. 5–20.

Drucker, Peter F. *Management: Tasks, Responsibilities, Practices.* New York: Harper & Row, Publishers, 1974, chaps. 16–19 and 33–39.

Fiedler, Fred E. "The Contingency Model—New Directions for Leadership Utilization." *Journal of Contemporary Business,* vol. 3, no. 4 (Autumn 1974), pp. 65–80.

Hall, Jay. "To Achieve or Not: The Manager's Choice." *California Management Review*, vol. 18, no. 4 (Summer 1976), pp. 5–18.

Herzberg, Frederick. "One More Time: How Do You Motivate Employees?" *Harvard Business Review*, vol. 51, no. 3 (May–June 1973), pp. 162–80.

Koontz, Harold. "Management Control: A Suggested Formulation of Principles." *California Management Review*, vol. 2, no. 2 (Winter 1959), pp. 50–55.

Machiavelli, N. *The Prince*. New York: Washington Square Press, 1963.

McClelland, David C., and Burnham, David H. "Power Is the Great Motivator." *Harvard Business Review*, vol. 54, no. 2 (March–April 1976), pp. 100–110.

Morse, John J., and Lorsch, Jay W. "Behind Theory Y." *Harvard Business Review*, vol. 48, no. 3 (May–June 1970), pp. 61–68.

Robbins, Stephen P. "Reconciling Management Theory with Management Practice." *Business Horizons*, vol. 20, no. 1 (February 1977), pp. 38–47.

Roche, W. J., and MacKinnon, N.L. "Motivating People with Meaningful Work." *Harvard Business Review*, vol. 48, no. 3 (May–June 1970), pp. 97–110.

Tannenbaum, Robert, and Schmidt, Warren H. "How to Choose a Leadership Pattern." *Harvard Business Review*, vol. 51, no. 3 (May–June 1973), pp. 162–80.

Tosi, Henry L., Rizzo, John R., and Carroll, Stephen J. "Setting Goals in Management by Objective." *California Management Review*, vol. 12, no. 4 (Summer 1970), pp. 70–78.

Vancil, Richard F. "What Kind of Management Control Do You Need?" *Harvard Business Review*, vol. 51, no. 2 (March–April 1973), pp. 75–86.

Webber, Ross A. "Career Problems of Young Managers." *California Management Review*, vol. 18, no. 4 (Summer 1976), pp. 19–33.

Zalenik, Abraham. "Power and Politics in Organizational Life." *Harvard Business Review*, vol. 48, no. 3 (May–June 1970), pp. 47–60.

FROM CONCEPTS TO CASES: PRACTICING AT BEING A MANAGER

PART II

Chapter 8
Case Analysis: Its Role and Method

8 CASE ANALYSIS: ITS ROLE AND METHOD

I keep six honest serving men
(They taught me all I knew);
Their names are What and Why and When
And How and Where and Who.

Rudyard Kipling

Management is an action-oriented activity. It requires doing to achieve proficiency. Managers succeed or fail not so much because of what they know as because of what they do. A person cannot expect to succeed as a manager and become a "professional" simply by studying excellent books on management—no matter how thoroughly the text material is mastered nor how many As are earned at exam time. Moreover, just as a golfer needs to practice at being a better golfer, a person who aspires to become a manager can benefit from practicing at being a manager.

Practicing Management Via Case Analysis

In academic programs of management education, students practice at being managers via case analysis. A *case* sets forth, in a factual manner, the conditions and circumstances surrounding a particular managerial situation or series of events in an organization. It may include descriptions of the industry and its competitive conditions, the organization's background, its products and markets, the attitudes and personalities of the key people involved, production facilities, the work climate, the organizational structure, marketing methods, and the external environment, together with whatever pertinent financial, production, accounting, sales, and market information upon which management had to depend. It may concern any kind of organization—a profit-seeking business, or a public service institution.

A good case offers about as live and effective a practice situation as can be achieved short of "the real thing." It puts the readers at the scene of the action and familiarizes them with the situation as it prevailed. As such, it is well suited as a pedagogical device for students practicing what they, as managers, would do if confronted with the same circumstances—and to do so without having to worry about inexperience and making amateurish or costly mistakes.

The essence of the student's role in the case method is to diagnose and size up the organization's situation and to think through what, if anything, should be done. The purpose is for the student, as analyst, to develop answers to a number of questions, the gist of which include: What factors have contributed to the organization's success (or failure)? What problems are evident? How would I handle them? What managerial skills are needed to deal effectively with the situation? How should they be applied? What actions need to be taken?

It should be emphasized that most cases are *not* intended to be examples of right and wrong, or good and bad management. The organizations concerned are selected neither because they are the best or the worst in their industry nor because they are average or typical. The important thing about a case is that it represents an actual situation where managers were obligated to recognize and cope with the problems as they were.

Why Use Cases to Practice Management?

> A student of business with tact
> Absorbed many answers he lacked.
> But acquiring a job,
> He said with a sob,
> "How *does* one fit answer to fact?"

The foregoing limerick was offered some years ago by Charles I. Gragg in a classic article, "Because Wisdom Can't Be Told," to illustrate what might happen to students of management without the benefit of cases.[1] Gragg observed that the mere act of listening to wise statements and sound advice about management does little for anyone's management skills. He contended it was unlikely that accumulated managerial experience and wisdom could effectively be passed on by lectures and readings alone. Gragg suggested that if anything has been learned about the practice of management, it is that a storehouse of ready-made answers does not exist. Each managerial situation has unique aspects, requiring its own diagnosis and understanding as a prelude to judgment and action. In Gragg's view and in the view of other case method advocates, cases provide aspiring managers with an important and valid kind of daily practice in wrestling with management problems.

The case method is, indeed, *learning by doing.* The pedagogy of the case method of instruction is predicated on the benefits of acquiring managerial

---

[1] Charles I. Gragg, "Because Wisdom Can't Be Told," in M.P. McNair, ed., *The Case Method at the Harvard Business School* (New York: McGraw-Hill 1954), p. 11.

"experience" by means of simulated management exercises (cases). The biggest justification for cases is that few, if any, students during the course of their college education have an opportunity to come into direct personal contact with different kinds of companies and real-life managerial situations. Cases offer a viable substitute by bringing a variety of organizations and management problems into the classroom and permitting students to assume the manager's role. Management cases therefore provide students with a kind of experiential exercise in which to test their ability to apply their textbook knowledge about management.

Objectives of the Case Method

As the foregoing discussion suggests, the use of cases as an instructional technique embraces four chief objectives.[2]

1. Helping you to acquire the skills of putting textbook knowledge about management into practice.
2. Getting you out of the habit of being a receiver of facts, concepts, and techniques and into the habit of diagnosing problems, analyzing and evaluating alternatives, and formulating workable plans of action.
3. Training you to work out answers and solutions for yourself, as opposed to relying upon the authoritative crutch of the professor or a textbook.
4. Providing you with exposure to a range of firms and managerial situations (which might take a lifetime to experience personally), thus offering you a basis for comparison when you begin your own management career.

If you understand that these are the objectives of the case method of instruction, then you are less likely to be bothered by something that puzzles some students: "What is the answer to the case?" Being accustomed to textbook statements of fact and supposedly definitive lecture notes, students often find that discussions and analyses of managerial cases do not produce any "answer." Instead, issues in the case are discussed pro and con. Various alternatives and relevant aspects of the situation are evaluated. Usually, a good argument can be made for one decision or another, or one plan of action or another. When the class discussion concludes without a clear consensus, some students may, at first, feel cheated or dissatisfied because they are not told "what the answer is" or "what the company actually did."

However, case descriptions of managerial situations where answers are not clear-cut are quite realistic. Organizational problems whose analysis leads to a definite, single-pronged solution are likely to be so oversimplified and rare as to be trivial or devoid of practical value. In reality, several

---

[2] Ibid., pp. 12–14; and D. R. Schoen and Philip A. Sprague, "What Is the Case Method?" in M. P. McNair, ed., *The Case Method at the Harvard Business School* (New York: McGraw-Hill, 1954), pp. 78–79.

feasible courses of action may exist for dealing with the same set of circumstances. Moreover, in real-life management situations when one makes a decision or elects a particular course of action, there is no peeking at the back of a book to see if you have chosen the best thing to do. No book of provably correct answers exists; in fact, the first test of management action is *results.* If the results turn out to be "good," the decision may be presumed "right"; if not, then, it was "wrong." Hence, the important thing for the student to understand in a case course is that it is the exercise of managerial analysis and decision making that counts rather than discovering "the right answer" or finding out what actually happened.

To put it another way, *the purpose of management cases is not to learn authoritative answers to specific managerial problems but to become skilled in the process of designing a workable (and, hopefully, effective) plan of action through evaluation of the prevailing circumstances.* The aim of case analysis is not for you to try to guess what the instructor is thinking or what his solution is. Rather, it is to see whether you can support your views against the counterviews of others in the group or, failing to do so, whether you can accept the merits of the reasoning underlying the approaches of others. Therefore, *in case analysis you are expected to bear the strains of thinking actively, of making managerial assessments which may be vigorously challenged, and of defending your analysis and plan of action.* Only in this way can case analysis provide you with any meaningful practice at being a manager.

In sum, the purpose of the case method is to initiate you and encourage you in the ways of thinking "managerially" and exercising responsible judgment. At the same time, you should use the cases that follow to test the rigor and effectiveness of your own theories about the practice of management and to begin to evolve your own management philosophy and management style.

Preparing a Case for Class Discussion

Given that cases rest on the principle of learning by doing, their effectiveness hinges upon *you* making *your* analysis and reaching *your* own decisions and then in the classroom participating in a collective analysis and decision-making process. If this is your first experience with the case method, you may have to reorient your study habits. Since a case assignment emphasizes student participation, it is obvious that the effectiveness of the class discussion depends upon each student having studied the case *beforehand.* Consequently, unlike lecture courses where there is no imperative of specific preparation before each class and where assigned readings and reviews of lecture notes may be done at irregular intervals, *a case assignment requires conscientious preparation before class.* You cannot, after all, expect to get much out of practicing managing in a situation with which you are totally unfamiliar.

Unfortunately, though, there is no nice, proven procedure for studying cases which can be recommended to you. There is no formula, no fail-safe step-by-step technique that we can recommend. Each case is a new situation and you will need to adjust accordingly. Moreover, you will, after a time, discover an approach which suits you best. Thus, the following suggestions are offered simply to get you started.

A first step in understanding how the case method of teaching/learning works is to recognize that it represents a radical departure from the lecture/discussion/problem classroom technique. To begin with, members of the class do most of the talking. The instructor's role is to solicit student participation and guide the discussion. Expect the instructor to begin the class with such questions as: What is the organization's strategy? What do you consider to be the real problem confronting the company? What factors have contributed most to the organization's successes? Its failures? Which manager is doing a good job? Are the organization's objectives and strategies compatible with its skills and resources? Typically, members of the class will evaluate and test their opinions as much in discussions with each other as with the instructor. But irrespective of whether the discussion emphasis is instructor-student or student-student, members of the class carry the burden for analyzing the situation and for being prepared to present and defend their analysis in the classroom. Thus, you should expect an absence of professional "here's how to do it," "right answers," and "hard knowledge for your notebook"; instead, be prepared for a discussion involving what do *you* think, what would *you* do, and what do *you* feel is important.[3]

Begin your analysis by reading the case once for familiarity. An initial reading should give you the general flavor of the situation and make possible preliminary identification of issues. On the second reading, attempt to gain full command of the facts. You may wish to make notes about apparent organizational goals, objectives, strategies, policies, symptoms of problems, problems, root causes of problems, unresolved issues, and roles of key individuals. Be alert for issues or problems which are not necessarily made explicit but which nevertheless are lurking beneath the surface. Read between the lines and do not hesitate to do some detective work on your own. For instance, the apparent issue in the case might be whether a product has ample market potential at the current selling price while the root problem is that the method being used to compensate salespeople fails to generate adequate incentive for achieving greater unit volume. Needless to say, a sharp, clear-cut "size-up" of the company and its problems is an essential function of management: one cannot devise sensible solutions to an organization's troubles until the troubles have first been correctly identified. In short, before a company's problems can be solved, they must be understood; they must be analyzed; they must be evaluated; and they must be placed in proper perspective.

To help gain this perspective, put yourself in the position of some manager

---

[3] Schoen and Sprague, "What Is the Case Method?" p. 80.

or managerial group portrayed in the case and get attuned to the organizational environment within which the manager or management group must make decisions. Try to get a good feel for the "personality" of the company, the management, and the organizational climate. This is essential if you are to come up with solutions which will be both workable and acceptable in light of the prevailing environmental constraints and realities. Do not be dismayed if you find it impractical to isolate the problems and issues into distinct categories which can be treated separately. Very few and significant real-world management problems can be neatly sorted into mutually exclusive areas of concern.

Most important of all, you must arrive at a solid evaluation of the company, based on the information in the case. Developing an ability to evaluate companies and size up their situations is *the key* to case analysis. How do you evaluate a company? There is no pat answer. But in general you need to identify the firm's strategy, evaluate its competitive position and financial condition, pinpoint external threats and opportunities as well as internal strengths and weaknesses, and assess its future potential. For more specific suggestions consult Table 8–1.

TABLE 8–1
Checklist for Evaluating a Company's Present Position and Future Potential

A. Product Lines and Competitive Position
   1. How do the firm's products (or services) stack up against those of rival firms? Has the firm been successful in differentiating its products from those of its rivals and in carving out a viable market niche for itself? Does the firm enjoy a position of market advantage and, if so, what is the basis for this advantage?
   2. How do customers and potential customers regard the company's products? What market shares does it have and how firmly does it hold them? Have market shares been increasing or decreasing? Is the company dependent on a few large customers for the bulk of its sales?
   3. What are the firm's profit margins? Have these been increasing or decreasing? Are the firm's margins above or below those of the industry? Is the firm in a position to be competitive on price?
   4. Where do the company's chief products stand in the life cycle? Is the industry young or mature? Are the markets for the firm's products expanding or contracting, and at what rates? How is the company's business affected by upswings and downswings in the economy? Is the firm's target market big enough to generate the revenues needed to be profitable?
   5. Is the company confronted with increasing competition? What is the nature of this competition and how vulnerable is the firm's strategy to new competition? Is entry into the industry easy or hard? Has the firm demonstrated an ability to compete effectively?
   6. Is the company a leader in its market area? Is the company being forced into head-to-head competition with proven leaders? If so, does the company have the competitive artillery it needs or is it trying to go to war with a popgun? Is the firm relying on a "me too" or "copycat" strategy?
   7. What are the strengths and weaknesses of the company's marketing strat-

TABLE 8-1 (continued)

egy? How well do its marketing efforts compare with those of rival firms? Is there a capability for exploiting new products and developing new markets? Does it have the necessary distribution channels or the ability to develop them?

8. If the firm is diversified, then are its product lines compatible? Is there evidence of strategic fit? Is the diversification plan well thought-out or has the company been seduced by the illusions of glamour products and glamour technology?

What is your summary evaluation of the firm's product line and competitive position? What are its particular strengths and weaknesses and how important are these to the firm's ultimate success or failure?

B. Profitability and Financial Condition

1. What is the trend in the firm's profitability as concerns total profits, earnings per share, return on sales, return on assets, return on total capital investment, and return on equity investment? How does the firm's profitability compare with that of other firms in the industry? What is the "quality" of the firm's earnings?

2. How is the company viewed by investors? What is the trend in the company's stock price, its price-earnings ratio, dividend payout, and dividend yield on common stock?

3. Is the firm liquid and able to meet its maturing obligations? What trends are evident in the firm's current ratio and quick (or acid test) ratio? See Table 8-2 for a summary of how these ratios are calculated and what they indicate.

4. To what extent is the firm leveraged? What are the trends in the firm's debt ratios, its times-interest-earned coverages, and its fixed charge coverages? (See Table 8-2 for a summary of how these ratios are calculated and what they indicate.) Has the firm exhausted its debt capacity? Does it have the ability to raise new equity capital?

5. How effectively is the firm employing the resources at its command? What problems are revealed by such ratios as inventory turnover, accounts receivable turnover, fixed asset turnover, total asset turnover, and average collection period? (See Table 8-2 for a summary of how these ratios are calculated and what they indicate.)

6. Is cash flow adequate to supply the company with working capital? Is the company (or some of its businesses) a "cash hog" or a "cash cow?" (A "cash hog" business uses more cash than it generates, whereas a "cash cow" business generates more cash than is required to finance working capital and expansion needs.)

7. Is the company well-managed from a financial standpoint? Does it have adequate financial controls and careful cash planning? Have capital investment decisions been based on thorough calculations?

What strengths and weaknesses are evident in the firm's overall financial condition? How do these relate to the company's present competitive situation and strategy?

C. Operations and Internal Organization

1. How well do the firm's resources and capability match its strategy in the marketplace? Does the firm have the talent, the knowhow, and the finan-

TABLE 8-1 (continued)

cial strength to succeed in executing its strategy? Does the company have the resources to make a commitment to see its strategy through to a successful implementation?

2. To what extent is the firm's manufacturing strategy, marketing strategy, R&D strategy, and financial strategy integrated, coordinated, and compatible? Are the organization's goals, objectives, and strategies suited to its skills and resources?

3. Is the firm threatened by new technological developments? Does it have enough R&D capability? What is its track record in innovation?

4. Is the firm large enough to take advantage of economies of scale? Is it efficient in its manufacturing and production activities? Are its equipment and facilities modern? Have capital expenditures been either inadequate or excessive with regard to ensuring future operating efficiency?

5. How vulnerable is the company to adverse shifts in raw material supply and labor supply conditions? Is there a major problem with unions or a history of poor union-management relations?

6. Is the firm developing the kinds of information it needs to solve its problems? Do operating-level managers have solid, pertinent, and timely data on the status of current operations? Is too much reliance placed on unsupported opinion or management hunch or seat-of-the-pants guestimates?

7. Does the firm have adequate knowledge about costs? Do its costs appear to be in line with other comparable firms? Is it generating the right kind of cost information?

8. How strong is the company's financial management? Are its inventory controls adequate? Are its purchasing procedures adequate?

9. Is the organization adequately staffed? Do key personnel appear knowledgeable and capable in performing their jobs?

10. Are the firm's pay scales and overall reward structure adequate? Is motivation a problem? Is there ample opportunity to promote good people? Are performance appraisals made on a regular basis? Does the company appear to treat employees fairly?

What distinctive competence(s) has the firm developed ? How important has this been in accounting for the firm's success (or failure)? What distinctive competence(s) is it missing?

D. Management Capability
1. Is the firm well-organized? Is the organization structure supportive of strategy?

2. Does the firm's present management have a good track record? How well has it handled past problems and crises? Have previously set goals and objectives been achieved on schedule?

3. How capable are each of the firm's key management personnel? Do they have the necessary qualifications and experience? Do they appear to know their jobs well and are the areas for which they are responsible functioning smoothly?

4. Are policies and control procedures in the various departments adequate? Is the organization efficient? Does it take too long for key decisions to be made?

5. Is the organization overly dependent on one person? Is there enough management depth for the type of business being run?

TABLE 8-1 (continued)

6. How good a job has top management done in selecting, training, and developing lower level management personnel? Have the right kinds of people been selected to fill new or vacant positions?
7. Is top management's leadership style adequate for the firm's situation and needs? Do the firm's managers know how to manage people? Do the managers have the respect of the people they supervise?
8. Does the extent to which the firm has diversified present undue problems of coordination and control to the present management?
9. Has management given evidence of an ability to adapt the firm and the organization structure to meet changing needs, priorities, and competitive conditions?
10. Does management have the respect of the financial community?

What is your summary evaluation of the company's management? What are its strengths and weaknesses and how do these weigh upon the firm's performance?

E. Prospects for the Future
1. Has the firm developed (or is it in a position to acquire) the technological proficiency it needs to remain competitive over the long run?
2. If the firm's competitive position is weak or is slipping, is it in a position to "play catch-up"? What are the chances that it can make up lost ground?
3. What is the future market potential for the firm's chief products? Will it need to diversify in the near future and, if so, does it have the financial and organizational strength to make new acquisitions or to build new businesses from the ground up?
4. What are the basic "facts of life" about product-market-technology and competitive trends in the firm's industry over the next decade? Will the company need to make fundamental revisions in its strategy in the near future?
5. What do the trends in the firm's profitability and overall financial condition suggest regarding the firm's prospects for growth and success? Does the firm have adequate long-range financial plans?
6. How adequate is management for coping with the challenges of the future?
7. Which factors have contributed most to the organization's successes? Its failures? How will these factors affect the firm in the future?
8. In view of the firm's overall strengths and weaknesses, and the challenges it faces, what are the odds that it will survive? At what level of success? Will it have to succeed by diversifying out of its present lines of business?

Source: Adapted with major revisions and additions by the authors from Robert B. Buchele, "How to Evaluate a Firm," *California Management Review*, vol. 5, no. 1 (Fall 1962), pp. 5-17.

Uppermost in your efforts, strive for defensible arguments and positions. Do not rely upon just your opinion; support any judgments or conclusions with evidence! Use the available data to make whatever relevant accounting, financial, marketing, or operations analysis calculations are necessary to support your assessment of the situation.

Lastly, be wary of accepting *everything* stated in the case as "fact." Sometimes, information or data in the case will be conflicting and/or opinions contradictory. For example, one manager may say that the firm's organizational structure is functioning quite effectively, whereas another may say it is not. It is your task to decide whose view is more valid and why. Forcing you to make judgments about the validity of the data and information presented in the case is both deliberate and realistic. It is deliberate because one function of the case method is to help you develop your powers of judgment and inference. It is realistic because a great many managerial situations entail conflicting points of view.

Once you have thoroughly diagnosed the company's situation and weighed the pros and cons of various alternative courses of action, the final step of case analysis is to decide what you think the company needs to do to improve its performance and to set forth a workable plan of action. This is a crucial part of the process of case analysis since diagnosis divorced from corrective action is sterile; but bear in mind that making a decision and jumping to a conclusion are not the same thing. One is well-advised to avoid the infamous decision-making pattern:"Don't confuse me with the facts. I've made up my mind."

On a few occasions, some desirable information may not be included in the case. In such instances you may be inclined to complain about the lack of "facts." A manager, however, uses more than facts upon which to base his or her decisions. Moreover, it may be possible to make a number of infer- ences from the facts you do have. So, be wary of rushing to include as part of your recommendations "the need to get more information." From time to time, of course, a search for additional facts or information may be entirely appropriate but you must also recognize that the organization's managers may not have had any more information available than that presented in the case. Before recommending that a final decision be postponed until addi- tional facts are uncovered, be sure that you think it will be worth while to get them and that the organization could afford to wait. In general, though, try to assess situations based upon the evidence you have at hand.

Again, remember that rarely is there a "right" decision or just one "opti- mal" plan of action or an "approved" solution. Your goal should be to find a practical and workable course of action which is based upon a serious analy- sis of the situation and which appears to you to be right in view of your assessment and weighing of the facts. Admittedly, someone else may evalu- ate the same facts in another way and thus have a different "right" solution, but since several good plans of action can normally be conceived, you should not be afraid to pursue your own intuition and judgment. One can make a strong argument for the view that the "right" answer for a manager is the one which he or she can propose, explain, defend, and make work when it is implemented.

The Classroom Experience

In experiencing class discussions of management cases, you will, in all probability, notice very quickly that you will not have thought of everything in the case that your fellow students think of. While you will see things others did not, they will see things you did not. Do not be dismayed or alarmed by this. It is normal. As the old adage goes, "two heads are better than one." So, it is to be expected that the class as a whole will do a more penetrating and searching job of case analysis than will any one person working alone. This is the power of group effort and one of its virtues is that it will give you more insight into how others view situations and how to cope with differences of opinion. Second, you will see better why sometimes it is not managerially wise to assume a rigid position on an issue until a full range of views and information has been assembled. And, undoubtedly, somewhere along the way you will begin to recognize that neither the instructor nor other students in the class have all the answers, and even if they think they do, you are still free to present and hold to your own views. The truth in the saying that "there's more than one way to skin a cat" will be seen to apply nicely to most management situations.

For class discussion of cases to be useful and stimulating you need to keep the following points in mind:

1. The case method enlists a maximum of individual participation in class discussion. It is not enough to be present as a silent observer; if every student took this approach, then there would be no discussion. (Thus, do not be surprised if a portion of your grade is based on your participation in case discussions.)

2. Although you should do your own independent work and independent thinking, don't hesitate to discuss the case with other students. Managers often discuss their problems with other key people.

3. During case discussions, expect and tolerate challenges to the views expressed. Be willing to submit your conclusions for scrutiny and rebuttal. State your views without fear of disapproval and overcome the hesitation of speaking out.

4. In orally presenting and defending your ideas, keep in mind the importance of good communication. It is up to you to be convincing and persuasive in expressing your ideas.

5. Expect the instructor to assume the role of discussion leader; only when the discussion content is technique-oriented is it likely that your instructor will maintain direct control over the discussion.

6. Although discussion of a case is a group process, this does not imply conformity to group opinion. Learning respect for the views and approaches of others is an integral part of case analysis exercises. But be willing to "swim against the tide" of majority opinion. In the practice of management, there is always room for originality, unorthodoxy, and unique personality.

7. In participating in the discussion, make a conscious effort to *contribute* rather than just talk. There *is* a difference.

8. Effective case discussions can occur only if participants have "the

facts'' of the case well in hand; rehashing information in the case should be held to a minimum except as it provides documentation, comparisons, or support for your position.

9. During the discussion, new insights provided by the group's efforts are likely to emerge, thereby opening up ''the facts'' to reinterpretation and perhaps causing one's analysis of the situation to be modified.

10. Although there will always be situations in which more technical information is imperative to the making of an intelligent decision, try not to shirk from making decisions in the face of incomplete information. Wrestling with imperfect information is a normal condition managers face and is something you should get used to.

11. Ordinarily, there are several acceptable solutions which can be proposed for dealing with the issues in a case. Definitive, provably correct answers rarely, if ever, exist in managerial situations.

12. In the final analysis, learning about management via the case method is up to you; just as with other learning techniques, the rewards are dependent upon the effort you put in to it.

Preparing a Written Case Analysis

From time to time, your instructor may ask you to prepare a written analysis of the case assignment. Preparing a written case analysis is much like preparing a case for class discussion, except that your analysis, when completed, must be reduced to writing. Just as there was no set pattern or formula for preparing a case for oral discussion, there is no ironclad procedure for preparing a written case analysis. With a bit of experience you will arrive at your own preferred method of attack in writing up a case and you will learn to adjust your approach to the unique aspects that each case presents.

Your instructor may assign you a specific topic around which to prepare your written report. Common assignments include (1) identify and evaluate company X's corporate strategy; (2) in view of the opportunities and risks you see in the industry, what is your assessment of the company's position and strategy? (3) how would you size up the strategic situation of company Y? (4) what recommendations would you make to company Z's top management? and (5) what specific functions and activities does the company have to perform especially well in order for its strategy to succeed?

Alternatively, you may be asked to do a ''comprehensive written case analysis.'' It is typical for a comprehensive written case analysis to emphasize three things:

1. Identification (of strategic issues and problems).
2. Analysis and evaluation.
3. Presentation of recommendations.

You may wish to consider the following pointers in preparing a comprehensive written case analysis.[4]

Identification. As the checklist in Table 8–1 suggests, there are five vital areas in an organization which form an integral part of any comprehensive analysis: (1) its product line and basic competitive position, (2) its profitability and financial conditions, (3) its operations—production, personnel, organization structure, controls, and so on, (4) the caliber of top management, including not only management's past record but also its adequacy to cope with what lies ahead, and (5) the company's prospects for the future. A comprehensive analysis must survey all five of these areas, with a view toward identifying the key issues and problems which confront the organization. It is essential that your paper reflect a sharply focused diagnosis of these key issues and problems and, further, that you demonstrate good business judgment in sizing up the company's present situation. Make sure you understand and can identify the firm's corporate strategy. You would probably be well advised to begin your paper by sizing up the company's situation, its strategy, and the significant problems and issues which confront management. State the problems/issues as clearly and precisely as you can. Unless it is necessary to do so for emphasis, avoid recounting facts and history about the company (assume your professor has read the case and is familiar with the organization!).

Analysis and Evaluation. Very likely you will find this section the hardest part of the report. Analysis is hard work! Study the tables, exhibits, and financial statements carefully. Check out the firm's financial ratios, its profit margins and rates of return, its capital structure and decide how strong the firm is financially. (Table 8–2 contains a summary of the various financial ratios and how they are calculated.) Similarly, look at marketing, production, managerial competences, and so on, and evaluate the organization's strengths and weaknesses in each of the major functional areas. Identify the factors underlying the organization's successes and failures. Decide whether it has a distinctive competence and, if so, whether it is capitalizing upon it. Is the firm's strategy working? Why or why not? Assess opportunities and threats, both internally and externally. Determine whether objectives, strategies, and policies are realistic in light of prevailing constraints. Look at how the organization is hedging its risks. Evaluate the firm's competitive position. Review the checklist in Table 8–1 to see if your have overlooked something—you may also want to review the checklists in Tables 4–1, 5–1, and 7–1.

---

[4] For some additional ideas and viewpoints, you may wish to consult Thomas J. Raymond. "Written Analysis of Cases," in M. P. McNair, ed., *The Case Method at the Harvard Business School* (New York: McGraw-Hill, 1954), pp. 139–62. In Raymond's article is an actual case, a sample analysis of the case, and a sample of a student's written report on the case.

TABLE 8-2
A Summary of Key Financial Ratios, How They Are Calculated, and What
They Show

Ratio	How Calculated	What It Shows
Profitability ratios:		
1. Gross profit margin	$\dfrac{\text{Sales} - \text{Cost of goods sold}}{\text{Sales}}$	An indication of the total margin available to cover operating expenses and yield a profit.
2. Operating profit margin	$\dfrac{\text{Profits before taxes and before interest}}{\text{Sales}}$	An indication of the firm's profitability from current operations without regard to the interest charges accruing from the capital structure.
③. Net profit margin (or return on sales)	$\dfrac{\text{Profits after taxes}}{\text{Sales}}$	Shows aftertax profits per dollar of sales. Subpar-profit margins indicate that the firm's sales prices are relatively low or that its costs are relatively high or both.
④. Return on total assets	$\dfrac{\text{Profits after taxes}}{\text{Total assets}}$ or $\dfrac{\text{Profits after taxes} + \text{Interest}}{\text{Total assets}}$	A measure of the return on total investment in the enterprise. It is sometimes desirable to add interest to aftertax profits to form the numerator of the ratio since total assets are financed by creditors as well as by stockholders; hence it is accurate to measure the productivity of assets by the returns provided to both classes of investors.
5. Return on stockholders' equity (or return on net worth)	$\dfrac{\text{Profits after taxes}}{\text{Total stockholders' equity}}$	A measure of the rate of return on stockholders' investment in the enterprise.
6. Return on common equity	$\dfrac{\text{Profits after taxes} - \text{Preferred stock dividends}}{\text{Total stockholders' equity} - \text{Par value of preferred stock}}$	A measure of the rate of return on the investment which the owners of common stock have made in the enterprise.

TABLE 8–2 (continued)

Ratio	How Calculated	What It Shows
7. Earnings per share	Profits after taxes − Preferred stock dividends / Number of shares of common stock outstanding	Shows the earnings available to the owners of common stock.

Liquidity ratios:

Ratio	How Calculated	What It Shows
1. Current ratio	Current assets / Current liabilities	Indicates the extent to which the claims of short-term creditors are covered by assets that are expected to be converted to cash in a period roughly corresponding to the maturity of the liabilities.

$$\text{Std} = 2.0$$

Ratio	How Calculated	What It Shows
2. Quick ratio (or acid test ratio)	Current assets − Inventory / Current liabilities	A measure of the firm's ability to pay off short-term obligations without relying upon the sale of its inventories.

$$\text{Std.} = 1$$

Ratio	How Calculated	What It Shows
3. Inventory to net working capital	Inventory / Current assets − Current liabilities	A measure of the extent to which the firm's working capital is tied up in inventory.

Leverage ratios:

Ratio	How Calculated	What It Shows
1. Debt to assets ratio	Total debt / Total assets	Measures the extent to which borrowed funds have been used to finance the firm's operations.
2. Debt to equity ratio	Total debt / Total stockholders' equity	Provides another measure of the funds provided by creditors versus the funds provided by owners.
3. Long-term debt to equity ratio	Long-term debt / Total stockholders' equity	A widely used measure of the balance between debt and equity in the firm's long-term capital structure.
4. Times-interest-earned (or coverage) ratios	Profits before interest and taxes / Total interest charges	Measures the extent to which earnings can decline without the firm becoming unable to meet its annual interest costs.

TABLE 8–2 (continued)

Ratio	How Calculated	What It Shows
5. Fixed charge coverage	$\dfrac{\text{Profits before taxes and interest + Lease obligations}}{\text{Total interest charges + Lease obligations}}$	A more inclusive indication of the firm's ability to meet all of its fixed charge obligations.
Activity ratios:		
①. Inventory turnover	$\dfrac{\text{Sales}}{\text{Inventory of finished goods}}$	When compared to industry averages, it provides an indication of whether a company has excessive or perhaps inadequate finished goods inventory.
2. Fixed assets turnover	$\dfrac{\text{Sales}}{\text{Fixed assets}}$	A measure of the sales productivity and utilization of plant and equipment.
3. Total assets turnover	$\dfrac{\text{Sales}}{\text{Total assets}}$	A measure of the utilization of all the firm's assets; a ratio below the industry average indicates the company is not generating a sufficient volume of business given the size of its asset investment.
4. Accounts receivable turnover	$\dfrac{\text{Annual credit sales}}{\text{Accounts receivable}}$	A measure of the average length of time it takes the firm to collect the sales made on credit.
⑤. Average collection period	$\dfrac{\text{Accounts receivable}}{\text{Total sales} \div 365}$ or $\dfrac{\text{Accounts receivable}}{\text{Average daily sales}}$	Indicates the average length of time the firm must wait after making a sale before it receives payment.
Other ratios:		
1. Dividend yield on common stock	$\dfrac{\text{Annual dividends per share}}{\text{Current market price per share}}$	A measure of the return to owners received in the form of dividends.
2. Price-earnings ratio	$\dfrac{\text{Current market price per share}}{\text{Aftertax earnings per share}}$	Faster growing or less risky firms *tend* to have higher price-earnings ratios than slower growing or more risky firms.

TABLE 8-2 (concluded)

Ratio	How Calculated	What It Shows
3. Dividend payout ratio	$\dfrac{\text{Annual dividends per share}}{\text{Aftertax earnings per share}}$	Indicates the percentage of profits paid out as dividends.
4. Cash flow per share	$\dfrac{\text{Aftertax profits} + \text{Depreciation}}{\text{Number of common shares outstanding}}$	A measure of the discretionary funds over and above expenses available for use by the firm.

Note: Industry-average ratios against which a particular company's ratios may be judged are available in *Modern Industry* and *Dun's Reviews* published by Dun & Bradstreet (14 ratios for 125 lines of business activity), Robert Morris Associates' *Annual Statement Studies* (11 ratios for 156 lines of business), and the FTC-SEC's *Quarterly Financial Report* for manufacturing corporations.

In writing your analysis and evaluation, bear in mind that:

1. You are obliged to offer supporting evidence for your views and judgments. Do not rely upon unsupported opinions, overgeneralizations, and platitudes as a substitute for tight, logical argument backed up with facts and figures.
2. You should indicate the key factors which are crucial to the organization's success or failure; i.e., what must it concentrate on and be sure to do right in order to be a high performer.
3. While some information in the case is established fact, other evidence may be in the form of opinions, judgments, and beliefs, some of which may be contradictory or inaccurate. You are thus obligated to assess the validity of such information. Do not hesitate to question what seems to be "fact."
4. You should demonstrate that your interpretation of the evidence is both reasonable and objective. Be wary of preparing an analysis which omits all arguments not favorable to your position. Likewise, try not to exaggerate, prejudge, or overdramatize. Endeavor to inject balance into your analysis. Strive to display good business judgment.

Recommendations. The final section of the written case analysis should consist of a set of recommendations or plan of action. The recommendations should follow directly from the analysis. If they come as a surprise, because they are logically inconsistent with or not related to the analysis, the effect of the discussion is weakened. Obviously, any recommendations for action should offer a reasonable prospect of success. *Be sure that the company is financially able to carry out what you recommend;* also your recommendations need to be workable in terms of acceptance by the persons involved, the organization's competence to implement them, and prevailing market and environmental constraints. Unless you feel justifiably compelled to do so, do not qualify, hedge, or weasel on the actions that you believe should be taken. Furthermore, state your recommendations in sufficient detail to be meaningful. Avoid using panaceas or platitudes such as "the organization should implement modern planning techniques" or "the company should be more aggressive in marketing its product." State *specifically* what should be done and *make sure your recommendations are operational.* For instance, do not stop with saying "the firm should improve its market position," continue on with exactly *how* you think this should be done. And, finally, you should indicate how your plan should be implemented. Here, you may wish to give some attention to leadership styles, psychological approaches, motivational aspects, and incentives that may be helpful. You might also stipulate a timetable for initiating actions, indicate priorities, and suggest who should be responsible for doing what. For example, "Have the manager take the following steps: (1) _____, (2) _____, (3) _____, (4) _____.

In preparing your plan of action, remember that there is a great deal of difference between being responsible, on the one hand, for a decision which may be costly if it proves in error and, on the other hand, expressing a casual opinion as to some of the courses of action which might be taken when you do not have to bear the responsibility for any of the consequences. A good rule to follow in designing your plan of action is to *avoid recommending anything you would not yourself be willing to do if you were in management's shoes.* The importance of learning to develop good judgment in a managerial situation is indicated by the fact that while the same information and operating data may be available to every manager or executive in an organization, it *does* make a difference to the organization which person makes the final decision.[5]

It should go without saying that your report should be organized and written in a manner that communicates well and is persuasive. Great ideas amount to little unless others can be convinced of their merit—this takes effective communication.

Keeping Tabs on Your Performance

Every instructor has his or her own procedure for evaluating student performance so, with one exception, it is not possible to generalize about grades and the grading of case analyses. The one exception is that grades on case analyses (written or oral) almost never depend entirely on how you propose to solve the organization's difficulties. The important elements in evaluating student performance on case analyses consist of (*a*) the care with which facts and background knowledge are used, (*b*) demonstration of the ability to state problems and issues clearly, (*c*) the use of appropriate analytical techniques, (*d*) evidence of sound logic and argument, (*e*) consistency

---

[5] Gragg, "Because Wisdom Can't Be Told," p. 10.

between analysis and recommendations, and (*f*) the ability to formulate reasonable and feasible recommendations for action. Remember, a hard-hitting, incisive, logical approach will almost always triumph over seat-of-the-pants opinions, emotional rhetoric, and platitudes.

One final point. You may find it hard to keep a finger on the pulse of how much you are learning from cases. This contrasts with lecture/problem/discussion courses where experience has given you an intuitive feeling for how well you are acquiring substantive knowledge of theoretical concepts, problem-solving techniques, and institutional practices. But in a case course, where analytical ability and the skill of making sound judgments are less apparent, you may lack a sense of solid accomplishment, at least at first. Admittedly, additions to one's managerial skills and powers of diagnosis are not as noticeable or as tangible as a loose-leaf binder full of lecture notes. But this does not mean they are any less real or that you are making any less progress in learning how to be a manager.

To begin with, in the process of hunting around for solutions, very likely you will find that a considerable knowledge about types of organizations, the nature of various businesses, the range of management practices, and so on has rubbed off. Moreover, you will be gaining a better grasp of how to evaluate risks and cope with the uncertainties of enterprise. Likewise, you will develop a sharper appreciation of both the common and the unique aspects of managerial encounters. You will become more comfortable with the processes whereby objectives are set, strategies are initiated, organizations are designed, methods of control are implemented and evaluated, performance is reappraised, and improvements are sought. Such processes are the essence of strategic management and learning more about them through the case method is no less an achievement just because there is a dearth of finely calibrated measuring devices and authoritative crutches on which to lean.

CASES IN STRATEGIC MANAGEMENT

PART III

A. The General Manager: Tasks, Functions, Responsibilities

1. United Products, Inc.*

Having just returned from lunch, George Brown, president of United Products, Inc., was sitting in his office thinking about his upcoming winter vacation—in a few days he and his family would be leaving from Boston to spend three weeks skiing on Europe's finest slopes. His daydreaming was interrupted by a telephone call from Hank Stevens, UPI's general manager. Mr. Stevens wanted to know if their two o'clock meeting was still on. The meeting had been scheduled to review actions UPI could take in light of the company's sluggish sales and the currently depressed national economy. In addition, Brown and Stevens were to go over the financial results for the company's recently completed fiscal year—they had just been received from UPI's auditors. Although it had not been a bad year, results were not as good as expected and this, in conjunction with the economic situation, had prompted Mr. Brown to reappraise the plans he had for the company during the upcoming year.

COMPANY HISTORY

United Products, Inc., established in 1941, was engaged in the sales and service of basic supply items for shipping and receiving, production and packaging, research and development, and office and warehouse departments. Mr. Brown's father, the founder of the company, recognized the tax advantages in establishing separate businesses rather than trying to consolidate all of his operations in one large organization. Accordingly, over the years the elder Mr. Brown had created new companies and either closed down or sold off older companies as business conditions seemed to warrant. As of the mid-1960s, his holdings consisted of a chain of four related sales distribution companies covering the geographic area from Chicago eastward.

In 1967, feeling it was time to step aside and turn over active control of the business to his sons, the elder Mr. Brown recapitalized and restructured his companies, merging some and disposing of others. When the restructuring process was completed, he had set up two major companies. United Products, Inc., was to be run by his youngest son, George Brown, with its headquarters in Massachusetts, while his other son, Richard Brown, was to operate United Products Southeast, Inc., headquartered in Florida.

---

* Prepared by Prof. Jeffrey C. Shuman, Babson College.

Although the Brown brothers occasionally worked together and were on each other's board of directors, the two companies operated on their own. As George Brown explained, "Since we are brothers, we often get together and discuss business, but the two are separate companies and each files its own tax return."

During 1972, United Products moved into new facilities in Woburn, Massachusetts. From this location it was thought that the company would be able to serve its entire New England market area effectively. "Our abilities and our desires to expand and improve our overall operation will be enhanced in the new specially designed structure containing our offices, repair facilities, and warehouse," is how George Brown viewed the role of the new facilities. Concurrent with the move, the company segmented the more than 3,500 different items it carried into eight major product categories:

1. *Stapling machines.* Manual and powered wire stitchers, carton stitchers, nailers, hammers, and tackers.
2. *Staples.* All sizes and types (steel, bronze, monel, stainless steel, aluminum, brass, etc.) to fit almost all makes of equipment.
3. *Stenciling equipment and supplies.* Featuring Marsh hand and electric machines, stencil brushes, boards, and inks.
4. *Gummed tape machines.* Hand and electric, featuring Marsh, Derby, and Counterboy equipment.
5. *Industrial tapes.* Specializing in strapping, masking, cellophane, electrical, cloth, nylon, and waterproof tapes made by 3M, Mystik, Behr Manning, and Dymo.
6. *Gluing machines.* Hand and electric.
7. *Work gloves.* All sizes and types (cotton, leather, neoprene, nylon, rubber, asbestos, and so on).
8. *Marking and labeling equipment.*

In a flyer mailed to United Products' 6,000 accounts announcing the move to its new facilities, the company talked about its growth in this fashion:

> Here we grow again—thanks to you—our many long-time valued customers . . .
>
> Time and Circumstances have decreed another United Products transPLANT—this time, to an unpolluted garden-type industrial area, ideally located for an ever-increasing list of our customers.
>
> Now, in the new 28,000-sq. ft. plant with enlarged offices and warehouse, we at UNITED PRODUCTS reach the peak of efficiency in offering our customers the combined benefits of maximum inventories, accelerated deliveries, and better repair services.

By 1974, the company had grown to a point where sales were $3.5 million (double that of four years earlier) and 34 people were employed. Results for 1973 compared to 1972 showed a sales increase of 22 percent and a 40 percent gain in profits. Exhibit 1 contains selected financial figures for 1971, 1972, and 1973, in addition to the fiscal 1973 balance sheet.

EXHIBIT 1
Selected Financial Information, United Products, Inc.

	11/30/71	11/30/72	11/30/73
Current assets	$ 862,783	$ 689,024	$ 937,793
Other assets	204,566	774,571	750,646
Current liabilities	381,465	223,004	342,939
Net worth	685,884	750,446	873,954
Sales	n.a.*	2,830,000	3,450,000

Statement of financial
condition, November 30, 1973:

Cash on hand	$ 46,961	Accounts payable	$ 321,885
Accounts receivable	535,714	Notes payable	20,993
Merchandise in inventory	352,136		
Prepaid insurance, interest,			
taxes	2,980		
Current assets	$ 937,791	Current liabilities.	$ 342,878
Fixtures and equipment	$ 42,891	Retained earnings	$ 471,655
Motor vehicles	49,037	Capital stock	519,800
Land and buildings	658,768	Surplus	354,154
Total assets	$1,688,487	Total liabilities ...	$1,688,487

* n.a.: Not available.

COMPETITION

George Brown indicated that UPI does not have clearly defined rivals against whom it competes head-on with respect to all of its 3,500-plus items:

> It is hard to get figures on competition since we compete with no one company directly. Different distributors carry lines which compete with various of our product lines, but there is no one company which competes against us across our full range of products.

On a regular basis, Mr Brown receives Dun & Bradstreet's *Business Information Reports* on specific firms with which he competes. Mr. Brown feels that since the rival firms are, like his own firm, privately held, the financial figures reported are easily manipulated and, therefore, are not a sound basis on which to devise strategies and plans. Exhibit 2 contains comparative financial figures for two competing companies, and Exhibit 3 contains D&B's description of their operations, along with D&B's comments about two other firms operating in UPI's New England market area.

MANAGEMENT PHILOSOPHY

When Mr. Brown took over UPI in 1967 at the age of 24, he set a personal goal of becoming financially secure and developing a highly profitable business. With the rapid growth of the company, he soon realized his goal of financial independence and in so doing began to lose interest in the company.

EXHIBIT 2
Financial Information on Rival Firms

East Coast Supply Co., Inc.—Sales $1 million:

	Fiscal December 31, 1971	Fiscal December 31, 1972	Fiscal December 31, 1973
Current assets	$ 88,555	$132,354	$ 163,953
Other assets	16,082	18,045	27,422
Current liabilities	41,472	47,606	74,582
Net worth	63,165	102,793	116,793

Statement of financial condition, December 31, 1973:

Cash	$ 42,948	Accounts payable	$ 39,195
Accounts receivable	86,123	Notes payable	27,588
Merchandise in inventory	34,882	Taxes	7,799
Current assets	$163,953	Current liabilities	$ 74,582
Fixtures and equipment	$ 15,211	Capital stock	$ 10,000
Deposits	12,211	Retained earnings	106,793
		Total liabilities	
Total assets	$191,375	and net worth	$ 191,375

Atlantic Paper Products, Inc.—Sales $6 million:

	June 30, 1970	June 30, 1971	June 30, 1972
Current assets	$884,746	$1,243,259	$1,484,450
Other assets	93,755	101,974	107,001
Current liabilities	574,855	520,572	1,120,036
Net worth	403,646	439,677	471,415
Long-term debt	0	384,984	

"I became a rich person at age 28 and had few friends with equal wealth that were my age. The business no longer presented a challenge and I was unhappy with the way things were going."

After taking a ten-month "mental vacation" from the business, George Brown felt he was ready to return to work. He had concluded that one way of proving himself to himself and satisfying his ego would be to make the company as profitable as possible. However, according to Mr. Brown, "The company can only grow at approximately 20 percent per year, since this is the amount of energy I am willing to commit to the business."

In 1974, at age 31, Mr. Brown described his philosophical outlook as "very conservative" and surmised that he ran UPI in much the same way as his 65-year-old father would. In describing his managerial philosophy and some of the operating policies he had established, he said:

> I am very concerned about making UPI a nice place to work. I have to enjoy what I'm doing and have fun at it at the same time. I cannot make any more

money, since I'm putting away as much money as I can. The government won't allow me to make more money, since I already take the maximum amount. I like to feel comfortable, and if we grew too quickly it could get out of hand. I realize the business doesn't grow to its potential but why should I put more into it. . . . The company could grow, but why grow? Why is progress good? You have to pay for everything in life and I'm not willing to work harder. . . .

Another thing, I am a scrupulously honest businessman and it is very hard to grow large if you're honest. There are many deals that I could get into that would make UPI a lot of money, but I'm too moral of a person to get involved. . . .

To me, happiness is being satisfied with what you have, I've got my wife, children and health: why risk these for something I don't need? I don't have the desire to make money because I didn't come from a poor family; I'm not hungry.

I have never liked the feeling of owing anything to anyone. If you can't afford to buy something, then don't. I don't like to borrow any money and I don't like the company to borrow any. All of our bills are paid within 15 days. I suppose I've constrained the business as a result of this feeling, but it's my business. The company can only afford to pay for a 20-percent growth rate so that's all we'll grow.

EXHIBIT 3
Descriptions of Major Competitors

East Coast Supply Co, Inc.
Manufacturers and distributes pressure sensitive tapes to industrial users throughout New England area on 1/10 net 30-day terms. Thirty-four employed including the officers, 33 here. Location: Rents 15,000 square feet on first floor of two-story building in good repair. Premises are orderly. Nonseasonal business. Branches are located at 80 Olife Street, New Haven, Connecticut and 86 Weybosset Street, Providence, Rhode Island.

Atlantic Paper Products, Inc.
Wholesales paper products, pressure sensitive tapes, paper specialities, twines and other merchandise of this type. Sales to industrial accounts and commercial users on 1/10 net 30-day terms. There are about 1,000 accounts in eastern Massachusetts and sales are fairly steady throughout the year. Employs 60, including officers. Location: Rents 130,000 square feet of floor space in a six-story brick, mill-type building in a commercial area on a principal street. Premises orderly.

The Johnson Sales Co.
Wholesales shipping room supplies, including staplings and packing devices, marking and stencil equipment. Sells to industrial and commercial accounts throughout the New England area. Seasons are steady. Terms are 1/10 net 30 days. Number of accounts not learned, 15 are employed including the owner. Location: Rents the first floor of a two-story yellow brick building in good condition. Housekeeping is good.

Big City Staple Corp.
Wholesales industrial staples, with sales to 2,000 industrial and commercial firms, sold on 1/10 net 30-day terms. Territory mainly New Jersey. Employs ten including the officers. Seasons steady and competition active. Location: Rents 5,000 square feet in one-story cinder block and brick structure in good condition, premises in neat order. Located on well-traveled street in a commercial area.

ORGANIZATIONAL STRUCTURE

Upon returning to the company from his "mental vacation" in 1971 George Brown realigned UPI's organizational structure as shown in Exhibit 4 (the company does not have a formal organizational chart; this one is drawn from the case researcher's notes). With respect to the way his company was organized, he remarked:

> We have to have it on a functional basis now. We are also trying something new for us by moving to the general manager concept. In the past when I was away, there was no one with complete authority; now my general manager is in charge in my absence.

EXHIBIT 4
Organization Chart—December 1974

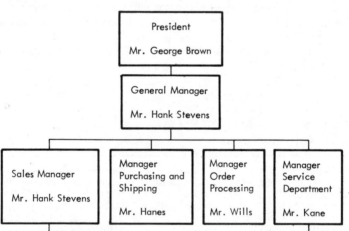

In discussing the new structuring of the organization. Mr. Brown was quick to point out that the company has not established formalized job descriptions. "Job descriptions are not worth anything. My people wear too many hats, and besides, we're too small to put it in writing." At present the company employs 34 people, including Mr. Brown.

Mr. Brown is quick to point out that he has never had a personnel problem. "All my people enjoy working here." He believes that "nobody should work for nothing" and has, therefore, established a personal goal of seeing to it that no one employed by UPI makes less than $10,000 per year. Mr. Brown commented on his attitude toward his employees as follows:

The men might complain about the amount of responsibility placed on them, but I think it's good for them. It helps them develop to their potential. I'm a nice guy who is interested in all of my people. I feel a strong social obligation to my employees and have developed very close relationships with all of them. My door is always open to them no matter what the problem may be.

I make it a policy never to yell at anyone in public; it's not good for morale. Maybe it's part of my conservative philosophy but I want everyone to call me Mr. Brown, not George. I think it's good for people to have a Mr. Brown. Although I want to run a nice friendly business, I have learned that it's hard to be real friends with an employee. You can only go so far. Employers and employees cannot mix socially; it just doesn't work out over the long run.

This is not your normal business. I am very approachable; I don't demand much and I allow an easy open dialogue with my employees. Seldom do I take any punitive action. I'm just not a hard driving, tough guy . . . I'm an easygoing guy.

It would take much of the enjoyment out of the business for me to come in here and run this place like a machine.[1]

I find it hard to motivate the company's salesmen. Since we have so much trouble finding good capable men, I'm not likely to fire any that I have. This situation makes it hard for me to put pressure on them to produce.

The bonus system, if you want to call it that, is I guess what you'd call very arbitrary. I have not set up specific sales quotas, or targeted goals for my inside people so, as a result, I base my bonus decisions on my assessment of how well I feel an employee performed during the past year.

Recently, I've given some thought to selling the company. I could probably get around $3 to $4 million for it. If I did that, I'm not sure what I would do with my time. Besides my family and UPI there is not much that I am interested in. A couple of years ago when I took my extended vacation I got bored and couldn't wait to get back to the company.

UPI'S PLANNING PROCESS

George Brown claims to be a firm believer in planning. "I find myself spending more and more time planning for the company. Currently, I'm averaging about 50 percent of my time and I see this increasing." As he described it, the planning process at United Products is really a very loose system:

We have no set way as to how we do the planning. Basically, the process is directed at ways of increasing the profitability of the company. I look at the salesmen's performance on a weekly and monthly basis, and use this information in the development of the plans.

Since we have a very informal planning process, we only forecast our one year at most. The company's plans are reevaluated each month and, if neces-

---

[1] When the case researcher arrived at the plant one afternoon, he observed Mr. Brown running around the office deeply involved in a water fight with one of his office girls. By the way, he lost.

sary, new plans are set. Only on rare occasions have we ever planned beyond one year. However, I think the current economic and political situation may force us into developing plans that cover a two-year period.

I am familiar with commonly accepted theory about planning systems, but I do not feel it is necessary for UPI to institute, in a formal manner, any of those I've read about. We perform many of the activities advocated in the planning models, but we do them in a relaxed, casual fashion. For example, I am a member of many organizations connected with my business and receive industry newsletters on a regular basis. In addition, I receive input from friends and business associates both inside and outside my line of business. Since we do not have a formal process, planning tends to be a continuous process at UPI.

Although goals are not formally developed and written down, Mr. Brown said he established targets for the company to achieve in the areas of sales, profits, and organizational climate:

1. Increase sales volume of business by 20 percent per year.
2. Increase gross profit margin 0.5 to 1 percent per year.
3. Make UPI a friendly place to work.

Mr. Brown feels that the company has been able to grow at about 20 percent a year in the past and should be able to realize that level in the future. In addition, he believes that sales growth is a necessary evil: "Those companies that don't grow are swallowed up by the competition, and besides, given the level of energy I'm willing to exert, I think 20 percent is a reasonable level of growth."

In the area of profits, the company actually sets no specific targeted figures other than simply an increase in the gross profit margin (as stated above). Mr. Brown observed:

> We do not set a goal because we would not have a way of measuring it. I have no way of knowing how much money I am making until the end of the year, without considerable time and effort.

When asked about UPI's strengths and weaknesses, Mr. Brown indicated that the company had four areas of strength:

1. The number of different products carried.
2. The quality of its employees, particularly salesmen.
3. The absence of any debt.
4. Purchasing capabilities.

The major weakness he viewed as an inability to get and train new personnel—primarily in the area of sales.

SALES FORCE

UPI's salesmen are not assigned a sales quota for the year, but rather are evaluated based on Mr. Brown's assessment of the particular salesman's territory and initiative. He feels his salesmen make more than the salesmen of his competitors. Several of UPI's ten salesmen have earned as much as $40,000 in a single year. All salesmen are compensated on a straight, sliding-scale commission basis calculated as follows:

8 percent for first $180,000 in sales.

7 percent for next $60,000.

6 percent for next $60,000.

5 percent for all sales over $300,000.

Mr. Brown is pleased with the sales success of his company and feels that United Products' greatest strength is its ability to "sell anything to anybody." Still, he perceives UPI's main problem as finding good salesmen. "There just aren't good salesmen around and this is a problem because salesmen are the lifeblood of our business."

UPI'S MANAGEMENT TEAM

At the time of the company's reorganization. Hank Stevens was brought in as general manager and assistant to the president. Over the past several years, Mr. Stevens' areas of responsibility have grown to an extent where they now comprise approximately 80 percent of the activities that were formerly done by Mr. Brown. As a result of this, George Brown sometimes finds himself with little to do and often works only five hours per day. As he described it:

> Hank's management discretionary power has increased steadily since he has been here—partly as a result of the extent of responsibility I've placed on him and partly due to his aggressiveness. As it now stands, he makes almost all of the daily operating decisions for the company, leaving me with only the top management decisions. Let's be realistic, there just aren't that many top-management decisions that have to be made here in the course of a day. A lot of the time, I walk around the plant checking on what other people are doing and, I guess, acting as a morale booster.

When asked about the management capabilities of Hank Stevens, Mr. Brown responded by saying, "Hank probably feels that he is working at a very fast pace, but when you evaluate the effectiveness of his actions, he is actually moving forward at what I would consider to be a very slow pace. However, everything else considered, Hank is the best of what is around. I guess if I could find a really good sales manager, I would add him to the company and relieve Hank of that area of responsibility."

Hank Stevens

Hank Stevens, 32, joined UPI at the time of the reorganization in 1970 after having graduated from a local university with a B.S. in economics. As general manager, Mr. Stevens' responsibilities included planning, purchasing, and sales management, as well as involvement in other decisions that affected UPI's policies. Mr. Stevens feels that he has been fortunate in that "Ever since I came to UPI, I've reported to the president and in essence have had everyone else reporting to me."

When asked about the goals of UPI, Mr. Stevens responded that, "As I see it, we have goals in three major areas: profitability, sales level and personal relationships." In discussing his own personal goals, Hank explained that he hoped that the organization would grow and as a result he would be able to grow along with it. Since Mr. Stevens works so closely with Mr. Brown, he has given considerable thought to his boss's business philosophy:

> I feel that George's business philosophy is unique. I guess the best way to describe it is to say that above all he is a businessman. Also, he has very high moral values and as a result of that he is extremely honest and would never cheat anybody. Actually, the company would probably look better financially if it was run by someone who didn't operate with the same values as George.

When asked about the sales force at UPI, Mr. Stevens commented that "when a new salesman starts with the company, he does so with full salary. After a period of about two years, we change him over to a commission basis." As has always been the case, UPI concentrated its sales efforts on large customers. Mr. Stevens noted that "on the average the company processes approximately 105 orders per day, with an average dollar value per order of roughly $132. It's not that we won't write small orders, we just don't solicit business from small accounts. It just makes more sense to concentrate on the larger accounts."

Jim Hanes

Jim Hanes, 24, has been with UPI for over six years and during that time has worked his way up from assistant service manager to his current position as the number-three man in the company—manager of purchasing and shipping. Jim is responsible for the front office, repair work, and the warehouse. He feels that his reporting responsibility is approximately 60 percent to Mr. Stevens and 40 percent to Mr. Brown. "Since I have responsibility for all merchandise entering and leaving the company, I get involved with both Hank and George, and, therefore, I guess I report to both of them."

In talking about where he would go from his present position, he explained that:

> I guess the next step is for me to become a salesman so that I can broaden my background and move up in the company. However, I am a little worried; I don't think the salesmen in our company are given the right sales training. As the system works now, a new man is assigned to work with an experienced salesman for about six weeks—after which time he is given his own territory.

Perhaps if our sales manager had more experience as a salesman, then he would handle the training differently.

In commenting on his understanding of Mr. Brown's philosophy, Jim summed up his position thusly, "George is a very open person. I think he is too honest for a businessman. He certainly gives his people responsibility. He gives you the ball and lets you run with it. I don't think enough planning is done at UPI. At most, it appears that we look ahead one year, and even then what plans are developed are kept very flexible."

UPI'S CORPORATE STRATEGY

When asked about UPI's current strategy, Mr. Brown responded that "the company is presently a distributor in the industrial packaging equipment, shipping supplies, and heavy duty stapling equipment business. In the past when we've wanted to grow, we have done one or both of the following: either add new lines of merchandise or additional salesmen. For example, this past year I got the idea of what I call a contract sales department. It is a simple concept. I took one man, put him in an office with a telephone and a listing of the *Fortune* top 1,000 companies, and told him to call and get new business. You would be surprised at how easy it was to pick up new accounts."

Mr. Stevens looks at UPI as being in the distribution and shipping of packaging supplies business. "In order for UPI to reach the goals that have been set we have to sell more products. That is, we can grow by adding new salesmen, adding more product lines, purchasing more effectively, and undertaking more aggressive sales promotion."

Mr. Brown believes that UPI should try to maximize the profit on every item sold. To do this the company tries to set its prices at a level which is approximately 10 percent above the competition. Mr. Brown explained his pricing philosophy:

> I don't understand why people are afraid to raise prices. If you increase the price, you will pick up more business and make more money. That allows you to keep the volume low and still make more money. In addition, although the customer may pay more, he gets more. The higher price allows me to provide top notch service to all my customers.

In his view, UPI is an innovative company. "Until very recently we were always innovating with new products and new applications. Now I think it's again time that we started to look for additional new and exciting products."

Brown was aware that UPI's strategic emphasis on service, together with his business philosophy, had resulted in UPI's organization being larger than it had to be, given the level of business. Mr. Brown explained the reasoning behind this condition. "I know the organization is bigger than it has to be. We could probably handle three times the present volume of business with our present staff and facility. I think it's because of my conservative attitude:

I've always wanted the organization to stay a step ahead of what is really needed. I feel comfortable with a built-in backup system and, therefore, I am willing to pay for it."

In December 1974, Mr. Brown talked optimistically about the future. He felt that sales should reach the $6–7 million range by 1978. "Looked at in another way, we should be able to grow at 20–25 percent per year without any particular effort." He went on to say:

> I want to grow and, therefore, I am making a concerted effort. I am constantly looking for possible merger avenues or expansion possibilities. I do not want to expand geographically. I would rather control that market area we are now in.
>
> I recently sent a letter to all competitors in New England offering to buy them out. Believe it or not, no one responded.
>
> I do not see any problems in the future. The history has been good, therefore, why won't it continue to happen?
>
> Growth is easy. All I have to do is pick up a new line and I've automatically increased sales and profits. Basically we are distributors, and we operate as middle-men between the manufacturers and users.
>
> In light of what has been happening in the market. I feel that supply and demand will continue to be a problem. Therefore, I am giving serious thought to integrating vertically and becoming a manufacturer. This will guarantee our supply.[2]
>
> Actually, I don't want to do the manufacturing. I think it would be better if I bought the manufacturing equipment and then had someone else use it to make my products.

THE FUTURE

Nevertheless, after reviewing with his accountant the results for the just-completed fiscal year, Mr. Brown was concerned about UPI's future course. "I know changes have to be made for next year as a result of this year, but I'm not sure what they should be." Mr. Brown continued:

> I think this next year is going to be a real bad year. Prices will probably fall like a rock from the levels they reached during 1974 and as a result those items that would have been profitable for the company aren't going to be, and we have much too large of an inventory as it is. It isn't easy to take away customers from the competition. As a result of this, I feel we have to step up our efforts to get new lines and new accounts. Recently, I've given some thought to laying off one or two people for economic reasons, but I'm not sure. I will probably give raises to all employees even though it's not a good business decision, but it's an ingrained part of my business philosophy.

---

[2] Refer to Exhibit 5 which contains minutes of a United Products sales meeting held at the end of 1973.

When asked if he had informed his employees of his concern about the future, Mr. Brown referred to the minutes of a sales meeting that had been held in November 1974:

. . . Mr. Brown then presided at the meeting, and announced that Al King had won the coveted award of "Salesman of the Month." This was a "first" for our Al, and well deserved for his outstanding sales results in October. Congratulations and applause were extended him by all present. The balance of the meeting was then spent in a lengthy, detailed discussion, led by Mr. George Brown, of the general, overall picture of what the future portends in the sales area as a result of the current inflationary, recessionary and complex competitive conditions prevailing in the economy.

The gist of the entire discussion can be best summarized as follows:
1. Everyone present must recognize the very real difficulties that lie ahead in these precarious economic times.
2. The only steps available to the salesmen and to the company for survival during the rough period ahead are as follows:
   A. Minimize the contacts with existing accounts.
   B. Spend the *majority* of time *developing new accounts* on the less competitive products: and *selling new products to established accounts.*
3. *Concentrate on and promote our new items.*
4. Mr. Brown and inside management are making and will continue to make every, concentrated effort to find new products and new lines for the coming year.

EXHIBIT 5
Minutes of UPI's Sales Meeting, December 5, 1973

Mr. Brown presided at the meeting. His opening remarks highlighted the extraordinary times our country and our company are going through as far as the general economy and the energy crisis are concerned, and the extraordinary effects of these unusual crises on people and businesses, including our company and our sources of supply.

He thanked all present for the many thoughtful, considered and excellent suggestions which they had offered in writing as to how best the salesmen and their company might handle the gasoline crisis without incurring an undue loss of sales and profits, and still maintaining the high standards of service to which UNITED PRODUCTS' thousands of satisfied customers are accustomed.

The whole situation, according to Mr. Brown, boils down to a question of supply and prices. Mr. Brown reported that on his recent trip to the Orient, there were very few companies who wanted to sell their merchandise to us—rather, THEY WANTED TO BUY FROM US MANY OF THE ITEMS WE NORMALLY BUY FROM FOREIGN COMPANIES, i.e., carton-closing staples, tape, gloves, et cetera . . . and at inflated prices!!! The Tokyo, Japan market is so great that they are using up everything they can produce—and the steel companies would rather make flat steel than the steel rods which are used for making staples. A very serious problem exists, as a result, in the carton-closing staple field not only in Japan, but also in Europe and America.

Mr. Brown advised that every year the company's costs of operating increase just as each individual's cost of living goes up and up yearly. Additional personnel, increased group and auto insurance premiums, increased Social Security payments, new office equipment and supplies, new catalogues, "Beeper system" for more salesmen—all of these costs accumulate and result in large expenditures of money. Manufacturers cover their increased operating costs by pricing their products higher—but to date, UNITED

EXHIBIT 5 (continued)

PRODUCTS has never put into their prices the increased costs resulting from increased operating expenses. Last year, the 3 percent increase which the company needed then was put into effect by many of you. HOWEVER, in order for the company to realize that additional profit, this 3 percent price increase had to be put into effect ACROSS THE BOARD . . . all customers . . . all items!

THAT DID NOT HAPPEN!!!

Mr. Brown advised that UNITED PRODUCTS got LAMBASTED when all of the sources of supply started to increase their prices. When SPOTNAILS, for example, went up 10 percent, the salesmen only increased their prices 7 percent, et cetera. We did *not get the 3 percent price increase above the manufacturers' price increase*—and we needed it then and need it even more NOW.

Eliminating the possibility of cutting commissions, there are three possible solutions for the problem of how to get this much needed and ABSOLUTELY IMPERATIVE additional 3 percent PRICE INCREASE ACROSS THE BOARD to cover the constantly growing operating costs for running a successful, progressive-minded and growing business whose high standards of service and performance are highly regarded by customers and sources of supply alike, namely:

a.   A 3 percent increase on all items to all customers across the board.
b.   A surcharge on all invoices or decrease in discounts allowed off LIST.
c.   A GCI charge (government cost increase) on all invoices.

Considerable discussion regarding these three possibilities resulted in the following conclusions concerning the best method for obtaining this special 3 percent ACROSS THE BOARD PRICE INCREASE, as follows:

a.   A new PRICE BOOK should be issued with all new prices to reflect not only the manufacturers' new increased prices, but in addition the 3 percent UNITED PRODUCTS PRICE INCREASE. All of the salesmen agreed that it would be easier to effect the additional 3 percent price increase if the 3 percent was "Built in" on their price book sheets.
b.   This new PRICE BOOK will be set up in such a way that prices will be stipulated according to quantity to item purchased . . . with no variances allowed. WITH NO EXCEPTIONS, the Price of any item will depend on the quantity a customer buys.
c.   Some items will continue to be handled on a discount basis—but lower discounts in order to ascertain that UNITED PRODUCTS is getting its 3 percent price increase.
d.   Until these new PRICE BOOKS are issued, all salesmen were instructed to proceed IMMEDIATELY to effect these 3 percent price increases.

TEN NEW ACCOUNTS CONTEST

Seven of our ten salesmen won a calculator as a result of opening up 10 new accounts each . . . a total of 70 NEW ACCOUNTS for our company!!! However, both Mr. Brown and Mr. Stevens confessed that the dollar volume amount stipulated in the contest had been set ridiculously low, as a "feeler" to determine the success and effectiveness of such a contest. All the salesmen voiced their approval of all of the contests offered to them—and agreed that they had enjoyed many excellent opportunities of increasing their personal exchecquers.

NEW CUSTOMER LETTERS

Mr. Brown again reminded all present that we have an excellent printed letter, which is available for sending to every new customer—and urged all to take advantage of this service by the office personnel by clearly indicating on their sales and order slips "NEW CUSTOMER." The procedure is but another step towards our goal of becoming more and more professional in our approach with our customers.

EXHIBIT 5 (concluded)

NEW CATALOGS

Mr. Brown advised that by the first of the new year, hopefully, all our hard-cover catalogs with their new divider breakdowns will be ready for hand-delivering to large accounts. These catalogs cost the company over $5 and should only be distributed by hand to those customers who can and will make intelligent and effective use of them.

EXCESSIVE ISSUANCE OF CREDITS

As a result of a detailed study made by Mr. Brown of the nature and reasons for the ever-increasing number of credits being issued, he instructed all of the salesmen to follow these procedures when requesting the issuing of CREDITS:

a. Issue the CREDIT at the right time.
b. Do not sell an item where it is not needed.
c. NEVER PUT "NO COMMENT" for the reason why merchandise is being returned. EVERY CREDIT MUST HAVE A REASON FOR ITS ISSUANCE.

The ever-increasing number of CREDITS being issued is extremely costly to the company: (1) new merchandise comes back 90-plus days after it has been billed, and frequently, if not always, is returned by the customer FREIGHT COLLECT; (2) CREDIT 9-part forms, postage for mailing, and extra work for both the Bookkeeping and Billing and Order Processing Departments mean higher expenses for the Company. More intelligent, considered and selective selling, plus greater care on the part of the Order Processing personnel, according to Mr. Brown, could easily eliminate a large percentage of these CREDITS.

In preparation for his meeting with Hank Stevens, Mr. Brown had drawn up a list of activities to which Hank should address himself while running UPI during George's upcoming vacation. Mr. Brown believed that upon his return from Europe his activities at UPI would be increasing as a result of the problems caused by the uncertain economic conditions. The first item on the list was a possible redefinition of UPI's marketing strategy. Mr. Brown now believed that UPI would have to be much more liberal with respect to new products considered for sale. "I'm not saying we are going to get into the consumer goods business, but I think we need to give consideration to handling consumer products which require no service and which carry a high-profit-margin factor for the company."

As he sat at his desk thinking about possible changes which he could make in UPI's planning process, Mr. Brown was convinced that if he hadn't done some planning in the past, the situation would be more drastic than it was. Yet at the same time, he wasn't sure that a more structured and formalized planning process would put UPI in any better position to face the more difficult times that he saw ahead.

2. Steadman Realty Company*

I think that there are certain fundamental principles involved in all forms of selling, and they apply especially to selling homes. You must develop a reputation for dependability and trustworthiness, and in the long run this can only be achieved by being dependable and trustworthy. In the end the willingness to provide the degree of service and attention to detail which this involves will determine the success or failure of a realtor.

So stated Henry Steadman, a successful realtor located in the town of Hendrix. Using this philosophy he had, in ten years of doing business, built Steadman Realty into one of Hendrix's leading real estate enterprises. Now, he had reached a critical stage in the growth of his firm and was considering what steps to take to ensure its continued profitable growth.

THE REAL ESTATE INDUSTRY

The typical real estate firm offers a variety of services involving detailed knowledge of the real estate market. By far the main activity of small real estate firms is assisting families in buying and selling residential properties. Other segments of the real estate market include property management, sale of commercial real estate, operation of a rental agency, and syndication of real estate transactions. In general, the larger a firm is, the more of these activities it will undertake.

The demand for the services of realtors is affected by the rate of turnover in the occupancy and ownership of residential dwellings and by the rate at which the local economy is growing. These in turn are influenced by population, occupations within the community, general credit conditions, income levels, changing land use patterns, industrial growth rates, attractiveness of the area to tourists, availability of recreation facilities, and so on. On a nationwide basis, the dollar volume of real estate transactions has grown at annual rates averaging 8 percent for the past decade.

Industry Structure. The predominant form of business organization in the real estate industry is the small proprietorship having fewer than ten sales associates. Most recently, though, corporate organizational forms have be-

---

* Prepared by Richard I. Levin and Ian Cooper, Graduate School of Business Administration, the University of North Carolina at Chapel Hill.

come more numerous, especially in the case of enterprises doing large volumes of business and offering a full range of real estate services. In between these two organizational forms in both size and number are partnerships.

The strongest constraint of the growth of the individual firms has, in the past, been geographical. The vast majority of firms operate in a single community, out of one office or a small number of branch offices. Since the lifeblood of a realtor's business tends to be reputation and contacts within the community, this mitigates against large, multiunit, multilocational firms. With increasing transiency and impersonality, however, there is now more opportunity for large firms to exist, and affiliation with national chains like Century 21 and Gallery of Homes has recently become more popular in some areas of the country.

Entry into the Industry. A realtor must be licensed by the state as a real estate broker. This requires passing an examination which tests knowledge of many aspects of real estate, including construction, financing, appraisal, and law. Realtors usually are members of local boards of realtors, which, in turn, are affiliated with the National Association of Realtors; the latter association often requires additional training to meet higher standards than those required by the state licensing agency. The real estate salesperson must also be licensed by the state, but the requirements are less stringent than those for the broker.

The financial costs to enter the real estate field are fairly low, involving only sufficient funds to carry the expenses of maintaining an office and covering expenses for advertising, signs, and incidentals. As sales volume builds up, these expenses tend to be readily covered by the broker's sales commissions. The National Association of Realtors tries to maintain professional standards in the industry, but the ease of entry and exit means that there are many "marginal" firms doing business in the industry.

Marketing. The service of the realtor is bought by the prospective seller who "lists" his or her property with the firm. Upon sale of the property he pays to the broker a commission, calculated as a percentage of the sale price. Listings are generally secured as a result of personal contacts, advertising, contacting owners who are trying to sell their homes without the services of a realtor, and recommendations from satisfied clients. One of the most important elements in securing listings in reputation. The successful realtor endeavors to build a reputation for being able to sell his listings, for providing a high level of service, and for reliability. Ideally, such an image should be held by both buyers and sellers of homes, so marketing efforts tend to be aimed at both of these groups.

Competition. Most realtors share listings with others, either through a formal multiple listing service or on an informal basis. If a property is listed by one realtor and sold by another, they split the commission. Therefore, a high degree of cooperation and interchange often exists between firms doing business in the same location. Commission percentages do not usually vary between realtors, so the main competitive element is the degree of service offered. Since service is largely a subjective concept, there can be considerable diversity in the ways in which individual realtors operate their organizations.

Income. The total commission on a transaction is usually about 6 percent of the selling price on improved property, 10 percent on unimproved land, and often negotiated on large commercial transactions. The individual who secures the listing, whether it be the broker or a salesperson, receives a listing fee. Normally this is between 10 percent and 20 percent of the total commission (between 0.6 percent and 1.2 percent of the selling price of the house). The rest of the commission is then customarily split about equally between the broker and the salesperson who sold the property. Various other systems of salesperson compensation involving such schemes as quotas and bonuses also exist. In the case of co-brokering (the situation where a property listed by one firm is sold by another), the two firms generally each take half of the commission. The selling realtor then splits his half with the salesperson who sold the property, and the listing realtor pays the lister his listing commission and keeps the rest. In the case where he obtains the listing himself, the listing realtor keeps the entire 3 percent. The realtor's commission income is highly dependent on changes in the housing market, financial conditions, and the skill of the broker and his salespersons in securing listings and selling property.

Costs. All personal expenses involved in selling (car, entertainment) are borne by the individual salesperson, whose pay is often entirely in the form of commissions. The broker himself bears the cost of maintaining the office: rent, secretarial and clerical staff, advertising, utilities, telephone, and so on. The income of the broker comes from his share of the commissions net of these office costs. Since the office maintenance costs are relatively fixed, the broker's net income can be subject to considerable variation as the firm's volume varies.

Typical income and cost figures for a small realtor office might be:

Total commissions	100%
Salespersons' share of commission	50
Income to broker's office	50
Costs as percentage of income to office	
Legal and professional	3
Telephone	6
Salaries:	
Clerical	15
Managerial	10
Promotion, entertainment, travel	5
Rent and utilities	6
Car and depreciation	5
Supplies and maintenance	5
Advertising	15
Other	5
Net profit	25

The figures above are adapted from a realtor periodical, *Real Estate Today*, and apply to an office with one broker and about a dozen salespersons. The profit figure is, of course, the income to the broker.

Organization. The typical proprietorship has at least a secretary and a bookkeeper, as well as the broker and the salespeople. Larger firms have a sales manager and other staff to take care of customer service and areas of business other than residential sales. The hours which sales personnel work tend to be irregular, and evening and weekend work is common. The payment of sales personnel purely by commissions, the fact that real estate selling is a part-time position for many of them, and the growing number of women in sales generates a high rate of turnover among salespeople. This situation is exacerbated because entry to the profession does not have the heavy formal requirements of many other professions.

Key Trends. Just as in other industries, local realtors find that the nature of the business is changing somewhat. Decreasing personal contact and increasing transiency are lowering former barriers to size. The average size of real estate firms is increasing, and the corporate form of organization is becoming more common. With these changes is coming a desire by realtors to be recognized as a profession and to regulate standards of business practice within the industry.

To retain more professional personnel and to increase their control over the sales force, some brokers are beginning to pay their sales staff partially by salary. This also permits more formalized organizational structures, further enabling the growth of these firms.

There is increasing government involvement in the financing, construction, and planning of real estate. Large corporations from other industries are also moving into the field, and the future of realtors may lie in increased size, professionalism, more effective service, and ability to compete. Nonetheless, there are no strong signs, as yet, that the small local real estate firm is an endangered species.

HISTORY AND BACKGROUND OF STEADMAN REALTY

Mr. Steadman had moved to Hendrix in the early 1960s to work in an industry closely allied to real estate. In the course of his work he discovered that the realtors engaged in selling hourses in Hendrix were generally content with the status quo and not innovative in the services that they offered. Such complacency in the face of steadily demand for realtor services led Mr. Steadman to believe that there was a good opportunity for a new realtor in in the town.

In August of 1963, Mr. Steadman rented an office in Hendrix and opened Steadman Realty. His initial investment consisted of a few hundred dollars for supplies and furnishings and enough money to carry the modest operating expenses of the office until it could become self-supporting. The risk of the decision was considerable, however, since it involved giving up his job and being prepared to support himself and his family for the six months he estimated it would require for the business to become profitable.

From the start Mr. Steadman decided to specialize in helping families sell their individual homes. In 1974, 90 percent of the income of the firm still came from commissions on residential sales. At first business was slow, but as the town expanded and the reputation of the firm grew, the volume of transactions at Steadman Realty steadily increased. In 1967, the general economic recession hit the Hendrix real estate market rather hard, and Mr. Steadman was forced to retrench—a move which, in part, led to the dismissal of two salespersons out of the total of five who had joined the firm as it expanded.

From 1967 on, the business grew rapidly, except for a dip in activity caused by another economic recession in 1970. Operating statistics for the years 1970 to 1974 are given in Exhibit 1. By 1974, the commission income of

EXHIBIT 1
Operating Statistics, 1970–1974

	Years Ending August 31				
	1970	1971	1972	1973	1974
Total commission income	$140,000	$149,000	$204,000	$296,000	$316,000
Costs as a percentage of total commission income:					
Sales commissions	43.4%	34.0%	39.2%	46.5%	47.3%
Office salaries	6.1	6.7	6.0	7.0	9.6
Advertising	8.0	6.0	4.6	4.2	5.8
Telephone	2.5	2.7	2.3	2.1	2.3
Insurance	0.6	0.9	0.6	0.7	0.7
Rent	2.3	2.2	1.9	2.0	2.2
Customer service	2.9	4.6	3.2	2.1	1.4
Office supplies	1.1	0.6	1.4	1.5	1.3
Miscellaneous	6.2	6.0	6.5	5.7	6.1
Percentage total	73.1%	63.7%	65.7%	71.8%	76.7%
Percentage profit and salary to owner	26.9	36.3	34.3	28.2	23.3

the firm had grown to $316,000, and the number of salespeople to eight. This fast growth had been achieved by gaining an increasing share of an expanding market, and in 1974, Mr. Steadman estimated that he had a market share between 20 and 30 percent of the total residential home sales in Hendrix in which realtors were involved. This represented a substantial share since there were 20 real estate firms in Hendrix.

The office staff of the firm had grown along with the sales personnel. Mr. Steadman had begun with a single employee acting as a combination secretary and bookkeeper. As business had grown, these responsibilities were split between two employees. Three further staff members had been added at various times. The latest addition to the staff had been in 1973, when a young woman was hired to take over advertising and certain customer service responsibilities.

THE TOWN OF HENDRIX

In 1974, Hendrix was a town of 40,000 people; the major employers were several large research facilities that either were part of or did work for medical organizations, technical firms, and the government. The population of the town was diverse in geographic origin, well educated, and predominantly white collar. Income levels were high, but the career demands on the skilled research workers often meant that they would not stay permanently in the town. Most of the people buying houses in Hendrix could be expected to stay between 4 and 12 years in those houses.

As more research facilities located in Hendrix during the 1960s, the population grew at an average annual rate of 7 percent. To accommodate this growth there had been a boom in building activity in the town, and this had continued into the early 70s. Despite the new homes coming onto the market, vacancy rates were extremely low, and property values remained high. In addition to single-family homes, there were many apartments in the town, and in recent years apartments and condominiums had formed an increasing proportion of total dwelling units. Some statistics on the population and housing characteristics of the town are given in Exhibit 2.

EXHIBIT 2
Market Profile of Town of Hendrix, 1973

1973 population	37,900
Annual population growth rate (1963–74)	7%
Number of households	9,500
Annual growth rate of households (1963–73)	7%
Number of houses	5,900
Number of apartments	3,600
Number of residential homes sold 1973	610
Annual growth in number of homes sold (1963–73)	10%

COMPETITION AND LOCAL REALTY PRACTICES

In 1974, there were about 20 realtors in Hendrix who acted as agents for the sale of individual homes. Few concentrated on this one activity as exclusively as Mr. Steadman, and other common areas of involvement were commercial real estate, insurance, property management, and large subdivision developments of new homes. The number of houses sold in Hendrix grew at an average annual rate of 10 percent from 1964 to 1974, and the price of homes had risen at about 8 percent annually throughout the period. In 1974, the tight money situation had caused a decline in the number of houses sold, but housing prices nonetheless rose almost 15 percent in 1974 alone—to about $45,000. In 1973, just over 600 houses changed hands in Hendrix; probably 10 percent to 15 percent of these transactions were carried out without the aid of a realtor.

All realtors in Hendrix charged a 6 percent commission on their sales. Traditionally there had been little competition in the degree of service which they offered. This, Mr. Steadman felt, was still true of many of the realtors in Hendrix. As an example, he cited the lack of care taken by some of the realtor firms to ensure that all details of the transaction (deeds, contracts, inspections, financing, homeowner's insurance, etc.) were completed before the final "closing" of the sale. He considered such attention to detail essential, and took great care to ensure that his sales personnel went to their closings with all these details finalized. Steadman also insisted that his salespeople prepare their clients for the closing with pre-closing statements and conferences.

Prospects for buying homes came from several sources, including the various research institutes. Often when a prospective employee would come to Hendrix on a job interview, the employer would make arrangements with one of the real estate firms in Hendrix for the visitor to be toured through the town and its residential areas. Many of these visits would not result in a sale for the realtor, and sometimes the newcomer would not even take the job in Hendrix, but nevertheless, this was the largest single source of contacts with prospective buyers of homes in the community. Mr. Steadman always tried to accommodate such requests, and arrange motel reservations if necessary, so that he could maintain the good relationship of his firm with the employers in the town.

The realtors in Hendrix did have a local board of realtors, but this tended to be a loose federation with little impact. It made no attempt to collect and distribute data, or to influence the conduct of any individual firm, nor did it undertake any institutional advertising to increase the proportion of house sellers employing the services of professional real estate firms.

STEADMAN REALTY'S PHYSICAL FACILITIES

The offices of Steadman Realty were located close to downtown Hendrix in an area predominantly occupied by small professional businesses. Each of the eight salespersons occupied a desk in one of four offices, two to an office. The secretary, the bookkeeper, and the three staff assistants each worked in separate offices, the secretary's area also being the reception area outside Mr. Steadman's office. There were other rooms in the same building which were available to Mr. Steadman if he wanted more space.

ORGANIZATION AND STAFFING

In 1974, there were 13 people employed by Steadman Realty, excluding Mr. Steadman. Eight of these were salespersons, compensated entirely by commissions. The other five included a secretary, a bookkeeper, a young woman responsible for advertising and post-sale customer service, and two young men. The two men were beginning to develop areas of business new to the firm. The most promising of these was the growing opportunity for putting together limited partnerships for various real estate investment purposes. Although this operation was not currently covering its costs, Mr. Steadman was confident that it would make a profit for the firm in 1975.

The other young man was acting as a property manager for a number of single-family homes and for a new housing project currently being rented. Mr. Steadman did not think that the income to his firm from the housing project service would warrant the time and effort put into it. Nevertheless, he was committed to staying with the program due to promises which he had felt obliged to make, and was prepared to carry the operation until other arrangements could be made.

All staff reported directly to Mr. Steadman, and relations within the office were very informal. He kept closely in touch with the work of the staff, and sometimes became involved in minor details. This enabled him to make sure that the concern for quality in the work of the firm was maintained, but Mr. Steadman realized that it was holding him back from other things that he should be spending time on. Although each employee was becoming more capable with experience, Mr. Steadman did not think that he could relax this close supervision. The basic problem in this respect was that, although the staff was well motivated, they sometimes lacked a business perspective on problems. For instance, when the advertising employee needed certain office supplies, she went to a retail office supply outlet rather than to one of Hendrix's wholesale supply firms. This fact came to Mr. Steadman's attention during a discussion with her of details of a project on which she was working, and enabled him to alter office purchasing procedure to solve the problem.

SALES PERSONNEL

The sales associates operated more independently than the office staff, but Mr. Steadman still monitored the details of their work. He did not think that they resented his supervision of their activities:

> I might walk past someone's desk and see a pile of papers, so I will just ask what they are. There is probably no reason for me to know, but I can't help being interested in the things that are happening in the office, and they understand that. Many an important detail has been brought to light by such casual observation. That doesn't speak well for my management style, but that's the way it is. The employee may not think it is important, but I often see something I might never have known about otherwise and, recognizing its importance, can do something about it before it is too late.

The sales associates were all women and had been with the firm for periods varying up to six years. Most were former homemakers who had come to Steadman Realty from another firm in Hendrix. The eight salespeople varied in both age and personality, and differences in individual productivities could not be accounted for by any readily identifiable personal characteristics. Mr. Steadman hired people whose personalities he felt would fit in with the philosophy of the firm, and who, he felt, would be compatible with the other employees. In one case of a bad personality clash between two of the saleswomen, he had thought it necessary to discharge one to preserve the harmony of the group. In this particular case Mr. Steadman, himself, had no difficulty getting along with either of the two people involved.

The saleswomen recognized the ability of Mr. Steadman to cope with difficult situations, and often came to him when they had a problem which they could not resolve. For instance, an overlooked detail might necessitate asking a favor of a lawyer involved in a sale; a buyer might have difficulty with financing and need to come to a special arrangement with the seller; or an obstinate seller might refuse a good offer for the sake of a few hundred dollars. In some cases the problems could be very personal and require a high level of diplomacy and understanding, qualities which had contributed considerably to Mr. Steadman's personal success as a realtor.

Some realtors in the town were interested in hiring away successful salespeople from the other firms. This was not a problem, however, for Steadman Realty, since the close personal relationships encouraged loyalty. On a purely business level, Mr. Steadman thought that his employees considered Steadman Realty to be the best in town to work for and wanted to be identified with it.

Prospective purchasers referred to him by personal contacts were each interviewed by Mr. Steadman. He would talk with them for about a quarter of an hour to discover general background information such as family size and financial means. From his assessment of the prospect's situation and needs, together with his knowledge of the number of clients and work load of each saleswoman, Mr. Steadman would then match the client with the saleswoman he thought most suitable. He had discussed with the sales staff whether it would be fairer to allocate prospective purchasers to them on a purely arbitrary rotational basis, but they had agreed that they preferred the present system.

The saleswoman's function at this point was to work with the customer to crystallize his needs and financial ability and to select properties which were on the market and might be suitable. Over a period of time, often limited by the amount of time that the client would be in town, the saleswoman would show the properties to the customer. This would often involve evening or weekend work for the saleswoman. Most of Steadman's saleswomen tried to take an active interest in each customer's situation and to develop a sense of rapport. Sometimes, however, a saleswoman would fail to follow up adequately a lead which she thought would not produce a sale, and Mr. Steadman tried to stay on top of each situation so he would know when to step in and make sure that sufficient care was being taken to ensure that a qualified buyer was not neglected.

Each week there was an hour-long sales meeting during which Mr. Steadman would inform all the staff of new listings, problems with clients, changes in policy, and any new developments in the firm. It was difficult to get all the sales staff to attend, since some would have appointments at the time of the meeting. Mr. Steadman had never made a big issue of these absences, however, since the saleswomen had to tailor their schedules around the availability of their clients. Feedback from the staff at these meetings was generally good, and most of the staff were quick to raise objections to anything with which they disagreed. A few of the saleswomen, though, did not consider the meetings very important, and Mr. Steadman was seeking ways to increase their enthusiasm and involvement.

MARKETING

A reputation for good service was the firm's most important marketing tool. Satisfied buyers, new to Hendrix, often talked to others about their experiences in buying their home, and the personal recommendations of satisfied buyers was, according to Mr. Steadman, strong encouragement for other prospective buyers to want to deal with the Steadman firm. Moreover, satisfied buyers who had dealt with Steadman were more likely to list their property with Mr. Steadman when the time eventually would come for them to sell. For these reasons, Mr. Steadman stressed the importance of taking care of all details of a sale, even if it involved spending part of the commission to improve minor defects in the property before the new owners moved in.

The saleswomen seemed to appreciate such details, but sometimes did not follow up the sale in the way Mr. Steadman considered necessary:

> We give a small gift to each purchaser after they move in, as a gesture of welcome. The saleswomen were not getting these delivered quickly after the sale, so I made it a firm policy that they would not get their commission check until the gift was out. Now we have no problem.

Some of the duties of maintaining post-sale contacts with home buyers had recently been taken over by the new female employee Steadman had hired to make follow-up contacts with clients, help with customer service, and oversee the firm's advertising program. Mr. Steadman considered that keeping in touch with previous buyers was one of the most important elements in the continuing growth of the firm and in developing a competitive edge over the other realty firms in Hendrix.

Mr. Steadman was very active in civic affairs in Hendrix, and had good relationships with both community groups and major employers in the town. Steadman felt obliged to maintain a visible civic profile because none of his other employees seemed inclined to assume this role. In Steadman's view, consistent public exposure, combined with a good selling reputation, was what drew most listings to the firm. When sellers called to inquire about listing their property, they would usually ask to speak to Mr. Steadman, who would then personally conduct the appraisal and discuss with the seller the specific features affecting the potential sale of the property.

Steadman Realty marketed its services in traditional ways. Generally, all listed properties were advertised in the local paper; this not only brought properties to the attention of potential buyers but it also made sellers feel that they were getting market exposure. It was Steadman's policy to take out ads in any local publication in which the majority of the realtors in Hendrix advertised—so as to neutralize any competitive advantage they might otherwise gain. One area of advertising where the firm did differ from others in the town was its heavier use of radio spots. Escalating rates were beginning to make this expensive, but Mr. Steadman believed radio was an effective medium to help convey the personalized service approach he was trying to achieve. To help reinforce that image, the firm did its own radio spots rather than using local announcers.

COSTS AND FINANCIAL DATA

Steadman Realty was organized as a corporation partly as a device for reducing Mr. Steadman's personal income tax on the profits he was reinvesting in the business and partly to give Mr. Steadman some flexibility in controlling the tax bracket of the firm through adjustments in the amount of salary that he drew. Exhibit 3 presents a percentage breakdown of the firm's costs for fiscal 1974 and shows how Steadman's percentages compared with similar operating percentages for a large, successful, multioffice realtor firm with over 50 sales associates. The proportion of the total commissions

EXHIBIT 3
Comparison of Operating Statistics of Steadman Realty for 1974 and a Large Successful Realtor Firm

Operating Statistics	Steadman Realty	Large Firm
Total commissions:	100.0%	100.0%
Sales staff share	47.3	51.5
Income to realtor's office	52.7	48.5
Costs as a percentage of commission income to the realtor's office:		
Advertising	11.0	12.0
Office staff	18.5	15.9
Sales management	0.0	21.3
Telephone	4.4	5.2
Rent	4.2	4.9
Supplies	2.5	2.6
Customer service	2.7	2.5
Other	12.8	13.7
Total percentage	56.1	78.1
Net income to broker	43.9	21.9

Source: Statistics reported in *Real Estate Today.*

earned by Steadman Realty which was paid to the saleswomen tended to be lower than for other firms since Mr. Steadman did most of the listing, and the listing fee thus accrued directly to the firm. In 1973 and 1974, the proportion of commissions paid to saleswomen was higher than for previous years because a larger fraction of Steadman's sales had involved other realtors' listings.

Steadman's salespeople earned gross commissions of between $10,000 and $25,000 each year, but there was only limited consistency in the level of earnings of each sales associate from year to year. The top salesperson one year could be number three or four the next year because of fluctuations in the percentage of clients who would actually buy a house—fluctuations which were not always within the salesperson's ability to control.

Staff costs comprised the largest category of overhead expense. Before Mr. Steadman hired a new staff member, he tried to make sure he had a large enough commission revenue to support the permanently increased level of overhead. Uncertainty about what kind of year 1975 would be made him wary of taking on more staff, but he knew that if he did so it would have to be during the slack period from November to January, so that he would have time to spare to train the person.

The selling costs Steadman Realty incurred in advertising, promotional efforts, and telephone costs were not always closely tied to the firm's sales volume. For instance, in slack years selling costs might actually be increased (as well as rising percentagewise) in an attempt to stimulate sales and try to keep commission income high enough to cover office overhead and salaries.

CONTROLS

No formal budget or sales goals were set by Mr. Steadman. Recording and filing systems had been developed as the firm grew, and were modified or expanded as new needs for information arose. The bookkeeper prepared monthly financial statistics, and Mr. Steadman studied these regularly to see how well costs were being kept in line. The number of closings planned, and the average price of these transactions, provided Mr. Steadman with a good indicator of how well the firm's income was being maintained. Annual comparative figures of monthly sales were of limited value, however, since the timing of sales activity in the market was likely to vary from year to year.

Mr. Steadman insisted that fairly comprehensive records be kept on prospective buyers and sellers; for example, the sales associates were expected to maintain a "client prospect card" on each buyer they were handling. From time to time, Mr. Steadman would go through these cards with his salespeople and check their progress with each customer he had assigned to them. Since the saleswomen were "independent contractors" and were compensated entirely by commissions, Mr. Steadman found that it was sometimes difficult to get them to adhere to his policy of keeping good records and updating files; some complained that they did not see these "duties" as being directly related to their job of selling or as being worth the time and effort it took. In responding to these complaints, it was usually sufficient for Mr. Steadman to emphasize that record-keeping and buyer follow-up were integral parts of the personalized and professional touch he was trying to create and that he wished them to adhere to policy. Chronic cases of nonadherence presented Mr. Steadman with a difficult choice as to whether to press the issue. Sometimes he did and sometimes he did not. On the issue of getting the gifts to the buyers promptly he had drawn a hard line but so far he had not thought it worthwhile to press the issues of slackness in recording customer data following closings and nonattendance of sales meetings.

The atmosphere in the office was generally relaxed, and the saleswomen seemed to enjoy working for the firm. On one occasion, though, a saleswoman remarked to Mr. Steadman that he criticized her faults but did not praise her good work. Mr. Steadman's response was "If you couldn't do your work I would take you aside and show you how. But you can do it, and are very good at it, so when you make a mistake you deserve criticism and constructive suggestions."

Managing the nonselling staff employees was easier; they were all salaried employees and reported directly to Mr. Steadman. He tended to supervise their work closely in an effort to get them used to paying attention to detail. Although Mr. Steadman felt that his office staff at times lacked commitment and initiative, the staff's conversations with the casewriter indicated that this might be due to the tight rein which Mr. Steadman tried to maintain over their work assignments. When informed of these views, Mr. Steadman commented to the effect that he did not think he could afford to give office staff enough responsibility to learn by making mistakes, since this would damage the image of the firm which had taken him so much time to build.

STEADMAN'S WORK LOAD AND TIME ALLOCATION

Mr. Steadman estimated that 20 percent of his time was spent working with sales associates, helping them with problems, giving them information, or discussing their work. As much, if not more, time was spent with the office staff dealing with day-to-day operations of the firm and supervising the special projects that each employee was assigned.

Another time-consuming activity was securing listings. Mr. Steadman personally obtained about 80 percent of the listings of the firm, because of his extensive contacts in the community and because the saleswomen were not either motivated or aggressively inclined to go out and secure listings on their own initiative. This was the case even though the salesperson received the listing fee when she got a seller to list property with Steadman Realty. Originally, Mr. Steadman had taken no listing fee out of the commission for the listings he secured and, in return, the sales associates had performed extra duties such as appraisals which were not directly part of their obligation. Eventually, he had decided that the money he was losing by not taking the listing fee himself was not sufficiently compensated by these extra services. He had, in the face of opposition from the sales staff, started to retain a 10 percent listing fee on the listings he secured. Even so, he still did not think that this was sufficient, and hoped eventually to raise it to 20 percent. He was cautious of this change, however, since he knew it would provoke strong opposition from the sales staff.

Mr. Steadman had several reasons why he did not want to give up the responsibility for dealing with prospects seeking to list their homes with Steadman Realty. He was convinced that many of the sellers who listed with the firm did so because of his own reputation for handling listings personally and because of the fine record of the firm in being able to sell its listings. Second, Mr. Steadman believed that the time he spent working with charities and community groups brought him into contact with potential buyers and sellers and gave the firm needed public exposure. His community involvement was a key factor in distinguishing between his role in the firm and that of the sales associates. He considered civic activities to be an essential function of anyone who would take over some of his responsibilities, and did not think that it was possessed by any of his current staff or saleswomen. Mr. Steadman saw a major difference between the way he was committed to the firm and the way his sales staff was committed:

> The sales staff are dedicated, but not in the same way as I am. Right now one of them is out scraping down shelves in a house into which the new owners are moving tomorrow. She couldn't find the workmen to do it, so she is doing it herself. But if she wanted to go to the beach this weekend, she would just take off. I can understand that, since she has to fit in with her husband's schedule; but if a problem comes up someone must be here, and I'm the one who does that.

A third reason why Mr. Steadman continued to do the listing himself was the income it brought in to the firm rather than being paid out to the sales associates. If he assigned the seller to one of the saleswomen to perform the appraisal and take the listing, the listing fee would go to the salesperson instead of the firm. These fees formed a large part of the salary of the person hired to supervise advertising and to develop new business through customer follow-up.

A final reason that Mr. Steadman wanted to continue taking listings personally was that he enjoyed the process of talking to the sellers and discussing with them the best way to market their house. Moreover, tactful and sophisticated sales strategies often had to be used to convince potential sellers that he, as a realtor, was genuinely seeking to market their house in an effective, professional manner and that he was not merely after the financial gain. This same enjoyment of dealing with people was a reason why Mr. Steadman also took time to talk to prospective buyers before passing them on to the sales staff. Mr. Steadman remarked that he derived a great deal of nonfinancial satisfaction from helping people who were in the market of buying or selling a home fulfill their housing needs and solve problems related to something as important to them as their home.

Another indication of the involvement of Mr. Steadman in his profession was his policy of continuing to maintain a business phone in his home. He explained the reason for this:

> If that phone rings on the weekend it might mean a listing or a sale. It was put in when I couldn't afford to let opportunities like that go by. Now I keep it because I don't want to disappoint people by them not being able to reach someone on the weekend. My secretary has offered to have a phone put in her home for the weekend calls, and I might do that, since it would help her to feel important to the firm.

GROWING PRESSURES ON MR. STEADMAN'S TIME

Mr. Steadman viewed his main problem during the summer of 1974 as an increasingly severe pressure on his own time. The height of the selling season extended from March to September, and during this period he put in extremely long hours. He knew that if the local real estate market was very active in 1975 that his personal work load would be unduly heavy. Several alternatives for action seemed possible, but all had their drawbacks.

An obvious possibility was to hire a manager to take over either the sales management or the office management function. Mr. Steadman had, in the past, considered this step and had even checked into the backgrounds of some people who might be suitable. He had concluded, however, that the closeness of the working relationship and the considerable amount of time he would have to invest in training the person made it unwise to employ anyone about whom he had the slightest reservations. Since he had not found anyone suitable, he had never made a serious move to try to hire a sales or office manager. The characteristics which he required above all were that the person be committed to a real estate career, responsible, and a firm believer in the same professional and personal approach to real estate sales which he himself had. Mr. Steadman was not sure that he could identify the right kind of person for the job without first getting to know him (or her) very well, and, there again, the time involved was a major problem. He knew of people working for other realtors in the town who might meet the qualifications he had in mind, but it was his long-standing practice not to attempt to hire employees away from rival firms.

Another difficulty with employing a good managerial assistant was the high salary required and the added burden to overhead which this would entail; more overhead, felt Steadman, made the firm's profits more vulnerable to a market slump and he was not sure that such risk exposure was warranted. A final repercussion of hiring a manager related to the effect it would have on the firm's personnel. The two young men on the office staff might feel that it demonstrated a lack of confidence in them, and this could have serious consequences for their attitudes toward their jobs. Mr. Steadman thought that the sales staff might also react negatively:

> If I do take on someone with whom I can work, I may lose a couple of sales associates who cannot work with him. What do I get in return for that loss?— time, peace of mind, and the opportunity to pursue other work I have to do. That's the choice I am faced with.

A second alternative to relieve the pressure on his time was for Mr. Steadman to delegate some of his responsibilities to the existing personnel. Yet, Steadman knew that he did not want to stop handling listings personally and that his commitment to quality service meant that he could not relax his close supervision of the work of his employees. While he could, perhaps, reduce the amount of time he spent with prospective buyers, Mr. Steadman did not think that this would be a significant saving, owing to the importance he attached to maintaining close personal involvement with as many customers as possible.

Nor did Steadman believe that the alternative of turning away potential business made good sense. Refusing listings or a deliberate lack of interest in clients would, Steadman felt, undermine the image and growth of the firm— and, eventually, would erode Steadman Realty's strong market position.

In the long run, Steadman saw a need for the firm to get more involved in land developments and speculative homebuilding; while he had a growing interest in pursuing these activities, he did not foresee his having the time it would take unless he made some managerial changes. The pressures of day-to-day operations had, in addition, kept Mr. Steadman from making progress on some internal projects which he had in mind. For instance, he wanted to investigate and possibly institute the use of a policy manual, but he had never found enough free time to devote to this project.

A more immediate and potentially troublesome problem was that one or two of his sales personnel were consistently below par in either their sales performance or their adherence to the firm's selling philosophy. Although circumstances were not so serious that Mr. Steadman felt forced to discharge them, he was alert to the major task he would face in finding better replacements:

> If my secretary or bookkeeper leaves her job, then the firm cannot function until I find a replacement. So I make time and get it done. But if there is a deficiency in the sales force and it is not sufficiently pressing to make a big difference in performance, I will not force myself to free the time to find a new employee.

A major difficulty Steadman encountered in planning the growth of the firm was the unpredictability of the real estate market. He had not found any practical way to predict from year to year what course it would take, and thus forecasting or projecting commission revenues was not very productive. Mr. Steadman did not make any formal business plan, and felt that even if he did it would turn out to be of marginal value in planning the growth of the sales staff:

> If I want to hire a new saleswoman and I take her on before the work is there for her to do, the others will complain that I am taking work away from them. So I just have to wait until they are all working at capacity, and then they can see the need as well.

FUTURE OUTLOOK

Despite his large share of the residential real estate market in Hendrix, Mr. Steadman thought that there was still room for his firm to increase commission revenues from residential sales. Even when his market penetration in Hendrix topped out, he thought that the firm could still expand by entering the markets in nearby towns. One town, about half the size of Hendrix and located 20 miles away, looked particularly promising. Mr. Steadman was confident that if he opened an office there, it would be making money within a few years.

One of the most rapidly expanding segments of the real estate market in Hendrix was apartments. However, meeting the needs of landlords and apartment tenants required as much time and energy as for single-family homes, and under the pressure of time from other activities, Mr. Steadman had elected not to focus very heavily on property management. For similar reasons, he had also decided to stay out of the insurance field.

Commercial real estate sales lacked the personal involvement of residential sales and had, therefore, never appealed much to Mr. Steadman. The most interesting and potentially promising field of new involvement was, in Steadman's view, acting as a selling agent for local contractors and speculative homebuilders. He had been approached several times about entering into such a relationship but had turned them down because he was not sure that this was the best use of his time.

Mr. Steadman had sufficient contacts in all these fields to ensure him a good volume of business if he ever wholeheartedly took the plunge toward any of them. It was, again, lack of time which held him back from doing so, although he admitted that if a very lucrative offer came along he would have to think very hard before turning it down. Nonetheless, he was still not sure how best to proceed. Each course of action had sufficient drawbacks to prevent him from committing himself, but he knew that the problem was not one which would work itself out unless he took positive action. As a first step, he had studied his organization and reviewed how he used his time, endeavoring to correct inefficiencies in the way he operated personally in the office. Yet, he knew this was only a delaying action and would not solve the long-run problem. The ultimate solution was undoubtedly in making more fundamental kinds of changes.

3.1 Ivie Electronics, Inc. (A)*

In March of 1970, Ray Ivie was reflecting on the problems and accomplishments of the past five years and considering future directions for growth and progress of the company he had founded. He was concerned about making the kind of financing, manufacturing, and marketing arrangements which would help lead to rapid and widespread utilization of some unique new high-performance and low-cost communications equipment he had developed. Moreover, he wanted to proceed in a way that would not only be financially profitable for himself and the other stockholders of the company but also would provide the resources and time for him to develop to a workable stage a number of other radically new concepts in electronic communications equipment.

COMPANY BACKGROUND

Ivie Electronics was incorporated in Ogden, Utah, in January 1965 by Ray Ivie, H. Leon Ivie (Ray's father), and Robert A. Larsen, a friend. The company planned to engage in research and development work in electronics, and manufacture, distribute, sell, and service electronic and mechanical equipment. The specific project which led to the formation of the company was the development of an extremely compact and efficient solid-state communications transceiver. Ray Ivie had been working on the basic circuits and design of the transceiver for several years prior to organization of the company.

Ray Ivie had long been interested in electronics, obtaining his amateur radio operator's license in 1951 while still in high school. Several years later, while at college, he developed a five-watt transceiver. His paper on that transceiver won the 1962 IEEE student paper contest and a trip to the Seattle World's Fair.

In 1963, Mr. Ivie graduated from Brigham Young University with a bachelor's degree in engineering science. He then worked for the Boeing Company in Seattle and in Huntsville, Alabama, on the Saturn 5 space program. While at Huntsville, he designed and built one of the first 5,000-watt static power inverters ever made and which has since been in use as the

* Prepared by Prof. Melvin J. Stanford, Brigham Young University. Copyright © 1974 by Brigham Young University. Reprinted by permission.

emergency power source for research facilities at the Huntsville space flight center.

From the beginning of the company, Ray Ivie served as president and manager. His father, H. Leon Ivie, a retired government auditor and school-teacher, kept the books for the company and provided his garage for initial operations. In November 1967 Ivie Electronics moved to Orem, Utah, where development operations were carried on in an old house on five acres of land which the company had purchased on contract.

PRODUCTS

The Timp Transceiver, which Ray Ivie had developed from his first efforts on the five-watt transceiver, was believed to be unique in its field, with performance capabilities that far exceeded any equipment on the market. It was very small, just 1½ inches by 2½ inches by 4 inches, and weighed only 16 ounces. Despite its small size and weight, it boasted 28 watts of power, 24 channels, and a range of 15 to 20 miles. Transmissions between the transceiver and a larger base station unit could be heard loud and clear over much longer distances. Power for the transceiver could be provided in several ways, with detachable power sources for use in an automobile, for home or office, or for carrying on the person. The lightest personal power source was a series of small batteries, weighing 14 ounces, fastened into a lightweight vest which could also contain an antenna.

The Timp Transceiver contained 16 separate, highly compact, solid state electronic modules, all of which had been completed and were functional by 1970. Most of the mechanical tooling for making cases, channel select knobs, neoprene strain reliefs, extrusions and the like also had been completed. As of spring 1970, remaining work on the transceiver consisted largely of building test jigs for each module, combining the modules, and optimizing the component values through extensive field testing. Ray Ivie estimated that it would take another 15 months to get the transceiver ready for a pilot production run of 100 units.

Other portable transceivers in the industry had power outputs of from 1.5 to 14 watts and sold in a price range of $600 to $2,400. No available equipment, however, was anywhere near as light and compact as the Timp Transceiver, and Ray Ivie did not think that anyone else even had workable designs which would compete on the basis of size and weight and the power and performance which the Timp Transceiver offered.

Mr. Ivie intended to file a patent application on the Timp Transceiver just prior to marketing it and then file periodic revisions to delay issuance of the patent (so the circuit diagrams could not be seen by competitors) until the company became firmly established in the market. In order to prevent someone from copying the actual transceiver, Mr. Ivie planned to encase the modules in an epoxy resin which would make it practically impossible to break down the module without damaging the component parts and circuitry beyond analysis. However, he felt that his best protection would be the continuous development of new technological elaborations and improvements, some of which he already had basic designs for. Ivie realized that owing to rapid progress in the field of electronics he would have to keep his innovations moving from concept through development to actual product with little delay, or someone else might come up with similar ideas. Some of these improvements were applied to the transceiver in the developmental stage. While this delayed the completion of the product, it made it even better. For example, Ray Ivie already had developed a way to fit a 100-watt, 100-channel transceiver into the same size package as the Timp Transceiver.

Another significant product of Ivie Electronics was a new type of audio amplifier system for home and commercial stereo systems. Ray had found a way to split the amplification of the audio frequency spectrum into three parts and to amplify each part separately. The result was far less distortion of sound than achieved by most of the equipment on the market. Moreover, using innovative circuitry techniques similar to those in the Timp Transceiver, it was possible to make all three amplifiers at a cost significantly less than the manufacturing cost of a single, average quality amplifier. Three amplifiers were combined with 12 speakers, all mounted in a large speaker box unit. A pair of these units could be built to sell at a price competitive with medium-priced units on the market, and yet the Ivie units, together with a preamplifier and a signal source (such as a radio tuner, turntable, or tape deck), could offer markedly superior performance. Several functioning prototypes of these units had been completed by late 1969, but Ray Ivie had not done anything further with them because of the urgency he felt to keep the work going on the Timp Transceiver. He did plan to apply for a patent on the audio circuits, and a patent search had been completed.

MARKETING OPPORTUNITIES

The Timp Transceiver had attracted considerable attention as word of its potential spread among some knowledgeable professionals in the field of electronics and communications. In 1967 and 1968, representatives from Litton Industries talked with Ray Ivie and offered him a job at Litton, at an attractive salary, to complete the development of the transceiver, using Litton's facilities. Litton further expressed an interest in obtaining a license to manufacture and sell the transceiver, as soon as it was completed, at a royalty to Ivie Electronics of 4 percent to 5 percent of gross sales. Litton spoke of an estimated first-year sales potential of from 10,000 to 20,000 units at $1,000 per unit, based in part on the strong interest the U.S. Army had shown toward the transceiver in discussing its performance with Litton. The transceiver was well-adapted to military needs and would outperform all other military portable transceivers with greater reliability and lower cost.

Patents in Ray Ivie's name would be obtained by Litton covering all of the patentable innovations in the Timp Transceiver. Mr. Ivie felt, however, that once Litton started manufacturing the transceiver there would be nothing to prevent the engineers of such a large company from developing similar designs for other products, which without patent infringement could still utilize enough of the technical concepts to pose a competitive threat to the unique innovative direction in which he seemed to be moving by himself. Largely because of his concern for this kind of threat, Ray Ivie did not go with Litton. He felt that he would have the transceiver completed on his own within 6 to 12 months and did not forsee any obstacles to so doing.

Subsequently, other companies in the electronics industry expressed an interest in manufacturing and/or marketing the transceiver when it was ready. Ray Ivie also received frequent telephone calls from potential users of the transceiver, such as the police chief of Birmingham, Alabama, who realized the value of the Timp Transceiver for police work and was eager to order a number of units. As of the spring of 1970, however, no marketing arrangements had been made by Ivie Electronics, and completion of the transceiver was still more than a year away. This was caused partly by the need for technical refinements that had come up from time to time as well as some delay resulting from the company's taking a contract to manufacture 10,000 circuit boards.

MANUFACTURING EXPERIENCE

In the fall of 1968, Ivie Electronics had obtained a $129,000 contract with JayArk Instrument Corporation for 10,000 AU-10, 10-watt audio circuit boards, which JayArk used in a portable audio-visual unit designed for sales presentations. Ray Ivie had hesitated to take the contract, because he knew it would delay the work on his transceiver. However, the contract was expected to yield a profit of more than $50,000, which was urgently needed, and it would enable Ivie Electronics to gain some valuable manufacturing experience. Accordingly, Mr. Ivie went ahead with the contract, hired several production workers, and began manufacturing the circuit boards.

The JayArk order was completed early in 1970, but as of March there remained an unpaid balance of $56,000 overdue from JayArk on the contract. Unfortunately, it appeared that JayArk was in financial difficulty and headed for bankruptcy.

FINANCES

From the first it had been a constant struggle for Ivie Electronics to keep enough money on hand to support the developmental work. Ray Ivie and his father had put what cash they could into the company, and most of those funds were spent for electronic equipment. Friends and relatives provided additional resources from time to time in order to help keep the work going. For his designs, services, and cash investment, Ray Ivie had been issued stock which, in March 1970, amounted to 59,330 shares of a total of 129,390 shares outstanding. H. Leon Ivie, then corporate treasurer, held 15,900 shares, and other friends and relatives owned the remainder of the stock. No individual stockholder other than Ray and Leon Ivie, however, held more than 10 percent of the stock outstanding. Total stock authorized was increased in February 1970 to 500,000 shares. At that same time a ten-for-one stock split had taken effect, resulting in an increase of the shares outstanding from 12,939 to 129,390 (see balance sheet, Exhibit 1 and addendum, Exhibit 2).

EXHIBIT 1

IVIE ELECTRONICS, INC.
Balance Sheet
December 31, 1969

Assets

Current assets:

Cash	$ 1,211.53	
Accounts receivable— JayArk Instrument Corporation (part of this receivable has become past due and owing)	56,463.20	
Inventory—materials, work in process and finished goods, estimated (note 1)	25,100.00	
Total current assets		$ 82,774.73
Property, plant and equipment:		
Land	$ 42,760.00	
Equipment (note 2) ... $25,098.66		
Less accumulated depreciation ... 8,272.39	16,826.27	
Total property, plant and equipment		59,586.27
Other assets:		
Advances to suppliers		900.00
Transceiver circuits, designs and processes (note 3)		51,147.00
Total assets		$194,408.00

Liabilities and Stockholders' Equity

Current liabilities:

Accounts payable	$ 19,709.17	
Notes payable—First Security Bank	10,000.00	
Land contract payable—Sanford Bingham (note 4)	22,260.00	
Land contract payable—Ray Ivie (note 4)	13,500.00	
Note payable—Ray Ivie	7,280.00	
Accrued payroll	112.00	
Accrued payroll taxes	738.08	
Total current liabilities		$ 73,599.25
Unearned revenue		800.00
Stockholders' equity:		
Capital stock, common, $1 par value, 12,939 shares issued and outstanding	12,939.00	
Paid-in surplus	128,216.39	
Retained earnings	(21,146.64)	
Total stockholders' equity		120,008.75
Total liabilities and stockholders' equity		$194,408.00

See accompanying notes (Exhibit 3) to financial statements.

EXHIBIT 2

IVIE ELECTRONICS, INC.
Addendum to Balance Sheet
December 31, 1969

The increase in authorized capital and ten-to-one stock split authorized by the shareholders on January 28, 1970, affect the capital section of the company's balance sheet as follows:

Stockholders' equity:

Capital stock, common $1 par value, 129,390 shares issued and outstanding	$129,390.00
Paid in surplus	11,765.39
Retained earnings (as of balance sheet dated December 31, 1969)	(21,146.64)
Total stockholders' equity (as of 12/31/69)	$120,008.75

See accompanying notes (Exhibit 3) to financial statements.

EXHIBIT 3

IVIE ELECTRONICS, INC.
Statement of Income and Retained Earnings
Six Months Ended December 31, 1969

Sales		$ 68,461.10
Cost of sales (note 5)		27,823.97
Gross profit		$ 40,637.13
Expenses:		
Salaries and wages	$17,643.19	
Payroll taxes	2,038.35	
Depreciation	2,944.15	
Amortization of incorporation expense	200.00	
Freight	252.95	
Office supplies and postage	90.83	
Utilities	480.17	
Repairs and maintenance	189.02	
Interest	157.50	
Travel	262.40	
Professional services	80.00	
Keyman term insurance	100.61	
Books and publications	3.65	
Donations	18.68	
Miscellaneous	28.74	
Total expenses		24,490.24
Net income		$ 16,146.89
Retained earnings, June 30, 1969		(37,293.53)
Retained earnings, December 31, 1969		$(21,146.64)

Notes to Financial Statements

Note 1: The company has not taken a physical inventory of materials, goods in process, and finished goods. Inventory balances for June 30, 1969, and December 31, 1969, are estimates furnished by the corporation president, Ray Ivie. Net income for the period is directly dependent upon the accuracy of these estimates and can be relied upon only to the extent that said estimates may be relied upon.

Note 2: Includes tooling, test and office equipment depreciated over eight years on a straight-line basis.

Note 3: At the inception of the corporation, 5,683 shares of stock were issued to Ray Ivie which were recorded on the books of the corporation at $1 par value only, representing

EXHIBIT 3 (continued)

money and equipment put into the company by Ray Ivie. It was subsequently determined by the board of directors that the books did not accurately reflect the value of transceiver circuits, designs and processes obtained from Mr. Ivie at the time of incorporation. They were valued by the board at $51,147.00, representing the difference between par value and the selling price of the stock at the time of incorporation. Outside this original transaction, the corporation has issued no stock at a price under $10.00 per share.

Note 4: Sanford Bingham and Ray Ivie are stockholders and directors of the company. They originally acquired the purchasers' interest in three adjoining parcels of land abutting 1200 South and 400 West in Orem, Utah, in their names under contracts with the original owners. The company now has the purchasers' interest in these parcels under contracts with Sanford Bingham and Ray Ivie.

Note 5: Direct labor costs have been included in salaries and wages since the books and records of the company have not to date segregated manufacturing labor from administrative labor.

During the six months ended December 31, 1969, Ivie Electronics had earned a net income of $16,146 (see income statement, Exhibit 3). However, due to the developmental expenses of several prior years, the retained earnings account still showed a deficit of $21,146 at the end of 1969. With a low cash balance and the large receivable from JayArk in question, new funds were needed to continue the work on the transceiver and the audio system units. Prior to 1969 Ray Ivie had not received a regular salary. Since January 1969 he had been receiving a salary of $1,000 per month. He got married in February 1969.

Mr. Ivie had learned in early 1969 that there was a good possibility of obtaining $500,000 to $1,000,000 in new capital, through stock or debt, from some eastern financial sources. This amount of money would enable him to build a new research and manufacturing building and accelerate the development and completion of the transceiver. By taking such a course at that time, the company could move more rapidly toward providing local employment and economic growth, toward which Ray Ivie was dedicated. However, he wanted to maintain control of his company and avoid dilution for the stockholders. Moreover, he felt quite reluctant to borrow such a large amount of money from far-away sources and with any strings attached. Consequently, he did not investigate substantial financing further at that time.

Mr. Ivie figured that the company would need in excess of $90,000 to keep things going from March 1970 until sales revenues on the transceiver and other products started coming in by mid-1971. He listed those needs as follows:

Parts, material and labor—audio system units	$21,740
Working capital for completion of transceiver	15,000
Payments on land contracts	25,000
First wing of new plant building	30,000
Total	$91,740

To raise this amount, he was preparing an offering circular for a private placement of stock among a small group of local investors who knew of the unique quality of the company's products. He felt that he could get the $91,740 by selling stock directly at $3 per share without paying any commissions and without any purchaser buying what would amount to more than 10 percent of the new number of shares outstanding.

Preliminary estimates by Mr. Ivie indicated that after the transceiver was completed, from $750,000 to $1,500,000 would be needed to build and equip manufacturing facilities and to market the product effectively. While such funds could probably be borrowed from eastern capital sources, Mr. Ivie felt inclined to consider a public stock issue in 1971 to raise the needed funds.

If Ivie Electronics manufactured the transceiver in its own plant, Mr. Ivie estimated the per unit cost of parts to be about $100, labor from $35 to $50, and overhead not more than $50, depending on volume of production. He planned that the unit would retail for about $800 initially. Normal markups from factory to dealer in the industry were in the range of 35 percent to 45 percent of retail on small quantity orders. Sales volume of the Timp Transceiver was estimated by Mr. Ivie at 10,000 to 20,000 units the first year, with an increase to 30,000 to 40,000 per year within three or four years. He based these estimates partly on information he had seen in some market surveys on portable communications transceivers and partly on his own appraisal of the performance features of equipment already on the market in comparison with what his transceiver could do.

Ray Ivie had not determined what the marketing costs might be for distribution by Ivie Electronics. If distribution were handled by an established company in the industry, Ivie Electronics would not be as directly concerned with marketing management and expense but would undoubtedly sell in larger quantities to the distributing company although at a greater discount than if to dealers.

FUTURE OUTLOOK

Ray Ivie realized that his best capabilities were highly technical and he preferred to spend most of his time in research and development. With limited management experience, he knew that the technical strength of his unique products had helped the company survive thus far. It was also quite clear that a sizable organization would have to built and managed in order for the firm to manufacture and market the transceiver and other products. Mr. Ivie felt, however, that he would need to continue to spend a great deal of time developing his new concepts in order to keep on the leading edge of the state of the art.

Licensing opportunities were still available. Litton was still interested, along with several other well-known companies in the field, in discussing either a licensing or marketing arrangement. Mr. Ivie was confident that if he chose to license an established company such as Litton to manufacture and market the transceiver he could probably get better terms and higher royalties than had been discussed in the past, and he intended to negotiate for a royalty of 10 percent on retail selling price if he decided to grant a license at all. If the problem of other companies being in a position to learn perhaps too much about the basic circuit designs could be overcome, licensing could probably get the products to market more rapidly and at the same time provide substantial revenue to Ivie Electronics. This could be done without investment in manufacturing or marketing facilities, providing income to the stockholders and supporting new research and development.

In considering the various possibilities, Ray Ivie felt that it was important that a definite direction be established and specific plans made so that when the Timp Transceiver was fully completed and tested, Ivie Electronics would be ready to get it produced and marketed in a way befitting the high quality and advanced design of the product.

3.2 Ivie Electronics, Inc. (B)*

During the two years between March 1970 and the spring of 1972, Ivie Electronics, Inc., (IE) developed two new products and continued the development of its unique communications transceiver and stereo amplifier equipment. None of these products had yet been marketed in significant quantities. Ray Ivie and Robert Larsen were still managing the company as president and executive vice president, respectively.

With the assistance of some MBA students from a nearby university, the company prepared in May 1972 a three-year operating plan, which included details of marketing, production, finance, organization, and personnel. The summary of that plan is shown as Exhibit 1.

A balance sheet for the company as of December 31, 1971, is shown in Exhibit 2, and an income statement for the six months then ended is shown in Exhibit 3. The Cinegraphic account receivable was the balance of the uncollected amount due on the JayArk account. When JayArk went bankrupt, Ivie Electronics attached a JayArk receivable from Cinegraphics in an attempt to secure payment of what JayArk owed Ivie Electronics. A financial backer in Cinegraphics was considering making good all or a portion of its financial obligations including the amount payable to Ivie Electronics. The expected collection of this account had been included in IE's cash flow projections.

The cash balance of IE was $7,400 as of March 31, 1972. A line of credit was available at a local bank in the amount of $20,000, plus $10,000 more with additional collateral pledged. Guarantees for loans of up to $300,000 through the Small Business Administration had been arranged, and several investment bankers in Salt Lake City had indicated that they would like to underwrite a public stock offering for Ivie Electronics.

PRODUCTS AND MARKETS

The four unique products of Ivie Electronics were as follows:

1. Timp Transceiver—a powerful self-contained two-way radio using modular construction. The unit has its own test equipment built in and will have a 1,000 channel capability.

---

* Prepared by Prof. Melvin J. Stanford, Brigham Young University. Copyright © 1974 by Brigham Young University. Reprinted by permission.

EXHIBIT 1

Ivie Electronics Summary Sheet 1972–1974; Pessimistic, Expected, and Optimistic Sales Levels

	Pessimistic Sales Levels			Expected Sales Levels			Optimistic Sales Levels		
	Year 1	Year 2	Year 3	Year 1	Year 2	Year 3	Year 1	Year 2	Year 3
Marketing (units):									
Timp Transceiver	0	1	19	0	13	46	0	46	103
Stereo amplifier	16	80	72	146	306	410	198	410	602
Chapel P.A. system	3	15	13	9	24	42	17	31	48
Concoder II	1	10	18	2	17	22	10	22	33
Income statement:									
Sales	$ 58,825	$175,800	$326,550	$126,400	$404,700	$632,050	$250,725	$773,550	$1,141,725
Cost of goods sold	17,431	44,295	84,731	32,810	106,928	161,688	60,239	195,125	284,727
Operating expenses	81,907	94,993	95,979	81,907	97,715	105,882	81,907	109,443	133,873
Profits before tax	(40,513)	36,512	145,840	11,683	200,057	364,480	108,579	468,982	723,125
Balance sheet:									
Assets	$181,008	$184,520	$301,493	$210,892	$360,314	$551,871	$322,362	$568,970	$947,450
Liabilities	62,048	29,283	22,218	14,548	20,783	30,218	16,748	28,983	46,018
Capital	118,960	155,237	279,275	196,344	339,531	521,653	305,614	539,987	901,432
Cash flows:									
Total receipts	$ 48,500	$170,125	$309,175	$133,963	$380,350	$614,300	$255,184	$646,300	$996,000
Total disbursements	101,726	133,519	194,660	123,463	139,311	437,676	163,957	524,245	760,428
Cumulative borrowings ...	48,100	12,100							
Financial ratios:									
Break-even (dollars)	$111,747	$128,898	$140,872	$111,399	$147,420	$167,151	$112,632	$174,573	$225,333
ROI (percent)	(22.0)	30.5	79.9	6.2	72.9	53.6	55.8	76.7	66.9
Total employment	8	8	12	9	13	15	11	16	20
Administration	2	2	2	2	2	2	2	2	2
Production	1	1	4	2	5	7	4	8	12
Marketing	3	3	4	3	4	4	3	4	4
R&D	2	2	2	2	2	2	2	2	2

EXHIBIT 2

IVIE ELECTRONICS, INC.
Balance Sheet
December 31, 1971

Assets

Current assets:

Cash		$ 18,281.88
Accounts receivable, cinegraphics	$42,733.94	
Less allowance for doubtful accounts	17,546.29	25,187.65
Job orders receivable		31,642.00
Inventory		48,713.08
Total current assets		$123,824.61

Property, plant, and equipment:

Land		42,760.00
Equipment	$36,195.59	
Less accumulated depreciation	13,618.43	22,577.16
Total property, plant, and equipment		$ 65,337.16

Other assets:

Transceiver circuits, designs, and processes		51,164.75
Total assets		$240,326.52

Liabilities and Stockholders' Equity

Current liabilities:

Notes payable		$ 800.50
Land contract payable, Sanford Bingham	$22,260.00	
Interest accrued	4,735.82	26,995.82
Land contract payable, Ray Ivie	$ 3,350.00	
Interest accrued	712.71	4,062.71
Accrued payroll		4,000,00
Taxes payable		590.51
Total current liabilities		$ 36,449.54
Warranty reserve, Temple project		3,000.00
Total liabilities		$ 39,449.54

Stockholders' equity:

Capital stock, common, $1 per value, 176,273 shares issued and outstanding		$176,273.00
Paid-in surplus		106,623.39
Retained earnings		(82,019.41)
Total liabilities and stockholders' equity		$240,326.52

2. Triplex Stereo—a three amplifier sound system that provides quality sound reproduction at low cost.

3. Concoder II—an automatic control center capable of operating 16 different devices simultaneously. The unit is programmable.

4. Remote P.A. System—expensive sound system amplifiers than can be mounted in burglarproof and tamperproof areas of buildings. The entire system is fully controlled by a remote plug-in device which fits in the palm of the hand.

EXHIBIT 3

IVIE ELECTRONICS, INC.
Statement of Income and Retained Earnings
For the Six Months Ended December 31, 1971

Sales		$46,667.05
Cost of goods sold, per job orders:		
Warranty reserve	$ 3,000.00	
Direct materials and supplies	6,201.32	
Materials from stock	2,185.89	
Direct labor	13,683.89	
Application of overhead	7,933.11	33,004.21
Gross profit		$13,662.84
Operating expenses:		
Administrative labor and labor taxes	$ 1,846.11	
Depreciation expense	1,731.75	
Utilities	669.40	
Travel and transportation	912.16	
Repairs, maintenance, and small tools	1,487.59	
Rent on R&D shop	360.00	
Office and engineering supplies	266.34	
Taxes and licenses	226.96	
Professional services	465.90	
Westcon convention, seminar, trade books and magazines, and miscellaneous expenses	650.61	
Total overhead expenses	$ 8,616.82	
Applied to job orders	7,933.11	
Unapplied overhead		683.71
Net profit on operations		$12,979.13
Other income and expense:		
Interest expense	$ 5,697.56	
Less interest income	250.00	5,447.56
Net profit		$ 7,531.57

The total U.S. market potential for radio equipment in general was estimated from industry sources to exceed $500 million per year in the commercial section (see Exhibit 4). Transceivers sold separately were valued at about $85 million in 1970; this segment of the market included airborne, marine, and ground usage. Ray Ivie believed that the Timp Transceiver would be used mostly in the ground market, which showed a sales increase of 27 percent in 1969 and 9 percent in 1970 (a year of economic recession) to a 1970 level of $29 million.

It was intended that the Timp Transceiver be initially produced in a 28-watt model for the citizens band market, which included:

Reserve teams.	Power companies.
Physicians.	Telephone companies.
Construction.	Railroads.
Forest Service.	Taxicabs and limousines.
Oil companies.	

EXHIBIT 4
Market for Radio Equipment 1969 to 1974 ($ millions)

	1969	1970	1971	1972	1973	1974
Radio equipment (except microwave)	$ —	$ 21.6	$ 23.2	—	—	$ 37.7
Citizen band equipment	35.4	34.2	36.0	—	54.0	45.8
Land mobile radio equipment	212.0	216.1	225.4	—	—	256.0
Marine radio equipment	23.5	24.7	26.1	—	33.7	35.9
Airborne radio equipment	144.2	149.3	141.0	—	197.0	202.5
General radio equipment	548.7	559.3	569.3	—	76.6	745.9
Military communication equipment						
Army	603.0	315.0	273.0			
Navy	474.0	386.0	305.0			
Air Force	426.0	429.0	301.0			
Total	$1,503.0	$1,130.0	$879.0			

Source: *Predicasts Annual Cumulative Edition*, published quarterly by Predicast Inc., 10550 Park Lane, University Circle, Cleveland, Ohio 44106. Issues: No. 46, published Jan. 28, 1972; Cumulative 1971, published 1971; Cumulative 1970, published 1970.

The U.S. market outlook for citizens band transceivers was estimated from published industry sources as follows:

1971	$ 9 million
1972	$11 million
1973	$14 million
1974	$12 million

The citizens band market was very competitive. Major producers with more than $100,000 annual sales decreased from nine in 1968 to six in 1969; in 1970 there were seven. The largest of these were Motorola and Bendix, whose 1970 total sales of $796 million and $1.44 billion, respectively, included a wide range of products.

The Timp Transceiver used a skillful engineering design that gave it both miniaturization and increased power output. For its size, it was a powerful transceiver, its outstanding characteristic. The advantages of the Timp Transceiver were:

1. Compact size.
2. Advanced design giving:
    a. A modular construction for ease of disassembly and repair.
    b. A self-contained speaker and mike.
    c. Increased power output and range.
    d. Low input power requirements.
    e. A rugged design that resists shock and corrosion of components.
3. Versatility—The Timp could be plugged into an antenna and power supply in a car, boat, plane; used as a base station in an office; or carried on one's person.

There were no other transceivers currently on the market that had all of the above characteristics. The price of the Timp, because of the above features, was quite high compared to other transceivers. The Timp would sell for $700 to $800 compared to $6.50 to $330 for other citizen band transceivers. Thus the Timp would appeal to a special segment of the citizen band market.

Ray Ivie predicted that the citizens band version of the Timp Transceiver would be ready for sale by the summer of 1973, with sales of 100 units the first year and 1 percent to 2 percent of that market in following years.

Specific sales forecasts were:

	1973	1974	1975
In dollars:			
Optimistic	80,000	236,000	254,000
Expected	40,000	118,000	127,000
Pessimistic	20,000	59,000	63,500
In units:			
Optimistic	100	296	318
Expected	50	148	159
Pessimistic	20	74	78

Several contingencies were recognized. The Timp Transceiver was designed to have a power output of 28 watts. Some of the citizens band equipment was used by unlicensed operators and was restricted to five watts power output. If a large part of the Timp market segment was found to contain this class of users, then Ivie would want to switch over to development of the government model immediately. The government agencies are not limited to a five-watt output.

The possibility also existed that shortly after the transceiver was introduced, someone would duplicate it. If this occured, then Ivie intended to immediately license the production of the transceiver to a larger firm like Motorola, which would be able to market the transceiver on a nationwide basis through already established marketing organizations.

The government and military markets were much larger than the citizens band market. Prices were also higher: $1,200 to $2,200 for police and public safety transceivers, and $1,500 to $5,000 for army transceivers. Ray Ivie intended to do further research on government specifications and then begin development of a government-military transceiver, with up to 1,000 channels in January 1973. By March 1974, he planned to submit a model to the federal government so that testing could begin in July 1974. He hoped to begin production for government agencies in October 1975.

The stereo amplifier was also unique in its field. Ray Ivie had split the audio spectrum into three segments, with a separate amplifier for each segment. For stereo, the Ivie system had six separate amplifiers; the system did not need expensive loudspeakers to attain high quality output of 100 watts per channel. Ivie would price it at $200 wholesale and $300 retail. Competing amplifiers were the Maranz (140 watts per channel) and the MacIntosh (105 watts per channel), both of which sold for $495 retail and required expensive loudspeakers. Industry publications listed total U.S. sales of audio amplifiers as $23 million in 1968, $18 million in 1969, and $22 million in 1970.

The Concoder II was an encoder-decoder device used to control many other functions, such as dimming lights, turning on a projector, and starting a tape recorder. The Concoder II would be good for multimedia presentations needing to be carefully timed and controlled. Some of the organizations that could use the Concoder were:

a. Sales promotion organizations.	*e.*	Tourist bureaus.
b. Sales convention facilities.	*f.*	University and school
c. State, trade, and world fairs.		auditoriums.
d. Visitor centers.	*g.*	Theaters.

There was no other 16-channel concoder on the market. A competing eight-channel concoder sold for $3,200. Ivie's concoder could be sold with from 2 to 16 channels and was priced at $800, plus $50 per channel. A few Concoders had been sold by Ivie and were operating well. Production of additional units would be undertaken as orders were received. Without any market data to go on, future sales of the Concoder II were estimated by Ivie at:

Pessimistic...............	25 per year
Expected	50 per year
Optimistic	75 per year

Public address systems were usually purchased by sound contractors who installed them in churches, schools, clubs, live theaters, television studios, and conference rooms. Industry sources indicated $224 million in U.S. sales of commercial sound systems, with a forecast of $206 million for 1971. Ray Ivie planned to sell initially in the church market. He believed that the remote and self-adjusting features of his public address system would enable IE to build a sales volume rapidly. Market shares of competitors making conventional P.A. equipment were not known. Ray Ivie intended to complete and test the working model of his remote system so as to begin production in July 1972.

OBJECTIVES AND PHILOSOPHY

Ray Ivie's principal objective was to make IE profitable. He also wanted to achieve a tenfold increase in the price of IE stock within a five to ten-year period and eventually reach a multimillion-dollar level of sales. Moreover, Ray Ivie wanted to be able to employ 500 Utah people in the IE company. His research and development goals were toward unique, high performance products of high quality and reasonable cost. Ray Ivie did not wish to compete with big business in established markets.

Ivie Electronics, Inc., had a corporate philosophy strongly oriented toward social responsibility. As stated by Ray Ivie:

> In the midst of a technological expansion in this fast-moving world, Ivie Electronics is not content to keep abreast of current technology but is forging ahead as a leader in design of highly sophisticated miniature circuitry. Over the past eight years Ivie Electronics has developed some unique, highly efficient communications circuitry that promises to revolutionize the industry.
>
> The decision of Ivie Electronics to build its research and development facilities as well as its manufacturing plant in Utah Valley, near Brigham Young University and the Utah State Technical College, is the result of the basic philosophy that recognizes the mutual benefits and advantages accruing to the company and its employees and to the educational institutions and their students through the exchange of facilities and resources. In addition to the manpower resources of the students and faculty of a nationally prominent electrical engineering department at BYU, the Utah State Technical College will soon build its new facilities adjacent to the Ivie Electronics plant. This will provide qualified students of both the university and the trade tech an opportunity to bridge the gap between classroom theory and practical application. This action is in keeping with a significant industrial trend to locate near institutions of higher learning.

Utah Valley is a fast growing and progressive area that still has a happy rural feeling. The family orientation in this area results in a highly educated and dependable labor force which is vital to the success of the company. The natural, cultural, and civic advantages which make this a desirable place to live will make it possible to attract and keep the highest type of qualified engineers.

Continuous research and development in the electronics field coupled with close cooperation within the company of those charged with the physical and technical applications of production will result in the design, manufacture, and marketing of highly desirable quality products at realistic prices. Such production will provide management, capitalists, and employees with ample reward and will result in a significant economic benefit to all of Utah Valley.

4. L. L. Bean, Inc. (B)*

In late 1974, Leon A. Gorman, president of L. L. Bean, Inc., reviewed the results of the company's performance during the seven years since the death of his grandfather, L. L. Bean. In its first 53 years, the company had built sales of its outdoor clothing and equipment to the $3.8 million level by 1966. About 80 percent of sales were made through the company's direct-mail catalog and 20 percent through a third-floor retail store in Freeport, Maine. Since 1966, sales had increased at an average rate of almost 27 percent per year (Exhibits 1 and 2) and the following changes were recorded:

	1966	1974 (fiscal year ending 2/28/74)
Sales	$3,858,000	$20,403,000
Profit	$ 85,000	$ 1,330,000
Percentage of profit	2.2%	6.5%
Return on investment	6.7%	25.8%
Number of employees	160	400
Names on mailing list	550,000	1,400,000

Over this same time period, several national measures of outdoor activity and recreation expenditures indicated a considerably lower growth rate, and total sales by direct-mail houses increased at less than half the average rate achieved by L. L. Bean (Exhibit 3).

Although he was pleased with L. L. Bean's record, Mr. Gorman felt that he, as a manager, had two major unresolved issues. First, he questioned whether his own administrative style was appropriate for the company L. L. Bean had become. Secondly, he was uncertain as to which direction the company should take in the future. In August 1974, he had sent out a letter (Exhibit 4) in search of a number 2 person for the company. He felt that in conjunction with selecting this key person, he would have to have a better understanding of the kind (and size) of company L. L. Bean might be in five or ten years.

EXHIBIT 1
Yearly Sales, Profits, and Retained Earnings ($000)

	1975*	1974*	1973*	1972*	1970	1969	1968	1967	1966
Total sales	$24,710	$20,403	$15,748	$12,786	$9,933	$7,338	$5,947	$4,755	$3,858
Cost of goods sold	15,263	12,072	9,365	7,416	5,993	4,336	3,648	2,887	2,378
Gross profit	9,447	8,331	6,383	5,370	3,941	3,002	2,299	1,868	1,480
Operating expenses	7,230	5,701	4,595	3,770	2,999	2,242	1,754	1,483	1,351
Operating income	2,216	2,629	1,788	1,599	942	760	545	385	129
Other Income, net	58	78	75	65	22	29	26	2	21
Income before income taxes and extraordinary items	2,269	2,703	1,863	1,664	964	789	571	387	150
Federal and state income taxes	1,142	1,373	941	821	484	429	298	180	65
Net income before extraordinary items	1,127	1,330	922	843	480	360	273	207	85
Write-off of goodwill, etc.	—	—	—	—	—	—	—	150	—
Net income	1,127	1,330	922	843	480	360	273	57	85
Retained earnings, beginning of year	4,408	3,172	2,320	1,535	1,135	814	963	941	837
Cash dividends declared	109	94	70	59	51	39	31	35	31
Stock split in form of dividend	—	—	—	—	—	—	390	—	—
Retained earnings, end of year	5,426	4,408	3,172	2,320	1,564	1,135	814	963	941

* Year ended February 28. The 1971 year consisted of only two months. Prior years were on a calendar basis.
Source: Company records.

EXHIBIT 2

L. L. BEAN, INC.
Balance Sheets
February 28, 1975, 1974, and 1973

	1975	1974	1973
Assets			
Current assets:			
Cash	$ 40,634	$ 5,868	$ 126,714
Certificates of deposit	600,000	1,600,000	500,000
Accounts receivable, net of allowance for doubtful accounts of $54,000, $18,000 and $11,000	473,472	181,738	124,169
Inventories	5,710,428	4,898,139	3,960,284
Refundable federal income tax	213,222	—	—
Prepaid federal income tax	20,600	—	—
Prepaid expenses and other assets	303,112	319,280	182,864
Total current assets	$7,361,468	$7,005,025	$4,894,031
Property, plant and equipment, at cost:			
Land	98,192	98,192	$ 106,336
Buildings	375,947	375,427	601,391
Leasehold improvements	151,831	—	—
Machinery, furniture and equipment	814,253	504,436	406,404
	$1,440,223	$ 978,055	$1,114,131
Less accumulated depreciation	409,544	349,880	305,913
	$1,030,679	$ 628,175	$ 808,218
Prepaid pension expense	28,602	13,751	—
Total assets	$8,420,749	$7,646,951	$5,702,249
Liabilities and Stockholders' Equity			
Current liabilities:			
Accounts payable	$1,232,541	$1,418,669	$ 945,919
Mortgage note payable	—	9,400	27,540
Dividends payable	62,400	—	—
Accrued liabilities:			
Federal and state income taxes	$ 189,561	$ 535,338	$ 193,289
Payroll	403,274	255,616	223,015
Payroll taxes	44,346	31,965	27,162
Pension and profit-sharing expenses	268,108	200,033	129,846
	$ 905,189	$1,022,952	$ 573,312
Total current liabilities	$2,200,130	$2,451,021	$1,546,771
Deferred federal income tax	$ 13,829	$ 6,700	$ —
Mortgage notes payable, less current portion	—	—	202,509
Stockholders' equity:			
Common stock, par value $100 per share, 8,000 shares authorized, 7,800 shares issued	$ 780,000	$ 780,000	$ 780,000
Capital contributed in excess of par value	800	800	800
Retained earnings	5,425,990	4,408,430	3,172,169
Total stockholders' equity	$6,206,790	$5,189,230	$3,952,969
Total liabilities and stockholders' equity	$8,420,749	$7,646,951	$5,702,249

EXHIBIT 3
Selected National Statistics, 1966–1973

	Disposable Personal Income ($ billions)	Percent Increase over Prior Year	Recreation Expenditures ($ billions)	Percent Increase over Prior Year	Fishing Licenses Issued (millions)	Percent Change over Prior Year	Hunting Licenses Issued (millions)	Percent Increase over Prior Year
1966	2,599		28.9		19.6		26.3	
1967	2,745	5.6%	30.9	6.9%	20.2	3.1%	27.1	3.0%
1968	2,945	7.3	33.6	8.7	20.9	5.0	28.8	6.3
1969	3,130	6.3	36.9	9.3	21.6	3.3	29.9	3.8
1970	3,376	7.9	40.7	10.3	22.2	2.8	31.1	4.0
1971	3,603	6.7	42.7	4.9	22.9	3.2	32.4	4.2
1972	3,816	5.9	47.8	11.9	22.9	3.0	33.0	1.9
1973	4,195	9.9			22.2			

Source: U.S. Department of Commerce, *Statistical Abstract of the U.S.* (various issues).

Sales of U.S. Mail-Order Houses

	($ million)	Percent Increase over Prior Year
1967	2,763	
1968	3,236	17.1%
1969	3,499	8.1
1970	3,846	9.9
1971	4,258	10.7
1972	4,722	10.9
1973	5,384	14.0

Source: U.S. Department of Commerce, *Survey of Current Business* (various issues).

EXHIBIT 4
Mr. Gorman's August 1974 Letter

L.L.Bean

INCORPORATED

Hunting...
Fishing and Camping
Specialties

Freeport. Maine 04032

Tel (207) 865-3111

August 12, 1974

Mr. Edward D. Rowley
Ass't Director of Alumni
  Placement
Harvard Business School
Soldiers Field Road
Boston, MA 02163

Dear Mr. Rowley:

We are presently looking for a qualified person to serve as our Merchandise
Manager. We would like to consider a graduate of the Harvard Business School.
I am enclosing the following information in the hopes that you will advise us
of any of your alumni who might be qualified for and interested in this position.

We are in the retail sporting goods and outdoor apparel and footwear business.
We do 80% of our business through mail order catalogs and 20% of our business
at our Freeport store. We are growing at a rate of about 25% annually and have
done so for six years. Our volume last year was slightly over $20 million.

Our Merchandise Manager would be in charge of all buying and buyers for our catalog and retail store, as well as product development, testing, and evaluation.
He would also be in charge of our retail store operations. In addition, he
would assist myself in advertising and in long range marketing planning. He
would report directly to me and should have sufficient capability in other areas
of business to act as my understudy, being capable of running the business in
the event of my death or disability. I am 39, so there is no guarantee he will
succeed me - only that he should have the ability to do so if something unfore-
seen happens to me. Consequently, we would like a "top" professional.
He needs to have had significant management experience in retailing,
especially in merchandising, and, hopefully, in store operations. Experience in men's sports apparel would be desirable, as well as in sporting
goods. This man also has to have demonstrated success in working through
and with people and in developing them.

He must have a strong, personal, and proven interest in some of our outdoor
sports such as fly fishing, upland game or duck hunting, family camping,
backpacking, canoe camping, or cross country skiing. Plus an interest in
country living. A job with Bean's in Maine should really "turn him on".

And he should have a "low key" personality. Age shoud be from early 30's
to early 50's. College degree essential and M.B.A. desirable. Salary
around $35 thousand.

I would appreciate any help you can give us and will be glad to answer
any additional questions about this position.

Yours truly,

/S/ Leon A. Gorman

LAG:HS   Leon A. Gorman
                                          President

PRODUCT LINE

The L. L. Bean catalog had changed very little since Mr. Bean's death (Exhibit 5 and 6). About 11,000 different items were offered (counting color and size variations), and almost 20,000 were carried in the store. Many small items (under $5) were carried in the store but not considered economical to list in the catalog. Mr. Gorman said, "We carry some souvenir-type items for summer people who are not outdoors people, but who would be disappointed if they couldn't spend their money on something."

EXHIBIT 5
Sample 1967 Catalog Page

Bean's Bird Shooting Pants

As a result of considerable research we developed this number over 30 years ago and it has been a best seller ever since. 100% all new wool reversed whipcord — one of the hardest wearing wool fabrics. Briar resistant. It looks and feels like highest grade serge. Leather trimmed pockets are made of extra heavy drill. Legs are cut full for ease in rough walking.

We have never sold a more durable woolen pant that is so neat in appearance. For bird shooting, Spring fishing or wherever a warm, hard wearing pant is required.

Color, Forest Green. Weighs 26 oz.
Waist sizes 30 to 50. Inseams 29", 31" and 33".
Price, $18.50 postpaid. Send for free sample.

Bean's Checked Wool Shirts

One of the most popular shirts in our line. 100% pure new wool in ⅛ inch check. 10 oz. weight. Well tailored with two breast pockets with button flaps.

An attractive sporting pattern, made in regular long tail shirt style. Machine washable. Weighs 17 oz.

Two colors: Black and White.
Red and Black.

Sizes 14½ to 19.

Price, $11.65 postpaid. Send for free samples.

Cold Weather Hunting Coat

Outershell of rugged Appalachian cotton poplin, windproof and water repellent. Body and arms insulated with Jen-Cel-Lite®, a blend of virgin white fleece wool and polyester fibers as specified by U. S. Navy for survival suits. Provides dry, healthy warmth at 15° below Zero, yet comfortable to 50° above.

A top quality coat with bi-swing back, rugged two-way zipper, two breast pockets, two bellows side pockets, and two hand-warmer pockets. Mouton pile lined collar, leather bound cuffs with knit wristers. Weighs about 3 lbs. 4 oz.
Color, Taupe.
Sizes 36 to 50. Body length 31".
Price, $31.00 postpaid.

Matching Insulated Storm Hood. Price, $4.90 postpaid.
Detachable Game Bag-Dry Seat. Fully rubberized and bloodproof, expanding bellows design. Opens fully to make seat. Order by coat size.
Price, $4.80 postpaid.

(Fall 1967)   **L. L. Bean, Inc. Freeport, Me.**   **19**

EXHIBIT 6
Sample 1974 Catalog Page

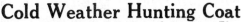

Cold Weather Hunting Coat

Insulated with DuPont's new 9 oz. polyester Fiberfill II®. Provides a uniformly soft and lofty heat retaining barrier. (Insulating quality of 1.4 pounds of Fiberfill II® equals that of one pound of goose down.) Warm at 15° below Zero and comfortable to 50° above. Fiberfill II® is non-allergenic, breathable and long lasting (won't break down with use).

Outershell of strong, polyester-cotton Appalachian poplin. Windproof and water repellent. Comfortable, non-restricting bi-swing back; sturdy two-way zipper; two breast pockets; and two bellows side pockets with outside handwarmer pockets. Cushioned recoil pads on shoulders, knit wristers inside sleeves and acrylic "fur" pile collar. Weighs about 3 lbs. 6 oz.

Color, Soft Tan. Body length about 31".
Sizes: Small (36-38), Medium (40-42), Large (44-46) and Extra Large (48).
1423 Cold Weather Hunting Coat, $50.00 postpaid.
1424 Matching Insulated Storm Hood, $6.00 postpaid.

Detachable Game Bag-Dry Seat. Fully rubberized and bloodproof, expanding bellows design. Opens fully to make seat. One size fits all.
1425 Detachable Game Bag-Dry Seat, $8.00 postpaid.

Bean's Trooper Cap

Has been popular and practical for cold weather comfort for many years. Tan polyester-cotton twill with Brown lambskin. Lined with quilted, foam insulation. Lambskin earlaps and visor fold down to protect neck, ears and forehead in extremely cold and windy conditions. Weight 6 oz.
Color: Tan with Brown lambskin. Men's sizes 7 to 7½.
1255 Trooper Cap, $7.35 postpaid.

Johnson Guide Pant

The famous Vermont-made wool trousers long used in Northern New England by guides, hunters and woods workers. Heavy weight 24 oz. fabric of 80% new wool and 20% nylon is warm and unusually durable. Can be dry cleaned.

Standard cut for comfortable, non-binding fit. Reinforced stitching at stress points and sturdy drill pocket linings and waistband. Front and rear pockets, suspender buttons and 1½" belt loops. Weight about 2 lbs.
Color, Spruce Green.
Men's even waist sizes 30 to 46. Inseams 29", 31" and 33".
1857 Johnson Guide Pants, $15.00 postpaid.

Bean's Navy Blue Shirt

We have been listing this shirt for over 35 years. Made of medium weight, all wool "fadeless" Navy Blue flannel it provides warmth and durability for active sporting usage. In addition, its fine appearance makes an attractive leisure shirt.

Lined, neckband collar, two flapped pockets and long, tuck-in tails. Dry cleanable. Weight about 18 oz.
Sizes S (14), M (15), L (16), XL (17), XXL (18) and XXXL (19).
1635 Navy Blue Shirt, $18.00 postpaid.

(Fall 1974)   **L. L. Bean, Inc. Freeport, Me.**   37

About 25 percent of the items accounted for 75 percent of the sales. The original Maine hunting shoe had always been the highest-volume item, although the chamois shirt was not far behind. Mr. Gorman felt that the number of items he offered was considerably less than the number offered by most retail operations, but he preferred to offer high-quality, carefully selected individual items that generated a lot of volume. While many mail-order catalogs featured "break-through" or "fad" items, the L. L. Bean catalog consisted of high-quality staple items that generally remained unchanged, year after year. Mr. Gorman made a major commitment of his time in product selection. He regularly read the catalogs of every other mail-order company in the recreation field, noting what products were currently being promoted.

While Mr. Gorman did not apply any rigorous formula of sales dollars per catalog page, he used rough rules of thumb as to what he should achieve for each advertised item. For example, for soft goods, he expected to sell $3,000 per page in the spring catalog and $4,000 in the fall catalog, (although in 1974 he felt these benchmarks should probably be doubled). The company might get half these amounts from hard-goods items, where the obsolescence was less and orders could be placed for smaller quantities. For soft goods, the company typically had to commit itself to a season's purchases well in advance in somewhat larger quantities (due to color and size variations).

In spite of a low sales volume, some items were carried because Mr. Gorman believed they were good items. For example, for many years the company had offered what he considered to be superior fishing flies and lures, and although sales were not in proportion to other sales, Mr. Gorman had no intention of dropping these items from the Catalog.

Color pages in the catalog often generated double the sales of black-and-white pages. This further complicated the product-selection process. When asked if he had ever considered printing more pages in color, Mr. Gorman replied, "The local printer who has always done our work has the capacity to print only one out of each four pages in color. Unless we can persuade him to invest some $200,000 on a larger press, I guess we are sort of stuck with our present number of color pages."

CUSTOMER SERVICE

Mr. Gorman felt that L. L. Bean was "50 percent product and 50 percent service." A no-questions-asked refund policy resulted in what Mr. Gorman felt was an above-average return rate of 5 percent. The company even refunded the $1.75 purchase price of a never-worn shirt bought 32 years ago. Only 1 out of 20 returns was due to a defect (most defects having been caught before shipment). The other returns were for incorrect size or what Mr. Gorman called "customer preference"—a change of mind when the customer viewed the actual merchandise and then decided he didn't want it.

Letters from customers were sorted into "priority" and "routine" status, and routed to one of five service specialists (clothing, footwear, tackle, camping, and miscellaneous). Returned merchandise was reported by item number and reason for return—fit, customer option (no special reason), delayed shipment, unsatisfactory, too large, too small, or other. Once a month, monthly and year-to-date totals were calculated for each item number and compared to the number of units sold. This report was sent directly to Mr. Gorman and the buyers.

In spite of what he considered to be excellent customer relations, in 1974 Mr. Gorman hired a consultant who specialized in mass letters. The consultant felt that timeliness and accuracy were the most important factors in answering customer complaints or questions; the customer should be given an accurate, fast answer, even if the response was on a preprinted form letter. The consultant recommended eliminating desks and using benches (with no drawers) instead. A large tag with the day the letter was received was stapled to the top of each letter. The colors of the tags were changed each week so that a supervisor could walk through the department and tell at a glance if there were any letters received last week and still not answered.

THE MAILING LIST

The mailing list was increased by coupon advertising (Exhibit 7), through customer referrals, and by store customers' leaving their names. In 1973, $200,000 was spent for advertisements in 64 magazines. A different street number on Main Street was used in each magazine advertisement to measure the number of catalog requests received from each advertisement. Usually, an item was offered for sale in the coupon ad. Any orders received with the inquiry were deducted from the cost of the ad, and a "net cost per inquiry" calculated. Response from some magazines was so good that a "negative cost" was generated. Mr. Gorman looked forward to the day when the original advertisement code would stay with a customer's name in the computer, and a running total of dollar sales generated for each advertisement. He felt that while most mail-order houses generated a "cost-per-inquiry" figure, very few knew how many actual dollars of sales they ultimately received from each advertisement. He expected to find a considerable difference between the number of inquiries and the number of actual orders received from some magazine advertisements.

About 25 percent of new catalog recipients bought something within a year. The rest were dropped from the mailing list. Once a person purchased something, he was left on the mailing list until he failed to reorder for a three-year period.

Unlike most direct-mail companies, L. L. Bean did not sell its list, or trade the list with other mail-order houses. If there was an overproduction of catalogs. Bean might exchange some names with a company like Orvis or Carroll Reed to use up the extra catalogs.

A "match code" was generated by the company for each name in the mailing list. The code was composed of the zip code and certain characters of the person's name and address. Whenever a new name was added to the list, the match code was compared to all the other match codes on the list. If a duplicate match code was found, both names were printed so that a clerical

EXHIBIT 7
Sample Magazine Advertisements

Bean's Outdoor Sporting Specialties

Flannel Pajamas

A good pair of flannel pajamas for cold winter nights. 100% combed cotton. Amply cut and comfortably warm. Sanforized®. Tops have button front with breast pocket. Bottoms have drawstring waist. Three colors: Red, Light Blue, Tan. Sizes A (110–135 lbs.), B (135–165 lbs.), C (165–185 lbs.), D (185–210 lbs.). Price $8.75 (Postpaid).

☐ Send Free Catalog
☐ Ship—   Flannel Pajamas @ $8.75 postpaid

Size _____ Color _____

Name _____

Address _____

Zip _____

L. L. Bean, Inc.
315 Main St., Freeport, Maine 04032

Bean's Outdoor Sporting Specialties

FREE Spring Catalog

120 fully illustrated pages featuring camping, fishing, hiking and canoeing equipment. Also includes practical, long-wearing apparel and footwear for the outdoors man or woman. Many items of our own manufacture. Our 63rd year of providing dependable, high-grade sporting specialties. All guaranteed to be 100 percent satisfactory or your money back. ☐ **Send Free Catalog.**

Name _____

Address _____

_____

Zip _____

L. L. Bean Inc.
409 Main Street, Freeport, Maine 04032

employee could compare them and determine if an actual duplication existed.

Leo Yokum, a mailing-list consultant, was hired in the summer of 1974 to attempt to eliminate duplicate names that were not identified through the match-code system. For example, if every child in a single family ordered a Bean catalog, as long as his first initial was different, a different match code would be generated. Yokum was able to eliminate 69,000 additional duplicate names on the 1.4 million mailing list. Since the company mailed out four times each year (two catalogs and two special flyers) at a cost of about 30 cents per mailing (including postage), Yokum's efforts resulted in annual savings of over $80,000.

PERSONNEL

Mr. Gorman was pleased with the 400-person work force. There was no union and little turnover. The average age of all employees was 42, compared to an average of 63 when he became president in 1967. Only one small group in the manufacturing area (hand shoe stitchers) were on piecework. All other employees (not counting supervisors) were on straight hourly earnings, averaging $3.11. The company provided substantial benefits, including the payment of up to 3/4 of the Blue Shield-Blue Cross plan, a bonus plan based on profits (which averaged 7.5 percent of wages in 1973), and a savings plan (up to 15 percent of an employee's earnings could be saved, with the company contributing 25 cents for every dollar saved). After two years, an employee entered the pension plan. It was calculated so that at retirement, the amount of the pension plus Social Security would equal 80 percent of the average pay for the five years preceding retirement.

Mr. Gorman identified the introduction of new management people as one of his most important responsibilities. Since the summer of 1973, after bringing in Joseph Callanan as the data processing supervisor, Mr. Gorman had utilized the services of Dr. Mahoney, an industrial psychologist in Portland, in assessing managerial candidates. At the supervisory level, prospective employees took a basic aptitude test and a personality test. At the management level and the department-head level, there was also an interview with Dr. Mahoney. Prospective employees were asked such questions as, "Who was your favorite boss and why?" and "Who was your least favorite boss and why?"

Mr. Gorman felt that the feedback from Dr. Mahoney was surprisingly "accurate."[1] Even for those individuals whom he had not interviewed, Dr. Mahoney was able to describe them quite well and see aspects of people quite clearly which Mr. Gorman had not completely recognized before. For example, the number 2 man who had left the company in the fall of 1974 had been hired before Dr. Mahoney's employment. This man had turned out not to have the administrative abilities that Mr. Gorman originally thought he had.

Mr. Gorman emphasized that Dr. Mahoney did not say that people were "good" or "bad," but rather whether there was a match between characteristics of an individual and the job he had to fill. Dr. Mahoney tried to match an applicant's personality to the specific needs and the personalities within the Bean organization, giving special consideration to the close personal relationships which existed.

A personnel policy manual had been in the writing for three years but had never been completed. Mr. Gorman described the organization as "fluid," but "most people understood who they report to." When drawing the orga-

---

[1] However, Mr. Gorman stated, "Dr. Mahoney did not find many characteristics of a successful chief executive in me."

EXHIBIT 8
Organization Chart

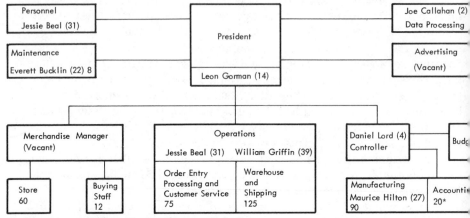

Figures in parentheses = Number of years at L. L. Bean.
Other figures = Number of employees
* William Griffin is also the buyer of hunting equipment and fishing tackle.
Source: From an original chart by Leon A. Gorman.

nization chart (Exhibit 8), Mr. Gorman said it was not specific as to whether the manufacturing department head reported to him or to the controller.

DATA PROCESSING

In 1969, a service bureau was employed to generate inventory and sales-by-product reports. Bean employees punched all the data to be processed on Friden Flexowriter paper-tape machines. In the same year, the mailing list was put on a local bank's computer. The bank had been the low bidder among nine others. The 25 employees who had previously addressed catalogs by hand were transferred to other areas within the company as the business grew.

In August 1974, an IBM System 3 (Model 10) was installed in the new warehouse facility to handle the order entry process. Joe Callanan had been working for a full year on the systems and programs prior to installation. Until August, every packing slip and back order had been manually extended and handwritten. The computer was expected to reduce costs from the time of its installation, especially since it would eliminate the need to add on up to 40 extra people for order entry during the peak buying season just before Christmas (Exhibit 9). The mailing list was not scheduled to be put on this computer until some later time.

Both Mr. Gorman and Joe Callanan felt that the employees had a healthy attitude toward the computer. "The Bean Scene," a company newsletter, quoted Mr. Callanan as finding "Bean employees eager to cooperate, recep-

EXHIBIT 9
Projected Annual Cost and Savings from Installation of IBM System 3 (Model 10),
prepared by Joseph Callanan

Cost (equipment rental)

Data entry equipment		$ 24,400
Central processor 64K		34,224
Printer and controller (600 LPM)		12,348
Disks (7.5 m. bytes)		5,304
2 tape drives		9,432
Communication terminal		1,100
Card reader		3,492
Data recorders...		1,140
Language rental (RPG 11)		1,996
One-time changes (programming A/R)	$2,000	
Three-months rental of connecting software	360	
	$2,360	$ 93,436

Savings (direct)

Additional order writers (1973 cost)		41,400
Flexowriter maintenance contract		6,000
Cost of processing at service bureau (IC)		10,000
Paper cost for order sets		22,508
Equivalent labor reduction costs (A/R)		25,000
		$ 104,908

Savings (indirect)
More efficient picking
Current backorder status (automatic B/O label)
Faster order processing (less paper and paper handling)
More complete look-up information on each order set
Standardized item description
More accurate cost of inventory by timely addition of
  receipts and new costs
Current merchandise demand information

Order sets used in last fiscal year	698,201
Back order used in last fiscal year	119,240
	817,441
× 25% increase...	1,021,801
× $50.00 per 000 (estimate)	$ 51,090
New 2-part form including back order	698,201
× 25% increase...	872,751
× $32.75 per 000 (actual)	$ 28,582

tive to change at all levels, and a spirit of cooperation that is outstanding. He
notes that Bean's is a business that is growing fast and no one seems to feel he
or she is going to be put out of a job by computerization." He went on to
state that "the computer would NOT take away any of the personal touch
between the customer and Bean's. The computer will be a tool of the Customer Service Department, not the master, and if there are any questions
about the order, *Customer Service* will personally contact the customer."

Some people were not as enthusiastic about the computer. For example,
Callanan had an appointment with a Portland doctor for a physical examination. When the doctor learned of his type of work and his new association

with L. L. Bean, he shook his head sadly, and said, "I was afraid when they put carpet on those stairs, sooner or later it would come to the introduction of a computer."

THE WAREHOUSE

In 1971, Mr. Gorman brought in industrial engineers to redesign the shipping operation and consider added space requirements. A year later, an architect was selected to begin designing a warehouse that would become economically feasible when sales reached $25 million. (Sales at this time were between $12 and $16 million.) To determine the space requirements at various sales levels, Dan Lord, the controller, calculated the cubic space for every item in inventory.

Sales increased considerably faster than expected, and ground was broken for the new warehouse in the fall of 1973. Completed in August 1974, the warehouse had 95,000 square feet of ground floor area, a mezzanine of 22,000 square feet, 32-foot ceilings, and an employees' lunchroom. The building itself cost $1.2 million, but purchase of land and an existing building of 60,000 square feet (converted to order entry, data processing, and manufacturing, with space left over) and site preparation brought the total cost to $2 million. While Mr. Gorman did not feel the new building would necessarily save the company any money, it would be more convenient to have all the inventory in one place instead of three scattered locations. Furthermore, the new warehouse would be sufficient for growth to $45 million, and more space could be added on to handle sales of $75 million. "We have taken a major step," noted Mr. Gorman, "which we could back off only with difficulty. Prior to this step we owned only the Main Street buildings and rented all other space used for growth. That meant we could always have 'pulled in our horns' if circumstances required."

The new building was owned by a limited partnership of 18 equal partners, consisting of every adult Bean stockholder and all department heads. Mr. Gorman and Dan Lord were the general partners, although they received nothing extra for their added responsibility. Each partner had to contribute $5,000. A local bank had agreed to loan $5,000 to any partner, secured by his interest in the partnership. The balance of the building cost was 100 percent financed, and the building leased by the partnership to L. L. Bean, Inc.

With the warehouse at a half-mile distance, the retail store had to carry its own inventory for all items. Its target was to keep two months' supply on hand for each item.

REPORTING AND CONTROL SYSTEM

The company did not have any profit planning or formal budgets. The store and the factory were set up as separate cost centers, but overhead was not allocated to either. Each buyer was asked to set up his own "budget" by estimating the sales of each of the items he handled. These estimates were based on a fixed percentage increase over last year's sales, and adjusted up or down for individual items which might deviate from this average. These figures were used as a guide for purchasing and forecasting cash requirements.

While Bean had no formal cost-control system, Mr. Gorman felt that he had a very good indication of how things were going by comparing the current year's figures to those achieved last year. For example, every morning the mail-room figure of orders received was posted against the number of orders received last year on the corresponding day (Exhibit 10). He felt that

EXHIBIT 10
Mr. Gorman's Record of Number of Orders Received

		1973	1974	
OCTOBER	(10/1)	3009	4029	(9/30)
		1182	928	
		1617	1919	
		1854	2528	
		1811	2183	
	TOTAL	9473	11587	+22.3%
	(10/8)	1391	4586	(10/7)
		2429	1352	
		976	1754	
		2036	2088	
		2067	1735	
	T	8899	11515	+22.7%
	(10/15)	3113	1577	(10/14)
		1104	2574	
		1534	1185	
		1906	2536	
		1486	2080	
	T	9143	9956	+8.9% +20% M-T-D
	(10/22)	1395	4267	(10/21)
		2364	1390	
		1504	2372	
		1896	2397	
		1915	2005	
	T	9074	12431	+36.9%
	(10/29)	3262	1538	(10/28)
		1436	3033	
	(11/1)	2021	1247	
		2585	2123	
		2534	2700	
	T	11838	10641	−10.1%
NOVEMBER	(11/5)	5765	5327	(11/4)
		1642	1677	
		3265	2853	
		4438	3082	
		4160	3751	
	T	19270	16690	−13.4%
	(11/12)	8255	7308	(11/11)

Source: Leon Gorman's notebook.

the workload for 75 percent of the employees (e.g., order entry, pickers, and packers) related directly to the number of orders received. Since most orders were shipped in 36–48 hours, department heads were in a position to forecast their work requirements for the next day by the number of orders received each day. However, Mr. Gorman doubted that they used the information for that purpose.

Each morning, Mr. Gorman also received reports from order entry, shipping, accounting, and customer service indicating which day's work they were currently working on. He would enter this data on a spread sheet so that he could tell at a glance how currently each area was operating. Since he spoke to each department head informally at least once each day, he could question unusual delays in any area.

Once each month, Mr. Gorman received an employee census for the week which included the 12th day of the month (Exhibit 11). For each department, the number of employees, regular hours worked, overtime hours worked, and gross pay for the week were compared to the same week for the prior year.

The monthly expense report (Exhibit 12) compared the current month with last year's month for each expense account, and included an "expense variance report" prepared by the controller (Exhibit 13). The employee census report, expense report, and the monthly profit-and-loss statement were distributed to all department heads. No formal monthly meeting was scheduled to discuss these reports, although Mr. Gorman generally reviewed them with each department head.

Although there were no specific limits on what a department head might spend without authorization. Mr. Gorman felt that expenditures under $200 would ordinarily be made without asking for his approval. "But five years ago," he said, "department heads would not have spent $50 without seeing me first." Mr. Gorman did approve all new requisitions for hiring, however.

OWNERSHIP AND CONTROL

In late 1974, ownership of the common stock (the only class of stock outstanding) was still entirely within the Bean family. A buy-back clause attached to the stock forbade selling to anyone outside the family, although Mr. Gorman was not certain that this clause would hold up in court. Precise stock ownership was unclear, since over 51 percent of the stock was tied up in Mrs. L. L. Bean's estate. Mr. Gorman owned 4 percent of the stock, and could conceivably end up with as much as 20 percent when the estate was settled.

During Mrs. L. L. Bean's lifetime, Mr. Gorman had his grandmother's full support in all company matters. He wondered what might happen in the future as the interests and financial requirements of the family members changed. Already, one of Mr. Gorman's brothers had children of college age with tuition to finance. Mr. Gorman said, "Of course, they could always

EXHIBIT 11

Employee Census August 1973 and August 1974 (based on the week including the 12th day of the month)

Department Section	Function	1973 Active	Regular Hours	Over-time	Gross Pay	1974 Active	Regular Hours	Over-time	More or Less	Gross Pay
01–01	Administration	4				4				
	Office services									
02–01	Mail department	7	158.00	.50	$ 554.06	10	238.75	—	+ 3	$ 883.43
02–02	Order entry	19	556.50	—	1,656.66	34	981.25	7.25	+15	3,667.41
02–03	Sec. services	8	268.75	.50	1,462.42	8	301.75	22.25	—	1,280.29
02–04	Switchboard	2	72.00	—	228.00	1	40.00	—	– 1	118.00
	Department totals	36	1,055.25	1.00	3,901.14	53	1,561.75	29.50	+17	5,949.13
03–01	Order processing	5	174.50	—	556.98	4	153.25	6.00	– 1	772.98
03–02	Order expeditors	3	77.50	—	259.31	4	143.75	5.50	+ 1	657.40
03–03	Order writers	6	187.50	—	482.19	10	210.50	—	+ 4	538.91
03–04	Filing clerks	6	176.50	—	778.70	9	200.75	—	+ 3	599.78
03–05	Sample clerk	—	—	—	—	1	37.00	—	+ 1	96.20
03–06	Phone clerks	7	211.75	10.75	657.63	11	288.00	8.00	+ 4	1,043.52
03–07	Back order clerks	2	78.00	—	198.90	3	80.00	—	+ 1	220.00
	Department totals	29	905.75	10.75	2,933.71	42	1,113.25	19.50	+13	3,928.79
	Office Service totals	65	1,961.00	11.75	6,834.85	95	2,675.00	40.00	+30	9,877.92
04–01	Personnel	2	30.00	—	115.90	2	42.50	2.50	—	153.13

EXHIBIT 12

Expense Report, Month September 1974 and Year to Date

Department Section Code	Type of Expense	Current Month	This Month Last Year	$ Variance + or (−)	Percent Variance + or (−)	YTD Current Year	YTD Last Year	$ Variance + or (−)	Percent Variance + or (−)
	Processing and customer service labor								
6021	Incoming mail	$ 3,916	$ 2,619	$ 1,297	49.5	$ 22,240	$ 17,795	$ 4,445	25.0
6022	Order entry	20,489	7,028	13,461	191.5	100,492	53,134	47,358	89.1
6031	Order processing	4,248	2,161	2,087	96.6	22,030	16,578	5,452	32.9
6032	Order expediting	2,257	1,175	1,082	92.1	17,208	11,718	5,490	46.9
6033	Order writers	196	3,644	(3,448)	(94.6)	19,431	18,887	544	2.9
6034	File clerks	2,988	2,661	327	12.3	20,881	18,364	2,517	13.7
6036	Phone orders	3,391	2,899	492	17.0	26,637	22,000	4,637	21.1
6037	Back orders	1,053	1,123	(70)	(6.2)	10,007	6,972	3,035	43.5
		$38,538	$23,310	$15,228	65.3	$238,926	$165,448	$73,478	44.4
	Material handling labor								
6050	Physical distribution	$ 848	$ 667	$ 181	27.1	$ 6,739	$ 5,881	$ 858	14.6
6051	Receiving and warehousing	2,904	2,863	41	1.4	24,318	31,535	2,783	12.9
6052	Order picking	9,182	7,021	2,161	30.8	54,091	48,217	5,874	12.2
6053	Order packing	8,179	7,362	817	11.1	48,261	42,861	5,400	12.6
6054	Postal unit	2,851	3,600	(749)	(20.8)	28,650	20,646	8,004	38.8
6055	Housekeeping								
6056	Stock clerks	9,532	8,330	1,252	15.0	65,987	59,546	6,441	10.8
6057	Order analysis	2,414	1,904	510	26.8	15,213	13,247	1,966	14.8
6058	Fourth class rec. clerks	2,948	1,905	1,043	54.8	19,348	14,561	4,787	32.9
6059	Shipping support service	1,438		1,438		12,313		12,313	
6150	Warehouse plan and relocation					1,227		1,227	
		$40,296	$33,652	$6,694	19.9	$276,147	$236,494	$49,653	21.9

Source: Dan Lord, controller.

EXHIBIT 13
Expense Variances, September 1974

A/C	6058	4th Class Rec. Clerk Labor One additional employee assigned to this department. Six employees FY 1974—5 employees FY 1973.	Variance $1,043.
A/C	6250	Warehousing supplies and equipment	Variance $4,346.
	$1,321.00	Charged to account in error. This was for 5 storage cabinets for fishing tackle and should have been charged to fixed assets. Correction made in October 1974.	
	$1,065.00	15 stock cart ladders purchased from James Wiltsie Company.	
A/C	6370	Office supplies and expense	Variance $6,961.
	$1,118.00	Various office expense items purchased from G. E. Stimpson Company	
	$1,230.00	Stock receipt forms from Standard Register.	
	$2,593.00	Refund checks from Standard Register.	
	$1,054.00	Supplies from 3M Company.	
A/C	7091	Advertising—Direct Mail space	Variance $44,885.
		September 74 paid 7 invoices from Ad agency— Last year paid none during month of September.	
A/C	8240	Factory—Manufacturing Supplies	Variance $238.
	$114.00	Paid for rubbish removal	
	$ 52.00	Paid for small tools purchased from Plymouth Div.	
	$ 63.00	Paid for 4 stools purchased from Lewiston Shoe Machinery Company.	
A/C	9421	Legal Services	Variance $1,302.
	$968.00	of Variance is for Services of Dr. Mahoney charged to this account in error. Should have been A/C 9423, consulting services. Correction made in October. Balance of variance is increase in retainer fee paid to legal counsel this year.	

Source: Dan Lord, controller.

borrow against their L. L. Bean stock, but this may not be the satisfactory answer."

Once the estate was settled, Mr. Gorman felt that a decision had to be reached as to whether they should continue as a family company, "go public," or sell out to a major company. (There were many suitors interested in this third alternative.)

In the summer of 1974, in anticipation of the settlement of Mrs. Bean's estate, three new family members (one of Leon Gorman's brothers, an aunt, and a cousin) were added to the board of directors. Other directors were Mr. Gorman, his other brother (who was Bean's traffic manager) and two nonfamily members, Daniel Lord, the controller, and William Griffin, a department head.

MR. GORMAN'S MANAGEMENT STYLE

Mr. Gorman questioned whether or not his own management style was appropriate for the size of company L. L. Bean had become. While the company was now over six times its size just eight years ago, his day had hardly changed at all. He still worked from 8 A.M. to 6 P.M. each day, plus Saturday morning. In addition, he usually brought work home at night, and took only one or two weeks' vacation each year. He was not proud of these hours, feeling that a successful administrator should be able to do his job on only 10 or 15 hours per week.

One explanation of Mr. Gorman's long hours was his concern with details in many areas of the company. For example, he gave a "pep talk" to the women who were being transferred to the new computer department. He felt that when people from different areas of the company were brought together in a new department, they were inclined to maintain loyalties to their former groups. He pointed out this possibility to the new computer-department employees, and explained to them how important their new jobs were to processing orders and maintaining proper inventory levels.

Mr. Gorman knew most if not all of the individual production workers by name. On a trip through the factory, he commented to a visitor about a delicate aspect of a cobbler's handling of the leather, and pointed out second- and third-generation Bean employees.

Mr. Gorman tried to work through department heads and managers rather than going directly to people. He felt that management visibility was important, and insisted that all department heads spend half of their time in the warehouse building and half of their time in the main building. He did not want the main building to be seen as an "executive tower."

Mr. Gorman's third-floor office was not pretentious. It had inexpensive paneling, and the only air-conditioning was a large fan positioned at the corner of the office. There were three books on his desk—*Profit Planning and Control, Marketing Handbook,* and *Duck Hunters Are Nuts.* The company did not have a Xerox machine or bond-paper copier.

Concerning the future, Mr. Gorman thought there were three major areas where the company might expand. First of all, they could increase manufacturing to more than the 20 percent of products sold they had historically maintained. In 1974, they manufactured only shoes, some leather items, and canvas tote bags. There were plentiful supplies of labor and manufacturing space in the area, since several shoe companies had recently closed. Secondly, they could expand their retail operations. Eddie Bauer, perhaps Bean's closest competitor, had opened six retail outlets in the mid- and far-West, plus one in Toronto, since being acquired by General Mills.

A third alternative was to allow customers to use credit cards (such as

MasterCharge, BankAmericard, or American Express) to make purchases. (In 1974, over 98 percent of all sales were for cash.) If credit sales were accepted, knowledgeable people in the industry estimated that sales might increase by as much as 50 percent. Mr. Gorman stated, however, "I doubt if we could finance that kind of growth in a single year."

Mr. Gorman felt that there were other, more important unresolved issues facing the company. In the short run, the general economic malaise that had hit the country in 1974 was apparently affecting L. L. Bean. In September, as the company moved into its highest-volume season, weekly sales suddenly dropped off by more than 10 percent, in contrast to several years of moving up by over 20 percent. Over the long run, he was concerned with the significant postage-rate increases announced for July of 1975, and increasing United Parcel Service rates. He wondered whether the company should continue its policy of shipping merchandise without adding on shipping charges.

Despite these concerns, Mr. Gorman was quite happy in his work. He felt a great deal of personal satisfaction by performing what he thought were the critical elements for success in his business—selecting and pricing merchandise, writing advertising copy, selecting key personnel, and corporate planning. In a philosophical mood, he said, "Sometimes I feel a little like my grandfather, who had said he was already eating three meals a day, and couldn't eat a fourth. At some point I will not be motivated by largeness. Perhaps at that point, it will be time for me to step aside."

5. Wall Drug Store*

Ted and Bill Hustead, primary owners and managers of Wall Drug Store, found themselves confronted with several key strategic issues in the winter of 1973. Should they invest aggressively in inventory for the tourist season of 1974, anticipating an increase in business, or should they buy conservatively? Should they continue to expand Wall Drug in the future or should they seek out new business alternatives? Although Wall Drug had been an unqualified success for the last 27 years and had been written up in newspapers and magazines on numerous occasions, times suddenly seemed more precarious. Rising gasoline prices, the prospect of a long-term fuel crisis, confrontation with the American Indian Movement (AIM) at Wounded Knee, and the highway beautification laws governing the location of Wall Drug's famous roadside signs all combined to pose new threats to tourist travel in South Dakota and to Wall Drug in particular.

COMPANY BACKGROUND

Ted Hustead majored in pharmacy at the University of Nebraska and graduated in 1929 at the age of 27. Less than three years later, in December 1931, Ted and his wife Dorothy (who grew up in Colman, South Dakota) bought the drugstore in Wall, South Dakota for $2,500. Dorothy and Ted, and their four-year-old son Bill, lived in the back 20 feet of the store for six years during the height of the Great Depression. Business was not good (the first month's gross revenue was $350) and Ted was not able to maintain a separate home and still keep the store going.

One writer described Wall in 1931 as follows:

> Wall, then: a huddle of poor wooden buildings, many unpainted, housing some 300 desperate souls; a 19th century depot and wooden water tank; dirt (or mud) streets; few trees; a stop on the railroad, it wasn't even that on the highway. US 16 and 14 went right on by, as did the tourists speeding between the Badlands and the Black Hills. There was nothing in Wall to stop for.[1]

---

* Prepared by Profs. James D. Taylor, Robert L. Johnson, and Gene B. Iverson of the University of South Dakota.

[1] Dana Close Jennings, *Free Ice Water: The Story of the Wall Drug* (Aberdeen, S. D.: North Plains Press, 1969), p. 26.

Neither the drugstore nor the town of Wall prospered until Dorothy Hustead conceived the idea of placing a sign beside the highway promising free
ice water to anyone who would stop at their store. The sign read "Get a
soda/Get a beer/Turn next corner/Just as near/To Highway 16 and 14/Free ice
water/Wall Drug." Ted put the sign up on a blazing hot Sunday afternoon in
the summer of 1936 and no sooner had he done so than the first cars started
turning off the highway to go to Wall Drug. This seemingly simple advertising effort marked a turning point in the Wall Drug's business strategy—and
in the success of the enterprise as well.

With the value of highway advertising thus made dramatically apparent,
Ted began erecting novel signs along all the highways leading to Wall. One
sign read "Slow down the old hack/Wall Drug Corner/Just across the railroad track." The distinctive, attention-catching signs were a boon to Wall
Drug's business and the town of Wall prospered, too. In an article in *Good
Housekeeping* in 1951, the Hustead's signs were called "the most ingenious
and irresistible system of signs ever devised."[2]

Just after World War II, a friend traveling across Europe for the Red Cross
got the notion of putting up Wall Drug signs overseas. The idea caught on
and small Wall Drug plaques were subsequently carried all over the world by
South Dakota GIs who were familiar with the store's advertising techniques.
A number of servicemen even wrote the store requesting signs. One sign in
Paris announced "Wall Drŭg Store 4,278 miles (6,951 kilometers)." Wall
Drug signs have appeared in Shanghai, Amsterdam, the Paris and London
subways, the 38th Parallel in Korea, the North and South Pole areas, and on
Vietnam jungle trails. The Husteads sent more than 200 signs to servicemen
in Vietnam. The worldwide distribution of Wall Drug signs led to news
stories and publicity which further nurtured the unique image and reputation
of the store.

In the late 1950s, *Redbook Magazine* carried a story about Wall Drug
which was later picked up and condensed in *Reader's Digest*. Since then, the
newspapers and magazines carrying feature stories or referring to Wall
Drug have included:

National Enquirer, November 11, 1973.

Grit, October 28, 1973.

Las Vegas Review—Journal, September 22, 1973.

Senior Scholastic Magazine, October 4, 1973, p. 11.

Congressional Record, September 11, 1973, Si6269.

The Wall Street Journal, September 5, 1973.

Omaha World-Herald, May 15, 1972.

Elsevier (Dutch magazine), February 12, 1972.

---

[2] Ibid., p. 42.

Rapid City Journal, April 12, 1970.

A Cleveland daily paper, May 16, 1971.

The New York Times, Sunday, January 31, 1971.

Oshkosh, Wisconsin, *Daily Northwestern,* August 2, 1969.

Sunday Picture Magazine, Minneapolis Tribune, September 21, 1969.

America Illustrated, U.S. Information Agency in Poland and Russia, June 1969.

Ojai Valley News and Oaks Gazette, August 14, 1968.

Chicago Tribune, Norman Vincent Peale's syndicated column, "Confident Living," October 8, 1966.

Norman Vincent Peale's book, *You Can If You Think You Can,* p. 34.

San Francisco Examiner, February 12, 1966.

Women's Wear Daily, September 16, 1966.

Coronet Magazine, April 1964.

Cleveland, Ohio, *The Plain Dealer,* date not known.

The June 1969 issue of *America Illustrated,* a U.S. Information Agency publication distributed in the Soviet Union and Poland, featured a story entitled "The Lure and Fascination of Seven Fabulous Stores," by Mal Oettinger. The seven stores were Macy's, Wall Drug Store, Rich's, L. L. Bean, Inc., Neiman-Marcus, Gump's, and Brentano's.

GROWTH AND DEVELOPMENT OF WALL DRUG

The sales and square footage of Wall Drug have grown steadily since the 1940s. From 1931 until 1941, Wall Drug was located in a 24- by 40-foot rented building on the west side of Main Street. In 1941, an old lodge hall, which acted as the gymnasium in Wasta (15 miles west of Wall), was bought and moved to the east side of Main Street across from the original store. It then became the site of Wall Drug; the store now occupies over an acre, taking up the better part of one side of Wall's block-long business district.

When World War II ended, tourist travel to the Badlands and Black Hills picked up considerably and Wall Drug's highway signs attracted so many people to the store that the Husteads claim they were embarrassed because the facilities were not large enough. There were no modern rest rooms even. Sales in the late 1940s ranged from $150,000 to $200,000 per year.

In 1951, the Hustead's son Bill graduated from South Dakota State College at Brookings with a major in pharmacy and returned to Wall to join his father in managing Wall Drug. Ted and Bill proceeded to initiate a series of expansions of the business. In 1953, a storeroom on the south end of the building (see Exhibit 1) was remodeled and became the Western Clothing Room. The next year, a new area adjacent to the Western Clothing Room was added. Sales increased about 30 percent to around $300,000 per year as a result of these two expansions to the store. In 1956, a self-service cafe was

EXHIBIT 1
Layout of Wall Drug

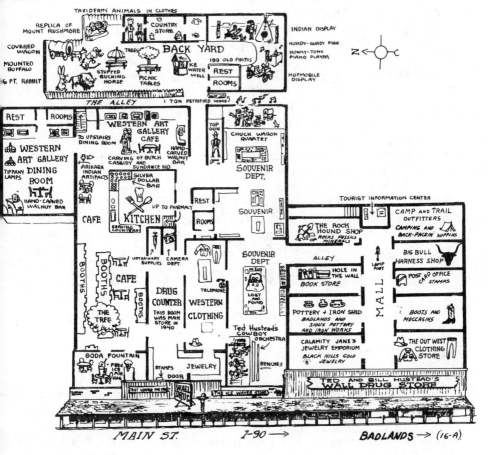

installed on the north side of the premises. By the early 1960s, sales had climbed to $500,000.

In the early 1960s, Ted and his son Bill began seriously thinking of moving Wall Drug out to the highway. The original Highway 16 ran by the north side of Wall, about two blocks from the store. But later Highway 16 was rerouted to the south side of Wall, though still only two blocks away from the drugstore. In the late 1950s and early 1960s, a new highway was built running by the south side of Wall paralleling the revised route. Ted and Bill Hustead were considering building an all new Wall Drug, along with a gasoline filling station, adjacent to the new highway just where the intersection to Wall was located.

They decided to build the gasoline station first, and did so, calling it Wall Auto Livery. But when the station was finished, they decided against moving the drugstore and, instead, elected to continue expanding the old store in downtown Wall. This proved fortunate, since soon after that a new interstate highway (I-90) replaced the new Highway 16 route and the new I-90 interchange ran right through the site of the proposed new Wall Drug.

Once the Husteads decided to keep the store in downtown Wall, expansion was continued. In 1963, a new fireproof construction coffee shop was installed where the present soda fountain is—see the store layout in Exhibit 1. In 1964, a new kitchen, again of fireproof construction, was added in back of the cafe and main store. In 1964 and 1965, offices and the new pharmacy were opened on the second floor over the kitchen. In 1968, the back dining room and backyard across the alley were added. This was followed in 1971 with the Western Art Gallery Dining Room. These expansions helped push annual sales volume to $1 million.

In 1971, the Husteads bought the theater that bordered Wall Drug on the south and continued to operate it as a theater through 1972. In early 1973, they closed the theater and began to convert the location into a new addition called the "Mall." By the summer of 1973, the north part of the Mall was open for business. The south side was unfinished. That year, Wall Drug grossed $1,600,000—an increase of about 20 percent over 1972. Bill attributed the increase to the new Mall addition. Currently, Wall Drug covers almost 32,000 square feet and is air-conditioned; the facility also contains 960 square feet of office space, and almost 12,000 square feet of storage space.

THE MALL

For about five years prior to starting construction, Bill Hustead thought about and planned the concept of the Mall. The Mall was conceived as a town within a large room. The strolling mall was designed as a main street with two-story frontier Western stores on either side—in the fashion of a recreated Western town. The shop fronts were reproductions of building fronts found in old photos of western towns in the 1880s. On the inside, the stores were paneled with such woods as pine from Custer, South Dakota, American black walnut, gumwood, hackberry, cedar, maple, and oak. Many photos, paintings, and prints lined the walls. The shops stocked products that were more expensive than the souvenir merchandise carried in other parts of Wall Drug and, in many respects, were like Western boutiques. The northern half of the Mall opened for business in July 1973. But Bill was uncertain as to whether to go ahead with construction of the south side.

The construction of the Mall prompted a distinct change in the financing strategy of Wall Drug. All previous expansions had been funded out of retained earnings or with short-term loans. But the Husteads built the Mall by borrowing approximately $250,000 for ten years. Part of this money was also used to erect 20 large new signs standing 660 feet from the interstate highway.

THE DRAWING POWER OF WALL DRUG

The Husteads operated Wall Drug and Wall Auto Livery as two separate corporations. Both businesses were heavily dependent on tourist travel and in 1973 the sales of each were at an all-time high. The economic base of Wall (1970 population, 786) consisted of 11 motels and a number of service stations—all keyed to the tourist traffic drawn by Wall Drug. The town's business district was one block long. Nearly a third of the labor force worked at Wall Drug. The president of the Chamber of Commerce once observed that without Wall Drug the town would dry up and blow away.

EXHIBIT 2
South Dakota: Location of Wall in Relation to the Black Hills, Badlands, Interstate 90, Rapid City, and Sioux Falls

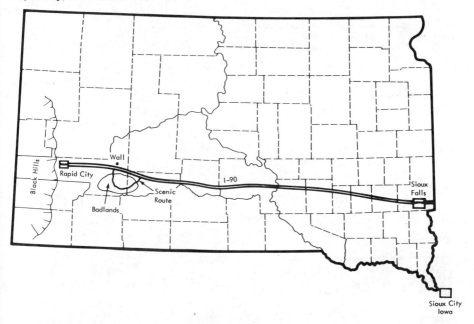

Wall is situated right on the edge of the Badlands (see Exhibit 2) and is 52 miles east of Rapid City, South Dakota's second largest city (1970 population, 43,836). For miles in either direction, travelers are teased and tantalized by Wall Drug signs. Along one 45-mile stretch of interstate highway leading to Wall, travelers encounter 53 Wall Drug signs. As tourists approach the town (those westbound usually after driving 40 miles or more through the Badlands), they are greeted by a large Wall Drug sign on the interchange and an 80-foot high, 50-ton statue of a dinosaur (see Exhibit 3).

As many as 10,000 people might stream through Wall Drug on a busy day. In the summer of 1963, a traffic count made on the highway going by Wall

EXHIBIT 3
The Wall Drug Dinosaur

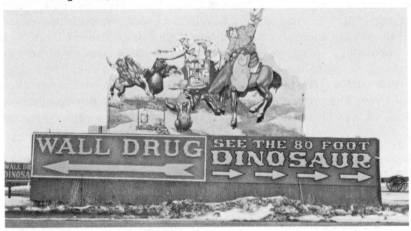

showed that 46 percent of the cars were eastbound and 54 percent were westbound. Of the eastbound traffic, 43 percent turned off at Wall. Of the westbound traffic, 44 percent turned off at Wall. On another occasion, a survey of state licenses of autos and campers parked in front of Wall Drug and in the camper and trailer park one block from Wall Drug between 8 A.M. and 10 A.M. on Wednesday, June 4 resulted in the following percentages:

Neighboring states and South Dakota (nonlocal)	37%
South Dakota, local county	32
Balance of states and Canada	31

THE MAIN ATTRACTION

The Husteads have made Wall Drug a place of amusement and family entertainment, a gallery of the West, a cultural display of South Dakota history, and a reflection of the heritage of the West. Some even say Wall Drug has become a South Dakota institution. Nostalgia addicts have a "field day" in the store and children delight in animated, life-size singing cowboys, a tableau of an Indian camp, a stuffed bucking horse, a six-foot rabbit, a stuffed buffalo, old 10-cent slot machines that pay out a souvenir coin, statues of cowboys, a coin-operated, quick-draw game, and souvenirs by the roomful.

Free ice water is still one of Wall Drug's biggest attractions. Ted Hustead, in his 70s but still on the job every day, estimated that the store gives out 5,000 glasses of water a day, plus filling and icing water jugs free of charge. The store has $30,000 worth of ice-making equipment with a capacity of one and one-half tons of ice per day—a far cry from earlier years when Ted cut winter ice from nearby farm ponds and stored it for summer use. Another of the store's traditions is a nickel cup of coffee and a breakfast of two eggs and a slice of toast for 25 cents. However, rising costs have since upped the price of the breakfast to 49 cents (as of 1973). On a busy day, patrons consume 250 dozen eggs and 6,000 homemade donuts.

The dining rooms are decorated with wood paneling and paintings of Western art; diners are entertained with Western music. Patrons can select from a moderately priced menu that includes buffalo burgers, roast beef, steak, and select wine, beer, or a "Jack Daniels" at a rustic, American walnut bar. The original soda fountain has been expanded into a 475-seat cafe built around a huge cottonwood tree growing up through the roof.

STORE OPERATIONS

Wall Drug does most of its business during the summer months. In 1973, sales for June were $258,000; July, $423,000; and August, $414,500. April sales totaled about $40,000 and in May were $100,000. Late tourists and hunters traveling through typically generate a modest volume of business in September and October. About one fourth of Wall Drug's sales consist of food; beverages and soda fountain sales account for another 5 percent to 10 percent (although these percentages do vary with the weather). The remaining portion of sales revenue is distributed among jewelry items (10–15 percent), clothing and hats (15 percent), souvenirs (35–40 percent), and drug sundries and prescriptions (5–10 percent). Both Ted and Bill are registered pharmacists and they fill at least 20 prescriptions a day.

During the summer the store is staffed by a crew of about 150 people, working seven days a week in two shifts from 5 A.M. to 10 P.M. About 40 to 50 percent of the employees are college students recruited especially for the summer months. The students are housed in ten homes that over the years have been bought and converted into dormitory apartments. The students pay $8 per week rent, but if they stay through Labor Day, they get a $5 per week refund as an incentive to stay the full summer. There is a modern swimming pool for their use. The Husteads set curfews of 11:30 P.M. on weekdays and 1:30 A.M. on weekends for their student residents; according to Bill, now the general manager, "It's hard work, and we feel they need a full night's sleep to do a good job. Besides, auto accidents can happen late at night and we want to send our kids back home in one piece."[3] About half of the student workers return each year for another season.

When the student employees arrive at the beginning of a new summer season, they are given a cram course in the history of the Badlands and the Black Hills and are told to memorize the mileage from Wall Drug to other tourist attractions such as Mount Rushmore. Then, to make sure the information has been learned, the students are given a quiz. According to Ted Hustead such procedures are used because "If tourists remember Wall Drug, it won't be because we have such a great store but because of the people who waited on them. We want them to be cheerful and helpful."[4]

MERCHANDISE ORDERING

The inventory in Wall Drug varies from around $300,000 in the summer to a low of around $80,000 in the off-season. Ordering for the following summer season begins the preceding fall. Orders begin arriving in December, but most of the merchandise arrives in January, February, March, and April. Many large souvenir companies postdate their invoices until July and August. Each year brings new offerings from souvenir companies and other suppliers. Wall Drug generally buys its souvenir merchandise directly from the producers or importers. The same is true of photo supplies and clothing. Most of the purchasing is done by Bill and Ted, who admit they rely on trusted salesmen of their suppliers to advise them on merchandise purchases. Many of these companies have supplied Wall Drug for 20 years or so. In addition, the Husteads rely on their department managers for buying

---

[3] As quoted in *The Wall Street Journal*, September 5, 1973, p. 12.
[4] Ibid.

help. The manager of jewelry, for instance, will recommend on the basis of last year's orders and experience with customer reaction how much to order for the next season. All ordering is approved by Bill and Ted.

Years ago, much of what Wall Drug bought and sold was imported or made by manufacturers in the eastern United States. In recent years much more of the merchandise has been made locally and regionally. Nearby Indian reservations now have small production firms and individuals that supply handcrafted items to Wall Drug. For example, Wall Drug stocked items made by Sioux Pottery, Sioux Moccasin, and Milk Camp Industries.

The merchandise carried ranges from the usual drugstore items to steer skulls, cowboy boots, snakebite serum, lariats, Levis, leather chaps, as well as tourist souvenirs. One of the best selling items was a snake ashtray made from plaster of paris and painted to resemble a rattlesnake: these were obtained from a resident of the Black Hills who used live rattlers to make the molds for casting the ashtrays. Another feature item was jack-a-lopes (stuffed jackrabbits sporting antelope horns), made by a local taxidermist.

PROMOTION

As indicated earlier, Wall Drug relied heavily on roadside signs to bring people to the store. By 1968 there were about 3,000 signs displayed along highways and roads in all 50 states. The company utilized a truck and two men working nine months a year to maintain the store's signs in South Dakota and adjoining states; however, many signs were put up by volunteers. The store gives away approximately 14,000 six-by-eight-inch signs and 3,000 eight-by-twenty-two-inch signs a year to people who request them. The signs are plastic and weather resistant. Many people have sent in photographs and snapshots showing a Wall Drug sign displayed in some unusual place: these are prominently posted in the store for visitors to see. Making new signs keeps two professional sign painters busy; in 1973 Wall Drug had a $100,000 budget for new signs.

In the mid-1960s, the Highway Beautification Act was passed by Congress and signed into law by President Johnson. The act regulated the use of outdoor billboards along interstate highways and posed a threat to the Hustead's continued reliance upon extensive highway advertising. However, Bill and Ted believed that the media publicity about Wall Drug, together with their sign giveaway program, would help offset the possible reduction in highway signs. Nonetheless, the Husteads felt that it was very important for Wall Drug to gain as much attention and publicity as possible. Subsequently, small ads were placed in New York City's Greenwich Village publication *The Village Voice* advertising 5 cent coffee, 49 cent breakfasts, and animal health remedies at Wall Drug. These ads resulted in a telephone call, several letter inquiries, an article about Wall Drug in *The Village Voice,* and some attention from other media sources. An article in the *New York Times* and some other publicity led to Bill Hustead's appearance on Garry Moore's television program "To Tell the Truth." Wall Drug's posters in the London subway produced a 20-minute, taped telephone interview with Ted by the British Broadcasting Company. Shortly thereafter, several British newspapers carried stories about Wall Drug because of the signs on the London Underground trains. Posters and signs were also erected in the Paris Metro subway (in the English language) and on the dock in Amsterdam in full view of people boarding sight-seeing boats.

Recently, the Husteads began printing two brochures: (1) *Motel Guide for South Dakota*, and (2) *South Dakota Campground Directory of Privately Owned and Operated Campgrounds and Trailer Parks*. Over 200,000 of these guides were given away to Wall Drug visitors each summer. The Husteads hoped that each of the motels and campgrounds in the brochure would reciprocate by displaying a Wall Drug sign on their premises, if asked to do so. This "we'll promote you if you promote us" approach, however, was in the initial stages and its success undetermined. Bill and Ted had plans for erecting Wall Drug signs which could be seen when travelers turned off the interstate at exits on either side of Wall; such signs on roads leading off the interstate, if appropriately located, were not under jurisdiction of the Highway Beautification Act.

FINANCE

Until December 1973, all of Wall Drug's expansion programs were financed with internally generated funds, supplemented with short-term borrowing. In effect, each addition was paid for as it was built (or soon thereafter). However, to fund construction of the Mall, a ten-year, $250,000 loan in the form of a real estate mortgage was negotiated. Payments on this loan, including 8 percent interest, were $34,000 in 1974 and $37,000 annually from 1975 through 1983.

The company generally financed inventory purchases for the upcoming season with short-term loans if internal funds were inadequate. However, seasonal billings by a number of suppliers obviated the need for heavy financing of inventories. Of course, the company was vulnerable to a cash squeeze if a large inventory was left unsold at the end of any tourist season. This potentiality was aggravated by the fixed annual repayments on the long-term loan.

Exhibits 4 through 10 present the financial condition of both Wall Drug and Wall Auto Livery.

EXHIBIT 4

WALL DRUG STORE, INC.
Balance Sheet
As of December 31

	1973	*1972*
Assets		
Current assets:		
Cash on hand	$ 1,037	$ 946
Cash in bank	2,450	138
Investment in commercial paper, at cost	70,000	—
Accounts receivable—trade.............................	12,121	7,183
Accounts receivable—officers and employees	4,300	3,323
Accounts receivable—income tax refund	—	19,824
Inventories	144,013	86,890
Accrued interest receivable	463	—
Prepaid insurance	9,455	9,068
Total current assets	$ 243,839	$127,372
Investment and other assets:		
Bonds, at cost	$ 1,675	$ 1,675
Organization cost, at cost	972	972
Total investments and other assets	$ 2,647	$ 2,647
Property, plant and equipment, at cost:		
Land	$ 70,454	$ 50,079
Buildings, building improvements, and parking lot improvements	692,488	527,456
Equipment, furniture, and fixtures	366,651	303,108
	$1,129,593	$880,643
Less accumulated depreciation	427,866	369,743
Depreciated cost of fixed assets	$ 701,727	$510,900
Goodwill, at cost:	$ 31,386	$ 31,386
Total assets.................................	$ 979,599	$672,305

EXHIBIT 4 (continued)

	1973	1972
Liabilities and Stockholders' Equity		
Current liabilities:		
Notes payable—Wall Auto Livery, Inc	$ 20,000	$ 50,000
Notes payable—bank	—	20,000
Current maturities of long-term debt	20,058	—
Accounts payable—trade	22,709	30,979
Income taxes payable	11,161	—
Accrued taxes payable	25,880	18,457
Profit sharing contribution payable	30,542	18,231
Accrued payroll and bonuses	40,073	28,559
Accrued interest payable	2,573	255
Total current liabilities	$ 172,996	$166,481
Long-term debt:		
Real estate mortgage payable	$ 232,742	—
Contract for deed payable	11,200	—
Total long-term debt	$ 243,942	—
Stockholders' equity:		
Preferred stock, $100 par value, 4%, cumulative, nonvoting, 1,000 shares authorized, 300 shares outstanding	$ 30,000	$ 30,000
Common stock, $100 par value, Class A, 500 shares authorized, 480 shares outstanding	48,000	48,000
Common stock, $100 par value, Class B, nonvoting 4,500 shares authorized, 400 shares outstanding	40,000	40,000
Retained earnings	444,661	387,824
Total stockholders' equity	$ 562,661	$505,824
Total liabilities and stockholders' equity	$ 979,599	$672,305

The accompanying notes (Exhibit 7) are an integral part of these financial statements.

EXHIBIT 5

WALL DRUG STORE, INC.
Statements of Income and Retained Earnings
Years Ended December 31

	1973	1972
Net sales	$1,606,648	$1,335,932
Cost of goods sold	805,827	687,613
Gross profit	$ 800,821	$ 648,319
General and administrative expenses	690,461	577,767
Income from operations	$,110,360	$ 70,552
Interest income	2,946	188
Rental income	3,647	4,248
Trailer park income	6,020	4,600
Theater income	—	5,197
Gain on sale of assets	176	4,286
Other income	747	902
	$ 123,896	$ 89,973
Other deductions:		
Interest	$ 19,735	$ 4,072
Theater expense	—	2,689
Trailer park expense	4,223	3,433
Loss on sale of assets	—	1,674
Loss on demolition of theater building	—	13,860
	$ 23,958	$ 25,728
Income before income taxes	$ 99,938	$ 64,245
Provision for income tax—current year	40,701	20,176
Net Income	$ 59,237	$ 44,069
Retained earnings:		
Beginning	387,824	343,755
	$ 447,061	$ 387,824
Dividends paid	2,400	—
Ending	$ 444,661	$ 387,824
Earnings per share	$ 65.95	48.71

The accompanying notes (Exhibit 7) are an integral part of these financial statements.

EXHIBIT 6

WALL DRUG STORE, INC.
Statements of Changes in Financial Position
Years Ended December 31

	1973	1972
Financial resources were provided by:		
Net income	$ 59,237	$ 44,069
Add income charges not affecting working capital in the period:		
Depreciation	58,723	43,862
Demolition loss on theater building	—	13,860
Working capital provided by operations	$117,960	$ 101,791
Proceeds from borrowings	264,000	—
Basis of property and equipment sold	625	2,750
Total resources provided	$382,585	$ 104,541
Financial resources were used for:		
Acquisition of land	$ 21,000	$ 5,799
Acquisition of building	165,031	149,924
Acquisition of equipment and signs	64,144	50,636
Reduction in long-term debt	20,058	—
Dividends paid	2,400	—
Total resources used	$272,633	$ 206,359
Increase (decrease) in working capital	$109,952	$(101,818)
Working capital:		
Beginning	(39,109)	62,709
Ending	$ 70,843	$ (39,109)
Increase (decrease) in components of working capital:		
Current assets:		
Cash	$ 2,403	$ (1,850)
Investment in commercial paper	70,000	—
Marketable securities	—	(59,375)
Accounts receivable—trade and other	(13,909)	684
Inventories	57,123	7,204
Other current assets—net	850	(3,650)
Total assets	$116,467	$ (56,987)
Current liabilities:		
Note payable—banks and others	$ (50,000)	70,000
Current maturities of long-term debt	20,058	—
Accounts payable—trade	(8,270)	12,891
Income tax payable	11,161	(32,272)
Other current and accrued liabilities—net	33,566	(5,788)
Total liabilities	$ 6,515	$ 44,831
Increase (decrease) in working capital	$109,952	$(101,818)

The accompanying notes (Exhibit 7) are an integral part of these financial statements.

EXHIBIT 7
Notes to Financial Statements

Note 1. Summary of Accounting Policies
   Accounting Method. The corporation uses the accrual method of accounting for income tax and financial statement purposes.
   Inventories. Inventories are generally valued at the lower of cost or market on a first-in, first-out basis computed under retail method.
   Fixed Assets. Fixed assets are stated at cost. Depreciation is calculated under the straight-line method, 150 percent declining balance method and 200 percent declining balance method. The same depreciation methods are used for financial and tax purposes. The useful lives selected for the assets are as follows: Buildings and building improvements. 15 to 40 years; parking lot, 8 years; and furniture, fixtures and equipment, 5 to 10 years. The provision for depreciation for 1973 of $58,723 and 1972 of $43,862 was charged to operations.
   Repairs and maintenance costs are generally charged to expense at the time the expenditure in incurred. When an asset is sold or retired, its cost and related depreciation are removed from the accounts and a gain or loss is recognized on the difference between the proceeds of disposition and the undepreciated cost as the case may be. When an asset is traded in a like exchange, the cost and related depreciation are removed from the accounts and the undepreciated cost is capitalized as a part of the cost of the asset acquired.
   Income Taxes. The provision for income taxes is based on the elements of income and expense, as reported in the statement of income. Investment tax credits are accounted for on the "flow-through" method, which recognizes the benefits in the year in which the assets which give rise to the credit are placed in service.

Note 2. Long-Term Debt
   The real estate mortgage is an 8 percent mortgage dated December 3, 1973 and due October 1, 1983. The mortgage is to be paid in annual installments of principal and interest as follows:

   10/1/74 .... $34,035.28

   10/1/75 and thereafter $37,257.50

   The Drug Store in downtown Wall is pledged as security on this real estate mortgage.
   The contract for deed payable is a 7 percent contract for deed, dated January 16, 1973 and is due January 16, 1978. The contract is to be paid in annual installments of $2,800 plus interest. This contract is for the purchase of approximately 202 acres of land which is the security for the contract for deed.

Note 3. Profit Sharing Plan
   The company has a profit sharing plan for all full-time employees who meet the qualification requirements. The company contributed $30,542 in 1973, and $18,231 in 1972 to the profit sharing trust.

EXHIBIT 8

WALL AUTO LIVERY, INC.
Balance Sheets
As of December 31

	1973	1972
Assets		
Current assets:		
Cash on hand	$ 100	$ 100
Cash in bank	14,590	19,916
Marketable securities, at cost	58,715	—
Notes receivable—Wall Drug Store, Inc	20,000	50,000
Accounts receivable—trade	1,967	8,205
Credit cards	2,010	—
Miscellaneous receivables	—	75
Inventory, at lower of cost (Fifo) or market	8,462	9,261
Prepaid insurance	1,557	1,469
Accrued interest receivable	729	247
Total current assets	$108,130	$ 89,273
Property and equipment:		
Land	$ 7,367	$ 7,367
Buildings	103,133	103,133
Equipment	26,297	26,076
	$136,797	$136,576
Less accumulated depreciation	57,685	52,548
Depreciation cost of fixed assets	$ 79,112	$ 84,028
Total assets	$187,242	$173,301
Liabilities and Stockholders' Equity		
Current liabilities:		
Current maturity of long-term debt	$ 5,000	$ 5,000
Accounts payable—trade	754	5,696
Income taxes payable	7,286	2,774
Accrued profit sharing contribution	2,666	2,446
Accrued payroll and sales taxes	840	756
Accrued interest payable	125	250
Total current liabilities	$ 16,671	$ 16,922
Long-term debt:		
Note payable noninterest bearing contract payable to F. M. Cheny maturing March 1, 1976	$ 5,000	$ 5,000
Note payable—6 percent to Perpetual National Life Insurance Company maturing in annual installments of $5,000 plus interest	—	5,000
Total long-term debt	$ 5,000	$ 10,000
Stockholders' Equity:	Common stock, $100 par	
Common stock, $100 par value, 2,000 shares authorized, 444 shares outstanding	$ 44,400	$ 44,400
Retained earnings	121,171	101,979
Total stockholders' equity	$165,571	$146,379
Total liabilities and stockholders' equity	$187,242	$173,301

The accompanying notes (Exhibit 7) are an integral part of these financial statements.

EXHIBIT 9

WALL AUTO LIVERY, INC
Statements of Income and Retained Earnings
Years Ended December 31

	1973	1972
Net sales	$191,969	$172,195
Inventories—beginning of year	$ 9,261	$ 9,467
Purchases	132,698	124,399
Freight	35	—
	$141,994	$133,866
Inventories—end of year	8,462	9,261
Cost of goods sold	$133,532	$124,605
Gross profit	$ 58,437	$ 47,590
General and administrative expense	44,568	41,443
Income from operations	$ 13,869	$ 6,147
Interest income	5,441	2,436
Rental income	17,917	15,440
Miscellaneous income	—	1,434
	$ 37,227	$ 25,457
Other deductions:		
Interest expense	$ 510	$ 775
Rent expense—depreciation	3,005	3,128
	$ 3,515	$ 3,903
Income before federal income tax	$ 33,712	$ 21,554
Provision for income taxes	$ 14,520	$ 7,574
Net income	$ 19,192	$ 13,980
Retained earnings:		
Beginning	101,979	87,999
Ending	$121,171	$101,979
Earnings per share	$ 43.23	$ 31.49

The accompanying notes (Exhibit 7) are an integral part of these financial statements.

EXHIBIT 10

WALL AUTO LIVERY, INC
Statements of Changes in Financial Position
Years Ended December 31

	1973	1972
Financial resources were provided by:		
Net income	$19,192	$13,980
Add income charges not affecting working capital in the period:		
Depreciation	5,137	5,390
Working capital provided by operations	$24,329	$19,370
Financial resources were used for:		
Acquisition of equipment	$ 221	$ 3,310
Reduction of long-term debt	5,000	5,000
Total resources used	$ 5,221	$ 8,310
Increase in working capital	$19,108	$11,060
Working capital:		
Beginning of year	73,352	61,292
End of year	$92,460	$72,352
Increase (decrease) in components of working capital:		
Current assets:		
Cash	$ (5,326)	$15,394
Marketable securities	58,715	(58,087)
Notes receivable	(30,000)	50,000
Accounts receivable	(6,238)	3,371
Credit cards	2,010	—
Miscellaneous receivables	(75)	(57)
Inventory	(799)	(206)
Prepaid insurance	88	73
Accrued interest receivable	482	40
Total assets	$18,857	$10,528
Current liabilities:		
Accounts payable—trade	$ (4,942)	$ 1,064
Income taxes payable	4,512	(1,925)
Other current and accrued liabilities	179	329
Total liabilities	$ (251)	$ (532)
Increase in working capital	$19,108	$11,060

The accompanying notes (Exhibit 7) are an integral part of these financial statements.

6. Bright Coop Company, Inc.*

When a number of East Texas farmers got into the business of raising chickens on a mass production basis in the early 1950s, Charles Bright and his brother N. G. Bright, quite by accident, stumbled upon an opportunity to supply low-cost coops for transporting the birds to market. Prior to 1951, live poultry transporters used custom-built coops that required two men to load onto trucks; the coops were rented from coop builders rather than being owned outright by the truckers. The Bright brothers, upon discovering that there was a sizable market for a low-priced wooden poultry coop, wasted little time in setting up Bright Coop Company as a manufacturer of wooden coops, with operations in Nacogdoches, Texas.

From 1952 to 1975, Charles, 48, and N. G., 59, periodically expanded their factory to the point where the Nacogdoches firm was producing an average of 2,000 coops per day. In 1975, Bright Coop was the largest wooden coop manufacturer in the United States; its coops were shipped all over the United States and into Mexico and Canada as well. Many of Bright Coop Company's customers were of the opinion that no other coop producer matched Bright on the combined features of competitive price, quality, and service.

HISTORY AND BACKGROUND

Prior to forming Bright Coop Company, the Bright brothers owned a grocery store and had a sideline business making wooden chairs in Nacogdoches. In April 1951, a load of building materials for the construction of 500 chair parts overturned and a local live poultry hauler asked the Brights to construct chicken coops out of the ruined material. The Brights agreed and spent much of their time from November 1951 to the end of January 1952 completing the project. They received $2.25 each for 168 coops. Even though the Bright brothers ended up losing money on that first project because they underestimated the amount of manual labor that it would take to make the coops, they felt there was good business potential in constructing coops for sale to poultry haulers. The East Texas broiler industry was beginning to grow rapidly and when the word spread in the poultry community that the Brights were producing coops, additional orders came in unsolicited.

Although, at first, the Bright brothers had a very limited knowledge of the woodworking business, they learned quickly and in 1953 began to make tools that would allow them to increase coop production more efficiently. At the

* Prepared by Prof. B. G. Bizzell and Prof. Ed D. Roach of Stephen F. Austin University.

time, coop-building tools and machinery were nonexistent. The Brights were clever enough to design and assemble most of the equipment they needed. They were also innovators in the design of their product. The Bright Coop Company introduced the first "one-man" coop which cut the loading and unloading costs of poultry haulers in half. Haulers liked the Bright's innovative coop design (aside from the laborsaving feature it had over the standard "two-man" coops) and orders increased steadily. As fast as they were able, the Brights moved to a more automated production of coops, thereby both saving substantially on labor costs per coop and increasing the daily production rate.

In 1959, the Brights diversified into wooden turkey coops and metal racks. This required a different coop design because whereas chicken coops were stacked on flatbed trailers for shipping, the greater size and weight of turkeys required a larger coop, together with metal racks for support. In 1963 the production of wooden turkey coops was curtailed in favor of producing just metal racks.

In the mid-1960s, the lumber market changed drastically and the company had difficulty in finding acceptable quality hardwood for its coops. Supplies were so tight that the two brothers accepted odd-lot shipments of hardwood lumber of different grades; large amounts of these shipments proved unsuitable for coop production. In an effort to find some use for the leftover lumber, the Brights began constructing wooden pallets for sale to chemical and shipping firms. Soon this business, too, prospered and pallet construction was continued as a regularly offered product.

In 1966, the company moved another step toward completely fulfilling its motto, "Complete Poultry Truck Outfitters," by commencing the production of trailers capable of hauling coops and related equipment. Shortly thereafter, Bright expanded into all kinds of accessories for transporting coops including straps, loaders, pallets, and chains. These last additions made Bright a full-line producer of items needed by haulers of live poultry.

THE MARKET FOR COOPS

From the time the company was started in 1952, Bright Coop's sales grew every year until late 1974. During the last five months of 1974, Bright Coop found itself caught in the midst of the bust phase of the poultry cycle, an economic recession, and an emerging demand for plastic coops as a substitute for wooden coops. Brights' sales fell from nearly 2,000 coops daily to 450 per day. Almost 40 percent of Bright's work force had to be laid off. Whereas Bright had used 40,000 board feet of lumber a day during the peak sales periods of early 1974, its lumber usage fell to less than 20,000 board feet during the first half of 1975. Most of the lumber was purchased from lumber mills in the Nacogdoches area.

Studies of ups and downs in the poultry business indicate an approximate five-year "boom to bust to boom" cycle—especially as concerns the broiler, roaster, egg, turkey, and rock cornish hen segments of the poultry industry. The most recent appearance of the bust phase began in the third quarter of

1972 and was accelerated by historically high broiler production, coincident with high beef production. The competition between beef and poultry for the consumer's meat dollar resulted in a 12 percent to 15 percent contraction in poultry sales, with the broiler and turkey market segments being hit hardest.

These events resulted in a sharp downswing in Brights' sales of coops. Processors who had a large inventory of coops to draw down stopped ordering new coops for several months. Others simply cut back on the size of their coop orders. As an illustrative example of how changes in the demand for poultry can affect the sales of coops over the course of the poultry cycle, suppose that a processor uses 100,000 coops in his operation during average production periods. Further suppose that 1,000 coops wear out each week and are replaced by ordering 1,000 new coops per week from Bright. Then if the processor's production rate falls by 20 percent such that only 80,000 coops are needed, the processor has a 20-week coop inventory on hand and will not need to order any more coops for 20 weeks. On the other hand, if and when the processor increases production back to normal, he will need to order 20,000 coops on a one-time basis and then cut back to the normal 1,000 replacement amount. Such boom-to-bust swings in coop orders prompted Bright to try to respond quickly to such market shifts and was also a motivating factor in Bright's earlier diversification moves.

While the boom-to-bust cycle was taking its toll on Bright, two other factors were also at work. One was the appearance of the severe economic recession in late 1974 which further undermined the poultry industry in general and coops sales in particular. The second was a surge of enthusiasm for plastic coops as a substitute for wooden coops. A number of haulers were persuaded by the plastic coop manufacturers to give plastic coops a try. The combination of these three factors was believed by the Brights to account for why the bottom literally fell out of the company's coop sales in late 1974. However, in the spring of 1975, the poultry market began a recovery and, according to prognosticators, the long-run outlook for coop sales was for a gradual expansion during the next five years.

PRODUCT LINE

In 1975, Bright Coop introduced a new wood-plastic combination coop to compete with the increasingly popular plastic coop. According to the company's promotional brochures, the new coop represented a "perfect marriage of wood and plastic." (See the illustration in Exhibit 1.) Other Bright products as of 1975 included the Bright pullet and poultry harvester, the live turkey harvester, the specially designed drop-frame poultry trailer in two styles, and hen floors. These items are displayed in Exhibits 2, 3, and 4.

PRODUCTION FACILITIES

All of Bright Coop's production facilities were located in Nacogdoches, Texas. The facilities included a coop manufacturing plant, a pallet manufac-

EXHIBIT 1

EXHIBIT 2

BRIGHT'S
Live Turkey Harvester

You, Mr. Turkeyman.... should be given full credit for the origination of the BRIGHT LIVE TURKEY HARVESTER. It was your continued constructive criticism, and suggestions, on how the present day loaders could be and should be built, to enable you to reduce your live loading cost in the field. We at BRIGHT COOP COMPANY want to thank you, and express our appreciation to all the industrymen who helped us design, build and field test our Turkey Harvester. With your help and our knowledge of building machinery for endurance, and workability, we have produced a loader we both can be proud of.

"BE BRIGHT   BUY RIGHT   BUY BRIGHT'S" has always been more than just a slogan.

BRIGHT COOP COMPANY
Complete Poultry Truck Outfitters
803 WEST SEALE ST. / DAY OR NIGHT PHONE (713) 564-8378 / NACOGDOCHES, TEXAS 75961

EXHIBIT 3

BRIGHT'S SPECIALLY DESIGNED LIVE POULTRY
TRAILERS hitch you to GREATER PROFITS

BRIGHT'S HI-TENSILE DROP-FRAME FLOAT

WHY?

Why is Bright Coop Company in the trailer business?. . . . Everyday at Bright Coop Company, we load our customers' trailers from all over the country. After studying these trailers we have designed a trailer with many "built in" features designed for the hauling of live poultry. We have improved the stability of our trailer. To solve the top heavy load problem in hauling live poultry we have placed the center I-Beams wider than usual, this gives more rigidity against twisting. This is also aided by the pipe braces from the center I-Beams to the cross members near the side rail.

See the other features that have been incorporated into these live haul trailers.

BRIGHT COOP COMPANY
COMPLETE POULTRY TRUCK OUTFITTERS
803 West Seale Street
Day or Night Phone 713/564-8378
NACOGDOCHES, TEXAS 75961

EXHIBIT 4

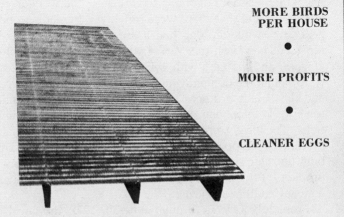

turing plant, and a building for assembling harvesters and trailers. The trailers were not manufactured by Bright; rather, they were built to specification by a trailer manufacturer and then outfitted by Bright in Nacogdoches.

MARKETING AND SALES

Bright's marketing efforts were concentrated in 11 poultry-producing states: Texas, South Carolina, Florida, Tennessee, Alabama, Mississippi, Georgia, Arkansas, Kentucky, North Carolina, and California. In addition, coops were exported to Canada and Mexico. The company estimated that it had a market share of about 40 percent in the wooden coop market segment as of 1974 and that there were roughly 1.5 million wooden coops in use. In general, a wooden coop had a life of about one year before it had to be replaced; however, this varied with how many times a coop was used, the climate, and the care with which it was handled.

Although the company had only a one-man sales force, both the salesman and the Bright brothers maintained extensive personal contacts with customers via telephone, periodic trips to customer facilities, and at conventions. The Bright brothers were both personally acquainted with nearly 90 percent of the poultry haulers and processors in the United States, having built up their associations over 24 years. The company had exhibits for its products at three different national conventions and advertised regularly in a national poultry magazine.

From July 1, 1974 through June 30, 1975 (the latest full fiscal year), the company's sales breakdown by product line was as follows:

Sales of coops	$1,400,000
Sales of crates, pallets, and hen floors	1,221,000
Turkey-related items	349,000
Trailer sales (6 units)	650,000
Total sales	$3,620,000

The company made sales forecasts for six months in advance for planning purposes.

COMPETITION

When the Brights first entered the coop business in 1952 there were 26 other wooden coop manufacturers. As of 1975, there were only five; of these, Bright was the largest and the company did not encounter intense competition from any of the other four firms. Bright's strongest competition came from the 11 plastic coop manufacturers. Plastic coops first appeared in 1966 but had not made major inroads until the 1972–74 period when significant market gains were made. The plastic coop producers touted their product as lasting for three years, although this had not been substantiated in actual use situations. The main benefit of plastic coops was a reduced airflow as compared to wooden coops.

The plastic coop had undergone many modifications in its short existence, owing to a series of different problems relating to strength, rigidity, and design. One problem in particular was that when plastic coops were stacked on top of each other, they had a tendency to shift and slide. In some instances, this shifting had caused trucks in transit to overturn. Inability of the plastic coop manufacturers to solve the various structural problems was creating some customer dissatisfaction and in 1975 Bright Coop regained some of its former business lost to plastic coop firms.

Bright had been contacted by plastic coop manufacturers to take on a plastic coop line. However, with all the problems attending plastic coops, Bright elected to wait and see if the problems with plastic coops could be ironed out. Actually, both Bright brothers felt that the plastic coop would "fade out" in the future.

FINANCIAL INFORMATION

The Brights organized their operations into three distinct companies: Bright Coop Co. stood as one entity; the trailer business was set up as Bright Sales Company; and a third company owned the land where all the plant facilities were located. Excluding the land and buildings, the total book value of the entire business was in the range of $150,000 to $200,000 (as of 1975).

The two brothers did not operate on the basis of a budget but they had plans to do a budget later in 1975. "We just spend what we need and then some," said one of the managers. To judge how well they were doing, the brothers compared their sales standing for the current year to date with that of comparable periods in years past.

To meet the rising volume of government regulations, the company had had to spend a combined total of about $300,000 over the past several years. Weekly payroll costs amounted to $10,000. Bright's bad debt ratio averaged about 0.5 percent of sales. A condensed income statement is presented below:

	Fiscal Year		
	1974	1973	1972
Sales	$2,635,927	$2,974,892	$3,034,049
Costs of goods sold	2,096,482	2,379,737	2,419,556
Gross profit	$ 539,445	$ 595,155	$ 614,493
Operating expenses	334,634	335,648	350,258
Net Income (excluding officers salaries, income taxes, and depreciation)	$ 204,811	$ 259,507	$ 264,235

An estimated balance sheet is presented in Exhibit 5.

EXHIBIT 5

COMBINED BRIGHT COOP AND BRIGHT SALES COMPANIES
Estimated Balance Sheet
(extrapolated from interviews with Charles and N. G. Bright)

Current assets:

Inventory (includes material work-in-process and finished goods)	$431,000	
Accounts receivable	217,000	
Cash	12,000	
Total current assets		$660,000
Fixed assets:		
Trucks	$272,000	
Plant and equipment	256,000	
Total fixed assets	$528,000	
Less accumulated depreciation	358,000	
Net fixed assets		$170,000
Total assets		$830,000
Current liabilities:	$ 81,000	
Long-term debt:	256,000	
Total liabilities		$337,000
Owners' equity		493,000
Total liabilities and owners' equity		$830,000

ORGANIZATION

Charles and N. G. assume most of the company's management responsibilities. They are assisted in day-to-day operations by Joe Biggerstaff, the
plant supervisor. Doug Swearingen, who is the Bright's brother-in-law, is in
charge of sales. An organization chart is shown in Exhibit 6. The Bright
brothers do not view the organization of the company as being tightly structured; those with line authority are left relatively free to manage in their own
ways and to carry out their own ideas.

EMPLOYEE RELATIONS

Bright Coop was proud of the relationship it had with employees. Many of
the employees had been with the company since its inception and Charles
Bright took special care to get to know each employee personally. In 1975,
Bright had 125 employees; eight months previous the work force totaled 160
persons, but the sharp downturn in sales in late 1974 forced layoffs of 35
persons. Both Charles and N. G. felt badly about having to lay off workers
because they felt a strong sense of obligation and responsibility to the community for providing job opportunities.

It was company policy to employ handicapped persons whenever a suitable job was available. Bright Coop had three blind workers on its payroll in

EXHIBIT 6
Bright Coop Company Organization

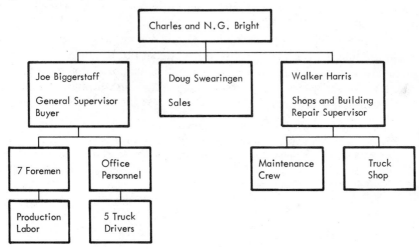

1975. At the same time, the company endeavored not to force a worker to retire. Rather a job was found or created for older employees who wanted or needed to continue work. Two of Bright's employees were 86 and 90 years old, respectively.

There was no union representation at Bright Coop Company. There had been previous attempts to unionize Bright's employees but each attempt had failed.

Workers were paid by the hour or by piece rate. Hourly wages ranged from $2.30 to $3. Personnel charts were kept on each employee, including information on number of days absent and production performance. A "merit system" keyed to absences and production was used as the basis for calling back employees who had been laid off.

FUTURE PLANS AND OUTLOOK

Although coop sales had been slack for the last six months, sales of pallets had increased to the point where plans were being developed to move the pallet plant to a new location having more operating space. The Bright brothers were also looking into several other expansion possibilities. There were plans to improve the broiler and turkey coops. Consideration was being given to adding a mulcher to the company's woodcutting process if and when coop sales increased to prior levels; a mulcher would enable the company to use 100 percent of its wood purchases, since scrap pieces could then be mulched and sold to poultry farmers as litter or desicants. Some thought had been given to producing wooden picnic tables, even though other picnic table producers had just recently managed to earn a profit. The Bright brothers were undecided about entering the plastic coop market because of the cost of tooling up for plastic coop production and because of the problems haulers were encountering with plastic coops.

But despite Bright Coop's being a leader in the poultry outfitting industry and the dominant producer of wooden coops, the Bright brothers were unsure how to go about improving and strengthening the company's position in the months and years ahead. Some of the major uncertainties bothering the two brothers were summed up by Charles Bright:

> I don't know what direction the company should take. I don't feel that plastics give the service offered by wood and the cost to produce is much higher. On the other hand, environmental requirements may make the wood coops obsolete— they may be difficult to clean. Yet, I am not sure I want to invest the capital required to tool up for a plastic product.

7. Itty Bitty Machine Company*

THE IDEA

It all started one Friday night in February 1976 when Jim Andrews and his neighbor friend, Bob Dulek, went out to dinner. It was then that Bob told Jim about a new field that was suddenly exploding. Bob wanted to start a new business in this brand new industry of personal computing.

A year before, the first practical home computer system had been announced in *Popular Electronics,* an electronics hobbyist magazine. The company, MITS Inc., was suddenly deluged with orders for its Altair 8800—a computer kit costing just under $500. Within almost a matter of weeks, a number of other new companies jumped on board announcing products that could be used with the Altair. By fall there were several competing systems; a nationally distributed magazine, *Byte;* and one or two retail computer stores.

The sudden explosion of the market for microcomputer kits and systems was impressive. For the same kind of money people spent on photography or hi-fi or other sports and hobbies, they could have their own computer for entertainment, education, or their profession. All kinds of people seemed to be getting involved for all kinds of reasons.

During their long evening at dinner, Bob, a systems analyst at a bank, explained all this and more to Jim. Bob proposed opening a retail computer store in the Chicago area.

At the time, Jim, who already had his MBA and lived alone with his father, was working on a law degree and feeling disenchanted with his job in one of the nation's largest financial companies. He began to get excited about the prospects of computer systems that were practical for the individual at home or on the job.

Within a few weeks, they had discovered a few more kindred souls. First there was Ted Nelson. Ted was a gifted writer who had written several articles and a book on the future of home computing. The book was an imaginative and rather unusual production in typography and editorial style. It did an unusually good job of explaining many computer concepts in every-

* Prepared by Prof. Charles F. Douds of DePaul University. The names in the case are disguised.

day language. It communicated a real sense of enthusiasm about what you could do with your own computer. This had been a favorite theme of Ted's for several years. When he lectured to an audience, as he frequently did, many would come away deeply intrigued with his ideas. Now it seemed that he was a prophet—what he had been predicting had come to pass. The technology for the hardware was now in place and the electronic boards and boxes were being produced.

Ted's book, *Computer Lib/Dream Machines*, made clear to the reader what computer specialists already knew. A computer is no smarter than the programs within it. The programs—the software—had yet to be written that would make his visions come true.

Through Ted another member came to the group. Gerald Courrington was a professor in a university computer science department. He was very knowledgeable in electronic engineering as well as programming. He had built computer circuits from the ground up and had practical experience as a consultant to companies designing and using such things. Ever since the invention of the transistor in 1955, the semiconductor industry had been characterized by extremely rapid technological advances. It was difficult for anyone to keep up with it, but Gerald had done so in computer applications.

It seemed like an ideal group to start the first microcomputer store in the Chicago area. Jim with a MBA had an overall knowledge of business and law; Bob worked with computer information systems in a bank; Gerald was a technological expert; and Ted not only had a wide-ranging overview of the market, but had written a successful book that communicated effectively to laymen.

Their discussions became serious. A computer store had opened near a university less than 200 miles away in a neighboring state and held the distinction of being the fourth computer store in the nation. Jim and Bob flew to California to visit the three computer stores in San Francisco and three in the Los Angeles area. They spent four hours talking with Dick Heiser, the founder of the very first retail computer store. From there, they flew to Albuquerque to the Altair Computer Convention at the end of March. Of course, the only products on display were Altairs, but there were sessions for prospective store owners as well as the tutorial and technical sessions for the 1,000 hobbyists attending.

A store in Knoxville, Tennessee had been running big ads in *Byte* indicating a wide range of services, so Jim went on to see it. After considerable difficulty locating the front door, he found two young men crowded into two rooms hardly bigger than 12' × 12' each with equipment, boards, and boxes piled every which way. In this business with companies springing up overnight when a couple of electronic engineers decided to make the plunge, it was not surprising to find a production operation looking like this; but it was surprising for a retail store. Jim realized there was nothing you could take for granted in this fledgling industry.

SETTING UP THE CORPORATION

After the trips, the group really got serious. The major problem was capital. Money would be needed for rent, utilities, and salaries, as well as inventory. The store would need demonstration systems, computers in stock, circuit board kits, parts, books, and magazines. Several expensive instruments would be needed for servicing equipment. It would be many months before the company could expect to break even.

To finance the venture, the group decided to sell stock and convertible debentures, with each of the principals subscribing to $15,000.

They incorporated as the Itty Bitty Machine Company and found a store in a good location in Evanston—one of the bedroom communities for executives and middle managers from the many corporations in Chicago. Twenty-nine investors subscribed, typically for $1,000. For each $5 of stock they received $95 in 6 percent convertible debentures. Most investors had a data processing background. A few were lawyers or relatives. Matthew Davis, the owner of a computer store in the next state, also became a stockholder. Davis's experience consisted of having been in the computer store business for five months. Itty Bitty's initial capitalization was $126,500.

Itty Bitty's officers consisted of the major stockholders and counsel:

> Bob Dulek—president.
>
> Ted Nelson—vice president.
>
> Jim Andrews—treasurer-secretary
>
> Walt Benson—attorney.

All four were also on the board of directors, along with Dr. Gerald Courrington, Matthew Davis, and a retired insurance agency owner.

The four officers decided to work together as a group. Mutually they agreed each one would spend one day a week working in the store. While some of them were tied up with their regular jobs during normal working hours, the store would be open four evenings a week and Saturdays.

They also decided that the board would actively manage the corporation. There was a great deal of work to be done. Not only was there the store, but it was clear to them that "applications software" was needed. Ted had discussed that at length in his book and knew just the computer language that would be ideal for this purpose. Gerald knew about a new microprocessor coming on the market that had very powerful capabilities. Equipment would be needed to exploit it and, of course, "operating systems" were needed for the computers. At that time, there was much more available in the way of hardware than software. Systems sales would soon drop off if the programs needed to make microcomputers do useful or entertaining things were not available. It was clear that the board had a great deal to do.

They met twice a month in long sessions that lasted from 6 P.M. until well after midnight. None of them was bashful; they all enjoyed a good argument.

Each had his own point of view and was willing to express it. With each person having strong views and interests of his own, they felt that it would be best to rotate the meeting chairmanship. The officers along with Gerald Courrington became very good friends. Even when they were not working, they tended to socialize together. Mr. Davis was not considered to be a part of the "inside" group.

A SECOND PROJECT—THE NEW COMPUTER LANGUAGE

Almost from the start, Ted was talking about the computer language, TRAC, he had discussed in his book. A computer language such as BASIC, COBOL, or FORTRAN is usually used to write the programs people or businesses actually use (applications software). The board had discussed how programs for entertainment or practical use would be needed to help sustain future computer sales. Ted was enthusiastic, as always, about the power and versatility of TRAC for such applications.

The language could be licensed from its creator for $200 plus royalty. However, it would have to be rewritten and adapted to the small computer systems. They would need a programmer and a computer for him to work with. This could not be a microcomputer system because for part of the work he needed capabilities only a larger computer could provide.

Ted had lots of ideas about how to do this. He wanted to get a LSI-11 minicomputer, a Diablo printer, and a video terminal—first class. Gerald immediately argued that this would be too expensive. While the LSI-11 itself started at $1,500, by the time you got everything else needed, the cost would be nearly $10,000. Of course, they realized that Gerald also wanted money to be available for the computer equipment projects he was talking about.

Among the many possibilities discussed, the Board eventually decided to rent time on a large computer through a time-sharing service. As the various parts of the program were developed, they would be tested out on one of the store's systems. Ted said TRAC would be up and running by the end of August at a cost of $1,500. Dan Rountree, the programmer he had located, impressed them as being a very sharp fellow and a nice person.

STARTING THE STORE

Stock was needed for the store. MITS, Inc., makers of the Altair, was only accepting exclusive MITS dealerships. They decided not to get locked into one company so they ordered 100 computer kits from IMSAI, MITS' major competitor. There were two or three other companies advertising complete computers, but it was obvious that it would be some time before the products would be shipped—and then how good would they be? Computers, even microcomputers, were not simple devices. The delivery schedule from IMSAI was 25 in July, 25 in August, and 50 in September. Ted was sure that they would all be sold by the end of September. Another reason for ordering 100 computers now was that a manufacturers' price increase of $100 was to be announced soon.

Price to the dealer was a particularly troublesome issue. The industry had started on a direct mail order basis. The pricing structure did not include provision for dealer markups. As the business grew, it was possible for the well-established manufacturers (those that had been in business for six months or longer) to buy their parts in quantity, and so to reduce their costs. However, few of these new companies knew much about manufacturing methods, and they did not have the capital to invest in efficient production techniques. It was difficult for them to adjust their retail prices upward to normal retail markups. They simply had little room in which to establish adequate dealer discounts.

The store needed many other items as well. Once a person bought a microcomputer he could tailor it to his particular needs by buying circuit boards to plug into it. Inventory was difficult to obtain because the companies manufacturing the circuit boards were small, rapidly growing, cash-tight companies. Financing terms were invariably COD plus freight charges.

They ordered a variety of kits to test the water and see which ones would sell. This aspect of the business was pretty much an unknown to the old computer hands on the Board. As software types they had no background of experience with hardware. Gerald was the only one with appropriate experience, but he could not make judgments from advertisements alone. He needed a microcomputer and the equipment itself in order to test it adequately. But that would only provide part of the answer. Of course, it would be desirable—necessary, as he argued in the Board meetings—to test as many of the products as quickly as they became available.

As store manager, Jim did the actual ordering. The variety of equipment and advertising claims was a bit bewildering. However, Mr. Davis was getting practical experience with the equipment and the business practices of the manufacturers, so Jim was able to get a lot of good advice from him.

The Itty Bitty Machine Company opened on June 14 with little fanfare. But the word spread, helped along by an announcement at the local 200-member computer club. A steady stream of people showed up. Many came back when new items arrived at the store—word seemed to spread like wildfire even to Milwaukee and beyond. Itty Bitty was the tenth computer store in the nation to open its doors.

Gerald built one of the ISMAI computers for the store, but it was several weeks after the store opened before it was available for demonstration. Jim found that there were more and more questions he could not answer adequately.

Gerald often called to find out if a new item had arrived. He would often borrow it for evaluation. His comments were helpful to Jim, but he could never be sure when the item would come back and it was rarely that the manuals with their technical details ever returned. Gerald had several projects going on in his shop at home. These were sometimes discussed at the board meetings, but the Board members had difficulty following his technical discussion.

In their travels to the West Coast computer stores, they had noted that many of the clerks were quite young. Bright high-school youths quickly learned the intricacies of computers and programming. They would work for low wages just to have the chance to be around the equipment. Ted felt and kept saying that the personal computers would sell themselves and he believed in youth, so they hired several sharp high-school students as part-time salesmen.

Jim, who had quit his job, wanted to learn more about the equipment and store operations. Mr. Davis was quite willing to have him spend time at his store so Jim began driving the 200 miles to spend days at a time there. To cover for him, the board hired an assistant manager—a high-school teacher familiar with computer programming. From June to October, Jim spent about one third of his time at Mr. Davis' store learning a great deal about the operations there.

Sales were slow during June and July, but by August they began to pick up a bit. A lot of people had been coming in to browse, but finally a few came back to buy. By the end of August they had sold 8 of the 50 IMSAI computers they had received. Jim was not drawing any salary—it was being deferred. Not only were there the clerks and the CODs, but Dan and the time-sharing service had to be paid for the work on TRAC, the new computer language.

TRAC IN THE STORE

Dan was frequently in the store for long hours working on the TRAC project when he was not at his regular job. The Board had decided that the store should have three working demonstration systems of different types, but only one of these was suitable for Dan's work. Without it there was little else he could do; his time would be wasted. During the afternoons the system would sometimes be changed around as boards were removed or inserted to try something new or to test an item repaired for a customer. Of course, sometimes such activity would take its toll on the system itself. Occasionally, the system would not work properly. Naturally, Dan, devoted to his programming work, found it most irritating when this happened. The TRAC project was supposed to be finished by the end of August and it was becoming more and more obvious that it would not be. So when the system quit working, it was upsetting to him and he wanted it fixed right away no matter what others were doing. His irritation did not make the best impression on customers.

But even when the system was working well—which actually was a high percentage of the time he was there—Dan's presence at the equipment created a difficulty for the store. There rarely were two other working systems. There was little space in the back of the store to do repair work. It usually wound up being done in the front and one system invariably would get involved in it.

For one reason or another, the third system never seemed to actually exist. One time when it did it was sold to an electronics laboratory of a major firm that wanted an assembled system. This nicely increased the store's margin on the sale. They had bought it at the dealer's discount as a kit and it had been assembled by a person whose salary they had to pay anyway. (Even if they hired a person to assemble the kit, it still would cost them less and they would get it sooner than buying it assembled from the factory.)

The net result was that there was usually only one working system to be used in demonstrations to customers. It was right by the front window where it could be seen by passers-by; but during the times when there were the most customers in the store, Dan was usually at it. Absorbed in his work, he was oblivious to the hubbub of the clientele and to the salesmen—the "kids," as he called them. It was only with evident reluctance that he would relinquish the console when Jim wanted to demonstrate the system to a good prospect.

TED'S CATALOG AND A CONVENTION

Ted's imagination was very fertile and always at work. Even before they incorporated he was talking about franchising the operation. Never one to be concerned about details, he painted colorful and profit-filled word pictures of the variety of ways in which they could expand nationwide. Each of them on the board had their own visions, and while not all of them were as facile with words as Ted, they were all eager to talk about their ideas and to seek ways to move closer to carrying them out. In the board meetings the eight of them would attempt to deal with the nuts and bolts of running a business, and each had his own ideas on that, too, but it did make it rather difficult to arrive at specific decisions.

Jim, spending a great deal of time at Mr. Davis' store, saw the need for a catalog. Ted got quite excited when he saw Jim's draft. Yes, a catalog was a great idea—and he knew how to do it. He was the one who had the pulse of the marketplace. The draft, full of technical descriptions, was nearly complete. Jim decided to turn it over to Ted for his creative touch.

The catalog Ted turned out created a minor sensation. It was written up in a magazine distributed nationwide to computer professionals. Because of it, first one of the city newspapers and then another did major stories on the store. The newspaper stories led to TV coverage on the local news.

The catalog was in narrative form chatting about personal computing, the manufacturers and products, and the kind of people you would find in a computer store. It was warm, human, and responsive to many of the better values of the youth movement that characterized the 1968–72 period. A number of humorous and wordless cartoons graced its pages. The last page is shown in Exhibit 1.

EXHIBIT 1

AND NOW SOME PREVIEWS...

Frankly, folks, the engineering hasn't been done yet, but we are holding deposits pending availability of ...

HEAVEN - 11™?

That, friends, is what we are calling our package of the LSI-11* with power supply and ALTAIR BUS.

That is why we are calling it the Heaven-11: It's the world's finest computer, effectively a PDP-11*, which few of us can afford; set up for the myriad weird and super accessories of the Altair world.

Our tentative price (kit, incl. LSI-11): FIFTEEN HUNDRED BUCKS.

Now some of you may want a computer that looks really zippy. We are considering styled packages for the Heaven-11 that include—

A JUKE BOX!
AN ART DECO SKYSCRAPER!
SWEPT-LINE RACER STYLING!

and for you who like vans, we hope to produce the

HEAV - ON - WHEELS™

which offers optional power brakes and steering, positraction, shag rug interior, terminal, and van. May be financed through local automotive dealer.

*A registered trademark of Digital Equipment Corporation.

"From the Dream to the Nitty Gritty—
TAKE THE TRIP
at Itty Bitty"

ABOUT MAIL ORDER:
You will not find an order blank. We're not dumb and neither are you, if you've gotten this far. Write a note. Or even CALL COLLECT to order: 312/328-6800. (We reserve the right to discontinue this policy.)

Prices, specifications and availability subject to change without notice. Customers will be notified when merchandise cannot be shipped immediately.

Shipping weight and charges are such a nuisance that we presently send freight-collect.

Illinois residents please add 5% sales tax.

Is it a book?
Or is it a way of life?

The answer is — YES!

THIS IS A TIME WHOSE BOOK HAS COME.

IT'S **COMPUTER LIB**
by Ted Nelson
$7 postpaid.

(for quantity discounts contact Hugo's Book Service, Box 2622, Chicago IL 60690.)

"The best damned book on computer science I've ever seen."
— Carl M. Ellison, Professor of Computer Science, University of Utah

---

ASK ABOUT
OUR FRANCHISE

We think Ittybitty is going to go over big.

Can you get in on it?

Yes. If you qualify.

If you qualify, you can open a Second-Generation Computer Store in your city.

(In fact, guess who can come to your opening IN PERSON! Why, Itty and Bitty™ the Computer Clowns, Bill Juggler™ and Captain Computer™ himself!) *

The cost of opening an Ittybitty franchise depends on the location but is comparable to a small fast-food outlet store.

Our package of franchise information is $3 by mail. We regret charging for what is scarcely more than a pamphlet, but we do not want to have to send it to the idly curious.

* Clowns and other personnel subject to availability.

"From the Dream to the Nitty Gritty—
CARRY IT THROUGH
at Itty Bitty"

Thank you for looking at this catalog. Now we'd like to hear from you. We've told you our interests and ideas —how about yours?

Whether you are a hobbyist, a customer, or a passerby; whether you join our clubs and services or just look in now and then; or whether you actually join the Ittybitty family with an outlet of your own— we appreciate your interest, and we care about your problems.

The brief item on the last page headed "Ask about Our Franchise" says that the cost would be comparable to a small fast-food store. An information package was available for $3. It nicely and openly concluded: "We regret charging for what is scarcely more than a pamphlet, but we do not want to have to send it to the idly curious."

Even the physical form of the catalog was novel. It was printed on 22" × 34" glossy stock folded to 8½" × 11". To read it you unfolded it lengthwise in a convenient manner. There were eight pages of text which left the reverse side free for a full-size poster cartoon Ted had drawn.

The catalogs arrived from Ted printed at a cost of about $6,000 for 10,000 of them. The items described in Jim's original version were mentioned in one-sentence descriptions that included the price, but absolutely no technical information.

The Personal Computing Convention had been announced for the end of August in Atlantic City. It seemed that all the manufacturers would attend and that it would draw a good crowd. Ted was to be one of the featured speakers. Sales on the exhibition hall floor would be allowed, so in June the Board had decided that the store should purchase a booth and take merchandise to sell.

The convention was a rousing success with over 10,000 people attending. The catalogs seemed to be a big hit. Needless to say, working the store's booth was exhausting with such a crowd, but $6,000 of the merchandise brought in a rented truck was sold. Of the eight IMSAIs sold by the end of August, three were sold here. They felt the trip had been worthwhile.

SEPTEMBER

Bob, president of the corporation, spent a week of his vacation in the store. Like other board members he really had not lived up to the vow of working there one day a week. It was an illuminating experience. He really began to appreciate how much he did not know about the products and prices. He found that the youthful sales staff really did a pretty good job, but with high school getting started they were not available all the time to help him out.

The week of his family's out-of-town vacation gave him a chance to really think things over. He was particularly concerned about the diverse ways things seemed to be going. The TRAC project was still going full blast. It always seemed as if he were getting different information about it. Ted never seemed to say the same thing about where it was going or how it was coming along. Gerald seemed to be generating useful information with his projects, but how did they all tie together? Here, too, he felt he was getting different stories. But maybe that was not it. Maybe the information was not really all that different. Perhaps he just did not understand the technical laguage and its implications well enough.

After he came back from vacation, he began sharing these thoughts with

Jim. Jim was quite concerned too. The financial situation was not good even though sales were picking up. As Jim put it, these projects of Ted and Gerald "were beginning to take on a life of their own." Bob felt that he was making too many poor decisions because he was getting too many different stories. As he finally concluded, perhaps it was more that he did not know how to adequately interpret and weigh what he was being told.

OCTOBER

At the first board meeting in October Bob announced that he was resigning as president. This took the board by surprise. After a long discussion, they elected Jim to the post.

Jim said it was only because he could quote all the prices and margins from memory (see Exhibit 2). Actually, he had been doing a lot on the

EXHIBIT 2
Retail Prices of Representative Microcomputer Boards (May 1976)

Dutronics 8K memory	$285 kit	
IMSAI 4K memory	$165 kit	($299 assembled)
Processor Technology 3P+S I/O	$135 kit	
Processor Technology video display	$179 kit	
Polymorphic video display	$185 kit	($260 assembled)

paperwork and had been becoming more and more specific with the figures in the September meetings. He was still the only one working fulltime for the corporation; the rest had their regular jobs.

They never really had gotten a decent bookkeeping system set up because of all the work in getting the store started, the convention, and Ted's promises about what TRAC would be able to do.

The bills for the convention totalled $6,000, the same amount they had grossed there. The margin on the items averaged 19 percent. They had lost $4,860 on the trip, not counting the catalogs given away.

The catalog had cost $6,000. They had yet to receive one mail or phone order from it even though about 5,000 were in circulation. It had taken $126 in postage alone to answer all the franchise inquiries—just to say that the information package was not yet available. With no package in sight, despite Ted's enthusiasms, there would have to be another round of letters returning the $3 payments.

But the biggest things were Ted's TRAC project and Gerald's activities. Not only were these taking on a life of their own, as he had remarked to Bob, but they were expensive. As best he could figure out, Gerald had about $8,000 of the store's equipment at home—7 percent of their initial capitalization. The consulting fee for Dan and the time-sharing service were running

EXHIBIT 3

ITTY BITTY MACHINE COMPANY
Income Statements

	2 Months (7/1/76-8/31/76)	As a Percent of Net Revenue	1 Month (9/1/76-9/30/76)	As a Percent of Net Revenue	1 Month (10/1/76-10/31/76)	As a Percent of Net Revenue
Revenue	$11,514.88	101.4%	$19,042.55	100.3%	$21,509.95	100.2%
Less returns	(18.90)	0.2	(59.70)	0.3	(4.07)	
Less discounts	(138.28)	1.2	-0-		(44.65)	
Net Revenue	$11,357.70	100%	$18,982.85	100%	$21,461.20	100%
Cost of goods sold:						
Beginning inventory	$ -0-		$36,213.77		$36,213.77	
Purchases	44,060.12		15,149.25		24,583.28	
Ending inventory	(36,213.77)		(36,213.77)		(44,057.31)	
	$ 7,846.35	30.9%	$15,149.25	79.8%	$16,739.74	78%
Gross profit on sales	$ 3,511.35	69.1%	$ 3,833.60	20.2%	$ 4,721.46	22%
Operating expense:						
Selling expense	$ 4,263.19	37.5%	$ 4,338.59	22.9%	$ 7,022.98	32.7%
General and administrative expense	4,601.27	40.5	4,659.11	24.5	5,742.11	26.8
	$ 8,864.46	78.0%	$ 8,997.70	47.4%	$12,765.09	59.5%
Net income	$(5,353.11)	(47.1)%	$(5,164.10)	(27.2)%	$(8,043.63)	(37.5)%

EXHIBIT 4

ITTY BITTY MACHINE COMPANY
Balance Sheet
October 31, 1976

Assets

Current assets:

Cash		$ 17,572.72	
Accounts receivable inventory:		7,594.22	
Computers	$26,434.20		
Boards	10,318.10		
Books	3,111.10		
Software	789.00		
Other	3,404.91		
		44,057.31	
Total current assets			$ 69,224.25
Fixed assets:			
Organizational costs		$ 2,225.00	
Fixtures		5,007.65	
Test and repair equipment		1,579.75	
Demonstration equipment		18,437.21	
Development		17,137.75	
Total fixed assets			44,387.36
Other assets			6,600.77
Total assets			$120,212.38

Liabilities and Stockholders' Equity

Current liabilities:		
Accounts payable	$ 7,320.79	
Notes payable	2,800.00	
Taxes payable	1,290.00	
Unearned income	862.43	$ 12,273.22
Long-term liabilities	—	—
Total liabilities		$ 12,273.22
Common stock	$ 6,325.00	
Convertible debentures 6 percent	120,175.00	
Retained earnings	(18,560.84)	
		107,939.16
Total liabilities and stockholders' equity		$120,212.38

about $5,000 per month, to say nothing of the aggravation and impact on sales they were causing in the store. So far the project had cost $15,000.

He got these figures with the supporting data into writing and had them ready for the second October board meeting.

Sales were going up encouragingly but their capital was being eaten up and their cash position was getting to be more and more of a problem (see Exhibits 3 and 4). He needed cash to pay for the goods coming in. It was becoming clear that their industrial customers would take 30 to 60 days to pay. At least sales to individuals were paid immediately.

He had been checking with the banks about loans. Sales growth was encouraging—but the bankers would not be convinced. They could not see how selling computers to individuals would be viable in the long run. None of the principals had any prior experience running a small business nor in retail sales. No loan could be arranged.

Perhaps a merger? But with whom? It would take months to work out a deal even if an interested party could be found. They had to do something about the situation!

Shortly before the board meeting he was at his desk (*his* desk—he shared it with everyone!) when he heard Dan once again impatiently demanding that the system be fixed while a customer was in the store. As soon as the customer left he walked out firmly and said, "Dan, pack up all your things, get out, and stay out of the store. You and Ted figure out where you'll work!"

He knew the next board meeting would be . . . perhaps "stimulating" was the word for it. He had better be really primed for it.

8. Builders Homes, Inc. *

On May 1, 1970, Builders Homes, Inc. (BHI) of Dothan, Alabama, officially became a wholly owned subsidiary of U.S. Land and Shelter Company, a large national firm (NYSE) specializing in all aspects of the real estate and shelter fields. Jay Bragg, BHI's president and founder, was excited about the prospects that the merger offered. As he saw it, the essential elements of the merger deal were:

A sales price of $4.8 million, payable in the form of 5 percent in cash and 95 percent in U.S. Land and Shelter stock. The selling price had been at the center of negotiation—U.S. Land and Shelter wanted to price the acquisition at ten times fiscal 1970 pretax earnings plus an "earnout" of five times incremental earnings each year for five years, after allowing for a minimum of 15 percent compound annual rate of growth in pretax earnings of BHI. The final terms ended up at 12 times initial earnings plus an earnout multiple of 3.

U.S. Land and Shelter would financially support Mr. Bragg's plan of constructing and operating a large modular home manufacturing plant. Support was agreed upon in two major areas:

1. The parent firm would guarantee a lease between BHI and the city of Dothan, Alabama. On the basis of the guarantee of a financially strong NYSE firm, the city was agreeable to selling up to $2.5 million in industrial revenue bonds which would then be used to acquire land and build a modular factory to BHI's specifications.
2. The parent company would provide $1 million in cash for working capital purposes during the start-up phase of the modular housing facility.

Already plans were rapidly moving ahead on the construction and start-up of the modular housing factory—located on an 80-acre site south of Dothan. The expected date for the first house to come off the assembly line was May 1971—just 11 months away.

---

* Prepared by Carle M. Hunt, Oral Roberts University, and Richard C. Johanson, University of Arkansas.

COMPANY HISTORY AND BACKGROUND

BHI was Alabama's largest volume builder of low to moderate income single family dwellings. Jay Bragg engineered BHI into this position in only seven years. He began in 1963, with his wife and a construction superintendent as the only employees; most of the actual construction work was subcontracted out. Bragg found, however, that the heavy reliance on subcontractors presented problems; the work was sometimes sloppily done and there were repeated "no-shows" on days work was supposed to be done. To circumvent these problems and delays, Bragg gradually increased the size of his own construction crews. As of 1970, BHI had become a sizable "scattered-lot" homebuilding company with over 300 people on its payroll.[1] BHI did 95 percent of all of its construction work with its own crews (including excavating, concrete and foundation work, plumbing, wiring, and both framing and finish carpentry). The company operated in a market area that included a 50-mile radius from corporate headquarters in Dothan, Alabama, and a branch marketing location in Albany, Georgia.

Two points in the short history of the firm are notable. The first was in 1965 when many things "came together" (see financial statements in Exhibits 1 and 2) and the number of homes sold jumped to 230 units (Exhibit 2). This was the year in which the low income housing programs of the Federal Housing Administration (FHA), the Veterans Administration (VA), and the Farmers Home Administration (FmHA) really began to stimulate rapid growth in low income housing construction. Jay anticipated the opportunity and built an 8,000-square-foot housing component shop where wall sections, roof trusses, and cabinets were built using mass production techniques. Availability of financing for customers plus the production capability of the component shop resulted in BHI averaging nearly one house per day in fiscal 1966 (based on 250 working days per year). Second, in fiscal 1969 when the Albany, Georgia marketing branch became fully operational, the number of units built, sold, and closed more than doubled.

Prior to the formation of the home-building company in 1963, Jay Bragg had pursued employment in the automobile business and in the vacation/ leisure home industry. For several years he was quite successful first as a salesman and then as a sales manager. In each of these jobs Jay learned about meeting needs of people who were his customers or his employees. While in the leisure home business, his responsibilities required travel throughout the southeastern United States developing dealers to sell prefabricated cottages and cabins. It was his contacts and knowledge gained from these prior experiences that allowed Jay to see a hole in the market in the geographical area encompassing southeast Alabama, southwest Georgia, and northwest Florida. He chose Dothan, Alabama, as his headquarters; it was a

---

[1] A scattered-lot homebuilder builds primarily or solely on single lots in small towns and in the rural countryside, as opposed to mass production in subdivisions.

EXHIBIT 1

BUILDERS HOMES, INC.
Statements of Financial Position,
Fiscal Years Ending April 30, 1965 and 1970

	1970	1965
Assets		
Current assets:		
Cash	$ 102,255	$ 53,625
Receivables, accounts	38,118	16,622
Notes receivable	20,921	25,596
Due from employers	122,660	19,752
Inventories:		
Raw materials	1,913,620	377,385
Work-in-process	1,659,186	344,389
Finished goods	133,400	34,671
Prepaid insurance	20,947	13,524
Other prepaid items	11,250	10,530
Deferred costs	241,713	–
Total current assets	$4,264,070	$ 896,094
Fixed assets:		
Land	$ 50,000	$ 15,000
Building and fixtures	1,298,169	326,310
Machinery and equipment	349,035	75,915
Furniture and fixtures	58,254	11,616
Model homes and exhibits	118,307	35,490
Automobiles and trucks	349,411	13,545
Less allowance for depreciation	430,440	100,446
Total assets	$6,917,686	$1,474,416
Liabilities and Net Worth		
Current liabilities:		
Notes payable		
Bank	$2,500,000	$ 300,000
Other	15,100	—
Accounts payable		
Trade	1,689,943	423,145
Other	54,630	9,264
Accrued expenses		
Salaries and wages	94,691	11,436
Taxes	44,458	6,972
Other		
Customers' Deposits	94,730	37,353
Total current liabilities	$4,493,552	$ 788,170
Long-term liabilities and net worth:		
Long-term notes payable		
J. Bragg	700,000	150,000
Others	150,000	180,000
Common stock of $1 par value per share, authorized 400,000, outstanding 250,000 shares	250,000	250,000
Additional paid-in capital	450,000	—
Retained earnings (deficit)	874,134	106,246
Total liabilities and net worth	$6,917,686	$1,474,416

EXHIBIT 2
Selected Financial and Operating Statistics, 1966–1970 (fiscal years ending April 30)

	1970	1969	1968	1967	1966
Net sales	$12,811,700	$8,910,000	$3,744,800	$2,895,900	$3,335,000
Cost of sales	10,365,300	7,119,100	2,827,300	2,148,800	2,524,600
Gross profit	2,449,400	1,790,900	917,500	747,100	810,400
Marketing and selling expenses	929,400	659,300	228,400	194,000	233,400
Depreciation and interest	409,900	499,000	123,600	86,900	226,800
General administration	710,000	680,000	445,500	187,300	176,500
Total overhead	2,049,300	1,838,300	797,500	468,200	636,700
Operating profit	400,100	47,400	120,000	278,900	173,700
Other income	0	115,200	8,600	0	0
Net income before tax	400,100	162,600	128,600	278,900	173,700
Income tax	192,600	68,700	54,000	131,100	77,500
Net income	$ 207,500	$ 93,900	$ 74,600	$ 147,800	$ 96,200
Number of units sold and closed	756	550	248	197	230
Average sales price (not including land which averages $2,500) ..	$ 16,950	$ 16,200	$ 15,100	$ 14,700	$ 14,500

growing, progressive community of 40,000 population serving as the trade center for another 250,000 people located within a 75-mile radius.

ORGANIZATION

During May 1970, Jay Bragg had been quite busy in his new role as president of the subsidiary. His first priority, after finalizing the merger deal, had been to restructure his organization and to bring in additional staff to strengthen the management of the newly created division. Exhibit 3 shows BHI's organization chart at the time of the merger.

In early May, he hired Conley Harris as vice president of corporate development. Harris had been with a consulting firm that had been retained to help negotiate the merger. Jay liked the way Harris thought and handled things, and offered him a sufficient challenge and pay package to get him to move to the south. In addition, Bragg had hired two other people during May:

Marion Smith—modular plant manager (production only). Houses were to be "transferred and sold" to the marketing branches (currently, Dothan and Albany, Georgia, located in southwest Georgia), which in turn would market to the final consumer.

Ben Brown—financial vice president. His major responsibilities were to find mortgage money for all the potential BHI customers, and manage Homeowners Insurance Co., a small insurance agency owned by BHI. He had no responsibility related to the modular housing facility.

EXHIBIT 3
Organization Chart as of May 1, 1970

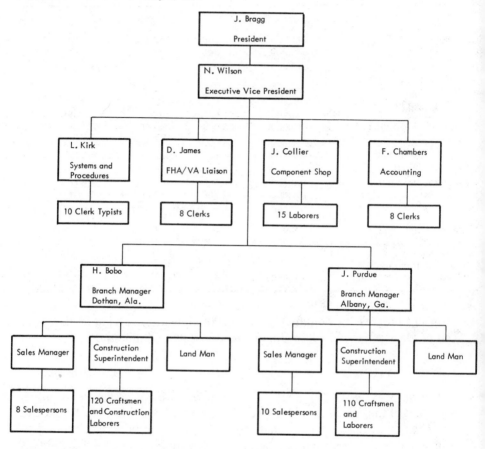

Most recently, Braggs had hired Victor Gladden as marketing vice president, effective June 1, 1970. Since the beginning of the month was always set aside as divisionwide management meeting day, Gladden was able to meet and talk to the two branch managers, Hal Bobo of Dothan and Jim Purdue of Albany, Georgia. It was explained by Bragg that the vice president of marketing was to be a division staff position supporting the branch managers and their sales managers.

COMPANY PHILOSOPHY AND OPERATIONS

Since there were several new people at the June management meeting, Jay Bragg took a few minutes to share (as he had many times in the past) company philosophy, mission, and the general way BHI was operated. He began:

From the very beginning, this company has used the KISS principle (*Keep It Simple, Sir*). All we do around here is five simple steps:

1. *Find customers.* There are over 350,000 people living within a 15-mile radius of Dothan, Alabama. A large percentage of these people are low- to moderate-income families who live in the rural areas.

2. *Find money.* Most of our homes are 1,000 to 1,200 square feet in size and are priced at $13,500 to $14,500, plus land at about $2,500. This price range appeals to low to moderate income families. However, most cannot qualify for mortgage loans under conventional loan programs at banks or savings and loan associations. So, we find lenders, usually mortgage bankers who lend mortgage money under one of the U.S. government underwritten and/or subsidized programs—FHA 235, VA, or Farmers Home Administration. Many requirements must be met and much red tape is involved, but we have become experts at government paperwork. We go to Birmingham so often to cut through red tape that we have worn out two company cars in the last five years.

3. *Find land.* We are a scattered-lot builder, which means we have no subdivisions and no land development. We have a land man in each branch, whose only job is to find single lots for our customers who do not own land. He also helps customers who have land to bring their abstracts up to date using our attorney.

4. *Build houses.* Rarely do we build a house on speculation (before it is sold). Over 95 percent of our houses have a contract on them before they are started. From the day we lay out the house and dig the footings until the day we clean up, landscape, and completely finish, there have been 20 to 22 working days elapse or, to put it another way, including weekends we put up a house in a month. Because we travel over such a wide area (75-mile radius from each branch), we are required to hire our own crews of craftsmen and laborers. We do not subcontract any major job except brickwork. This is the reason that our present employment level is over 300 employees. We have our own component shop and cabinet shop located behind the Dothan marketing branch. We are currently making the exterior wall sections, interior partitions, and roof trusses for four houses per day.

5. *Close the sale.* This involves bringing it all together—a qualified customer approved by the government agency, the mortgage banker with his money, the lawyers with their contracts, deeds and mortgages, and titles.

To sum it all up, Builders Homes is a people business. It is our objective to satisfy our customers with the best house available for the money; to make contributions to the communities in which we serve by being good corporate citizens; to provide opportunities for our employees to grow to their potential; and to make a profit so that we can continue to achieve the other objectives.

Bragg ended his introductory remarks with a rhetorical question: "I wonder if we can continue to operate with these five simple steps after the modular housing facility begins operations?"

GLADDEN'S FIRST ASSIGNMENT

At the end of the meeting, Bragg met briefly with Victor Gladden and asked him to take on the following assignment:

> In the next 11 months I want you to develop and implement a plan that will handle the entire output of the new modular housing plant—10 houses per day or 2,500 houses per year. Last fiscal year our present component shop and two marketing branches built, sold, and closed 750 homes. We are currently producing and selling at a rate of about 1,000 homes per year, based on last month's sales report just received. I would like your fiscal 1972 marketing plan and strategy by August 1, 1971, in time for our corporatewide planning sessions to be held on September 1, 1971, which in turn must meet the parent company's budgeting and planning sessions scheduled for October 1, 1971.

Before Gladden left the corporate offices, Bragg gave him a copy of a rough draft of BHI's long-range plan which he was working on for the parent company's strategy meetings in October (see Appendix—The Strategic Plan).

During the next 60 days, Mr. Gladden talked to a lot of people, both inside and external to the company. On August 1, he presented his marketing plan and strategy for 1972 to president Bragg. See Exhibit 4 for the text of Gladden's strategic marketing plan.

EXHIBIT 4
1972 MARKETING STRATEGY AND PLANS (by V. Gladden, Vice President of Marketing)

I. BACKGROUND
   A. Guidance and direction for fiscal year 1972 (May 1, 1971–April 30, 1972) strategy and plans for Builders Homes has been spelled out. The message is—"Sell single-family housing!"
      The company's basic objective for fiscal 1972 is to sell and close a total of 2,500 single-family housing units through the present two marketing branches, plus two new branches proposed to be located in Mobile, Alabama, and Pensacola, Florida.

Marketing Division	Number of Units	Total Sales Revenue (including land)
Albany, Georgia	750	$14,400,000
Dothan, Alabama	750	13,912,500
Mobile, Alabama	500	9,050,000
Pensacola, Florida	500	9,475,000
Totals	2,500	$46,837,500

These preliminary figures are subject to change, and the final projections will be adjusted in accordance with the overall corporate plan.

II. THE GENERAL MARKETING STRATEGY
   A. Marketing's role is to provide the advertising and promotion support in order to bring sufficient numbers of prospects into our sales offices and

EXHIBIT 4 *(continued)*

model complexes to make the projected number of sales for each division, and

B. To provide the necessary merchandising tools in the way of reception area materials, color coordination rooms, projection rooms, furnished models, brochures and other material to make the sale easier to consummate, and

C. To provide the proper advice and counsel in the areas of sales recruiting, sales training and retraining, sales manuals, sales incentives, etc. to insure the ever presence of a good sales force with high morale and motivation in all sales branches, and

D. To provide the necessary market, competitive and customer preference research to insure that our sales force is armed at all times with readily salable products in the field.

III. ADVERTISING AND PROMOTION
General Advertising and Promotion Plan

A. Goals and Objectives

1. To develop prospects in both sufficient quantity and quality to enable Builders Homes to establish a solid foundation of "straight" or non-subsidy sales in order to level out peaks and valleys in our sales curve.

   It is Marketing's contention that the market for low-priced nonsubsidy housing is large enough for adequate growth potential and that subsidy programs such as FHA 235, Farmers Home Administration and Veterans Administration should be the "frosting on the cake" rather than the main thrust of our sales efforts. Heretofore, 90 percent of the company's sales have been to low income families qualifying under one of the above government underwritten and/or subsidized programs.

2. Goal for 1972 will be 25,000 prospects broken down by divisions as follows:

Division	Weekly Goal	Monthly	Annually
Albany	200+	875	10,500
Dothan	125+	540+	6,500
Mobile	115+	500	6,000
Pensacola	92+	400	4,800

This formula has, of course, been set up on a ten prospects for one good sale basis and will be adjusted in total according to changes in divisional goals. However, it is believed that with our new furnished models, etc., the 10-to-1 ratio is a realistic prospect goal. We will be attracting a lot more "shoppers" than we have in the past.

B. Budget

1. Regular Budget. It is recommended that our regular budget be established as one percent of gross, i.e., $460,000 based on projections of $46,837,500. The regular budget would be utilized for on-going media campaigns for the actual cost of TV, newspaper, radio and outdoor advertising.

2. Contingency Budget. It is recommended that a contingency budget of $60,000 be established. This budget would be used for opening the two new branches in Mobile and Pensacola.

EXHIBIT 4 (continued)

3. Distribution. Budget distribution for both regular and contingency should be by divisions based on the individual division's objectives and expenditures, i.e., regular budget should be one percent of projected gross sales; production charges should be made on a formula based on each division's projected gross sales and expenditures for open houses; and other special events should be charged directly to the division staging same.

C. Theme Development

   1. It is of major importance that suitable advertising themes be developed in order to:

      a. Project an image of a quality home builder capable of producing single-unit housing for both subsidized and nonsubsidized low and moderate income families.

      b. Project our image of size and stability as an operating division of U.S. Land and Shelter Co.

      c. Project our capability of subdivision building as well as scattered lot building.

      d. Project our dedication to "servicing what we sell"—our regular call-backs and customer service backup.

      e. Project our image of being a "one-stop shopping center" for the home buyer—the lot, the home, the financing, and the insurance.

   2. Specific themes will be developed to cover the above situations, such as:

      a. "We build the best home for your money."

      b. "Builders Homes—A U.S. Land and Shelter Co."

      c. "Quality homes—on your lot or ours."

      d. "Where service after the sale is a certainty."

      e. "We take care of all details—You just provide the living" or, when possible to show visually (as on TV) mother and child or family groups, "We take care of all details—You just provide the love."

      f. "Where putting you in a home of your own is the major goal."

      g. Possible adoption of a trade name.

   3. Music

      a. Logo. A special BHI musical bridge or logo will be developed as a background for local division office tags.

      b. Jingles. Special BHI jingles for use primarily on radio will be developed. These will be built around adopted themes.

D. Media

   1. Constant study will be made on media in all our markets to make sure that we have the proper media mix to bring in prospects and that we are getting the best buy for our media dollar.

   2. Each marketing division must be treated as a separate entity, because each is different. TV may always be the best medium for Dothan, for example, but newspaper might prove better for Mobile. Our new prospect reporting system will be a big help in determining this factor; but we must also use other means, such as market surveys to gauge our advertising effectiveness.

E. Relationship with Agencies and Consultants

   1. We will aim toward the development of our own in-house capability to produce all of our advertising and merchandising needs with an eye toward establishing our own recognized advertising agency in order to

EXHIBIT 4 (continued)

have better speed and flexibility and to take advantage of available commissions and discounts.

2. Agencies and consultants will continue to be utilized until we are certain that adding to overhead expenses via additional payroll and expense is the best way and the proper talent is available.

IV. MARKET RESEARCH

Customer Preference Research

A. Internal Research

Customer preference and profile information will be constantly gleaned from our company sales prospect cards. However, this in-house research, although important, tells us only history. We must develop the capability for future development of desired product.

B. External Research—Field Research of Customer Preferences

1. This is to be accomplished by interview of individuals and groups of people, particularly women, in shopping centers, home economics classes, women's clubs, garden clubs, etc.

2. Field research will be accomplished, also, by customer reaction to units set in Sears parking lots and through pretesting of models built in the field prior to establishment as a permanent part of the product line in model complexes.

C. Subdivision Feasibility Research

1. Total Company Owned. Research will be conducted on land areas planned for purchase and development as a totally owned company subdivision and recommendations provided company management in this regard.

2. Lots Bought from Others. Research will be performed and recommendations offered to management regarding purchase of ten or more lots in subdivisions developed by others. Recommendations regarding purchase of individual lots or groups of lots 1 to 9 will be made by division Land Development Directors and division General Managers.

D. Competitive Research

1. Present Marketing Divisions. Constant updating of competitive research will be performed by Marketing to keep on top of competitive factors affecting present marketing divisions.

2. Future Marketing Divisions. Although present strategy plans do not include opening additional marketing divisions in 1972, Marketing will continue to develop basic data on adjacent market areas such as Macon, Georgia; Tallahassee, Florida; and Montgomery, Alabama.

V. SALES MANAGEMENT

Sales management is a very critical and vital area in the company and needs constant attention, immediately as well as in 1972. The sales force should be the spawning ground for the development of future executives in a sales oriented company such as BHI. However, in our efforts to become more professional in our business operations and to become more sophisticated in our marketing approach, we have increased the communications gap between the Executive and Corporate Staff and the people in the field "where the action is."

It is imperative that we begin immediately to make every effort to improve the caliber of our sales force in all divisions for the accomplishment of our

EXHIBIT 4 (continued)

goals and objectives and the development of future division sales and general managers. It is Marketing's recommendation that a General Sales Manager be recruited and brought on board immediately as an important arm of the total marketing team. This individual would have the following responsibilities:

A. Sales Recruiting. To recruit, in conjunction with division sales and general managers, qualified, by education and experience, Sales Counselors as needed with special attention to real estate commission requirements for sales of homes and/or lots in all of our marketing areas.

B. Sales Training and Retraining. This individual would be responsible for the backup of division sales managers in general and special sales training courses and sessions to improve our skills in this area. He would also be responsible for necessary retraining as financing and qualification changes are made in the various present programs and when new ones are added.

C. Sales Compensation. It would be an additional responsibility to keep constant check on our method of sales compensation and how it compares with plans used by our competitors in housing and general real estate. And, also, our competitors from other fields for talented sales personnel. He would also make sure that whatever compensation plans BHI utilizes would keep our cost of sales percentage in line.

D. Sales Incentive. He would develop incentive programs that would continually revitalize our sales force, prod them on to new sales heights and keep morale high.

E. Project Input. He would work with divisional sales managers and Market Research in assisting the Marketing Department in formulating plans and recommendations for necessary present product redesign and introduction of new product.

VI. DESIGN AND MERCHANDISING

A. Design. Marketing, with in-house capability and help of outside consultants, U.S. Land and Shelter staff people and others, will constantly review BHI floor plans, exterior elevations, materials, and color selections being used in order to keep our product line new, fresh, and competitive. Recommendations will be submitted on a regular basis on design changes, new product designs and material and color suggestions.

B. Merchandising. With internal capability and use of outside aid, as needed, Marketing will keep close watch on our model home interiors and exteriors to make sure these are always clean, fresh and in order. The same applies to sales office reception areas and color selection rooms. These areas are where we make our first impression on prospects, and first impressions are the lasting ones.

VII. COMMUNICATIONS

A. Public Relations and Publicity. Constant attention will continue to be given to increasing our quantity and quality of information to the local and trade press. This is a vital link in our overall communications effort because it keeps our buying public, the communities we serve, our trade allies, and our employees informed as to who we are, what we are doing, and what we have to sell.

B. Presentations. With staff and outside aid, when needed, Marketing will continue to improve its capabilities in the preparation of slide, film, and film strip presentations for sales theater, industry, governmental agency,

EXHIBIT 4 (concluded)

and community presentations. Resource files will be developed and up-dated on industry and other vital information necessary for aid in assisting in the preparation of speeches and presentations to be given by top management personnel. This is most important in accomplishing our goal of presenting a more professional approach to our business and improving our overall company image.

C. Marketing will provide necessary aid and assistance in the publication of necessary employee handbooks, customer books, etc., as well as constantly striving to improve content and format of employee publications. Deadlines and publication schedules will be *set* and *met* in order to continually improve the information flow and communications to our employees in all divisions and areas of operations.

APPENDIX: BUILDERS HOMES, INC. (a subsidiary of U.S. Land and Shelter Company)

THE STRATEGIC PLAN FOR 1972

(submitted by Jay Bragg, September 1971)

I. FORECAST OF ENVIRONMENT

From all the recognizable signs, it is apparent to me that inflation will continue to be a problem in the economy for the next five years. Money costs will continue to be high; however, I feel interest rates will maintain or decrease slightly from their present levels. We estimate that within the next two years, the Viet Nam War will have reached a point whereby a greater flow of funds will be diverted to domestic programs. We forecast that a greater absolute dollar amount, as well as a greater percentage of these funds will be available for the housing industry and the mortgage market. I feel that we are on the threshold of a housing boom at this moment. Although I am very optimistic about the prospects of housing within the next five years, I feel the United States will continue to be engaged in similar conflicts such as the Viet Nam War.

The effects of the Administration's fight on inflation has resulted in other economic problems, especially unemployment. This particular situation of unemployment will continue to put pressure on Congress to subsidize more and more housing. In turn, this will contribute to a greater effective demand for this sector of the housing market. Real household income should continue to grow, allowing a good portion of the population to enjoy prosperity as this country has never seen before. Regardless of the trend of real income, however, there will always be the lower twenty percent of the income strata.

In certain geographical areas of our country where land is available at reasonable cost, the single family dwelling will continue to dominate the market at all income levels. This market should definitely not be overlooked by those of

APPENDIX: BUILDERS HOMES, INC. *(continued)*

us in a position to serve it. I am particularly optimistic about the demand for low-cost housing where land is available at reasonable costs. I anticipate that sixty to seventy-five percent of all housing starts within the next five years will be subsidized in one form or another by government housing programs.

During the next five years, I forecast that multi-family starts will continue to account for about fifty percent of our total housing needs. This market segment includes apartments, condominiums and condominium type living, such as mobile home parks and single family dwellings designed around the planned unit development concept. I feel that mobile homes, as such, will take a smaller part of the market than they have in the past several years. However, I believe that the mobile home type of living will continue to be an acceptable life style of a certain segment of the market.

There will be a market for vacation or seasonal housing or second homes which will be created by the prosperity enjoyed by our populace. However, I believe that this is not a market in which a high volume, mass-housing producer can take advantage. My experience indicates that people use second homes as luxury dwelling units. They particularly want it customized and are not willing to pay the price that is necessary to obtain a desirable profit by our company. However, I do believe that the development of land for this purpose is a good business and will continue to be in great demand.

Technological innovation and adaptation will progress rapidly during the next five years in the housing industry. Conventional stick building techniques will be obsolete. They will be replaced by component construction, prefabrication and modular construction techniques. All knowledgeable builders will take advantage of these opportunities because of inherent economy and higher quality of output. By the end of the five-year period, we foresee the possibility of modular type construction supplying as much as fifty percent of total production in all types of housing construction in this country. Factory built housing will yield greater quality control as well as management control of the production process. As most of us know we are in an industry that has one of the most antiquated methods of production. I believe that we have finally awakened to the fact that there are better ways of producing houses and that they are being brought to the forefront, not only by the private sector, but by our government.

It is apparent that this company has taken the role of a giant in the industry. It is easy to see that the industry is pointed in this direction. However, there are numerous types of organizations that would be useful to identify in terms of competition. *First,* we have organizations put together that consist of only building and real estate development companies. They normally consist of five or six building operators and are located over a wide geographical area; for example, U.S. Home and Development Company. This type of company has definite advantages in that the people joined together have wide and varied experiences in the building and development business. However, they lack expertise in the field of mortgage banking, sophisticated financing, joint ventures, syndications, innovation in building methods, products and systems. The *second* type of organization is that of the large multi-industry industrial or service company of which building is a division or arm. An example of this type of organization is Levitt of IT&T. Picture what would happen to this type of

APPENDIX: BUILDERS HOMES, INC. (*continued*)

company when there are reversals in the building industry or perhaps when they stub their toe; they would become a pawn of the industrial or service company and perhaps be spun-off for some other more enticing profit center. I feel that, because of the nature of the larger company's primary interest, a building division would not be supported when the going gets tough. A *third* type of organization also falls within the classification of a conglomerate. Builders, land developers, mobile home people, cookie makers and furniture manufacturers are put together primarily for financial advantage by promoters and money managers. It would appear that the primary objectives for this type of organization are capital gain and financial leverage in the stock market. It is only a matter of time before we see these types of organizations leave the industry because they do not have the final consumer in primary perspective. Both types of conglomerate organizations will perhaps be very strong competitors in the short run because of their financial strength, but in the long run I feel they will not be as strong a competitor as the type of organization exemplified by the first type mentioned. The *fourth* type of organization would be a firm composed of several builders, mortgage bankers, land developers, and mobile home park developers, etc., merged with a building products manufacturer whose primary interest is to build products that would enhance a better living environment of all people. This type of orgaanization is composed of knowledgeable people in all fields related to real estate and homebuilding. Competition from this type of organization will be directed toward resources as well as for markets. They provide products and services more closely aligned with our company. They have the objectives to provide decent living environments for all people and possess the financial strength that is necessary to fulfill the objectives. *Fifth,* we have the small builder who will always be on the American scene and who will continue to contribute. However, it will become more and more difficult for this builder to compete other than in high priced custom homes. *Finally,* we have large independently owned building companies that will continue to grow and be part of this industry. Again, it will be more and more difficult for these people to compete because of their limited financial resources and lack of flexibility to cope with the changing economic and social environment. I think our organization should strive to be the leader in the building industry and real estate field. We have the resources and the desire to reach such a position, because we: (1) have the financial stability, (2) are experts in building techniques, (3) are experts in land development, (4) are experts in mortgage banking, (5) are proficient in marketing. Perhaps the greatest advantage of our type of organization is our dedication to the proposition of providing a decent living environment for all people.

II. RESOURCE ANALYSIS

The greatest resource that we have is our people. The growth and accomplishments that we have reached thus far can be attributed directly to the people who are leaders in this company. We must continue to create an organizational environment which allows our people to:

Manage their time effectively.

Identify important objectives.

APPENDIX: BUILDERS HOMES, INC. (*continued*)

Plan and implement programs to accomplish results.

Cooperate and coordinate their activities with other people in this company and in other external organizations.

It is of particular importance that the entrepreneurship of these people be recognized as the greatest asset that this company has; our growth and development shall be limited to the degree that this asset is allowed to develop. The inability of these people to use this quality in taking advantage of our association with U.S. Land and Shelter will determine our future to a large degree. We will be able to open many doors that were not available to us heretofore because of the prestige and financial possibilities that are necessary for the development and growth of this business.

III. FUTURE SCOPE OF OPERATION

The following is a list of businesses that I think we should be in:

Land speculator

Land planner (planning use of our own land)

Construction company

Total land developer and builder

Mortgage banker

Manufacturer

Mobile home parks developer

Condominium promoter, developer and builder

We should be specialists, builders, developers, owners, operators, etc. of all types of government guaranteed low income housing. I don't think we should operate apartments; only in those cases where it is necessary to properly merchandise the sale of them. We should not operate hotels, restaurants, golf courses, casinos, curios or spas. It would be all right to sponsor a training program for underprivileged residents to low income housing projects as long as sponsorship was profitable. We should definitely give consideration to being our own subcontractor in all fields, but this can only be determined by the prevailing circumstances in each area. Present information we now have available to us indicates that there is no economical advantage in being our own supplier. As a general rule, we should not be in any other business than those primarily connected with the building of shelter. There are advantages as previously pointed out on being geographically diversified, and I would encourage our continuing to explore the possibilities of expanding as such on *our own* and with local builders on a joint venture basis.

IV. OBJECTIVES

In general, we should work toward developing a volume of business that would be commensurate with the developed talents of our present organization and the financial resources from which to draw in order to accomplish the

APPENDIX: BUILDERS HOMES, INC. (*continued*)

objective that might be set. All the prevailing conditions that might affect our volume of business would be recognized by our people if they have the proper tools with which to work and they are the proper people for the positions they hold within our company.

Our profit should be relative in a dollar amount as to the amount of business that we would do controlled by the above formula; however, ten percent profit before taxes on sales would be fair to expect in most circumstances. Return on investment in the normal run of business should be approximately thirty percent. In all circumstances the return on investments should be measured by the amount of risks and the level of risks involved. New types of projects that we may undertake should be done only after thorough analyses have been made and with our feeling that we have the capacity of management.

From 25 to 50 percent of our corporate growth should be a result of moving into new divisions or new segments of this business through acquisition and joint ventures.

V. STRATEGY

Growth Strategy. Taking into consideration that the alternatives in light of our analyses of environment, our analyses of resources, our competitive position, our desired future scope of operations, we, as a company, view the continental United States as our area of operation in the next five years and should take an approach that will allow us to attract and employ the top management team in the country for the home-building industry. We should take these people and exploit the plans and opportunities available to us and what will be made available to us from time to time. We should become actively engaged in joint ventures and acquisitions to the degree that would be necessary to fulfill those goals that we concurrently establish.

I do not think that this company should enter into any new business that is not directly concerned with the furnishing of shelter for people within the degree and scope in which we are now operating. We should enter into as many new businesses in any one year as we can profitably manage with the sources of personnel and finances available.

Any acquisitions that we might undertake should be related to our current operations. The criteria we should use in judging an acquisition or a new business should be growth rate, return on investment, reportable profit, possible contribution of management to our company, the need of their profits or parts of the market they are in that would help us to become oriented easier on a profitable basis.

We should orient our group toward being a provider of shelter with all its inherent many-faceted services. We should, in all cases, evaluate the alternative of acquisition versus our starting operation ourselves and the things to be considered should be as follows:

Personnel and their ability to manage.

Finances and our ability to provide.

APPENDIX: BUILDERS HOMES, INC. (*concluded*)

Organizational growth should be through promotion and development of our own personnel. This has proven the best type of growth and lends to the development of organizations more expediently than any other. The best possible way to developing organizations with the entrepreneurship that is so necessary in business today is to train our own people. Sometimes it is necessary to employ outside people who have needed experience, or are specifically trained for a required position, or who represent "new blood" and do not have preconceived conceptions of the organization and its operations.

The corporate staff should be a group of people joined together with experience in all phases of operations that can plan, set policies, establish procedures, fix guidelines, and set objectives. The staff, under certain circumstances, will have to implement their plans, policies, etc. with the division people, but should primarily be available for major decision-making and consultations.

It is according to each particular situation as to whether or not we function on a centralized basis. In general, it is best that we operate with each particular profit center being autonomous as long as the autonomy fits into the general scope of policies, objectives, profitability, philosophy, etc. There should be a close enough rapport between the staff and various divisions of the company that ideas may flow so that all concerned will profit.

Compensation strategy should be adapted where people are compensated commensurate with their contribution. Compensations should be determined also in light of particular patterns of compensation established for the area, type of work and environment in which this particular person is working. It is the policy of our company to pay extra good for extra good performance of extra good people.

9. Indian Cashew Processors, Ltd.*

Indian Cashew Processors, Ltd. (ICP) was a cashew nut processor located near the city of Quilon, in the Indian state of Kerala. ICP consisted of two major divisions: (a) a packaging division and (b) a cashew nut processing division. Practically all cashews were exported. Sales of this division in 1974 had reached 10 million rupees (about $1.3 million)—equivalent to 1 percent of India's 58,000 metric tons of cashew nut exports.

Early in 1974, N. Singh, the sole proprietor of ICP, became increasingly concerned about the competitive situation of India's cashew nut processing industry vis-a-vis the recently installed mechanized plants in Africa and Brazil. ICP, as all other Indian cashew nut processors, was largely dependent on raw nut imports from Africa because India's own raw nut crop only satisfied about one third of the industry's needs. However, with the newly installed processing capacity in African countries (Kenya, Mozambique) that had traditionally been important raw nut suppliers to India, competition for raw nuts was expected to intensify. African governments would probably favor their own processing industries, leaving India with fewer cashews to process. Furthermore, India's present customers, cashew nut brokers and food marketers in the developed countries, might shift their buying in favor of the newly created African processors. If ICP was to survive as a major cashew nut processor, Mr. Singh had to find a solution to neutralize the threat of losing its major raw material source and its access to the major consumer markets.

THE CASHEW NUT

Cashew nuts grow on cashew trees in the tropical climates of Africa, Latin America, and India. The tree grows wild to about 30 to 40 feet in height with a thick green foliage. Trees grow in a density of about 100 trees per one hectare of land, and grow well even on poor soil. They bear their first fruits after about three years. Commercial harvesting usually starts after four to five years, or one or two years after the first fruits developed. Today, there are very few plantations of cashew trees. Most of the world's crop comes from wild trees. Only recently has there been an interest on the part of some African and Latin American countries to develop large scale plantations.

---

* Prepared by Prof. Jean-Pierre Jeannet of Babson College.

The cashew tree is probably one of the few trees where the nut grows outside its fruit, called the apple (see drawing below). This apple, occasionally referred to as "false fruit," can be used for jams, fruit juices, or even for the production of alcoholic beverages. It can be eaten just as a regular apple.

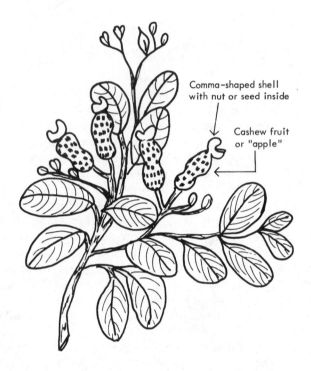

Comma-shaped shell with nut or seed inside

Cashew fruit or "apple"

The fruit, or apple, matures before the nut, and since the nut has a far greater commercial value, the nut is usually detached when the apple no longer has any use. Cashew nuts are highly nutritional, containing vitamins, iron, calcium, and phosphorus. Because of its superior value, most commercial efforts concentrate solely on the cashew *nut*.

The raw cashew nuts are harvested mostly in India, East Africa, and Brazil. Since the trees grow wild, the only cost involved in harvesting is labor. During harvesting time, collecting cashew nuts creates jobs for thousands of otherwise unemployed or underemployed persons.

Harvesting seasons differ according to climate and geographical location. For the major producing areas, the harvest takes place during the following months:

India	March to May, also small crop October to November
Mozambique	November to January
Tanzania	October to November
Kenya	October to November
Brazil	May to July

The raw cashew nut itself consists of a hard, thick, and green shell accounting for about half of the raw nut's total weight (see drawing). This hard shell

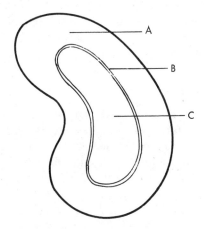

(layer A) contains a reddish-brown viscous liquid called "Cashew Nut Shell Liquid," or CNSL. This liquid has a high commercial value due to numerous applications in industry. This liquid consists of two naturally produced phenolic compounds, an acardic acid (90 percent) and cardol (10 percent). The liquid is used, among other things, as a protective agent for anticorrosive paints to be used on metal or wood. The largest importers of CNSL are the United States, the United Kingdom, and Japan.

The ivory white cashew nut (C) is surrounded by a tight thin reddish covering (B). The cashew nut (C) is very brittle and will easily break as a result of shock or pressure. One of the major tasks of the cashew nut processing industry is to remove the first two layers without breaking the nut (C). A broken nut loses between 25 to 35 percent of its regular commercial value depending on the size of the broken pieces.

STRUCTURE OF WORLD CASHEW NUT INDUSTRY

Traditionally, the industry has consisted of three major groups of participants:

1. *Raw material producers.* Located in countries like India, Mozambique, Kenya, Tanzania, and Brazil. Countries that could potentially become raw material producers in the future are most West African countries, Ceylon, Cambodia, Malaysia, Indonesia, Phillipines, Thailand, Guatemala, Colombia, and Venezuela.
2. *The cashew nut processors.* Until a few years ago, only India had an efficient processing industry for cashew nuts. During processing, the nut shell is cracked and peeled to get to the inner core. The process is very labor intensive. Only recently have some of the African nations bought equipment that will perform the same process. With the arrival of such

cashew nut peeling machinery, India has lost its monopoly over processing. In 1973–74 India still processed 75 percent of all cashew nuts.
3. *The cashew nut consumers.* Cashew nut consumers are dispersed
throughout the world. They consist primarily of importers and food
companies in industrial countries such as the United States, USSR,
Canada, the United Kingdom, and Japan.

The Raw Material Producers

This industry started about 50 years ago in India. Originally, only small
amounts of processed nuts were exported to the United States and the
United Kingdom. As demand increased, India's raw material sources were
not sufficient to satisfy demand. As a result, a flourishing import trade based
on African raw nuts developed. Today, the following countries lead in raw
nut harvesting:

Country	Crop Year	Raw Nut Production (000 tons)	Raw Nut Exports (000 tons)
India	1973	105	—
Mozambique	1973	216	181
Tanzania	1974	120	95
Kenya	1974–75	25	15

These figures clearly show that India, which produces no more than 30
percent of total raw nut production, retains all of its production for further
processing. Other countries export most of their production to India for
processing.

Due to the high commercial value of the cashew nut, many countries try
to promote the harvesting and processing of these nuts. As a result, the
supply of cashew nuts is expected to increase further with many additional
countries entering the market as suppliers.

The Cashew Nut Processing Industry

In 1974, Indian exporters sold 57,976 metric tons of processed nuts valued
at $130 million. With the advent of mechanized processing, some African
countries have also begun to install processing equipment.

Country	Year	Installed Processing Capacity	Actual Local Processing
		Tons of Raw Nuts (000)	
India	1973	(unlimited)	282
Mozambique	1973	130	35
Tanzania	1974	35	25
Kenya	1974–75	10	10

In India, about 200 private companies account for the bulk of cashew nut processing. These processors use little machinery; instead, they depend on 300,000 workers who are able to handle the nuts skillfully to avoid cracking during processing. Most of these processors are concentrated in the Quilon district of the state of Kerala, in the southwest of India. The average factory employs between 800 and 1,500 employees, 80 percent of whom are women.

Indian cashew nut processors perform six distinct steps:

Step 1: Raw Nut Burning I. All raw nuts are thrown into an open fire for about five to seven minutes. The CNSL contained in the shell helps burn the external cover.

Step 2: Shelling. Burnt nuts while still warm are distributed to workers in the shelling department. Workers use a wooden hammer to crack the shell. Expertise is necessary since excess pressure will break the nut.

Step 3: Raw Nut Burning II. The cracked nuts are heated in an oven at 100°F for another eight to ten hours. This helps loosen the grip of the closely attached thin cover to the nut.

Step 4: Peeling. The warm nuts are sent to the peeling department where the skin is removed by hand. The use of any sharp instruments, even fingernails, is prohibited since marks might be left on the surface or the nut could even break.

Step 5: Grading. The grading department sorts the ivory colored nuts into 24 different qualities depending on size of pieces. The sorting skills of the employee are crucial at this stage due to large price differences between the higher and lower quality grades. In 1975, the highest quality grade sold for $1.16 per pound compared with 30 cents to 40 cents per pound for the lowest quality.

Step 6: Packing. The graded nuts are packaged into 25-pound tin cans. Two cans are called a case.

Processors who extract CNSL perform this operation before the initial burning process. One ton of raw nuts yields about 500 pounds of processed nuts of various quality grades (exact composition depends on crop quality and country of origin).

So far, only India has developed a large processing industry that entirely depends on the skill of its labor force. Attempts to teach these skills to Africans were unsuccessful. As a result, these nations looked for automated processing equipment. This equipment is being supplied by Italian and U.K. manufacturers. Supposedly, the U.K. machinery is superior.

The minimum capacity of such a plant is 1,250 tons of raw nuts per annum. Such a plant sells at $320,000 f.o.b. British port and requires a minimum labor force of 25. In March 1975 the World Bank granted Tanzania a $10 million credit to install a pilot plant to process cashews. Many units, large and small, are rapidly being installed throughout Africa. Even the small nation of Dahomey installed a 1,500-ton-per-year factory in May 1975. In Latin America it is primarily Brazil that has encouraged the development of its cashew nut processing industry. Brazil now has a processing capacity in excess of its own raw nut production resulting in heavy buying from African raw nut producers.

The manufacturers of cashew nut processing machinery claim that the processing costs of a mechanized plant equal those of India's hand operated factories. The African producers, however, incur no freight charges on their raw material as their Indian competitors do. Shipping costs of raw nuts from East Africa to India average $22 to $30 per ton. The major disadvantage of the mechanized units is the large proportion of broken nuts with a low commercial value. This revenue loss combined with the high financing costs tends to bring the total unit costs about in line with those of the Indian processors of $114 per ton. There is one difference still, and that is the easy access of African processors to raw nuts.

As long as African nations did not have any processing capacity, these countries were ready to sell any quantity to Indian processors. However, with the installation of a number or processing plants to Africa and Brazil, plus increased world demand for cashew nuts, competition for raw nuts has intensified resulting in higher prices.

East African Raw Nut Prices (average price per ton c.i.f. Cochin Port, India)*

1962	$124
1965	199
1968	200
1973	216
1974	288

* C.i.f. means the price paid for the raw nuts, including insurance and freight to Cochin Port, India.

The Cashew Nut Consumers

The majority of processed cashew nuts are consumed by the developed countries of the Western world (United States, United Kingdom, Canada, Germany, Japan) and the USSR (see Exhibit 1). As indicated by the table below, the United States accounts for more than half of all cashew imports.

Country	Imports (metric tons)	Percent of World Imports
United States	48,996	52%
USSR	20,400	22
Canada	6,703	7
United Kingdom	3,420	4
Japan	3,289	3.5
		88.5%

EXHIBIT 1
Cashew Nut Imports (metric tons)

	Australia	Belgium	Canada	France	Germany (Federal Republic)	Holland	Japan	New Zealand	Sweden	United Kingdom	United States
1946		—	1,148							1,838	13,561
1947		—	697							3,860	14,395
1948		11	835							3,237	15,745
1949			964							1,663	16,625
1950		12	706					105	25	2,902	21,993
1951		61	954					90	1	4,385	22,908
1952		11	1,035			38		50	19	7,697	19,116
1953		3	1,233			41		75	13	7,107	21,619
1954	260	16	1,043			133		75	75	3,451	25,651
1955	577	43	1,141			286		79	256	3,209	30,116
1956	463	129	1,191			413		121	340	3,518	25,528
1957	650	65	1,480			...		118	192	3,109	26,489
1958	685	113	1,507			...		134	223	2,717	30,286
1959	566	107	1,363			202		79	205	2,260	28,737
1960	1,103	86	1,543		352	229		151	157	2,525	29,083
1961	1,218	111	1,760		1,163	287		166	135	3,317	26,703
1962	1,416	161	1,570		1,413	419		186	218	2,551	29,248
1963	1,547	148	1,892		1,483	505		210	199	2,554	34,355
1964	1,928	119	1,788		1,326	577		207	202	3,468	31,529
1965	1,536	147	1,882		1,071	449	515	170	142	3,265	29,761
1966	1,554	240	1,439		883	574	602	122	127	2,479	30,752
1967	2,198	204	1,944	514	972	655	658	110	147	2,747	33,043
1968	2,024	196	2,272	184	1,174	777	514	210	176	3,150	42,234
1969	2,317	198	2,604	896	1,460	946	868	170	165	2,559	37,607
1970	1,739	224	2,787	800	1,817	1,156	1,311	212	179	1,573	42,943
1971	2,339	280	5,778	959	2,105	1,679	1,735	171	163	2,305	44,229
1972	2,853	323	7,678	1,059	2,479	2,094	2,370	326	232	3,157	48,443
1973	2,422	391	6,703	1,164	3,004	2,616	3,289	254	197	3,420	48,996
1974	3,264	222	4,397	512	2,064	2,013	1,887	276		3,058	31,292

The majority of these cashews are imported by bulk importers for further processing in their plants (either for frying in oil with salt added or for roasting with chemicals added). These bulk importers sell cashews under their own brand names marketed through the typical distribution channels for food products. Cashews are generally consumed as a snack food during cocktail parties. Some of the lower qualities are used by the confectionary industry.

A rather interesting development in the international cashew market is the recent strong buying by Russia. Russia's imports have risen faster than United States imports in recent years and now stand at 22 percent of total world imports. Due to low consumer income in Russia, it is generally believed that these cashew nuts are not bought for the same purposes as in Western countries. Furthermore, Russian imports tend to consist exclusively of the lower-quality cashews (broken pieces of whole cashews). Since cashews contain 21 percent vegetable proteins (on a par with meat, milk, or eggs) as well as numerous vitamins (B, B2, B6, PP, A, D, and E) it is believed the Russians use these cashews as supplement for some basic foods such as bread.

Not only has Russia concentrated all its imports on low-grade cashews, but it has also exclusively imported from Indian sources. In the past, Russian buyers have offered Indian processors much higher prices than other countries' buyers for certain grades. Low-quality nuts that might sell for 30–40 U.S. cents per pound in the open world market could be sold for 60–70 cents per pound to Russian buyers.

Many observers of the cashew industry believe the Russian buying practice has political overtones. For one, since 1965 India has moved closer to Moscow politically and cashew nuts represent an important export earning for India. More important, some experts argue, India's cashew nut industry with its 300,000-strong labor force is centered entirely in the southern state of Kerala, the only Indian state to vote consistently communist for years. Russia's exhorbitant prices represent, adopting the reasoning of these experts, a handsome subsidy to Kerala.

The world market has adapted to these trends. Indian exporters now ship much of their available products to Russia. Furthermore, the United States and other Western nations have diversified their sourcing. U.S. buyers buy their lower-grade cashews exclusively from non-Indian suppliers to avoid price competition with Russian buyers. This trend is clearly illustrated in the table below:

Percentage of U.S. Cashew Imports by Country of Origin

	1965	1970	1974
Brazil	1%	10%	13%
India	86	60	42
Mozambique	8	21	38

International Trade in Processed Cashews

Most Indian and African exporters do not directly deal with the food products marketers in the various countries. Instead, they deal through their agents in major buying centers such as New York or Hamburg. The agent maintains communication between suppliers and importers on pricing and shipping arrangements. Usually, the agent works on the basis of a 2.5 percent commission to be paid by his principal. Importers generally buy in bulk—500 to 2,000 cases per deal depending on shipping costs. Before a deal is consumated the importer will open a letter of credit in favor of the supplier who will in return discount the bill immediately upon delivery of the shipment at the supplier's port. The governments usually act as quality control to protect the importer. The majority of the sales are closed on a four- to five-month forward cycle. Since it is the importer who generally has to take the risk of changing price conditions in the future, and because of the considerable working capital required (2,000 cases at present prices represents a value of $100,000 or more), cashew nut buying is restricted to a few larger buyers. Exhibits 2 and 3 show the recent prices of cashews with Quality 320 being the quality usually found in an expensive can of mixed nuts.

EXHIBIT 2
Quality/Price Level for Cashews in 1975

Quality	Price per Pound (US $)	Discount Premium (grade 320 as base)
210	$1.16	5.45%
240	1.11	1.8
320	1.10	0
450	1.08	−1.8
SW	1.02	−7.27
Splits	0.70	−36.0
SP	0.40	−63.0

EXHIBIT 3
Average Prices of Processed Cashews New York, Quality 320*

1958	$0.47/pound
1960	0.56
1965	0.60
1970	0.75
1973	1.20
1973	1.15
1975	1.10

* Includes cost, insurance, and freight to New York.

BRIEF HISTORY OF INDIAN CASHEW PROCESSORS

Mr. Singh founded Indian Cashew Processors, Ltd. in 1942. Originally, ICP was a trading company only. Following the expansion of demand for cashew nuts in the post World War II period, ICP expanded into processing as well. In 1974, the company successfully expanded into the packaging industry through the production of tin containers and wood cases.

Mr. Singh, now aged 58, had little formal education. He tightly controlled all six subunits of the company, consisting of the various processing units and the packaging division. All submanagers reported directly to him on a daily basis. This heavy dependence on Mr. Singh had caused some problems in the past. When he traveled to the United States in 1972 for a major cashew nut promotion, all units incurred losses and production ground to a halt within ten days.

Most members of the company's managerial staff were of about the same age as its owner. With the exception of the general manager, who had earned a B.S. in Commerce degree, the managers did not have a formal education beyond high school. Most of the managers and staff members were Mr. Singh's former classmates or relatives. His son, N. Singh, Jr., had recently attended several universities and earned a Bachelor of Commerce from the University of Kerala, India, a Bachelor of Communication and a Master of Business Studies from the National University of Ireland, and was expected to earn, by the end of 1974, an M.B.A from Babson College in the United States. Mr. Singh, Jr., was expected to join ICP early in 1975. Despite his absence from India, Mr. Singh, Jr., was closely involved in the company's affairs.

ICP operated three processing facilities employing close to 2,000 persons. Mr. Singh had been successful over the years and his net worth was estimated at 5 million rupees (or about $625,000).

ICP'S COMPETITIVE SITUATION AS A PROCESSOR

There were about 200 cashew nut processing factories in India, most of these located in the state of Kerala. Only 40 to 50 of these could be considered as established exporters. Since all the cashew nut processors in India used similar technology in processing and packaging, costs were relatively uniform. None of the companies had any complex organizational structures or exceptional managerial skills. Raw nuts were imported through the State Trading Corporation of India (STC), a government-sponsored organization, and allocated to each processor according to capacity. Prices charged were uniform. State laws existed to keep labor cost the same for processors in Kerala.

As a result, a processor's success depended on two key factors:

1. A high yield of whole nuts from a ton of raw nuts (this depended largely upon the skills of the employees and effective supervision).

2. Accurate forecasting of market demand for different grades of cashews in foreign markets.

ICP'S STRENGTH AND WEAKNESSES

Mr. Singh's son believed ICP had a number of strengths:

1. *Expertise.* Mr. Singh's personal knowledge of the world cashew industry based upon his 30 years of experience in trading and processing.
2. *Access to Raw Material.* ICP had an assured quota of both the Indian imports of raw nuts as well as of India's own local crop.
3. *Financing.* Mr. Singh enjoyed solid financial backing in India. However, there was little chance to export any capital for ventures abroad.
4. *Reputation.* Mr. Singh's reputation as a businessman and exporter was excellent. He could exert influence on a local level. He was known among the few buyers in the United States as a reliable contract shipper and his relationship with his major New York broker dated back to the 40s.

ICP was not without weaknesses, however. These weaknesses were listed by Mr. Singh, Jr., as:

1. *Consumer Contact.* ICP shipped processed nuts in large quantities to brokers and marketers in industrialized countries who sold these cashews under their own brand names. As a result, ICP or its management knew little about the ultimate consumer.
2. *Dependence on Russian Orders.* Due to the high prices Russian buyers paid for lower grades, ICP had sold a growing proportion of its output to the USSR. This had weakened the company's traditional ties with brokers in the Western world.
3. *Absence of Home Market.* Despite India's large population, no real market for cashew nuts had developed. This was largely due to the high prices of the cashews and India's low per capita annual income of $116.
4. *Control over Raw Material.* ICP had no control over its raw material sources. All supplies originated from India's state agencies where ICP enjoyed an annual quota. Prices were set by the buying organization. In addition, revenue was subject to fluctuations of cashew world market prices.
5. *Management.* ICP was overly dependent on its owner, Mr. Singh, for all decisions. The only successor in sight was his son, who actually preferred to live abroad.

Most of these strengths and weaknesses were not limited to ICP alone. They were faced by India's cashew nut exporters who, after all, faced the same competitive threats.

ALTERNATIVES

Mr. N. Singh, Jr., believed ICP had two major alternatives: (*a*) backward integration, or (*b*) forward integration.

To ensure a constant supply of raw material, ICP could invest in company-owned plantations. However, the capital requirements were beyond the firm's financial capabilities. Also, it was felt that the political risks were too high for such an investment in Africa. And, in areas where cashew nuts grew wild, acquiring a controlling interest would not be feasible.

To start or buy out existing processing facilities in East Africa was also considered. Capital needs would be very high, though not as high as for a plantation. But most African countries discouraged ownership by foreign investors, and Asians in particular had been subject to discrimination in countries such as Uganda or Tanzania. In general, backward integration was considered too expensive or too risky. It was for these reasons that ICP's owner was investigating forward integration into consumer markets.

The second alternative was to integrate forward and start to market directly to consumers in some countries. ICP would have to set up an additional processing unit to fry and salt cashews. These cashews could then be sold under ICP's brand name in major consumer markets or else sold under private label. Since this called for a relatively modest capital outlay in countries of solid investment climate, ICP decided to further investigate this course of action.

MAJOR WORLD MARKETS FOR CASHEWS

United States. The United States was the largest importer of cashew nuts and therefore the most important consumer market. Other than cashews, the United States was also a major importer of Brazil nuts and pistachios.

Total imports of edible nuts for 1971 amounted to 74,846 tons valued at $90 million. The following nuts accounted for the bulk of all imports:

	Percentage of Imports by Volume
Cashews	59%
Pistachios	16
Brazil nuts	15
Chestnuts	4
Hazel nuts	3
Others	3
Total	100%

Eighty percent of the cashews were used in the consumer market. The remainder was sold to industrial users such as the confectionary industry, bakeries, ice cream manufacturers, etc. These users, however, consumed only the lowest grades and represented a small segment of the market when measured in sales volume.

For the consumer market, the imported natural cashews were retailed in three basic forms:

1. *Fried*—fried in vegetable oil with salt added.
2. *Roasted*—dry roasted with chemicals added (primarily for weight watchers).
3. *Natural*—without any further processing.

It was generally agreed that cashew nuts were consumed as snack foods, particularly with cocktails.

The U.S. cashew import trade was characterized by a large degree of concentration. There were about 30 major importers of cashews. Most of these were processors as well, performing their own roasting and frying. A few were wholesalers only selling to small regional processors. All of these importers imported in bulk. Five hundred cases (one case equalled 50 pounds) was the minimum transaction handled by brokers, and in general, Indian exporters also did not ship below 500 cases. This required that the importer handle an annual volume of at least 5,000 cases. There was a high uncertainty in importing quality-grade cashews because the exporter may not ship the correct grades. Usually, payment for the shipment was made when the cashews had been loaded onto the ocean vessel. By the time the importer had a chance to inspect the merchandise in the United States, the shipment had already been paid for. Prices were quoted five to six months ahead, adding a new risk for the importer.

All of these factors made the cashew trade a "big-boy's business" requiring solid financial backing, good contacts, and a keen understanding of international laws, shipping, and even politics.

Three fourths of all U.S. imports were estimated to be handled by three New York brokers:

Richard Franco Co.

Frank Crauss & Co.

Mitchell Beck Company, Inc.

Among the 30 importers, the following companies accounted for the bulk of the volume:

Planters Peanut Division (18 percent of volume).

CPC International.

A&P Food Stores.

Planters was also the only company selling its brand in more than one country (United States, Canada, and the European Common Market). Planters was the leading brand in the United States. In most regions, such as New England, 10 to 12 smaller regional brands existed. These brands were marketed by small- to medium-sized companies offering a variety of nuts besides cashews. The same was true for Planters. A third group of competitors consisted of large supermarket chains selling private brands. These chains did not have their own processing and production facilities. Their processing was done on a contract basis.

Whole cashew nuts were packaged in three different forms:

1. Pull-tab aluminum cans in two standard sizes (6-oz. and 12-oz); this form was primarily used for fried cashews.
2. Glass bottles, normally 7-oz. size; used primarily for dry-roasted cashews.
3. Plastic or polyethylene bags, in sizes of 3- to 12-oz; primarily for fried and natural cashews.

Prices and retail margins differed by packaging type and size. The following retail prices were considered typical for their respective categories:

```
6-oz. can (fried cashews) ...............  $1.00 to 1.20
12-oz. can (fried cashews) ..............   1.80 to 1.95
7-oz. bottle (dry roasted) ..............   1.20 to 1.35
3-¾ oz. plastic bag....................   0.69 to 0.89
```

On a per-pound basis, cashews selling in small plastic bags were more expensive than those selling in cans or bottles. Marketing cashews in plastic bags caused higher handling expenses. Therefore, retail margins averaged 25 to 30 percent for plastic bags compared to 25 percent for cans or bottles. Usually a food broker was used to contact wholesalers and retailers at an additional cost of 5 percent of sales.

Presently, cashews were not directly advertised to the consumers. Planters heavily advertised its peanuts and peanut butter, thereby creating a strong brand image that influenced sales of all nuts sold under the Planters brand. Regional brands were promoted to the trade through special discounts and liberal credit policies on the part of processors. The industry usually refrained from price competition.

United Kingdom.   The U.K. market had traditionally imported large amounts of nuts. But cashew imports into the United Kingdom had remained small averaging only 2,500 tons annually (1967–71). Over the period 1961 to 1971, imports even declined by 14 percent.

The reason for this market decline was generally believed to be the high prices for cashews. Peanuts, the major processed nut consumed in the United Kingdom, could be imported at $340 to $510 per ton c.i.f. U.K. port.[1] This compared favorably with a price of $2,000 to $2,200 per ton for

---

[1] C.i.f. stands for cost, insurance, and freight. In other words, the price for a ton of peanuts included the shipping to a U.K. port.

cashews. However, the market declined primarily in the consumer segment. Consequently, nearly 60 percent of total imports of cashew nuts were absorbed by industrial users, 90 percent of which went to the confectionery industry.

The U.K. market consumed nuts valued at £19 million ($40 million). Peanuts accounted for 80 percent of the total volume, followed by cashews. The following brands were the market share leaders:

Brand	Market Share
K.P. Nuts	45%
Smith's Big D	15
Golden Wonder	14
Sun Pat	5
Private Labels	12
Others	9

K.P. Nuts and Sun Pat were also market leaders in Scandinavia and Ireland. Both held strong positions in other European Common Market (ECM) countries.

Retail prices in the United Kingdom equaled those of the United States. Considering the British per capita income, cashews were comparatively more expensive for the British housewife.

Exporters in India and Africa who had to pay the freight charges on their shipments often preferred to deal with U.K. importers despite low volumes because shipping charges to the United Kingdom were less than those to the United States by nearly one dollar a case. And, as pointed out by N. Singh, Jr., $1 per case was a considerable difference for an exporter in a country where the cost of living was so much lower than in the United States. Presently, all imports into the United Kingdom were charged with a 2.5 percent duty (standard for all European Common Market countries).

Continental European Markets. For both Germany and France, distribution patterns and packaging were similar to the United Kingdom. Retail prices were higher in Germany, averaging $3.50 per pound. There was a high emphasis on quality and service in the German market. Moreover, the German consumer tended to favor German products rather than foreign brands.

Japan. Very little was known about the Japanese market for cashews. 1973 imports amounted to 3,289 metric tons. Japan assessed a duty of 16 percent on the c.i.f. value of cashew imports. Plastic bags retailed from 900 to 1,300 yen with the prices of cans averaging 1,300 to 1,700 yen (300 yen = U.S. $1).

Canada. Canadian imports reached 6,703 tons in 1973. In general, Canadian importers dealt directly with the exporters abroad, that is, there was no broker involved. Cashews entered Canada duty free. Prices for plastic bags ranged from $2.50 to $5 per pound. When sold in cans, prices averaged from $2.40 to $3.17 per pound.

This general market information had been assembled by N. Singh, Jr., as a basis for ICP's investment decision. As a rule, N. Singh, Jr., concluded, retail prices of cashews were at least double the c.i.f. imported price in all countries.

ALTERNATIVE MARKETING AND LOCATION STRATEGIES

Mr. N. Singh, Jr., felt that forward integration invariably required an additional processing unit. Such a unit could either fry or roast the cashews or both, and use various types of packaging. Because both glass bottle and aluminum can packaging required a larger amount of capital investment, he was leaning toward the plastic bag as a package. This automatically ruled out the sale of dry-roasted cashews.

A major decision was now to find a location for this proposed processing facility. It was said that while India would be advantageous because of cheap labor costs, such attempts had failed in the past. One of the biggest problems was the availability of good packaging material in India. Also, ICP management believed that Indian food products were not very well accepted by the consumer, particularly in the United States. Since cashews shipped in polyethylene bags could not be vacuum packed (both glass and aluminum can allowed vacuum packing), the quality of the products tended to suffer during the four to six weeks it took to ship cashews by ocean vessel. Furthermore, shipping costs per pound nearly doubled when cashews were shipped in retail packages rather than in bulk.

For these reasons, N. Singh, Jr., argued for a location closer to the major markets. As major markets he considered the United States and the USSR, with Europe rapidly gaining in importance.

Based on personal research, N. Singh, Jr., liked the investment climate of both Ireland and Luxemburg, but ruled out the latter country for lack of a port facility. Ireland was considered as particularly appealing because Irish food products were accepted in all markets. Some Irish agricultural products were said to have an excellent reputation, such as potatoes in the United States or beef and cheese in the United Kingdom and other European Community markets.

N. Singh, Jr., listed additional advantages for Ireland:

1. Tax and government incentives for export oriented industries, such as financial grants, free marketing services, and technical assistance.
2. Import duties were low (member of ECM) and amounted to 15 percent. Import duties on exports would be refunded. Due to an ECM agreement with Tanzania, cashews could be imported duty free from that particular country.
3. No direct competition in local market since Ireland did not have a local importer or processor of cashews.
4. Irish labor costs were among the lowest in Europe with a current hourly maximum of $2.05 (including fringe benefits).

5. Political neutrality resulting in good relations with Moscow, trade ties with Japan and Middle East.
6. Low packaging material costs—both cans and bottles were equal or below U.S. prices, and lower volume purchases were possible (U.S. minimum order for printed aluminum cans was 50,000 units). Quality was up to international standards.
7. Cost of living in Dublin was one of the lowest among capital cities.
8. Due to easy access to many markets, the marketing risk could be spread among the United States, Canada, the United Kingdom, and ECM.

But Ireland as a location for a processing plant was not without its disadvantages. Mr. N. Singh, Jr., felt there were two major factors that had to be mentioned:

1. Absence of direct shipping connections from India to Africa to Ireland, and from Ireland to the United States or Canada. All cargo had to be transshipped via U.K. ports.
2. Limited home market of 3 million people and low awareness of cashews as a product.

Exhibit 4 presents N. Singh, Jr.'s, preliminary cost calculations on the feasibility of locating a small processing unit in Ireland.

Since the United States was the largest market for cashews, Mr. N. Singh, Jr., also worked up some price-cost estimates for this particular market. The Northeast alone consumed 11,000 pounds of cashews in plastic packages per week. Based on price elasticities studies on other food products as a result of a 13 percent price reduction (69 cents for a 3-oz. bag instead of 79 cents) a market share of 10 to 15 percent could be expected. The margins were computed under the assumption that a food broker would be used to contact wholesalers and retailers. All warehousing and transportation expenditures in the United States were to be paid by ICP.

```
Selling price: $.69 for 3 ounces or $3.68 per pound.
  Retail price ...........................    $3.68 (per lb.)
  Retail margin (−28%) ...................      .81
  Wholesale price .......................      2.87
  Wholesale margin (−4% of retail price) ...   .15
                                               2.72
  Broker margin (−5% of wholesale price) ..   −.14
  Net revenue ICP .......................    $2.58 per pound
  Warehousing and transportation expenditures: $200 maximum
                                               per 1,000 lbs.
```

ICP's management needed to decide what to do about investing in a new processing unit and, if so, where to locate it. At the same time, the decision on the processing plant needed to be coordinated with how and where to market the processed nuts.

EXHIBIT 4
Cost Estimates for Irish Plant

Unit: Located in Ireland
  Processing minimum 2,000 pounds per month
  Total investment $40,000
  Processing fried cashews and packaged in plastic
Fixed costs (per month, U.S. dollars)

Depreciation on machinery	$ 250
Rent*	180
Salaries management	350
Interest on capital at 15 percent†	500
Total fixed costs	$1,280

Variable costs (per 2,000 pounds)

Labor: 30 hours at £1.0	$ 64.50
Oil and salt :	37.50
Raw material c.i.f. Dublin $1.15 per lb.	2,300.00
Customs and delivery imports	15.00
Export costs	30.00
Shipping costs Dublin to Boston	250.00
Insurance (estimate)	100.00
Packaging materials	
plastic films	32.00
Cardboard and belts	30.00
Total variable costs	$2,859.00

* Processing facility consisted of a frying unit and a packaging unit and comprised only 1,000 square feet.

† A total investment of $40,000 would be required. Most of these funds could be borrowed locally in Ireland at low rates. The 15 percent represented the target return for ICP.

10.   The Southland Corporation*

In 1978, the world's largest chain of convenience food stores was 7-Eleven markets, a division of the Southland Corporation. The 7-Eleven chain started from very humble beginnings in 1927 to surpass the $3 billion sales figure in 1978. Southland showed all indications of continuing its 15 percent annual growth rate and capitalizing on consumer acceptance of convenience shopping. As the president of a rival chain expressed it, "I think it has to be said that Southland is one of the great retailing stores of our time."

COMPANY HISTORY

In 1924, Jodie Thompson wanted to get married, but his $40-a-week salary from a Dallas ice-making firm was not enough to support a wife and family. From working on the ice docks and overseeing sales that summer, Thompson came upon the solution—chilled watermelons. No one had ever tried to sell chilled watermelons (or any other retail item for that matter) off the ice docks in Texas. Thompson's boss was initially very skeptical, but finally gave approval to try the idea. The venture was a success, and, by the end of the summer, Thompson had made $2,300.

In the summer of 1927, one of the dock managers of the Southland Ice Co. found that he could do a much brisker business by staying open 16 hours a day, seven days a week. He also noted that late-hour ice customers often complained about there being no place to pick up a loaf of bread or a bottle of milk. The dock manager persuaded Mr. Thompson, who by then was secretary-treasurer and a director of Southland Ice Co., to finance an inventory of bread, milk, and eggs and stack them on the dock. The items sold well, and shortly thereafter, when Thompson became president, all the company's ice docks were stocked with grocery items and the enterprising dock manager was assigned the task of finding new store sites. At the advice of a local advertising agency, Thompson named the stores 7-Eleven because they were open from 7:00 A.M. to 11:00 P.M.

By the mid-1950s, Southland had expanded to about 300 stores, mostly in Texas and Florida. As the United States became more urbanized, with many people commuting to work from the suburbs, Thompson and his two oldest

* Prepared by J. W. Brown, M.B.A., 1979, at The University of Tennesee, under the direction of Prof. John Thiel.

sons believed that Southland could move into and redefine the niche once dominated by mom-and-pop corner grocery stores; they felt that selling customers convenience in the form of accessible hours, handy locations, big parking lots, and well-selected merchandise would translate into a competitive edge and accelerate a shift of buyer patronage from the rapidly failing corner groceries to Southland's convenience food store concept. Southland's store expansion program began in earnest about 1960.

SOUTHLAND'S CURRENT BUSINESS STRUCTURE

In 1978, Southland's business interests were organized into three major groups. The Stores Group was the world's largest operator and franchiser of convenience stores with 6,599 7-Eleven stores in 42 states, the District of Columbia, and 5 provinces of Canada. Its three distribution centers served 3,916 7-Eleven stores with approximately 50 percent of their merchandise needs. Food Centers, located at each distribution center, prepared a variety of sandwiches for distribution to 7-Eleven and other customers. Other retail operations included 109 Gristede's and Charles & Company food stores and sandwich shops in metropolitan New York, 383 R. S. McColl confectionery, tobacco, and news stores, and 7 7-Eleven units in the United Kingdom. Southland also had an equity interest in 5 Super Siete stores in Mexico and 23 Naroppet stores in Sweden. An additional 279 7-Eleven stores were operated by area licensees in the United States, 559 in Japan, 5 in Canada, and 12 in Australia.

The Dairies Group, another part of the Southland Corporation, was a major processor of dairy products which were distributed under 11 well-known regional brand names in 34 states and the District of Columbia.

The Special Operations Group included the Chemical, Reddy Ice, Hudgins Truck Rental, and Tidel Systems which manufactured money handling devices for retail operations. In addition, Chief Auto Parts, a retail automobile supply chain of 119 stores in Southern California, was added to the Group in late 1978.

Exhibit 1 gives a breakout of the sales revenues and operating profits of these three groups. Exhibit 2 provides a corporatewide financial summary and Exhibit 3 is a condensed statement of consolidated earnings.

EXHIBIT 1
Revenues and Operating Profits by Major Business Segment (all dollar figures are in millions)

	1978		1977		1976		1975		1974	
Revenues:										
Stores Group	$2,791.0	90%	$2,271.9	89%	$1,857.5	88%	$1,556.0	87%	$1,405.4	87%
Dairies Group	253.4	8	236.5	9	236.1	11	208.3	12	184.0	11
Special Operations Group	40.9	2	33.7	2	26.0	1	25.0	1	22.6	2
Corporate	4.8	—	3.3	—	2.4	—	1.5	—	2.2	—
Total	$3,090.1	100%	$2,545.4	100%	$2,122.0	100%	$1,790.8	100%	$1,614.2	100%
Operating profits:										
Stores Group	$ 142.7	92%	$ 115.7	90%	$ 92.3	86%	$ 80.8	88%	$ 68.5	85%
Dairies Group	6.7	4	6.0	5	8.6	8	10.1	11	8.1	10
Special Operations Group	6.0	4	6.7	5	6.4	6	.9	1	4.0	5
Total	$ 155.4	100%	$ 128.4	100%	$ 107.3	100%	$ 91.8	100%	$ 80.6	100%

Source: Company records.

EXHIBIT 2
Southland Corporation Financial Summary

	1978	1977	1976	1975	1974
Operations (Note 1):					
Total revenues (in 000s)	$3,090,094	$2,545,415	$2,122,023	$1,790,805	$1,614,188
Increase over prior year	21.40%	19.95%	18.50%	10.94%	15.47%
Net earnings (in 000s)	$57,097	$45,317	$37,849	$32,068	$27,167
Increase over prior year	25.99%	19.73%	18.03%	18.04%	25.85%
Per revenue dollar	1.85%	1.78%	1.78%	1.79%	1.68%
Return on beginning shareholders' equity	17.30%	15.62%	14.56%	13.72%	13.16%
Assets employed (Note 1):					
Working capital (in 000s)	$141,633	$136,693	$101,536	$80,196	$72,495
Current ratio	1.54	1.66	1.63	1.58	1.55
Property, plant, and equipment including					
capital leases (net) (in 000s)	$677,284	$567,442	$506,190	$447,392	$406,486
Depreciation and amortization (in 000s)	67,724	61,735	55,029	47,974	43,078
Total assets (in 000s)	1,134,476	942,531	799,261	696,107	639,599
Capitalization (Note 1):					
Long-term debt (in 000s)	$261,460	$195,520	$153,093	$119,911	$105,609
Capital lease obligations (in 000s)	211,342	192,547	178,556	163,380	155,918
Shareholders' equity (in 000s)	374,467	329,952	290,142	259,940	233,659
Total capitalization (in 000s)	847,269	718,019	621,791	543,231	495,186
Shareholders' equity to total capitalization	44.20%	45.95%	46.66%	47.85%	47.19%

Per share data (Notes 1 and 2):

Primary earnings	$2.83	$2.26	$1.92	$1.63	$1.42
Earnings assuming full dilution	2.74	2.19	1.85	1.58	1.35
Cash dividends	.68	.55	.44	.36	.30
Shareholders' equity	$18.55	$16.48	$14.68	$13.23	$12.21

Other data:

Cash dividends (in 000s)	$13,627	$10,961	$8,660	$7,033	$5,834
Dividends as a percent of earnings (Note 1)	23.87%	24.19%	22.88%	21.93%	21.47%
Stock dividends	3%	3%	3%	3%	3%
Average shares outstanding (Note 3)	20,181,879	20,015,512	19,761,788	19,642,947	19,137,414
Average diluted shares (Note 3)	21,129,981	21,028,143	20,911,047	20,883,719	20,854,737
Market price range (Note 3)					
High	$33¾	$25⅞	$26⅛	$26¼	$18⅞
Low	21½	19¼	19⅛	14	11⅜
Year-end	26¾	24⅝	25½	20⅜	14¼
Number of shareholders	8,627	8,764	8,881	9,093	9,351
Number of employees	37,000	34,000	31,000	28,600	28,200

Notes:
(1) The years 1974 through 1977 have been restated for the change in the method of accounting for leases to comply with the privisions of Statement of Financial Accounting Standards No. 13 which was adopted early in accordance with the requirements of the Securities and Exchange Commission
(2) Based on average shares outstanding adjusted for stock dividends
(3) Adjusted for stock dividends
Source: *1978 Annual Report.*

EXHIBIT 3

Consolidated Statement of Earnings (all figures are in 000s of dollars except the per share data)

	1978	1977	1976	1975	1974
Revenues:					
Net sales	$3,076,532	$2,536,109	$2,115,769	$1,787,928	$1,609,257
Other income	13,562	9,306	6,254	2,877	4,931
	$3,090,094	2,545,415	2,122,023	1,790,805	1,614,188
Cost of sales and expenses:					
Cost of goods sold, including buying and occupancy expenses	$2,311,024	1,903,791	1,577,141	1,323,799	1,184,835
Selling, general, and administrative expenses	619,519	510,337	435,687	374,234	348,797
Interest expense	15,804	13,540	9,707	7,936	8,674
Imputed interest expense on capital lease obligations	19,325	18,064	15,388	13,969	12,982
Contributions to employees savings and profit sharing plan	11,714	9,726	8,346	6,995	5,899
	$2,977,386	2,455,458	2,046,269	1,726,933	1,561,187
Earnings before income taxes	$ 112,708	$ 89,957	75,754	63,872	53,001
Income taxes	55,611	44,640	37,905	31,804	25,834
Net earnings	$ 57,097	$ 45,317	$ 37,849	$ 32,068	$ 27,167
Per share					
Primary earnings	$2.83	$2.26	$1.92	$1.63	$1.42
Earnings assuming full dilution	$2.74	$2.19	$1.85	$1.58	$1.35

Source: *1978 Annual Report.*

CUSTOMER PROFILE OF SOUTHLAND'S 7-ELEVEN STORES

Approximately 5.4 million people patronized 7-Eleven stores daily in 1978. Based upon a study it conducted that year, Southland came up with a profile of its customers:

69.8 percent male
80.2 percent in 18–49 age group
80.9 percent live/work in area
4.3 average trips a week
30.1 percent shop weekends
50.2 percent shop 1 P.M. to 10 P.M.
$1.54 average purchase
822 customers daily per store

On the average, the typical customer spent less than $2—and three to four minutes—at the store, and often made at least one unplanned impulse purchase. Though these small unplanned purchases did not amount to much extra expense for the individual customer, they resulted in significant extra sales and profits to Southland, given that over five million customers a day were involved.

According to a reporter for *The Wall Street Journal:*

> Southland's 7-Elevens are successors of the old-fashioned mom-and-pop grocery, but they prosper by catering to the modern urge for instant gratification. Their customers fill their pantries at the supermarket but dash instead to the closest 7-Eleven to fill their latest desire for, say, cigarets or cold beer. Indeed, well over half the goods a 7-Eleven sells are consumed within 30 minutes . . .[1]

The same article quoted a 7-Eleven customer who lived in Dallas:

> I usually stop by on the way to work to get a roll, in the afternoon to pick up a TV dinner and sometimes during the day to get a coke. I'm a bachelor and it's quick and convenient.

This view reflected management's own perceptions that Southland was really in the convenience business rather than in the retail grocery business.

STORE GROWTH AND LOCATIONS

Southland's management looked upon convenience as "giving customers what they want, when they want it, where they want it." As a consequence, in 1978, 5,407 of Southland's 6,599 7-Elevens were open around the clock and 91 percent were open beyond the traditional 7 A.M. to 11 P.M. hours. Moreover, Southland emphasized easily accessible neighborhood locations and quick, friendly service; its product lines included popular fast foods selections and, at 30 percent of its locations, self-serve gasoline.

---

[1] Gerald F. Seib, "Despite High Prices and Sparse Selection, 7-Eleven Stores Thrive," *The Wall Street Journal*, May 1, 1979, p. 1.

In recent years, Southland has opened about 500 new 7-Eleven stores per year. The net gain in stores has been smaller, however, because population shifts, changes in traffic patterns, lease expirations, and relocations to newly available and more desirable sites have resulted in some existing stores being closed. The number of store openings and closings since 1972 are shown in the table below:

	New Stores Opened	Existing Stores Closed	Total 7-Eleven Stores
1972	424	83	4,455
1973	426	80	4,801
1974	n.a.	n.a.	5,171
1975	566	158	5,579
1976	528	154	5,953
1977	658	254	6,357
1978	550	308	6,599

Southland used a meticulous store site selection system; the primary criteria included such factors as (1) the traffic count in front of the site, (2) the ease with which passing cars could enter and leave the site, (3) the site's visibility from the street or road, (4) the number of people living within a one-mile radius, (5) the site's proximity to apartments, subdivisions, and high-traffic commercial establishments, (6) the adequacy of parking space, and (7) whether the site was a "natural" stopping-off point in the traffic flow by the site. To make sure its small 2,400-square-foot stores were readily seen from approaching traffic, they were carefully positioned in a heavy traffic area where they could be seen easily and were convenient to passers-by. Traffic patterns and flows were so crucial that stores had failed because a street was made one-way or because the opening of new streets and subdivisions had shifted traffic away from a site. Southland extensively studied potential sites and used a computer to estimate a proposed store's sales for its first five years.

John Thompson, Southland chairman, recently indicated that when a store starts looking like a loser, "We would rather close then and take our licks." The poor performers were identified by computerized analysis; by merely punching the store number into a computer terminal, executives could call up on a terminal display the store's current sales and earnings and tell how close it was to its budget. The company's management kept a close check on each store's operating performance.

In 1977, Southland started opening central-city stores. Located in high-density metropolitan residential areas, Southland saw them as filling a genuine need for walking customers. The company now has central-city stores in Philadelphia, Boston, San Francisco, and New York City; more are planned. According to Thompson, the central-city stores "open up a whole new market area we haven't yet been able to serve. We will attempt to build and merchandise stores according to their neighborhoods.

PRODUCT LINES AND MERCHANDISING

Southland continually experimented with the product mix offered in the stores. Some products, like the frozen concoction "Slurpee," became huge successes. Others, like 7-Eleven beer, turned out to be quiet flops.

One Southland executive stated, "There's little risk involved in experimenting. We have a built-in market base of 5 million customers a day. Things that don't work out we can throw out after a week or two. Things that catch on in one store we can try nationwide. Our computers in Dallas can tell us overnight about any new market trends."[2]   7-Eleven stores carried 3,000 different items, about 23 percent of them Southland's own house brands. The larger percentage of brands available in a 7-Eleven store were nationally recognized brands; however, each item was located in a space predetermined by a Southland computer in Dallas. One Southland executive indicated:

> There is no room to store a lot of different brands of the same product. Our customers don't have time to make choices anyway. We usually put on our shelves only the top one or two sellers of every product line and we put them in the area of the store where we think the customer would like to find them. It's all been researched and market tested. I can walk into most stores blind-folded and find any item you want.[3]

Through 1977, Southland's biggest selling item was tobacco—cigarettes primarily—followed closely by groceries, beer and wine, soft drinks, nonfood items such as magazines and Kleenex, and dairy products (see Exhibit 4). However, tobacco products dropped from number one in 1978, the change primarily due to increased gasoline sales. 7-Elevens have at times sold shotgun shells, television tubes, watermelons, and cancer insurance. Among the stores' best selling items today are fast-food sandwiches, disposable diapers, and *Playboy* magazines (of which 7-Eleven sell far more than any other retailer). In general, the items carried were products that would be needed on a fill-in basis or else bought on impulse.

By the end of 1978, self-service gasoline accounted for 60 percent of all gasoline sales in the United States and showed every indication of increasing beyond that figure, according to industry sources. In response to this demand, 7-Eleven provided self-service gasoline at 1,857 locations. A substantial increase in volume at existing units, as well as the addition of gasoline at 284 stores during 1978, resulted in a 70 percent gasoline sales increase for the

---

[2] "7-Eleven Creates a Mood of Convenience at a Price," *The Washington Star*, November 27, 1978.

[3] Ibid.

EXHIBIT 4
7-Eleven Store Sales by Principal Product Category*

	1978	1977	1976	1975	1974
Groceries	13.4%	14.0%	14.6%	15.3%	17.1%
Gasoline	13.4	9.8	6.8	3.9	2.7
Tobacco products	12.9	14.2	14.7	15.6	15.7
Beer/wine	12.9	13.7	14.4	14.8	14.1
Soft drinks	10.9	11.0	10.7	11.5	11.5
Nonfoods	9.4	9.9	10.2	9.5	9.3
Dairy products	8.9	9.3	9.6	9.5	10.5
Other food items	5.5	4.7	4.7	4.2	3.9
Candy	4.7	5.0	5.4	5.7	5.3
Baked goods	4.6	5.0	5.3	5.7	5.9
Health/beauty aids	3.4	3.4	3.6	3.9	4.0
Total	100.0%	100.0%	100.0%	100.0%	100.0%

* The Company does not record sales by product lines but estimates the percentage of convenience store sales by principal product category based upon total store purchases.
Source: *1978 Annual Report.*

year. The availability of gasoline also led to the generation of additional sales, as more than 30 percent of 7-Eleven's gasoline customers in 1978 purchased other merchandise.

One merchandising trend of particular import was that of adding higher-margin items to each store's product line to try to boost store profitability. Fast-food items like sandwiches, pizza, soup, coffee, fruit punch, and draft soda (like "Slurpee") carried gross margins in the 40 percent range. Nonfood impulse items, which had margins in the 35 percent range, were also being added. Both compared favorably with Southland's recent storewide margins of 25 percent to 27 percent. Southland's fast food division, which in 1978 experienced a 30.5 percent sales gain, produced approximately 30 sandwiches marketed under the 7-Eleven and Landshire labels. These were distributed either fresh or flash-frozen for reheating in microwave or infrared ovens. The division in 1978 sold approximately 80 million sandwiches to 7-Eleven stores, other retailers, and institutional customers; it also furnished 7-Eleven stores with more than 1 million gallons of Slurpee syrup.

Southland's management was optimistic about the potential for increasing its share of the food-away-from-home market. Projections called for this segment to increase its share of the consumer's total food dollar owing to greater numbers of women entering the workforce, higher family incomes, smaller families, and more single people—all of which acted to reinforce the lifestyle where a higher percent of disposable personal income would be spent for food prepared outside the home.

PRICING

According to Southland's marketing research director, people just about everywhere are willing to pay a little extra for the convenience a 7-Eleven offers—especially when the consumer is hit by an urge to buy. Most of the items in a 7-Eleven are therefore prices some 10 to 15 percent above the levels in most supermarkets. But, as shown in Exhibit 5, a few items, like milk, are priced more competitively.

As one 7-Eleven customer put it:

> There's a lot I don't like about 7-Eleven stores. They look tacky. They charge too much. They sell stuff that isn't good for you, and they always seem to be getting robbed. But yes, I do shop there. They're so convenient.[4]

So far, though, no consumer activist groups had targeted 7-Eleven for either its high prices or its line of merchandise.

EXHIBIT 5
Sample Comparisons of Prices at 7-Eleven Stores and Safeway Supermarkets in 1978

Item	7-Eleven	Safeway
Cascade (20 oz.)	$ .98	$ .89
Shredded wheat (12 oz.)	.93	.75
Tuna (chunk light, 6 oz.)	1.19	.99
Campbell's chicken noodle soup	.36	.30
Jello instant pudding (4 oz.)	.40	.35
Log Cabin maple syrup (12 oz.)	1.15	.93
Hellman's mayonnaise (16 oz.)	1.23	.99
Franco-American spaghetti (14 oz.)	.39	.34
Domino sugar (5 lbs.)	1.59	1.49
Wesson oil (16 oz.)	1.19	.99
V-8 juice (46 oz.)	1.09	.85
Maxwell House instant coffee (6 oz.)	4.29	3.79
Kellogg's corn flakes (12 oz.)	.85	.69
Hydrox cream-filled cookies	1.19	1.09
6-pack of Budweiser (12 oz.)	2.33	1.99
6-pack of Schlitz Light	2.34	1.99
Gallo burgundy wine	2.23	1.99
6-pack of Pepsi (16 oz.)	2.02	1.89
7up (32 oz.)	.71	.63
Hostess cup cakes (2)	.35	.33
White bread (22 oz.)	.73	.40
Hostess powdered doughnuts (12)	.99	.99
Dozen eggs (grade A large)	.89	.79
Minute Maid orange juice (quart bottle)	.85	.75
Philadelphia cream cheese (3 oz.)	.43	.34
Salt (26 oz.)	.35	.30
Bayer aspirin (50 tablets	1.19	.89
Heinz ketchup (14 oz.)	.79	.61
French's mustard (9 oz.)	.55	.43
Carton of Winston cigarettes	4.79	4.49
10 Briggs hot dogs	1.69	1.39
Half-gallon milk	.91	.91
Total (32 items)	$40.97	$35.55

Source: *The Washington Star,* November 26, 1978.

---

[4] "Southland is the Best Example I Know of Modern Capitalism," *The Washington Star,* November 26, 1978.

Southland seemed to have discovered, and was helping perpetuate, its own market segment—a world of customers caught in a time crisis, willing to pay extra to save themselves a few seconds waiting in line. A Wall Street analyst said:

> It is perplexing to us why Southland's revenue growth has accelerated when rising prices have stretched the consumer's budget to a considerable extent. Perhaps it is time rather than money which is the precious commodity to most Americans at present. The appeal of convenience stores has nothing to do with price. It has to do with people's lifestyles and their constant need for fill-ins. The more tightly the pocketbook is pinched, the less frequently the housewife shops at her supermarket, and the more need she has for last minute fill-ins.[5]

FRANCHISE ACTIVITIES

Of the 6,599 7-Eleven stores operating at the end of 1978, 4,056 were company operated and 2,543 were franchised. The typical franchise agreement allowed for the company to lease the property and equipment to a franchisee in exchange for a fee of $10,000 plus roughly half the store's profits. Southland allowed new franchises a 120-day grace period to pull out of their contracts without losing their initial investments. Most of the franchisees were couples with children and the family typically worked in the store.

SOUTHLAND'S ADVERTISING FOR 7-ELEVENS

In January 1978, Southland introduced its first prime-time network 7-Eleven commercial to the largest audience in television history prior to Super Bowl XII. Product awareness messages featuring Hot-to-Go coffee, Egg Hamlette, Chili Dog, Slurpee, or sunglasses reached 58 million households each broadcast week. In addition to the network television commercials, advertisements were aired on approximately 500 radio stations and published in more than 200 newspapers nationwide.

During 1978, broadcasts remained the company's major advertising vehicle with spot radio getting 30 percent, network television 35 percent, spot television 25 percent, newspapers 4 percent, and outdoor advertising 6 percent. Total television advertising increased 22 percent during the first half of 1978, compared with the same period in 1977.

7-Eleven stores are decidedly male-oriented. However, due to the increased buying power of women in today's society, Southland's advertising had begun to be geared specifically toward women.

---

[5] "7-Eleven Creates a Mood of Convenience."

DISTRIBUTION CENTERS

Southland's 7-Eleven stores were served by distribution centers in Florida, Virginia, and Texas that were specifically designed to meet the needs of 7-Eleven for a reliable and efficient source of supply, frequent delivery, and a high in-stock position. The system also enabled the stores to have the flexibility to respond quickly to customer preferences and seasonal changes in demand, as well as to implement promotional programs and introduce new products. The centers serviced 3,916 7-Eleven stores at the end of 1978.

Store stock lists, which are compiled and updated monthly by computer, were tailored to the merchandise specifications of each store, enabling personnel to easily determine their restocking needs. The store orders were then transmitted through a network of computer terminals located at 7-Eleven district offices and connected to the computer center in Dallas, which assimilated the orders and transmitted them to printing terminals at the appropriate distribution center. From these printed lists, the store orders were then "picked" and assembled for delivery. Custom-designed trucks with separate compartments for dry, chilled, and frozen merchandise followed computer-planned routes to achieve maximum savings of energy and time.

Southland's concept of delivering prepriced merchandise in less-than-case-quantities eliminated overstocking, assured fresh merchandise on the store shelves at all times, promoted more productive use of selling space, and improved store profitability. The importance of stores not having to order full cases of merchandise was highlighted by Southland's manager of information services: "Can you imagine how long it would take to sell 48 cans of tomato paste in a 7-Eleven? Now we can give them three cans and keep it fresh." During 1978, the computerized inventory control system enabled the stores to achieve an average inventory turnover of 23 times while maintaining a 99 percent order fill rate.

In many cases, store managers did not even bother to order groceries; that was done by warehouse employees whose only job was visiting each 7-Eleven twice a month to take inventory and order merchandise.[6] The computer then took over, sending hundreds of orders to a warehouse, deciding which orders to ship on what truck, and telling employees how to stack goods inside the truck to fill it to the brim. The trucks were able to begin delivering only hours after the warehouse got the order. Southland's computer also helped analyze the layout of merchandise in the store—by keeping track of what items sold well in which shelf locations.

FINANCING

The long-term policy of Southland was to finance expansion from retained earnings, although other methods of raising funds were used when neces-

---

[6] Seib, "Despite High Prices."

sary. In late 1978, the company offered $50 million of unsecured 9⅜ percent Sinking Fund Debentures, due December 15, 2003. These debentures, as well as a 1977 8⅜ percent issue, were rated A by both Moody's and Standard & Poor's and were listed on the New York Stock Exchange.

In April 1978, the annual cash dividend rate was increased 20 percent to 72¢ per share. Cash dividends have been paid each year since 1957, and the annual rate has been raised seven times in the last eight years, providing shareholders an average compound growth rate of 20.7 percent. In addition, for the 13th consecutive year, a 3 percent stock dividend was distributed.

In recent years, Southland has been forced to increase its debt burden to finance corporate expansion—especially the growth in the number of 7-Eleven stores. To open a new store, Southland had to invest more than $180,000. This included land costs of about $50,000, a store building costing an average of $70,000, equipment installation of $46,000, and initial inventory costs of $18,000 to $25,000. In the case of franchised stores, Southland advanced most of the up-front investment, with the exception of the $10,000 franchise fee.

The capital costs of financing 400–500 new stores per year had exceeded Southland's retained earnings and internal cash flow capabilities during recent years; the resulting debt increases were in such an amount as to cause a steady decline in Southland's equity capitalization percentage (see Exhibit 2).

Although a 41-year-old Southland official expressed the view that the company would be adding a net of 300–400 stores per year for the rest of his lifetime, it was not clear that Southland could continue to finance such an ambitious store expansion program without adversely affecting earnings. Higher site and construction costs and higher interest rates were becoming significant factors; so was the move to increase store size from 2,400 square feet to the 2,700 to 3,000 square feet range. In 1977, Southland spent an estimated $75.3 million to open 658 stores; in 1978, the figure exceeded $95 million for 550 new stores.

Nor was it clear that such a rate of expansion was consistent with market opportunities. Already there were over 33,000 convenience food stores in the United States—approximately one for every 6,600 persons. Prime sites were becoming hard to find and were increasingly expensive. According to one industry trade publication, several factors were at work:

> Munford executives, like most in the business, have set their sights on prime corner locations with high visibility and heavy traffic counts. Because Munford is selecting former gas station sites for its new units, traffic counts have replaced household density, once the sacred cow of the industry's site selection procedure.
>
> In fact, one Majik Market is making $7,000 per week in food sales—the industry average is $5,257—without a house within a five-mile radius of the store.
>
> Secondary sites, mainly at the mouths of suburban subdivisions and in

shopping malls, are a thing of the past. "The suburban, residential convenience store is doomed," explains Tom Ewens, vice president of real estate for Houston-based National Convenience Stores Inc., "because the sales volume that those units produce simply can't keep pace with the costs of land, construction and operation."

But the recently sought-after, first-rate corner spots are getting harder for convenience store chains to find due, in part, to increased competition from other retailers for the same locations. As store sizes creep up to the 3,000-square-foot mark, and lot sizes expand to allow for increased gas and parking facilities, convenience stores are looking for roughly the same size lot that a fast-food unit, drug store, bank or gas station might want. This means that the sector's traditional strength of flexibility in site selection is being somewhat impaired.

And in some markets, notably parts of Arizona, Texas, and Florida, where convenience stores already account for 10 percent–12 percent of grocery sales, there just aren't that many choice spots to be found.

John C. Nichols II, senior vice president and chief financial officer of Convenient Industries of America Inc., reveals that the Louisville, Kentucky-based operator of Convenient Food Marts is having to look at more sites today than in the past to find good ones, like its industry counterparts. Three years ago a site might have been selected from two or three. Now it's more likely that seven or eight are considered before a choice is made.

What's happening is that convenience stores are pinning their hopes for higher sales volumes and profits on primary locations, while coping with higher real estate and operations costs than they faced at former sites.

This means that convenience stores' profit and loss statements will likely get tighter and tighter, the line between a winning and losing location more thinly drawn.[7]

Exhibits 6 and 7 contain additional financial data on Southland.

RECENT TRENDS IN THE CONVENIENCE FOOD INDUSTRY

In 1957, the industry consisted of 500 stores with an annual volume of $75 million. Ten years later, there were 8,000 convenience stores with combined sales of $1.3 billion. In 1978, the corresponding figures were some 33,000 stores and an annual sales volume of $8.7 billion. Average annual sales growth during the last five years was about 17 percent. Sales volumes in convenience food stores were approaching 5 percent of total U.S. grocery sales, up from 1.7 percent in 1967. Many industry sources predicted favorable sales growth for convenience food stores for the years ahead. Sales revenues were projected to increase at a 15 percent annual rate and volume was expected to reach 8 percent of total grocery sales by 1980.

For the extra convenience and service they offered, convenience food stores took higher mark-ups on the items they sold. Whereas conventional

[7] "What's Down the Road for Convenience Stores," *Chain Store Age Executive*, June 1979, pp. 23–24.

EXHIBIT 6

SOUTHLAND CORPORATION
Consolidated Balance Sheets

	December 31 1978	December 31 1977
Assets		
Current assets:		
Cash and short-term investments	$ 82,745,504	$ 65,903,801
Accounts and notes receivable	78,968,103	75,171,378
Inventories	161,254,967	126,913,578
Deposits and prepaid expenses	26,777,392	21,436,624
Investment in properties	55,857,419	53,319,492
Total current assets	$ 405,603,385	$342,744,873
Investments in affiliates	27,364,352	26,717,136
Property, plant, and equipment	479,554,364	389,251,583
Capital leases	197,730,040	178,190,671
Other assets	24,223,652	5,627,054
	$1,134,475,793	$942,531,317
Liabilities and Shareholders' Equity		
Current liabilities:		
Accounts payable and accrued expenses	$ 211,920,848	$168,894,391
Income taxes	18,636,987	15,481,417
Long-term debt due within one year	13,254,868	4,142,055
Capital lease obligations due within one year	20,157,217	17,533,856
Total current liabilities	$ 263,969,920	$206,051,719
Deferred credits	23,235,908	18,460,424
Long-term debt	261,460,472	195,520,000
Capital lease obligations	211,342,074	192,546,677
Committments for operating leases		
Shareholders' equity		
Common stock $1 par value, authorized 40 million shares, issued and outstanding 20,200,557 and 19,557,287 shares	202,006	195,573
Additional capital	242,339,822	223,499,143
Retained earnings	131,925,591	106,257,781
	374,467,419	329,952,497
	$1,134,475,793	$942,531,317

Source: *1978 Annual Report.*

supermarkets had an average gross margin of 22.4 percent in 1978, the gross margins in convenience food stores were typically 28 to 30 percent. Exhibit 8 gives a breakdown of the 1976 gross margin, expenses, and net profits for the representative convenience food store.

Recently, industry observers had become concerned with the increased competition that supermarkets seemed to be initiating. Specifically, the trends of many supermarkets toward longer hours, Sunday openings, and express-lane checkouts had the potential of eroding the market shares of convenience food stores. In response, some convenience chains were keeping prices on selected high volume items as close to those of supermarkets as possible. Munford's Majik Market stores, Southland's biggest competitor,

EXHIBIT 7

SOUTHLAND CORPORATION
Consolidated Statements of Changes in Financial Position
Years ended December 31, 1978 and 1977

	1978	1977
Sources of working capital:		
From operations:		
Net earnings	$ 57,097,109	$ 45,317,241
Expenses charged to earnings which did not require outlay of working capital:		
Depreciation and amortization	46,839,875	41,991,861
Amortization of capital leases	20,884,330	19,743,097
Deferred income taxes and other credits	6,552,597	3,415,874
Working capital provided from operations:	$131,373,911	$110,468,073
Long-term debt	70,658,506	61,534,160
Capital lease obligations	41,907,748	37,409,857
Retirements and sales of property	13,555,200	12,774,857
Retirements and sales of capital leases	1,397,049	6,191,948
Issuance of common stock		
Conversion of notes	—	2,690,000
Acquisitions	—	2,310,000
Key employees incentive plan	470,992	462,278
Employee stock options	704,463	97,343
	$260,067,869	$233,938,516
Uses of working capital:		
Property, plant, and equipment	141,438,084	96,324,184
Capital leases	41,907,748	37,409,857
Reduction of capital lease obligations	23,112,351	23,419,196
Payment of long-term debt	4,718,034	16,862,491
Cash dividends	13,627,443	10,960,976
Net noncurrent assets of businesses purchased for stock and cash	29,180,394	9,111,552
Retirement of long-term debt upon conversion of notes	—	2,690,000
Investments in affiliates	647,216	1,061,359
Other	366,089	836,640
Cash paid in lieu of fractional shares on stock dividend	130,199	105,267
	$255,127,558	$198,781,522
Increase in working capital	$ 4,940,311	$ 35,156,994
Changes in working capital:		
Increases in current assets:		
Cash and short-term investments	$ 16,841,703	$ 39,504,544
Accounts and notes receivable	3,796,725	7,788,618
Inventories	34,341,389	21,884,637
Deposits and prepaid expenses	5,340,768	1,482,830
Investment in properties	2,537,927	9,342,429
	$ 62,858,512	$ 80,003,058
Increases (decreases) in current liabilities:		
Accounts payable and accrued expenses	43,026,457	38,624,253
Income taxes	3,155,570	4,442,417
Long-term debt due within one year	9,112,813	(611,614)
Capital lease obligations due within one year	2,623,361	2,391,008
	$ 57,918,201	$ 44,846,064
Increase in working capital	$ 4,940,311	$ 35,156,994

Source: *1978 Annual Report.*

EXHIBIT 8
Breakdown of 1976 Margins, Expenses, and Net Profit for the Representative Convenience Store*

Sales	100.0%
Cost of goods sold	71.2
Gross margin	28.8
Employee wages	10.6
Employee benefits	1.9
Advertising and promotion	0.7
Property rentals	3.3
Utility expenses	3.2
Other expenses	5.7
Total expenses.....................	25.4
Net profit before taxes	3.4

* Determined by trade sources from industrywide data.
Source: *Convenience Stores,* September–October 1977, p. 44.

recently adjusted the prices of some 25 of its best-selling items to be competitive with supermarket prices.

In addition to competition from supermarkets, competition from other retail sectors was emerging. Fast-food chains, liquor-delis, gas stations carrying food items, and discount and drug outlets with newly added food items were a new competitive threat. These types of firms were expected to expand their convenience food lines and to begin to carry high-traffic nonfood items. Furthermore, many of the drug stores were staying open longer hours and opting for locations with many of the same features of convenience stores.

7-ELEVEN'S COMPETITORS IN CONVENIENCE FOODS

7-Eleven in 1978 was more than seven times the size of Munford, its nearest competitor. (Munford is the only other convenience chain listed on the New York Stock Exchange.) In recent years, while 7-Eleven had been booming, Munford had been having more than its share of problems. While in the process of closing marginal and unprofitable units, earnings and sales for Munford suffered accordingly. In addition to their stores group, Munford experienced problems with Farmbest Foods, a dairy operation acquired in 1975. The Farmbest operation lost money in 1977 due to unsettled industry conditions in Florida and Alabama.

A new merchandising concept being tried by Munford, in order to catch up with the industry, was to join forces with major oil companies such as Texaco, Gulf, and Amoco by putting Munford's Majik Market convenience stores at existing gasoline station sites. The executives of Munford felt that there were many advantages for this concept, because they were convinced

EXHIBIT 9
Sales and Earnings of Convenience Chains

Company	Sales ($000)			Earnings ($000)		
	1978	1977	1976	1978	1977	1976
Southland	$3,089,000	$2,544,414	$2,121,146	$57,000	$45,348	$40,277
Munford	378,950e	340,174	334,770	6,090	(770)	3,427
Circle K	363,783	302,603	262,362	8,196	6,912	5,122
National Convenience Stores	263,705	233,208	212,606	5,011	3,536	2,652
Utotem Group	221,423	206,041	192,499	9,658	8,788	8,822
Convenient Industries of America	177,732	146,598	123,368	1,148	896	857
Sunshine-Jr. Stores	93,553	81,225	68,899	1,622	1,432	1,387
Shop & Go	82,729	70,136	60,780	2,271	1,655	1,650
Hop-In Food Stores	31,714	22,739	14,077	658	392	280
Lil' Champ	22,727	21,006	18,807	778	647	592
Grand total	$4,725,316	$3,968,144	$3,409,314	$92,432	$68,836	$65,066

Note: Include sales and earnings from operations other than convenience stores where applicable.
e Estimated.
Source: *Progressive Grocer*, April 1978.

that the consumers were accepting the idea of buying gasoline at convenience stores very well.

Another competitive factor in the convenience store field was Circle K. For a period of four years through 1977, Circle K virtually halted its store expansion program in favor of remodeling and renovating older, existing stores. The Circle K chain, like Munford and others, entered the gasoline business, but with a basic difference from Munford. Circle K's strategy was to retain its recognition and image as convenience first and gasoline second. For this reason, Circle K chose to add gasoline pumps to their existing stores, not vice versa, as Munford did. Circle K planned to add 60 to 70 stores a year through the mid-1980s.

A third competitor of 7-Eleven was the National Convenience Stores chain. In 1976, a young, dynamic man named Pete Van Horn became president of National Convenience. Not being fettered by the bonds of tradition in the industry, Van Horn slashed the number of stores, lowered personnel turnover, increased sales in remaining stores and, in general, put National Convenience on a sound footing. Van Horn was anxious to try out his ideas about store layout, merchandising and expansion; his goal at the end of 1977 was to double earnings in the next four years.[8]

Exhibit 9 presents comparative sales and earnings for ten leading convenience food chains. Exhibit 10 contains per store sales and profit statistics for the 1974–1978 period.

EXHIBIT 10
Average Sales and Profit Statistics for Top Ten Publicly Held Convenience Food Store Chains

	1978	1977	1976	1975	1974
Yearly sales per store	$274,115	$263,895	$240,828	$232,140	$213,89
Weekly sales per store	$5,257	$5,061	$4,606	$4,452	$4,113
Profit on pretax sales	3.65%	3.48%	3.64%	3.32%	3.39%
Profit on aftertax sales	1.98%	1.8%	1.92%	1.71%	1.77%
Yearly pretax profit per store	$10,026	$9,194	$8,762	$7,723	$7,242
Yearly aftertax profit per store	$5,431	$4,752	$4,523	$3,978	$3,789

Source: "Eighth Annual Dollars-per-Day Survey of Small Food Store Industry," as published in *Chain Store A Executive*, June 1979, p. 26.

SOUTHLAND'S DAIRIES AND SPECIAL OPERATIONS GROUPS

Initially, the Dairies and Special Operations groups were formed to vertically integrate their activities with 7-Eleven. The Dairies Group processed and distributed milk, ice cream, yogurt, juices, eggnog, dips, and toppings; in 1978, it served 5,295 of Southland's convenience stores and supplied 66 percent of all the dairy products sold in all 7-Eleven stores. The group

---

[8] "The Convenience Stores," *Financial World*, November 1, 1977.

included 28 processing plants and 86 distribution locations. However, more and more of the Dairies Group sales volume was coming from outside Southland. In 1978, 65 percent of the unit's $400 million sales revenues were to food retailers such as Denny's and Wendy's. The expansion of sales to outside companies was being pursued through the development of new high-margin novelty items such as sundae-style yogurts, cheeses, and frozen dairy items like Big Deal, Gram Daddy, and Big Wheel.

A similar trend was evident in the special operations group. While this division supplied other Southland units with food ingredients, ice, Slurpee concentrate, preservatives, sanitizers, and cleaning agents, in 1978 a total of 72 percent of sales were to outside customers. In 1978, the chemicals unit was expanded by the acquisition of a New Jersey fine chemicals plant; this acquisition allowed Southland to market a broader line of products to customers in the agricultural and pharmaceutical industries. The division's Hudgins Truck Rental unit was expanding its efforts to provide full-maintenance truck leasing to national and regional customers, as well as to Southland operations; in 1978, its outside sales were up 10 percent and accounted for 68 percent of revenues. In 1978, a new unit called Tidel Systems was added to the special operations group; it manufactured an innovative money-handling device designed to reduce losses from robberies and to increase store-site cash handling efficiency. While Southland planned to install the device at its 7-Eleven stores, there was an even greater potential for sales to other retailers and a nationwide sales and maintenance organization was being assembled.

THE ACQUISITION OF CHIEF AUTO PARTS

In December 1978, at a cost of $20 million, Southland acquired the assets of Chief Auto Parts, a chain of 119 retail automobile supply stores in southern California. A typical Chief store was 2,000 square feet in size, open seven days a week, and located in a neighborhood shopping center close to homes or businesses. The stores sold approximately 7,500 replacement parts and accessories and carried both national brands and private-label products. The average purchase was $5 and a large percentage of sales were on weekends when most do-it-yourselfers had time to service their cars. Chief also had a modern warehouse in Los Angeles from which it supplied its stores.

There was some thought that the Chief acquisition signaled a move by Southland to diversify into small store retailing, particularly those kinds of retail businesses which had operating characteristics similar to those of 7-Eleven stores.

FUTURE OUTLOOK

Southland management's view of the future for its 7-Eleven stores was exemplified by John Thompson, chairman:

We believe that the growth opportunity in the convenience store area is great. I'm very bullish on the future. There are many parts in the U.S. that are not saturated with convenience stores, and I would say that Texas and Florida are the two most saturated areas. Even in those states we can go 20 to 40 more stores a year, depending on housing. But in the rest of the United States, there is relatively much less saturation, so that as far as we're concerned we think we can build 500-plus stores a year for a long time. Why, the Northeast is a great area. We haven't really saturated that market at all. And the Midwest? Well, we've hardly gotten started there. And California? Well sure we have 900 stores in California, but you can build forever in that state. I guess you could say the future for us looks marvelous.[9]

However, in 1979, several industry observers were taking a more cautious stance and asking if the industry was not on the verge of maturity.

---

[9] "Southland Is the Best Example."

11. Coca-Cola Wine Spectrum (A)*

Albert Killeen, general manager of Coca-Cola's newly formed Wine Spectrum division, was concerned about mounting delays in a "revolutionary" comparative advertising campaign for Taylor California Cellars wines. Not only was this the first major campaign of the Wine Spectrum division involving the California Cellars winery, the Taylor name, and bottling by Coca-Cola of New York's Franzia subsidiary, but issues had also arisen over the legality of comparative taste tests for wines. After three months of discussions with lawyers and federal officials, Mr. Killeen had still been unable to get a ruling. Basically, it all boiled down to: "Do we wait for, probably, another year or go ahead and risk legal actions?"

Prior to the 1977 acquisition of Taylor Wine Company by Coca-Cola, Inc., Taylor management had promoted the concept that wine was right for any time and any place in "Taylor territory." They had also worked to educate consumers to appreciate New York wines by using the "answer grape." Since California wines were blended into Taylor products, a later campaign used the term "Californewyork" to try to broaden the appeal of Taylor wines. However, Taylor's marketing organization had never seen wine commercials quite like the introductory campaign proposed by their new advertising agency (see Exhibit 1). The new ads were based on a comparative taste test which not only named Taylor California Cellars as the best, but named the competing wines.

The problem with the new ad campaign was that of determining whether comparative advertising of wine was allowed under federal regulations. The federal Bureau of Alcohol, Tobacco, and Firearms (BATF) had regulatory powers over the industry's advertising, but officials had refused to give any determination. The courts had also refused to hear the case prior to action being taken by Taylor. BATF was reviewing its regulations on the wine industry but contended that only after running the ads would competitors bring forward the evidence necessary for them to make their judgment. BATF would not protect Coca-Cola or Taylor from legal consequences should they be found in noncompliance with regulations. While it was generally known that misleading or disparaging ads were not permitted, specific

---

* Prepared by William R. Boulton and Phyllis G. Holland. Copyright © 1979 by University of Georgia. Reprinted by permission.

EXHIBIT 1
Comparative Taste Test Advertisement Script

Program: "San Francisco Wine Test"	*Client:* Taylor Wine Company

VIDEO	AUDIO
OPEN ON: Taster (male) inspecting glass and sniffing	*ANNOUNCER V/O:* a new California Rhine wine is judged against its competitors. Twenty-seven wine experts gather in San Francisco
CUT TO: MASTER SHOT	
TITLE: JULY 22, 1978	
CUT TO: Taster (male) sniffing	to compare four
TITLES:	
A-C. K. Mondavi Rhine B-Taylor California Cellars Rhine C-Almaden Mountain Rhine D-Inglenook Navalle Rhine	
CUT TO: Taster (male) sniffing	California Rhine wines.
CUT TO: Four glasses and hand writing	Which was judged best?
CUT TO: Tasters in foreground, Judge and Nationwide Consumer Testing Institute Representatives in background	"Ladies and gentlemen, the wine you have judged best is
TITLES: A, C, and D OUT REMAINING: B. Taylor California Cellars Rhine	Wine B."
CUT TO: Four glasses. Hand places Taylor bottle in front	*ANN'R V/O:* Wine B. New Taylor California Cellars Rhine
TITLE: OUT	Taylor California Cellars
TITLE: Taylor Label	
CUT TO: Glass A	
TITLE: C. K. Mondavi Rhine	*ANN'R V/O:* Judged better than C. K. Mondavi
Pan to: Glass C	
TITLE: Almaden Mountain Rhine	Better than Almaden
Pan to: Glass D	
TITLE: Inglenook Navalle Rhine	Better than Inglenook
CUT TO: Taylor Label	*TASTER (male) V/O:* "An interesting wine.
TITLE:	*ANN'R V/O:* But when you cost a little more, you better be better.

guidelines on comparative taste tests in wines were not expected for another year.

THE WINE INDUSTRY IN THE UNITED STATES

In 1972, wine prices were rising dramatically and there was great interest in entering the industry. New wine grape acreage soared, with more new acreage planted in 1971, 1972, and 1973 than the total of all previous plantings. In addition, speculators observed that foreign wines selling for $25 per case in the 1950s were selling for $500 to $1,000 per case and began to put bottles in storage. The 1972 vintage was bad and did not sell well, and the 1973 harvest was the largest in history. The increased supply led to a decline in prices which accelerated when the speculators put the hoarded wine on the market. By the time the first wine from the new plantings hit the market in 1974, inventories were at an all-time high and the oversupply was further increased by another large harvest in 1975. In 1972, the average return to a California grower per ton of grapes crushed was $217. In 1974 the return dropped to $131 and to $100 in 1975.[1]

By 1976 conditions were improving. Inventories were slowly being worked off and more grape vines were taken up than planted. Even though prices began to rise, producers were still cautious. In describing the future direction of the market, Taylor management indicated in 1976:

> In general, 1974 and 1975 were characterized by large grape harvests throughout the United States. It is believed that adverse weather conditions caused a smaller crop in 1976. However, increased grape harvests in the future may be anticipated as a result of substantial grape acreage which was planted in 1971 through 1974 and should mature approximately four years after planting. Grapes are a commodity which will continue to be affected by weather conditions, diseases and grower practices, which cause uncertainty for the crop until each annual harvest is near. Despite increases in many production costs, the abundance of grapes and large wine inventories have generally restricted wine price increases on an industrywide basis. Furthermore, as discretionary income is believed to impact directly on wine consumption, recent economic conditions have contributed to relatively level industry sales.

WINE CONSUMPTION IN THE UNITED STATES

Wine consumption in the United States was increasing both in absolute amounts and per capita. In 1977, 6 percent more wine entered distribution channels than in 1976 and the same advance was predicted for 1978. Wine consumption was 400 million gallons in 1977 or 1.85 gallons per capita, as compared to 1.7 gallons in 1976:

> Wine sales in the foreseeable future should grow 8 percent a year, versus less than 3 percent for distilled spirits, according to Marvin Shanken, editor of

---

[1] Gigi Mahon, "Everything's Coming Up Rosés," *Barron's*, vol. 56 (June 7, 1976), pp. 11–16.

Impact, a widely respected liquor industry newsletter (soft drink sales are growing 7 percent annually). By 1980, says Shanken, wines will overtake distilled spirits in gallons.[2]

Per capita consumption in the United States varied geographically, with the highest consuming states being on the east and west coasts. Highest per capita consumption was 5.41 gallons in Washington, D.C.—a far cry, though, from the Italian average of 26 gallons or the French average of 24. Twenty-two percent of the wine sold in the United States was sold in California, 10.6 percent in New York, 5.1 percent in Illinois, followed by New Jersey with 4.5 percent and Florida with 4.3 percent.

Wine consumption was greatest in the 21–40 age group (which was growing as a percentage of the population) and was also greater among the more affluent income groups. Factors underlying increased wine consumption were said to be a growing preference for lighter, drier beverages; the availability of broadcast media to efficiently create a nationwide market, and growing purchases by women. A *Forbes* article stated that wine is

> increasingly purchased by women right along with the groceries. According to *Progressive Grocer,* the trade publication, 35 percent of all wine is sold in supermarkets. In addition more wine (particularly dry white wine) is now being sipped before dinner—as a fashionable substitute for the Martini and Bloody Mary.[3]

WINE PRODUCTION IN THE UNITED STATES

In 1976 Taylor management noted several facts about U.S. wine production:

> California is the largest wine producing area in the United States, with New York State being the second largest producing area. Based upon the latest available industry estimates, California production increased 47 percent from 239.6 million gallons in 1969 to 351.9 million gallons in 1975. During this same period, wine production in New York increased approximately 32 percent from 26.3 million gallons to 34.7 million gallons. Based upon the most recent industry estimates, during 1975, 84 percent of U.S. wine produced (but not necessarily sold) was produced in California and 8 percent in New York. Taylor and many other non-California wine producers use California wines for blending purposes to achieve certain flavor characteristics.

In 1977 there were 615 wineries in 30 states, an increase of 41 percent from 435 in 1970. California had the largest number with 353, followed by New York with 39. Ohio, Oregon, Michigan, and Pennsylvania each had 16. Average production was 20,000 gallons per year as compared to Gallo's production of 100 million gallons annually. Many of the smaller wineries were still

---

[2] "Beverages: Basic Analysis," *Standard & Poor's Industry Surveys,* October 19, 1978, p. B-71.

[3] "Coke Takes a Champagne Chaser," *Forbes,* vol. 118 (October 15, 1976), p. 66.

EXHIBIT 2
Major U.S. Wineries

Company	Brands	Ownership (date of acquisition)	1977 Wine Sales ($000)
E&J Gallo	Gallo	Private	$370,000*
United Vintners	Colony Italian Swiss Colony Inglenook	Heublein (1969)	$201,751
Franzia-Mogen David	Franzia Mogen David	Coca-Cola Bottling (N.Y.) (1970, 1973)	$ 59,900
Almaden Vineyards	Almaden	National Distillers (1967)	$ 88,023
Canadaigua Wine Co.	Richard's Wild Irish Rose	Public	$ 35,605
The Taylor Wine Co.	Taylor Great Western	The Coca-Cola Co. (1976)	$ 59,600
Paul Masson Vineyards	Paul Masson	Seagram (1945)	$ 70,000†
Mont La Salle	Christian Brothers	Private	$ 50,000*

* Where companies are privately owned, sales figure is based on statement of owner.
† Casewriter's estimate

waiting for their first vintage. Exhibit 2 shows the ownership of major brands in the wine industry.

Independent wineries are seldom publicly held and are rapidly being acquired by large firms who are increasingly aggressive marketers. Profiles of major competitors are included in Exhibit 3. At the same time, small mom-

EXHIBIT 3
Profiles of Major Competitors in the Wine Industry

E&J Gallo

With a sales volume nearly double its closest competitor, Gallo has more influence in the wine industry than any other U.S. company. Because Gallo purchases 40 percent of the California grape harvest, the company is in the position of impacting grape prices throughout California. In addition to the winery, Gallo operations include vineyards, apple orchards, one of the West's biggest bottling plants, one of California's largest trucking companies, and several big wine distributors. The founders of the winery, Ernest and Julio Gallo, are active in the firm; Julio oversees the wine-making and Ernest looks after everything else.

Gallo is the only large winery which doesn't offer tours and Ernest is noted for his secrecy about operations. At the same time, Gallo has served as a training ground for many vintners who have gone on to other companies.

In recent years, Gallo had upgraded its product line and its prices. Once known for pop wines like Thunderbird, Ripple, and Boone's Farm, the company stopped advertising these wines and began to emphasize the higher priced varietal and proprietary wines. Although sales and market share temporarily suffered, profits increased steadily.

Exhibit 3 *(continued)*

Gallo is noted for producing a quality wine at a low price. Hearty Burgundy has been called the best wine ever made for the money and because of the cost advantage of the bottling plant, Gallo has sometimes been in the position of selling wine below cost while making a profit on the bottles.

United Vintners

United Vintners is 82 percent owned by Heublein, Inc., the major U.S. producer of vodka (Smirnoff) and the owner of Kentucky Fried Chicken. The range of products of UV included pop wines (Annie Green Springs, T. J. Swann), Colony, Italian Swiss Colony, Inglenook table and dessert wines, and high quality wines from Beaulieu Vineyards. The company also distributed Lancer's wine from Portugal.

United Vintners has been in the wine industry since the late 60s and is the second-largest seller of wines. Sales totaled $226.1 million in 1976, but fell to $201.8 million in 1977. Recent advertising campaigns have emphasized the personality of the drinker rather than attributes of its wines.

Franzia-Mogen David

Coca-Cola Bottling Company of New York purchased Mogen David in 1970 and Franzia Brothers in 1973. The former is known for sweet table, fruit, and specialty wines while the latter produces a range of California dry red and white wines, table wines, rose, sparkling, and dessert wines, and brandy. In addition to bottling and distributing soft drinks (Dr Pepper and 7up in addition to the Coca-Cola line) the company's subsidiaries produce Igloo plastic coolers and other plastic products. The company owns two steamboats, Mississippi Queen and the Delta Queen, and a TV station. It is one of the largest independent soft drink franchises in the world.

In 1977 wine sales of Mogen David and Franzia brands totaled almost $60 million, down slightly from $60.8 million in 1976; the operations of the Franzia unit were not profitable in 1977. Recent Mogen David commercials urged consumers to drink Mogen David because of its taste—even though it lacked "snob appeal."

Almaden

National Distillers and Chemical Corporation acquired full ownership of Almaden in 1977. One of the four largest distillers in the United States, National Distillers was also active in chemicals, petrochemicals, brass mill products, and textiles.

Almaden had sales of $88 million and operating profit of $14 million in 1977; in 1978 sales increased to $117.5 million and operating profits rose to $17.2 million.

Canadaigua Wine Co.

Canadaigua sold primarily dessert wines and one product, Richard's Wild Irish Rose, accounted for over two thirds of its sales. The company owned wineries in New York, California, South Carolina, and Virginia and its 1977 sales were in the $35 million range.

Paul Masson Vineyards

Seagram Company Ltd., of which Paul Masson is a division, was in 1977 the world's largest producer and marketer of distilled spirits and wines. Case volume of Paul Masson wines was reported to be growing about 15 percent annually. The Paul Masson brand enjoyed a good reputation in the industry and was one of the better known brands among customers.

EXHIBIT 4
Market Share by Origin of Wine (1977)

Origin		Share	Volume Increase (decrease) from 1976
Domestic		82.8%	
California	86.1%		6.0%
Others	13.9		(4.1%)
	100.0%		
Imports		17.2%	
Italy.....................	43.0%		29.1%
France	19.4		12.2
Germany	15.3		18.5
Spain	9.4		(6.1)
Portugal................	8.6		3.0
Other	5.0		
	100.0%		

and-pop wineries have proliferated in the premium wine segment with sales going to local communities. There is little chance that they can expand beyond restricted market areas because of their small size, legal restrictions on interstate wine sales, and the wide variations in their product quality.

Most wine sold in the United States is produced in California. Exhibit 4 shows market share by origin of wine. Import prices have generally increased more than domestic prices because of inflation and the devaluation of the dollar. The packaging of some French wine in flexible plastic film pouches is one effort to maintain competitive costs.

Some wineries own grapevines while others buy from independent growers. For those depending on outside growers (Almaden uses 85–90 percent

EXHIBIT 5
Storage Capacities of 12 U.S. Wineries

Winery	Storage Capacity (millions of gallons)
E&J Gallo	226
United Vintners (Heublein)	110
Guild Wineries	57
Vie Del Co.	37.1
Bear Mountain	36
Taylor (Coca-Cola)	31.3
Sierra Wine Corp.	30
Almaden (National Distillers and Chemical)	29.4
Franzia Bros. (Coca-Cola, N.Y.)	28.3
Paul Masson (Seagram)	28
The Christian Brothers	27.5
A. Perelli-Minette & Sons	20

outside grapes and Taylor 90 percent) relationships with growers are very important. In hard times, the vintner buys grapes to subsidize the growers in order not to jeopardize future supplies. This practice can lead to large inventories and make storage capacity an important factor. Aging requirements for premium and sparkling wines also add to storage requirements. White wines require significantly less aging than red wines of comparable quality. Exhibit 5 shows storage capacities of 12 U.S. wineries which account for 73 percent of the storage capacities of the 100 largest wineries. All except Taylor are in California.

ADVERTISING

The entry of large companies into the wine industry has been accompanied by an increase in advertising budgets and the advent of mass marketing techniques. Almaden has increased advertising by 100 percent since 1974 while Taylor's advertising has increased 33 percent. The largest advertiser, Gallo, on the other hand has increased its ad budget only about 9 percent. In 1977, however, Gallo spent over $12 million on advertising while Taylor and Almaden spent about $2 million. Since all segments of the alcoholic beverage industry compete to some extent, the level of wine advertising is partly affected by promotion of beer and spirits.

REGULATION

Wine is subject to regulation from all levels of government. State and local governments regulate the sales of alcoholic beverages and in some states legislation has been proposed to regulate packaging. At the federal level, the Treasury Department's Bureau of Alcohol, Firearms, and Tobacco (BATF) regulates advertising and labeling. New advertising guidelines were expected late in 1979 and new labeling requirements were to take effect in January 1983. These requirements state that if place of origin (e.g., California) is identified on the bottle, 75 percent of the grapes must be from that place and if a viticultural area is identified (e.g., Napa Valley), 85 percent of the grapes must be from there. These standards match those prevailing in the European Common Market.

In addition to regulation, wine is subject to taxation from all levels of government. Federal excise tax is 17 cents per gallon on table wines, 67 cents per gallon on dessert wines, and $3.40 per gallon on sparkling wines.

THE TAYLOR WINE COMPANY

The Taylor Wine Company, at the time of acquisition by Coca-Cola, was a leading domestic producer of premium still and sparkling wines, marketed under the Taylor and Great Western labels; it was also the largest producer of premium domestic champagnes. The record of Taylor Wine Company from

1972 to 1976 reflected the cyclical swings in the industry during that period. In 1973, record sales of $51 million registered an 18 percent increase over 1972, with profits up 25 percent to $6.8 million or $1.57 per share. In 1974, sales increased to $56 million while profits increased to $6.9 million or $1.58 per share. Results worsened as Taylor reported sales and profits of $57.6 million and $5.4 million, or $1.24 per share, in 1975 and $59.6 million and $5.6 million, or $1.30 per share, in 1976. In explaining these results, Taylor's management said:

> During the four years 1969–1972, the volume of wine entering U.S. marketing channels increased 10–14 percent per year. As a result of this growth and anticipated continued growth, substantial vine plantings and wine production occurred during the period 1971–1974. However, due to economic conditions in 1973 through 1975 the expected rate of growth in wine sales was not realized, and the industry faced a period of surplus wine inventories and grape crops. Taylor believes that its sales for the fiscal years 1975 and 1976 were adversely affected by competitive pricing conditions attributable to the foregoing factors. In its effort to maintain profit margins, Taylor has generally held or slightly increased its prices to distributors during this period, even though, based upon retail prices, it is believed that a number of wine producers have reduced prices. However, inflationary pressures, which increased costs, resulted in reduced profit margin percentages in fiscal 1974 and 1975. A decrease in some material costs and improved cost controls resulted in a modest improvement in profit margins for 1976, although gallons sold declined slightly.

Taylor's *1976 Annual Report* stated that the company had "successfully weathered the recession of the past two years and is in a strong position to take advantage of the recovery the wine industry appears to be experiencing." In addition to the recovery, 1976 also marked the end of the Taylor family's participation in the company's management and its merger with the Coca-Cola Company.

MERGER WITH COCA-COLA

On August 6, 1976, Lincoln First Bank of Rochester, New York, put out a preliminary prospectus for sale of 603,000 of the 900,000 shares of Taylor stock it held for trust customers. The motive for the sale was to raise cash for the trusts involved and Taylor was informed of the proceedings because 10 percent of the outstanding stock was involved. Several companies responded to the prospectus including Coca-Cola, PepsiCo, Beatrice Foods, Norton-Simon, and five private investors headed by Marne Obernauer (a former Taylor director and owner of Great Western before it was purchased by Taylor). Coca-Cola was interested in more than the 603,000 shares so when Coca-Cola and the Bank reached an agreement, the secondary offer was withdrawn and Coca-Cola entered into merger talks directly with Taylor.

After the Taylor board's approval of the proposed merger, Taylor's president, Joseph Swarthout, explained to the shareholders in the December 2, 1976 prospectus:

> The U.S. wine market has never been more competitive. As I stated at our Annual Shareholders' Meeting in September, our major competitors are stronger than ever. In several cases they have significantly stronger financial backing that we have. Under these conditions, it becomes increasingly difficult to improve, or even maintain, our share-of-market.
>
> I have had the pleasure of being an employee of this company for more than thirty years. I have been a corporate officer since 1955. They have been interesting years of growth and opportunity. It is now my firm belief that The Taylor Wine Company would enjoy substantially greater opportunities for success in the future through the financial strength and diversity of The Coca-Cola Company.

Industry observers speculated that Taylor management was frightened by several of the "unfamiliar" companies showing interest in the 603,000 shares of Taylor's stock and looked at the Coca-Cola merger as a way of preventing a greater evil. There did however appear to be possibilities for strategic fit with Coca-Cola, as indicated in Coca-Cola's description of its business:

> The Coca-Cola Company is the largest manufacturer and distributor of soft drink concentrates and syrups in the world. Its product, "Coca-Cola," has been sold in the United States since 1886, is now sold in over 135 countries as well and is the leading soft drink product in most of these countries.
>
> In 1978, soft drink products accounted for 76 percent of total sales and 87 percent of total operating income from industry segments. Soft drink products include Coca-Cola, Fanta, Sprite, TAB, Fresca, Mr. PiBB and Hi-C. Brand Coca-Cola accounts for over 70 percent of all Company soft drink unit sales, both in the United States and overseas.
>
> The worldwide soft drink operations of The Coca-Cola Company are organized into three operating groups: the Americas Group, the Pacific Group and the Europe and Africa Group. The Company's largest markets within its Americas Group are the United States, Mexico and Brazil. The largest markets within the Pacific Group are Japan and Canada. The largest market in the Europe and Africa Group is Germany. In 1978, overseas markets accounted for some 62 percent of total soft drink unit sales.
>
> In the United States, 67 percent of soft drink syrup and concentrate is sold to more than 550 bottlers who prepare and sell the products for the food store, vending and other markets for home and on-premise consumption. The remaining 33 percent is sold to approximately 4,000 authorized wholesalers who in turn sell the syrup to restaurants and other retailers. Overseas, all soft drink concentrate is sold to more than 900 bottlers. Approximately 90 percent of the syrup and concentrate is sold for further processing outside the Company before sale to the ultimate consumer, both in the United States and overseas. The remaining 10 percent is converted into consumable soft drinks before being sold by the Company.
>
> Through the Foods Division, the Company manufactures and markets Minute Maid and Snow Crop frozen concentrated citrus juices, Minute Maid

chilled juices and related citrus products, and Hi-C ready-to-serve fruit drinks and powdered drink mixes. The Foods Division also markets coffee and tea under the "Maryland Club," "Butter-nut" and other brands, as well as to private label and institutional accounts.

Exhibits 6, 7, and 8 show the combined pro forma summaries of operations, net profits, and balance sheet statements for the merged companies.

Under the terms of the merger agreement approved by stockholders of both companies in January 1977, all outstanding shares of Taylor stock were converted into shares of common stock of Coca-Cola at the rate of one share of Coca-Cola stock for each 3.75 shares of Taylor stock. No changes in Taylor management were planned and the company was to operate as a wholly owned subsidiary of Coca-Cola with Coca-Cola officials on its Board of Directors. Exhibit 9 shows the stock price movements for Coca-Cola and Taylor.

TAYLOR WINE COMPANY OPERATIONS

At the time of the merger proposal, Taylor described its operations as follows:

> Taylor is a leading domestic producer of premium still wines. It is also the largest domestic producer of sparkling wines using the traditional French method of fermentation in the bottle, as contrasted with the bulk process in which the wine is fermented in large volume.
>
> Taylor's 63 types of sparkling and still wines are produced and marketed exclusively under two trade names representing its two wine divisions. The Pleasant Valley division, the successor to the Pleasant Valley Wine Company, acquired by Taylor in 1961, produces and markets its wines under the Great Western name. Historically, these divisions have utilized separate production and marketing techniques, and the wines produced by each division traditionally have had different characteristics and consumer brand loyalties. As a result, they have continued as separate divisions since 1961 and presently maintain their own advertising, marketing, productive and storage capacity, and operational staffs, although legal, financial, accounting, personnel, and other functions are performed at the corporate level.
>
> Wines are classified as either still or sparkling. Still wines containing 14 percent or less alcohol are generally referred to as table wines and those containing 14–21 percent alcohol are generally referred to as dessert wines. Sparkling wines are those which are effervescent and contain not more than 14 percent alcohol.

EMPLOYEES

Taylor employed approximately 670 full-time employees. Due to increased use of mechanized harvesting equipment, the number of seasonal workers hired by Taylor had declined in recent years. Approximately 15 seasonal workers were employed during the 1976 grape harvest as compared

EXHIBIT 6

THE COCA-COLA COMPANY AND SUBSIDIARIES
AND THE TAYLOR WINE COMPANY, INC.
Pro Forma Combined Summary of Operations
(Unaudited) ($000 except per share amounts)

	1971	1972	1973	1974	1975	Six Months Ended June 30 1975	Six Months Ended June 30 1976
Net sales	$1,772,029	$1,927,242	$2,201,410	$2,579,754	$2,932,457	$1,476,764	$1,508,416
Cost of goods sold	949,124	1,021,889	1,179,168	1,576,068	1,745,238	904,183	835,472
Taxes on income	165,270	179,661	194,007	173,899	226,750	106,372	129,008
Net profit (Note 1)	173,238	197,004	221,862	201,365	224,951	122,344	144,483
Per share:							
Net profit (Note 1)	$2.85	$3.24	$3.64	$3.30	$4.01	$2.00	$2.37
Cash dividends declared	1.58	1.64	1.80	2.08	2.30	1.15	1.32
Average number of shares outstanding (Note 2)	60,730,000	60,860,000	60,937,000	60,996,000	61,050,000	61,049,000	61,078,000

Notes:

(1) In 1974 The Coca-Cola Company adopted the last-in, first-out accounting method for certain major classes of inventories as explained in Note B to the financial statements of The Coca-Cola Company and subsidiaries. For the year ended June 30, 1975, Taylor also adopted the last-in, first-out method of valuation for all its inventories as explained in Note (a) to the Taylor statement of income. These accounting changes had the effect of reducing pro forma net profit for 1974 by $32,329,548 ($.53 a share).

(2) The pro forma average number of shares outstanding represents the average number of shares of The Coca-Cola Company outstanding during each period after giving retroactive effect to the average number of Taylor shares outstanding during each period converted into shares of The Coca-Cola Company on a .267-for-1 basis.

(3) Estimated expenses of this proposed merger will be approximately $700,000. These expenses, which have not been included in the above pro forma presentation, will be deducted from operations of the resulting combined company for the period in which they are incurred.

THE COCA-COLA COMPANY AND SUBSIDIARIES
AND THE TAYLOR WINE COMPANY, INC.
Pro Forma Combined Net Profit and Per Share Data
(Unaudited)

	1971	1972	1973	1974	1975	Six Months Ended June 30 1975	Six Months Ended June 30 1976
Net profit ($000):							
The Coca-Cola Company historical	$167,815	$190,157	$214,981	$195,972	$239,305	$119,762	$141,763
The Taylor Wine Company, Inc. historical	5,471	6,847	6,881	5,939	5,646	2,582	2,720
Pro forma combined	$173,286	$197,004	$221,862	$201,365	$244,951	$122,344	$144,483
Net profit per common share:							
The Coca-Cola Company:							
Historical	$2.82	$3.19	$3.60	$3.28	$4.00	$2.00	$2.37
Pro forma combined (Note A)	2.85	3.24	3.64	3.30	4.01	2.00	2.37
The Taylor Wine Company, Inc.							
Historical	$1.29	$1.57	$1.58	$1.24	$1.30	$ .59	$ .63
Pro forma combined (Note B)	.76	.86	.97	.88	1.07	.53	.63
Cash dividends declared per common share:							
The Coca-Cola Company historical	$1.58	$1.64	$1.80	$2.08	$2.30	$1.15	$1.32
The Taylor Wine Company, Inc.:							
Historical	$ .48	$ .50	$ .56	$ .60	$ .62	$ .30	$ .31
Pro forma combined (Note B)	.42	.44	.48	.56	.61	.31	.35
Book value per common share:							
The Coca-Cola Company:							
Historical						$21.57	
Pro forma combined (Note A)							22.13
The Taylor Wine Company, Inc.:							
Historical						$13.67	
Pro forma combined (Note B)							5.90

Notes:

(A) Pro forma combined amounts per share for The Coca-Cola Company are based on average number of shares outstanding during each period and as of June 30, 1976 after giving retroactive effect to the conversion of Taylor shares into shares of The Coca-Cola Company on the basis of the exchange ratio for the merger, at .267 shares of The Coca-Cola Company for each share of Taylor.

(B) Pro forma combined amounts are based on .267 shares The Coca-Cola Company exchanged for each share of Taylor.

Source: Prospectus.

EXHIBIT 8

THE COCA-COLA COMPANY AND SUBSIDIARIES
AND THE TAYLOR WINE COMPANY, INC.
Pro Forma Combined Condensed Balance Sheet
As of June 30, 1976
($000, unaudited)

	The Coca-Cola Company	Taylor	Adjustment (Note)	Pro Forma Combined
		Assets		
Current assets:				
Cash	$ 78,571	$ 1,173		$ 79,744
Marketable securities	229,793			229,793
Trade accounts receivable—net	250,947	4,366		255,303
Inventories	374,920	41,766		416,686
Prepaid expenses	28,467	180		28,647
Total current assets	962,698	47,475		1,010,173
Property, plant, and equipment—net	647,684	26,462		674,146
Other assets	209,641	902		210,543
Total	$1,820,023	$74,839		$1,894,862
		Liabilities and Stockholders' Equity		
Current liabilities:				
Notes payable including current maturities of long-term debt	$ 24,891	$ 3,037		$ 27,928
Accounts payable and accrued accounts	337,129	3,656		340,785
Accrued taxes including taxes on income	121,763	1,729		123,492
Total current liabilities	483,783	8,422		492,205
Long-term liabilities and deferred taxes	44,092	6,904		50,996
Stockholders' equity:				
Common stock—no par value The Coca-Cola Company	60,485		$ 1,173	
Common stock—$2 par value The Taylor Wine Company, Inc.		8,707	(8,707)	
Capital surplus	87,938	9,930	7,534	105,402
Earned surplus	1,159,090	40,876		1,199,966
Treasury shares	(15,365)			(15,365)
Total stockholders' equity	1,292,148	59,513		1,351,661
Total	$1,820,023	$74,839		$1,894,862

Note: The pro forma adjustment reflects the issuance of 1,161,000 common shares of The Coca-Cola Company upon conversion of each of the presently issued common shares of Taylor for .267 common shares of The Coca-Cola Company pursuant to the terms of the merger.

EXHIBIT 9
Comparative Stock Prices

	Taylor Common Stock		The Coca-Cola Company Common Stock	
	High Bid Price	Low Bid Price	High Sale Price	Low Sale Price
1974				
First quarter	$38.25	$23.75	$127.75	$109.50
Second quarter	24.25	16.50	118.375	98.375
Third quarter	17.75	12.25	109.00	48.00
Fourth quarter	13.75	9.25	68.75	44.625
1975				
First quarter	20.875	10.125	81.50	53.25
Second quarter	19.50	16.00	93.50	72.75
Third quarter	18.375	11.00	92.00	69.625
Fourth quarter	15.375	10.75	89.75	69.875
1976				
First quarter	17.50	13.50	94.25	82.00
Second quarter	15.50	12.25	89.00	77.625
Third quarter	19.375	12.875	89.625	82.875
Fourth quarter				
November 20, 1976	20.25	16.875	86.25	76.25

The Coca-Cola Company announced that it had entered into merger negotiations with Taylor on September 8, 1976, and preliminary agreement on the exchange rate was announced on October 14, 1976.

with approximately 200 such workers employed during the 1967 harvest. A few additional seasonal workers were sometimes employed at the winery for the grape pressing operations. Taylor maintained a pension plan to which it made annual contributions and which allowed employees to make voluntary contributions; it also provided group life and medical benefits for its regular full-time employees. The employees of Taylor were not represented by any unions, and Taylor believed that its employee relations were satisfactory.

MARKETING

Taylor's wines were sold throughout the United States. Both Taylor and Pleasant Valley advertised through television, magazines and newspapers. In addition, each division provided promotional materials to its customers for eventual use by retailers. In recent years, advertising, sales promotion and selling expenditures by Taylor approximated 17 percent of net sales.

In 1976 the Taylor and Great Western product lines were marketed by 64 and 34 salesmen, respectively. Taylor's products were sold primarily to 490 wholesale distributors and through 27 brokers. With few exceptions, Taylor and Great Western wines were handled by different distributors in the respective geographic locations. Brokers were primarily used by Taylor to sell its products in states where no distribution agreements existed and in some of the 15 "control" states where Taylor's customer was the local or state agency that controlled the purchase and distribution of alcoholic beverages. In some control states, such as Pennsylvania, sales were made directly by Taylor to the appropriate governmental agency. (A distributor purchases Taylor's products for resale to retailers, whereas brokers act on behalf of Taylor on a commission basis.) Taylor maintained one price list for all purchasers (f.o.b. the winery) and did not engage in selective discounting.

In 1976, no distributor accounted for more than 7 percent of Taylor's net sales, and no state control agency accounted for more than 10 percent of Taylor's net sales except Pennsylvania which accounted for 11 percent. The largest markets, by state, for Taylor's products were New York, Pennsylvania, New Jersey, and Illinois. In addition to the wine sold through the distribution channels outlined above, a small volume of wine was sold by Taylor directly to airlines and exported to United States armed forces, embassies and consulates abroad, and some foreign countries.

Taylor's sales volume was seasonal and was affected by price adjustments and the introduction of new products. Normally, sales volume was greatest in the last calendar quarter and smallest in the third calendar quarter. Sales volume for the first and second quarters was normally about the same. Preannounced price increases and new product introductions typically resulted in anticipatory buying by Taylor's customers. In addition to normal and continuous product advertising, it was Taylor's practice to conduct individual promotional programs at various times during the year for certain of its wines and brands.

The vast majority of Taylor's products were bottled in one-fifth gallon (25.6 oz.) and 1.5 liter (50.7 oz.) sizes. Metric conversion was legally required as of January 1, 1979, and, at that time, the one-fifth gallon size was expected to be converted to a .75 liter (25.4 oz.) size. In early 1976, Taylor converted the half-gallon (64 oz.) size to 1.5 liter size. Taylor did not produce wine for bulk sale to other wineries. Exhibit 10 shows the market sizes and Taylor's position in the table, dessert, and sparkling wine segments.

WINE PRODUCTION

During the last five years, vineyards owned and operated by Taylor supplied approximately 10 percent of its annual grape requirements. Taylor had over 850 acres of vineyards in production, with an additional 450 acres of such plantings not yet in full bearing. Of the 450 acres, 420 acres overlooking Seneca Lake, the largest of the Finger Lakes, were recently purchased and planted and were expected to be in full bearing by 1980. The balance of Taylor's annual grape requirements was supplied by more than 450 independent growers from approximately 11,500 acres, located principally in the Finger Lakes region of New York State. A portion of Taylor's grape requirements was purchased from counties in the far western part of New York State.

EXHIBIT 10
Marketing of Wines in the United States (000 gallons)

	1971	1972	1973	1974	1975
Table wines*					
U.S.-produced	159,510	182,640	190,469	201,634	219,171
Foreign-produced	26,356	37,741	45,658	42,153	40,524
Total	185,766	220,381	236,127	243,787	259,695
Taylor	2,840	3,504	4,574	5,123	5,264
Taylor market share†	1.5%	1.6%	1.9%	2.1%	2.0%
Dessert wines*					
U.S.-produced	87,551	86,976	82,637	78,447	80,659
Foreign-produced	8,023	7,325	7,487	7,437	6,867
Total	95,574	94,301	90,124	85,884	87,526
Taylor	4,420	4,465	4,577	4,752	4,683
Taylor market share†	4.6%	4.7%	5.1%	5.5%	5.4%
Sparkling wines					
U.S.-produced	22,005	20,323	18,935	18,008	18,424
Foreign-produced	1,877	1,976	2,081	1,804	1,928
Total	23,882	22,299	21,016	19,812	20,352
Taylor	1,697	1,738	1,763	1,688	1,605
Taylor market share†	7.1%	7.8%	8.4%	8.5%	7.9%
Total of all categories					
U.S.-produced	269,066	289,939	292,041	298,089	318,254
Foreign-produced	36,156	47,042	55,226	51,394	49,319
Total	305,222	336,981	347,267	349,483	367,573
Taylor	8,957	9,707	10,914	11,563	11,552
Taylor market share†	2.9%	2.9%	3.1%	3.3%	3.1%

* Still wines with less than 14 percent alcohol have been included in table wines and those with greater than 15 percent alcohol have been included in dessert wines.
† Taylor as a percentage of total.
Source: Wine Institute Statistical Reports for other than Taylor statistics.

Taylor had contracts with all independent growers from whom it purchased grapes, and a large number of these growers had been supplying Taylor for many years. These contracts required Taylor, on or before August 1 of each year, to announce the prices it would pay for grapes to be purchased in the Fall harvest as well as the quantities it would purchase. Taylor financed its grape purchases through short-term financing. Harvesting generally occurred for approximately eight weeks in September and October. Growers had the right to cancel their contracts during the first two weeks of August; and during November of each year, either the grower or Taylor could cancel the contract. In the past five years, four growers exercised their cancellation rights. On July 30, 1976, Taylor announced it would purchase approximately 70 percent of the grape tonnage purchased in 1975; this was the first time that the announced quantities did not constitute substantially the entire crop of its growers under the contract. The average per-ton price paid to growers for grapes for the 1976 harvest was approximately 86 percent of that paid in the 1975 harvest. The company maintained an advisory service program for its independent grape growers, providing them with information with respect to fertilization, cultivation, soil analysis, disease control and planting. In addition, it conducted experimental work in its own vineyards and in conjunction with the New York State Agricultural Experiment Station located in nearby Geneva, New York.

Taylor purchased about 25 percent of its wine needs from several California suppliers for blending purposes and also bought ingredients for certain wines the flavor characteristics of which were derived from grapes not grown in the Eastern United States. In addition, wine spirits, sugar and other ingredients, and packaging materials were obtained from several sources. The company believed its sources of supply were adequate and anticipated no shortage in the foreseeable future of grapes supplied by independent growers or of land suitable for growing the varieties and quality of grapes required for its wines.

Taylor's current manufacturing facilities had a total bottling capacity of approximately 4,070 cases per hour. Aging of Taylor's sparkling and still wines normally took up to two years, although wines could be stored for substantially longer periods. As a result of this aging process, and to guard against crop shortages, Taylor, like many companies in the wine industry maintained inventories that were large in relation to sales and total assets. The company's inventories usually peaked in late October shortly after the grape harvest. In October 1975, Taylor's wine inventories totaled 25.2 million gallons. This figure declined to 20.7 million gallons in July 1976 and then rose again to 25.5 million gallons in October 1976. Taylor had approximately 31.1 million gallons of wine storage capacity, of which 24.7 million gallons was tank storage and 6.4 million gallons was bottled storage. Because of operating limitations, the effective tank storage capacity was limited to approximately 85 percent or 21 million gallons. On June 30, 1976 the cost (Lifo basis) of Taylor's inventory of still wines in bulk and sparkling wines in process was approximately $30.8 million.

ACQUISITION BY COCA-COLA

Analysts on Wall Street identified several factors that seemed to make the Taylor acquisition a bargain for Coca-Cola. By maintaining premium prices while others were cutting prices, Taylor had maintained its profitability and its record of increasing dividends. Although not investing heavily in such capital projects as a bottle factory, the company had kept its facilities up to date and in good shape. The slipping market share and lack of national image for Taylor were the kind of problems that Coca-Cola's $387 million in cash could solve. Taylor was not deep in debt, was profitable, and in a position to capitalize on what Coca-Cola saw as another wine boom.

Coca-Cola's decision to enter the wine industry was discussed in its publication, *Refresher USA:*

Our Company's figurative foray into the vineyards came only after a very careful study of the market, a study which revealed some extremely positive indication of growth potential for wine in this country.

The study's major conclusion was that the wine boom that began in the United States in the 1960s will continue through the 1970s and beyond. In other words, the popularity of wine is here to stay.

"More than 60 percent of the adult U.S. population now consumes wine, which has become an everyday dinner beverage in many households," says Thomas Muller, manager of administration and development for the Wine Group (Changed to Wine Spectrum in 1978). "And as distribution expands from specialty stores to supermarkets, women are becoming an increasingly important group of purchasers as well as consumers of wine."

Another major factor favorable affecting sales, says [Albert] Killeen [president of the Wine Spectrum] "is an accelerating general cultural interest in wine. There's almost an art form to it that could be called 'winesmanship' as people gain more knowledge about wine.

"There's great interest in such activities as wine tasting, vineyard tours, and wine with food. Many people are studying how to develop a wine cellar, the ritual of chilling, de-corking, decanting, and serving wine."

"Among college students there is a decided preference for wine over other alcoholic beverages," observes Grant Curtis, vice president and marketing services manager for Taylor Wine. "To give you an idea of what an important growth factor that is, there are 28 million college graduates in the United States today; by 1985, there will be nearly double that number—45 million. And these young adults are carrying their preference for wine into their post-college lives."

BUILDING THE WINE SPECTRUM DIVISION

After the Taylor acquisition, Coca-Cola purchased two California vineyards. Sterling Vineyards was the 100th largest winery in the U.S. with a capacity of 60,000 cases per year. Sterling president Michael P. W. Stone described his product:

> We are one of the half-dozen or so of the smaller California wineries which seek to position their products at the extreme upper spectrum of the premium line of wines. Wines generally are classed as standard, medium-range and premium: we are aiming to be what you might call "super-premium."

The winery's four red and four white wines were grown and bottled on premises and were classified as estate-bottled, vintage wines. Mr. Killeen commented on plans for Sterling:

> Sterling Vineyards' development as a wine growing and producing enterprise will remain unchanged. It will continue to have as its objective the production of the finest Napa Valley premium estate bottled wines in the United States. Production will continue to be restricted and the uncompromising practices

that have made Sterling Wines highly respected will be continued by the existing staff at Calistoga.[4]

The purchase of the Monterey Vineyard near Gonzales, California was announced by Coca-Cola in November of 1977. Monterey County was one of the last regions in California to be planted in wine grapes and its wines have been characterized as having "an intense varietal flavor, thinner body, and more fruitiness and crispness." Monterey was completed in 1975 and much of the production equipment was designed by its president, Richard Peterson, a Ph.D. in agricultural chemistry and former employee of Gallo and Beaulieu. The construction of the winery was somewhat unorthodox—the foundation was laid, then the production equipment was installed, and finally the walls and roof were put up. Monterey owned no vineyards and produced eight varietals and one blend. Production capacity was 7 million cases and storage capacity was 2.2 million gallons.

Taylor, Great Western (Pleasant Valley), Sterling, and Monterey became the components of the Wine Spectrum Division of the Coca-Cola Company; together, these wine operations made Coca-Cola the fifth largest factor in the U.S. wine industry. Albert E. Killeen served both as executive vice president of Coca-Cola and president of the Wine Spectrum. He had responsibility for directing and coordinating the company's wine interests and served as chair of the board of directors of each winery. He had previously served as corporate marketing director and executive vice president for marketing at Coca-Cola.

Killeen assessed the strengths of the components of the Wine Spectrum as follows:

> Taylor is the keystone of the Company's wine business because of its reputation for quality, its strong distribution system, and its fine sales organization. The Sterling and Monterey wineries add geographic balance as well as new brands of varietal wines to our product mix. We now have really the best of both worlds—the distinguished tradition of wine-making from the Finger Lakes region of New York State known for its fine champagne and sherries, and the fresh and exuberant ambience of the California growing regions, known for their table wines. Even the two California wineries were carefully chosen to balance one another. One is in a region that produces a very fine Cabernet Sauvignon grape, for example; the other in a much cooler region, fosters some of the best Johannisberg, Riesling and Grüner Sylvaner grapes available anywhere. So our combination of vineyards puts us in a prime position for taking advantage of opportunities to produce a wide variety of high-quality American-grown wines for optimum acceptance among American consumers and consumers around the world.[5]

---

[4] "The Coca-Cola Company Acquires Sterling Vineyards," Coca-Cola Press release, August 8, 1977.

[5] *Refresher, USA*, vol. 4 (1977), p. 15.

The importance of the Taylor name to Coca-Cola was illustrated in the following news item:

> Walter S. Taylor, a grandson of the founder of the giant Taylor Wine Company, must take his last name off the labels of bottles containing wine produced by his own company, Bully Hill.
>
> So said Federal Judge Harold Burke in the United States District Court in Hammondsport, N.Y. yesterday. The judge upheld a request by the Coca-Cola Company, of Atlanta, for an injunction forbidding Mr. Taylor to use the name because of confusion over the wine made by Taylor Wine Company, which Coca-Cola had purchased last year.
>
> Mr. Taylor had been a vice president of Taylor Wine, but left some years before Coca-Cola acquired control.
>
> Mr. Taylor said he planned to appeal the ruling. However, he added, the family name will be scratched out by hand on the Bully Hill bottles, pending resolution of the case. The "Walter S." will stay.[6]

NATIONAL STATUS SOUGHT FOR TAYLOR

The immediate result of Coca-Cola's acquisition was the introduction of a new line, Taylor California Cellars. The line was composed of four generic wines—chablis, rhine, rose, and burgundy—which were developed and blended by Dr. Peterson of Monterey Vineyards. The wines were bottled at Franzia Brothers, a subsidiary of Coca-Cola of New York. Taylor provided the label name and the distribution system. Prices for California Cellars were set slightly higher than other premium generic wines. The introductory ad campaign for California Cellars became the reason for the BATF dispute.

Taylor's advertising agency had commissioned a national consumer group to conduct a series of taste tests to compare the new wines with more established names in California premium wines. The results of the tests placed three California Cellars wines in first place in generic categories and one in second place (see Appendix). Their results were used as a basis for the introductory ad campaign for the fall of 1978 in the East and in Southern California.

Comparative advertising was a break with traditional wine advertising and there was some question also about whether it was allowed under federal regulations. Taylor sought clearance to use the ads from the Bureau of Alcohol, Tobacco, and Firearms, but was refused. The BATF also refused to prohibit the ads. Taylor then sought court action to gain approval for its commercials but the court ruled that there were no grounds for suit because the ad had not been ordered stopped. Part of the problem resulted from the fact that the Bureau was about to review advertising regulations and new guidelines were not expected for a year after the California Cellars campaign was scheduled to begin. The Bureau was unwilling to pre-clear taste test

---

[6] "People and Business," *The New York Times*, August 16, 1977, p. 58.

advertising until it had held hearings and developed standards for review. Prohibitions against taste test ads were based on a 1954 ruling dealing with beer. One BATF official stated:

> It is not the Bureau's position that all comparative taste test advertising is misleading and therefore prohibited. It is the Bureau's position that misleading advertising of wine be prohibited.[7]

The decision as to whether or not Taylor's ads were misleading was to be left until the ads were aired and complaints were filed. In view of the uncertainty surrounding the campaign an alternate series of introductory ads was prepared which did not use taste test information.

Penalties for improper advertising ranged from a "letter of admonition" to suspension of vintners' license to criminal prosecution. The possibility of suits from competitors was also present.

STRATEGIES AND FUTURE OUTLOOK

Regarding the prospects for the Wine Spectrum division, Coca-Cola stated the following in its *1978 Annual Report:*

> The United States wine market is expected to grow at a healthy rate in the years ahead; annual growth in table wines alone may surpass 10 percent. United States wine consumption today is at only 5 percent to 10 percent of the per capita levels of many European markets. Production, packaging, marketing, merchandising, advertising and promotional programs are now being developed to take advantage of this unique growth opportunity.
>
> The Wine Spectrum units are attempting to exceed industry growth by following these strategies: (1) establish strong production and distribution bases; (2) develop a balanced industry position with quality products from both coasts of the United States; and (3) employ strong and innovative marketing merchandising, and advertising programs targeted at both the trade and the consumer.
>
> These strategies have already resulted in a unit sales increase of more than 10 percent in 1978.

APPENDIX: BACKGROUND INFORMATION ON THE ADVERTISING CAMPAIGN FOR "TAYLOR CALIFORNIA CELLARS"

> The advertising for the introduction of Taylor California Cellars is based on a scientifically structured and carefully monitored wine tasting test, a study which relied on the objective ratings of a panel of 27 recognized wine experts

---

[7] Richard C. Gordon, "Try Taste Test Ads, Taylor Told, But U.S. Won't Give Prior OK," *Advertising Age,* vol. 49 (August 21, 1978), pp. 1, 70.

APPENDIX (*continued*)

---

and which clearly establishes this new brand of premium generic wine as one of the finest of its genre.

To insure the validity and accuracy of the competition, Kenyon & Eckhardt, agency of record for Taylor California Cellars, commissioned the Nationwide Consumer Testing Institute, Inc. (NCTI) to design and implement the tasting test.

The NCTI project sought to determine the rank preference of four brands of California wine in four different categories.

Specifically, the wine tasting competition included the following four tasting tests:

    A. *Chablis tasting*
        Almaden Mountain White Chablis
        Inglenook Navalle Chablis
        Sebastiani Mountain Chablis
        Taylor California Cellars Chablis
    B. *Rosé tasting*
        Almaden Mountain Nectar Vin Rosé
        Inglenook Navalle Vin Rosé
        Sebastiani Mountain Vin Rosé
        Taylor California Cellars Rosé
    C. *Rhine tasting*
        Almaden Mountain Rhine
        Inglenook Navalle Rhine
        C. K. Mondavi Rhine
        Taylor California Cellars Rhine
    D. *Burgundy tasting*
        Almaden Mountain Red Burgundy
        Inglenook Navalle Burgundy
        Sebastiani Mountain Burgundy
        Taylor California Cellars Burgundy

II. *Panel of Experts*

    To reach the highest standards of integrity, the tasting tests required a panel of qualified and unbiased wine tasters, in a blind study, to rank each wine according to preference.

    Careful and detailed screening procedures governed the search for the wine tasters to participate in the test. NCTI specified, for instance, that no taster could have any financial interest in or affiliation with: a wine producer (wholesale or retail); any publication dealing with wine or reviewing the quality of wine; or a restaurant. Nor could any participant be associated with an advertising agency or market research firm.

    As a further requirement, each participant had to have a minimum of five years' tasting experience and was required to average at least 12 tastings per year.

    NCTI chose the San Francisco Vintners Club, a nonprofit private wine tasting group, as a starting point for recruitment because of its reputation

APPENDIX (*concluded*)

within California wine tasting circles. The club also is not affiliated with any wine producer and its members routinely participate in weekly wine tastings, generally organized according to the identical principles and 20-point Davis rating system the NCTI intended to use in its own study.

Sixty-four percent of the 27-member panel was chosen from this group. The remainder was composed of other serious wine tasters who were members of such other respected wine tasting societies as Les Amis du Vin, Knights of the Vine, and Berkeley Food and Wine Society. Like the tasters from the Vintners Club, each participant was chosen for his or her experience and familiarity with tasting protocol.

The resulting lineup of participating tasters far exceeded those initial qualifications. Most of the respondents had well over 5 years of tasting experience and several had 20 years or more. In fact the 27 panel members averaged 12.3 years of wine tasting experience.

Likewise, the frequency with which each panel member participated in wine tasting tests averaged 50 per year, far exceeding the minimum standards established by NCTI.

III. *Test procedure*

The details of the testing procedure itself were no less demanding than those governing the selection of the panelists. The wine tasting format of the Vintners Club was chosen as the model to be followed by NCTI, specifically because of the club's meticulous and established protocol, including the use of the 20-point Davis rating system.

The tastings were conducted on July 22, 1978, in San Francisco at the Stanford Court Hotel.

Identical settings and procedures were replicated for each of the four wine tastings. All wine was served in odorless glasses marked only by A, B, C, or D.

In accordance with standard tasting procedures, the panelists moved from tasting the drier wines first to the sweeter wines. Within this order—chablis, rosé, rhine, burgundy—the individual wines were also rotated so that, for example, Glass A contained a different brand of wine in each test.

Great care was also taken in the purchase of the competitive wines to ensure that the competitive wines in the tasting were also recently bottled. Naturally, each of the wines was served at the appropriate temperature.

IV. *The results*

Using the 20-point Davis rating system, the tasters evaluated ten different properties of each wine and ranked the four wines in each test in order of preference.

When the results were tabulated, Taylor California Cellars was judged superior in the rosé, burgundy, and rhine tastings and a very close second in the chablis testing.

C. Reappraising Strategy and Corporate Direction

12. The Devil's Own Wine Shoppe*

Bruce Nelson looked around the handsome wine store and remarked to his wife Mary Lee, "We may have given the old saying, 'in vino veritas,' a new and even more sardonic meaning. In the end, this wine shop may have provided us with an education in the ways of business but—oh my!—at a cost of $10,000." It was difficult for the Nelsons to think about the likelihood of such a loss, but events required that they face the possibility.

Just that morning, Bruce's boss, the sales manager of a large Chevrolet dealership, had called Bruce to his office for a talk. He explained to Bruce that he had a good deal of confidence in his ability as a salesman and felt that Bruce could become one of the agency's most productive salesmen if he would only give undivided attention to selling as his work. The sales manager knew that the Nelsons had opened a wine shop about nine months earlier and that Bruce was working at the wine shop when he did not have floor duty at the dealership. The sales manager believed that the extra time and worry of the wine shop was affecting Bruce's performance as a salesman and, not unpleasantly, suggested that a choice between working at the dealership or the wine shop ought to be faced by Bruce.

There were other reasons for deciding what to do about the wine shop quite soon. The Nelsons had a $15,000 bank loan and the bank was asking for repayment to begin and for agreement about a schedule of regular payments even though the wine shop was operating at a loss. In personal terms, the Nelsons had two small children and the present necessity for one of the Nelsons to be at the wine shop when it was open was disrupting their home life and, they felt, unfavorably affecting them as parents. Bruce himself had several classic symptoms of "nerves." At times he had a rash on his body and hands and found it difficult to relax or be at all still. He knew that he was tense; he was, in his own words, "obsessed with his problems."

PERSONAL BACKGROUND

"My dream—my goal—has been to have my own business," Bruce explained to a fellow car salesman who was sympathizing with him and trying to understand how Bruce had gotten himself into his present difficult situa-

---

* Prepared by Profs. Eleanor Casebier and Manning Hanline, the University of West Florida.

tion. "My father was an independent hardware store owner in Pontiac, Michigan, and, as I was growing up, I recognized that I wanted the kind of life that can come from having a successful, personal business." To Bruce that meant not only having a degree of independence but, frankly, it also meant being successful in economic terms. If he had not read tales of Horatio Alger, he nevertheless had acquired similar values and hopes from his home background.

Bruce was the oldest of three boys all of whom had grown up helping in the hardware store. "Why didn't you stay in Pontiac and continue in business with your father?" the car salesman asked. Bruce answered: "I might have except that the Vietnam War took me away from Pontiac and other events also occurred to keep me from returning permanently.

"I joined the Marines in 1964 and, after training, was sent to the Pensacola, Florida, Naval Air Station for duty. I met and married my wife while stationed at NAS. She was born and reared in Pensacola. After leaving the Marines, I went to work for the Gulf Power Company in Pensacola for a short period of time but returned to Pontiac to help my father who was critically ill.

"We stayed in Pontiac for two years and during that time my father died. I may as well be frank about my relations with my mother. She and my wife did not get along well. I offered to stay and help with the business but only if I could acquire part ownership. I would not work for my mother.

"As it turned out, my 'middle' brother stayed to help with the hardware store. However, he has left the business and is teaching school. My mother runs the business now and my youngest brother is helping her.

"My wife and I came back to Pensacola and I began to work here selling cars. I really do like to sell and, in a way, I've always felt that I would have mastered a real challenge if I were to be a successful new-car salesman. It is so different from other work I've done and I've had no particular training for it as I find it being done here. Nevertheless, my dream of having a personal business led to our opening the wine shop last fall."

The fellow car salesman wondered, "If you wanted your own business, why didn't you open a hardware store? I can understand that you returned to Pensacola because it's your wife's hometown."

"It would take somewhere between $60,000 and $75,000 for inventory alone to open a good hardware store," Bruce observed. "There were also two other factors that I considered. The hardware business is a 'cut-rate or discount' business these days. It's extremely competitive. In addition, I know from hard experience that it can be a 'dirty' business. Customers expect you to take their greasy tools or what-have-you—or even their bathroom fixtures—and find parts for them. You might spend a half-hour finding one small ten-cent bolt for something-or-other."

"On the other hand, my wife and I became interested in wine; the subject appealed to us. It's certainly a 'clean' business and a first-rate wine store doesn't require nearly the inventory investment that a hardware store does."

STORE LOCATION

A regional economic analysis for the Pensacola Standard Metropolitan Statistical Area (SMSA) was prepared by planning consultants aided by a federal grant in 1973. This study indicated that growth and change were to be expected in the Pensacola area. The city had a population of about 80,000; the SMSA, about 245,000. Population was expected to grow at a faster rate than in the nation as a whole. According to the study, "The general area possesses a viable economy, an adequate natural resource base, and abundant geographical and climatic amenities." The Pensacola SMSA had made impressive gains in per capita income over the past ten years and had experienced, and was expected to continue to experience, a substantial growth rate in the higher income ranges.

The study stated that the economy of Pensacola SMSA was well balanced with activity including manufacturing, government (largely military, including substantial repair facilities), tourism, and some oil drilling and refining, in addition to a representative share of retail trade, construction, transportation, finance, insurance, and real estate. According to the analysis, the area had "the potential to be a primary tourist center."

The Devil's Own Wine Shoppe was located in a "mature" shopping center first opened in 1958. The center was "L-shaped" in design and was the type where storefronts were connected by an outside walkway with a roof overhead. There was a large parking area between the two legs of the "L."

The center had experienced a considerable turnover in stores and a noticeable reduction in customer traffic during the past two years—mainly because three larger, enclosed shopping malls and several other smaller shopping centers of the open type had recently opened in Pensacola. However, there was a branch store of a large, regional department store in the shopping center and a respectable variety of stores and shops in the center. The general look of the center was not one of prosperity, though, and Bruce knew that businesses in the center were having a difficult time. (It was satisfying to Bruce that other store owners and managers had come to accept him as a compeer in the nine months he had been in business and to confide their business concerns to him.)

A particular feature of the shopping center was that it included a five-story office building which housed various professional and service organizations. The office building was connected to the center by a patio-type roof. Attractive planters had been placed in the area between the center and the office building. The Devil's Own Wine Shoppe was situated in the shopping center at the point that it was connected to the office building (the front corner; at the end of the longer leg of the "L," in effect) and, therefore, overlooked both the planted patio area and the parking lot.

In making the decision to locate in the shopping center, Bruce relied upon the following factors:

1. The shopping center was near the "center of population" of the Pensacola area and located at one of the busiest intersections of the city.
2. Relative to possibilities in other shopping centers, lease costs were lower. One of the enclosed malls wanted $1,000 a month for a space just slightly bigger than the present location of The Devil's Own Wine Shoppe. Another wanted $750 a month and a percentage of sales plus requiring the payment of dues to an association of tenants and an amount for maintenance of the common area of the center. This same mall wanted $5,000 to prepare the site (for carpeting, doors, a sign, and so on).
3. He could locate no acceptable building with adequate parking that was not in a shopping center. Many retail businesses had moved out of downtown Pensacola; it had obviously been affected by the competition of the newer shopping malls and centers as the following local newspaper story illustrated:

Business Association Decides "Down" Is Out And "In" Is In

Downtown Pensacola is no longer "down" but "in" as members of the Intown Business Association (IBA) seek to change the downtown image to intown Pensacola.

The IBA, formerly the Downtown Development Association met Tuesday in the San Carlos Hotel to announce to merchant members that they are changing the name of the organization.

President Bob Smith says the new name is designed to keep downtown alive, because many of the nation's downtown areas are plagued with desertion, leaving the impression of being really "down."

The Nelsons had signed a three-year lease on August 3, 1974, to pay rent at $369 a month. Utilities were furnished by the leasee.

ECONOMIC CONDITIONS

The economic recession of the mid-1970s in the United States was a matter of record. The state of Florida developed a rate of unemployment 2 percent to 3 percent higher than the national average during this period. The Pensacola area felt the effects of recession more gradually than either the state or nation, but by the third quarter of 1974 had exceeded the national average rate for unemployment while remaining somewhat under the state average rate.

As reported by the Department of Commerce, state of Florida, in its "Pensacola SMSA Labor Market Trends," which included statistics for the surrounding two-county area, the unemployment rate was 10.1 percent as of June 1975.

Local economic optimism during this time centered on tourism. Tourist trade as reflected by such informal indexes as tourists' requests for help and motel occupancy rates continued strong. The main attraction in the Pensacola area was the beautiful, open beach along the Gulf of Mexico but historical attractions and museums were also emphasized and publicized.

COMPETITION

The Devil's Own Wine Shoppe was unique in Pensacola; that is, it was the only store offering wine and related products exclusively. All grades of wines from the least expensive to the very expensive were stocked. Both domestic and foreign wines were carried but the Nelsons attempted to promote and develop a clientele for California wine.

Outside of wine, a limited number of wine racks and wine glasses were carried. The initial wine inventory cost approximately $10,000; there had not been money for party or other complementary items, according to Bruce.

Wine was available in Pensacola, however, from a variety of sources: grocery stores, drugstores, and liquor, or package, stores. It was Bruce's understanding (gleaned from wholesaler salesmen) that three of the four largest wine accounts were grocery supermarket chains and the fourth, a drugstore chain. Their volume came from sales of less expensive domestic wine.

For this type of wine, retail price competition was strong. Wholesalers offered the same volume-discount pricing structure to all customers. The large-volume grocery and drug chains bought selected items at the lowest wholesale prices and marked them up little, if at all. Bruce was convinced that one drug store chain had begun a policy of selling its limited variety of domestic wine at wholesale cost simply to attract customers into its stores; subsequently, another local drug store had been spurred to discount its wine at prices equivalent to a 10 percent markup. These wine prices were regularly advertised in the local newspaper by both the grocery and drug outlets.

There was other competition, especially from a local liquor (package) chain which did extensive advertising in the newspaper and on radio. In one campaign, it labeled itself as "the ubiquitous package store" easily available to all; in another, it claimed to carry the "greatest selection of imported and domestic wines" in northwest Florida.

The Nelson's pricing policy was to mark up the relatively inexpensive, domestic wine by 20 percent–25 percent over wholesale cost; to mark up the middle range of wine by 40 percent; and the very best by 50 percent. Bruce estimated that his average gross profit was 28 percent.

Figuring out how to price against the discount wine stores was not the Nelson's only dilemma. Bruce had come to believe that "advertising is fantastically expensive." He had signed a contract with an advertising agency prior to opening the wine shop and, in 1974 with the help of the agency in preparing copy and placing ads, spent almost $1,100 on advertising. He had purchased spot announcements on three AM radio stations and on two FM stations. He had advertised in the local newspaper. Copy featured The Devil's Own Wine Shoppe as a distinctive place to buy wine but also contained specials at competitive prices.

Bruce had not been able to measure directly the effect of this type of advertising on sales or to notice any accumulative positive effect. For these reasons, and because of its high cost, he had almost stopped advertising. On the advice of the advertising agency, he was evaluating the technique of direct-mail and had compiled a list of doctors, lawyers, and other professional persons by using the yellow pages of the telephone book. He was not convinced, however, that present circumstances justified expenditures for postal permits and mailing.

The advertising agency had charged The Devil's Own Wine Shoppe very little in fees; it hoped to develop the account into a larger one in the future. It had supplied Bruce with a copy of a research report on the wine industry. (See Exhibit 3 at end of the case.)

FINANCIAL CONSIDERATIONS

On their own, the Nelsons had invested $7,000 in The Devil's Own Wine Shoppe. To add to this, they had obtained a loan of $15,000 from a local bank with interest at 9.85 percent. At the time the Nelsons arranged the loan, the prime rate of interest was 12 percent, as Bruce recalled the circumstances. (Florida had a usury law which prohibited lending at over an annual percentage rate of 10 percent.)

The loan officer of the bank explained his reasons for granting the loan: "The decision to lend Bruce the money was based on several factors. He had reasonable capital in the form of family money, and had both the enthusiasm and training to be successful with what we felt, and still feel, was a unique idea. He had nearly completed an M.B.A. degree program and was reasonably skilled in bookkeeping and accounting." The loan officer might have added, but did not, that Bruce and the vice president in charge of the Loan Division of that bank were close acquaintances, having gotten to know one another as fellow students in the M.B.A. degree program.

The loan officer further explained that the wine inventory and store fixtures of The Devil's Own Wine Shoppe were required as collateral. "While loans of this type usually are made by the bank for a 90-day period," he said, "in this instance the loan was drawn so that it could extend up to five years." During the first 90 days, Bruce was to have decided what size payments he would make and in effect thereby determine the term of the loan. Actually, at the end of 90 days, Bruce asked for an extension and the loan officer agreed to it. Other 90-day extensions followed; however, the last extension carrying The Devil's Own Wine Shoppe through May 1975, was for 60 days.

He did not worry about losing money on the loan, the loan officer stated, because of the collateral but did recognize the high "mortality rate" among new, small businesses. "Only about 1 percent of the amount we lend goes to new businesses," he said. "Had Bruce requested $50,000, for example, the decision could very well have been different. We're aware of the disturbing statistics showing that, except for those with exclusive franchises, seven out of ten new businesses fail. Often, the symptoms of failure are apparent as early as, say, six months and most often are quite clear within two years."

Both the loan officer and the vice president of the Loan Division were pleased that Bruce had regularly and voluntarily stopped by the bank to discuss his situation. On these occasions, they expressed their confidence in his ultimate success.

They did not feel that his difficulties were due to location. They felt that Bruce's analysis of alternatives before choosing his site was sound and that relocation would be expensive and simply not solve what they felt was his problem. It was, they thought, the type of competition that the wine shop faced, especially for low-cost wines. They recommended that The Devil's Own Wine Shoppe should increasingly emphasize fine wines for which there was much less, in fact very little, competition.

The bankers made several allied suggestions to Bruce which would indicate that he should supplement both his present promotional and retail store activities. They suggested consideration of the following:

1. Arrange wine-tasting parties. Wholesalers would provide the wine; local country clubs might be willing to host such parties.
2. Begin to solicit business by telephone. Bruce and Mary Lee could utilize the time they are at the wine shop and not busy otherwise for this.
3. Convince banks and other business firms to give Christmas baskets filled with different types of wines, priced around $25. There was a large market for the Christmas business gift and wine might be considered to be more aristocratic than whiskey, the current vogue in commercial "giving."

The bankers claimed that data were available proving that sales of liquor stores had continued to be good, if in fact they had not increased, during the economic slump. "People drink when they are happy and when they are sad, it would seem," one said. In any event, they did not consider general economic conditions to be an important factor when considering the problems of The Devil's Own Wine Shoppe.

COSTS AND OPERATIONS

When planning the layout of The Devil's Own Wine Shoppe. Bruce designed a special rack to display the most expensive wines and a U-shaped counter not only for use in waiting on customers but also for storing supplies, records, display material, and so on. He had these built to order by a cabinetmaker. In addition, he purchased standard wall shelves, floor display racks, a cooler, and a cash register. All together, fixtures cost $4,415, as itemized below:

Cash register	$ 400
Custom fixtures	848
Wine island floor fixtures	1,026
Wall fixtures	458
Shelving fixtures	749
Finishing fixtures	153
Lumber for shelving	157
Cooler	624
	$4,415

Expenditures by the Nelsons for leasehold improvements, largely to carpet the store and to buy and have signs installed, included:

Carpeting	$ 743
Store sign	650
Window signs	174
Parking lot sign	130
Lumber	46
	$1,743

TABLE 1
Sales in 1974*

Week Ending	Monday	Tuesday	Wednesday	Thursday	Friday	Saturday	Weekly Total
8/16 (Sunday)							$ 40.4:
8/17	$ 58.22	$ 54.33	$ 18.86	$ 18.73	$ 60.44	$216.69	427.2:
8/24	41.74	71.26	45.02	69.76	68.40	88.79	384.9:
8/31	70.11	130.43	22.13	68.77	134.57	182.45	608.4(
9/7	Holiday	74.86	41.66	26.40	81.99	58.67	283.5:
9/14	64.70	63.19	35.65	48.31	68.97	50.61	331.4:
9/21	38.06	38.20	50.73	48.06	73.35	160.82	409.2:
9/28	149.90	11.87	38.33	52.87	156.02	303.67	712.6(
10/5	10.29	70.02	58.44	52.67	73.32	75.47	340.2'
10/12	20.05	8.01	15.66	36.63	279.48	72.54	432.3:
10/19	187.04	60.42	55.92	55.39	49.23	73.55	481.5:
10/26	85.67	238.54	73.95	66.59	95.37	53.59	613.7'
11/2	141.40	45.17	61.58	43.39	61.72	55.03	408.2:
11/9	21.62	47.69	23.66	28.33	136.44	24.21	281.9:
11/16	39.82	10.81	24.41	67.99	97.49	121.91	362.4:
11/23	91.66	32.60	67.65	31.76	74.60	82.87	381.1<
11/30	119.63	62.69	245.44	Holiday	66.36	85.32	579.4<
12/7	34.65	52.04	31.38	109.78	120.84	83.34	432.0:
12/14	40.64	41.34	121.30	67.17	111.69	106.08	488.2:
12/21	53.06	186.79	130.97	76.47	230.55	263.84	941.6:
12/28	255.73	297.79	Holiday	47.27	70.09	42.12	713.0(
12/31	79.63	128.61	Holiday				208.24

* Daily sales data include 4 percent Florida sales tax.

In June 1974, the Nelsons purchased a Chevrolet van which was carried on the accounts of The Devil's Own Wine Shoppe. The down payment was $176; monthly payments were $97.

Wine purchases in 1974 totaled $15,316; to date in 1975, wine purchases amounted to $3,024. Miscellaneous purchases of merchandise for sale amounted to $1,323 in 1974, and to $26 so far in 1975. For daily sales from the time the store was opened in August 1974 to May 1975, see Tables 1 and 2.

Outlays of cash not provided for in the foregoing accounting data in 1974 totaled $8,011; in 1975, $4,319. These outlays are itemized below.

Other Outlays of Cash in 1974

Rent	$1,476	Telephone	$ 219
Chamber of Commerce dues	47	Labor	2,143
Licenses and taxes	265	Social Security	124
Supplies	164	Withholding tax	251
Utility deposits	60	Payroll tax	245
Freight	399	Florida sales tax	264
Postage	78	B. Nelson, drawing	350
Repairs and maintenance	29	Advertising	1,080
Bank charges	81	Accounting	60
Insurance	384	Donations	7
Interest on bank loan	285		$8,011

Other Outlays of Cash in 1975

Rent	$1,845	Telephone	$ 182
Supplies	8	Labor	21
Repairs and maintenance	17	Social Security	1
Insurance	10	Payroll tax	24
Interest on bank loan	682	Florida sales tax	366
Janitorial service	40	Advertising	235
Child care	888		$4,319

These cash outlays were ordinary, but the circumstances calling for several of them were singularly related to The Devil's Own Wine Shoppe.

The Nelsons had not intended that Mary Lee should work in the wine shop when they opened it. At the beginning, they hired a full-time clerk (a younger girl in her early 20s) at a salary of $500 a month. Bruce planned to be at the shop during lunch-hours and late in the afternoons. The girl was laid off in the middle of December 1974, and Mary Lee began to work regularly. From then on, she and Bruce shared being at the shop. They enrolled their preschool child in a nursery and hired a baby-sitter to watch over their other school-age child after school until Mary Lee could get home.

The Nelsons carried fire insurance on the contents of The Devil's Own Wine Shoppe. They did not carry burglary insurance because, Bruce reasoned, the shopping center was well lit at night and guarded by armed security men and trained dogs. An inventory as of the end of 1974 showed the wholesale value of wine and other merchandise for sale on hand to be $8,038. Cash on hand was $102.

TABLE 2
Sales in 1975*

Week Ending	Monday	Tuesday	Wednesday	Thursday	Friday	Saturday	Weekly Total
1/4				$ 53.01	$ 31.38	$111.02	$195.41
1/11	$ 31.67	$ 75.68	$31.60	19.66	100.59	137.96	397.16
1/18	31.94	18.22	70.82	47.63	53.92	18.67	241.20
1/25	63.30	39.95	26.39	16.27	47.92	63.00	256.83
2/1	25.98	85.43	92.21	74.34	57.32	142.64	477.92
2/8	20.95	48.60	30.90	115.61	34.87	399.96	650.89
2/15	127.81	53.83	17.68	137.31	163.16	122.70	622.49
2/22	43.49	46.94	40.13	30.67	91.25 .	202.39	454.87
3/1	47.79	50.89	78.20	24.22	83.32	98.40	382.82
3/8	30.68	23.44	50.48	48.27	50.78	101.45	305.10
3/15	23.47	12.74	14.36	39.03	123.17	130.55	343.32
3/22	3.54	20.83	18.02	12.58	115.78	147.19	317.94
3/29	14.63	113.22	41.75	27.68	133.86	135.76	466.90
4/5	44.36	139.72	35.71	22.25	64.76	31.79	338.59
4/12	11.46	0	43.61	102.04	133.09	134.42	424.62
4/19	28.34	64.12	59.82	24.95	67.69	141.84	386.76
4/26	118.38	23.87	41.99	16.33	28.07	48.44	277.08
5/3	37.35	10.42	44.89	26.80	74.15	32.85	226.46
5/10	35.22	25.00	14.88	20.78	56.52	66.19	218.59
5/17	32.69	27.66	33.12	55.67	74.01	72.30	295.45
5/2	7.48	20.22					27.70

* Daily sales data include 4 percent Florida sales tax.

ASSESSING THE SITUATION

With his background, Bruce did not have difficulty thinking in a traditional way about the financial condition of The Devil's Own Wine Shoppe. He wondered, though, if the newer quantitative techniques which he had learned in operations research and management science would be helpful. He set out to try them with help from a mathematically skilled friend. In fact, his friend became so interested that he prepared the following report for Bruce:

An analysis of costs, volume, and profit relationships reveal that you have sound reasons for concern, Bruce.

In an effort to use the normal curve to make predictions, daily sales were plotted. There are 239 days for which data are available. The first six classes plot something like a normal curve. The frequency polygon shows extreme skewness with a few very good days causing a tailing out toward the right. (See Table 3 and Exhibit 1.)

It was assumed without rigorous statistical testing that additional data on daily sales would fully justify the assumption that the distribution could be described by a normal curve. The average monthly sales were $1,888 and the standard deviation was $394. With the mean, standard deviation, and an assumption about the distribution of the random variable (sales), it was possible

TABLE 3
Frequency Classification of Daily Sales

Class	Frequency
$ 0 and under $20	24
20–40	54
40–60	51
60–80	43
80–100	14
100–120	12
120–140	19
140–160	6
160–260	11
260–360	4
360–460	1
	239

EXHIBIT 1
Frequency Polygon of Daily Sales

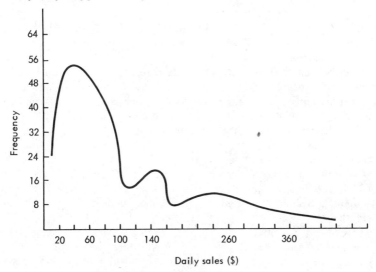

Daily sales ($)

to use normal curve areas and assess the probability of sales reaching certain desirable levels. (See Table 4.)

Costs per month were computed with and without a salary for you, Bruce. This made it possible to find a level of sales which would permit you to break even given the present arrangement, and also makes it possible to determine what volume would permit you to quit your job and devote full time to the business. First without considering money withdrawn by yourself, expenses have averaged $1,330 a month. This figure was computed as follows: Total ordinary expenses were $12,330 for the nine months of operation. This amount

TABLE 4
Monthly Sales, August 16–May 15

Year	Month and Day	Sales
1974:	8/16–9/15	$ 2,076
	9/16–10/15	2,142
	10/16–11/15	1,779
	11/16–12/15	2,003
1975:	12/16–1/15	2,576
	1/16–2/15	2,128
	2/16–3/15	1,486
	3/16–4/15	1,641
	4/16–5/15	1,166
	Total	$16,997

Average monthly sales (rounded) = $1,888 = $\bar{X}$
Standard deviation of monthly sales (rounded) = $394 = \sigma$

Note: Sales data were available from August 16, 1974, to May 20, 1975. In order to use as much of the available data as possible, sales are shown from the middle of one month to the middle of the following month. Four days have been omitted at the end.

was reduced by the amount shown in the drawing account ($350), and the total expenses used is $11,980 which amounts to approximately $1,330 a month for the nine months.

Markup on sales is estimated at 28 percent. This is an estimated overall markup consisting of a 20 percent–25 percent markup on low-priced items and higher markups on more expensive wines. Since sales of low-priced items have the greatest volume, an average markup seems to be justified. (You have estimated that the average price per item sold is $3.)

With a 28 percent markup on average monthly sales of $1,888, there is a $528 contribution available to cover costs. With ordinary cash outlays of $1,330 a month, the business has been losing money at the rate of about $802 a month. However federal income tax refunds—which you have gotten—based on losses amounted to about 25 percent, so these losses can be reduced by $200 to $602 a month.

However, it is obvious that the matter of the bank loan cannot be ignored indefinitely. Also, Bruce, you are overextending your energies, so that you either have to hire someone to operate the business or give up your job and devote all your attention to it. The maximum length of the loan was to have been five years. Repayment of principal, then, would amount to $250 monthly.

With a monthly expense of $1,580 which included payments on principal of $250, but no salary for you, a sales volume of $5,642 a month would be required to break even. This represents a 28 percent contribution and includes sufficient income to cover normal costs of operating the business as well as repayment on the principal of the loan. Your salary at the auto dealership averages $1,000 a month, you have said. If this is included in the calculation, the expenses go to $2,580, and a sales volume of $9,214 a month would be required to break even.

The original intent was to use the normal curve areas and assess the proba-

EXHIBIT 2
Normal Curve Showing Mean and Break-Even Point

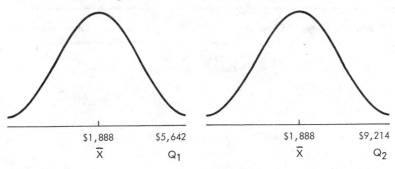

$1,888	$5,642	$1,888	$9,214
$\bar{X}$	Q_1	$\bar{X}$	Q_2

bility of breaking even or making a profit. This can be shown as the probability of $X > Q$, where X is monthly sales and Q is break-even point. As a picture, this is represented in Exhibit 2.

A Z value can be computed as follows:

$$Z = \frac{Q_1 - \bar{X}}{\alpha} = \frac{5.642 - 1.888}{394} = \frac{3.754}{394} = 9.52$$

Thus, there is almost no likelihood using normal curve areas and present data that the business will reach a break-even point sufficient to cover expenses excluding a salary for you. Obviously, there would be even less likelihood including that amount.

Data do not indicate that the outlook for the future of the wine shop is good, Bruce. A monthly trend line shows that sales are declining at the rate of $115 a month. Acknowledgement is made that trend analysis is designed for long-term annual data. Of course, such data are not available for the wine shop. Also, it is quite obvious that there is a strong seasonal influence on sales, with the peak occurring around the holidays at year's end. Since data are available for only nine months, they do not lend themselves to a statistical computation of seasonal influence. Recognizing all these factors a trend line was computed, and it is as follows:

$$Y' = 1,888 - 115X$$
Origin – 1/1/75
X in months
Y in sales dollars.

WHAT TO DO?

"It's decision time," Bruce said to Mary Lee, "things just aren't righting themselves." Mary Lee agreed. Even with agreement, they found decision making to be hard because in their case it involved dreams, economics, home life, career; all in all, a way of life.

EXHIBIT 3
Profiles on Leading Categories of Business

Size of Business. Consumer expenditures and gallonage for recent years:

	Expenditures (Supermarketing)	Gallons (Wine Institute)
1974	$2,200,000,000	370,000,000
1973	1,944,000,000	347,317,000
1972	1,700,050,000	336,985,000
1971	1,545,500,000	305,221,000

Types of Wine. Of 1973 sales, 84.1 percent were domestic brands (69.6 percent California), and 15.9 percent imported. Of the imports, Italy supplied 26 percent, France 24.3 percent, Spain 17.2 percent, Portugal 14.9 percent, Germany 10.3 percent, all other countries 7.3 percent. Table wines were 55.1 percent of sales, followed by dessert wines (20 percent), flavored wines (17.2 percent), champagne and sparkling wines (6 percent), and vermouth (2.9 percent) (*Wines & Vines*, April 1974).

When Business Occurs. Wine sales by months (*1973 Wine Marketing Handbook*):

January	7.0%	May	7.2%	September	7.1%
February	7.6	June	7.7	October	8.6
March	7.2	July	8.5	November	10.3
April	9.8	August	6.1	December	12.9

Where Sold. Liquor stores 60 percent, food stores 33 percent, others 7 percent (*Supermarketing,* liquor store magazines). Average liquor store stocks 79 domestic and 151 imported types.

Place of Consumption. A Trendex survey found 84.7 percent of wine drinkers last had wine at home, 8.1 percent in someone else's home, and 7.7 percent in a restaurant or bar. A 1972 *Food Service Magazine* survey found 55 percent of restaurants serving wine, but only 26 percent of adults ever order wine when dining out. By demographics:

Sex:	Men	26%	Income:	$15,000+	38%
	Women	24		$10,000–14,999	28
				$ 7,000– 9,999	25
				$ 5,000– 6,999	15
				Under $5,000	16
Age:	18–34	32%	Region:	Northeast	31%
	35–49	30		North Central	19
	50+	16		South	17
				West	40

Why People Drink Wine. Like taste, 60 percent; be sociable, 45 percent; celebrate an occasion, 41 percent; stimulates appetite, 35 percent; helps one relax, 27

EXHIBIT 3 *(continued)*

percent; habit, 17 percent; thirst-quenching, 5 percent (*Beverage Industry*, March 24, 1972).

Reason for Last Specific Purchase (Women). Dinner, 26 percent; regular use, 18 percent; party or celebration, 15 percent; special dinner, 13 percent; gift, 11 percent, other, 17 percent (*Family Circle*, 1973). For buying specific brand; personal experience, 59 percent; husband's influence, 40 percent; friends/relatives influence, 29 percent; other, minor.

Most Recent Usage. *Newsweek* survey asked last time wine was:

	Personally Consumed	Bought
Within past week	57.6%	32.1%
Within past four weeks	22.8	29.5
Within past six months	14.9	25.2
Longer ago, don't recall	4.7	13.2

Wine Drinking Occasions. The *Time* survey found 85 percent of wine users serving it during dinner, 50 percent before dinner, 31 percent after dinner, 10 percent other times. The *Newsweek* survey found 72 percent agreeing with the statement "meals generally taste better when accompanied by wine"; also 72 percent agreeing that "wine should be served whenever you have guests for dinner," 66 percent substituted wine for liquor on occasions (*Time*).

Buying Habits. A survey for the French government found 47.3 percent had discovered their favorite wine from a friend's suggestion, 31 percent from a wine-tasting session, and 10.7 percent from a waiter; 86.4 percent had decided to buy before entering a package store, and three out of four had already chosen the country of origin; 63.7 percent had decided on a specific brand or type; 13.8 percent considered vintage dates very important and 24.9 percent fairly important (*Wines & Vines*, September 1971). The *Time* survey found for home use, that men decide brands 51 percent of the time, women 22 percent, together or equally 38 percent. Men make the purchase 53 percent of the time, women 23 percent, together or equally 24 percent. The *Newsweek* survey found the decision on type to buy made before the shopping trip 66.1 percent of the time, in the store 26.6 percent; 53.7 percent decided brands before shopping and 35.6 percent in the store; 79 percent sometimes change brands, 8 percent never do, and 12 percent don't buy by brand name (*Time*). When women shop alone, 83 percent made final decision on type/brand (59 percent unaided, 24 percent somewhat influenced by others).

Gift Market. The *Time* survey found 55 percent having given wine as a gift within the past year, while 58 percent received wine as a gift; 11 percent of women had made their last purchase as a gift (*Family Circle*).

Prices. Forty-nine percent of brands are less than $1.25 a bottle, 43 percent between $1.25 and $3.50, and 8 percent more than $3.50 (*Ad Age*, October 23, 1972); 22 percent in the *Time* survey found price "very much" a factor, 50 percent said "somewhat," 28 percent "little importance."

Demographics. The 1972 *Time* survey (done in large markets only) found wine drinkers to have the following characteristics:

EXHIBIT 3 (concluded)

Sex:	Men 73%		Income:	Over $25,000 .... 38%
	Women 27			$15,000–24,999 38
				$10,000–14,999 16
				Under $10,000 8
Age:	Under 25 3			
	25–34 16			
	35–49 39			
	Over 50 42			

Young Adult Market is important for "pop wines . . . about 25 percent of today's sales; 70 percent consume wine, of which 61 percent drink wine at least once a week; 50 percent use table wines, 33 percent fruit wines, 17 percent "pop" wines. Most important purchase factors: type 43 percent, brand 33 percent, price 23 percent. Average weekly expenditure on wines is $4 (ABC-FM Stereo Rock Market Study, fall 1971). A *Redbook Magazine* survey found 83 percent serving wine at home; 39 percent use it for drinking, 6 percent for cooking, 55 percent both. The respondent (mostly women 18–34) buys the wine 67 percent of the time. Factors influencing brand choice include others suggestions (50 percent), advertising (36 percent), price (27 percent), and taste (17 percent). Occasions for guest use: dinners, 46 percent; when guests ask for it, 10 percent; before dinner, 7 percent; holidays, 7 percent. A National Educational Adv. Services survey found half of college students drink wine; one out of seven at least once a week.

They especially wondered about two questions. Would the market for wine in Pensacola support an all-out effort by them? Were they, themselves, committed enough to being in business to sacrifice what it would involve to make the all-out effort?

Bruce indicated that they had five options:

1. Sell the store.
2. Merge with a sandwich shop, or cheese store, to introduce wine to more people and to make it generally more available at more times.
3. Have Bruce quit his job and devote full-time to the wine shop, emphasizing the introduction of new promotion and selling activities.
4. Close the store and liquidate the assets.
5. Declare bankruptcy.

13. Northern Scrap Processors, Inc. (A)*

In January 1975, David Longer, owner and president of Northern Scrap Processors, Inc., learned that an outside firm had approached the local city government with a proposal to take over the municipal trash collecting operations. Although Mr. Longer's business was presently confined to processing scrap metals for recycling, he feared that the initial intrusion into the local waste removal business by this outside firm could eventually lead to an undue amount of competition in the local scrap market. Therefore, he was considering whether to make a counterproposal to the city, and if so, what the terms of such a counterproposal might be. At the same time, he had to consider the implications of this decision for his scrap business which was facing new competitive pressures from other important sources.

COMPANY BACKGROUND

Mr. Longer had bought Northern Scrap Processors in late 1969 and assumed control of operations on January 1, 1970. Northern Scrap, which served a growing northwestern city (population 50,000) and neighboring areas, was in the business of processing all common kinds of scrap metals. The company did not deal in nonmetallic materials. The main business of Northern Scrap was salvaging old automobiles, washing machines, and similar durable goods as well as industrial scrap. This raw scrap was separated into various categories and processed into different grades of reusable materials. Then, it was sold, generally through brokers, to various iron and metal manufacturers.

When Mr. Longer, a professional engineer with considerable experience in defense-related industries, took over the business in 1970, it was unprofitable and in a run-down state. (See Exhibit 1). One of his early moves was to find a new site for his metals processing and storage operation in a different part of the city. The site he chose had a railroad siding and was large enough to provide for eventual expansion of the business. A metals house was erected on the site. This house served as secure storage for the more valuable metals (copper and brass) as well as office space. The layout of Northern Scrap's new site is shown in Exhibit 2.

---

* Prepared by Richard S. Harrigan and Burnard H. Sord, the University of Texas at Austin. The firm's name and location are disguised.

EXHIBIT 1

1969 Federal Income Tax Return Information for Northern Scrap Processors (year prior to purchase by Mr. Longer)

IMPORTANT—All applicable lines and schedules must be filled in. If the lines on the schedules are not sufficient, see instruction M.

GROSS INCOME	1	Gross receipts or gross sales .... Less: returns and allowances	152,321.18
	2	Less: cost of goods sold (Schedule A) and/or operations (attach schedule)	125,016.24
	3	Gross profit	
	4	(a) Domestic dividends	
		(b) Foreign dividends	
	5	Interest on obligations of the United States and U.S. instrumentalities	
	6	Other interest	
	7	Gross rents	
	8	Gross royalties	
	9	Gains and losses (separate Schedule D, Form 1120S)—	
		(a) Net short-term capital gain reduced by any net long-term capital loss	
		(b) Net long-term capital gain reduced by any net short-term capital loss (if more than $25,000, see instructions)	
		(c) Net gain (loss) from sale or exchange of property other than capital assets	
	10	Other income (attach schedule)	
	11	Total income, lines 3 through 10	27,304.94
DEDUCTIONS	12	Compensation of officers (Schedule E)	
	13	Salaries and wages (not deducted elsewhere)	34,847.25
	14	Repairs (do not include capital expenditures)	5,620.01
	15	Bad debts (Schedule F if reserve method is used)	
	16	Rents	117.00
	17	Taxes (attach schedule)	6,092.86
	18	Interest	4,024.00
	19	Contributions (not over 5% of line 28 adjusted per instructions—attach schedule) . . .	
	20	Casualty or theft losses (attach schedule)	
	21	Amortization (attach schedule)	
	22	Depreciation (Schedule G)	1,581.08
	23	Depletion (attach schedule)	
	24	Advertising	455.38
	25	(a) Pension, profit-sharing, stock bonus, annuity plans (attach Form(s) 2950)	
		(b) Other employee benefit plans (see instructions)	
	26	Other deductions (attach schedule)	21,729.37
	27	Total deductions on lines 12 through 26	74,466.95
	28	Taxable income, line 11 less line 27	(47,162.01)
TAX	29	Income tax: (a) On capital gains (Schedule J)	
		(b) Surcharge—enter 10% of line 29(a) (Fiscal year corporations: see instructions for Schedule J)	-0-
	30	Credits: (a) Tax deposited—Form 7004 application for extension (attach copy) . . .	
		(b) Credit for U.S. tax on nonhighway gas and lube oil (attach Form 4136) .	
	31	TAX DUE (line 29 less line 30). See instruction G for Tax Deposit System . . . . →→	-0-
	32	OVERPAYMENT (line 30 less line 29) . . . . →→	

EXHIBIT 1 (continued)

Schedule L—BALANCE SHEETS (See instructions)

ASSETS	Beginning of taxable year (A) Amount	(B) Total	End of taxable year (C) Amount	(D) Total
1 Cash		11,464.55		761.34
2 Trade notes and accounts receivable	11,415.73		101.60	
(a) Less allowance for bad debts		11,415.73		101.60
3 Inventories		14,187.02		15,000.00
4 Gov't obligations: (a) U.S. and instrumentalities . .				
(b) State, subdivisions thereof, etc.				
5 Other current assets (attach schedule)				
6 Loans to shareholders				
7 Mortgage and real estate loans				
8 Other investments (attach schedule)				
9 Buildings and other fixed depreciable assets . . .	128,213.42		96,236.79	
(a) Less accumulated depreciation	121,899.09	6,314.33	89,666.99	6,569.80
10 Depletable assets				
(a) Less accumulated depletion				
11 Land (net of any amortization)		3,850.00		1,200.00
12 Intangible assets (amortizable only)				
(a) Less accumulated amortization				
13 Other assets (attach schedule)		258.30		
14 Total assets		24,560.83		23,632.74
LIABILITIES AND SHAREHOLDERS' EQUITY				
15 Accounts payable . (payroll taxes)		414.96		513.89
16 Mtges., notes, bonds payable in less than 1 yr. . .		36,975.00		38,400.00
17 Other current liabilities (attach schedule)				
18 Loans from shareholders		315,170.36		370,153.70
19 Mtges., notes, bonds payable in 1 yr. or more . .		12,473.35		2,200.00
20 Other liabilities (attach schedule)				
21 Capital stock . . . . ◦ . .		10,000.00		10,000.00
22 Paid-in or capital surplus (attach reconciliation) .				
23 Retained earnings—appropriated (attach schedule) .				
24 Retained earnings—unappropriated		(350,472.84)		(397,634.85)
25 Shareholders' undistributed taxable income . . .				
26 Less cost of treasury stock		( )		( )
27 Total liabilities and shareholders' equity . .		24,560.83		23,632.74

Schedule M–1—RECONCILIATION OF INCOME PER BOOKS WITH INCOME PER RETURN

1 Net income per books	(47,162.01)	7 Income recorded on books this year not	
2 Federal income tax		included in this return (itemize)	
3 Excess of capital losses over capital gains . .		(a) Tax-exempt interest. $	
4 Taxable income not recorded on books this year			
(itemize)			
		8 Deductions in this tax return not charged	
5 Expenses recorded on books this year not de-		against book income this year (itemize)	
ducted in this return (itemize)			
		9 Total of lines 7 and 8	
6 Total of lines 1 through 5	(47,162.01)	10 Income (line 28, page 1)—line 6 less line 9	(47,162.01)

Schedule M–2—ANALYSIS OF UNAPPROPRIATED RETAINED EARNINGS PER BOOKS (line 24 above)

1 Balance at beginning of year	(350,472.84)	5 Distributions out of current or accumulated	
2 Net income per books	(47,162.01)	earnings and profits: (a) Cash	
3 Other increases (itemize)		(b) Stock	
		(c) Property . . .	
		6 Current year's undistributed taxable income	
		or net operating loss (column 6, Schedule K) .	
		7 Other decreases (itemize)	
		8 Total of lines 5, 6, and 7	
4 Total of lines 1, 2, and 3	(397,634.85)	9 Balance at end of year (line 4 less line 8) . .	(397,634.85)

EXHIBIT 2
Layout of Facilities

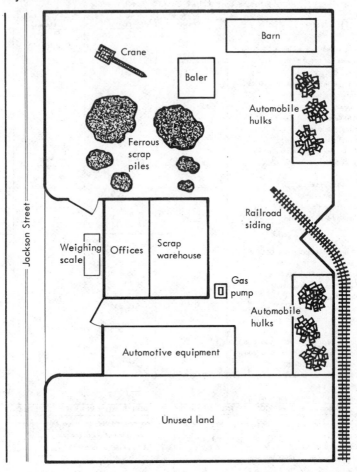

In 1970, Northern Scrap had a dozen employees. Among these were a truck driver, a crane operator, several torch cutters, and a foreman. Problems with the foreman resulted in Mr. Longer doing a substantial amount of personal supervision. By mid-1972, Mr. Longer had found a competent and dependable foreman; as a consequence, he was able to spend more time in the office and less time in the yard.

By early 1975, Mr. Longer could look back over five years of steady growth. His sales for 1974 had been $1,556,453, his employees numbered 18 skilled people, his new site was operational, and his company was gaining stature in the community though, in his words, "it had a long way to go."

THE INDUSTRY

The environmentally fashionable industry of resource recovery actually had its origin in the much older business of waste processing. Waste processing embraces three relatively exclusive categories based on the physical state of the untreated waste when it is deposited into the environment: (1) gas, (2) liquid, and (3) solid. With the increase in the regulation of systems that inject "pollutants" into the environment, and a change in the economics of recovering resources rather than relying on virgin materials, distinct competitive markets developed around each of the three waste categories. The technology, type of competition, and the specific firms in each market vary widely.

The solid waste business involves both processing solid wastes such as trash and garbage for ultimate disposal, and reclaiming junked automobiles and other metal equipment (scrap processing).

One of Northern Scrap's competitors gave the following view of solid waste processing:

> The industry offers an unusual speculative opportunity to the investor willing to cope with a high-risk undertaking. If a firm can gain control of technology that would make its process more profitable than competitors', it could lead to substantial growth and provide the keystone to establishing a large, diverse corporate entity from humble beginnings. The elements of the speculation are:
>
> 1. Energy costs will remain high.
> 2. The demand for the products extracted from today's waste will remain constant or increase.
> 3. The composition of solid waste will not change radically in the near future.
> 4. Legal and physical control can be obtained over processes, providing a clear advantage in separating and processing economically recoverable elements of solid waste.
> 5. The world economy will remain healthy enough to sustain basic material demands worldwide.

Social pressures for environmental policing and the perception of dwindling world reserves of raw materials, combined with an increasing materials usage, produced added pressure for sophisticated, efficient, and effective recycling programs. Post-consumer solid wastes amounted to 125 million tons, or 3,132 pounds per day per person in 1971. When firms package their wares using wasteful designs, such as individually wrapped portions, the cost of disposal soars. In 1966, for example, American consumers paid $25 billion for 52 million tons of packaging material, 90 percent of which was eventually discarded. Packaging wastes were 75 million tons in 1975, and were projected to increase to a level of 89 million tons by 1980.

The relative components of this national waste are given in Exhibit 3. Projected demand for key raw materials and related data can be found in Exhibit 4.

EXHIBIT 3
The "National Garbage Can"

It takes a heap of garbage . . .

Type of waste	Percentages
Paper	31
Yard wastes	19
Food	18
Glass	10
Metals	10
Wood	4
Plastic	3
Rubber and leather	3
Textiles	1
Miscellaneous	1

Every American generates roughly 1,000 pounds of solid waste a year, according to the Environmental Protection Agency. The country's trash, as measured by weight, consists of the varied items listed above.

RAIL RATES

Mr. Longer indicated that the bulk of all of Northern's scrap shipments to steel mills or other users was made by rail. Barge transportation, being cheaper, was used by some scrap dealers in areas accessible by large rivers or lakes. Since Northern's market area was not adjacent to rivers or lakes, Mr. Longer considered the Interstate Commerce Commission's (ICC) regulation of rail freight rates for scrap steel to be critical to his business.

Rail rates for scrap steel were substantially higher than the corresponding rates for shipping iron ore, despite the fact that the pure iron recovered from a given quantity of scrap was substantially greater than the pure iron recovered from a corresponding quantity of iron ore. Moreover, rail freight rates for scrap steel had risen sharply over recent years. In 1969, the cost of shipping one gross ton from Mr. Longer's yard to one of his key customers was $4.25. In 1974, the rate was $8.97 per ton.

Northern Scrap belonged to the Institute of Scrap Iron and Steel, Inc., an association that was actively lobbying with the ICC and the railroads to get the rate differential between iron ore and scrap reduced. When asked

EXHIBIT 4
Projected Usages of Key Materials and Estimated Scrap Recovery Rates

	1960	1980	1990	2000
Selected metals (comparative usage— 1960 = 100)				
Aluminum	100	360		1000
Copper	100	198		390
Zinc	100	190		355
Steel	100	172		285
Lead	100	158		230
Tin	100	130		180
Aluminum (millions of tons)				
Projected consumption:				
Low		3.4	4.9	6.6
Medium		5.6		14.4
High		10.1	18.7	31.1
Relative consumption (percent of total metals):				
Low		10.9%	12.5%	16.8%
Medium		11.2	11.6	17.0
High		13.5	15.8	18.2
Projected secondary recovery from obsolete scrap:				
Low		0.48	1.02	1.68
Medium		0.61	1.50	2.94
High		0.94	2.55	4.94
Copper (millions of tons)				
Projected consumption:				
Low		2.2	2.5	2.8
Medium		3.6	5.2	6.8
High		5.2	9.6	14.0
Relative consumption:				
Low		2.1%	2.1%	2.2%
Medium		2.2	2.3	2.4
High		2.1	2.3	2.5
Projected secondary recovery:				
Low		1.3	1.3	1.4
Medium		1.4	1.6	2.0
High		1.5	2.0	2.9
Aluminum: projections (medium) of markets (millions of tons):				
Building and construction		1.60	2.49	4.25
Electric power construction		0.16	0.22	0.32
Consumer durables (except autos)		0.51	0.84	1.41
Products durables (except transport equipment)		0.55	0.84	1.32
Containers and packaging		0.70	0.97	1.22
Transportation equipment		2.04	3.71	6.07
Defense and miscellaneous		0.09	0.11	0.13
Net and end-use consumption		5.65	9.18	14.72
Steel: projections (medium) of markets (millions of tons):				
Heavy structural shapes	5.2	6.5		7.0
Oil-country goods	1.5	3.0		5.5
Nails and staples	0.2	0.2		0.2
Galvanized sheet	3.8	7.5		12.1
Railroads	8.7	13.8		20.2
Concrete reinforced bars	2.1	4.1		6.3
Line pipe	2.7	5.0		5.7
Total	24.2	40.1		57.0

whether he felt that the scrap industry was winning or losing the rate battle. Mr. Longer replied:

> We have won a few, but recently there have been a few decisions that indicate that we are not winning. Not long ago, one group of environmentalists instituted a suit to prevent the further increase of scrap steel rates. The basis for this suit was the tenet that scrap and iron ore are competitive—a fact which to me seemed self-evident. The ICC came up with a study to support the position that they are not competitive. It seems just ridiculous. This ICC study was recently upheld by the courts, and scrap freight rates were raised by $1 per ton.

SOURCES OF SCRAP

Mr. Longer indicated that Northern dealt primarily with two types of scrap—industrial scrap (or by-product scrap) and obsolete scrap (old autos, washing machines, and so on). When Mr. Longer took over Northern Scrap in 1970, industrial scrap constituted about 10 percent of his incoming scrap. By 1974, that figure had increased to 25 percent, Mr. Longer attributed this increase primarily to an improved local market image of Northern Scrap and, to a lesser degree, to growth in the area's industrial base and the resulting larger amount of industrial scrap that stemmed from this growth. According to Longer, Northern's improved image was due to two things: "First, we now have reliable, efficient materials handling. Second, we have our containers at our customers' places of business."

Approximately 90 percent of the "obsolete scrap" which Northern obtained was brought to the yard by individuals seeking a small salvage value. Since Mr. Longer had one local competitor, the price he was willing to pay for scrap was quite important in determining the extent of his volume in the "obsolete" segment of the local scrap market. He used a pricing formula that was based on the prices being offered to him for processed scrap. Currently, he was buying ferrous scrap for $56 a gross ton. He estimated that on the average he was being paid $68 to $70 for a gross ton of processed scrap; such a spread, he felt, gave him a pretax profit margin of between 8 percent and 10 percent of sales.

COMPETITION

Northern's ability to attract scrap was also affected considerably by the actions of its competitors. In addition to one local competitor. Northern had to contend with a very aggressive competitor based in a city about 50 miles away—Yakima Scrap, Inc. Recently, Yakima had invested in a shredder—a sophisticated piece of scrap processing machinery that was designed primarily to process crushed cars at the rate of one car every 45 seconds. Scrap processed by a shredder was of purer quality and presently sold for about $88 a ton, as compared to Northern's baler processed scrap, which sold for about

$68 a ton. This differential allowed Yakima Scrap to offer to pay more for old autos than Northern Scrap. After Yakima installed the shredder, Northern experienced a 40 percent decline in its volume of junked auto bodies. Moreover, because of the high cost of shredders (generally in excess of $1 million), Yakima had a strong incentive to utilize it as fully as possible. In an effort to build up the utilization of its shredder, Yakima Scrap invested in a car crusher unit costing about $60,000. (Northern currently owned neither a car crusher nor a shredder.) The car crusher unit consisted of a large front-loading device, a piece of machinery that flattened auto hulls, and a long platform truck on which the two were loaded. Essentially, the purpose of the car crusher unit was to compress old cars and make them economical to haul. Yakima had begun sending its car crusher into junkyards[1] in Northern's immediate market area for the purpose of crushing cars, and then hauling them away to its own shredder. This "invasion" caused Mr. Longer considerable consternation. "I know I will have to take some action to avoid having scrap bled away from me to a catastrophic degree," he said.

In 1972, Mr. Longer asked one of the large manufacturers of shredders to do a market survey in his locality in an effort to determine if there was sufficient scrap available to justify an investment in a shredder. At the same time, Mr. Longer did a survey of his own. Both surveys led to the same conclusion—there was not sufficient potential now or in the foreseeable future to justify the presence of a shredder in Mr. Longer's area.

Nevertheless, the shredder question continued to reassert itself. Shredders were being installed in an increasing number of scrap yards throughout the country. The number of shredders in the state in which Northern operated had increased by a factor of five over the past three years. Longer was concerned whether his business could survive over the long term without a shredder.

Yakima Scrap was not the only organization encroaching on Northern Scrap's market area. Some steel mills made deliveries of finished goods in Northern's vicinity. Rather than having the delivery trucks return to the mill empty, the management of the mills decided that these trucks could pick up old autos from junkyards and haul these back to the mill. Over the past couple of years, an increasing number of small and intermediate size steel mills had begun to backhaul scrap, apparently because they viewed this to be a more economical source of supply. Mr. Longer knew of one steel mill located about 150 miles away which had invested in a shredder. He had driven by the mill several weeks earlier and said he had seen "acres and acres of cars" waiting to be processed.

The trucks that Mr. Longer currently owned were physically capable of hauling cars from a junkyard to his processing site. However, the cost of using these trucks to haul uncompressed cars was so high that, with few

---

[1] Junkyard as used here refers to an establishment that stores inoperative autos and sells parts and finally sells the hulk for salvage. Such junkyards do not process metal.

exceptions, Mr. Longer did not employ the trucks for that purpose. Consequently, 90 percent of the autos processed by Northern Scrap were brought to the yard by their owners.

Longer figured that if he purchased a car crusher, he could then haul cars more economically, being able to transport 16–20 cars on each trip as opposed to 2 or 3 per trip using his present equipment. After crushing the cars which he could buy from junkyards at a price ranging from $30 to $35, he had two options. First, he could process them into steel bales at his own yard using his baler. Alternatively, he could sell the crushed cars directly to Yakima where they would be shredded. Yakima was currently offering $65 a ton for crushed cars because of its ability to sell shredded output at a considerable premium.

For Northern to realize full utilization of a car crusher, Longer judged that he would have to hire an additional truck driver (expected wage, $4.50 an hour) and two additional workers (expected wage, $3.50 an hour). Alternatively, he could rely on his present work force and simply use the crusher on a part-time basis.

SCRAP PROCESSING

For processing purposes, it was Northern's practice to divide its scrap supplies into two categories—nonferrous and ferrous. Nonferrous scrap, which consisted of copper, brass, aluminum, car radiators, and similar items, represented about 30 percent of Northern Scrap's total sales volume. Workers using small metal shears grade, sort, and cut these nonfoerrous materials into convenient sizes and shapes for shipping. Since this scrap was of considerable value on a per pound basis, the great majority of it was kept inside the metals house until time for shipping.

In processing ferrous metals, the "old standby" piece of equipment was the flame-cutting torch. The torch was used to separate certain nonmetallic parts from the metallic parts of purchased scrap as a prelude to further processing, as well as to separate various grades of ferrous material such as the body tin of an auto from the "dirty" cast of the engine. All workers at Northern Scrap were required to know how to use a torch. Mr. Longer said, "A good torch-man is worth considerable money because there is an art to rapid, yet efficient, torching.

Northern Scrap also had a hydraulic shear that could be used for shearing car bodies into "slabs." "From time to time, there is a market for this type of steel," Mr. Longer added.

"One of the key pieces of equipment in the scrap yard," Mr. Longer explained, "is the baler." Cars and other scrap were loaded into the baler by means of a crane. At that point, hydraulic mechanisms compressed the scrap into small bales which were usable by steel mills, Mr. Longer had the following comments about his baler:

We will undoubtedly need to give some thought to getting a better baler one of these days. The baler we have now has had eight years of hard life. It was a marginal baler to begin with. If continuously fed, it can process one car body every six minutes. It is capable of processing 5 tons an hour, but the inability of feeding it continuously means that we can only get 25 tons a day maximum. It has paid for itself a number of times over. If we want to have the widest possible market for our bales, we need a better quality baler.

Our current market is quite limited because of the marginal quality of our bales. Specifically, there are two problems with our current bales. First, the size of the bales put out by our machine tends to be large. Our smallest bales are 2 by 2 by 3 feet, but many of our bales are 3.5 to 5 feet long, which is awfully long. Second, the density of our bales is not what it should be. Steel mill specifications generally require a minimum density of 75 pounds per cubic foot. We are just barely capable of reaching that density, and there are many times that we don't reach it. A good baler operator can do much toward improving the size and the density of the bales.

The steel mills operate using a batch process. They have a pot of a given size, and, the greater the weight of scrap iron that they can put in that fixed pot size, the more efficient their operation is. When the steel industry is slack, they shun the poorer quality bales. In boom periods, they are interested in all qualities of bales.

Mr. Longer added that there were balers on the market that would process 50 tons a day of consistently high-quality bales. The downtime on his present baler was still negligible. It was currently used about 50 percent of the time; of this, 30–50 percent was spent processing car bodies.

Mr. Longer explained that labor was the high-cost item in the scrap business. The skills needed were truck drivers, crane operators, torch cutters, men experienced in the sorting of nonferrous metals, men who could operate the baler or the shear, and a mechanic to help maintain the equipment. Men who had combined skills were, of course, more valuable. When a man was hired, considerable effort was made to broaden his skills. Because the work was dangerous, insurance costs ran about 16–18 percent of total labor costs.

Since the demand for scrap and the prices offered by the mill were currently reaching all-time highs and the unemployment rate in Mr. Longer's city was around 1 percent, he had difficulty in finding good employees. Mr. Longer said, "We have our share of unreliables." However, he felt many of his labor problems could be worked out with time.

PURCHASERS OF PROCESSED SCRAP STEEL

Northern Scrap sold ferrous scrap through brokers almost without exception. Dealing through brokers was typical in the scrap industry. The exceptions to this practice were a very few large scrap processors who sold directly to local mills. Mr. Longer dealt primarily with two brokers from a large, nearby metropolitan area and one other broker who specialized in sales to the Canadian market. His dealings with the brokers were explained as follows:

> At the beginning of a month, the major steel mills announce a price. This price, which can be found in various publications, is telephoned to me informally by my brokers. I then must tell them how much I want to sell. I am then bound to make delivery on that amount by the end of the month. They, in consideration, are bound to the announced price.
>
> If I were to decide later in the month that I want to sell more than the original amount, I don't know what price it can be sold for, or if it can be sold at all.

Northern Scrap was too small to exercise any leverage with steel mills on the matter of price. Mr. Longer pointed out that sometimes larger scrap processors did exercise some leverage with steel mills. These yards "secured a special deal for themselves," and it worked to the detriment of other scrap processors.

Mr. Longer was asked if he ever held on to inventories of scrap metals in anticipation of higher prices. He replied, "A couple of years ago, the answer was 'without qualification, we never do.' In 1974, the steel market was hectic. By that, I mean there were many peaks and valleys. Nevertheless, I felt the intrinsic value of scrap was on an upward trend, so I accumulated a large inventory of scrap and later sold it at a higher price.

"Lately our average inventory has been higher than it was in the more distant past. In earlier years, we simply didn't have the operating capital to allow us to hold an inventory."

Regarding whether scrap dealers' speculative holding of inventories affected the price at which steel mills would buy, Mr. Longer stated, "I don't think any one dealer is big enough to alter the price, except possibly in the special case where there is only one scrap dealer in a given area and also one steel mill, and there are no other dealers within a 200-mile radius. In my area, we have several aggressive, competitive dealers."

CITY TRASH COLLECTION CONTRACT

Prior to 1960, the city in which Northern Scrap was located conducted its trash collection through a contract with local businessmen. However, the reliability of the collection service deteriorated considerably over time. Consequently, the city passed an ordinance in 1960 prohibiting commercial trash collection by anyone except the city. For reasons unknown, the ordinance also stipulated that the rates charged by the city for trash collection could not exceed 75 percent of the cost of providing the service.

The rates were set by the superintendent of sanitation. Theoretically, the rates were supposed to vary as the amount of service required varied. A cursory check by Mr. Longer revealed that this was not the case. Some industrial and commercial establishments were having their trash hauled for

$5 a month and certain other establishments were having their trash hauled for "literally zero." Mr. Longer attributed this deficit policy more to "lethargy and inertia" than to "politics."

In early 1972, Mr. Longer approached the city commission about the possibility of letting Northern Scrap get into the trash collection business. In contrast to the city operation which consisted of manually emptying trash cans into a dump truck, Mr. Longer proposed a service whereby he would install a more durable, sanitary container at the customer's place of business and would schedule pickups more in accordance with customer's needs. Using one of two large, roll-off trucks, which he had already bought for the purpose of serving his industrial scrap customers (see Exhibit 5), he would dispatch a driver to the customer's location where the driver would mount the large container onto the roll-off truck using hydraulic power, transport the container to a dumping site, empty it, and return the empty container to the customer's place of business.

In preparation for making his proposal to the city commission. Mr. Longer conducted a survey of local businessmen, and found some interest in having this more efficient roll-off service. The city took a cursory survey which drew a more pessimistic picture of the desire for roll-off service and decided to reject Longer's offer.

When, in late January 1975, Mr. Longer learned that an outside firm had proposed a trash collection contract to the city, he knew that he had to look into whether Northern Scrap should, once more, consider a trash collection contract with the city. Mr. Longer believed that if the other company was awarded the contract and entered his locality to haul trash, then they might soon begin to haul scrap also. Other considerations shaped Mr. Longer's thinking as well. The scrap business, in his view, was a volatile business subject to periodic recessions. The trash business, on the other hand, was unlikely to exhibit these same mercurial shifts in volume and could thus serve as an economic base to buffer the company from the ups and downs of the scrap business.

Another factor Longer had to deal with was whether and how to increase the utilization of equipment that Northern already owned. In 1972, he had bought two large roll-off trucks and a number of containers in order to serve industrial scrap customers. In January 1975, Northern was only getting 30 percent utilization of this equipment.

REAPPRAISAL

Mr. Longer recognized that submitting a bid for the city trash collection contract meant confronting these and a number of other fundamental issues. One such issue concerned the minimum length of time for which the trash contract should run. Longer, of course, preferred any contract to span a time period long enough for him to recover whatever investment would have to be made in trash hauling equipment.

EXHIBIT 5

The issue of the time length of the contractual period led directly to a second issue—should Northern undertake to provide front-loader trash collection service? Front-loader service was considerably more efficient than roll-off service. Special front-loader trucks (see Exhibit 6) were dispatched to the customer's place of business, where special garbage containers (provided to the customer as a part of front-loader service) were emptied into the front-loader truck by means of a hydraulic mechanism and then returned to their original position. Inside the truck, a compactor mechanism compressed the garbage in order to increase the truck's carrying capacity. The key advantage of front-loader service was that many customers could be serviced before the truck had to make a trip to the dumping site—as opposed to roll-off service which necessitated that each customer's container be brought to the dump individually and returned to its origin before another customer could be serviced.

If the front-loader option were chosen. Longer estimated that it would be necessary to buy at least two front-loader trucks in order to insure reliable service. New trucks retailed for about $30,000 apiece. Mr. Longer would have to hire one truck driver, in addition to those he currently employed.

EXHIBIT 5 *(continued)*

DETACHABLE CONTAINERS

The DEMPSTER-DINOSAUR is a new system of materials handling that employs small or large detachable containers ranging up to 40 cu. yd. capacity, with larger containers available for special situations. Only one man, the driver, operates the system which, in most situations, will do the work of several trucks. All operations are hydraulic and handled from simple controls in the cab. Over-the-road gross loads up to 30,000 lbs. may be handled. In off-the-road applications, weight and container size is limited only by the size of the truck. Uses of the DEMPSTER-DINOSAUR in the refuse collection, materials handling and scrap collections industries are almost endless.

HOW IT WORKS

The DINOSAUR is of extremely simple design, consisting of a tipping frame, two hydraulic raise-lower cylinders and a "U" shaped bail which is moved back and forth by a double-acting cylinder. Containers are mounted on a base which has a guide rail with recessed lifting hooks spaced from front to back at intervals to coincide with the length of the bail cylinder stroke. As illustrated in photos **70** through **73**, the bail enters and engages the first lifting hook. The cylinder pulls the container up on the tipping frame, then moves back to engage the bail in the second hook. This forward and backward ratcheting action is repeated and the frame is lowered until the container base is pulled into carrying position and locked. Progress of the bail is shown by white circles. To put container off on ground, dock or legs, the action is reversed with the bail pushing against the back of the lifting hooks. Photos below show pickup of an actual container.

Wages for truck drivers of this type were generally $4–$5 an hour. The trucks would require liability insurance, registration fees, and collision insurance during their early life. Containers for customers would cost in the range of $200 to $400 apiece, depending on the size of the container and Northern's ability to order them in truck-load lots—the most economical order quantity. A truckload of containers consisted of 6 to 22 units, depending on the size of each unit.

In looking into the issue of front-loaders. Longer learned of a place where he could acquire two used front-loader trucks. The price for both trucks would have to be negotiated, but indications were that the total price would range between $18,000 and $25,000. These trucks were currently inoperable. They could be towed to the Northern Scrap yard for a cost of $1,000. Mr. Longer estimated that there was a 50 percent chance that the repairs necessary to bring these trucks into operable condition would cost $10,000, a 25 percent chance they would cost $12,500, and a 25 percent chance they would cost $15,000. However, the useful life of these trucks should be at least three years and they could last up to ten years.

EXHIBIT 6

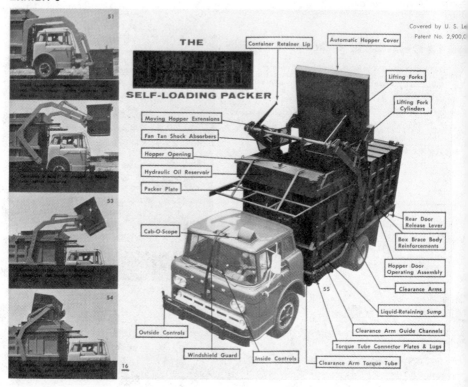

Based on conversations with prospective customers, city officials, and citizens of similar cities where a private trash collection program was currently in use, Longer developed a schedule of service charges which he believed would be acceptable to all of the parties concerned (see Exhibit 7). He estimated that there were roughly 300 prospective commercial customers and 20 prospective industrial customers for pickup service. He figured no more than 20 percent of the commercial customers would need more than 1 pickup per week or a container larger than 4 cubic yards but he thought the industrial customers would probably need an average of 3 pickups per week and containers with a 30 or more cubic yard capacity.

Longer was aware that if Northern entered into a contract with the city to haul industrial and commercial trash, then the city might eventually want Northern to take over the hauling of trash from private residences. Longer viewed this possibility unenthusiastically, but it had to be weighed against having Northern Scrap undertake the task or allowing an outsider to do the job.

EXHIBIT 7
Estimated Monthly Service Rates for Containerized Waste Collection and Disposal Service

Commercial size (front-loader) containers:

Container Capacity		No. of 20-Gallon Trash Cans	Monthly Rates for Basic Service* (pickups per week)						Per Additional Pickup
Cubic Yards	Gal-lons		1	2	3	4	5	6	
3..........	480	24	$22	$35	$ 48	$ 61	$ 75	$ 88	$3.50
4..........	640	32	30	47	65	82	100	100	4.50
6..........	960	48	34	58	73	97	121	145	6.75
8..........	1280	64	44	77	103	130	150	176	9.00

Industrial size† (open top, roll-off) containers:

Container Capacity (cubic yards)	Monthly Rates for Basic Service* (pickups per month)				Per Additional Pickup
	1	2	3	4	
15 or 20	$ 66.50	$ 87.00	$107.50	$128.00	$20.50
25	78.00	104.50	131.00	157.50	26.50
30	89.50	122.00	154.50	187.00	32.50
40	101.00	144.50	188.00	231.50	43.50

* Basic service provides for:

    Standard front-loader and open-top roll-off containers of selected size.
    Pickup within three-mile radius of corner of Main Street and Central Avenue.
    Commercial pickup during regular route runs.
    Industrial pickup during regular working hours.
    Waste to consist of benign materials, only: no free liquids.
    Absence of unusual location conditions which increase cost of pickup.
    Standard contract period (not temporary service).

    The basic service rates are in compliance with city permit and ordinances. Rates are subject to changes as may be approved by the city.

    † The rates for industrial size containers are exclusive of the city landfill dumping charge ($2.50 per load).

Finally, if Northern did enter into a contract with the city, there was the issue of how best (if at all) to promote this new service. Should Longer hire a PR man or contract with an ad agency? Should he rely completely on phone calls and personal selling? Should he mail brochures or use local radio and TV?

The city council was meeting in one week to consider, among other things, the issue of trash collection. Mr. Longer had to make his decision and, if the decision on trash collection was affirmative, then to submit a written proposal to the council. Yet, he knew that his decision on the trash collection issue must be coordinated with his decisions regarding investments in new equipment such as a car crusher, a new baler, or a shredder.

EXHIBIT 8

NORTHERN SCRAP PROCESSORS, INC. (A)
Income Statements, 1973 and 1974

	1974	*1973*
Sales of recyclable materials	$1,556,453	$719,568
Environmental protection revenue	65,892	699
	$1,622,345	$720,267
Cost of recyclable materials	1,015,406	418,136
Gross profit	$ 606,939	$302,131
Salaries and wages	$ 163,458	$ 69,068
Depreciation	39,365	13,892
Transportation expense	62,606	12,274
Maintenance	40,327	28,155
Insurance	12,334	10,975
Property and other taxes	19,929	9,364
Other expense	87,928	31,521
Total operating expense	$ 425,947	$175,249
Profit from operations	$ 180,992	$126,882
Interest expense, net	18,076	16,992
Profit before federal income tax	$ 162,916	$109,890
Federal income tax	57,367	0
Net income after tax	$ 105,549	$109,890
Retained earnings beginning of period	($ 271,622)	($381,512)
Net income per books	105,549	109,890
Federal income tax adjustment	(12)	—
Retained earnings at end of period	($ 166,085)	($271,622)

EXHIBIT 9

NORTHERN SCRAP PROCESSORS, INC. (A)
Balance Sheets, 1973 and 1974

	1974	1973
Current assets:		
Cash	$ 78,803	$ 5,216
Accounts receivable	1,277	0
Inventory	28,554	89,417
Income tax deposits	85,000	—
Construction contract deposit	10,000	—
Other current assets	466	907
Total current assets	$204,100	$ 95,540
Land, buildings, and facilities	$421,547	$243,565
Reserve for depreciation	(76,067)	(38,461)
Fixed assets, net of depreciation	$345,480	$205,104
Total assets	$549,580	$300,644
Current liabilities:		
Federal income tax payable	$ 57,367	—
Other current liabilities	462	$ 1,213
Current portion of long-term notes payable	62,251	16,400
Total current liabilities	$120,080	$ 17,613
Long-term portion of notes payable	$200,131	$159,199
Common stock, $100 par value, 100 shares issued and outstanding	$ 10,000	$ 10,000
Additional paid-in capital	385,454	385,454
Retained earnings (or deficit)	(166,085)	(271,622)
Net equity	$229,369	$123,832
Total liabilities and equity	$549,580	$300,644
Working capital	$ 84,020	$ 77,927

14.   Grant Industrial Corporation (A)*

As Bill Anthony, president of Grant Industrial Corporation (GIC), drove to his office on Monday morning his thoughts were more on the 10 o'clock meeting with his management team than on rush hour traffic conditions in Wilmington, Delaware. Contract negotiations were scheduled to begin the next day with the United Metalworkers (UMW), who represented the hourly employees at the Engineering and Manufacturing Division of his company. In spite of the fact that the division had three years of heavy losses, he was sure that the UMW would be more interested in the economic status of its members than the economic status of his company. Hopefully, the meeting with his management group would produce some strategic solutions to the serious problems confronting the division, as well as a bargaining approach to deal with the union.

As Bill Anthony parked his car in the GIC parking lot, he recalled a phrase about the work force that once had been common around the company during his father's and grandfather's days; "An ounce of loyalty is worth a pound of cleverness." The phrase no longer seemed applicable, particularly given what he perceived as the lack of worker loyalty during the past year. There was no doubt that the work force was changing. Over one third of the 55 employees had been with the company at least 30 years, whereas another one third had been hired since 1970. In Anthony's opinion these recent hires never had shown the kind of loyalty that traditionally had characterized the work force. Bill Anthony had been wanting for some time to change the paternalistic approach to labor that had characterized the family business for many years. Maybe now was the time to begin the change and to tie these changes into the new strategic moves that would be necessary to make the division profitable again.

COMPANY BACKGROUND

In 1911, Henry B. Anthony, Sr., a former governor of Delaware, began to establish a network of family businesses throughout Delaware. The governor had a wide range of business interests and was a tough executive. By the 1950s, he had established family businesses that included a construction company, a manufacturing company, a truck dealership, a farm, a small

CATV company, and a construction equipment dealership. By this time, he had become one of Delaware's most prominent citizens.

The forerunner of Grant Industrial Corporation had been started in 1917 when James Blaine and Matthew Carpenter formed a small metalworking company, Blaine and Carpenter Engineering Company. In the 1930s Henry B. Anthony, Sr. had become co-owner of the company with Blaine, having bought out Carpenter's interest. At that time, the company had become known as Blaine Engineering Company and specialized in the manufacture of textile frames used for moving yarn among the various work areas in textile plants.

In 1934, after the death of James Blaine, Henry Anthony had become the sole owner of Blaine Engineering Company. He had continued to make textile frames; however, the company had begun to make proprietary earth-digging equipment designed by a friend of the governor. The arrangement with the designer had made Anthony the only manufacturer of trenchers in the eastern United States; the designer had become the sole manufacturer for the western half of the country.

In the late 1940s, at the death of the designer, another individual had paid $100 for the designs of the trenchers which never had been patented. As a result of this purchase, several competitors had sprung up in the West, some quite large in size.

In 1949, Henry Anthony's company had been renamed Grant Engineering and Manufacturing Company. Shortly thereafter, several family operations had begun to merge, ultimately forming in 1974 the Grant Industrial Corporation. Grant Engineering and Manufacturing Company became one of four divisions (Exhibit 1).

BILL ANTHONY

Bill Anthony, second oldest of Henry Anthony's grandsons, became president of Grant Industrial Corporation in 1974. His success, as well as that of his other brothers, had been attributed in part by their mother to "relative ability." Nonetheless, he had not achieved his position without proving himself. He had dropped out of college in the mid-1960s and gone into the Army for several years. During this period, his father died, leaving the family businesses to his sons.

When Bill had left the Army in 1969, he had been offered a position with Grant Industrial Corporation by general manager, John Rawlins. The position was that of salesman for the textile line of the engineering division. The offer had included a salary of $6,000 a year and no car. At the time, there had been no salesmen in the field, and sales had amounted to $250,000 a year, generating a profit of $15,000.

Bill Anthony had begun calling on textile manufacturers throughout the South. One year later, sales for the division had increased to $750,000 with profits of $200,000 for the corporation. In 1970, Bill had been made sales

EXHIBIT 1
Organization Chart

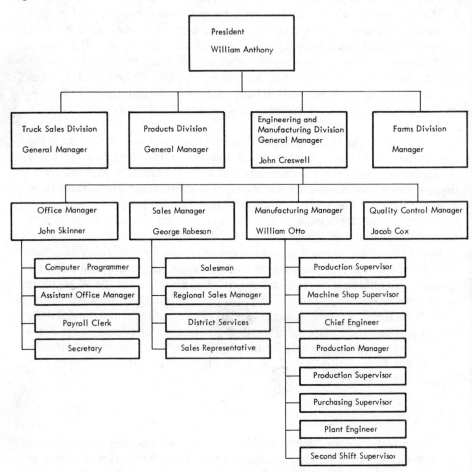

manager for the engineering division. In 1971, he had become vice president
for Corporate Affairs for Grant Industrial Corporation with special responsibility for marketing the trenchers. According to him, it was a job in which
"You couldn't do anything. We had it (the eastern market) all." Although he
did explore the possibility of a national distributorship for the line, he had
soon focused his attention on another area that he considered to have greater
potential for the company. In late 1971, he had suggested to his family that
they consider establishing a distributorship to handle all television supplies.
It seemed a natural expansion for the family, given the fact that they were
already into the television industry and were supplying heavy equipment to
the industry as well. Bill's idea had been to supply everything from cable to
heavy equipment to electronic equipment. The initial reaction on the part of

the family had not been favorable. Finally, according to Bill, "The chairman, my brother, said, 'Do it on your own time.'" Bill had asked what would be in it for him and was told he would have one half of the profits. Since his salary was then $12,000 a year, the prospects had appeared attractive.

According to Bill, there had been "an absolute vacuum" in the industry. In its first year of operation, the new distributorship had generated sales of $2.1 million and profits of $120,000. Sales continued to grow; in 1975, they reached $10.5 million and profits were in excess of $700,000. The rapid growth was attributed in part to Bill's large discounts on supplies. According to him, "I upset the game. I could have made more money, but I didn't know how the game was played." As a result of the close relationship between suppliers and CATV companies, Bill had been seen as the upstart who was upsetting the cozy arrangement that had developed over the years. According to Bill, the result had been to close a lot of doors that might have been open to him otherwise.

Because of Bill's success as vice president of corporate affairs and in establishing the distributorship, he had been made president of Grant Industrial Corporation in 1974. As such, he was responsible for all divisions of the corporation except engineering and manufacturing. Although he had been given financial responsibility for the engineering and manufacturing division, his older brother retained operating control. It was not until 1975 that Bill obtained full responsibility for the engineering and manufacturing division. But by that time the company had assets of $16 million, sales of $17 million, and a loss of $141,000 (Exhibits 2–4).

"THE FACTORY"

By 1975, the engineering and manufacturing division consisted of one plant near Wilmington, Delaware, commonly known as "the Factory." A major part of the existing plant was as old as the company itself, dating from 1917. The production area was designed as a large job shop with such key areas as a machine shop, welding, assembly, shipping, and finishing, which included both painting and plating.

The engineering and manufacturing division had two major activities: (1) metal products and (2) equipment for CATV, utilities and the construction industry. The metal products were specialized items consisting principally of custom-engineered materials-handling equipment for the textile industry. The Factory also specialized in resistance-welded wire products, chrome plating, electropolishing of stainless steel, and zinc plating. Although the division had tried to branch out into consumer products, such as wire coat hangers, tie racks, and towel racks, Bill thought that these products had not sold well because the company lacked experience in marketing consumer goods.

Until the 1940s, the metal products line had included stackable baskets for use in the textile industry. In the 1950s the product had become somewhat

EXHIBIT 2

GRANT INDUSTRIAL CORPORATION (A)
Balance Sheet
December 31, 1974

Assets

Current assets:

Cash	$	144,625
Accounts receivable		
Trade		1,080,884
Affiliates		513,059
Other		115,817
		$ 1,709,760
Refundable federal and state income taxes		—
Inventories		
Raw materials and supplies		1,356,291
Communications parts and supplies		1,358,533
Truck and equipment parts		535,415
Work in process		381,903
Finished goods: trucks and equipment		1,261,819
Grain and livestock		160,341
		$ 5,054,308
Prepaid expenses	$	29,918
Total current assets		$ 6,938,611
Investments in affiliated companies		4,910,460
Property, plant and equipment, less accumulated depreciation of $1,109,536 in 1974		2,327,366
Aggregate lease payments receivable		1,538,202
Cash surrender value of officers' life insurance		103,855
Other assets		84,717
Total assets		$15,948,211

Liabilities and Shareholders' Equity

Current liabilities:

Notes payable	$	1,350,360
Current portion of long-term debt		295,765
Accounts payable, trade and other		2,339,933
Accounts payable—affiliate		—
Accrued expenses		224,843
Federal and state income taxes		—
Deferred income taxes		19,000
Total current liabilities		$ 4,493,901
Long-term debt		$ 5,972,799
Accounts payable—affiliate		—
Deferred income taxes, noncurrent	$	516,087
Common stock, no par, stated value $50, authorized and issued 10,000 shares	$	500,000
Paid-in capital		79,216
Retained earnings		4,576,738
		$ 5,155,954
Less 4,184 treasury shares, at cost		541,410
Total shareholders' equity		$ 4,614,544
Total liabilities and shareholders' equity		$15,948,211

EXHIBIT 3

GRANT INDUSTRIAL CORPORATION (A)
Statements of Operations
December 31, 1974

	1974
Sales	$16,812,657
Cost of sales	15,193,860
Gross profit	$ 1,618,797
Selling, general and administrative expense	1,696,944
Income (loss) from operations	$ (78,147)
Other income (expense)	
Interest expense, net of interest income of $70,108	(360,952)
Other income	35,960
Equity in income of affiliated companies*	390,876
	$ 65,884
Income (loss) before income taxes and extraordinary credit	$ (12,263)
Provision (credit) income taxes	(128,400)
Income (loss)	$ (140,663)

* Since GIC owned 10.8 percent of CATV company's stock and 40 percent of construction company's stock in 1974, these figures represent corresponding percentages of their respective net income.

more sophisticated as the baskets were put on wheels. It was after Grant introduced wheels on the baskets that Grant's sale had begun to increase.

To compete in the textile industry, a major supplier, such as Grant, had to design as well as manufacture its products. In general, the industry was interested in custom metal-working products. Because the equipment needed to move the materials was such an insignificant cost relative to the total investment in a new textile plant, most companies did not consider the cost or method of moving materials until after the facility had been built. Then they would approach a custom metal-working company to design a system for them to use to move yarn or tubes. Since aisle space and processes also frequently differed from one plant to another, there was very little standardization within the industry.

In the custom metal-working industry that supplied textile manufacturers, cost was the key competitive weapon, with very little repeat business. Although there were no major competitors for Grant, there were a significant number of small competitors who were often very successful. Small welding shops throughout the South were considered to be Grant's prime competitors. It was not uncommon for small welding shops to bid low in an effort to secure a contract and then produce the product that had been designed by Grant as part of its bid effort. Because Grant's labor rates were approximately 30 percent higher than the average welding shop in the South and because it incurred approximately 10 percent higher transportation cost because of its location, it sometimes had difficulty competing with the small,

EXHIBIT 4

GRANT INDUSTRIAL CORPORATION (A)
Statements of Changes in Financial Position
December 31, 1974

	1974
Uses of working capital:	
Loss for the year	$ 140,663
Items not involving working capital:	
Depreciation and amortization	(222,281)
Equity in income of affiliated and associated companies	390,876
Deferred income taxes, noncurrent	139,650
Working capital used in operations	$ 448,908
Reduction of long-term debt	1,047,125
Decrease in noncurrent accounts payable to affiliates	—
Additions to property, plant and equipment	1,284,343
Aggregate lease payments receivable	1,583,202
Acquisition of shares:	
CATV Company	923,851
PSE	82,750
Other	978
Total uses of working capital	$5,371,157
Sources of working capital:	
Proceeds from sale of property, plant and equipment, exclusive of	
net gains included in loss for the year	$ 256,618
Additions to long-term debt	4,252,630
Increase in noncurrent accounts payable to affiliates	326,839
Dividends received from CATV Company	188,530
Disposition of investments:	
Sale of CATV	
Company common stock	—
Conversion of CATV	
Company convertible subordinated debentures to common	
stock.	—
Decrease (increase) in cash surrender value of officers' life insurance	(13,318)
Decrease in other assets	25,603
Total sources of working capital	$5,036,902
Decrease in working capital	$ (334,255)
Components of decrease in working capital:	
Cash	$ 37,723
Accounts receivable	(165,106)
Refundable federal and state income taxes	—
Inventories	929,578
Prepaid expenses	(2,980)
Notes payable and current portion of long-term debt	(729,549)
Accounts payable	(161,233)
Accrued expenses	(98,621)
Accrued and deferred income taxes	(144,067)
Net decrease in working capital	$ (334,255)

fly-by-night operators. Consequently, Grant accounted for only 20 percent of industry sales but developed 50 percent of the products used by the textile industry.

In 1974, 40 percent of the Factory's sales were attributable to the textile line. A typical order for the textile metal-products line was approximately 100 to 200 units, each selling for $150 to $400; the average price for such a "buggy" was approximately $200. A typical order was in the range of $30,000 to $50,000. A large company, such as Du Pont, might place an order for 500 to 1,000 units. Although Grant sold some products to textile plants in other countries, almost all of its sales were to U.S. firms. Even its few foreign sales usually were to subsidiaries of U.S. companies.

The second product line of the engineering and manufacturing division was utility and construction equipment. For this line, Grant made ditch digging equipment, used extensively by CATV, electric, and power construction companies. In addition, Grant made some post-driving equipment used by the guard-rail construction and the fence industries. Most of these large earth digging trenchers were custom made and proprietary in design, although there were only six basic models.

There was very little trencher competition for Grant in the East but a great deal in the West. In fact, from Maine to Virginia and west to Chicago, Grant accounted for 90 percent of the market for such equipment. In the rest of the country, however, Grant accounted for only 10 percent of the market. The price range for trenchers was $20,000 to $40,000, with the average being approximately $30,000; some units cost as much as $200,000, particularly when mounted on a chassis. The cost to the company of a $200,000 trencher was approximately $100,000. Break-even on the largest units was not reached until five units were sold.

Since 1947, Grant had manufactured approximately 1,200 trenchers; 1,000 of these were still in active service in 1975. This made the sale of parts a significant part of this line's revenue, sometimes as much as 60 percent of new sales. In 1974, however, 60 percent of the Factory's sales were attributable to trenchers and approximately $100,000 of that was from parts. The company continued to manufacture parts for many pieces of equipment that had been discontinued years before. Because the products division was the main distributor for Grant earth-digging equipment, accounting for 58 percent of trencher sales, the company could reduce the 20 percent markup that other distributors used in the industry and give the customer a direct discount. This enabled the company to make a profit on the sale of the unit and then continue to make money from the sale of parts.

A comparison of cost breakdowns between the two product lines illustrated a significant difference. Labor accounted for 25 percent of the cost of a trencher, materials 75 percent; for custom metal work, by contrast, labor and materials were both 50 percent. Direct-labor cost was estimated to be $4.80 per hour. Indirect labor was approximately 22 percent of direct, and fixed overhead was 130 percent of direct labor. An additional 52 cents per hour was charged for expendable tools. Thus, in most contracts, the Factory estimated labor to cost approximately $12.50 per hour. Actual labor and material costs by product were unknown.

LABOR BACKGROUND AT THE FACTORY

The work force at the Factory was stable, as indicated by several factors: (1) Between 1948 and 1959, there had been no new hires at the plant. (2) there had been only one strike in the company's history (1949); (3) there had been very few arbitration cases; and (4) the local union had elected the same president, George Boutwell, every year for the past 20 years.

In spite of the stability that had characterized the work force over the past two decades, the composition of the work force had begun to change in recent years. In 1967, for example, the average employee in the 40-man work force had over 20 years of seniority; by the mid-1970s it was approximately 10. Many of the older employees had come to GIC during the Great Depression or soon thereafter and were very loyal to the Anthony family. These employees were described by one manager as "firm believers in the work ethic." According to a common expression around the Factory, "An ounce of loyalty is worth a pound of cleverness." By the mid-1960s, however, this view and the attitudes of employees were beginning to change. The employees were described as "increasingly radical," and there was a growing emphasis on money, as opposed to security, during contract negotiations.

One indication of the increasing instability of the work force was that George Boutwell, in his most recent election, had won by only one vote, after being challenged by a younger worker. The heir apparent to the presidency was Local 492's vice president, a 27-year-old stockroom attendant with nine years of seniority. It appeared that he would soon succeed George Boutwell, who had indicated an unwillingness to run again.

FACTORY PROBLEMS

The problems facing Bill Anthony in the fall of 1975 had been evolving for some time. In the late 1960s and early 1970s the Factory had been managed by John Rawlins, a former personnel executive from a nearby CATV company. Rawlins had grown increasingly concerned about the way the work force had been treated in the past. He had been particularly concerned about the relatively low level of wages. Consequently, in negotiations with the union, he had agreed to significant wage increases and for the first time agreed to pensions and Blue Cross/Blue Shield coverage. Although he had been felt to be doing an acceptable job in running the Factory, he had been increasingly criticized for his leniency with the work force; he had been considered unduly accessible to the workers and had often been seen on the plant floor. References to "Rawlins' Giveaway Program" had not been uncommon. During Rawlins' tenure Factory wages had risen from below the Wilmington average to well above the average.

In the early 1970s, John Rawlins had quickly "gotten in over his head" when he had assumed responsibility for both the Factory and the products division. In an effort to straighten out some problems in the products division, he had spent less and less time managing the Factory. As the Factory began to slide in efficiency, he had also encountered problems in the products division where he wanted to fire a number of office and sales people who had been with the company for many years. Although Bill Anthony prevented the firings, his dissatisfaction with the general manager had mounted. The Anthony family soon became aware of a local plant manager, John Creswell, who was becoming bored at his job and had indicated an interest in making a move.

John Creswell, a 45-year-old graduate of a well-known eastern business school, had "impeccable references." In 1973 he had been running a textile plant in the Wilmington area for a large textile corporation and had been active in community affairs. A few years earlier he had been responsible for building and getting the facility on line. He had done so in record time and now, with the benefit of a 25-year sales contract with a *Fortune* 500 company, was generating an annual $3 million profit on sales of $30 million. Although he had established a good reputation within his own organization, he had established an unfavorable reputation among many of the contractors who had been involved in the plant construction. He was known as a man who would push very hard for what he wanted. When Bill Anthony had made a sales call on Creswell's plant, he had sensed Creswell's dissatisfaction. In November 1973, Anthony fired Rawlins and replaced him with Creswell.

Creswell's philosophy was that an increase in sales[1] was the key to the success of the Engineering Division. This meant a gradually increasing work force and at the same time an unwillingness to take a strike. Consequently, wages had been increased approximately 12 percent during his first labor negotiations in 1974.

In late 1974, there had been considerable discontent among the management and staff of the Factory. Although production was increasing from 5 trenchers per month in early 1974 to 10 per month in 1975 and there were plans to increase to 15 per month in the near future, there had been rumors of dissatisfaction among the management staff. Good engineers were leaving the organization, more and more people were complaining about the lack of planning in the daily affairs of the Factory, and there were conflicts between the production and engineering departments.

Directly in the middle of these problems was William Otto, the soft-spoken 44-year-old manager of manufacturing. Otto was a very competent engineer who enjoyed solving technical problems. He had joined the firm in

---

[1] A sale to the products division was not treated as a sale until it left the corporation but a sale to the distributor was recognized when it left the Factory.

1969 after working 15 years on the engineering staff of Du Pont. Otto was torn between his responsibilities to the general manager, his concern for his own career, and his interest in the viability of the family corporation. His relation with Creswell had become increasingly strained. At one point, Otto had proposed that more planning be done in the affairs of the Factory, and suggested an in-process report to help eliminate or at least pinpoint the source of problems between production and engineering. He was concerned that there was no way of telling the exact status of any order without a visual check on the factory floor. He had designed a system that would let management keep better track of in-process work, but Creswell had rejected his system. Otto also had proposed that standards be developed for better costing of production runs since the Factory continued to rely heavily on gut feel for bidding. Another of Otto's problems was the request by Creswell that he develop a new trencher that would be a slight modification of an old design and yet would be able to do considerably more difficult work than the previous model. After extensive study, Otto concluded that the old design was unsound for the kind of work envisioned for the new model. Creswell rejected Otto's advice and ordered that the new trencher be produced. Otto commented later that it was very embarrassing to have to go to an industry show where the product was being demonstrated in the presence of knowledgeable people. He felt that the company had been the laughing stock of the show. On another occasion, Otto had resisted sending a trencher to the customer because it had not been completely checked out. Creswell insisted that it be sent anyway. Ultimately the trencher had to be sent back for additional work.

The problems between Otto and Creswell had reached a head in the fall of 1974; Creswell had stripped Otto of most of his production responsibilities and assigned him solely to an engineering function. Being relieved of some of these administrative tasks to focus more time on engineering functions would have been viewed positively by Otto under different circumstances. But, by this point, he had begun looking for a new job, because of his concern with what was happening to the organization. He and other members of the staff continued to ask themselves, "When will the family wake up? When are they going to see what is happening?" In late 1974, Bill Anthony had told them informally that he was indeed aware of what was going on and that things would be taken care of. A major concern to Bill was that although he did not have operating control over the Factory, in 1974 the Factory had lost $960,000 on sales of $2 million.'

In the summer of 1975, Grant Industrial Corporation not only had profit responsibility for the Factory but, at brother Henry's request, Bill was given total managerial responsibility. Bill immediately asked Creswell to produce pro-forma statements for the next six months. The optimistic statements indicated that sales would increase and that the company would make a profit for 1975. Nevertheless, Bill asked Creswell not to make any more products for inventory and to consider the possibility of reducing costs by firing some of the staff people at the Factory.

EXHIBIT 5
Article X–Seniority

(a) Seniority is defined to mean length of continuous service with the Company and will apply in event of a plant-wide or general layoff. Departmental seniority of the regular employees shall prevail with respect to layoffs and re-employment after layoffs when ability and qualifications are equal and shall apply to departmental situations; for the purpose of this agreement, the departments shall be as outlined in Appendix "A".

(b) The Company agrees to furnish the Union Committee, from time to time, with a list of all new employees under the jurisdiction of the Union, together with the starting date.

(c) Seniority will be considered broken under the following conditions:

1. When an employee is discharged for cause and not reinstated.
2. When an employee voluntarily terminates employment.
3. When an employee fails to report the cause of absence from work within three (3) working days from the start of such absence unless there is reasonable excuse for such absence and for failure to notify the Company. However, this shall not excuse an employee from his or her responsibility to notify the Company of an absence from work that is less than three (3) days nor will it excuse an employee from disciplinary action that may result from such failure to report an absence.

(d) Employees in their first forty-five (45) days of employment do not have seniority rights (however, if an employee with less than forty-five (45) days' service is laid off and subsequently re-employed within two (2) years, he will receive credit for the time actually worked prior to layoff for purposes of the trial period referred to in Article I, paragraph [m]). Employees with more than forty-five (45) days' service shall lose seniority rights if laid off and not re-employed within two (2) years.

(e) For layoff and re-employment purposes only, an employee's seniority accumulates while not working during his layoff period. This in no way affects or modifies the vacation schedule otherwise provided for in this agreement.

(f) Employees who have been laid off shall be accorded seniority rights in the matter of re-employment.

(g) They shall be notified by certified mail sent to the last known address to report for work and failing to report for work in three (3) days within, and five (5) days outside, the Wilmington Postal Delivery Area, shall lose seniority except for reasons beyond their control in which case notice within periods shown above shall be given to the Company explaining the situation.

(h) It is understood and agreed that temporary transfers may be made without recourse to seniority.

(i) An employee who has, or may be, promoted by the Company to a job excluded from the Bargaining Unit, and later returns to the Bargaining Unit, shall retain his seniority which he held when he left the Bargaining Unit.

Within two months, it was clear to Bill that Creswell's projections were overly optimistic. Not only had he not been able to meet early targets, but a key outside distributor for trenchers had cancelled his arrangement with the company after having been pressured by Creswell to accept six new trenchers. In addition, Bill learned that a $40,000 trencher on a $40,000 chassis had been sent to Alaska in anticipation of a sale that had not been firm. When Bill had asked if in fact the sale had been made, he was told by the general manager that it had. Bill also learned that no staff personnel had been fired and that the Factory was continuing to build inventory in anticipation of increased sales. This was in spite of the fact that the construction industry had been in a severe recession for the past few years.

In late October 1975, it was clear that the Factory was going to lose almost as much money as it had the previous year. A projected loss of $720,000 was now forecast on sales of $2.1 million. In addition, there were 31 trenchers at various points in the pipeline; none of these had firm sale orders. Eleven of the units had been assigned to the Products Division with the remainder allocated among the 24 distributors. It was rumored that the remaining 20 units had been shipped to the distributors with an understanding between Creswell and the distributors that the units could be returned to the Factory. Furthermore, there were only $30,000 to $40,000 worth of firm orders on the books, most which were from the textile industry. Although there were a few thousand dollars worth of trencher parts' sales there had been no new trencher sales in recent months.

On November 1, 1975, Bill Anthony knew that drastic action had to be taken. Several key decisions had to be made. Foremost among them was whether or not the Factory could be saved. If the Factory was to be saved, a number of steps would have to be taken at once. One of the problems facing the Factory was the absence of a good control system that would tell him the true cost of his products. In addition, he was concerned about the size of the staff and the size of the work force at the Factory. In discussions with William Otto, he had learned that only some 50 people in the hourly work force were working on real orders. The rest were continuing to build inventory. If any employees were to be laid off, he would have to determine how many and which ones, following the terms of the contract as closely as possible (Exhibit 5). In addition, he was of the opinion that the 44 management and office employees could be reduced drastically if necessary. An additional concern was that within a few months, the work force was entitled to a wage increase of 30 cents per hour over the current average rate of $4.80 an hour. He was uncertain whether or not the company could afford such an increase. As Bill pondered the problems before him, it seemed that one possible alternative that at least should be explored was the possibility of liquidating the entire operation. A major drawback to such an alternative was that finished-goods inventory would be worth only 10 percent of market value if scrapped.

15. Anheuser-Busch Companies, Inc.*

BACKGROUND OF THE FIRM

In 1852, Georg Schneider opened the Bavarian Brewery on the south side of St. Louis, Missouri. Five years later, the brewery faced insolvency. In 1857, it was sold to competitors who renamed it Hammer and Urban. The new owners launched an expansion program with the help of a loan from Eberhard Anheuser, a successful soap manufacturer at the time. By 1860, the brewery had faltered once again and Anheuser assumed control. Four years later, his son-in-law, Adolphus Busch, joined the brewery as a salesman. Later Adolphus became a partner and finally president of the company. Busch was the driving force behind the company's success and in 1879, the company name was changed to Anheuser-Busch Brewing Association.

An important reason for the brewery's success was Adolphus Busch's innovative attempt to establish and maintain a national beer market. In 1877, he launched the industry's first fleet of refrigerated freight cars. He also pioneered the application of a new pasteurization process. Busch's talents were not limited to technology alone; he concurrently developed merchandising techniques to compliment his technological innovations. By 1901, annual sales had surpassed the million-barrel mark for the first time.

August A. Busch succeeded his father as president of Anheuser-Busch in 1913. With the advent of Prohibition, he was forced to harness the company's expertise and energies into new directions (i.e., corn products, *con* baker's yeast, ice cream, commercial refrigeration units, truck bodies, and *centric* nonalcoholic beverages). These efforts kept the company from collapsing during the "dry" era. With the passage of the 21st Amendment, Anheuser-Busch was back in the beer business. To celebrate, a team of Clydesdale horses was acquired in 1933—the Budweiser Clydesdales. *single product*

In 1946, August A. Busch, Jr., became president and chief executive officer. During his tenure, the company's beer operation flourished. Eight breweries were constructed and annual sales increased from 3 million barrels in 1946 to more than 34 million in 1974. The corporation also diversified

---
* Prepared by Douglas J. Workman, Neil H. Snyder, Rich Bonaventura, John Cary, Scott McMasters, and Karen Cook of the McIntire School of Commerce of the University of Virginia.

469

extensively, adding family entertainment centers, real estate, can manufacturing, transportation and a major league baseball franchise.

August A. Busch III was elected president in 1974 and chief executive officer the following year, making him the fifth Busch to serve in that capacity. Thus far under his direction, Anheuser-Busch has accomplished the following: opened its 10th brewery; introduced "Michelob Light," "Anheuser-Busch Natural Light," and "Würzburger Hofbräu"; opened a new Busch Gardens theme park; launched the largest brewery expansion projects in the company's history; vertically integrated into new can manufacturing and malt production facilities; and diversified into container recovery, soft drinks, and snack foods.

THE INDUSTRY AND COMPETITION

Ninety percent of Anheuser-Busch's sales come from beer products. (Generically, the term *beer* refers to any beverage brewed from a farinaceous grain.) The type of beer consumed in America today originated in the 1840s with the introduction of lager beer. Lager beer is bottom fermented (meaning yeast settles to the bottom during fermentation). The beer is then aged (or lagered) to mellow, resulting in a lighter, more effervescent potation. Prior to 1840, Americans' tastes closely resembled British tastes (i.e., heavily oriented toward ale, porter and stout). The influx of German immigrants in the 1840s initially increased the importance of lager beer because of the influence of German tastes and brewing skills.

By 1850, there were 430 brewers in the United States producing a total of 750,000 barrels per year, and by the end of the decade, there were 1,269 brewers producing over 1 million barrels per year. At that time, brewers served relatively small local areas. In the latter half of the 19th century, several significant technological advances were adapted to the beer industry, including artificial refrigeration, mechanized bottling equipment and pasteurization. The latter innovation enabled brewers to ship warm beer and store it for a longer period of time without refermentation. With developments in transportation technology, the 20th century saw the rise of the national brewer. The combined impact of these technological advances resulted in greater emphasis on marketing as the primary instrument of competition.

The modern era of the brewing industry begins with the end of World War II. Prior to that time, only a few brewers sold beer nationally, and they primarily operated out of a single plant. To offset additional transportation costs not incurred by local or even regional brewers, the national firms advertised their beers as being of premium quality and charged a premium price. This structural change in the industry (from predominantly local or regional to national producers) in the post-World War II time period has resulted in a steady decline in the number of brewers and plants and an increase in the market concentration of the large national brewers. (See Exhibits 1 and 2.)

In the period following World War II, annual beer sales hit a record high in 1947 and then declined and stagnated until 1959. Exhibit 3 shows per capita demand trends in beer, packaged beer and draft beer for this time period.

Many analysts blamed the lack of growth in demand upon demographic factors. According to *Brewers Almanac 1976* (p. 82) past industry surveys have shown that persons in the 21–44 age group account for about 69 percent of beer consumption. Since this age group exhibited little growth during 1948–59, population demographics offer a good explanation for stagnated demand during this period. However, other factors must be introduced to account for post-1959 growth because beer sales grew more than twice as fast as the number of people in this age group.

EXHIBIT 1
Number of Breweries and Brewery Firms, 1946–1976

Year	Plants	Firms
1946	471	
1947	465	404
1948	466	
1949	440	
1950	407	
1951	386	
1952	357	
1953	329	
1954	310	263
1955	292	
1956	281	
1957	264	
1958	252	211
1959	244	
1960	229	
1961	229	
1962	220	
1963	211	171
1964	190	
1965	179	
1966	170	
1967	154	125
1968	149	
1969	146	
1970	137	
1971	134	
1972	131	108
1973	114	
1974 (June)	108	
1976	94	49

Sources: for 1946–74: *Brewing Industry Survey* (New York: Research Company of America, 1973, 1974); for 1947–72: U.S. Bureau of the Census, *Census of Manufacturers;* for 1976: *Brewers Digest Brewery Directory, 1977.*

EXHIBIT 2
National Beer Sales Concentration Ratios, 1935–1977
(percentages)

Year	4-Firm	8-Firm
1935	11	17
1947	21	30
1954	27	41
1958	28	44
1963	34	52
1966	39	56
1967	40	59
1970	46	64
1972	52	70
1973	54	70
1974	58	74
1975	59	78
1976	59	80
1977	63	83

Sources: For 1953–72: U.S. Bureau of the Census, *Census of Manufactures;* for 1973: *Brewing Industry Survey (1974);* for 1974–75: *Advertising Age,* November 3, 1975, and December 27, 1976; for 1976–77: *Modern Brewery Age,* Feb. 14, 1977, and Feb. 13, 1978, by permission.

Data for 1935–72 based on value of shipments; for 1973–77, on sales data.

Economies of Scale

A major reason for the growth of national firms is the economies of scale obtained in their plant operations. Economies of scale in plant size enable brewers to obtain the lowest possible unit cost. According to one authority on the brewing industry, Dr. Kenneth G. Elzinga of the University of Virginia, the minimum efficient size (MES) plant capacity for the brewing industry is 1.25 million barrels per year. Cost savings accrue from water-processing equipment, sewage facilities, refrigeration equipment, management, laboratories, and custodial cost reductions. Scale economies from most of these sources continue to plant capacities of 10 million barrels per year, but beyond the size of 4.5 million barrels, cost savings are negligible. Exhibit 4 shows one method used to estimate the extent of economies of scale: the survivor test.

Economies of scale played a central role in the restructuring of the brewing industry which led to the demise of hundreds of breweries between 1945 and 1970. Moreover, according to Charles F. Keithahn of the Bureau of Economics of the Federal Trade Commission, an analysis based solely on economies of scale would indicate a decline in firm concentration over the 1970s (in a world in which all plants are of minimum efficient size but no larger). Exhibit 5 shows the minimum market share a firm with MES plants would need for survival.

EXHIBIT 3
Per Capita Beer Demand in the United States, 1935–1963

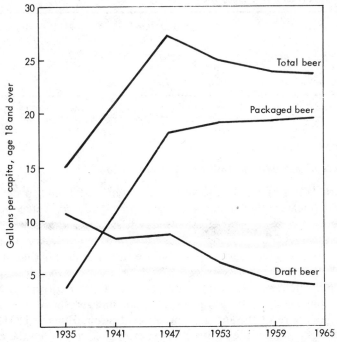

Source: John G. Keane, "An Analysis of Per Capita Beer Demand in the U.S. 1935–1963," University of Pittsburgh.

EXHIBIT 4
Surviving Breweries by Capacity, 1959–1973

Listed Annual Capacity Barrels (000)	1959	1961	1963	1965	1967	1969	1971	1973
0–25	11	9	8	7	3	3	2	2
26–100	57	51	46	44	33	23	19	11
101–250	51	44	39	30	26	23	19	11
251–500	40	37	33	24	18	14	14	10
501–750	14	15	13	12	13	15	12	5
751–1,000	16	19	20	20	22	20	20	15
1,001–1,500	14	14	12	13	15	13	13	13
1,501–2,000	4	5	5	3	3	8	8	7
2,001–3,000	5	6	6	7	5	6	9	9
3,001–4,000	3	3	4	5	5	3	3	3
4,001+	2	2	3	3	4	7	7	11

Source: Compiled from plant capacity figures listed in the *Modern Brewery Age Book* (Stamford, Conn.: Modern Brewery Age Publishing Co., various years), and industry trade sources. These figures do not include plants listed only on a company-consolidated basis (in the case of multiplant firms) or single-plant firms not reporting capacity in the *Blue Book*. Most plants list their capacity.

EXHIBIT 5
Economies of Plant Scale Expressed as a Percentage of Total Industry Production for 1970, 1975, 1980

	Production (million barrels)	MES Plant as a Percent of Production
1970	134.7	.9%
1975	150.3	.8
1980 (est.)	176.8	.7

Source: Dr. Willard Mueller, testimony before the Subcommittee on Antitrust and Monopoly of the Committee of the Judiciary, U.S. Senate, 95th Congress, 2nd session, 1978.

The Effects of Mergers on Industry Concentration

Leonard Weiss of the University of Wisconsin at Madison developed a means of delineating the impact on mergers on an industry's structure. Using his methodology, Dr. Elzinga found that mergers accounted for a negligible amount of the concentration occurring in the brewing industry. In fact, concentration trends in the brewing industry are rather unique in that most of the increased concentration was brought about by internal expansion rather than by merger or acquisition. Strict enforcement of the antitrust laws by the Justice Department (DOJ) is the reason that mergers have accounted for such a small share of the increase in concentration. But the DOJ, through its rigid enforcement of the antitrust laws, may have promoted the end result it was seeking to prevent, increased national concentration. With the elimination of the merger route, the national brewers were forced to expand internally. They built large new breweries, which were more efficient than the older, smaller ones. If mergers had been permitted, the national firms might have acquired old small breweries and might have grown slower than they actually did.

The Effect of Advertising

Forced to expand internally in a capital-intensive industry (it costs between $25 and $45 for each additional barrel of capacity), the national firms sought to ensure a steady demand for their products. The need for larger markets resulting from increased capacity coincided with the development of television, which led to an increase in the firm's desired level of product identification. Advertising, particularly television spots, became the key to product differentiation in an industry where studies have shown that under test conditions beer drinkers cannot distinguish between brands. (See Exhibits 6 and 7).

In the last decade, a new rivalry has developed among major national brewers (this time at the instigation of Miller Brewing Company). In 1970, Philip Morris completed an acquisition of Miller, and according to Dr. Wil-

EXHIBIT 6

Barrelage Sold, Measured Media Advertising Expenditures, and Advertising Expenditures, Per Barrel, Ten Leading Brewers, 1972–1977

	Year	Barrels (000)	Advertising[1] (000)	Advertising per Barrel
Philip Morris-Miller	1977	24,410	$42,473	$1.74
	1976	18,232	29,117	1.60
	1975	12,862	20,894	1.62
	1974	9,066	12,140	1.34
	1973	6,919	10,002	1.45
	1972	5,353	8,400	1.57
Anheuser-Busch	1977	36,640	$44,984	$1.23
	1976	29,051	25,772	.89
	1975	35,200	19,237	.55
	1974	34,100	12,359	.36
	1973	29,887	12,936	.43
	1972	26,522	14,808	.56
Schlitz	1977	22,130	$40,830	$1.85
	1976	24,162	33,756	1.40
	1975	23,279	23,173	1.00
	1974	22,661	17,977	.79
	1973	21,343	16,615	.78
	1972	18,906	17,782	.94
Pabst	1977	16,300	$10,843	$ .67
	1976	17,037	9,112	.53
	1975	15,700	9,007	.57
	1974	14,297	7,711	.54
	1973	13,128	6,422	.49
	1972	12,600	6,142	.49
Coors	1977	12,824	$ 3,966	$ .25
	1976	13,665	1,626	.12
	1975	11,950	1,093	.09
	1974	12,400	801	.06
	1973	10,950	699	.06
	1972	9,785	1,332	.14
Olympia (Hamm 1975)	1977	6,831	$ 8,470	$1.24
	1976	6,370	5,430	.85
	1975	5,770	5,555	.96
	1974	4,300	2,764	.64
	1973	3,636	2,323	.64
	1972	3,330	2,491	.75
Heileman (Grain Belt 1975)	1977	6,245	$ 4,636	$ .74
	1976	5,210	3,616	.69
	1975	4,535	2,864	.63
	1974	4,300	2,329	.54
	1973	4,420	2,243	.51
	1972	3,675	2,260	.61
Stroh	1977	6,114	$ 7,212	$1.18
	1976	5,765	5,017	.87
	1975	5,133	3,950	.77
	1974	4,364	3,477	.80
	1973	4,645	3,145	.68
	1972	4,231	3,567	.84
Schaefer	1977	4,700	$ 4,219	$ .90
	1976	5,300	2,516	.47
	1975	5,881	2,637	.45
	1974	5,712	2,308	.40

EXHIBIT 6 (continued)

	Year	Barrels (000)	Advertising[1] (000)	Advertising per Barrel
	1973	5,500	2,438	.44
	1972	5,530	2,994	.54
C. Schmidt.....................	1977	3,571	$ 3,912	$1.10
	1976	3,450	2,703	.78
	1975	3,330	2,269	.68
	1974	3,490	3,035	.87
	1973	3,520	2,916	.83
	1972	3,194	2,104	.66

[1] Advertising expenditures in six measured media as reported in *Leading National Advertisers,* various issues.

Source: Company sales for 1970–76 from *Advertising Age,* various issues; 1977 sales, Table 1.

lard F. Mueller of the University of Wisconsin, Philip Morris' multiproduct and multinational operations in highly concentrated industries enabled it to engage in cross-subsidization of its brewing subsidiary. This capacity, coupled with the relatedness of the marketing function between Philip Morris and Miller, provided a powerful vehicle for industry restructuring. Miller adopted aggressive market segmentation and expansion strategies, thus increasing their capacity five-fold between 1970 and 1977. According to Dr. Mueller, a doubling of 1977 capacity is planned by 1981. Exhibit 8 shows comparative financial data on Philip Morris and the rest of the leading brewers.

In 1975, Miller found a successful method for promoting a low-calorie beer, Lite, which they had purchased from Meister Brau Inc., of Chicago in 1972. They spent heavily, about $6 per barrel, to introduce it nationwide. However, Lite's success was not wholly attributable to heavy advertising. Low-calorie beers were promoted in the past with a notable lack of success. Through marketing research, Miller discovered that a significant portion of the beer market is comprised of young and middle-aged men who are sports fans with dreams of athletic prowess. In advertising Lite, Miller relied predominantly on retired athletes renowned for their speed and agility. The message was that one could drink a lot of Lite and still be fast, not that one should drink Lite to keep from getting fat.

By 1975, Schlitz, and to some extent Anheuser-Busch, began to increase their own advertising expenditures and had made plans to enter the low-calorie beer market. This was done not only as a response to Miller's aggressiveness, but also because of a general lack of growth in demand in the face of increasing industry capacity. By 1978, nine of the ten largest brewers had light brands on the market. Exhibit 9 through Exhibit 11 show brand shipment breakdowns for the three major brewers.

Currently the only company with the financial resources to battle Miller and its multinational conglomerate backer is Anheuser-Busch, the industry

EXHIBIT 7

Relative Media Advertising Effectiveness By Beer Brand, 1975–1978

	Media Advertising Expense ($ million)	Total Barrels (million)	Advertising Expense per Barrel	Barrel Change 1978 versus 1974	Advertising Expense per Incremental Million Barrel
Premium category					
Budweiser	$71.5	100.2	$ 0.71	1.1	$65.00
Miller High Life	60.5	61.3	0.99	13.5	4.48
Schlitz	70.4	59.3	1.18	(5.2)	NA
Light category					
Lite	63.8	22.9	2.79	8.4	7.60
Anheuser-Busch					
Natural Light	24.0	3.8	6.32	2.3	10.43
Michelob Light	6.5	0.9	7.22	0.9	7.22
Schlitz Light	30.3	3.6	8.42	0.7	43.29
Superpremium category					
Michelob	35.9	23.0	1.56	4.3	8.35
Lowenbrau	29.4	1.7	17.29	1.2	24.50

Source: C. James Walker III, *Competition in the U.S. Brewing Industry: A Basic Analysis.* Shearson Hayden Stone, Inc., 14 Wall Street, New York, New York 10005, September 26, 1979.

EXHIBIT 8
Assets, Sales, Net Profit, Net Income on Stockholders' Investment, and Total Advertising Expenditures, 1977 ($ millions)

Company	Assets	Sales	Net Profit	Total Profit on Equity	Total Advertising
Philip Morris (Miller)	$4,048	$3,849*	$335	19.8%	$277
Anheuser-Busch	1,404	1,838	92	13.5	79
Joseph Schlitz	727	937	20	5.5	55
Pabst Brewing	396	583	22	8.1	27
Adolph Coors	692	593	68	12.2	15†

* Excludes U.S. and foreign excise taxes.
† Estimate.
Source: "500 Largest Industrials," *Fortune*, May 1977; advertising data reported in individual company SEC Form 10-K reports for 1977.

EXHIBIT 9
Estimated Anheuser-Busch Brand Breakdown, 1974–1978, Shipments in Barrels (millions)

	1978	1977	1976	1975	1974
Budweiser	27.5	25.4	21.1	26.2	26.4
Michelob	7.4	6.4	5.0	4.2	3.1
Michelob Light	0.9	—	—	—	—
Busch	3.5	3.3	3.0	4.8	4.6
Natural Light	2.3	1.5	—	—	—
Total	41.6	36.6	29.1	35.2	34.1

Source: C. James Walker III, *Competition in the U.S. Brewing Industry: A Basic Analysis*. Shearson Hayden Stone, Inc., 14 Wall Street, New York, New York 10005. September 26, 1979.

EXHIBIT 10
Estimated Miller Brewing Brand Breakdown, 1974–1978, Shipments in Barrels (millions)

	1978	1977	1976	1975	1974
High Life	21.3	17.3	13.5	9.2	7.8
Lite	8.8	6.4	4.6	3.1	0.4
Lowenbrau	1.2	0.5	0.1	0.0	—
Other	0.0	0.0	0.2	0.5	0.9
Total	31.3	24.2	18.4	12.8	9.1

Source: C. James Walker III, *Competition in the U.S. Brewing Industry: A Basic Analysis*. Shearson Hayden Stone, Inc., 14 Wall Street, New York, New York 10005. September 26, 1979.

EXHIBIT 11
Estimated Schlitz Brewing Brand Breakdown, 1974–1978, Shipments in Barrels (millions)

	1978	1977	1976	1975	1974
Schlitz	12.7	14.3	15.9	16.8	17.9
Old Milwaukee	4.3	4.9	5.5	5.2	3.9
Schlitz Light	0.7	1.3	1.4	0.2	—
Malt Liquor	1.7	1.4	1.3	1.0	0.8
Primo	0.2	0.2	0.1	0.1	0.1
Total	19.6	22.1	24.2	23.3	22.7

Source: C. James Walker III, *Competition in the U.S. Brewing Industry: A Basic Analysis.* Shearson Hayden Stone, Inc., 14 Wall Street, New York 10005. September 26, 1979.

leader. Anheuser-Busch responded aggressively to Miller's program. In 1977 Anheuser-Busch surpassed Miller and Schlitz in advertising expenditures by spending over $44,000,000. (See Exhibit 12.)

Clearly, Anheuser-Busch's and Miller's growth has been at the expense of the regional brewers and the faltering national brewers (Schlitz and Pabst). C. James Walker III, an industry analyst for Shearson Hayden Stone, Inc., estimates only 2.7 percent per year industry growth for the early 1980s. The capital-intensive nature of the industry, coupled with huge advertising outlays, make it very unlikely that any firm will be able to challenge the two leaders. To quote August Busch III, "This business is now a two-horse race."

ORGANIZATION OF ANHEUSER-BUSCH

Effective October 1, 1979, Anheuser-Busch, Inc., became a wholly owned subsidiary of a new holding company, Anheuser-Busch Companies, Inc., and the outstanding shares of Anheuser-Busch, Inc., were exchanged for an equal number of shares of the holding company. Concerning this change, August A. Busch III said,

The holding company's name and structure will more clearly communicate the increasingly diversified nature of our business, thereby reflecting not only our position of leadership in the brewing industry, but also our substantial activities in yeast and specialty corn products, family entertainment, transportation, can manufacturing, real estate, and other businesses. The new structure will also provide management with increased organizational and operational flexibility.

Each of our businesses can eventually be operated as separate companies under Anheuser-Busch Companies, Inc., with responsibilities divided among management personnel.

This reorganization will help facilitate our long-range plan to not only continue to grow in production and sales of beer but also to continue to expand and diversify into other areas which offer significant opportunities for growth.

EXHIBIT 12
Market Share Performance

	Barrel Shipments (millions)	Market Share	Barrel Increment (millions)	Percent Increase (Decrease)	Barrel Shipments (millions)	Market Share	Barrel Increment (millions)	Percent Increase (Decrease)
		1978				1977		
Anheuser	41.6	25.1%	5.0	13.7 %	36.6	22.9%	7.5	25.8 %
Miller	31.3	18.9	7.1	29.3	24.2	15.2	5.8	31.5
Schlitz	19.6	11.8	(2.5)	(11.3)	22.1	13.9	(2.1)	(8.7)
Pabst	15.4	9.3	(0.6)	(3.8)	16.0	10.0	(1.0)	(5.9)
Coors	12.6	7.6	(0.2)	(1.6)	12.8	8.0	(0.7)	(5.2)
Top 5	120.5	72.7%	8.8	7.9 %	111.7	70.0%	9.5	9.3 %
All others	41.7	25.2	(3.5)	(7.7)	45.2	28.3	(3.0)	(6.2)
U.S. industry	162.2	97.9%	5.3	3.4 %	156.9	98.4%	6.5	4.4 %
Imports	3.45	2.1	0.8	30.8	2.6	1.6	0.2	8.3
All beer	165.6	100.0%	6.1	3.8 %	159.5	100.0%	6.7	4.5 %

	Barrel Shipments (millions)	Market Share	Barrel Increment (millions)	Percent Increase (Decrease)	Barrel Shipments (millions)	Market Share	Barrel Increment (millions)	Percent Increase (Decrease)
		1976				1975		
Anheuser	29.1	19.0%	(6.1)	(17.3)%	35.2	23.4%	1.1	3.2 %
Miller	18.4	12.0	5.6	43.8	12.8	8.5	3.7	40.7
Schlitz	24.2	15.8	0.9	3.9	23.3	15.5	0.6	2.6
Pabst	17.0	11.1	1.3	8.3	15.7	10.4	1.4	9.8
Coors	13.5	8.8	1.6	13.4	11.9	7.9	(0.4)	(3.3)
Top 5	102.2	66.9%	3.3	3.3 %	98.9	65.8%	6.4	6.9 %
All others	48.2	31.5	(1.5)	(3.0)	49.7	33.1	(3.3)	(6.2)
U.S. industry	150.4	98.4%	1.8	1.2 %	148.6	98.9%	3.1	2.1 %
Imports	2.4	1.6	0.7	41.2	1.7	1.1	0.3	21.4
All beer	152.8	100.0%	2.5	1.7 %	150.3	100.0%	3.4	2.3 %

	Barrel Shipments (millions) 1974	Market Share 1974	Increased Barrel Shipments (millions)	Market Share Point Change 1974–1978	Compounded Annual Shipment Growth
Anheuser	34.1	23.2%	7.5	+ 1.9	5.1 %
Miller	9.1	6.2	22.2	+12.7	36.2
Schlitz	22.7	6.2	(3.1)	− 3.6	(3.3)
Pabst	14.3	9.7	1.1	− 0.4	1.9
Coors	12.3	8.4	0.3	− 0.8	0.4
Top 5	92.5	63.0%	28.0	+ 9.7	6.8 %
All others	53.0	36.0	11.3	−10.8	(4.9)
U.S. industry	145.5	99.0%	16.7	− 1.1	2.7 %
Imports	1.4	1.0	2.0	+ 1.1	24.9
All beer	146.9	100.0%	18.7	0.0	3.1 %

Source: C. James Walker III, *Competition in the U.S. Brewing Industry: A Basic Analysis.* Shearson Hayden Stone, Inc., 14 Wall Street, New York, New York 10005. September 26, 1979.

KEY EXECUTIVES

August A. Busch III was born June 16, 1937, attended public and private schools in St. Louis, the University of Arizona, and the Siebel Institute of Technology, a school for brewers in Chicago.[1] He is chairman of the board and president of Anheuser-Busch Companies, Inc., and he bagan his career with the company in 1957 in the St. Louis Malt House. Since that time, he has worked in practically every department of both the Brewing and Operations Divisions. In 1962, he moved into Marketing, working in the field with wholesalers as well as company-owned branches in all areas of the country. Returning to St. Louis, he was promoted to assistant sales manager-regional brands and later was named sales manager for regional brands where he was responsible for the marketing of Busch throughout the product's marketing area.

Mr. Busch was named a member of the company's board of directors and appointed vice president of marketing operations in 1963. He became general manager in July 1965, executive vice president and general manager in April 1971, president in February 1974, chief executive officer in May 1975, and chairman of the board in April 1977.

Fred L. Kuhlmann, a native of St. Louis, is vice chairman of the Board of Directors and executive vice president of Anheuser-Busch Companies, Inc. He joined Anheuser-Busch, Inc., in August 1967 as general counsel and was elected a vice president in January 1971, senior vice president of administration and services and member of the board of directors in February 1974, executive vice president of administration in June 1977, and was elected to his present position in October 1979.

Kuhlmann received his A.B. degree from Washington University in St. Louis and his LL.B from that institution's School of Law. He also has an LL.M degree from Columbia University School of Law in New York. He has been active in a number of business and civic groups and serves as a director of the St. Louis National Baseball Club, Inc., and Manufacturers Railway Company. He is also a director of Boatmen's National Bank of St. Louis, Civic Center Redevelopment Corporation and St. Louis Regional Commerce and Growth Association.

Dennis P. Long, 44, president of Anheuser-Busch, Inc., has extensive experience spanning more than 25 years at Anheuser-Busch both in brewing and nonbrewing areas, and he attended Washington University in St. Louis, Missouri. After serving as national price administrator in beer marketing from 1960–64, he was promoted to assistant to the vice president of beer marketing operations and worked in the field with the nationwide beer wholesaler network as well as with company-owned branch distribution centers. He was promoted to assistant to the vice president and general manager in 1965.

---

[1] The information presented in this section was obtained from the corporate headquarters of Anheuser-Busch Companies, Inc.

In 1972 Long was elected group vice president responsible for the Busch Gardens and industrial products divisions and Busch Properties, Inc. Under Long's leadership, the industrial products division became the nation's leading producer of bakers yeast; the division's sales of both yeast and corn products and its profitability increased to record proportions. He also headed the transition of Busch Gardens from beer promotional facilities to a separate profit center. Since then a new Busch Gardens has been opened in Williamsburg, Virginia, and that division also operates profitably. Since taking charge of Busch Properties, Inc., the real estate subsidiary has embarked further into residential and resort development in addition to the commercial-industrial field, and the performance of Busch Properties has improved markedly.

In June 1977, Long became vice president and general manager of the Beer Division and since that time has embarked upon a strong effort to increase beer sales volume and profitability. His efforts include new and expanded marketing efforts, increased productivity in brewing and packaging, and a strong cost-control and cost-reduction effort.

PRODUCTS OFFERED BY ANHEUSER-BUSCH

Over the past five years, Anheuser-Busch's beer division has accounted for approximately 90 percent of consolidated net sales. The beer division of Anheuser-Busch produces Budweiser, Michelob, Busch, Michelob Light, Classic Dark, and Anheuser-Busch Natural Light. The remaining 10 percent of the consolidated net sales come from family entertainment (Busch Gardens Division), can manufacturing, container recycling, transportation services (St. Louis Refrigerator Car Company and Manufacturers Railway Company), major-league baseball (St. Louis Cardinals), real estate development (Busch Properties, Inc.), and the manufacture and sale of corn products, brewer's yeast, and baker's yeast (industrial products division). Anheuser-Busch is the nation's leading producer of baker's yeast with a market share well over 40 percent. Exhibit 13 presents data by product line.

During 1978, Anheuser-Busch made significant progress in redefining its diversification objectives as a means of building for the future. A corporate policy was established to concentrate initially on developing new food and beverage products which are compatible with the existing capabilities and also, where possible, on distributing these products through the company's existing wholesaler network. The company is presently working on developing a line of snack foods, reportedly called "Eagle Snacks," which would also be compatible with existing production and distribution facilities.

The company began test marketing Würzburger Hofbräu beer in the United States early in 1979. This full-bodied, premium, German beer will be brewed in Wurzburg, West Germany, and shipped in large insulated barrels to the United States where it will be bottled by Anheuser-Busch and distributed through the company's wholesaler network.

EXHIBIT 13
Anheuser-Busch Revenue Breakdown by Product Class (000)

	1978	1977	1976	1975	1974
Consolidated sales............	$2,701,611	$2,231,230	$1,752,998	$2,036,687	$1,791,863
Federal and state beer taxes	441,978	393,182	311,852	391,708	378,772
Consolidated net sales	$2,259,633	$1,838,048	$1,441,146	$1,644,979	$1,413,091
Beer division	2,056,754	1,691,004	1,282,620	1,480,481	1,271,782
Percent of consolidated net sales	91%	92%	89%	90%	90%
Other divisions*	$ 202,879	$ 147,044	$ 158,526	$ 164,498	$ 141,309
Percent of consolidated net sales	9%	8%	11%	10%	10%

* All other divisions include: Industrial Products Division, Busch Gardens Division, Busch Properties, Inc., Transportation, and the St. Louis Cardinals.
Source: Annual reports.

Anheuser-Busch has a new installation in St. Louis, Missouri, which annually produces 1.8 million pounds of autolyzed yeast extract, a flavoring agent for processed foods. As the only producer of the extract in the United States with its own captive supply of brewer's yeast, Anheuser-Busch entered this new venture with a decided competitive advantage.

Anheuser-Busch's well-known family of quality beers includes products in every market segment. Budweiser has been brewed and sold for more than 100 years. Budweiser, available in bottles, cans, and on draught nationwide, is the company's principal product and the largest selling beer in the world. Michelob was developed in 1896 as a "draught beer for connoisseurs." Super-premium Michelob is sold nationally in bottles, cans and on draught.

With a greater percentage of the population entering the weight conscious 25–39-year old range, Anheuser-Busch has introduced Michelob Light. It has 20 percent fewer calories than regular Michelob. When introduced in 1978, it was the first superpremium light beer. In order to capitalize on this by transferring the consumer appeal for Michelob to Michelob Light, Anheuser-Busch communicates "the heritage of Michelob and the taste of Michelob Light" in its advertising. Michelob Light is available nationwide in cans, bottles, and on draught. Anheuser-Busch also offers Natural Light for weight conscious beer drinkers.

Busch Bavarian beer was introduced in 1955 as a low-priced beer in direct competition with subpremium regional beers. In April 1978, a smoother, sweeter, and lighter Busch beer was successfully test marketed in New

England as a premium-priced brand to capitalize on anticipated growth of the premium segment of the market in future years. In 1979, with new package graphics and advertising, premium Busch was introduced in areas where the company previously marketed Busch Bavarian.

Anheuser-Busch's expanding corporate programs of vertical integration into can manufacturing and barley malting play an important role in overall beer division activities and profitability. The company's various vertically integrated enterprises provide an added advantage in controlling the cost and supply of containers and ingredients. Vertical integration helps to reduce cost pressures in brewing operations and to insure continuity and quality of supply.

Metal Container Corporation, a wholly owned subsidiary of Anheuser-Busch Companies, produces two-piece aluminum beer cans at facilities in Florida, Ohio, and Missouri. Container Recovery Corporation, another wholly owned subsidiary of Anheuser-Busch Companies, operates container recovery facilities in Ohio and New Hampshire which are actively involved in collecting and recycling aluminum cans.

The company's Materials Acquisition Division is responsible for purchasing all agricultural commodities, packaging materials, supplies and fuel. Its objective is to increase stability and flexibility in the procurement of commodities and materials. This division investigates alternative methods of supply, analyzes vertical integration opportunities available to the company and monitors the supply and cost of all commodities purchased by Anheuser-Busch.

Anheuser-Busch processes barley into brewer's malt at plants in Manitowoc, Wisconsin (total capacity of 8.5 million bushels annually), and Moorhead, Minnesota (annual capacity of 6.4 million bushels). These two malt production facilities provide the company with the capability to self manufacture approximately one third of its malt requirements.

The Industrial Products Division produces corn syrup and starch for numerous food applications, including the processing of canned frozen foods and the manufacture of ice cream and candy. Additionally, the division markets starch and resin products used in the manufacture of paper, corrugated containers, and textiles. The company's corn processing plant in Lafayette, Indiana currently has a grind capacity of 11 billion bushels of corn yearly.

The company's brewer's yeast food plant in Jacksonville, Florida, has a yearly capacity of 3 million pounds. The debitterized brewer's food yeast is sold to health food manufacturers for use in a variety of nutritional supplements. Busch Entertainment Corporation, the company's family entertainment subsidiary, operates theme parks in Florida and Virginia. Unique blends of natural beauty and family entertainment activities and attractions are featured in both locations. Busch Properties, Inc., is the company's real estate development subsidiary. It is currently involved in the development of both residential and commercial properties at sites in Virginia and Ohio. St.

Louis Refrigerator Car Company, Manufacturers Railway Company, and five other companies compose Anheuser-Busch's transportation subsidiaries. They provide commercial repair, rebuilding, maintenance, and inspection of railroad cars, terminal railroad switching services, and truck cartage and warehousing services.

Philosophy — brand consciousness

MARKETING

Anheuser-Busch has a coast-to-coast network of eleven breweries which are selectively situated in major population and beer consumption regions. Once the beers leave the breweries, distribution to the consumer becomes the responsibility of 959 wholesale distribution operations and eleven company-owned beer branches which provide the company with its own profit centers within the distribution system. The beer branches perform sales, merchandising, and delivery services in their respective areas of primary responsibility. The company's beer branches are located in Sylmar and Riverside, California; Denver; Chicago; Louisville; New Orleans; Cambridge, Massachusetts; Kansas City, Missouri; Newark, New Jersey; Tulsa; and Washington, D.C.

The beer industry has always been a highly competitive industry. Success depends on volume, and sales by the nation's top five brewers account for an estimated 70 percent of the total market. There is intense competition between the industry leaders. According to Value Line, it is expected that by 1980 the top five brewers will account for approximately 80 percent of the market.

Competitive pressures have led Anheuser-Busch to take an aggressive stance in its marketing strategy. Anheuser-Busch is the country's largest brewer in terms of barrel sales per year and the 34th largest national advertiser. The 1978 annual report of Anheuser-Busch said that marketing efforts were "the most extensive and aggressive in company history," stressing product and packaging innovations, brand identity, and off-premise merchandising. The company is entering the 1980s with new packaging innovations and new marketing programs. The aggressive packaging is aimed at further market segmentation and penetration. Presently, the company sells more than 80 basic packages.

Anheuser-Busch's advertisements have traditionally been aimed at communicating the quality of the company's beer products, which appeal to virtually every taste and price range. Television advertisements and sports sponsorships continue to be the major focal point for marketing the company's beer brands. Television advertisements focus on prime-time programming and sports. To increase its presence on college campus, Anheuser-Busch utilizes a unique marketing team of 400 student representatives at major colleges and universities across the country.

Anheuser-Busch has enlarged its marketing staff in the beer division. A field sales task force has been established to provide immediate and concentrated assistance in markets needing a sales boost. The national accounts sales department was created to provide better marketing coordination and communication between the company's sales staff and large national chain accounts such as grocery stores, convenience stores, fast food outlets, hotels, motels, liquor chains, and athletic stadiums. The marketing services department coordinates and expands activities in the areas of sales promotion, merchandising, special markets, point-of-sale, and incentive programs.

PRODUCTION FACILITIES

Reviewing the production facilities utilized by Anheuser-Busch provides insight into the growth pattern of the organization. Devotion to investment in plant capacity has been extensive in the past decade, and the future capital expenditure program allows for further expansion and modernization of facilities.

The largest subsidiary of Anheuser-Busch Companies is the beer production sector. Exhibit 14 is a listing of the geographically dispersed breweries

EXHIBIT 14
Anheuser-Busch Production Facility Locations and Capacities

	Capacity (millions of barrels)	Beginning Year of Shipment
St. Louis	11.6	1880
Los Angeles	10.0	1954
Newark, New Jersey	4.7	1951
Tampa, Florida	2.2	1959
Houston, Texas	2.6	1966
Columbus, Ohio	6.2	1968
Jacksonville, Florida	6.5	1969
Merrimack, New Hampshire	2.8	1970
Williamsburg, Virginia	7.5	1972
Fairfield, California	3.5	1976
Baldwinsville, New York	6.0	1982

Source: Company annual reports, various years.

with their corresponding annual capacity in millions of barrels and dates of first shipments. As can be seen from this exhibit, many of the beer production facilities are quite new. Plants in St. Louis and Newark have undergone extensive modernization programs to upgrade older plants and equipment and ensure consistent quality regardless of brewery location. In 1980, Anheuser-Busch purchased a brewery formerly owned and operated by Schlitz. The seller was forced to close the plant as a result of declining sales due to competitive pressures.

Commitments to plant expansion have been extensive in the past few years. For example, capital expenditures will approach $2 billion for the five years ending 1983, with 93 percent for beer-related activities, according to industry analyst Robert S. Weinberg. Expansion is currently being undertaken at several of the eleven breweries. At the Los Angeles plant, the largest expansion project, capacity is being increased by more than 6 million barrels. Capacity in Williamsburg, Virginia, is being increased threefold.

Plant expansion in the areas of can manufacturing and industrial products manufacturing is being conducted at rapid rates. Vertical integration into can manufacturing and malt production is requiring substantial increases in plant investment. Can production facilities were completed in Jacksonville, Florida, in 1974, in Columbus, Ohio, in 1977, and a new plant will be completed in 1980 in Arnold, Missouri. Nearly 40 percent of cans used will be provided internally by 1980.

Conglomerate, - 4th Stage development
Divisional

RESEARCH AND DEVELOPMENT

R&D funds are currently being used to develop new food and beverage products which are consistent with the company's production and distribution capabilities. The organization has a Corn Products Research Group which recently developed a number of new and very profitable modified food starches. In addition to these, Anheuser-Busch's research on possible new beer products helped to place Michelob Light and Anheuser-Busch Natural Light beers on the market.

Along with research on new and profitable products, the company is striving to cut packaging costs by doing research in the production of aluminum. Anheuser-Busch paid $6 million in 1978 to a major international aluminum company, Swiss Aluminum Ltd., for access and participation rights in this company's ongoing research on the development of certain new technologies in aluminum casting.

Besides product and container research, Anheuser-Busch's R&D departments are studying matters of social concern. The company conducts this type of research, first, in order to remain active in its social responsibility as a public corporation, and, second, to strengthen its influence in reducing government regulations and thus avoid possible costly restrictions to its operations. Research to determine the causes of alcoholism and develop effective treatment and prevention programs, in cooperation with the U.S. Brewers Association, is one example of the company's effort here. Other examples relate to environmental matters. In an independent effort toward developing and utilizing alternative energy systems other than scarce natural gas an oil, Anheuser-Busch is researching solar energy. In 1978, the company installed a new pilot-project at its Jacksonville, Florida, brewery. At this plant, solar energy is being tested in pasteurizing bottled beers. In addition to this, the company is developing new land-application programs aimed at soil enrichment and energy conservation. Under these programs, rich soil nutrients are taken from the breweries' liquid wastes and used to grow various crops, primarily sod, grass, and grains.

FUTURE

In his letter to the shareholders in the 1978 annual report, August A. Busch III discusses Anheuser-Busch's expansion and diversification plans. He writes,

> We continue to commit substantial resources to provide the capacity necessary to support our planned sales growth and to maintain our industry leadership. Future growth and profitability also depend, however, on our willingness to commit funds and energies to the development of new products and new areas of business activity.
>
> For a number of years, we have been investing considerable sums of money and a great deal of effort in the area of vertical integration of our beer business . . . new can and malt plants and, more recently, in exploring the possibility of producing our own aluminum sheet used in the manufacture of cans. These activities have proved to be successful in controlling costs and we will continue to pay close attention to vertical integration.
>
> We are also exploring opportunities to diversify into other business ventures which are not beer related. We can do this either through acquisitions or through internal development of new products. At the present time we are emphasizing a program aimed at maximizing use of existing capabilities. We are in the process of developing internally a line of soft drinks and other consumer products which can be distributed through our wholesaler network. We recognize from the outset that we may not achieve success in every one of these new ventures. However, the financial risks are relatively small and the potential rewards are considerable.

C. James Walker III, industry analyst, believes that Anheuser-Busch expects a 1981 shipment level of 55 million barrels, indicating 9.2 million barrel growth in the 1979–81 period. This is comparable to what should be achieved in 1977–79. However, without the presence of a visible new major category similar to light in size, Walker doubts that growth in the 1980s can match the expansion of the late 1970s. According to Walker, new brands such as Würzburger and Busch Premium seem unlikely to garner the growth that Natural Light and Michelob Light may attain. Exhibit 16 shows Walker's estimates for 1981, which would make Anheuser-Busch fall 6 percent shy of its goal of 98 percent capacity utilization.

Busch, on the other hand, is more optimistic. He writes,

> In anticipation of what we can expect to encounter in the marketplace, we have developed strong and aggressive marketing and promotion programs to enhance our position as industry leader. We will be introducing more new products and new packages to keep Anheuser-Busch in the forefront of market segmentation. And, we will be intensifying our emphasis on the quality of our products.

EXHIBIT 15
Ten-Year Financial Summary ($000, except per-share and statistical data)

	1978	1977	1976	1975	1974	1973	1972	1971	1970	1969
Consolidated summary of operations:										
Barrels sold	41,610	36,640	29,051	35,196	34,097	29,887	26,522	24,309	22,202	18,712
Sales	$2,701,611	$2,231,230	$1,752,998	$2,036,687	$1,791,863	$1,442,720	$1,273,093	$1,173,476	$1,036,272	$871,904
Federal and state beer taxes	441,978	393,182	311,852	391,708	378,772	333,013	295,593	271,023	243,495	205,295
Net sales	2,259,633	1,838,048	1,441,146	1,644,979	1,413,091	1,109,707	977,500	902,453	792,777	666,609
Cost of products sold	1,762,410	1,462,801	1,175,055	1,343,784	1,187,816	875,361	724,718	658,886	579,372	490,932
Gross profit	497,223	375,247	266,091	301,195	225,275	234,346	252,782	243,567	213,405	175,677
Marketing, administrative and research expenses	274,961	190,470	137,797	126,053	106,653	112,928	108,008	108,087	92,660	84,113
Operating income	222,262	184,777	128,294	175,142	118,622	121,418	144,774	135,480	120,745	91,564
Interest income	11,693	7,724	10,304	10,944	9,925	4,818	3,299	3,102	3,715	3,604
Interest expense	(28,894)	(26,708)	(26,941)	(22,602)	(11,851)	(5,288)	(6,041)	(6,597)	(7,104)	(7,401)
Other income net	751	4,193	1,748	1,816	4,840	5,287	4,855	4,065	3,420	5,171
Loss on partial closing of Los Angeles Busch Gardens (1)			(10,020)							
Income before income taxes	205,812	169,986	103,385	165,300	121,536	126,235	146,887	136,050	120,776	92,938
Income taxes	94,772	78,041	47,952	80,577	57,517	60,658	70,487	64,412	58,227	47,627
Income before extraordinary item	111,040	91,945	55,433	84,723	64,019	65,577	76,400	71,638	62,549	45,311
Extraordinary item (2)							4,093			
Net income	111,040	91,945	55,433	84,723	64,019	65,577	72,307	71,638	62,549	45,311

Per share (3)										
Income before extraordinary item	2.46	2.04	1.23	1.88	1.42	1.46	1.70	1.60	1.40	1.02
Net income	2.46	2.04	1.23	1.88	1.42	1.46	1.61	1.60	1.40	1.02
Cash dividends paid	37,013	32,036	30,646	28,843	27,041	27,037	26,109	23,784	18,991	17,843
Per share (3)	.82	.71	.68	.64	.60	.60	.58	.53	.425	.40
Dividend payout ratio	33.3%	34.8%	55.3%	34.0%	42.3%	41.1%	36.0%	33.1%	30.4%	39.2%
Average number of shares outstanding (3)	45,138	45,115	45,068	45,068	45,068	45,063	45,020	44,887	44,686	44,616
Book value per share	16.71	15.07	13.72	13.17	11.93	11.11	10.25	9.20	8.02	7.03
Balance sheet information:										
Working capital	236,396	188,069	194,814	268,099	145,107	82,352	88,711	92,447	85,102	80,963
Current ratio	1.9	1.9	2.2	2.7	2.3	1.8	2.1	2.2	2.1	2.3
Plant and equipment, net	1,109,243	951,965	857,073	724,914	622,876	541,236	491,671	453,647	416,660	387,422
Long-term debt	427,250	337,492	340,737	342,167	193,240	93,414	99,107	116,571	128,080	134,925
Debt to debt plus total equity	34.5%	31.7%	34.0%	35.6%	25.7%	15.3%	17.2%	21.4%	25.6%	29.2%
Deferred income taxes	153,080	125,221	99,119	80,748	66,264	54,281	41,456	34,103	27,274	23,212
Deferred investment tax credit	58,053	48,371	43,174	24,293	21,157	17,225	14,370	14,276	13,563	12,577
Shareholders' equity	754,423	680,396	618,429	593,642	537,762	500,784	461,980	413,974	358,476	314,121
Return on shareholders' equity	15.1%	14.2%	9.2%	15.0%	12.3%	13.6%	16.5%	18.6%	18.6%	15.1%
Other information:										
Capital expenditures	228,727	156,745	198,735	155,436	126,463	91,801	84,217	73,214	65,069	66,396
Depreciation	66,032	61,163	53,105	51,089	45,042	41,059	38,970	34,948	33,795	30,063
Total payroll cost	421,806	338,933	271,403	268,306	244,437	221,049	190,517	176,196	156,576	133,872
Effective tax rate	46.0%	45.9%	46.4%	48.7%	47.3%	48.1%	48.0%	47.3%	48.2%	51.2%

Notes:

(1) In December 1976, the company decided to close a portion of the Los Angeles Busch Gardens and convert the remainder to a sales promotion facility. Closing a portion of the Gardens resulted in a nonoperating charge of $10,020,000 (before reduction for income tax benefits of approximately $5,000,000). This nonoperating charge, which reduced earnings per share by $.11, has been reported in accordance with Accounting Principles Board Opinion No. 30 which was effective September 30, 1973.

(2) In December 1972, the company decided to close a portion of the Houston Busch Gardens and convert the remainder to a sales promotion facility. Closing a portion of the Gardens resulted in an extraordinary after-tax charge against 1972 earnings of $4,093,000, or $.09 per share, net of applicable income tax benefits of $4,006,000.

(3) Per share statistics have been adjusted to give effect to the two-for-one stock split in 1971.

EXHIBIT 16
Estimated Volume by Brewer 1978 and 1981

	1978		1981E		1978–81	
	Barrel Shipments (millions)	Market Share	Barrel Shipments (millions)	Market Share	Barrel Increment (millions)	Compounded Annual Rate of Growth
Anheuser-Busch	41.6	25.1%	51.5	28.7%	+9.9	7.4%
Miller	31.3	18.9	44.9	25.0	+13.6	12.6
Schlitz	19.6	11.8	17.2	9.6	−2.4	(3.8)
Pabst*	15.4	9.3	14.7	8.2	−0.7	(1.2)
Coors†	12.6	7.6	17.2	9.6	+4.6	11.1
Top 5	120.5	72.8%	145.5	81.1%	+25.0	6.6%
All others	41.7	25.2%	28.4	15.8%	−13.3	(9.7)%
U.S. industry	162.2	97.9%	173.9	97.0%	+11.7	2.3%
Imports	3.4	2.1%	5.4	3.0%	+2.0	16.5%
All beer	165.6	100.0%	179.3	100.0%	+13.7	2.7%

* In 1981 the operations of Blitz-Weinhard are included with Pabst; in 1978 about 600,000 barrels of Blitz in the all-other group.

† Coors in a 16-state market in 1978 and an estimated 19-state market in 1981 (additions: Arkansas, Louisiana and Minnesota).

Source: *Competition in the U.S. Brewing Industry: A Basic Analysis* by C. James Walker III. Shearson Hayden Stone, Inc., 14 Wall Street, New York, New York, 10005; September 26, 1979.

Competitive pressures will demand the most dedicated and creative efforts that we can muster, but we are confident that with:

—our strong sales momentum,
—our quality products,
—our great wholesaler family, and
—the team effort of our employees,

we will have another successful year and will continue to build a solid corporate foundation for future growth and profits.

16. A Note on the World Petroleum Industry*

The business of supplying crude oil and petroleum products is not only economically crucial but it is also one of the largest, if not the largest, businesses in the world. Worldwide sales of crude oil and petroleum products in 1980 were well in excess of $1 trillion and petroleum consumption averaged about 60 million barrels per day. Billion-dollar oil companies are commonplace and no nation is without at least one truly large-scale oil company. In the United States 11 of the 20 largest industrial corporations are primarily petroleum companies—Exxon, Mobil, Texaco, Standard Oil of California, Gulf, Standard Oil of Indiana, Atlantic Richfield, Shell, Conoco, Tenneco, and Sun. Exhibit 1 presents selected statistics on the free world's largest oil companies.

THE EMERGENCE AND GROWTH OF THE MAJOR OIL COMPANIES

The oil industry in the early post-Civil War years consisted principally of small firms specializing in one function. Gradually, however, larger firms began to emerge and some started to integrate backward and forward from their original operation. Outstanding in both the size of its operations and its growth via horizontal and vertical integration was The Standard Oil Company, incorporated in 1870 by John D. Rockefeller, his brother William, and three other partners. From the outset, Rockefeller stressed the importance of large capacity and efficient operations as means of reducing costs and increasing profits. The company discovered, as early as 1884, that by concentrating 75 percent of its production in three big refineries its average refining costs per barrel fell to 0.534 cents compared to 1.5 cents for the rest of the industry. Standard Oil's rise to a position of market dominance is business legend. So also is the Supreme Court's historic declaration that the Standard Oil was an illegal monopoly under the Sherman Act of 1890 and, consequently, had to be dissolved.

From the time of the Standard Oil breakup until the present, seven companies have dominated the world petroleum industry: Exxon, Royal Dutch/ Shell, British Petroleum, Gulf, Texaco, Mobil, and Standard Oil of California

---

* Prepared by Arthur A. Thompson, Jr., The University of Alabama, with the assistance of Victor Gray.

EXHIBIT 1
Comparative Statistics on the World's Leading Oil Companies, 1978 and 1979 ($ millions)

Company	Sales	Assets	Net Income	Percentage Return on Stockholders' Equity	Number of Employees
Largest U.S. Companies*					
1. Exxon	$79,106	$49,490	$ 4,295	19.0%	169,000
2. Mobil	44,721	27,506	2,007	19.1	213,500
3. Texaco	38,350	22,992	1,759	16.5	65,800
4. Standard Oil of CA	29,948	18,103	1,785	19.2	39,700
5. Gulf Oil	23,910	17,265	1,322	15.2	57,600
6. Standard Oil of IN	18,610	17,150	1,507	18.0	52,300
7. Atlantic Richfield	16,234	13,833	1,166	19.1	50,300
8. Shell Oil†	14,431	16,127	1,126	16.1	36,400
9. Conoco	12,648	9,311	815	21.6	40,500
10. Tenneco	11,209	11,631	571	17.1	107,000
11. Sun	10,666	7,461	700	18.6	40,100
12. Occidental Petroleum ..	9,555	5,560	562	38.4	34,200
13. Phillips Petroleum	9,503	8,519	891	20.9	30,300
14. Standard Oil of Ohio‡ ..	7,916	9,209	1,186	38.4	22,100
15. Amerada Hess	6,770	4,899	507	26.7	7,815
Largest Foreign Companies§					
1. Royal Dutch/Shell Group	$44,045	$42,422	$ 2,084	12.8%	158,000
2. British Petroleum	27,408	26,533	853	11.1	109,000
3. National Iranian Oil‖	22,780	15,147	15,178	278.3	67,000
4. ENI (Italy)	12,566	20,917	(368)	(13.7)	120,900
5. Francaise deo Petroles ..	12,510	11,537	60	2.4	44,000
6. Petroleas de Venezuela ..	9,137	8,376	1,449	20.5	29,800
7. Petrobras (Brazil)	9,131	11,227	1,214	20.8	58,000

* All statistics are for 1979.
† Shell Oil is the U.S. subsidiary of Royal Dutch/Shell Group.
‡ Standard Oil of Ohio was acquired by British Petroleum in 1979.
§ All statistics are for 1978.
‖ Government owned.
Source: *Fortune*, issues of August 13, 1979, p. 194 and May 5, 1980, pp. 276–77.

or Socal (which markets under the Chevron brand name). These seven companies—five American, one British, and one Anglo-Dutch—were all major companies prior to the 1920s and have often been referred to as "the Seven Sisters" because of their long-standing cooperation and closeness. The Sisters' cooperation and closeness goes back over 50 years. In 1928 British Petroleum, Royal Dutch/Shell, Exxon, and Mobil entered into what became known as the "Red-Line Aggreement." The agreement provided for the four partners to share all oil discovered in the new, developing fields of the Middle East and included provisions which minimized any competition in production, refining, or securing concessions within the area. The effect was to monopolize the supply (according to oil industry critics) or to steady an unstable situation (according to the companies). A second 1928 agreement called upon the major oil companies (1) to accept and maintain their relative shares of world petroleum markets; (2) to avoid unnecessary duplication of new facilities; (3) to draw supplies for a given market from the nearest producing area; (4) to avoid use of surplus crude production from any geographic area to upset the price structure in any other area; and (5) to eliminate measures that would materially increase costs and prices.[1]

After the end of World War II, the Sisters expanded the number of jointly owned production companies and also entered into numerous long-term mutual supply contracts. Socal, Texaco, and Gulf joined the other four in their Middle East understandings.

In 1952, a Federal Trade Commission study entitled "The International Petroleum Cartel" eventually led to an out-of-court consent decree whereby the Seven Sisters agreed to certain modifications in their practices. Irrespective, though, of the alleged cartel and monopoly activities among the Seven Sisters, many new oil companies became active and successful in international oil in the 1950s and 1960s:

	1950	1960	1970	1974
Largest international companies	7	7	7	7
U.S. independents	10	18	30	34
Foreign independents	2	4	31	41
Foreign government entities		2	13	17
Total	19	31	81	99

One critic has summarized and portrayed the Seven Sisters' behavior thusly:

> In Pittsburgh the solid stone monument of Gulf, with a pyramid on the top, has dominated the city for 40 years, still linked with the wealth of the first Pittsburgh family, the Mellons. In San Francisco the tower of the Standard Oil Company of California, or Socal, looms over the bay like a fortress, the richest company in the city. In New York two of the sisters face each other across 42nd Street, but with almost opposite viewpoints; Texaco, inside the Chrysler building, cultivates a reputation for meanness and secrecy, while Mobil over the road is the most loquacious and extrovert of them all, churning out explanations, complaints and counterattacks through the TV channels and newspaper. Across the Atlantic in London, the headquarters of BP rises up from its own piazza, announcing with its name Britannic House that here is an oil company that is part of the nation's patriotism, half-owned by the government.
>
> Within these corporate citadels there was little doubt that they were competing ferociously with each other. Their inhabitants seem to belong not so much to the world of "oildom" as of Mobildom or Gulfdom, and with some coaxing they could be persuaded, I found, to criticise each other. Yet each had been linked to all the others through a web of joint ventures and concessions across

---

[1] David I. Haberman, *Hearings before the Senate Subcommittee on Multinational Corporations,* 1974, part VII, p. 14.

the globe, from Alaska to Kuwait: sharing now with one partner, now with another, in different permutations. It was this strange cavorting of the sisters, competing one moment and conniving the next, which had made them such an enduring subject of suspicion and investigation by politicians, economists and nationalist leaders.[2]

THE STRUCTURE OF THE INDUSTRY

The petroleum industry spans a wide range of geographically separate and technically distinct activities relating to getting oil from the ground to the final user. The main stages in the process are (1) finding and producing the crude oil, (2) transporting it to the point of processing, (3) refining it into marketable products,[3] (4) transporting the products to regions of use, and (5) distributing them at retail. However, in the search for oil, producing companies are inadvertently or contingently involved in the production, use, and sales of natural gas. Thus many of the major oil companies are also major suppliers of natural gas.

In the United States over 10,000 companies are involved in oil and gas exploration and production. No one firm accounts for more than 11 percent of oil and gas production. Over 80 percent of total U.S. crude oil output comes from Texas, Louisiana, California, Alaska, and Oklahoma, with almost 33 percent from Texas alone. It moves mainly through 68,000 miles of gathering lines and 81,000 miles of trunk pipelines, as well as on oceangoing tankers, river barges, railroad tank cars, and trucks, to some 310 operating refineries, with a total 1980 capacity of 17.4 million barrels per day. These refineries are operated by approximately 140 companies; in 1974 the top four companies accounted for 31 percent of refining capacity, and no one company had more than 9 percent. In 1979, about 100 pipeline companies were engaged in transporting crude oil and refined products on an interstate basis; additional companies operated intrastate. The top four pipeline companies accounted for about 24 percent of total volume moved, with the largest having a share under 7 percent.

The greater proportion of these products move from the refinery to the final customer via one or more intermediate storage facilities. Although residual fuel oil, for example, may go to large utility and industrial customers directly from the refinery, most products go first to large terminals, located generally at the outlet of a pipeline, or on a river, lake, or coastal port, where they can take barge or tanker delivery. By far most of these terminals are owned by refiners, although independent wholesaler-owned terminals take a substantial portion of the distillate and residual oils. Most gasoline and home heating oils go next to still another storage facility, the so-called bulk

---

[2] Anthony Sampson, *The Seven Sisters* (New York: The Viking Press, 1975), p. 7.

[3] A barrel of crude when refined breaks out roughly as 44 percent gasoline, 1.2 percent kerosene, 12.0 percent residual fuel oil, 2.9 percent asphalt, 6.6 percent jet fuel, and 33.3 percent gas, oil distillates, and miscellaneous products.

plant—although some is sold directly to large commercial, industrial, and governmental users. The bulk plants are generally smaller than the terminals and are located near the final customers. From the bulk plants, the gasoline is transported to service stations and the heating oil to the storage tanks of homes and commercial establishments. However, in the case of gasoline it is not uncommon for terminal operators—mostly within the marketing departments of the refinery companies—to bypass bulk plants and ship directly to the service stations. This development was made possible by the construction of large-volume retail outlets and the use of increasingly efficient truck carriers.

In 1975, there were about 15,000 wholesale distributors, and about 190,000 service station retailers (down from a peak of 226,000 in 1972). These figures do not include an indeterminate number (more than 100,000) of other outlets such as convenience food stores, motels, and car washes that also retail gasoline as a secondary activity. The large oil companies own less than 10 percent of the retail outlets which they supply; most are owned (or leased) and operated by wholesalers and retail resellers who established their own prices and operating practices.

The table below summarizes the structure and extent of concentration in the industry as of 1974:

Concentration Ratios, 1974 (percent)

	Top 1	Top 4	Top 8
Production:			
Oil (net liquid hydrocarbons)	10.0%	31%	49%
Gas (net)	10.7	29	44
Refining capacity	8.4	31	55
Marketing:			
Retail branded gasoline sales	8.1	30	52
All petroleum products	10.7	31	52
Petroleum pipelines (interstate; by volume)	6.9	24	43
All U.S. manufacturing average		39%	60%

VERTICAL INTEGRATION IN THE OIL INDUSTRY

As early as 1900–11, vertical integration had become a part of the oil industry's way of life insofar as the large, successful companies were concerned. The dissolution of Standard Oil added impetus to vertical integration because a number of the newly created companies had major gaps in their business operations. During the next decade or so, with the demand for petroleum products increasing, with sales of automobiles beginning to mushroom, and with alternating periods of crude oil shortage and oversupply, nearly all of the major companies found it less risky (and sometimes essential for competitive survival) to integrate both vertically and geographically. In the case of a refiner-marketer, there was always the threat that the feast of new crude oil discoveries would be followed by famine if and when the fields ran dry or demand increased faster than supply. So, both to preserve their profitability in the case of mushrooming supplies and to guard against possible shortages, it was desirable to integrate backward, part or all the way. This meant cultivating the good will of producers and drillers and making continued exploratory efforts attractive by constructing gathering lines and storage facilities as rapidly as possible and in sufficient volume to handle whatever was offered. It also meant going into production whenever and wherever necessary.

Crude oil producers, in turn, could escape their feast-famine dilemma only by developing their own markets outlets, integrating forward into both refining and retail distribution. Without assured markets, producers were necessarily subject to the randomness of crude oil discovery and the ease of competitive entry in drilling and exploration. In both situations vertical integration contributed to the stability of the integrating company, first by providing some security against market fluctuation and instability and, second, through greater certainty of profit margins associated with a continuous utilization of producing capacity, pipelines, refinery facilities, and marketing outlets. In general, the oil companies which chose to integrate appeared to be seeking a degree of balance in their operations so as to protect them against what they perceived as an uncertain profit and competitive position associated with heavy fixed costs and with being heavily dependent on uncontrolled intermediate markets. By maintaining a balance in each of the stages in which they did business, the operations at each stage tended to become mutually reinforcing and, thus, a contributor to greater operating efficiency and stability.

According to the classic study of integration and competition in the petroleum industry by Professors de Chazeau and Kahn in 1959, the following composite paraphrase represents a rough consensus of how the executives of almost all the leading oil companies viewed the importance of vertical integration:

> We certainly try, in general, to keep a balanced operation. We will not ordinarily make major investments in one level without seeing that we are pretty well covered at other levels. So we do not expect to make the same return from our investments in production, refining and marketing. As a general rule we will not demand as high a return from prospective investments that put us in balance as from those that put us out of balance. We have a going organization, with substantial commitments at all levels; we cannot shift from one to the other with each short-term fluctuation of returns; we have to protect the positions we already have.[4]

De Chazeau and Kahn also concluded as a result of their study that:

> The only places where it seemed monopoly profits could still be locked in between, say, 1911 and 1935, were in pipeline transportation, where entry was

---

[4] Melvin G. de Chazeau and Alfred E. Kahn, *Integration and Competition in the Petroleum Industry* (New Haven, Conn.: Yale University Press, 1959), p. 114.

not easy and an integrated company could at least for a time hold ,
difference between the pipeline costs and rail tariffs; in the adoption of
cracking, where patent control blocked access of independents; and pos,
undertaking distribution of one's own branded gasoline through the con
tion of one's own service stations. In each instance . . . the high pron
returns materialized, but could not be preserved definitely. These areas
come the new foci of integration and investment decisions because chang
circumstances made these the operations a large company had to control for \
own protection—if only temporary and partial—against the eroding influence,
of free markets.[5]

Of these three possibilities, pipeline transportation was the most attractive.
A refiner who had control over the pipelines in a given oil field was in a good
strategic position to convince producers that their most profitable alternative
was to sell their oil at the wellhead or to pay the charges which pipeline
owners insisted upon to carry their oil.

However, in 1935 when the states in which large crude oil supplies were
being found began to exercise control over the amount of oil produced from
each well each year (via a system called "prorationing"), production became
the strategic area for almost the first time in the history of the U.S. oil
industry. Control over production meant that the tyranny of a highly unstable and inelastic supply of crude oil could be curbed, allowing the crude
market to be effectively stabilized and the profits of successful producers
made less uncertain. Integration of marketing, refining, and pipelines alone
no longer offered the only promise of market stability. Pipeline owners found
it far more difficult to give preference to their own producing wells in periods
of excess supply; and nonintegrated refiners and marketers were confronted
with the somewhat uncomfortable situation of buying in a market where
prices were relatively stable compared to the retail markets in which they
sold. In such an environment, it was not surprising that the major companies,
already committed to an appreciation of advantages of vertical integration,
began to work hard at improving the balance between their producing and
their downstream operations.

Currently, about 50 petroleum companies in the United States can be
classified as vertically integrated in that they operate in at least three
stages—production, refining, and marketing. However, since even the
largest oil companies are not so integrated as to be self-sufficient in all stages
of operation, significant markets for crude and for refined products exist.
Almost every oil company to one extent or another buys or sells crude and
refined products to balance out its operations; this results in oil companies
engaging in numerous transactions with one another.

These transactions (called exchange agreements) occur for several reasons:

1. To help lower transportation costs.
2. To give refiners greater flexibility in securing appropriate quality cru

---

[5] Ibid., pp. 116–17.

3. To help reduce inventory and operation costs and supply interruptions caused by temporary surplus/shortage situations at refineries or terminals.

For example, when a company's crude is of the desired type and is geographically close to its refinery, the company will arrange transportation from the oil field to the refinery. If the company owns more crude than it needs in its refinery, it will sell the volumes least attractive to it. If its crude is not the proper type or is remote from its refinery, the company can arrange to exchange with another refiner who can run this crude economically. Through exchanges and purchases and sales, companies are able to minimize transportation and refining costs, thus providing lower cost products to the consumer.

As another example, short-term disruptions may create a need for spot or emergency exchanges. Pipelines or refineries may be shut down for several days due to fires, a mechanical failure, process upsets, and so on; tankers or barges may be delayed due to weather conditions, strikes, or operating problems. The short-term disruption can be solved if another company makes a spot or emergency exchange. For instance, Company A might lend 5,000 barrels of product to Company B whose shipments have been delayed. Then a few days later when its shipment arrives, Company B can return the barrels. An exchange of this nature may save many miles to costly trucking from a distant terminal and allow uninterrupted service to consumers.

Many oil industry critics, however, see vertical integration as a monopolistic element. To the extent that firms are integrated, they are insulated in part from demand-supply changes at each of the processing stages; this, in turn, results in prices which may not be completely responsive to market conditions. Critics also allege that vertically integrated firms are able to put a squeeze on independents by shifting profits to their production operations, thereby keeping marketing and refining profits artificially low so as to discourage entry and further expansion of nonintegrated independent refiners and marketers. Insofar as exchange agreements are concerned, critics see these as being, on some occasions, a way to exchange information and promote relaxed competition and, on the other occasions, as being a vehicle for squeezing or punishing maverick firms—especially independents. Exhibit 2 shows how the 1975 assets of the U.S. Sisters were distributed among the various vertical stages.

EXPLORATION AND PRODUCTION

In recent years, exploration and production activities have occupied center-stage in the oil industry. Heightened awareness that existing oil reserves are being used up faster than new reserves are being discovered, together with the public spotlight on energy supplies in general, has stimulated worldwide increases in capital outlays for drilling and exploration. In

HIBIT 2
tribution of Assets among the Various Vertical Stages, U.S. Sisters Only, 1975 ($ millions)

mpany	Production Amount	Per-cent*	Transporta-tion Amount	Per-cent	Refining† Amount	Per-cent	Marketing Amount	Per-cent	Other Amount	Per-cent	Total Assets
xon ...	$8,487	33%	$4,275	16%	$7,693	29%	$4,374	17%	$1,263	5%	$26,092
•lf	5,326	45	1,023	9	3,170	27	1,667	14	700	6	11,886
♭bil	4,524	38	1,371	12	3,287	28	2,426	21	187	2	11,795
cal	4,925	48	1,032	10	2,713	27	1,406	14	161	2	10,237
xaco ..	7,345	53	1,186	9	3,173	23	1,974	14	164	1	13,842

* May not add to 100 percent due to rounding.
† Refining includes chemical operations.
Source: U.S. Treasury Department, *Implications of Divestiture*, staff study (Washington, D.C., June 1976).

the United States, for example, expenditures totaled $10.0 billion in 1978, as compared to $2.6 billion in 1970 and $2.4 billion in 1960. The total number of free world oil wells drilled and completed rose from 36,465 in 1970 to 61,222 in 1978. The results have been less than spectacular, however. World reserves of crude oil fell from a high of 712 trillion barrels to 641 trillion barrels in 1979 (about a 28-year supply at current consumption rates). In the United States, estimated reserves fell from the all-time high of 39 trillion barrels in 1971 to 27.8 trillion barrels in 1979.

Looking at the U.S. petroleum industry and comparing 1978 with 1956 (in many respects a record year for exploration activity), the statistics reveal some striking facts:

Domestic demand for refined products—up 115 percent.
Domestic production of crude oil—up 17 percent.
Imports of crude oil—up 58 percent.
Imports of refined products—up 300 percent.
Crude oil price index—up 323 percent.

Exploratory wells drilled—down 34 percent.
Wildcat wells drilled—down 25 percent.
Total wells drilled—down 23 percent.
Rotary rig activity—down 14 percent.
New reserves proved during year—down 55 percent.
Total producing oil wells—down 6 percent.
Total proved oil reserves—down 3 percent.

Of course, much of the increased expenditures for drilling and exploration is a reflection of inflation and higher operating costs. For instance, between 1967 and 1977, the average cost per well drilled in the United States rose

EXHIBIT 3
Statistical Summary of U.S. Petroleum Supply and Demand, 1946–1978 (000 barrels per day)

Year	Domestic Production			Imports				Total Supply	Petroleum Demand		
	Crude Oil	Natural Gas Liquids	Total	Crude Oil	Refined Products	Total	Other Sources		Domestic	Export	Total
1946	4,751	322	5,073	236	141	377	—	5,450	4,912	419	5,331
1950	5,407	499	5,906	487	363	850	2	6,758	6,509	305	6,814
1955	6,807	772	7,579	782	466	1,248	34	8,861	8,493	368	8,861
1960	7,035	930	7,965	1,015	799	1,814	146	9,926	9,807	202	10,009
1965	7,804	1,210	9,014	1,238	1,230	2,468	220	11,702	11,523	187	11,710
1966	8,295	1,284	9,579	1,225	1,348	2,573	245	12,397	12,095	198	12,293
1967	8,810	1,410	10,220	1,128	1,409	2,537	292	13,049	12,569	307	12,876
1968	9,096	1,503	10,599	1,290	1,550	2,840	348	13,787	13,404	231	13,635
1969	9,238	1,589	10,827	1,409	1,757	3,166	340	14,333	14,148	233	14,381
1970	9,637	1,660	11,297	1,324	2,094	3,418	355	15,071	14,709	259	14,968
1971	9,463	1,692	11,155	1,681	2,245	3,926	439	15,520	15,225	224	15,449
1972	9,441	1,744	11,185	2,216	2,525	4,741	444	16,370	16,379	223	16,602
1973	9,208	1,738	10,946	3,244	3,012	6,256	485	17,687	17,321	231	17,552
1974	8,774	1,688	10,462	3,477	2,635	6,112	491	17,065	16,666	220	16,886
1975	8,362	1,633	9,995	4,105	1,920	6,025	527	16,547	16,322	210	16,532
1976	8,125	1,605	9,730	5,265	1,985	7,250	660	17,640	17,461	223	17,684
1977	8,245	1,618	9,863	6,615	2,193	8,808	568	19,239	18,431	243	18,674
1978	8,708	1,567	10,275	6,356	2,008	8,364	492	19,131	18,847	362	19,209

Source: U.S. Energy Information Administration, *Annual Petroleum Statement.*

from $72,000 to $229,200—a 212 percent increase. Exhibit 3 contains some additional statistics on the U.S. petroleum market.

PIPELINE OPERATIONS

Most interstate pipelines in the United States are owned by more than one company. This stems from exceptionally large economies of scale (see Exhibit 4) which extend the efficient volume of a pipeline beyond the level which a single company can utilize. Moreover, the risk capital required for a large pipeline project can be immense; for instance, the Trans-Alaska Pipeline system is the largest single capital project ever undertaken by private enterprise.

Pipeline owners may require throughput guarantees or some other provision for the recovery of costs incurred before they will connect a new shipper to the system. The cost of a new connection may include laying a pipeline to the new shipper or installing new metering facilities to account for shipments or building additional working tankage. Throughput guarantees commit the shipper who is requesting the connection to either ship sufficient volumes or pay sufficient tariffs to provide some reasonable assurance that

EXHIBIT 4
Relative Pipeline Costs versus System Throughput

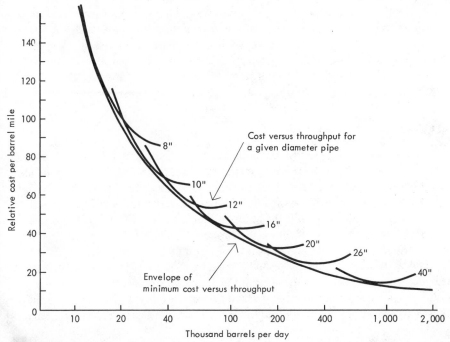

Source: Exxon Company, U.S.A.

the added investment by the pipeline owner will be paid off. The Interstate Commerce Commission (ICC) has authority to address any abuses, including the prevention of excessive throughput guarantees. Small nonowner firms are guaranteed access to pipelines on an equal basis with large owner-users and thus crude and product transportation is available to producers, refiners, and marketers alike.

Pipeline practices such as minimum tender requirements are dictated by considerations of efficiency. Crude oils vary greatly in quality, as do the different types of refined products. To minimize mixing and contamination at the interface between sequential batches of crude or product, the pipeline sets minimum batch sizes. When a full batch is accumulated, it is pumped through the pipeline.

Whenever common carrier pipeline capacity is inadequate to meet volumes tendered, government regulations require that available capacity be allocated equitably. Pipeline proration rules allocate capacity in proportion to recent shipments or current tenders of new shippers and historic shippers alike. Deviation from the pipeline's proration rules in favor of an owner company is a violation of the law. Under ICC regulations and the common carrier status of the interstate pipelines, users have the right to appeal for relief to the ICC if they feel they have been treated unfairly. The ICC has broad remedial powers in the event that a pipeline fails to conduct its operations as a true common carrier.

Pipeline tariffs are regulated by the ICC and have fallen steadily since the early 1950s, mainly because new technology has allowed larger and larger diameter pipelines with their resultant economies of scale and greatly reduced costs. According to ICC statistics, the average industry revenue per barrel moved 1,000 miles fell from 65 cents in 1955 to 50 cents in 1971. Pipeline tariffs tend to be competitive with alternative transportation modes, such as Gulf/East Coast tankers and Mississippi barges.

REFINING

Historically, the refining segment of the oil business has been the least profitable. Nonetheless, refining capacity has continued to expand in step with market demands. From 1950 through 1973 about 80 refineries were built with a total capacity of about 3 million barrels per day; about one fourth of this new capacity was built by independent refiners. In 1951 the largest 20 refiners had 81 percent of total U.S. capacity; as of 1974 these same refiners had only 75 percent of capacity and the number of refiners with capacity of 50,000 barrels per day or more had grown from 20 in 1951 to 38 in 1974. U.S. oil companies expanded their refining capacity by 63 percent during the 1967–80 period; total operable capacity as of January 1980 was 17.4 million barrels per day, up from 10.7 million barrels in 1967 and 13.7 million barrels in 1973.

At the same time, the use of ever more capital-intensive refining technology has made refinery construction an expensive proposition. Between 1946 and 1955 the cost of building a new refinery increased from approximately $575 to $872 per daily barrel of crude oil capacity. As of the late 1970s the per barrel cost of new refinery capacity was approximately $2,000, up from about $1,000 per barrel in the late 1960s. Oil company executives accounted for the growing investment in refinery facilities as necessary to maintain balanced operations, even though the return on new refinery investment was subpar. In their view, the requirements of their marketing divisions had to be met and the growth in the allowable crude oil production had to be matched. To do otherwise meant possible loss of market share. Moreover, firms that expected to remain competitive in selling their branded refined products had to invest in whatever refinery improvements and technological advances were available and to otherwise stay in the forefront of refinery knowhow.

New technology has significantly improved refining efficiency. From 1950 to 1972, wage rates tripled, fuel costs doubled, and an increased proportion of higher-quality products (higher-octane gasoline, lower-sulfur distillate fuels, better lubricants) demanded additional processing and higher costs. Nonetheless, the industry held its operating cost increases to about 2 percent per year and wholesale prices in real terms were kept almost constant, reflecting both technological improvements and competition. Probably the most dramatic technological advances in refining in the last 25 years have been the large scale introductions of new processing facilities such as catalytic cracking and reforming, alkylation, and hydrocracking. These have allowed refinery yields and product qualities which would not otherwise have been possible or economically feasible. For example, without catalytic reforming, gasoline octanes would probably be lower than they are today, the compression ratios of internal combustion engines would be correspondingly lower, and automobiles would be less efficient.

MARKETING

More than any other branch of the petroleum industry, the distribution and marketing of refined products is the domain of small enterprises. Over the years, of course, there has been tremendous change in the character, location, and operation of distribution and retail facilities (see Exhibit 5), but even more important, perhaps, there has been intense rivalry for consumer patronage—until the late 1970s when gasoline supplies were tight and a sellers' market prevailed. The major companies loom large in most of the markets in which they operate. Their brands command wide and reasonably loyal public acceptance. Usually, they are disposed to channel their competitive efforts away from price and more towards quality of service, reliability, and dependability.

However, independent refiner-marketers have typically been more willing to use price as a competitive weapon, either when demand was slack or as a

EXHIBIT 5
How U.S. Retail Marketing Is Changing

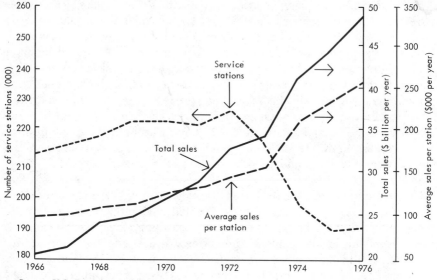

Source: U.S. Department of Commerce.

substitute for the full range of services and lack of a reputation and image. To some extent, the independents have also evidenced a greater willingness to experiment and to innovate, in order to offset the strategic advantages and possible operating efficiency of the larger majors. Because the independents are outsiders and because their situation tends to be so different from the integrated majors, the presence of the independents, according to many observers and especially the critics of the large firms, makes it difficult for the 10–15 largest oil firms to rig the market to their own advantage and to otherwise collude on price. Industry analysts generally agree that the independents add an important competitive element to the retail marketing part of the oil business—primarily because they offer a different type of service to the consumer (called intratype competition, as opposed to intertype competition). The so-called independents or nonmajor brand marketers accounted for 30.1 percent of the market in 1974, compared to 22.8 percent in 1968.

THE EMERGENCE OF OPEC

In August 1960, due to an oversupply of crude oil on the world market, Exxon announced a 10 cent per barrel reduction in its offer price for crude oil; this followed an 18 cent per barrel reduction the previous year. Other companies, though some did so reluctantly, followed Exxon's example and before long all the Seven Sisters were offering and paying the same lowered price for crude oil—an outcome which disgruntled the governments of the foreign oil-producing nations since it reduced the tax revenues which they received on each barrel of crude produced. Prior to this time, the major producing nations had met to considered uniting into some form of combined front against the Seven Sisters, but no action had resulted. However, the second reduction in the posted crude oil price catalyzed a further conference of the oil-producing countries, the objective of which appeared to be to form a cartel to confront the cartel. Whether this was indeed the objective, the result nonetheless was exactly that and precipitated the formation of the Organization of Petroleum Exporting Countries (OPEC). OPEC's first resolution was to indicate clearly its stance as a foe to the Seven Sisters and their kin.

Initially, the new organization had little effect, but as time passed it gained greater internal strength. By 1970–71, many of the religious and linguistic barriers, conflicting political goals, and internal economic priorities had been settled to such an extent that OPEC began to be a factor with whom the major oil companies had to reckon. The 1971 Teheran Agreement, which involved the Seven Sisters and the major Middle East oil producers, outlined significant changes in the crude oil prices which producers would be paid by the oil companies.

As is well known, the strength of OPEC reached a new plateau in November 1973 when a complete embargo was undertaken of nations which were considered unfriendly to OPEC. The balance of power had shifted from the companies to the OPEC cartel. A number of nationalization moves by various OPEC members cut the Seven Sisters' holdings in crude oil reserves. The new owners continued to deal with the major oil companies but with a new purpose. The oil companies' role was to supply the expertise in logistics and provide the essential refining-distribution-retailing network needed to support OPEC's crude oil production targets. The OPEC nations sought to limit production to match demand at the price they, the producers, set—see Exhibit 6 for the trend in OPEC prices. OPEC's power in the world petroleum market derived not from its newly asserted ability to control the major companies, but from the dependence of the consuming nations on OPEC oil. World demand for crude had grown to the point where the major consuming nations have to depend on imports as a source of supply—because domestic sources are no longer adequate. The growing worldwide importance of OPEC oil is suggested by Exhibits 7 and 8.

As of the mid-1970s, OPEC countries accounted for roughly 95 percent of the non-Communist country trade in international crude oil. The OPEC nations met regularly to determine the cartel's price of crude oil and, since they controlled two thirds of the world's oil reserves (see Exhibit 7), there seemed little doubt over their continued ability to control the world market to their own advantage—barring major new discoveries outside their borders.

EXHIBIT 6
How OPEC Crude Oil Prices Have Risen

Country	Crude Type	Crude Oil Price ($ per barrel)						
		August 1970	November 1973	January 1975	January 1977	October 1979	April 1980
Saudia Arabia	Arabian light	$1.80	$5.18	$11.25	$13.00	$18.00	$26.00
Iran	Iranian light	1.79	5.34	11.48	13.77	23.71	35.87
Iraq	Basrah light	1.72	5.12	11.28	n.a.	19.96	27.96
Kuwait	Kuwait blend	1.59	4.96	11.15	n.a.	21.43	27.50
Abu Dhalic	Murban	1.88	6.11	11.69	13.44	21.56	29.56
Qatar	Marine	1.83	5.56	11.61	13.98	21.23	29.23
Venezuela	Tia Juana	2.19	7.56	14.13	n.a.	20.90	28.90

n.a.: Not available.
Source: *Petroleum Intelligence Weekly* and *Oil and Gas Journal*, various issues.

EXHIBIT 7
The Growth of OPEC Crude Oil Reserves Annually as of January 1 (million barrels)

Year	Total OPEC	OPEC as Percent of Free World Total	OPEC as Percent of World Total
1960	196,500	75.6%	67.8%
1970	391,750	83.3	73.8
1971	431,900	84.5	70.7
1972	425,251	79.6	67.2
1973	463,623	81.9	69.8
1974	421,815	80.5	67.3
1975	484,970	80.7	68.1
1976	449,879	81.1	68.4
1977	440,395	81.7	68.8
1978	439,915	80.3	68.1
1979	444,936	81.2	69.3
1980	435,591	79.0	68.0

Source: *Oil and Gas Journal*, "Worldwide Report" issue, 1980.

EXHIBIT 8
The Growth of OPEC Crude Oil Production (000 barrels per day)

Year	Total OPEC	OPEC as Percent of Free World Total	OPEC as Percent of World Total
1960	7,874	44.6%	37.6%
1970	22,134	58.4	48.3
1971	25,092	62.9	51.9
1972	26,711	63.7	52.6
1973	30,989	67.5	55.5
1974	30,747	67.8	54.5
1975	27,200	65.4	50.9
1976	30,558	67.5	52.8
1977	31,115	66.6	52.8
1978*	29,898	64.2	49.6

* Preliminary
Source: U.S. Energy Information Administration and *Oil and Gas Journal*.

THE U.S. ECONOMY AND ENERGY

As Exhibit 9 indicates, there has been a close historical relationship in the United States between increases in growth and increases in energy use. Equally significant is the fact that the United States, with only six percent of the world's population, consumes about one third of the world's annual

EXHIBIT 9
Energy Use and Economic Growth in the United States

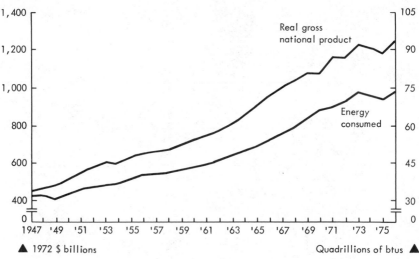

▲ 1972 $ billions   Quadrillions of btus ▲

energy supplied and produces almost one third of the world's total output of goods and services. Exhibit 10 provides an indication of the relative importance of oil as an energy source in the U.S., both now and as projected. Comparative energy consumption and production patterns among various nations are shown in Exhibits 11 and 12.

Consumption of petroleum products in the U.S. reached an all-time high in 1978, averaging 18.8 million barrels daily, up 15.3 percent over the 1975 average of 16.3 million b/d. Motor gasoline consumption was 7.4 million barrels daily, up from 6.7 million in 1975. Imports provided nearly 8.4 million b/d, or 44.4 percent of 1978 U.S. oil consumption. Crude oil imports averaged nearly 6.4 million barrels daily, up from 4.1 million in 1975 and 1.0 million in 1960; imports of refined products totaled 2.0 million b/d as compared to 1.92 million in 1975 and 1.2 million in 1960.

Just how long the world's crude oil reserves will last is debatable. In 1977 the Carter Administration presented studies that the world only had about 20 years of proven reserves and would run out of crude oil supplies by the year 2000. Other observers discounted the significance of the government study since it did not allow for new discoveries; some estimates of the remaining

EXHIBIT 10
Percentage Share of U.S. Energy Market by Energy Source, with Projections to 1990

Energy Source	1920	1973	1980	1990
Oil	18%	46%	47%	32%
Gas	18	31	26	22
Coal	78	18	20	19
Nuclear	—	1	4	22
Hydro and other	4	4	4	5
Total energy	100	100	100	100

EXHIBIT 11
Energy Consumption per Capita, 1973 (barrels oil equivalent)

	Population (millions)	Total Energy Consumption (million barrels)	Energy Consumption per Capita (barrels per year)
United States	210.2	13,434	64
Canada	22.2	1,365	62
Sweden	8.14	359	44
Netherlands	13.48	535	40
Belgium/Luxembourg	10.09	391	39
Denmark	5.02	168	34
United Kingdom	56.01	1,787	32
West Germany	62.04	1,966	32
Australia	13.22	419	32
Switzerland	6.49	181	28
U.S.S.R.	249.93	6,584	26
France	52.19	1,323	25
Japan	108.35	2,676	25
Italy	54.78	1,122	21
Spain	34.83	399	12
Argentina	24.28	248	10
Saudi Arabia	7.5	62	8
Mexico	54.48	373	7
Iran	30.55	186	6
Brazil	101.69	348	3
Turkey	37.94	121	3
India	575.89	649	1

Source: Hearings before the Senate Subcommittee on Multinational Corporations, 1976.

EXHIBIT 12
World Crude Oil Production, 20 Leading Nations, 1978 (000 barrels)

Nation	Production Total	Barrels Per Day	Percentage of Free World Production	Percentage of Total World Production
1. U.S.S.R.	4,093,475	11,215	—	18.5%
2. United States*	3,175,927	8,701	18.5%	14.3
3. Saudi Arabia	3,113,470	8,530	18.1	14.0
4. Iran	1,900,555	5,207	11.1	8.6
5. Iraq	959,585	2,629	5.6	4.3
6. Venezuela	790,418	2,165	4.6	3.6
7. People's Republic of China	731,825	2,005	4.3	3.3
8. Libya	727,445	1,993	4.2	3.3
9. Nigeria	697,150	1,910	4.1	3.2
10. Kuwait	680,725	1,865	4.0	3.1
11. United Arab Emirates	668,680	1,832	3.9	3.0
12. Indonesia	597,505	1,637	3.5	2.7
13. Canada*	483,260	1,324	2.8	2.2
14. Algeria*	447,125	1,225	2.6	2.0
15. Mexico*	440,555	1,207	2.6	2.0
16. United Kingdom	394,930	1,082	2.3	1.8
17. Qatar	176,537	484	1.0	0.8
18. Neutral Zone	170,090	466	1.0	0.8
19. Egypt	169,360	464	1.0	0.8
20. Argentina	165,195	453	1.0	0.8
Total Free World	17,195,001	47,105	100.0	77.6
Total World	22,158,251	60,708	—	100.0

* Includes lease condensate.
Source: U.S. Energy Information Administration, *World Crude Oil Production Annual.*

recoverable reserves indicated adequate supplies would be available for several centuries.

Prof. Ross Wilhelm, a business economist at the University of Michigan, observed that:

> If you go back and study our history you will discover that in each year over the past 50 years we have had about 20 years of proven reserves of petroleum products on hand. Yet we did not run out of petroleum then and the evidence indicates we need not do without petroleum for the next 200 years, even if we do not undertake a preservation program.
>
> The energy crisis is not a crisis that arises from inadequate potential supplies of energy. The energy crisis for the American people is that they feel the prices of energy are too high and they would like to see them come down.
>
> The only way to bring about lower prices over the long run is to begin to increase supplies now. President Carter's program does not adequately provide for increasing supplies now.[6]

---

[6] *Automotive News,* June 20, 1977, p. 15.

Wilhelm argued that it was economically unsound for producers to search out and maintain more than about 20 years of proven reserves of crude oil. But irrespective of whomever's estimates one chose to believe, it was clear that all of the estimates depended on (1) the rapidity with which new sources of energy were developed and their relative costs, (2) discoveries of new reserve deposits, (3) OPEC's willingness to use up its oil reserves to meet world demand, (4) the rates of worldwide economic growth, (5) the success of conservation measures, and (6) governmental energy policies—to mention only the more important.

OUTLOOK FOR THE 1980s

In 1980 several energy realities relating to the world petroleum industry were fairly clear:

The OPEC countries held more than 80 percent of proved oil reserves in the non-Communist world and accounted for almost 50 percent of total worldwide production.

Even with the development of the North Sea, two thirds of Europe's oil consumption would likely come from OPEC sources by 1985. Japan might have to depend almost 100 percent on OPEC oil by that same time.

The United States, once self-sufficient, had been using 6 to 10 times as much oil, and twice as much natural gas, as it had been discovering in recent years.

While coal and nuclear energy would likely begin to cut into the rising demand for oil sometime in the 1980s, oil would likely still account for approximately one half of the world's energy consumption in the 1990s.

Anything which slowed down the displacement of oil by other fuels would increase the free world's reliance on OPEC oil.

The world prices for crude oil and refined petroleum products would continue to rise at a sharp pace.

17. Exxon Corporation*

In 1979 Exxon Corporation ranked number one in sales, number one in assets, and number one in aftertax profits on *Fortune's* list of the 500 largest U.S. industrial corporations. Insofar as a worldwide ranking among all corporations of all types, Exxon was number one in sales, number two in assets, and number two in aftertax profits. In the first three months of 1980 Exxon's sales were $27.6 billion (an annual sales rate of $110 billion) and profits were $1.9 billion—the all-time quarterly records for a privately owned company anywhere in the world. Although Exxon was clearly a giant corporation by any standard, its overall profitability in terms of percentages rather than absolutes was more modest compared to other *Fortune 500* companies. The company's aftertax return on stockholder's equity was 19.0 percent in 1979, good enough only for a rank of 122 among the *Fortune 500*; its growth rate in earnings per share during 1969–79 period was 14.8 percent, which ranked just 129th out of 500; and the company's total return to investors (dividends plus capital gains) from 1969 through 1979 was 12.1 percent—which yielded a ranking of 118.

Exxon Corporation and its subsidiaries and affiliated companies operated in the United States and nearly 100 other countries; the firm was an acknowledged leader in the world petroleum industry. Exxon's business interests included exploring for and producing crude oil and natural gas, marine and pipeline facilities for transporting both crude and refined products, refining and marketing, petrochemicals, coal mining and development, uranium mining and nuclear fuel, various energy ventures, office equipment and information systems, and energy-saving equipment and technology. Exhibits 1, 2, and 3 provide a financial and operating overview of the company.

COMPANY HISTORY AND BACKGROUND

Exxon Corporation is the surviving parent company from the legendary breakup of the Standard Oil Company of New Jersey in 1911. The Standard Oil Company, of course, was headed by the man who dominated the oil industry in its early years and who became a symbol for both the sins and the virtues of capitalism—John D. Rockefeller. Rockefeller, his brother William,

---

* Prepared by Prof. Arthur A. Thompson, Jr., The University of Alabama, with the assistance of Victor Gray.

EXHIBIT 1

EXXON CORPORATION
Financial Summary, 1975–1979
($ millions)

	1975	1976	1977	1978	1979
Sales and other operating revenue:					
Petroleum and natural gas					
Petroleum products	$33,040	$36,867	$40,739	$45,216	$59,458
Crude oil	9,548	8,474	9,628	10,340	11,968
Natural gas	1,262	1,509	1,791	2,123	2,517
Other	979	1,106	1,225	1,429	2,219
Total	$44,829	$47,956	$53,383	$59,108	$76,162
Chemical products	2,594	3,238	3,578	4,034	5,807
Other	373	432	568	754	1,586
Total sales and other operating revenue	$47,796	$51,626	$57,529	$63,896	$83,555
Interest, earnings from equity interests and other revenue*	968	966	931	990	1,254
Total revenue	$48,764	$52,592	$58,460	$64,886	$84,809
Costs and other deductions:					
Crude oil and product purchases	$21,702	$26,776	$29,274	$31,408	$40,831
Operating expenses	4,347	4,658	5,378	6,395	8,482
Selling, general and administrative expenses	2,628	2,719	2,955	3,640	4,292
Depreciation and depletion	1,471	1,392	1,494	1,678	2,027
Exploration expenses, including dry holes	485	527	642	775	1,052
Income, excise and other taxes					
Income	7,285	5,182	5,643	5,759	8,449
Excise, duties and other	8,047	8,318	9,948	11,757	14,643
Interest expense	385	396	399	425	494
Foreign exchange loss/(gain)*	(165)	(105)	186	186	103
Income applicable to minority interests	123	114	98	100	141
Total deductions	$46,308	$49,977	$56,017	$62,123	$80,514
Net Income	$ 2,456	$ 2,615	$ 2,443	$ 2,763	$ 4,295
Net income per share	$ 5.49	$ 5.84	$ 5.45	$ 6.20	$ 9.74
Cash dividends per share	$ 2.50	$ 2.725	$ 3.00	$ 3.30	$ 3.90
Net income to average shareholders' equity (percent)	15.4%	15.1%	13.1%	14.0%	20.1%
Net income to total revenue (percent)	5.0%	5.0%	4.2%	4.3%	5.1%
Property, plant and equipment, less reserves	$16,115	$18,593	$20,491	$22,806	$26,293
Total additions to property, plant and equipment	$ 3,461	$ 4,002	$ 3,563	$ 4,187	$ 5,859
Working capital	$ 4,660	$ 4,531	$ 4,619	$ 4,328	$ 4,595
Ratio of current assets to current liabilities	1.50	1.43	1.43	1.36	1.29
Long-term debt	$ 3,451	$ 3,697	$ 3,870	$ 3,749	$ 4,258
Shareholders' equity	$16,638	$18,058	$19,121	$20,229	$22,552
Shareholders' equity per share	$ 37.18	$ 40.30	$ 42.74	$ 45.60	$ 51.39
Average number of shares outstanding (000)	447,315	447,744	447,898	445,915	440,843
Number of shareholders at year-end (000)	689	684	684	695	686
Research and development costs	$ 187	$ 202	$ 230	$ 290	$ 381
Wages, salaries, and employee benefits	$ 2,694	$ 2,661	$ 2,893	$ 3,405	$ 4,182
Average number of employees (000)	137	126	127	130	169

* Foreign exchange loss/(gain) related to companies accounted for on the equity method is included in "Interest, earnings from equity interests and other revenue".

Source: *1979 Annual Report.*

EXHIBIT 2

EXXON CORPORATION
Consolidated Balance Sheets
December 31, 1978 and 1979
(in $000s)

	1978	1979
Assets		
Current assets:		
Cash, including time deposits of $1,360, $181,000 and $1,755,758,000	$ 1,992,573	$ 2,515,964
Marketable securities	2,763,375	1,991,644
Notes and accounts receivable, less estimated doubtful amounts of $95,774,000 and $120,293,000	6,725,741	9,011,237
Inventories		
Crude oil, products and merchandise	3,726,938	4,789,936
Materials and supplies	570,030	690,758
Prepaid taxes and expenses	590,094	1,478,809
Total current assets	$16,368,751	$20,478,348
Investments and advances	$ 1,533,078	$ 1,474,601
Property, plant and equipment, at cost, less accumulated depreciation and depletion of $12,748,577,000 and $14,307,410,000	22,805,824	26,292,952
Deferred charges and other assets	823,151	1,244,063
Total assets	$41,530,804	$49,489,964
Liabilities and Shareholders' Equity		
Current liabilities:		
Notes and loans payable	$ 1,400,735	$ 1,867,924
Accounts payable and accrued liabilities	9,115,451	11,845,361
Income taxes payable	1,524,545	2,170,130
Total current liabilities	$12,040,731	$15,883,415
Long-term debt	$ 3,749,241	$ 4,258,018
Annuity and other reserves	1,099,722	1,413,881
Deferred income tax credits	3,436,848	4,385,082
Other deferred credits	95,264	104,925
Equity of minority shareholders in affiliated companies	880,400	892,692
Total liabilities	$21,302,206	$26,938,013
Shareholders' equity	20,228,598	22,551,951
Total liabilities and shareholders' equity	$41,530,804	$49,489,964

Source: *1979 Annual Report.*

and three other partners formed the Standard Oil Company in January 1870; the company was capitalized at $1 million and John D. Rockefeller was elected the first president.

When the Supreme Court ruled in 1911 that Standard Oil of New Jersey constituted a monopoly in restraint of trade, the company was given six months to divest part of its business and create 33 new companies. The stocks of each of the 33 new companies were distributed on a pro-rata basis

EXHIBIT 3
Functional and Geographic Breakout of Earnings and Investment

	Earnings (in $ millions)			Average Capital Employed*		
	1970	1978	1979	1970	1978	1979
Earnings from operations						
Energy operations						
Petroleum and natural gas						
United States						
Exploration and production .	$ 517	$1,202	$1,438	$ 2,418	$ 5,871	$ 6,372
Refining and marketing	103	294	108	2,372	2,741	2,669
Foreign						
Exploration and production .	579	1,282	1,579	2,374	4,987	5,178
Refining and marketing	187	563	1,504	5,058	5,349	6,248
International marine	112	(31)	—	581	1,676	1,518
Coal mining and development . . .	(1)	(20)	(13)	24	271	314
Uranium mining and nuclear						
fuel fabrication	(4)	(51)	(25)	7	201	211
Other energy	9	10	15	71	194	308
Total energy operations	$1,502	$3,249	$4,606	$12,905	$21,290	$22,818
Chemical operations						
United States	22	154	202	410	1,052	1,258
Foreign	23	114	254	865	1,160	1,247
Minerals mining and development . . .	(2)	(23)	(28)	1	90	200
Other operations	(7)	(11)	(7)	221	290	1,319
Earnings from operations	$1,538	$3,483	$5,027	$14,402	$23,882	$26,842
Corporate general and						
administrative costs	(53)	(241)	(359)			
Corporate interest income	31	158	210			
Interest expense	(130)	(221)	(304)	649	3,291	2,611
Foreign exchange loss	(19)	(316)	(138)			
Minority interest	(55)	(100)	(141)			
Net income	$1,312	$2,763	$4,295			

* Capital employed consists of shareholders' equity, debt and minority interest. Average capital employed includes $2,523 million and $2,549 million for the years 1978 and 1979, respectively, applicable to companies accounted for under the equity method. Exxon's ownership percentage operating earnings of such companies is included in "Earnings from operations." The other categories include amounts applicable to consolidated companies as well as those companies accounted for under the equity method. Transfers of crude oil, products and services between business activities are at estimated market prices.

Source: *1979 Annual Report.*

to the 6,000 shareholders of Standard Oil. The effect of divestiture on the Standard Oil Company of New Jersey management was immediate. John D. Rockefeller resigned as president; William Rockefeller and his son, William G. Rockefeller, also stepped down from their positions in the company.

However, except for changes in officers and directors, for many years there was little indication that much had happened. Each company retained its original corporate name with the result that there were now eight Standard companies: Standard Oil Company (New Jersey)—now Exxon Corporation; Standard Oil Company (Indiana); Standard Oil Company (Kentucky);

Standard Oil Company (New York); Standard Oil Company (California); Standard Oil Company (Kansas); Standard Oil Company (Nebraska); and Standard Oil Company (Ohio). The name Standard was so well known to consumers that these companies felt it unwise to change their names. For this reason, even though the companies were separate and independent, the general public often failed to make any distinction and many people continued to think of them as a single company.

In many respects this was accurate. The same seven individuals who had held a majority of stock in Standard of New Jersey held a majority of stock in each of the other 33 companies. Each of the marketing companies continued to market in the territory originally assigned to it, and for some years they did not actively compete with one another. Active competition did not immediately develop because there was no particular incentive to invade the marketing territory of another company, given the rapidly growing demand for petroleum products and the fact that each company had plenty of business available within its own territory. Equally as important, as long as the old Rockefeller men managed the various companies, there was a community of interest, a friendly feeling, and no overall benefits from invading one another's territory.

But with the passage of time, market circumstances prodded the Standard units into competition with one another. The primary reason for this was that most of the companies, not being integrated fully, were in a somewhat insecure position. Some had an immense investment in refining facilities but were without a crude oil supply or pipelines; others were large marketing companies without refineries or pipelines; and others had pipelines but no refineries or marketing organizations. The companies discovered, in time, that they had to integrate to survive and to make their investments secure.

For more than 50 years the Humble Oil and Refining Company was the chief domestic operating unit of the Standard Oil Company (New Jersey); it engaged in producing, transporting, refining, and marketing petroleum products in the United States. Its trademark, ESSO, was one of the best known in the world and was a recognized symbol. The company was originally organized in Texas in 1917 as a successor to the Humble Oil Company. In 1917 Humble was the fifth-largest producer in Texas and also operated a small refinery and topping plant; in 1918 it began building a marketing division. Humble's producing prospects were promising, but the company was badly in need of working capital. Standard Oil (New Jersey), which had ample funds, an inadequate producing capacity, and an interest in securing a foothold in Texas, approached Humble about merger. On January 29, 1919, Humble signed an agreement calling for the sale of a 50 percent interest in the company to Standard Oil (New Jersey) for $17 million.

In 1960 Standard Oil (New Jersey) merged a number of its subsidiaries into Humble, placing the parent company in a position to market nationwide through Humble. With the merger, Humble adopted a uniform design for its service stations. Since the nationwide use of ESSO as a trade mark had been ruled by the courts as inappropriate, owing to conflicts with other Standard Oil trademarks, Humble adopted the brand name ENCO (from ENergy COmpany). However, in the east the company continued to market its products under the ESSO brand; in the southeast, depending on the state, both ESSO and ENCO were used; in Ohio the name Humble was used. ENCO was used principally in the west and the southwest. In 1960, Humble, as a result of other Standard Oil (New Jersey) subsidiaries having been merged into it, was marketing in 35 states. That same year, Humble announced its intention to market nationwide and to adopt a uniform design for its service stations. In 1972, after almost 35 frustrating years of trying to establish a single trademark under which to market and advertise nationwide, Standard Oil (New Jersey) and its domestic operating subsidiary, Humble Oil and Refining Oil Company, announced that they would, henceforth, use the name EXXON as their single primary trademark on a nationwide basis. Subsequently, Standard Oil (New Jersey) became known as Exxon Corporation, and Humble Oil and Refining Company became known as Exxon Company, U.S.A.

One other episode in Exxon's growth deserves mention because of the significance it has come to have presently—some have even referred to it as the most important strategic decision in the company's history. In 1960, when Monroe J. Rathbone started his five-year stint as Exxon's CEO, the industry and the company were enjoying ample supplies of cheap crude oil. Even if the markets for refined products were occasionally torn by price wars, Exxon with its cheap crude sources in Saudi Arabia and Venezuela was able to make up at the wellhead what it lost at the retail pumps. Nonetheless, Rathbone saw trouble ahead; he believed that the demand for oil, rising faster than new discoveries, would one day convert a glut to a scarcity and that the Middle East oil-producing countries would be able to charge much higher prices for their crude. Thus, even though Exxon then had more crude than its refined-products markets could absorb, Rathbone persuaded the company's board to approve major outlays for a search for oil outside the Middle East. Rathbone set up a brand new subsidiary called Esso Exploration and sent geologists and drilling crews into new areas of the world; Exxon's existing subsidiaries were ordered to begin combing their territories for more oil. In the period 1964–67 Exxon spent nearly $700 million on exploration, mostly in non-OPEC areas. Other major oil companies indicated their amusement at Exxon's move by declining to follow suit on any large scale. Mobil, for instance, with the greatest lack of crude oil reserves of any major U.S. company, spent just $267 million for exploration during the same period. Nonetheless, Exxon's decision paid off. As of 1977, Exxon had more proven oil reserves outside the Middle East than any other major company. For his role and foresight in engineering Exxon's move, *Fortune* in 1975 named Monroe J. Rathbone to its Business Hall of Fame—he was one of four living executives so chosen (together with 15 other deceased laureates, among whom was John D. Rockefeller).

ORGANIZATION AND MANAGEMENT

Exxon adopted the principle of decentralized management of its operations in the late 1920s. Since then its volume of business has grown some 20 times and its operations have become substantially more complex. Generally speaking, policy formulation, planning, and coordination were functions of Exxon Corporation's senior management and staff. Activities such as drilling wells, running refineries, and marketing products were delegated to local and division managements close to the scene of these activities. Management positions in Exxon's foreign affiliates and subsidiaries were, with few exceptions, almost entirely staffed by nationals of those countries.

Prior to 1966, some 40 affiliated companies were reporting directly to corporate headquarters in New York. Feeling that this system was becoming unwieldy and inefficient, Exxon reorganized its divisions and companies into a small number of regional and operating units. The top officials in each of these subunits were given broad responsibilities and their own staffs in an effort to permit quicker response to changing conditions and, further, to reduce the number of people reporting to corporate headquarters. Some of these subunits were given responsibilities for certain parts of the world, such as the United States, Europe and Africa, Latin America, and the Far East. Others had worldwide responsibilities for particular segments of Exxon's business, such as chemicals or research. As of 1980 there were 13 such subunits, each headed by a senior executive: Exxon Company, U.S.A., Esso Middle East, Exxon Chemical Company, Exxon International Company, Esso Eastern Inc., Esso Europe Inc., Esso Exploration Inc., Esso Inter-America Inc., Exxon Enterprises Inc., Exxon Research and Engineering Company, Imperial Oil Limited (70 percent owned by Exxon), Exxon Production Research Company, and Reliance Electric Company.

In 1980 the principal link between the Corporation and each regional or operating subunit was provided by one of seven senior management officials (either a senior vice president or the corporation president) who were on Exxon's board of directors. The officer-director was designated as the contact executive for at least one of the regional or operating subunits. The concept of "contact" responsibilities was, according to Exxon, a significant innovation when introduced in 1943. A contact executive's responsibilities were implicit rather than precisely defined, but his chief role was to provide policy guidance to the subunits for which he was responsible. When he did so, it was understood that he spoke for the chief executive officer. The contact executive endeavored to stay well informed about the plans of the regional or operating subunits and the problems they faced. They consulted him on any matter they expected to review with the corporation's management committee (composed of all seven officer-directors) or the compensation and executive development committee (known informally as the COED committee and having the same membership as the management committee). On many matters the contact executive had final review authority. From time to time, the contact assignments of the officer-directors were rotated so as to provide new viewpoints and broaden their own experience.

In 1980 Exxon's board chairman was Clifton C. Garvin; he had been board chairman since August 1975 and a director since 1968. Mr. Garvin began his career with Exxon in 1947. A graduate of Virginia Polytechnic Institute, he joined Exxon as a process engineer at Exxon's Baton Rouge refinery and became operating superintendent in ten years. Later, he moved through a series of positions in Exxon Company, U.S.A., gaining experience in other major functions of the oil business. In 1964 he went to New York as executive assistant to Exxon's president. During the three years prior to his election as a director, he headed Exxon Chemical, U.S.A. and then Exxon's worldwide chemical organization. Mr. Garvin regularly consulted with the corporation's management committee composed of all eight employee directors; he was chairman of this committee and was also chairman of the COED committee which was primarily concerned with the continuity and quality of Exxon's management. The COED committee directly concerned itself with about 200 senior management positions around the world and indirectly kept an eye on another 400 top management jobs in affiliated companies and subsidiary operations. The COED committee met weekly.

Exxon's president was Howard C. Kauffmann; he served as vice chairman of both the management committee and the COED committee. Mr. Kauffmann started with Exxon as an engineer trainee in Oklahoma in 1946. He spent 11 years in Exxon's U.S. producing operations. During the next 11 years he held a series of positions concerned with Exxon's operations in Latin America, including assignments in Peru and Columbia. In 1966, he became president of Exxon's then newly established regional organization for Latin America. In 1968, he moved to the United Kingdom as executive vice president of the regional organization for Europe and became its president in 1971. He was elected a director of Exxon in 1974 and president in 1975.

Anthony Sampson, in describing each of the Seven Sisters, said the following about Exxon and its management:

> In the middle of Manhattan, in the line of cliffs adjoining the Rockefeller Center, is the headquarters of the most famous and long-lived of them all: the company known in America as Exxon, and elsewhere as Esso, and for most of its hundred years' existence as Standard Oil of New Jersey or simply Standard Oil. It is a company which perhaps more than any other transformed the world in which we live. For much of its life it was automatically associated with the name of Rockefeller, and some links still remain. The family still own two percent of the stock; Nelson Rockefeller once worked for it in Venezuela; and the desk of the founder, John D. Rockefeller I, is still preserved as a showpiece at the top of the building. But Exxon has long ago outgrown the control of a single family. It is, by assets, the biggest company in the world. It has 300,000 shareholders, its subsidiaries operate in a hundred countries, and in 1973 its profits were a world record for any company in history; $2.5 billion.

The tranquil style of Exxon's international headquarters seems to have little in common with the passionate rhetoric of Arab politicians in Algiers. Beside a bubbling fountain and pool on Sixth Avenue, the fluted stone ribs soar up sheer for 53 storeys, and inside the high entrance hall is hung with moons and stars. On the 24th floor is the mechanical brain of the company, where the movements of its vast cargoes are recorded. A row of TV screens are linked with two giant computers, and with other terminals in Houston, London and Tokyo, in a system proudly named LOGICS (Logistics Information and Communications Systems). They record the movement of 500 Exxon ships from 115 loading ports to 270 destinations, carrying 160 different kinds of Exxon oil between 65 countries. It is an uncanny process to watch: a girl taps out a question on the keyboard, and the answer comes back on little green letters on the screen, with the names of ships, dates and destinations across the world. From the peace of the 24th floor, it seems like playing God—a perfectly rational and omniscient god, surveying the world as a single market.

Up on the 51st floor, where the directors are found, the atmosphere is still more rarefied. The visitor enters a high two-storey lobby with a balcony looking down on high tapestries; the wide corridors are decorated with Middle East artifacts, Persian carpets, palms, or a Coptic engraving. It is padded and silent except for a faint hum of air-conditioning, and the directors' offices are like fastidious drawing rooms, looking down on the vulgar bustle of Sixth Avenue. It all seems appropriate to Exxon's reputation as a "United Nations of Oil."

But in this elegant setting, the directors themselves are something of an anticlimax. They are clearly not diplomats, or strategists, or statesmen; they are chemical engineers from Texas, preoccupied with what they call "the Exxon incentive." Their route to the top has been through the Texas pipeline—up through the technical universities, the refineries and tank farms. The Exxon Academy, as they call it, is not a university or a business school, but the giant refinery at Baton Rouge, Louisiana. Watching the Exxon board at their annual meeting, I found it hard to imagine them as representatives of a world assembly. It was true that there were, in 1974, two foreign directors—Prince Colonna, the former commissioner of the Common Market, and Otto Wolff, the German industrialist; and there was also one director, Emilio Collado, with experience of government. But the core of the board was made up of the engineers, enclosed in their own specialised discipline.

Ken Jamieson, the chairman and chief executive, a tall cliff of a man with a wide deadpan mouth, was brought up a Canadian, in Medicine Hat, the son of a Mountie; but Texas has since become his adopted home, and he will soon retire there. Jim Garvin, the president, an engineer from Virginia, worked his way up through chemicals and Texas, insulated from the world outside oil; he is expected to be chief executive for eight years. Mike Wright, the chief executive of Exxon, U.S.A., began as a roughneck in Oklahoma before he, too, went down to Texas, where he now lives: a wiry outspoken champion of the fight for free enterprise. Tom Barrow, a short, thick-set man, comes from an old Texan oil family with a shareholding in Exxon: he studied geology in Texas and California, made his name in exploration, and came back to Texas as president of Exxon, U.S.A.; he is likely to be Garvin's successor. George Piercy, the Middle-East negotiator, is the director who is most constantly concerned with diplomacy and foreign countries: he has a combative look, with a quiff of hair and a bulldog face, as if built to battle over barrels. He too came up through the pipeline: he became a chemical engineer in Minnesota, and graduated at the Bayway Refinery.

Within their own citadel these men seem confident enough, with some reason: they are directors of a company that has survived for a century, they have acquired great expertise, and they each earn over $200,000 a year. They move in a world enclosed by the rules of Exxon, which belongs to them. "I think of it as a proprietory relationship," said Garvin in 1973, "Like running a company of which I am the owner. It is not just my duty, but my deep personal desire, to keep it in the best shape possible for the men who will come after me. But once outside their own territory, their confidence easily evaporates. Confronting their shareholders they seem thoroughly nervous, sitting in a row, their fingers fidgeting and their cheekbones working, as they listen to questions about Exxon's African policy, Exxon's salary policy, Exxon's kidnap policy, Exxon's Middle East policy. They know well enough that their company, while one of the oldest, has also been the most hated.

It is in Texas, not New York, that the Exxon men feel more thoroughly at home: and it is the Exxon skyscraper in Houston, the headquarters of Exxon, U.S.A., which seems to house the soul of the company. At the top is the Houston Petroleum Club, with two entire storeys making up a single room, where the oilmen can lunch off steak and strawberries every day of the year. They like to show visitors the view, of which they are justly proud. The flatlands stretch in every direction, broken only by the jagged man-made objects: the domes and tower-blocks in place of cliffs and hills; the curving freeways instead of rivers; the giant road-signs instead of trees. The glaring gasoline signs stick up from the desolate landscape, like symbols leading to some distant shrine: Exxon, Texaco, Shell, Gulf, Exxon. The fluid which has wrought all these changes is concealed from the view: around Houston, there are only a few little pumps nodding in the fields, a few piles of pipelines, to indicate the underground riches. But no one needs reminding: it was all done by oil.[1]

EXXON'S PETROLEUM BUSINESS: AN OVERVIEW

Approximately 90 percent of Exxon's revenues and earnings are concentrated in petroleum and natural gas. Exhibit 4 provides a summary of recent operating statistics regarding this part of Exxon's business. Although a review of the figures in Exhibit 4 indicates that the unit volume and size of Exxon's petroleum business has remained relatively flat since 1975, sales revenues have grown by 70 percent, reflecting the sharp rise in prices.

Exploration and Production. In 1979 Exxon's worldwide production of crude oil and natural gas liquids declined to about 4.6 million barrels a day (1 barrel equals 42 gallons)—down from the 1976 record high of 5.6 million barrels per day. Declining production in the United States, the Middle East, and Africa could not be offset by the increases realized from Venezuela and

---

[1] Anthony Sampson, *The Seven Sisters* (New York: The Viking Press, 1975), pp. 8–10. Quoted with permission.

EXHIBIT 4

Operating Summary of Selected Petroleum and Natural Gas Activities of Exxon, 1975–1979

	1975	1976	1977	1978	1979
Net production of crude oil and natural gas liquids and petroleum supplies available under special agreements (000 of barrels daily)					
United States	846	812	795	829	791
Canada	171	149	143	130	140
Other Western Hemisphere	947	18	16	14	13
Europe	14	26	49	93	154
Middle East and Africa	90	109	109	97	77
Australia and Far East	181	188	196	220	248
Total consolidated affiliates	2,249	1,302	1,308	1,383	1,423
Supplies available under long-term agreements with foreign governments	1,313	1,498	1,438	1,333	1,127
Proportional interest in production of equity companies	899	1,073	1,160	1,031	1,126
Subtotal	4,461	3,873	3,906	3,747	3,676
Oil sands production—Canada	3	5	5	8	20
Other supplies available under special agreements	495	1,447	1,180	936	748
Worldwide	4,959	5,325	5,091	4,691	4,444
Refinery crude oil runs					
United States	1,182	1,277	1,339	1,426	1,320
Canada	394	412	415	416	449
Other Western Hemisphere	689	394	368	406	370
Europe	1,564	1,737	1,694	1,646	1,691
Middle East and Africa	110	125	86	67	52
Australia and Far East	392	414	446	466	472
Worldwide	4,331	4,359	4,348	4,427	4,354

Petroleum product sales

Aviation fuels	292	316	322	343	350
Gasoline, naphthas	1,421	1,457	1,459	1,540	1,534
Home heating oils, kerosene, diesel oils	1,319	1,470	1,461	1,533	1,520
Heavy fuels	1,389	1,523	1,426	1,383	1,316
Specialty products	569	587	598	591	599
Total	4,990	5,353	5,266	5,390	5,319
United States	1,561	1,830	1,748	1,736	1,667
Canada	433	456	443	463	476
Other Western Hemisphere	580	473	488	510	505
Eurpoe	1,812	1,943	1,918	2,015	2,019
Other Eastern Hemisphere	604	651	669	666	652
Worldwide	4,990	5,353	5,266	5,390	5,319
Natural gas sales (million cubic feet daily)					
United States	4,937	4,673	4,476	4,348	4,007
Canada	410	376	361	343	367
Other Western Hemisphere	104	41	50	54	76
Europe	4,776	5,111	5,057	5,015	5,168
Other Eastern Hemisphere	418	477	544	608	563
Worldwide	10,645	10,678	10,488	10,368	10,181
Tanker capacity, owned and chartered (000 deadweight tons, daily average)	24,400	27,005	27,840	26,160	24,140
Pipeline throughput (thousands of barrels daily)	6,491	5,836	5,854	5,609	5,490

Source: 1979 Annual Report.

wells in the North Sea near Norway and Britain. Exxon's Iranian supplies were cut off completely when the Iranian government embargoed all sales to U.S. companies and their affiliates.

Exxon drilled 2,420 wells in 1979, up from 1,728 in 1978 and 1,553 in 1970. At year end 1979, Exxon had drilling and exploration rights to some 424 million acres, up from 405 million in 1978 but down from 443 million acres in 1970. The company spent almost $1 billion for leases on new properties in 1979—the largest single-year total in Exxon's history.

In an August 1976 auction of oil and gas leases held by the U.S. Department of the Interior for drilling rights in the Baltimore Canyon area 50 miles off New Jersey's shore, Exxon paid $343 million for rights on 171,000 acres, nearly one third of the acreage leased by the industry. In reporting on the bidding a *Business Week* reporter wrote

> . . . Exxon repeatedly brought gasps with its enormous bids. "Clobbered," moaned one oil man, his companion nervously gulping Rol-Aids, as an Exxon bid was opened and read off by the auctioneer—$51.3 million, double the highest competing bid. On another tract, Exxon overwhelmed a $12.4 million bid with $86.4 million. "They left $74 million on the table on that one," Mobil's Hohler remarked wryly.
>
> All told Exxon made bids totalling $730 million, nearly three times as much as Shell, the next highest bidder. And it won on $343 million in bids, almost 4 times the outlays of Mobil, the second biggest winner. Said a government staffer: "Exxon just hit everyone over the head with their money."[2]

However, the risks which Exxon took in making its bids are well-illustrated by its drilling experience in the Baltimore Canyon. As of 1980 Exxon had drilled four wells without significant shows of oil. It had an ownership interest in the drilling of three other wells, one of which was a gas discovery near discoveries announced by other companies. But otherwise, it had nothing to show for its $343 million lease investment except the added costs of the testing and drilling.

According to the president of another oil company, Exxon was obliged to bid heavily at every lease sale "because any major oil company with a huge investment in refineries like Exxon can't afford not to have an oil supply."[3] Even so, Exxon's managers were considered as superior bidders at leases; in recent years Exxon has compiled a 20 percent success rate in finding oil and/or gas on new tracts where it has obtained drilling leases—compared to an industry average of 10 percent. Exxon, U.S.A.'s senior vice president of exploration indicated that there was no real alternative to anteing up and rolling the dice: "You have nightmares going into these things, but an exploration man has to learn early that it's better to try and fail than not to try and have nothing."[4]

---

[2] "Exxon's High Roller in Oil Lease Sales," *Business Week*, September 20, 1976, p. 116.

[3] Ibid., p. 120.

[4] Ibid.

To try to reduce the risk on tracts on which auctions were to be held, Exxon, like other oil companies, sent out seismographic teams to assess the probability of discovery. In the case of Baltimore Canyon, 31 companies banded together to drill a test hole to determine if the geological structure had the necessary porosity to qualify as a reservoir where oil might have collected with perhaps 70 percent probability. But the hole was too shallow to test for hydrocarbon source rocks—limestone and shell—at the depth required for oil or gas. And it was drilled adjacent to rather than on top of the area up for lease. In fact, the oil companies did not want to find oil prior to the auction because of the likely reluctance of Congress to let the tract go if any oil had been found before the auction. The U.S. Geological Survey used a complex computer program called the "Monte Carlo System" to estimate the average amount of oil and/or gas which each parcel up for auction might be expected to produce; their estimates for the Baltimore Canyon area ranged from 400 million to 1.4 billion barrels of crude oil and from 2.6 trillion to 9.4 trillion cubic feet of natural gas. But oil men irreverently called this estimating approach the SWAG ("Scientific Wild Ass Guess") method.[5]

Exhibit 5 presents a profile of Exxon's exploration and production activities.

Refining and Marketing.   In refining, Exxon was the world's largest, with a capacity of just over 6 million barrels per day—nearly double the capacity of the next largest refiner, Texaco. In 1979 Exxon's refineries ran at about 80 percent of capacity overall in the United States and at about 75 percent of capacity overseas. Earnings from this segment of Exxon's business declined in the United States because along with reduced crude oil supplies prices for major products did not keep pace with rising raw material and operating costs. In 1979 Exxon earned $108 million on its refining and marketing operations in the U.S. (equal to a 4.0 percent return on capital) compared to $1.5 billion in the foreign segment (a 24.1 percent return on capital).

During the 1970s there was a significant shift in market demand away from heavy fuel oil to light products such as gasoline, heating oil, and jet fuel (Exhibit 4). Slower-than-anticipated growth in consumption led to substantial refining overcapacity in some areas. The reduction of lead in motor gasoline in North America, stricter environmental requirements, the trend to heavier, higher sulfur crude oil feedstocks and a several fold increase in energy costs all posed severe challenges.

To deal with some of these changes, Exxon utilized technology which permitted the conversion of heavy fuel oil to light products. The company was also using refinery equipment in ways quite different from those originally intended. In Europe, for instance, idle pipestills were converted to visbreakers to produce heating oil and gasoline out of fuel oil. In 1979, a $30 million project of this kind was completed at Milford Haven, Wales, and construction began on similar projects at four other European refineries.

[5] Ibid., p. 116.

EXHIBIT 5
Summary of Exploration and Production Operations, Exxon Corp., 1970, 1978, 1979

	1970	1978	1979
	\$ Millions		
Earnings from operations			
United States	517	1,202	1,438
Foreign	579	1,282	1,579
Total	1,096	2,484	3,017
Average capital employed			
United States	2,418	5,871	6,372
Foreign	2,374	4,987	5,178
Total	4,792	10,858	11,550
Capital and exploration expenditures			
United States	368	1,523	2,359
Foreign	370	1,884	2,378
Total	738	3,407	4,737
Research and development costs	18	61	71
	Percent		
Return on average capital employed			
United States	21.4	20.5	22.6
Foreign	24.4	25.7	30.5
Total	22.9	22.9	26.1
	000 Barrels Per Day		
Net production and supplies—liquids			
Net production			
United States	946	829	791
Foreign	2,272	554	632
Long-term agreements with governments	429	1,333	1,127
Proportional interest in production of equity			
companies.......................................	1,142	1,031	1,126
Oil sands production—Canada		8	20
Supplies available under other special agreements	663	936	748
Total	5,452	4,691	4,444
	Million Cubic Feet Per Day		
Natural gas sales			
United States	5,488	4,348	4,007
Foreign	2,003	6,020	6,174
Total	7,491	10,368	10,181

Source: *1979 Annual Report.*

Improved catalysts developed by Exxon made it possible to upgrade refinery yields and product quality without major investment in new equipment. The company's conversion capacity in Europe has increased by 30 percent in the past decade.

Another project to convert heavy fuel oil to light products came on stream at Exxon, U.S.A.'s Baton Rouge, Louisiana, refinery. A $94 million isomerization unit was started up at the Bayway refinery in Linden, New Jersey, to produce high-octane motor gasoline blending stocks. This unit and two hydrofiners put on line at the Baton Rouge plant increased the company's capacity to make both leaded and unleaded gasoline with octane levels suitable for current automobiles.

The company continued to reduce energy consumed in its refining operations. Process changes, improved insulation and other measures taken over the past six years have cumulatively saved more than 100 million barrels of oil, or enough energy to heat half a million average homes in the northeastern United States throughout those years. The energy efficiency of Exxon refineries has been improved by 21 percent in that period, and further operating changes combined with significant investments are aimed at an improvement of 17 percent over 1979 levels by 1982.

Marketing programs designed to reduce costs and improve efficiency in plants and terminals through job content studies and computer automation were accelerated in 1979. The company continued its long-term program to improve the efficiency and profitability of its retail service station chain, disposing of over 800 owned and leased service stations with marginal prospects during the year. From 1969 to 1980, the number of service stations selling Exxon products declined by 28 percent to 65,600, even though the volume of motor fuel sold through retail outlets increased by 38 percent.

Exhibit 6 provides a more detailed breakdown of the profitability of Exxon's foreign and U.S. operations in the areas of refining and marketing.

International Marine Transportation. As a result of reductions in the world tanker surplus and increases in freight rates, Exxon's international tanker operations broke even in 1979, as compared to operating losses of $31 million in 1978. However, the results were far below the earnings levels of 1970:

	1970	1978	1979
Earnings/(losses) from operations	$ 112*	$ (31)	—
Average capital employed	581	1,676	$1,518
Capital expenditures	162	48	69
Research and development costs	3	4	3
Return on average capital employed	19.3%	(1.8%)	—
Average capacity, owned and chartered†			
Owned vessels	8.1	17.3	16.6
Chartered vessels	10.6	8.9	7.5
Total	18.7	26.2	24.1

* All dollar figures in millions.
† Capacity in millions of deadweight tons.

EXHIBIT 6
Summary of Refining and Marketing Operations, Exxon Corp., 1970, 1978, 1979

	1970	1978	1979
	$ Millions		
Earnings from operations			
United States	$ 103	$ 294	$ 108
Foreign	187	563	1,504
Total	290	857	1,612
Average capital employed			
United States	2,372	2,741	2,669
Foreign	5,058	5,349	6,248
Total	7,430	8,090	8,917
Capital expenditures			
United States	315	271	294
Foreign	577	606	748
Total	892	877	1,042
Research and development costs	33	56	71
	Percentage		
Return on average capital employed			
United States	4.3%	10.7%	4.0%
Foreign	3.7	10.5	24.1
Total	3.9	10.6	18.1
	000 Barrels Per Day		
Petroleum product sales			
United States	1,753	1,736	1,667
Foreign	3,931	3,654	3,652
Total	5,684	5,390	5,319
Refinery crude oil runs			
United States	989	1,426	1,320
Foreign	4,281	3,001	3,034
Total	5,270	4,427	4,354

Source: *1979 Annual Report.*

In 1979, Exxon contracted with a shipyard in the Far East for construction of four crude oil carriers of 88,700 deadweight tons each intended for service between the Caribbean and U.S. east and Gulf coast ports where restricted draft bars larger vessels. In addition to the latest safety and antipollution features, the ships will incorporate a number of fuel-saving improvements. Scheduled for delivery beginning in mid-1981, the ships will achieve fuel savings estimated at 20 percent above comparable vessels built in 1978.

CHEMICAL OPERATIONS

Exxon Chemical Company increased its worldwide earnings 70 percent in 1979 on revenues of $6.7 billion, up 44 percent over 1978. Foreign chemical earnings more than doubled as feedstock shortages and strong demand caused a recovery of depressed industry margins, particularly in Europe and

EXHIBIT 7
Summary of Chemical Operations, Exxon Corp., 1970, 1978, 1979

	1970	1978	1979
	$ Millions		
Earnings from operations			
United States	$ 22	$ 154	$ 202
Foreign	23	114	254
Total	45	268	456
Average capital employed			
United States	410	1,052	1,258
Foreign	865	1,160	1,247
Total	1,275	2,212	2,505
Capital expenditures			
United States	47	359	246
Foreign	54	111	187
Total	101	470	433
Research and development costs	31	40	51
	Percentage		
Return on average capital employed			
United States	5.4%	14.6%	16.1%
Foreign	2.7	9.8	20.4
Total	3.5	12.1	18.2

Source: *1979 Annual Report.*

Canada. U.S. chemicals earnings rose 31 percent, due primarily to increased sales volumes aided by a strong export market.

A brief profile of Exxon's chemical operations is shown in Exhibit 7.

EXXON'S PROJECTIONS OF U.S. ENERGY DEMAND

In 1975 Exxon projected that total U.S. energy demand would increase from an estimated 36.6 million barrels per day of oil equivalent in 1976 to about 54 million barrels per day in 1990—an average annual growth rate of just under 2.9 percent per year but significantly below the average growth of 4.0 percent during 1960–73 (prior to the Arab oil embargo). Exxon attributed the lower growth rate to changing consumption patterns and to a more efficient use of energy brought about by government initiatives and higher energy costs. Nonetheless the projected growth rate in demand represented a 50 percent increase in demand over the period and convinced Exxon of a genuine need to continue development of U.S. energy supplies.

Exxon forecasted that future discoveries of oil and gas would be barely sufficient to offset the decline in U.S. production from existing reserves for many years. For this reason, nuclear fission and coal and, eventually, synthetic fuels from oil shale and coal, solar, and nuclear fusion were viewed by the company as increasingly important energy sources needed to meet these projected energy demands. The exact distribution of these energy supplies was difficult to project and varied depending upon what economic, political, and environmental assumptions were made. The company believed that its projections, while not necessarily exact, still demonstrated a clear need to develop energy sources other than oil and gas.

Exxon estimated that in 1990 domestic coal output would approach 1.5 billion tons a year, more than double production levels in the late 1970s. About 6 percent of coal production in 1990 was expected to be used to produce synthetic oil and gas. Synthetic oil from coal and oil shale was pegged at about 2 percent of total oil demand by 1990. Synthetic gas from coal was projected to be over 3 percent of total gas demand in that year. Nuclear energy sources were expected to increase almost fivefold between 1976 and 1990, a growth rate of 12 percent per year. The company believed that slower-than-forecast growth in domestic supplies of coal, nuclear, synthetic fuels, or any form of indigenous energy, unless accompanied by reductions in consumption, would translate directly into additional oil imports, which Exxon estimated would climb to 12 to 13 million barrels per day in the 1980s, or about half of expected total oil demand in the United States. The company believed that by 1985 imported oil could account for about 28 percent of total energy usage in the United States, compared with 17 percent in 1975.

In the company's view, the United States needed to develop all viable domestic energy sources to the fullest so as to limit growing reliance upon foreign oil supplies. In so doing, the vulnerability to future embargoes and to OPEC pricing decisions would be reduced, balance of payments strains would be mitigated, and the inevitable transition from oil and gas to other fuels would begin sooner. The company took the position that legislation which impeded energy development without generating compensating benefits would have significant adverse effects on the nation's future wellbeing.

Furthermore, studies made by the company indicated that from 1976 to 1990 cumulatively, in order to provide the domestic energy capabilities necessary to realize the projected outlook, the United States would need to add the equivalent of over 210 large coal mines (5 million tons per year each); 2,700 unit trains (100 cars each); 7 oil shale synthetic plants (50,000 barrels per day each); 7 coal gasification plants (250 million cubic feet per day each); 3 coal liquefication plants (50,000 barrels per day each); and 30 uranium mining and milling complexes (2 million pounds per year each); all in addition to more than 450,000 new oil and gas wells and 31 new refineries (150,000 barrels per day each). The capital requirements associated with these facilities amounted to an average of about $30 billion per year in constant 1976 dollars, compared with an average of less than $8 billion per year in captial expenditures for such facilities for the ten-year, preembargo period of 1963 through 1972.

EXXON'S STRATEGIC SHIFT TO BECOME AN
ENERGY COMPANY

The foregoing trends and statistics were not new to Exxon's management. As far back as the 1960s the company had begun to sense that oil and gas reserves would be inadequate to meet the world's need for energy. It was with this in mind that Exxon started laying the groundwork for a major strategic shift from being just a petroleum company to becoming an energy company.

Exxon's strategic move into alternate energy sources was motivated by two factors: (1) projections that all types of new and existing energy sources would be needed to meet a growing U.S. and world demand for energy and (2) the conviction that Exxon could meaningfully contribute to meeting these needs in a fashion that served both consumers and shareholders. Top management was convinced that the skills needed to develop these energy sources were similar to those Exxon had acquired in its existing business. Randall Meyer, president of Exxon Company, U.S.A. and vice president of Exxon Corporation, described Exxon's assessment of the desirability of diversifying thusly:

> Over many years Exxon has regularly prepared energy supply/demand outlooks for both the United States and the world. In the early 1960s we were projecting that oil and gas demand would continue to grow at about the same rate as the total demand for energy; however, it was not clear just where in the long term these supplies would come from. It appeared to us at that time that domestic production of both oil and gas could peak during the 1970s. We were also aware that there were very substantial reserves of oil and gas located overseas; however, like others, we were becoming increasingly concerned over the national security aspects of increased imports. Thus, we concluded at this early date that there could be substantial future needs for synthetic oil and gas. It also appeared that, since coal reserves are so plentiful in this country, a high percentage of the synthetic fuels would be made from coal . . . .
>
> Another important conclusion reached by our appriasals during this period was that use of electricity was going to grow about twice as fast as the demand for total energy. The high projected growth rate for electricity led to our interest in uranium. Looking ahead toward 1980, it appeared to us that nuclear power would play a significant and increasingly important role in meeting the electric utility demand growth . . . .
>
> An important question which had to be answered before we made a decision to enter either the coal or uranium business was the availability of resources . . . . Our studies indicated that of this amount of potential reserves, approximately 65 percent were not owned or under lease by any company then producing coal . . . .
>
> In the case of uranium, the reserves situation was quite different. Because uranium is difficult to find, it has a very high discovery value. This resource had been much more actively sought after than coal, and all known reserves were controlled by companies which were already active in the business. We be-

lieved, however, that the Company's accumulated oil and gas exploration skills would offer a good start toward discovering new reserves . . . . most of the known uranium deposits in the United States occur in sedimentary rocks. Since oil and gas occur in a similar environment, we had a great deal of geological expertise which could be applied to uranium exploration. Also, Exxon, U.S.A. had an extensive library of geological and geophysical information that had not yet been examined with the objective of locating uranium deposits. Many of the areas of the United States containing known or potential uranium deposits had been explored in the course of our oil and gas exploration effort. It seemed possible that rock samples and detailed geological information could be reexamined for guides to locating uranium deposits. In addition, the Company held mineral leases which covered not only oil and gas but also other minerals, including uranium. For all these reasons, we believed we could contribute to uranium discovery.

In addition to our exploration capabilities, we had other strengths which could be effectively used in establishing a position in the nuclear fuel and coal businesses. For example, we had developed over the years considerable expertise in processing hydrocarbons in our refineries. We believed that much of the research and development work we had done in refining would prove useful in developing processes for converting coal to gas or liquids.

It was determined at an early date that, to be successful, the coal and nuclear fuel businesses would require sizable amounts of front-end capital. Another important factor was that our Company had considerable experience in the area of high-risk, capital-intensive, long-lead-time ventures. In short, we concluded that the needs to be met in these energy fuel areas were compatible with the capabilities of our Company.[6]

EXXON'S ENTRY INTO COAL

Exxon's studies in the 1960s, which utilized reports published by the U.S. Geological Survey and the Bureau of Mines, estimated economically recoverable domestic coal reserves, at then current costs and technology, to be in the range of 200 billion tons. When compared to annual coal production at that time of about half a billion tons, these reserves represented more than a 400-year supply. Since coal was plentiful, it was expected to be a raw material for production of synthetic fuels. And, synthetics were believed to be a likely future raw material for Exxon's refineries and chemical plants, or to be substitutable as retail products.

Since coal was a fuel with ready marketability regardless of the success or failure of synthetic research, it offered an opportunity for Exxon to broaden its primary business of energy production and sale. When this was coupled with Exxon's considerable experience in such commercial undertakings as land and resource management, the wholesale marketing of fuels, and activities involving core or directional drilling, logging, fracturing, and trans-

---

[6] Testimony before Senate Committee on Interior and Insular Affairs, December 6, 1973.

porting, Exxon's management concluded that the company had the internal capabilities required to compete effectively in the coal business.

Exxon's coal activities became the responsibility of a subsidiary, the Carter Oil Company. The purchase of undeveloped coal reserves began in 1965; bituminous coal reserves were purchased in Illinois, West Virginia, and Wyoming and lignite reserves were obtained in Arkansas, Montana, North Dakota, and Texas. Once the general availability of leasable coal was established, the company still had to conduct a substantial amount of core hole drilling and testing to define the exact location, extent, and quality of these deposits. Considerable effort was spent assembling blocks of reserves of sufficient size to develop in order to compete effectively in coal markets.

Exxon's management maintained that large blocks of mineable reserves were needed to realize economies of scale in coal mining and to be price competitive on coal supplied to large electric utilities. A large mine, for example, could produce in sufficient quantities to justify assembling unit trains traveling *direct* from the mine to a utility's coal-fired generating plant; unit trains were a substantially more economical mode of transportation. Also, potential coal suppliers had to have adequately large coal reserves if they wished to compete for the long-term contracts desired by utilities; many utilities wanted assured coal supplies of known quality for a major portion of the useful life of their new plants before committing the capital for such generating facilities. (For instance, a 1,000 megawatt coal-fired plant requires about 3 million tons of coal per year.)

Exxon's coal marketing activities began in 1967. Initially, coal from the Illinois reserves offered the best prospects for marketing because of its proximity to major markets. In 1968 a sales contract was negotiated with Commonwealth Edison of Chicago, and Monterey Coal Company, a Carter subsidiary, was formed and began development of its first mine. Located in southern Illinois near Carlinville, this mine commenced production in mid-1970. It employed about 500 people, had a maximum capacity of about 3 million tons of coal per year, and was one of the largest and most modern underground mines in the country. A second mine was opened in 1977 to supply coal to the Public Service Company of Indiana; its capacity was 3.6 million tons per year. Additional markets for Exxon's Illinois coal, which had a sulfur content of 3 to 4 percent, were limited by air pollution regulations. However, as commercial equipment became available for removing sulfur from coal, either directly during combustion, or from smokestacks after combustion, the prospects for marketing the company's Illinois coal were expected to improve greatly.

In May 1974 the Carter Oil Company signed an agreement with Columbia Coal Gasification Corporation exchanging a 50 percent interest in certain Illinois lands containing coal reserves for a 50 percent interest in a like amount of Columbia's West Virginia land. This agreement allowed development of the lower sulfur coal in West Virginia and committed some of Exxon's high-sulfur coal in Illinois to a possible gasification project when the economics and technology were commercially demonstrated.

The Carter Mining Company, another subsidiary of the Carter Oil Company, developed Exxon's coal reserves in the West. In January 1974 Carter announced plans for its first surface mine in Wyoming to employ 250 people, and to produce 12 million tons per year by 1980. Although Exxon maintained that land reclamation would assure negligible long-term environmental impact, and despite a favorable Final Environmental Impact Statement issued by the Department of the Interior in October 1974, progress on this mine (and on others in the area) was delayed by a court injunction obtained by the Sierra Club and others against the Department of Interior. The injunction prohibited the Secretary of the Interior from issuing mining permits and approving mining plans. The suit sought development of an extraordinary regional environmental impact statement. Ironically, the company's western coal reserves, development of which was held up by the environmental suit, had a lower sulfur content than Illinois coal and could more easily meet environmental regulations. After over a year of litigation, Exxon was allowed to proceed. The company had, as of 1980, two surface mines in operation near Gillette, Wyoming.

From 1967 to mid-1976 Exxon made over 600 sales contacts and 25 formal bid proposals, and had entered into 4 long-term sales contracts. In addition, the company had one short-term agreement to sell coal. Exxon was striving to negotiate more sales contracts which could lead to the opening of additional mines. Exxon's underground coal mine productivity in 1975 was 23 tons per man-day compared with 17 tons per man-day for all underground mines in Illinois (1974), and less than ten tons per man-day for all U.S. underground mines (1975).

Even so, Exxon's coal business did not become profitable until 1979, nine years after the first mine was opened in Illinois. Exhibit 8 shows operating statistics for Exxon's coal mining and development business. Exxon projected its coal production levels would reach nearly 28 million tons a year by 1984.

Coal Research and Synthetics. Exxon and its affiliate, Exxon Research & Engineering Company, have had active coal research programs since 1966. The emphasis has been on removing sulfur and nitrogen oxides in coal burning processes, and especially on processes for manufacturing synthetic gas and oil from coal. Exxon had spent more than $120 million in coal synthetics research through 1979 and turned up some promising processes for gasifying and for liquefying coal, each of which had been tested in small pilot plants. The company was awarded several multimillion dollar government contracts to develop synthetic fuels processes; these involved further testing of the Exxon Donor Solvent liquefaction process, development of a new catalytic coal gasification process, building a one-ton-per-day pilot plant for gasifying coal using a catalytic process invented by Exxon, and an evaluation of the applicability of its proprietary coking technology to coal liquefaction residues.

EXHIBIT 8
Summary of Coal Mining and Development Operations, Exxon Corp., 1970, 1978, 1979

	1970	1978	1979
		$ Millions	
(Losses) from operations, after tax			
Operating mines	—	2	8
New business and mine development costs	(1)	(22)	(21)
	(1)	(20)	(13)
Research and development costs	—	4	3
Average capital employed	24	271	314
Capital and exploration expenditures	13	87	57
		Millions of Short Tons	
Recoverable reserves	7,000	9,500	9,500
Production	.3	5.2	8.6
Design capacity			
Existing operations	3.0	26.6	26.6
Under construction	—	1.0	1.0
		Number	
Mines			
In operation	1	4	4
Under construction	—	1	1

Source: *1979 Annual Report.*

In 1979, construction was 90 percent completed on a 250-ton-per-day pilot plant to make liquid fuels from coal. The total pilot plant program, including operations and associated research, had a cost of $250 million and was jointly financed with the Department of Energy and a group of private investors; Exxon was underwriting 23 percent of the cost and was acting as program manager and plant operator.

Exxon was also working on two development programs utilizing fluid bed technology (a technique pioneered by Exxon in petroleum) for the clean combustion of coal in utility boilers and in major industrial fuel burning units. The first involved burning high sulfur coal in fluid beds of coal and limestone. The second program, sponsored by the Department of Energy, was a fluid bed combustion system in which steam generating coils were immersed directly in a fluid bed of coal and limestone. Exxon operated a six-ton-per-day pressurized fluid bed pilot plant, and had demonstrated the feasibility of fluid bed combustion and simultaneous limestone regeneration.

EXXON'S ENTRY INTO NUCLEAR ENERGY

As far back as the mid-1960s, Exxon's analysis of the energy situation indicated that use of electricity was to grow about twice as fast as the demand for total energy; Exxon believed that nuclear power would play an increasingly important role in meeting this future electric utility demand. The most recent nuclear power generation projections had indicated that nuclear power would grow from less than 10 percent of U.S. electric energy supply in 1976 to about 30 percent in 1990—an outcome which would greatly increase uranium demand and make diversification into uranium mining and nuclear fuels a profitable business opportunity.

As Exxon saw it, the nuclear fuel business consisted of several distinct activities—uranium exploration, mining and milling; uranium enrichment; fabrication of enriched uranium into nuclear fuel assemblies; chemical reprocessing of the spent fuel assemblies to recover uranium and plutonium for recycling into the fuel cycle, thus reducing requirements for new uranium supply and enrichment services; and ultimate safe storage and disposal of nuclear wastes.

Exploration, Mining, and Milling.   Exxon initiated its uranium exploration program in the United States in 1966. By 1977, the company had made two uranium discoveries that had been brought into production and two others that were in varying stages of evaluation. The first commercial discovery was made in 1967 in south Texas and was a relatively minor deposit. The second discovery was made in 1968 in eastern Wyoming and was a much larger deposit having substantial proven commercial potential. Exxon's petroleum activities played a key role in both of these discoveries: the Texas discovery was located on a lease which was originally obtained as a petroleum prospect; the discovery in Wyoming resulted, in part, from information gained during geophysical exploration for hydrocarbons. Exxon estimated that in 1977 it had about 5 percent of the uranium reserves in the United States. Those reserves that had been assessed as commercially viable were already committed under contract to the utility industry. The company's uranium exploration program was believed by company officials to be among the more significant in the industry.

Nuclear Fuel Fabrication.   Besides mining and milling activities, Exxon entered into uranium marketing and into the design, fabrication, and sale of nuclear fuel assemblies to electric utilities with nuclear-generating plants. The company also began to provide a range of fuel management and engineering services to electric utility firms. Responsibility for these activities rested with Exxon Nuclear, Inc., a wholly owned and separately managed affiliate of Exxon Corporation.

Exxon Nuclear competed only in the market segment for refueling nuclear reactors. About two years after start-up, a nuclear reactor is refueled just about annually over its 30- to 40-year life. At each such refueling, a portion of the fuel core is discharged and replaced with a batch of fresh "reload" fuel. Exxon Nuclear's rivals in the replacement fuel market were Westinghouse, General Electric, Combustion Engineering, and Babcock and Wilcox. Exxon Nuclear was the only fuel fabricator not engaged in selling nuclear reactors and supplied about 6 percent of the domestic fuel fabrication market.

In Exxon's view, the primary challenge confronting nuclear fuel suppliers was the improvement of processes and technology which would (1) reduce the requirements for massive capital investments, (2) conserve uranium as a vital energy fuel resource by achieving greater energy output per unit of new ore mined, and (3) demonstrate acceptable solutions to the nuclear waste management need. Exxon's nuclear research and development activities were aimed at meeting these perceived needs, and its programs concentrated on emerging, potentially more efficient technologies such as centrifuge enrichment and isotope separation by lasers.

These efforts had, by 1979, begun to show some promise. After several years of research, a joint venture between Exxon Nuclear and Avco Corp. had produced a proprietary laser process for uranium isotope separation—at a cost of $65 million. The process had the ability to increase fissionable material recovery and thereby extend uranium reserves. A review panel of independent experts advised Exxon and Avco that the domestic deployment of this process for the production of low-enriched uranium would be consistent with U.S. nuclear nonproliferation objectives. Although logical development of the process called for construction of a pilot plant and a development program (at a projected cost of $165 million), the U.S. government indicated that it did not intend to permit private industry investment in the enrichment and reprocessing phases of the nuclear fuel cycle. Exxon Nuclear and Avco therefore offered to build the plant under government auspices—but as of 1980 the offer had not been accepted.

Overall, though, Exxon's nuclear energy business was not profitable as of 1979; according to the company's management:

> Operating losses continued in Exxon's uranium production and fuel assembly manufacturing businesses, primarily due to higher-than-expected costs which have occurred since the early 1970s, when many current contracts were signed. Negotiations are continuing with a number of customers to obtain contract modifications allowing for these unexpected cost increases, with about half of the contracts renegotiated to date.
>
> New orders for fabrication of future reload fuels reached the highest level since 1975. They were about equally split between reactors currently operable and those under construction. Production from Exxon's nuclear fuel fabrication facilities was at a new high.

Exhibit 9 summarizes the recent operating results of Exxon's ventures into uranium mining and nuclear fuel fabrication.

EXXON'S OTHER DIVERSIFICATION EFFORTS IN ENERGY

Exxon's diversification into other energy areas was motivated by some of the same factors that motivated its diversification into coal and nuclear fuel. As of 1977, Exxon's total expenditures on these other diversification efforts were small relative to coal and nuclear fuel expenditures. The company's efforts were designed to learn about emerging technologies, to contribute to their development, and to position the company so that a competitive com-

EXHIBIT 9
Summary of Uranium Mining and Nuclear Fuel Fabrication Activities,
Exxon Corp., 1970, 1978, 1979

	1970	1978	1979
		$ Millions	
(Losses) from operations, after tax			
Operating results	(3)	(33)	(11)
Exploration costs	(1)	(18)	(14)
	(4)	(51)	(25)
Research and development costs	1	25	23
Average capital employed	7	201	211
Capital and exploration expenditures	10	74	66
Revenue	1	142	179
		Million Pounds	
Production of uranium concentrates	—	3.3	3.4
		Number	
Mines			
In operation	—	3	3
Under development	1	—	—

Source: *1979 Annual Report.*

mercial contribution could be initiated when and if market demand led to profit opportunities that appeared to be commensurate with the risks involved.

Oil Shale. Oil shale from deposits in Colorado, Utah, and Wyoming represents a potential source of supplemental liquid and gaseous fuels many times that of the proved domestic reserves of crude petroleum. While considerable shale lands are held by oil companies, the vast majority—about 80 percent—of potential reserves are federally controlled.

Exxon's oil shale activities were relatively limited.[7] During the early 1960s, Exxon acquired a number of small tracts of patented land and mining claims in the oil shale area of Colorado. These holdings, however, were

---

[7] The same was true for most other companies. The large amount of federally controlled oil shale reserves were placed under a lease moratorium in 1930. It was not until 1968 that the Department of Interior, in recognition of the possible need for future shale oil production, undertook to evaluate industry interest in federal lands by offering selected tracts for lease sale. Suitable offers were not received and no sales were made. In 1971 the government initiated a second leasing effort aimed at encouraging the development of commercial operations on a controlled basis to allow an assessment of the economic cost and environmental impact of shale oil production. This prototype lease sale culminated in early 1974 in the sale of four tracts—two in Colorado and two in Utah, each about 5,000 acres. Terms were designed to encourage purchasers to proceed with serious development of commercial facilities. Even then, there was a tremendous range of bids, demonstrating the asymmetry of oil company interests, and the need to encourage these different assessments of potential energy sources in order to insure their most optimal development.

widely scattered and would have to be consolidated to form mineable blocks. Exxon's expenditures in oil shale totaled more than $16 million as of 1977. Of this, $8.8 million went to acquire oil shale reserves in the early 1960s, $4.9 million was spent on research, and $2.8 million on core drilling, administrative expenses, and the like. Exxon believed that, in addition to the major environmental and cost problems, the lack of a government policy concerning this potentially significant energy source was a significant factor in the delay of its commercial development.

Solar. Exxon has been investigating commercial uses of solar energy since 1970, when a research program was initiated to develop advanced low-cost photovoltaic devices. Throughout the 1970s, Exxon and other companies worked at developing terrestrial applications for photovoltaic devices, such as for use in microwave transmitters and ocean buoys. In 1979 Exxon's Solar Power Corporation recorded a 33 percent increase in unit sales of its solar photovoltaic products. It also obtained government contracts for several major demonstration projects in amounts sufficient to assure that 1980 sales would more than double the 1979 total.

Batteries and Fuel Cells. Recognizing the increasing electrification of energy and the need for efficiently storing solar-generated electricity, Exxon was carrying out research in electrochemistry. Fuel cells (devices that convert special fuels such as hydrogen to electricity) had been under study in Exxon Research & Engineering since 1960. In 1970 Exxon Enterprises entered a joint development effort with a French electrical equipment manufacturer to develop a more efficient power supply for electric vehicles, and to replace generators driven by engines or gas turbines. Program costs through 1975 exceeded $15 million, but technical progress had not met expectations.

Exxon Enterprises also initiated a battery development program in 1972 based on concepts developed by Exxon Research and Engineering Company. Batteries with increased energy densities were viewed as being useful as storage devices to help utilities meet peak electricity demands and as potential power sources for electric vehicles. Company experts felt the technological challenge was to develop new batteries that would store from two to five times more energy per unit weight than conventional batteries and be rechargeable hundreds of times without deterioration.

In 1978 Exxon's advanced battery division began selling a titanium disulfide button battery for use in watches, calculators, and similar products.

Laser Fusion. Exxon Research and Engineering Company was one of the sponsors of a program at the University of Rochester begun in 1972 to study the feasibility of laser-ignited fusion of light atoms (e.g., deuterium, tritium) for the economical generation of power. Out of an estimated program cost of $5.8 million through August 1975, Exxon Research and Engineering Company had contributed about $917,000. This included the cost of Exxon scientists on direct loan to the University.

The figures below give a brief profile of the financial extent of Exxon's efforts in these other-energy ventures:

	1970	1978	1979
		(in $ millions)	
Earnings from operations, after tax			
Operating results	$ 9	$ 20	$ 26
Business development cost	—	(10)	(11)
	9	10	15
Research and development costs	$ 1	$ 38	$ 61
Average capital employed	71	194	308
Capital expenditures	14	49	231

EXXON'S ACQUISITION OF RELIANCE ELECTRIC COMPANY

During 1979 Exxon acquired 100 percent ownership of the Reliance Electric Company of Cleveland, Ohio, at a cost of $1.2 billion. With 31,000 employees and principal operations or subsidiaries in 16 states and 14 foreign countries, Reliance and its affiliates were in the business of developing, manufacturing, marketing, and servicing a broad line of industrial equipment. The company's principal domestic operating organizations were: a rotating machinery group, which made electric motors; a drives and systems group, which made motor controls; a mechanical group, which made mechanical power products and components; a weighing and controls group, which was composed primarily of the Toledo Scale subsidiary; a telecommunications group, primarily a supplier to the telephone industry; and Federal Pacific Electric, a subsidiary which manufactured and marketed electric power distribution equipment.

Exxon's principal purpose in making the acquisition was to obtain the means for rapid development and marketing of a new energy-saving technology called alternating current synthesis (ACS). According to Exxon management, the technology promised a low-cost, efficient and reliable means of converting standard utility alternating current electricity into variable voltage and variable frequency electricity with resulting savings in power consumption. The new technology, which grew out of Exxon's research efforts on an electric car, had the potential for cutting the energy required by a standard industrial electric motor as much as 50 percent (the equivalent of 1 million barrels of crude oil a day)—there were an estimated 20 million electric motors in industrial use. Exxon felt it needed to acquire a well-established electrical equipment manufacturer to manufacture and market the ACS device with a high probability of success. Reliance Electric in 1978 had sales of $966 million and profits of $65 million; about 12 percent of its sales were in electric motors.

Exxon was also interested in Reliance Electric because of Exxon's high priority research into a new power system for automobiles. In 1979 Exxon had reached the prototype stage in its efforts and had come up with a hybrid car powered by both a battery-driven motor and a small gasoline engine. The electric motor, equipped with the new ACS device, provided the power for acceleration and steep grades; the gasoline engine took over on level stretches and served to recharge the batteries. Exxon felt the new system would be very fuel efficient even on larger cars.

EXXON ENTERPRISES

Exxon Enterprises, officially known as the new-business-development arm of Exxon, as of 1979 had invested over $500 million in some two dozen small new ventures, either by joining other investors in additional venture-capital deals or by funding new businesses created and run by its own employees. Most of these fledgling firms were far removed from Exxon's traditional business. Only two involved the energy industry—Solar Power and Daystar, both of which made equipment for collecting solar energy. Scan-Tron sold scholastic tests that were automatically graded by its own machine; Environmental Data produced instruments for measuring air pollution; Qyx marketed computer-controlled office typewriters; Graftek made graphite shafts for golf clubs and fishing rods; Delphi had developed a way to store voice messages in a computer; Zilog manufactured microprocessors to transmit and process data; Qume made high-speed printers; Vydec produced word-processing display terminals and text-editing systems; and Periphonics made switching computers. Other companies that were a part of Exxon Enterprises included Amtek, Xentex, Qwip, Micro-Bit Corporation, Magnex Corp., Intecom, and Optical Information Systems.

The corporate role of the Exxon Enterprises division was to develop options for Exxon's future, mainly in case Exxon's diversification into other energy sources was curtailed by political forces and also to take up the slack from the eventual decline of the oil business. Unlike other oil companies such as Mobil and Atlantic Richfield which chose to diversify by acquiring well-established companies, Exxon opted for buying ownership interests in small entrepreneurial companies which were just getting started and which appeared to have products capable of achieving $100 million in sales. The idea was to grow up with a new industry as opposed to entering an established industry. In addition, Exxon had a longer time horizon, less aversion to risk, more money, and a greater determination to "stick with the winners" than many other venture capital firms.

In 1980 Exxon Enterprises made a major move to consolidate its several ventures in the office equipment and office systems field. Fifteen of the small "startup" companies were molded into a new unit called Exxon Information Systems; the combined sales of these companies totaled $200 million in 1979 and nearly all were experiencing rapid growth (though none were profitable). A drive was also launched to recruit senior executives away from other information processing companies—IBM and Xerox in particular. *Business Week* quoted Ben Sykes, senior vice president of Exxon Enterprises, as saying, "We intend to be the systems supplier to the office market." The strategy seemed to be one of becoming a major supplier of advanced office systems equipment within three to five years using a "supermarket approach"—offering customers a wide variety of products (typewriters, word processors, fast printers, electronic files, voice-input devices, message units, and so on—see Exhibit 10) with the potential of computer-controlled coordination. Most industry observers believed that Exxon intended to challenge IBM and Xerox head-on in the office automation market which, by the end of the 1980s, was projected to be a $150–$200 billion industry.

Exxon indicated that while some of the companies in the Exxon Information Systems unit should be profitable in 1980, revenues would probably have to reach $1 billion before EIS as a whole became profitable. Management was prepared to be patient in integrating the 15 companies into a single systems company and in "growing" the unit into a profitable and highly competitive market position. Already though, EIS revenues placed it among the top 25 producers in office equipment and 1980 sales were expected to reach $400 million—nearly double 1979 sales.

Outside Exxon, opinions were mixed about the future role and success of the Exxon Information Systems unit:[8]

"Exxon Enterprises has the right pieces for the office of the future but they don't have the management to make it come together."

"It seems likely that the [office systems] business they are building now will rival, if not surpass, their oil business ultimately."

"The base of oil and gas operations is so big that even if [the information business] is spectacularly successful, it won't make much difference for a long time."

"I don't think Exxon senior management has even focused on the idea that the office automation business might be bigger than the oil business [or that this is] a realistic possibility."

"There are only one or maybe two other companies that have all the pieces that Exxon has. And even those two—IBM and Xerox—don't have them in the quantity and quality that Exxon has."

"Exxon doesn't have forever to get organized. In the next few years there are going to be a lot of significant announcements in office automation, and unless Exxon does something soon, they might not be one of the first ones in there."

"When you think of the resources that IBM throws into integrating its products, I don't see how Exxon can hope to be competitive."

"One thing Exxon has is a lot of cash. And that's one thing this market is going to need."

---

[8] The quotes are taken from "Exxon's Next Prey: IBM and Xerox," *Business Week*, April 28, 1980, pp. 92–103.

EXHIBIT 10
Examples of Exxon's New Office Products

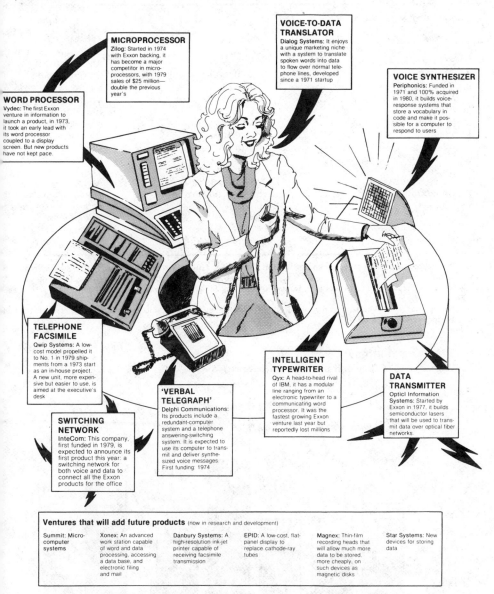

VOICE-TO-DATA TRANSLATOR
Dialog Systems: It enjoys a unique marketing niche with a system to translate spoken words into data to flow over normal telephone lines, developed since a 1971 startup

MICROPROCESSOR
Zilog: Started in 1974 with Exxon backing, it has become a major competitor in microprocessors, with 1979 sales of $25 million—double the previous year's

VOICE SYNTHESIZER
Periphonics: Funded in 1971 and 100% acquired in 1980, it builds voice-response systems that store a vocabulary in code and make it possible for a computer to respond to users

WORD PROCESSOR
Vydec: The first Exxon venture in information to launch a product, in 1973, it took an early lead with its word processor coupled to a display screen. But new products have not kept pace.

TELEPHONE FACSIMILE
Qwip Systems: A low-cost model propelled it to No. 1 in 1979 shipments from a 1973 start as an in-house project. A new unit, more expensive but easier to use, is aimed at the executive's desk

INTELLIGENT TYPEWRITER
Qyx: A head-to-head rival of IBM, it has a modular line ranging from an electronic typewriter to a communicating word processor. It was the fastest growing Exxon venture last year but reportedly lost millions

DATA TRANSMITTER
Optical Information Systems: Started by Exxon in 1977, it builds semiconductor lasers that will be used to transmit data over optical fiber networks.

'VERBAL TELEGRAPH'
Delphi Communications: Its products include a redundant-computer system and a telephone answering-switching system. It is expected to use its computer to transmit and deliver synthesized voice messages. First funding: 1974

SWITCHING NETWORK
InteCom: This company, first funded in 1979, is expected to announce its first product this year: a switching network for both voice and data to connect all the Exxon products for the office

Ventures that will add future products (now in research and development)

Summit: Micro-computer systems	Xonex: An advanced work station capable of word and data processing, accessing a data base, and electronic filing and mail	Danbury Systems: A high-resolution ink-jet printer capable of receiving facsimile transmission	EPID: A low-cost, flat-panel display to replace cathode-ray tubes	Magnex: Thin-film recording heads that will allow much more data to be stored, more cheaply, on such devices as magnetic disks	Star Systems: New devices for storing data

Source: *Business Week,* April 28, 1980, p. 94.

EXHIBIT 11

Top 16 Companies in Each Energy Source (1975 production)

Crude Oil and Natural Gas	Coal	Uranium
1. Exxon	Peabody	Kerr-McGee
2. Texaco	Conoco	Utah International
3. Standard of Indiana	Amax	Anaconda
4. Shell	Occidental	Union Carbide
5. Gulf	Pittston	Exxon
6. Mobil	U.S. Steel	Un. Nuclear
7. Arco	Ashland/Hunt	Rio Algom
8. Standard of California	Bethlehem	Homestake
9. Union	Peter Kiewit	Conoco
10. Sun	North American	Cotter
11. Getty/Skelly	Sohio	Dawn
12. Phillips	American Electric Power Co.	Pioneer
13. Cities Service	Westmoreland	Atlas
14. Conoco	Eastern Association	Western Nuclear*
15. Tenneco	Gulf	Federal Resources/ American Nuclear*
16. Marathon	Freeman-United	Getty/Skelly*

* These three companies were ranked in the top 16 in 1974. However, the mills owned by Getty/Skelly and by Western Nuclear were shut down during 1975, and the Federal/American mill tolled for Utah International during 1975. Sources: For crude oil and natural gas, *Annual Reports* and *Statistical Supplements*.

For coal, *Keystone News Bulletin*.

For uranium, Exxon estimate based upon ERDA mill production figures by state, annual reports, press releases, and mill capacities reported by ERDA.

EXHIBIT 12

1975 Concentration Ratios (percent)

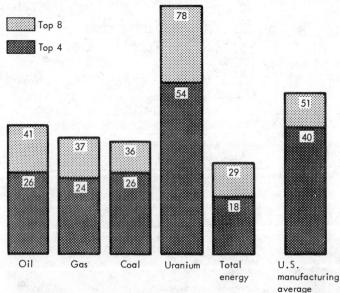

Source: Exxon, U.S.A.

Nevertheless, it was clear that Exxon was on the verge of a major effort to penetrate the market for information systems. The *1979 Annual Report* contained the following discussion:

> Vydec, Inc., the first venture of Exxon Enterprises to market a commercial product (in 1973), announced two new display-aided text editing products in 1979. The Model 2000 communicates with a broad range of computer and communicating terminals. The 4000 Series offers all features of the Model 2000 and is the only text editing machine which provides a full two-page display.
>
> Qwip Systems led the industry in shipments of telephone facsimile machines in the United States in 1979 and significantly increased sales in the international market. The number of QWIP units installed worldwide rose to over 55,000.
>
> The QYX electronic typewriter was Exxon Enterprises' fastest growing venture in 1979. The QYX division also introduced a sixth model, called Level One Plus.
>
> Sales of ZILOG microcomputer components and systems more than doubled, spurred by the successful introduction of the company's Z-8000 microcomputer "chip," which is the most advanced device of its type on the market.

OUTLOOK FOR THE FUTURE

Despite its diversification efforts, Exxon's future was by no means well charted. Barring major new oil and gas discoveries (which, even then, would only postpone the inevitable), its main business seemed on the verge of long-term decline. Oil and gas reserves were being depleted at a rate exceeding new discoveries and this condition was held by many industry experts and government officials as unlikely to change. Environmental regulations and price controls were making petroleum exploration ventures either difficult or unattractive financially—at least according to industry officials. So also was the windfall profits tax legislation passed by Congress in 1980.

Equally important was the fact that many members of Congress and a substantial portion of the general public were hostile to the major oil companies in general and in particular to oil companies like Exxon diversifying into other energy sources. In their view, allowing the giant oil companies to diversify and become "energy companies" was to risk the emergence of substantial monopoly control over energy on the part of these companies— see Exhibits 11 and 12.

18. Mobil Corporation*

Mobil began the 1970s as a company with assets of $8 billion, annual earnings of less than $500 million, and capital expenditures, exploration, and other outlays under $900 million. It ended the decade with assets of $28 billion, earnings of $2 billion, and outlays of nearly $4 billion. Mobil Corporation is the parent holding company of three operating units: Mobil Oil Corporation, Montgomery Ward, and Container Corporation of America. The Mobil Oil division accounted for the major portion of corporate revenues (almost 85 percent in 1979), but the nonenergy divisions had an important role in Mobil's total corporate strategy. In 1979, Mobil Corporation had business interests in more than 100 countries and employed 215,000 people; it ranked as the third-largest industrial corporation in the United States and the fifth largest in the world. Exhibit 1 provides a five-year financial summary of Mobil's operations.

History and Background

In 1866, Matthew Ewing, a carpenter, persuaded Hiram Bond Everest, a grocer, to invest in a venture to produce kerosine by distilling crude oil in a vacuum. Ewing believed his method would produce higher kerosine yields than the conventional distillation at atmospheric pressure. The increased yields did not transpire but an important difference did result; because of the lower temperatures used in the vacuum process, the residual undistilled oil proved to be of better lubricating quality than other oils on the market produced by the normal process. Ewing's method was patented in October 1866, and the Vacuum Oil Company was formed to capitalize upon it. Within a number of years, Vacuum Oil became a recognized leader in the industrial lubricant field.

The activities of the company attracted the interest of John D. Rockefeller, who purchased a controlling interest in 1879. In 1882, the Standard Oil Company of New York (Socony) was formed and became part of Rockefeller's Standard Oil Trust. When Rockefeller's Standard Oil empire was

---

* Prepared by Prof. Arthur A. Thompson, Jr., The University of Alabama, and Victor Gray.

EXHIBIT 1
Financial Summary (amounts are in $ millions except per share figures)

Year ended December 31	1979	1978[a]	1977[a]	1976[a]	1975[a]
Revenues	$ 48,241	$ 37,331	$ 34,443	$ 28,046	$ 22,355
Operating and other expenses	40,927	32,805	29,592	23,865	18,934
Interest and debt discount expense	459	420	397	315	224
Income taxes	4,848	2,975	3,428	2,893	2,374
Total costs and expenses	46,234	36,200	33,417	27,073	21,532
Net Income	2,007	1,131	1,026	973	823
per share, based on average shares outstanding ($)	9.46	5.34	4.85	4.69	4.04
Cash dividends	541	456	413	364	346
per share ($)	2.55	2.15	1.95	1.75	1.70
Return on average shareholders' equity	20.5%	13.0%	12.8%	13.3%	12.3%
Return on average capital employed[b]	16.0%	10.4%	9.9%	10.5%	10.0%
Net income per dollar of revenue	4.2¢	3.0¢	3.0¢	3.5¢	3.7¢
Energy earnings per gallon sold	4.4¢	2.4¢	2.1¢	2.0¢	1.6¢
Capital expenditures, exploration, and other outlays[c]	3,812	2,175	1,786	2,485	1,469
At December 31					
Current assets	11,889	9,800	9,174	8,157	6,160
Current liabilities	11,170	8,686	7,632	6,844	5,226
Working capital	719	1,114	1,542	1,313	934
Investments and long-term receivables	2,030	1,844	1,657	1,504	1,998
Net properties, plants, and equipment	13,103	10,816	9,973	9,366	6,885
Total assets	27,506	22,880	21,182	19,323	15,257
Long-term debt	2,962	3,047	3,310	3,214	2,172
Shareholders' equity	10,513	9,037	8,358	7,739	6,897
per share, based on shares outstanding at end of year ($)	49.54	42.63	39.45	36.56	33.86
Number of shares outstanding (000)	212,229	211,978	211,852	211,663	203,729
Number of shareholders	274,200	268,000	268,100	265,200	229,000
Number of employees	213,500	207,700	200,700	199,500	73,200

Mobil's 54% voting interest in the Marcor companies was accounted for on the equity method through July 1, 1976, when Mobil became the 100% owner of these companies.

(a) Restated to reflect adoption of FAS 19, Financial Accounting and Reporting by Oil and Gas Producing Companies. Per-share amounts and shares outstanding have been adjusted for the two-for-one stock split.

(b) Net income plus income applicable to minority interests plus interest expense net of tax divided by the sum of average shareholders' equity, debt, capital lease obligations, and minority interests.

(c) Includes capital expenditures of majority owned unconsolidated companies and acquisitions.

Source: 1979 Annual Report.

broken up in 1911, Socony emerged as one of the 33 individual companies, with Vacuum as another. From 1911 until 1931, Socony and Vacuum separately set about building, acquiring, and expanding their operations. Vacuum's interests were toward additional refining capacity, while Socony sought production interests—since the break-up left it devoid of production facilities. Vacuum was recognized worldwide for its industrial lubricants. Socony had marketing operations throughout the United States and the Far East, but mainly in the field of fuels. The interests, operation, and facilities of the two companies complemented each other, and a court-approved merger was consummated in July 1931, with a new name being chosen: Socony-Vacuum Corporation. In 1934, the company's name was changed to Socony-Vacuum Oil Company, Inc. By 1955, the brand name for Socony-Vacuum's gasoline and lubricants—Mobil—had become so well recognized that the company decided to include it in its corporate name. The firm's name was thus changed to Socony-Mobil Oil Company, Inc.

When the Suez Crisis of 1956 led to the closing of the canal, the traditional route of Middle East oil to its major markets in Europe had to be changed. The oil industry's reaction in developing alternative patterns of supply was such that in 1957, when the canal was reopened, the world-market was oversupplied. The glut reduced prices and earnings of the major oil companies, and several were forced to revise their strategies. Socony-Mobil retrenched and reorganized, after posting combined earnings declines of nearly $100 million in 1957 and 1958. In 1959, its four U.S. subsidiaries were merged into two major divisions: Mobil Oil Company, which operated in the United States and Canada, and Mobil International Oil Company, which had responsibility for operations throughout the rest of the world. In 1960, a new division was added: the Mobil Chemical Company.

A further name change was made in 1966, to Mobil Oil Corporation. In 1976, when Mobil acquired Montgomery Ward and Container Corporation of America, it was deemed desirable to form the Mobil Corporation as the holding company for all the various Mobil interests.

INTERNAL RESTRUCTURING

In 1959, Mobil—under the leadership of Albert J. Nickerson, president and later chairman—reorganized its corporate structure. Divisions were organized as profit centers with an increase in authority for decision making. From 1959 to 1966, 11,000 U.S. employees were removed from the payroll, many through attrition or early retirement. Looking back at the reorganization, Nickerson commented:

> . . . the company had become noncompetitive. Costs were too high. There was confusion as to accountability, and lines of communication were unclear.
> We created a new organization structure, centralized policy formulation, decentralized administration, and reduced expenses . . .

Along with the organizational changes, management renewed its dedication to improving the ability of Mobil to achieve planned profitable growth. Ten years later, Nickerson, then chairman of the board, was able to report to the stockholders these improvements during the ten-year period: an increase in sales revenues from $3.5 billion to $7.1 billion, a gain in total assets from $3.3 billion to $6.9 billion, and an increase in dividend payments from $97 million to $207.5 million. Mobil's earnings per share rose 135 percent during the ten-year period, the largest increase of the five leading U.S. based international oil companies. In addition, in 1969, Mobil alleged it had:

1. A lean, purposeful organization well structured to take on the problems of the 1970s and 1980s.
2. A management succession "pipeline" filled with high-potential individuals.
3. Heightened skill in planning and in seeking out and evaluating investment opportunities.

Mobil, in trying to manage change more effectively, claimed a strong commitment to long-range analysis and strategic planning. The company stated that its planning group was responsible for projecting and anticipating "technological, social, economic, governmental, and population factors that may affect Mobil's business as much as 30 years ahead."

In 1966, Mobil Oil realized substantial additions to its crude oil supplies, mainly in Canada and the Middle East. Gross output of crude oil was more than double 1956 production levels. A new impetus in refining operations was also evident in 1966. Modernization of a number of plants was begun to allow production of additional higher value products and more efficient manpower utilization. It was anticipated that the modernization would reduce both maintenance and operating costs, as well as allow for the installation of antipollution equipment. Mobil Chemical achieved record sales during 1966 and introduced Hefty plastic bags for home food storage; its chemical business ranged across industrial chemicals, plastics, paints, packaging material, agricultural products, and gases.

During 1958–69, Nickerson continued Mobil's efforts to strengthen its crude oil exploration and production segments and bring supply capabilities more in line with the company's refinery capacity. For many years, Mobil had had the lowest self-sufficiency ratio of the Seven Sisters and it had a long-standing reputation in its production and exploration efforts of "arriving in the oil patch too late with too little."

In 1969, the company withdrew from the domestic retail fertilizer business, selling a major portion of its retail fertilizer assets and business to Swift and Company at a loss of $22 million or 22 cents per share. In explaining the company's move, Mobil's chairman observed, "We didn't do the proper analysis we should have. We didn't buy competent management, and when they left, we were oil men running a business we didn't know much about."

MOBIL'S NEW MANAGEMENT TEAM

In 1969, Mobil got a new top management team: Rawleigh Warner, Jr., chairman (Exhibit 2) and William P. Tavoulareas, president (Exhibit 3). Warner has been described as a man who appears to be a diplomat rather than a business man. He is an urbane, trim, dapper executive who gets

EXHIBIT 2

Rawleigh Warner, Jr.:
- 1921   Born, Chicago. Father, chairman of Pure Oil Company.
- 1943   B.A. (cum laude), Princeton University.
- 1946   Secretary-treasurer: Warner-Bard Company.
- 1948   Continental Oil Company, various positions; left as assistant treasurer.
- 1953   Joined Mobil as assistant to the financial director of Socony-Vacuum overseas supply company.
- 1958   Manager of economics department.
- 1959   Regional vice president for Middle East.
- 1960   Executive vice president of Mobil International.
- 1963   President of Mobil International.
- 1964   Director, executive vice president, and member of executive committee, responsible for Mobil International and Mobil Petroleum Company, Inc.
- 1965   President of Mobil.
- 1969   Chairman of the board of directors and chief executive officer.

Director of Time, Inc., American Telephone and Telegraph Company, American Petroleum Institute, Caterpillar Tractor Company, Chemical New York Corporation and Chemical Bank, American Express Company. Republican.

EXHIBIT 3

William P. Tavoulareas:
- 1919   Born, Brooklyn. Father a butcher.
- 1941   B.B.A. St. John's University.
- 1947   Joined Mobil as an accountant.
- 1948   J.D., St. John's University.
- 1957   Manager of Middle East accounting department of Middle East Affairs.
- 1959   Manager of corporate planning and analysis department.
- 1961   Vice president of plans and programs of Mobil's international petroleum division.
- 1963   Vice president of supply and distribution and international sales.
- 1965   Director, member of the executive committee and a senior vice president Mobil.
- 1967   President of North American Division.
- 1969   President and vice chairman of executive committee of Mobil.

Director of Bankers Trust Company, General Foods Corporation. Democrat.

intricately involved in the day-to-day operations of the company. Warner maintains an active role in Mobil's financial and legal affairs and has taken a special interest in the public relations of Mobil, particularly those dealing with government. Regarding Mobil's public relations, Warner explained the company's strategy:

> Our posture of reacting when we were not properly treated has made our adversaries think a second time about zinging us. They may still zing us, but with facts and not emotions.

After he became chairman and chief executive in 1969, Warner surprised many people in the oil world by appointing William P. Tavoulareas as president of the company. Unlike Warner, whose father was an oil man, Tavoulareas was the first in his family to enter the oil industry. One observer described Tavoulareas as "an irreverent, fast-talking numbers man who has the crucial Rockefeller talent for lightning arithmetic." Another described him thus:

> Tavoulareas is now widely regarded as the ablest of the major oilmen. He sits in shirt-sleeves, talking at top speed, blinking, twitching, and staring, running to the telephone like an imp let loose; saying "gimme" and "lemme," "whadda ya want?" In the Middle East, Tav was determined to increase Mobil's share, and was much more prepared to consider new partnership arrangements, which antagonized the other sisters, but also brought him closer to the producers; and he formed a close friendship with Yamani in Saudi Arabia.[1]

Mobil is regarded as one of the best managed companies in the oil business, with much of Mobil's success being attributed to Warner and Tavoulareas. The company has been described as a financier-lawyer-businessman type company rather than an oilman-geologist company. The people Warner has chosen to work with him talk in terms of *managing assets* and *portfolios*. A term used by Mobil to describe the Marcor acquisition was *risk aversion investment*. Some suggest these terms are not the typical jargon of the oil industry. Warner has developed within the company a strong commitment to planning, and many analysts see planning as Mobil's strongest management characteristic. Tavoulareas said of planning:

> The real virtue of centralized planning is that it provides a person whose main responsibility is to question what the operator is doing. By his very nature, the person charged with day-to-day operations doesn't have time to worry about tomorrow's problems. The planner, on the other hand, can look over his shoulder and try to anticipate what kind of environment we will be operating in the future and how we can take advantage of it. In the end, his decisions will help the operator do his job better.[2]

---

[1] Anthony D. Sampson, *The Seven Sisters* (New York, N.Y.: The Viking Press), p. 193.

[2] As quoted in *Dun's,* December 1972, p. 38.

Under Warner and Tavoulareas, Mobil continued the search for additional crude to try to bring crude oil supplies into better balance with refinery capacity. Exploration and production outlays rose from 19 percent of Mobil's capital expenditures in 1969 to 67 percent in 1979—see Exhibit 4. Even

EXHIBIT 4
Mobil's Capital Expenditures, 1965–1979 ($ millions)

Function	1965	1970	1971	1972	1973	1974	1975	1976	1977	1978	1979
Exploration	95	124	127	150	148	189	243	208	280	253	358
Production	167	244	266	360	559	753	466	567	499	715	793
Marine	23	49	64	78	160	95	139	65	28	41	81
Refining	67	160	244	268	215	334	242	151	168	233	298
Marketing	116	226	256	252	190	113	114	102	122	162	186

Source: *Annual Reports, 1965–1979.*

so, Mobil's crude reserves declined slightly in both 1978 and 1979—an outcome which tended to reinforce the company's long-standing short position in crude oil. And, like other transnational oil companies, Mobil had to scramble to maintain its sources of crude oil supply in foreign countries, particularly in the volatile OPEC nations. Exhibit 5 is indicative of the extent

EXHIBIT 5
Mobil's Loss of Holdings in Foreign Countries

Country	Mobil's Interest
Iraq	Nationalized 1972/73.
Libya	Nationalized 51 percent in 1973.
Nigeria	55 percent interest sought by national government.
Qatar	Mobil's 11.875 percent of Qatar Petroleum Co. Ltd. nationalized 1976.
Venezuela	Nationalized 1976.
Saudi Arabia	Arabian government moved to gain full control of Mobil's 15 percent interest in Aramco.
Iran	20-year agreement of oil supplies whereby the participating companies acquire oil at prices that will substantially increase Iran's take from the operation. Mobil's share, 7 percent.

Source: *1976 Annual Report.*

to which Mobil has encountered diminishing control over its foreign investments. The following statement in Mobil's *1979 Annual Report* highlights the risks involved:

> Since the early 1970s many producing country governments have assumed an increasing control of the oil industry within their jurisdictions. In several countries terms of ownership and operation are not settled as yet.

In Saudi Arabia negotiations contemplate government acquisition of substantially all of Aramco's assets and the establishment of future arrangements. Under these proposed arrangements Aramco will provide management and technical services, will conduct an exploration program for the government, and will receive certain payments. Also, the U.S.-owner companies will have access through Aramco to substantial volumes of crude oil at a competitive price under a long-term contract.

In Iran the government has taken over all producing and refining operations and in effect has announced that it considers the prior arrangements to be no longer operative.

In Nigeria the government's participation in Mobil's exploration and producing operations was increased from 55 percent to 60 percent effective July 1, 1979. The amount of compensation remains to be settled.

In addition, producing country governments have nationalized or negotiated a participation in Mobil's producing, refining, and pipeline assets and operations in Venezuela (100 percent), Qatar (100 percent), Abu Dhabi (60 percent), Libya (51 percent), and Iraq (100 percent). Compensation has generally been based on net asset values used for local tax purposes.

In all of these countries except Iran and Iraq, Mobil or its affiliate has continued as the concession operator or is providing management and technical services for stated payments, and, except in Iran and Venezuela, has access to quantities of crude oil under equity agreements and/or at competitive prices under long-term contracts.

. . . Mobil is hopeful that the ultimate compensation received will be at least equal to the carrying value of the assets that have been, or will be, given up. It is clear the ultimate compensation will be substantially less than the economic value of the reserves that have been, or will be, given up.

Tavoulareas cited two major objectives for Mobil's oil business: (1) to increase crude supplies all around the world so as to bring the company closer to self-sufficiency in supplying its refineries with crude oil and (2) to maximize the efficiency with which the supplies of crude were carried to refineries, and refined products to their marketing areas. To assist in achieving these objectives, Tavoulareas indicated that Mobil's "exploration program around the world is proceeding above historical levels." Nonetheless, between 1965 and 1979, 60 percent of Mobil's capital expenditures were in the United States, and a significant part of its foreign exploration and production efforts were in the Middle East, especially Saudi Arabia. According to one of Mobil's directors:

> It makes sense to put your investment where the oil is, and Saudi Arabia's reserves are far larger than any other country's. The money we invest in Saudi ventures should help assure our access to this crude in the years ahead when oil supplies are tighter. Mobil has had more than 30 years of mutually beneficial relationships with the Saudis.

Examples of key Mobil projects in Saudi Arabia include:

1. A 1-million-barrel-a-year lube oil refinery, a 30–70 Mobil/Saudi venture.
2. A 700,000-barrel-a-year petrolube plant, a 29–71 Mobil/Saudi project.

3. A 250,000-barrel-a-day export refinery, a 50–50 Mobil/Saudi deal.
4. A 750-mile, 48-inch crude pipeline, designed, constructed, and managed by Mobil but 100 percent Saudi-owned.
5. A petrochemical complex, a 50–50 Mobil/Saudi investment.
6. A dry cargo shipping company, a 60–40 Mobil/Saudi project.

These ventures may prove to be even more beneficial to Mobil. In 1980, Saudi Arabia increased its efforts to refine and market its oil rather than just selling its crude direct to the major oil companies; the Saudi government began offering its oil on a priority basis to companies who were willing to finance a joint petrochemical venture with them—reportedly the Saudis were offering the right to buy 1,000 barrels daily for every $2.5 million in equity investment. Because Mobil had been active in organizing partnerships with the Saudis, it seemed to be in a position to be hurt least by the Saudi effort to integrate forward into the industry.

Among the Seven Sisters, only Royal Dutch/Shell was more active than Mobil in the Middle East. And although Mobil's foreign exploration program was not as extensive as that of the other major companies, it had come close to maintaining its access to crude reserves and supplies (see Exhibit 6). In

EXHIBIT 6
Mobil's Production of Crude Oil and Natural Gas Liquids (000s of barrels a day)

	1978	1977	1976	1975	1974
U.S. onshore	297	296	311	330	351
U.S. offshore	72	66	64	68	69
Total U.S.	369	362	375	398	420
Foreign	1,748	2,008	1,781	1,842	2,042
Worldwide	2,117	2,370	2,156	2,240	2,462

Source: *1978 Annual Report.*

1974, Mobil was successful in negotiating an increase in its ownership share of Aramco (a joint venture of Mobil, Texaco, Exxon, Socal, and Saudi Arabia) from 10 percent to 15 percent—a move which as of 1980 gave Mobil access to about 540,000 barrels daily of Saudi crude without the risk of exploration (albeit did carry risk of a loss of Mobil's $223 million investment in Aramco in the event of nationalization). Outside the Middle East, Mobil's foreign exploration efforts were focused in the North Sea (where in 1980 Britain and Norway raised their oil production tax rates to 70 percent and 82 percent respectively), in the Canadian Atlantic (where Mobil was rumored to be on the verge of important new discoveries), off Cameroun in West Africa, in Tunisia (North Africa), and in West Germany.

Mobil's exploration expenditures in the United States have produced mixed results. For example, wells in Prudhoe Bay in Alaska yielded an increase of some 200 million barrels of crude reserves to Mobil—the company has a 5 percent ownership in the Trans-Alaska Pipeline System. In 1979, a promising gas discovery was made offshore Alabama in Mobile Bay. On the other hand, Destin Anticline, in the Gulf of Mexico, cost Mobil $227 million in lease bonuses; the increase to crude reserves: zero. Mobil's efforts in the Baltimore Canyon area have also resulted in dry wells.

Moreover, despite Mobil's record expenditures for exploration, industry experts regard Mobil's approach to exploration and development as one of the less adventurous in the industry. The company has employed a strategy of maximizing recovery of oil from fields already in production through expanded use of technology such as waterflooding and thermal recovery. About 70 percent of Mobil's U.S. production of crude oil in 1976 came from fields where improved recovery processes were used. Mobil's lack of bold effort is suggested by the number of exploratory wells it drilled in the United States in 1976 relative to other majors: Texaco 647, Gulf 629, Exxon 613, Mobil 377. When the companies which do not have interests in the Middle East are included in the comparison, Mobil's efforts faded even further (for example: Standard Indiana, 781; Shell [United States], 715). On the list of companies drilling the "very risky" wildcat wells in 1976, Mobil was not among the top ten drillers.

Joint ventures have frequently been favored by Mobil in its exploratory programs and in bidding for leases on undeveloped properties:

> Mobil prefers to bid jointly with other companies both large and small because it believes it is prudent to hedge against the risk of failure by seeking a smaller interest in many tracts rather than a larger interest in a few, and limited capital is available for investment in exploration and producing because of the high risk nature of offshore investment.
>
> In selecting partners with whom to bid, primary consideration is given to the financial capabilities of the company as well as to the potential partners' technical expertise. With the initiation of leasing high cost frontier areas, it is increasingly important that a company be financially capable of providing its share not only of the lease bonus, but also of the subsequent expense for wildcat drilling and development if hydrocarbons are found. The ability of a company to add data and expertise to the joint venture is very important given the risky nature of offshore exploration. The interpretation of data available at the surface as a means of predicting the state of nature many miles below the surface is not an exact science, and interpretation by other qualified geologists and geophysicists is important.[3]

UPSTREAM ACTIVITIES FROM CRUDE PRODUCTION

To complement its crude supplies, Mobil had, over the years, acquired a substantial fleet of tankers. The company had been able to reduce its trans-

---

[3] From a statement by Mobil to the House Subcommittee on Monopolies and Commercial Law, 1976. (Serial No. 48, Part 1, Joint Ventures, p. 235.)

portation cost by the use of 18 large crude carriers (VLCCs) and good access to low-cost charter vessels. Plans were underway to convert the company's larger VLCCs from steam turbine to more cost-efficient diesel propulsion. In recent years, Mobil's tanker fleet had operated profitably.

Mobil's involvement in pipelines ranks fifth behind the other four U.S. Sisters, with approximately a 6.8 percent share of the market. Mobil ranked fourth in 1951, with 8.4 percent of the total U.S. market in interstate oil pipeline movements. In 1976, the company had a complete or partial interest in 24,000 miles of crude oil, natural gas, natural gas liquids, and product pipelines in the United States and 17,500 miles in foreign countries.

In 1976, Mobil had 7 U.S. refineries, along with 10 wholly owned and 21 partly owned foreign refineries located in 21 different countries. During the late 1970s, Mobil ranked as the industry leader, in both the United States and worldwide, in upgrading refining facilities to increase yields of gasoline and distillate fuels, including home heating oil.

After the 1911 split-up of Standard Oil, many of the new companies had concentrated marketing operations in clearly defined areas of the United States. Mobil's home ground and strong area for 20 years following the split was Connecticut, Maine, Massachusetts, New Hampshire, Rhode Island, Vermont, and New York. Mobil's claim to these areas was through its Standard of New York (Socony) subsidiary. Texas and Oklahoma were also major areas, through the wholly owned subsidiary of the Magnolia Petroleum Company. By and large, these areas still remain the company's retail marketing stronghold. Exhibit 7 shows Mobil's share of gasoline sales in recent years.

Mobil has always been an industry leader in lubricants, and this is a continuing strategic goal. In April 1976, the company introduced into the U.S. market Mobil 1, a synthesized engine lubricant for passenger vehicles, and Delvac 1 for commercial vehicles. Both lubricants improve gas mileage, reduce engine wear, and provide faster cold-weather starts. Demand has been strong since their introduction, with U.S. sales increases of 135 percent and 250 percent, respectively, in 1979. Mobil Super Unleaded gasoline was introduced in 1978 and has received wide acceptance among motorists needing a higher-octane unleaded fuel for satisfactory performance. Mobil's management feels that through these two new products, especially the synthesized lubricants, they have obtained an edge on the competition.

In recent years, Mobil's overall marketing strategy has been to restrict marketing investment in new outlets to areas where significant growth would be likely; older, less-efficient outlets have been closed, and self-serve stations have increased. At year end 1979, there were 17,749 Mobil retail outlets in the United States; abroad, the total was 20,088. Both totals reflected a continuing downward trend. However, the average annual gasoline sales in Mobil's U.S. stations increased 33 percent during the 1975–78 period—a reflection of Mobil's success in upgrading throughputs and profits in its retail outlets.

EXHIBIT 7
Top 20 U.S. Companies' Percentage of Gasoline Sales

Company	1970	1972	1973	1974*	1975
Texaco	8.12%	8.15%	8.09%	8.07%	7.89%
Shell	7.85	7.20	7.52	7.39	6.85
Exxon	7.41	6.86	7.62	7.38	7.32
Standard of Indiana	7.30	6.96	6.99	6.99	7.05
Gulf	7.12	6.50	6.73	6.55	6.22
Mobil	6.59	6.41	6.53	6.54	6.00
Socal	4.63	4.67	4.79	4.90	4.58
Arco	5.54	4.89	4.41	3.98	3.95
Phillips	3.96	4.07	4.05	3.81	3.90
Sun	4.14	3.84	3.72	3.72	3.48
Union	3.28	2.95	3.16	3.11	3.13
Continental	2.34	2.34	1.81	1.81	1.78
Cities Service	2.05	1.80	1.69	1.70	1.66
Marathon	1.73	1.58	1.52	1.49	1.49
Ashland	1.26	1.49	1.37	1.32	1.35
Standard (Ohio)	1.45	1.21	1.22	1.14	1.01
Clark	0.66	1.14	1.26	0.99	1.00
Amerada Hess	0.64	1.01	0.98	0.92	0.89
Tenneco	0.93	0.83	0.80	0.91	0.95
American Petrofina	0.64	0.63	0.80	0.85	0.99
British Petroleum Oil	1.40	1.12	0.66	0.54	0.63
Kerr-McGee	0.77	0.29	0.30	0.36	0.34
Murphy	0.75	0.66	0.62	0.67	0.64
Top Four	30.7	29.2	30.2	29.8	29.11
Top Eight	54.6	51.6	52.7	51.8	49.86
Top 20	80.0	76.7	77.5	75.9	71.49

* Ranked by 1974 sales.
Source: National Petroleum News, *Factbook Issues.*

DIVERSIFICATION

Following the corporation's internal reorganization during the late 1950s and early 1960s, the top management of Mobil determined that one corporate objective should be some kind of meaningful diversification. Mobil's performance had been questioned and criticized by some petroleum analyists for the small proportion of its earnings derived from domestic operations; for instance, from 1973 through 1975, domestic earnings averaged only 35 percent of total earnings. Moreover, Mobil, like many companies in the industry, fully realized that at some point the opportunity to productively spend dollars on petroleum exploration would diminish. The question thus became where to invest the company's cash flow of some $1.5 billion. In addressing this issue, Mobil's chairman, Rawleigh Warner, stated:

> . . . The oil industry in the past few years has been undergoing major changes in its relations with government in practically every country where it operates. Governments are interfering. The U.S. government certainly is. The Federal

Energy Administration tells us to whom we must sell our crude and what we can charge. They threaten us with a federal oil company that will be a yardstick to how effective we are. There are 3,000 bills before Congress, each of which will do something to the oil industry . . . an alert management doesn't ignore changes or challenges.

We concluded that there was a lot of wisdom in diversifying into a large business completely apart from the energy industry because we could see the government becoming more and more involved in energy activities . . . so we went out, picked an area in which we believed the government is not as interested as it is in the energy field.[4]

Mobil's acquisition interests were directed toward companies which (1) were not subject to the same business cycles and risks as the petroleum industry and (2) were not likely to attract as much government intervention. Mobil's executive vice president for planning and economics, Lawrence M. Woods, headed the team created in 1968 that searched for a company which would fit Mobil's diversification strategy. During a five-year search, Mobil considered over 100 different firms in 25 industries. Eventually, Woods reported that Marcor, Inc. (the merged parent of Montgomery Ward and Container Corporation of America) appeared to satisfy the major criteria that Mobil had set: a low price/earnings multiple, a large share of earnings from U.S. operations, a large enough firm to impact Mobil's earnings, a management team whose track record (in this case turning the sagging business of Montgomery Ward around) was satisfactory.

In 1973, Warner obtained approval from Mobil's board to purchase 4.5 percent of Marcor's common stock. The purchase was to be made in a brokerage house's name in an effort to take a closer look at the company as a potential investment without revealing Mobil's interest. After having secretly bought 1,235,000 shares at an average price of $20 per share, Mobil approached the management of Marcor about increasing the investment to 51 percent. On June 14, 1974, Warner and Tavoulareas flew to Chicago to meet with the management of Marcor. Leo H. Schoenhofen, Marcor's chairman, had a previous engagement, but the company's president, Edward S. Donnell, and Gordon R. Worley, the vice president, met with the two Mobil executives. Commenting on the meeting, Warner said:

We told them we had one thing we wanted to tell them and one thing we wanted to propose to them. They were very surprised, just as I would be if someone walked into my office and told me they owned 10 million shares of Mobil. But it was all very cordial and businesslike . . . we told them we had financial resources that may be helpful to them, that we don't want to run their business, but we would be very interested as investors.[5]

Marcor's management was receptive and formal negotiations were initiated.

---

[4] As quoted by H. Lee Silberman, "Appear to Reason," *Finance Magazine*, November 1975, pp. 9–13.

[5] As quoted by *Business Week*, June 29, 1974, p. 29.

In an effort to get to know the company from the inside, four Mobil executives were appointed to the Marcor board. They reported no surprises, and in fact reported some strengths that had not previously been identified. An acquisition agreement was reached whereby 3,577,970 shares of Mobil Corporation's common stock and $673 million principal amount of Mobil Corporation's 8.5 percent debentures due 2001 were issued to Marcor shareholders. The total cost to Mobil of acquiring Marcor was $1.7 billion, approximately 13 times Marcor's 1975 earnings. The merger became effective on July 1, 1976.

The merger had an appeal to both companies. Short-term loans for working capital at that time were costing Marcor up to 16 percent and since part of Mobil's tender included $200 million for a new series of Marcor's voted preferred stock, this gave Marcor a cash inflow of $200 million at 7 percent. From Mobil's point of view, for the equivalent of one year's cash flow, Mobil had obtained two companies which in 1976 would add roughly $150 million to its net income from domestic operations.

Mobil made it plain from the beginning of new operations that it had no plans to continually pump further working capital into Marcor. Mobil intended for the two major companies which comprised Marcor (Montgomery Ward and the Container Corporation of America) to stand on their own feet. Addressing the question of autonomy, Warner said,

> I don't see an operating role for Mobil in Ward for one fundamental reason. We are not retailers; we learned that a long time ago, that you can't anoint someone and expect him to do an effective job in a business that he doesn't know. You can question a commitment to autonomy if we took over another oil company, but retailing is a unique exercise. We have not been involved in it except for gas, which is totally different . . .
>
> When our diversification quest finally led us to Ward, we told our board and management committee that we weren't deep enough to divert our energies to another business. We weren't broadbased in our management skills, so any acquisition had to have good management.[6]

Edward S. Donnell, the President of Marcor, said,

> [We] will check our management style against theirs. We will have financial counsel and advice, and a lot of good, hard pragmatic questions in planning areas. But there will be full freedom in operating areas. Mobil people aren't retailers and they don't have the people to run the business; we're people intensive and they are capital intensive.[7]

After the merger, Frederick H. Veach, Ward's vice president for corporate planning, expressed it in a different way:

> We wondered if we would get the mushroom treatment. First, they [new owners] put you in the dark. Then they cover you with manure. Then they cultivate

---

[6] As quoted by *Chain Store Age Executive*, September, 1976.

[7] Ibid.

you. Then they let you steam for a while. Finally, they can you. We have been looking for evidence, but haven't found any of these steps. Maybe it's too early, but we can depend on everything they have said. I have faith and confidence, naive as this may be.[8]

Formalized planning has been a strong feature at Mobil and Mobil's management quickly pressed Marcor's management to formalize its planning. "We want them to format what they have already been doing and what we have institutionalized since 1959. This will make things more understandable to us," said Woods. On the subject of long-range planning, Veach said,

> There's always resistance to formal planning. First, line managers see it as a threat to their authority. Second, they feel their business instincts will take care of problems better. Third, they don't really want to be as open as they think they have to be. Fourth, most incentive compensation plans are based on short-term results, so they couldn't care less about the future. And finally, managers aren't interested in long range plans because they get promoted or otherwise judged on the basis of what happens this year. These are generic obstacles.[9]

MARCOR, INC.

On October 31, 1968, when the stockholders of Montgomery Ward and Container Corporation of America voted to combine the assets and managements of the two companies, they created Marcor, Inc., a diversified, marketing-oriented, multibillion dollar company that brought together two leaders of the merchandising and packaging industries. Montgomery Ward was a primary marketer of consumer goods and services, with sales of almost $2 billion and profits of $33 million. Container Corporation provided a variety of packaging materials for consumer and industrial products; it had 1968 sales of $469 million and profits of $31.6 million.

After the merger, Marcor implemented no basic changes in the names, administration, or operation of its two subsidiaries. Montgomery Ward and Container continued to have their own boards of directors, officers, administrative staffs, and service functions. And each continued its own programs of growth and expansion in merchandising, marketing, and manufacturing.

The role of Marcor executives in the operation of Ward and Container was a blend of outside counselor and parent. While they expected to preserve what was best in each of the companies, they believed Marcor would introduce a new degree of objectivity and independent scrutiny, permitting a fresh look at both operations. Marcor's management planned to remain small and "free form" so that it could respond quickly and effectively to new problems. It planned to draw freely on the management capabilities of both Ward and Container from time to time, assembling task forces to tackle

---

[8] Ibid.
[9] Ibid.

particular projects, and disbanding or reshaping the force as each problem was solved or redefined. Marcor's officers expected the parent company to experience almost continuous restructuring and augmentation as its role evolved. Marcor's executives concentrated their effort and attention on developing and implementing broad corporate objectives.

One of the most direct and immediate benefits Marcor wanted to produce was the infusion of many of the specialized management skills and techniques of each company into the other's management force. Marcor executives would direct and channel the available management talent into critical areas first, while evaluating additional opportunities in all parts of both operations. Marcor also served as a focal point for determining what management resources of one company were available for the other.

Part of Marcor's task was to combine the development programs of each of the subsidiaries to provide "cross training" of the management. Exhibit 8 shows financial highlights of Marcor for three years prior to the Mobil's acquisition.

MONTGOMERY WARD

Ward was founded in 1872 by Aaron Montgomery Ward and his brother-in-law, George R. Thorne. The company was exclusively a mail order sales firm until 1926 when it opened the first of the chain of retail stores in Marysville, Kansas. Following World War II, when competitors undertook giant building and modernization programs, Ward—under the direction of Sewell Avery—refrained from store expansion for fear of impending return to the depressionary era of the 1930s. For 16 years, no new stores were opened—a strategic decision which has become one of the legendary mistakes in all of business history. In 1957, new management began the tremendous task of rebuilding what had become an outdated and outmoded chain and trying to regain the last ground that Sears had easily captured.

From 1958 to 1969, Ward invested $500 million in modernizing and moving the thrust of its retail operations from the small town to the metropolitan suburb, while developing and installing computerized systems for reducing costs and improving efficiencies in handling catalog sales. The company's diversification program added new markets to its operations.

At the time of its acquisition, Ward was the third-largest catalog and nonfood retail merchandiser in the United States, trailing Sears and J. C. Penny (see Exhibit 9). In 1976, the company sold through 2,300 retail and catalog outlets and employed approximately 100,000 employees. The company operated 439 retail stores having more than 58 million square feet of gross space, over half of which was in retail selling areas.

Ward semiannually published two large general merchandise catalogs, together with a number of small seasonal catalogs. Catalog sales were made through direct mail, catalog order desks in retail stores, 550 catalog stores, and some 1,300 independently owned sale agencies. A support network of

EXHIBIT 8
Summary of Marcor Operations, 1973–1975 (prior to acquisition by Mobil)

Summary of Earnings ($ millions)

	1975	1974	1973
Net sales	$4,822.3	$4,667.5	$4,077.4
Costs and expenses:			
Cost of goods sold	$3,517.8	$3,379.9	$2,951.5
Operating, selling, administrative and research expenses	902.6	886.6	818.3
Interest expense	145.6	174.9	127.5
Provision for taxes on income†	121.1	105.7	83.4
Net earnings before change in accounting policy*,†	$ 135.2	$ 120.4	$ 96.7
Effect of change in accounting policy related to store pre-operating expense	—	4.7	—
Net earnings*,†	$ 135.2	$ 115.7	$ 96.7

Financial Data ($ millions except per share amounts)

	1975	1974	1973
Accounts receivable—parent and consolidated subsidiaries	$ 440.6	$ 339.2	$ 369.6
Accounts receivable—owned by credit subsidiary	2,075.7	1,880.1	1,512.7
Inventories	942.6	958.4	850.1
Net investment in properties and equipment	1,146.2	1,087.1	984.3
Additions to properties and equipment	179.9	214.8	202.6
Depreciation and amortization	87.7	80.0	75.9
Long-term debt	827.3	742.4	741.1
Stockholders' equity*,†	1,392.9	1,309.4	1,028.9
Book value per share‡	31.12	28.77	26.60
Primary earnings per share*,†	3.60	3.40	3.01
Fully diluted earnings per share*,†	2.85	2.63	2.32
Cash dividends per common share‡,§	1.00	0.97½	0.87½

Market History (calendar-year basis)

	1975	1974	1973
Market price range of common shares (high–low)‡	29⅛–13⅞	28⅛–13¼	29⅝–17¾
Closing price year-end‡	28⅞	13⅞	20
Year-end price-earnings ratio (fully diluted earnings)	10	5	9

* Net earnings for 1974 includes a net loss of $4.5 from the sale of Pioneer Trust & Savings Bank. As of the beginning of 1974, the company adopted the Lifo method of determining inventory cost for a substantial portion of its domestic manufacturing inventories. This change in accounting had the effect of reducing net earnings for 1974 by $9.1.

† Amounts prior to November 1, 1968 have been reduced by the portions applicable to Container Corporation shares exchanged for debentures at that date.

‡ Adjusted for two-for-one stock split June 9, 1970.

§ Dividends prior to November 1, 1968 are those paid on common shares of Montgomery Ward & Co., Incorporated.

Source: Marcor's *Annual Reports, 1973–1975.*

EXHIBIT 9
Comparative Statistics of Montgomery Ward, 1946–1976

Year	Sales ($ million)	Net Earnings ($ million)	Retail Stores	Catalog Stores	Catalog Sales Agencies
1946	974.2	52.3	628	215	—
1950	1,170.4	74.2	614	250	—
1955	969.9	35.2	566	301	—
1960	1,248.9	15.0	529	627	—
1965	1,748.4	23.9	502	864	287
1966	1,894.1	16.5	493	793	569
1967	1,879.0	17.4	475	719	632
1968	1,985.6	33.3	468	695	804
1969	2,155.2	39.6	464	669	894
1970	2,226.9	34.6	462	660	961
1971	2,376.9	36.8	465	644	1,014
1972	2,640.0	42.3	458	590	1,184
1973	3,231.0	54.9	449	419	1,239
1974	3,623.0	44.3	446	460	1,253
1975	3,779.3	67.7	443	555	1,288
1976	4,020.0	89.0	439	550	1,314

Source: Montgomery Ward, *Annual Reports,* various years.

nine catalog distribution centers shipped some 100,000 items of merchandise to consumers throughout the country. Credit sales were a major portion of Ward's business, accounting for more than half of its sales in 1975. At many of its urban and suburban store locations, Ward offered such services as auto and appliance repairs, driver education, interior design systems, kitchen planning, home cleaning and painting, pest control, key making, utility bill payment, postal services, tax return preparation, notary public service, ticket reservations for theatrical and sporting events, photocopying, and beauty, optical, and hearing aid shops. Exhibits 9 and 10 show details of Montgomery Ward's performance prior to its acquisition by Mobil.

EXHIBIT 10
Sales-Profit Comparisons of Top Three Leading Catalog Retailers, 1970–1976
($ millions)

Year	Sears Roebuck		J. C. Penney		Montgomery Ward	
	Sales	Net Income	Sales	Net Income	Sales	Net Income
1970	$ 9,262	$464.2	$4,150	$114.1	$2,227	$34.6
1971	10,006	550.9	4,812	135.7	2,376	36.8
1972	10,991	614.3	5,529	162.7	2,640	42.3
1973	12,306	679.9	6,243	185.8	3,231	54.9
1974	13,101	511.4	6,935	125.1	3,623	44.3
1975	13,639	522.6	7,678	189.6	3,779	67.7
1976	14,950	695.0	8,354	228.1	4,020	89.0

Source: Annual reports of the companies.

Montgomery Ward—Since the Acquisition.   In the three years following the acquisition, Ward's performance has been mediocre:

Year	Revenues	Earnings	Assets
1977	$5,047*	$ 94	$3,343
1978	5,474	105	3,569
1979	5,652	54	3,746

* All figures in $ millions.

Exhibit 11 provides some additional operating statistics for these three years.

EXHIBIT 11
Montgomery Ward's Operations since Its Acquisition by Mobil

	1979	1978	1977
Retail stores	419	411	427
PAATS* stores	238	230	209
Catalog stores	264	284	298
Catalog sales agencies	1,394	1,373	1,354
Electronic cash register terminals	16,104	14,351	12,061
Credit customers	8,800,000	8,300,000	7,700,000
Auto Club members	1,109,000	1,151,000	925,000
Retail sales per square foot	$145	$144	$133
Catalog sales as a percent of total	22.07%	21.80%	21.7%
Credit sales as a percent of total	56.8%	56.4%	55.4%
Value of life insurance policies in force ($ millions)	$5,354	$4,703	$3,853

* Paints, appliances, automotive accessories, tires, service.
Source: Mobil *Annual Report, 1978* and *1979.*

Mobil attributed Ward's 1979 profit decline to a fall off in durable goods sales in the last nine months of 1979 and to higher financing and operating costs. Nonetheless, Ward was proceeding with its store construction program. According to the *1979 Annual Report:*

> Retail store selling space was increased by 1.9 million square feet to a total of 31.1 million, with the opening of 11 large Ward Stores and 10 in the Jefferson/Ward operations. Retail stores, including newly constructed and renovated stores acquired from others, totaled 419 at year-end, a net increase of 8. During the year, 13 retail stores were closed.
>
> Expansion of Jefferson/Ward operations will facilitate economical entry into some of those major metropolitan markets in the East where Wards has never had retail representation. The concept for Jefferson stores is to maintain lower operating costs, yet provide customers with both private-label and a national-brand merchandise that equals Ward's quality standards. The interiors and exteriors of these self-service stores acquired in 1979 are being redesigned to

make them attractive as well as convenient. The Jefferson/Ward operations increased the number of stores from 11 to 21, and others are scheduled to be added during 1980.

Substantial progress was made by Montgomery Ward's merchandising group during 1979 to upgrade product quality and supplier services, as long-term buying agreements were signed with many of the nation's top-ranked manufacturers. An increasing proportion of Ward's private-label merchandise is not coming from industry leaders.

Continuing the practice of making the widest selection of goods and services available to its customers, Wards during 1979 became the first U.S. department store chain to offer legal and family health-care services. The first legal services clinics were opened at four stores and the first family health-care center was opened at one. There are now six dental clinics in Ward Stores.

To serve urban consumers more effectively, Wards is accelerating its program for new retail stores within the city limits of many of its major urban markets.

CONTAINER CORPORATION OF AMERICA

The other company Mobil obtained in the Marcor acquisition, the Container Corporation of America, was founded in 1926 and grew through internal expansion and acquisition to become a major factor in the packaging industry. A corollary to its development of packaging products was Container Corporation's innovation in the application of marketing and packaging design services, where the company's influence extended far beyond its own industry. Its design and market research laboratories, established in the mid-1940s, were the industry's first to use programmed application of market research, design, and scientific testing in the development of more effective consumer packaging.

By 1976, Container Corporation, with a total workforce of more than 21,000, was the nation's largest producer of paperboard packaging and the second largest manufacturer of paperboard. In 1975, it operated 90 facilities throughout the United States. Its overseas affiliations employed 8,000 employees in 56 different operations in Colombia, Mexico, Venezuela, Italy, Spain, and the Netherlands.

Finished packaging products, which represented over 80 percent of container sales, included corrugated shipping containers, folding paper cartons, composite cans, fiberboard and drums, and industrial plastic containers. Production of paperboard in 1975 totaled almost 2 million tons, of which 1.5 million tons were produced by domestic mills. Allied to its paperboard packaging, the company offered packaging services including graphic design, structural design, market research, packaging testing, packaging machinery development, and manufacturing. To supply its operation in 1976, the corporation owned or controlled over 744,000 acres of timberlands and had a 49 percent interest in the T. R. Miller Lumber Company, Inc. This company owns almost 200,000 acres close to the company's Alabama paperboard mill.

Container also had short-term cutting rights to timber on some 103,000 acres. The company had a continuing policy of increasing its holdings in timberlands.

Container Corporation had an operating characteristic similar to that of Mobil. They were timber-shy, just as Mobil has been crude-shy. Warner observed, "There is a kind of affinity between Container Corporation and ourselves . . . I suppose we were attracted to someone who has to live by their wits like we have had to do."

Container Corporation in 1975 collected more than a million tons of waste paper for recycling. Approximately half this collected material was used by its own domestic recycling mills, and the balance was sold to other countries. Exhibits 12 and 13 present summary financial information for Con-

EXHIBIT 12
Container Corporation's Financial Information for Ten-Year Period Ended December 31, 1967
(prior to becoming a subsidiary of Marcor)

	1967	1966	1965
Net sales ($000)	$463,135	$460,365	$405,689
Earnings before income taxes ($000)	58,773	62,181	50,159
Provision for income taxes ($000)	25,867	27,950	22,858
Earnings for the year ($000)	$ 32,906*	$ 34,231	$ 27,301
Per share	$ 2.95*	$ 3.06	$ 2.42
Percent return on shareholders' equity	14.7%	16.8%	14.2%
Total common stock dividends ($000)	$ 14,555	$ 13,996	$ 12,848
Per share	$ 1.30	$ 1.25	$ 1.15
Property additions and improvements ($000)	$ 50,060	$ 44,032	$ 36,540
Depreciation and depletion ($000)	20,752	19,593	18,454
Current assets ($000)	$125,230	$133,214	$114,279
Current liabilities ($000)	53,725	67,971	48,583
Working capital ($000)	$ 71,505	$ 65,243	$ 65,696
Current ratio	2.33 to 1	1.96 to 1	2.35 to 1
Property, less reserves ($000)	$247,401	$236,251	$211,866
Deferred income taxes and other liabilities ($000)	19,660	17,421	12,850
Long-term debt ($000)	71,882	69,484	59,832
Shareholders' equity ($000)	241,105	223,417	203,717
Book value per share	$ 21.64	$ 19.95	$ 18.19

* Excludes extraordinary earnings of $1,065,000 or 10 cents per share.

tainer Corporation for three years prior to becoming a subsidiary of Marcor and for selected years after acquisition by Marcor.

Container Corporation's Progress since the Mobil Acquisition. In 1979, Container Corporation's U.S. sales exceeded $1 billion although profit margins were depressed and operating earnings were essentially unchanged from 1978. International sales were up 26 percent, however, and foreign earnings rose 41 percent, with each country in Latin America and Europe where the company operated reporting improvements. Several new products were successfully introduced in each of the first three years following acquisition.

EXHIBIT 13
Highlights of Container Corporation's
Performance since Acquisition by Marcor
($ millions)

Year	Sales	Earnings
1968	$469	$31.6
1969	510	27.7
1970	527	30.1
1971	559	24.1
1972	624	33.7
1973	755	50.0
1974	965	74.6
1975	953	64.0
1976*	995	53.9

* 11-month period.
Source: Container Corporation's *Annual Reports, 1968–1976.*

Container increased its timberland holdings in the southeastern United States by 122,000 acres in the 1977–79 period. Exhibit 14 summarizes some of Container Corporation's recent operating highlights.

EXHIBIT 14
Container Corporation's Operating Highlights, 1975–1979

	1979	1978	1977	1976	1975
Paperboard produced worldwide (000 tons)	2,478	2,382	2,183	2,224	1,995
Folding cartons shipped worldwide (000 tons)	389	378	345	334	294
Corrugated containers shipped worldwide (billion square feet)	20.2	19.9	18.7	17.9	16.5
U.S. timberland owned or under long-term lease (000 acres)	860	839	781	744	716
Recycled paperboard as percent of paperboard produced worldwide	49%	49%	51%	49%	47%

Source: Mobil's *1979 Annual Report.*

But despite these gains, earnings have failed to increase:

	$ Millions		
Year	Revenues	Earnings	Assets
1977	$1,145	$45	$1,205
1978	1,284	5	1,279
1979	1,476	35	1,382

EXHIBIT 15
Distribution of Earnings and Assets Summary ($ millions)

	1979	1978*	1977*	1976*†
Segments:				
Energy				
Revenues				
Nonaffiliated				
Refined petroleum products	$27,317	$20,266	$18,100	$16,259
Crude oil	5,890	4,702	5,176	4,371
Natural gas	1,803	1,136	930	763
Other	3,944	2,900	2,599	2,303
Intersegment	287	207	199	196
Earnings.........................	2,021	1,060	938	848
Assets	20,942	16,933	15,846	14,455
Chemical				
Revenues				
Nonaffiliated	1,633	1,282	1,155	1,066
Intersegment	85	79	48	41
Earnings.........................	113	86	85	81
Assets	1,160	955	835	739
Retail merchandising				
Revenues—nonaffiliated	5,652	5,474	5,047	2,514
Earnings.........................	54	105	94	86
Assets	3,746	3,569	3,343	3,021
Paperboard packaging				
Revenues—nonaffiliated	1,476	1,284	1,145	540
Earnings.........................	35	5	45	38
Assets	1,382	1,279	1,205	1,119
Other				
Earnings.........................	(68)	(35)	(59)	(13)
Assets ....:.	229	45	(8)	10
Geographic:				
United States				
Revenues				
Nonaffiliated	18,400	15,317	14,315	10,520
Intergeographic	508	345	238	139
Earnings.........................	736	569	626	605
Assets	13,696	11,386	10,733	9,900
Canada				
Revenues				
Nonaffiliated	685	587	567	424
Intergeographic	38	47	61	137
Earnings.........................	100	82	73	85
Assets	788	690	618	524
Other foreign				
Revenues				
Nonaffiliated	28,765	21,140	19,270	16,872
Intergeographic	2,990	1,569	1,937	1,695
Earnings.........................	1,319	570	404	350
Assets	13,716	11,225	10,457	9,398

* Restated to reflect adoption of FAS 19, Financial Accounting and Reporting by Oil and Gas Producing Companies.

† Mobil's 54% voting interest in the Marcor companies was accounted for on the equity method through July 1, 1976, when Mobil became the 100% owner of these companies.

The sharp decline in 1978 was attributable to $42 million in charges against earnings for settlements in two antitrust class-action lawsuits involving folding cartons and shipping containers. In addition, the company attributed its lackluster profits to a profit squeeze brought on by the failure of prices to keep pace with rising costs.

MOBIL'S CHEMICAL DIVISION

Mobil's diversification into the chemical industry in 1960 was a move that many other large petroleum companies also pursued. In 1979, the chemical division produced 5.6 percent of Mobil's net income on only 3.4 percent of the total revenues. In 1977, the Mobil Chemical Company had 49 plants in operation in eight countries. It was the largest U.S. manufacturer of disposable plastic products, including (1) polyethylene, one use of which was the material for Mobil's Hefty Bags, (2) polystyrene, which is the base for foam containers, and (3) polypropylene, which is the transparent packaging film used in many industries. The company in 1977 had a capacity to produce almost 3 billion pounds of petrochemicals per year. In addition, it ranked as the third-largest producer of phosphate rock, sources of phosphorous chemicals, and fertilizer in the United States. The chemical division's profits for the years 1973 to 1979 were $36, $106, $89, $81, $85, $86, and $113 millions, respectively—see Exhibit 15.

MOBIL: THE LAND DEVELOPER

A less obvious diversification move was the company's involvement in land development. One such venture was a 13,000-unit condominium apartment complex in Hong Kong which housed 70,000 people. In 1970, Mobil created a real estate company, named Mobil Oil Estates Limited, which was involved in real estate development in California and Texas. Another major venture was a San Francisco Bay project at Redwood Shores, a residential community covering 1,300 acres. In October 1974, Mobil reached an understanding with majority owners on a bid to purchase the Irvine Company, owner of 77,700 acres of land in Orange County, California, approximately 73,000 acres of which were undeveloped. However, after two years of litigation and the entry of two other firms into a bidding war for Irvine, Mobil disengaged from its attempts at acquisition.

Since the abortive attempt to acquire Irvine, Mobil has made no further diversification attempts. In 1979, Mobil did acquire the oil and gas operations of General Crude Oil Company for $792 million. According to Lawrence Woods, a Mobil director (as well as an executive vice president and project leader for the Marcor acquisition), Mobil's strategy in investing in Montgomery Ward, Container Corporation, and land development was not an attempt to become a conglomerate:

When we acquired Montgomery Ward and Container Corporation of America we merely implemented a diversification policy established a decade ago. Our goal with this policy was to increase Mobil's domestic revenue and earnings base, and to engage in activities subject to different business cycles and regulatory climates than the energy companies. We believe these objectives have been met, and we are not actively seeking other major diversifications. We see ourselves essentially as a diversified energy company.

Whether Mobil could seriously be considered as a diversified *energy* company as of 1980 was debatable, however. Mobil did own an estimated 3.7 billion tons of coal reserves, but it had no operating mines; construction on Mobil's first coal mine was tentatively scheduled to start in 1981, with initial deliveries in 1983. The company's first uranium plant (with only a 325-ton annual capacity) went into production in mid-1979. Mobil was engaged in a joint venture with Tyco Laboratories to develop high-efficiency solar cells, but commercial sales were not expected until "the more distant future." Mobil had sizable shale holdings in Colorado and tar sand holdings in Canada. Work was progressing on a methanol-to-gasoline catalytic process to be used in a commercial New Zealand facility (with natural gas as the hydrocarbon source), and in a pilot plant being built in West Germany (with coal as the hydrocarbon source). These activities, as of 1980, constituted most of Mobil's noteworthy energy investments outside of petroleum and natural gas.

MOBIL'S PUBLIC RELATIONS PROGRAM

Mobil had long been known, as Warner put it in 1976, "as a good gray Republican company. Some of us began to think around here that maybe there were two sides of the street to walk down and maybe we ought to walk down the other side of the street."

Herman J. Schmidt, vice chairman of Mobil, said in February 1977,

> Ten years ago, top management in a company such as Mobil could spend a minimal amount of its time communicating with the media, with legislators, and with the general public. Management in most companies could generally meet what seemed their public-affairs responsibilities by having the chief executive or some other senior officer go to Washington once in a while to talk with a few people or to testify before a congressional committee. He could grant an occasional interview to an essentially friendly reporter and make a speech now and then to an audience with which he felt comfortable.
>
> Today, however, large-scale communication has become a prime requirement of business—and not just big business. It is a major element in the time of even the most senior people in our company, and by that I mean our chief executive officer, our president, other of our employee directors and officers and managers below the directors' level.
>
> In retrospect we can see that our approach in the mid-1960s was a mistake. Those of us in top management should have paid greater attention to public

opinion and to the media and to members of the Congress and of the state legislatures. We should have worked to establish greater credibility, which would have stood us in good stead when the going got tough. People seldom heard from us until we were in trouble, and by then it was usually too late.

Mobil in the 1950s and 1960s, like most petroleum companies, had few friends in the ranks of ardent Democrats, but did have some support in the House and Senate. As Warner put it,

> We had fellows like Lyndon Johnson, Sam Rayburn, and Bob Kerr in the Senate and in the House who, coming out of that Southwestern area, were very close to the oil industry. Every time the industry got in trouble, they would run to these four or five fellows. What we forgot as an industry was that those fellows weren't planning on living forever! The decision was made; Mobil crossed the line from a low profile to public.[10]

In a speech, Warner described the company's advertising practice:

> We published, a quarter-page advertisement virtually every Thursday, year-round, on the page opposite the editorial page of *The New York Times*—called, as you might deduce, the Op-Ed page. This is the only space the Times will sell on those two pages. It therefore has pretty high visibility, which we try to enhance with an off-beat approach. The space gives enough room for essay-type ads similar in tone to other material appearing on those two pages.
>
> We try to surprise readers of the *Times* with our selection of subject matter, our headlines, and our brisk and often irreverent text. We try to be urbane but not pompous. We try to talk to ourselves and we accept that we can never tell the whole story in any one ad.
>
> Our ads have ranged over a wide gamut—the energy crisis in its ramifications, the role of profits, earnings as expressed in rate of return, capital requirements and capital information, the need for national energy policies . . . why we support the New York Public Library, public television, the United Negro College Fund, the Better Business Bureau . . . the need for economic growth . . . the dangers of simplistic knee-jerk reactions . . . the need to conserve energy, and ways to use less gasoline. The list is a long one.
>
> We try to help people understand what options are open to them and what sort of costs are involved in the various trade-offs. The response has been strong and generally favorable, though in addressing ourselves to opinion leaders we deliberately opted for a rather thin cut of the total public. We believe we have had some impact and that we have been reaching people other than just those already wedded to the free market, but we realize we have not yet done enough to reach the public at large. In sum, we think the exercise has been useful, albeit somewhat expensive *in toto*, and sufficiently productive to continue.

Exhibits 16, 17, and 18 present samples of Mobil's ads.

Herbert Schmertz, Mobil's vice president, has been the chief architect of Mobil's media campaign. According to one company source,

---

[10] As quoted by *Fortune*, September 1976, p. 109.

EXHIBIT 16
Sample of a Mobil Ad

Yes, $2 billion is a lot of money, but...

Mobil earned a lot of money in 1979: $2 billion, or 78 percent more than in 1978.

Having said that, we need to add these basic points to put our earnings in perspective:

1. Our profits have not—we repeat, not—been a major factor in the higher price of such petroleum products as gasoline and heating oil. These products are more expensive because of steadily rising costs, particularly for crude oil.

2. Our profits are not excessive in relation to what companies in other industries earn on investment.

3. Our profits and more are being used to finance the development of more energy the nation needs so badly.

On pricing, here are the key facts:

During 1979, we estimate the average price of regular gasoline in the U.S. rose about 37 cents a gallon, heating oil almost as much. But Mobil's after-tax energy profits during the year rose only about three-quarters of a penny a gallon to 3.3 cents a gallon sold in the U.S. and 2 cents a gallon to 4.4 cents a gallon sold worldwide.

On profitability, here are key points:

Our rate of return on average shareholders' equity last year was 20.8 percent. When the average rate of return for all U.S. manufacturers is computed, ours may well be higher, but we were usually below the average for many years. For comparison, the rate of return for the 12 months ended September 30, 1979 looked like this for some of the companies in other industries:

- Hilton Hotels, 31.6 percent.
- MGM, 31.0 percent.
- The Washington Post Company, 27.9 percent.
- American Broadcasting Company, 24.6 percent.
- McDonald's, 23.3 percent.
- Pepsico, 22.3 percent.
- IBM, 22.1 percent.
- General Electric, 21.2 percent.
- CBS, 20.7 percent.

Our thought: Oil profits are big, in terms of the number of dollars, simply because we operate with huge volumes. They are not excessive, however, when measured by rate of return.

On the cost of new energy supplies:

Big as our profits are, we consistently spend more than we earn to find and develop new sources of energy. Although Mobil earned $6 billion from 1975 through 1979, we spent $11.7 billion—considerably more than our profits—on exploration activities and new investment, mostly to develop more energy.

Finding and producing energy anywhere in the world isn't cheap.

- Just one North Sea producing platform can cost as much as $2 billion.
- A new refinery can cost over $1 billion to build.
- A New Zealand natural gas-to-gasoline plant will cost more than half a billion dollars.
- A 100,000-barrel-per-day coal-to-oil synthetic fuel plant would cost $4 billion to $6 billion—and America would need 80 of these simply to replace the foreign crude the U.S. currently imports.
- One linear foot of well drilled in the U.S. cost $46.82 in 1977, 195 percent more than in 1967. The oil industry drills about 230 million feet per year in this country.

The message is clear:

While our profits are large in terms of the number of dollars involved, they are only a small factor in the price of our products. Our profitability, when compared with U.S. industry in general, has hardly been excessive. And the tasks we face, in terms of finding and developing new energy sources, require all our earnings and more.

These are the facts, as clear as we can make them. We hope we've made the subject as simple as big numbers and a complex industry permit.

Mobil®

This ad appeared in *The New York Times* on January 24, 1980.

EXHIBIT 17
Sample of a Mobil Ad

can't tell the seven sisters apart?
we're the one with extra dimension

One of the seven largest international oil companies. But more than that.

The right diet of investments in recent years has filled us out. Made us a balanced, diversified energy company. With the flexibility to move ahead in the United States as well as abroad. In petroleum. Or in other businesses.

Our diversifications, begun in the '60s, are now rounded out. Container

Corporation of America, the nation's leading maker of paperboard packaging. Montgomery Ward. Mobil Chemical, grown to a billion dollar business. Among other virtues, it's America's largest manufacturer of disposable plastic products.

Sure, we're still big abroad. With substantial shares in the North Sea's largest oil field and the huge Arun gas

field in Indonesia. Both Mobil discoveries. And we're working closely with Saudi Arabia on a number of major projects.

But we're even stronger in the U.S. Where our diversifications are centered. Where our petroleum production in the Gulf of Mexico is growing. Especially natural gas.

So forgive us, sisters, if we think we're special.

Mobil®

Exhibit 18
Sample of a Mobil Ad

"I'm from the government and I'm here to help you"

While the Chinese have their Three Ways of Listening and their Four Rules of Morality, Americans have gone one step further and codified the Three Great Lies.

First: "Your check is in the mail."

Second: "The delivery is on the truck."

Third: "I'm from the government and I'm here to help you."

Behind this sardonic humor is a failure of faith, a wry expectation of betrayal, a rising belief in America that you can't trust your government. And while distrust of creditors and merchants represents an ancient source of wit and pathos, there's bitter irony that citizens of the world's foremost, and most emulated, democracy should be distrusting their government. If Americans—with all their liberties, their Bill of Rights, and their careful balance of federal powers—have become cynical about Washington, must we conclude that government of, by, and for the people is becoming an idle dream?

That, of course, carries cynicism too far. But a government that is increasingly seen as a nuisance, a pain, a meddling, nagging, obtrusive, petty, nit-picking, and troublesome pest has obviously managed to get itself deep into the rough. Whatever the Founding Fathers had in mind, it surely was not a sprawling bureaucracy that busied itself with the sugar on cornflakes, the shape of toilet seats, and the content of television commercials. Who can forget the government's insistence on a standard that would have required computerized braking systems for trucks—until balking

truckers made it clear that this would likely do more harm than good?

Even an internal audit of the Department of Energy noted that, with the Administration and Congress changing energy signals every few weeks, "...it is as if the Super Bowl game were being played while the referees were arguing about and making up the rules and the players were still being selected." And now, the energy companies caught in this frantic milling are being hit with federal penalties for not understanding well enough the confusing rules that have resulted. "We've had about all the help we can take from the Feds," said Georgia's Governor George Busbee recently. "What we need is a little less help...and a little more incentive."

There is, of course, an obvious cure for the meddling disease. And that would be for Congress and the Administration to reduce all this mucking about in inconsequential matters—to reduce it drastically, imperiously, and quickly. That is hardly likely to occur in an election year—but would a moratorium on further meddlesome regulation be out of the question, too? From that small beginning, perhaps we could look for an overhaul and gradual reduction of the present regulatory establishment. If no respite can be achieved, distrust of government may no longer be a joking matter. For the power over our lives will have been transferred from elected representatives to a huge, faceless, and infinitely meddlesome bureaucracy. And that, we think, would be pretty sick humor.

This ad appeared in the *New York Times* on February 28, 1980.

One of the things that Herb brought was an ability to talk to the Democratic side of the House and Senate and to know some of those people—particularly some of those people that we never, never would see before—the liberal element of the Democratic side.[11]

The op-eds were started on an infrequent basis in October 1970, but by mid-1971 it was determined that they would be a regular feature. It took Schmertz and his staff six months of experimentation and preparation to complete the 20 backup ads necessary to insure that the most relevant topic would be included each week. In January 1972, Mobil was ready for a weekly column. It has been a regular feature since then. Mobil made it a policy to pay for advocacy ads from profits rather than to expense them as operating costs.

The production of the op-ed ads involves considerable collective effort. The Schmertz staff and, on occasion, Warner and Tavoulareas are involved in the initial theme selection; the final draft always requires approval of either Warner or Tavoulareas.

As to whether Mobil's advocacy ads have had the desired impact, one top official stated:

> We have learned in the intervening years that unless we win our case with the general public, we stand little chance of winning it in the halls of Congress. Accordingly, we in Mobil have taken our case to the people, through the newspapers of the country and through local television and radio stations, as well as directly to congressmen and senators and others in Washington. This has required a sustained effort to the highest levels of management and throughout the organization but we are persuaded it has been worthwhile and may well represent the shape of the future for all business.
>
> Mobil has put a number of executives through special training and sent them on media blitzes across the country during which they appear on numerous TV and radio programs, in addition to meeting newspaper editors. In all, we have had as many as half a dozen traveling around the country at one time. We also tape interviews for syndication.
>
> In the last two years, Mobil representatives have appeared on a total of 365 television shows, 211 radio shows, and have had 18 newspaper interviews.
>
> We know we have stiffened every employee's morale and that our people have been greatly pleased to see management stand up and fight for what they believe to be right. We have indications that many of our shareholders feel the same way.

Warner has also defended Mobil's approach:

> There is no way we can measure what we have accomplished with the program we have been following. If we hadn't done it, we would have left all of the media to our critics. And I have to assume we would be worse off today. Somebody had to answer, and thus, that's what we have tried to do.
>
> We will continue as a matter of established policy to use every opportunity

---

[11] Ibid., p. 108.

to point to the real energy problems and propose solutions. We will continue to oppose ill-conceived and counterproductive government programs such as price controls and allocations, which can only result in less available energy, not more.

FUTURE DIRECTIONS AT MOBIL

In December 1976, Warner summed up Mobil's strategic position as follows:

Mobil is one of the world's largest companies. Energy is and will remain, our primary business, but a carefully balanced program begun in 1968 has broadened and strengthened our earnings base. . . .

For 16 consecutive years, Mobil has increased the size of its dividends. It is a record of which we are proud—one we are determined to improve. . . .

In the past, Mobil has been known primarily as an international oil company. Today, diversification has created an earnings mix which retains our ability to grow in the petroleum industry while offering attractive new earnings sources in fields that are subject to different economic cycles and less stringent government regulations. . . .

A result of this strategy has been to strengthen our U.S. earnings base. In 1976, more than half of Mobil's earnings are coming from domestic sources. And our diversification has been accomplished without weakening our position in energy. . . .

Mobil is beginning to benefit from the results of strategic petroleum exploration and production investments that were made overseas during the earlier years of the decade, improving the company's already strong position internationally with as diversified a base of oil and gas supply as possible. . . .

Nothing is more basic to Mobil's business than the search for energy.

Wherever energy is to be found—as oil, gas, coal, shale, shale oil, uranium, the sun—Mobil is prepared to lead in its development. . . .

Mobil Oil's exploration and production division was recently reorganized on a worldwide basis to provide effective response to energy opportunities so investment can be channeled to those that are most promising. . . .

Mobil Oil Corporation is totally integrated from the research laboratory to the gasoline pump. . . .

Mobil prides itself on having management in depth. We encourage our people to innovate, whether in the laboratories or refineries or in planning marketing or supply strategies.

We stress dynamic planning. Each year, managers of the Mobil group of companies at all levels, from domestic refineries to marketing operations in the South Pacific, develop assumptions about conditions likely to be encountered. They set objectives, not just for the year ahead but for the next five years. They develop a profit plan, then capital and operating budgets to implement these objectives.

At each level, this dynamic planning process is refined. Hard choices in investments and economies are made. Ultimately, top management has the information and the perspective necessary to make the broad decisions; to map not just year-by-year tactics, but long-term strategy. . . .

Montgomery Ward and Container Corporation bring to Mobil similar, sophisticated management processes adapted to their special needs. . . .

However, three years later in Mobil's *1979 Annual Report,* Warner's message to the shareholders suggested more of a strategic emphasis on petroleum than on either energy or further diversification:

> For the years immediately ahead, when industry supplies of oil and gas will become less abundant and higher priced, we expect to follow a multipronged strategy. We will continue heavy investments in exploration and producing, seeking in particular to expand and develop promising discoveries made in the 70s and investigating new prospective areas identified by our advanced exploration technology. Priority will continue to be given to finding new U.S. reserves. At the same time, we will build on our industry leadership in the United States and abroad in upgrading refinery yields to obtain greater proportions of high-value fuels, and we will continue our expansion into high-value chemicals. We intend also to seek attractive opportunities to build synthetic-fuel plants, looking toward the day when significant volumes of synthetic fuels can be produced on a commercial basis.
>
> Although Mobil has achieved some diversification into businesses subject to different economic cycles and less government regulation, our main thrust will continue to be as an energy company. Evidencing this was the $792 million purchase of General Crude Oil Company's exploration and producing operations in 1979.
>
> In the years immediately ahead, we should be able to realize significant earnings improvement from the capital projects started in the 1970s, especially our large producing ventures and the new manufacturing facilities of Mobil Chemical Company.

In the section of the *1979 Annual Report* on "Prospects in the 80s," Mobil made no mention of any of its diversification investments or any of its energy activities other than petroleum, natural gas, and petrochemicals. The company's 1980 internal available cash flow was estimated to be $3.6 billion.

19. Dresser Industries, Inc.: Acquisition of Jeffrey Galion, Inc.*

In 1973, Dresser Industries, Inc., a billion-dollar manufacturer of high-technology products for the natural resource and energy related markets, was considering the acquisition of Jeffrey Galion, Inc., a major manufacturer of heavy construction vehicles—road rollers, motor graders, earth movers and cranes—and a leading producer and innovator in the underground coal mining machinery industry. The first section of this case will be concerned with the background, operations, and strategies of Dresser Industries; the second section will focus upon Jeffrey Galion's operations and financial status as an acquisition candidate.

COMPANY HISTORY

In 1880, S. R. Dresser pioneered the production of a new pipe coupling necessary for the development of the rapidly expanding oil industry. This leak-free coupling was used in the construction of the first gas pipeline operated in the United States.

During the century since that historic invention occurred in Bradford, Pennsylvania, Dresser Industries has developed into a leading supplier of high technology products and services to the energy and natural resource industrial markets. Through diversification and acquisition, Dresser has expanded into an industrial giant with sales topping $1 billion in 1973. Financial data from the past five years indicate steady sales growth, a stable cash dividend, and a strong earnings-per-share comeback following a dramatic decrease in 1971. Exhibits 1 and 2 present the balance sheet at October 31, 1973, and the income data for the period 1969–73.

CURRENT OPERATIONS

Dresser Industries, Inc., now headquartered in Dallas, Texas, has offices located in Europe, the Far East and across the United States. Management is continuously looking abroad for growth possibilities and has enjoyed an

---

* Prepared by A. J. Strickland with the assistance of research MBA Fellow Ken Voelker, both of The University of Alabama.

expanding presence in the international marketplace. According to Rex Sebastian, senior vice president of Operations, a Dresser executive with very considerable experience in international operations:

> Dresser over the years has been committed to international business. We compete in world markets against both U.S. and foreign companies. We can help to bridge the gap between the developing nations and the industrial world through the transfer of technology, capital, and management techniques if we are able to achieve a return on our investment commensurate with the risks.

At the end of 1973, 23 percent of revenues came from international operations while 14 percent of total net assets were outside of the U.S.

EXHIBIT 1

DRESSER INDUSTRIES
Consolidated Balance Sheet
October 31, 1973
$000

Assets

Current assets:

Cash	$ 33,114
Marketable securities—at cost (approximate market)	9,566
Notes and accounts receivable	224,825
Less allowance for doubtful receivables	(5,729)
	219,096
Inventories—at lower of cost (principally average cost) or market	
Finished products and work in process	175,642
Raw materials and supplies	67,030
	242,672
Prepaid expenses	4,289
Total current assets	508,737

Investments and other assets:

Investments	
Unconsolidated subsidiaries and affiliates	
National Equipment Leasing Corporation (including notes receivable of $1,315,000)	5,655
Others (including advance of $3,038,000)	20,575
Other securities—at cost (approximate market)	1,263
Notes and accounts receivable	4,418
Common shares of Dresser held for deferred compensation—at cost	4,263
Excess of cost over net assets of businesses acquired	22,494
Other assets	11,110
Total investments and other assets	69,778

Property, plant and equipment—at cost:

Land, land improvements, and mineral deposits	24,711
Buildings	115,486
Machinery and equipment	351,456
	491,653
Less accumulated depreciation and amortization	(264,169)
Total properties—Net	227,484
Total Assets	$805,999

EXHIBIT 1 (continued)

Liabilities and Shareholders' Investment

Current liabilities:

Notes payable	$ 38,894
Accounts payable, etc.	55,710
Advances from customers on contracts	7,405
Accrued compensation	23,155
Accrued taxes, interest, and other expenses	50,298
Estimated warranty costs	6,812
Federal, state, and foreign income taxes	12,456
Current portion of long-term debt	11,816
Total current liabilities	206,546
Long-term debt	163,005
Deferred compensation	9,601
Deferred income taxes	20,930
Minority interests in consolidates subsidiaries	1,354
Shareholders' investment	
Convertible preferred shares, without par value, stated at $1.00 a share	
$2.20 Series A (liquidating preference $152,395,000)	3,366
$2.00 Series B (liquidating preference $68,871,000)	1,673
Common shares, $0.25 par value	2,547
Capital in excess of par or stated value	96,581
Reserve created out of retained earnings for foreign business risks (classified as a reserve and excluded from share holders' investment in reports to shareholders)	5,000
Retained earnings	295,396
Total shareholders' investment	404,563
Total liabilities and shareholders' investment	$805,999

Dresser's manufacturing and service operations are high-technology oriented and can be broken down into four categories:

1. Petroleum group—Dresser's oil-related products serve every phase of the horizontally integrated oil industry. These products range from Ideco drill rigs to Wayne self-service gasoline pumps. Additionally, Dresser is a leading innovator in the well-site instrumentation field of the petroleum industry. As this industry continues to move toward increasingly scientific and precise drilling techniques, these highly sophisticated monitoring and logging services were expected to generate increased profits.

2. Machinery group—A wide line of compression and pumping systems, power systems and environmental control systems are designed and manufactured by Dresser. These systems and accompanying equipment are demanded by a wide range of industrial markets primarily related to energy. Clark compressors, Pacific pumps and Roots boosters are standards in their respective market segments and demonstrate the consistent quality of Dresser machinery.

3. Refractories and minerals group—The developing need for refractory products has resulted in a dynamic and expanding market in high temperature processing industries. Harbison Walker Refractories is a leading

EXHIBIT 2

Dresser Industries
Consolidated Statement of Income
Year Ended October 31, 1969–1973
($000)

	1969	1970	1971	1972	1973
Net sales and service revenues	$700,148	$789,137	$805,234	$906,947	$1,025,217
Cost of sales and services	465,273	530,709	548,589	619,799	701,905
Selling, engineering, administrative and general expenses	$234,875	$258,428	$256,645	$287,148	$323,312
	161,245	184,114	195,403	215,214	241,984
	$ 73,630	$ 74,314	$ 61,242	$ 71,934	$ 81,328
Other income (deductions)					
Interest expense	$ (8,912)	$ (14,725)	$ (14,974)	$ (14,766)	$ (16,904)
Interest earned	3,197	3,346	2,345	1,553	2,417
Royalties earned	3,702	3,268	3,526	3,364	2,985
Other income	4,511	5,591	5,721	3,552	2,470
	$ 2,498	$ (2,520)	$ (3,382)	$ (6,297)	$ (9,032)
	$ 76,128	$ 71,794	$ 57,860	$ 65,637	$ 72,296
Income taxes	37,112	31,587	24,584	26,656	28,273
	$ 39,016	$ 40,207	$ 33,276	$ 38,981	$ 44,023
Minority interests in (earnings) losses of subsidiaries	(963)	(687)	(233)	(48)	173
Net earnings	$ 38,053	$ 39,520	$ 33,043	$ 38,933	$ 44,196
Provision for preferred dividend requirements	10,967	10,969	10,970	10,970	10,900
Net earnings available to common shareholders	$ 27,086	$ 28,551	$ 22,073	$ 27,963	$ 33,296
Average common shares outstanding (000)	9,339	9,513	9,758	9,780	9,839
Earnings per common share	$2.90	$3.00	$2.26	$2.86	$3.38
Earnings per share on a fully diluted basis	$2.65	$2.72	$2.23	$2.62	$2.98
Cash dividends per common share	$1.40	$1.40	$1.40	$1.40	$1.40

supplier of refractory products to the steel, aluminum, copper, glass, cement and petrochemical industries. Coal gasification processes are being researched extensively by Dresser technologists in attempts to make this technique economically feasible.

The minerals division of this group mines and processes both metallic and nonmetallic ores nationally and internationally. The output from these operations is employed in a host of industrial applications ranging from gas-well drilling fluids to the production of animal feed.

4. Industrial specialties group—Dresser produces a wide variety of industrial and consumer tools and equipment which is grouped in this category. Some better known brands and products include Ashcroft instruments and gauges, Consolidated safety valves, S-K hand tools, and Dresser pipe coupling and fittings.

The total sales and profit contribution by product groups is presented in Exhibit 3.

CORPORATE GOALS

Growth, both internally and externally, has been and continues to be a prime task of the management at Dresser Industries. Internal growth has historically centered upon increasing earnings levels and profits. According to John V. James, president and chief executive officer:

> Over the years, we have very deliberately built a unique company whose future is tied closely to activities within a broad spectrum of the energy industries throughout the world. Our assessment of future energy demand, combined with the increased efforts that will be required to meet the world's needs, makes us quite optimistic as we view the future. A few years ago, we established an average annual earnings growth objective of 10 to 15 percent. I believe this objective is still viable and attainable, even from our large base. I don't expect the problems of the future to be significantly different from the past—inflation, too much government, and continuing international uncertainty.

The dominant strategy for external growth has been horizontal diversification followed by vertical integration utilizing the synergistic effect of the organization. Dresser has searched worldwide for new products and services, developing markets, joint ventures and acquisitions which mesh properly with existing Dresser capabilities. The ideal fit for an acquisition candidate occurs, according to Dresser, when the aggregate profits of two companies combined grow at a faster rate than the respective profits of each company would grow separately. Dresser has used acquisitions to broaden and strengthen their product and service line by striving for diversification without dilution.

The management network employed by Dresser to achieve these internal and external goals is even more diverse than its product line. The corporate office in Dallas houses five vice presidents who have functional horizon-

EXHIBIT 3
Product Group Contributions ($ millions)

	1969		1970		1971		1972		1973	
Sales contribution*										
Petroleum group	$259.5	36%	$296.7	37%	$322.7	40%	$323.5	35%	$ 362.2	35%
Machinery group	192.3	27	207.2	26	199.4	24	233.4	26	253.2	24
Refractories and minerals group	140.9	20	163.1	20	149.0	18	150.3	16	184.0	18
Industrial specialties group	123.6	17	139.3	17	144.5	18	205.7	23	246.2	23
Total	$716.3	100%	$806.3	100%	$815.6	100%	$912.9	100%	$1,045.6	100%
Profit contribution†										
Petroleum group	$ 31.8	33%	$ 30.2	30%	$ 28.0	32%	$ 30.4	32%	$ 33.2	30%
Machinery group	15.3	16	13.0	13	13.2	15	12.9	13	16.3	15
Refractories and minerals group	27.0	28	33.7	34	20.0	23	16.9	18	22.7	21
Industrial specialties group	22.9	23	23.1	23	25.8	30	36.0	37	37.1	34
Total	$ 97.0	100%	$100.0	100%	$ 87.0	100%	$ 96.2	100%	$ 109.3	100%

* Sales contribution data are before elimination of intergroup sales.
† Profit contribution data are before general corporate expenses, income taxes, minority interests in earnings of subsidiaries, and intergroup eliminations and adjustments.

tal responsibility for finance, industrial relations, accounting and administration, and operations. Seven individual divisions are headed by presidents who are vertically responsible for the product activity in their respective division. (See Exhibit 4.) All of these officers report directly to John V. James, president and chief executive officer, and John Lawrence, chairman of the board.

THE MINING EQUIPMENT INDUSTRY

The mining and energy related equipment industry is not very well defined. No specific company compares with Dresser, but instead, various divisions of many companies compete with the various groups within the Dresser Family. The nearest competitors are listed below for 1973 and in millions of dollars:

	Mining	Industrial	Construction
Joy	$145.9	$ 84.8	—
Galion	36.7	91.8	$ 95.0
International Harvester	—	1,355.6*	513.8
John Deere	—	465.0	—

* Includes agricultural sales.

Industry sources reported that the large firms in the industry each have their own strength but taken as a whole all have excellent products. For example, John Deere is known for its excellent tractors while Galion is known for its conveyor systems as well as earth moving equipment. Joy is known best for its deep mine equipment.

ACQUISITION EVALUATION

Throughout Dresser's history aggressive acquisition has been the battle plan for growth. In 1944, when large firms were not as aquisition minded as they are now, Henry N. Mallon was asked "what is Dresser Industries?" He replied that Dresser was

> . . . a group of related companies in related industries. To be a member of the group (an acquisition target) each member company must contribute something to the whole so that the group is stronger because of that member company's contribution . . . (It) must be so related to the group that it itself gains by membership in the group. In other words, our Dresser Industries organization makes sense only if it can offer advantages to each operating company and, if at the same time, each operating company adds strength to Dresser Industries.

As a preface to its acquisition philosophy, Dresser has published general guidelines which provide a framework for determining desirable acquisition candidates. These guidelines appear in Exhibit 5.

EXHIBIT 4
Organization Chart

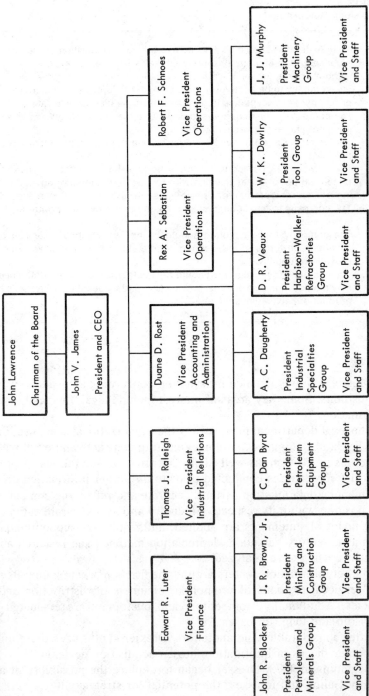

John Lawrence
Chairman of the Board

John V. James
President and CEO

Edward R. Luter
Vice President
Finance

Thomas J. Raleigh
Vice President
Industrial Relations

Duane D. Rost
Vice President
Accounting and
Administration

Rex A. Sebastian
Vice President
Operations

Robert F. Schnoes
Vice President
Operations

John R. Blocker
President
Petroleum and
Minerals Group

Vice President
and Staff

J. R. Brown, Jr.
President
Mining and
Construction
Group

Vice President
and Staff

C. Dan Byrd
President
Petroleum
Equipment
Group

Vice President
and Staff

A. C. Daugherty
President
Industrial
Specialties
Group

Vice President
and Staff

D. R. Veaux
President
Harbison–Walker
Refractories
Group

Vice President
and Staff

W. K. Dowlry
President
Tool Group

Vice President
and Staff

J. J. Murphy
President
Machinery
Group

Vice President
and Staff

EXHIBIT 5
Acquisition Guidelines

1. No time or effort should be devoted to a potential acquisition of a leading firm in a concentrated industry or a firm with sales or assets in excess of $10 million without prior approval in writing and preliminary antitrust screening.
2. The company to be acquired should be one that furnishes competitive products or has market acceptance in a market having a high growth rate.
3. The company to be acquired should be one that has a history of efficient management and as a low-cost producer.
4. The company to be acquired should be one that has a proprietary product(s) position.
5. The company to be acquired should be one that provides, or could provide, penetration of overseas markets with respect to manufacturing and/or marketing of Dresser's product or service lines—in addition to its own situation.
6. The company to be acquired should be one that provides opportunity for scale economies.
7. The company to be acquired should be one to which Dresser can offer an advantage in terms of engineering, marketing, or administrative skills for improved profitability.
8. The company to be acquired should be one that has a new product line serving new markets and also one that provides secondary benefits to Dresser's existing product or service lines.

Dresser requires detailed information concerning all aspects of proposed acquisitions. Some key areas of interest include legal, financial, and market information.

The legal department must review the organizational structure, Securities and Exchange Commission filings, existing contracts and employee benefit programs of the firm, as well as any antitrust considerations. A preliminary antitrust screening is conducted prior to any other information collection.

Financial data must be current, accurate and reflect the company's financial position within its respective industry and as a separate entity. All relevant financial statements are audited, and significant accounting policies—such as inventory valuation, depreciation methods and research and development costing—are analyzed.

Market information centers around the firm's marketing mix: its products and services, methods of promotion, channels of distribution and pricing policies. Additionally, competitors and customers are evaluated on both short-run and long-run bases.

After considerable time and effort, Dresser synthesizes these and countless other pieces of information into an acquisition decision.

Beginning in 1973, Dresser began to explore the possibility of acquiring Jeffrey Galion and to assess the potential for strategic fit.

JEFFREY GALION, INC.

Company History.   Jeffrey Galion's chief predecessors were Jeffrey Manufacturing Company, a mining machinery manufacturer founded in Columbus, Ohio, in 1877, and Galion Iron Works, founded in Galion, Ohio, in 1907. The company gradually evolved into a leading manufacturer of motor graders, road rollers, rough-terrain hydraulic cranes, and various types of power transmission equipment and coal mining machinery. As of 1973 Jeffrey Galion had three foreign subsidiaries in operation: British Jeffrey-Diamond Limited, Jeffrey Manufacturing Company Limited, and Jeffrey Manufacturer Mexicana, S.A. The balance sheet for 1973 and the income statement for the years 1969–73 are shown in Exhibits 6 and 7.

Current Operations.   Jeffrey Galion's operations consisted of three lines of business: construction equipment, industrial equipment, and mining machinery. The following section presents products and markets for each of these lines.[1]

Construction Equipment.   The principal Jeffrey Galion construction equipment products, marketed under the Galion trademark, were motor

EXHIBIT 6

Jeffrey Galion
Consolidated Balance Sheet
December 31, 1973
($000)

Assets

Current assets:	
Cash, including certificates of deposit $1,308	$ 9,420
Marketable securities	218
Receivables:	
Accounts—trade, including retainages of $1,768	46,200
Notes—trade	9,667
Other	1,317
	$ 57,184
Less:	
Unearned interest	$ 339
Allowance for doubtful receivables	1,706
	$ 2,045
Net receivables	$ 55,139
Inventories:	
Finished goods and parts	$ 32,878
Raw materials and work in process	54,331
Total inventories	$ 87,209
Prepaid expenses	386
Total current assets	$152,372

---

[1] This section is drawn heavily from Dresser Industries, Inc., *Prospectus,* dated March, 1974.

EXHIBIT 6 (continued)

Other assets:

Notes receivable due after one year, net of unearned interest of $416	$ 4,882
Investment in unconsolidated foreign subsidiaries, at cost	2,598
Investment fund, at cost, which approximates market	3,099
Other	1,452
Total other assets	$ 12,031

Property, plant, and equipment, at cost:

Land	$ 3,617
Buildings	24,306
Machinery, equipment and fixtures	51,591
Rental equipment	3,585
	$ 83,099
Less accumulated depreciation	41,069
Net property, plant and equipment	$ 42,030
Total assets	$206,433

Liabilities and Shareholders' Equity

Current liabilities:

Current installments of long-term debt	$ 229
Notes payable to banks, unsecured	16,339
Due to foreign banks on notes and open credit	2,344
Accounts payable	10,134

Accrued liabilities:

Salaries, wages and commissions	2,463
Taxes, other than federal and foreign taxes	4,287
Interest	595
Other	7,977
	$ 15,322
Federal and foreign income taxes	$ 3,579
Total current liabilities	$ 47,947

Deferred:

Federal income taxes	838
Compensation	680
	$ 1,518

Long-term debt, less current installments:

Notes payable—revolving credit	$ 20,000
6¾% loan of foreign subsidiary, guaranteed by the company, due May 1980, payable in annual installments of $140	840
Other	118
Total long-term debt	$ 20,958
Minority interest in subsidiaries	$ 444

Shareholders' equity

Common stock of $1 par value. Authorized 4,000,000 shares; issued 3,004,835 shares, of which 4,835 shares are held in treasury by subsidiary at nominal value	$ 3,000
Additional capital in excess of par value	5,747
Retained earnings	126,819
Total shareholders' equity	$135,566
Total liabilities and shareholders' equity	$206,433

EXHIBIT 7

JEFFREY GALION

Consolidated Statements of Income
Years Ended December 1969–1973
($000)

	1969	1970	1971	1972	1973
Net sales	$ 133,773	$ 151,639	$ 171,679	$ 170,914	$ 223,501
Cost of sales	95,069	109,421	128,879	128,760	164,558
	$ 38,704	$ 42,218	$ 42,800	$ 42,154	$ 58,943
Selling, engineering and administrative expenses	21,717	22,943	24,804	25,189	33,521
Operating income	$ 16,987	$ 19,275	$ 17,996	$ 16,965	$ 25,422
Other income (expense):					
Interest income	$ 1,060	$ 1,075	$ 1,178	$ 1,091	$ 1,458
Interest expense on short-term borrowing	(199)	(198)	(483)	(269)	(1,832)
Interest expense on long-term borrowing	(185)	(139)	(139)	(191)	(512)
Miscellaneous, net	435	525	667	493	449
Foreign currency exchange gain (loss)	—	—	229	(948)	562
	$ 1,111	$ 1,263	$ 1,452	$ 176	$ 125
Income before income taxes and extraordinary item	$ 18,098	$ 20,538	$ 19,448	$ 17,141	$ 25,547
Income taxes	$ 9,915	$ 10,002	$ 7,945	$ 8,117	$ 12,604
Charge equivalent to realized net operating loss carryforward of foreign subsidiaries	—	471	702	401	—
	$ 9,915	$ 10,473	$ 8,647	$ 8,518	$ 12,604
Income before extraordinary item	$ 8,183	$ 10,065	$ 10,801	$ 8,623	$ 12,943
Extraordinary item—tax benefits realized from net operating loss carryforward of foreign subsidiaries	—	471	702	401	—
Net income	$ 8,183	$ 10,536	$ 11,503	$ 9,024	$ 12,943
Net income per share:					
Income before extraordinary item	$ 2.73	$ 3.35	$ 3.60	$ 2.87	$ 4.31
Extraordinary item	—	0.16	0.23	0.13	—
Net income	$ 2.73	$ 3.51	$ 3.83	$ 3.00	$ 4.31
Dividends per share	$ 0.91	$ 0.92	$ 1.07	$ 1.12	$ 1.14
Average number of shares of common stock outstanding	3,000,000	3,000,109	3,001,505	3,003,543	3,001,480
Depreciation	$ 3,930	$ 4,218	$ 4,485	$ 4,383	$ 5,029

graders, road rollers, rough-terrain hydraulic cranes, and components for these products, which were manufactured in the United States at Galion and Bucyrus, Ohio. Sales of spare parts averaged approximately 19 percent of construction equipment sales over the past five years and were more profitable than sales of new machines.

Galion motor graders, which ranged in size from 62 to 190 horsepower, were used principally for maintenance of roads, highways, airports, and mining haulways and for snow removal. Approximately 80 percent of sales of motor graders were to governmental agencies, primarily at state and local levels.

Galion road rollers ranged in size from 3 to 14 tons. Jeffrey Galion manufactured two-axle tandem, three-wheel, pneumatic tire and vibratory road rollers. Road rollers were used in the maintenance and construction of highways, airports, parking lots, and other surfaced areas. Principal users of road rollers were governmental agencies and private contractors, with sales divided approximately equally between the two.

Galion rough-terrain hydraulic cranes, ranging in lifting capacity from 8 to 15 tons, were used in warehousing, yard storage, oil refinery, pipeline and other construction, aircraft maintenance, heavy in-plant materials handling, and a wide range of other applications. Jeffrey Galion also manufactured a truck-mounted crane and a pedestal crane.

In 1974, Jeffrey Galion expected to commence production of a road planer, which used a cutting drum with replaceable teeth to mill off old road pavements without preheating the road surface and permitted year-round pavement removal even in cold climates. British Jeffrey-Diamond Limited had produced a similar planer since 1972.

Galion construction equipment was sold by approximately 80 independent domestic distributors and approximately 135 foreign distributors (who also had sales and service agreements with other manufacturers of construction equipment). In 1973, the five distributors with the largest volume accounted for approximately one third of domestic sales of construction equipment.

Several major manufacturers produced competing lines of construction equipment which were broader than Jeffrey Galion's product lines, and a number of smaller companies offered certain products which competed with various Galion products. However, Jeffrey Galion considered itself to be a major competitive factor in each of its lines of construction equipment.

The market for motor graders and road rollers used in new construction was thought to be affected by factors such as the level of government funding for highway construction and possible shortages of petroleum-based asphalt. A significant portion of Galion motor graders and road rollers (including most of these sold to government agencies, approximately 80 percent in the case of motor graders and approximately 50 percent in the case of road rollers) was used for road and highway maintenance, and to this extent sales were less subject to declines in new construction. Declines in state gasoline tax revenues, or in highway usage, as a result of the gasoline shortage could, of course, result in reduced expenditures for highway maintenance.

Principal items purchased by Jeffrey Galion from outside suppliers for use in the manufacture of Galion products were steel, axles, transmissions, torque converters, engines, tires, electrical equipment, and bearings. Currently, certain items—transmissions, torque converters and axles—were supplied by one manufacturer. This manufacturer had advised Jeffrey Galion of a proposed limitation in availability of transmissions, torque converters, and axles. While Jeffrey Galion was endeavoring to obtain an assurance that deliveries of these components would continue at required levels, such a limitation in availability would impair the ability of Jeffrey Galion to meet production schedules and adversely affect construction equipment sales and income. To date, deliveries of these components had been adequate. There was no alternate supplier of transmissions and axles which could meet Jeffrey Galion's current requirements. Management was also aware that one of this manufacturer's major collective bargaining agreements was to expire in April 1974.

Industrial Equipment. Jeffrey Galion's industrial equipment products were divided into two product categories: mechanical power transmission equipment and conveying and processing products and systems.

Prior to 1973, Jeffrey Galion's mechanical power transmission equipment line consisted of engineering-class chain and sprockets. In 1973, Jeffrey Galion acquired three units of the Power Transmission Division of Litton Industries, Inc.: Whitney Chain, with headquarters and manufacturing facilities in Hartford, Connecticut; Foote-Jones, with headquarters and several plants in the Chicago area; and Electra Motors, with headquarters in Anaheim, California, and manufacturing facilities in Anaheim and Ashland, Virginia. Whitney Chain manufactured precision roller chain. Foote-Jones manufactured a broad line of in-line and parallel-shaft speed reducers, worm gear reducers, gear motors and related products. Electra Motors manufactured small worm gear motors, worm gear reducers, small motors, and custom designed drives. Profit margins on some products produced by the acquired operations had been below other industrial equipment margins.

Principal users of mechanical power transmission equipment included pulp and paper mills, chemical plants, steel mills, mines, and mining equipment manufacturers.

Jeffrey Galion's conveying and processing products and systems included conveying machinery, processing equipment, and engineered systems. Conveying machinery was manufactured at plants located at Belton, South Carolina, Fort Worth, Texas, and Columbus, Ohio. These products included belt conveyors, components for belt conveyors, apron conveyors, bucket elevators, and screw conveyors. Conveying machinery was marketed principally to users in the primary metals, stone, glass, coal, and chemical industries. Screw conveyors were purchased primarily by food, grain, and chemical processors and air pollution control equipment manufacturers. Processing equipment was manufactured in Woodruss, South Carolina, and Columbus, Ohio and included crushing and shredding machines and vibratory and other processing equipment sold to a broad range of mining and manufacturing end users.

Engineered systems incorporating conveying and processing products and equipment were custom-designed, manufactured and, in certain instances, installed by Jeffrey Galion personnel to meet the requirements of specific users. Typical applications included foundry conveying systems and major components for water, sewage, and solid waste treatment plants. In some cases, engineered systems were installed under fixed-price contracts.

Industrial equipment products were marketed in the United States through approximately 100 field sales engineers with offices serving most major industrial cities, complemented by a network of approximately 300 independent distributor outlets.

Jeffrey Galion's industrial equipment products competed with those of a number of other manufacturers, both larger and smaller than Jeffrey Galion. Competition was primarily on the basis of price, warranty, and customer service.

Mining Machinery. Jeffrey Galion's mining machinery products, marketed under the Jeffrey trademark, included continuous mining machines, self-propelled vehicles for the transfer of materials from the mine face to main line haulage, crawler mounted loading machines, electric and battery powered mine locomotives, ventilation fans and chain conveyors. Sales of spare parts averaged approximately 42 percent of mining machinery sales over the past five years.

Principal users of domestically produced Jeffrey Galion mining machinery were domestic operators of underground bituminous coal mines. Sales of mining machinery were made directly to users through company sales engineers and support personnel in the country's major coal-producing areas. Parts warehouses were maintained in the principal coal fields. Some of this equipment was adaptable to and had been sold for use in mining underground deposits, potash, salt, and other friable materials, both in the United States and abroad. In 1973 Jeffrey Galion's five largest customers for mining machinery accounted for approximately 30 percent of its mining machinery sales from the United States.

Increasing consumption of electric energy and growth of the steel industry had resulted in increased demand for coal. Sales of mining machinery tended to fluctuate with coal industry capital spending cycles and with tonnages of deep-mined coal produced. Since 1971 sales had declined slightly as a result of environmental protection regulations affecting the use of high sulphur coal and greatly increased mine operating costs resulting from Federal safety regulations. Continuing demand for replacement parts, which were significantly more profitable than new machines, moderated the effect of fluctuations in sales of new machines. Another factor at work was the expiration of the United Mineworker's collective bargaining agreement with the coal industry in November 1974. Consumption of replacement parts would be severely reduced for the duration of any mineworkers strike, and deliveries of new machines could also be delayed.

British Jeffrey-Diamond Limited's mining machinery products, which accounted for approximately 30 percent of Jeffrey Galion's mining machinery sales in 1973, consisted principally of shearer-loaders, used extensively in long-wall coal mining, and replacement parts. Approximately 90 percent of British Jeffrey-Diamond Limited's sales of mining machinery were to the National Coal Board. The recently settled strike by the National Union of Mineworkers resulted in a significant decrease in sales during the period of the strike.

While Jeffrey Galion believed that it was a significant factor in the underground mining machinery market, this market was characterized by a small number of manufacturers and purchasers, and competition was intense.

Net sales and profit contribution by each of these product lines for the past five years is presented in Exhibit 8.

Foreign Activities. Jeffrey Galion's enterprises abroad included direct export sales, sales to foreign distributors, and sales by manufacturing subsidiaries and licensees. The company had operating interests in Australia, Belgium, Brazil, Canada, Japan, Mexico, South Africa, the United Kingdom, and West Germany. Revenues generated through export sales and foreign operations are presented below:

	1969	1970	1971	1972	1973
Export and foreign sales ($ millions)	$45.1	$50.2	$52.6	$60.5	$63.5
Percentage of net sales	33.7%	33.5%	20.7%	35.4%	28.4%

While Galion was subject to the typical risks of unsettled political conditions, adverse govermental action, exchange control and currency problems inherent in international operations, there was no currently effective restriction on repatriation of foreign earnings which had a material effect on its operations as a whole.

Employees. On December 31, 1973, Jeffrey Galion had approximately 7,550 employees, 5,250 in the United States. Approximately 54 percent of the U.S. employees were members of collective bargaining groups. Jeffrey Galion considered its employees relations to be generally satisfactory. Union contracts covering a total of 966 employees expired in 1974.

Property. Jeffrey Galion had 24 manufacturing plants, ranging in size from approximately 41,000 square feet to approximately 885,000 square feet and totaling some 3.5 million square feet. These plants were located in the United States, Canada, and various foreign countries.

EXHIBIT 8
Product Group Contributions

	1969		1970		1971		1972		1973	
Sales contribution:										
Construction equipment	$ 65.6	49%	$ 72.6	48%	$ 68.5	40%	$ 77.0	45%	$ 95.0	43%
Industrial equipment	44.3	33	49.5	33	67.8	39	59.8	35	91.8	41*
Mining machinery	23.8	18	29.5	19	35.4	21	34.1	20	36.7	16
Total	$133.7	100%	$151.16	100%	$171.7	100%	$170.9	100%	$223.5	100%
Profit contribution:										
Construction equipment	$ 14.5	75%	$ 17.0	77%	$ 15.2	72%	$ 15.5	82%	$ 21.9	73%
Industrial equipment	4.6	24	3.3	15	1.8	8	1.2	6	5.3	18*
Mining machinery	.1	1	1.8	8	4.2	20	2.2	12	2.7	9
Total	$ 19.2	100%	$ 22.1	100%	$ 21.2	100%	$ 18.9	100%	$ 29.9	100%

* Before income taxes, extraordinary items, allocation of general corporate expenses, interest on corporate borrowings, and certain intercompany eliminations which are not material.

STRATEGIC CONCERNS ABOUT ACQUIRING GALION

In trying to evaluate the pros and cons of acquiring Jeffrey Galion, Dresser's management raised a number of strategic questions and concerns:

1. What was the long-term attractiveness to Dresser of increasing its participation in the construction equipment, industrial equipment, and mining machinery businesses? Should Dresser have a strategic interest in expanding its efforts in these particular product markets?
2. Assuming Dresser should consider entering these product markets, was Jeffrey Galion a logical company to try to acquire?
3. How much should Dresser be willing to pay for the acquisition of Jeffrey Galion? What should the terms of an acquisition offer be?

R. H. Jeffrey's reaction to an acquisition "feeler" from Dresser was favorable:

> There is no question in my mind that acquisition by Dresser might prove beneficial to Jeffrey Galion's business. As a large public company, Dresser has access to the financial resources which will be needed to support the rapid growth which Jeffrey Galion is planning for the future and which would eventually exceed the limited means of a private company.

20. The Ditch Witch and the Sky Witch*

INTRODUCTION

On June 1, 1970, Dan Garner, general sales manager of Charles Machine
Works (CMW) requested that the executive committee of the company
schedule a meeting in the near future to discuss the Sky Witch Work-Lift
Platform, one of the products manufactured by CMW. The purpose of the
meeting was to establish top management's long-range objectives concerning
this product so that Garner could develop a comprehensive marketing program. In preparation for this meeting Garner reviewed the history of CMW
with particular consideration for the position of the Sky Witch relative to the
growth of CMW.

COMPANY BACKGROUND AND MAIN PRODUCT LINE

In 1907, the same year that Indian Territory and Oklahoma Territory
became the State of Oklahoma, Charles F. Malzahn and his son Charles
opened a blacksmith shop in Perry, Oklahoma (about 50 miles north of
Oklahoma City). As more and more oil derricks appeared on the horizon,
Charles Malzahn placed a growing emphasis on the repair of oil-field equipment. The Charles Machine Works was officially established. In the late
1940s, a third-generation member of the family, Ed Malzahn, a graduate
engineer, entered the business. His engineering training was the basis for
broadening even further the activities of the company.

One day, watching a pipeline being installed in Perry, Oklahoma, Ed
Malzahn saw a large-wheel trenching machine sitting idle, its use in digging
the main-line trench having been completed. Meanwhile, two men with
shovels dug smaller trenches for installing service lines to surrounding
houses. From Malzahn's observation of this situation and his recognition of
the need for a maneuverable, relatively inexpensive, small trenching machine were born a new product and enterprise expansion. The first Ditch
Witch trencher was produced in 1949. A pouring of resources into engineering modification and into further development has resulted in six basic models that provide a complete line of fully self-propelled trenching machines,
each with varying degrees of capability. Other CMW products include the

---

* Prepared by Dennis M. Crites and James M. Kenderdine, University of Oklahoma.

Roto Witch, a boring unit for continuing trenching operations under streets, sidewalks, and similar surface obstructions. The Sky Witch (the principal subject of this case) is a portable hydraulically powered work platform and is handled largely as a separate sales division of the company. Another CMW product is Geronimo, an escape device for oil-field derrick workers, made exclusively by CMW and used almost universally in the drilling industry.

The first Ditch Witch trenchers were produced in the original plant of the Charles Machine Works. In 1959 a site was purchased west of Perry, and a new 24,000 square-foot manufacturing facility was constructed. Since that time, with demand continuing to grow each year, the plant has undergone seven different expansions, the latest of which gives a total of 250,000 square feet of plant space, with an additional 24,000 square feet in office and clerical space. Behind the plant is the company airstrip, where company planes are in constant operation helping solve the sales and production problems which occur across the nation.

Although the small utility-type trenching machine was envisioned by CMW and has been pioneered into a major national product, greatly increased competition has marked the growth. Rival manufacturers quickly noted the initial success and geared themselves to produce competitive products. Today, there are approximately ten manufacturers actively competing with Ditch Witch for a share of the national market.

Ditch Witch equipment is sold by independent businessmen-dealers, authorized by CMW to provide sales and service in geographical territories all over the United States and abroad. Together, there are more than 100 dealers in all 50 states, Canada, Latin America, Europe, Australia, and Japan. The Ditch Witch dealer and his employees receive complete and continuing training by the factory to assure that they are experts in all phases of trencher sales, operation, maintenance, and repair. The dealer is on call at all times to deliver a part or provide emergency service to keep each customer's equipment on the job. A total of 16 district marketing and maintenance representatives keep in constant touch with the activities in the field. Millions of miles of travel are annually logged by marketing personnel, in their company airplanes and on regular air carriers, to all parts of the world where Ditch Witch equipment is sold. Representatives of the Ditch Witch marketing team demonstrate their product at practically every major trade and industrial show in America.

The company, in a brochure entitled *The Ditch Witch Story,* proudly points out:

> The combination of advanced engineering design, an aggressive marketing program, and an enthusiastic national and international dealer organization have made it possible for Ditch Witch to claim well over 50 percent of the total annual sales for this type of equipment.

A roster of Ditch Witch customers would include some of the most famous names in American business as well as a large number of small companies, contractors, municipalities, governmental agencies, and rental companies. Major American power companies and utilities mark the list, along with major oil companies and giant contracting firms. Another important segment of the Ditch Witch market is represented by the Bell Telephone System and major independent telephone companies. Along with electrical utility companies throughout America, they are engaged in a massive program to place all telephone and power cables underground in new residential and commercial developments.

PERSONNEL AND ORGANIZATION

Operations of CMW are the product largely of the personal leadership of the president, Edwin Malzahn, and the policy guidance developed by Malzahn and his fellow members of the board of directors; the board also serves as the company executive committee. The engineers, draftsmen, skilled craftsmen, assembly-line workers, secretaries, and clerks that make up the home office and factory work force now total over 400 employees. Practically all of them were born and educated in the Perry area.

Despite the size to which the company has so rapidly grown and the complexity of its operations, Malzahn and other officials in the company direct its activities on a largely informal, family-like basis. For example, Malzahn does not believe in organization charts and the company does not have one. (Exhibit 1 is a rough representation by the case writers of the principal positions and departments and the relationships among the persons directing them.) *The Ditch Witch Story,* describing the major tasks carried on by the work force, indicates: "Perhaps the most important operation is the initial one—the design of the machine." It continues: "From the engineering

EXHIBIT 1
Charles Machine Works, Inc.—Organization Chart

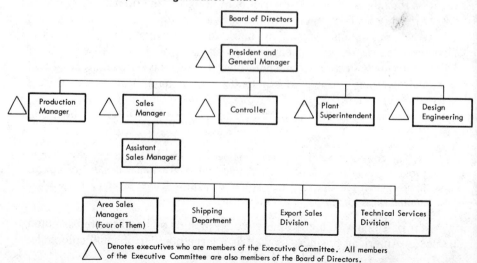

Denotes executives who are members of the Executive Committee. All members of the Executive Committee are also members of the Board of Directors.

department . . . comes a continuing research and development program to help maintain the Ditch Witch position of leadership." On the part also of all employees, the brochure notes their industriousness, resourcefulness, adaptability, and versatility.

The Ditch Witch Story, describing "people who market the product," asserts: "Without question, one of the major reasons for the company's sales superiority can be attributed to the local dealer organization." Efforts of the local dealer are backed up by "a highly-trained, efficient marketing department maintained in the Perry headquarters" . . . including "the national sales and merchandising specialists who plan and coordinate the entire sales picture." Edwin Malzahn, on the last page of The Ditch Witch Story, expresses: (1) pride in the product, plant, people, and pioneering role that mark the company's story; (2) a pledge of "a united team effort to continue to build the finest trenching equipment possible;" (3) a pledge of "every resource toward a constant program of design improvement;" and (4) goals of leading " in the development of new tools to serve our customers . . . and to make every product we manufacture the finest available."

THE SKY WITCH

CMW's first association with work-lift platforms occurred in 1957 when the marketing arm of the company agreed to distribute a platform manufactured by another company. As demand from customers increased for platforms that had additional capabilities, CMW determined in 1958 to design and manufacture its own work-lift platform, the Sky Witch. By 1962 sales of the Sky Witch totaled $83,500 for 38 units. In 1958 CMW began to experience even greater success in the manufacture and distribution of its line of chain trenching machines. Trencher sales continued to increase impressively, growing from about $1 million in 1959 to $16 million in 1969 (see Exhibit 2). Trencher sales consistently amounted to more than 97 percent of total company sales. Quite understandably almost all company resources

EXHIBIT 2
Sales Data*

Year	Total Company Sales ($ millions)	Sky Witch Sales ($ 000)	Sky Witch Percent Increase over Last Year	Sky Witch Percent of Total Sales
1969	16.9	260	22	1.5
1968	12.8	212	−11	1.6
1967	9.0	232	67	2.6
1966	7.8	138	5	1.7
1965	5.6	132	9	2.3
1964	3.9	121	67	3.1
1963	3.1	71.6	−12	2.3
1962	3.1	83.5		2.6
1959	1.0			

* Data have been disguised. Relationships are approximately correct.

and efforts were directed towards the production and marketing of the trenching machine. Sky Witch sales, meanwhile, were growing somewhat erratically; there was a 67 percent increase in 1964 and again in 1967. However, there had been a 12 percent decrease in 1963, relatively small yearly increases between 1964 and 1967, and an 11 percent decrease in 1968 (see Exhibit 2). Sky Witch sales reached $260,000 in 1969, but the percentage of total CMW sales dropped from a high of 3.1 percent in 1964 to 1.5 percent in 1969. Profit as a percent of sales was acceptable in view of company objectives and compared favorably with percent profit from trencher sales.

THE PRODUCT

The Sky Witch is a portable, hydraulically actuated, scissors-arm-type work-lift platform. Various models and options are available for different lifting capacities, elevated heights, power sources, and type of mounting (see Exhibits 3 and 4). A total of seven basic models with over 150 different options are available to meet varied customer requirements and permit custom design. The different models (see Exhibit 3) provide load capacities of 750, 1,000, or 2,000 pounds and maximum platform heights of 9 feet, 15 feet 6 inches, 21 feet 6 inches, or 16 feet. Power options provide for 110-volt a.c. electric motor, hand-operated pump, gasoline engine, and explosion-proof electric or air motor-driven power units. Mounting options make the Sky Witch available as skid mounted (for truck mounting), caster mounted, or four-wheel mounted. Larger models are available with both ends steerable for maneuverability. Manually operated leveling jacks and out-riggers provide stability at elevated work heights. A width to elevated height ratio of one to three is maintained to comply with the safety codes of various states and good design practice. Before it leaves the factory, each machine is load tested at two times its rated capacity.

Almost no changes have been made in the basic design for several years. However, a self-propelled unit was developed in mid-1969 in response to market demand. Problems soon developed with the solenoid valves used on the electric-motor-driven self-propelled models and sale of electric self-propelled models was discontinued. Considerable customer dissatisfaction was expressed also because the chain driving the self-propelled units had to be taken apart to tow the machine to work locations. At the present time design engineering has promised to develop a shiftable drive unit, when it can be worked in. A new structural design was developed and partially tested in the summer of 1969 when an engineering instructor worked at CMW for three months. Testing has not been completed nor fully pursued.

THE SKY WITCH CUSTOMER

The user of the Sky Witch can be almost anyone who needs to place people and equipment at variable work heights between 9 and 30 feet. Ex-

EXHIBIT 3
Sky Witch Models and Prices, February 27, 1968 (all prices f.o.b. factory)

Mountings	Power Units				
	Hand-Operated Hydraulic Pump	Electric Motor (std. 110-volt a.c.)	Gasoline Engine Driven Pump	Explosion Proof Electric (110-volt a.c.)	Air Motor Driven Pump
Model 7-710					
Skid mounted	$1,600	$1,800	$1,800	$2,050	$1,800
Caster mounted	1,700	1,900	1,900	2,150	1,900
4-wheel mounted steer 1 end	1,800	2,000	2,000	2,250	2,000
Optional extras					
Guard rails					
1 each side	15				
1 end	15				
Telescoping ladder		65			
Leveling jacks (4)			140		
Outriggers				75	
Hand pump aux. to power pump					200
Model 10-1117					
Skid mounted	$1,800	$2,000	$2,000	$2,250	$2,000
Caster mounted	1,900	2,100	2,100	2,350	2,100
4-wheel mounted steer 1 end	2,150	2,350	2,350	2,600	2,350
4-wheel mounted steer both ends	2,300	2,500	2,500	2,750	2,500
Optional extras					
Guard rails					
2 each side	15				
1 each end	15				
Telescoping ladder		70			
Leveling jacks (4)			160		
Outriggers (2)				100	
Hand pump aux. to power pump					200
Model 10-1624					
Skid mounted	*	$3,450	$3,450	$3,700	$3,450
4-wheel mounted steer 1 end	*	3,800	3,800	4,050	3,800
4-wheel mounted steer both ends	*	3,950	3,950	4,200	3,950
Optional extras					
Guard rails					
3 each side	15				
1 each end	15				
Telescoping ladder		85			
Leveling jacks (4)			160		
Outriggers (2)				100	

* Not recommended.

EXHIBIT 3 (*continued*)

Mountings	Hand-Operated Hydraulic Pump	Electric Motor (std. 110-volt a.c.)	Gasoline Engine Driven Pump	Explosion Proof Electric (110-volt a.c.)	Air Motor Driven Pump
			Power Units		
Model 20-1117					
Skid mounted	*	$2,450	$2,450	$2,700	$2,450
Caster mounted	*	2,550	2,500	2,800	2,550
4-wheel mounted steer 1 end	*	2,800	2,800	3,050	2,800
4-wheel mounted steer both ends	*	2,950	2,950	3,200	2,950
Optional extras					
Guard rails					
2 each side		15			
1 each end		15			
Telescoping ladder			70		
Leveling jacks (4)				160	
Outriggers (2)					100
Model 20-2117					
Skid mounted	*	$3,400	$3,400	$3,650	$3,400
4-wheel mounted steer 1 end	*	3,750	3,750	4,000	3,750
4-wheel mounted steer both ends	*	3,900	3,900	4,150	3,900
Optional extras					
Guard rails					
3 each side		15			
1 each end		15			
Telescoping ladder			70		
Leveling jacks (4)				160	
Outriggers (2)					100
Model 20-2124					
Skid mounted	*	$5,300	$5,300	$5,550	$5,300
4-wheel mounted steer 1 end	*	5,650	5,650	5,900	5,650
4-wheel mounted steer both ends	*	5,800	5,800	6,050	5,800
Optional extras					
Guard rails					
4 each side		15			
1 each end		15			
Telescoping ladder			85		
Leveling jacks (4)				160	
Outriggers (2)					100
Model 20-2430					
Skid mounted	*	$5,900	$5,900	$6,150	$5,900
4-wheel mounted steer 1 end	*	6,250	6,250	6,500	6,250
4-wheel mounted steer both ends	*	6,400	6,400	6,650	6,400
Optional extras					
Guard rails					
5 each side		15			
1 each end		15			
Telescoping ladder			110		
Leveling jacks (4)				160	
Outriggers (2)					100

* Not recommended.

EXHIBIT 4
Models Sold*

Year	Total Units Sold	Model 10-1117		Model 20-1117		Model 10-1624		Total Percent
		Number Sold	Percent of Total	Number Sold	Percent of Total	Number Sold	Percent of Total	
1969	99	36	37	9	9	38	39	85
1968	80	32	40	11	14	25	31	85
1967	84	18	21	6	7	29	35	63
1966	75	19	25	9	12	29	39	76
1965	56	24	42	3	6	16	28	76
1964	56							
1963	42							
1962	38							

* Data have been disguised. Relationships are approximately correct.

amples are found in construction, maintenance, and service work. Municipalities use the platform for tree trimming, painting, and overhead maintenance. Contractors use the Sky Witch to install electric lights, airconditioning duct work, wiring and conduit, piping, painting, and any overhead equipment. Maintenance crews in large manufacturing plants, chemical plants, refineries, and power plants find the Sky Witch a labor-saving piece of equipment. Maintaining and servicing the nation's airliners is another application for the Sky Witch. Construction crews use the Sky Witch to strip forms and paint bridges and overpasses. A great many rental yards have lift platforms among their stock of rental goods.

Many customers desire features that are peculiar to their industry. For example, the airlines require a machine that cannot cause an explosion and one that is padded where contact can be made with the airplane. Many contractors feel that their particular application is different and that a standard model won't quite do the job. A contractor is also quite likely to need immediate delivery, having been sold on the fact that labor savings on the current job will pay for the Sky Witch. As labor rates continue to rise, certain features are desired by more and more customers. Some competitive machines have one or more of these features. The fact that the self-propelled machine usually reduces the size of the crew by one worker makes it highly desirable. Wanted also is the ability to move the machine while elevated instead of from the lowered position. This creates serious problems concerning safety and liability. Along with operating the machine from the platform goes the need for hydraulically operated out-riggers or leveling jacks. Smaller turning radii are often requested. Many customers want outlets provided to plug in electric or air tools on the platform. Inquiries have been received concerning a direct current battery-powered unit. In certain situations, alternating-current power or compressed air is not available, but a gasoline engine cannot be used because of the carbon monoxide fumes. Inquiries have been received for a lift that would elevate to 40 feet. Some customers have said that the Sky Witch is not as appealing to the eye as more streamlined competitive units. Also, complaints have been received that the wearing surface of the scissor arms wears and scars easily.

In discussing these customer wants and problems with the design engineering section, Garner found that no insurmountable obstacles were involved with the possible exception of making the machine mobile from an elevated height. The problem was rather one of allocating scarce engineering resources to the many projects demanding attention. He was encouraged by the fact that the design engineering staff had been increased from three to seven people in the past 18 months; but this was only one engineer for each $2 million in yearly sales. This meant that Sky Witch could only expect 1½ months of design engineering time per year. The customers had not expressed concern about a reasonable price for the features they wanted, and Garner wondered if added engineering investment on the Sky Witch might not be easily recovered through expanded sales and more expensive machines. He noted that while the self-propelled option added $1,250 to the list price of the machine, this was less than two months pay for a construction worker or electrician. Also, similar capacity competitive machines with additional features were listing for $2,500 more than Sky Witch. Further talks with design engineering developed these estimates of increases in list prices for the following optional features:

1. Self-propelled with shift $1,500.00
2. Hydraulic out-rigger 500.00
3. Power steering of both ends 200.00
4. Platform plug-ins for tools 150.00
5. Battery operated d.c. unit 600.00

COMPETITION

Some 10 or 12 companies manufacture a unit that competes with the Sky Witch. Most of these companies sell fewer units per year than CMW and generally seem to lack adequate resources to develop full market potential. The typical competitor is a company with sales under $1 million per year and none to date have gained a commanding position. CMW has national distribution experience and financial resources that can be considered significantly superior to that of its competitors. The fact remains, however, that several competitors are growing and are experiencing considerable success in some geographical area and with certain market segments. This is because of their ability, versatility, and willingness to provide the options wanted by certain customer groups. Selma Manufacturing Company of Selma, California, has placed an estimated 300 units in rental yards on the west coast in the last 18 months. Their latest model features platform controls, brakes, hydraulic out-riggers, propane, diesel, or battery power, self-propelled mobiling, 31 foot work height, 1,250 pounds capacity, and power source for hand tools on the platform. The unit lists for over $8,000. (See Exhibit 3 for Sky Witch prices.) Stampco, Inc. of Dunbar, West Virginia, manufactures the Skyfold platform in eight basic models that are either battery powered or 110-volt a.c. powered. Options include self-mobiling and hydraulic outriggers. The Get Smart lift is giving Selma competition on the West Coast. Another West coast firm, American Manufacturing Company, manufactures a line of material-handling scissor lifts, including a man-lift for plant maintenance work. Their products are marketed nationally but the man-lift has not been serious competition for CMV. Ballymore Company of West Chester, Pennsylvania, custom-engineered both fixed and variable height work platforms for specific applications such as aircraft maintenance. One manufacturer has just started advertising a lift that will lift to 40 feet working height.

Very little specific information on the competition has been gathered relating to rivals' financial situation and growth capabilities. Garner is convinced that CMW could take a commanding position in the work-lift platform market if the resources are committed to that objective.

DISTRIBUTION AND DEALERS

The CMW Sky Witch is sold by 21 dealers in 16 states. These dealers are typically material-handling equipment companies or construction supply companies which represent a large number of manufacturers of various kinds of equipment. Most maintain a warehouse and a large stock of items. Dealers are given 30 percent or 25 percent off list price, depending on whether or not they are a stocking dealer. This percentage is higher than that on most items the dealer handles. The three largest distributors, one of whom is also a trencher dealer, account for approximately 25 percent of total sales, as shown in Exhibit 5.

EXHIBIT 5
Distribution Data

	Percentage Sold*			
Year	CMW Direct to Customer	Trencher Dealers	3 Largest Sky Witch Dealers	Balance of Sky Witch Dealers
1966	19	34	34	19
1967	30	35	27	21
1968	31	56	20	17
1969	14	35	27	17

* Percentages add to more than 100 percent because one trencher dealer is one of the three largest Sky Witch dealers.

The trenching machines are sold through a dealer organization of 70 dealers in the 50 states and Canada. These dealers are serviced by 16 district representatives and a home office staff. Speaking of the CMW distributors and representatives, one local resident says, "Some of the most able people in Perry have gone out and taken over some of the CMW selling areas." Most of the dealers are handling CMW trenching equipment exclusively and the handling of other items is strongly discouraged. The selling of trenchers and Sky Witches by the same dealer does not create a complementary situation. However, nine trencher dealers are official Sky Witch distributors and other dealers frequently sell a Sky Witch. These trencher dealers account for 35 percent plus of Sky Witch sales. District representatives are encouraged to answer Sky Witch inquiries in their area but trencher sales effort is to receive priority.

Prior to 1968 no factory sales representative was assigned exclusively to Sky Witch sales for more than a few months at a time. From time to time a salesman would set up a dealer somewhere or answer some customer inquiries. Little effort was made to develop distributors or satisfy customer needs. When a backlog of several units was created, delivery time became longer as output was not increased at a level equal to sales. Sales effort then was discontinued. Both production effort and sales effort were constantly strained as the trencher market grew.

In 1968 an extremely able district representative was assigned to Sky Witch sales full time. His efforts in adding distributors were quite successful, but delivery problems soon severely hampered his accomplishments. Delivery time gradually increased. In the first quarter of 1969 delivery time was about 60 days. By the third quarter of 1969 delivery time was above 90 days. Many customers canceled their orders when delivery was later than originally promised. Others simply weren't interested when they were told that delivery could be no sooner than 75 days. Distributors soon lost interest when they found that they had to wait 90 days to replace a standard machine on their floor. As customers were sought out there were more and more requests for options not available on Sky Witch machines. Some might have purchased a standard machine if immediately available but would not wait 90 days for a machine that did not have all the features they wanted.

By late 1969, Garner decided that the present production capacity of the Sky Witch department would not justify a full-time salesman. The salesman was returned to trencher sales, and it was hoped that the distributor organization that had been developed would sell all the units CMW could produce. Inquiries and sales continued strongly through the first quarter of 1970. Delivery time remained at about 90 days. The production department made some methods improvements and added manpower so that production capacity reached 13 to 15 units per month.

By mid-May new orders were down to about one a week. It now appeared that by July 1, all orders would be shipped and that units manufactured would be going into stock. Also, while trencher sales were ahead of the last year, the production department was not operating at full capacity. A plant expansion in 1969 had provided a 50 percent increase in shop floor space. Production capability in all areas was better than at any time in several years. Another major expansion was being added to the factory and was scheduled to be ready for production in January 1971.

PROMOTIONAL METHODS

The Sky Witch has been advertised in leading trade journals such as *Plumbing, Heating, Cooling; Electrical Contractor New Equipment Digest;* and *Oil and Gas Equipment.* News releases frequently appear in *New Equipment Digest* and *New Products.*

National mailing lists were used to send descriptive literature to general, air-conditioning, plumbing, heating, electrical, painting, and prefab building contractors. Mailers were also sent to oil refineries and aircraft companies. A high return of 5 percent was received from 100,000 sent out over a four-year period. The inquiry was answered, literature was sent, and the Sky Witch distributor in that area was notified, if there was a representative. If no report of a sales call had been received from the distributor, a follow-up letter was mailed with a return enclosed. The card was to be returned to CMW.

The Sky Witch was taken to two or three trade shows annually. Those attended included the National Plant Engineering Show, the Western Plant Engineering Show, the National Electrical Contractors Association Show, the American Rental Association Show, and the National Plumbing, Heating and Cooling Contractors Show. The advertising manager and the assistant sales manager both feel that the interest generated by Sky Witch at these shows was quite exceptional. The extent to which sales leads were followed up was not known. The total dollar amount spent on advertising and trade shows is estimated at $10,000 per year. This amount on a percentage basis is more than that being spent on trencher advertising.

THE POTENTIAL MARKET

Garner's quantitative data about the total national demand for work-lift platforms was rather limited. Experience told him that sales effort had in the past generated more demand than could be met by the production department. The Sky Witch salesmen had put together a figure of $1.5 million in sales of Sky Witch type lifts for the calendar year 1968. Selma had sold 300 units in 18 months, most of them in California. Interest at trade shows and response to advertising indicated that potential demand was present. Because the Sky Witch can be used by such a diversified group of customers, Garner wants many more outlets than CMW has for trenchers. In studying data or models sold he noticed that despite the clamor for special features over 75 percent of Sky Witch sales were of three basic models. (See Exhibit 4.) Also, two of these, the 10-1117 and the 20-1117 were built on the same size frame. Garner surmises that two markets really exist. One is for a standard work-lift platform that has features available which many customers want. The other is a market for custom-engineered, material-handling work-lift systems.

The rapid advance of wages in the construction trades is stimulating interest on the part of contractors. Hourly rates for skilled journeymen of $7 to $10 per hour make the adoption of labor-saving equipment mandatory.

Garner had requested a special meeting of the executive committee devoted exclusively to the Sky Witch because the regular meetings of the committee always seemed to end before fully dealing with the problems of the Sky Witch. Somehow the other members of the committee did not seem to get very excited over problems associated with the Sky Witch, and they usually seemed willing to pass them by or to deal with them in an off-hand manner. The only reason he could think of to explain this attitude was that the committee felt that there was nothing the company was doing with regard to the Sky Witch that could be considered "wrong." The product was profitable to the firm; it was selling at a higher rate now than when it had been introduced; and even if design-engineering time were at a premium within the firm, the Sky Witch was continually being improved and developed. He felt it might be better, in the long run, simply to wait until specific problems regarding the Sky Witch did appear.

But if the executive committee could be persuaded that the time to make changes and adjustments was before problems developed, then Garner felt that there were really three courses of action open to the firm. The first and most logical would be to spin off the Sky Witch operation from the main operation of the firm as a completely separate operating division, headed by its own top-level executive. This way a design-engineering team interested solely in the Sky Witch could be created, and a sales force and distributor organization totally oriented to the Sky Witch could be created.

A second course of action would be somewhat less drastic than the first and would involve setting up only a separate sales organization and distribution structure for the Sky Witch. Although the customers for the Sky Witch and the Ditch Witch overlapped to some extent. Garner felt that the Sky Witch might differ enough in terms of applications to justify a somewhat different approach than that developed for the Ditch Witch. For one thing, the customers for the Sky Witch tended to be somewhat larger firms than those purchasing the Ditch Witch and it might, therefore, be possible to sell the Sky Witch directly to them, eliminating the need for many small independent distributors.

The final course of action that Garner felt was available to the company was also the most drastic of the three—sale of the Sky Witch operations to another firm. While there were no offers on his desk, Garner felt confident that he could find a buyer for the Sky Witch at terms quite favorable to the firm. Several times during the past couple of years, executives of other lift-platform companies had told him at trade fairs that if the company ever "got tired of trying to sell the Sky Witch to call them." Garner had always felt that these men were trying to do three things at once—pick up a very respected brand name, eliminate a powerful competitor, and acquire a very profitable product. Thus, he was quite sure that if the executive committee wanted to dispose of the Sky Witch, he would be able to do so.

21. Bishopric, Inc.*

In March 1977, Bishopric, Inc., a holding company located in Cincinnati, Ohio, was approached by ACI Industries regarding the possibility of Bishopric being acquired by ACI. During the past year Bishopric had acquired and revitalized several food processing equipment companies, and ACI hoped that Bishopric could turn around ACI's floundering Crown Division, a producer of specialty food processing equipment. Whereas ACI had a sales volume of $500 million and its Crown Division did a volume of $30 million, Bishopric's 1976 sales were about $15 million.

Although Tom Layton, Bishopric's president, had rejected ACI's initial offer, during the next few weeks Layton and John Davies, Bishopric's chairman, began to consider plans for acquiring the Crown Division from ACI. Tom Layton explained:

> Being approached by ACI expanded our thinking. Here was a large company coming to us saying that we could turn around one of their divisions that was twice our size.
>
> Well if they had that much confidence in us, then why shouldn't we buy the Crown Division and have us realize the benefits of our efforts? The Crown Division fits our plans and strategies like a glove. The only problem is that Crown is twice our size. The thought of taking over a company that is larger than us is somewhat risky, but on the other hand, I feel that we have the skills to manage the Crown Division.
>
> In fact, my main concern is not whether we can manage Crown, but that the acquisition may precipitate too rapid a reorganization of Bishopric, Inc. We have been growing so fast over the past few years that I'm not sure if our organization will be able to handle so much change and growth in so short a period of time.

COMPANY BACKGROUND

The Bishopric Products Company was founded in the early 1900s and originally engaged in numerous areas related to the construction industry. Over time, however, the company's activities became more narrowly focused on the production of large storage tanks for food and beverage com-

---

* Prepared by Prof. Richard Hamermesh of Harvard University. Copyright © 1977 by the President and Fellows of Harvard College. Reprinted by permission. All rights reserved.

panies. Bishopric had entered the tank business shortly after World War II and was immediately successful in this endeavor. By 1977, the Bishopric Products Company was the largest subsidiary of Bishopric, Inc., and was one of the leading manufacturers of lined steel and stainless steel tanks in the United States.[1]

Growth during the 1950s and 1960s was unspectacular but steady and the company reported satisfactory profits. Nevertheless, as a third-generation family-run company, Bishopric faced the problem of having its ownership dispersed among several family branches and members, with only one family member, John Davies, working in the company. John Davies noted some of the problems:

> There are really very few successful family companies. And I guess that's because families tend to mess up the decision making process.
>
> I am a firm believer in having a strong board of directors because I feel I need a Board as a check on me, and because a board can help set the overall direction of a company. With our family situation, too many of our directors represented family factions or were bankers representing trusts. The result was that I was blocked from doing many of the innovative things which I wanted to do with the company.
>
> I decided that I had to find a way to gain control of the company and to get the bankers off my board. It took me about three or four years to work it out, but finally I figured out a way of getting the family and the bankers out of the business.

By 1975, John Davies had acquired 80 percent of Bishopric's stock. To accomplish this, Bishopric purchased the shares of several family members for 20 percent more than its book value, while other family members exchanged their stock for debt. These transactions substantially depleted Bishopric's net worth, but gave John Davies control of the company.

At about this same time, the holding company, Bishopric, Inc., was established. The motivation for forming Bishopric, Inc., was to provide the financial and organizational flexibility to acquire other companies. In 1969 John Davies had wanted to acquire a fiberglass boat company, but the proposal was rejected by Bishopric's board of directors. The boat company subsequently became extremely successful, so John Davies wanted to form the holding company so he could take advantage of similar opportunities in the future.

Bishopric Products. The Bishopric Products Company was the foundation around which Bishopric, Inc., was built. Even though Bishopric, Inc.'s five-year plan called for several acquisitions, Bishopric Products was expected to remain the largest subsidiary within Bishopric, Inc.

During the past several years Bishopric Products had enjoyed spectacular growth. Since 1972 sales had increased at an annual rate of 30 percent, while

---

[1] The distinction is a confusing, but important one. The Bishopric Products Company was a subsidiary of the parent company, Bishopric, Inc.

operating profit grew at over 50 percent annually. The success of the company seemed to illustrate John Davies' dictum that, "I'd rather own a small gold mine, than a large silver mine." (See Exhibits 1 and 2 for financial information.)

EXHIBIT 1

BISHOPRIC, INC.
Profit and Loss, 1972–1976 ($000)

	1972*	1973	1974	1975	1976
Sales	$5,220	$6,218	$9,652	$17,763	$14,70
Cost of goods sold	4,128	5,460	8,007	13,312	10,48
Gross profit	1,092	758	1,645	4,451	4,22
Administration and selling expense	631	616	802	1,125	1,28
Operating profit	461	142	843	3,326	2,93
Other income*	133	445	327	225	19
Profit before taxes	594	587	1,170	3,551	3,13
Profit after tax	305	322	625	1,832	1,59

* All fiscal years end on September 30.
** Throughout the October 1, 1971 to September 30, 1976 period, Bishopric, Inc. had only one subsidiary, Jense Fittings, Ltd., whose performance was recorded using the equity method.

Although Bishopric Products manufactured storage tanks for a wide number of food and beverage companies, the majority of its business was done with the brewing industry. In fact, it was estimated that Bishopric enjoyed a 75 percent share of the beer storage tank business. Bishopric's dominance in this area could be attributed to a long history of successfully meeting the needs of the brewing companies as well as to some important innovations. For example, Bishopric Products had pioneered in the development of large temperature controlled storage tanks which could be placed outdoors. Prior to this, most beer was stored in smaller tanks which were installed in multistoried refrigerated buildings.

As shown in Exhibit 3, Bishopric Products' tanks were extremely large. The company had made tanks with up to 300,000 gallons of capacity. As a result, Bishopric manufactured some of the tanks in its factory, but over half of the tanks were "field erected." In addition, for some applications, the tanks were lined with a resin that would prevent deterioration of the stored product. Bishopric's lining activities were also carried out in their factory or in the field.

Bishopric Products had enjoyed considerable success in the tank business. John Davies explained some of the reasons:

> One of our advantages just comes from the fact that we do a lot of business with the breweries—Anheuser-Busch, Schlitz, Miller, and so on. Not only have these companies been growing quite rapidly, but these firms are also cash rich.
>
> As a result we get a lot of advance payment from our customers—25 percent when we sign a contract and 25 percent when the materials to build the tanks

EXHIBIT 2

BISHOPRIC, INC.
Balance Sheets
As of September 30
($000)

	1972	1973	1974	1975	1976
Current assets:					
Cash	$ 158	$ 162	$ 234	$ 236	$ 189
Certificates of deposit	435	815	3,020	3,700	4,050
Accounts receivable	1,220	901	875	1,834	1,712
Inventories	300	1,422	3,881	2,032	2,715
Prepaid expenses	72	75	470	102	89
Total current assets	$2,185	$3,375	$ 8,480	$7,904	$ 8,755
Property, plant and equipment:					
At cost	$2,081	$2,335	$ 2,721	$2,910	$ 3,926
Less accumulated depreciation	1,180	1,261	1,380	1,536	1,748
net	$ 901	$1,074	$ 1,341	$1,374	$ 2,178
Other assets	$1,248	$ 774	$ 760	$ 618	$ 612
Total assets	$4,334	$5,223	$10,581	$9,896	$11,545
Current liabilities:					
Notes and accounts payable	$ 916	$ 485	$ 682	$1,130	$ 1,299
Advance billings	94	985	5,418	2,066	2,812
Accrued liabilities	266	315	382	1,070	854
Income taxes payable	102	202	272	1,680	1,763
Total current liabilities	$1,378	$1,987	$ 6,754	$5,946	$ 6,728
Long-term notes payable	—	—	—	$1,271	$ 1,245
Deferred income taxes	35	50	75	128	166
Shareholders' Equity:					
Common stock	126	126	126	74	238
Paid-in surplus	44	44	44	25	25
Retained earnings	2,751	3,016	3,583	2,451	3,141
Total equity	$2,921	$3,186	$ 3,753	$2,550	$ 3,404
Total liabilities	$4,334	$5,223	$10,581	$9,896	$11,545

arrive at Bishopric. Since we can usually build a tank fairly quickly, we can run the tank business with little working capital. This enables us to reduce our cost of capital and to be more competitive.

In terms of competition there is really no one in the country who does all the things we can do in the tank business and our prices are always competitive. No one builds in quality and performance like we do, and our customers know that.

In line with this, I tell all of our customers that I will show them the basis on which we compute our bids, because as a percent of sales our margins are quite small. But to me, return on sales isn't the important number, it's the cash flow and ROI that count.

In many ways we are in a perfect size industry, what I call an in-between

EXHIBIT 3
Bishopric Products Storage Tanks

Over 50,000 barrels of fermenting capacity was furnished by Bishopric on this job for Miller Brewing Co., Milwaukee, Wisconsin. The eight 6,250-barrel units are stainless steel.

industry. Our industry is too big and requires too much investment for fly-by-night operators to enter. But it's too small to be of much interest to the really large companies.

In addition to these factors, Bishopric Products also had a number of operating practices which management believed contributed to the success of the company. For example, John Davies believed that "people should be over worked and over paid," and as a result Bishopric's salaried employees were paid considerably higher than industry averages. Of the nearly 60 executives working with Bishopric, Inc., 20 earned more than $60,000 in 1976.[2] Also, beginning in 1968 Bishopric began a restricted stock option plan. By 1977 over 20 employees had been included in the plan. Although Bishopric Products' workers were represented by the Boilermakers Union, the company made extensive efforts to create a fair, open, but tough work environment. As a result, Bishopric's employees were quite loyal and during the natural gas shortages of January and February 1977, the workers chose to work in the factory which was at 19 degrees, rather than to close the plant.

---

[2] In total, Bishopric had about 300 employees.

Management Style. Bishopric, Inc., was headed by the two-person team of John Davies, chairman, and Tom Layton, president. John Davies, 49, had joined Bishopric after attending the Harvard Business School and the University of Chicago. John Davies had a wide variety of interests and was a very fast and innovative thinker over a broad range of topics. John enjoyed both his position as an entrepreneur and the success that his business had brought him, but he was also spending more time on projects away from his business. The following comments are representative of John Davies' thinking:

> I believe that a small company is better than a large company, and that a private company is better than a public company. Fortunately the tax laws now favor private ownership, so I am in no hurry to sell this business. When and if we sell, it will be for cash and for the amount that the company is worth.
>
> How can you expect good work if you don't pay people well? I noticed the other day that Riklis was making $600,000 a year while he was ruining Rapid America. If that's what a man gets paid for ruining a company, what should the President of the United States be paid?
>
> I believe that a CEO is no better than the team which works for him. And that extends beyond employees to your board, lawyer, insurance people, and accountants. And although we are a private company, I like to run this as a public company in terms of management practices. I feel that our books and record keeping and organization policies are as good as those of any public company.
>
> I personally think that cash flow is the best measure of a business's success. To me the name of the game is how much more cash you have at the end of the year than at the beginning. Unfortunately, public companies aren't valued that way.
>
> I don't want to work six days a week anymore, so I'll let Tom Layton and his team grow the company and I'll just be involved in the fun parts of the business and the important decisions. There are a lot of other things I want to do. I want to do a number of community things which are important to me, to put some things back into this world. Personally I have all the money I want, and I have long felt that money is only important if you don't have enough. Although I am only 49, I've seen too many people wait until they are too old, and then not have the energy to get involved in new projects or to do the things they have dreamed of all their working lives.

Tom Layton, 40, had joined Bishopric, Inc., as its president in January 1976. Tom could best be described as a thoroughly professional manager who had held a number of operating positions. After receiving his undergraduate degree in chemistry, Tom joined Owens Chemical[3], a midwestern chemical company. One of Tom's first assignments was to develop Owens' business in Texas. One of the accounts which Tom Layton called on was a fledging electronics company, Texas Instruments. Within a year and a half, Texas Instruments was Owens' largest account.

---

[3] Disguised names.

In 1970 Tom Layton accepted the position of president of a medium-size firm located in Cincinnati. Shortly thereafter the company was acquired by B. D. Hudson[4], a large pharmaceutical company. Tom Layton reflected on his experience in this larger corporate structure in which he became quite active:

> Besides being president of one of Hudson's subsidiaries, I had a number of other titles. For example, I was chairman of the Executive Committee of their worldwide chemical group. I guess the point is that Hudson gave me the experience of working in a large, cumbersome, bureaucratic company. In a sense, I've been there and have played that game.
>
> You see, Owens Chemical was a very innovative company, and as a younger manager I was sent to a lot of outside seminars and conferences. As a result I was exposed to MBO and strategic planning and a lot of new management techniques very early in my career. But at Owens, although we were interested in these innovations, we were always very pragmatic and practical and made sure that these programs had bottom line results.
>
> Hudson, on the other hand, had gone in for some outlandish job enrichment and communication programs. The company was managed by committees and consensus and things were most cumbersome. I hope that you get the gist of what I'm saying. I consider myself to be very sensitive to organizations and to the skills needed to implement organization change. But I still believe very strongly that business firms should be efficient.
>
> I had known John Davies through the Young Presidents organization for the past three years, but I didn't know him terribly well. My thoughts were that he was a very intelligent, creative, and expansive manager and person. I visited Bishopric on a Tuesday and continued my discussions with John at a party on Saturday. Over the weekend, I studied five-year financial figures and on Monday we shook hands.

THE HOLDING COMPANY AND DIVERSIFICATION

Bishopric's first attempts at diversification were in the late 1960s, before John Davies had gained control of the company and before the formation of Bishopric, Inc. John Davies explained his interest in diversification and acquisitions:

> Because of the way we operate, Bishopric Products doesn't need a lot of cash to maintain its growth. Our shareholders don't need cash, and besides, paying large dividends would be unwise given the double taxation situation. So for some time, I have felt that we should be putting our cash flow to work by entering additional businesses.

Bishopric's first venture was the purchase of a 50 percent interest in a construction company which built and developed mobile home parks. Although this venture was successful, in time Bishopric felt that its partner had been deceptive in reporting the results of the business. Since the original

---

[4] Disguised names.

agreement had a buy-sell clause, requiring either party to accept a purchase price or to buy out the other partner at the same price, Bishopric sold its interest in the business in 1972 and made about $1 million on the deal. Shortly thereafter, the mobile park industry underwent a severe shakedown.

Another early attempt at diversification was the purchase of a company which made ladders and barrels for the beer industry. Within a year and a half, Bishopric sold the company back to the original owner because of conflicts between Bishopric's management and the owner's son.

In contrast to these ventures, in 1969 Bishopric acquired Jensen Fittings, Ltd., a Canadian firm which made sanitary fittings for the food and beverage processing industry. At the time it was acquired Jensen's sales were $200,000. By 1976 sales approached $800,000.

Efforts within Bishopric Products. Within Bishopric Products efforts had also been made to diversify. John Davies explained:

> Despite our success with breweries, some things made me quite uncomfortable. For example, 95 percent of our sales come from tanks sold to the beverage industry, and only 5 percent from other applications. Well just on principle it is not a good idea to have all of your eggs in one basket. And moreover we can see the day when the breweries will not be building at anywhere near the same rates they had been sustaining in the past. So the question is what can we do to spread our risks a bit.

Support for John Davies's concerns came from industry analysts who were forecasting future average annual barrelage growth of 3.5 percent, compared to a rate of almost 5 percent which had been experienced in recent years.

Two of the most important new activities of Bishopric Products were the production of tanks for nuclear power installations and the development of an aseptic food storage system for food processing companies. For the nuclear power industry, Bishopric Products manufactured auxilliary equipment, such as tanks and pool liners for the chemical and radiation waste systems. Although there were many similarities between Bishopric's traditional tanks and those which were made for nuclear applications, there were also some important differences. One difference had to do with quality assurance. All manufacturers of equipment for nuclear power facilities had to be certified. The certification was referred to as an "N-stamp." Al Hucke, executive vice president of Bishopric Products, commented:

> To receive an N-stamp required us to have much better control and information systems. For example, we have to be able to trace where every one of the materials came from, in case there are any problems. But this has had a good effect on our operation. Now our entire reporting system has been improved and I believe it has helped the quality control of our brewery operations.

Other differences with nuclear equipment were the large volume of sales made to engineering consulting companies and the stage of development of the industry. The future of the nuclear power industry was most uncertain, which was in marked contrast to the beer industry.

Bishopric Products' other new product area was in aseptic (germ-free) storage systems. Bishopric's aseptic system had been developed in conjunction with a research team at Purdue University and the company held several patents for its system. In 1976, Bishopric was awarded the Food Technology Industrial Achievement Award and the Putnam Award for its aseptic bulk food storage system.[5]

Basically, Bishopric's aseptic food processing system enabled food processors to store large quantities of concentrated food products in large aseptic storage tanks for extended periods of time. The process involved pulping the food products, heating the product through a series of rapid temperature changes to achieve sterilization, cooling the product, and storing the product in large tanks which were capable of maintaining asepsis.

Although the basic principles behind Bishopric's system were simple, developing a commercial system was not. For example, every valve, tube, tank, and other piece of equipment with which the food product came in contact had to be totally aseptic. Bishopric had spent over $500,000 to develop its system and was continuing to fund research for its system. Bishopric's aseptic system had many unique characteristics, including the ability to store a wide range of concentrates. Some larger companies, such as H. J. Heinz and Hunt-Wesson, had previously developed their own aseptic processing systems, but these systems lacked the features of Bishopric's and had failed to meet management's earning projections. As a result, Bishopric's management felt that it had no real competition in the aseptic food processing field.

The advantages of aseptic food storage to a food processor were considerable. Currently all processing and packaging of food products was made during the short picking season. For tomatoes, for example, all of the decisions regarding product—paste, sauce, puree, juice—and size and type of container were made during an 8- to 12-week period. Bishopric's system enabled food processors to smooth production by merely withdrawing and processing stored concentrate as it was needed during the year. In addition, Bishopric had developed aseptic tanks which could be shipped to widely dispersed processing plants.

Although Bishopric's aseptic food processing system drew on the firm's strength in storage tanks, the system also engaged the company in the food processing equipment industry. The sterilization unit, chilling unit, valves, and numerous other products used in the system were all developed by Bishopric. By 1977, Bishopric Products had installed three aseptic systems. Al Hucke commented on the future prospects of both the aseptic system and the nuclear tank business:

---

[5] These awards were sponsored by the Institute of Food Technologists and by *Food Processing* magazine.

Currently we are doing about $2 million of sales in each of these businesses. Of course, the nuclear power industry is in somewhat of an upheaval and the food processing companies have hit such hard times that they haven't had much money available for capital expenditures.[6] But in the long run the prospects for both businesses are excellent and I see no reason why both won't be doing $10 million within five years.

The Current Plan. When Tom Layton was hired in January 1976 as president of Bishopric, Inc., he faced the two-fold task of learning about and becoming involved in the Bishopric Products Company and of developing an overall plan for Bishopric, Inc. Tom Layton recalled:

When I joined the company, I guess my conclusions were that I had great respect for John Davies, I knew the company had a good name and that it was profitable. I knew that John Davies did not want to work full-time in the business, but that he was willing to back creative plans for managing and growing the business. I knew John wanted his business to grow, but that he was not desperate for growth and we could do what we felt was right. Also I was intrigued by the food processing equipment, but I had no idea of its potential. I was impressed that the company had obtained N-stamp certification because it meant that they must have excellent quality control and information on the manufacturing process. In summary, I felt that Bishopric was a good company, but basically that it was a four times earnings metal fabrication company.

Well during the next several months I began to read trade journals, attend trade shows, and got to know the people in our company. By the spring of 1976 my impressions had changed. At first, I had no idea what our potential in the food business might be. But I soon realized that it was considerable, say $50 million a year. In fact, Bishopric needed additional food processing products to complete its product line. I also realized that our potential in the nuclear business was vast. My best estimate is that the total market for our products in all of the nuclear power plants currently on the drawing boards is $263 million. Of course we will have to compete for this business and those plants will be built over a number of years. But the potential is vast.

I also discovered that Ed Steinebrey, our controller, had an outstanding financial mind. I also found that our attorney and accountants were absolutely outstanding. Given that I was already thinking of going into acquisitions, it was very important that I have these assets. Also within the organization, I identified six to eight people with high potential who were operating at 60 percent to 75 percent of their capacity. So in the spring of 1976, I began to feel that Bishopric, Inc., was a strong company that was probably worth nine or ten times earnings or about $15 million.

By the end of the summer of 1976, we had formulated our basic plan for the company. Given our strong financial team, the capabilities of a number of people within the organization, and our strong financial position, we became convinced that we could use our stock to acquire other companies. In particular, we wanted to acquire firms in the food and beverage processing equipment industries to expand and round out our capabilities in those areas. Given our

---

[6] See Exhibit 4 for financial data on selected food processing companies.

plans and capabilities, I now believe that Bishopric, Inc. is worth 15 times current earnings.

The cornerstones of Tom Layton's plans for Bishopric, Inc. were judgments that there were substantial growth opportunities in the food processing equipment industry and that it would be possible to acquire companies for stock in a privately held company.

Food processing equipment was a $2 billion industry which had been growing at an annual rate of 9.6 percent since 1967.[7] Future growth was forecast at even higher rates due to the necessity of using processed foods to feed the world's population and because of the growing importance of fast and convenience foods in the United States.[8]

EXHIBIT 4
Financial Data of Selected Food Processing Companies (all figures $ million, except return on equity)

	Sales	Net Income	Capital Expenditure	Return on Equity (5-year average)
Del Monte				
1975	$1,430.4	$53.20	$36.62	13.8%
1972	946.5	26.01	34.55	
Green Giant				
1975	$ 455.39	$ 5.72	$10.56	8.6%
1972	341.81	7.70	10.70	
H. J. Heinz				
1975	$1,888.30	$73.96	$34.68	11.9%
1972	1,205.91	41.55	48.32	
Stokely-Van Camp				
1975	$ 470.2	$ 9.04	$ 8.42	8.1%
1972	316.7	8.22	10.39	

Source: Standard & Poor's stock report.

There were, however, some obstacles facing the food processing equipment industry, such as consumer resistance to new processed food products. For example, aseptic milk, which could be purchased by the consumer in larger quantities and stored at room temperature prior to refrigeration and use, had been on the European market for almost ten years and had made only modest inroads. Also, the food processing companies tended to lack the marketing expertise to develop markets for new food products, and were often either too conservative or cash poor to experiment with new processing techniques. Some observers felt that some of the large packaged goods

---

[7] Domestic market only. Some estimates placed the worldwide market for food processing equipment as much as four times the size of the domestic market.

[8] In 1976, 36 percent of all food expenditures were made at restaurants. Many expected that percentage to reach 50 percent by 1985.

companies might enter the food industry, as Procter and Gamble had with its brand of Pringle potato chips.

The food processing equipment industry was highly fragmented with almost 700 firms. Many of these firms were small companies, started by an engineer with an idea for improving a particular part or piece of food processing equipment. For these companies distribution was crucial and there had been a trend toward consolidation in the industry. Although price was an important factor in purchasing food processing equipment, a reputation for quality and reliability was equally important.

Since Bishopric was a privately held firm, acquiring companies for Bishopric stock posed some serious obstacles. To provide a return to minority shareholders, Bishopric began paying dividends in 1976 of 10 percent of net earnings and planned to increase its payout rate to 15 percent within five years. In addition, all Bishopric acquisitions were made on a book value basis, that is, Bishopric would issue shares whose book value equaled the book value of the acquired company. Since Bishopric's book value per share in 1976 was about $14 a share, while EPS was $7, the acquired firm's owners were obtaining Bishopric stock at a "price" of only two times earnings. Of course one other problem with acquiring companies for stock was that it would dilute John Davies's ownership position. Although John accepted this as necessary, provisions were made to enable John Davies to elect a minimum number of directors to constitute a majority of Bishopric, Inc.'s Board.

John Davies and Tom Layton had developed a number of criteria to guide their acquisition strategy and the selection of specific companies. These included:

1. Only acquiring companies at the right price and at the right time, and only those companies which met Bishopric's needs. Bishopric did not have an acquisition timetable.
2. Companies with high quality, proprietary products in the food and beverage processing industries that would enable Bishopric to develop processing systems.
3. Never buy a company which is "for sale."
4. Only companies with "our kind of people."
5. The companies should have some operating problems.
6. The companies would probably have less than $5 million in sales.

Recent Acquisitions. Bishopric's first acquisition under its guidelines and strategy was Fran Rica Mfg., Inc. Fran Rica fit closely with Bishopric's strategy. The company manufactured a variety of food processing equipment and was providing total processing systems for a number of food products including tomatoes, french fried potatoes, fish fillets, fruit concentrates, and fried onions. Significantly, Fran Rica was located in Stockton, California, giving Bishopric access to the largest agricultural market in the United States. Besides manufacturing a number of proprietary product lines, Fran Rica also did a substantial engineering consulting business in which it would design entire processing facilities for a customer. Tom Layton described how the acquisition came about:

> We knew of Fran Rica through the trade and knew that they had a great reputation. They made food processing equipment that would fit very well with the research we were doing on aseptic storage of food products. We got a Dun & Bradstreet on them, and found out that the year before they had done $4½ million of sales and had made $790,000 in profits before taxes. However, we later found that those figures were somewhat misleading and that they really were earning 5–6 percent pretax profit. I was very straightforward with Al Rica when I met him and I told him that we wanted to buy his company. He was equally honest with me and told me that he owed the IRS $240,000 and thus he would be interested. But he added that he was not going to be pushed into making a sale and would rather take the company through bankruptcy proceedings than to make a bad deal. I think this impressed us about Al, knowing how tenacious he was. As we proceeded, a few other things impressed me about this business and its managers. First the company had young management. Their only problem was that they did not know much about how to manage the administrative aspects of a business and they had been given some bad financial advice along the way. It seemed to me that this would make the company a perfect fit with our skills and abilities. In the end we acquired the company for 15,000 shares of Bishopric stock.

In early 1977, Bishopric, Inc., made another acquisition, RL Industries. RL was one of the leading manufacturers of fiberglass storage tanks in the United States and had been the first company licensed by DuPont to make teflon coated tanks. Since RL Industries had a high level of expertise in synthetic building material technology, it was felt that RL added an important dimension to Bishopric's basic business of storing foods and beverages.

Since the acquisitions of Fran Rica and RL were consummated in fiscal 1977, their results had not been included in Bishopric's financial statements. If Fran Rica, RL, and Jensen Fittings' figures had been included in 1976's totals, sales would have passed $20 million and net profit would have reached about $1¾ million. Table 1 shows a pro forma breakdown of 1976 performance.

The Five-Year Plan. In February 1977, John Davies, Tom Layton, Ed Steinebrey, and the key managers of each of Bishopric's subsidiaries met to

TABLE 1
1976 Contribution to Total Performance

Subsidiary	Percent of Total Sales	Percent of Total Net Profits
Bishopric Products	72%	91%
Jensen Fittings	4	2
Fran Rica Mfg........................	20	2
RL Industries	5	4

Figures may not add to 100 percent due to rounding.

develop a five-year plan for the company. Although Tom Layton had done a great deal of background work, the purpose of the meetings was to encourage each of Bishopric's managers to think strategically about his business. By the end of the meetings a specific five-year plan had been developed. For example, it was expected that total sales would reach $60 million by 1982. Although the plan included buying four more small companies during the next five years, it was felt that Bishopric could meet most of its objectives solely from internal expansion. Bishopric expected that by 1982 sales of food processing equipment would equal those to the beer industry and that nuclear power equipment would be about one fifth the size of the other businesses. Although the five-year plan called for substantial growth, the company did not foresee the need for additional long-term borrowings to finance its growth.

COMPANY OPERATIONS

Given Bishopric's plans for growth and acquisition, it is important to understand the internal systems, skills, and resources which management believed would enable Bishopric to continue to prosper. These are discussed below.

Organization. As noted earlier, Bishopric had grown quite rapidly during the 1972–76 period. Nevertheless, John Davies had noted some potential problems:

> In some ways we were quite lucky to make it through our period of rapid growth without a major disaster. We had been growing so rapidly that we were short of managers and lacked any management depth. You know a smaller firm doesn't have the luxury of training lots of people and of being sure that they are ready for promotion.

In some instances, the process of developing and bolstering Bishopric's organization could proceed rather quickly. Other organizational changes took longer to implement. Among the organizational changes that had been made were the hiring of Tom Layton as president of Bishopric, Inc., the hiring of additional engineers to design food processing equipment and systems at Bishopric Products, the creation of a four-person quality control department at Bishopric Products, the creation of a personnel department at Bishopric Products, and the hiring of additional estimators for Bishopric Products' nuclear business. In fact, for the first time an organization chart was developed for the entire Bishopric organization (see Exhibit 5).

Other organization changes took longer to implement because of either the scope of the change or the human problems which could be encountered. Tom Layton noted:

> I realize that some people are in the wrong positions at Bishopric Products, but I am only slowly making those changes. You have to be careful not to throw

EXHIBIT 5
Organization Chart

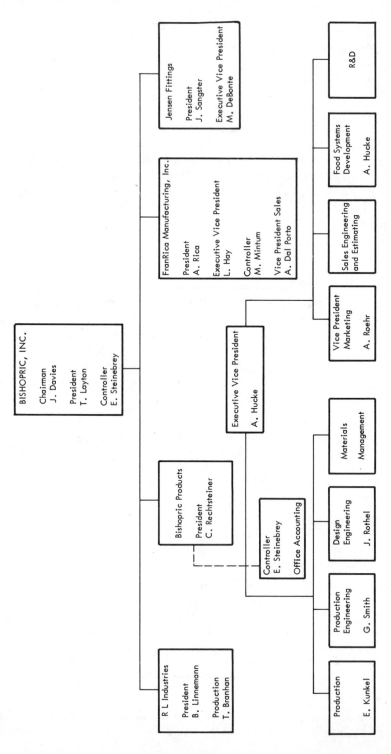

BISHOPRIC, INC.

Chairman
J. Davies

President
T. Layton

Controller
E. Steinebrey

R L Industries

President
B. Linnemann

Production
T. Branhan

Bishopric Products

President
C. Rechtsteiner

FranRica Manufacturing, Inc.

President
A. Rica

Executive Vice President
L. Hay

Controller
M. Mintum

Vice President Sales
A. Dal Porto

Jensen Fittings

President
J. Sangster

Executive Vice President
M. DeBonte

Executive Vice President

A. Hucke

Controller
E. Steinebrey

Office Accounting

Production

E. Kunkel

Production
Engineering

G. Smith

Design
Engineering

J. Rothel

Materials

Management

Vice President
Marketing

A. Roehr

Sales Engineering
and Estimating

Food Systems
Development

A. Hucke

R&D

the baby out with the bath water, so I am grooming the organization to accept change and will only slowly make changes.[9]

In terms of longer range organizational issues, the question of how Bishopric, Inc., would be organized after several more acquisitions was a nontrivial one. Since all of Bishopric's subsidiaries served the same industries with closely related products, the opportunities for rationalization seemed great. For example, whereas Bishopric Products maintained one sales force to sell its products to the beverage, food, and nuclear industries, another subsidiary, RL Industries, did not have a sales force and instead relied on customer referrals and solicitations to attract business. Although some attempts had been made to have Bishopric salesmen mention the existence of RL Industries, all contacts were then referred to RL Industries. Within Bishopric Products, plans for segregating the sales force by end user were being formulated and a separate food systems division, headed by Al Hucke, was established. Exactly how the food systems division would relate to Fran Rica or future food processing equipment subsidiaries was still un-

EXHIBIT 6
Employee Roster

Name	Position	Years with Bishopric or Subsidiary	Current Age
Bishopric, Inc.			
John Davies	Board chairman	28	49
Tom Layton	President	1½	41
Ed Steinebrey	Controller	7½	35
The Bishopric Products Company			
Carl Rechtsteiner	President	31	59
Al Hucke	Executive vice president	24	55
Al Roehr	Vice president—marketing	20	52
Bill Kunkel	Manager of production	20	56
Jim Rothel	Manager of design engineering	2	32
Chuck Smith	Manager of production engineering	13	41
Jensen Fittings			
John Sangster	President	14	58
Marinus DeBonte	Executive vice president	18	51
R L Industries			
Bob Linnemann	President	10	37
Tom Branhan	Production manager	7	33
Fran Rica Mfg., Inc.			
Al Rica	President	10	46
Lloyd Hay	Executive vice president	10	41
Mike Mintum	Controller	4	44
Allan Dal Porto	Vice president—sales	2	36

---

[9] See Exhibit 6 for a roster of key employees.

clear. Tom Layton saw the problem of developing an appropriate organization structure to be closely related to the need for more professional general managers:

> The difference between how I might like to organize our subsidiaries, and how I actually can organize them can be great. For example, we currently do almost $2 million in the tank lining business, even though that business is somewhat of a side activity for us. I'd like to assign one person to be general manager of that business and then let that person go out and develop the business. The problem is in finding that person.

Although there were some questions as to how to organize Bishopric's subsidiaries, there were no plans to expand the staff of Bishopric, Inc.'s corporate office beyond the three-person team of John Davies, Tom Layton, and Ed Steinebrey. Tom Layton explained:

> In terms of general management, professional management, and legal and financial skills, we have all the expertise at the top of the company that we will need. Other skills such as market research or new product development should be contained in the operating subsidiaries.

One organizational issue which Tom Layton and John Davies hoped to resolve soon was the problem of finding appropriate positions for some Bishopric Products managers who had made significant contributions to the company when it was much smaller, but who were somewhat "overwhelmed" by the increased size and complexity of the business. Currently, the idea of transferring some of these managers to other positions within the corporation was being given consideration.

Control. Ed Steinebrey was the third member of Bishopric's management team. In addition to serving as controller of Bishopric, Inc., he was also controller at Bishopric Products and RL Industries. In time, Ed hoped to concentrate solely on his responsibilities at the parent company.

Bishopric had four mechanisms for maintaining financial and operating control over its subsidiaries. The first was a series of financial incentives. For example, Bishopric, Inc., loaned funds to its subsidiaries at a rate of 1 percent higher than prime. This mechanism enabled Bishopric to keep close tabs on the indebtedness of each subsidiary. In addition, all acquisitions were made with bonus agreements which enabled the previous owners' personal earnings to increase rapidly after certain earnings targets had been achieved.

Bishopric, Inc., also received various operating statements from its subsidiaries. For example, on a weekly basis Bishopric, Inc., received statements of the cash position, accounts receivable, new orders, and order backlogs of each subsidiary. On a quarterly basis, complete profit and loss and balance sheet statements were required of each subsidiary except for Jensen which supplied the data semiannually. Beyond these standard reports, Bishopric tailored its information requirements from each business. Ed Steinebrey explained:

> From Bishopric Products, we get a weekly job progress report which shows our labor utilization rates and whether jobs are on schedule. The business does not warrant a monthly profit and loss statement because the company seldom completes an order in just one month.
>
> We used to get a monthly P&L from Fran Rica, but now we only get them every quarter. We found that we just weren't using the information.
>
> You know, I spend a lot of time at the divisions understanding their control and financial systems. I work on special projects reviewing how their overhead rates are set and how they calculate prices. It's that information, plus the day-to-day communication and phone calls, which establishes control.
>
> Right now, I think the information we're getting is sufficient and that any more information would not be worth the cost required to collect it. Of course, as the company gets bigger we may have a need for more detailed information on our subsidiaries.

Another form of control at Bishopric was the classification of certain actions which could not be taken by a subsidiary without approval from Bishopric, Inc. These included all personnel additions, all pay raises, all contracts, all R&D expenditures, and all borrowings from Bishopric, Inc.

Finally, Bishopric's executives felt that their willingness to learn the details of their businesses and to get their hands dirty provided the most useful form of control. Tom Layton explained:

> I think that personal involvement in planning is the best form of control and am not afraid to get personally involved in the activities of our subsidiaries. For example, just last week I was at RL Industries and personally costed a portion of their inventory. The president of the company asked me why I was spending my time on clerical activity. I told him that I wanted to know enough about his business so that I could help him, and now that I understood how they kept their inventories I would be able to help him if he should ask me any questions about their inventory policy. I should mention, of course, that just by checking out their system I had a few suggestions to make.

Turnaround Skills. Since one of Bishopric, Inc.'s acquisition guidelines was to acquire companies with operating problems, a key requirement was for Bishopric to correct these deficiencies. Although Bishopric's financial incentives and strong cash position could help to solve some operating problems, Tom Layton noted a number of other skills which he felt enabled Bishopric to turn around its subsidiaries:

> One of the skills which we have is that John Davies, Ed Steinebrey, and I simply have a far better understanding of profit and loss and balance sheet statements than most people. We can get to the bottom of the figures and ask the tough questions. Also we are not afraid to get in and learn about the businesses which we acquire. I honestly feel that I now know and understand as much if not more about our subsidiaries' businesses than the people who are running them. I understand how they keep their books, the nature of their

expense numbers, their costing systems, and their pricing systems. Moreover, I am not too proud to read trade journals and to go to trade shows regularly. I am always trying to learn about our business in a first hand way.

Also, we do not change the top management of the firms we acquire. We acquire companies that we feel have potential in the marketplace and that have people at the top who we can train to be good managers. I always try to size up the top management of the companies that we're going to acquire and check three things about them. First, do they have the basic intelligence or gray matter to run their business? Second, do they understand their industry? And third, do they have the tenacity to make it? Of course, above all these things I try to determine if I like that person, if we can get along with them. My personal criteria is that I do not want anyone working in this company who I would not be willing to take home and have dinner with my wife and family.

In terms of making a manager out of these people the task is relatively simple. First, through Ed, we are able to establish a professional, well-organized financial information system. And secondly, through the questions that John Davies and I ask we are able to get the managers to think more strategically about their business. We also provide the important service of giving them someone to whom they can talk about their management problems. I don't think most people realize what a problem this is for the managers of small companies. They have no one to talk to for advice or simply a person to talk to about their concerns and plans for the business. Sometimes it's nice to have someone around who merely reassures you that you are indeed on the right track. In short, we speak the same language as the managers of the companies which we acquire, we understand them, and we've been there before.

THE CROWN DECISION

In March 1977 Tom Layton was contacted by Carl Brady, a top executive of ACI Industries. Mr. Brady had heard of Bishopric through trade sources and had been impressed with Bishopric's record of turning around Fran Rica Manufacturing and of developing the business of Jensen Fittings. One of the subsidiaries for which Brady was responsible was the Crown Division, a manufacturer of specialized food processing equipment. During the four years after ACI acquired Crown[10], Crown's performance had fallen off considerably and the division had even lost money in 1974. Mr. Brady hoped to have ACI Industries acquire Bishopric, Inc., and then to have Bishopric manage the Crown Division. Tom Layton commented on his meeting with Carl Brady:

> It was amazing for me to meet Brady. He is the type of person who is enamored with flying in the company plane, the size of his company, his title, his responsibility, and his status. But he has not taken the time to learn about the businesses which he is managing. He suggested $10 million in cash for Bishopric, Inc. I told him that he was right in that we would only consider cash

---

[10] ACI had paid about $9 million in stock for Crown.

offers, but that in my view the company was worth three to four times what he was offering. Brady responded by telling me about all of the advantages and perks which I would enjoy as a high ranking executive of a big company. I guess that he hadn't checked into my background enough to find out that I had already worked for a large company.

After meeting with Brady, Tom Layton and John Davies tried to amass as much data as possible about ACI and Crown through their numerous contacts in the trade. (See Exhibit 7 for financial information.) Among other

EXHIBIT 7
Selected Financial Data on ACI Industries and the Crown Division

	ACI Industries ($000)			
	1973	1974	1975	1976
Sales*	$280,000	$370,000	$460,000	$535,000
Net income	13,000	22,000	24,000	35,000
Working capital	79,000	77,000	93,000	115,000
Net fixed assets	51,000	70,000	102,000	109,000
Shareholders' equity	115,000	128,000	147,000	170,000
Earnings per share	$1.17	$2.05	$2.30	$3.30
Number of employees	8,100	9,000	11,100	10,300

	Crown Division ($000)			
	1973	1974	1975	1976
Sales	$ 36,000	$ 28,000	$ 30,000	$ 30,000
Net income	1,000	(100)	100	350
Working capital	1,000	1,500	1,200	1,200
Net fixed assets	6,500	7,500	7,400	7,400
Number of employees	860	820	740	700

* Over half the sales increase was due to acquisitions.

things they found that Crown's owners had sold the business out from under the management of the business and that the old management had had difficulty in relating to ACI's methods of doing business. Both the Crown name and the division's management had an excellent reputation in the trade. At the time of the Crown acquisition, ACI indicated its intentions to enter more specialized industrial markets, but apparently ACI lacked the skills to manage more narrowly defined businesses and Crown had been unable to meet ACI's financial goals.

For Bishopric, the main appeal of Crown lay in its product line and management personnel. Crown's line of small capacity heat exchangers was among the best in the industry and the company also manufactured a complete line of sanitary valves and fittings which would compliment Jensen Fittings' products. Also, Crown did a large portion of its business with dairies, a market which Bishopric had planned to serve. From a number of sources, Bishopric learned that Crown's management was competent, but frustrated at being a part of ACI.

By the end of March 1977 Tom Layton and John Davies felt they had reached an important crossroads in their negotiations with ACI Industries. Several days previously Carl Brady had written Davies and Layton explaining that ACI was willing to increase its offer for Bishopric and that Layton or Davies should contact him if they were interested. This confronted Davies and Layton not only with the problem of determining at what price they may be willing to sell to ACI, but also with determining a specific counter proposal to purchase the Crown Division themselves. Since both Layton and Davies wanted to meet with Crown's management and to evaluate Crown's products and technology first hand, they knew that they would have to make a reasonable first offer to Carl Brady. On the other hand, Davies and Layton could simply reject ACI's offer and not pursue Crown, and follow their original strategy. John Davies reflected on his options and Bishopric's current position:

> This company has come a long way and I'm convinced that the strategy which we are following is a good one. The impact of the two acquisitions that we have made has been to increase our sales by 30 percent and our earnings by 15 percent, and it's only taken 10 percent of the equity of this company to do this.
>
> Tom Layton and his team really want to make this company grow and I concur. Layton is the future of this company, is a very organized planner and professional manager, and is chomping at the bit to have this company grow.
>
> I believe that it is very important to keep your options open and to have the flexibility to go in a half-dozen different directions. This deal with Crown and ACI is sort of typical. Sure running a $30 million company would be a challenge to us. But if we could purchase Crown on the right terms, I have no doubt that we would be able to manage the business and to improve its profits. There are other options, however, which I am also considering. For example, I would like to know how much more ACI would be willing to pay Bishopric. There is a point at which I would sell the business, and I think it's a little lower than Tom's [Layton]. Finally, we could drop all of our discussions with ACI and just pursue our original strategy.

22. Alabama Power Company*

In early 1979 management officials of Alabama Power Company (APCo) were awaiting a decision by the newly elected Alabama Pulbic Service Commission on the company's filing for a record $283 million increase in electric rates. Earlier the Commission had rejected APCo's request for an *emergency* rate increase of roughly 30 percent, although it did grant the company a 9.5 percent *temporary* increase, pending its July 1979 decision on the company's $283 million rate hike request.

Alabama Power had earnings in 1978 of $42.9 million, down 63 percent from a $117 million profit in 1977 (see Exhibit 1). The company's present return on equity investment was barely 4 percent and, in the absence of a rate increase, this was projected to fall to zero by September 1979. The company's cash flow problem was so critical that the comptroller was relieved of other duties to devote full time to the firm's cash flow "crisis."

In view of both company officials and outside experts, Alabama Power's financial situation was serious. According to a top security analyst of Paine Webber Mitchell Hutchins, Inc.:

> Alabama Power Company is a company in the midst of a financial crisis, and is only a step away from jeopardizing its ability to service customers because of its depressed level of financial integrity.

Several factors justified this conclusion. APCo's 1978 profits of $42.9 million were far below its dividend obligations of $108.8 million. The company was confronted with financing roughly a $3 billion construction program over the next four to six years to meet the electric power needs of customers in its service area; yet declining profitability, rising interest rates, and inflation were making the task of raising this much capital for construction virtually impossible. Equally important, however, was the politically and emotionally charged atmosphere in the state which, in the last two years, resulted in the power company being generally known as "public enemy number one" and becoming a frequent target of the governor, the state attorney general, and nearly every candidate for public office. Public attitudes toward the company were strongly hostile because of rising electric bills, thereby making it political suicide to be pro power company. With feelings against Alabama Power running so high and with the three members

---

* Prepared by Prof. Arthur A. Thompson of The University of Alabama.

EXHIBIT 1

ALABAMA POWER COMPANY
Statements of Income
($000)

	1978	1977	1972	1968
Operating revenues, electric	$1,014,443	$968,693	$325,700	$212,126
Operating expenses, electric:				
Fuel	$ 295,186	$250,409	$ 63,528	$ 26,499
Purchased and interchanged				
power (net)	161,602	183,746	32,061	21,536
Other operation and maintenance . . .	198,596	160,725	71,882	44,259
Depreciation and amortization	109,315	69,938	37,253	25,722
Taxes other than income taxes	63,737	47,887	24,950	13,885
Federal and state income taxes	25,080	89,161	20,327	29,429
Total operating expenses	$ 853,516	$801,866	$250,001	$161,330
Operating income, electric	$ 160,927	$166,827	$ 75,699	$ 50,796
Other income:				
Allowance for funds during				
construction				
Debt and equity	—	—	14,954	$ 2,237
Equity	38,927	53,168	—	—
Other (net)	5,965	4,268	1,728	1,737
Income before interest charges	$ 205,819	$224,263	$ 92,381	$ 54,770
Interest charges:				
Long-term debt and other				
interest expense	$ 169,645	$137,678	$ 42,709	$ 19,511
Allowance for funds used during				
construction—debt	(19,207)	(27,624)	—	—
Income-tax effect of debt portion				
of allowance for funds used				
during construction	(18,741)	(26,953)	—	—
Net interest charges	$ 131,697	$ 83,101	$ 42,709	$ 19,511
Net Income	$ 74,122	141,162	$ 49,672	$ 35,259
Dividends on preferred stock	31,219	23,886	9,027	3,591
Net income after dividends on				
preferred stock	$ 42,903	$117,276	$ 40,645	$ 31,668

Source: *1978 Annual Report.*

of the PSC being elected by the voters (although one commissioner had been appointed by Governor Wallace when a former PSC member was convicted of bribery), the regulatory environment was clearly adverse in terms of getting approval of rate increases.

Moreover, the situation in the summer and fall of 1978 was further complicated by the election of a new governor to succeed George Wallace and the election of two new PSC members (neither of the two incumbents chose to stand for reelection and the third member, whose term was not up, was running for another state office). Alabama Power's management delayed filing for a major rate increase until after the elections partly, it was suspected, to avoid further political controversy—see Exhibit 3 for a chronology of other rate-related events. But in late 1978, Alabama Power found itself in a severe cash flow bind and without hope of action on its newly filed $283 million rate hike request until mid-July 1979 when the new PSC would render a decision. In January 1979, construction work at all new generating plants was suspended. Approximately 2,700 craft workers were laid off at the job sites, most of whom were employed by construction firms having contracts to build the new facilities for Alabama Power. In addition, the company initiated drastic cutbacks in its coal purchases; all spot purchases of coal, approximately 100,000 tons per month, were stopped and reductions in deliveries from long-term contractors were sought in the amount of 150,000 tons per month. The reduction in coal purchases was projected to conserve

EXHIBIT 2

ALABAMA POWER COMPANY
Balance Sheets
December 31, 1978 and 1977
($000)

	1978	1977
Assets		
Utility plant		
In service and held for future use, at original cost	$3,543,626	$3,070,210
Less accumulated provision for depreciation	709,123	610,943
	$2,834,503	$2,459,267
Nuclear fuel, at amortized cost	$ 63,670	$ 65,170
Construction work in progress		
Nuclear	465,144	347,928
Other	270,633	415,149
	$3,633,950	$3,287,514
Other property and investments	$ 19,372	$ 19,042
Current assets:		
Cash	$ 9,283	$ 3,234
Temporary cash investments, at cost	8,507	—
Receivables, less accumulated provision for uncollectible accounts of $811,000 in 1978 and $440,000 in 1977	88,347	78,542
Refundable federal income tax	—	25,985
Fossil fuel stock, at average cost	127,684	89,838
Materials and supplies, at average cost	20,415	18,377
Prepayments	11,389	2,970
	$ 265,625	$ 223,946
Deferred charges:		
Deferred cost of cancelled plant	$ 26,404	$ 32,363
Debt expense, being amortized	6,378	5,492
Miscellaneous	16,177	13,099
	$ 48,959	$ 50,954
	$3,967,906	$3,581,456

EXHIBIT 2 (continued)

Capitalization and Liabilities

Capitalization:

Common stock equity	$ 952,648	$ 971,626
Preferred stock	384,400	384,400
Long-term debt	1,851,394	1,652,013
	$3,188,442	$3,008,039

Current liabilities:

Notes payable to banks	$ 219,253	$ 53,690
Long-term debt due within one year	42,958	29,747
Accounts payable ....:.............	109,968	83,886
Revenues to be refunded	2,547	15,402
Interest accrued	44,359	34,671
Customer deposits	16,600	14,633
Dividends declared	7,805	6,939
Taxes accrued		
Federal and state income	7,507	2,057
Other	6,396	5,633
Miscellaneous	5,652	6,864
	$ 463,045	$ 253,527

Deferred credits, etc.

Accumulated deferred income taxes	$ 263,675	$ 248,718
Accumulated deferred investment tax credits	39,054	60,102
Miscellaneous	13,690	11,070
	$ 316,419	$ 319,890
	$3,967,906	$3,581,456

Source: *1978 Annual Report.*

EXHIBIT 3

Chronology of Recent Events Involving APCo's Rates

Date	Event/Actions Taken
November 26, 1975	The company filed new schedules of rates with the Alabama Public Service Commission (PSC), asking for increases totaling $106.8 million in residential, commercial, and industrial rates.
June 25, 1976	The PSC issued an order denying the company any portion of the $106.8 million increase request. The company appealed the PSC decision to the Montgomery County Circuit Court, and also asked the court that the company be allowed to place into effect, subject to refund, the entire $106.8 million rate increase.
June 28, 1976	The Circuit Court refused to allow the company the right to put into effect, subject to refund, the $106.8 million rate increase. The company renewed this request with the Circuit Court.
August 11, 1976	The Circuit Court remanded the case to the PSC with instructions to the PSC to establish rates which would give the company sufficient earnings to finance construction.

EXHIBIT 3 (continued)

August 23, 1976	The PSC interpreted the court order to require a rate increase of $23.3 million of the original $106.8 million requested. The PSC ordered the $23.3 million into effect. The company appealed the PSC's order to the Montgomery County Circuit Court.
October 12, 1976	The Circuit Court allowed the company to place into effect, subject to refund, $30.1 million in rates, in addition to the $23.3 million allowed by the PSC on August 23, which was not subject to refund. The company appealed the Circuit Court's order to the Alabama Supreme Court, and also asked that the Supreme Court allow the company to place into effect, subject to refund, $53.4 million in increased rates. The $53.4 million represented the balance of the original $106.8 million request.
October 15, 1976	The company filed new schedules of rates with the PSC asking for increases totaling $173.9 million on an annual basis in residential, commercial, and industrial rates.
December 2, 1976	The Alabama Supreme Court denied the company's request to place into effect $53.4 million in increased rates, under bond, subject to refund.
December 6, 1976	The company requested that, on an emergency basis, the retail electric rates filed on October 15, 1976, be permitted to become effective in the form filed at the earliest possible date and in no event later than January 15, 1977. The company requested that these rates continue into effect until the final findings and order in this case. By this means, some $60.6 million could be expected to be made available between January 15 and May 15 (the end of the suspension period).
January 20, 1977	The PSC granted the company a $47.2 million emergency rate increase for a four-month period ending May 15.
April 26, 1977	The PSC granted the company a $61 million rate increase and made permanent $30 million collected subject to refund since October, 1976.
August 29, 1977	Governor George Wallace initiated through the PSC a complaint proceeding alleging that Alabama Power Company's rates were too high.
October 16, 1978	Following 14 months of hearings and testimony, the complaint proceeding was completed with the filing of reply briefs and was submitted for order by the PSC.
November 8, 1978	During a formal PSC meeting, Commissioner Jim Zeigler presented a proposal to grant immediate rate relief to Alabama Power based on testimony and evidence presented in the complaint proceeding. A witness for Governor Wallace had previously testified that the company was entitled to approximately a 12 percent return on its investment. The company was asking for a 15 percent return. The meeting adjourned with no action taken.
	Attorney General Bill Baxley filed suit in Montgomery County Circuit Court asking that the PSC be prohibited from granting a rate increase to the company.

EXHIBIT 3 (continued)

November 15, 1978	Following arguments before Circuit Court Judge Phelps on Baxley's suit to halt action by the PSC, Judge Phelps denied the request for a temporary restraining order. He cited the fact that the PSC had not, in fact, granted a rate increase. Therefore, a temporary restraining order would be premature.
November 22, 1978	The PSC stated that the investigation proceedings forced it to make a determination as to the adequacy and reasonableness of the rates and earnings of the company and that the evidence had proved such rates to be unreasonably low. It was further ordered by the commission . . . "that the company file with the commission forthwith rate schedules to reflect the surcharge herein fixed." Alabama Power complied by filing a schedule of rates in response to the directive of the commission. The PSC issued a second order in response to the rate schedule filed by the company with the commission. The PSC approved the rate schedules and ordered a 25 percent rate surcharge "effective for bills due on November 22, 1978, and thereafter except for bills in January and February, 1979, which will be subject to a 12.5 percent rate surcharge."

Alabama Power appealed the PSC rate increase order to the Alabama Supreme Court, pointing out in the appeal that the PSC order granted an inadequate revenue increase. Other conditions in the order making the appeal necessary were: (1) the reduction in residential rates to 12.5 percent during January and February, (2) a freeze on salaries in excess of $25,000, (3) a limit on increases in salaries less than $25,000 to 7 percent, (4) a limit on company expenditures to 7 percent above 1978 levels throughout 1979, except with special permission of the PSC, (5) submission of plans for cutting back or postponing construction. Attorney General Baxley and Governor Wallace filed Supplemental Complaints in Montgomery County Circuit Court seeking a temporary restraining order to suspend the enforcement of the rate increases ordered by the PSC. Alabama Power put into effect the increased rates as ordered by the PSC on all bills due on or after November 22, 1978.

November 28, 1978	Judge Phelps ordered that the rate increase granted by the PSC on November 22, 1978, be "hereby temporarily restrained and stayed pending the further order of the [Circuit] Court." Alabama Power immediately ceased billing at the increased rate and continued its normal billing cycle at the old rate.
November 29, 1978	The company filed petitions in the Alabama Supreme Court asking the court to set aside the temporary restraining order issued on November 28, 1978, by Judge Phelps. The company also asked the court to rule that the Circuit Court had no jurisdiction to act on the complaint filed on November 22, 1978, by Governor Wallace and Attorney General Baxley.

EXHIBIT 3 (concluded)

December 6, 1978	The Supreme Court refused to set aside the temporary restraining order issued by the Circuit Court on November 28, 1978.
December 7, 1978	Judge Phelps extended his temporary restraining order until December 13, 1978, when he would again consider the matters before the court.
December 19, 1978	Judge Phelps ruled that the PSC had no legal authority to grant the company a 25 percent rate increase on November 22, 1978, and that the order granting the increase is "void and of no effect."
December 20, 1978	The company filed a formal rate increase with the PSC for $282.9 million in its retail rates and appealed the December 19 ruling by the Montgomery County Circuit Court to the Alabama Supreme Court, requesting that the 25 percent surcharge be collected under bond.
January 4, 1979	The Alabama Supreme Court refused (1) to set aside the lower court order and (2) to allow the company to collect the 25 percent rate increase under bond.
January 8, 1979	The PSC set July 19 as the date by which it must rule on the company's $282.9 million rate increase. During this six-month period, the commission would hear testimony on the merits of the case and, by law, could act anytime within that six-month timetable. The company filed emergency testimony asking that the rate increase be put into effect on an emergency basis.
January 18, 1979	The Alabama Supreme Court dismissed the company's appeal of the Circuit Court order. The November 22 order of the PSC was voided, and the company was directed to pursue any rate increase through the PSC.
January 24, 1979	PSC members, Alabama Power Company officials, held closed-door session in Gov. Fob James' office.
January 25, 1979	James pubicly asked PSC to reconsider power company's emergency application. PSC scheduled hearings on emergency request to begin Feb. 14.
January 30, 1979	Legal Service Corporation of Alabama filed motion to dismiss the emergency rate application. Motion filed with PSC. Claimed meeting in James' office violated open meeting law and compromised PSC ability to fairly and impartially hear request. The corporation is nonprofit, supported by federal funds and represents indigent clients.
February 14, 1979	PSC hearings began on company's request for emergency hike of $282.9 million.
March 6, 1979	The PSC granted Alabama Power a 9.5 percent rate increase on a temporary basis, pending its final order in mid-July 1979.
March 7, 1979	Company officials indicated that the emergency increase was not sufficient to permit construction work to resume.

$5 to $7 million in cash each month and would reduce the company's coal stockpile to a 45-day supply, well below the normal objective of a 60-day supply. Management also announced efforts to limit company expenditures only to those necessary for continued emergency operation.

COMPANY BACKGROUND AND GENERAL DESCRIPTION

Alabama Power Company is engaged in the generation, transmission, distribution, and sale of electricity; it serves 56 of Alabama's 67 counties (parts or all of 11 counties in north Alabama are served by TVA). As of 1979, APCo distributed electric power at retail to customers in over 700 communities, as well as in rural areas, and at wholesale to 16 municipalities, 11 rural electric cooperatives, and 1 generating and transmitting cooperative. Total population in the company's service area was approximately 2.3 million persons. The company owned substantial coal reserves near its Gorgas steam-electric generating plant and used the output of coal from these reserves in its generating plants.

APCo also sold electric appliances through its own outlets—in addition to cooperating with dealers in selling electric appliances. The company's overall market share of the electric appliance business throughout its service territory was an estimated 5 percent.

As of 1979, Alabama Power owned and operated 13 hydroelectric dams, 7 coal-fired generating plants, 1 nuclear generating plant, and 2 combustion turbine plants. It was part owner of two other coal-fired generating plants. The rated capacity of all of APCo's generating plants was 7,705,675 kilowatts, of which 1,342,225 (17.4 percent) was hydro capacity.

Relationship to The Southern Company. Alabama Power is a wholly owned subsidiary of The Southern Company, the largest electric utility firm in the United States in terms of assets. The Southern Company is a regulated public utility holding company and is the parent firm of Alabama Power Company, Georgia Power Company (serving almost all of Georgia), Gulf Power Company (serving the western part of the Florida Panhandle), and Mississippi Power Company (serving southeastern Mississippi). Each of the four operating affiliates has its own president and board of directors and issues first mortgage bonds and preferred stock in its own name. Southern Company issues common stock in its name (traded on the NYSE), but does not issue any long-term debt securities; Southern's common stock is the most widely held electric utility stock in the nation and is among the ten most widely held corporate stocks in America. The Southern Company system also includes Southern Services, Inc., which provides engineering, financial, R&D, statistical, technical, and management services, at cost, to Southern's four operating affiliates.

Selected operating and financial statistics for The Southern Company are shown in Exhibit 4. As was the case with Alabama Power, Southern Company's profits were down sharply in 1978 from the previous year and per

EXHIBIT 4
**Financial and Operating Highlights of The Southern Company, Parent Firm of
Alabama Power Company ($000)**

	1978	1977	Percent Increase (decrease)
Operating revenues	$ 2,906,672	$ 2,652,085	9.6
Operating expenses	$ 2,433,803	$ 2,222,349	9.5
Consolidated net income*	$ 201,568	$ 245,067	(17.7)
The Southern Company common stock data:			
Earnings per share on average number			
of shares outstanding	$ 1.45	$ 1.95	(25.5)
Dividends paid per share	$ 1.54	$ 1.48	4.1
Book value per share (year-end)	$ 17.05	$ 17.21	(0.9)
Market price (year-end closing)	$ 13.50	$ 17.75	(23.9)
Shares outstanding:			
Average	139,005,117	125,845,666	10.5
Year-end.............................	142,102,123	136,771,988	3.9
Number of stockholders (year-end)	342,482	328,135	4.4
Construction expenditures	$ 1,082,431	$ 1,218,404	(11.2)
Net investment in utility plant (year-end)	$ 8,642,951	$ 7,919,839	9.1
Maximum peak-hour demand*	18,173	16,974	7.1
System capability*	23,356	21,988	6.2
Total kilowatt hour sales†	87,035	85,354	2.0
Average kwh sales per residential			
customer	11,035	10,944	0.8
Total number of customers served at			
year-end.............................	2,472,646	2,415,939	2.3

* Thousands of kilowatts.
† Millions.
Source: *1978 Annual Report.*

share earnings of $1.45 were below the annual $1.54 dividend. Nonetheless, in 1978 Southern's board of directors voted to increase the dividend from the 1977 level of $1.48, making 1978 the 24th consecutive year in which the company paid higher per share dividends.

A major feature of Alabama Power's relationship with its sister companies in the Southern Company system was the benefits that accrued from coordinated planning, diversity of loads, and mutual assistance in supplying power to each other. Specific economies arose from

1. Staggered construction of generating plants so that each of the four operating companies could take advantage of building the maximum optimum-size generating units.
2. Locating their respective hydroelectric operations so as to capitalize upon the diversity among various watersheds in the Southeast.
3. Combining and programming their energy loads in such a manner as to fully utilize hydro-resources at a time of high water flows.
4. Coordination of maintenance operations.

5. The opportunity of the companies to implement a computerized, coordinated dispatch of power from all generating plants based on the relative efficiencies of different generating units, the relative fuel costs at each plant, and the transmission line losses, all on an incremental (marginal cost) basis.

This latter advantage—the power pool—is of particular importance to Alabama Power because it is known as a "short company," meaning that it does not have the generating capability to meet the demand for electricity in its service area all of the time.[1] In 1978, for example, Alabama Power purchased a net of 5.2 billion kwh from other utilities to supply its customers' electricity needs—an amount equal to 15.5 percent ot total kwh generation. The average cost for APCo-generated electricity was 1.61 cents per kilowatt hour (from steam plants), compared to 2.37 cents per kilowatt hour for purchased power.

In 1978, the combined growth and expansion plans of the companies in the Southern Company system entailed a construction program totaling almost $1.1 billion, down slightly from $1.2 billion in 1977. The sources of funds for new construction were

	$ Millions	
	1978	1977
Debt financing	$ 593	$ 303
Sale of preferred stock	—	114
Sale of common stock	81	233
Sale of property	33	324
Internal sources	375	244
Total	$1,082	$1,218

In financing construction expenditures, The Southern Company had as its present goal a consolidated capital structure of 55 to 57 percent long-term debt, 10 to 12 percent preferred stock, and 31 to 33 percent common equity. To maintain this capital structure and help its operating divisions finance the contemplated construction program of $1.5 billion in 1979, $1.6 billion in 1980, and $1.6 billion in 1981, Southern's management expected to have to issue new shares of common stock on an annual basis. From 1970 to 1978, the number of shares of common stock outstanding increased from 51.6 million to 139.0 million—all as a result of new issues to raise equity capital to

---

[1] Even though APCo's nameplate generating capacity of 7,705,605 kilowatts in 1978 exceeded its all-time maximum peak-hour demand of 6,670,700 kilowatts, the hydroelectric capacity could not be depended upon in the hot summer months when rainfall was often insufficient to generate a reliable pool of water in the reservoirs behind the dams. In addition, the coal-fired and nuclear units were not 100 percent reliable, so that in the event of unexpected breakdowns and "outages," the company could not achieve an output equal to its nameplate capacity. It is for reasons such as this that it was common practice for electric utilities to try to maintain a 15–20 percent reserve margin of nameplate capacity over the anticipated peak-hour demand for electric power.

finance construction. The proceeds of the common stock issues were used to supplement the capital raised in the operating divisions through their sale of new preferred stock issues and the issuance of new first mortgage bonds.

The following tabulation indicates the additional generating facilities expected to be placed in operation in the Southern Company system during the 1978–80 period:

Plant and Location	Capacity Kilowatts (nameplate)	Type Fuel	Planned Commercial Operation Date	Estimated Construction Cost ($ millions)	Estimated Cost Per Kilowatt
Miller No. 1— Alabama	660,000	Coal	August 1978	$334	$506
Wansley No. 2— Georgia	462,775	Coal	May 1978	111	239
Hatch No. 2— Georgia	410,820	Nuclear	November 1978	261	636
Combustion Turbines—Georgia	300,000	Oil	1979–80	64	213
Farley No. 2— Alabama	860,000	Nuclear	1980	647	753
Harris Hydro Plant—Alabama	135,000	Hydro	1980	93	688
Wallace Dam— Georgia	321,300	Hydro	1979–80	178	553

The higher capital costs for nuclear facilities were offset to some extent by sharply lower costs for nuclear fuel per kilowatt-hour generated, as suggested by Southern's record of fuel costs for its facilities:

	Average Cost (in mills) of Fuel per Net KWH Generated				
	1973	1974	1975	1976	1977
Coal	4.47	7.67	10.64	10.63	12.00
Oil	13.59	24.79	25.85	29.28	32.12
Gas	5.98	7.33	10.06	15.35	17.04
Nuclear	—	—	—	2.10	3.21
Overall Average	4.94	8.69	11.08	11.29	12.71

The fuel costs for hydroelectric generation are essentially zero, since there is no operating cost attached to the water in the dam reservoir once the dam is built and the hydroelectric generators are in place.

As of year-end 1977, Southern's generating capabilities were divided among hydroelectric, fossil fuel (largely coal but some fuel oil and natural gas), and nuclear as follows:

Company	Hydroelectric Stations	Fuel-Electric Stations		Total
		Fossil	Nuclear	
Alabama Power	1,342,225	4,333,610	860,000	6,535,835
Georgia Power	430,380	9,613,090	405,810	10,449,280
Gulf Power	—	1,469,400	—	1,469,400
Mississippi Power	—	1,965,760	—	1,965,760
Segco	—	1,019,680	—	1,019,680
Total	1,772,605	18,401,540	1,265,810	21,439,955

Capacity—Kilowatts (nameplate).

GENERAL PROBLEMS OF THE ELECTRIC UTILITY INDUSTRY

During the 1970s the electric utility industry experienced problems in a number of areas: (1) sharp increases in operating costs and construction costs owing to high inflation rates in the economy, (2) major increases in the cost of fuel for generating electric energy, (3) escalating interest rates on long-term securities, (4) difficulties in trying to raise exceptionally large amounts of both debt and equity capital to finance new construction programs, (5) difficulty in earning a sufficient rate of return on invested capital and in securing adequate and timely rate increases, (6) difficulty in meeting coverages on long-term bonds and preferred stock, as required in mortgage agreements and charters, (7) rising costs associated with complying with environmental regulations, (8) licensing and other delays affecting the construction of new facilities, (9) the effects of energy conservation and economic recession on the use of electric energy.

Alabama Power Company and the other operating affiliates of The Southern Company system experienced these problems in varying degrees and during the 1975–79 period made substantial reductions in previously planned construction programs. The reductions were prompted by difficulties in financing, new estimates of increased construction costs, inadequate earnings coverages on securities, and an apparent slowdown in the rate of growth in the demand for electric energy.

ASPECTS OF POWER GENERATION AND POWER SUPPLY

An electric system consists of one or more generating plants interconnected by transmission lines which carry electricity to distribution lines through substations and other voltage transformation facilities. The distribution facilities, in turn, are connected to the electric facilities and equipment of various residential, commercial, and industrial customers. Unlike other enterprises, electric utilities are less able to regulate production rates and sales volumes. Users of electricity can change the demands upon a utility's electric system and utilize more or less electric energy by simply pushing a button, pulling a switch, or otherwise exercising their freedom to operate (or not to operate) a particular electrical device or series of equipment or machinery. Customers are also free to add new equipment and facilities activated by electric energy without prior notification. The degree to which customers place their electricity-using equipment in operation varies widely with the hour of the day, the day of the week, and the month of the year. Peak loads are typically encountered between 11:00 A.M. and 3:00 P.M. on a daily basis, during weekdays rather than on weekends, and in either summer or winter, depending on whether the utility is in a hot or cold climate. Alabama Power Company, along with its other affiliates in The Southern Company, experiences summer peaks due to the heavy use of air conditioning in its service area.

Alabama Power Company, like other electric utilities, took the position that it *must* be ready and able to meet the energy load imposed upon its electric system. This policy existed mainly out of a desire and legal responsibility to serve the full needs of customers and secondarily to protect the company's electric system from "brownouts" and damage that would necessitate extended and expensive repair work. Electric generators are constructed with characteristics which cause them to cease turning if the load or drag becomes greater than their capacity. Thus, if at any given time the total demand upon an electric system exceeds its capacity, the generating plants, unless otherwise disconnected from the load, will become overtaxed, cease operating, and discontinue supplying any electric energy to the system. The system can be reactivated only when a balanced relationship is restored between customer demand and supply capability. As a general rule of thumb, electric utilities seek to maintain a generating capability (nameplate-rated capacity) at least 15 percent greater than the maximum peak demand load they expect to encounter. This 15 percent margin provides not only a measure of safety against an unusually large peak load but also allows the firm to meet peak demands even if it should experience a breakdown in one of its generating units. In 1978, The Southern Company had a 22.2 percent reserve margin, down slightly from 22.9 percent in 1977. Alabama Power's reserve margin in 1978 was just under 15 percent.

REGULATION

In 1920 the Alabama legislature passed a bill creating the Alabama Public Service Commission and giving it the authority to regulate Alabama Power Company with respect to the issuance of securities, the extensions of its electric plant, the rates and charges for the service it provides, and related matters concerning the exercise of its public utility responsibility. According to Alabama law, the Public Service Commission is responsible for seeing that every utility under its jurisdiction:

> shall maintain its plant, facilities and equipment in good operating condition and shall set up and maintain proper reserves for renewals, replacements and

reasonable contingencies. Every utility shall render adequate service to the public and shall make such reasonable improvements, extensions and enlargements of its plants, facilities, and equipment as may be necessary to meet the growth and demand of the territory which it is under the duty to serve.

Alabama Power is precluded from constructing any plant, property, or facility for production, transmission, delivery, or furnishing of electricity except ordinary extensions of its existing system in the usual course of business without first obtaining approval from the Commission and being issued a certificate of convenience and necessity. A public hearing must be held before the PSC may issue such a certificate. In addition, Alabama Power is prohibited from issuing securities (preferred stock and/or first mortgage bonds) without PSC approval.

Although the Public Service Commission was directly responsible for regulating APCo's retail rates and charges for services, the law stated that the retail rates set by the Commission " shall be reasonable and just to both the utility and the public." Further, the law stated that every utility

> shall be entitled to such just and reasonable rates as will enable it at all times to fully perform its duties to the public and will, under honest, efficient, and economical management, earn a fair net return on the reasonable value of its property devoted to the public service.

It directed that the Commission

> shall give due consideration, among other things, to the requirements of the business with respect to the utility under consideration, and the necessity, under honest, efficient, and economical management of such utility, of enlarging plants, facilities and equipment of the utility under consideration, in order to provide that portion of the public served thereby with adequate service.

The Federal Energy Regulatory Commision has jurisdiction over the rates charged by Alabama Power Company in selling electric power at wholesale, such as sales to municipal and rural electric cooperative systems, and where transactions involve the use of electric facilities interconnected with electric facilities located in other states. Section 201 of the Federal Power Act declares

> that the business of transmitting and selling electric energy for ultimate distribution to the public is affected with a public interest, and that Federal regulation of matters relating to generation . . . and . . . the transmission of electric energy in interstate commerce and the sale of such energy at wholesale in interstate commerce is necessary in the public interest.

Section 202 confers specific powers upon the FERC

> for the purpose of assuring an abundant supply of electric energy throughout the United States with the greatest possible economy and with regard to the proper utilization and conservation of natural resources.

Alabama Power must also obtain licenses from the FERC to build and operate hydroelectric facilities. When such licenses expire, the federal government, by act of Congress, may take over the project or the FERC may relicense the project either to the original licensee or to a new licensee. In the event of takeover or relicensing to another, Alabama Power would be entitled to recover its net investment in the project (not in excess of the fair value of the property taken) plus reasonable damages to any other property directly associated with loss of the hydroelectric facilities.

As with other corporations engaged in interstate commerce, the Securities and Exchange Commission maintains continuous surveillance over the financing activities of Alabama Power Company. APCo is required to register the sale of all of its securities with the SEC and it is prohibited from issuing or selling any bonds, preferred stock, or common stock that do not comply with SEC policies and regulations.

Alabama Power is required to comply with the regulations of the Nuclear Regulatory Commission in constructing and operating nuclear plants. The NRC has dominion over matters concerning the public health, safety, and environmental impact of a proposed nuclear plant; the NRC is also empowered to investigate the benefits of nuclear plants relative to other means of power generation as a basis for deciding whether to issue construction permits. Issuance of operating licenses by the NRC may be conditioned upon requiring changes in operating techniques or upon the installation of additional equipment to meet safety or environmental standards; moreover, opportunity is provided for interested parties to request a public hearing on health, safety, or environmental issues.

Alabama Power is also subject to regulation by the Corps of Engineers, the Alabama Water Improvement Commission, the Alabama Air Pollution Control Commission, and Alabama Public Health Department with respect to the construction and operation of plant facilities which could have an impact upon the environment.

RATE REGULATION BY THE PSC

When Alabama Power requests permission to alter rate schedules, it is customary for the Public Service Commission to inquire into the factors which have influenced the company to seek changes in its rate schedules. The company must furnish whatever pertinent information is requested and, in particular, must present in public hearings justification for its request. This justification includes an analysis of all costs incurred in its electric service operations during a particular time frame, usually referred to as a *test year,* and a determination of what level of revenue would have been required during the test year to cover the company's costs and also provide a fair net return on the compamy's property devoted to its electric service operations.

Company officials offered the following explanation of how its electric rates were determined:

> Three main steps must be taken in applying the fair-rate-on-fair-value rule of rate making. First, the rate base must be determined. The rate base represents

the value of utility property and assets devoted to electric service less depreciation. Second, the utility's operating expenses which will be incurred in providing electric service must be determined. Finally, the fair rate of return must be determined. This is the rate—in percentage form—which is applied to the rate base to give the dollar amount of return allowed to the utility as a profit on its operations to serve the public. The difference between the dollar amount of return allowed and the dollar amount of return earned during the test period equals the dollar amount of return deficiency for the test period.

In its 1978 regular session, the Alabama Legislature amended Act 850 of the 1975 Code of Alabama so as to define the reasonable value of a public utility's property to be used as the rate base in fixing utility rates. This amendment eliminated the amount of new investment to be added in the year immediately following the test period. The act prescribes a formula for the rate base as the "original" cost thereof less accrued depreciation as of the most recent date available."

Another important factor in determining a reasonable rate of return is cost of capital, the cost to a utility of obtaining the capital it needs to go into business and stay in business. Cost of capital includes the interest expense associated with debt, dividends on preferred stock, and a return on common equity investment, for which dividends and appreciation of stock value are expected. As a company's earnings drop, long-term investors see a greater risk in the company's ability to pay back the loan with interest. This concern causes a lower bond rating resulting in a higher cost of interest. Furthermore, when depressed earnings bar a company from issuing first mortgage bonds or preferred stock, for instance, the company must depend on its short-term credit line for financing. In the past few years, short-term borrowing has often been a higher cost of capital than long-term borrowing. In addition, the use of short-term debt subjects the company to more risk than does long-term debt because of changing market conditions.

It is generally considered that a healthy business and one which is attractive to investors must have sufficient earnings to cover all expenses of operation and to provide a reasonable return to its common stockholders—the owners of the business. The common stockholder takes a certain risk in letting a business use his money. In effect, he says that he believes the company is efficiently managed and has a record indicating that he will receive a return on his investment. He takes the risk that there will be something left over for him after all expenses (including interest, taxes, mortgage payments, and preferred stock dividends) are paid. The common stockholder expects a portion of this leftover (or earnings) to be reinvested in the business to help support the growth necessary to meet increased demand. Whether this has or has not been done materially affects the potential investor's opinion of the company and the consequent cost of capital.

A third important factor considered in a rate case is attraction of capital, a major measure of reasonableness in determining a rate of return. The final test that any utility enterprise has to meet, if it is to continue in business, is whether it can sell its securities in the investment market. In fixing a reasonable rate of return, the commission must take into account the sound business reality that the return should be sufficient to enable the company to go into the money markets on a favorably competitive basis.

A fourth major factor which is beginning to be considered by some regulators in determining a reasonable rate of return is economic conditions. Since rates based upon historical data are used in the future, it has been generally accepted that prevailing economic conditions and discernible trends for the future are factors affecting the rate of return allowed. If a so-called prosperity period is accompanied by continuous and prolonged price increases, as in a period characterized by rapid inflation, public utilities are likely to be adversely affected by the price changes in a way which is called *regulatory lag*.

Regulatory lag is the situation created by the time interval between the initiation of a request for a change in rates and the final action by the commission on that request. The rate increase may be justified and eventually granted. However, if the company must suffer financially from the delay involved in the regulatory process of granting the rate increase, it has lost earnings which it cannot recoup. Though commissions throughout the country are not agreed on whether this lag should result in a somewhat higher or "catch-up" allowance, there has been some recognition of this problem in recent rate cases for a few commissions.

Suppose a utility has a property fairly valued and adjusted to indicate a rate base of $1 million. Assume that its operating expenses are $250,000 a year. These expenses would not include any construction costs or interest paid on construction loans. If the regulatory agency found that a five percent rate of return on the property value, or rate base, was fair and reasonable, this would result in a dollar amount of return of $50,000 on such a rate base. It also means that the charges for service will have to produce a revenue requirement of $350,000 a year in order to cover the expenses ($250,000) plus about twice the amount of return allowed ($50,000). To achieve the return of $50,000 it is necessary to bill revenues of approximately $100,000 above expenses because of federal, state, and local taxes.

The PSC, in testing the company's rates, uses an historical test period of 12 months in calculating the statutory rate base on property devoted to electric service, as well as the company's operating revenues, operating expenses, and operating income. Because it takes three to four months for the company to compile test-period data, the test period often begins 15 to 16 months prior to the filing date.

Data used in preparing the test year is normalized and annualized where necessary. For instance, if two different schedules of rates were in effect during the test year, then the revenue figures are adjusted to normalize for the approved rates in effect at the end of the test year on an annual basis. If a lack of rainfall caused abnormally low hydroelectric generation during the test year, adjustments are made to recognize normal hydro generation. If union wages are slated to increase, an upward adjustment in expenses is made in the test-year data. If a new generating plant was on line during one month of the test period, then the effect of that plant on both revenue and expenses is calculated on a 12-month basis and included as a normalization adjustment.

These are but a few of the many normalization and annualization adjustments which are made before a twelve-month period can be more accurately considered as a test period. These adjusted test-period figures are then used to calculate the statutory rate base as well as operating revenues, operating expenses, and operating income for the purpose of rate making.

The rate base is separated into retail and wholesale for resale jurisdiction through the use of a detailed cost-of-service study. Operating expenses are also separated into the two jurisdictions. Revenues are separated without a study since each jurisdiction has its own rate schedules.

Once a rate of return on investment has been determined, then the company files a schedule of rates which when applied to the test-year sales would generate this rate of return. After the new schedule of rates is approved, the commission orders the increase into effect on a certain date. On that specified date, the new rates are the only legal rates that the company may charge its customers.

Given that a rate of return is to be reasonable, there are several factors on which testimony and evidence focus during a rate case. One of these is an examination of the utility's expenses. In reviewing a company's expenses, the regulators, in essence, are determining the efficiency of the company's operation. The objective of a commission's review of expenses, then, is to see that those expenses which are allowed for rate making are both reasonable and necessary so that rates, in turn, may be kept as low as possible.

It should be noted that this is an area in which commission authority can easily encroach upon the function of utility managerial judgment. When the company feels this happens, it has recourse to the courts. Court decisions have frequently contained restrictions on commission jurisdiction over expenses by specifying that such authority should not interfere with the functions of management. Expenses are the responsibility of the company, just as rates are the responsibility of the regulatory commission. Each directly affects the other.

In the early days of Alabama Power Company's operations, when its customers were scattered and fewer uses were made of the company's electric service, most residential customers utilized electric energy for lighting purposes only. The unit cost of electric service was relatively high. However, as electric service became more popular during the 1920s, 1930s, and 1940s, and the company's service became available on a broader scale, more and more people began to utilize electricity for a growing range of purposes. With the increased utilization and improvement in the density of electric consumers, along with improvements in the art and technology of providing electric service, definite economies were achieved, with the result that during the 1920s and continuing into the 1960s, Alabama Power Company followed a general pattern of filing for and obtaining rate decrease after rate decrease.

It was not until 1968 that the company first filed an application for a general increase in its retail electric rates. Exhibit 5 summarizes APCo's rate increase requests and the amounts granted by the Alabama PSC.

Despite the rate increases granted Alabama Power during the 1970s, the company's rates for residential, commercial, and industrial customers compared favorably with those charged by other utilities. According to testimony by John Burks, Manager—Rates and Regulatory Matters for APCo, at the 1979 public hearings held by the PSC on APCo's $283 rate increase request:

> The Edison Electric Institute (EEI), the trade organization of investor owned electric companies, sends out a quarterly report of typical electric bills,

EXHIBIT 5

Summary of Retail Rate Increase Requests and Actions Taken

Date filed	2/27/68	11/6/70	6/9/72	6/14/74	11/26/75	*	10/15/76
Revenue asked	$7,396,981	$19,946,600	$29,873,474	$64,484,114	$106,804,188	—	$201,606,704
Revenue allowed	$6,994,981	$16,923,364	$26,985,378	$54,182,268	0	$23,331,752	$ 91,130,111
Percent increase (of retail revenue)	3.6%	7.2%	9.8%	13.9%	0	4.2%	14.91%
Date of Commission's order	4/28/69	4/29/71 5/3/71	12/13/72	1/14/75	6/25/76	8/23/76	4/26/77
Date effective	9/1/68	4/29/71 5/3/71	12/13/72	1/14/75	—	8/23/76	4/28/77
Rate of return allowed on rate base	6.28%	6.92%	6.6%	6.526%	6.37%	—	7.33%

* PSC ordered a $23.3 million increase in rates after remand from the Montgomery County Circuit Court.

covering essentially the entire investor owned electric industry. The latest such report (October 1, 1978) lists residential bills from 226 such companies. With the highest bill being number 1, Alabama Power Company ranks 174th of the 226 based on 1,000 kwh usage. If the proposed rates were in effect, the company would be 70th in the listing. It must be remembered, however, that rate increase proceedings are pending for a majority of these companies. The EEI Rate Action Survey for January 1979 shows that 41 companies filed for increases in the last quarter of 1978 and that 122 requests for rate increases were pending from previous quarters. Also, 51 increases were granted during the last quarter of 1978. Thus, these numerous increases, asked for and granted, could well put Alabama Power Company in the lower half of the typical electric bill report even with the approval of the new rates. The Rate Action Survey shows that requested increases of $3.8 billion were pending at December 31, 1978 and that, during the year 1978, there were approved 200 increase applications amounting to $2.4 billion in additional revenues.

In the EEI typical electric bill study as to commercial and industrial service, Alabama Power Company normally ranks around 145th of the 226 in the commercial field and around 130th in the industrial field.

It is standard practice throughout the electric utility industry to have separate rate schedules for residential, commercial, and industrial users. Typically, industrial users pay a much lower rate per kilowatt-hour because of their higher volume of use and because it costs less to serve them than it does other users (in terms of investment in distribution facilities and the expenses of servicing the accounts). Exhibit 6 provides additional information on Alabama Power's rates and customer usage of electricity.

The Fuel Adjustment Clause. Fuel costs (for coal, natural gas, oil, and nuclear fuel) and net purchased power currently account for over 50 percent of Alabama Power's operating expenses. Because fuel costs have fluctuated in the last decade, regulatory agencies across the country have approved a mechanism, usually referred to as fuel cost adjustment, to allow utilities to recover this significant, fluctuating expense on a current basis. As an illustration, APCo was paying in 1979 about five times as much for coal as it was in 1970. The company purchased about 10.5 million tons of coal annually; 1978 total fuel costs were $295.2 million, up from $26.5 million in 1968.

A complex formula is used in calculating the fuel cost adjustment each month. The PSC staff audits calculations the company makes in arriving at the fuel cost adjustment factor, and the PSC reviews the matter at a public hearing each month. PSC auditors also check company records relating to the adjustment determination.

Several variables account for the change in the fuel cost adjustment from month to month: quantity and cost of fuel used, the amount of energy produced by hydroelectric plants, and the amount and cost of net purchased energy. For instance, during a period of little rainfall, the company has to cut back its hydroelectric generation in order to keep its reservoirs at the required levels. With less hydro generation available, more coal is burned and more purchased power is required—thus increasing the fuel cost factor.

EXHIBIT 6

Alabama Power Company Data on Rates and Customer Usage

Item	1967	1972	1975	1976	1977	1978
Average annual kwh usage per customer:						
Residential	6,279	9,285	9,954	10,223	10,840	10,939
Commercial	25,157	38,053	43,398	43,849	45,887	46,237
Industrial	3,121,838	3,493,603	3,319,631	3,476,637	3,628,669	3,834,133
Revenue per kwh (in cents):						
Residential	1.69¢	1.90¢	2.97¢	3.08¢	3.90¢	3.87¢
Commercial	1.83	1.97	3.05	3.21	4.12	4.03
Industrial	0.80	1.02	1.94	2.03	2.65	2.59
Overall average	1.17	1.41	2.46	2.56	3.27	3.23
Annual revenue per customer (in $):						
Residential	$ 106.02	$ 176.25	$ 295.85	$ 315.26	$ 422.51	$ 423.24
Commercial	460.38	749.07	1,322.76	1,406.23	1,891.69	1,864.80
Industrial	25,044.82	35,495.24	64,297.90	70,503.66	96,218.93	99,386.22

These variations occur, then, even if there is no change in the basic cost of fuel. If the actual figures differ from the estimates, an adjustment up or down is made in the next month's factor.

In April 1977, the PSC altered APCo's fuel adjustment clause for the fifth time. A portion of the monthly fuel charge was "rolled into" the base rates charged by the company, making the total fuel costs included in the residential base rate equal to $11.50 per 1,000 kwh. In the 21 months since that charge, the average monthly fuel adjustment charge (separate from the base rate) has been $1.89 per 1,000 kwh. For 6 of those 21 months, the fuel adjustment was a negative figure, meaning a reduction in each customer's bill; this was attributable mainly to increased generation at the company's Farley nuclear plant.

APCO'S CONSTRUCTION PROGRAM

During the 1970–78 period, Alabama Power spent $3.33 billion on construction of new facilities. Such heavy expenditures were required because of the very high capital-intensive nature of the electric utility business. APCo had a fixed asset investment of $3.58 for each dollar of sales revenue it was generating (by way of comparison General Motors has a fixed asset investment of about 16 cents per dollar of sales revenue and Exxon has an investment in property, plant, and equipment of about 36 cents per dollar of sales revenue). Prior to the shutdown of its construction program in 1979 due to lack of financing, Alabama Power had budgeted construction expenditures from 1978 through 1982 of approximately $3 billion—an amount which would increase the company's investment in facilities by 75 percent (from $4 billion to $7 billion) in just five years.

APCo's estimated construction additions for 1979, 1980, and 1981 were 1698 million, $633 million, and $585 million, respectively. However, in December 1978, the board of directors ordered a cutback in construction as a result of inadequate earnings and insufficient cash. The company, in its *1978 Annual Report,* said the following about the length and impact of the construction shutdown:

> Its duration will depend on the speed with which the company is allowed to bill at adequate rates. The extent to which the planned in-service dates and final costs of major projects will be affected by the shutdown cannot be predicted at this time.
>
> Following testing and pre-operational procedures during the summer and autumn, Unit no. 1 of Plant Miller began commercial operation on October 12, 1978. The newly completed 660,000 kilowatt (kw) installation provides an increase of approximately 9 percent in the Company's total generating capacity. Planned for Plant Miller are three additional coal-fired 660,000-kw units. Unit 2 was about 22 percent complete at year's end. Before shutdown, Unit 2 was scheduled to be operational in 1981; Unit 3 in 1982; and Unit 4 in 1983.
>
> At year's end, Unit 2 of Plant Farley near Dothan was about 75 percent

complete. Before the shutdown, this unit was scheduled to go into commercial service in 1980.

Work also continued on construction of the Harris Dam located on the Tallapoosa River in Randolph County near Wedowee and Lineville. This hydroelectric project will have two generating units with a total installed capacity of 135,000 kw and will create a lake covering about 10,600 acres. At the end of 1978, the project was 52 percent complete. Before the shutdown, Units 1 and 2 were scheduled to go into commercial service in the spring of 1980.

The reconstruction of Bouldin Dam began July 11, 1977. At year's end, the construction work was 56 percent complete. Before the shutdown, the plant was scheduled to be operational in late summer of 1979.

Construction on redevelopment of Mitchell Dam began early in 1978 on temporary facilities. At year's end, the project was 10 percent complete. Before the shutdown, the project was scheduled to be completed by the end of 1981.

Additional remedial construction at Logan Martin Dam and Electric Generating Plant started on June 6, 1978. The purpose of the work is to ensure the continued integrity of the dam and reduce leakage. The scope of the work will entail filling upstream forebay sinkholes and constructing a large trench-drain bolster in the flood plain downstream of the east plain and dike. At year's end, the job was 57 percent complete; it is expected to be finished by the end of 1979.

FINANCIAL CONSIDERATIONS

A key factor affecting the ability of Alabama Power to finance its construction program was the ratio of earnings to interest costs and to preferred stock dividends. These ratios are sometimes referred to in financial circles as "coverages." The mortgage indenture entered into by Alabama Power in 1942 (which the company has no authority to change without the consent of all bondholders) provided in effect that before the company could issue additional first-mortgage bonds, its before-tax operating profit had to be great enough to cover pro forma annual interest charges on all such securities outstanding by at least two times. Hence APCo could not raise capital through first-mortgage bonds if a new issue would cause its coverage to fall below two times earnings (nor, of course, could it issue any new bonds if its coverage was already below the 2.0 level).

For the issuance of new preferred stock, APCo's charter required that the company have sufficient operating profits before interest charges, but after taxes, to cover pro forma annual interest charges on all debt plus preferred stock dividends (including any new issues) by at least one and one-half times. Hence, new preferred stock issues were forbidden if earnings were less than 1.5 times the total charges on indebtedness and on preferred stock dividend requirements. In both cases the coverage requirements had to be met for a period of 12 consecutive months within the 15 calendar months immediately preceding any proposed new issue. The figures below show the coverage ratios which the company maintained in recent years:

Year Ended December 31	Earnings Coverage on First-Mortgage Bonds	Earnings Coverage on Preferred Stock
1958	5.11x	2.63x
1964	4.70	2.58
1969	4.26	2.41
1970	3.31	2.03
1971	2.73	1.87
1972	2.23	1.61
1973	2.51	1.72
1974	1.66	1.36
1975	2.29	1.57
1976	1.69	1.39
1977	2.49	1.49
1978	1.51	1.14

The deterioration in the company's coverages stemmed from higher interest rates on new securities issues, the large volume of new financing required to finance such a large, continuing construction program, and lagging earnings. For example, whereas until the late 1960s the company was able to sell first mortgage bonds at interest rates in the 3–5 percent range, its most recently issued first mortgage bonds carried interest rates in the 8¼ to 10⅞ percent range. These increases, together with the fact that APCo's long-term debt increased by $1.46 billion during the 1968–78 period, resulted in an increase in interest charges on long-term debt from $19.5 million in 1968 to $169.6 million in 1978 (see Exhibit 7). Likewise, the dividend yields on APCo's preferred stock issues, which ran between 4 and 5 percent until the late 1960s, rose to as high as 11.0 percent in the 1970s. Between 1968 and 1978 Alabama Power issued $302 million in new preferred stock. As a consequence, APCo's preferred stock dividend payments jumped from $3.5 million in 1968 to $31.2 million in 1978 (see Exhibit 7).

Alabama Power's capital structure for selected years of the 1965–78 period was:

Year Ended December 31	Long-term Debt	Preferred Stock	Common Equity
1965	53.7%	10.6%	35.7%
1970	56.0	9.7	34.3
1975	55.9	10.9	33.2
1978	58.1	12.0	29.9

Through 1978 The Southern Company had invested a total of $960,500,000 in the common equity capital of APCo, of which $625,700,000 had been invested since 1970.

Exhibit 8 shows the sources used by APCo to generate the funds for plant additions during 1974–78. The table below summarizes several other financial statistics of Alabama Power Company:

	1974	1975	1976	1977	1978
income (000s)	$48,995	$77,782	$59,664	$117,276	$42,903
te of return on average equity investment	8.61%	11.60%	6.92%	12.07%	4.50%
vidends declared on common stock (000s)	$46,800	$60,000	$60,000	$94,900	$108,800
vidend payout ratios	95.52%	77.14%	100.56%	80.92%	253.60%
pital contributions from The Southern Company (000s)	$115,000	$67,000	$150,000	$95,000	$47,200

At the hearings on its $283 million rate increase request, expert witnesses for Alabama Power testified that the company needed a 15 to 15.5 percent return on its equity investment to be able to attract the needed capital for new construction and to give the stockholders a fair and reasonable return on their investment.

Also of major concern to APCo's management was the ratings on its first mortgage bonds and preferred stock. In 1975 and in early 1976, pending the decision by the Alabama PSC on the company's $106.8 million rate increase request, Moody's downgraded APCo's preferred stock from A to Baa in December 1975. Standard & Poor's rated both types of securities A−. However, following the PSC denial of the increase both agencies promptly downgraded their ratings on APCo's first mortgage bonds: Moody's to Baa (lower medium grade) on both first-mortgage bonds and on seven pollution-control issues, and S&P to BBB on first mortgage bonds. The downgrading of the company's bonds from A (investment grade) to Baa not only meant higher interest rates on new bond issues but also the loss of a significant part of the market for the company's securities. A number of institutional investors (pension funds, insurance companies, savings banks) were precluded by law or by company policy from investing in securities below investment grade. In 1979 Moody's reduced Alabama Power's preferred stock rating to Ba.

Testimony given by Elmer Harris, senior vice president, at the 1979 public hearings held by the Alabama PSC regarding the $283 million rate increase request revealed some additional aspects about the company's financial picture:

> During most of 1976 and the first half of 1977, the company was barred from the long-term security markets by the coverage restrictions contained in its first mortgage indenture and charter. During this period of time, the company was forced to rely on short-term bank borrowings in order to continue to carry on needed construction. By June 1977, the company had over $390 million of short-term debt (the short-term debt limit imposed by the SEC was $400 million and the lines of credit available totaled $405 million), the vast majority of which was due March 31, 1978. In July 1977, the company was finally able to sell first

EXHIBIT 7
Summary of Selected Financial and Operating Statistics (all $ figures are in 000s)

	1978	1977	1972	1968
Capitalization—end of Year:				
Common stock	$ 224,358	$ 224,358	$ 224,358	$ 187,3•
Other paid-in capital	625,700	578,500	86,500	—
Premium on preferred stock	461	461	338	1•
Earnings retained in the business	102,129	168,307	115,613	87,0•
Preferred stock	384,400	384,400	150,400	82,4
Long-term debt	1,894,352	1,681,760	738,418	438,9•
Utility plant				
Total utility plant—end of year	$ 4,372,725	$ 3,903,164	$ 1,759,520	$ 1,114,7
gross additions	483,430	540,076	257,338	81,3
Operating revenues, electric:				
Residential	$ 351,644	$ 339,393	$ 126,355	$ 78,6•
Commercial	213,059	208,864	74,758	47,6•
Industrial	357,691	338,007	104,427	71,4•
Other	73,543	62,535	15,053	11,6•
Total revenues from electric sales—territorial	$ 995,937	$ 948,799	$ 320,593	$ 209,4•
Nonterritorial Sales	10,534	12,496	1,981	5•
Other operating revenues	7,972	7,398	3,126	2,0•
Total operating revenues, electric	$ 1,014,443	$ 968,693	$ 325,700	$ 212,1•
Electric sales:*				
Residential	9,088,856	8,804,755	6,656,760	4,649,0•
Commercial	5,282,746	5,121,461	3,797,751	2,628,9
Industrial	13,799,043	12,845,489	10,278,181	8,934,2•
Other	2,604,616	2,467,159	2,015,945	1,575,7•
total electric sales— territorial	30,775,261	29,238,864	22,748,637	17,787,8•
Nonterritorial	342,302	615,423	104,303	67,0•
total electric sales	31,117,563	29,854,287	22,852,940	17,854,8•
Electric customers—end of Year:				
Residential	841,781	821,599	729,840	657,9•
Commercial	115,208	112,691	101,613	90,9•
Industrial and other	4,451	4,286	3,564	3,2•
Total	961,440	938,576	835,017	752,1•

* Thousands of kilowatt-hours.
Source: *1978 Annual Report.*

EXHIBIT 8
Sources of Funds for Gross Property Additions ($000)

	1978	1977
Net income	$ 74,122	$ 141,162
Less:		
Dividends on common stock	108,800	94,900
Dividends on preferred stock	31,219	23,886
Reinvested earnings	$ (65,897)	$ 22,376
Principal noncash items:		
Depreciation and amortization	140,087	75,675
Deferred income taxes, net	25,151	86,456
Investment tax credits	—	26,185
Allowance for funds used during construction	(58,134)	(80,792)
	$ 41,207	$ 129,900
Changes in net current assets, other than long-term debt due within one year and interim obligations:		
Cash and temporary cash investments	$ (9,556)	$ 3,933
Receivables	(9,805)	(7,514)
Refundable federal income taxes	25,985	(13,985)
Fossil fuel stock	(37,846)	(34,954)
Materials and supplies	(2,038)	2,279
Accounts payable	26,082	(7,679)
Revenues to be refunded	(12,855)	8,682
Interest accrued	9,688	9,903
Taxes accrued	6,208	605
Other, net	(6,798)	11,904
	$ (10,935)	$ 26,826
Other, net (includes allowance for funds used during construction)	$ 24,753	$ 47,097
Total internal sources	$ 55,025	$ 150,171
Sale of securities:		
First mortgage bonds	$200,000	$ 300,000
Less		
Bonds retired	10,345	10,740
	$189,655	$ 289,260
Preferred stock	—	99,000
Capital contribution by parent company	$ 47,200	$ 95,000
Pollution control obligations	26,565	30,185
Obligations under capitalized leases	(754)	51,699
Sales of property, net book value	176	10,671
	$262,842	$ 575,815
Increase (decrease) in interim obligations	$165,563	$ (185,910)
Total external sources	$428,405	$ 389,905
Gross property additions	$483,430	$ 540,076

Source: *1978 Annual Report.*

mortgage bonds again by reason of earnings improvement resulting from emergency rate relief effective in early 1977 and permanent rate relief granted in April 1977. The company was able to sell $500 million of first mortgage bonds and $99 million of preferred stock on a crash basis by March 1978.

That brief period of minimal coverage has ended, and once again the company is barred from the long-term security markets because of inadequate coverages resulting from completely inadequate earnings. This places the company in the position of drawing on short-term lines of credit to finance construction of long-term capital assets.

The company's short-term revolving credit agreement with our banks is based upon the prime interest rate. The company is currently paying approximately 14 percent on the funds borrowed under this agreement. The 14 percent excludes fees payable on the unused portion of the $500 million credit line. These fees can be substantial. For example, the company has paid over $10 million in such fees since the execution of the previous revolving credit agreement on March 31, 1976. Additionally, the company has paid, on an annual basis, approximately 18 percent in interest and fees on funds borrowed under the current revolving credit agreement during the period October 1, 1978 through January 31, 1979.

The company cannot currently issue first-mortgage bonds due to inadequate earnings and coverages. Since 1976, the company has been downgraded on its first-mortgage bond rating. To achieve financial integrity, the company should, as a bare minimum, have an A rating on its first-mortgage bonds. If the company's earnings were increased to the point that it could issue first-mortgage bonds with A ratings, the interest rate on such bonds would be approximately 10 percent or lower. The company is, therefore, currently paying in excess of 4 percent more for funds under the revolving credit agreement than it would be paying if the company were able to issue A-rated first-mortgage bonds. This 4 percent increase in interest amounts to approximately $10 million of increased cost annually on $250 million of borrowed funds. Assuming full utilization of the $500 million available to the company under the revolving credit agreement, this 4 percent increase in costs for funds amounts to approximately $20 million annually.

Allowance for Funds Used During Construction.   One key financial factor which merits special mention is the quality and makeup of APCo's net profits, particularly the impact of the component labeled "allowance for funds used during construction" or AFUDC (see Exhibit 1). AFUDC is an accounting procedure whereby interest charges on the debt and equity capital used to finance new construction are capitalized and later included in the book value of utility plants, once the construction is completed and the new facilities are in service. The accrual of AFUDC is in accord with established rate-making procedures and accounting policies of the industry, but it does not represent current cash income. In 1978 APCo's AFUDC was $38.9 million, or 90.7 percent of APCo's net profit of $42.9 million. This compared to a 1968 AFUDC amount of $2.3 million on net profits of $31.7 million (7.1

percent). Because AFUDC represents a bookkeeping profit entry rather than current cash income, in the minds of security analysts and investors, the higher the percentage of AFUDC in net profit the lower the quality of a utility's earnings. And because AFUDC has the effect of raising current profits above what they would otherwise be (see Exhibit 1), the effect upon rate payers is to defer the (higher) rates necessary to cover construction financing costs until later when the plants under construction come into service—in other words, by using AFUDC accounting procedures, a company's rates are structured such that customers pay for the costs of financing new plant construction over the period the facilities are in service rather than paying the financing costs during the time of construction.

MARKETING AND ENERGY SERVICES

After the appearance of the energy crisis in late 1973, Alabama Power's marketing efforts underwent significant change. When the Alabama PSC turned down the entire rate increase request in June 1976, it also refused to consider advertising costs as an allowable expense in assessing APCo's rate of return. Company officials responded by announcing the cancellation of all media advertising, including ads which informed customers of ways to save on energy. But even before this, the company had stopped actively promoting greater usage of air-conditioning because of the uneven load balance it created on the generating system between summer and winter months. During the 1960s and early 1970s, sharp increases in the use of air-conditioning (both residential and commercial) caused the company to build new generating capacity to handle summer loads; however this capacity went largely unused during the remaining months. To counter this, Alabama Power aimed its marketing efforts at increasing off-peak loads so as to increase utilization of its facilities and to increase the revenues from its fixed investment. For example, APCo strived to promote electric heating to increase its wintertime load factor and dusk-to-dawn security lighting to increase its nighttime load factor.

The marketing significance of trying to balance the winter and summer peaks and to increase the overall load factor was that any resulting improvement in the utilization of existing facilities reduced fixed costs per kilowatt hour and paved the way for lower rates. In recent years the company's load factor has been in the 56–59 percent range.

Because of higher rates, energy conservation efforts, and the state of general flux in the entire energy market, APCo was making regular surveys of its customers. A summary of the results of the company's 1977 survey of residential customers is presented in Exhibit 9. Another change which indicated the company's shift in marketing focus was the change in the name of the marketing department to the energy services department in 1978.

EXHIBIT 9
Highlights of 1977 Survey of Residential Dwelling Construction and Energy Conservation Efforts

Demographic and Related Data

1. The ratios of single family swellings, apartments and mobile homes compared to total dwellings have remained relatively constant over the last seven years.
2. Dwelling ownership, household income, energy usage and conservation practices tend to increase with the increase in dwelling size.
3. New dwelling construction tends to have substantially higher levels of insulation and to be occupied by families with substantially higher income.
4. The lower the household income and the smaller the size of the dwelling the greater the percentage of customers who make no effort to practice conservation. Of total residential customers surveyed, approximately 25.2 percent had made no effort to conserve energy.
5. Of the dwellings with any type of air conditioning, partial or total, 41.0 percent were single family and owned by the occupant. This group of customers could benefit most from higher energy efficient dwellings. Approximately 90 percent of this group needed to be upgraded.
6. Owned single family dwellings represent 69.6 percent of the total residential market. This group represents the primary market potential for upgrading dwelling energy efficiency levels.

Dwelling Construction

1. The average size of all dwellings, based on conditioned space, was 1321 square feet. By type of dwellings, the breakdown was single family—1429 square feet, apartments—788 square feet, and mobile homes—784 square feet.
2. Approximately 70.8 percent of residential customers in single family dwellings acknowledged that, in their opinion, their dwellings were inadequately insulated.
3. Of the existing electrically heated dwellings, about 93.0 percent do not meet the present dwelling energy efficiency standards. About 42.6 percent of these dwellings are owned and single family.
4. The larger the dwelling the greater the tendency to use storm doors, storm windows, and higher levels of insulation.

Energy Conservation

1. Customer conservation practices increased in all appliances and equipment categories since the 1975 survey.
2. Approximately 74.8 percent of total residential customers made efforts to conserve energy.
3. 11.1 percent of all customers spent money in some way to upgrade their dwellings to conserve energy during the past five years, and 26.8 percent raised their thermostats in the summer. For night setback a significant 60.4 percent of customers lowered their thermostats.
4. The following percent of customers indicated that they practiced energy conservation in the use of the following:

Electric range .... 37.4 percent   Electric dishwater .... 13.0 percent
Electric water heater . 18.4 percent   Electric dryer .... 30.3 percent

Again these percentages increased substantially with the increase in the size of dwelling and household income.
5. The older the dwellings the greater the percentage of dwellings that were upgraded for conservation purposes during the past five years.

EXHIBIT 9 (continued)

6. About 18.0 percent of customers in single family dwellings equipped with heat pumps spent money to upgrade dwelling energy efficiency levels during the past five years. This follows from the fact that most of these dwellings already had higher than average insulation levels, and these customers were more aware of the benefit of higher energy efficient construction. Overall 11.1 percent of our customers made conservation expenditures.
7. Customers with any air conditioning made a substantial effort to conserve energy. The effort was greater for dwellings with heat pumps and central units than the window units.

OPERATIONS

Alabama Power's operating organization is divided into three major functional categories: operations services; fuel supply; power supply and power delivery. The operations services department has responsibility for:

A. Coordinating communications related to operating matters with regulatory agencies and negotiation of interconnection and coordination agreements with other utilities and agencies.
B. Generation and transmission system planning.
C. Electric system operation, including dispatch of the hydroelectric and thermal-electric generating resources and transmission facilities.
D. The application, installation, operation, and maintenance of protective and supervisory control systems to APCo's transmission and generating plant substation facilities.

The fuel department is responsible for acquiring adequate fuel for the generating plants of the company. Fuel is purchased in sufficient quantities to meet the respective requirements of each generating unit, and of sufficient quality to meet environment regulations. The fuel department is responsible for both long-term and short-term fuel planning and acquisition. The department is responsible for negotiating long-term fuel contracts and purchasing fuel in the spot market with the fundamental objective of achieving the lowest practicable fuel cost consistent with having an adequate and reliable fuel supply.

The power supply department has primary responsibility for:

A. The operation and maintenance of the company's electric generating plants, including hydro, fossil-fueled, and nuclear-fueled plants, and the engineering evaluation of systems and equipment applicable to such plants, as well as the responsibility for the manning and training of personnel to operate such plants.
B. The installation, operation, and maintenance of protective and control devices within the company's generating plants.

C. Administration of quality assurance efforts relating to the design, construction, and operation of generating plants.
D. The securing of environmental permits and the development and analysis of technical studies involving air and water quality conditions.

The power delivery department is principally concerned with:

A. The design and construction of bulk power transmission facilities.
B. The effective implementation of policies and practices necessary to assure the availability, economic operation and maintenance of transmission lines, substations, distribution systems, and other devices related to delivering energy from sources to customers.

The day-to-day operation and maintenance activities of the company and a significant amount of construction work are performed by field units organized into six operating divisions. Each division is headed by a vice president who has responsibility for operations within the respective division. Each division is subdivided into districts where district managers and their staffs have direct contact with customers in the company's 37 districts and 13 subdistricts. Each division has engineers, supervisors, and crews assigned to it to operate and maintain the company's transmission and distribution systems.

OPPOSITION TO HIGHER ELECTRIC RATES

> While asking for increased revenues is an unpleasant task for us and our customers, the alternative is to jeopardize the economic future of the state, which must have an adequate and reliable supply of electricity both today and in the future.

So said Joseph Farley, president of Alabama Power Company. Yet, beginning in 1975 when a $106.8 million rate increase request was filed, the company was continually confronted with vigorous opposition. In fact, APCo's rate hike requests became a political football, involving Governor George C. Wallace, State Attorney General Bill Baxley (who was a candidate to succeed Governor Wallace in the 1978 election), Lieutenant Gov. Jere Beasley (also a candidate for governor in 1978), the PSC (two new members of which were elected in 1978), the courts, various state legislators, a number of the state's largest industrial users of electricity (U.S. Steel, Kimberly-Clark, Olin Corp., Uniroyal, Diamond Shamrock, Ideal Basic Industries), the Alabama Textile Manufacturers Association, the United Steelworker's Union, and several protesting consumer groups. Newspaper reporters and TV newsmen regularly covered and reported on events involving the company and its management.

So strong was the public outcry over rising electric bills that the state legislature enacted a bill authorizing the expenditure of $100,000 to conduct a management study and financial audit of Alabama Power. After signing the bill into law, Governor Wallace appointed a three-member committee which subsequently recommended Price Waterhouse & Co. to conduct the audit. In their 410-page report to the committee and the Governor made in April 1978, the auditors said their

> . . . overall conclusion from the management study is that Alabama Power Company is an effectively managed company, and that Southern Company Services effectively manages the principal services it renders to the company.

Other major findings of the report included the following:

Alabama Power Company's rates for electricity "compare favorably with those of other electric utilities" in the United States "and are well below the national average. . . ."

The principal factors which have caused electric rates "to increase so rapidly lie beyond the company's sphere of control."

The company is organized "in a logical manner and staffed with competent and knowledgeable personnel at all levels of management."

The company's methods and procedures for load forecasting and for generation and transmission planning "are among the most advanced in the utility industry."

Major forces exerting pressure on the company's operations are general inflation, "substantial increases in the cost of long-term capital funds," and "burgeoning expansion in governmental regulation."

The company "has an excellent policy governing conflicts of interest."

The Southern electric system power pool "insures that, except during system emergencies, the company's customers are supplied with the lowest cost energy which is available."

The company is providing a relatively high level of service to its customers at a cost which is less than the average expended per customer by other utilities.

Current methods and procedures for controlling the costs of constructing new generating units "are adequate."

The company's construction costs are comparable to those of other electric utilities.

Financial management and the company's accounting and financial reporting systems are adequate.

For both capital and raw materials (coal), the input categories which unquestionably are the most significant financially, the company has used its resources effectively.

The report concluded that

> . . . considering the effect of the upward pressures which inflation, capital costs, and regulatory requirements continue to exert on the company, it is unrealistic to expect even a small reduction in electric service rates.

One of the major issues over rates related to how any rate hike would be distributed among residential, commercial, and industrial customers. In this regard, a spokesman for Diamond Shamrock was quoted as saying:

> Diamond Shamrock is willing to pay its fair share of any increase granted to Alabama Power Company by this Commission, provided the increase is applied against all three classes of customers on a equitable and fair basis . . .
>
> Diamond Shamrock would vigorously oppose any changing of the percentages as between residential, commercial, and industrial customers. The percentages were changed to favor the residential customers by this Commission in two prior cases, and Diamond Shamrock is of the opinion that any such additional change would result in an unfair, inequitable, improper and discriminatory rate . . .
>
> The evidence is clear that industry is already paying more than its fair share, and there should not be placed on industry an even heavier share of the increase.

A spokesman for the Uniroyal plant in Opelika, Alabama, made the following remarks regarding how the proposed increases in industrial rates might affect the plant's costs and operations:

> The Opelika Plant, unlike the older Uniroyal tire plants, was built with the concept to be highly automated, well ventilated, partially air conditioned and well lighted in order to improve the efficiency of the worker and to make the plant a safer and healthier place to work. Also, extensive use of cooling towers for process cooling water has minimized water usage and thermal pollution of this natural resource, together with air pollution control equipment making this manufacturing facility one of the cleanest. These features cause the Opelika Plant to use 33 percent more electrical energy than other Uniroyal plants.
>
> Since the advent of the radial tire and the recent recession, all tire companies have suffered from reduced sales which in turn has caused reduced production. This means that because of over capacity, top management is having the tires made at the plants which have the lowest operating cost. Therefore, if the Opelika Plant's operating cost is greater than its sister plants, Opelika's production would be shifted to one of its sister plants in another state.

The purchasing agent for the cement division of Ideal Basic Industries, which operates a cement plant in Mobile, explained why his company could not cost-justify generating its own electric energy requirements and why industrial rates ought to be lower than rates for other customers:

> First, the utilities have historically designed their rates based on the true cost of serving their customer loads at various levels of usage. In this respect, you could say they supply a cost-plus product. Under this type cost-allocation and rate design condition, I do not feel that the potential benefits of generating our own electric energy (previously mentioned) could offset the savings of purchasing our power requirements from a utility. Second, steady high load factor users such as Ideal and the other industries represented here are an economic benefit to Alabama Power Company and its other customers, first

because their consistent year round power usage prevents deep valleys of unused generating capacity from occurring during off-peak seasons of the year and, second, because we provide a volume of usage to the system that allows Alabama Power Company to buy and operate at lower production costs which are a benefit to every customer.

. . . industries such as Ideal, in purchasing electricity from Alabama Power, cause other customers' bills to be lower than they would be if Alabama Power did not have industrial customers such as Ideal to level their load. Industrial customers are also very important to Alabama Power Company because of the basically low investment Alabama Power has in industrial customers, minimal expenses incurred by Alabama Power in servicing industrial customers, and the higher rate of return which Alabama Power receives from its industrial customers.

A representative of the Alabama Textile Manufacturers Association said:

The company has proposed equal rate increases for each class. It is the position of the Alabama Textile Manufacturers Association that any increase which may be granted by the Commission should be spread so that each class of customer receives an equal percentage increase. This would be a fair, equitable and nondiscriminatory increase.

The director of manufacturing-industrial production for Olin Corporation's McIntosh plant testified that approximately 50 percent of the total costs of the plant were for electricity (Olin's plant at McIntosh was Alabama Power's third-largest industrial customer) and further stated:

Our basic position is that we are willing to pay our share of the company's total cost of service. Of course, we would like to see our rate for electricity as low as possible. But we recognize that costs may be going up and we do not ask to be subsidized by any other users. In turn, we feel that the intense competition between our location and other locations in the Southeast and elsewhere in the country make it important that our rate be held as low as possible, consistent with recovering the cost of serving us.

Exhibit 6 contains an indication of the differential rates between residential, commercial, and industrial users. At both the prevailing and the proposed rates, APCo had a substantially higher profit margin on its sales to industrial customers than it had on residential customer sales. This was true even though the average price per kwh paid by industrial users was considerably lower than for residential customers (see Exhibit 6)—an outcome which reflected sizably lower costs per kilowatt hour in serving industrial customers.

DEMAND TRENDS AND PROJECTIONS

Like most other electric utilities, Alabama Power's sales of electric energy in 1974–75 declined abruptly from the steady upward trend of previous years. However, by 1978 the usage of electric energy appeared to be returning toward its former growth rate; kilowatt-hour sales were up significantly in all three major customer groups—residential, commercial, and industrial—during the 1976–78 period (see Exhibit 6). In 1978 the peak demand was 10.1 percent higher than in 1977. The following table shows the company's actual and projected generation requirements:

Year	Maximum Peak Hour Load (in kilowatts)		Sales of Energy (million kilowatt-hours)
1970	4,175,500	actual	22,236.8
1971	4,420,000		23,264.6
1972	4,922,600		25,384.7
1973	5,326,700		27,428.4
1974	5,493,300		25,263.8
1975	5,644,800		27,748.3
1976	5,880,500		29,782.3
1977	6,060,300		31,983.8
1978	6,670,700		33,604.2
1979	6,783,000	projected	35,241.0
1980	7,192,000		37,167.0
1981	7,632,000		39,307.0
1982	8,094,000		41,551.0
1983	8,542,000		43,923.0
1984	8,985,000		46,315.0
1985	9,452,000		48,740.0
1986	9,928,000		51,263.0
1987	10,422,000		53,876.0
1988	10,937,000		56,610.0

A comparison of APCo's kilowatt-hour sales and Alabama's Gross State Product (GSP) revealed that total electric energy usage rose an average 2.28 percent for each 1 percent increase in real growth of the state's economy during the 1960–75 period. This was equivalent to 3.64 billion kwh in additional energy sales for each $1-billion increase in Alabama's constant-dollar GSP. In the industrial sector of Alabama's economy, APCo's kilowatt-hour sales to industrial customers rose an average of 2.87 billion kwh for each $1-billion increase in constant-dollar output in mining and manufacturing. Residential consumption of electricity rose 533 kilowatt hours for each $100 increase in real personal income per capita during the 1960–75 period.

The economic likelihood of further increases in the demand for electricity in Alabama Power's service area was outlined thusly by an economist:

> I would expect demand for electricity in Alabama Power's service area to increase. There are several reasons for this. First, Alabama's industry-recruiting successes of the past are likely to spill over into the future, at least for a foreseeable time, and this means a greater demand for electricity in the industrial sector. Alabama needs new industry and more high-skill, high-wage jobs in manufacturing, both to provide jobs for new entrants into the labor force and for the unemployed and to open up better job opoprtunities for

workers who have the skills and abilities to upgrade themselves. More and better manufacturing jobs are Alabama's key to closing the gap between the living standards and material well-being of its residents and those of other states. This means ensuring that the state has enough electric power to offer and to supply to new firms—otherwise their locating in Alabama is automatically foreclosed.

Second, expansion in the industrial sector can be expected to stimulate expansion in the trade and service industries and, in turn, to expand commercial demand for electricity.

Third, as incomes rise in Alabama, there is ample reason to expect further increases in residential demand for electricity. To begin with, growing numbers of builders and developers are installing electric heat and electric appliances in new homes and apartments under construction. Moreover, there is certain to be more widespread use of air-conditioning and electrical appliances in Alabama households as incomes and purchasing power rise.

All three major components of electricity demand—residential, commercial, and industrial—have inherent built-in features to increase as the level of economy activity goes up and as the material well-being of the population improves. This is particularly true in states like Alabama where there is economic catching up to do. In other words, in a less-developed economy like Alabama's, there are stronger demand-pull pressures being exerted for electricity than tends to be the case in a mature economy. Hence, there is solid economic reason to expect a higher demand for electricity to materialize in Alabama Power's service area over the next several years. The only question is how much the demand for electricity will increase and the extent to which higher electric rates will take some of the steam out of demand.

With regard to whether higher rates for electricity would reduce the need for Alabama Power to construct new generating facilities, the economist concluded:

> Although a great number of studies have been done all over the country to try to figure out what higher prices for electricity will do to electric energy demand both in the short run and in the long run, the results are not consistent and the answer remains quite uncertain. Such studies are necessarily based on historical or past data. The past may or may not be a reliable guide to the future. While it does appear that in 1974 and 1975 the demand for electric energy did not grow at the same pace of previous periods, the nation was, during this time, in the midst of its most serious recession since World War II; there was rampant inflation which struck hard at consumer purchasing power; and there was much publicity in the media and elsewhere about the need to conserve energy. These factors, along with higher prices for electricity, dampened the consumption of electricity. But, continued growth in electric energy usage can still be reliably expected—as the company's 1976–78 experience readily confirms. We can, however, expect the growth rate to be slower, perhaps in the range of four to six percent per year instead of the previous trend of six to eight percent per year.
>
> If the lead times in constructing new generating capacity were not so long, then it would be a simple matter to wait until the course of the demand for

EXHIBIT 10
Territorial Load Trend Curves

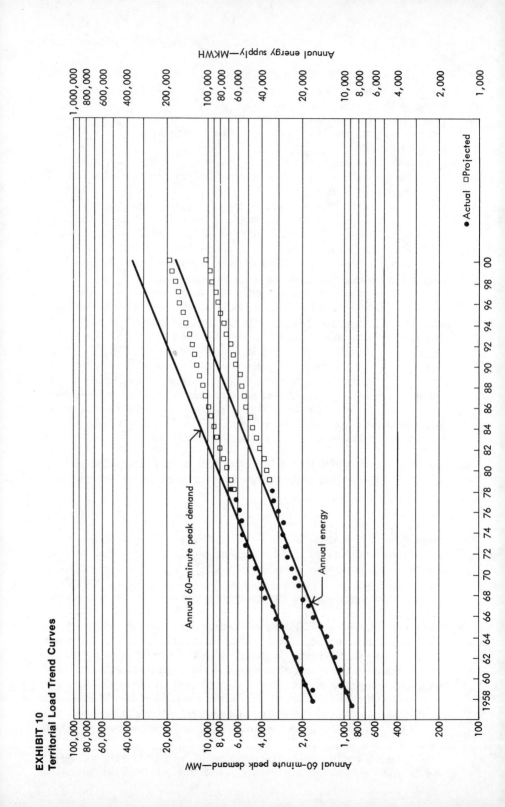

electricity became more certain and then build capacity accordingly. Unfortunately, though, this is not feasible. Long lead times are a reality and construction plans must be made and work begun now to be ready for 1985 and beyond.

In my judgment, given these lead times and given the inherent uncertainties in demand forecasts, there is far more risk of damage to the state's economy from having too little capacity than from having a slight excess over needed reserves. In other words, if the demand for electricity materializes as forecast by the company, or is even a bit higher for whatever reason, and if ample generating capacity is not available, then the effect will be to choke off economic expansion that otherwise could have taken place. Some new industries that might have located in Alabama will go elsewhere. Expansions of existing operations may have to be delayed or else shifted to plant locations in other states. Construction of new homes and commercial buildings may be adversely affected. At the same time, consumers who are in a position to improve their living standards are thwarted from doing so. Of course, Alabama Power may be able to relieve its shortages partially by purchasing excess power from surrounding utilities if they should have extra generating capacity, but it is to be expected that the marginal costs of obtaining power in this manner will be higher and that such costs will have to be passed on to ratepayers in one way or another.

Exhibit 10 depicts the company's load trend curves and indicates how the projected loads are expected to fall below the historical trend of the 1958–74 period.

THE FUTURE OUTLOOK

In commenting on the recent turmoil over the company's proposed rates and reflecting on its future prospects, Joseph Farley, APCo's president, said:

> If ever a year could be described as eventful at Alabama Power Company, 1978 certainly would meet all the criteria . . . . There is nothing pleasant about a rate increase. The entire process in the past year has been made more difficult for all by the actions and rhetoric of some elected officials and their representatives. In this respect, today—more than at anytime in recent years—perhaps we have a cause for optimism. All we ask or expect is objectivity, reasonableness, and a cooperative spirit in working for the good of our state, our customers, and our stockholders.

Mr. Farley was hopeful that the new members of the PSC (along with a newly hired executive director for the PSC), the new governor and lieutenant governor, and the generally changed political climate that accompanied the beginning of the new state government administration in 1979 would result in Alabama Power's being able to secure needed rate relief. If this did not occur, the outlook for the company was indeed cloudy and uncertain.

D. Strategy Implementation and Administration: Converting the Strategic Plan into Results

23. Narragansett Bay Shipbuilding and Drydock Company (A)*

It was a typically cold, wet, and windy New England day as Jim Butons reclined in his chair and looked out the window at the bay and the cluster of shops, dry docks, and building bays near the water's edge. He well remembered those days before he became general manager, when he fought the wet, bitter cold as a young engineer on the waterfront. As he reflected on those days, it brought back pleasant memories of the camaraderie that existed in the shipyard as they built and delivered the "90-day wonder" ships during the war.

Pat Woods, his secretary, interrupted, "Bob Doyle is returning your call."

"Yes, Bob," Jim said, as he snapped back to reality. "I've been looking over the new design package with some of my management engineering people and I think we ought to have a staff meeting to discuss our strategy as it will apply to this effort. I want you there as engineering director. I would also like you to bring the managers of your design departments so we can get their feelings on reorganizing to meet this new effort. As you know, we're going to attempt to break from the traditional design approach and try what we're calling the Seaborne method. I think this presents quite a challenge, but with proper organization we should be able to handle it."

"I agree Jim, but don't you think Bill Moore should also attend to represent the shipyard, since he is director of operations?"

"You're right, Bob, especially since our ultimate product will be production-oriented drawings rather than the traditional system-oriented drawings.[1] Let's see if we can get together next Wednesday and try and brainstorm some alternatives for organizing the design effort."

---

* Prepared by Prof. Louis K. Bragaw, U.S. Coast Guard Academy, and Prof. William R. Allen, University of Rhode Island, in collaboration with Daniel J. McCarthy and Robert Ames.

[1] Production-oriented drawings sought to facilitate land-based prefabrication of entire ship sections whereas traditional system-oriented drawings emphasized the working system around which the ship would be built.

"Sounds good to me, Jim. We'll do some preliminary work here and get a good handle on what it will take to get production-oriented results. See you Wednesday."

COMPANY BACKGROUND

Narragansett Bay Shipbuilding and Drydock Company (NBSD) was established around the turn of the century. Although some of its first work was commercially oriented, it soon developed a close association with the Department of Defense, and the Navy in particular. Navy contracts continue to be the company's primary source of business.

The company was particularly proud of its contribution in developing ships as a major weapons system. NBSD, in fact, participated with the Navy as lead design shipyard on many ship designs. During the rapid development of nuclear ships during the 1950s and 1960s, the company had participated in a number of different innovations relating to the Navy's search for such things as optimal speeds, more effective offensive and defensive weapons systems, quietness, and other operating improvements. Out of this participation NBSD developed an extensive engineering design department that operated under the general manager almost completely independent of the rest of the shipyard.

During the mid-1960s, NBSD was invited by the Institute for Defense Analysis to participate in a program to develop a new missile system for the 1980s. This program was to be unlike anything previous, and the Institute for Defense Analysis wanted to spur competition between the Army, Air Force, and Navy for the best system. This led to a challenging and active period for NBSD's advanced engineering department as it departed from conventional approaches and tried to blaze new trails for the future. Every time NBSD conceived of a novel idea it was then dissected thoroughly by the Institute's design, economic, and threat divisions.[2] Over a period of several years numerous concepts were analyzed, including truck borne missiles proposed by the Army, airborne or flying platforms by the Air Force, and stationary undersea platforms on the Continental Shelf by Navy sources. However, in the late 1960s, NBSD was successful in winning the competition with a ship-type launch platform.

The design contract was long term and would likely provide NBSD with stable work, including construction, through the 1970s and into the 1980s. However, it was also at this time that both the Department of Defense and Congress were seeking more participation in design by contractors, with the government maintaining an overview position. This was a departure from tradition (see Exhibits 1 and 2) and was the reason that NBSD was faced with its present problem of accommodating the government's wishes and at the

---

[2] The threat division would try to show how vulnerable or threatening to the safety of the United States the concept could be.

EXHIBIT 1
Traditional Ship Design Evolution

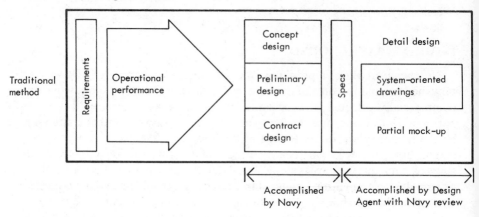

EXHIBIT 2
The Seaborne Design Method

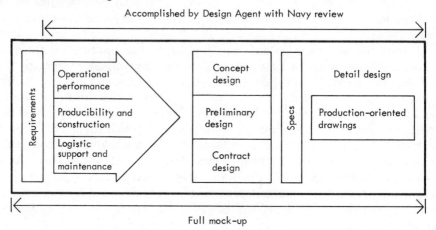

same time designing and constructing one of the most sophisticated ships ever built.

ORGANIZATIONAL PROBLEMS POSED BY THE NEW CONTRACT

In the week since Jim Butons and Bob Doyle had talked, the weather had been typically New England—unpredictable. While spirits had risen with the prediction of a clear day, it had been snowing since late Tuesday night. Jim Butons thought how lucky he had been to schedule the meeting for midmorning since this would give everyone a chance to fight the snow and get to work.

Dan Hall, manager of advanced engineering, met Jim on the way to the conference. "What a day, Jim! The weather sure changes fast here on the Bay!"

"It's liable to do most anything," responded Jim, "and even after 30 years here, I'm still not used to it!"

As they entered the conference room, Jim scanned the table hoping that everyone was present. Bob Doyle was at one side flanked by his staff managers: John Wilson of marine engineering, Carl Anderson of electrical engineering, Joe Harrington of naval architecture, and Tom Parker of arrangements.[3] Bill Moore was in deep conversation with Paul Michaud of industrial relations (which Jim surmised related to union problems); George Blanchard of management engineering was seated drawing block diagrams—as he always seemed to be doing.[4]

Jim took his place at the head of the table and began immediately, "Good morning, gentlemen! I trust you have all been informed as to why we are here. Basically, we're here to discuss our ability to respond effectively to our new ship design contract for the Seaborne project. As you know, we're calling this the Seaborne method. Seaborne is going to be our bread and butter for the next 10 or 15 years, and I want to ensure that we don't underestimate the scope of the job or overestimate our ability to perform."

John Wilson interrupted, "I don't see any big problem here, Jim. We've been designing ships here for years. Why, I can remember that as we struggled with our first nuclear design we had plenty of problems, but each engineering discipline responded and the problems were solved without too much difficulty."

"I agree!" interjected Joe Harrington. "Our department has always been responsive and, to my recollection, there have never been any design problems we couldn't solve."

As the others were talking, Dan Hall started giving each person at the table a schematic arrangement of the traditional and Seaborne methods of design evolution (see Exhibits 1 and 2).

"I'm not sure you're seeing the problem, gentlemen," Jim responded. "I'm not trying to belittle the ability of your organizations or their historical contribution to the company.[5] What I'm trying to evaluate is their effectiveness in the present situation. Perhaps Dan, who has been working on the Seaborne concept since the competition phase, can shed some light on what I'm driving at."

---

[3] The arrangements staff was charged with locating various equipment and other items within the vessel so as to enhance convenience and functional effectiveness.

[4] Management engineering participated in all organizational changes in an effort to smooth the transition and provide advice on how to improve the engineering department's management structure.

[5] See Exhibits 3, 4, 5, 6, and 7 for the design engineering functional organizations.

"Right, Jim," said Dan, as he completed passing the schematic arrangements around the table. "Traditionally, the Navy would state its requirements and operational performance objectives to its own team within the civilian department of the Navy. This portion of the Navy organization would work on the concept design, preliminary design, and contract design, with the end product being a set of ship's specifications."

"Sure, Dan," interrupted Bob Doyle, "but my people also participated."

"Agreed, Bob, but generally on a very small scale. The Navy would call and say they would like, let's say 20 designers, for the contract design phase and you would pick as required from your organization. But let me emphasize that up to the ship's specification stage our participation was minimal."

"I see your point," Bob responded.

"After the ship's specifications were written," Dan continued, "the Navy would award the detail design contract and the design agent, typically ourselves, would be off and running. We would then allocate to our functional design departments that part of the ship design which fell within their responsibility and they would ultimately produce ship's drawing."

"And that's one of my problems," Bill Moore of operations interjected. "Nowhere in this scheme has a serious attempt been made to consider our construction problems. The first time my organization is considered is when the plans are delivered to the shipyard."

EXHIBIT 3
Management Organization Chart

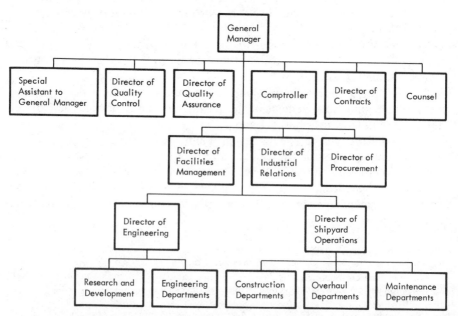

"Well, I think with the Seaborne system we can alleviate some of those problems," Dan continued. "As you can see in the Seaborne method we, as the design agent having won the competition, will participate from the inception, with the Navy playing a minimal role as a review activity. We will integrate the Navy requirements and operational performance objectives, logistic support, and maintenance objectives before we begin concept design.[6] We will then enter the concept design, preliminary design, and contract design phases, ultimately writing the ship's specifications. The end product of this method should be a set of production-oriented drawings, which is what I think you're after, Bill. Right?"

"Yes, Dan, it certainly sounds like it would help our end of the operation," Bill replied.

EXHIBIT 4
Marine Engineering Organization Chart

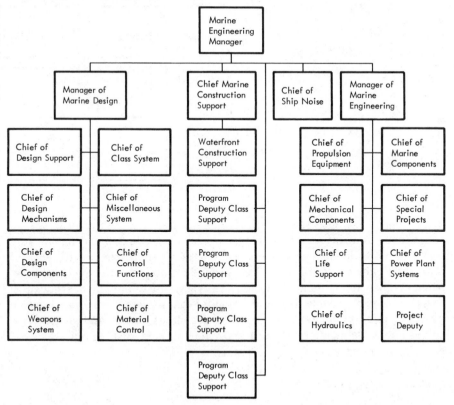

---

[6] After a certain period of deployment at sea, it was customary for ships to return to a shipyard for upkeep, logistics support, and maintenance. Maintenance was considered in the design stage in an effort to minimize the time that ships would have to be "off station."

EXHIBIT 5
Electrical Engineering Organization Chart

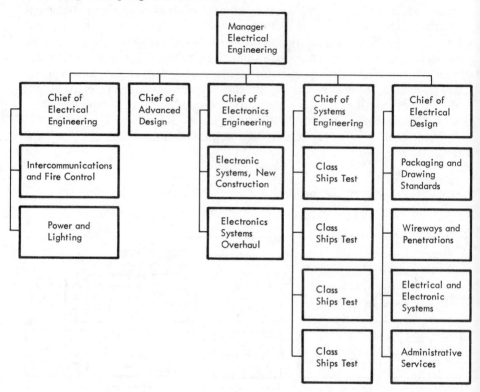

"Thank you, Dan," said Jim Butons as he stood up. "As you can see we can expect total involvement in this Seaborne method, but I'm not sure we're organizationally geared up for it. I don't think we can expect our functional engineering organization to handle this task effectively as independent units. In my mind I envision a restructuring of our engineering effort to be more responsive to this new method. What I'd like is for you fellows to go back, think about what we have to accomplish, and talk among yourselves about viable alternatives. I know this may be pushing but I'd like to reconvene in one week."

INTERIM MEETING

Recognizing the necessity to act with some degree of haste, Bob Doyle called a meeting of his staff managers shortly after Jim Buton's meeting.

"Gentlemen," Bob began, "I'd like to start by reassuring you that the problem at hand is in no way a reflection on yourselves or on the way in which your organizations have performed. You've performed satisfactorily in the past, as I would expect you to do in the future. I only mention this because we need some fresh thinking here, and I don't want our discussions influenced by attempts to unnecessarily fight change to protect existing organizations."

"Does this mean that we've already ruled out handling Seaborne with our present structure," Carl Anderson interrupted.

"I didn't say that, Carl," Bob responded. "I just don't want to get bogged down defending our existing structure."

EXHIBIT 6
Naval Architecture Organization Chart

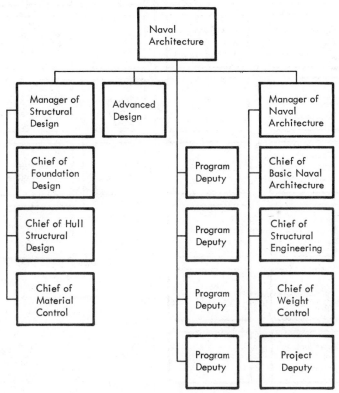

"Let's see where we stand today," John Wilson began, as he leaned forward in his chair and put his pipe down next to the yellow pad he had been staring at. "I think we are all in agreement that we have the in-house technical expertise to handle the design phase of this project."

The others at the table nodded agreement.

"I also think we have competent management people within the company to handle the administrative end," John continued. "The problem would appear to be how to more effectively utilize this talent."

EXHIBIT 7
Engineering Services Organization Chart

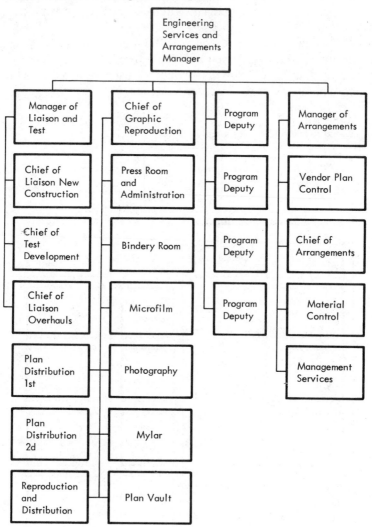

"Our present experience up to the awarding of the detail design phase of the contract has been minimal," Tom Parker interjected. "It would seem to me that this would be our weakest area."

"I agree, Tom," Bob replied, "and I think this is the area we should concentrate on. When we get to the detail design phase I'm confident we can perform adequately, but getting to that point may prove somewhat of a problem."

Joe Harrington cleared his throat and stood up. "I don't think our individual organizations would be responsive to a total involvement approach—independently—without a significant potential for duplication of effort.''

"I think you're right, Joe," Bob interjected.

Joe continued, "What I can envision is the need for a project office which would act as a point of contact with the Navy and direct our effort here."

"Yes, Joe," Carl interrupted, "but you know the difficulty we have pulling people from the functional organizations for project-type organizations. When the project ends they are usually on their own and find their positions within the original organizations filled. This has traditionally made it hard to get top-notch people for project-type organizations. If we want top-notch people for this effort, we may have a problem unless we also consider what will happen as the project dissolves, if we go that way."

"You've got a good point, Carl," Joe replied as he sat down.

"Well, gentlemen, I think the single point of contact is a good idea, and I think the project approach, in some form, is the way we should point this effort," said Bob Doyle as he stood and paced the floor. "I also think we will have to face the traditional problem with staffing a project organization. One way to circumvent this problem would be to establish a small project on the general manager staff level which would pool from the existing functional areas as required on a temporary basis."

"Would this retain the present functional organizations?" Carl Anderson asked.

"Yes, Carl," Bob responded. "Another approach would be to break off and establish a new organization to exclusively handle the project up to the detail design phase, at which time we would dissolve it and continue the design essentially as we do now. This project would be the single point of contact with the Navy and have total responsibility for this effort."

"I can see that if we draw this organization from the existing functional organizations it might also be a good time to reorganize their efforts in preparation for the detail design phase," Tom Parker interjected.

"Good point, Tom," Bob replied, "Any more ideas?" Bob scanned the table and there were no replies. "Okay, let me work up these ideas for a presentation at Jim Buton's next meeting. Thank you for your help," said Bob, as he gathered his notes and started to leave the conference room.

THE ALTERNATIVES

The weather had stayed cold and the snow was still on the ground as Jim Butons reconvened the meeting.

"Well, gentlemen, let's get down to business," Jim began, "I trust you've all had an opportunity to think the situation over and come up with some viable alternatives."

"I think I can best speak for the group," Bob Doyle interjected.

"Fine, Bob, let's see what you've got," Jim replied.

"First, let me say that it hasn't been easy to analyze this situation objectively," Bob began. "As the name implies, our traditional design approach has in its course caused functionally oriented departments to emerge which are justly proud of their accomplishments and skills. As such, the thought of change is not easy to swallow. However, after much discussion I think we all realize our approach should change as the design approach changes. Once we agreed on this we were able to narrow our viable options to the following.

"One option would take someone from Dan Hall's advanced engineering group who has been familiar with the Seaborne program, and, with a small group of subordinates, coordinate the Seaborne method within the existing functional design departments. He would have the right to pool talent as required or delegate task-type contracts to the functional organizations.[7] He would report directly to the general manager and be the sole point of contact with the government. This option would cause a minimum reorganization and would give a single controlling position (see Exhibit 8).

"Another option would entail the creation of an entirely new department. The project would be headed by a director of Seaborne design and construction. He would pull the cream of the crop from the existing functional departments to form his own organization (see Exhibit 9). This department would handle the design phase up to and through the ship's specification phase, at which point the detail design would revert to the functional organization. In that this option would draw from the functional organizations it would also be a good time to reorganize the functional departments and eliminate duplication of effort as they prepare for the detail design.

"It's our opinion, Jim, that these are the only real viable alternatives. We must choose one of these if we are to handle the Seaborne design contract effectively."

---

[7] A task-type contract is one where services for one specific task (or job) are requested from the technical departments.

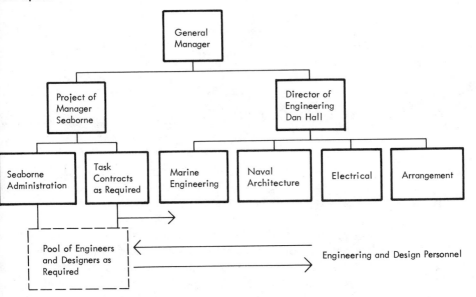

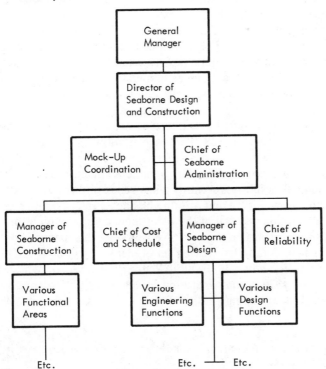

EXHIBIT 9
Second Option

24. The A. L. Garber Company*

The name of the United Board and Carton Corporation was changed to the
A. L. Garber Company, Inc., at a special stockholders' meeting on December 28, 1971. The purpose of changing the name was to more accurately
identify the company's new business strategy. A. L. Garber was the name of
United's Ashland subsidiary, which was purchased in 1969. A. L. Garber,
which was founded in 1879, had established an outstanding reputation for
fine-quality printing and packaging. After the name change of United, the
Ashland plant remained a subsidiary until March 31, 1972, when it was
merged into the A. L. Garber Company.

After making a study of the company David L. Summers became president in the latter part of February 1971. In an effort to correct serious
operating losses, Mr. Summers rapidly made some drastic changes in the
company, including such actions as eliminating the purchasing department,
closing two paperboard plants, and firing the sales service manager and 50
percent of his staff.

Mr. Summers announced first-quarter 1971 earnings of $81,550 in a letter
to stockholders dated May 28, 1971 (see Exhibit 1).

After spending several months rearranging company operations and disposing of the paperboard mills, Mr. Summers began to devote more time to
the development of future operating plans based on the new strategy of being
in the specialty packaging and printing business. In November 1971, he held
a three-day meeting with all of the plant managers, at which they set objectives for the next year and the next five years. At this meeting, projects were
also established. A detailed written set of plans was prepared. The summary
of these plans is shown in Exhibit 2, the first page of which includes a
comparison of 1970 actual operating losses with 1971 estimated and 1972
target sales and operating profits. Exhibit 3 shows 1971 and 1972 data by
plant.

---

* Prepared by Prof. Melvin J. Stanford with the collaboration of Prof. J. Weldon Moffitt,
both of Brigham Young University.

EXHIBIT 1
Letter to Shareholders

 UNITED BOARD & CARTON CORPORATION
Corporate Office · 600 Union Street · Ashland, Ohio 44805 · 419-322-1111

May 28, 1971

Dear Fellow Shareholder,

     We are pleased to report that our company earned $81,550, or $.12 per common share, on sales of $3,775,859 for the first quarter ended March 31, 1971, compared with a loss of $4,600, or $.01 per share, on sales of $4,249,311 for the first three months last year.

     Favorable operating results were achieved even though economic conditions in those market areas we serve have yet to recover fully from the general decline of 1970.

     Our strategy of streamlining operations and concentrating in those businesses where we have a distinctive competence - primarily the manufacture and marketing of folding cartons, and commercial printing in the specialty packaging area - has yielded positive results.

     Our outlook for the second quarter and the remainder of 1971 is encouraging, especially if the current economic recovery continues.

                  Best personal regards,

                  David L. Summers
                  President and Chief
                  Executive Officer

EXHIBIT 2
1972 Strategy

Basic Strategy:

ALG's basic strategy is to become the most profitable company, with the best growth rate, in the business of designing, manufacturing, and marketing of specialty printing and packaging.

Definition of Basic Business

ALG's basic business is the design, manufacture, and marketing of specialty printing and packaging. The major product lines of the company are folding cartons, record jackets, direct mail advertising, magazine inserts, specialty publications, and general commercial printing. Folding cartons and specialty printing represent 80% and 20%, respectively, of total sales.

Profit Objectives—1972

ALG's profit objectives for 1972 are as follows:

	1972 ($000)	1971 Est. ($000)	Percent 1972 over 1971	1970 ($000)
Sales	$16,572	$15,150	9.4%	$16,615*
Net income—after tax operations	615	515	19.4%	(589)*
Extraordinary—NOL carry forward	465	68		
Net income—after extraordinary	1,080	583	85.0%	(3,516)
Net income as a percent of sales	3.7%	3.4%		
Earnings per share before extraordinary	92¢	77¢	19.5%	(88¢)
Earnings per share after extraordinary .	$ 1.62	87¢	86.2%	($5.26)
Return on shareholders' equity (including debt)				
Before extraordinary	9.5%	8.3%		
After extraordinary	16.7%	9.3%		

* Restated to exclude discontinued operations.

We believe the above objectives are reasonable in light of the significant changes in operating strategy and the many changes in personnel at our plant locations. The estimate for 1972 is further complicated by the present wage and price controls and how much we will be able to raise prices relative to labor costs.

The following outline illustrates in part the nature and significance of the changes made at ALG during the past 11 months:

ALG Corporate

The company redefined its basic business and discontinued the unsuccessful strategy of functioning as an integrated paperboard and packaging company, and initiated a new strategy to operate as a specialty printing and packaging company. Two paperboard mills were liquidated and over 300 people terminated.

EXHIBIT 2 (continued)

The management structure of ALG was changed from a centralized and staff-oriented company to a lean, line, nonstaff, decentralized profit-center type of organization.

Those unnecessary staff functions which did not measurably improve or assist the profit centers of the company were eliminated.

Ashland

A new sales manager was appointed and one third of the sales force was replaced by more capable people.

The account profile of Ashland was screened by profitability and over $1 million of sales volume was eliminated. A new system of charging higher prices for specialty service was installed. An overstaffed administrative organization was significantly reduced.

Sandusky

The general manager and office manager were replaced by high-talent people.

The basic business and competence of Sandusky were negatively impaired due to the transfer of a large amount of equipment from the closing of the Springfield, Ohio, and Ridgefield Park, New Jersey plants. This equipment was poorly maintained and should have been junked. Excessive manufacturing costs, quality problems and lower profits resulted. Significant dollars were spent to improve this equipment.

Victory Mills

The general manager, sales manager, plant manager, sales service manager, and 40 percent of the sales force were replaced by more capable people.

An excessive and almost disastrous inventory, both in-process and finished goods, had to be reorganized and a program for its reduction implemented.

Terms of sale relative to price, terms of payment and inventory maintenance had to be modified significantly in favor of ALG and its shareholders. The result has been the elimination of a significant number of undesirable accounts and a loss in sales volume.

Syracuse

Syracuse was the only division where significant changes have not been made during the 1971 period.

ALG's Areas of Distinctive Competence

The basic operational strengths of ALG are as follows:

People—ALG has a group of very capable professional line managers who are highly motivated and personally involved in the daily management of their businesses.

Plant locations—ALG's four plants are geographically well positioned in good labor markets and have ready access to customers in those industries we serve. The plants are totally profit oriented, lean staffed, and have lower overhead burdens, by most industry comparisons.

EXHIBIT 2 (continued)

In the folding-carton sector of our business, ALG provides fast service, outstanding quality, a significant range in size and types of cartons, and accurate control over costs and selling prices which enable the company to obtain higher profit margins than most competitors in the industry.

In the commercial and specialty printing sector, which is done primarily at the Ashland Division, the company provides outstanding quality, great service, and a wide range of manufacturing capability unique in the industry. The product lines at Ashland include direct mail printing, record jackets, folding cartons, educational games, magazine inserts, periodicals, annual reports and other commercial printing.

ALG's Operational Weaknesses

The basic operational weaknesses of ALG are as follows:

The previous method of compensation, opportunities for growth, and general management environment at ALG did not attract high talent people. We have thus been forced to make major personnel changes and have hired several talented managers to solve this problem.

ALG had a relatively poor image as a nongrowth company in most of its market areas. Our improvement in operations and the ability to attract high talent people has been of significant value in overcoming this problem in 1971.

The company had an extremely weak and nonsophisticated approach to sales and market planning. We have made significant progress in improving this problem, and the new managers that have been attracted to ALG have had significant impact in this area.

The standard, commodity-oriented folding carton industry is not attractive from a growth and profitability viewpoint. The industry in the 1960–70 period grew at an average of approximately 3 percent. The industry forecast for 1970–80 is for an annual growth of approximately 4 percent. The industry averages approximately 3 percent profit after taxes on sales. The general commodity-oriented printing industry is also not attractive, being plagued by poor management, low prices, overcapacity and generally unsatisfactory profits and return on invested capital.

However, the operating strategy of ALG to concentrate in the specialty segments of the packaging and printing industries have permitted the company to achieve outstanding improvements in profits in 1971 and future profitable growth in the specialty areas appears very promising.

EXHIBIT 2 (concluded)

1972 Strategy and Profit Plan Financial Summary ($000)

	1969 (Re-stated)	1970	1971 (Est. Actual)	1972 Budget	1973	1974	1975	1976
Net sales	$17,431	$16,615	$15,150	$16,572	$18,225	$20,045	$22,055	$24,275
Percent annual growth	n.a.	(4.68)	(8.82)	9.38	9.97	9.99	10.03	10.07
Operating income (loss) before taxes	(149)	(295)	991	1,182	1,369	1,630	1,937	2,303
Percent of sales	—	—	6.54	7.13	7.51	8.13	8.78	9.49
Net income (loss) after taxes and discontinued operations before extraordinary	(53)	(589)	515	615	712	848	1,007	1,198
Percent annual growth	—	—	—	19.42	15.77	19.10	18.75	18.97
Net income (loss)	(169)	(3,516)	583	1,080	1,105	848	1,007	1,198
Operating return on debt and equity	—	—	8.26	9.53	n.a.	n.a.	n.a.	n.a.
Net return on equity	—	—	12.31	18.57	n.a.	n.a.	n.a.	n.a.
Working capital ratio	2.67	1.83	2.92	3.31	n.a.	n.a.	n.a.	n.a.
Accounts receivable 12/31	2,676	2,701	1,868	2,043	n.a.	n.a.	n.a.	n.a.
Inventories 12/31	3,137	2,741	2,085	2,242	n.a.	n.a.	n.a.	n.a.

n.a. = not available.

EXHIBIT 3
Consolidated Statements of Income for the Years Ended December 31, 1972 and 1971 (000 omitted, except employees)

	Ashland		Sandusky	
	1972	1971	1972	1971
Net sales	$9,680	$8,715	$2,400	$2,288
Cost of sales	7,550	6,747	1,949	1,880
Gross profit	$2,130	$1,963	$ 451	$ 408
Selling expense	$ 583	$ 504	$ 181	$ 158
Administrative expense	492	614	91	88
Subtotal	$1,080	$1,118	$ 272	$ 246
Net operating profit before taxes	$1,050	$ 850	$ 179	$ 162
Provision for taxes	504	408	86	78
Net profit before extraordinary income	$ 546	$ 442	$ 93	$ 84
Credit for income tax due to net operating loss carryover	402	—	86	78
Net profit	$ 948	$ 442	$ 179	$ 162
Employees		361		132

John Rymell, vice president and manager of the Syracuse plant, in discussing the plans, said,

> These are projects we feel we can do. From that point it is up to us to make these things come true. The projections are made by deciding how much business this plant can handle. We know the business is in the area, so by adding one or two salesmen we know we can do it. First of all, Dave Summers knows what this plant can do and we know what he expects of us. I am more enthused about the company now than I have ever been. Being able to do the kind of job you are capable of, knowing what the plans are, and that we are all a part of the future is just great. I'm sure A. L. Garber will be the leader in its field within five years.

A growth strategy for the company was also developed in written form at the November 1971 meetings (see Exhibit 4).

The cash balance at the end of 1971 was $533,000, with total current assets of $4,519,000, current liabilities of $2,493,000, and long-term debt of $618,000. Mr. Summers had continued his practice of sending to the stockholders brief quarterly reports in addition to the regular annual report. Operating data from the second and third quarters of 1971, year-end 1971, and first quarter 1972 are summarized in Exhibit 5. Investor reaction to Garber operations in 1971 was reflected in the stock price, which traded that year at a low of 8 ⅜ and as high as 12.

Syracuse		Victory Mills		Home Office		Consolidated	
1972	*1971*	*1972*	*1971*	*1972*	*1971*	*1972*	*1971*
$1,940	$1,725	$2,552	$2,422	$ —	$ —	$16,572	$15,150
1,471	1,300	2,080	2,014	—	—	13,050	11,941
$ 469	$ 425	$ 472	$ 408	—	—	$ 3,522	$ 3,209
$ 95	$ 90	$ 192	$ 218	—	—	$ 1,056	$ 970
65	60	140	80	496	406	1,284	1,248
$ 160	$ 150	$ 332	$ 298	$ 496	$ 406	$ 2,340	$ 2,218
$ 309	$ 275	$ 140	$ 110	$(496)	$(406)	$ 1,182	$ 991
148	132	67	53	(238)	(195)	567	476
$ 161	$ 143	$ 73	$ 57	$(258)	$(211)	$ 615	$ 515
148	132	67	53	(238)	(195)	465	68
$ 309	$ 275	$ 140	$ 110	$(496)	$(406)	$ 1,080	$ 583
	64		121		8		

John Rymell further observed that, "Dave Summers knows what he wants to do and he doesn't waste time getting things done. He treats you nice and gives you credit for what you do. He gives you the authority to go ahead and run your own division as long as you do the right kind of job with it." Mr. Wood, director of sales at the Ashland plant, said:

> One day Mr. Summers came in with his little hatchet and turned this place upside down and inside out. He quickly earned the support of all of us. He's a tiger. I've learned an awful lot working for all these guys. He's a heck of a nice guy and very calm and quiet. He's a good man. I've learned an awful lot by being around him. The first month he had thrown out the computer. He's a man of action and he did the kinds of things needed. We're making money and that's our objective. We have a heck of a lot better image in the market. The suppliers and competitors cannot believe the change in our image. He came in at a time when they were all headed in the wrong direction and he stopped them. We'd have gone down the drain quickly. He motivated us by letting us know we were on the winning side. And that we were not ready to die. We are very bright, vibrant, and alive. And he means it. We believe and he believes what he says and he makes no bones about it. If you fear him, you fear for good reason.
>
> When Dean Bartosic came in as president at Ashland, things really changed. The first week he was here, we had a press that was falling apart. I told him we would need to spend about $4,000 to fix it. He'd say, "Well, go ahead and fix it." You couldn't believe the difference. Here's a guy, you said you needed

EXHIBIT 4
Growth Strategy, 1972

Concept

The basic growth concept of ALG is to obtain profitable entry into areas of packaging and printing where design, style, uniqueness, service, and merchandising capabilities of the package and printed material form the basis for the purchasing decision. The market position of these businesses will not be "commodity-oriented" and will function independently of any raw material base, distribution channels or present businesses in which ALG participates. Our current experience with a number of these companies that participate in this segment of the packaging and printing industry indicates that those companies that fulfill the merchandising needs of the buyer achieve excellent profit levels. These profits appear to relate primarily to the merchandising capability of the package and printed material and have limited relationship to the cost of the raw material used in the package.

General Description of Qualifying Companies

The nature of the service, design, and profit-making requirements generally limits the size of "specialty" printing or packaging companies to annual sales of $1MM to $15MM. There are exceptions to this size limitation, but generally this range will include most companies.

The majority of these companies are privately held and, many times, family owned businesses.

Method of Entry

Our growth in specialty packaging and printing will be primarily through acquisition during 1972. The creative variables of the specialty packaging and printing business of design, service, established image and reputation and the relatively narrow industry profile tend to make acquisition the more practical method of entry. We probably will expand internally a number of these businesses in order to increase sales opportunity on a broader geographic basis, as a number of these companies appear capable of expanding their market coverage.

Viability of Growth Strategy

There are a number of valid reasons why we feel that ALG is an excellent vehicle to seek, bring together, and acquire a number of these specialty companies:

ALG is currently participating in the specialty printing and packaging industry and achieving good profit levels. We understand the critical variables and the controls required for success in the industry.

ALG is a public company, listed on the American Exchange, with a relatively small number of shares issued.

The specialty companies previously described are profitable and many times develop very attractive shareholders' equity levels. However, the owners and family members find that this "net worth" is not liquid in that it is tied up in the company. Their alternatives to make this net worth more liquid are to take the company public, sell the business, or merge with a larger public company.

The strategy of taking these small companies public is not really viable. The specialty nature and requirements of the business precludes any major growth because if the business does grow on a large scale, larger companies will enter the business and a general reduction in profitability occurs. The OTC public issue for these companies does not really make their estates more liquid as they cannot quickly sell large blocks of this stock without loss in market value—if buyers can be found for large blocks of stock of this type.

These companies have problems merging with larger public companies due to a reluctance on the part of larger firms to acquire companies that require "special management" and do not fit broad and standard type markets.

EXHIBIT 4 (*continued*)

We believe that a number of these special "higher achievers than industry average" profitable companies can obtain significantly improved returns on their equity by becoming a part of ALG. Thus, combining their earnings with other profitable companies or divisions and the combined profits can have a significant impact on the earnings capability and value of ownership in ALG.

Specialty Packaging Businesses

The major classifications of the businesses which ALG may possibly enter are as follows:

Paper packaging—folding cartons, set-up boxes, oval boxes, and specially designed boxes for the cosmetic, pharmaceutical, and other industries.

Specialty labels—metal, paper, plastic and other labels, used with highly merchandised packaging for cosmetics, liquor accessories, and general pressure sensitive labels.

Glass packaging—glass containers for the cosmetic, distilled spirits, pharmaceutical, and other industries.

Plastic packaging—plastic containers for the cosmetic, pharmaceutical and toy industries, and some custom flexible packaging areas.

Metal packaging—round metal cans, pails and aerosol cans for cosmetics, specialty foods, and other products.

Package machinery—specialty packaging machinery such as label making and applications, shrink film, and other specialized packaging machinery.

Metal and plastic tubes—metal and plastic tubes for the cosmetic and pharmaceutical industries.

Partial Listing of Acquisition Prospects

We are currently negotiating the acquisition of two companies—the Salem Label Company, a specialty pressure-sensitive label company, located in Salem, Ohio. Salem Label was founded in 1862 and is one of the oldest names in the label industry. We are also negotiating with the Greenfield Printing Company of Greenfield, Ohio, a printer of specialty publications.

A partial listing of other target companies we will be evaluating in 1972 is as follows:

Carton Companies
Barger Packaging Corporation, Elkhart, Ind.
Southern California Carton Co., Gardena, Calif.
The Central Carton Company, Cincinnati, Ohio
S. Curtis & Son, Sandy Hook, Conn.
Sheboygan Paper Box Co., Sheboygan, Wis.

Label Companies
A. M. Steigerwald, Chicago, Ill.
Andrew H. Lawson, Sharm Hill, Pa.
Package Products Co., Charlotte, N.C.
U.S. Tape & Label, St. Louis, Mo.
Marklite Tape & Label, Wheaton, Ill.
Anchor Continental, Columbia, S.C.

Printing Companies
Stecher-Traung-Schmidt, San Francisco, Calif.
F. M. Howell & Company, Elmira, N.Y.

Metal Companies
Burdick & Sons, Albany, N.Y.
Freind Can Company, Chicago, Ill.

Plastic Companies
Gilbert Plastics Inc., Kenilworth, N.J.
U.S. Cap & Closure Chicago, Ill.
Tower Products Inc., Chicago, Ill.

Glass Companies
Lancaster Glass Company, Lancaster, Ohio
Bauer Glass Company, Millville, N.J.

EXHIBIT 5
A. L. Garber's Recent Financial Data

	6 Months* Ended 6/30/71	9 Months* Ended 9/30/71	Year Ended 12/31/71	3 Months* Ended 3/31/72
Net sales	$7,668,401	$11,346,959	$15,223,000	$3,969,311
Net operating income	425,517	374,215	926,000	203,551
Net income after taxes	251,517	388,715	556,000	128,781
Earnings per share	.37	.58	.83	.18

* Unaudited.

something and he gave it to you. The people downstairs wouldn't believe it when I told them. This attitude permitted us to run the show the way we wanted to run it. I started a meeting with all of the foremen once each week, and for the first time some of them got to know each other. We got to working as a team. I feel that you need people at your flank because there are always people taking pot shots at you. I wanted people around me that were looking after my best interests. I figured that if we had a group that looked out for each other, we would eventually be successful.

We're not afraid now to turn a machine down rather than to run at a loss. Dean is not afraid to do things. He cut some fat out of the office. He's willing to back you up. He's got a lot of backbone and the men don't want to let him down.

Most of the marketing conditions that would have affected us would have been adverse the past two years. Look at our peers. They are going downhill. We can act faster and we carry a very big stick because we can go faster. We had a meeting in November at which time we planned and outlined what we were going to do. We set at that time a goal of $1 million profit. So far, we are ahead.

In discussing the changed management philosophy for A. L. Garber, Dean Bartosic, vice president and manager of the Ashland plant, described it this way:

I think business is easy and we make it difficult and we get to thinking it is then difficult. Basically, I think it is easy to understand. I don't think the previous management made business easy. I think they made it difficult and I think that is part of what was wrong. For an example, there are economists running all over the country saying that if you have two shifts of a plant running, you're going to make more money if you just bring breakeven business to fill up the third shift. This has to do with absorption of operating costs and overhead in business. That's true, but it doesn't mean anything once you know it because you then go out and start pricing business on a breakeven basis that becomes a habit with you, and you price the stuff you run in the first and second shift the same way. The competitor will probably decide to meet the price the same way. The basic philosophy of marketing that the previous management did not have was that if a customer wants to do business with you, he will find a way to do business with you and price is not so important, or if he doesn't want to do business with you, the lowest price in the world won't get you that business. That is why some of these guys would come and say there is no business out there. We haven't really had any significant changes in the people here except for a number of people who were not needed. In a company there is a tendency to get more people than we need. It's like cancer, because sooner or later it will eat the best out of everybody. This plant was no exception. The plant was reduced by some 75 people. We are now doing less business because we are picking and choosing. We also tightened up and made the people work a little harder. In fact, the remaining people are working harder because they are getting paid more for what they do and hopefully they see a better future here. In fact, it would amaze me if there were an employee in this whole company who didn't think his future were better now than they thought it was three years ago.

A couple of years ago we used to determine bids by a rate on every machine which included total cost except salesman cost. It was based on a 50–50 material-to-conversion ratio. That was so stupid, because the cost came out of a guy back at the plant who had never seen the marketplace in his life. You just can't price things in the marketplace that way. You have to decide how intricate is your product, how much peril there is in making it, and how competitive you can be with other companies.

Jim Hallinan, the general manager at Victory Mills, was with American Can before joining UB&C. When contacted by Mr. Summers, he wasn't dissatisfied with American Can, but he wasn't satisfied either.

Dave Summers told me really about Dave Summers. He told me UB&C was a lousy company, which I already knew. It wasn't the type of company I was used to. The way I would describe it, Dave told me about his own development and background. He felt that an awful lot of acquisitions made in recent years by the industry were fine companies when acquired and then in two years were lost. He felt that adding a huge burden of a corporate staff, depersonalization of management, and a focus on the corporation rather than on the acquisition were the problems or the reason for the failure of so many of these acquisitions. He rationalized this way, "You're a very fine small company; for tax reasons and other reasons you really need public stock, so you merge into a big company. All of a sudden, what made your company fine is no longer there." He felt this way, that if we could make a large company out of many small family companies, that you could maintain the advantages of a family-run company and still have the benefit of the larger corporation—financial advantages, etc.

So David's concept as I understood it was that each small company remain a totally decentralized operation, it would be like a family-run company. If he acquired a company that had been developed by a family and they were good operators, they would continue to run it. If not, we would bring in professional managers who would take the place of the family, but act pretty much as if they were in their own business. This is the way I understood it then, and it is still the way I see it.

It's very obvious to me, I see this division as my company. I'm running it as if it were my own. At American Can, no individual ever made a decision. All decisions were made by groups and many recommendations that were filtered in by others. By the time a decision is reached, it is almost evident what the decision will be. Its very rare that I had to say go or no go. Maybe they do indirectly, but always there was a big umbrella over all decisions. In other words, no accountability. This is one of the big shortcomings of American Can Company.''

In addition to making numerous operational changes, Mr. Hallinan had to develop an entirely new management group at Victory Mills. Extensive changes were made in the sales force, and management began experimenting with a wider range of production capability. Jim said:

> In our system, it's very clear where the accountability is. I was very much aware of this when we decided to go ahead on the building of that four-color press into a five-color press. I talked to as many people as I could and got as many opinions as I could, but finally, there was only one person to make that decision, and it wasn't Dave Summers. Dave could veto that decision after a final study, but really the decision was purely mine. I enjoy that. I like the accountability. In large corporations you have a lot of responsibility but very little accountability. Because things went very quickly when Dave became president, he saw a need to get rid of the plant manager and then the sales vice-president. I don't know if these were good men or not. At this time the company was in the red. Things were going from bad to worse. The quality was terrible, service was terrible, the plant manager and sales manager were barely on speaking terms. Dave came in with a big broom and cleaned it all out. I knew that the company was no good or not very good when I came on. I think I'm particularly good at problem solving and organizing. Some of these changes Dave made were not right from my standpoint but were probably essential from his standpoint. Oh, probably I'd do a few things differently, not major things but individual situations. Now it's a matter of building the proper foundation. The morale today is fantastic. The sales department is eager and hard-working. They are working together with a lot of team effort. The morale in the whole plant is very good. We've got an enthused team.

When asked what problems he saw now with Dave's philosophy, Jim replied:

> There are problems I see. One of them we'll have a meeting on this coming week. Decentralization is a great concept and now that we've gone under one name, it's even more magnified. Let me give you an example. My plant is in Victory Mills, my sales program is in New York, but Ashland also has a New York office. They have two salesmen in New York and are considering the addition of a third man. They're calling on some of the same accounts we're calling on. They are competitors of ours. For example, last week I received a call from American Brands. The purchasing director of Americans Brands is a man I've known for 10 or 12 years. He said, ''We have a problem. Your company has four salesmen calling on me. We like all of these guys, but we don't have the time to see all of these salesmen. Not only do you have four salesmen, but they each have different policies. One salesman will do one thing and allow one thing and another takes a totally different approach. We're confused.''
> You see, American Brands has acquired companies that various divisions of

UB&C have sold to over the years. These are now gradually being pulled in, so Ashland was calling on the company, Syracuse was calling on them, and I had two people calling on them. So this is another problem with commission men. It's harder to switch accounts around. So this is one problem I see. I don't think we have truly recognized that some of our customers are now part conglomerates, or could be tomorrow.

The other problem—or I shouldn't call it a problem—is the lack of development. We've been doing the same thing in all the divisions for years. You copy your competitor. . . . . I'm not saying that we should have a research and development department, but I'm interested in new things and I like to see creativity, I like to see new ideas and concepts. I don't think we have to create them necessarily, but I do think we should be versatile enough to climb on board. Let me give you an example—stretch pack. This is a package device for which we've been able to become a licensee. The license is a minimum royalty of $5,000 per year plus we have to buy at least one machine. You're talking over $12,000 there, so you're talking $17,000 the first year and $5,000 each subsequent year. That $5,000 comes out of product sales. If you don't sell any products you have to pay, but if you sell the products you don't have to pay. If all of our plants went into that and sold $5,000, there would only be $12,000 left. So if I could convince the other three plants that this would be a good thing, we could get into it very economically. Like the whole company for $5,000, which would be nothing, but for me with my profit and loss, I can't afford it, but yet I think it would be a good direction to go. My whole background is this way, and 20 years of training you just don't wipe out. I've sent all the materials and brochures to all of the divisions, and as of today, I don't have a single response from any one of them. It's not my job to tell them what to do. Obviously, I'm in the weakest position—I make the least amount of money. Let's face it, they're running better operations than I am, but I see this as a lack. What are we going to be doing tomorrow?

The other lack—we aren't taking advantage of our corporate purchasing power. I'm buying better than we've ever bought with a corporate headquarters. That's because we didn't have good management. We met with Federal Paper Board yesterday; we want to buy paper from them. They give us their price and we say no, we want a lower price. Well, how much can we buy, is their question. So we give them our annual figures, but just for our little plant. I'm sure that if we could take two or three mills, we could put leverage on it to a point that we could get much better prices. Yesterday I found I could buy cut boards very, very economically, and as soon as I get the details, I will latch onto the Syracuse mill because I think he could use the same narrow board. But if I don't let John know about it, he'll never know about it. Now, what does John know about that I don't know about? We all depend totally on Dave to carry the word, but I don't write Dave telling him about the price of narrow board. I think what Dave might do, well, I'd like to see a little strengthening.

Well, I'd say those are the principal concerns I have. They aren't too serious. I'm handling a lot of these myself. I think that's part of my job as a general manager. But maybe someone is sharper than I am in certain areas, and I would like to take advantage of that sharpness.

Larry Church became manager of the Sandusky plant in September 1971.

Previously he had sold against UB&C for the Packaging Corporation of America in the Cleveland area and had known United before and after Dave Summers came. He saw UB&C as an easy company to sell against except for price:

> They had brought in a couple of hot dogs who proceeded to do what this business is famous for—cutting prices and quality and thinking they were going to make it up on volume. So my impression of UB&C was a Shylock House, a big zero. I told Dave before coming that drastic changes would have to be made. We've gone through a tremendous problem of raising prices and concentrating our attention on improving quality, and I have had to reorganize the scheduling so that we can become more believable to our customers. With present plant and equipment, we should go from $2½ million to $4½ million in sales in 3 years. The customer image of our quality has already improved tremendously. Among the peers in the business, people would probably say the company isn't very strong but they have good people and they seem to be coming up. Our low-price image has now changed to a good-quality, higher-price, and good-product image. I think all of our general managers are highly regarded, as competitors quite feared. We are on the come.

VERITONE ACQUISITION

Garber acquired Veritone from Rand McNally in April 1972. A memo regarding the acquisition is shown in Exhibit 6.

Rand McNally wanted to sell Veritone, its Chicago-based printing company, for several reasons. First, RM had the worst profit year in its 114-year history in 1971 and wanted to free up some cash. Second, printing companies in Chicago were having a hard time making a satisfactory profit. Third, the general manager of Veritone was 64 and wanted to retire. RM didn't want to put one of its own people into a situation where it had no growth strategy for Veritone. Finally, most of RM's own printing done at Veritone could be handled at its other printing plants in the East and South.

Veritone's sales were at about the $5 million annual level. A. L. Garber's marketing strategy for Veritone is shown in Exhibit 7.

Following the Veritone acquisition, Dave Summers began to contemplate what further changes he needed to make in A. L. Garber's strategy and in its management.

EXHIBIT 6
Memo re Acquisition of Veritone

On April 13, 1972, the A. L. Garber Company purchased from the Veritone Company (a wholly owned subsidiary of Rand McNally) Veritone's operating assets (current assets and machinery and equipment, but excluding the land and buildings) subject to liabilities other than liabilities of Veritone to Rand McNally, for a purchase price of $703,000. Of this, $100,000 was paid on April 13, 1972, and the balance of $603,000 is to be paid with respect to $50,000 in four annual installments beginning April 14, 1973, and with respect to $553,000 in monthly installments, with interest of 8 percent, beginning November 14, 1973, and ending February 14, 1977 (five years from the closing).

Concurrently with this transaction, Veritone sold its land and buildings to a third party, and we leased these premises for a period of 20 years at an annual basic rental of $132,000.

The Veritone Company, located in Melrose Park, Illinois, is a high-quality offset lithographer, and we intend to expand the scope of this business to include our capabilities in specialty printing and packaging.

After the sale of the land and buildings, Veritone's financial statement appeared as follows:

Current assets	$1,020,000
Current liabilities	541,000
Working capital	479,000
Machinery, equipment at book value	410,000
	889,000
Purchase price	703,000
Excess assets acquired over purchase price	$ 186,000

The excess of the net book value of assets acquired over the purchase price was assigned to the machinery and equipment and will be reflected in income through reduced depreciation over the remaining lives of the assets.

700

EXHIBIT 7
ALG's Marketing Strategy for Veritone

The marketing profile of Veritone would approximate the schedule outlined below.

Sales Categories	1972	1973	1974	1975
Commercial printing	70%	69%	70%	68%
Rand McNally	30	18	14	12
Standard packaging*	—	7	8	9
Specialty packaging*	—	3	4	5
Miscellaneous packaging*	—	3	4	6
	100%	100%	100%	100%
Sales increase (1972 = 100)	100	100	117	123
Estimated net profit before tax (M = 000)	$247M	$425M	$530M	$650M

* Approximate percentages.

We believe the above projected marketing plan for Veritone will achieve the following:

Increase Veritone's sales and profits.

Increase Veritone's utilization of its pressroom and assist in covering fixed costs.

Avoid the dependence on only the commerical printing market and limit wide swings in sales volume.

Assist in more effective utilization of all equipment and the labor force.

In order to achieve these advantages we would have to install finishing equipment for both paper and paper board. This would involve approximately three pieces of finishing equipment for the first five-year plan. The cost of equipment will be minimal as we can transfer one of the required die cutters from the Ashland Division and the other two can be purchased as used equipment from sources we have already explored.

Rand McNally has agreed to purchase $4MM worth of printing from Veritone over the next four years. This is to be a minimum of $1MM for each year. [MM = million]

25. Riverview Apartments*

Riverview Apartments, consisting of five buildings of 18–24 apartments each, were built during 1970–71 in Academe, home of State University, in response to continued demand for off-campus housing. Student enrollment at the university had increased almost 120 percent between 1960 and 1970.

LOCATION AND CONSTRUCTION

The apartment site is located three blocks from the university. Sidewalks exist for two of the three blocks. Since Academe had no bus service, there was a parking problem in the university area. Riverview Apartment residents, however, could walk to the campus.

The apartments are one-bedroom units, with living room, kitchen area, and bath. They have all modern features except dishwashers, including central heat and air conditioning, carpets, and drapes. Ninety-eight units are furnished, 80 with twin beds and 18 with double beds. The manager's apartment includes a double bed, and one unit was designated as a storage area. Coin-operated washers, dryers, and vending machines are located in a service building. A large swimming pool is the central recreation theme.

The first buildings were available for occupancy in September 1970, one week after university registration began. The managing realtor attempted to mollify future tenants because of the postregistration availability, and in several instances arranged motel accommodations for students who were unable to stay for several days with friends until the buildings were completed. The second building was ready for occupancy one week later. Despite the problems attendant with the completion date of the first two buildings, all 46 units were occupied by October 15, 1970. Seventy-four paved parking spaces were available.

Work continued on the third, fourth, and fifth buildings during winter, spring, and summer 1971. Owing to other construction activities, the swimming pool could not be completed until August 1971; no landscaping was done, and inspection of building features was hampered because tenants were waiting to occupy each unit as soon as it was completed.

The university changed its registration date in fall 1971, so that the fall semester would be completed prior to the Christmas holidays. Classes began

* Prepared by Leon Joseph Rosenberg, the University of Arkansas at Fayetteville.

on August 25, three weeks earlier than previous years. Final exams ended on December 22 and registration for the spring semester began on January 10. This change resulted in a three and one-half week winter vacation instead of the former two weeks.

The third, fourth, and part of the fifth Riverview buildings were completed in October 1971, five weeks after the fall semester began. Despite their late completion, 36 units were rented in October. The remaining units were finally finished late in February 1972, almost 18 months after the first apartment unit was completed.

MANAGEMENT AND OPERATIONS

The corporation that owned the apartments was headquartered in Capitol City, 175 miles from Academe. The managing realtors, who had a sizable position in the owning corporation, were also located in Capitol City. Further, the prime contractor, similarly located in Capitol City, was a principal investor in the ownership corporation. The prime contractor used the services of a number of subcontractors, several of whom were located in Academe.

Riverview's management policy called for the complex to be managed by a married graduate student couple. The managers were given an apartment and a salary of $200 per month. This was above the compensation level provided managers of other student apartment complexes in Academe. An extended recruiting and selection process resulted in the hiring of Jack Brite, a public administration student and his wife, Peggy, to manage the complex during the academic year 1970–71. Jack was a full-time graduate student; Peggy took one course each semester.

The managing couple was totally responsible for the Academe operation, including renting, advertising, and inside and outside housekeeping. Plumbers, electricians, and heating and air conditioning service companies were called when necessary. However, as long as construction continued, the prime contractors, having an ownership interest, provided necessary mechanical maintenance.

Owing to onsite construction activities, the swimming pool was not completed until the end of the summer of 1971. Despite Riverview's lower summer rental rate, a number of tenants moved to apartments with completed pools. The number of students attending the university during the summer was traditionally lower than during the regular academic year, so finding an available apartment presented no problem to the 1971 summer school students.

Jack and Peggy Brite received little guidance from the Capitol City property management office. The divisional manager of apartment residences was responsible for the operation of 25 complexes in Capitol City plus 3 located in towns near his headquarters office.

The successor management couple to Jack and Peggy were selected after numerous interviews, with Jack and Peggy participating in the selection. Bill Roberts, a pre-law senior undergraduate, and his wife, Ann, were employed. None of the other applicants for the position seemed to be as fully qualified for the managerial position. Jack and Peggy were continued on the payroll, and in an apartment, for four weeks to help train the new managers. Ann and Bill were both enrolled as full-time students.

The supervisor from Capitol City headquarters visited Academe after Bill and Ann were hired. A number of Riverview's tenants moved out at the end of the 1971 summer session. Bill and Ann rented many of the vacant units, but in October an additional 36 units became available—at just about mid-semester. Thirty-three units were rented, but the vacancy ratio of 12 percent in mid-October increased to 23 percent in mid-December (see Exhibit 1).

EXHIBIT 1
Occupancy Record

	Units*	Vacancy†	Percent Vacancy		Units*	Vacancy†	Percent Vacancy
1970				**1972**			
September	22	1	4%	January	91	18	20%
October	46	0	0	February	97	22	23
November	46	0	0	March	97	25	26
December	46	2	4	April	97	24	25
1971				May	97	6	6
January	46	0	0	June	97	1	1
February	46	0	0	July	97	2	2
March	46	0	0	August	97	1	1
April	46	1	2	September	97	1	1
May	46	0	0	October	97	4	4
June	46	5	11	November	97	5	5
July	46	2	4	December	97	11	11
August	46	10	22	**1973**			
September	46	5	11	January	97	22	23
October	82	10	12	February	97	22	23
November	82	12	15	March	97	27	28
December	83	19	23	April	97	27	28
				May	97	33	34
				June	97	0	0
				July	97	1	1

* Riverview's first two buildings (24 units each) were opened during September 1970; more buildings were completed between October 1971 and March 1972.
† Monthly vacancy rates for 1970 and 1971 are based on an analysis of monthly statements; 1972 and 1973 data are taken from weekly occupancy reports, at mid-month.

Although weather slowed construction in December 1971, and January 1972, the last nine units were completed. Meanwhile, since the new academic schedule resulted in a winter holiday break of three and one-half weeks between semesters, a number of tenants forfeited their damage deposit ($50 per apartment), moved out and either returned one month later, or moved into competitive apartment units.

When the total Riverview complex, consisting of 98 units plus the managers' apartment, and an apartment for storage or an assistant manager, was completed, there was a minimum of onsite inspection by the owning corporation representatives. Due to the weather, no action was taken on landscaping. Approximately 110 parking places were provided for the 100 apartment units, which had an average occupancy of 1.8 tenants† per unit. No street parking was permitted by the city. At that time a maintenance manager, who was given no salary but was provided a rent-free apartment, was added to Riverview's managerial staff.

RENTAL RATES

Most of the occupants were students; they were asked to sign a nine-month lease at $155 per apartment, due on the first day of each month, during the fall and spring semesters. If they signed a 12-month lease, and remained during the summer, they were billed at $100 per month during June, July, and August. Although a number of students moved out during summer 1971, some of the vacancies were rented at $155 per month to students who lived in dorms, fraternities, sororities or other units during the regular academic year. Nonetheless, failure to complete the proposed swimming pool seemed to be the prime reason why 10 of the 46 units then available were vacant in August 1971 (see Exhibit 1).

The vacancy rate for the 1972 spring semester was 20 percent in January, 23 percent in February, and 26 percent in March. The managing realtor decided to replace the manager and his wife, Bill and Ann Roberts, since it

EXHIBIT 2
Student Enrollments, Dormitory Construction, and Multiresidence Building Permits

	Student Enrollment (fall semester)	Dormitory Construction	Multiresidence Building Permits	
			Value	Number
1960	10,862		$ 90,000	5
1961	12,388	2	40,000	2
1962	12,867	2	150,000	4
1963	14,326	3	330,000	9
1964	14,912	4	1,209,000	40
1965	18,268	2	167,000	8
1966	18,973		694,000	18
1967	20,423	2	1,265,000	15
1968	20,549		2,289,330	45
1969	22,081		6,311,832	25
1970	23,709		5,697,472*	48
1971	24,131		6,004,756†	99
1972	23,804		7,855,400	109

* Includes first Riverview buildings.
† Includes fourth and fifth Riverview buildings.

was felt they were not working hard enough to keep the complex fully rented. The supervisor flew from Capitol City, fired the managing couple (who then decided to rent an apartment in the complex) and hired a young man who had registered with the State Employment Service. The terminated managers were given a month's severance salary. The new manager moved into the complex, and the supervisor flew back to Capitol City the following day. A new salary of $250 per month, plus apartment, was established.

The vacancy rate of 26 percent in March 1972 fell to just 25 percent in April. At that time it was discovered that the personal activities of the new manager were unsatisfactory, so Bill and Ann Roberts were rehired.

In an effort to fill the vacant apartment, a summer rate of $100 per unit was established. The vacancy rate dropped to 6 percent in May and averaged only 1 percent during the summer months.

The Roberts graduated in August 1972, and two male students, John Hall and Frank O'Brian, the former of whom was known by the Capitol City management realtor, were employed as co-managers. University enrollment declined slightly in fall 1972—to 23,804, down from 24,131 the previous fall.

The vacancy rate in fall 1972 averaged 4 percent, until mid-December when the long holiday vacation began. The vacancy rate jumped to 11 percent in December, 23 percent in January, 28 percent in April, and dropped to 0 percent in mid-June, when a 1973 summer rate of $110 was established.

At that time, one co-manager graduated and the other, Frank O'Brian, got married. The O'Brians stayed on as managers of Riverview, but Frank took a full-time job and attended some classes; Frank's wife was a part-time student. The Capitol City realtor supervisor was agreeable to the arrangement which was worked out in a long-distance phone call. However, subsequent efforts to talk with the new managerial couple by phone were largely unsuccessful. They were usually unavailable. Further, they went on trips almost every weekend. On some occasions the maintenance manager was available to handle problems, but he did not show apartments to prospective tenants during the 1973 fall semester.

ADVERTISING

An ongoing advertising program was maintained, at an annual cost of about 3 percent of rentals. This was comparable with similar apartments, according to the Capitol City realtor. The local newspaper, two student newspapers, and three local readio stations were utilized. Most students and townspeople knew about the Riverview Apartments.

INVESTMENT

The owner's total capital investment in Riverview Apartments approximated $800,000 and required about $90,000 annually in debt retirement payments. Studies made by the Capitol City supervisor indicated that over 90 percent of the Riverview Apartment expenses were fixed; only a few items were dependent upon the occupancy ratio. Gas and electric usage varied more with temperature than with the number of occupied units. The expense of water was also dependent upon the occupancy rate, but the large items, such as real estate taxes, management fee, and debt retirement, were fixed.

An operating statement summary for the period May 1972, through April 1973 showed that the complex incurred an annual loss in excess of $9,000 (see Exhibit 3). The corporation's treasurer prepared a breakeven analysis

EXHIBIT 3
Operating Statement Summary, May 1972—April 1973

Month	Receipts	Disbursements	Profit (Loss)
1972			
May	$ 9,801	$ 10,890	$(1,089)
June	8,148	10,994	(2,846)
July	10,597	10,911	(314)
August	7,241	13,891	(6,650)
September	12,748	18,208	(5,460)
October	14,811	10,131	4,680
November	12,489	10,154	2,335
December	14,523	10,639	3,884
1973			
January	10,210	10,568	(358)
February	10,900	11,146	(246)
March	9,880	10,996	(1,116)
April	9,587	11,532	(1,945)
Total	$130,935	$140,060	$(9,125)

during the spring of 1973, using an academic year rent of $155 and a summer rent of $110. He determined a 90 percent occupancy rate would result in a breakeven operation.

ATTEMPTS TO FIND THE PROBLEM

The spring semester final exam period ended May 14, 1973. Many students left the campus, including a number who planned to attend summer school. There was a three and one-half week vacation between the end of the regular academic year and summer school. A number of tenants forfeited their $50 damage deposit, and broke their leases by not returning after the holiday. Since summer occupancy had averaged about 97 percent during the previous two summers, the special summer rate was increased to $110 from $100 during the preceding summers.

In June 1973, the chief executive officer of the real estate firm and the senior vice president. Ernest Jones, determined that an intensive analysis should be conducted of the marketing program and general operation of Riverview Apartments. Though the apartments were incurring a significant dollar loss, their time was taken with other investment negotiations and a consultant was hired to conduct the necessary research and prepare a set of recommendations.

The consultant undertook a number of actions. Competitive apartments that appealed to the student market were visited, pictures taken of each, and rental schedules were secured (see Exhibit 4). Locations of the various apartments were plotted on a map of the city. None of the apartments were in excess of two miles from the campus, though most students who lived over six blocks from the campus preferred driving to the campus and searching for one of the inadequate number of parking spaces. There appeared to be no relationship between monthly rental and distance of the various apartments from the campus.

EXHIBIT 4
Rental Schedule Comparison

Apartment	Fall/Spring	Summer	Remarks
Riverview	$155	$110	Includes all utilities.
Howe Hill	135	135	(Only several one-bedroom units.) Plus utilities.
Sherman Woods	185	135	Plus utilities.
Francis Jett	155 (monthly basis) 149 (9-month lease) 140 (12-month lease)	143	Plus electricity. Gas air conditioning.
University Terrace	110	110	Plus utilities.
Glover Creek	135	110	Plus electricity. Gas air conditioning.
Contemporary Arms	140 (9-month lease)	143	Plus electricity (six weeks, $200). Gas air conditioning.
	150 (12-month lease)	143	Includes dishwasher and shag carpets. If 12-month lease signed prior to September 1, $20 per month *less*.
Hale	140	143	Plus electricity (six weeks, $200). Gas air conditioning.
Hale II	150	143	Same as Hale. Both Hale and Hale II, 12-month lease $20 per month *less*.
Lee Gardens	160	120	Plus electricity. Gas air conditioning.
Silvia	150	150	Plus electricity. Gas air conditioning. If 12-month lease, last month reduced by $60, or equivalent to $145 month.
Joe-Ann	142 (monthly basis) 136 (9-month lease) 122 (12-month lease)	136	Plus electricity. Gas air conditioning.

Occupancy figures of the other apartment complexes were unavailable. While completing the rental survey of competitive apartment complexes (Exhibit 4), visual inspection of the various apartments led to the conclusion that most were more attractive, better landscaped, and had more parking per unit than did Riverview. Further, housekeeping standards of Riverview's grounds and parking areas were unsatisfactory. When a representative from Capitol City made several attempts to mention this to the managers of Riverview, neither the manager nor his wife were available. On each occasion, nontenant children who lived in the neighborhood were swimming in the pool, beverage cans were on the ground, and dog deposits were much in evidence.

Newspaper advertisements of Riverview and of its competitive apartments were reviewed as to content, size, and frequency. No significant differences were apparent.

Two questionnaires were designed to obtain present and past tenant input. The first set of questionnaires (Exhibit 5), each accompanied by a business reply envelope addressed to the residential property manager in Capitol City, was given to the manager to distribute to tenants who were living in Riverview at the time. Though several demanding phone calls were required before he distributed the questionnaires, the assignment was accomplished and replies were received from 48 percent of the tenants living in the various units of Riverview Apartments.

The consultant realized that a certain favorable bias might characterize the responses to the survey. The manager had copies of the questionnaire and could have urged friends to reply favorably, and might have failed to deliver a copy to a tenant whom he thought was dissatisfied with the managers. Nevertheless, in the interest of speed and cost, it was decided to take the risk since replies went to the Capitol City office.

A second questionnaire was prepared and sent to the hometown address of 45 tenants who had lived in the apartments until the end of spring 1973. Replies were received from 25 percent of the former tenants (Exhibit 6).

The consultant prepared an analysis of the 1972–73 annual rental rate of $1,725 and its relationship to the break-even occupancy rate, coming up with the following:

Annual Rental Rate	Break-Even Occupancy Percentage
$1,620	95
1,695	90

During the almost two years the apartments had been occupied, the owners had been adding additional funds to cover the negative cash flow of funds.

Color pictures of Riverview Apartments and competitive apartments were taken and sent to the realty firm in Capitol City. For information purposes, a

EXHIBIT 5
Riverview Apartments: Questionnaire Results, Present Residents

We would appreciate you answering a few questions which will enable us to do a better job managing Riverview Apartments to your satisfaction. Your name is not necessary since we will tabulate and analyze the answers. Most questions just ask that you check the appropriate blank.

1. Please rate the following items:

	GOOD	AVERAGE	POOR
Cleanliness	17	23	3
Parking	1	10	29
Pool	13	21	9
Laundry	18	21	5
Grounds	12	24	9
Furniture	29	13	2
Carpet	23	15	4
Management	7	21	6
Stove	19	13	8
Refrigerator	15	10	11

2. What do you dislike about the Riverview Apartments?   16 Inadequate parking
   15 Maintenance
   8 Plumbing

3. What do you like about the Riverview Apartments?   29 Location
   14 Summer rental rate
   11 Pool
   7 Furnishings

4. Did you live in the Riverview Apartments in Spring 1973?

   Yes 14   No 29

5. Do you plan to live in Riverview Apartments during the academic year of

   1973–1974?   Yes 14   No 25   Undecided 6

   If not, why not?   8 Rent too high
   7 Leaving Academe
   4 Moving back to sorority or fraternity house
   4 Moving back to dormitory

6. What can we do to make living in the Riverview Apartments more fun for you?
   11 More parking
   8 Have game room, shuffleboard, parties around pool, college
   atmosphere
   7 Improve and speed up maintenance
   5 Prevent non-tenant children, dogs and cats around pool
   4 Nicer landscaping
   3 New diving board, lawn chairs beside pool, basketball goal

EXHIBIT 5 *(continued)*

7. How many people occupy your apartment?

   One _11_   Two _62_   Three _9_   (45 apts. completed
                                              questionnaires)

8. Are you, or all of you: (82 individuals live
                                              in the 45 apts.)
   Married _18_   Single _64_

9. Occupants in your apartment.

   Couple _20_   One Man _6_   Three Women _6_
   Two Men _18_   One Woman _5_   Two Parents & Child ___
   Two Women _24_   Three Men _3_   One Parent & Child ___

10. Age of Occupants: Age   M   W

Age	M	W
17		1
18	2	2
19	7	8
20	5	12
21	12	9
22	2	6
23	3	6
24		
25	1	
26	2	
27	1	
28		
29		
30		1
32	2	
Totals	37	45

EXHIBIT 5 (concluded)

---

11. (a) Are occupants in your apartment:

_12_	Nonstudents	_2_	Student and Husband
_11_	One Student	_6_	Student and Wife
_42_	Two Students	_9_	Other (please specify)
			(3 students)

(b) If students, are you:

_4_	Freshman	_6_	Graduate
_8_	Sophomore	_1_	Law
_20_	Junior	___	Medical
_31_	Senior	___	Special

(c) Expected date to receive degree?

Number	Date
4	Aug. 73
11	Dec. 73
21	May 74
15	Dec. 74
11	May 75
5	May 76

Thank you for completing this questionnaire. Please return it to us in the attached envelope.

Residential Property Manager
Beasley, Gibson, Inc.
111 Marion Avenue
Capitol City, Blank

---

number of the replies to the different sets of questionnaires were routed across the desk of the realty firm's senior vice president. He continued to be involved in a major negotiation and could not take time to visit the apartments in Academe. He requested that the consultant furnish a completed report, with substantiated recommendations, to him and the chief executive officer of the realty firm. He said they wanted an actionable report that would permit them to make recommendations to the officers of the corporation that owned the apartment complex.

EXHIBIT 6
Riverview Apartments: Questionnaire Results, Past Residents

June 4, 1973

Dear _____

We are very interested in the service you received while a resident of Riverview Apartments in Academe. You can help us do a better job next fall by answering a few questions and returning in the enclosed postpaid envelope.

1. Please rate the following items:

	GOOD	AVERAGE	POOR
Cleanliness	5	6	
Parking	8	1	2
Pool	10	1	
Laundry	9	2	
Grounds	6	5	
Furniture	7	4	
Carpet	5	5	1
Manager	7	4	
Stove	6	4	1
Refrigerator	4	3	4

2. What did you dislike about the Riverview Apartments?   3 Parking
2 Refrigerators

3. What did you like about the Riverview Apartments?   8 Location
4 Manager
3 Size

4. What was the reason you moved? 8 Home for summer
2 Lower rent

5. Do you plan to live in the Riverview Apartments during the academic year of 1973–1974?   Yes ____   No 9   Undecided 2

If not, why not? 2 Winter rent too high
2 Not returning to Academe
2 Too small for three people

EXHIBIT 6 (continued)

6. (a) Were occupants:

_1._ Nonstudents		____ Student and Husband
_1_ One Student		_1_ Student and Wife
_5_ Two Students		____ Other (Please specify)
_3_ Three Students		

(b) If students, were you:

_3_ Freshman		____ Graduate
_6_ Sophomore		____ Law
____ Junior		____ Medical
_1_ Senior		____ Special

Sincerely,

Beasley, Gibson, Inc.
Bill Cook
Property Manager

26. Lincoln County Welfare Services*

Dr. John Anderson, Lincoln County Welfare Commissioner, was not surprised at the findings of the New York State Office of Child Support Enforcement (OCSE) review team. Anderson had known for the past year that the arrangements for Lincoln's program to locate absent parents and make them pay court-ordered support for their children (Title IV-D) were not exactly done as OCSE wanted them, but he had had little support from the local welfare board of supervisors in creating new positions for the IV-D program.

TITLE IV-D PROGRAM

Title IV-D is a federal-state-local intergovernmental system for locating absent parents of families receiving welfare payments and collecting court-ordered child support from them, thus reducing the amount paid out in welfare. In New York State the program is operated by the Office of Child Support Enforcement, utilizing county welfare departments as the direct implementing agents.

The counterpart to the IV-D program is IV-A, which is the classic welfare system. Title IV-A is associated with giving aid to dependent children (ADC). The dramatic increases in aid to dependent children is a result of changing family structures. Fathers are leaving the families at an increasing rate, which has resulted in a greater dependence on welfare. For example, the absent father-figure has risen from 45.5 percent in ADC cases in 1948, to 66.7 percent in 1961, and to 85 percent in 1975.

Corresponding to this dramatic rise has been the percentage of recipients who are born out of wedlock: 11 percent in 1948, 24 percent in 1961, 35 percent in 1977. Illegitimacy creates the problem of determining paternity in order to set support payment levels, making such cases additionally troublesome.

Title IV-D was created in the belief that absent parents should be located and made to pay the court-ordered support for their children. Title IV-D was expected to collect at least as much money from these parents as it expended for staff, office, and expenses. It was realistically expected to show a profit. To achieve effective enforcement, the program alters in some basic ways the

---

* Prepared by Prof. Jeremy F. Plant of George Mason University.

overall ADC approach. It requires the establishment of a single organizational unit within the local welfare department concerned solely with child-support enforcement functions and supervised by an official reporting directly to the local social services commissioner. A major change from the past is in the assignment of support payments by the resident parent to the state/local social services department. In the past, child-support payments were ordered by Family Court to be paid directly to the family, with ADC payments dependent on the level of that support, which was counted as income. Now the government is in the position of the creditor. The ADC family signs over its support rights and then is assured of 100 percent funding, regardless of whether the absent parent actually pays the support that has been ordered.

While the core agency for the implementation of the Title IV-D program is the local Child Support Enforcement Agency, the program requires other agencies to become involved as well.

The IV-A agency is responsible for administering the ADC program, including determination of eligibility for welfare, disbursement of funds to eligible recipients, monitoring of ADC cases, and reporting results to state and federal authorities. In addition, the IV-A agency is required to refer cases to the IV-D agency once assignments of rights and guarantee of cooperation by the welfare recipient have been granted.

The IV-A and IV-D agencies are then required to communicate with each other concerning all changes in the status of absent parents of ADC families or any other information pertinent to the case that may arise.

The Family Court retains a central role in the IV-D program. Family Court judges still have total discretion in awarding levels of support payments. The attitudes of the judges, the level of their workloads, and the interest of local law enforcement and probation agencies in enforcing court orders all help to determine the total levels of support returned to the government under the program. Law enforcement agencies serve court orders and apprehend delinquent parents for nonsupport.

THE IV-D PROGRAM IN NEW YORK STATE

Implementing the IV-D program in New York State is the responsibility of the Office of Child Support Enforcement (OCSE). The basic mission of the operational staff of OCSE is to assist the local IV-D agencies in developing programs which comply with federal and state guidelines. Basic to this mission are the on-site visits by OCSE staff to examine local IV-D operations. Each year one or two OCSE child support specialists visit each county for two to three days and prepare a report on the county program, noting discrepancies from the Child Support Manual or noncompliance with state and federal regulations. A copy of the report is sent to the local commissioner of welfare services, who is expected to note the discrepancies and prepare a written response outlining steps being taken to insure compliance.

In its on-site reviews, OCSE concentrates on organizational and procedural questions. Especially stressed are the federal requirements that a separate IV-D unit be established, with its director reporting directly to the local commissioner; that all IV-D personnel (including the director) be engaged only in IV-D functions; that proper record keeping in the manner prescribed by federal statute be established; and that accounting procedures and reimbursement of collected support payments to the federal and state levels of government be administered by the local unit in accordance with established procedure. OCSE audits do not attempt to set quotas on collections and/or casework closings by a local unit; they tend to concentrate more on adherence to procedure than on measurements of performance or productivity.

Within the guidelines, there is much latitude as to the level of staffing and the division of labor to be employed by the IV-D agency. Some IV-D agencies concentrate on investigation: finding the absent parent, either by utilization of the automated state and federal Parent Locator Systems (PLS) or through field investigation. (Many absent parents do not go far from their former residence and remain in the same community or general area.) Others concentrate on clerical tasks: efficient processing of new cases and accounting and filing procedures mandated by the state guidelines. Others work on enforcement: making sure that absent parents are actually fulfilling their court-ordered payments. The task of enforcement requires that the IV-D agency work closely and effectively with the Family Court and probation department and other law enforcement agencies who serve Family Court orders, since IV-D investigators are not peace officers and cannot serve these functions without making special arrangements.

In the final analysis, the kind of IV-D program that a county in New York will have is largely a decision of the county political officials, who will determine funding and staffing levels in the county budget; of the local commissioner of social services, who will determine the priority within the welfare system given to IV-D and select the officials who will work under him on the program; and of the county IV-D coordinator, who will be able, as the specialist on IV-D, to work within the constraints of guidelines and politics to flesh out the particulars of the county program.

LINCOLN COUNTY IV-D PROGRAM

As Dr. Anderson, Lincoln County welfare services commissioner, studied the recent review of his IV-D program (see Exhibit 1), he knew that for at least a year the arrangements for Lincoln's IV-D program were somewhat makeshift, but armed with the latest review, he hoped he could make headway with his board.

Jack Wells, Anderson's deputy, was the administrative brains in Lincoln County Welfare Department and had helped in setting up the original bookkeeping, records, and assignments of personnel, but his time had had to be

EXHIBIT 1
Report of Inspection/Staff Visit

Purpose: Inspection	Period: April 12–14, 1976	File Number: 77–1–36	Date of Report: May 4, 1976
Reporting Unit: Upstate Operations		County: Lincoln	

Reference:
   Initial Inspection—1976

Summary:

1. There is no single organizational IV-D Unit.
2. The IV-D function is not under full-time supervision.
3. The IV-D supervisor is performing IV-A and other non-IV-D duties.
4. Referrals from IV-A to IV-D are not appropriate IV-D cases.
5. The IV-A to IV-D referral form does not contain all required information.
6. The IV-A Unit is not furnishing IV-D with all required documentation.
7. There is no separate IV-D case file.
8. IV-D files do not reflect current status of the case.
9. The Central Registry file is not separated into Known and Unknown section.
10. Initial Location investigations are not completed within 30 days.
11. The military is being contacted directly for location assistance.
12. No attempts are made to obtain voluntary resumption of support payments.
13. No efforts are made to determine parents' ability to support.
14. There is no adequate monitoring of support orders.

In addition, the following problem area recommendations are submitted:

1. IV-D case files should be established and maintained by the absent parent's last name.
2. A IV-D Unit should be established, designated The Child Support Enforcement Unit or the Office of Child Support Enforcement.

Distribution:		Reporting Staff:
Commissioner, LCWS	2	Janice Stevens, Sr. Child Support Specialist
Director, OCSE	1	Gordon Harper, Sr. Child Support Specialist
Systems	1	
Fiscal	1	
Local Agency Manpower	1	Jeffrey G. Sterngold
File	1	Director, OCSE

divided between IV-D and other assignments in the department. Wells had not had the time to sit down with the sheriff, the probation director, or Family Court judges to explain the impact of the program on them, and the job of coordination had simply not been done. Wells's attempts to integrate IV-D tasks and personnel with those of the IV-A program blurred the distinctions between the two and did not square with the OCSE report. The initial organizational structure is shown in Exhibit 2.

Even more fundamentally, Dr. Anderson himself did not know where the program should be heading. What goals should be set in terms of collections,

EXHIBIT 2
Lincoln County IV-D Organization

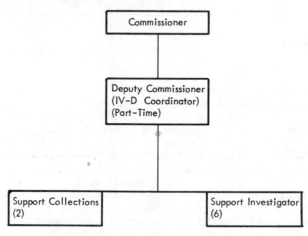

number of cases to be closed, and net benefits to the county? The program needed a full-time director, and Dr. Anderson decided that his first priority in changing the Lincoln program would be the hiring of a IV-D coordinator.

After advertising the position and letting the word out to friends around the state that the county was looking for such an individual, Dr. Anderson narrowed the choice down to two individuals: Joe Roberts and James Jones. Both men looked promising but differed widely in background and orientation. Roberts, 35, was a former investigator in the Lincoln County sheriff's department who was currently employed as an insurance claims adjustor. Jones, 32, was a case supervisor in the Lincoln IV-A unit, a ten-year employee of the Lincoln Social Services Department.

Dr. Anderson chatted briefly with each candidate during the interviews and described the findings of the OCSE review. His question to each man was simple: given these deficiencies and a probable increase of no more than one or two staff positions, what could you do to improve Lincoln's IV-D program? Where would you start? Dr. Anderson realized that neither man was as yet an expert on all the details of the program, but each had some experience in related program areas and could be expected to have some views on what to do as IV-D coordinator.

Roberts was interviewed first. He had some definite opinions on the role of the IV-D unit. It was a mistake to see the IV-D program as a part of the welfare system, in his opinion. He saw it as part and parcel of the criminal justice system, dependent for its success on close dealings between IV-D and the enforcing agencies: Family Court; probation; and police agencies, especially the sheriff's department. As coordinator, Roberts would spend much of his time working to develop closer relations with these agencies and would appear himself in Family Court when needed to press for sound decisions on support judgments. Roberts recalled that Family Court warrants "were used to line the desk drawers" when he was in the sheriff's department; they were the lowest-priority enforcement item to be acted upon by the department. He would urge the commissioner to allow him some leeway in the use of his IV-D personnel to work with the law enforcement agencies to keep tabs on absent parents. In addition, he would use new staff positions to increase the clerical staff competence, since the success of his system required constant surveillance of records on payments to insure maximum dollar intake for the unit. His measure of productivity would be net cost. He did not want to "build an empire" of his own at IV-D but felt that a small staff, working closely with enforcement agencies, could clear the maximum profit for the unit. Investigations using either field work or the available state/federal automated locator systems, he felt, required a great deal of paperwork and staff time for limited ends. Solving the maximum number of cases would be secondary to showing a profit.

Jones was familiar with the IV-D program by virtue of his work on IV-A. Jones made no attempt to conceal from Dr. Anderson his feelings concerning the present state of the IV-D unit, which were apparently shared by much of the social services department. He felt IV-D to be floundering because the assigned personnel did not see their role in the broader perspective of the welfare system. His criticism of IV-D was also managerial in tone: IV-D personnel needed to be directed more efficiently so that the maximum number of absent parents could be located. Jones felt that the Lincoln IV-D program could pay its own way or show a profit for the county through a combination of effective investigations and efficient administration. The major goal he set for the IV-D agency was to become a model of efficiency for the rest of the county Social Services Department. He had strong views on the program deficiencies noted by the state review team: he would clear up overlaps with the IV-A unit yet insist that each unit work closely with the other to process new ADC cases efficiently and smoothly. Managing the flow of paperwork required by the unit would be one of his chief problems, as well as determining the proper workload responsibility for the staff.

When informed by Dr. Anderson that new staff positions might be hard to come by, Jones voiced his hope that a new position could be created for research and analysis of county trends in ADC cases to develop such data as the characteristics shared by absent parents, the cases that tend to be closed and those which tend to remain open, and the levels of support ordered by the Family Court. To Jones, the IV-D program was a means of learning more about the entire ADC program. Investigation of each and every case as thoroughly as possible was the key to the success of the unit. His own role, he told Dr. Anderson, would have to be largely internal management: making certain that the staff worked smoothly, with an equitable distribution of cases, that guidelines were adhered to, and that proper filing and reporting procedures were established. In his view paperwork, in and of itself, was not the problem. The emphasis should be on staff understanding and acceptance of operating systems. When Dr. Anderson asked about external relationships, Jones wondered if he meant dealing with the IV-A unit, since to him these seemed to involve the greatest number of overlaps in case processing. Jones had little understanding of the overlaps between IV-D, the judicial system, and law enforcement agencies.

After much deliberation Dr. Anderson selected Jones and sent him the letter shown in Exhibit 3.

Shortly after his appointment, Jones sent the memorandum shown in Exhibit 4 to his staff.

EFFECTS OF THE STAFF MEETING

Not surprisingly to Jones, the morale of the investigators was low, and it showed at the staff meeting. Four of the six investigators had come to the IV-D agency from IV-A when the program began in 1975; they had no training or experience in investigative work. Two others were recent college graduates with no special training in investigations. The two support collectors had two-year college degrees—one from a local community college, in criminal justice, the other from a business school.

In the course of the meeting, Jones gathered that little specialization was evident in the operations of the unit. The six investigators divided up the caseload alphabetically and tried as best they could to keep up with their cases from start to finish. The two support collectors worked entirely on the enforcement of court-ordered payments. Al Smith, with the degree (and interest) in criminal justice, worked as liaison with the Family Court and tried to get enforcement of court orders in delinquent cases. Liz Golden monitored the flow of support funds and generally supervised the paperwork and accounting procedures.

Jones discussed the comparative figures on Lincoln's program vis-a-vis other counties and then opened the floor for "gripes." It didn't take much effort to get a wide-open discussion started:

> Our work is to find the absent parents, but when we do, we have no guarantee that they'll pay or that the court will try to make them.

> There's no way you can make money from these deadbeats. They're generally unproductive, and even if you find them, they don't have much to offer.

> The usefulness of the Parent Locator Service is more than offset by the paperwork reporting that is required on each request. What good are 1975 addresses and job information for finding a guy in 1977?

> You can't handle 300 cases at one time and do a thorough job. If we had the staff to handle 75 apiece, we could show a tremendous net gain in productivity.

EXHIBIT 3

Office of the Commissioner
County of Lincoln

July 1, 1976

Mr. James Jones
1 Main Street
Lincoln, New York

Dear Jim:
  I am pleased to inform you that I am recommending your appointment as Coordinator, Child Support Enforcement Activities, Lincoln County Department of Welfare Services. I was very impressed with your appreciation of the current problems of the IV-D agency and your suggestions for possible ways to improve operations.
  Once you get yourself settled in, let's meet and discuss some changes you think are needed to get the IV-D program rolling. I'd also like your help in drafting a letter to OCSE outlining the changes we'll be making to comply with their recent review.
  Congratulations, and I look forward to working with you.

                              Sincerely,

                              John Anderson, D.S.W.
                              Commissioner

JA/jfp

The IV-A people don't understand IV-D and don't want to do their required part in it. We have to handle the assignments and get information directly from the mothers, or we'll never get it.

This is not a welfare program; it's law enforcement. Let's move over to the courthouse so we can keep in touch with enforcement. This program doesn't relate to social services.

You can't collect from them until you find them.

We're not appreciated by the rest of the people in the department.

Despite the criticisms, Jones came away from the meeting impressed with the possibilities of revitalizing the program on the basis of the enthusiasm that came out during the meeting. He called Dr. Anderson and got approval for organizing the staff into teams, with three investigators and one support collector per team. In addition to serving as a way of dividing the workload, the teams were each asked to come up with their own ideas on how best to orient the total Lincoln IV-D program. Jones was especially pleased to hear from Dr. Anderson that the County Board had heard through the grapevine that the IV-D program might finally get off the ground. Dr. Anderson implied

EXHIBIT 4

MEMORANDUM

To: IV-D Staff

FROM: J. M. Jones

SUBJECT: Staff Meeting 7/8/77

I.   I'm calling a "get acquainted" meeting for July 8, 1977, to discuss the IV-D
     program in Lincoln. I'm interested in getting your views on where we should be
     going and the best way of getting there. Please feel free to prepare questions
     for me on what options are open to us. I'm including some material I hastily put
     together (see Table 1) comparing our program in a number of important areas
     with those of some similar counties (in population) upstate. As you can see, we
     don't stack up too favorably.

II. I guess you know that there will be some changes taking place soon in our unit.
     I hope this meeting will establish some priorities we can all agree upon. I would
     especially like to know:

     1. What indicators should be used to allocate and evaluate your work as inves-
         tigators, i.e., number of locations made, total amount collected, and num-
         ber of assigned cases?
     2. What is the proper caseload per investigator? Currently it runs about 250
         per investigator. I'm looking forward to getting your views as to the rea-
         sonableness of the workload.
     3. What is the best organization for the unit? Should we organize on the basis
         of specialties or should we apportion cases in some equitable fashion and
         handle them from start to finish?

III. Of course, I'm depending on you to let me in on all the inside dope on IV-D I
     couldn't get across the hall. Feel free to air your pet gripes so we can get
     Lincoln up near the top for IV-D programs in New York.

---

that, with the proper nurturing, this might lead to some additional staff for
the program.

Jones spent much of the first few months gathering data on the IV-D
program in Lincoln and comparing what he found there with data on other
counties in New York State. If he were given even one additional staff
position, he wanted to know the best way of utilizing it. In addition, he gave
a good deal of thought to a policy problem that bothered him: should the
success of IV-D be measured in cost/effectiveness terms or in terms of its
mission, which presumably is to locate and secure legally-required payment
from all absent parents of ADC families? The more he thought about it, the
more the two criteria seemed incongruous. Paring the staff to a minimum
might be the most cost-effective approach. Some absent parents would always remain close enough to be found without full-blown investigations, and

TABLE 1
Comparison of IV-D Programs in Upstate Counties

County	Caseload	Collections	Average Number of Cases Receiving Collections	Percent of Cases Receiving Collections	Expenditures	Ratio of Collections to Expenditures
Albany	3,197	$ 434,000	627	20	$ 369,000	1.18:1
Broome	1,500	316,000	469	31	99,000	3.19:1
Clinton	490	125,000	132	27	61,000	2.05:1
Columbia	398	39,000	53	13	51,000	1:1.31
Dutchess	2,494	220,000	602	24	317,000	1:1.44
Rensselaer	1,495	306,000	300	20	112,000	2.73:1
Schenectady	1,995	353,000	388	19	105,000	3.36:1
Saratoga	940	247,000	259	28	49,000	5.04:1
Lincoln	1,500	160,000	200	13	110,000	1.45:1
Statewide less NYC	115,220	$9,923,000	17,868	16	$9,217,000	1.08 :1

a small clerical/accounting staff might be all that would be needed to process voluntary payments and account for dollars. The totals would be small but the ratio impressive. Investigation was a costly enterprise, since there was no guarantee that once found the individual would pay or even that a reasonable support settlement would be required by the court.

On the other hand, it seemed to Jones that an increase in investigative staff would overcome the inertia in the Lincoln program. If the caseload were 75–100 rather than 250 per investigator, the results would be impressive, since the investigator would have no backlog of cases and could process new cases faster, get support collections earlier, and in addition maintain a follow-up capability for continuing cases. Jones was disturbed that many parents were found, reported missing again, and then refound in a seeming endless cycle. As he saw it, a caseload of 250 created communications problems between his investigators and the IV-A staff. Adding staff positions was the only approach that offered a feasible solution to those problems.

The staff concurred. Each team, working independently, stressed the addition of staff. The team idea was quite well received, but the teams differed in regard to the proper breakdown of cases. Team A argued that each team should get 50 percent of the cases and handle them to completion. Team B toyed with the idea of team specialization, with one team concentrating on initial processing and investigation, the other on follow-up work. The support collection function was felt by one individual (a support collector, not surprisingly) to be worthy of a team in itself, which would also work with the Family Court, probation, and police. Jones was pleased with the constructive tone of the suggestions and considered them carefully.

At the end of Jones' fourth month as coordinator, he assessed the changes in the statistical picture of the Lincoln program. They were as follows:

	Cases	Cases Receiving Collections	Percent Receiving Collections	Total Collections
July	1,500	200	13	$160,000
October	1,600	320	20	185,000

Jones was pleased by the increase in cases resulting in collections, since he regarded this as the most important index of the program's effectiveness. However, he still compared Lincoln, with its small staff, to other counties in the hope of determining the effect that adding staff might have on collections. Statewide, the relationship of staff to collections was ambiguous, and no clear figures could be derived to point up the marginal benefit of a new staff position in terms of the collections/expenditure ratio. Even the relatively small increase in locations had begun to tax the docket of Family Court, and the collections-to-locations ratio that Jones tabulated went down somewhat. More staff meant more locations, but it wouldn't necessarily mean a straightline increase in collections as well.

Jones was troubled by the implications of the figures. He recognized only too well that his unit had little real control over the collection function, yet it would be evaluated in terms of total collections by outside analysts. He arranged to meet with Steve Will, the county probation director, to talk over the problem of collections. Will was moderately knowledgeable about the IV-D program and very knowledgeable about one aspect of it: namely, that the reimbursement by the federal government did not cover agencies like his that were involved in the program but not under the formal organizational heading of the IV-D program. Will mentioned his own understaffing problems to Jones and offered little hope for strenuous support of the IV-D program. Jones called Sheriff Roy Brown a short time later and again was told that "my boys are doing the best that can be done under the circumstances." Jones decided to continue these discussions with outside parties involved in enforcement on a more regular basis. He knew that, though they were outside his control, he could not afford to make enemies by leaning too hard on them for priority treatment. The pleas of overwork and understaffing, he knew, were well founded; he experienced them first-hand in his own unit.

A further external problem was the poor communications with IV-A people. Two of his investigators complained that IV-A staff were slow in assigning support rights and referring cases and were not cooperative when it came to sharing information that might be of some use to the investigators. For example, one investigator had followed up some leads on an absent father that had come through the PLS, and once he found the individual, he learned that a IV-A staffer had been given the same information at the time of assignment but had not transmitted it to him. Other complaints centered on the unwillingness or inability of the IV-A staff to require the active cooperation of the ADC recipient in IV-D investigations. Jones discussed the problem with the head of the IV-A office but expected little change. He remembered his own attitudes toward IV-D in the past. When he met the IV-A director, he was greeted by the question, "How does it feel to be a cop?"

All these issues came to a head when Jones received the following memorandum from Dr. Anderson.

MEMORANDUM

To: James Jones

From: John Anderson

Subject: IV-D Budget

As you know, the time is fast approaching when our budget requests have to be developed and discussed with the board of supervisors. The IV-D budget is, quite frankly, a troublesome item to me. Don't get me wrong—the board is as impressed as I am with the measures you have taken to improve the morale and performance of your unit. This may actually be our problem. At least one board member (I think you know who he is) has told me that he expects Lincoln to top the state average for the collection/expenditure ratio. He said, "There's two types of people I don't much care for—welfare bureaucrats and welfare cheaters. If you have to have the first, they should be there to find the cheaters." Great, but it means I have to have some definite plans from you on how to incorporate new staff into your program.

Jim, let me give it to you straight. You're probably going to get two new positions at $12,000 apiece. In return the program is going to have to show a return of $3 for every dollar spent. What I need as soon as possible from you is a plan which shows how you propose to organize the unit with this expansion, the emphasis you are going to put on the various elements of the program, and a fairly accurate date when you might reach the 3/1 ratio. Remember, this isn't a contract, but it's as close to one as you can get. You may want to spend some time discussing the problem with the Family Court judges and the probation people. I have confidence that you can reach the 3/1 figure and surpass it.

Give me a battle plan within a week or two. Good luck.

27. Mr. Gatti's Pizza*

"I guess I was born an entrepreneur," said James R. Eure, describing how he came to go into the pizza business. A product of the Depression, Eure recounted how, even at an early age, he displayed signs of being a potential entrepreneur.

> During the depression, I would grow peanuts off the farm and sell them for 5 cents per bag, which was pretty good money in those days. When I graduated from high school in 1936, it was in the midst of the depression and there was little hope of going to school that year.
>
> My brother and I borrowed $75 and rented what had been an old drug store in this little drying up town in West Texas where we were living. With just $75 we put in what we called a confectionery—a little soda fountain, a little ice cream and school supplies, hamburgers, and some drugs and sundry items.
>
> But, typically I suppose, I didn't know what I wanted to be so I drifted from that to selling magazines and taking my pay in chickens (which I had to catch myself).

After bouncing around awhile, Eure decided to go into the Air Force. He spent 25 years in the service and retired with the rank of Lieutenant Colonel in 1964. His career in the Air Force was spent as a communications-electronics officer.

DEVELOPMENT OF MR. GATTI'S

When Eure retired from the Air Force, by his own account he did not have anything specific in mind. He was, however, determined that he would not let occupation determine where he would live. He wound up in Stephenville, Texas (population 7,000 with a small college), about 60 miles southwest of Ft. Worth. He and his wife built a new home with their own hands. Then he decided to think about going into the restaurant business.

> I knew that it was the one sure way for me to make some money. I knew that you can make money in any service business if you give good service. There is always a shortage of good things.

Eure managed to scrape up enough money to open a "hole in the wall" in Stephenville. Before that time, no one had ever tried to sell pizza there. Eure

---

* Prepared by Ed D. Roach and Jack D. Eure, Jr. of Southwest Texas State University.

indicated that at the time it was generally believed that pizza could succeed only in larger cities. In addition to pizza, the restaurant served charburgers and submarine sandwiches. Eure called his new business venture the Yucca Hut.

> The charburgers were a whole lot better than the pizza because I knew how to make a good hamburger. I didn't know the first thing about pizza. I figured that by the time I got opened I would learn how to make pizza. Sure enough, I didn't learn. The cheese companies, the tomato companies, etc., would give you all sorts of recipes to make pizzas. None of them worked and none of them was good.

Despite his failure to invent the perfect pizza by opening day, Eure indicated that the people in this small town were so hungry for something besides chicken-fried steaks and Dairy Queen hamburgers that they mobbed him the first day. In fact, the response was so unexpectedly large that he had run completely out of food before 6 o'clock.

> As bad as the pizza was, they even liked that. We had no idea of the people that were going to mob us. We weren't stocked, manned, or equipped. We had good intentions and that's about all. So we actually shut down. We put up a sign on the reader board saying "Oops, we goofed!! We will reopen in a few days." This was my first experience and worst.

After this rather unexpected start in business, Eure set about to deal with the surprising level of demand. While on a trip to Dallas to look for a used walk-in cooler, he met a person who was to change the course of his business. This individual was in the pizza business, and Eure noted that he "had some sharp-looking methods." Eure asked for help to learn the pizza business. For a modest contract, essentially based on 2 percent of sales in two years, this pizza entrepreneur agreed to share some of his secrets with Eure and to furnish the spices to mix the pizza sauce. He showed Eure how he did everything except the spices.

Yucca Hut apparently was a tongue-twister for the people of Stephenville and after a few months, everyone had more or less changed the name to Pizza Place. In the meantime, Eure had purchased the property next door with the anticipation of building a restaurant large enough to accommodate the ever-increasing demand for his pizza, charburgers, and submarine sandwiches. He closed his restaurant on the last day of school and began preparation for building and moving to the property next door. With this restaurant, Eure started on a long journey of growth and innovation in the pizza business that was to change his life drastically.

THE PIZZA PLACE AND ATMOSPHERICS

By Eure's assessment, the Pizza Place was pretty innovative for the town and the time.

That was my first venture into split-level dining and to my little privacy booths and to the showing of old movies. I found that people loved to go up and down steps. They seemed to go first to the available seating which was hardest to get to. I also found that people like lots of privacy. People are territorial. The more that a customer can stake out his territory and say "This is mine," the more comfortable he will be. So it's not so much privacy as the satisfying of the territorial urge.

Eure observed that the little privacy booths came to be one of his most important gimmicks. Eure believes that gimmicks are very, very important.

You have to create a gimmick to create good advertising. You have something that generates your own advertising by making people talk about you. You have something different and they will go and say, "You should go to that place; they even have this." So you try to put something that is different in each one.

For the size of town, Eure believed the Pizza Place to be very successful. However, in 1968, because of school problems of his handicapped son, he leased the business and moved to Austin, Texas. Exhibit 1 shows a sketch of the first "Pizza Place."

FROM PIZZA PLACE TO MR. GATTI'S

After a brief and unsuccessful attempt at selling real estate, Eure decided that he would "back his ears and get back into the kitchen making pizza," so he picked a spot in Austin.

I don't know why I picked it except that the rent was cheap. It was a location which many of my subsequent locations have been—dismal failures—but these are the locations you can get on your own terms. It was originally to be a Utotem Store [a chain of small, convenience stores] and it was a different design. Utotem had a 15-year lease for $300 per month and a 7-Eleven had already opened around the corner. There was an informal arrangement between 7-Eleven and Utotem that they wouldn't get that close to each other. Anyway, Utotem never opened the store, and I got it cheap.

Eure indicated that he knew immediately that the new pizza operation would be a success; but it was not an immediate, raging success. Within six months, however, traffic was very heavy. Too many people were coming in, in Eure's opinion, for the size of the restaurant. Therefore, he started looking for a second location, thinking more of an overflow to take some pressure off the first than to put in a second restaurant to "make lots of money." Number 2 was opened one year after the first Austin Pizza Place in a shopping center store front. The location had just failed as a pizza operation. About this time Eure began to see, according to his accounts, the potential for growth and expansion. He was, however, determined to do it very cautiously and to do it only out of cash flow.

EXHIBIT 1
The First Pizza Place in Stephenville, Texas

1571 West Washington - Stephenville, Texas
Phone 968-2512

One year after the opening of number 2, additional space was leased to double the seating capacity of this unit. Sales grew from first-month sales of $6,800 to better than $15,000 monthly sales within a relatively short time span. Number 3 was soon opened opposite the main gate of the Air Force base located on the outskirts of Austin. It was housed in a building which had seen a succession of failures in its five-year life. Its immediate success prompted negotiations for a larger facility.

> Before number 1 had been open a year we had three places opened. In opening number 3 I discovered how easy it was to open a pizza restaurant. If you have a central commissary, you can put in an oven and some tables and chairs and some refrigerators. Then you send some people that you have taught how to put pizzas together. You control the quality in the commissary.

Number 4 was opened 16 months after number 1 opened. It also contained the first complete commissary, supplying other stores with preportioned and "idiot-proofed" supplies (see below for a discussion of the commissary concept). Its sales increased steadily from a first-month of $7,000+ to a volume in excess of $24,000 per month.

Number 5 opened in August 1971 in a large regional shopping center in Austin. Eure believes this to have been the first pizza operation in a shopping mall. Several of the better known chains now have mall locations. Eure noted that this store not only enjoyed a steady increase in sales but provided much publicity and recognition for other outlets. It quickly reached a volume of $20,000 per month in sales and was highly profitable.

Cautious expansion was continued in Austin. In addition, in September 1972, San Marcos number 1 was opened (San Marcos is a small city of about 20,000 population located 28 miles south of Austin). Second-month sales were $11,000 or approximately $10 per square foot.

Writing in 1973, James R. Eure observed that

> This business has easily survived the transition from "mom-and-pop" operation. After taking accelerated depreciation and every permissible write-off for tax purposes, our net profit is 13 percent. Our salaries and wages are equal to or above the industry average; salary and bonuses of the two top executives this year will total $84,000.

MR. GATTI'S

Eure indicated that the name "Pizza Place" was getting more and more confusing.

> I would call up somebody and say, "I'm 'so-and-so' with the Pizza Place." They would say, "Which one? The one over on Guadalupe?" "No," I'd say, "We don't have one on Guadalupe. That's Shakey's." "The one on so-and-so?" "No. That's Pizza Inn." So many people thought "pizza is pizza," and maybe some still do. That's one reason why we decided to change our name. I wanted to leave pizza completely out of the name. I wanted the name to be

"Mr. Gatti's," followed by a comma, and then in smaller print, "Pizza, etc." I was convinced the vagueness of the name "The Pizza Place" would hamper future expansion.

Eure explained that the name "Mr. Gatti's" was decided upon after reviewing names submitted by employees in a contest to rename "The Pizza Place." Gatti is the maiden name of Eure's wife. See Exhibit 2 for the logo of Mr. Gatti's, inset below a promotion of the privacy booths featured at the restaurants.

EXHIBIT 2
Logo for Mr. Gatti's

MANAGEMENT AND ORGANIZATION

Upon reaching the decision to go into business in Austin, Eure decided to ask relatives to enter a partnership with him. His sister and her nephew agreed to a partnership arrangement. They remained a partnership until January 1971 when a Subchapter S corporation was formed by the original partners. At the same time, David M. Danser, Jr., who had been accountant and operations manager, was permitted to buy stock equivalent to 1/7 ownership. The original three partners retained the remaining stock (2/7 each).

Eure used nothing but students and other part-time workers. In fact, four locations were in operation before the first full-time employee was hired.

> Nobody had any responsibility. I did all the scheduling and all the hiring. I didn't have a single person other than my wife who had any responsibility for the stores when they were not there. In other words, they came in and worked and then they went home.

As things began to get more and more complex with the addition of other locations, Eure decided that what he needed was someone whose main job it would be to figure what the stores needed each morning and figure up how much the commissary should make that day to get ready for the various locations. From the product delivered to them, this person should be able to calculate how much money should be in each restaurant.

> We had number 4 opened and this young man who had just graduated from the University of Texas with a degree in finance went to work for us. He had worked his way through college working at Shakey's. Prior to going to college he had been a naval pilot. He was a whiz at mathematics and accounting. He knew quite a bit about computers. He was very good for the business.
>
> We were a good combination. He never questioned philosophies and policies. If he didn't think that everything I wanted to do was the greatest he did not let on. He backed me 100 percent in everything.

Eure began to give more and more decision making authority to Danser, although at first it was very difficult to part with the authority.

> He had been given 95 percent of the decision making. But it took a long time for him to get to that level. Buying was the hardest thing for me to turn loose of. I wanted to buy everything. If we needed a pound of nails, I wanted to buy them. I soon found that I couldn't do all these things, and I gradually turned bigger and bigger things over to other people once I gained confidence in them.

The second full-time employee hired had the responsibility of going around and collecting the money and making the deposits. Then as the number of restaurants increased, stronger and stronger people were hired to work in the headquarters office. Eure desired that one headquarters person should be held responsible for about four stores.

Eure recognized himself to be a stern taskmaster, a perfectionist. He indicated that one of his faults was not to have enough confidence in people initially.

> I'm too much of a perfectionist. I don't give people enough credit for being able to do the job initially. Once they prove themselves to me then I'm inclined to give them too much leeway. I know I'm a very difficult person to work for. However, I'm very good to my people. I pay them well. On the other hand, I've given lots of thought as to why, the way I pay people, I can't get the same kind of longevity and loyalty and dedication that [some people get].

Knowing that people find him difficult to work for, Eure indicated that he tried to isolate himself two or three steps from employees. He said, "I put one trusted person who can put up with me between me and the employees."

STRATEGIC DEVELOPMENT

Eure described his business as a well-above-average pizza restaurant. Mr. Gatti's never did advertise cheap prices. Their prices, according to Eure, were known to be a little higher than the competition. As an above-average pizza restaurant, Mr. Gatti's sought to cater to a sophisticated, mature crowd.

> Steak and Ale and that type of restaurant is our competition. The better restaurants, the ones catering to a lively crowd, are our competition.

Eure indicated that he never was afraid of taking on the likes of Pizza Hut, Pizza Inn, and Shakey's. He gave the following account as to why.

> I once knew a fellow who had a little hamburger joint. I had a friend who owned the property and he asked me to go by and visit with this fellow and kind of evaluate his operation. So I did. The significant thing that came out of the conversation was that he was going to turn out a good product, but he was in no way going to attempt to be as good as McDonald's.
>
> I think that the big boys are sitting ducks for any single, quality operator. I mean you are not going to hurt them but you can operate all around them. You must take advantage of them because you are a single owner-operated enterprise, and you should be able to do so much better in quality, size, and product.
>
> So I don't think the little operator needs to fear the big boys if he knows this and applies it.

PRICE AND QUALITY

Gatti's, under Eure's direction, did not price according to competition. The best ingredients were figured into the product; the products were then priced to keep food costs around 20 to 25 percent. No resistance to the company's pricing policies has been encountered, according to Eure.

> At times we've had to raise the prices to maintain food costs and we have not hesitated one minute to do so. I did have a price-raising strategy. I leap-frogged prices. That is, I would never raise prices across the board. There were always some products that were dragging heels, some that were underpriced anyway. So those would go and become overpriced. I would leave some things alone. For example, one time I'd raise the price of small and leave the large and medium alone. Next time I would raise the medium and leave the small and large alone.

PRODUCT MIX

Eure stressed the philosophy of "keeping it simple" and doing what you do well. His strategy was not to try to satisfy everyone. The theme was to do what you do well and leave the rest up to somebody else. In the first Austin location, he started out with pizza only. He then added the submarine sandwich. However, he indicated that the submarine sandwich was not added until the pizza was established.

I haven't really developed a new product since Stephenville that succeeded. We have never sold a dessert because we have not come up with anything that would not take away from our efforts to sell pizza.

When Shakey's a few years ago first came out with their big announcement that they were going to serve fried chicken and mojo potatoes I laughed and said that was wonderful. I said that if they can't make pizza they sure can make pizza and chicken. And I was right in thinking that it would make their pizza worse, their service worse, and their business worse. People who think they have got to grab whatever somebody wants to eat think they are missing out if they're not there to satisfy them. We want our customers to go somewhere else to eat chicken.

ADVERTISING AND PROMOTION

In the early phases of operation, Gatti's was so small that the only promotion was through Welcome Wagon. After four locations opened, one-inch, one-column ads simply stating "Mr. Gatti's—South Congress" were run in the paper. These ads got larger as the number of stores grew. Seldom, however, was anything run in the newspaper except the logo and the name. The radio spots were kept as short as possible, never more than 30 seconds. Many of the spots were for 20 seconds. Eure indicated that he wanted the customers to be so happy that he wasn't "bugged for a whole minute" that they were left with a good feeling toward Mr. Gatti's. In other words, Eure said, "Give our name and what we do and then we're gone."

Promotion coupons that were handed out never used a discount or "you-buy-one-get-one-free" theme. The promotion coupons were always no strings attached. This was in keeping with the quality image which Mr. Gatti's tried to promote. "When we gave away beer, we would say, 'come in for a free Michelob.' That may cost us only one cent more."

OPERATIONS

James R. Eure expressed "a terrible fear of deterioration of products." This led him to develop two concepts which became a trademark of his operations. These two concepts were the "commissary principle" and "idiot-proofing," as he labeled it. Essentially this meant doing the important part of the food preparation in the back of the restaurant. Then the people who were to put the pizza together in the rush at night would have everything laid out for them. Eure observed that the important steps are cooking the sauce, mixing the dough, and even chopping the onions.

Eure found that he could get stable, permanent-type help from people who were looking for daytime work. Then, he relied on students and part-time help to put the pizzas together and cook them at night.

As noted previously, Eure did all of the hiring, interviewing, and scheduling for all the stores in the early history of Mr. Gatti's. At the stage where he had four restaurants, he bought a little pick-up and put a cooler on the back of it to haul the groceries. It was while doing this that Eure says that he "perfected the method of restocking the stores."

> The concept was to sell out. Theoretically, it meant they were not supposed to have a scrap of food left. But in practice they would have some left. The more perishable the item was the more often it was required that they run out of it. That was one of the biggest battles—overcoming the fear of running out of something. One of the most important things is running out of something often. If something has only a two-day shelf life and you are afraid of running out of it, you are going to be selling about 90 percent of the time a product which is on the tail-end of its shelf-life and is deteriorating. If you have enough before you run out, you have too much, and today when you like to be serving a nice, fresh product you are still serving yesterday's leftovers.

Another thing which Eure believed had made his operation profitable was the fact that he had no losses on products. He required that stock would be maintained at a level that they would run out of one size of pizza crust in a store every night. The attempt was made to schedule the run-out just after the rush hour. Eure scheduled his salads to run out at some point during the supper rush. He maintains that no one was offended if they ran out of salads.

The commissary principle and idiot-proofing allowed Eure to manage his operations in such a way that the people in the stores had nothing to do with how much merchandise was brought to a particular restaurant. The employees in a restaurant had nothing to do with scheduling and so on. Therefore, Eure alleges, "there was nothing to manage."

> Whoever got there first was the manager. Usually someone had already been there and put the stuff in the refrigerator for him before he got there.
>
> Eventually, we started the commissary at three or four in the morning and we had restocking procedures laid out. With brief calculations, we would know how much to start producing to build the stores back up to a Monday, Tuesday, stock level. It really worked quite well. It made each store identical. You could go into any one of them and get exactly the same quality food.

Eure's operations manager "knew computers." For a long time prior to the hiring of Danser, Eure had been interested in computers and in "teaching a computer how to stock and control his restaurants." The type of control he ultimately was able to achieve he attributes to the use of computers and to Danser's knowledge of how to use them.

FINANCE

Consolidated balance sheets and income statements are shown for Mr. Gatti's in Exhibits 3 and 4.

GROWING PAINS AND OTHER PROBLEMS AT MR. GATTI'S

Reflecting upon the strains that almost any business experiences that has been successful enough to grow, James R. Eure rather philosophically observed:

EXHIBIT 3
Consolidated Balance Sheets

Assets	1969	1970	1971	1972	1973	1974
Current assets						
Cash	$ 2,620	$ 7,395	$ 13,713	$ 28,253	$ 52,760	$ 39,879
Accounts receivable		1,342	2,532	3,346	5,637	26,823
Inventories	951	8,471	12,385	14,251	37,734	106,003
Other current assets			23,392	4,639	25,507	24,288
Total current assets	$ 3,571	$17,208	$ 52,022	$ 50,489	$ 96,131	$196,993
Loans to shareholders					5,000	9,609
Building and other fixed depreciated assets	12,199	68,196	129,349	331,791	586,828	732,370
Land			2,000	12,958	32,317	32,317
Other assets	2,370	6,173	5,244	8,112		10,314
Total assets	$18,140	$91,577	$188,615	$403,350	$745,783	$976,603

Liabilities and Capital	1969	1970	1971	1972	1973	1974
Current liabilities						
Accounts payable		$25,551	$ 27,183	$ 65,658	$ 97,064	$354,362
Notes payable in less than 1 year		25,424	17,545	17,655	48,651	41,775
Other current liabilities			27,078	44,175	81,250	92,502
Total current liabilities		$50,975	$ 71,806	$127,488	$226,965	$488,639
Notes payable in more than 1 year		40,602		73,986	125,275	179,471
Partner's capital	$18,140					
Capital stock			64,890	64,890	69,890	66,640
Paid-in or capital surplus			22,730	22,730	48,840	37,270
Retained earnings unappropriated			(1,094)	(3,294)	44,457	73,443
Shareholder's undistributed taxable income previously taxed			30,283	117,550	230,356	131,140
Total liabilities and shareholders' equity	$18,140	$91,577	$188,615	$403,350	$745,783	$976,603

EXHIBIT 4
Consolidated Profit and Loss Statements

	1969	1970	1971	1972	1973	1974
Net sales	$70,871	$313,981	$479,426	$1,050,791	$1,772,123	$2,952,548
Cost of sales	20,166	92,240	124,760	271,644	480,201	805,077
Gross profit	$50,615	$221,741	$354,666	$ 779,147	$1,291,922	$2,147,471
Total expenses	39,405	193,371	302,641	658,982	1,119,581	1,875,042
Taxable income	$11,210	$ 28,370	$ 52,025	$ 129,165	$ 172,341	$ 272,429

I know many businesses have been a booming success as a single operation and they make good money and have decided to expand. They didn't take into consideration that they and their families were doing a large share of the work. They often use the family automobile and their personal tools to fix things and are able to do all the repairs. They use their garage for their warehouse. You do your own bookkeeping, etc. When you start growing suddenly you have to hire someone to do your maintenance and you have to buy them a set of tools and a truck and rent a warehouse. You suddenly stop working and start spending. Labor and capital become strained.

In the specific case of Mr. Gatti's, Eure noted that he ultimately got up to 18 stores. The pressures and the work resulting from such a large number of stores made Eure wonder about the desirability of continued expansion when he was already making more money than he "really wanted to spend." He remarked, however, how that it was difficult to stop once the venture is started and some talent is attracted by the expansion.

You are committed from then on. You can't stop because the minute you stop everybody will abandon ship. So I had this pressure of "You got to keep rolling." We had passed the "one-at-a-time-we-conceive-one-build-it-finish-it-and-open-it" stage. At one time we had four big ones going, and this was at the time the recession [of 1973] hit. We had construction delays and we had other problems.

Among those "other problems" was the loss of Eure's key man, David Danser. Along toward the latter part of his tenure with Mr. Gatti's, Danser, according to Eure, began wanting to inject himself into advertising, design, and so on. These were areas in which Eure felt himself particularly qualified in the case of Mr. Gatti's, and even more that Danser lacked proven expertise in.

He came back from a restaurant show once with a whole bunch of propaganda. He wanted us to hand out buttons to everyone saying "Pizza Makes Me Passionate." Also, he wanted to hand out balloons for the kids. I said, "Dave, we are not Shakey's; we are not Pizza Hut." This is an important thing. A business has to decide who it is, who are you, and constantly—everything you do—to work toward that image. We worked to be a quality place and we deliberately avoided gimmicks, give-aways, promotions, and the like, such as balloons and things to encourage kids to come in.

When Danser left he took two or three of Eure's top people with him. By the time Danser decided to leave, Eure had got almost completely out of operations. He was leaving the "nuts and bolts" up to Danser and concentrating upon the strategy and policy side of the business.

At this stage, Eure began to search for a replacement for Danser. He ran ads in paid publications such as *The Wall Street Journal*. He got numerous applications from all over the country. He read through the piles of resumes and sorted out those which appeared to have any promise at all.

I'd get on the phone and talk to them. I'd go to Denver and then swing over to New York City and talk to them. . . . I'm a great pessimist. People who are looking for jobs—you don't want to hire them.

Eure began to assess the situation. He was nearing age 60. He began to balance the desire to build a financial empire at the expense of enjoying life. Eure looked at the construction delays and the impact which the energy crisis would have on the eating-out habits of Americans. He thought again of his naturally pessimistic nature.

As he reflected upon the direction he ought to take, Eure thought about the earning capacity of the business and the volume it was doing. Perhaps, he thought, he should look for a quality buyer, someone whom he thought would continue the business as it was intended to be. Should he decide to sell, he wondered about the asking price he should attempt to establish for the business.

APPENDIX: A NOTE ON THE PIZZA INDUSTRY

A BRIEF HISTORY OF PIZZA

Pizza has become as American as hot dogs and hamburgers, but it didn't start out that way. Pizza goes back in history many years. Naples and Sicily, Italy, were responsible for developing the pizza in the forms we are now familiar with. From the 1700s until the 1940s, pizza traveled the length of Italy picking up local refinements and embellishments. Meat was added in Rome, mushrooms were added in Sicily, anchovies were added in Italian fishing areas, and so on. The crust varied from region to region, with the extremes being the very thin Neapolitan crust and the one-inch-thick Sicilian crust.

Somewhat later, some of the Italian chefs traveled to France because the King of France had heard about how delicious Italian food was, and he wanted to try it. These Italian chefs taught the French chefs how to cook Italian foods, and before long they became world famous for "French cooking." Eventually, some of these French chefs traveled to the United States, and that's how pizza made the journey to our country and became one of our favorite foods.

Pizza may have arrived in the United States as early as the 1890s, but America's passion for pizza is only about 20 years old. It was originally sold by peddlers from wagons and pushcarts or from corner stands in immigrant Italian neighborhoods, mostly along the Atlantic coast from New York City to Providence, Rhode Island. This early American pizza was just a slice of bread, already baked, over which the peddler ladeled fresh tomato sauce.

According to Henry Weil, the first chef to bake bread and topping together—or so he insisted—was the late Frank Pepe, an immigrant from near Salerno who opened a pizzeria in New Haven, Connecticut, in 1925. Pepe claims his place was the first sit-down pizzeria in America and the first to make a king-sized shareable pizza. None of this can be documented; but Pepe's is at least known to be the first American pizzeria to be granted a beer license.

Until the early 1950s, a non-Italian person had to go to an immigrant community to get a pizza. Then, suddenly, pizza's popularity in America erupted. In 1954, Sherwood (Shakey) Johnson founded Shakey's in Sacramento. Four years later, Frank and Don Carney started Pizza Hut. The first Pizza Hut

APPENDIX: (*continued*)

restaurant opened on June 15, 1958. Their tiny Pizza Hut restaurant became an almost overnight success.

REGIONAL DIFFERENCES IN PIZZA

America's taste for pizza varies regionally. Mid-America and the two coastal markets are complete extremes from one another. In the Southwest a different kind of dough is used. The sauce is put on top of the cheese in Pennsylvania. The people in Milwaukee cut pizza into little pieces. A Greek style is prepared in Boston. Deep dish is the "thing" in Chicago. Only Sicilian pan pizza sells well in New York, and San Francisco serves yet another version.

Americans also vary in the type of toppings they prefer. Most Americans prefer a thin crust with cheese and pepperoni or sausage, though the Southwesterners like to liven things up a bit with jalapeno peppers.

According to a 1978 survey, cheese pizza is the biggest seller nationally, and per capita consumption of cheese pizza in Philadelphia is higher than any other city in the country. Cheese pizza is least popular in Minneapolis. Sausage pizza is the second-most popular type of pizza nationally and the leader in the Midwest. The entire Northeast is at the bottom of the barrel for sausage pizza sales. Pepperoni pizza has found the greatest intensity of demand in the South, but can scarcely be found in large cities like New York and Chicago. The beef-raising states prefer hamburger pizza, but very little of it is on sale in the Northeast. Denver and Seattle residents buy more deluxe combination pizzas than any other city, and a variety on the rise in the Northwest is Canadian bacon.

THE PIZZA INDUSTRY

Americans ate a mere $700 million worth of pizza at restaurant chains in 1974, but spent $1.6 billion on the dish in 1978. Projections called for more than 20 percent growth in 1979. Pizza Hut is the undisputed leader of franchised pizza operations, with 2,820 units in 1977. It accounts for 22 percent of total sales for pizza-only chain restaurants.

Exhibit A–1 gives some detailed information about some selected leading pizza chains and the top 20 pizza chains in the United States. Pizza Hut dominates the pizza-chain market even more than McDonald's does the hamburger market. "However, pizza is more fragmented and less chain-dominated than the hamburger segment," says Michael Esposito of Bache-Halsey-Stuart-Shields, Inc. "In 1975, there were 5,000 units of pizza chains but 23,000 hamburger-chain units. By 1977, pizza had grown about 15 percent to 7,250 units, while hamburger increased almost 9 percent—to 25,070 units."

Exhibit A–2 shows the growth rates in sales at franchise restaurants. Sales of franchise pizza chains are increasing faster than those of any other type except seafood in the most recent year. Five of the leading pizza chains are owned by other corporations—PepsiCo owns Pizza Hut; Hunt Resources International, Shakey's; Saga, Straw Hat; LSB (conglomerate), Mr. Gatti's; and Campbell Soup, Pietro's. Even though the major chains have a lower cost advantage, the smaller regional chains have bigger sales in the ethnocen-

APPENDIX: (continued)

Exhibit A-1
Selected Leading Pizza Chains

Chain Headquarters	Year Founded	Past and Current Estimated Fiscal Year Sales ($ millions)	Past and Current Fiscal Year Estimated Net Income ($ millions)	Average Estimated Per-Year Sales ($000)	Average Estimated Per-Person Ticket	Number of Units	Number of New Units Projected 1979	Main, Extra, and Test-Menu Items
Pizza Hut (Wichita)*	1958	$650–$850	$25–$20	$225	$2.25	3,700	450	Super-style pizza, chili, soups, desserts salad bar
Pizza Inn (Dallas)	1960	125–160	2.1–n.a.	240	2.05	730	155	Gourmet pizza, taco pizza, salad bar
Shakey's (Dallas)†	1954	130–145	(−1)–1	320	2.10	500	40	Spaghetti, sandwiches, salad bar
Straw Hat (Dublin, Calif.)‡	1943	56–65	n.a.	310	2.50	220	25	Hot Hat sandwiches deli sandwiches, salad bar

Pasquale's (Birmingham, Ala.)	1962	50–65	0.6–n.a.	225		275	50	Salads
Mr. Gatti's (Louisville)§	1974	25–38	1–1.5	350	2.00	105	90	Sandwiches, salad
Noble Roman's (Bloomington, Ind.)	1969	25–30	2–2.5	525		55	20	Deep-dish pizza
Papa Gino's (Needham, Mass.)	1958	20–25	1–1.2	350		75	18	Hamburgers, desserts
Cassano's (Dayton, Ohio)	1953	18–21	1–n.a.	250	2.75	95	10	sandwiches, seafood, soup
Gigi's (Atlanta)	1959	8–8	n.a.	375	n.a.	20	0	Sandwiches, sausages
Pietro's (Seattle)‖	1964	n.a.	n.a.	500	2.75	15	10	Wines, salad bar

n.a. = Not available.
* Owned by Pepsico.
† Owned by Hunt Resources International.
‡ Owned by Saga Corporation.
§ Owned by LDB, Incorporated (Texas).
‖ Owned by Campbell Soup.
Source: *Restaurant News*, January 8, 1979, p. 123.

APPENDIX: (*continued*)

EXHIBIT A-2
Percent Increase in Sales of Franchise Restaurants by Major Activity, 1975–78*

	1976 Sales ($ thousands)	1975–76	1976–77	1977–78
Seafood	$ 439,762	48.7	49.1	39.2
Pizza	1,091,534	18.1	20.3	22.7
Mexican (taco, etc.)	309,113	13.4	17.4	21.8
Hamburger, hot dog, roast beef	8,030,623	18.8	17.7	20.3
Pancake and waffle	464,462	23.8	12.5	17.0
Steak and full-menu	2,585,786	17.0	13.0	15.2
Chicken	1,609,270	17.1	9.0	10.2
Sandwich and other	75,763	39.8	22.5	48.0
Total	$14,606,313	19.1	16.9	19.4

---

* Estimated by respondents for 1977–78.
Original data source: National Restaurant Association.

tric areas of the United States. The national chains have another problem caused by large corporate structures. To state it simply, the problem is a lack of capable managers.

Regional and medium-sized pizza chains appear to be taking an increasing share of the market from the big three chains (Pizza Hut, Pizza Inn, and Shakey's). But, inflation has slowed their growth, at least in absolute numbers. Most of the small regional pizzerias plan to open only a few (0–10) stores in the near future, whereas the larger chains have been very aggressive in their growth attempts (almost 100 per year). This situation may be a blessing in disguise for the "little guys." Growing pains may have gotten the best of a couple of the larger chains. Costs are rising rapidly, and they are eating away at the marginal profitability of the newly opened pizza restaurants. The regional chains, by restricting their growth to familiar areas, may achieve a higher profitability per store.

Because regional differences are so wide, it is hard for any single chain to customize one product on a nationwide basis. This pattern of pizza acceptance is so diverse and decisive that it would be next to impossible for any company in the business—even the large ones—to achieve market saturation. For these reasons, the small independent pizzeria has an advantage over a national chain operation.

INDEPENDENTS

There are more independent operators of pizza parlors than national chains in the United States. This is because of regional differences in taste. (It is not feasible for chain operators to differentiate their pizzas for all regions.) Independents have the advantage of superior quality in their pizzas because of the individual attention given to each pizza. It is harder to make pizza in multiples than it is hamburgers or chicken. Therefore, most chains make compromises

APPENDIX: (*continued*)

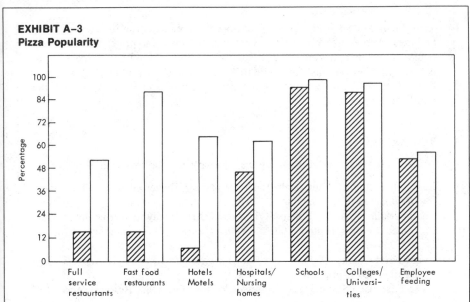

EXHIBIT A-3
Pizza Popularity

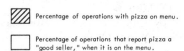 Percentage of operations with pizza on menu.

Percentage of operations that report pizza a
"good seller," when it is on the menu.

Source: "1978 Menu Census," *Institutions,* January 1, 1978, p. 81.

with their dough. For this reason some people feel the national chains' pizza is somewhat plastic, and they prefer "home-made" pizza.

The independents' main disadvantage is that their pizza's quality is not consistent. They are not standardized like the big chains because the quality of the ingredients they buy is not constant. Many experts do believe that pizza is likely to taste better in an independent's restaurant than at a chain's unit. But the independents pay for that advantage with higher food costs. "The food cost at Pizza Hut may be 22 percent or at Shakey's may be 32 percent—there's a difference in weight and the toppings used," says one observer. "An independent operator may run a food cost of 40–45 percent using all fresh, made-to-order methods."

PIZZA POPULARITY

Pizza's mass appeal makes it an American concept. No longer just a teenage favorite, pizza appeals to all age groups. Sales growth over the years has been steady, and the percentage of the population raised on pizza keeps increasing. This gives an added dimension to pizza's popularity growth. Exhibit A–3 gives an indication of its popularity.

APPENDIX (*concluded*)

In final analysis it can be said that pizza varies significantly by geography and meal. People like variety in flavors, crusts, sizes, and prices because pizza is fun as well as nutritional. Pizza is not about to knock off hamburgers as the nation's number one fast food. (In 1978, Americans spent about $11 billion at hamburger restaurant chains.) But pizza, according to trend watchers, has more room to expand.

BIBLIOGRAPHY

The note on the pizza industry was drawn from the following sources:

Bernstein, Charles. "Regionals Push Giants for Bigger Slice of Pizza Pie." *Restaurant News,* January 8, 1979, pp. 122–24.

Chamberlain, Ross. "Italian-Style Foods Are Ready to Move into Wide-Open Central United States." *Quick Frozen Foods,* January 1978, pp. 22–26, 69.

"Fast-Food Chains—Which Fast Foods are Best?" *Consumer Reports,* September 1979, pp. 508–13.

"The Fast-Food Stars: Three Strategies for Fast Growth." *Business Week,* July 11, 1977, pp. 56–68.

"Institution's 400." *Institutions,* July 15, 1979, pp. 64, 321.

Martin, Sam. "Frozen Pizza Preferences by City Drawn from Household Purchases." *Quick Frozen Foods,* April 1979, pp. 14–25.

Moffett, Barbara S. "Hamburgerized Society Takes Time Out for Pizza." Pottsville, Pennsylvania *Republican,* March 21, 1979, p. 28.

National Frozen Food Association, Inc. "State of the Industry." *Mainstream,* April 19, 1978, pp. 8–10.

North American Pizza Association. *A Brief History of the Pizza.*

"Pizza Kitchens' Italian Menu Shifts from Pasta to Full-Dinner Concepts." *Institutions,* January 1, 1978, p. 81.

Richard, Carval R. "Born Again Fast Food Fan Lets Chains Defend Product." *Reno, Nevada, State Journal,* February 10, 1979.

"Study Shows Frozen Pizza Is Protein-Rich with Excellent Vitamin and Mineral Content." *Quick Frozen Foods,* April 1979, pp. 31–32.

Weil, Henry. "Mom, the Flag, Apple Pie, and Pizza." *Good Housekeeping,* May 1979, pp. 20–21.

Wiley, Judy. "Pizza." *Institutions/Volume Feeding,* May 5, 1978, pp. 31–34, 39.

28. Dover Municipal Hospital*

I knew the hospital either made money or lost it based on its professional services. And I knew that you came in contact with the whole hospital through those services; so I said that's what I want to run. I also knew that professional services was filled with the biggest prima donnas on the staff–radiologists, biochemists, cardiologists—each more difficult than the others, and that my predecessor, at age 28, had developed a bleeding ulcer and left.

Chuck Graham, Assistant Administrator
Dover Municipal Hospital

So thought Chuck Graham when he had accepted responsibility for professional services at Dover Municipal Hospital in Delaware. The past few months had given him a much better insight into just how difficult it was to manage those prima donnas, and now, he had to decide whether or not, how, and how tightly, to put the lid on this business of sending tests to outside laboratories.

THE DOVER MUNICIPAL HOSPITAL

The Dover Municipal Hospital (DMH) was a complex of five buildings located in one of the poorest sections of Delaware's capital city. Constructed mostly in the 1930s, the physical plant was drab, and security was tight. After 5 o'clock in the evening, heavy chains and padlocks secured the doors to passageways leading from one building to another. Nearly all of DMH's patients arrived via the hospital's emergency room, and most of the remainder came through its ambulatory care unit. The Dover police department brought DMH most of the hospital cases it picked up; and other hospitals sent their "dump jobs"—indigent, uninsured patients that these hospitals were "too full" to accommodate.

---

* Names and locations have been disguised.

Prepared by Prof. John R. Russell of Boston University's Public Management program, with the help of Terrence Briggs, research assistant.

Throughout its history, DMH had been a teaching hospital, and was currently affiliated with Delaware University's medical school. The hospital was staffed entirely by residents and interns who worked under a salaried senior medical staff that provided both teaching and supervision. No physicians in private practice had staff privileges. All the senior medical staff committed only one quarter to one half their time to the hospital. They were paid an administrative salary by the city, which was all that third-party reimbursers would pay for, and which was only a fraction of what a doctor could earn in private practice or from a full-time job at a private hospital. Most of the physicians augmented their DMH salaries with teaching stipends from the university, salaries received as principal investigators on research grants, jobs managing outside laboratories, and other means. In addition, a special physicians' billing corporation culled the hospital's records to identify patients with third-party reimbursement resources, such as commercial medical insurance, that could be billed for the doctors' services. According to one observer, these arrangements created friction:

> The city wants to pay for clinical care for indigent patients. It doesn't want to pay for research or teaching, or try to make DMH a great research center. The medical staff, on the other hand, are the kind who are willing to give up the money available in private practice because they *are* researchers. And this is where they expect to do their research and their teaching.

The breakdown of billing for inpatient care was Medicare, 20 percent; Blue Cross, 3 percent; Medicaid, 40 percent; commercial insurance, 5 percent; and "self-pay," 35 percent. In practice, the hospital sent all its patients a bill, but did not expect to recover from any of the self-payers. Each year, DMH estimated the cost of the services it would deliver next year, subtracted the amount of third-party and self-paid reimbursements it expected, and submitted the remainder as its annual budget proposal to the city. The city usually cut several million dollars from this proposal, and it was up to the hospital to determine how to absorb the cuts. The current city share of hospital expenses was about $10 million.

At one time, the hospital's capacity had been about 750 beds, but demand for its services had slackened when the advent of Medicaid and Medicare gave many indigents the option of going to other Dover hospitals. Eventually, over half of DMH's beds had been delicensed. The staff currently numbered about 2,000, of whom approximately 150 were interns, residents, or senior medical staff; and the remainder were nurses, technicians, clerical help, maintenance people, messengers, orderlies, and so forth.

The *medical* staff was organized into two major departments—medicine (which included pediatrics, cardiology, gastrointestinal, hematology, pulmonary, and other internal medicine subservices) and surgery (which included obstetrics/gynecology). There was also an outpatient department. The hospital's *administrative* staff reported to an associate director and three assistant directors, one for medicine, one for surgery, and one for professional services. The assistant director for professional services had administrative responsibility for the laboratories and other diagnostic services as well as various support services such as medical records, admitting, social services, messenger, pharmacy, and transportation. (In a few instances, such as the biochemistry laboratory, these professional services subdepartments reported on medical matters to the department of medicine and on administrative matters to the assistant director of professional services.) Both the associate director and the heads of the two medical departments reported to the hospital director, who was hired by the city. The relative influence of the director, the associate director, and the medical staff depended on the individuals who occupied the various positions at a particular time.

CHUCK GRAHAM

In the spring of 1975, the old director of DMH retired and was replaced by Donna Breen. The two were a study in contrasts. Whereas her predecessor has been described as a wily and cautious civil servant who had managed, nevertheless, to alienate city hall, Breen was young, active, and had excellent relations with the city manager and his staff. She had just completed three years as Delaware's assistant commissioner for social services. Breen was without experience in medicine or the health system, but believed firmly that a hospital could be managed well by people who were good managers, but who were not necessarily doctors. She also believed in change and innovation. Good ideas should be tried and mistakes tolerated. Within a few days of Breen's arrival, the associate administrator resigned, and Breen herself decided to occupy the position until a suitable replacement could be found. In the weeks that followed, a great many junior administrators left DMH and others were shifted to new responsibilities. One of the latter was Chuck Graham.

Like Breen, Graham had no medical background. As an undergraduate, he had been a summer intern at DMH and decided he liked working in health. After three years as a Peace Corps volunteer in South America, he returned to DMH, this time as unit coordinator for three wards and the intensive care unit. In this capacity, he was responsible for administrative operations—that is, making sure the units were properly stocked with supplies, dealing with the demands and complaints of the physicians and nurses, supervising the secretaries, and handling other administrative chores. Graham characterized the work as middle management, which to him meant solving whatever problems came up in the wards, and "doing what head nurses used to do but don't want to do anymore." After six months, he had been promoted to assistant manager for the unit coordination department and, after a year, to head of the department. In a few months, he had been promoted again, to junior administrator in charge of 12 support service departments including messenger, transportation, housekeeping, mail, central supply, laundry, kitchen, and several others.

During the fall of 1975, Breen offered Graham any of the three assistant administrator slots, and Graham elected professional services:

> I went from managing 12 departments to managing over 20. They said I could give up transportation and messenger, but I decided to keep them. I knew if I wanted to make the labs work, I'd have to control the process from the time a specimen was drawn to the time the results were delivered back to the doctor.

The main additions to Graham's responsibilities were five large decentralized clinical laboratories and several small research labs that performed one or two tests of clinical importance to the hospital. The five were hematology, biochemistry, bacteriology, pathology, and the blood bank. They employed about 200 people. A physician had medical responsibility for each of the labs, and as administrator, Graham would "more or less," as he put it, be in charge of personnel and budget.

> If a lab wanted to buy a new piece of equipment, I'd have to sign off on it. On the other hand, if I wanted a lab to do a particular test, the doctor could say, "No, I won't do it." Or, he could say, "I'll do it, but it will cost you two technicians and $100,000 in equipment." In other words, the doctors controlled what went on in the labs. And I had to avoid practicing medicine.

Since the lab chiefs were there only part-time, the day-to-day operations were run by chief technicians who ordered supplies, signed documents, scheduled work, and trained other technicians. Bringing outside work into the labs (except under a contract to which the city was a party) was against the law. While the lab chiefs had the final say on hiring technicians, Graham, theoretically, could fire anyone, including the lab chief himself. In practice this was difficult, because replacing a lab chief for $15,000 to $20,000 meant finding someone in the area who had enough other activities to augment his DMH salary, but who still had enough time left to work one-quarter time for the hospital.

THE TEST LIST

During his early days on the job, Graham was plagued by his own ignorance of the labs and by a barrage of complaints from the doctors:

> The physicians, when they're unhappy with the administration, think their best leverage is to complain. Donna [Breen] was moving strongly to shift the balance of who ran the hospital—from the physicians to the administration—and the physicians were fighting it. One thing they did was to complain about the service they were getting from the labs and other support departments. What really was bothering them was Donna's demands that they devote more time to clinical work and less to their research and teaching. She didn't want to support those activities with public funds.

One discovery Graham made was that no one in the hospital knew every test that was offered by the laboratories. His predecessor had tried to compile a list, but failed. Graham decided to try for himself and visited each lab chief:

> They all said, "All we've got is a partial list." I said "May I see it?" and they said, "Sure, but it's out-dated. We've added a few tests and dropped a few others. Also, I'm short a few people because of layoffs, and I really don't have time to put a list together for you now."
>
> I began to think that most of the lab chiefs didn't want the administration to know what tests they could perform. It gave them more flexibility.

After two months of trying, Graham had virtually nothing of any value from biochemistry, pathology, or hematology. Bacteriology and the blood bank, on the other hand, had provided him with lists that he thought were complete.

> What I did was design a form [see Exhibit 1]. Then I said, "I want a completed form for every test you do. It's getting close to budget time; and if you give me ten tests, that's what I'll base your budget on. If you do 50 more on the sly, you'll have to find the funds on your own." Suddenly, I began to get a little cooperation, and the number of tests that everyone was doing began to go up.
>
> I also began to call the chief lab technicians into my office and deal with them because the physicians were only there part of the time.

It took almost six months, but at the end of that time Graham believed he had a collection of forms that represented, quite accurately, the tests currently being performed. He had also developed the following impressions of the five labs:

Hematology. The lab consisted of two units: the main hematology lab, where a staff of 30 technicians, blood drawers, and clerks provided round-the-clock service and performed the bulk of hematology testing, and an outpatient laboratory that ran simple tests on ambulatory patients. Little or no research was done in the lab.

The lab chief, who also ran the hematology lab at another Dover hospital, was extremely independent. Said Graham:

> If he feels like doing a test, he does it. If he doesn't feel like it, you're out of luck. He's very difficult to get along with, but he's a very skillful hematologist and he runs a quality lab. No matter what you want, though, it's push, shove, and toe-to-toe, and there's always a price attached to it.
>
> He runs the lab like a dictator, and the techs do what he tells them to. But he sends them home two hours early if he thinks that's good for them. And he won't let his techs help with some of the chores that all the other lab techs share.
>
> I've been told that he asks only for new equipment in his budget request, even when he knows some of the most vital older equipment will probably break down soon. Then when it does, you have to add money to his original budget so he can go on performing the tests.

EXHIBIT 1
Sample of Completed Test Inventory Form

LAB: Central Hematology

1. *Lab test name:*
   White Blood Count (WBC)
2. *What it does (What is its purpose? What does it test for? What sample (Blood, urine, etc.)? Is it a common test?):*
   Very common test
   Blood sample
   Test for:
   infection—leukemia—surgical conditions
3. *How many tests are done per year?:*
   85,000
4. *Is it part of a larger test (i.e., CMC, SMA 12)?:*
   Yes (CBC)—Usually done on Coulter Counter
5. *Charge of this test as of 8/25/76:*
   Manually—$ 4.00
   Coulter   —$10.00
6. *Cost of the test as of 10/1/76:*
   $0.50
7. *Automated or manual test (batches or individual)?:*
   Either—Automated = 95%
   Manual   = 5%
8. *How long does it take to perform?*
   Coulter —45 seconds
   Manually—10 minutes
9. *Emergency nature or routine (How quickly is it needed)?:*
   Either
10. *What reagents and equipment are used to perform this test?:*
    Reagents: 2% Acetic Acid—Manually (unopette)
                 Isoton—Lyse S—Coulter
    Equipment: Microscope—coverglass—counting chamber—Tally counter
                 (manually)
                 Coulter models
11. *The hours the test is offered (What is the turn-around time)?:*
    24 hours
    STAT Turn-Around Time—30 minutes or less
12. *Procedure used to perform the test (i.e., radioimmunoassay, etc.):*
    Manual Unit Count by Hand
    Particle Count on Coulter
13. *Who takes the specimen? What container is used? How is it transported?:*
    Phlebotomist—Lavender Top Tube (EDTA)
    By hand to tech—messenger service—pneumatic tube
14. *Amount of sample required:*
    At least half-filled Lavender Top Tube

Biochemistry. Staffed 24 hours a day, 7 days a week, biochemistry was the largest producer of tests in the hospital. It was also the biggest money maker and the best equipped. Daily operations were supervised by a Ph.D. in chemistry who presided over a staff of about 45 technicians and support personnel. There was also a consulting biochemistry lab which consisted of two people, on a normal 40 hour week, working on research grants and doing a few sophisticated clinical tests.

The chief of biochemistry was new at DMH. He had come to Graham with several requests from his technicians concerning longer lunch hours or shorter work days—all of which Graham had refused. He spent almost all his time either teaching or working on his research in the consulting biochemistry lab. The Ph.D. in chemistry appeared to run the laboratory.

Bacteriology. From a technical viewpoint, this was the showpiece laboratory. More than in the other labs, the work in microbiology—which involved planting specimens in culture media—was an art form. While the output of the hematology and biochemistry labs was sometimes criticized, the quality of microbiology's output was never questioned. The 40 technicians and bacteriologists worked a five-day week, and because bacteriologists would not read anything that someone else had planted, delays sometimes developed over weekends.

The lab had a degree of fiscal independence that the other labs did not. Almost two thirds of its budget came from a local foundation and another 15 percent from contracts to perform work for Memorial Hospital. DMH paid for only that part of the lab's budget that was not supported by these outside sources.

The lab chief was one of the DMH's medical statesmen. He stayed out of hospital politics and hospital administration, seemed always to have a good word for everyone, and made few demands of his own. When he did ask for something—such as a new piece of equipment—the request was invariably reasonable.

Pathology. Pathology, with about 90 people, was concerned with the analysis of disease. Its lab chief, who was to retire at the end of 1976, had earned a national reputation in anatomical pathology research. His fund-raising efforts had paid for most of the equipment in the building where the lab was housed, and his continuing success at acquiring research grants kept more than a dozen physicians working at the hospital, providing services for which the city did not have to pay. In return for these benefits and the high quality of his work, he expected to be given a budget and then left alone. No one on the Dover University medical staff, except the senior surgeons, ever set foot in the laboratory. Graham visited the area once, but discovered that most of the doors were locked and that keys were not available.

Blood bank. The blood bank managed DMH's inventory of blood and performed the simple tests necessary to dispensing that inventory properly. Nominally, one of the staff surgeons was the lab chief, but the bank was actually managed by a very pleasant and capable nurse.

THE FREE T-4 INCIDENT

As he was developing the list of tests and becoming more familiar with the laboratories, Graham learned that almost $150,000 in testing (10 percent of the total DMH lab budget) was being sent to labs outside the hospital. After securing a breakdown of these outside tests from the DMH accounting department (see Exhibit 2), he noted that over $20,000 was being spent annually just to perform Free T-4 tests at Memorial Hospital, Dover, where the biochemistry lab was run by a doctor who had recently left DMH. He asked several doctors why this was being done:

> Their answer was something like, "Well, young man, this is a superior methodology being used by a superior laboratory. We've done it that way for three or four years, and it's really none of your business."

Rather than let the issue drop, Graham asked other doctors about the Free T-4 test. He discovered that there was a more advanced method of doing the test that could be set up in the DMH biochemistry lab for an initial cost of about $20,000.

> So I went to my laboratory advisory committee (the group of doctors who advise me on the technical and medical aspects of the labs) and asked them if they thought it would be all right to switch to the new method. They said no. Then I went to biochemistry—since Free T-4s are basically biochemistry

EXHIBIT 2
Summary of Outside Laboratory Tests for January 1976

Test	Number of Tests	Price	Total
Ag titer to crystococcus	3	$ 20.00	$ 60.00
Alcohol level*	42	16.00†	672.00
Alkaline phosphatase-fractionated*	2	10.00	20.00
Alpha fetoglobin	2	11.00	22.00
Amino and organic acids	1	10.00	10.00
Aminophylline level	1	23.00	23.00
Analysis of kidney stone	2	9.50	19.00
Analysis of urinary calculus	2	9.50	19.00
Anti-mitochondrial antibodies	1	16.50	16.50
Anti-smooth muscle antibodies	1	16.50	16.50
Anti-toxoplasma antibodies	1	18.00	18.00
Australian antigen (HAA)	77	4.75	365.75
Barbiturate level	3	16.50	49.50
Calcium*	64	6.50	416.00
Carcinoembryonic antigen	11	30.00	330.00
Catecholamines	1	16.00	16.00
Chromosomes	1	100.00	100.00
Cortisol*	12	20.00	240.00
CPK—fractionated*	1	8.00	8.00
CPK—isoenzymes*	22	19.50	429.00
Digitoxin level*	1	25.00	25.00
Digoxin level*	19	21.00†	399.00
Dilantin level*	20	25.00†	500.00

EXHIBIT 2 (*continued*)

	Number of Tests	Price	Total
Dilantin and phenobarb level	1	$ 25.00	$ 25.00
Drugs of abuse	1	35.00	35.00
Elavil and thorazine level	1	20.00	20.00
Estradiol level*	13	38.00†	494.00
Fats*	1	6.00	6.00
Febrile agglutinins	1	10.00	10.00
Fluorescent treponema antibodies	1	9.00	9.00
Free T-4	90	18.00	1,620.00
FSH*	15	22.00†	330.00
Gamma glutamyl transpeptidose	1	10.00	10.00
Gastrin level	5	22.00	110.00
Histoplasma compliment fixation	1	29.25	29.25
Immunoglobulin E	1	15.00	15.00
17-Ketogenic steroids*	1	18.00	18.00
17-Ketosteroids*	1	12.00	12.00
Lap stain*	1	5.00	5.00
Latex fixation*	1	11.00	11.00
Leucine amino peptidose	1	5.00	5.00
LH	15	22.00†	330.00
Lithium level	1	9.00	9.00
Luteinizing hormone	1	19.50	19.50
Mercury level*	2	6.00	12.00
Metanephrine	1	20.00	20.00
Myoglobin	1	10.00	10.00
Mysoline level*	2	18.00†	36.00
Parathyroid hormone	13	49.50	643.50
Phenobarb level*	2	16.50	33.00
Phenothiazine screen	1	3.50	3.50
Phosphorus*	2	4.40	8.80
Pregnanetriol	13	23.00†	299.00
Progesterone*	15	24.00†	360.00
17-OH Progesterone	3	25.00	75.00
Prolactin assay*	13	30.00	390.00
Protein analysis*	1	38.50	38.50
Protein electrophoresis	1	24.00	24.00
Rast profile	1	70.00	70.00
Renin level*	16	25.00	400.00
Rubella	18	8.00	144.00
Salicylate level*	1	5.00	5.00
Semen analysis	1	10.00	10.00
Sensitivity to 5 FC	1	15.00	15.00
Sub B unit level	1	21.00	21.00
Sweat test*	1	35.00	35.00
Tegretol	1	18.00	18.00
Testosterone*	16	32.00†	516.00
Testosterone doxycortisol	1	20.00	20.00
Theophylline level	10	12.00	120.00
Toxic screen (blood)	70	13.00†	910.00
Toxic screen (urine, gastric)	35	13.00†	455.00
Valium level*	2	15.00	30.00
Zarontin level	1	15.00	15.00
	690		$11,634.30

* Can be performed at DMH.
† Average cost.

tests—and asked if he'd be willing to do them in-house. I was told that it was none of my business, that I wasn't a physician, that Memorial's method was much better, and that biochemistry reported to the department of medicine anyway.

I didn't buy it. I called an out-of-state friend who was a hospital administrator and talked to his clinical pathologist, and he convinced me that the new method was not only better, it was cheaper. He also said the Memorial Hospital method cost a lot less than they were charging us, which made me think our money was being used to support teaching and research over there.

I went back to biochemistry and said, "Will you do it?" But he wouldn't. So I talked to hematology, and he said he'd do it provided I gave him another $15,000-a-year technician.

THE OUTSIDE TESTING ISSUE

In the midst of his efforts to resolve the Free T-4 issue and to compile a complete list of tests, Graham received a phone call from the city's auditor. The auditor, too, was concerned about the amount of outside testing. What was even more disturbing to him, many of the outside labs that DMH used were receiving more than $2,000 in business. The law required that dealings of this amount be covered by a contract, and that these contracts be awarded on the basis of competitive bidding. None of DMH's outside sources were under contract.

In response to the auditor's prompting, Graham set out to learn, in detail, how the process worked. He found that physicians who wanted a test performed by an outside laboratory filled out a four-part form and delivered it (together with the specimen) to the secretary of one of the medical staff (see Exhibit 3). (There were about 10 or 12 secretaries throughout the hospital who processed these requisitions.) The secretary sent a messenger, with one copy of the requisition, to the invoice office where the requisition was assigned an invoice number, authorizing payment for the test. The invoice number was filled in on the remaining three copies, the secretary obtained a cab voucher, and the messenger delivered the specimen and two copies of the requisition, via cab, to the outside lab. The remaining copy stayed with the secretary and was eventually filed in the patient's record. When it had performed the tests, the lab returned the results and one copy of the requisition to the DMH secretary (who transmitted the results to the doctor) and retained the second copy for its records. Periodically, the lab submitted a bill to the DMH invoice office, listing all the tests it had performed by invoice number. The invoice office matched the numbers with its copies of the requisitions, paid the outside lab, and sent the requisition copies to the hospital's billing office, so the costs could be billed to patients and third-party reimbursers.

The system seemed to work reasonably well except for several problems. First, messengers from the outside labs who delivered test results (and sometimes picked up requisitions and specimens) often got lost in DMH and

EXHIBIT 3
Requisitions for Outside Laboratory Tests

DATE	NAME OF PATIENT

HOSPITAL NUMBER	MEDICAL SERVICE	WARD OR CLINIC

USE ADDRESSOGRAPH PLATE OR PRINT LEGIBLY

REQUISITION FOR SPECIAL LABORATORY TESTS

INDICATE SOURCE OF REQUEST:

OPD ☐   EMERGENCY FLOOR ☐   PED WALK-IN ☐   HOUSE PATIENT ☐

INDICATE IN WRITING LAB DESIRED	SERVICE ORDER NUMBER	TEST NUMBER	ESTIMATED COST

ATTENDING PHYSICIAN — EXTENSION NO.	AUTHORIZED BY
SPECIMEN SUBMITTED	TEST DESIRED (DO NOT ABBREVIATE)

● DIRECTIONS ●

Specimen containers must be properly labeled with patient and hospital identification prior to being granted a requisition no.

House officers are not to deliver specimens to labs in person, however it is incumbent upon them to specify the lab to which the specimen is to be sent.

Special Instructions

delivered material to the wrong location. Second, the invoice office's copy of the requisition frequently did not arrive in the billing office until long after the patient had been dismissed. Finally, there was no way for the invoice office to know if a test for which it was billed had actually been performed. It was standard practice for the invoice office to pay outside laboratory bills even if the invoice number could not be matched.

When a physician wanted a test done by one of the DMH labs, he obtained the specimen and filled out one of several different in-house, four-part requisition slips, depending on which lab did the test and what test it was (see Exhibit 4). He then stamped the requisition with the patient's name and

EXHIBIT 4
Samples of Requisition Forms for Tests Performed in DMH Laboratories

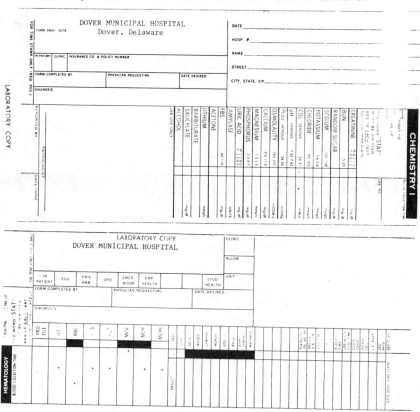

hospital number. One copy of the requisition stayed in the doctor's department for inclusion in the patient's record, and three copies, together with the specimen, were sent to the laboratory where the test was performed. The lab kept one copy of the requisition, sent one back with the test results, and sent the third to the DMH billing office so the patients and third-party reimbursers could be billed. (Instead of doing the work themselves, physicians could simply ask that a test be performed. In that case, a technician drew the specimen and a secretary filled out the requisitions.) The only substantial problem in this procedure occurred when a physician failed to provide the patient's name and number, or did so illegibly, so that subsequent billing was impossible.

Graham discovered several reasons why physicians sent tests to outside labs:

> Sometimes the senior staff just decided that it made sense to use tests we couldn't or hadn't been performing. We also had some senior staff who ran laboratories outside DMH, and they might say to the house officers, "When you need an Australian antigen, send it to my lab, because I know they do it the way I like it done." They might even ask—as they made their rounds with the house staff—why Australian antigen tests hadn't been ordered for some patients and direct that they be ordered.
>
> A lot of other tests went out because the physicians thought our labs did poor work or because they'd had a fight with the lab chief. The head of hematology had chewed out a lot of interns and residents for criticizing, so they tried to avoid his lab. Sometimes a fleeb (the person who draws the blood sample) would mix up specimens, so a physician would get wildly fluctuating results and conclude it was because the lab wasn't testing properly. Some of the newer interns and residents just didn't know what tests our labs could do.

Graham also discussed, with several house physicians and lab chiefs, the issue of contracting for outside laboratory services. They were all adamantly opposed to the concept.

> City Hall had suggested that we give all the outside work to one laboratory, but there were some reasons why this didn't make sense. If you go to the lowest bidder, you may get someone with poor quality control. Then, once they've got your contract, they may begin to cut corners or reserve their fastest service for other customers. We also were using some small specialty labs that were doing work for us almost as a favor, and the price at a big lab under contract would almost certainly be much more.
>
> I told all this to the auditor, but he wouldn't budge. He wanted everything over $2,000 under contract. He didn't care about the difficulties, and he didn't care if it cost more money. Those were my problems. He just wanted to satisfy the legal requirements for a contract.

29. Village Inn*

The Village Inn, located on Bermuda Boulevard in San Diego, was only a few blocks away from San Diego State University and was within several miles of some of California's largest tourist attractions. Visiting lecturers, speakers, professors interviewing for jobs, and people attending conferences at the university resulted in a considerable amount of business for Village Inn.

The Inn was also near a concentrated area of light and heavy industry. The largest shopping mall in San Diego was under construction across the street from the Inn. A relatively new VA hospital and the University Community Hospital were both located within one mile. The Inn's very favorable locational features, together with the fact that it was a franchise of a major national noted chain, had made it a profitable investment. During the past 12 months, the Inn had an average occupancy rate of between 65 and 70 percent, some 15 or more percentage points above the break-even occupancy rate of 50 percent.

Although the Village Inn had only modest competition from other hotel or motel facilities in the immediate vicinity, a new Travelodge Inn was under construction next door. The other closest competitors were nearly three miles away at the intersection of Bermuda Blvd. and Interstate 8. Village Inn offered a full range of services to its guests, including a restaurant and bar. The new Travelodge next door was going to have just a coffee shop. Insofar as its restaurant/bar business was concerned, the Village Inn's strongest competitor was the popular priced University Restaurant, two blocks away. Village Inn did not consider its own food service operations to be in close competition with the area's fast-food franchises or with higher priced restaurants.

OWNERSHIP OF VILLAGE INN

Mr. Johnson, a native of Oregon, opened the first Village Inn in San Diego in 1958. Since that time, he had shared ownership in 15 other Village Inns, several which were in the San Diego area. He opened the Bermuda Blvd. Inn in October 1966. Prior to his focusing on the motel and restaurant business,

---

* Prepared by Diana Johnston, Russ King, and Prof. Jay T. Knippen, the University of South Florida.

Mr. Johnson had owned and operated a furniture store and a casket manufacturing plant. A suggestion from a business associate in Oregon influenced his decision to seek out Village Inn franchises and get into the motel
business. In some of his Village Inn locations, Mr. Johnson leased out the
restaurant operations; however, the restaurant and bar at the Bermuda Blvd.
Village Inn was not leased out. Mr. Johnson felt that because the occupancy
rate at this location was so favorable it was more profitable to own and
operate these facilities himself.

MANAGEMENT OF THE INN

Mr. Johnson had employed Ms. Deeks as the innkeeper and manager of
the entire operation. She had worked in Village Inns for the past seven and
one-half years. Previously, Ms. Deeks had done administrative work for
Davis General Hospital and before that had been employed as a photo lab
technician for two years. Her experience in the motel/restaurant business
included working for several restaurants and lounges for five years as a
cocktail waitress just prior to joining Village Inns.

Ms. Deeks stated that her main reason for going to work for Village Inns
was because she felt there was more money to be made as a waitress than
anything else she had tried. Her formal education for her present position of
innkeeper consisted of a three-week training course at the Home Office
Training Center, in Louisville, Kentucky, and one-week refresher courses
each year at the Training Center.

Recently, the assistant innkeeper had been promoted and transferred to
another location. Both Mr. Johnson and Ms. Deeks agreed that there was a
pressing need to fill the vacancy quickly. It was the assistant innkeeper's
function to supervise the restaurant/bar area and this was the area which
always presented the toughest problems to management. Unless the food
was well prepared and the service was prompt, guests were quick to complain. Poor food service caused many of the frequent visitors to the area to
prefer to stay at other motels. Moreover, it was hard to attract and maintain
a sizable lunchtime clientele without having well-run restaurant facilities.
With so many restaurant employees to supervise, menus to prepare, and
food supplies to order, it was a constant day-to-day struggle to keep the
restaurant operating smoothly and, equally important, to see that it made a
profit. Ms. Deeks, with all of her other duties and responsibilities, simply did
not have adequate time to give the restaurant/bar enough close supervision
by herself.

While searching for a replacement, Mr. Johnson by chance happened to
see a feature article in the *Village Inn Magazine,* a monthly publication of the
Village Inns of America chain—copies of which were placed in all of the
guest rooms of the Inns, describing the operation of a successful Village Inn
in nearby San Bernardino. The article caught Mr. Johnson's attention because it described how the Inn at San Bernardino had gained popularity and

acclaim from guests because of the good food and fast service provided by the head chef of the restaurant operations. After showing the article to Ms. Deeks, Mr. Johnson wasted no time in getting in touch with the head chef of that Inn, Mr. Bernie, and persuading him to assume the new role of restaurant/bar manager for the Bermuda Blvd. Village Inn in San Diego.

FOOD SERVICE FACILITIES AND LAYOUT

Exhibit 1 depicts the arrangement of the lobby area and food service facilities at the Inn. A brief description of the restaurant/bar area follows.

EXHIBIT 1

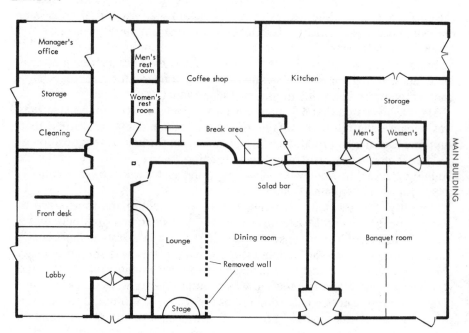

Restaurant. The restaurant itself consists of a dining room which seated 74 people, a coffee shop which seated 62 persons, and a bar which seated 35 people. The Inn's banquet facilities were just behind the main dining room and could seat 125 people.

The essential role of the restaurant and bar area was to provide pleasant and convenient facilities for the Inn's guests. The contractual franchise agreements with the national chain required all owners to provide these services in conjunction with the overnite accommodations. There were periodic inspections of the facilities by a representative from Village Inn's corporate officer. Village Inn required each franchisee to comply with minimum standards for its food service facilities in an effort to promote comparability and ensure attractiveness. Restaurant services were to be available to guests from 6:30 A.M. until 11:00 P.M.

Coffee Shop. The coffee shop was open from 6:30 A.M. to 11:00 A.M. to serve breakfast to motel guests. At 11:00 A.M. these facilities were closed and the main dining area was opened. The coffee shop was occasionally used beyond scheduled hours to serve customers for lunch and dinner when there was an overflow from the dining area. Tables in both the coffee shop and the dining room were decorated and set uniformly.

Dining Room. The dining area was open from 11:00 A.M. until 11:00 P.M. It was located next to the lounge and was physically separated from the coffee shop by a wall. The lunch and dinner offerings featured a salad bar along with menu items which were somewhat uniform with other Village Inns and which were prescribed by the franchise agreement. However, menu deviations were allowed if approved by corporate representatives from Village Inn's central office.

Bar. The bar, separated from the dining room by a partition, was open for business from 10:00 A.M. until 1:00 A.M. It had tables and booths and customers who preferred to do so could have their food served to them in the bar area. A small dance floor was located in front of the entertainer stage near the front window; a juke box furnished music when there was no live entertainment. A small bar stockroom was located at one end of the bar counter. The cash register area was centrally located to receive payments from customers in all three areas—dining room, coffee shop, and bar.

Kitchen. The kitchen facilities, located beside the coffee shop and dining room, had a stainless steel counter at the entrance door from the restaurant area. It was here that waitresses turned orders in to the cooks and that the cooks served the orders up to the waitresses. The cooking area was located in the center of the room and sinks were located along the sides of the kitchen.

RESTAURANT OPERATIONS

As was to be expected, customers' activity in the restaurant area fluctuated widely. Busy periods were generally at the traditional meal hours, but the peak load at any given mealtime period often varied by as much as an hour from one day to the next. At lunchtime, for example, customers sometimes seemed to come all at once, while on other days the arrival times were more evenly distributed throughout the 11:30 A.M. to 1:30 P.M. interval. Experience had shown that these peaks were hard to anticipate and that the staff had to be prepared for whatever occurred. Moreover, on Monday, Tuesday, Wednesday, and Thursday evenings, the customers were mostly business people, sales representatives, and university visitors, whereas on weekends there were more family travelers. Because of the Inn's location, its clientele consisted somewhat more of the former than the latter.

The Inn's restaurant business was also subject to some seasonal fluctuations. There were always a certain number of people who spent the winter in Southern California to escape the harsh northern and Canadian winters; these included not only winter tourists but also the "Canadian Snow Birds" who came to Southern California to work in the late fall and returned to Canada in March or April. In addition, the Inn's business picked up noticeably during the June graduation exercises at San Diego State University and during the week when the fall term opened. By and large, the daily fluctuations were harder to predict than the seasonal fluctuations.

RESTAURANT STAFFING

Because of the alternating between peak periods and slack periods, the employees in the food service area tended to work together, take breaks together, and eat their meals together. In commenting on the kind of people who tended to work in hotel-motel operations, Ms. Deeks indicated that employees were typically gregarious and were there because they wanted to be. They had to contend with an uneven work pace, a low-wage scale (often no more than the minimum wage), and irregular working hours. Since waitresses often earned only a token wage ($0.75 to $1 per hour) and relied mainly on tips for their income, they could not afford many "slow days" or "bad days" at work. Their livelihood and degree of service was dependent upon how well they greeted customers, a friendly smile, prompt service, and, in general, an ability to make customers feel satisfied with the attention they received. When the food was cold or ill-prepared or the service less than expected, customers left smaller tips and the waitresses' disgruntlement carried over to the kitchen staff, the hostess, and the busboys. But even more disruptive than the loss of tips were the customers who complained directly to the Inn's management; if this occurred frequently, then the pressure and anxiety felt by the restaurant staff increased noticeably. Ms. Deeks noted that people who could not adjust to the tempo and temperament of the restaurant business usually did not stay in it long. She noted further that it was extremely difficult to "standardize" the human service aspects of the restaurant business and that trying to attract and keep a good, experienced food service staff was a challenging task.

Ms. Deeks supplied the following job descriptions of the restaurant staff: these descriptions, however, came from her thoughts and perceptions and had never been formally set forth in writing to the Inn's employees:

Bartender. Cut up fruit for drinks, wash glasses, serve counter drinks, clean behind bar, stock liquor and mixes, stock bar, fill room service orders, ring up checks, balance register, and help with inventory.

Hostess/Cashier. Take room service orders, seat guests, deliver menu, direct seating, supervise waitresses and busboys, perform any functions within their prescribed area that speeds service, check out customers from dining area, check out register, file cash register receipts, and assign stations.

Waitresses. Take food orders, deliver order to kitchen, pick up and serve orders, serve food and beverages, and perform any function that speeds service as directed by the hostess.

Busboys. Bus tables, put clean place settings on tables, clean dining rooms, stock supplies, take ice to all areas, get supplies for cooks, help set up banquets, deliver room service orders, help with maintenance, and perform any function that will speed service as directed by the hostess and manager.

Dishwasher. Wash dishes, pots and pans, sweep and mop floors.

Cook. Prepare meals, schedule meals for prep cook, assist management in stock orders, receive food supplies, supervise and direct kitchen help, and assist management in menu changes. Report to management any changes or problems that occur.

Prep cook. Prepare all food that the cook needs for the dinner and evening meals. Assist cook in any meal preparation that is necessary to expedite service to guests. Inform cook of any problems that need attention and help cook see that facilities are clean at all times.

Breakfast Cook. Open the kitchen in the morning. Prepare breakfast food for motel guests. Provide information necessary to maintain in-stock supplies.

MR. BERNIE

When Mr. Bernie arrived to assume his new duties as restaurant/bar manager, he wasted no time in demanding and receiving total obedience from the personnel under his direction. He made it clear that he would not tolerate insubordination and that the consequence would be immediate discharge. Although Mr. Bernie stayed in his new job less than three months (from January to March), he nonetheless created an almost instantaneous climate of ill will and hatred with his subordinates. The intense dislike for Mr. Bernie was voiced by nearly every employee. One example of this was a statement by Elaine, the day hostess/cashier who had been employed in this capacity for the past two and one-half years: "I enjoy my job because I like people. But Mr. Bernie was something else! I generally do not use this term in my vocabulary, but Mr. Bernie was a bastard from the day he arrived until the day he left."

Mr. Bernie's unpopularity was further brought out by a busboy's impromptu comment. Elaine was trying to possibly justify Mr. Bernie's temperament by pointing out that he was not of American nationality. Unable to recall his nationality she inquired of a nearby busboy if he could remember. The busboy immediately and sincerely replied, "He crawled out from under a rock."

Mr. Bernie spent considerable time trying to impress upon his staff the "right way" (his way) of accomplishing tasks (see Exhibits 2 and 3). Most of

EXHIBIT 2
Memo 1 from Mr. Bernie to Food Service Staff

People,
   Please help keep the floor clean.
   If you drop something, pick it up.
   Wipe table off in a trash can.
   If you spill something the mops and brooms are outside.
   It's no fun scrubbing the floor Saturday, and if you don't believe it, be here Saturday night at 11:00 P.M.

Mr. "B"

EXHIBIT 3
Memo 2 from Mr. Bernie to Food Service Staff

March 11

TO ALL FOOD AND BEVERAGE EMPLOYEES:
   I wish to thank each and every one of you for the very good job you have done in the past two weeks. The service has greatly improved on both shifts. There has been a better customer/employee relationship, but there is a long way to go yet. We are nearing the end of our winter season so it is most important to all of us that we concentrate on more service in order to obtain a local year-round business. Appearance, neatness, and good conduct on the floor will obtain this, along with good food.
   A waitress and busboy are like salesmen. The hostess/cashier can determine the quality of service in this organization.
   I expect my waitresses while on duty to be on the dining room cafe floor at all times. I should find waitresses and busboys at the cashier stand only when getting a ticket or paying a check.
   I smoke myself—probably more than the rest of you put together. Your service area is beginning to look like a cigarette factory. I do not expect people to give up their smoking habit, but I do expect them to curtail to the rules and regulations of Village Inn, Inc., and those of the health department, "No Smoking on Premises." I would not like to enforce this law.
   In the last two weeks I have walked into the operation after a busy breakfast or dinner and found everyone sitting around the first three booths of the cafe. I do not say it cannot be used, but when I find no waitresses on either floor day or night and customers have to call for service because waitresses are off the floor, I believe each waitress and busboy on all shifts should ask themselves one thing: what kind of service would I like if I were a guest? There is only one thing I know, in this part of California when the tourist is gone, half of the employees are worked on a part-time basis, which is not good on anyone's pocketbook. Therefore, I say let's not be second best but let's be first.
   With regard to employees taking their meal breaks, I do not wish to schedule them but I cannot have everyone eating at once. Busboys will eat one at a time.
   Thank you once again for your good performance.

Mr. "B"

the employees resented Mr. Bernie's close supervision. Ann, a veteran employee and waitress, describing her resentment, said, "No one really needs to supervise us, especially the way Mr. Bernie stood over us. Usually the hostess is the supervisor, but all the old girls know what they are doing and everyone does their job."

Although an intense dislike for Mr. Bernie was foremost in the minds of the employees, he did manage to make a number of improvements and innovations. Physical changes became obvious within all departments under his authority. In the kitchen a general cleanup campaign was instituted, an order spindle was added, and new oven equipment installed. In the coffee shop and restaurant, new silverware, china, and glasses were purchased, and the menu was improved and complemented by the use of a salad bar. *Explicit* work duties were written and verbally defined to all employees under Mr. Bernie.

Mr. Bernie separated the cashier/hostess function into two distinct jobs. The cashier was confined to the cash register station and given instructions as to the duties she was to perform in that area. The hostess was given instructions to greet people, seat them, and supply menus. When Mr. Bernie was absent, he instructed the hostess to see that the waitresses and busboys carried out their jobs efficiently and effectively. According to Gay, one of the two-day hostesses:

> When Mr. Bernie was here I never had any employee problems. Waitresses and busboys did what I asked. But now if we have a busboy absent or we are crowded, some of the waitresses inform me they will not bus tables. Today there's no one in charge of anything. We need more employees here. It is always better to have more help than not enough. That's one thing Mr. Bernie did, he doubled the help the day he came.

The changes which Mr. Bernie instituted regarding the waitresses were significant in several aspects. All waitresses were required to wear fitted uniforms. This necessitated them driving across town for a uniform fitting. Mr. Bernie's detailed scrutinizing consisted of specific instructions on how to serve customers and which station locations each waitress would serve. He even went as far as to show them how to wrap the silverware and the napkins, and gave explicit instructions to veteran waitresses on how to fill out the order tickets.

Mr. Bernie had the wall between the dining room and bar taken down. He then brought in an entertainer who supplied dinner music for both the restaurant and bar guests. Today, the waitresses are getting some dysfunctional effects from this innovation; according to one:

> Mr. Bernie brought in an organ player. While this was conducive to a more pleasant dining atmosphere, the organist was not good enough to keep the people beyond their meal. But now that Mr. Bernie is gone, our new entertainer is causing some serious problems. For example, last night I had a family of five

sit at a table in my station for two and a half hours after their dinner. If people won't leave and they won't buy drinks, I can't make tips.

Mr. Bernie instilled an atmosphere of insecurity and day-to-day doubt in the minds of the employees as to how long they could weather the barrage of innovation and directives. To some, just remaining on the job became a challenge in itself. Elaine (the day hostess) phrased it in this manner:

> I have been employed with the Village Inn for almost two and one-half years. I have worked most of my life and have never felt insecure in any of my jobs. The last job I held was a swimming instructor for ten years with the Academy of Holy Names in San Diego. The reason I had to leave there was because of the change in the educational background requirement which called for a college degree.
>
> My children are all college graduates with highly responsible positions. They achieved this by hard work. I instilled this in their minds because I am a hard worker. But when Mr. Bernie was here, I experienced for the first time in my life the feeling of not knowing from one day to the next if my job would be there when I came to work. What few personnel he failed to drive away, he fired.

Linda, who was a bartender in the lounge area, commented further on Mr. Bernie's supervisory tactics:

> Bernie was a rover. When he walked into an area, including my area, the bar, he could not stand to see someone not involved with busy work. He even made me clean under the bar on the customers' side. I'm not a maid and I often wanted to tell him so. But the way he was hiring and firing employees, I just kept my mouth closed and did as he told me. My experiences with Mr. Bernie were nothing compared to the relationship he had with the busboys. From the bar he would sneak around and watch them in the dining area. If they did anything the least bit out of line, he would call them aside and give them lectures that could last for half an hour. He really treated the busboys like the scum of the earth. When the boys did get a break, they would come over to the bar and get a coke and ice. You know, he even started charging them 25 cents for that!

Sam, a cook hired by Mr. Bernie, offered a slightly different perspective view of Mr. Bernie:

> My wife was working here as a hostess and I used to bring her to work everyday. One day I came in with her and for some reason they were short of help in the kitchen. They needed a dishwasher. I was sitting in the coffee shop and Mr. Bernie walked over and asked me if I could use a job. I had been interested in cooking ever since I was in the Navy. There are two things you can do in your spare time in the Navy . . . drink and chase women, or find a hobby. I found a hobby, which was cooking. On my two days off I used to go down to the galley and help the cooks. There I learned everything I know today. When I got out of the service I worked as a prep cook in a restaurant in Pennsylvania for a year or so. My real specialty is soups, though. Anyway, I had been a dishwasher here for about two days when the cook walked off the

job after three years of service here. Mr. Bernie came in and asked how I'd like
to be the new cook and here I am today. Mr. Bernie really taught me a lot. He
taught me that a restaurant has three things it must give a customer: service,
good food, and a pleasing environment to dine. If you have these three, customers will return.

I've spent most of my working career in the automotive business doing such
things as driving trucks. But I'm really into this cooking thing. Mr. Bernie
taught me that about 50 percent of the customers who come in and order from
the menu have no idea what they are ordering. The menu is too complicated.
The customer doesn't know what he thinks he ordered and what you think he
ordered. Another thing that fascinates me is trying to think like the customer.
His definition of rare, medium, and well done is altogether different from my
idea of how it should be. One addition by Mr. Bernie was the salad bar. This is
a tremendous help to my job. If the waitress can get to the customer before they
go to the salad bar and take their order, this gives me plenty of lead time to be
sure the meal will be cooked right and served in the attractive manner that Mr.
Bernie was so particular about. This lead time is especially important on those
days that we are unusually busy. For example, I have prepared as many as
250 meals on some days and as few as 40 on others.

The employees who left or were dismissed by Mr. Bernie included two
hostesses, two waitresses (one had an employment record at the Inn that
dated back five years), and two busboys. Two of the personnel that Mr.
Bernie fired have since returned to their old jobs. One of the waitresses that
subsequently was rehired described her reason for leaving as follows:

> I really enjoy being a waitress and have been here for about five years. The
> work isn't really too hard and the pay is good. I took all the "directives" I
> could take from Mr. Bernie! A week before he left, I gave my resignation and
> took a vacation. When I returned, I learned of his departure and here I am
> again. I'm really glad things have worked out as they did.

Ms. Deeks opinion of Mr. Bernie's performance was one of general dissatisfaction with the way he handled his dealings with employees:

> Mr. Bernie was highly trained, but he was an introvert who stood over his
> subordinates and supervised everything they did. Cooks are a rare breed of
> people all to themselves. The help situation has changed greatly in the past few
> years. It used to be that you could give orders and tell people what they were
> supposed to do. Now, you have to treat them with "kid gloves" or they'll just
> quit and get a job down the street. This problem is particularly true with cooks.
> They are very tempermental and introverted and they expect to be treated like
> "prima donnas."
> Mr. Johnson and I really tried to work with Mr. Bernie during his 90-day
> trial period. We knew that terminating him without a replacement would be
> hard on us, but we had no choice. We are now without a restaurant/bar manager
> or assistant innkeeper. We have been looking for a replacement, but finding a
> person that is knowledgeable in both the hotel and restaurant management is
> something of a chore.

CONDITIONS AFTER MR. BERNIE'S DEPARTURE

Since Mr. Bernie had departed, the restaurant personnel were in general agreement that their operation was understaffed. Often guests were seated in both the dining area and coffee shop waiting to be served; even though the waitresses were apparently busy, many customers experienced waits of 20 to 30 minutes. Elaine, one of the two hostesses, explained the lack of prompt service as follows:

> The coffee shop is supposed to take care of the guests until 11 A.M. and then the restaurant part is to be opened. Mr. Bernie handled the situation differently than we do now. When he was here he would not open the dining hall in the morning no matter how crowded the coffee shop was. I can remember mornings when people were lined into the hallway and all the way outside the front door. I guess he knew two girls and two busboys could not handle two rooms.
>
> But today we handle the situations differently. If the coffee shop gets crowded or we have many dirty tables we open up both rooms. This really makes it hard on the girls trying to serve both rooms. What we generally have when this happens is poor service to all concerned and consequently some guests leave unhappy and without tipping the waitresses.

Ralph, a busboy, indicated the problem was not exclusively felt in the restaurant only. He seemed to feel the lack or absence of a manager was the primary problem:

> Ms. Deeks just can't run this operation by herself. It is physically impossible for her to be here seven days a week from 6:30 A.M. until 11:00 P.M. and manage the kitchen, restaurant, bar, coffee shop, front desk, maid service, and maintenance crew all at the same time.

Some of the employees perceived their duties and functions differently. For instance, the restaurant's two-day hostesses alternated work shifts. Elaine would seat customers, give them their menu, take beverages to customers to help out the waitresses, help out busing tables when it was very busy and had very little to say in supervising the waitresses and busboys. On the other hand, the other day hostess, Gay, would seat customers and give them menus but would not do what she perceived to be the duties of waitresses and busboys. Instead, she exercised supervisory authority over these personnel and when they were not able to get everything done, she would try to find out why not, rather than doing them herself.

There were similar discrepancies in the ways the waitresses and busboys performed their duties. In some cases, waitresses would help busboys clear tables during overcrowded periods and busboys would also help out the waitresses by bringing water and coffee to the people who were waiting to be served. The other side of the coin occurred also. Some of the waitresses, particularly those who had been employed for some time, felt that it was the busboys' responsibility to clear tables and would not lift a finger to help them. In these instances the busboys did not go out of their way to help the waitresses.

Gene, the other bartender, offered yet another view of the Inn's problems:

> You know, I could tell management a few things about the restaurant business if they asked me. I knew from the first day Mr. Bernie arrived that he wouldn't work out. But Mr. Bernie is not the only problem they had. One of the biggest problems they have with this restaurant is in the banquets they have. We have a luncheon here every week with such clubs as the Sertoma, Kiwanis, and the like. Their luncheons start at noon and last until 1:30 or so. Have you ever noticed how they park outside? Well, I'll tell you they park all over the front parking lot and when local people drive by they assume our restaurant is full and go on down the street. These businessmen tie up most of our help and yet the dining room may be empty. These banquet people don't buy drinks with lunch like the local businessmen do who take clients out to lunch and often have a bigger bar bill than their restaurant checks. There's only one successful way to have a banquet business and that's not next to your dining room. If the banquet room was on the opposite side of the restaurant, then it would be okay.

EMPLOYEE TRAINING

The Village Inn provided a minimal amount of job training for employees with the exception of the management staff. The contractual agreement between franchise owners and Village Inns of America required all innkeepers, assistant innkeepers, and restaurant managers to attend the Home Office Training Center within a year of being hired. They also had to attend refresher courses on a yearly basis.

The restaurant personnel, in contrast, were given little job training. Instead, efforts were made to hire cooks, waitresses, and bartenders who had previous experience in the field. But in practice this policy was not always adhered to—as was exemplified by the way Linda became a bartender:

> My training on the job was really short and sweet. Mr. Bernie came in one day and inquired, "How would you like to be a bartender?" At the same time he handed me a book on mixing drinks. I went home and studied it and "poof" I was a bartender.
>
> Within a short time on the job I began getting a lot of help and advice from the waitresses who came over to the bar for drink orders. Sometimes when we do get a drink mixup they are very nice about it. I've even had people from other departments in the Inn to help me when the situation called for it. One night I had two ladies in here, one from the "crazy house" and the other her bodyguard. After a few "shooters" as they referred to the drinks, they asked for their check. They wanted to use a credit card instead of paying cash. This was not a problem but so I would get my tip I offered to carry the check and credit card to the front desk. Then they said I would cheat them on their bill once I was out of their sight. The front desk man heard the hassle and came in and escorted the ladies to the desk. This type of working together happens here all the time. Ms. Deeks, my boss, is really a nice person to work for. She doesn't come around very much, except if she needs information or to advise me about something.

PAY SCALES

Management indicated that there was a shortage of good employees and that a low pay scale was characteristic of the restaurant business. Some of the employees expressed their awareness of this also.

(Bartender) Linda: The pay scale is really low compared to other areas. My first job as a cocktail waitress in San Diego was in a dive downtown. They paid us 50 cents an hour plus tips, but the tips were lousy. Here they're paying 80 cents an hour plus tips which is somewhat better, but it's still way below the wages elsewhere. I really don't feel like I'm suited for this work, but I make more money at the bar than I did as a cocktail waitress.

(Hostess) Gay: I make $2 an hour here. With all the responsibility and experience I've had, the pay scale here compared to other parts of the country is deplorable. The busboys make almost as much as I do. They make $1.45 an hour plus 15 percent of the waitress's tips. Even though the pay scale is low, there is always overtime available to most of all of the employees who want it. My husband who is a cook here has worked 145 hours so far in this two-week pay period and he still has five more days to go.

Barb, one of the waitresses, further substantiated the availability of overtime by saying she got at least one hour overtime each day. She attributed the extra hours of overtime to the fact that the Inn's restaurant staff always seemed to have at least one person unexpectedly absent each day.

The problem in the restaurant was apparently compounded by the fact that it was operating with a minimum number of employees. Timmy, a busboy, indicated the wide range of activities that were expected of him and the other busboys:

> We do everything; I clean and bus tables, sweep floors, and do janitorial work. I don't mean in just my area either. If the front desk needs a porter or runner, or if some type of room service is needed, I do that too. Mr. Bernie was really hard to work under but he always confined us to restaurant duties. When he was here we didn't do all those jobs outside our area. Those duties were handled by a front desk porter. But, I'd still rather have to do things all over the place than have to put up with Mr. Bernie.

SEARCHING FOR MR. BERNIE'S REPLACEMENT

In outlining her thoughts on trying to replace Mr. Bernie, Ms. Deeks stated:

> I really had a good track record with personnel before Mr. Bernie came along. I strongly objected to his dictatorial supervision. In my experience I have learned employees perform their jobs better when left alone most of the time. I once tried to set up off-job activities for my employees. I reserved a room at the hotel for employees to meet together after working hours to play cards and drink coffee. Unfortunately the room was not used enough to merit keeping it on reserve. However, I still support functions that the employees

suggest. We are presently sponsoring a bowling team that two of my waitresses belong to.

Most of the waitresses would rather work night shifts if they have their choice. Some of the girls have children and husbands that require them to be home at night. This balances the shifts real well. One reason I prefer to schedule the waitresses is because of peculiar problems which occur. For example; I have two extremely good waitresses that will not work on Saturdays and Sundays. The other waitresses do not know this and I feel if I were to allow the hostess to do the scheduling I would have some immediate personnel problems. To further complicate any benefits that might be derived by allowing the hostesses to make out schedules, it would be necessary to reveal my awareness of the slower waitresses we have which I schedule on Saturday and Sunday—our slower business days.

I am really more active in management and day-to-day problems than most of the employees realize. Any significant changes in rules or policies are usually passed in the form of a written memo. I prefer to handle communication in this way for two reasons: first, there is no room for distortion, and second, it does not give the employees a feeling that they are being closely supervised. However, I do need an assistant to help me manage this place. I have verbally put the word out to other Inns and motels. I'm really not concerned whether I get a restaurant manager or an assistant innkeeper so long as he has a knowledge of the food and beverage service. I'm really going to be cautious in the selection of this person as I don't want to jump out of the frying pan into the fire.

The absence of Mr. Bernie is now a well-known fact by all of the Inn's personnel. However, it was not known to everyone. One day, Mr. Trainor, a well-liked sales representative walked into the restaurant and inquired, "Where is Mr. Bernie today?" There was a hush of silence and then in answer to his own question he replied, "Why is everyone smiling?"

30. Hoosier Home Federal Savings and Loan Association*

In August 1978, Charles Sims, vice president in charge of Personnel, went into Lew Winter's office complaining about the high turnover rate in the Loan Division. "I thought we had finally solved our personnel problem in the Loan Division when we still had Dan Davis and Ed Smith a year after they were hired. After firing Davis two weeks ago and finding out today that Ed plans to take another job, I am back where I started from 18 months ago." Mr. Winters looked up from his work, gave a sneer and declared, "As long as we have the old man's nephew running that division, the situation will never improve. How in the hell does Spears expect to run this Association when the old man hands over the reins if he can't even keep one division operating smoothly?"

BACKGROUND

The Hoosier Home Federal Savings and Loan Association (HHF) is a medium-sized savings and loan association doing business in three contiguous counties in northern Indiana. In recent years, Hoosier Home Federal has experienced a sizable growth in assets (see Exhibit 1). Part of this growth is attributable to an increase in the tri-county population from 260,000 in 1965 to just over 350,000 in 1975. The continuing industrialization of this area was expected to result in a 5–10 percent annual increase in population over the next five years.

A second force behind HHF's growth was the adoption of more aggressive strategies. In the past, HHF had avoided the use of branch locations. It was estimated that a branch location required a capital outlay of between $75,000 and $150,000, depending on the cost of the land. In addition to the large capital outlay, John Curry, chairman of the board, did not like the idea of having three or four employees in any HHF branch with no senior officer around to supervise. Mr. Curry also felt HHF's policy of paying the highest interest rates on savings allowed by law eliminated the need for a branch network. At the end of 1977, Hoosier Home Federal had one branch and a main office. The branch was created when HHF moved into a newly constructed main office in 1969. After the move it was decided to keep the old main office as a branch.

---

* Prepared by Prof. W. Harvey Hegarty, University of Indiana.

EXHIBIT 1

HOOSIER HOME FEDERAL SAVINGS AND LOAN ASSOCIATION
Statement of Financial Position, 1975, 1976, and 1977

$000

Assets	1975	1976	1977
Cash & Other	$ 1,656	$ 1,799	$ 1,217
Government Securities	10,403	9,101	4,688
Federal Home Loan Bank Stock	1,050	1,050	2,204
First Mortgage Real Estate Loans	127,438	136,866	155,354
Collateral Loans	437	585	772
Property and Fixtures	4,135	4,772	5,895
Total	$145,119	$154,173	$170,130
Liabilities			
Savings and Investment Accounts	$118,463	$124,688	$139,861
Escrows and Loans in Process	8,051	9,741	9,799
Customer Collect & Accounts Payable	62	105	121
Advance Payments by Borrowers	149	162	158
Advances from F.H.L.B.	7,794	8,672	9,104
Reserve for Loan Losses	593	586	637
Capital and Surplus	10,007	10,219	10,450
Total	$145,119	$154,173	$170,130

During 1977, Irvin Spears was able to convince his uncle that if HHF did not provide branches for its customers, it would eventually lose customers to the three rival savings and loan associations in the area (see Exhibit 2). HHF opened its second branch in early 1978 in the fashionable western end of the county. Since its opening the branch had been very successful at attracting new customers. More important, 40 percent of HHF's business was coming from residents of the two adjacent counties.

EXHIBIT 2

Assets of Tri-County Banks and Savings and Loans for 1975, 1976, and 1977; and Number of Offices as of December 1977

Institution	Total Assets ($ millions)			Number of Offices
	12/31/75	12/31/76	12/31/77	12/31/77
American Bank and Trust Bank	$229	$251	$286	7
Citizens Trust Bank	227	257	295	5
Farmers Federal Savings and Loan	126	137	150	1
First National Bank	594	631	716	12
First Federal Savings and Loan	139	193	262	13
Hoosier Home Federal Savings and Loan	145	154	170	3
Merchants and Investors Bank	118	129	136	4
Peoples State Bank	74	89	86	2
Pioneer Federal Savings and Loan	87	102	116	3
Second National Bank	581	615	654	10

After reviewing the campaign's success, Mr. Curry agreed to spending most of HHF's advertising budget for TV spots.

During 1978, Spears developed a master plan for branch development which called for the addition of two new branches each year for the next five years. Two branches, to be opened in early 1979, were presently under construction—one in each of the two adjacent counties.

A second newly adopted strategy that had contributed to HHF's growth was the use of TV advertising. In the past HHF advertised exclusively in the financial section of the *News-Reporter*, a regional newspaper. The ads emphasized to the saver that HHF paid the highest interest rate allowed by the regulatory authorities. Mr. Curry considered TV advertising a waste of money and did not believe that it could attract new customers. However, Mr. Spears, with the help of Richard Holland, HHF's president, prepared a very persuasive presentation during 1977 that convinced Mr. Curry and the board of directors to try TV advertising on a trial basis. Mr. Spears was assigned the task of working with HHF's advertising agency to develop a TV campaign. The ads began in the fall of 1977 and were judged by management to be successful in creating consumer awareness of Hoosier Home Federal.

JOHN CURRY

Hoosier Home Federal was headed by John Curry, chairman of the board of directors. The Curry name had been affiliated with Hoosier Home Federal ever since it was established in 1899. Mr. Curry was a highly respected member of the financial community and possessed a great deal of knowledge about the savings and loan industry. He was regarded by the officers of HHF as an expert in his field. However, he was a very autocratic individual. It was often said that Mr. Curry believed there were two ways of doing things: his way and the wrong way. If he believed in a new idea, it was implemented; if he did not like an idea, it was dropped.

One case where his unilateral decision making may have proved costly was in data processing services. In 1976, HHF had to decide whether to update and modernize its existing data processing system, which it rented, or to buy computer services from an outside source. After listening to a sales presentation by Federal Home Loan Bank representatives, Mr. Curry decided to rent time from the FHLB. The FHLB representatives said they would be able to handle all of HHF's computer needs within nine months. No outside experts were consulted to determine what HHF's data processing requirements were and no systematic evaluation of the FHLB proposal was conducted to determine whether the service HHF would receive would really be adequate. Several of the associations's officers did express skepticism at the FHLB proposal but were ignored.

As it turned out, the data processing tie-in with the FHLB quickly proved unsatisfactory. Only half of Hoosier Home Federal's data processing could be accommodated by the FHLB and the service was slow; the rest continued to be handled in-house on HHF's outdated equipment. As a consequence, Hoosier Home Federal found itself burdened with the costs of using and maintaining two different data processing systems. To correct this, HHF had plans underway to modernize its own system. The Federal Home Loan Bank had been informed that as soon as HHF's new system was operational, their arrangement on computer services would be discontinued.

In addition to making the key decisions, Mr. Curry also believed in maintaining control over the board of directors. Mr. Curry handpicked the members of the board of directors; all of the present board members were respected businessmen in the county and most of them had retired from full-time positions at firms in the area. Their average age was 67 years.

The board met once a month and had the final say on any decision affecting the association. A major complaint by the loan officers was the number of loans that had to be taken to the board for approval and any loans that did not meet the guidelines had to be approved by the board. This policy required each loan officer, during peak loan demand, to prepare 15 or 20 loan files for the board's review. Board approval also had to be obtained for all nonroutine expenditures over $100.

RICHARD HOLLAND

Mr. Holland held the title of president and supervised the daily operations of HHF's five functional divisions (see Exhibit 3) for HHF's organizational chart). In the past this did not require a great deal of responsibility, but as Mr. Curry neared retirement more of the operating decisions were being made by Mr. Holland.

Mr. Holland had a degree in agriculture from Purdue University. Prior to joining Hoosier Home Federal in 1969, he had worked as a branch manager for a commercial bank for ten years. Mr. Holland's first assignment was as a mortgage loan officer. He progressed rapidly and was made a vice president in 1972; six years later he was promoted to executive vice president. In 1978, when Mr. Curry assumed the title of chairman of the board and chief executive officer, Mr. Holland was made president.

Mr. Holland's personality contrasted with Mr. Curry's. Holland was very friendly with everyone and never lost his temper with employees. He was very open minded and could be persuaded to adopt new methods and ideas if they were substantiated by convincing data. Holland had been instrumental in carrying the banner of change in the board of directors meetings—Holland and Curry were the only officers of HHF that were members of the Board.

Much of Holland's success at Hoosier Home Federal was due to his ability to work successfully with Mr. Curry. Holland knew when to push and when to keep quiet, and he clearly enjoyed Mr. Curry's confidence. Holland recognized that Mr. Curry was grooming his nephew, Irwin Spears, to eventually assume the leadership of Hoosier Home Federal. This did not bother

EXHIBIT 3
Organization Chart

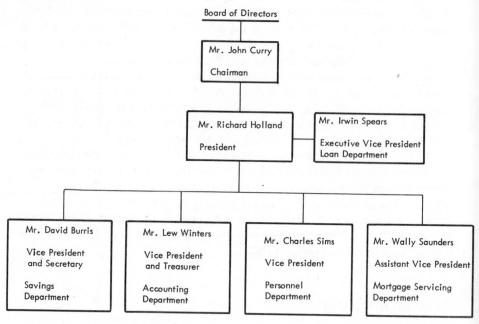

Mr. Holland, however, because he planned to retire in four years and did not feel Mr. Spears would have enough experience to take over the top spot before then. Mr. Curry was planning to retire in January 1980 when he reached the age of 70.

In his interview with the casewriter, Mr. Holland indicated that his worst experience as president at Hoosier Home Federal concerned the dismissal of Mr. Breedlove, age 57, who had been an assistant vice president in the mortgage lending area and who had been employed at HHF for 15 years. Breedlove had been fired at the insistence of Irwin Spears. Spears wanted Breedlove "out of the way" in his attempts to revise and improve HHF's mortgage lending procedures. In Holland's view, Breedlove had been a good employee—a bit crotchety perhaps, but amiable and hardworking. Holland had been greatly disturbed at firing an employee whom he had worked with as a fellow loan officer—especially under the circumstances.

THE LOAN DIVISION

HHF's loan division was responsible for generating loans for the deposits brought in by the savings department. Loan officers were responsible for a loan from the time of application until it was closed and a permanent file made. Exhibit 4 is a flowchart of a loan officer's duties. During the winter months, when loan demand was slack, the loan officers were assigned a

EXHIBIT 4
Flowchart of a Loan Officer's Duties

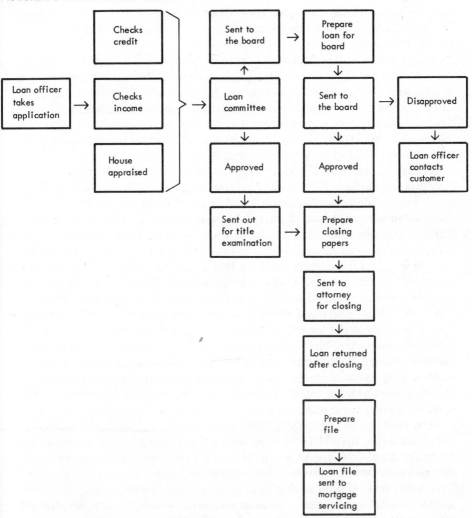

number of special projects, such as working on branch applications or conducting efficiency studies of the Loan Division.

Irwin Spears was in charge of Hoosier Home Federal's loan division. He had a B.A. degree from Butler University and an M.B.A. from Indiana State University. After graduation, he served two years in the Peace Corps before joining HHF in 1975. At the outset, Spears worked briefly in several of HHF's different departments to gain an overall knowledge of the business. He was soon assigned to the Loan Division as a loan officer.

Shortly after Mr. Spears joined the loan division, conflicts began to develop between him and the other loan officers. The loan officers resented Mr. Spears sometimes leaving work early to play golf and taking extra-long lunch hours with friends at the Riverview Country Club. Mr. Holland justified Spears' activities to the other loan officers by pointing out that he worked late several nights a week.

In January 1977, Mr. Spears was promoted to vice president in charge of the loan division. Two months later, Spears was the driving force behind the termination of Mr. Breedlove. Prior to his dismissal, Breedlove had indicated that he could not make ends meet with the salary he was receiving. Spears refused to recommend a raise for Breedlove; instead Spears had indicated to Mr. Holland that he could not gain complete control over the loan division unless Mr. Breedlove was removed.

During the fall of 1977, Spears set out to improve the operations of the loan division for the 1978 lending season. Most of HHF's home mortgage loans were made between March 1 and September 30, during the height of the residential real estate market. Mr. Spears took a number of steps to increase the efficiency of the loan division. A new phone system was installed that allowed secretaries to answer the phones of the loan officers. Two new secretaries were hired so that each loan officer would have a secretary. Electronic calculators were purchased for the loan officers that enabled them to avoid the time consuming task of doing calculations by hand. Plans were also made to bring a branch manager and several management trainees into the loan division during peak periods to help out the two new loan secretaries. Mr. Spears made one final alteration of the operation of the loan division. In an attempt to avoid risky loans on low quality housing, underwriting standards were raised. Under the new standards a house had to sell for at least $15,000 and be located out of a declining neighborhood before it would qualify for a loan.

In addition to the preceding changes in internal operations, Spears also attempted to improve HHF's image among the real estate brokers and builders in the area. Over the years, HHF had gained a reputation among builders and realty firms for giving "short appraisals" (where a house is appraised for a value less than its selling price). As a result, builders and real estate agents usually steered their customers to HHF's competitors. Mr. Spears discussed this problem with the firm that did HHF's appraising and received the firm's assurance that the problem would be eliminated.

A second step Spears took to improve HHF's relationship with realty firms and builders was the development of a newsletter. The newsletter was sent out monthly to real estate brokers and builders and highlighted Hoosier Home Federal's lending policies and the current mortgage interest rates. The response from the builders and realty firms was very favorable.

The addition in August of two new loan officers was particularly beneficial. Both Mr. Davis and Mr. Smith were young and aggressive individuals. Mr. Davis had completed two years of college and had worked at a small savings and loan in Chicago for three years prior to joining Hoosier Home Federal. Mr. Smith, on the other hand, was a spring 1977 graduate of Ohio

State University with a major in finance, and did not have any previous business experience. Both individuals were hard workers and took pride in doing their best.

In organizing the staff of the loan division, Mr. Spears adhered to the philosophy that competition increases productivity. With this in mind, he established two teams made up of a loan officer and a secretary. Each team was assigned a specific volume of loan closings. Data was kept on each team's performance and a total of the loans closed by each loan officer was announced at the end of the month. The team system worked out better than had been expected. During May 1978, Smith and Davis closed $2.4 million of loans and took a total of 135 loan applications. This was an all-time record for the loan division, and Spears was very satisfied.

The large volume of loans in May had required Davis and Smith to work 70 to 80 hours a week. Very rarely did one of them stay after work without the other also staying. Neither loan officer was compensated for the additional time he spent after work. Both loan officers realized that their future success at HHF was dependent on how the senior officers viewed their performance.

In early June several problems came to the attention of Mr. Spears. While reviewing a few of the loans that had been closed in May, Spears discovered a number of mistakes. As a result of these findings he decided to take a sample of ten loans from the loans closed by each loan officer during the month of May. Upon investigation, Spears discovered Davis had made mistakes on four of the ten loans he closed while Smith had made no mistakes. Three of the mistakes Davis made were of a serious nature. After talking to the loan officers about the situation, it became apparent they were both under a tremendous amount of pressure. Smith indicated that he had probably made a number of mistakes on files that were not checked.

Mr. Sims, vice president of personnel, brought a second problem to the attention of Mr. Spears. Mr. Sims informed Spears that Davis was turning off his phone at the switchboard so that he could get his work done. Mr. Sims said the switchboard operator came to him in tears recently because of the profane language customers would use when she told them Davis was not available. After talking to Mr. Smith, Mr. Spears discovered that Smith and a management trainee had been answering all of the information calls and had even been receiving calls from Davis's customers.

The final problem brought to the attention of Mr. Spears also came through Mr. Sims. Mr. Sims had indicated that Smith had come to him, disturbed about the situation in the loan division. Smith had two gripes that he wanted to get off his chest. The first gripe Smith had concerned the use of branch managers and management trainees in the loan division during peak periods. He thought it was an asinine idea, but was scared to tell Mr. Spears that one of his ideas was stupid. Smith said he was under enough pressure without having to train someone to handle mortgage loans. He indicated he spent more time fixing mistakes made by the branch manager than it would have taken for him to close the loans himself.

The second complaint Smith made concerned Mr. Davis. Smith said that during the month of May, Davis and he were running neck and neck in loan closings. Each loan officer knew whoever closed the most loans would hold the all-time record for loans closed in one month. Toward the end of May, Mr. Smith did not receive any title examinations from the title company and as a result closed only $1.13 million in new home loans. Davis went on to close $1.32 million in loans. In early June, Smith called the title company to find out why he was not receiving any title reports. The title company informed Smith that Davis had told them to expedite his examinations. This action had caused a delay in the processing of the title searchers requested by the other loan officers. Smith had indicated that Davis and he had almost come to blows over the matter one night when they were working late. Smith felt that he had been cheated out of the loan-closing record.

During the next weekly loan division meeting Spears went over the problems that had come to light. He emphasized the importance of accuracy in closing loans and indicated that everyone was working for the same team. He also warned loan personnel never to take complaints about the operations of the loan division to anyone expect himself. In order to eliminate the mistakes, Spears established a policy of having loan officers review the work of fellow loan officers before the loan was closed. He also hired a new loan officer in July to take the pressure off Davis and Smith. The new loan officer was a 1974 graduate of Indiana University. His addition brought the loan division up to three full-time loan officers, a management trainee, and a branch manager.

These changes were very effective. Mistakes declined; Davis and Smith were not required to work as much overtime. But the improvements turned out to be temporary. During the spring, Spears found it necessary to fire two secretaries for not performing their duties. One was terminated in February and her replacement was fired in June. Mr. Davis was also terminated in August, after he had argued with Mr. Spears over the quality of his work. Two weeks after Davis was fired, Mr. Smith gave his notice and said he had taken a job with a large commercial bank in Indianapolis.

Outside the present turnover problem in the loan division, Spears had compiled an impressive track record during his short tenure at HHF. He had developed a program to establish branches and was instrumental in establishing more effective advertising campaigns. In addition, Mr. Spears was behind reorganizing Hoosier Home Federal into separate operating divisions. Prior to the reorganization, the duties and functions of HHF's officers had not been clearly separated and defined; the overlapping and fuzzy lines of authority had created a lot of internal confusion and bottlenecks in paperwork.

TREASURER'S DEPARTMENT

The treasurer's department was headed by Lew Winters, a 1955 graduate of West Virginia University. Prior to joining HHF in 1969 Mr. Winters worked as a CPA for one of the "Big Eight" accounting firms. Mr. Winters occupied the position of vice president and treasurer of HHF and was responsible for the accounting function and cash planning in the association. The accounting functions at HHF were considered to be efficiently performed. Mr. Winters believed in training the people in his department to do two or three different jobs in order to avoid any disruption if an employee decided to quit. In the last two years the accounting department had lost only one employee. The employee who resigned was a degreed accountant who took a more rewarding position in a local manufacturing firm. After attempting for six months to replace this individual with a person of equal caliber, an employee was shifted from mortgage servicing to fill the opening.

The employees in accounting were very loyal to Mr. Winters and many considered him to be "the ideal boss." Mr. Winters had also developed good relationships with Mr. Davis and Mr. Smith who worked in the loan division. Outside the accounting group, however, Mr. Winters was considered to be very short tempered—he was not above swearing at employees who made mistakes. Mr. Winters was disliked by a large number of employees in the other divisions largely because of his position as financial watchdog for the association. For instance, Winters had instituted a strictly enforced policy that tellers could not leave work at the end of the day until they balanced their cash or found the mistake. In one case with a new teller, three employees worked until 8:30 at night helping the teller balance. Employees normally work from 9:00 A.M. to 4:00 P.M.

During 1978, Mr. Winters was concerned about HHF's liquidity position. Rising interest rates during the summer of 1978 had caused many customers to withdraw their savings to place them in higher-interest-bearing investments elsewhere. Winters had brought the deteriorating liquidity position to the attention of Mr. Curry, and suggested that HHF slow down its mortgage lending activities. However, Mr. Curry ignored the suggestion and continued to allow the loan division to operate at full capacity. For a period of two months, HHF was the leading savings and loan in the tri-county area in making loans.

At the end of July, the Federal Home Loan Bank Board finally forced Hoosier Home Federal to curtail making home loans. The FHLB had been lending money to HHF in order to help it maintain its liquidity position. On August 25 the FHLB took steps to improve HHF's liquidity position. One of the steps strongly suggested was a moratorium on all lending activities. Mr. Winters was very disturbed that the situation reached the point where outsiders were telling Hoosier's management what had to be done.

PERSONNEL

Mr. Sims was vice president in charge of the personnel division. He joined HHF in 1967 following his graduation from Western Michigan University where he majored in psychology. Sims was a very dedicated employee who was very conscientious about doing a good job.

Sims was responsible for hiring new employees and terminating those who did not work out. He was also responsible for resolving all personnel problems that arose in the association, except for those that occurred in the loan division. Mr. Spears insisted upon the right to hire and fire all the employees under his supervision—an insistence which produced conflicts between Mr. Sims and Mr. Spears. Spears believed that if an employee was not doing a good job, he should be terminated and a new employee hired. Mr. Sims, on the other hand, believed it was necessary to work with the employee in an effort to resolve the problem. Mr. Sims felt termination should be used only when other measures failed.

One of HHF's long-standing personnel policies was to start new employees off at a relatively low salary. All salary scales and raises were approved by the board of directors. The salary scales for nonofficer-level positions at HHF were between 10 and 15 percent lower than other financial institutions in the tri-county area. However, Mr. Curry was proud that HHF had been able to maintain proportionately lower salary expenses than other savings and loans in the area.

Mr. Sims took pride in Hoosier Home Federal's accomplishments in the area of equal employment and advancement of women. The assistant savings division officer, a branch manager, and two assistant branch managers were women. All four of these employees started their careers as tellers and had worked their way up. HHF had more women in middle-management positions than any other savings and loan in the area. Sims was also pleased with two personnel development programs which he instituted. The first program was an employee education program whereby HHF paid tuition for any employee who completed courses sponsored by the American Institute of Savings and Loan Associations. A total of 20 employees, 30 percent of HHF's work force, had participated in this program during the last five years.

The second program Mr. Sims had developed was a management training program. Under the program, management trainees were rotated through the different divisions in order to give them a broad exposure to HHF's various operations. In the future, he hoped new loan officers and branch managers would be chosen from the individuals who had completed this program.

SAVINGS DIVISION

David Burris, who was in charge of the savings division, had been with HHF since 1954. He was a graduate of Ohio State University and had a great deal of experience in the savings and loan industry. Prior to the reorganization Burris had split his time between mortgage lending and savings, but after the reorganization, he had been placed in charge of the savings division. Mr. Burris was a quiet and reserved type of person. He made a good first impression, enjoyed meeting people, and understood the importance of HHF's employees furnishing customers with friendly efficient service. Customers often came to Mr. Burris wanting him to make exceptions on deposits and withdrawals, even though the exceptions would break FHLB regulations. Mr. Burris' job was made easier by the fact that HHF always offered the highest interest rate allowed on each type of savings account. The success of the new branch, which was opened in early 1978, helped to bring in a substantial amount of new savings deposits.

Mr. Burris, in conjunction with Mr. Holland and Mr. Spears, established two new programs in 1977 which were very successful. The first program developed was a save-by-mail savings plan. Under this plan, HHF paid postage both ways for customers who mailed in deposits. This feature was very attractive to savers in rural areas who were not able to obtain an equally high return on their savings at banks or who found it more convenient to make their deposits via mail.

The second innovative program that was established in 1978 was a "dial-a-check" savings plan. Under this plan savings customers could call or write the assistant savings officer and authorize a transfer from their savings account to their checking account at a commercial bank. This program was very attractive to customers who held large balances in noninterest-bearing checking accounts. Hoosier Home Federal paid interest on its regular pass book accounts from the day of deposit until the day of withdrawal.

In addition to these new programs, Mr. Burris was optimistic about the impact of opening more new branches. Savings that came in through branch locations were, on average, deposited in lower-yield savings accounts; experience showed that new deposits at the branch offices were mainly in regular passbook accounts. The main office had a very high proportion of new deposits in savings certificates that carried generally higher interest rates. The overall average ratio of interest which Hoosier Home Federal was paying on its savings accounts was crucial because it directly affected the interest rate which had to be charged on new mortgage loans.

MORTGAGE SERVICING

The mortgage servicing department was run by Wally Saunders. Mr. Saunders had completed a two-year course in computer programming at United Electronics Institute before joining HHF in 1972. He was promoted to his present position in 1975 after spending three years in data processing. Mr. Saunder's department was responsible for collecting payments on the mortgage loans and for, in general, servicing the mortgage loan accounts. This included handling escrow agreements on homeowners insurance and property taxes, making sure monthly payments were made on schedule, and so on. The operations of Mortgage Servicing usually proceeded very smoothly, but in 1978 a few problems did develop.

In the summer of 1978, when Mr. Saunders was preparing to pay the property tax bills, he discovered his division did not have information on over 200 loans. Upon investigation he discovered that the loan division had been closing loans, and then not preparing a file. After talking to Mr. Curry, Mr. Saunders learned that the loan division had established closing loans as its top-priority duty and everything else came second. After Saunders explained the problems this policy created for mortgage servicing, Mr. Curry assigned several people to assembling files.

The only other difficulty that occurred in this division during 1978 was the departure of three employees. At the end of July, three of the seven clerks were new. Of the clerks replaced, two of them had quit and the third was fired. The majority of the clerks, tellers, and secretaries at HHF were younger than 25.

Although Saunders expressed satisfaction with his position at Hoosier Home Federal, he was uneasy about his future. He felt that Mr. Spears looked down on him because he was not a college graduate. Saunders knew that both Spears and Holland preferred to have college graduates in upper management positions.

THE FUTURE

As of late 1978 Mr. Holland was contemplating what steps to take regarding the problems that cropped up over the summer. He also realized that he needed to look ahead to 1979 and to map out some operating improvements. As he thought more about it, he saw three areas of particular concern:

1. The turnover problem both at the management level and among the staff employees.
2. How to deal with Irwin Spears, who in some respects had made some very positive contributions, but who on other fronts had been something of a disaster.
3. The whole idea of growth—the additional branches which were planned over the next five years offered some exciting possibilities for HHF, but he was not convinced that the Association was organizationally equipped to cope with the changes that more branches would bring.

31. Rick Montrose (A)*

Rick Montrose ordered another cocktail and then returned to his contempla-
tion over the situation in which he now found himself. Hired as an organizational consultant two months ago for a small but explosively growing plastics
firm, the day of his final report and recommendations was drawing near. He
realized that the facts that he had learned in the preceding eight weeks had to
be weighed carefully and that he must also consider his own aspirations and
career.

Having graduated from a large midwestern university two years before,
Rick had gone the corporate route immediately out of school because of the
advancement potential and the financial rewards. Starting from a staff engineering position he had risen rapidly to a middle-management line position.
Divisional financial difficulties, his supervisor's personality, top management's conservatism, and his own desires caused Rick to leave the corporate life with two years' tenure and to strike out on his own.

After finishing up a rather successful production consulting assignment,
Rick had taken advantage of his loose schedule to travel to Midvale, his old
college town, to visit some friends and get away from the big city. While out
drinking one night he had run into an old college flame, Robin Furnall, and
had been invited to stay with her at her apartment while he was in town.
This unlikely romantic rendezvous actually paved the way for his second
consulting job at the firm where Robin was employed as the personal secretary to the president, Jim Larton.

When Robin learned of Rick's background and expertise she had informed
her boss. This led to the initial interview the following week. This interview
showed the firm to be in need of policy guidelines, operating procedures,
organizational restructuring, and day-to-day leadership. After the customary
reference checks Robin had come home one day and informed Rick that he
was to be offered the job on a two-month contract with a renewal clause for
another two months if needed.

---

* Prepared by Frank Leonard under the direction of Prof. J. A. Barach, Tulane University
Graduate School of Business Administration. This case also appears in Jeffrey A. Barach, *The
Individual, Business and Society* (Englewood Cliffs, N.J.: Prentice-Hall, Inc., 1977.) Copyright
© 1974 Tulane University Graduate School of Business Administration. Reprinted by permission.

After confirmation of the offer from Mr. Larton, Rick had rented an apartment in town, despite Robin's generous offer to move in as her roommate for two months. Rick believed that work and play seldom mixed, and Rick wanted the job and experience too much to risk losing it on account of Robin (or any woman).

PLASTECH, INC.

The company, PlasTech Inc., now almost three years old, had grown from a basement operation of Mr. Larton's to its present sales volume of $2 million in its short history. Using shrewd long-term contracts, Mr. Larton had succeeded in profiting from the plastics market shortage situation the last two years. PlasTech was now both nationally and internationally recognized as an innovative researcher and reliable distributor of specialty plastics. Jim Larton not only relied on luck to prosper, but also was a brilliant inventor and strategist who always was one step ahead of his competitors in marketing techniques and product introductions.

The next stage of expansion now lay in the production of consumer plastic goods. Mr. Larton's tenth patent had just been approved and he was awaiting only capital and manufacturing facilities to move these inventions from the drawing board into production. He had just completed arrangements for the construction of a $500,000 factory and office complex to be located on the outskirts of Midvale and financed by an SBA loan. He had also taken an option on 800 acres of land in Arizona on which to eventually build a western research and warehousing facility when the Midvale plant was operational. Mr. Larton both understood the market potential in the western states for his new products and personally wanted to move his wife and three children "out of this cold, flat land."

The constant attention by Mr. Larton to the planning and design details of expansion had taken its toll on the day-to-day operations of the firm. The immediate problem solving had been ignored. There was a general lack of guidance, supervision, and direction that was causing some customer complaints, lost accounts, and severe internal problems. The inability and lack of interest to cope with these problems had been bothering Mr. Larton for some time. When Robin had come to work one Monday with the news that she had met a consultant whom she knew personally, he knew that this was what the firm needed—and two weeks later Rick Montrose was hired.

SIZING UP THE SITUATION

Rick spent the first three weeks learning the operation of the firm and becoming familiar with the plastics industry. As he learned more, Rick became very interested in the amount of innovation and excitement present in this small firm and in the dynamic, young industry. PlasTech employed 54 people (43 females) with an average age of 23. The formal organization (see

Exhibit 1) was of a horizontal nature, as was found in most rapidly growing firms, with all department heads reporting to Mr. Larton. Although he found several problem areas that were to be expected in such a rapidly growing firm (i.e., procedure documentation, policy formation, etc.), the functioning of the work force was being affected by something other than the present operating systems.

EXHIBIT 1
Organizational Chart

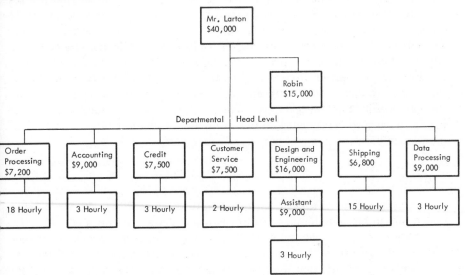

There seemed to be an underlying motivation and morale problem that was impairing the accomplishment of even the most trivial tasks. In order to get to the heart of the matter, Rick decided to interview all the employees during the fourth and fifth week to find out their individual views of the firm. Quite a few of those interviewed placed many confidences in Rick, which revealed the true nature of the power structure within the firm.

The subject of the majority of complaints and the source of most of the morale problem was Mr. Larton's secretary, Robin. Although probably the hardest working person in the firm, she had been using her position as Mr. Larton's secretary as a lever to gain power and to influence his decisions concerning internal affairs. In Mr. Larton's absence she had continually taken charge and made decisions that other department heads should have clearly made.

Because of his involvement with external problems, Mr. Larton had come to rely on Robin for advice on the functioning of the company. More than once Rick had heard, "you have to be on Robin's good side in order to get any place in this company." The employee's complaints to Mr. Larton seemed to have fallen on deaf ears and the influence of Robin had been the cause for several resignations and a real sore spot with most everyone. Several employees had confided in Rick that Robin had probably gotten a previous accountant fired because she disliked him and felt her power base was being threatened.

The singularly most discomforting fact that came from the interviews was that Robin and Mr. Larton seemed to have more than just a business relationship, many out-of-town trips and late nights at work serving more prurient interests than plastics. Robin had recently bragged at a party (while under the influence of alcohol) that Mr. Larton paid her a salary of $15,000 for her excellent services, third-highest only behind a design engineer and Mr. Larton himself. Their intimate relationship was common knowledge to the employees and this created a general atmosphere of mistrust, hard feelings, and insecurity. The only apparent way to a promotion or raise was through Robin, and the establishment of oneself on her good side was a prime concern to everyone. Relative competence and reliability was considered to play only a minimal part in advancement.

THE JOB OFFER

In the beginning of Rick Montrose's sixth week at PlasTech, Mr. Larton called him in for a conference. After the usual "how are things going?" Mr. Larton got straight to the point. He had checked on Rick's previous accomplishments, which, when combined with his outstanding performance to date, indicated to him that Rick had much potential in this industry. He was very impressed with Rick's grasp of the business and he wanted Rick to consider taking charge of the operation as general manager, so that Mr. Larton could devote himself more fully to research work.

Mr. Larton wanted to move out west as soon as the new plant was completed in Midvale and would leave Rick in charge of all eastern and central operations. He assured Rick of complete autonomy in any decision making plus absolute control of all phases of the firm from staffing to financing. In addition to a starting salary of $22,000 and a bonus program, Rick was offered a stock-option plan that would make him the second majority shareholder in five years (local businessmen, relatives, and employees owned 40 percent and Mr. Larton 60 percent of the stock outstanding).

Mr. Larton wanted Rick to take some time to think about the offer and to give him an answer when the consulting project was finished. Rick left Mr. Larton's office, walking past a glaring Robin. He was overwhelmed by the magnitude of the offer but overjoyed at the possibility to launch himself into a new and interesting career.

The two weeks following Mr. Larton's offer had only served to complicate Rick's situation. At the beginning of the seventh week he had heard a rumor that Robin was selling drugs (LSD, cocaine) to the boys in the warehouse although there wasn't any word as to whether it was on company property. Friday of that week, Rick had arrived at work to find a memo from Mr. Larton leaving him in charge of things until Robin and he got back in one week from an extended, urgent trip east.

The eighth week of work, in the absence of Mr. Larton and Robin, went very smoothly. Thursday, Robin called from the Baltimore airport saying that the trip would be lengthened until next Monday and that Mr. Larton wanted the final consulting recommendations and an answer to the job offer on his desk by Tuesday.

On the Friday of Rick's final week of consulting, following Robin's call, a call from Mrs. Larton was transferred to him. She wondered if he had heard from her husband and if he was still expected in that evening. When he replied that they would not be in until Monday Mrs. Larton had asked who "they" were since her husband had said that he was going on the trip alone. Rick managed to get out of it by saying that Mr. Larton might be bringing home a major client with him. She asked if there was a number where Mr. Larton might be reached. Rick had to tell her that Mr. Larton rarely informed anyone of his whereabouts, preferring to call in to check on things.

THE CONSULTING REPORT

That afternoon Rick completed the first part of his consulting report (see the Appendix) but was stumped as to how far to go on the final part of it. He was completely undecided whether to mention all the details about Robin or just some, to recommend her termination, to have her moved to another position (where?), or to ignore her completely. Further, he did not know whether Mr. Larton knew that he had spent ten days with Robin before taking the job.

Robin's and his friendship had completely disintegrated since coming to PlasTech, partly due to his moving out and his refusal to date her, and partly due to his increasing influence with the employees and the job offer. She had recently refused to even talk to him and had even ignored an official request for some data from Mr. Larton's files.

Rick had learned enough about Mr. Larton to realize that his affair with Robin was a tremendous ego boost to the 43-year-old man and that he not only enjoyed the sexual conquest but the envious remarks from his business cronies as to the "fine-looking office decorations" and "my wife would never let me get away with something like *that*."

Rick enjoyed the work and was enamored of the idea of becoming general manager. The financial benefits that would accrue would probably surpass his uncertain consulting fees and would allow him to pay off some of the bills left over from his consulting start. With five- to ten-years' experience as general manager of PlasTech, Rick knew that he would be groomed for a management job in any of several multinational chemical or plastic companies. Despite the handsome benefits of this job he also had to weigh the costs that were inherent in any such small and tightly held firm. Not only was there a plethora of personal problems evident in Robin's and Mr. Larton's relationship, but if the firm should fold, the mark on his record would be far from impressive. Rick considered the chance of the firm failing as approximately 2-in-10 odds, based on the newness of the venture, the aggressiveness of Mr. Larton, and the increasing competition that was developing in the industry.

Another perplexing problem that irked Rick was that he did not know where Mr. Larton drew the line between the firm and his "fun." Being majority shareholder and president, Mr. Larton was entitled to run the company anyway he felt, but Rick wondered exactly where the personal involvement ended and rationality began. Would Mr. Larton's conduct spill over into Rick's area of control and affect Rick's effectiveness in a period of change?

With these things in mind Rick sipped his drink and pondered the courses of action that were available to him and just how he should word his final report. He knew that the exact wording would have a definite effect on his ability to accept the job and on his working relationship with Mr. Larton, should he opt to accept the job. The final decision had to be weighed in light of his own personal feelings, his career aspirations, and his ethical sense of what was right to do in the situation as a professional and as a consultant.

APPENDIX: SUMMARY STATEMENTS OF
THE CONSULTING REPORT

There are two (2) major problem areas evident in the organization that are causing employee dissatisfaction, resentment, and job insecurity. The company is in turn being hurt by this in that work is being performed in less than an optimum fashion. The two areas and recommendations are as follows:

Salary Levels

The present pay system is both inadequate and unequal. Employees with the same tenure and relative position are being paid different amounts and in different ways. All personnel below a supervisory level should be paid on an hourly basis with the customary overtime for more than 40 hours. Evaluation sheets and reviews should be completed at least once a year (preferably semiannually) and raises should be given according to a standard formula. Raises should *never* be given according to subjective or personal feelings but should *always* be given on an objective basis. All employees should be made aware of their evaluation by their supervisor and praised for their strong points and told to improve on their deficient areas. The company must at all times be fair on ratings and raises since this will only lead to better employer-employee relations. All employees at a supervisory level or above should be paid on a salary basis. Like the hourly employees, all salaried personnel with similar responsibilities, and tenure should be paid similar wages.

If more than 40 hours per week is required, special time off in slack areas should be given. All salaried personnel should also be evaluated and a fair salary progression table established. Salaried (staff) employees would be expected to perform at a responsibility level above the hourly people but they also should be compensated for the difference. Under *no* and I emphasize *no*, circumstances should the management disclose, discuss, or divulge the wages of employees to other employees. This only leads to resentment, animosity, and a distrust or feelings of unfairness toward the company. If employees want to discuss wages on their own, then that is their business and consequences resulting from this will not involve the company in any way.

A primary and very important factor in good personnel management is that the company and its management must always appear to be impartial in its relationships with employees. Even though discrepancies will appear as a part of human nature, these differences *must* be concealed from the employees.

Working Hours

The required working hours of hourly people should be set and established. They should work only those number of hours that are required and if, because of business, more hours are required, they should be compensated at a fair and just level. The hours of supervisory personnel should *not* be rigidly set but should be determined by the individuals themselves. It is assumed that the person in a staff position has the intelligence and integrity to devote him or herself to the job and, if needed, will work the hours that are required to get the job done. In the past ten weeks a lot of time has been turned in by both the hourly and staff employees that has been unproductive because of the amount of work involved. The employees' attitude is harmed by requiring the presence of people when they are not needed. If the company is to be respected and trusted it in turn must trust its staff to get the job done. Any failure of an employee to get the job done when needed is a reflection on the company for hiring that person. Any termination of personnel should be done on a minimum time basis, that is, a two-week notice for hourly workers and a 30-day notice for staff. The company in turn would deserve the same consideration from its employees. The importance of the above cannot be stressed enough. Any employee who is deficient in his work or hours should be reprimanded but any employee who works longer or harder than required should be compensated.

Although financial gain is a prime motivator for many people, it is by far not the most important. Self-esteem and self-fulfillment is a very powerful force and overrides financial aspects for many people. Only when the company can present its employees with this type of job enrichment can it benefit from the great potential that is there.

32. Value Valve Company*

In the executive dining room at Value Valve Company, Dick Rogers flopped down into a chair for lunch. He was already tired from a hectic morning in his new job as group product-market analyst. He had picked a table where several of his previous associates in Corporate Industrial Relations and Personnel were already seated. Rogers was interested in finding out about the previous all-day meeting of the corporate and divisional industrial relations and personnel managers. He was particularly curious about the discussion as it related to a memorandum he had prepared as a favor for P. H. Wrigley, corporate vice president of industrial relations and personnel. The subject was management development, one of the functions Mr. Rogers had managed until six months ago under the supervision of Mr. Wrigley. When Rogers asked about it, the silence was deafening. Finally, two of the men reluctantly admitted that it had been a good meeting, but that the subject of management development had not been discussed. Rogers left the table both angry and disgusted: angry because he'd been asked to do unnecessary work and disgusted because any company that was so utterly disinterested in organization planning and management development would never be a company that could offer him much of a future.

COMPANY BACKGROUND

The Value Valve Company was originally a supplier of valves to oil companies. The valves were widely used in oil-well applications, refinery operations, and fuel transportation. With the increased emphasis on domestic oil production, the company had experienced substantial sales increases. The company had also acquired a number of companies, which had been established as separate divisions. Many of the products acquired had similar technologies, but the divisions were generally in unrelated industries. The organization had recently grouped some of the divisions together because of the similarity of their product lines and to provide better control than could be exercised by a few corporate officers over seven autonomous divisions (see Exhibit 1 for an organization chart, sales, and profits).

---

* Prepared by Prof. Roger M. Atherton and Prof. Dennis M. Crites of the University of Oklahoma.

Value Valve's strategic performance was somewhat below the average for similar companies; several of the divisions were doing quite well, but the Oil Valves Division was not performing up to the expectations of top management largely because of the problems of adjusting to the recent increases in sales.

THE NEW VICE PRESIDENT

About three years ago, as a result of company growth, Value Valve's president decided that the company needed a corporate vice president to be responsible for the industrial relations and personnel functions. A variety of corporate executives had been given responsibility for these functions, but only in addition to their primary duties, and none had had training or experience in industrial relations or personnel. Increasing pressures from the unions and rumors of discontent among salaried employees led the president

EXHIBIT 1
Organization Chart

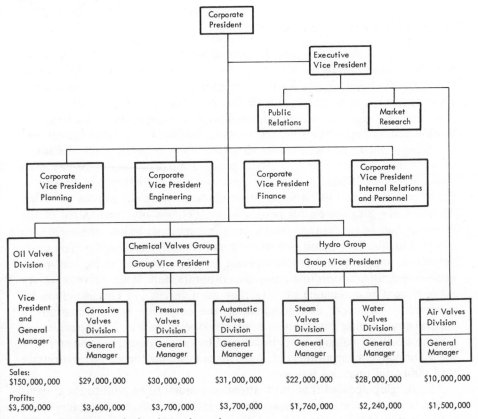

Source: Corporate organization chart and annual reports.

to believe it was time for one individual to be responsible at the corporate level for industrial relations (blue-collar workers and unions) and personnel (white-collar workers, engineers, and managers). Value Valve had a total of about 12,000 employees. The divisions all had directors of industrial relations whose primary responsibilities were blue-collar workers and their unions. The new position would serve to coordinate divisional industrial relations and establish a salaried-personnel function.

The person selected was Mr. Wrigley, previously the director of industrial relations for the largest manufacturing facility (approximately 12,000 employees) of Value Valve's principal competitor. He had a J.D. degree in law, an M.B.A., and was working toward a masters degree in law, at night school. His experience was almost entirely in industrial relations. Known to both management and union as being a firm, fair, and honest executive, his reputation as a negotiator was outstanding. The company he had been with was considerably more sophisticated in both industrial relations and personnel than Value Valve. It was therefore expected that Mr. Wrigley would not only be a good executive, but would also be aware of the latest approaches and techniques in both industrial relations and personnel.

MR. WRIGLEY'S DECISION

After six months of learning his way around and consolidating his position, Mr. Wrigley reviewed his organization. He had three subordinates who had been with the company for more than ten years. These subordinates had experience in, and were responsible for: (1) labor relations, (2) hourly benefits, and (3) wage and salary administration and supervisory training. All three acted as corporate staff representing headquarters management and providing various services to the divisions upon request. Each divisional director of industrial relations (DIR) handled most of the day-to-day divisional activities. When labor negotiations involved more than one division or the negotiations in one division were likely to have an impact on other divisions, the corporate staff people would become involved. Most of the divisions had labor contracts with the same national union, although with different locals. As a result, the fringe benefits (such as unemployment compensation, supplemental unemployment benefits, and the retirement plan) needed centralized coordination by the corporate staff. Wage surveys, salary surveys, and maintenance of data files on different job classifications by geographic area were also handled by the corporate staff. Occasionally supervisory training programs in human relations, motivation, communication, or decision making, some developed by other companies and some by the Value Valve's corporate staff, were made available through the corporate staff industrial relations function.

Mr. Wrigley decided that more attention needed to be paid to the organization structure, the strengths and weaknesses of individual managers, the long-run personnel requirements for professionals and managers, and the planned development of managerial and executive talent throughout the organization. He decided to establish an organization planning and management development function. He believed he needed an expert with significant experience and found a perfect candidate in D. M. Jones, who was employed at General Motors. Mr. Jones accepted Mr. Wrigley's offer and gave his termination notice to GM. He had not yet left GM, however, when Mr. Wrigley called a meeting of all seven divisional directors of industrial relations plus the three corporate staff personnel. Mr. Wrigley asked the new man to take a day's vacation and attend the DIR meeting so that Jones might meet those with whom he would be working most frequently. About two days after the meeting, Jones called Mr. Wrigley to inform him that he had decided not to accept the job after all, as it would involve more travel to the various locations than he had anticipated.

ESTABLISHING THE NEW FUNCTION

In the course of these hiring negotiations, a number of executives had made kidding remarks to Mr. Wrigley about his decision to hire someone from outside the company when he was supposed to be responsible for emphasizing internal promotion and development. After Jones changed his mind, Mr. Wrigley began to look at possible internal candidates. He selected Dick Rogers, 35 years old, who had an engineering undergraduate degree, an M.B.A., and had been serving as a product engineer and administrative assistant to the vice president of research and engineering for the oil valves division. Mr. Rogers, in order to learn about this new function, attended a number of American Management Association seminars plus several programs sponsored by different universities. After attending these sessions, Mr. Rogers wrote a salary position description (Exhibit 2) for his new job. Mr. Wrigley reviewed the description and returned it unchanged with the brief comment that it looked fine to him.

About a year later, Mr. Rogers prepared a more detailed written statement regarding his job and areas of responsibility. The major tasks he identified were as follows:

1. *To determine the numbers and kinds of college recruits required.* Since it takes a minimum of one to three years for these people to be adequately trained, our recruiting people must be working well in advance of our openings at the moment. We must know whether we should be looking for engineers or purchasing people. Instead of having the cyclical up-and-down requirements based on next year's business forecast, we would be working with long-term forecasts of divisional requirements.
2. *To determine the numbers of foremen required.* Since both the training and locating of such men takes time, this could be much more effectively done in anticipation of needs than the on-the-spot, hip-pocket approach taken now. Pre-foreman training could be implemented in time to produce a pool of qualified and capable candidates.

EXHIBIT 2

SALARY POSITION DESCRIPTION	Job Title: Manager-Organization
	Planning and Management
Division: Corporate	Development

Basic Functions:

The responsibilities of this position are to develop, administer, and coordinate inventory, appraisal, training, development, placement, counselling, and related programs to improve salaried employee potential and to provide a continuing flow of qualified management personnel.

Reporting Responsibilities:

Reports to vice president of personnel and industrial relations. Supervises director of college recruiting and secretary.

Typical Duties:

1. Supervise college recruitment, placement, and training. Approve salary recommendations, quota, trainee expenses, and colleges selected. Assist by interviewing both in plant and on campus.
2. Supervise professional-technical placement, approve advertising, salary recommendations, expenses, classifications, and use of agencies. Assist by interviewing, determining schedules, coordinating, and making recommendations; correspond with applicants as necessary.
3. Establish and supervise the maintenance of a skills inventory program. Promote the utilization and application of this system.
4. Supervise the administration of the educational assistance program.
5. Supervise the selection, arrangement, and administration of after-hours education classes at corporate headquarters.
6. Coordinate performance appraisal program. Train or instruct supervisors in implementation on request.
7. Coordinate studies of existing management manpower and possible replacements. Establish and maintain manpower inventory books to include replacement charts, training and development needs, manpower forecasting, young high potentials, and executive inventory records.
8. Determine needs and develop training programs for staff personnel. Prepare training material. Conduct training classes when required.
9. Maintain file and make recommendations on university executive management development programs.
10. Conduct continuing investigation of management training activities in other companies.
11. Review the literature and attend seminars to ensure the consideration of contemporary developments in organization and management development and the behavioral sciences. Make recommendations concerning new programs to top management. Develop, administer, and coordinate the implementation of accepted programs.
12. Coordinate with the vice president of planning and report on projected manpower requirements.
13. Counsel employees on personnel and personal problems.
14. Interpret policy on request.
15. Assist in developing or revising policy when requested.
16. Perform special assignments at the request of management.

3. *To determine the scope and need for professional recruiting.* By an examination of the levels, salary estimates, and departments indicating expansion we can anticipate needs, begin to build resume files, make valuable contacts with recruiting firms, and establish relationships with executive and professional search firms.

4. *To determine the kind and extent of the need for internal training and development.* We have a fairly good-sized group, already employed, which with proper training and development could be upgraded to new positions, as they occur. However, these people must be trained and prepared in advance of the need, or the temptation will be to recruit from outside the company. This is demoralizing, frustrating, and apt to result in high turnover of employees with potential. We have recently developed programs such as skills inventory, college recruiting, after-hours classes, and educational assistance, all attempting to attack this problem. We have given thought to such programs as job-rotation, interdivisional transfers, and staff assistantships, for the same purpose. We need to do much more work, but to do it we need to know what the divisions have and what they think they will need over at least the next five-year period.

5. *To put pressure on management to think about and spend time forecasting manpower before the need is apparent.* We attempted to do this with organization replacement charts and to a lesser extent with performance appraisals. Neither of these programs has been really successful, probably because management is not convinced of the need. We believe that by going through the relatively simple exercise of forecasting their manpower requirements, they will prove the need to themselves. Corporate staff can then come to their assistance with the proven techniques that have helped so many other companies. We purposely plan to ignore more detailed factors such as specific types of skills or skilled trades, classification levels, detailed departmental breakdowns, specific analysis of functional areas at the plant levels, attrition rates, estimates of retirements, and cyclical variations during the fiscal year because we believe it should be simple, brief, and reasonably easy to complete. Once the manager becomes aware of the overall problem and accepts it as worthy of his attention, he will be more willing to examine these specifics.

6. *To establish the size and depth of the overall work force, so that some intelligent planning can be done in terms of benefit programs, plant location, bargaining needs, dealing with the union, and predicting costs of concessions made during contract negotiations.* Several other new programs could, if there were sufficient need, be started. These might include working with career development centers, whose purpose it is to work with the disadvantaged minority groups. Also, we could set up in-house basic education programs to lift the typical educational levels of the hourly work force from less than fourth grade to eighth grade. We might want to open up after-hours education programs to hourly employees. We might want to consider educational assistance programs for hourly people. We might want to review our present policy of having educational assistance paid for by the man's department and change it to a policy of having corporate staff pay the expense, thereby eliminating much of the operating managers' reluctance to promote such education. We might consider a similar step with respect to seminars and supervisory training (including overtime pay). All

or any of these can only be intelligently reviewed and considered with adequate facts and a concerned management.

ROGERS' ACTUAL WORK EMPHASIS AND PERFORMANCE

At the end of his second year in this position, Mr. Rogers attempted to evaluate his performance in the organization planning and management development functions. The company seemed to be appreciative of his efforts, as he had received a 30 percent increase in salary over the two-year period and a bonus of 20 percent in each of the two years.

Mr. Rogers, however, was quite dissatisfied with the progress made. He found himself spending most of his time on professional-technical placement. He was very good at this function, had a very low failure rate, and was able and willing to respond quickly to urgent requirements. It was not unusual for him to find and hire people in four to six weeks as compared to the norm of eight to ten weeks. He also found that he was frequently the man to see when executives had a complex problem that they wanted to discuss or informally brainstorm. Top management was generally very critical of new ideas and proposals that had not been adequately thought through and developed. Mr. Rogers provided executives with an opportunity to expose their tentative ideas or thinking to critical review and to evaluate their subordinate's readiness for top management.

Mr. Rogers was also spending an increasing amount of time with the corporate vice president of planning, working on acquisition proposals, new-product planning, and both corporate and division five-year forecasts. All these additional tasks, coupled with a large number of professional-technical recruitment requests, left little time to do the management development and organization planning that he believed were his primary responsibilities. He recognized, however, that neither Mr. Wrigley nor the general managers of the seven divisions seemed to want any more services or assistance than was already available.

In fact, Mr. Rogers noted that there seemed to be developing a reluctance to do even as much as had been done in the past. Mr. Rogers believed this was the result of the fact that none of the material previously put together on the divisions had received much more than superficial attention from either Mr. Wrigley or the company president. This lack of use served to provide an excuse for division managers; they would argue that if it's not going to be used, then why should they bother to put it together? Mr. Rogers was quick to point out that its primary use was to be at the division. He argued that insight into their division's strengths and weaknesses, training and development needs, manpower replacement needs, organizational structure needs, and requirements in the long-run instead of just the short-run should be of great assistance in doing a better job of managing a division. Mr. Wrigley seemed reluctant to become involved, and whenever the subject came up, consistently argued that corporate industrial relations was a service function and should not dictate to the divisions.

Relations between Rogers and Mr. Wrigley were cordial, but there was very little close interaction between the two men, with Mr. Wrigley doing little or no checking or commenting upon Rogers' work. Mr. Rogers was never quite sure whether Mr. Wrigley believed he was doing a good job, just wasn't interested in his activities, or was focusing his attention on items of higher-priority importance than those in the management development and planning function.

A NEW ASSIGNMENT

About a month later, Mr. Rogers was promoted to the staff of the chemical valves group vice president to investigate the marketing potential of a new line of valves. Mr. Rogers suggested to Mr. Wrigley that his replacement be a trained, respected professional in the field of management development and organization planning. It was Rogers' belief that the function was very important to the future of the company. He thought that perhaps his inability to make the kinds of changes as rapidly as he wanted was because he was not looked upon as an expert but as a home-grown product that really knew only slightly more about the function than the other managers at Value Valve. In addition, Mr. Rogers had no real experience with applications. His knowledge was derived from readings, seminars, and talking with experts. A man with the theoretical knowledge, practical experience in applications, and a reputation which would be respected by the president and divisional DIRs, would be better able to establish and effectively administer a viable and expanding program. Mr. Wrigley, however, was not impressed with these points and decided not to fill the position immediately. He told Mr. Rogers that he would perform the function himself (except for the professional-technical recruitment, which he delegated to another member of the department.) He believed that by doing this he would get real insight into the problems, difficulties, and opportunities in the organization planning and management development functions. After six months or so, he felt he would be in a better position to decide whether he should hire an already established expert or train another man, as he had done with Mr. Rogers.

LATER DEVELOPMENTS

Six months later, Mr. Wrigley had still not filled the position. He had, however, scheduled a meeting of all the directors of industrial relations throughout the company. The primary purpose of the meeting was to exchange ideas and to review the results of the recently completed labor contract negotiations. Mr. Wrigley asked Mr. Rogers as a favor to put together a presentation on management development that Mr. Wrigley could use at this meeting. Mr. Rogers wrote a cover letter (Exhibit 3) describing his opinions and a memorandum (Exhibit 4) that provided additional discussion material. Mr. Rogers felt that any program could only be as effective as its implementation. He felt confident that a discussion of such implementation at the

EXHIBIT 3

To: P. H. Wrigley

From: D. R. Rogers

Subject: Management Development

The attached (see Exhibit 4) is a broad brush approach to management development in answer to your request for speech material. My own feeling is that we need to sell the concept of management development to the divisions. We must get more than lip service; we must get action. A basic appeal to reason is about all we can do at this particular meeting. However, to get things going, to stimulate participation, and to find out where we actually stand, it seems desirable to open up the meeting to a discussion on the subject. The objectives would be:

1. To determine why the divisions really haven't shown any real desire for management development. Is this because of cost, lack of commitment, lack of time, or insufficient staffing so that managers can't be spared? Depending on the reasons, we might want to request changes in present procedures such as the source of funds for such training.
2. We also need to get as many innovative ideas as possible. It will also make the DIRs feel they are a part of the management development effort, rather than having it imposed on them.
3. To determine what the divisions actually want. Perhaps they have all kinds of management development needs we have not been addressing ourselves to. This meeting offers an excellent opportunity for an exchange of information and feedback.

If we are going to have a meaningful management development effort at Value Valve we must:

a. Provide a service the divisions want and need.
b. Convince the divisions as well as top management of the need for management development.
c. Obtain the *active* support of both the divisions and top management.
d. Work closely with the divisions in developing such programs and providing such services as we *mutually agree* are necessary.

We will be unsuccessful if the divisions feel our efforts are not helpful to them, are unnecessary, or are solely used by the personnel department and not by top management. Every effort should be expended during this meeting to obtain the DIRs' cooperation, assistance, and active support of management development.

EXHIBIT 4
Management Development

I. *Introduction*

To insure the growth and effectiveness of the Value Valve Company, we must have programs for the development of all management personnel.

One of the shortages in our economy is that of competent executives. The success of the company, in the years to come, will at least to some extent, depend upon our ability to develop executives qualified to manage an expanded activity.

EXHIBIT 4 (*continued*)

A superior management group for both the present and the future can best be assured through a program of organization planning and executive development. This is a matter of such importance that it should not be left to chance. The same resourcefulness should be devoted to the development of executive talent that is used in other management activities.

II. *Objectives*
   A. General Objectives
       1. Long-range planning for organizing and motivating the development of executives to meet the needs of the company.
       2. To develop a philosophy and environment conducive to executive development.
       3. To develop the talents of executives for eventual top level responsibilities.
       4. To develop a reservoir of generally qualified executives who can be promoted within the company.
   B. Specific Objectives
       1. To enlarge an individual's appreciation and understanding of other functions within his own department, beyond the current area of his specialty and responsibility.
       2. To develop better appreciation and understanding of the needs and problems of other operating departments within his division.
       3. To develop a management perspective in evaluating problems for the overall good of the division.
       4. To develop an understanding of the important economic and social forces which affect the operation of a company.
       5. To develop a top management perspective in evaluating problems from the overall company viewpoint.

III. *Need*

Summary of Five-Year Manpower Requirements

	Present	Future	Increase	Percent
Factory				
Direct	6,574	10,631	4,057	62
Indirect	3,766	5,646	1,880	50
Supervision	454	685	231	51
Total factory	10,794	16,962	6,168	57
Functional				
Manufacturing	275	382	107	39
Engineering	194	297	103	53
Sales	92	153	61	66
Quality control	91	119	28	31
Finance-accounting	100	187	87	87
Industrial relations	47	58	11	23
Purchasing	69	88	19	28
Total functional	868	1,279	411	47
Total company	12,545	19,449	6,904	55

EXHIBIT 4 (*continued*)

These figures make no allowance for deaths, retirements, or other employee turnover, so they might be considered the absolute minimum of activity.

1. We are going to require more than 200 new supervisors. This will mean more supervisory training, greater efforts to find capable and interested people in our present work force, and perhaps innovations such as presupervisory training programs. We may have to rethink our past practices of foreman training on a man's own time. Many companies have obtained better results and found foremen far more receptive when the company shows its commitment to training by scheduling it on company time. In addition, if we assume that it is desirable to upgrade our supervisory force by recruiting some 50 percent through the college recruiting program, then we will have to increase our quota by 20 each year.

2. In the functional areas, we can see the need for about 400 people. Since these are largely professional, well-educated people, they are going to have to be obtained through the college recruiting program or through outside hiring. If we assume 50 percent through college recruiting, it will mean an increase of 40 new recruits each year. If we include the supervisory needs previously mentioned, the yearly total increase would be 60. Some of these are already being requested by the divisions but by no means all. We have increased our quota to 50 from the usual 15–20, but this is just a beginning. With the remaining 200 being sought from outside, we have a mandate to start building resume files, establish good contacts at employment agencies, and to continue developing good working relationships with executive and professional search firms. It also alerts top management to the impending high expenses of recruiting (typical fees running 10–25 percent of base salary). It further points to the importance of the promotion-from-within policy, and a possible need to install some meaningful way to enforce this concept.

3. The area of management competence also comes into focus because we are going to need additional qualified, capable, well-trained managers to run this corporation with a projected sales increase of 95 percent and an employee increase of 55 percent. We must give thought to new ideas such as inter- and intradivisional job rotation, staff and line assistantships, techniques to measure managers with respect to their management development activities, the possible contribution of psychological testing, and the recognition of young high potentials early in their careers. We must consider all kinds of innovations in order to stimulate this activity. Your suggestions and cooperation are sorely needed.

IV. *Installation of Program*
  A. *Description*
    1. *Personal Qualifications and Skills Inventory*
      This inventory has been obtained through the completion of an experience and educational questionnaire. Our efforts are now directed towards maintaining the program and promoting its use for internal promotions.
    2. *Performance Reviews*
      This program has been successfully installed at most locations. We are

EXHIBIT 4 (*continued*)

now working on improvements and modifications, such as management by objectives.

3. *Manpower Inventory Books*
   These books have been completed for most divisions. We expect the divisions to obtain more use of the books than we do. The intent is that you will be able to perceive your own strengths and weaknesses. The result should be that corrective action is taken without prodding from corporate staff.

4. *Training Programs*
   A number of such programs have been initiated at the supervisory level. It is our hope that we can now expand our efforts to include higher level managerial personnel.

B. *Divisional Responsibilities*
   1. Designate an individual to coordinate programs in each division.
   2. Coordinate completion of the personal qualification and skills inventory form.
   3. Evaluate executive performance and appraise executive potential.
   4. Determine development needs of individual executive.
   5. Notify the corporate industrial relations department of executive openings.

V. *Executive Development*
   The policy of the Value Valve Company has always been to promote from within. The environment in which a man works may encourage self development or it may stifle development potential. Each manager should help to provide individual development opportunities and do everything possible to make this a never-ending process.

1. *Company Environment*
   The greatest influence on an individual is his working environment including company policies, his associates, the way he is treated, the attitude of his superior and things the company emphasizes.

2. *Individualized Development*
   Executive development should be individualized. Every executive is a very different person and has different aims and goals, and the duties and responsibilities of his job are probably not like any other. If executive development is an individual matter then there must be a different development program for every man.

3. *Executive Development on Divisional Level*
   Through the use of the performance evaluation, development needs for executives will evolve between the man and his superior. Much of the development at this point will be on the basis that it is first a responsibility of the individual. Much of this can be done through individual reading and study. It should be possible to have small group development courses where the individual needs are the same, carried out at the location of the particular Division.

4. *Outside Executive Development Courses*
   These would include a wide range of educational opportunities for executive development including courses offered by universities; programs and activities offered by management societies.
   a. Executive development programs in universities.
   b. National Industrial Conference Board executive development.
   c. American Management Association executive development courses.

EXHIBIT 4 *(continued)*

VI. *Conclusion*

It is hoped that a philosophy and environment will be developed where executives will find an opportunity to develop for eventual top-level responsibility. The program that is developed at each division should be tailored to the local situation and divisional needs within the overall company policy and objectives.

The development of executives to provide for continuity of strong and effective management is just as important as operating results. These development activities are one means by which operating results can be effectively accomplished. Good current recruiting, selection, and placement will build toward the future. Each current vacancy should be filled with the best man available on the basis of ability and potential, thinking of the future as well as the present.

---

division level might help Mr. Wrigley see the importance of an improved and aggressive program and the necessity to hire a man with the reputation, knowledge, and skills to stimulate effective implementation.

When he heard that Mr. Wrigley failed to discuss this document at the meeting, Mr. Rogers concluded that the future for organization planning and management development at the Value Valve Company was not bright. It appeared that there would no longer be any planned effort directed at improving the organizational structure, developing long-range manpower needs, or formally developing managerial and executive potential.

E. Responding to Societal Priorities

33. Welgro Chemical Company, The EPA, and Other Environmentalists*

What follows is an excerpt from an August, 1976 report on the "CBS Evening News."[1]

Dan Rather: One of the familiar environmental themes a few years ago concerned phosphates, chemicals used in detergents and boycotted by environmentalists. In Florida's Polk County, another phosphate battle now is starting up, at the source. Bruce Hall reports.

Bruce Hall: It's called Bone Valley—5,000 acres strip mined every year. It's not the coal fields of West Virginia or Montana; it's the phosphate mines of Florida, the residue from pre-historic seas and creatures that left the area with one of the most bountiful supplies of phosphate in the world.

Florida produces 80 percent of the nation's phosphates, and more than a third of the world's supply. Phosphates are essential in the production of fertilizer, and have been mined here since the turn of the century. And it has grown into a $3-billion business that employs 61,000 people.

Now, however, because of pressure from many city and county officials, the Environmental Protection Agency has, in effect, called for a moratorium on new phosphate mining and plant construction until an environmental study of the area is completed. The study may take up to 18 months, and industry spokesmen say it is unnecessary.

Homer Hooks (Executive Director, Florida Phosphate Council): We opposed the EPA study from the outset because we felt that there—we know there are presently 16 studies being conducted in and about the industry by all levels of government.

Hall: The federal government ordered the environmental impact study after critics complained the industry's air pollution controls are inadequate; that too much land is being destroyed, left as huge barren gullies; that the industry's extremely heavy use of water is depleting the fresh water resources of the state; that the slime ponds filled with waste products have in the past collapsed, polluting nearby agricultural lands and streams. The phosphate producers claim all Federal standards for air and water pollution are being met, and further that they are now reclaiming much of the strip mine land. But a preliminary study by the EPA now indicates that many homes built on that reclaimed land are trapping

---

* Prepared by Profs. William B. Callarman, Denzil Strickland, and Victor J. LaPorte, Jr., of Florida Technological University.

[1] Reprinted by permission of CBS, Inc.

high levels of radioactive radon gas inside the structures. Radon is caused by the decay of uranium, which is often found with phosphates and can cause lung cancer. County, state and federal agencies are trying to measure the amount of radon in more than a thousand homes, but it will be at least the end of the year before any conclusive results are known.

Richard Guimond (EPA):   To tell you the truth, when we first came down here we really didn't expect to find as much radon, particularly in structures, as we did. From the standpoint of the average levels we've found in the structures so far, if someone was to live there on an annual basis, we would estimate that after approximately six to eight years, they could double their risk of lung cancer.

Hall: Industry spokesmen say the danger of radon has been blown out of proportion, and further, that homes are able to be built in a way to minimize the risk.

Hooks: We think that there are reasonably simple ways to handle this, such as, for instance, the construction of residences six or eight or ten inches above the ground to allow for ventilation. Air-conditioners would be a solution—anything to keep the air moving. Normal home ventilation might be the answer.

Hall: The phosphate industry concedes it has been a dirty business in the past, but isn't any more; that stiffer regulations could cause a fertilizer shortage, and raise world food prices. Nevertheless, state and federal agencies are expected to insist on tighter industry controls before any new land is mined.

HISTORY

The Product.   Phosphate is mined in Florida primarily in an area about 50 miles long and 40 miles wide in Polk and Hillsborough Counties. Roughly, this mining area lies between Tampa and Orlando, Florida.

Processed phosphate is used principally in high analysis fertilizers. In addition, phosphate is used in the production of food preservatives, cloth dyes, gasoline and oil additives, toothpaste, shaving cream, soap, and many other products.

World Market.   Morocco accounts for about one third of the world's exports and controls about two thirds of the world's known phosphate reserves. Morocco's reserves appear to be much larger than those in the United States and are believed to be sufficient to last for hundreds of years. (According to University of Florida Prof. David Anthony, statistics from the Bureau of Mines indicate that at the present mining rate the United States will be out of phosphates by the year 2000.)

According to a *Wall Street Journal* article in August 1976, Morocco seems to be headed toward a dominating position in the world phosphate market. In 1974, Morocco took a cue from the Organization of Petroleum Exporting Countries (OPEC) and successfully pushed the price of phosphate up as high as $68 a ton, compared to $14 a ton in 1973.

Prices soon returned to normal, however, as companies in the United States and elsewhere increased production. Also, consumption declined as farmers began to buy less phosphate because of the high prices.

Other major exporters of phosphate, besides Morocco and the United States, are the Soviet Union, Tunisia, and Jordan.

Mining Process. The phosphate mining operation itself is a gigantic operation beginning with prospecting and site surveys. The survey stage includes extensive planning for drainage and water supply requirements, waste disposal and electric power distribution systems, the mining layout itself, and railroad tracks and roads necessary for transportation.

The first step in mining is the removal of from 5 to 40 feet of sand lying above the phosphate deposits. This "overburden" is scooped up by mammoth electrically operated draglines and is deposited into an adjacent mined out area. After the overburden is stripped away, the dragline digs up the phosphate ore. Phosphate mining would be a simple matter if this ore were pure phosphate, but the phosphate deposits are actually a matrix of phosphate, sand, and clay. The remainder of the mining process, then, consists of separating the phosphate from the rest of the matrix.

The matrix is dumped into a shallow pit called a *sump* where high pressure water guns convert it into a fluid mixture known as *slurry*. The slurry is propelled by centrifugal pumps from the mining site through a pipeline to the phosphate washer and recovery plant. This plant may be located as far as five miles from the mining site.

At the plant, the slurry goes first through a washing operation. Basically, washing is a screening operation to clean and separate the larger phosphate pebbles from the slurry. These pebbles are conveyed to loading bins and the slurry is processed further. The finer particles of phosphate remaining in the slurry are removed by screening or chemical flotation processes.

Phosphate can be shipped in a wet rock or dry rock form. Wet rock is simply phosphate materials as they come out of the washing operation with no further processing. Dry rock is phosphate which has undergone drying in large rotary kilns to lower its moisture content, making it easier to use in chemical processes and easier to transport. In some cases, dried rock is sent to grinding plants to be ground to a specified size for the individualized needs of phosphate users. Modern methods of phosphate recovery have made it possible for companies to recover about two thirds of the phosphate in the ore.

Environmental Problems. Although contemporary phosphate processing is certainly more efficient than ever before, it has been the target of criticism because of historical environmental problems which have worried environmentalists for decades. To begin with, the strip-mining operation is far from aesthetically pleasing. As Orval Jackson, a writer for UPI, points out, from the air parts of southwest Florida look like the moon, with giant craters and mountains of barren grey earth. This provides a startling contrast to the rest of the area's subtropical greenery.

As can be readily noted from the description of the phosphate mining process, the industry uses great amounts of water in various stages of the mining and recovery operations. It has been estimated that it takes 10,000 gallons of water to mine one ton of marketable phosphate. Critics contend that the phosphate industry is thus depleting Florida water resources. They point to the lower water table levels in the area as proof of this contention.

Not only is there the fear that the water level is dropping, but also that existing water sources may be contaminated by the mining process. The major portion of the water used by the phosphate plant is pumped into clay settling ponds where contaminants are allowed to precipitate to the bottom over a period of time allowing the clean water at the top to be discharged and recycled for further use. Critics fear that spills from these ponds could contaminate fresh sources of water in the vicinity.

Although the mining of phosphate is not a major contribution to air pollution despite the vastness of the area that is mined, there has been some problem with the release of particulate matter into the air from the drying and grinding processes as well as gaseous emissions from the various chemical processes. Among the most harmful contaminants has been fluoride which attacks the bone structure of animals. In addition, critics of the industry have claimed that it can be harmful to plant life, including citrus, a mainstay of Florida economic life.

Perhaps ironically, the latest criticism of the industry has come about through its efforts to improve an earlier criticism. Following mining operations, the land which was disturbed is now required by Florida law to be reclaimed by grading with bulldozers and other earth moving equipment. It has been determined that associated with the phosphate deposits are low concentrations of uranium. Since the mining of phosphate disturbs the overburden, radioactivity contaminates the overburden used in land reclamation. The critical question is just how dangerous this radioactivity may be. Critics claim that any exposure to radioactivity is harmful because of its cumulative effects over the years.

In the face of the many criticisms, the phosphate industry has attempted to make major adjustments. An important voice for the industry in Florida has been the Florida Phosphate Council. Homer Hooks, executive director of the Phosphate Council, sees these adjustments as not only a reaction to environmental law but also an adjustment in environmental attitude.

> The old myths of the big, dirty, nasty phosphate industry, poisoning the air and the water and ruining the landscape—that's no more. Don't misunderstand—our hands were dirty for a long time, a very long time. But I think that's changed. Within the last ten years, since we've organized the Phosphate Council and pulled these companies together to improve what we do, there has been a marked change, both in our performance, and in our attitude. We are now complying with the environmental regulations.

THE PHOSPHATE COUNCIL

The Florida Phosphate Council is a nonprofit trade association organized and operated for the welfare of 11 phosphate mining and processing companies, and Welgro Chemical Company is 1 of those 11. The purpose of this council is to act as a public relations body for the member firms with respect to the citizenry, the press, and government. It is in the latter role as lobbyist that the Council does much of its most vital work. Routine functions of the Council include publication and distribution of *Environment Fact Sheets, Economic Fact Sheets,* a weekly summary of newspaper articles concerning the phosphate industry, and numerous miscellaneous brochures introducing the phosphate industry or presenting the phosphate industry viewpoint on given issues. Member companies depend on the Council to represent their best interests and serve as a point of contact in matters involving their mutual concern. In many respects, the Council has become the spokesman for the phosphate industry in Florida.

Gerald Sims, manager of the environmental control department at the Welgro Chemical Company, has this to say about the Council:

> (The Phosphate Council is) geared to the needs of local Florida operations . . . I would say they are . . . a watchdog on legislative matters on a country and state basis . . . They also sponsor tours; they are available for public-speaking engagements. They are principally PR.

An example of the work the Council has done in the past is their efforts in 1969 to lobby against a state imposed severance tax on the phosphate industry. A Phosphate Council publication at the time contended:

> A severance tax is the most serious threat to the continued growth of Florida's mining industries.
>
> Such a tax would not produce nearly as much money for the State as some persons predict. Any income realized from this source would be largely offset by losses in other tax producing areas.
>
> Phosphate, the largest segment of Florida's mining industry, is particularly vulnerable to such a tax.
>
> If Florida's phosphate deposits were the only ones in the world, or the biggest, or the richest, or the most strategically located, perhaps the industry could absorb a modest severance tax.
>
> But Florida has no monopoly on phosphate, and none of these advantages exists.

The severance tax came into effect in 1971.

The public relations efforts of the Council have not always stimulated the desired response in readers. In one case, a copy of the *Economic Fact Sheets 1976* spurred an editorial in the *Daytona Beach Journal* which labelled the publication as propaganda. Taking a hardline on the phosphate industry in general and the Phosphate Council in particular, the editorial concluded with:

> We hope that our legislators will take a hard look at who makes up the "Florida" Phosphate Council, look at the danger to this state its propaganda does not recognize, and decide that there is a need for further legislative action to control the situation.

WELGRO CHEMICAL COMPANY AND
ENVIRONMENTAL CONTROL

One of the important member firms of the Florida Phosphate Council is the Welgro Chemical Company. Welgro is an old and respected name in the fertilizer business with a history going back before the turn of the century. After several changes of ownership, Welgro Chemical is now a subsidiary company of The Bradford Companies of Fort Worth, Texas, a diversified company with assets of over $1.5 billion. Other major Bradford companies include Bradford Steel Company, Bradford Energy Company, Bradford Exploration Company, Bradford Pipe Line Company, and Bradford Realty Corporation.

Welgro is a completely integrated company in that it is involved in the phosphate mining and processing operations from the time the phosphate rock is removed from the ground until it is sold to consumers as Welgro fertilizer. Besides its rock mines in Florida, Welgro operates seven fertilizer production plants in the United States, along with many terminals and market outlets.

Corporate Attitude toward Environment. A Welgro publication details a number of voluntary public interest projects in which the company participates:

> Today Welgro has forest lands in Hillsborough and Polk counties that encompass some 45,000 acres under a scientific forestry program . . . . The harvesting of these forest products creates additional jobs, and generally adds to the local economy.
>
> The company is an active participant in the Nationwide "Tree Farm" Program. Since 1936, more than 11 million pine seedlings have been planted. Welgro Chemical Co. works actively with the U.S. Forest Services, Colleges, and forest industries in establishing test plantings and conducting forest fertilization research.
>
> Over the years Welgro Chemical Co. has donated and leased lands to various local civic, conservation and recreational groups . . . .
>
> Fields of grain, planting of citrus, forage for cattle, and beautiful forests stand in testimony of our interest in returning mined out land to useful production. The lakes, which accompany reclaimed lands are a veritable fisherman's paradise and offer unlimited recreation for people in central Florida.

Gerald Sims, manager of environmental control, commenting on regulation, says:

> We have a past history of cooperation with the (regulatory agencies) . . . .
>
> We don't entirely agree with all the rules and regulations . . . and in some cases we have actually gone to court action to rectify and correct some of those regulations . . . . Welgro . . . wishes to comply with any reasonable law that is promulgated by the EPA or the state.

Richard Guimond of the EPA agrees that Welgro is cooperative. He explains:

We began our study of the Florida phosphate industry in June 1974, with a meeting with the Florida Phosphate Council, the member companies, and the local government leaders. During the meeting we outlined the study plans and requested their cooperation.

Shortly after this meeting, we began environmental investigations in and around the facilities of several companies including Welgro. Since that time we have conducted field studies at Welgro's mines, benefication plant, drying plant, and phosphoric acid plant. . . . During each of these field trips, Welgro's management ensured that their staff answered all of our questions and provided us with access to any areas we required.

Further, since some of our equipment required electricity in remote areas along with other special needs, they made provision for these requirements.

In general, because of their excellent cooperation, we were able to gather much environmental data, and information in a very short period of time. Because of their assistance, we were able to devote time to our scientific investigation which otherwise would have been needed for logistical support.

Environmental Control Department.   In the late 1940s and 1950s, pollution projects at Welgro were assigned to personnel as required. In 1958, the company established a one-man pollution control department, and in 1964 a technician was added.

Presently five persons are assigned to the environmental control department. Also at each chemical plant there is a small staff responsible for pollution control, involving a total of 15 persons. In addition, one person is assigned to monitor water discharge at each mining location.

Budget for the corporate environmental control staff was about $150,000 in 1975. Welgro plans to budget from $3 million to $10 million per year for capital and maintenance of pollution control items in just its Florida operations.

RESPONSIVENESS OF INDUSTRY TO REGULATION

Dr. David Anthony, a University of Florida biologist, has said that the phosphate industry has had to be "dragged, kicking and screaming, into the 20th century. It has been consistently resistant to even minimal regulation. It has a history of reacting nonresponsibly."

Replies Phosphate Council director Homer Hooks:

> Dr. Anthony's statement does not hold up under examination of the facts of the past ten years. The industry worked closely with the State Department of Pollution Control in development and promulgation of the very strict dam construction and maintenance regulation in 1972. Other control regulations . . . have likewise been accomplished with industry cooperation and participation. . . . I am afraid Dr. Anthony was merely repeating old perceptions about the industry which are no longer true.

Still, those perceptions persist. Waldo Proffit, Jr., a writer for the *Sarasota Herald Tribune,* wrote in June 1976, that phosphate companies were not taking advantage of existing technology to reduce flouride emissions:

It would seem that an industry sincerely concerned about the public would exert every reasonable effort to reduce fluoride emissions below the liberal legal maximums. Especially when the technology to do it has been available for ten years and when those years have seen unparalleled prosperity in the industry.

The lesson for the Florida citizenry is clear. When discussing rules and regulations for any aspect of the phosphate industry, pay no attention to what the industry tells you it CAN do. Insist on a specific definition of what it MUST do.

Dr. Herschel H. Nelson, chairman of the social science division at Polk Community College, Winter Haven, agrees with the view of an industry resisting regulation. Commenting on the sincerity of the companies in the phosphate industry in attempting to correct environmental problems, he says:

They will do as little as they can up to the point where they are cornered and forced to take corrective measures. The nature of their business is to reduce expenses and maximize profits, so it is only when profits . . . are threatened by unfavorable publicity, boycott, expensive after-the-fact corrective measures, or fines in the form of penalties that they will respond effectively.

One *Sarasota Herald Tribune* writer wrote in early 1976 that the industry's attitude is "the public be damned." Not so, says James L. Cox of Lakeland, a phosphate management consultant for over 20 years:

I think the industry has got environmental religion. Some of it was not voluntary, but whether they got religion or not, they are going to church regularly. What I'm saying is that the indsutry is very responsive to community and social needs. It was not true 15 years ago.

"As for environmental religion," counters University of Florida biologist Anthony, "just get up in an airplane, look at the mining area and determine for yourself. Note, also, whether land reclamation is predominantly along major highways."

CONTEMPORARY ENVIRONMENTAL PROBLEMS

Reclamation of Land. Effective July 1, 1975, Florida law made it mandatory that mined land be restored to "an acceptable condition" after mining operation ended. This had been done in the past by phosphate companies on a voluntary basis. To help phosphate firms accomplish this restoration, the government paid between $8.5 and $9 million in 1975 in rebated severance taxes. But when it became known that this restored land was susceptible to radiation, the EPA stepped in to study the extent of the problem.

Wayne King of the *New York Times* described the land reclamation situation in this way:

According to Mr. Hooks (of the Phosphate Council) Florida, in essence, requires only that mined land be returned to some useful purpose. Thus, on the vast majority of land, little or nothing is done after mining, and it is still considered reclaimed. It may simply be dubbed a wildlife preserve, pasture land, or something similar. Even where the land is used for development, it may be left as it was, rutted and hilled, with the great mesas of sifted earth, ten stories high, still standing.

Mr. Hooks says this is more aesthetic, lending more interest to the landscape. Florida is very flat, as you know.

It is this restored land upon which dwellings had been built which concerned the EPA most, since the radioactive radon gas was felt to be especially dangerous when trapped in dwelling structures.

Richard Guimond of the EPA states:

> Based upon our present knowledge, we estimate that continuous occupancy of the structure with the highest average radon daughter level we have measured over the past year (0.1 working level) would double the occupant's risk of lung cancer after about 6–8 years of residence. Occupancy for longer periods would proportionately increase the risk. Ventilation is a very important factor in the radon daughter levels within a structure. Increasing ventilation by opening windows or otherwise diluting the indoor air with outdoor air can greatly reduce the indoor radon daughter concentrations in the air. Conversely, structures that are closed up will provide the opportunity for build up of the radiation levels in the structure. Concrete can provide a barrier to prevent radon from diffusing through the ground into a structure. However, the thickness and quality of the concrete are very important in determining the effectiveness of the barrier. If the concrete is very thin or has many cracks in it, the radon will be able to be transported through the floor into the structure.
>
> In general, the radiation problems in open areas are minimal because of the great diffusing power of the atmosphere. The primary concern in open areas is the potential uptake of radionuclides in food crops that may be grown on the land.

Welgro's Gerald Sims comments:

> They (the EPA) embarked on a one-year study. At the end of 5 weeks they had some results, and they issued a report from EPA to the Governor of the State of Florida on five weeks of a 12-month survey. This was preliminary data and the Governor in fact handled the situation very admirably, in that he indicated the State would not be moved into some decision that may be wrong down the road. We need more data.

Despite industry claims that the EPA's results were only preliminary, Hillsborough County imposed a temporary moratorium on residential construction on land reclaimed from phosphate mining in the summer of 1975.

Dr. Charlton Prather, the state health office, was quoted in the press as saying that there was no evidence of increased cancer caused by residing in phosphate mining areas. Scientists studying the problem made the suggestion that miners save the ten feet of top soil stripped from the land and replace it during the reclamation project. This would restore nature's protective blanket over any radioactive material.

Homer Hooks of the Phosphate Council pointed out that this was possible but that it would greatly increase reclamation costs. He added,

> First of all, we need to find out if it's necessary to do it. We're not convinced it is. If it's necessary, okay, this is one of the reclamation techniques we may have to adopt. . . . When we find out the scientific facts, we want to be prepared to take whatever remedial steps are indicated to assure safety to everybody.

Gerald Sims explained:

> I've read some reports from the EPA and from the state people where there's a possibility of air spacing from the foundation to the dwelling floors. . . . Shielding . . . these things have to be investigated. . . . They indicate that (concrete) does act as somewhat of a shield, but not a complete shield. They are talking about metal, lead, something of this nature. It would increase construction costs, but, again, I haven't seen any real firm figures on this at all.

With respect to the possibility of bringing topsoil in from a different area entirely, Mr. Sims replied:

> To translocate topsoil from another area, to our previously mined areas . . . that would be an impossibility. The economics there would not be justified. . . . I want to emphasize that you are talking about a tremendous acreage, and a tremendous earth movement by sorting the piles in our present mining, but to take from other areas would be an impossibility. . . . How would you move Hardee County into Polk County?

Richard Guimond of the EPA said of the control measures:

> With respect to potential control methods for precluding the problem of contaminated lands in the future, economic practicability of various control actions would be a valid consideration in determining the most suitable control means. However, at this time the Environmental Protection Agency has no authority to require specific types of mining or reclamation technology by industry in order to control this pollutant. . . . We can only make recommendations to the state of Florida and the local governments concerning acceptable radiation levels in structures and land contamination levels.

In July 1976, a symposium was held in Lakeland (Polk County), Florida to discuss the dangers of radiation on the populace of Central Florida. Few persons attended the symposium, however. Observed Dr. Nelson of Polk Community College and moderator of the panel:

> While radiation from reclaimed phosphate is measurable, it is not intense enough to arouse public alarm nor prompt public action to take measures to curtail it. . . . Unfortunately, not many people are trained in matters of radiation and need tangible, visible evidence to be convinced it poses a health problem. Even when long range effects of radiation damage add up to a cancer condition, the cause is in dispute and may be attributed to a variety of things that are more convincing in the minds of the public.

When asked how he felt county politicians viewed the radiation problem, Dr. Nelson replied:

> Commissioners are members of the public also and are subject to the same limitations in considering radiation damage—especially if economic advantages of an immediate nature outweigh arguments for spending money to limit radiation from reclaimed phosphate land. If it ever comes to a decision requiring drastic expenditures on the part of phosphate companies to correct radiation dangers, and these expenditures are coupled with economic penalties (increased cost of products, layoffs, closing of sections of the industry, etc.) county commissioners will minimize (the dangers of) radiation.

By late 1976, the phosphate industry was awaiting the results of the first phases of the EPA's radiation study.

Air and Water Pollution.   A recent brochure published by the Florida Phosphate Council makes the following points:

> The modern phosphate industry in Florida is a far cry from the operations of the early opportunists who saw, took and left. Today's industry is devoting time, money and total cooperation in making the term, "good business citizen," mean all that it should. . . .
> Air and water quality play an important part in phosphate operations. Dedicated and often voluntary efforts (at a cost of over $200 million in the past 10 years) have attacked the problems of pollution. . . . .
> Waterborne emissions have been cut by over 90 percent. And the industry's techniques of air pollution control are so successful they're studied as models by industries throughout the world.
> Preservation of our environment is vital. So is the production of phosphate. The environment nurtures us. Phosphate feeds us.
> We need both.

With few exceptions, the phosphate industry is meeting state and federal standards on permissible air and water emissions. In 1967, the Florida State Legislature passed the Air and Water Pollution Control Act which established a 5,500-pound-per-day level for fluoride emissions into the atmosphere. IMC Inc., a large phosphate producer, makes the following claim: ". . . by this time, the phosphate industry had voluntarily reduced its fluoride emissions to 3,000 pounds per day at full-production capacity, even though phosphoric acid production was rapidly increasing. Today, emissions are barely above 2,000 pounds."

In May 1972, the EPA approved an even more stringent Florida State Implementation Plan which required compliance by July 1, 1975. According to spokesmen for both the Atlanta regional office of the EPA and the Florida Department of Environmental Regulation (DER), the Florida phosphate industry is more than adequately meeting these standards.

However, the phosphate industry is far from being out of the woods with regard to air pollution. Constant monitoring is conducted by the DER and from time to time cases of noncompliance are uncovered. In June, 1976, the *Sarasota Herald Tribune* reported the following:

. . . the State Department of Environmental Regulation (DER) had filed suit in Hillsborough County Circuit Court seeking to shut down operations of the Gardinier Phosphoric Inc. phosphate processing plant at Gibsonton.

According to technicians of the Hillsborough County Environmental Protection Commission, the plant had registered 11 instances of excessive emissions since installation of the monitors in 1975. . . .

The water emission situation is very similar. In general, the industry is complying with state and federal standards. In 1972, the Florida Legislature enacted the Water Resources Act which established five water management districts within the state. The Southwest Florida Water Management District is responsible for the area where the bulk of the phosphate industry is located in Florida. In addition, corporate scientists constantly monitor water samples to assure compliance with published standards.

Most of the pollutants resulting from the phosphate mining process are contained in the clay solids which are separated from phosphate pebble. Because it takes as long as 10 to 15 years for the clays to stabilize in the industry's settling ponds, public concern is always present regarding the threat of a dam failure. In an article appearing in the *Tampa Tribune*, UPI writer Orval Jackson made the following observations:

. . . while in use these ponds pose the threat of pollution through spillage. (Homer) Hooks says new dam construction techniques minimize this danger. But twice in the last ten years, slime spills have turned the picturesque Peach River and part of Charlotte Harbor chalky and white and killed millions of fish before the waters cleared.

Hal Scott of the Florida Audubon Society expresses the opinion:

The phosphates present a real risk of water pollution. Considerable damage has been done to the Peach River over the years. With the expansion of the mining region, other areas will be threatened with the same thing.

Thomas Love, staff writer for the *Washington Star* summarizes the position of critics:

According to opponents of the industry, the mining operations pose a major pollution threat to Florida's beautiful and economically important rivers. They feed the estuaries which are dependent on the fresh water for their production of aquatic life.

Homer Hooks responds:

We raise families, send our kids to school, breathe the air, drink the water and enjoy the scenic beauties of Florida with everybody else. I'm a lifelong resident, and I'm not about to countenance the ruination of the place where I live. I'm not going to dirty my nest and I don't think anybody else in this industry wants to either.

Water Usage.   Perhaps more imperative than the long-standing debates over air and water quality is the recent controversy over water usage. Phosphate mining taps huge quantities of water from southwest Florida's supply. The Southwest Florida Water Management District says that phosphate companies draw 244 million gallons of water a day. This water comes from the huge underground freshwater reservoir which stretches the length and breadth of the state—the Floridian aquifer. Critics are quick to point out that the City of Tampa requires only 59 million gallons of water a day to supply its 320,000 residents.

The Florida Phosphate Council says that, through the industry's conservation practices, 85 percent of the water used by phosphate companies is recycled water, not water from the aquifer. In addition, the industry returns another 30 million gallons of water a day back into the Floridan aquifer by recharge wells. IMC, the industry's largest producer, is quick to point out the fact that:

> . . . in the last 15 years, approximately 115 fewer inches of rain fell than normal. This translates into some 20 billion gallons of water per day less than normal. . . . While industry might be thought to be the greatest water consumer, figures show it is not; irrigation for agriculture holds that distinction. . . . In a study of Consumptive (Water) Use in Florida conducted by Black, Crow and Eidsness, Inc., a firm of consulting hydrologists, irrigation accounted for 69 percent of the total water used, with municipal's share estimated at 13 percent, industry's 9 percent, and other usages 9 percent. . . . Presently IMC . . . recycles 89 percent of the water used at its four processing plants and withdraws 11 percent from the aquifer. However, IMC believes it can do better. Its goal is zero "consumptive" use of water from the aquifer. . . .

These future efforts are apparently unacceptable to critics who point out the present dangers of the situation. An editorial in the *Sarasota Herald Tribune* in June, 1976, expressed the opinion:

> We were blessed, in the month of May, with rainfall—more than in any May in recent memory.
> Watering bans imposed earlier in the spring get lifted now, and the temptation is to think that the water crisis has passed.
> But the improvement in our water situation is largely superficial. The problem is a long-term, continuing one. . . . And we are faced, in these counties, with proposals for unprecedented drawdowns of multibillions of dollars of fresh water from the Floridian aquifer in the next few years by phosphate mining and chemical processing companies.
> Data collected in May, district hydrologist Horace Sutcliffe, Jr., of the U.S. Geological Survey told the Manasota Basis Board this week, made it "very obvious the zone of closed contours has expanded considerably."
> A "zone of closed contours" is, in a manner of speaking, a subterranean sump—an area where the underground water supply has been so depleted that ground water from the surrounding areas in all directions tends to flow toward the sump.
> And this particular sump, from which too much water has been sucked, is in turn robbing water from an area covering about half of Manatee County where

a combination of over-use and rain-short years has caused the water table to drop to the average level of the Gulf of Mexico.

That, of course, means that sea water presses inland, rendering well water unfit for consumption and for crops. . . .

And as Sutcliffe warned the water board, the process is almost irreversible. It took all the millions of years since this peninsula emerged from the sea for our supply of ground water to accumulate.

We have been wastefully mining the essential resource.

And that must stop.

Gerald Parker, a recently retired hydrologist for the Southwest Florida Water Management District, also points out the dangers of salt water intrusion. He claims that the aquifer in Manatee County has dropped to ten feet below sea level 35 miles inland from the Gulf Coast. In Mr. Parker's words:

> If the present conditions continue, both Manatee and Sarasota Counties will be in serious trouble.

Homer Hooks agrees that great quantities of water are essential to the phosphate industry. But he points to studies which show that alternate mining methods are unfeasible. Dry mining, Hooks says, would increase the cost of the raw product and create a new pollution problem—dust.

Expansion into Other Areas. During the summer of 1976, Manatee County became the battleground for environmentalists and the phosphate interests. At issue: Would Beker Phosphate Corporation and Phillips Petroleum Company be allowed to mine phosphate in Manatee County?

In Manatee County, phosphate deposits were located about 50 feet below ground level. Before the recent increase in phosphate prices, the industry had not believed that mining in Manatee County would be particularly profitable.

"We've got everything going for us here," said vocal environmentalist, Sheila D. Leach, also the wife of the mayor of Brandenton. "It's a beautiful county. Don't we have a right to determine our destiny?"

One of the key points of contention in the controversy was the industry's use of water. Officials in adjoining Sarasota County pointed out that half of Sarasota's water supply came from reserves in Manatee County. Furth more, officials argued that the problem would worsen in future years because projections indicated that population in the Sarasota area would double in the next decade.

Also at issue was the detrimental effect that industry critics claimed mining would have on tourism, the largest industry in Manatee and Sarasota counties.

Much of the opposition indeed came from neighboring Sarasota County. In particular, the *Sarasota Herald Tribune* took a strong antiphosphate stance. The Sarasota County Commission also entered the antiphosphate fight as an interested party when Manatee County Commissioners granted Beker Corporation the first permit to mine in Manatee County.

So active were both of these phosphate opponents in their efforts that in

April Beker filed a $2 million lawsuit against the Sarasota County Commissioners, charging them with harrassment. A $10 million libel suit was filed against the Sarasota paper the same day. The suit against the paper was later dropped, but was then refiled in August.

In May, President Gerald Ford, in Florida during the 1976 campaign, was briefed by David Linsay, Jr., editor of the *Herald Tribune*. Later, at the president's request, the President's Council on Environmental Quality ordered an intensive and sweeping study of the environmental impact of phosphate mining in Florida.

Opposition to mining in Manatee County also came from environmental groups in Manatee County. The primary effort of these groups was to petition for a referendum on phosphate mining. In addition, one of the newspapers conducted a mail survey to determine the attitudes of Manatee County citizens toward phosphate mining. Over 95 percent of the respondents opposed mining in Manatee County, the paper later reported.

In July, in the eastern part of the county, a homeowner's association obtained 2,500 signatures on a petition protesting mining in the county.

Phosphate Council spokesmen were active as well during the summer: "I don't believe we need any kind of governmental restriction on mining," Homer Hooks was quoted as saying in an August newspaper article.[2] "The demand for food supply around the world requires that those of use who are in the food chain do the best job we can to feed these people." Hooks further observed:

> Those who say "Cut your mining rate in half and it will last twice as long"—well, that sounds good in theory, but who are we going to tell they cannot have phosphate fertilizer to grow a food crop? We can't play God. You've got people starving in Bangladesh, Pakistan, the Congo and other areas that desperately need food.

"If we are to keep feeding the world, expansion is necessary," Phosphate Council director of information Bobby Barnes told a Kiwanis Club.

Hooks was reported as saying in another interview:[3]

> World population is gaining at the rate of 200,000 persons every day. It will double early in the next century, and these people must be fed. Therefore, we have to mine the phosphate which the Lord put under the soil in Florida. It's simply a matter of the baby crop versus the food crop.

To counter arguments by critics that phosphate mining is harmful to tourism, Hooks often pointed out that Cypress Gardens is only 7 miles from an active phosphate mine and Disney World is 22 miles away from a mine.

As the expansion fight continued through the summer, many newspapers, government officials, and radio stations became active participants in the

---

[2] Orval Jackson, "Florida Phosphate Industry a Big Business," *Tampa Tribune*, August 17, 1976.

[3] Charles Patrick, "Phosphate Mining Involves Trade-offs," *St. Petersburg Tim s*, May 13, 1976.

controversy. Below is an excerpt from an August editorial aired by a radio station in Sarasota:

> In this coming election phosphate mining is becoming an issue. Most candidates are opposed to the mining of phosphate in Manatee County, They just simply do not want it anywhere around us. If you ask why they'll tell you it's ugly, how much water is used, the possibility of radiation, the possibility of the sludge contaminating our rivers. Everything is based on a possibility. Anyone being for phosphate mining now . . . is condemned.
>
> Well, the facts are these. According to the *St. Pete Times,* without artificial fertilizers food production in the United States would be cut 50 percent. The cost of food would more than double, millions of people here in America and overseas would go hungry and perhaps starve. . . . Suppose every area in the world took the same attitude on all mining and drilling. Where would we get coal, oil, iron ore, bauxite, uranium, copper and so on?
>
> . . . Here we sit in Manatee and Sarasota using all the world's goods—oil, steel, paper, food. Yes and even fertilizer in our agriculture products— tomatoes, oranges, etcetera. But we will not produce; we take, but we don't give. It's not right. It's not fair. It's unjust.
>
> We know we'll be heavily criticized for our attitude. But before you do we want everyone of you to stop using products that are grown from commercial fertilizer—tomatoes, bread, oranges, orange juice, all meat, all cereals, all vegetable, all fruit. Then when you do and give up these products forever we'll believe you are definitely against phosphate mining.

In late summer, the Manatee County Commission met to review the mining request of Phillips Petroleum Company.

WELGRO: EXPANSION STRATEGY

A major expansion program completed in 1975 included: a new 3.5 million-ton-per-year phosphate rock mine in Polk County mines; construction of a deep water terminal on Tampa Bay with loading facilities for phosphate rock; a new ammonia plant in Oklahoma; and, finally, a new urea plant in Arkansas.

Demand for Phosphate.   Welgro's president, Carl J. Martin, wrote in a Letter to Stockholders:

> Looking to the future, the industry prospects are favorable. Fundamental strength still stems from the increasing need for food. . . .
>
> In the United States during 1975, 574 million acres were used for crops, representing essentially all of the arable acreage available. Increased requirements for agricultural products, for both domestic consumption and for export, can be met only by increasing yields per acre. This will require progressively larger amounts of fertilizer.

Participation with Foreign Countries.   Welgro is currently participating in several foreign projects. Welgro is, through a 25 percent interest, participating in the Korean Seventh Fertilizer Complex. In addition, Welgro is a 25

EXHIBIT 1
Mining Site

EXHIBIT 2
Mining Site (dragline in center)

EXHIBIT 3
Reclaimed Land

EXHIBIT 4
Reclaimed Land

percent equity holder in a proposed phosphate project in Jordan. Welgro has a 30 percent interest in a proposed nitrogen venture in Pakistan.

According to Mr. Martin, other projects are being evaluated in Southeast Asia, Europe, South America, and the Middle East.

Expansion in the United States. Other expansion projects either underway or planned are a second ammonia plant in Oklahoma and facilities in Louisiana to permit the receipt of phosphate rock from Florida and the loading of ships with the finished product.

34. Cumberland Gasket Company, Inc.*

"It's my problem and I've got to live with it," said Fred Barlow, vice president and general manager of the Maryland division of Cumberland Gasket Co., Inc. "There are 30 people out there in the plant working with asbestos, and even with all of the precautions we have taken, some of them may develop symptoms of asbestiosis or lung cancer." Mr. Barlow went on to observe that the real moral issue for him was related to the fact that most of the scientific evidence of serious consequences from inhaling asbestos dust was based on asbestos miners and other workers around raw asbestos, while only a relatively modest amount of asbestos was used in the Maryland Division. "My trouble is," he said, "that I just cannot be sure how serious it is."

The Maryland Division of Cumberland Gasket Co., Inc., manufactured a wide range of gaskets, washers and other nonmetallic fittings and parts which were primarily used in petroleum processing equipment such as pumps and valves. Some of these parts and fittings were made of asbestos because of the latter's exceptional resistance to wear and heat. The parts were relatively inexpensive, but were unusually critical components of the equipment in which they were used. Failure of one of these small parts could shut down an oil well or cause serious oil spillage for example. Thus, Cumberland's products were of substantial importance. The parts in question were manufactured in two plants in Cumberland, Maryland. In 1977, the Maryland Division had sales of about $20 million. Cumberland, which in other plants in Michigan and California made parts for the automotive industry, had sales of about $60 million in 1977.

CUMBERLAND AND FRED BARLOW

Cumberland Gasket Co., Inc., had been formed in 1970 by the merger of three smaller companies. While the primary goal behind the merger was to enable the companies involved to serve better an increasingly dispersed nationwide market, the divisions, which were generally equivalent to the predecessor companies, retained a great deal of autonomy. The general man-

---

* This case was made possible by the cooperation of a business firm which remains anonymous. Prepared by Profs. Herman Gadon and Dwight R. Ladd of the University of New Hampshire.

agers of each division, who were vice presidents of Cumberland, were primarily responsible for the profitability of their divisions. Thus, Mr. Barlow had the authority to decide what was best for his division, although he would also be responsible for the consequences.

Fred Barlow had been vice president at the Maryland division of Cumberland Gasket for three years. His career had been marked by determination to do well and to move on to more challenge when he felt he had come to grips with the ones he faced when he first took a job. Now 34, he had gone to work for a bearing manufacturer after he had finished high school. He worked there for a year to get enough money to get through college, went to college for a year, ran out of money, went back to the bearing manufacturer and finished his Bachelor's degree at night. After completing college, he acquired an MBA in an evening program. When he was 22 he became works manager of the bearing company. At 24 he left that company and joined a larger one that made electromagnetic laminations and stampings. First employed as production control manager, he became manufacturing manager before he left at the age of 27 to manage a division of a company that sold to libraries. At the age of 30 he came to Cumberland Gasket Co., Inc., as manufacturing vice president. Two years later the company merged and he became a corporate officer and general manager of the Maryland division.

Shortly after he joined Cumberland, Mr. Barlow read a book entitled *The Expendable American,* by Paul Brodeur. The book described the hazards of breathing asbestos dust, and documented the long struggle to impose maximum exposure standards. The book convinced Fred Barlow that working with asbestos could be a major health hazard, and he concluded that dealing with that hazard should be one of his major responsibilities.

THE PRODUCTS

About 15 percent of the Maryland division's sales were of products containing asbestos. These products ranged from tiny washers and gaskets to relatively large vanes used in air compressors. All of these were parts which had to fit snugly with metal surfaces against which they moved, while also being resistant to heat and having a certain amount of give. The production process began with sheets of canvas and asbestos laminated with resin compounds which were purchased from another manufacturer. At the Maryland plants, the laminated sheets were sawed, cut or drilled into the desired shapes and sanded as necessary. These operations created the exposure to dust which concerned Mr. Barlow.

ASBESTOS

Asbestos is a mineral which is impervious to heat and fire, and which can be separated into fibres which, like wool, can be carded, spun and woven or felted. It can also be crushed into powder and mixed with other substances such as paint or patching plaster. These qualities of asbestos mean that it has a multitude of applications in industry and consumer products. Some commonplace applications are brake linings, electrical insulation, washers, gaskets, and shingles.

Asbestos was known and used in classical times—as lamp wicks, for example—but widespread use began with the industrial revolution. For some applications—automotive brake linings, for example—there is no known substitute for asbestos. Unfortunately, it has been generally known since the beginning of this century that asbestos—or more specifically, inhaled asbestos fibres—is a principal cause of certain, almost invariably fatal, diseases. One of these is asbestosis which is the scarring of the tissues of the lungs which ultimately results in the victim being unable to breathe. Lung cancer is also a likely result of inhaling asbestos, as is mesothelioma (malignant tumors of the lining of the chest cavity). Asbestos-related diseases are of the sort which, in the absence of regular medical checkups, appear only 20 or 30 years after exposure at which time they are generally untreatable. As yet, it is not known how much or how little exposure will cause one or another of these diseases, but it is believed that not a great deal of exposure is required and that build up of fibres in the body is cumulative and irreversible. Further, because asbestos fibres readily cling to other substances such as clothing or the skin, the dust can be widely dispersed. There is incontrovertible evidence that members of the families of asbestos workers have contracted these diseases in an abnormal degree even though they had never been near places where asbestos was handled.

REGULATION

Prior to 1972, the United States had no enforceable standard for maximum exposure to asbestos. In 1969, the American Conference of Governmental Hygienists recommended a minimum exposure standard of not more than 12 asbestos fibres longer than five microns in a cubic centimeter of air, over an eight-hour period.[1] In spite of its name, this organization was a privately funded, nongovernmental agency, and thus adherence to the standard was entirely voluntary.

In 1970 Congress passed the Occupational Safety and Health Act which, among other things, empowered the Secretary of Labor to set safety standards. The act also created the National Institute for Occupational Safety and Health (NIOSH), and, during 1970 and 1971, NIOSH publicized a number of earlier studies showing the health hazards associated with asbestos. Trade union officials and independent investigators urged that a minimum

---

[1] A micron is equal to 1/5,000th of an inch. It is about the smallest fibre length that can be measured without an electron microscope. It is estimated that the presence of two five-micron fibres in a cubic centimeter of air means the presence of up to 1,000 smaller particles.

The average person will breathe in about 8 million cubic centimeters of air in an eight-hour period.

exposure standard of two five-micron fibres per cubic centimeter be instituted by the Secretary. This, incidentally, was the standard adopted by the
British government in 1968. However, the Secretary chose, in early 1972, to
impose a standard of five fibres. After continued controversy and public
hearings, the two-fibre standard was promulgated in July 1975, and in 1977
OSHA proposed a new limit of one half five-micron fibre per cubic centimeter of air. NIOSH, at the same time, was urging adoption of a standard of
one-tenth five-micron fibre.

THE FABRICATION DIVISION

The Maryland division's operations were carried on in two separate
plants. One was housed in the original 19th-century factory where Cumberland began, but the other, in which most of the asbestos processing took
place, had been constructed in 1976. In the old plant, only some machines
were fitted with dust collectors, and therefore asbestos products could only
be worked on those machines—thereby considerably limiting flexibility in
scheduling. In the new, one-story, windowless plant, dust was collected
from all machines and deposited through a central evacuating system into
plastic sealable bags. This meant that products containing asbestos could be
worked on any machinery in the plant. Though more costly, the application
of dust collection to all equipment in the new plant provided a cleaner total
environment as well as more scheduling flexibility. The sealed plastic bags
were removed by a small independent contractor and buried within 24 hours
in the city's landfill dump.

Under OSHA regulations every employee working with asbestos was
required to wear a mask. Mr. Barlow insisted on rigorous enforcement of the
rules by decreeing that the supervisor of any employee working with asbestos
without a mask would be immediately suspended for a week. Though Mr.
Barlow made frequent inspections, no one had ever been found without a
mask. In the early days of Mr. Barlow's tenure, Cumberland's insurance
carrier had made annual surveys of dust conditions. In 1976, Mr. Barlow had
his own testing equipment purchased so that the plant could conduct its own
tests every month. In the three inspections by OSHA, particles of asbestos
at every machine in the two factories had always been below the OSHA
standard of two fibres. In accordance with OSHA regulations, any employee
working with asbestos was required to have his pulmonary functions tested
and chest X rayed under the direction of a physician at least once each year.
The company was required to keep records of these medical tests of each
employee for 50 years.

ATTITUDES ABOUT THE HAZARD

In spite of various precautions being taken, Mr. Barlow was not sure that
enough was being done, or whether any exposure to asbestos was accepta-

ble. Though scientific evidence of the effects of small dosage was still inconclusive, Mr. Barlow observed, "If a five-micron fibre is dangerous, why is a 4.9-micron fibre OK?"

Though his peers were aware of, and concerned about, the dangers of working with asbestos, there were differences of opinion among them about what more could or should be done. Some were resigned to the realization that hazards are all about us anyhow and in some minimum sense unavoidable. Others equated the risk with no more than occasional smoking and raised the question whether tests on animals of massive exposure to substances could really be used to evaluate effects of very small, albeit continuous, exposure of humans to those substances. By and large they had concluded from all the facts as they knew them, that Cumberland's precautions provided workers with sufficient protection as well as early warning through regularly scheduled pulmonary inspections. This opinion was strengthened by the results of a study of the medical records of retired Cumberland employees who had died during the preceeding 20 or so years. In no case was the cause of death apparently related to asbestos.

Mr. Barlow's greatest frustration was with the workers themselves, who, according to Mr. Barlow, "couldn't give a damn." Employees and others, Mr. Barlow felt, had seen so many ridiculous government regulations that they assumed that all government regulations were ridiculous.[2] Wiping the white asbestos dust off his finger after he had handled a small, in-process piece of asbestos-laminated sheet, a supervisor, showing the casewriters through the plant, shrugged his shoulders and said he had resigned himself to the exposure as an unavoidable part of his job, though he worried about the effect on his wife and children. He noted the thin layer of dust on all surfaces in the plant in spite of elaborate dust collection equipment, and reflected about the consequences of asbestos particles carried home on his clothes and transferred to the clothes of other family members in the family wash.

Most customers were primarily concerned that asbestos and asbestos products were becoming more expensive and harder to get, but did not otherwise appear to be overly concerned about the health hazard since they only installed parts and did not machine, sand or saw them.

THE MARKET

When Mr. Barlow took over management of the Maryland division, Cumberland Gasket Co., Inc., had two competitors for its asbestos-based products. About the time that the two-fibre OSHA standard was introduced in 1975, one of the competitors left the market for reasons not known to Mr.

---

[2] Mr. Barlow believed that, contrary to much popular opinion, OSHA was good and effective. He observed that while OSHA had promulgated some silly and widely publicized regulations about the shape of toilet seats and the like, there was incontrovertible evidence that industrial injuries and accidents had declined since OSHA had come into existence. He was confident that these declines would not have occurred without OSHA.

Barlow. Thus, in 1978, only Cumberland and one other company were supplying the market. Mr. Barlow thought that the other company reflected concern for the hazards of working with asbestos when they stopped selling trimmed asbestos sheet in 1977. (Trimming creates dust.) He had heard rumors from customers and other sources that the last competitor was planning to leave the market.

The market for the asbestos-based products made by Cumberland was dominated by a few large companies. In addition, there were 20 to 30 very much smaller customers. Mr. Barlow felt that the primary concern of these customers, especially in the replacement market, was with price and delivery. Early in 1977, the price of asbestos had increased by 16 percent following just six months after a 10 percent increase. Because there were now only two producers left, Cumberland and its one competitor, it was becoming increasingly difficult for customers to get timely delivery. Because of the general lack of concern about the hazards of asbestos, very little work had been done on developing a substitute. (There are hazards other than those related to workers. One estimate holds that 158,000 pounds of asbestos fibre is put into the air each year from the wearing down of automotive brake linings.) Nor could Cumberland, a relatively small company, afford to do much pure R&D on its own. DuPont had developed a substitute, which tends to be four to five times more expensive than asbestos, and was of inferior quality for some applications. The evidence of customer behavior was that they were unwilling to pay more for asbestos substitutes.

COMPANY POLICY AND ALTERNATIVES

In 1978, Cumberland's announced policy was to continue to manufacture asbestos as long as it could do so in compliance with OSHA or other standards, and as long as it could do so without further capital investment—unless the investment had a six-month or less payback. The investment limitation reflected management's view that standards very probably would be made more restrictive. Products using asbestos were always fully priced, including the costs of the air testing and special cleaning programs. Mr. Barlow would not discount products containing asbestos in order to promote other business. In his visits to and discussions with customers, he regularly tried to get them to try substitutes for asbestos, though with limited success. Mr. Barlow stressed the company's obligation to its customers and observed that Cumberland could not leave them without a source. Without Cumberland as a supplier, market demands could not be met. However, if the OSHA standard of one half of a fibre were introduced, Mr. Barlow thought that Cumberland could not continue without major changes.

One possible change would be to move to a complete "white room," space-age environment. This would involve isolating equipment used in making asbestos from the rest of the plant. Employees using the equipment would have to make a complete change of clothing and to shower before leaving the room. Masks would still be required. In addition to the costs associated with clothing changes, etc., the white room would mean serious underutilization of equipment, since the machines would only be used with asbestos material about 30 percent to 40 percent of the time. A white room would require an investment of three quarters of a million dollars and would raise operating costs by $100,000 a year. The fabrication division had $6 million in assets. Another alternative would be to process all asbestos under water or other liquid. However, since asbestos is absorbent, product properties could change. Thus considerable research would have to go into developing the liquid used and testing the properties of the product after it had been processed in a liquid.

Processing in a liquid would eliminate dust but would substitute asbestos-bearing sludges. Interestingly, neither OSHA nor the State had any regulations preventing the company from dumping sludge containing asbestos into the river. (Eventually, asbestos in the water would be washed up on the banks, dry out and enter the air.) The new Cumberland plant had a completely enclosed filtration system designed to prevent any discharge into the river. This system had not been required by law, but Mr. Barlow had included it when the plant was built, and even though it had added a substantial amount to the cost of the plant, top management had not questioned it.

The final option for Mr. Barlow and Cumberland was to leave the asbestos business entirely. As noted above, this would do irreparable harm to customers, and would raise the cost of many goods and services for society generally. Beyond this, there were serious financial consequences for the Cumberland company and its employees. Unless substitutes developed for asbestos-involved materials and processes which were adaptable to Cumberland's capabilities, jobs in the plant would inevitably be lost. Furthermore, the fabrication division was only marginally profitable and the contribution of products containing asbestos was considerable. Loss of the asbestos business would place the division in a loss position—and would jeopardize the profitability of other divisions within the company.

Though Mr. Barlow had given considerable thought to the moral and business issues involved in Cumberland's processing of asbestos materials, he still faced unresolved questions and concerns about the extent of the hazards to which Cumberland's workers were exposed and of the ways in which he should respond to them.

35. Asheville Foundries, Inc. (A)*

In June 1976, Adam Martin, assistant to the president of Asheville Foundries, Inc. (AFI), had been asked by the president, John Ridley, to prepare a proposal and specific recommendations concerning the closing of the company's large casting facility located in Greeneville, Tennessee. Martin had worked for AFI for only two months when he was given his assignment, and he was afraid that he had been handed a hornet's nest. Looking back through the files of the large castings foundry, he learned that the question of its closing had been considered many times during the last 12 years. Each time, "old-timers" at AFI had decided to keep the foundry open, for reasons Martin considered to be sentimental in nature.

In April 1976, OSHA (Occupational Safety and Health Agency) had issued citations on conditions at four of AFI's five foundries, including the large-castings foundry (called the Special Foundry by AFI) in Greeneville. This citation served as a stimulus for Mr. Ridley's request. Martin knew he would be expected to analyze the present and future markets for the special castings manufactured in Greeneville, as well as to analyze all other factors related to a possible shutdown of the facility. In particular, he would have to address the labor force and community relations problems. AFI was one of three major employers in Greeneville, and unemployment in the 45,000-population town had exceeded 11 percent since a large textile mill had closed its doors in the late 1960s. In spite of these considerations, Martin expected that Mr. Ridley would be most interested in an analysis of the cash flows associated with closing the foundry versus keeping it open.

Martin was concerned what effect his background might have on the top management task force set up to consider the closing of the foundry. (The task force included Mr. Ridley and five senior AFI officials from different parts of the company.) Since earning his M.B.A. at a large eastern business school in 1965, Martin had worked for a small electronics wholesaler for five years before coming to AFI's parent company, Acme Steel, as a financial analyst in the corporate office. His transfer to AFI was his first experience in the foundry business. He had, in fact, never seen a foundry until moving to Asheville.

---

* Prepared by Terry Allen under the supervision of Prof. Neil H. Borden, Jr. Copyright © 1977 by the Sponsors of The Colgate Darden Graduate School of Business Administration, University of Virginia. Reprinted by permission.

AFI, with 1975 sales of almost $200 million, had been a subsidiary of Acme Steel, headquartered in Dayton, Ohio, since 1967. The foundry company had operated almost completely autonomously of Acme control until John Ridley was named president of the subsidiary in 1973. Top Acme management considered itself to be at the vanguard of modern management techniques, and was particularly pleased with Mr. Ridley. He had established himself as one of Acme's most efficient and capable executives before being sent to "generate some cash" at the foundry. While AFI had always been profitable, Mr. Ridley had instituted some financial control systems which had helped the division double its profit rate inside of two years. In 1975, AFI was one of Acme's most profitable and fastest growing subsidiaries, accounting for 12 percent of Acme's sales and 26 percent of the parent's profits.

THE FOUNDRY INDUSTRY

The gray and ductile iron castings industry was composed of about 900 companies, most of which had fewer than 250 employees, and were located in the vicinity of their largest customer. The number of iron foundries had decreased to 900 from over 1,500 shortly after World War II, and the industry had grown steadily more concentrated during the postwar period (Exhibit 1). Slightly more than half the industry output was generated by "captive" foundries which produced castings primarily for use within their own company. The largest captive foundries were found in the automotive, construction equipment, and farm machinery industries. While independent foundries were more numerous (approximately 70 percent of all foundries), they were generally smaller, and accounted for only half of total iron castings.

Most U.S. foundries were built in the early 1900s, and continued to use rather simple production techniques. The production process generated a considerable amount of air and water pollution compared to many other industries. In the mid-1970s, outmoded manufacturing facilities and recent requirements of the Environmental Protection Act (EPA) and OSHA were forcing many smaller (mostly independent) foundries out of business. This contraction in the number of competitors had had a limited effect on total industry capacity because it primarily impacted upon the smaller operations with the least financial resources. Larger companies, such as AFI, were adding to capacity with technologically improved and environmentally clean facilities.

TYPES OF CAST IRON

Pure iron was a very soft metal which had few, if any, commercial applications. Combined with other elements, however, pure iron was transformed to one of five basic forms of commercially valuable materials—gray iron, white iron, malleable iron, ductile iron, and steel. The key element to these various iron forms was the carbon content.

EXHIBIT 1
Selected Foundry Industry Statistics

Industry Code	Industry and Year	Number of Companies	Value Added by Manufacturer ($ millions)	Total ($ millions)	Value of Shipments Percent of Total, Ranked by Company Size			
					4 Largest	8 Largest	20 Largest	50 Largest
3321	Gray Iron Foundries							
	1947	1,554	733	1,173	16	24	35	n.a.
	1958	1,199	811	1,435	24	33	47	61
	1963	1,062	1,169	1,985	28	37	51	65
	1967	969	1,543	2,638	27	36	50	61
	1972	893	2,257	3,877	34	45	59	71

n.a. = Not available.

Iron Products—Castings (000 short tons, gray and ductile iron shipments)

Year	Total	Noncaptive	Year	Total	Noncaptive
1947	12,755	7,314	1960	11,594	6,403
1948	13,207	7,381	1961	10,824	6,176
1949	11,050	5,787	1962	11,553	6,324
			1963	12,764	7,089
1950	13,725	7,324	1964	14,316	8,132
1951	14,989	8,453			
1952	12,869	7,372	1965	15,713	9,171
1953	13,708	7,495	1966	15,716	8,927
1954	11,532	6,323	1967	14,329	8,128
			1968	15,130	8,715
1955	14,838	7,967	1969	15,933	9,185
1956	13,861	7,960			
1957	12,665	6,876	1970	13,945	8,173
1958	10,358	5,849	1971	13,839	7,606
1959	12,308	6,994	1972	15,302	8,190
			1973	17,047	9,008
			1974	15,691	8,704

Gray iron was the oldest and most widely used cast iron. It contained a relatively high percent of dissolved carbon (graphite), a substance similar to pencil lead. The high graphite content in gray iron produced castings with the following qualities: (1) highly castable into intricate shapes; (2) easily machined (the graphite acted as a lubricant); (3) relatively simple to produce; (4) much cheaper than many other metals; (5) absorbed vibration better than other forms of iron or steel; (6) extremely brittle, with no elasticity; (7) strength, but not as strong as other forms of iron or steel; and (8) strongly corrosion-resistant.

White iron was harder than gray iron, but its low carbon content (below 3 percent) rendered it even more brittle and virtually unmachinable. (Gray and white iron derived their names from the color of the castings when fractured.) There were only limited applications for white iron—mostly in products which required exceptional resistance to abrasion or wear, such as grinding wheels.

Malleable iron was essentially white iron after undergoing an annealing process. This process, which increased the cost of the casting considerably, involved heating the white iron in a furnace well below the melting point for several days. The resulting iron was stronger and less brittle than gray iron, and could easily be machined (providing its name, malleable). However, malleable iron could not be used for larger castings, and its use was limited to situations where castings had to be machined, were resistant to shock, and had thin sections. Automobile door hinges were generally made of malleable iron castings.

Iron that contained 1 percent or less carbon was called steel. Castings made of steel were stronger than traditional iron castings, and were considerably more elastic and workable. However, steel castings could not be made into intricate shapes like gray iron. Steel castings generally required a large amount of machining, shaping, and welding after the casting had been made.

Ductile iron, discovered in the late 1940s, combined some of the best qualities of steel (strength, impact resistance) and gray iron (castability into intricate shapes, corrosion resistance, machinability). Due to the presence of graphite, ductile iron wore better than steel. An important advantage of ductile iron was that while a higher level of technology was involved, the production methods were similar to gray iron. Ductile iron was produced by removing most of the sulphur content from base iron, and adding magnesium while the iron was still molten. In this form, the iron would be worked or drawn (hence its name, ductile iron). Typical ductile iron applications included highway safety items such as automobile brakes, clutches, and power steering parts, as well as industrial crankshafts, valve bodies, and air-conditioning parts. Ductile iron capacity in the United States had increased by almost 20 percent a year since the early 1950s, and was expected by industry leaders to continue a 10–15 percent annual growth rate well into the 1980s.

Regardless of the type of iron being cast, there were four distinct steps in the manufacturing process for castings: melting the metal, making cores and molds, pouring iron into the molds, and finishing or cleaning the resultant casting. Most foundries performed the melting step in a cupola, a large vertical steel cylinder lined with refractory brick. Coke was used as fuel to melt a combination of pig iron, steel scrap, and limestone into molten iron. As the molten iron was removed or "tapped" from the cupola, new ingredients were continually added. In many foundries, two cupolas were operated in pairs with one running while the other underwent maintenance.

Cores and molds were used to form the shape of the casting. The core formed the openings inside the casting while the mold shaped the outside dimensions. Cores and molds were made of sand by one of three methods—green sand molding, shell molding, or no-bake molding. The green sand method was the oldest and most frequently used method. Green (uncured) sand was mixed with a binder and compacted around a steel pattern. In some cases the sand was mechanically thrown at high velocity onto the pattern, and in others it was jolted or squeezed to compact it. Shell molding used sand mixed with a resin which was heat-baked on a steel pattern. Asheville Foundries pioneered the shell molding method in the mid-50s. Shell molding was used to produce small castings at high-dimensional accuracy and excellent surface finish for grinding. No-bake molding was a new process just being developed in the late 1960s.

The third step in the manufacture of castings was pouring the molten iron into the cores and molds. Once the alloys were added and slag removed, the molten iron was put in a pour-off ladle which was tilted by the operator to pour into the molds. Depending on the size of the castings, the molds were either moved by conveyor belt to the pour-off ladle or for large castings, an overhead crane moved the pour-off ladle to a stationary mold.

Once the molten iron had cooled, the cores and molds were disintegrated by blasting with metal shot. The sand was reclaimed and used again to produce more cores or molds. The castings were inspected, weighed, and packed for shipment.

The manufacture of castings was generally considered to be a dirty business. Large amounts of smoke and ashes were produced by the process, and considerable amounts of water were filled with particles of dirt while cooling the cupolas and cleaning mold and core sand for reclamation. Dust released in the iron-melting process (fly-ash) was difficult and expensive to control. A cupola with an annual capacity of 10,000 tons (the size used in the Asheville Special Foundry) would release 160,000 pounds a year into the atmosphere when operating at capacity. Because of the intensity of the heat from the burning of the coke, and the air pressure introduced to raise the temperature of the coke, the air was too hot and fast moving to filter immediately upon exiting from the cupola. In order to control these emissions, the air had to be cooled first.

According to government tests, 80 percent of the dust which escaped through the stack was comprised of particles that were too heavy to travel beyond the immediate vicinity of the foundry. Many foundries had, for years, employed sweepers whose sole job was to sweep dust from the foundry roof. Smaller foundries had periodic sweeping days in which the foundry yard would be similarly cleaned. On windy days, the dust would inevitably escape to the surrounding neighborhood. Air pollution experts categorized 90 percent of the foundry industry's air pollution as "nuisance" (as distinct from gaseous pollution, which might be poisonous even in small quantities).

Recently OSHA and EPA requirements had forced many foundries to install expensive systems to safeguard workers, prevent smoke from polluting the air, and to keep dirty water out of the waterways. AFI spent almost $1 million a year from 1970 to 1975 to install such equipment. Many smaller foundries could not afford these kinds of investments, and were forced to suspend operations.

ASHEVILLE FOUNDRIES, INC.

AFI was established with $25,000 capital in 1902 with the sole purpose of manufacturing agricultural implements. The company soon branched out to other kinds of castings, and purchased a Greeneville foundry in 1905. In 1919, the company earned the Distinguished Service Award of the War Department for having aided materially in obtaining victory in World War I. During World War II, a second foundry was built in Asheville. A new mechanized molding unit enabled the company to mass produce small- and medium-sized gray iron castings critically needed for war purposes. Over the years, AFI employees were especially proud of the part they played in the making of the Panama Canal, several U.S. aircraft carriers, and the Apollo moon project. In 1967 Acme Steel of Dayton, Ohio, acquired AFI.

In 1976, AFI owned five foundries, three of which made small (under 100 pounds) castings, one which made medium castings (100–1,000 pounds), and the Special Foundry in Greeneville which produced large castings (1,000 to 60,000 pounds).[1] All but one foundry manufactured both gray and ductile iron. Exhibit 2 summarizes the locations, capacities, and markets served by AFI's foundries.

AFI had long been a technological leader in the foundry industry. A new $600,000 research facility was completed in 1975 to help insure continuation of this leadership. The company's largest foundry (Asheville 3) was completed in 1973, and was recognized as being one of the most modern, clean, and efficient foundries in the world. Almost half the employees in this foundry were women. In comparison, the Greeneville foundries had historically employed virtually no women in the manufacturing operations. Technolog-

---

[1] There were five separate foundry facilities, three in Asheville, two in Greeneville. Some central services supported all five foundries, while some other services supported either Asheville operations or the Greeneville foundries.

EXHIBIT 2
Summary of Production Facilities

	Markets*	Expected Annual Growth Rate (percent)	Foundry	Type Iron	Capacity†	1975 Production Capacity (percent)
Small castings— less than 100 lbs.	Internal combustion engines Automotive Air conditioning and refrigeration Farm machinery Valves and pumps	10–15%	Asheville 3	Gray and ductile	60,000	88%
Medium castings— 100–1,000 lbs.	Construction equipment Highway trucks Internal combustion engines Air conditioning and refrigeration Farm machinery Valves and pumps	4–8	Asheville 2	Gray and ductile	30,000	100
Large castings— 1,000+ lbs.	Construction equipment Machine tools Glass industries Chemical process Miscellaneous industry products	0–5	Greeneville Special	Gray and ductile	10,000	67

* Markets are not listed in order of importance.
† Capacity in annual tons based on normal five-day operation.
Source: Company records.

ical leadership, a high-quality product, and a base of hard-working loyal employees were considered by top management as being responsible for AFI's position as one of the largest noncaptive foundries in the United States. AFI maintained a position of price leadership in the industry. Because of its high quality and modern facilities, many companies with captive foundries used AFI as a second source of supply in spite of its generally higher prices.

Most of AFI's customers were among the largest 200 companies in the United States. The automotive market was AFI's largest volume customer for small castings. AFI made disc brake calipers, power steering components, automatic transmission parts, and air conditioner parts, and was normally the majority supplier to a particular automotive customer. Small castings were also sold to farm machinery, air conditioning, and industrial valve manufacturers.

The medium-size casting foundry (Asheville 2) primarily served the construction equipment industry. This foundry had been running at capacity since 1963. Medium castings were also sold for trucks, automobiles, air conditioners and refrigeration units, valves, and pumps.

Large castings made in the Greeneville Special Foundry were primarily sold to the construction equipment industry, with smaller amounts going for chemical process equipment and machine tool markets. Slow market growth, less than the real growth of GNP, had been projected by AFI top management for the large castings market.

THE CONSULTANT'S REPORT

In 1973, AFI had hired a leading management consultant firm to investigate AFI's customer image, and to project future sales of the Greeneville Special Foundry. The consultant had reported that AFI had an excellent reputation in the field, and was considered as one of the best commercial jobbing foundries in the country. Customers generally identified Greeneville with Asheville, and did not consider the foundries as separate entities. In the words of the consultant,

> "AFI is viewed as a first class operation, headed by an extremely capable management and technical group, dedicated to superior quality products. AFI had a near perfect delivery record going until the strike in the spring of 1973 forced the foundry to allocate orders and to fall behind in shipments. Although many customers have been irritated and inconvenienced by the allocation scheme, very few of them said that the temporary situation would cause them to look elsewhere for engineered castings.

The consultant firm had additional thoughts about the Greeneville Special Foundry:

> Greeneville has an excellent quality reputation, but the larger castings produced there are not priced competitively. If other capacity were available some of Greeneville's patterns would be pulled by existing customers and placed elsewhere. Other foundries that specialize in large engineered castings have upgraded their sand handling facilities and mold lines, and have become very competitive. Greeneville is the least cost competitive of the AFI facilities.

The consultant concluded that the major weakness of AFI was its lack of capacity. Customers had been forced to source their new parts at other domestic and foreign foundries, and to dual-source existing parts because they had been unable to place additional business with AFI. Many companies had indicated that as long ago as 1969, AFI had refused to quote on many parts because of lack of capacity.

The consultant projected sales for the Greeneville Special Foundry (Exhibit 3) and noted that the outlook for castings under 2,500 pounds was strikingly dissimilar to the outlook for castings over 2,500 pounds. Little or no growth was expected for large castings in most existing industry/product areas, and in glass grinding laps, a complete loss of business was projected. The float glass process had replaced the grinding process, and the one remaining glass plant that used laps was going to be closed within five years. On the other hand, demand for the smaller castings produced at the Greeneville Special Foundry was projected to increase steadily, at least until 1984.

THE GREENEVILLE SPECIAL FOUNDRY

Built in the early 1900s, the Greeneville Special Foundry was AFI's smallest and least technologically advanced foundry. The large castings made in Greeneville required the most highly skilled craftsmen in the company, and the methods of making cores and molds did not lend themselves to mechanization. Since large castings were generally stationary, conventional assembly line and conveyor systems of handling the castings could not be used. AFI engineers had concentrated on technological improvements in the small and medium casting foundries, particularly the three foundries in Asheville.

EXHIBIT 3
Consultant's Projection of Sales, October 1973—Opportunity for Greeneville Special Foundry (000 tons)

	Castings under 2,500 lb. Incremental			Castings over 2,500 lb. Incremental		
	Actual	Opportunity		Actual	Opportunity	
Industry	1972	1976	1982	1972	1976	1982
Valves	0.02	0.5	0.6	0	0	0
Construction machinery (except Eugene)	0.4	0.2	0.4	0	0	0
Pumps and compressors	0	0.5	0.8	0.1	0.1	0.2
Air conditioning and refrigeration	0.5	0.7	2.3	0.02	0.2	0.5
Engines	0.03	1.8	5.5	0	0	0
Electric motors	0.2	0.2	0.4	0.1	0	0
Machine tools	0.2	0	0	0.6	0	0
Glass grinding laps	0.1	0	0	2.1	0.2	0
Process equipment and miscellaneous	0.3	0.2	0.4	0.4	0	0
Subtotal	2.0	4.1	10.4	3.3	0.5	0.7
Eugene Tractor	4.6	0.8	0.2	0	0	0
Total	6.6	4.9	10.6	3.3	0.5	0.7

Source: Consultant's report.

The Special Foundry shipments in 1975 were as follows:

End-Use Industries	GSF Shipments 1975 (tons)	Percent of Shipments
Construction equipment	4,360	64%
Air conditioning and refrigeration	467	6
Pumps and compressors	51	nil
Large engine blocks	155	2
Large motors and generators	383	5
Machine tools	74	1
Chemical processing equipment	266	3
Industrial valves	199	2
Miscellaneous	777	17
Total	6,732	100%

A single customer in the construction equipment industry, Eugene Tractor, accounted for over half the Special Foundries shipments in 1975. Eugene had redesigned the earthmover that used AFI large castings, and would require 2,000 less annual tons from AFI after 1979.

Adam Martin asked the marketing department to analyze the markets for large castings manufactured in the Special Foundry. Their study showed AFI was price competitive on only 1 out of 15 representative castings (see Exhibit 4). For the other 14 items, AFI's customers were paying 15–100 percent more for AFI's castings than they would pay competitors. One of the reasons for the price discrepancy was that many of AFI's competitors had switched to the lower-cost no-bake method of making molds for large castings, while AFI had not yet made the change.

The marketing department made an industry-by-industry analysis of the market (Exhibit 5) which concluded that demand would be falling off as more large castings were made by captive foundries and customers switched to foundries offering lower prices. Based on this analysis, sales of large castings were forecast for the years 1976–80 (Exhibit 6). Martin thought that the forecasts developed by the marketing department were generally in line with the projections made by the consultant in 1973.

The marketing department's analysis of potential gains in market share, the competitive situation, and cost effectiveness is summarized in Exhibit 7.

OPTIONS

In preparation for a preliminary meeting with the task force, Martin spent a considerable amount of time with marketing, plant, and accounting personnel. After these discussions he developed four tentative alternatives for consideration:

Option 1. Continue the present operation, retain the existing casting mix, and make improvements (primarily a conversion to no-bake molding) to cause the foundry to be cost-competitive and to achieve government-

EXHIBIT 4
Greeneville Special Foundry Pricing

	Date	Part No.	Part Name	Weight (pounds)	Repre-sentative Quotations
Eugene*	12/4/75	2QR-12	Trans case, D.I.	318	30% high
	9/22/75	2QP-18	Sprocket	763	Competitive
	9/22/75	TF-1200	Wheel	580	Now fabrica-tion; cast-ing price is same
	4/25/75	FF-1407	Wheel	640	67% high
	1/6/75	QRP-16	Frame	1,020	56% high
	12/24/75	QZ-12-S	Case	450	100% higher than fabri-cation construc-tion
Consolidated	1/12/76	RF-24	Frame	735	25% high
Electric Systems	1/12/76	RF-80	Frame	876	25% high
World Tractor†	4/5/76	WT-8	Wheel	2,350	15–20% high
	4/5/76	WT-12	Wheel	2,215	15–20% high
	4/5/76	WT-18	Wheel	2,000	15–20% high
General Turbine	2/6/76		Pump cases	516	15–30% high
			Pump cases	550	15–30% high
			Pump cases	550	15–30% high
			Pump cases	830	15–30% high

* Competition is Cambridge and Ames Corporation and Pittsdown on G.I.
† Competition is Pittsburg Foundry.
Source: Company records.

EXHIBIT 5
Markets for Large Castings—Greeneville Special Foundry Marketing Department

Construction Equipment

This segment, particularly Eugene, has historically represented 40–60 percent of the Special Foundry shipments. Present shipments include tonnage for B.A. Indus-tries that is not as profitable nor stable as Eugene. Approximately 2,000 tons annu-ally from Eugene will be lost by the end of 1979 due to a complete redesign that eliminates the need for a casting. Eugene will have first refusal on any new casting that will fit their foundries. The trend is toward small quantity parts going to fabrica-tions. Eugene does not offer the potential for large castings as in the past. B.A. Industries placed work at Greeneville when they took out a sandslinger. We will not be able to keep all of this work long range at present cost structure. The ductile wheels for off-highway trucks that we produce for World-Tractor should continue. European Motors is jobbing castings in this country.

Air Conditioning and Refrigeration

Requires high quality and competitive pricing, particularly at General Air. At De Frost Compressor, high quality and reliable delivery will bring a premium price.

EXHIBIT 5 (continued)

Returns and allowances are high. With good quality and delivery, an opportunity exists at DeFrost for 1,000–1200 tons annually. General Air would buy more from AFI is prices were competitive with Chicago Industries (mechanized no-bake foundry). We are 20 percent high on the active part that we now make, and additional reorders are questionable at present prices. Screw compressor castings at Forster Equipment offer only small tonnage. Southington will never be a big factor in this market. There are few captive foundries in the air conditioning and refrigeration industry, and good current and growth potential is available to a quality, cost-effective foundry.

Pumps and Compressors

The three major producers all have captive facilities. We have produced for Claremont, but price and delivery caused them to move patterns locally.

Large Engine Blocks

Our experience with V.S. Auto was good from a quality standpoint, but pricing was 50–60 percent high. Lends itself to a foundry that specializes in heads and blocks.

Large Motors and Generators

Good continuing potential with Consolidated Electric and Universal. Growth will be limited, however, due to more and more being built special and the stator frame being fabricated.

Machine Tools

Highly captive—again, due to the custom made machines; there is excess capacity in this industry. In previous years, this industry would move patterns outside when they were busy and bring them back when the crunch was over.

Chemical Processing Equipment

Little long-range potential. Due to the exotic materials processed, most processing equipment has been changed to stainless steel and the demand for iron is limited.

Industrial Valves

Highly captive and highly fragmented—usually for special applications. Some of captive shops are not cost effective. Valves for Pratt, Malleable, and Scott Equipment.

Miscellaneous

Paper-making machinery—S-W Corporation has 60–70 percent of the market and has captive foundry.
Printing machinery—United Printing has a high percentage of the market, but is moving toward fabrications as more and more are custom made.

Source: Company records.

EXHIBIT 6
Shipments to Present Customers after Screening—Marketing Department Projections (tons)

	1976	1978	1980
Eugene	3,876	2,515	1,011
B. A. Industries	1,021	549	413
World Tractor	144	84	58
General Air	164	93	71
DeFrost Compressor*	589	442	349
Consolidated Electrical Systems	209	122	84
Universal Electric	255	148	107
Youngstown Consolidated	180	181	84
Scott Equipment	78	76	33
Malleable Corporation	32	8	12
Total	6,548	4,219	2,222

* Optimistic tonnages, although schedules for 1976 reflect over 1,000 tons.
Source: Company records.

mandated and socially desirable environmental changes. If this alternative were selected, top management estimated that $334,000 should be invested to improve the handling of sand (mixers, shakeout, and conveyors), $125,000 for the OSHA citation (exhaust system for the No. 1 cleaning shed), as well as $855,000 for other environmental systems (primarily exhaust systems) not presently required by OSHA (see Exhibit 8 for detail). There was a strong feeling throughout AFI headquarters that the current OSHA citation was only a beginning, and that eventually, OSHA would require that the full $855,000 be spent at the Special Foundry to improve the environment for production workers.

Option 2. Convert the present operation to 2,500 tons per year of select castings. This option was attractive because it involved shutting down the cleaning shed cited by OSHA, eliminating an expenditure of $125,000. Further, the Special Foundry would be manufacturing selected castings that were cost competitive, profitable to AFI, and growing in demand. Estimated environmental costs of $798,000 made this option almost as costly as option 1, however (see Exhibit 9 for details).

Option 3. Continue the foundry but without casting pots, laps, and pits, and only react when required to do so by OSHA. Only a small part of the foundry's output would be affected by discontinuing pots (large iron pots used to mix caustic chemicals), laps (being discontinued by the glass industry anyway), and pits (large iron molds inside of which pots were cast). The exhaust system for the No. 1 shed would be dropped (or at least delayed) since the shed would have reduced usage.

The OSHA citation was issued in January 1975, and AFI was given until January 1977, to remedy the situation in the No. 1 cleaning shed. The citation also included a fine and required that monthly progress reports be sub-

EXHIBIT 7
Additional Potential Business: Report from Marketing Department

An analysis of the market indicates that there is minimal additional business available that fits the Special Foundry.

The foundry has, through the years, relied heavily on Eugene as well as a wide range of industrial jobbing customers.

Technological change has eliminated the potential castings business in glass making, chemical pots, and pit molded compressor bases. Change in machine tool designs as well as change in the economy has allowed the machine tool manufacturers to produce most of their own castings.

In Eugene's Project 300 the two major castings that are currently produced at Greeneville will be designed out due to moving the location of the engine on the Model 10 bulldozer. This will eliminate over 2,100 tons annually from our schedule.

Market Share

With the exception of DeFrost Compressor and General Air, AFI already supplies almost 100 percent of customers' requirements in this type casting. At DeFrost, AFI currently supplies less than 10 percent of their requirements. An opportunity exists to supply up to 20 percent of their demand.

Competitors

Chicago Industries—quality foundry, produces in no-bake and supplies heavily to DeFrost and General Air.

Pittsburg Foundry—quality foundry, produces pit molded housings for Cleveland Motors. Produces for DeFrost.

Messner, division of Central Equipment—formerly a captive shop but has been supplying DeFrost for about two years.

Terry Foundries—produces quality castings up to 5,000 pounds.

Pittsdown Foundry—has first refusal on any new gray iron castings at Eugene.

Auto Castings—quality short-run foundry for castings up to 5,000 pounds.

Cambridge—gray and ductile iron up to 40,000 pounds.

Both LeMonde Foundry (owned by Eugene) in Belgium and a foundry in Brazil are tooled on Model 10 (Brazil supplied some during AFI's strike in 1973).

Cost Effectiveness

The Greeneville Special Foundry is old and not a cost-effective facility and will become even less so as capital monies for OSHA are added.

Source: Company records.

mitted to OSHA. These reports were to specify what had been done and what remained to be done to effect full abatement.

Martin thought that option 3 might be risky and could result in hundreds of top management hours being consumed in negotiations with OSHA officials. Martin believed AFI had maintained good relations with OSHA, especially compared to other foundries in the area, and Martin thought that Mr. Ridley would not want to jeopardize this relationship.

Option 4. Discontinue the Greeneville Special Foundry. Martin thought that the greatest disadvantage to this alternative was the matter of overhead presently being absorbed by the Special Foundry. This amounted to almost

EXHIBIT 8
Option 1—Continue Present Operation and Convert to No-Bake Molding

OPTION 1—Continue to operate the Special Foundry for at least five years with the present casting mix and at an output of 10,000 tons per year.

General Conditions of Operation

1. Use existing core, molding, pouroff, and cleaning facilities.
2. Ventilate building for pouroff by using roof ventilators and unheated makeup air. Exhaust to atmosphere. (This ventilation method is a risk in that it may not meet environmental control standards.)
3. New castings shakeout and exhaust system.
4. New cores shakeout and exhaust system.
5. Improvements to molding sand handling system.
6. New sand mixer for molding sand—30 tph capacity.
7. Air condition crane cabs on the four bridge cranes that serve the Special Foundry.
8. Exhaust System for No. 1 cleaning shed.

A. Core Making:
   Use present process and equipment. No capital improvements.

B. Molding:
   Use present process and equipment. No capital improvements.

C. Pouroff and Shakeout:

1—Castings shakeout (8′ × 10′—15-ton capacity)	$ 80,000
1—Castings shakeout exhaust system (75,000 cfm, including dust collector	270,000
1—Hot castings exhaust system (125,000 cfm, use same collector as shakeout exhaust)	50,000
1—Core shakeout (6′ × 8′—10-ton capacity)	50,000
1—Core shakeout exhaust system (50,000 cfm, including dust collector)	150,000
Subtotal	$ 600,000

D. Molding Sand System:

1—Bucket elevator	$ 23,000
1—Belt conveyor	10,000
1—Rotary screen exhaust system (exhaust to shakeout dust collector)	6,000
2—Sand storage silos (modifications)	22,000
1—Sand unloading conveyor (30″W × 24′L—30 tph)	25,000
1—Sand unloading conveyor (30″W × 12′L—30 tph)	16,000
1—Sand transfer conveyor (30″W × 28′L—30 tph)	27,000
1—Sand mixer and skip loader (30 tph)	75,000
1—Sand mixer exhaust system (2,000 cfm)	10,000
Subtotal	$ 214,000

E. Environmental:

1—Building ventilation system 2 million cfm to atmosphere	$ 275,000
4—Air condition bridge crane cabs	100,000
1—Exhaust system for No. 1 cleaning shed	125,000
Subtotal	$ 500,000
Subtotal, all items	$1,314,000
10% contingency	131,000
Grand total (Option 1)	$1,445,000

Source: Company records.

EXHIBIT 9
Option 2—Convert to 2,500 Tons per Year

OPTION 2—Convert present operation to 2,500 tons per year of select castings using green sand molding and combination of no-bake and oil sand cores.

General Conditions of Operation

1. Improve core making.
2. Use present molding and material handling facilities.
3. New sidewall exhaust system (and collector) for pouroff.
4. New castings shakeout and exhaust system (because of reduced tonnage of castings, this shakeout can also serve as core shakeout).
5. Hot castings exhaust system.
6. Improve molding sand system (sand handling storage).
7. New molding sand mixer (12 tph capacity).
8. Discontinue using the No. 1 cleaning shed (OSHA citation).
9. Clean castings in the No. 2 cleaning shed.

A. Core Making:
   1—Electric heater (50 KW; heat core boxes) . . . . $ 6,000
   1—Electric oven (125 KW; skin dry cores)   12,000
   1—Oil-fired oven (dry core blacking)   60,000
   1—Sand heater (120 KW; heat sand to 75°F)   12,000
   1—Sand mixer exhaust system (2,000 cfm; to atmosphere)   7,000
   1—Roller conveyor, powered (48'W × 40'L)   12,000
   1—Electric power supply system (300 KW)   21,000
   Relocate 2 core blowers and 1 bench station   10,000

   Subtotal . . . . $ 140,000

B. Molding
   No capital improvements.

C. Pouroff and Shakeout
   1—Pouroff exhaust system (400,000 cfm; ductwork and
      dust collector) . . . . $ 700,000
   1—Shakeout for castings and cores (8' × 10'—15-ton
      capacity)   80,000
   1—Shakeout exhaust system (75,000 cfm; use same collector
      as for pouroff exhaust)   25,000
   1—Hot castings exhaust system (125,000 cfm; use same
      collector as for pouroff exhaust)   50,000

   Subtotal . . . . $ 855,000

D. Molding Sand System
   1—Bucket elevator . . . . $ 23,000
   1—Belt conveyor   10,000
   1—Rotary screen exhaust system (exhaust to shakeout
      dust collector; 2,000 cfm)   6,000
   1—Sand storage silo (modifications)   11,000
   1—Sand unloading conveyor (30"W × 24'L—30 tph)   25,000
   1—Sand mixer and skip loader (12 tph)   55,000
   1—Sand mixer exhaust system (2,000 cfm)   10,000

   Subtotal . . . . $ 140,000

      Subtotal, all items $1,135,000
      10% contingency   113,000

         Grand total (Option No. 2) $1,248,000

Source: Company records.

$800,000 in 1975 (see Exhibit 10). Martin, working with the accounting people, estimated that slightly over half of this overhead was entirely fixed, and would continue if the Special Foundry were closed.

In an effort to compare the financial implications of options 1 and 4, Martin prepared the pro forma income statements listed in Exhibits 11 and 12. While he did not have time to prepare a pro forma for option 2, he had been assured by both marketing and accounting that a 35 percent gross profit could be earned on the 2,500 tons produced, and that the foundry would operate at full capacity. Martin did not try to estimate the cash flows which might result if option 3 were adopted.

Discounted at 13 percent, the present value of option 1 (continue to operate) was worth $410,000 compared to option 4 (discontinue), which was worth $330,000. While this made the continue-to-operate option worth $80,000 more than discontinuing, Martin thought that Mr. Ridley would be very much impressed by the large amounts of positive cash flow in the first two years if the foundry were closed down.

OTHER CONSIDERATIONS

If the discontinue option were to be seriously considered, Martin thought that the employee situation had to be investigated. In June 1976, the Special Foundry work force was as follows:

Categories	Number of Employees
1. Direct-hour employees	
Hourly employee age levels	
Age	
20–30	61
31–40	52
41–50	49
51–55	19
56–60	12
61–	6
	199
Hourly employee skill levels	
Unskilled	48
Semiskilled	111
Skilled	27
Highly skilled	13
	199
2. Supervisory	
Foremen	10
3. Service/maintenance hourly employees*	
All categories	25

* These employees were used at both Greeneville plants. The 25 figure represented the allocation to the Special Foundry.

EXHIBIT 10
Costs Allocated to Greeneville Special Foundry

Depreciation	$94,939
20% of cupola fixed	56,403
20% of cupola general plant per capita	4,080
20% of cupola general plant capital investment	37,200
20% bed coke	29,000
20% cupola lining	16,200
Special Foundry general plant per capita	179,184
Special Foundry general	282,072
20% burden on service labor	78,000
Total	$777,078

Source: Company records.

Martin understood that about 190 employees could be absorbed in other AFI foundries. About 105 employees could be absorbed in the other Greeneville Foundry which was undergoing an expansion, and another 85 might be offered a job if they would move 110 miles east to Asheville. AFI top management believed that since Asheville was a larger, more cosmopolitan city, many Greeneville employees might be eager to make the move, especially if they were offered work in the modern Asheville 3 Foundry. Many of the highest-skilled workers would not be needed in the other foundries, although they would most likely all be offered jobs at lower skill levels because of their seniority. The union contract prohibited reducing their wage levels, however.

The union contract provided that if a foundry were closed, all employees who were 55 years of age and had 15 years of service could retire with no reduction in retirement benefits. Normally, an employee had to have 30 years service before he could retire at age 55. Retirement benefits were $11 per month for each year of service (plus Social Security). Martin thought that no more than ten employees would elect early retirement if the foundry were closed. He was not certain as to the exact reaction the union, the employees, or the townspeople might have if the Special Foundry were closed, although he knew that it would not come as a surprise to many of them. During the past 12 years, word had somehow leaked out to the local newspaper every time a decision to close the Special Foundry was being considered.

Another implication of closing the foundry was the possible impact on AFI's customers who would suddenly be without a supplier. Martin learned that the Special Foundry's largest customer (who was also a major customer of AFI's other foundries) might be willing to expand its own captive foundry, and make its own large castings. Three customers (each representing about 4 percent of the Special Foundry's output) would be expected to have extreme difficulty finding another source of supply. These three customers did not purchase any other castings from AFI. Martin believed that a decision to

EXHIBIT 11

Option 3: Greeneville Special Foundry Projected Statement of Income, 1976–1986

	1976	1977	1978	1979	1980	1981	1982	1983	1984	1985	1986
Tons	6,548	8,163	4,219	3,082	2,222	2,355	2,500	2,650	2,800	2,975	3,000
Price per ton	$1,035	$1,067	$1,218	$1,385	$1,625	$1,723	$1,826	$1,936	$2,052	$2,175	$2,306
Gross sales ($ thousands)	$6,777	$8,713	$5,137	$4,268	$3,611	$4,058	$4,565	$5,130	$5,746	$6,471	$6,918
R&A	203	261	154	128	108	122	137	154	172	194	208
Net sales	$6,574	$8,452	$4,983	$4,140	$3,503	$3,936	$4,428	$4,976	$5,574	$6,271	$6,710
Variable cost	4,405	5,663	3,339	2,774	2,347	2,638	2,967	3,335	3,734	4,206	4,497
Start up cost (for no-bake)				250	200						
AFI margin	$2,169	$2,789	$1,644	$1,116	$ 956	$1,298	$1,461	$1,641	$1,840	$2,071	$2,213
Manufacturing fixed	$ 698	$ 771	$ 714	$ 847	$ 893	$ 932	$ 978	$1,029	$1,085	$1,149	$1,217
Manufacturing variable											
Hourly fringes	648	700	413	343	290	326	367	412	461	519	555
General plant	85	90	53	44	37	42	47	49	55	62	66
(total)	733	790	466	387	327	368	414	461	516	581	621
Inventory change	175										
Selling expense	35	46	27	22	19	21	24	25	28	32	34
General expense	128	170	100	83	70	79	89	93	104	117	125

Earnings before taxes	$ 400	$1,012	$ 337	$ (223)	$ (353)	$ (102)	$ (134)	$ 33	$ 101	$ 192	$ 216
Earnings after tax	$ 198	$ 502	$ 167	$ (111)	$ (175)	$ (51)	$ (66)	$ 16	$ 53	$ 95	$ 107
Working capital change		(188)	347	84	64	(44)	(49)	(55)	(59)	(70)	627
Depreciation		108	144	235	236	228	222	217	213	211	210
Capital expenditure											
New		(315)	(901)	(98)							1,892*
Maintenance		(150)	(150)	(150)	(158)	(165)	(174)	(182)	(191)	(201)	
Cash flow		$ (43)	$ (393)	$ (40)	$ (33)	$ (32)	$ (67)	$ (4)	$ 16	$ 35	$2,836
Present value factor @ 13%		.885	.783	.693	.613	.543	.480	.425	.376	.333	.295
Present value cash flow		$ (38)	$ (308)	$ (28)	$ (20)	$ (17)	$ (32)	$ (2)	$ 6	$ 12	$ 837
Capital cash flow	410										

* Assumes liquidation of business at book value in 1986.

Notes: *Startup costs* include costs of setting up the no-bake process, including higher cost per ton on the early part of the learning curve.
Manufacturing overhead includes fringe benefits on hourly workers which are mostly variable and an allocation of general overhead which is mostly fixed.
  General expense is an allocation of corporate overhead and is mostly fixed.
  Working capital change reflects increases and decreases in working capital.
  Capital expenditure includes amounts for new facilities and for replacement or overhaul of existing facilities.
  Source: Company records.

EXHIBIT 12

Option 4: Income and Cash Flow-Liquidation of Greeneville Special Foundry (12/31/77)

	1977	1978	1979	1980	1981	1982	1983	1984	1985	1986
Service and indirect labor........		$(484)	$(523)	$(565)	$(610)	$(659)	$(712)	$(768)	$(830)	$(896)
General plant allocation		(53)	(44)	(37)	(42)	(47)	(49)	(55)	(62)	(66)
Selling expense allocation		(27)	(22)	(19)	(21)	(24)	(25)	(28)	(32)	(34)
General expense allocation		(100)	(83)	(70)	(79)	(89)	(93)	(104)	(117)	(125)
Savings due to closing		222	239	258	279	302	326	352	380	410
Earnings before taxes...........	$1,012	(442)	(433)	(433)	(473)	(517)	(553)	(603)	(661)	(711)
Earnings after taxes	502	(219)	(215)	(215)	(235)	(256)	(274)	(299)	(328)	(353)
Working capital change	(188)	845								
Capital expense		418								
Depreciation	108	144								
Cash flow..................	$ 422	1,188	(215)	(215)	(235)	(256)	(274)	(299)	(328)	(353)
Present value factor @ 13%......	.885	.783	.693	.613	.543	.480	.425	.376	.333	.295
Present value cash flow........	$ 373	930	(140)	(132)	(128)	(123)	(116)	(112)	(109)	(104)
Total cash flow..............	339									

Notes: The first four lines represent the amounts of these categories of expense which are allocated to the Greenville Special Foundry. They are considered mostly fixed expense. However, if GSF were closed, certain amounts of these could be eliminated. My estimates of the possible reduction are shown on the fifth line.
  The amounts shown in the first four lines correspond to the figures for allocation of fixed costs included in Option 1 calculations.
  Working capital change shows the liquidation of working capital in 1978 if the plant is closed.
  Capital expense shows the after tax liquidation value of the fixed assets.
  Figures after 1980 for cash flow are adjusted for inflation.

phase out the Special Foundry would have an insignificant psychological effect internally on the total AFI company (and Acme as well), but it might disrupt relationships with some customers.

A final factor mentioned several times by Mr. Ridley was the question of whether AFI should attempt to operate a small foundry. Given the projected demand for large castings, the Special Foundry could only be expected to get smaller than it was at present. Mr. Ridley believed that almost as much management attention, concern, and time went into the Special Foundry as other foundries five or 10 times its size. Perhaps the beneifts to be derived from concentrating management attention on the expansion potential in larger markets were greater than the costs required to continue to operate the Greeneville Special Foundry.

THE TASK FORCE MEETING

Martin distributed some of his research and analysis (primarily Exhibits 3 through 12) to the task force several days prior to the preliminary meeting. Mr. Ridley, who had planned to chair the meeting, had been asked to visit Dayton at the last minute and could not attend. He told Martin to conduct the meeting without him.

Members of the task force included David Case, assistant plant manager at the Special Foundry, Douglas Leeds, treasurer, Harold Owens, vice president of engineering, Charles Shook, vice president of sales, and Robert Evans, vice president of manufacturing.

Excerpts of their conversation were as follows:

Douglas Leeds: I think we ought to close down the Special Foundry. The present value of the cash flow is only $80,000 less than keeping it open, and we can more than make up that much *each year,* just in the business we can transfer to our other facilities. I can think of a hundred better ways to spend $1½ million than to invest it in a dying market.

Robert Evans: I agree with you, Doug, about the lousy investment, but you forget that we are operating at full capacity in other facilities. There's no place to shift that business to. I think we ought to drag our feet on OSHA. What do those feds know about running a foundry? They go sniffing around the plant with their notepads and government manuals, and they'll always find something to complain about. I think we've got to face the facts. Those boys aren't going to be satisfied until all our people wear white uniforms and work in sterile conditions. They'll have us looking like a hospital before they're done. I don't think we should install one lousy fan unless they require it, and we should delay as long as possible before we get it done. The faster we clean things up, the sooner they'll be back with more requirements. We sure don't want to be the model for the industry—that would put us at a competitive disadvantage.

Harold Owens: I agree with your thoughts about OSHA, Bob, but why don't we close the place down and blame them for the whole thing? They are trying hard to avoid that kind of publicity, but they've got it coming. The citation is the perfect excuse to get ourselves out of a bad situation without getting the union on our backs. The Special Foundry has been a real dog for years, and it's going to get worse. We'll spend half our lives in Greeneville talking to OSHA if we keep the place open.

Charles Shook: I'm not so sure. I've got some salesmen out there who have worked years to establish good relationships with key customers. Now you want me to tell those customers to forget it? To go find another supplier? Some of those customers are regulars at the Asheville plants, also. That's a job I can do without. We'll also have a credibility problem with our customers in the other foundries. Here we are telling them to be patient on deliveries because we are operating at full capacity, and then we close a plant. It just won't make sense to them.

I'm an optimist at heart. Just because future demand doesn't look so good right now doesn't mean that it will be dead forever. New things might come along. Maybe we'll get some business for big coal-mining equipment in a couple of years. The energy situation and changing technology make a lot of forecasts nothing but guesses. There's no telling what new business might come along. We have been working on some pretty interesting large casting work, but it will probably be a few years before the fruit of this work breaks for us. If we close down, we'll never be able to get back in.

David Case: I've been listening to all you guys talk, and some of the comments make me sick. Have you got your heads in the sand? The big problem is that you're all here in Asheville ivory-tower offices, and you have no idea what's going on out there in the real world, especially at Greeneville. The reason we're not cost-competitive in the first place is because all the engineers like to play around in Asheville. We can't get them to come down where they're needed. Where have all the technological improvements been made—Asheville or Greeneville? We all know the answer to that one.

So you all look at the numbers, and make a decision based on some ridiculous projections. I'm no numbers genius, but if you add across the cash flows for closing compared to staying open, you will find that staying open yields a positive cash flow of $2,276,000, and liquidating shows a *loss* of over half a million dollars. Leave it to some business school graduate to make a half-million dollar loss seem like a better deal than a $2 million profit. And I'm talking about real dollars, not some type of accounting dollars.

Speaking about numbers, they're loaded in another way, too. Take out all the environmental expenditures except those in the citation and see what it does to your $80,000. Then take a poll of the workers in the Special Foundry, and see if they would prefer breathing the air they and their fathers have been breathing for 60 years or would they rather change jobs or be put out of a job. Just ask them. By adding in about $855,000 for fans we don't need, you make the answer come out to say what you want.

Furthermore, the figures for shutting it down don't include anything for the guys who'd get laid off. We might well have a dozen or 15 of those who are 55 or over take the early retirement. One or two would have the normally required 30 years service but on the average my guess is they'd have about 20 years service and wouldn't normally be eligible. So that's going to cost the company something. On top of that there will be well over 30—say maybe 40—we won't be able to absorb elsewhere in the company. These people would get severance pay, depending on length of service, but perhaps averaging $4,000 per person.

You guys don't know what it's like living in a town like Greeneville. With so

EXHIBIT 13
Planning Commission Letter

June, 1976

Dear Mr. Case:
It has come to our attention that Asheville Foundries, Inc. is again considering closing the Greeneville Special Foundry. We wish to register a strong protest to such a possibility; we believe a closure would be unwarranted and irresponsible.

AFI has considered closing the Special Foundry numerous times in the past. Each time we have protested such a move; several times the city has made certain concessions to the company, such as road improvements, new water service, and so forth. Each time the plant has not closed, and we assume it has run profitably for the company, the employees, and the community—in spite of the dire predictions made for it.

Our city can ill afford to lose the employment of over 50 people, many of whom have specialized and nontransferable skills. We had expected the Greenville expansion to help us in getting more people employed, not to be just a trade-off. Unemployment in the area is already at 15.5 percent, and many of the unemployed have exhausted their benefits and assets. The city's shrinking tax base is hard-pressed to accommodate the demands of such an unfavorable economic climate.

At a time when economic predictions are becoming brighter, AFI now brings up the closing question again. Surely a plant running at 80 percent or more of capacity is profitable, especially when that plant must be fully depreciated. What does AFI want now?

The city has been most liberal with AFI for years. No unreasonable demands have been made by us on your company. Sources close to us indicate that OSHA requests of you were most reasonable compared to several other firms within the city, and those other firms have no intention of closing down.

We have faith that AFI wants to be a good corporate citizen; and we trust you will again put aside thoughts of closing.

Sincerely,

Cortland Bayles
Chairman, Planning Commission

CB/cf

many people unemployed, there is likely to be big trouble if we close down the foundry. I've got relatives working in the foundry, and I know what it would be like. There are rumblings already. Don't be surprised if there is a wildcat strike that throws us all out of work, and I don't mean just the Special Foundry—they would close the other Greeneville plant and perhaps agitate in Asheville as well. We survived the strike in 1973, but that one lasted for only three weeks. What would happen if they stayed out for three months? We'd all be out of work, even the genius who put these numbers together.

You can't keep a question like this secret! I've already got a letter from a guy I know in the Planning Commission accusing us of irresponsibility or even worse [see Exhibit 13]. This kind of trouble will haunt us for years.

What if word got out that we closed the foundry because some kid who never saw a foundry before came up with some numbers that said that it might be more profitable for AFI if everyone in the Special Foundry stayed at home? Some of those men have worked here for 20, 30 years. They are skilled craftsmen. Sure, we might accommodate some of them in the other plant, but we really can't use their skills. There's no way that they will sweep floors for the rest of their lives, no matter what you pay them. There's going to be big trouble if we close down, believe me. You guys ought to get out there in the trenches and see what's it's like.

Martin was taken aback by Case's emotional outburst, and adjourned the meeting as soon as Case had finished. He returned to his office to think about what had transpired. Before the meeting, he had been leaning toward closing the facility, but he wasn't so sure any longer. He knew that Mr. Ridley would expect a final recommendation from him when he returned from Dayton in two days.

INDEX OF CASES

SUBJECT INDEX

*This book has been set VIP in 10 and 9 point
Times Roman, leaded 2 points. Part numbers are
24 point Times Roman Bold and chapter numbers are 72 point Caslon No. 540 Roman. Part
and chapter titles are 16 point Times Roman. The
size of the type page is 28 by 46½ picas.*